E 159-95

READER'S DIGEST

South African Cookbook

READER'S DIGEST

South African Cookbook

PUBLISHED BY THE READER'S DIGEST ASSOCIATION
SOUTH AFRICA (PTY) LIMITED, CAPE TOWN

First edition copyright © 1985
Reprinted © 1994
The Reader's Digest Association South Africa (Pty) Limited
130 Strand Street, Cape Town 8001

All rights reserved. No part of this book may be reproduced, translated, stored in a retrieval system, or transmitted in any form or by any means, electronic, electrostatic, magnetic tape, mechanical, photocopying, recording or otherwise, without permission in writing from the publishers.

® READER'S DIGEST is a registered trademark of The Reader's Digest Association, Inc. of Pleasantville, New York USA.

ISBN 0 947008 24 1

◆

Reader's Digest South African Cookbook
was edited and designed at
The Reader's Digest Association South Africa (Pty) Limited
Cape Town

EDITOR Vincent Leroux

ASSOCIATE EDITOR Alfie Steyn

ART DIRECTOR Elaine Partington

SENIOR DESIGNER Christabel Hardacre

PROJECT CO-ORDINATOR Dominique Emery Davis

CONCEPT RESEARCH Frances Howard

COPY EDITORS Alan Duggan, Ros Lavine, Jeremy Lawrence

TYPESETTER Mary Lacey

Chief Consultant
Phillippa Cheifitz

Copy Contributors
Renata Coetzee, Ina Paarman, Simon Rappaport,
Professor Leonie van Heerden

Recipe Contributors
Irma Barenblatt, Lynn Bedford Hall, Phillippa Cheifitz, Renata Coetzee,
Department of National Education, Gerti Easterbrook, Vivia Ferreira,
Ian Gallie, Sonja Garber, Gilbey Distillers and Vintners (Pty) Ltd,
Martine Israel, Pamela Lassak, Susan Long, Barbara Newman,
Ina Paarman, Ramola Parbhoo, Sue Ross, Betsie Rood, Sylvia Sieff,
Elizabeth Southey, Tafelberg Publisher's Ltd, Irna Turilli,
Magdaleen van Wyk, Peter Veldsman

Test Cooks
Vivien le Roux, Susan Long, Wendy Malleson

Photographers
Alain Proust,
Roger Bell, Jac de Villiers, Franz Lauinger, Anthony Johnson

Stylists
Sylvia Sieff, Phillippa Cheifitz

Illustrator
Felicity Harris

Script Designer
Drexler Kyzer

Contents

A World of Cooking in One Country *page 8*

How to Use this Book *page 11*

PART 1
The Recipes
page 12

Starters, Snacks and Savouries *page 14*

Soups *page 34*

Fish *page 52*

Meat *page 80*

Poultry *page 122*

Braaivleis *page 148*

Savoury Sauces, Stuffings and Dumplings *page 164*

Vegetables and Salads *page 182*

Pasta, Rice and Cereals *page 212*

Eggs and Cheese *page 226*

Pastries, Puddings and Desserts *page 246*

Breads, Cakes and Biscuits *page 288*

Preserves, Jams, Pickles and Sweets *page 318*

PART 2
Entertaining
page 342

PARTY TIME   *page 344*

SERVING WINE   *page 354*

DRINKS FOR ALL OCCASIONS   *page 358*

PART 3
The Practical Cook
page 366

GLOSSARY   *page 380*

INDEX   *page 384*

ACKNOWLEDGMENTS   *page 400*

A World of Cooking in One Country

WHICH DISHES come to mind when you think about South African cooking: sosaties braaied over an open fire; a thick bredie; a sweet Malay curry? You'd be right with all of these. But you would also be right if you thought of sweet and sour pork, spaghetti Bolognese, veal schnitzel, or even roast beef and Yorkshire pudding. The fact is that cooking in South Africa is as international as the ancestors of today's South Africans.

Visit an Italian kitchen and you would be hard put to find anything but pasta and veal; go to India and every meal that is served seems to be spicy; and everyone knows that most Englishmen are raised on a regime of meat-and-two-veg.

But take a peek inside the average South African kitchen and you are likely to find a veritable storehouse of international ingredients, most of them grown or prepared right here in South Africa.

Chances are that you will find pasta, probably several varieties; there will be a fairly decent selection of spices and herbs; and there will be tinned delicacies such as artichokes or the more ubiquitous sweetcorn.

You will also find a good selection of fresh vegetables, and there's bound to be all you need for making a nutritious fresh salad.

South African cooks are lucky: our rich heritage has given us a whole gamut of dishes upon which to draw. The output from a typical kitchen could range from a cottage pie on Monday, a pot of curry for the family on Tuesday, a steak with pepper sauce on Wednesday, ravioli on Thursday and a Chinese stir-fry on Friday. Assuming there is a braai on Saturday, you will probably find a 'boerekos' Sunday roast, with rice, sweet potatoes and pumpkin to add a really traditional South African flavour.

Home cooking in our pioneer past
South African cooking in the 1980s has come a long way from the kitchens of the early pioneers. New settlers brought their culinary traditions with them, adapting their favourite recipes to local ingredients. The final result is a fascinating mixture of European, Asian, African and even American cooking that is both nutritious and delicious.

Many South African culinary traditions began in the European kitchens of the 16th and 17th centuries, especially those of Holland, Germany and France, with an added contribution from the various Eastern peoples who came to South Africa during the early years of settlement.

All the recipes from these sources had to be modified to take account of ingredients available at the southern tip of Africa, far removed from the abundance and variety of ingredients to be found in Europe and Asia.

Some of these ingredients were ones used by the indigenous people of Southern Africa, for instance maltabella and biltong, which to this day remain favoured South African foods.

Other varieties of fresh vegetables and fruit were grown in the lush gardens of the early Cape to replenish the stores of the ships that plied their way between Europe and the East.

The influence of the Dutch on Cape cooking is especially noticeable in the extensive and varied use of vegetables.

The Dutch were the leaders in agricultural development in 16th century Europe. Many of the new ideas in farming originated in the Low Countries, where shortage of land had encouraged the inhabitants to embark on a system of intensive cultivation, and the techniques developed in this way were brought by Jan van Riebeeck to the Cape.

Butter and cheese at the Cape
A specialised dairy industry also came into being and cheese-making was introduced to the Cape as early as 1657. Butter was produced too, and the South African custom of serving cooked vegetables with a dab of butter and a sprinkling of nutmeg or cinnamon derives from that era – when the products most readily available at the Cape at the time were in fact vegetables, butter and spices.

Spices and herbs were also used in the preparation of meat and fish dishes, which were often marinated in wine, lemon juice, or an infusion of rose petals known as rose-water. (The preferred marinade of South African cooks today is wine rather than the rather mild-tasting rose-water!)

The German influence on South African cuisine is most clearly discernible in the wide variety of sausages that are available locally, especially of boerewors, favoured at traditional braais, the favourite way of entertaining in this country.

The French influence on local cooking derives from the domestic kitchens of 17th century France. The French Huguenots fled their homeland long before famous and sophisticated chefs such as Carême created their recipes, or the well-known restaurants of the 18th century opened their doors.

But even though it lacked lavish embellishments, French cooking brought a new flair to the established Dutch Cape kitchen. Foods were flavoured more delicately, with herbs and spices used sparingly. Surplus fat was drained from dishes; for example the hotpot, a stew from Holland, was made lighter and less rich, like the kind prepared in the south of France.

Later, the traditional Cape stew – which was much influenced by Malay cooking – was renamed 'bredie', and tomato bredie, quince bredie and waterblommetjie bredie became favourites. The waterblommetjie grows indigenously only in South Africa, and the bredie made from it has become something of a status-symbol dish, served and appreciated only by those well initiated into South African cuisine.

Among the Huguenot settlers were many skilled farmers who made an important contribution to the improvement of viticulture in their new homeland.

Also under their influence, good-quality apricots were cultivated and the drying of raisins was developed. The Cape delicacies 'boere-meisjes' and 'boere-jongens' (literally, 'farmer girls' and 'farmer boys') were made, consisting of apricots and raisins preserved in brandy and served as an apéritif or for dessert.

The introduction of courses
Another important innovation was that of serving dishes in sequence instead of simultaneously, therefore introducing the system of various 'courses'.

Formerly all the dishes were put on the table at once, and it was not unusual to count 50 different dishes at a banquet! The much tidier French style of menu-planning was introduced not only to the Cape at this time, but also to Europe.

Local cuisine was also enlivened by the influence of slaves brought to the Cape from the Eastern possessions of the Dutch East India Company towards the end of the 17th century.

The men, who were outstanding fishermen and hunters, introduced fish and game to the menu, while the women were expert cooks and introduced a variety of exotic oriental spices and seasonings: aniseed, fennel, turmeric, cardamom pods, ginger (both green and dried), cumin seeds, coriander, garlic, various mixtures of curry, mustard seeds, red peppers, saffron, saltpetre, sari leaves and tamarind.

The curry dishes from the East were skilfully flavoured by these knowledgeable cooks, and to this day curry is a favourite, making frequent appearances on South African menus.

Adapting to South African ingredients
Dishes were developed from available local produce, and where the Eastern spices such as cardamom pods, green ginger and saffron were not freely available, local flavouring agents such as dried apricots or orange leaves were used.

Typical South African dishes were developed, such as bobotie (a flavoured mincemeat dish), atjar (a piquant relish made with pieces of fruit), sambal (finely chopped vegetables or fruit steeped in salt and vinegar, and flavoured with chillies or other hot, spicy ingredients), blatjang (a strongly flavoured thick sauce made from fruit and flavourings) and 'funeral rice' (turmeric rice with raisins).

The Malay recipes for the preparation of Cape fish are mouth-watering, making imaginative dishes out of everything from galjoen, Cape salmon, maasbanker, mackerel, hottentot, elf, stumpnose and steenbras to stockfish and harder.

A snoek braai is popular at the Cape, especially when the snoek is served with a sweet syrup called 'moskonfyt' (made from the must produced during winemaking) and with sweet potatoes baked in the coals of the fire.

Although many Malay dishes such as bredies, sosaties, boboties, atjar, blatjang, sambal and various curry dishes like pienang (a mutton curry) are favourites in South Africa today, other traditional Malay foods are unknown to the average South African.

Through the centuries in which they have lived at the Cape the Muslim people have adhered to their traditions, and today still honour these at religious festivals and family celebrations.

Muslims eat only 'halaal' food, that is, food prepared or selected according to Islamic law. Meat, poultry, tinned products and other foods are often seen on supermarket shelves with the 'halaal' mark.

The variety of Cape cuisine was extended by the Trekboers, who had to develop new dishes suitable for their nomadic existence. Biltong (dried, salted meat) and rusks were popular foods and are still favourites with South Africans.

A new culinary influence was felt when the English arrived at the beginning of the 19th century. For the first time a leavening agent – which had the same chemical composition as smelling salts – was introduced. This meant that leavened cakes could now be baked, and these were immediately christened 'thick cakes'. Prior to the introduction of this leavening agent, sponge cakes were made using whisked egg white to enable them to rise.

The excitement of creating new textures in baked products inspired many women to develop new cake recipes. These abound in early handwritten cookbooks, together with many new recipes for baked puddings. Up until then the best-known dessert at the Cape was tart with various fillings, such as 'melktert' and fruit tart that had not required leavening.

The hearty English breakfast of bacon, eggs and toast also came into fashion and was enjoyed for many years before the introduction of the more prudent 'healthy' breakfasts of today.

The Company's Gardens at the Cape

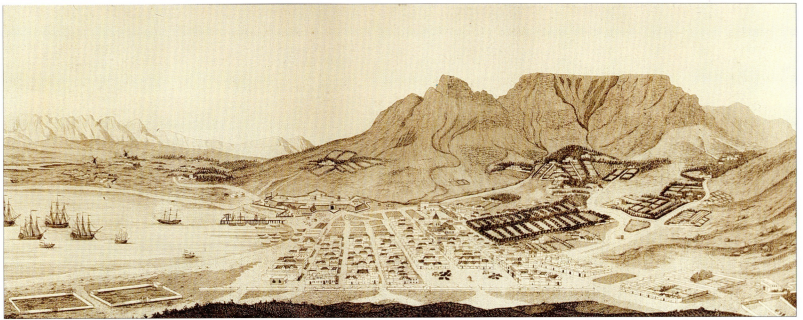

Jan van Riebeeck's task of growing fresh produce for the passing ships of the Dutch East India Company was carried out with such skill that his gardens – seen in the right-hand half of the above etching of 18th century Cape Town – soon achieved a world-wide reputation. The gardens were laid out in squares, separated by irrigation ditches and avenues of large bay and camphor trees. Produce from the gardens included grapes, figs, pomegranates, citrus fruit, chestnuts and cabbages.

A WORLD OF COOKING IN ONE COUNTRY

The typical Victorian kitchen owed its existence to the development of English food technology. At the turn of the 19th century, George Bodley, a Devon iron-founder, patented the first closed-top cooking range of cast-iron. This brought an end to open-hearth cooking, in Europe as well as in South Africa.

By the end of the 19th century an abundance of gadgets and labour-saving appliances was being manufactured overseas and imported into the country. Coffee-grinders, colanders, mincers, knife-polishers and percolators all aided the cooking process.

Numerous new restaurants were opening their doors, using all these 'modern appliances' to prepare food. The modern-day restaurant in South Africa has come a long way since food was first served to passing sailors at the Cape.

Today, the sophistication of local restaurants matches those of countries overseas. Many restaurants were founded by newcomers to South Africa, and so the local table was enriched with many ethnic dishes; some of these have become standard fare and can be purchased on supermarket shelves, reflecting the cosmopolitan nature of the South African population today.

The Italian community has contributed generously to our cuisine. Pastas, pizzas and ravioli have become household words. Special Italian cheeses, and a wide variety of pastas and flavourings are all readily available in South Africa.

Many Greek dishes are also entrenched in South African cuisine, such as moussaka, taramasalata and pastitsio. Lesser-known recipes such as spanakopitta and dolmades are also provided in this book in the hope that they, too, will gain a wider popularity.

The Portuguese population has contributed a number of recipes, including flavourful dishes containing tomato, onion, green pepper, peri-peri, oil and vinegar; these are served in many South African homes today. The Portuguese have also contributed some outstanding chicken and prawn recipes.

Although the kosher table of the Jewish people contains many delectable dishes, only a few restaurants serve traditional Jewish food.

Fish is a particularly popular food amongst the Jewish community and is traditionally served on the Sabbath, which begins at sunset on Friday. Three of the better-known fish dishes introduced into South African cuisine by the Jews are egg and lemon fish, gefilte fish and herring rollmops – all of which appear in the recipe section of this book.

The German influence on local cooking extends beyond just sausages and boerewors. The many types of smoked and cured meats available in supermarkets have a German origin, as have the speciality breads such as pumpernickel and rye bread. Delicious pastries and cakes, such as the well-known Black Forest cake, have found permanent recognition on South African coffee-house menus.

Although choux pastry, French bread and French salad-dressing are known in many South African households, only a few devotees are familiar with the wide range of delicately flavoured dishes typical of French cuisine.

An interest has been shown in 'nouvelle cuisine', especially by recent visitors to France, but in general French foods are mostly prepared in specialised restaurants in South Africa rather than in the home. The influence of the French Huguenots is seen in traditional fare like fruit preserved in brandy or as konfyt.

The important impact of the Orient
The Orient has made an important impact on our tastebuds. Indian spices are regularly purchased by visitors to Natal, where hot curries are especially popular. Poppadums and samoosas are Indian specialities now available in many food outlets throughout the country.

Delicately flavoured Chinese foods have also become part of the national food scene, judging by the popularity of Chinese restaurants. And the stir-fry of vegetables, rice or meat has even invaded the sacred braais of South Africa, in the form of 'Chinese braais'. Bean sprouts, bamboo shoots and soy sauce, popular ingredients in Chinese dishes, have now become standard commodities in most local supermarkets.

The Indonesian rice table is a latter-day contribution to local cuisine by the Dutch. Nasi goreng and other accompaniments are available in supermarkets for those who are energetic enough to prepare a complete *rijsttafel*.

From America come cheesecakes, cherry pies, salad dressings, brownies and chowders. (South African country cooking is remarkably similar to Pennsylvanian Dutch food.)

It is this cosmopolitan background that is reflected in the Reader's Digest South African Cookbook. Here is a book truly for South African cooks: not just a book about bredies and boboties, but one that uses the wealth of South African ingredients to create the wonderful international heritage of cooking that we have made our own.

How to Use this Book

The Reader's Digest South African Cookbook is more than a collection of delectable recipes: it also provides you with the information and skills you will need to tackle any culinary task with confidence – be it a basic family meal or an impressive buffet for 100 guests. The book consists of three parts:

Part 1 – *The Recipes* This part contains about 900 expertly tested recipes for every occasion. Each individual section opens with useful information about foodstuffs and advice on culinary skills, such as beating egg whites, kneading bread and carving meat – to mention but a few.

Part 2 – *Entertaining* This is a guide to catering for virtually every social occasion. It not only helps you create well-balanced menus for parties, but also gives information on serving wine with food and how to prepare other drinks.

Part 3 – *The Practical Cook* In this final part you will find basic information about storing and freezing food, the equipment you need to run an efficient kitchen, and many useful tips on buying food and appliances.

HOW TO USE THE RECIPES

Before you begin preparing a dish, read the recipe right through to ensure that you have all the ingredients and equipment required.

If any of the steps described in the recipe are unfamiliar, try referring to the practical section at the beginning of the particular recipe chapter. These sections contain essential information pertaining to each chapter.

The comprehensive glossary situated at the back of the book gives the meaning of many commonly used cookery terms.

From time to time you will notice an asterisk next to an ingredient or term, for example *flaky pastry**, or *2 large onions, peeled and chopped**. Asterisks indicate cross-references to other parts of the book. In the first example, the asterisk indicates that a recipe is given elsewhere in the book for flaky pastry; in the second example it means that there is a description of how to peel and chop onions. In both cases, refer to the index to locate the relevant information.

The following information, where applicable, is contained in the recipes:

Preparation and cooking time Each recipe gives the time needed to prepare and cook the particular dish. Use this as a rough guide to plan your meal: the time it takes to prepare a dish obviously varies from one cook to another, depending on the speed with which they can tackle the particular steps and whether they use time-saving devices, such as electric beaters or food processors.

Standing and marinating time If a dish (or part of it) needs to be left standing or marinating for 30 minutes or longer, this time has been listed separately to help you with planning. When the standing or marinating time is shorter than 30 minutes, the time is included in the preparation time.

Chilling and freezing time Some dishes need chilling or freezing as part of the preparation, or before they can be served. If these times are 30 minutes or more, they have also been listed separately from the preparation time. (These times should also be used as rough guides, since some refrigerators and freezers are more efficient than others.)

Yield Each recipe provided indicates how many people can be served with the given amount or, where more appropriate, the yield in grams, millilitres or quantities (for example, 40 biscuits). Although every effort has obviously been made to make these as accurate as possible, it is wise to use your discretion: a group of people who have just returned from a cross-country hike are probably likely to consume a much larger supper than they would in the evening following a hearty Christmas luncheon!

Serving suggestions Many of the recipes offer specific suggestions which you may wish to follow. It is advisable to read these suggestions before you begin the main recipe.

Variations Some recipes in this book can be varied to suit your personal taste, or because particular ingredients are out of season. Each variation that is given at the end of a recipe is denoted by a separate paragraph. They have all been tested as carefully as the main recipes. If you are a vegetarian, it is particularly worthwhile checking the variations for meatless options to the main ingredients.

ALTITUDE

All recipes in this book have been tested at sea level. Since altitude affects the temperature at which liquid boils, check the Rules for Sugar Boiling on page 325 before making sweets or boiled icings at higher altitudes. If you do not live at the coast, it may also be necessary to make slight adjustments to cake recipes – see The Altitude Factor on page 294.

MEASURES

Metric measurements have been used for volume and mass throughout the book. Where these correspond closely to cup or spoon measurements, these have been provided in brackets. The approximate equivalents are provided on the inside of the back cover.

Because scales are more accurate for measuring dry or solid ingredients, we have given these measurements in grams and kilograms, except where quantities are so small that any possible discrepancy is negligible (for example, 15 ml flour). For those cooks who do not have a kitchen scale, the chart of volume equivalents on the inside of the back cover gives the *approximate* mass of 250 ml (1 cup) of the most commonly used dry or solid ingredients.

TEMPERATURES

The temperatures in this book are given in degrees Celsius (centigrade). For those who have ovens that are still marked in Fahrenheit, or for those who use gas cookers, there is a simple conversion chart on the inside of the back cover.

Other useful temperatures can be found in the charts for cooking meat (page 85) and poultry (page 125).

INGREDIENTS

Where ingredients go by several names, we have used the most common South African name, for example brinjal instead of aubergine or eggplant, and naartjie rather than tangerine. The sections on fruit and vegetables will help with alternative names, while the section on spices gives some of the Indian names under which many spices are sold locally.

Sugar In recipes that specify only 'sugar', use granulated, white sugar.

Flour Where simply 'flour' is mentioned, use cake flour.

PART 1

The Recipes

The food in this book reflects the diversity of the country in which we live – and the spirit of adventure which has awakened in the South African kitchen in recent years. This first part explores many new culinary boundaries and also includes those traditional dishes which have endured through changes in lifestyles and eating habits. The recipes, whether new or traditional, have been contributed by some of the top cookery writers in South Africa. Experts have also provided food preparation tips which apply specifically to South Africa and have adapted many international classics so that local cooks can have everything of the best.

Starters, Snacks and Savouries

The correct choice of starter is crucial to the success of a meal, whether the occasion is formal or informal. If starting with a snoek pâté or crayfish cocktail, for example, do not follow with a fish main course. Similarly, try and avoid serving too generous a starter with a substantial main course: it should complement rather than overwhelm the dish that is to follow.

If possible, place the starter on the table just before your guests take their seats, and make sure that any vegetable garnishes are still fresh and crisp. Few things are more depressing than a 'tired' introduction to a meal.

You need not spend a lot of money in producing a tasty and attractive starter. Remember that it is intended primarily as an appetite stimulant – and visual appeal plays a great part in this. Be free with the use of fresh ingredients which provide a variety of tastes and textures.

Snacks and savouries open up a whole new culinary world for the imaginative cook. Once again, visual appeal is important: combine different ingredients on attractive platters; decorate plates with fresh lettuce leaves, chopped parsley, sliced tomatoes or sliced cucumber. When preparing snacks for parties, remember that cheese and pastry are quite filling. Keep the servings small, and bear in mind that they are snacks only, and not the constituents of a full meal for every guest.

The choice of snacks and savouries offers enormous scope. Try stuffing avocados with cream cheese and caviar, or with shrimps. Create patterns on a large platter with sliced melon and Parma ham, and experiment with dips and pâtés.

STARTERS, SNACKS AND SAVOURIES RECIPES · *PAGE 16*

SPECIAL FEATURES

FINGER FOOD TO FILL THE GAP · *PAGE 20*
MAKING THE MOST OF DIPS · *PAGE 28*

Making the Most of Avocados

Avocados are used in a large variety of dishes: they can be chopped for salads, puréed for mousses, used as a spread for sandwiches or even made into desserts.

•

Select 2-3 perfect ripe avocados. Split them lengthways, discard the pips and brush them with lemon juice in order to prevent discolouring of the flesh. Fill the centres with one or more of the following mixtures and serve with thin crisp slices of Melba toast*.

•

125 g cream cheese mixed with 30 ml (2 tablespoons) sour cream. Pipe swirls or spoon into the centres. Top with a spoonful of Danish 'caviar' and serve well chilled.

•

Mix together two sliced sticks of table celery, a thinly sliced (or chopped) green apple and 30 ml (2 tablespoons) chopped pecans with 60 ml (¼ cup) mayonnaise* and 60 ml (¼ cup) sour cream or natural yoghurt*, adding salt and freshly ground black pepper to taste.

•

Add 250 ml (1 cup) cubes of poached kingklip or monkfish (poach* in a court-bouillon*) tossed in lemon juice to the above filling, but leave out the nuts and use only half an apple.

•

Alternatively, use cubes of cooked chicken instead of fish, and include some nuts.

•

Mix 250 g cooked and shelled prawns* or cubes of boiled crayfish with 60 ml (¼ cup) sour cream, 15 ml (1 tablespoon) tomato sauce*, 2 ml (½ teaspoon) Worcestershire sauce, a small dash of Tabasco (chilli sauce) and a squeeze of lemon juice.

•

Fill the avocados with cooked and shelled prawns* or cubes of crayfish. Mix 125 ml (½ cup) very thick mayonnaise* with 50 g grated Gruyère cheese and fold in a stiffly beaten egg white. Spoon over the seafood and ensure that the avocados are completely covered. Bake at 200°C for 15 minutes or grill briefly until slightly puffed and pale golden. Dust with paprika and serve immediately.

•

Fill with scoops or swirls of smoked snoek* or tuna pâté*.

Chilled Grapefruit

THE REFRESHING, slightly bitter taste of a fresh grapefruit has long appealed to South Africans as the first course of their breakfast. However, it should not be forgotten that this fruit can also be a light, palate-clearing start to a rich dinner.

PREPARATION TIME: 15 MINUTES
CHILLING TIME: 2 HOURS

INGREDIENTS FOR FOUR
4 grapefruit
15 ml (1 tablespoon) castor sugar
15 ml (1 tablespoon) Van der Hum liqueur* or port
Fresh mint

Halve the grapefruit and carefully remove the flesh. Dice neatly, removing all traces of pith, and place in a bowl with any juice. Add the sugar and liqueur or port and toss gently to blend the flavours.

Divide the mixture and juices among four of the grapefruit halves. Top with sprigs of fresh mint. Seal well in plastic wrap and refrigerate until you are ready to serve the meal. Serve in a pretty bowl, or centred on an attractive plate.

VARIATION Peel and quarter the grapefruit lengthways, removing the seeds. Slice neatly into sections and arrange in concentric circles on a plate. Pour over the Van der Hum or port, then garnish with mint and chill (well wrapped).

Chilled Melon

A COOL, SWEET MELON makes an excellent start to a summer meal. When choosing a melon, make sure you buy a ripe, perfect fruit.

Shake the melon: if you hear the sound of liquid moving inside, the fruit is overripe, and may have begun to deteriorate. Avoid melons that are too soft, bruised or scarred. If in doubt, ask your greengrocer for advice.

PREPARATION TIME: 15 MINUTES
CHILLING TIME: 2 HOURS

INGREDIENTS FOR SIX
1 medium-sized melon
90 ml (6 tablespoons) port
Fresh mint for garnish

Wipe the melon with a damp cloth, then cut it into six equal-sized wedges and discard the pips. Carefully separate the fruit from the skin with a sharp knife, without removing it, and cut the fruit across into neat pieces. Keep the wedge shape intact on the base of the melon skin. Arrange the wedges on six plates and pour over the port: allow 15 ml (1 tablespoon) per serving. Wrap the wedges in plastic wrap and chill for about 2 hours. Garnish with fresh mint.

VARIATIONS Peel the melon and cut it into thin slices. Arrange these in concentric circles on a large plate. Pour over the port, garnish with mint, and refrigerate (well wrapped).

If you wish, use ground ginger instead of port.

Alternatively, arrange slices of peeled melon with paper-thin slices of Parma ham in a circle on individual plates. Cover them and chill. When serving, pass around a pepper grinder.

Snails in Mushrooms

THE CLASSIC FRENCH snail dish, *Escargots à la bourguignonne*, calls for hefty specimens from the vineyards of Burgundy, served sizzling in their shells with great quantities of rich garlic butter and fresh crusty bread.

The following recipe, while less traditional, provides a very good starter: the snails are baked on a large mushroom 'plate', topped with garlic butter and a sprinkling of breadcrumbs.

PREPARATION TIME: 20 MINUTES
COOKING TIME: 25 MINUTES
PRE-HEAT OVEN TO 200°C

INGREDIENTS FOR FOUR
1 tin (125 g) snails
4 giant mushrooms (the biggest you can get)
130 g butter
3 cloves garlic, crushed
15 ml (1 tablespoon) chopped parsley
A squeeze of lemon juice
Freshly ground black pepper
15 ml (1 tablespoon) fine breadcrumbs (optional)
Chopped parsley for garnish

Drain the snails and put aside. Rinse the mushrooms and dry them thoroughly. Trim the stalks, melt 30 g of the butter and brush it all over the mushrooms. Place them stalk-side up in individual oven-proof dishes. They should fit snugly. Cream the rest of the butter with the garlic and parsley, adding the lemon juice and a grinding of black pepper. Smear each mushroom with the garlic butter (keep some over for the snails).

Divide the snails among the mushrooms. Top each snail with a dab of garlic butter and sprinkle lightly with fine breadcrumbs (if used). Bake the mushrooms in the pre-heated oven for 25 minutes, or until they are just tender. Place the hot dishes on dinner plates and sprinkle their contents with parsley.

SERVING SUGGESTION Serve with fingers of fresh white or brown bread (trim the crusts).

VARIATIONS Leave out the snails and instead serve the piping hot mushrooms with chunks of crusty bread. You can, of course, use small black mushrooms, but in this case you should reduce the cooking time.

If you wish to serve snails in garlic butter, push the snails into shells and pack generously with garlic butter. Bake them in a very hot oven (230°C) and cook for about 10 minutes. If you want to do it 'properly', serve the snails in dimpled plates (called *escargotières*) and provide your guests with tongs for picking up the hot shells and special forks for twisting the snails out of the shells.

Cucumber and Prawn Mousse

CUCUMBERS BELONG to the gourd family of plants, and come in many shapes and sizes. They have been cultivated in the north-west of India for 3 000 years.

Prawns and cucumbers combined in a mousse make a very delicate, cool start to a luncheon on a hot summer's day.

PREPARATION TIME: 30 MINUTES
CHILLING TIME: 2 HOURS

INGREDIENTS FOR FOUR
125 g cream cheese
175 ml natural yoghurt*

STARTERS, SNACKS AND SAVOURIES

½ English cucumber
100 g small cooked and shelled prawns*
15 ml (1 tablespoon) lemon juice
15 ml (1 tablespoon) gelatin
125 ml (½ cup) chicken stock*
Salt and white pepper

For the sauce:
250 ml (1 cup) plain drinking yoghurt
30 ml (2 tablespoons) thick mayonnaise*
Salt and white pepper
30 ml (2 tablespoons) fresh chopped dill

Beat together the cream cheese and yoghurt until smooth. Reserve 4 thin slices of cucumber and a few prawns for the garnish. Peel and finely chop (or grate) the rest of the cucumber and add, with the prawns, to the cheese and yoghurt. Add the lemon juice.

Next, sprinkle the gelatin over the stock and heat, stirring until dissolved. Strain into the mousse mixture and stir well. Check the seasoning. Ladle into four ramekins or moulds (oiled or coated with a non-stick spray) and then refrigerate until fully set.

To make the sauce, mix the yoghurt with the mayonnaise, then add the seasoning and dill. Pour the sauce over four plates. Invert the moulds on to the puddles of sauce. Garnish with the reserved cucumber slices and prawns.

SERVING SUGGESTION Pass around slices of Melba toast*.

VARIATION For a less expensive mousse, prepare without the prawns.

COMPOSED GRAPEFRUIT SALAD *This simple salad derives much of its appeal from its attractive appearance.*

COMPOSED GRAPEFRUIT SALAD

AN ATTRACTIVE and tasty salad, with the pale pink of the grapefruit and smoked chicken contrasting against the pale green of the avocado and endive. Careful positioning of the food on the plate shows the influence of the 'nouvelle cuisine'.

PREPARATION TIME: 30 MINUTES

INGREDIENTS FOR FOUR
2 pink grapefruit
1 large avocado
Juice of 1 large lemon
Breast of a smoked chicken
75 ml (5 tablespoons) sunflower oil
Curly endive (or chicory)
5 ml (1 teaspoon) whole seed mustard
5 ml (1 teaspoon) honey
Salt and freshly ground black pepper
Snipped chives

Peel and quarter the grapefruit lengthways, remove the seeds, and slice them into neat sections. Peel and slice the avocado and soak it in the juice of the lemon. Remove the skin from the chicken breast, cut the skin into strips and crisp in 15 ml (1 tablespoon) hot oil. Drain well, then slice the chicken breast very thinly. Line four dinner plates with washed and well-dried endive (or leaves of chicory).

Arrange the grapefruit in an overlapping fan to take up one third of the plate, and do the same with the avocado and chicken slices. Mix the remaining lemon juice and oil with the mustard and honey, adding the seasoning. Sprinkle some snipped chives over the avocado and place the crisped skin over the chicken. Cover well with plastic wrap and refrigerate. Spoon over the dressing just before serving.

DOLMADES

THIS DISH of stuffed vine leaves is popular world-wide with its intriguing combination of flavours. In this country it is generally a starter for Greek meals.

You can also make dolmades with cabbage leaves, spinach leaves or fig leaves: choose young leaves with no holes.

Dolmades can be frozen successfully: drain and open-freeze them on a tray. Once they are hard, arrange them closely together in containers and separate the layers with freezer film.

PREPARATION TIME: 30 MINUTES
SOAKING TIME: UP TO 30 MINUTES FOR THE VINE LEAVES; 1 HOUR FOR THE CURRANTS
COOKING TIME: 30 MINUTES

STARTERS, SNACKS AND SAVOURIES

INGREDIENTS FOR ABOUT 40 DOLMADES
- 40 fresh young vine leaves (or 1 jar or tin of vine leaves)
- 35 g currants
- 30 ml (2 tablespoons) dry white wine
- 125 ml (½ cup) olive oil
- 2 medium-sized onions, chopped*
- 3 ml (¾ teaspoon) salt
- 1 ml (¼ teaspoon) pepper
- 200 g rice
- 375 ml (1½ cups) water
- Juice of 2 large lemons
- 60 ml (¼ cup) chopped parsley
- 40 g pine kernels
- 30 ml (2 tablespoons) chopped mint
- 3 ml (¾ teaspoon) dried origanum
- 1 ml (¼ teaspoon) allspice
- 3 ml (¾ teaspoon) cinnamon
- A few sprigs of parsley

Choose fresh, young vine leaves about the size of your palm. Before cooking, tie them into bundles and dunk in boiling water for 2 minutes, then drain. If you are using pickled vine leaves, first soak for 30 minutes to reduce the briny taste.

Tinned vine leaves are very delicate, and must be handled carefully to avoid tearing. After removing the compacted leaves from the tin, stand them in a large bowl of cold water for 15-20 minutes; then gently separate the individual leaves. Any broken leaves can be used to line the cooking pan and 'patch' holes.

Dry the leaves and spread them out on a large surface, with the undersides facing up and the stalks towards you. Cut off and discard the stalks. Soak the currants in the wine for about 1 hour.

Heat half the oil in a saucepan and gently fry the onions until tender and transparent. Add the salt and pepper, rice, water and half the lemon juice, and steam (covered) for about 10 minutes, or until the rice is tender.

Stir in the chopped parsley, pine kernels, currants, mint, origanum, allspice and cinnamon.

Spoon about 10 ml (2 teaspoons) of the mixture on to each leaf, wrapping them up securely. Place the dolmades side by side in a heavy-bottomed saucepan, interspersing them with sprigs of parsley.

Add the remaining olive oil and the juice of the remaining lemon. Weigh the dolmades down with a large plate, cover the saucepan and steam gently for 20 minutes. Lift out the vine parcels with a perforated spoon, arrange them on a warm serving dish and serve immediately.

SERVING SUGGESTIONS Natural yoghurt* or avgolemono sauce* make good accompaniments.

VARIATIONS Dolmades can also be eaten cold. When they are cool, sprinkle them with a little lemon juice, olive oil and freshly ground black pepper, or simply serve with lemon wedges.

HOT SPINACH AND BACON SALAD

SPINACH HAS BEEN CULTIVATED for thousands of years, and is eaten in many ways. It contains a high proportion of calcium and iron, and is rich in magnesium and potassium.

This unusual spinach salad, garnished with bacon and croûtons, makes a tasty and attractive addition to the dinner table. Prepare as much of the recipe as possible ahead of time, then quickly complete the final stages before serving.

PREPARATION TIME: 40 MINUTES
COOKING TIME: 20 MINUTES

INGREDIENTS FOR SIX
- 2 slices stale bread
- 600 g spinach leaves
- 250 g rindless bacon, diced
- 125 ml (½ cup) olive oil
- 1 large clove garlic, crushed
- Juice of 1 large lemon
- Freshly ground black pepper
- Salt

Lightly toast the bread, trim the crusts and cut into small cubes. Wash the spinach leaves very well and cut away any thick stalks. Leave small, young leaves whole or shred them coarsely. Dry the leaves very well. Cook the bacon in its own fat until crisp, then remove with a slotted spoon.

Add the cubes of bread and fry in the bacon fat until golden, adding a little oil only if necessary.

Heat the olive oil in a clean pan and add the spinach. Cook gently until it turns bright green (it should be limp and glistening with oil). Add the crushed garlic and lemon juice and turn the spinach into a heated dish. Then add the bacon and croûtons and toss together. Add a grinding or two of black pepper and a little salt.

HOT SPINACH AND BACON SALAD *is an unusual flavour combination.*

LETTUCE AND CHICKEN LIVER SALAD

THIS SALAD OFFERS interesting contrasts in taste, texture and even temperature. Be sure to prepare the cold ingredients first, as proper timing is essential for successful results.

If butter lettuce is unobtainable, use an ordinary lettuce – but make sure it is crisp.

PREPARATION TIME: 25 MINUTES
COOKING TIME: 5 MINUTES

INGREDIENTS FOR FOUR
- 1 large (or 2 small) butter lettuce
- 4 spring onions, finely chopped
- 15 ml (1 tablespoon) chopped parsley
- 100 ml sunflower oil
- 60 ml (¼ cup) cream
- 30 ml (2 tablespoons) white wine vinegar
- 5 ml (1 teaspoon) French mustard
- 1 small clove garlic, crushed
- Salt and freshly ground black pepper
- 250 g chicken livers, cleaned and trimmed
- 1 tomato, skinned* and cut into strips
- 1 stick celery, cut into 'matchsticks'
- 1 leek (white part only), thinly sliced

Rinse the lettuce leaves and dry well. Place them in a salad bowl with the spring onion and parsley. Beat together 75 ml (5 tablespoons) of the oil with the cream, vinegar, mustard and garlic. Add seasoning to taste.

Quickly sauté the chicken livers in the remaining oil until well browned outside, but still pink inside. Season them lightly and slice thinly. Add the livers to the salad bowl with the dressing, tomato, celery and leek, and toss together. Check the seasoning and serve immediately.

Vegetable Terrine

The preparation of this terrine is somewhat complicated, but the end result is very satisfying – it looks and tastes delicious. You can use any vegetables in season, but make sure that they are sufficiently tender to slice easily before being layered in the dish and baked. Arrange the colours and flavours to achieve maximum taste and eye appeal.

Because this is a time-consuming dish, it could be suitable as a starter for a large dinner party, or simply as a party dish on its own. Use a container with a capacity of 2 litres.

If it is to be served cold, it can be made a day ahead. It is not suitable for freezing.

Preparation Time: 2 hours
Cooking Time: 1½ hours
Standing Time: 30 minutes
Pre-heat Oven to 180°C

INGREDIENTS FOR TEN
*300 g brinjal, peeled, halved lengthways and sliced across
5 ml (1 teaspoon) salt
125 ml (½ cup) oil
200 g white mushroom caps, wiped
3 large sweet red peppers, wiped
300 g leeks, with green part removed and halved lengthways
250 g green asparagus, trimmed
250 g spinach, well washed and with stalks removed
4 extra-large eggs, beaten
250 ml (1 cup) thick cream
Salt and freshly ground white pepper
Grated nutmeg*

For the sauce:
*125 ml (½ cup) cream, whipped
60 ml (¼ cup) hot leek or chicken stock*
10 ml (2 teaspoons) lemon juice*

For the garnish:
*Lemon slices
Chopped chives or chervil
Chopped hard-boiled eggs**

Vegetable Terrine *A variety of fresh vegetables is combined in a terrine and topped with a hot, creamy sauce.*

Sprinkle the brinjal with salt and leave for an hour so that the bitter liquid drains off. Rinse, pat it dry and fry in oil until soft and golden. Remove from the pan with a slotted spoon and drain on a paper towel. Add a little oil to the pan (if necessary) and stir-fry the mushroom caps for 1 minute. Drain them on a paper towel.

Skin the peppers*, quarter them lengthways, seed and wash and dry them.

Cook the leeks in salted water until tender (about 20 minutes). Drain them in a colander – reserving about 60 ml (¼ cup) liquid for the sauce – and refresh under cold running water. Drain off as much water as you can, pressing the leeks with the flat of a knife, and then press them between layers of paper towels to absorb the extra moisture. Cook the asparagus* for 5-7 minutes, or until tender. Drain, refresh and dry well.

Blanch the spinach in boiling salted water for 1 minute, drain and refresh, and squeeze out as much moisture as you can. Turn on to a clean tea towel and squeeze out any remaining moisture.

Now arrange your terrine. Lay the asparagus neatly on the bottom of a well-greased glass or ceramic loaf pan. Then layer with the brinjal, red peppers, spinach and mushrooms, and end with a layer of leeks. Mix together the eggs and cream, then season to taste with salt, pepper and nutmeg. Pour the egg mixture over the vegetables, allowing it to seep between the layers. Set the loaf pan in a pan of hot water (it should reach halfway up the sides of the terrine) and bake for 1½ hours: it is ready when a knife inserted in the centre comes out clean.

Do not allow the water in the pan to boil; if it seems likely to bubble, add ice cubes to lower the temperature. When done, remove the loaf pan from the water and leave it to stand for 30 minutes before turning out the terrine on to a platter.

Make the sauce by whisking together the whipped cream, hot leek or chicken stock and lemon juice until frothy.

Cut the terrine into slices 1 cm thick. Ladle some of the sauce on to warm plates and top each with a slice of terrine. This shows up the different layers of vegetables most attractively. Garnish with a twisted slice of lemon, chopped chives or chervil and finely chopped hard-boiled egg.

VARIATIONS Turn out the terrine and chill it, lightly covered in plastic wrap, for 4-5 hours. Serve sliced with the sauce (also chilled) and any of the above garnishes.

Although this dish is best when prepared with fresh vegetables, you can cut down the preparation time by using frozen spinach and tinned red peppers.

As the asparagus season is rather short, you could replace the asparagus with extra leeks or tinned asparagus.

~ Finger Food to Fill the Gap ~

Drinks somehow taste better and go further when accompanied by an appetising snack. Choose attractive but substantial little titbits that can be held comfortably. When entertaining, allow 8-10 individual snacks per person.

TINY QUICHE

Quick Bites

Parma Ham and Melon or Fig Wrap thin slices of Parma ham or smoked beef around fingers of ripe melon, or place ham slices on top of halved ripe figs.

Stuffed Celery Sticks Make short, equal-length sticks of celery crisp by placing them in a bowl of iced water. After 30 minutes (or less), pat dry and fill with piped swathes of cream cheese or smooth cottage cheese. Top with lumpfish 'caviar', coarsely chopped salted nuts or slices of radish.

Cream Cheese Bites Pipe a swirl of cream cheese on a triangle of buttered wholewheat* or pumpernickel bread. Top with a smoked oyster or mussel or a strip of tinned pimento.

Egg and Caviar Bites Roughly mash together 3 hard-boiled eggs*, 15 ml (1 tablespoon) finely chopped onion* and 15 ml (1 tablespoon) mayonnaise*. Season with salt and freshly ground black pepper and spread on ovals of sliced buttered pumpernickel bread or Melba toast*. Top with a swirl of piped whipped cream and a sprinkling of lumpfish 'caviar' (red or black).

Snoek Fingers Pound 250 g flaked smoked snoek or a 200 g tin of drained tuna. Add 30 ml (2 tablespoons) mayonnaise* and 30 ml (2 tablespoons) whipped cream or smooth cottage cheese, a good squeeze of lemon juice and plenty of seasoning. Spread on fingers of buttered pumpernickel bread. Dust with a sprinkling of paprika or garnish with diced cucumber.

Smoked Salmon Nibbles Place thin slices of smoked salmon on buttered pumpernickel or wholewheat bread*. Flavour with lemon juice and freshly ground black pepper.

PARMA HAM AND FIG

HAM CRESCENTS

DOLMADES

SMOKED SALMON NIBBLES

CHINESE CHICKEN WINGS

STUFFED EGGS

Tasty Snacks

Fish Croquettes Make a thick white sauce* with 30g butter, 30g flour and 300ml milk. Mix 350g cold cooked, minced or finely chopped white or smoked (or tinned) fish with the white sauce, 30 ml (2 tablespoons) freshly chopped parsley, 15 ml (1 tablespoon) chopped chives, 5 ml (1 teaspoon) lemon juice, and salt and pepper to taste. Chill and divide into 30-40 small balls or cork shapes.

Roll each one in flour, then in beaten egg mixed with 15 ml (1 tablespoon) water. Dip in dry breadcrumbs, patting the crumbs well on to each croquette. Chill for 30 minutes, then deep-fry in hot sunflower oil until golden. Drain on paper towels and serve with tartar sauce*.

Bacon-Wrapped Chicken Livers (or prunes or dried apricots) If you use prunes or dried apricots, plump them overnight in water. Simmer until tender, drain and wrap in thin rashers of streaky bacon. If you use chicken livers, trim off any fatty tissue and wrap bundles of liver in rashers of bacon. Just before serving, grill or bake (at 200°C for 15-20 minutes) until the bacon is crisp. Serve speared on a cocktail stick.

Ham Pinwheels Spread 125g ham*, thinly sliced (about 10 slices), in a single layer on a flat working surface. Mix 200g cream cheese with 5 ml (1 teaspoon) finely chopped gherkin and 15 ml (1 tablespoon) chutney, and season with salt and black pepper. Spread over the ham slices. Roll up each slice, cover and chill for at least 2 hours. To serve, cut into 2 cm thick slices and spear with a cocktail stick.

Cheese Whirls Unroll a 400g packet of puff pastry and cover with thinly sliced rashers of streaky bacon. Top with grated cheese, then re-roll the pastry to its original shape. Freeze or chill until firm. Slice into 1-2 cm thick rings. Arrange them side by side on a baking sheet and grill under a medium-high heat until golden. Turn and grill the second side until golden.

Chinese Chicken Wings Cut the tips from the chicken wings and discard. Cut each wing in half at the joint and arrange the pieces side by side in an oiled baking tin. Brush over them a sauce made from 30 ml (2 tablespoons) sunflower oil, 15 ml (1 tablespoon) Worcestershire sauce, 30 ml (2 tablespoons) fruit chutney, 30 ml (2 tablespoons) soy sauce and 30 ml (2 tablespoons) tomato sauce*.

Grill until golden-brown, turn and brush the other side, and grill again – about 10 minutes on each side, or until tender and crisp. Serve warm.

Anchovy Fingers For 30 pastries, roll out a 500g piece of ready-made puff pastry to a strip 15 cm wide. Cut in half lengthways. Trim the edges and brush one rectangle with beaten egg. Lay drained anchovy fillets on it (crossways) at 3 cm intervals.

Place the second rectangle of pastry on top and press down gently with a fingertip to outline the anchovies. Brush with beaten egg and cut between the fillets to form fingers. Decorate the tops of the fingers with a criss-cross marking made with the back of a knife.

Transfer the pastry fingers to a dampened baking sheet. Chill for 15 minutes, then bake at 220°C for 8-12 minutes, or until puffed and golden. Lift on to a wire cake rack to cool. Eat the fingers the day they are made. Alternatively, the pastries can be frozen, baked or unbaked, for up to 6 months.

Chicken Liver Puffs For 40 pastries, melt 30g butter and fry 1 finely chopped* medium-sized onion until soft. Add 250g chicken livers, trimmed, and sauté until lightly brown outside but still pink inside.

Add 30 ml (2 tablespoons) brandy, a pinch of cayenne pepper and plenty of seasoning, and continue to cook for another minute. Leave to cool, then chop. Roll out 500g ready-made puff pastry to a strip 15 cm wide. Spoon the chicken liver mixture on to one half of pastry, but not too near the edge. Brush the edge of the pastry with beaten egg.

Fold over one side to meet the other, covering the chicken liver mixture. Press the edge and seal. Trim the edges, brush with beaten egg and cut into 2-3 cm long pieces. Bake at 220°C for 8-12 minutes until puffed and golden. Cool on a wire cake rack.

Ham Crescents To make about 50 pastries, roll 500g ready-made puff pastry to a strip about 15 cm wide and trim the edges. Cut in half lengthways, then cut each half into 7-8 cm squares. Cut each square into triangles and put 5 ml (1 teaspoon) finely chopped cooked ham (mixed with a little Worcestershire sauce) in the centre. Roll up the triangles, starting at the long edge. Shape into a crescent and arrange on a dampened baking sheet. Brush with beaten egg and bake at 220°C for 8-12 minutes, or until golden.

Cheese Beignets Crisp little cheesy bites, deep-fried in hot sunflower oil, are made from a choux pastry. Melt 75g butter in 180 ml water with a pinch of salt. Bring to the boil and add 110g sifted flour.

Remove from the heat and beat vigorously with a wooden spoon to make a smooth mixture that forms a ball in the saucepan. Beat for a further 30 seconds, then leave to cool for 10 minutes. Beat in 3-4 beaten eggs, little by little, to make a very shiny paste that just falls from the spoon.

Stir in 100g finely diced Gruyère cheese, a pinch of dry mustard and plenty of seasoning. At this stage the dough can be covered and kept in the refrigerator for up to 6 hours. Just before using, heat a deep pan of sunflower oil to 180°C – a cube of day-old bread dropped into it should turn brown in 1-1¼ minutes – and drop in 1-2 cm balls of choux. Do not fry too many beignets at once, as they will swell.

While you cook, increase the temperature slightly until the beignets puff and become a light golden colour. Cook for about 4-5 minutes, then drain well and keep warm in a moderate oven with the door ajar while frying the remaining dough.

Filled Cases

Hollowed-out vegetables (such as tomatoes or cucumbers), pastry, cocktail rolls or sliced buttered bread pressed into tartlet tins (and baked until crisp) make ideal cases for savoury fillings.

*Stuffed Eggs** One of the simplest snacks is stuffed halved hard-boiled* eggs. See the recipes in the Eggs and Cheese section for suggestions for fillings.

Cucumber Boats Peel the cucumbers and split them lengthways. Scoop out the seeds by running your index finger down the length of each half. Make a filling of cream cheese mixed with cooked shellfish or smoked flaked fish.

Spoon this mixture into the cucumber halves and leave them in the refrigerator for about 1 hour, or until crisp. With a sharp knife, cut the cucumber into 3 cm lengths.

*Dolmades** This traditional Greek and Turkish recipe – also referred to as stuffed vine leaves – makes an excellent cocktail snack. If vine leaves are not available, cabbage leaves may be used.

Tiny Quiches Roll shortcrust pastry* (made from 225g flour) or 450g ready-made puff pastry on a floured surface to a thin (3 mm thick) sheet. Cut 24 rounds to fit 5-6 cm tartlet tins. Press the dough rounds into the tins and add a quiche filling*. Use a double quantity of quiche custard* to fill the tartlets, and garnish with an asparagus tip, a strip of tinned pimento, a slice of black or green olive or a small shrimp. Bake at 220°C until puffy and golden (about 20 minutes).

STUFFED CELERY STICKS

STARTERS, SNACKS AND SAVOURIES

FOLDING SAMOOSAS

Cut the prepared dough into 8 cm-wide strips, each about 25-30 cm long. With the strip hanging over your left hand, bring the bottom left corner across to lie flush with the right side of the strip.

Fold the point of the dough across the strip to lie flush with the left side: you now have a small pocket or 'envelope', in which you place the filling.

Holding the dough in your left hand, bring the long back strip over the top to close the pocket, ensuring that you seal off the two top corners. Bring the dough across the triangle and fold it over the far end.

Trim the edges neatly and seal the samoosa with a mixture of flour and water, taking care that the three corners are completely closed.

SAMOOSAS

ALTHOUGH OFTEN ASSOCIATED with the Cape Malay community, samoosas are actually of Indian origin. These savoury triangles of spiced mince or vegetables in crisp pastry are usually bought ready-made, but can – with patience and practice – be made successfully at home. The pastry can also be bought ready-made, but you may have to ask around, as it is a home industry.

If you are using a food processor to chop the garlic, ginger and chillies, chop the meat and onions at the same time.

PREPARATION TIME: 3 HOURS
COOKING TIME: 10 MINUTES
PRE-HEAT OVEN TO 230°C

INGREDIENTS FOR 24 MEAT OR VEGETARIAN SAMOOSAS

For the dough:
375 g flour
5 ml (1 teaspoon) salt
250 ml (1 cup) cold water
5 ml (1 teaspoon) lemon juice or vinegar
Ghee* or sunflower oil
Sunflower oil for frying

For a meat filling:
500 g mutton, lamb or chicken, minced
2 ml (½ teaspoon) turmeric
5 ml (1 teaspoon) salt
5 ml (1 teaspoon) garlic and ginger paste, or 1 large clove garlic and an equivalent-sized piece of fresh green ginger, pounded together
10 ml (2 teaspoons) well-chopped coriander (dhania) leaves
5 green chillies, well-pounded
2 medium-sized onions, finely chopped*
15 ml (1 tablespoon) ghee* or butter
4 spring onions, finely chopped
2 ml (½ teaspoon) garam masala

For a vegetarian filling:
45 ml (3 tablespoons) sunflower oil
1 large onion, grated
5 medium-sized carrots, cooked and minced
150 g rice, cooked*
1 medium-sized potato, cooked and mashed*
10 ml (2 teaspoons) garam masala
2 ml (½ teaspoon) turmeric
2 ml (½ teaspoon) salt
10 ml (2 teaspoons) garlic and ginger paste, or 2 large cloves garlic and an equivalent-sized piece of fresh green ginger, pounded together
2 small to medium-sized green chillies, pounded together
10 ml (2 teaspoons) well-chopped coriander (dhania) leaves
8 spring onions

To make the dough, sift the flour and salt and add sufficient cold water to make a fairly stiff dough. To make the dough more elastic, add the 5 ml (1 teaspoon) lemon juice or vinegar. Knead the dough gently, then divide it into 12 portions and roll each portion into a ball, using the palm of your hand.

Roll out six of the balls on to a floured board, shaping them into discs with a diameter of 9-10 cm. Brush the tops of the discs with melted ghee or oil and sprinkle with flour as you stack them, leaving the surface of the upper disc ungreased and unfloured.

Roll out the stack of discs with light rolling movements into one large, flat, very thin disc and cut the sides evenly to form a square. Place an ungreased baking tray in the pre-heated oven until it is hot, then remove. Place the dough square on the hot baking tray. Turn the square over lightly several times on the baking tray to loosen the layers. If this is done quickly, no speckles will appear on the dough.

As soon as the layers show signs of loosening (this should occur after 3-4 minutes), remove them from the baking tray. Prepare the remaining six balls in the same way. When the layers have cooled slightly, cut and fold as illustrated.

To make the meat filling, cook the mutton, lamb or chicken in a saucepan with the turmeric, salt, garlic and ginger, coriander leaves and chillies. When the mixture is nearly dry, add the onions and cook until the liquid has evaporated. Stir frequently to prevent the meat from forming lumps. Add the ghee or butter. The final product should be fine and dry (like breadcrumbs). Allow it to cool, then add the spring onion and garam masala.

To make the vegetable filling, heat the oil, add the onion and sauté until it becomes transparent. Mix the carrots, rice and mashed potato together and add them to the onions, then stir and cook until they are crumbly (remove from the heat as soon as it reaches this stage; do not overcook). Add the garam masala, turmeric and salt; cook for a few more minutes, stirring to blend. Remove from the heat and allow the filling to cool, then add the garlic and ginger, chillies, coriander leaves and spring onions. Stir well to mix. It is important that you allow the filling to cool before it is folded into the dough and fried.

Allow 10 ml (2 teaspoons) of either mixture for each samoosa filling. When filled, the samoosas should be left for a while in a cool place before they are fried. Fry the samoosas in hot oil, turning often, until they are a golden colour. Remove from the oil and drain in a colander.

SERVING SUGGESTIONS Chutney and slices of lemon make good accompaniments.

BLINI WITH 'CAVIAR'

BUCKWHEAT PANCAKES, known as blini, have been made in Russia for over a thousand years. In western Russia, during a spring festival called 'Mother-in-Law's Day', it was the custom for every young husband to go to his mother-in-law's house to eat blini.

The inclusion of 'caviar' as an accompaniment makes this a particularly appealing blini dish.

PREPARATION TIME: 25 MINUTES
RISING TIME: 1½ HOURS
COOKING TIME: 20 MINUTES

INGREDIENTS FOR SIX

1 ml (¼ teaspoon) sugar
300 ml warm milk
15 g fresh yeast
225 g buckwheat or wholewheat flour
A pinch of salt
25 g butter, melted
1 egg white, whisked until stiff
2 onions, coarsely chopped*
250 ml (1 cup) sour cream
1 small jar (about 100g) Danish 'caviar'
1 lemon
Sunflower oil for frying

Dissolve the sugar in the warm milk and use 30 ml (2 tablespoons) of the liquid to mix

STARTERS, SNACKS AND SAVOURIES

BLINI WITH 'CAVIAR' *Freshly fried buckwheat pancakes are served with 'caviar', chopped onion, sour cream and lemon.*

the yeast to a smooth, thin paste in a large, warmed mixing bowl. Stir in the remaining milk. Add about two-thirds of the flour and the salt and whisk to make a smooth batter. Cover with plastic wrap and stand in a warm place to rise for 1 hour.

Add the remaining flour and the butter to the batter, and beat well. The mixture should have the consistency of thick cream; if it is too stiff, add a little extra warm milk. Fold the egg white into the batter. Cover and allow to rise again for 30 minutes.

Meanwhile, put the onions in a serving bowl. Spoon the sour cream and 'caviar' into two serving bowls. Wash the lemon, cut it into segments and arrange them in another bowl. Chill until you are ready to serve.

Brush the inside of a large, heavy-based frying pan with oil and heat it until it exudes a slight haze. Cook three blini at a time, allowing a full tablespoon of batter for each. Fry gently for about 2 minutes, until the surface has just dried out and is a mass of small holes, then turn the blini over to brown the other sides for about 2 minutes. Cover the cooked blini with foil and keep warm until you are ready to serve.

When serving, place two or three blinis on each plate and pass around the bowls of onions, cream, 'caviar' and sliced lemon.

VARIATIONS For different flavours, try the blinis with thinly sliced smoked salmon or chopped hard-boiled eggs*.

'CAVIAR' TART

THIS RICH AND COLOURFUL tart features a base of cracker crumbs topped with layers of snoek pâté, avocado and cream cheese topped with Danish 'caviar'. Each layer has a distinctive colour, thus creating a strong visual appeal when the tart is cut.

PREPARATION TIME: 1 HOUR
CHILLING TIME: 1 HOUR

INGREDIENTS FOR EIGHT
100 g cream cracker crumbs
125 g butter, melted
1 ripe avocado
30 ml (2 tablespoons) thick mayonnaise*
15-30 ml (1-2 tablespoons) finely chopped onion*
15 ml (1 tablespoon) lemon juice
Salt and pepper
250 g savoury cottage cheese
30 ml (2 tablespoons) sour cream
400 g smoked snoek pâté*
1 small jar (about 100 g) Danish 'caviar'
2 hard-boiled eggs*

Mix the cracker crumbs with the melted butter and pat into a 23 cm pie dish (choose a deep dish) coated with a non-stick cooking spray, or oiled. Refrigerate while preparing the filling. Mash the avocado and mix with the mayonnaise, onion and lemon juice; season to taste. Mix the cottage cheese with the sour cream to create a good spreading consistency.

Spread a layer of snoek pâté over the bottom of the chilled crust. Cover with the avocado mixture, then the cheese. Top with 'caviar' and garnish with finely chopped egg yolk and egg white.

Chill in the refrigerator, covered with plastic wrap.

'CAVIAR', EGG AND ONION STARTER

STRICTLY SPEAKING, the term 'caviar' should be applied only to the salted roe of the sturgeon, a fresh caviar marketed mainly by Russia and Iran. However, there is a far cheaper substitute – the roe of the Arctic lumpfish – sold as 'Danish caviar'.

This dish consists of an egg, onion and mayonnaise base topped with whipped cream and 'caviar'.

PREPARATION TIME: 20 MINUTES
CHILLING TIME: 1 HOUR

INGREDIENTS FOR SIX
6 hard-boiled eggs*, chopped
1 small onion, very finely chopped*
30 ml (2 tablespoons) thick mayonnaise*
Salt and freshly ground black pepper
125 ml (½ cup) cream, whipped
1 small jar (about 100 g) Danish 'caviar'

Mix the eggs with the onion and mayonnaise. Season lightly with salt and pepper. Pat into a thick layer on a serving plate. Spread with a layer of the whipped cream. Cover loosely with plastic wrap and chill for an hour. Just before serving, spoon over the 'caviar'. Cut into wedges for serving.

SERVING SUGGESTIONS Serve with slices of Melba toast* or triangles of hot toast.

VARIATIONS Instead of the 'caviar', cover with a lattice of split anchovies (first soaked in milk for 10 minutes to remove excess saltiness) and thin strips of marinated or tinned red pepper (pimento).

Cleaning and Serving Oysters

Most of our oysters come from the Knysna area, where strict rules control the collection and marketing of these delicately flavoured shellfish. When serving oysters as an hors d'oeuvre, you should allow six per person.

To open an oyster, hold it firmly in your left hand with the flat side facing up and wrap a tea towel round your hand and most of the shell, leaving the hinge showing. Hold the shell level to avoid losing juice. Insert the point of a short strong knife (or a special oyster knife) in the crack between the upper and lower shells, near the hinge.

Once the knife has penetrated the crack, ease it about until you feel it cut the muscle attaching the oyster to the flat upper shell. Then twist the knife firmly to prise the shell apart. Keep the flat side uppermost. Remove the flat top half of the shell to reveal the oyster and its juice held in the deeper half.

Make a bed of cracked ice on each plate. Arrange the oysters in their deep shells on top, and serve with lemon quarters and brown bread and butter.

Crayfish Cocktail

Although this starter is featured on many restaurant menus, it is all too often a colourful but disastrous waste of money.

The following recipe describes a basic crayfish cocktail with a sauce that will enhance rather than 'kill' the delicate crayfish flavour, and suggests ways in which it could be presented.

Preparation Time: 20 minutes

Ingredients for Six
3 crayfish, boiled*
125 ml (½ cup) mayonnaise*
20 ml (4 teaspoons) tomato sauce*
75 ml sour cream
A dash of Tabasco (chilli sauce)
A dash of Worcestershire sauce
Salt to taste
Small pinch cayenne pepper
A squeeze of lemon juice
Lettuce
Fresh herbs for garnish

Remove each crayfish tail from the body (reserve the bodies in the freezer for use in fish stock). Use a very sharp knife to cut the tail lengthways through the shell. Remove the alimentary canal and discard the shell.

Rinse the flesh under cold running water and pat it dry (it is not necessary to wash away the yellowish substance, as it imparts an appealing flavour to the sauce). Crack the claws and antennae, remove the meat and slice the tails into bite-sized pieces.

Mix together the mayonnaise, tomato sauce, sour cream, Tabasco, Worcestershire sauce, salt, cayenne pepper and lemon juice, then pour over the crayfish and toss gently to coat all the pieces. Shred some lettuce and place it in a cocktail glass, add the crayfish and garnish with fresh herbs.

VARIATIONS For a composed crayfish salad, use six pretty side plates or fish plates and pour a pool of sauce on to each. Arrange the crayfish in the sauce in overlapping circles. Cut carrots, celery and cucumber into matchstick slices and sprinkle them over the crayfish. Chop and sprinkle fresh dill or parsley over the vegetables or decorate with sunflower sprouts*.

This recipe also works well with cooked shelled prawns*, tinned shrimps, cold poached* monkfish and kingklip.

Grilled Black Mussels

Black mussels are plentiful along South Africa's shores, but there are various provincial regulations controlling their collection. You are advised to check with the relevant authorities whether you need a licence, and how many mussels you are allowed to remove at a time.

When collecting mussels, you must ensure that they are alive: if you are in any doubt, discard the suspect mussels. These and other shellfish can be poisoned by a 'red tide', making them dangerous for human consumption, so it is a good idea to contact the relevant authorities before collecting them.

Soaking Time: 2 hours
Preparation Time: 1 hour
Cooking Time: 15 minutes
Pre-Heat Oven to 200°C

Ingredients for Six
60 fresh mussels
250 g butter, softened
1 large clove garlic, crushed
45 ml (3 tablespoons) finely chopped parsley
1 slice white bread, crumbed (optional)

Soak the mussels in a basin of fresh water for one or two hours and scrub the shells thoroughly.

Place the mussels in a 200°C oven for 10 minutes (to open), then remove them, discard the empty half shells and remove the 'beards'. Arrange the mussels in the half shell on a baking tray. Mix the butter, garlic and parsley to form a soft paste and spoon 5 ml (1 teaspoon) on to each mussel. Sprinkle with breadcrumbs (if used) and place them under a grill until golden-brown.

SERVING SUGGESTION Serve with hot crusty French bread.

VARIATIONS Prepare the mussels as described but replace the garlic butter with a different sauce, made up by combining 1 clove crushed garlic, 250 ml (1 cup) mayonnaise* and 5 ml (1 teaspoon) dried thyme or 10 ml (2 teaspoons) fresh thyme, finely chopped.

If fresh mussels are not available, this recipe will work well with tinned mussels: remove from the tin, rinse gently, open the shells and discard the empty halves.

Smoked Salmon Blintzes

Crisply fried and served off the pan with a dollop of sour cream, savoury blintzes make a most delicious starter. You can also bake them in the oven with excellent results when making larger quantities.

Make these savoury blintzes a day ahead of time and refrigerate, or keep in a freezer for weeks. This recipe allows two blintzes per serving.

Preparation Time: 1 hour
Cooking Time: 20 minutes

Ingredients for Six
2 eggs
375 ml (1½ cups) water
125 g flour
A pinch of salt
125 ml (½ cup) sunflower oil
60 g butter
Butter and sunflower oil for frying
250 ml (1 cup) sour cream (smetana)

For the filling:
250 g smoked salmon, finely chopped
250 g smooth cottage cheese
2 ml (½ teaspoon) dried dill or 10 ml (2 teaspoons) fresh dill (optional)
A squeeze of lemon juice
Freshly ground black pepper

Lightly beat the eggs, add the water, and then the flour and salt. Beat well until the mixture is smooth (you could also use a liquidizer). If the mixture is too thick, add a little water very gradually until it has the consistency of thin cream. Strain the batter into a jug: this may be refrigerated for a few hours before making.

Heat a buttered or oiled pan and pour in a thin layer of the batter. The pan must not be too hot as the blintz should set without browning. It is ready when the edges curl. Cook it on one side only and turn it out on to a clean tea towel to cool.

Combine the ingredients for the filling and place a spoonful of the mixture on the cooked side of each blintz. Fold the ends over the filling and roll them up. Fry the blintzes in a mixture of hot butter and oil until they are crisp and golden.

Drain on a paper towel and serve piping hot with dollops of sour cream.

STARTERS, SNACKS AND SAVOURIES

VARIATIONS Try baking the blintzes instead: place them in a buttered oven-proof dish and pour over 250 ml (1 cup) cream. Bake them (uncovered) at 200°C for 20 minutes, or until they are bubbly and browned.

Pour over 250 ml (1 cup) thin cheese sauce* before baking.

Use the cream, but sprinkle with grated Gruyère and Parmesan cheese before baking.

Use a tin of well-drained and boned salmon instead of smoked salmon. Combine the salmon and cheese with a fork rather than a food processor, or the mixture will be too runny.

SMOKED FISH PASTES

THE EXCELLENCE of smoked fish pastes depends primarily upon the quality of fish used, so choose a superior fish wherever possible. Pastes made from kippers, smoked haddock or smoked trout are excellent as a first course (serve with Melba toast*) or as a sandwich filling. Bland fish can often be improved by adding fresh grated horseradish.

PREPARATION TIME: 30 MINUTES
COOKING TIME: 15 MINUTES

INGREDIENTS FOR SIX
*4 kippers, or 2 large smoked
   haddock fillets, or 2 smoked
   trout**
125 g soft butter
Juice of 1 lemon
Freshly ground black pepper
Salt
Clarified butter*

Cook the kippers in water, the smoked haddock in milk and water, until the fish is tender (about 10-15 minutes). The trout need not be cooked further. Remove the skin and bones. Small kipper bones will be well broken up, so it is not necessary to remove these.

Put the fish and butter in a blender with half the lemon juice and pepper and blend until smooth. Check the seasoning and add salt (the trout will need most). Beat in the rest of the lemon juice if needed. Pot the paste, sealing with clarified butter. Do not keep too long before eating – fish pastes taste best when eaten fresh.

SALMON MOUSSE WITH CUCUMBER SAUCE

A FINE PARTY DISH that uses a generous amount of canned salmon for maximum flavour. Canned salmon comes in several grades, the bright red variety usually being the best. The addition of a cucumber sauce to this dish provides an interesting taste and texture. A mousse should be chilled for several hours before serving.

PREPARATION TIME: 40 MINUTES
CHILLING TIME: 4 HOURS

INGREDIENTS FOR SIX
*2 tins red salmon (about 220 g
   each)*
15 ml (1 tablespoon) gelatin
60 ml (¼ cup) cold water
*¼ English cucumber,
   peeled and finely diced*
1 stick celery, diced
30 ml (2 tablespoons) lemon juice
60 ml (¼ cup) mayonnaise*
1 ml (¼ teaspoon) salt
*A few drops of Tabasco (chilli
   sauce)*
60 ml (¼ cup) cream

For the sauce:
*½ English cucumber, peeled
   and finely diced*
*250 ml (1 cup) sour cream or
   natural yoghurt**
1 small onion, finely chopped*
A squeeze of lemon juice
Salt and pepper

Drain the salmon. Discard any skin and large bones and flake the fish. Sprinkle the gelatin over the cold water in a small heat-proof dish, then dissolve it over a saucepan of simmering water, stirring until the liquid is clear. Mix the salmon, cucumber, celery and lemon juice in a food processor or liquidizer until smooth.

Stir in the mayonnaise, salt and Tabasco, strain in the dissolved gelatin and mix well together. Whip the cream and fold it in. Spoon the mousse into 6 small moulds (coated with a non-stick cooking spray) and refrigerate until set.

Mix the ingredients for the sauce (retain a little cucumber for garnishing) in a food processor or liquidizer until smooth. Check the seasoning and chill well.

Turn the 6 moulds out on to a serving platter, loosening the edges with a small spatula. Garnish with the chopped cucumber and serve it with the cucumber sauce.

VARIATIONS Try serving this salmon mousse accompanied by lemon wedges or an avocado sauce*.

Set the mousse in a large mould instead of 6 individual moulds.

SALMON MOUSSE WITH CUCUMBER SAUCE *A rich dish that benefits from the slightly bitter taste of the cucumber sauce.*

Fish Terrine with Sour Cream Sauce

THIS DISH MAKES a very pretty start to a sumptuous dinner. The array of colours in the multi-layered terrine is sure to delight your guests, as will its special combination of flavours.

The recipe calls for sufficient ingredients to make a substantial terrine, so you may choose to serve it as the first course rather than an appetiser.

PREPARATION TIME: 45 MINUTES
COOKING TIME: 1¼ - 1½ HOURS
PRE-HEAT OVEN TO 180°C

INGREDIENTS FOR TWELVE

For the terrine:
500 g kingklip or monkfish, skinned and filleted*
250 g soles, skinned and filleted*
2 eggs
10 ml (2 teaspoons) salt
5 ml (1 teaspoon) white pepper
1 ml (¼ teaspoon) grated nutmeg
90 ml lemon juice
500 ml (2 cups) fresh white breadcrumbs
500 ml-750 ml (2-3 cups) cream
125 g smoked salmon
250 g frozen spinach
Boiling water

For the sauce:
Cooking juices from terrine
250 ml (1 cup) sour cream
125 ml (½ cup) fresh cream
10 ml (2 teaspoons) horseradish
5 ml (1 teaspoon) mild mustard
5 ml (1 teaspoon) lemon juice
Salt and white pepper

FISH TERRINE WITH SOUR CREAM SAUCE *A rich and colourful combination of puréed fresh fish with a savoury cream sauce.*

Line a bread tin or terrine (1,5 litre capacity) with aluminium foil and butter it generously.

Place the kingklip (or monkfish) and sole together in a food processor and blend until smooth, then remove the lid and add the eggs, salt, pepper, nutmeg, lemon juice, breadcrumbs and 500 ml (2 cups) of the cream.

Mix these ingredients until they are thoroughly blended, then test for the right consistency: peaks should just hold their shape. If the mixture is too firm, add more cream until you achieve the correct consistency. Taste for seasoning and assemble.

Process about 45 ml (3 tablespoons) of the mixture with the smoked salmon until smooth, adding more cream if the mixture becomes too stiff and dry.

Process another 45 ml (3 tablespoons) of the mixture with the spinach until it is well blended, then divide the remaining white fish mixture into three equal portions. Arrange the terrine in layers: first, a white layer of the mousse mixture, then green, white, pink, and finally another white layer. Use a wet spoon to smooth down layers and achieve an even spread.

Butter a piece of wax paper and place it, buttered side down, on top of the terrine. Cover the terrine with aluminium foil and place it in an oven-proof dish. Pour in enough boiling water to come half-way up the baking dish. Bake at 180°C for 1¼ -1½ hours, depending on the shape of the tin: if it is long and narrow, it will take the shorter time, but if it is short and deep, it can take up to 1½ hours. When it is almost ready, the mousse will start rising.

Remove the terrine from the oven, pour off and retain the juices, and turn it out on to a serving dish. It will keep in the oven for up to 10 minutes while you mix the sauce ingredients (keep it covered with the bread tin or terrine). It may be cooked the day before serving and re-heated in a *bain marie**. Serve the terrine with the sour cream sauce, the latter made by combining the ingredients in a bowl and mixing well.

VARIATIONS Instead of spinach, use sorrel or watercress, or both, and add finely chopped watercress to the sour cream sauce.

To serve cold, remove the dish from the water. Pour off the juices and allow the terrine to cool. Cover it with plastic wrap and place it in the refrigerator. The terrine will keep for two or three days. Terrine to be served cold should be slightly over-seasoned, as it becomes less strong on cooling.

STARTERS, SNACKS AND SAVOURIES

POTTED SHRIMPS

THE TRADITIONAL MENU for an English 'shrimp tea' includes potted shrimps, thin slices of brown or white bread, spread with butter and accompanied by a large plate of watercress.

Shrimps, heated in butter and spices, then sealed in small pots with clarified butter and served with traditional accompaniments, make a delicious starter.

PREPARATION TIME: 20 MINUTES

INGREDIENTS FOR FOUR
450 g frozen cooked and shelled shrimps (or small prawns)
125 g butter
1 ml (¼ teaspoon) ground mace
1 ml (¼ teaspoon) cayenne pepper
Salt and freshly ground black pepper
Clarified butter*

Defrost the shrimps and pat quite dry. Melt the butter over a moderate heat. Add the shrimps, mace and cayenne pepper. Season with salt and pepper. Heat through but do not allow the shrimps to boil, as this toughens them. Stir while heating them.

Put into small pots, seal with clarified butter, and leave them to chill in the refrigerator.

SMOKED SNOEK PÂTÉ

THIS PÂTÉ, made simply by blending smoked snoek with cream, butter, lemon juice and spices, is probably the best-loved starter of its kind in South Africa, and is featured on many restaurant menus. Pre-packaged smoked snoek is available at most supermarkets and delicatessens long after the snoek fishing season has ended. Snoek pâté freezes very well. Divide the pâté into smaller quantities before freezing. Thaw in the refrigerator before serving.

PREPARATION TIME: 20 MINUTES
CHILLING TIME: 20 MINUTES

INGREDIENTS FOR SIX
250 g smoked snoek, boned and flaked
60 ml (¼ cup) thick cream
60 g soft butter
15 ml (1 tablespoon) lemon juice
Salt and freshly ground black pepper

Pound the ingredients together (or blend in a food processor) to form a smooth paste. Add a grinding of black pepper (you may not need to add salt). Check the seasoning and adjust if necessary. Pack into small individual dishes and chill the pâté until ready to serve.

SERVING SUGGESTIONS If you wish, garnish with fresh herbs and lemon slices. Serve with home-baked wholewheat bread*, hot brown toast or thin crackers.

VARIATIONS Use tinned (drained) tuna or salmon instead of snoek and add a little finely chopped onion*.

Pack it into scooped-out lemons for an unusual presentation.

Substitute savoury cottage cheese for the cream and butter.

CHOPPED HERRING

CHOPPED HERRING (gehackte herring) is usually associated with traditional Jewish cooking, and at most Jewish parties or functions the menu would not be considered complete without this dish.

Salt herring was a staple food of the Ashkenazi Jews of Poland and Russia, from where the dish's popularity spread throughout the world.

SOAKING TIME: OVERNIGHT
PREPARATION TIME: 35 MINUTES

INGREDIENTS FOR SIX
2 salt herring, cleaned and heads removed
5 hard-boiled eggs*
1 medium-sized onion, finely grated
2 green apples, peeled and cored
10 Marie biscuits
75 g sugar (or to taste)
80 ml white vinegar (or a few drops tartaric acid)
A dash of pepper
A dash of cinnamon
Fresh parsley for garnish

Soak the herring overnight in cold water, changing the water once. Remove the herring skins and as many of the bones as possible, dry the fish well and mince them into a large mixing bowl with three of the eggs, onion, apples and biscuits. Slowly add the sugar and vinegar, tasting the mixture to achieve the flavour you desire (some people like it sweeter than others). Season with pepper and cinnamon and spoon it on to a flat serving platter. Grate the remaining eggs and use them to decorate the dish. Garnish with fresh parsley.

SERVING SUGGESTION Serve as an hors d'oeuvre with crackers or the traditional Jewish kichel (a thin, crisp biscuit).

VARIATIONS Try leaving out the onion: you will find that the mixture is much firmer.

You can substitute day-old kitke for the Marie biscuits.

For a somewhat cheaper dish (herring have become a fairly expensive delicacy), mince 1 large tin (about 400 g) of middle cut with 4 hard-boiled eggs, 4 small apples, 1 onion, 6 Marie biscuits (soaked in vinegar) and a pinch of pepper and serve in the same way as chopped herring.

TARAMASALATA

TARAMASALATA, A FISH ROE PÂTÉ, is a popular Greek appetiser. Tarama, the main ingredient, is smoked fish roe (typically obtained from grey mullet or cod). It is bright orange and salty, and should be beaten with the other ingredients until pale pink, and light and creamy in texture.

PREPARATION TIME: 15 MINUTES
CHILLING TIME: 1 HOUR

INGREDIENTS FOR SIX
75 g smoked cod roe
4 thick slices white bread, crusts removed
80 ml (⅓ cup) milk
1 clove garlic, crushed
150 ml olive oil
60 ml (¼ cup) lemon juice
Freshly ground black pepper

Beat the tarama in a food processor or blender, or with an electric beater, until it is smooth. Soak the bread in the milk for a few minutes and add to the smoked cod roe with the garlic. Beat well together, then beat in the oil, alternating with the lemon juice, a little at a time. Add a grinding or two of black pepper. If the mixture is still salty, beat in a little milk. Chill the taramasalata until ready to serve.

SERVING SUGGESTIONS This dish may be accompanied by quarters of pitta bread* or hot toast.

VARIATION Instead of using the white bread and milk, mix the tarama with 100 g cream cheese and 60 ml (¼ cup) thick cream and use this mixture as a dip for crisp raw vegetables.

SERVING SMOKED SALMON

Many people consider smoked salmon to be the prince of smoked fish and some believe the only salmon worth eating are those caught in Scottish waters, while others maintain those found in Norwegian waters are best. Whatever the origin, avoid any salmon with a darker than normal orange or red colour, as this usually indicates over-cured or dyed fish.

Use a very long, flexible knife to cut the salmon (it must be very sharp, with a serrated edge), and cut across the grain, working from the shoulder towards the tail. The slices should be as thin as possible.

Serve it generously, with finely cut slices of brown bread and butter. If you wish, season it with sprinklings of lemon juice and freshly ground black pepper. For a colourful presentation, try serving rolled-up salmon with red lettuce leaves and twists of lemon.

Use the trimmings, pounded finely, as a filling for omelettes, little pastry cases and vol-au-vent.

A most luxurious notion, thought to have originated in eastern Europe, is to serve smoked salmon with bagels* and a covering of cream cheese.

~ MAKING THE MOST OF DIPS ~

Dips are quick to make and can be enjoyed as a casual snack with drinks (or as the first course), leaving the hostess free to serve only the main course and dessert at the table. They also make very good party fare, as they can be made beforehand and refrigerated.

AVOCADO DIP

PREPARATION TIME: 15 MINUTES

INGREDIENTS FOR SIX TO EIGHT
1 large ripe avocado
60 ml (¼ cup) smooth cottage cheese
30 ml (2 tablespoons) thick mayonnaise*
15 ml (1 tablespoon) sour cream (smetena) or natural yoghurt*
15 ml (1 tablespoon) lemon juice
Salt and freshly ground black pepper

Scoop out the flesh of the avocado. Mash it with the rest of the ingredients adding salt and pepper to taste. Mix the ingredients together until they are smooth and creamy.
Spread a layer of sour cream over the surface of the dip to prevent discolouring.

CHICK-PEA DIP

PREPARATION TIME: 15 MINUTES

INGREDIENTS FOR SIX
1 tin hummus (about 320 g)
15 ml (1 tablespoon) lemon juice
30 ml (2 tablespoons) natural yoghurt*
1 clove garlic, crushed
Salt and freshly ground black pepper
Paprika
Finely chopped parsley

Mix the hummus (another name for a prepared chick-pea dip) with the lemon juice, yoghurt and garlic. Add seasoning to taste and more lemon juice if it is needed. Turn the mixture into a small bowl and sprinkle it with paprika and parsley. Refrigerate the dip until it is to be served.

CREAM CHEESE DIP

PREPARATION TIME: 15 MINUTES

INGREDIENTS FOR SIX
250 g cream (or cottage) cheese
30 ml (2 tablespoons) thick mayonnaise*
30 ml (2 tablespoons) sour cream (smetena)
15 ml (1 tablespoon) chopped parsley
15 ml (1 tablespoon) snipped chives
1 clove garlic, crushed
Salt and freshly ground black pepper
30 ml (2 tablespoons) chopped toasted cashew nuts
15 ml (1 tablespoon) toasted sesame seeds

Mix the ingredients, except for the nuts and seeds. Check the seasoning and pack the mixture into a dish just large enough to hold the dip. Sprinkle the nuts and seeds over the dip and press them in gently. Refrigerate the dip until it is to be served.

LIPTAUER CHEESE DIP

PREPARATION TIME: 15 MINUTES

INGREDIENTS FOR SIX
250 g smooth cottage cheese
1 ml (¼ teaspoon) paprika
2 ml (½ teaspoon) caraway seeds
2 ml (½ teaspoon) dry mustard
2 ml (½ teaspoon) chopped capers
2 ml (½ teaspoon) snipped chives
15 ml (1 tablespoon) natural yoghurt*
10 ml (2 teaspoons) beer (optional)
Salt and freshly ground black pepper

Mix the ingredients very well together, adding seasoning to taste. Chill the mixture in the refrigerator until ready to serve.

BRINJAL DIP

PREPARATION TIME: 15 MINUTES
COOKING TIME: 30 MINUTES
PRE-HEAT OVEN TO 200°C

INGREDIENTS FOR SIX
2 medium-sized brinjals
15 ml (1 tablespoon) lemon juice
15 ml (1 tablespoon) natural yoghurt*
2 ml (½ teaspoon) dried origanum
1 clove garlic, crushed
30 ml (2 tablespoons) olive oil
Salt and freshly ground black pepper

Bake the brinjals on an oiled baking sheet for 30 minutes or until very soft. Leave until cool enough to handle, then halve them and scoop out the flesh. Mash (or use plastic blade of food processor) this flesh with the lemon juice, yoghurt, origanum and garlic. Gradually blend in the oil. Add seasoning to taste and beat until smooth and creamy. Refrigerate until required for serving.

CHICK-PEA　　　AVOCADO

YOGHURT AND CUCUMBER DIP

PREPARATION TIME: 15 MINUTES
STANDING TIME: 1 HOUR

INGREDIENTS FOR SIX
250 ml (1 cup) natural yoghurt*
125 ml (½ cup) chopped English cucumber
Salt
1 clove garlic, crushed
15 ml (1 tablespoon) olive oil
15 ml (1 tablespoon) lemon juice
Salt and freshly ground black pepper

Turn the yoghurt into a colander and allow the whey to drain off to ensure that the yoghurt will be really thick. Turn the cucumber into another colander or a strainer and salt it, then weight it down and leave it to drain. After about an hour mix these ingredients together, adding the garlic, oil and lemon juice. Season the dip to taste and chill it until it is required for serving.

TUNA DIP

PREPARATION TIME: 15 MINUTES

INGREDIENTS FOR EIGHT
1 tin (200 g) tuna
250 g smooth savoury cottage cheese
30 ml (2 tablespoons) thick cream
15 ml (1 tablespoon) thick mayonnaise*
15 ml (1 tablespoon) lemon juice
15 ml (1 tablespoon) finely chopped onion*
A dash of Tabasco (chilli sauce)
Salt and freshly ground black pepper

Drain and flake the tuna. Mix it quickly with the remaining ingredients until it is smooth and creamy, using the plastic blade of a food processor to prevent over-mixing. Check the seasoning and refrigerate it until it is needed for serving.

SMOKED SNOEK

SMOKED SNOEK DIP

PREPARATION TIME: 20 MINUTES

INGREDIENTS FOR SIX
250 g smoked snoek
1 clove garlic, crushed
1 thick slice wholewheat bread*
60 ml (¼ cup) natural yoghurt*
30 ml (2 tablespoons) lemon juice
60 ml (¼ cup) sunflower oil
Salt and freshly ground black pepper

Skin the snoek and remove the bones. Flake the fish and place it in the bowl of a food processor or blender with the garlic. Remove the crusts from the bread, crumble it into the yoghurt and mash them together.
    Add this mixture to the snoek and blend them together. Add the lemon juice, then gradually add the oil. Beat all these ingredients well together. Add pepper to taste, and salt only if it is needed. Refrigerate the dip until it is required for serving.

SMOKED OYSTER DIP

PREPARATION TIME: 10 MINUTES

INGREDIENTS FOR SIX
1 tin smoked oysters
250 g smooth cottage cheese
15 ml (1 tablespoon) lemon juice
30 ml (2 tablespoons) thick cream
A dash of Tabasco (chilli sauce)
Salt and freshly ground black pepper

Drain the oysters very well, then chop them fairly finely. Mix them by hand with the rest of the ingredients, adding salt and black pepper to taste. Refrigerate until required for serving.

IDEAS FOR DIPPING

A large variety of foods in different forms is suitable for dipping in the accompanying dishes, ranging from raw vegetables to crackers and bread. If you are using raw vegetables, first soak them in iced water in the refrigerator to make them really crisp. Fresh asparagus spears, florets of broccoli and cauliflower should be blanched* before use.

SUITABLE RAW VEGETABLES INCLUDE:
Whole baby carrots (or sticks of carrot)
Sticks of table celery
Strips of cucumber
Strips of red, yellow or green peppers
Small radishes (whole)
Baby mushrooms
Tufted baby tomatoes
Wedges of fennel
Strips of baby marrow
Young spring onions

OTHER IDEAS FOR DIPPING:
Large crisps
'Corn' crisps
Prawn crackers
Melba toast* (made from French loaf)
Fingers of wholewheat or rye toast
Wedges of pitta bread*
Crisp crackers

CREAM CHEESE

TUNA

STARTERS, SNACKS AND SAVOURIES

HERRING ROLLMOPS

Rollmops, or pickled herring, can be bought in jars, but preparing them at home has an advantage in that you can vary the pickling spices to suit the family's taste.

This very good appetiser is particularly popular in eastern Europe, Germany and Holland, where fresh herring are salted and preserved in barrels. They need to be soaked to remove excess saltiness.

SOAKING TIME: 48 HOURS
PREPARATION TIME: 45 MINUTES
PICKLING TIME: 3-4 DAYS

INGREDIENTS FOR SIX

6 salt herring, filleted
A few milk roes
100 g sugar
500 ml (2 cups) white vinegar
3 onions, thinly sliced*
36 peppercorns
24 allspice
8 bay leaves

Soak the herring and milk roes together for 48 hours, changing the water occasionally. Cream the roes with the sugar, stir in the vinegar and strain into a jug.

Place the herring fillets skin-side down, scatter some onion rings over the fillets and roll them up, securing the rolls with toothpicks.

Pack the herring in a glass jar, layering them with onion rings, peppercorns, allspice and bay leaves. Pour over the vinegar mixture (to cover) and refrigerate for a few days before serving.

SERVING SUGGESTION Serve the rollmops with the onion rings and a little of the marinade from the jar, garnishing with pickled cucumbers. Pass around slices of rye bread* and butter.

VARIATION Pickle the flat herring fillets. Drain them well and place on a shallow dish. Slice a fresh onion* and green apple very thinly and arrange the slices over each fillet. Pour over cream (fresh or soured) and chill, well covered, for an hour or more.

CHICKEN LIVER PÂTÉ WITH PORT

A HOME-MADE PÂTÉ, butter-smooth and well-matured, is one of the most delicious and successful ways of starting a meal. It is also one of the simplest dishes that one can make.

This pâté should preferably be refrigerated for two or three days before it is eaten. As long as it is protected from the air, it will keep in the refrigerator for several weeks. Fill several small pots rather than one large pot, as the pâté keeps best if well sealed. A pot of pâté makes a welcome gift, is good on hot toast with morning tea, and – if served with pickles, mustard and puffy crisp rolls – also makes an appetising lunch.

PREPARATION TIME: 1 HOUR
COOKING TIME: 20 MINUTES
CHILLING TIME: 12 HOURS

INGREDIENTS FOR SIX

500 g chicken livers
250 g soft butter
½ medium-sized onion, peeled* and grated
30 ml (2 tablespoons) brandy
30 ml (2 tablespoons) port
1 clove garlic, peeled and crushed
5 ml (1 teaspoon) dry mustard
3 ml (¾ teaspoon) dried thyme
1 ml (¼ teaspoon) mace (or nutmeg)
Salt
Clarified butter*

Clean the livers very carefully, paring off any greenish parts, which may impart a bitter flavour to the pâté. Melt 50 g of the butter in a frying pan and sauté the grated onion until soft, then remove it from the pan and put it to one side.

Add a little more butter if necessary and then sauté the livers, whole, for about 5 minutes (they should be cooked on the outside but still pink in the centre). Remove the livers from the pan and pour in the brandy.

Heat the brandy until it bubbles, then add the port, garlic, mustard, thyme and mace, and cook for a minute.

Put the livers, onion, pan sauces and remaining butter into a food processor or blender and blend to a smooth paste, then add salt to taste.

CHICKEN LIVER PÂTÉ *A delicately flavoured pâté that makes a wonderful snack.*

Spoon the mixture into small pots and top with clarified butter to seal: the butter should be 3-5 mm thick. Cover the pots with foil and chill the pâté thoroughly before eating.

You can freeze this pâté for about six weeks, but the texture may coarsen during this time.

SERVING SUGGESTIONS Serve the pâté very cold with hot toast or warm, sliced French bread (this is a rich pâté, and no butter is necessary).

Otherwise, spread it thickly on toast and pop it under a hot grill until the pâté bubbles. Serve immediately, topped with a spoon of thick sour cream.

VARIATION If you do not have a food processor or blender, you can use a baby-food mouli or alternatively pound the various ingredients in a mortar.

CHOPPED LIVER

IT IS WIDELY BELIEVED that Jewish poultry farmers in Strasbourg were the first to produce the famous pâté de foie gras.

This traditional Jewish dish of finely minced chicken livers, though less ambitious, is nevertheless tasty and very popular: it frequently starts the formal Friday night Sabbath meal, the left-overs ending up more casually on a rye bread* sandwich the following day.

PREPARATION TIME: 20 MINUTES
COOKING TIME: 15 MINUTES
CHILLING TIME: 1 HOUR

INGREDIENTS FOR SIX
500 g chicken livers
2 medium onions, thinly sliced*
45-60 ml (3-4 tablespoons) chicken fat (or a vegetable substitute)
Salt and white pepper
4 hard-boiled eggs*
Cinnamon

First trim the livers and pat them dry. Fry one and a half onions in about 45 ml (3 tablespoons) heated chicken fat until lightly browned. Add the chicken livers and fry them until nicely browned. If there appears to be too much liquid, reduce it by increasing the heat, then season with salt and pepper.

Mince the chicken livers (or process them very carefully) with the remaining raw onion and two of the hard-boiled eggs. Check the seasoning and add a little cinnamon to taste. Mash the mixture together with a fork and, if necessary, add a little more chicken fat to bind it.

Turn the liver on to a serving platter and press it down with a fork to make a shallow layer. Decorate it with the remaining hard-boiled eggs, separating the yolks and whites and chopping them very finely. Chill before serving.

SERVING SUGGESTIONS Add a border of thinly sliced pickled cucumbers and half-slices of tomato. Serve with slices of Jewish challah bread, a plaited egg-enriched white loaf, or with rye bread*.

VARIATION Calf liver may be used instead of chicken liver. This is more often grilled than fried, in which case you will need more fat to bind the mixture.

VENISON PÂTÉ

FOR MANY SOUTH AFRICANS, making a venison pâté is merely a sensible thing to do with the left-over meat. It is often more of a spread or paste than a true pâté. However, by using raw meat and applying a little effort, the home cook can create a real pâté which offers a variety of subtle flavours, and is certain to win compliments.

PREPARATION TIME: 1 HOUR
COOKING TIME: 1 HOUR
CHILLING TIME: OVERNIGHT

INGREDIENTS FOR EIGHT
1 kg boneless venison
150 g bacon
1 bay leaf
3 juniper berries (optional)
2 cloves
2 whole allspice
4 onions, finely chopped*
3 leeks, finely chopped
5 young carrots, sliced
25 ml lard
Salt and freshly ground black pepper
1,5 litres (6 cups) basic stock*, heated
50 g mushrooms
50 g butter
50 g flour
125 ml (½ cup) sour cream (smetena)
30 ml (2 tablespoons) quince jelly*
45 ml (3 tablespoons) sweet dessert wine
Clarified butter*

Cut the meat into cubes. Chop the bacon finely. Tie the bay leaf, juniper berries (if used), cloves and allspice together in muslin cloth and crush them. Place the bacon, onions and leeks in a saucepan and fry over a medium heat until the onions are transparent, then add the sliced carrots and fry for another 2-3 minutes.

Remove the mixture and put on one side. Add the lard to the same saucepan and fry the meat, a few pieces at a time, until it is well browned.

Return the bacon and vegetable mixture and all of the meat to the saucepan and season to taste. Add the stock and spices, bring to the boil, then reduce the heat and simmer for 45-60 minutes without covering the saucepan. Pour off 1 litre (4 cups) of the stock (this may be retained for making soup or sauce) and remove the crushed spices.

Fry the mushrooms in the butter, season to taste, add the flour and fry for 1 minute. Add the mushrooms to the meat and simmer until the sauce is very thick.

Remove the saucepan from the heat and stir in the sour cream, jelly and wine. Check the seasoning.

Liquidize the mixture and pour it into a terrine. Spoon the clarified butter over the pâté. Place the terrine in the refrigerator until set.

SERVING SUGGESTIONS Serve with toasted wholewheat bread, or with French bread.

VARIATIONS Replace the sour cream with crème fraîche* and spoon the mixture into a shortcrust pastry* case. Cover with a lattice of pastry and bake it as a tart. Serve it with pickles and a salad of lettuce, cucumber and green pepper.

If using left-over cooked meat, liquidize the meat with cream and wine. For a more textured pâté, layer the terrine with strips of pre-cooked venison. Line the terrine with slices of cold tongue or cooked spinach before adding the meat.

ANTIPASTOS – AN ITALIAN TREAT

These Italian favourites should be arranged on giant eye-catching platters if you plan to entertain a crowd, or on attractive plates for individual servings. Serve with chunks of crusty bread to mop up the tasty marinades.

To make a cold marinade, mix together 160 ml olive oil, 80 ml (⅓ cup) wine vinegar, 1 large clove crushed garlic, 5 ml (1 teaspoon) origanum, salt and freshly ground black pepper to taste.

Pour the marinade over thinly sliced raw mushrooms, wedges of tomato, onion rings, quarters of fennel, julienne strips* of baby marrow, cooked butter beans, calamari rings (simmered in lightly salted water until opaque), chunks of tuna, ripe black olives, tinned artichoke hearts, anchovies and slices of skinned red, yellow and green peppers*.

To make a hot marinade, simmer (for 5 minutes) 125 ml (½ cup) sunflower or olive oil, with 125 ml (½ cup) wine vinegar, 1 or 2 cloves crushed garlic, a few sprigs of parsley, 1 bay leaf, 5 ml (1 teaspoon) origanum, 12 coriander seeds (optional), 4 peppercorns and 2 ml (½ teaspoon) salt.

Pour the marinade over the following hot, lightly cooked vegetables: whole green beans, thick slices of baby marrow, strips or rounds of carrot, small whole mushrooms, florets of cauliflower and broccoli, cubes or slices of brinjal and quarters of freshly boiled artichokes. Leave the vegetables in the marinade for 2-3 days before serving.

Other good antipastos include paper-thin slices of Parma ham wrapped around wedges of melon or peeled ripe figs, thinly sliced mortadella, and slices of salami.

STARTERS, SNACKS AND SAVOURIES

TERRINE OF DUCK WITH ORANGE

THIS IS A RATHER special dish, suitable for an important occasion – hence the generous proportions specified in the ingredients. Although the recipe appears long and complicated, it is really very simple. Skinning and boning the duck is quite easy. It is important that the breast is neatly removed and sliced, but for the rest it does not matter how the flesh is removed from the carcass, as it will be minced anyway.

A proper lidded terrine makes cooking easier, but any attractive, fairly deep oval or loaf-shaped oven-proof dish will do. Make an aspic jelly with the duck carcass (lightly flavoured with orange and sherry) or use a jellied stock made with chicken stock cubes, and flavoured the same way.

PREPARATION TIME: 1½ HOURS
MARINATING TIME: OVERNIGHT
COOKING TIME: 1½ HOURS
CHILLING TIME: 3 DAYS
PRE-HEAT OVEN TO 190°C

INGREDIENTS FOR EIGHT
1 medium-sized duck
   (not too fat, about 2 kg)
60 ml (¼ cup) brandy
60 ml (¼ cup) medium sherry
30 ml (2 tablespoons) dry
   vermouth
80 ml (⅓ cup) fresh
   orange juice
1 small onion, finely chopped*
3 ml (¾ teaspoon) dried thyme
3 ml (¾ teaspoon) dried sweet
   basil
3 ml (¾ teaspoon) dried sage
15 ml (1 tablespoon) chopped
   parsley
2 bay leaves, crumbled
5 ml (1 teaspoon) grated rind of
   orange
125 g liver (use the duck liver and
   make up the weight with
   chicken livers)
125 g lean veal
250 g unsalted back bacon
1 large egg, beaten
Salt and freshly ground black
   pepper

For the garnish:
Orange, sliced thinly
250 ml (1 cup) aspic*

TERRINE OF DUCK WITH ORANGE *The duck breast is marinated in sherry, brandy and orange before being set in the terrine.*

Skin and fillet the duck, removing any excess fat. Cut the breast into long, thin strips about 1cm wide. Marinate the breast strips overnight in the brandy, sherry, vermouth, orange juice, onion, herbs and orange rind. Mince together the rest of the duck meat, liver, veal and the lean of the bacon (keep the fat to line the terrine).

The next day, stir the liquid in which the breasts were marinated into the mince mixture, and mince again. Add the beaten egg, mix well and season with salt and pepper. A good way to test the seasoning is to fry a little mince, then taste and correct.

Line the terrine with half the bacon fat, press in half of the mince mixture and top it with neatly arranged duck slices. Cover these with another layer of mince and top with the remaining strips of bacon fat.

Cover the terrine with the lid (if you are not using a lidded terrine, cover with a double layer of foil, neatly tucked around the dish). Place the terrine in a pan of hot water (it should reach halfway up the sides of the terrine).

Bake at 190°C for 1½ hours, remove it from the oven and take off the lid. Place a weighted plate on the terrine to compress it and leave it to cool. It can be frozen (for 6-8 weeks) before the bacon fat has been removed and the aspic added.

When cold, remove the meat from the dish, carefully remove the bacon fat and replace the meat in the clean dish. Garnish it with thin overlapping slices of orange, and pour over aspic jelly. Cover with foil and leave the terrine to set and mature in the refrigerator for three days.

SERVING SUGGESTIONS Serve the sliced terrine as a starter, garnished with fresh sweet basil or parsley, or as part of a cold buffet.

VARIATION The terrine can also be made with chicken, which gives a lighter, less rich dish that is almost as delicious.

STARTERS, SNACKS AND SAVOURIES

SHAPING SAUSAGE ROLLS

Roll the pastry to a thickness of 3 mm, keeping it in the shape of a neat rectangle. Place a roll of sausage meat 3 cm from the top end of the dough, then brush a 1 cm wide strip of water or beaten egg directly under the meat.

Grip the top end of the pastry and fold it over the sausage. Press down firmly on the dampened portion to seal the edges and cut along the edge through the bottom layer.

Brush the top of this long roll with a little beaten egg (to provide a glaze) and then cut it up into 2,5 cm long rolls. Decorate them by making two diagonal slashes across each sausage roll.

SAUSAGE ROLLS

POPULAR AS PARTY snacks and even as meals in themselves, sausage rolls have long been a favourite food for South Africans. They are very easy to make when pre-prepared pastry is used, but this homemade version, that makes use of sour cream flaky pastry and a spicy sausage meat filling, will yield noticeably superior results.

PREPARATION TIME: 1¼ HOURS
COOKING TIME: 30 MINUTES
PRE-HEAT OVEN TO 220°C

INGREDIENTS FOR 20 SAUSAGE ROLLS
For the filling:
250 g beef, minced
250 g pork, minced
5 ml (1 teaspoon) salt
A pinch of ground cloves
A pinch of ground coriander
A pinch of grated nutmeg
A pinch of freshly ground black pepper
10 ml (2 teaspoons) vinegar
Sour cream flaky pastry* using 250 g flour

Lightly mix the ingredients for the filling, then roll into 1,5 cm-diameter sausage shapes. Roll these sausage shapes in a little flour and leave in the refrigerator to firm while you are preparing the sour cream flaky pastry.

Roll out the flaky pastry and shape the sausage rolls as illustrated in the panel alongside, place them on a lightly greased baking sheet (allow 1 cm space between the rolls) and then bake in the pre-heated oven for 30 minutes.

VARIATIONS For the filling, you can use raw home-made or bought sausages such as beef, pork or boerewors. However, Viennas and Russian sausages are also equally successful. You must skin the sausages before use.

Slice Vienna sausages lengthways, spread with mild mustard and sandwich a thin strip of cheese into the sausage.

Alternatively you can roll a slice of lean streaky bacon over the sausage meat of your choice.

You could also add some interesting flavours by rolling the pork sausages in chopped sage, or the beef sausages in chopped thyme.

CAMEMBERT EN CROÛTE

CAMEMBERT, an internationally popular soft cheese created by a French farmer's wife in the late 1700s, lends itself to combination with a large variety of ingredients. This recipe is for Camembert in a pastry shell, served hot.

PREPARATION TIME: 1 HOUR
FREEZING TIME: 1-2 HOURS
CHILLING TIME: 2 HOURS
COOKING TIME: 20 MINUTES
STANDING TIME: 30 MINUTES
PRE-HEAT OVEN TO 220°C

INGREDIENTS FOR FOUR
A 125 g Camembert cheese
120 g flour, sifted
A pinch of salt
60 g smooth cottage cheese
60 g butter
1 egg yolk, beaten

Place the Camembert cheese in the freezer for an hour or two before you make the pastry. Sift the flour and salt together, then add the cottage cheese and butter, and rub lightly together until the mixture resembles coarse crumbs. Knead the mixture very slightly, form the dough into a ball, and refrigerate (covered) for 1 hour.

Roll out the dough (not too thinly) on a lightly floured board. Cut out a circle large enough to enclose the base and sides of the cheese. Place the cheese in the centre of the circle and bring the pastry up around the side and 2 cm over the top of the cheese. Cut a circle of dough to fit the top of the cheese, moisten the edges with egg yolk and press to make a seal. Decorate the top of the cheese with leaf and rose shapes* cut from the remaining pastry. Refrigerate for about an hour, then brush with the remaining egg yolk and bake at 220°C for 20 minutes or until golden. Allow the baked Camembert to stand in the warming drawer for at least 30 minutes before serving.

SERVING SUGGESTIONS Serve on a platter with a radish and spring onion or garnish it with a sprig of parsley.

Prepare crunchy raw vegetables (celery sticks, young carrots, mushrooms, cauliflower florets, radishes and spring onions) for dipping into the melted cheese.

VARIATIONS Place frozen Camembert cheese on five layers of phyllo pastry*, first brushing each layer of pastry with melted butter. Fold the edges of the pastry up around the cheese, then cover the top with six sheets of pastry, once again brushing each sheet with melted butter. Tuck the ends of the pastry under the cheese, and freeze for 10 minutes or longer before baking. Brush all over with more melted butter and bake.

CAMEMBERT EN CROÛTE *Crisp pastry wrapped around ripe Camembert.*

Soups

Soups provide subtle taste sensations that few other foods can match. They can be consumed hot or cold, thin or thick, and lend themselves to combination with a huge variety of dishes.

Home-made soups are far preferable to the tinned or dehydrated variety, which have no comparable flavour or texture. If you are seeking optimum quality, use a good home-made stock rather than a commercial stock cube.

Iced soups are perfect for entertaining on a hot summer's night. They should be *really* cold, so you are advised to chill the bowls as well as the tureen. Garnish a chilled soup with parsley or other chopped herbs and add a swirl of cream.

Thick soups make more substantial dishes, and are often served as meals in themselves. They are generally cooked more slowly than other soups, and are simmered for longer to soften cheaper cuts of meat and blend the flavours of the vegetables – usually root vegetables.

The classic soups such as vichyssoise, Scotch broth or minestrone need not conform exactly to the original. Try varying the ingredients; experiment with cream, lemon juice and extra vegetables, and alter the texture of the soup by using a sieve or blender.

For an impressive presentation, serve your guests a rich pumpkin soup in the pumpkin shell. For an exotic treat, make a Chinese won-ton soup, or an ice-cold gazpacho. Offer your family a nourishing split-pea soup flavoured with bacon, onion and a little Worcestershire sauce, or a different variation with the fresh tang of mint. The possibilities are endless, and the results thoroughly rewarding.

ADVICE ON BASIC STOCKS AND SOUPS · *PAGE 36*

SOUPS RECIPES · *PAGE 40*

Advice on Basic Stocks and Soups

Stocks

Whatever soup you are making, it will taste better if its base is a home-made stock. Stock is the liquid in which meat and vegetables have been cooked, and which has taken in their flavour. Sauces and gravies are also improved when made with good stock.

Making your own stock is simple and straightforward: you can use scraps of meat, bones, poultry carcasses, vegetable trimmings and left-overs that might otherwise be thrown away.

Cooking Equipment

Most stock needs long simmering to produce the best flavour. Make it in a large, heavy-based saucepan with a well-fitting lid. A pressure cooker will reduce the amount of time and fuel needed to make the stock, while a slow-cooking pot will reduce the amount of electricity used.

Main Types of Stock

Choose the stock that best suits the dish you are making. Many ingredients will give your stock flavour, but its greatest nutritional value comes from gelatin. The best source of this is bones: there is eight times as much gelatin in bone as in meat. To extract the most goodness, break up the bones to expose as much of their surface to the liquid as possible. You can either break them yourself with a hammer, or ask a butcher to do it for you. Simmer the bones until they are pitted with small holes. They will give an even better flavour if they are roasted before being simmered.

Household stock

For use as an economical all-round base in family soups and dishes. Use cooked and uncooked scraps of meat, bones and poultry carcasses, giblets, meat juices, gravy and pieces of fresh vegetables or clean peelings.

Chicken and other poultry stock

For use in soups and casseroles. Use a raw or cooked carcass, the trimmings, giblets and feet. Cover the feet with boiling water for 5 minutes, and skin before use.

For making small amounts of stock you can use the giblets from the bird, barely covered with water and flavoured with onion and seasonings. Simmer for 1 hour.

Chinese chicken stock

This distinctively flavoured stock is used in a variety of Chinese soups and other dishes.

Preparation Time: 15 minutes
Cooking Time: 2¼ hours

Ingredients to Yield 2 litres
1 chicken
3 litres cold water
2 or 3 slices fresh green ginger
6 spring onions, sliced

Place the well-washed chicken in a large pot. Add the water and quickly bring to the boil on high heat. Remove any scum, then reduce the heat, add the ginger and spring onions and allow to simmer (covered) for at least 2 hours. Strain and reserve the chicken meat for another use.

If you prefer, concentrate the stock by boiling to reduce it by half – allow the stock to cool before refrigerating. Remove any fat and impurities before using.

Fish stock

For use in fish soups and sauces. Use fish heads, skins and trimmings, or cheap white fish. Do not use oily fish.

Preparation Time: 15 minutes
Cooking Time: 40 minutes

Ingredients to Yield 1,5 litres
1 kg fish heads, bones and trimmings
1 onion, peeled and sliced*
1 carrot, sliced
1 stick celery or a few stalks soup celery, chopped
Bouquet garni*
1,5 litres water
125 ml (½ cup) dry white wine (optional)
5 ml (1 teaspoon) salt

Rinse the fish bits and pieces very well before placing in a saucepan with the vegetables, herbs, water and wine. Add the salt. Bring gently to the boil.

Remove the scum as it rises. When there is no scum left, half-cover the saucepan and simmer for about 30 minutes. Strain and allow to cool before refrigerating or freezing.

Clear stock

For use as a clear soup. Use only fresh uncooked meat and vegetables. Simmer the meat (such as shin of beef or chicken) for 3 hours before adding the vegetables. It is essential to make this stock in advance so that every particle of fat can be removed when it has set.

Brown stock

For use in brown meat or vegetable soups, and in casseroles and sauces. Use the same ingredients as you would for a basic, household or vegetable stock, but fry the solid ingredients lightly in a little butter or dripping* until golden-brown before adding to the liquid. Heat the fat before starting the frying, so that the surface of the meat or vegetables is sealed as soon as it touches the pan, and does not absorb too much fat.

White stock

For use as the basis of a white cream soup, or in chicken, rabbit and veal dishes. Also use it in galantines and other dishes that require jellied stock. Use the knuckle and feet of veal (first plunge into boiling water for 2-3 minutes to ensure thorough cleansing) and, if possible, some meat from a chicken.

A basic stock

You can vary the first ingredient in the following recipe to suit what you have available, and the dish you are making. Keep the proportions of roughly 500 g solid ingredients to 2 litres liquid. This will make about 1 litre stock. For a larger amount, increase all the ingredients in proportion.

Preparation Time: 15 minutes
Cooking Time: 5¼ hours

Ingredients to Yield 1 litre
500 g bones and meat (beef, poultry and so on)
2 litres cold water
5 ml (1 teaspoon) salt
2 large carrots, well scrubbed and cut into large pieces
1 large onion, peeled* and halved
2 sticks table celery, well washed, or a bunch of soup celery

If you wish to intensify the flavour and colour, roast the bones before use. Cut the meat into large cubes. Place the meat and bones in a large, heavy-based saucepan with water and salt. Bring slowly to the boil and remove any white scum that forms on the surface. Cover with a well-fitting lid and simmer gently for 3 hours. Add the carrots, onion and celery, cover again and simmer for another 2 hours.

Strain through a sieve, taste, and if the stock lacks flavour, boil it rapidly to reduce its volume and concentrate its flavour. Pour into a bowl, and allow to get quite cold. Remove any fat from the surface with a slotted spoon. Cover the bowl and store in a refrigerator. Use the stock within 1 week, or freeze it.

Vegetable stock

To make this simple vegetable stock, use well-washed stalks and vegetable peelings which you would normally throw away. Avoid cabbage and cauliflower leaves and stalks, as these impart a very strong flavour when boiled. Store vegetable trimmings and off cuts in a plastic bag in the refrigerator until you have a good bagful (1 kg or more). The stock provides a good base for delicious soups and sauces. Store it in convenient-sized quantities in the freezer.

PREPARATION TIME: 20 MINUTES
COOKING TIME: 1 HOUR

2 medium-sized onions, cut in half but not peeled
2 medium-sized carrots, scrubbed and cut in half lengthways
2 sticks table celery, broken into short lengths (and a few celery leaves), or a bunch of soup celery
10 ml (2 teaspoons) salt
10 ml (2 teaspoons) black peppercorns
Large bouquet garni* which includes 2 bay leaves
30 ml (2 tablespoons) soy sauce

Vegetable trimmings such as:
Tips of green beans and baby marrows
Pea pods
Spinach and parsley stems
Carrot ends (especially green tops)
Trimmed ends of leeks
Brussels sprout trimmings
Turnip, swede or parsnip trimmings
Potato and butternut peelings

Place the onions, carrots, celery and vegetable trimmings in a large saucepan and cover generously with water. Add the salt, peppercorns, bouquet garni and soy sauce, cover and simmer for 45 minutes. Cool and strain: the stock is now ready for use, or for freezing.

COOKING STOCK IN A PRESSURE COOKER

Place the stock ingredients, with lightly salted water, in the pressure cooker (it must not be more than two-thirds full). Bring to the boil and remove the scum from the surface before fixing the lid.

Lower the heat and bring to a pressure of 80 kPa. Reduce the heat quickly and cook steadily for 35 minutes. Strain the stock and remove the fat.

STORING STOCK

Most stocks can be kept covered in a refrigerator for up to 1 week. Cooks with a freezer can prepare any kind of stock in bulk and divide it into suitable quantities for freezing. Stock loses flavour if stored in a freezer for more than 2-3 months. A fish stock should not be frozen for longer than 2 months. If your freezer space is limited, reduce stocks by half prior to freezing. However they are kept, stocks must be brought to the boil again before they are used.

REMOVING THE FAT

If you intend to cook and use the stock on the same day, try to make it a few hours in advance to give it time to cool and so that any fat that has risen to the top can solidify: it is then easy to lift off the layer of fat. If speed is essential and there is no time for the fat to harden, let the stock stand for a few minutes so that the fat rises to the surface, then draw paper towels across the surface to absorb the fat.

Essential Points in Stock-Making

1. All ingredients must be clean and sound.
2. Use a heavy-based saucepan with a well-fitting lid.
3. Cook bones and meat for 2-3 hours before adding vegetables. Once the vegetables are cooked they will start absorbing the flavour from the liquid, so do not leave them in the liquid for too long either during or after cooking.
4. Do not cook fish stock for more than 45 minutes.
5. Use a balanced mixture of vegetables so that none predominates.
6. Cook vegetables in large pieces.
7. Do not use too many green vegetables, or the stock will have a bitter taste.
8. Use herbs and spices in very small amounts. If you add too much, the stock is almost certain to taste bitter.
9. Starchy ingredients, such as potato or thickened gravy, will make the stock cloudy and can give it a sour taste, so do not use too many of them.
10. The liquid in which bacon or salt beef has been cooked is not suitable for stock, as it is much too salty.
11. Remove any white scum that rises during cooking, but do not remove brown scum; this is nourishing protein that has set in the hot liquid.
12. As soon as the stock is cooked, strain it into a clean china or plastic bowl. Leave it to cool and remove the fat before covering and storing in a refrigerator or freezer.
13. Never keep stock standing in a saucepan. It will develop a sour flavour and stain the saucepan.

MEAT GLAZE

Any brown meat stock can be made into a delicious glaze for cold meats. Measure out 300 ml stock from which all fat has been removed. Pour it into a saucepan and boil it briskly (uncovered). From time to time, skim off any scum that has formed. Let the stock boil until it has greatly reduced in volume.

Watch it carefully, and stir continuously at this stage, as it can quickly burn. When the glaze is as thick as treacle, take it off the heat and let it cool before spooning it over cold meat or poultry. If it is not intended for immediate use, pour it into separate small containers, cover, and store in a refrigerator for up to 1 week.

ASPIC

This is a jelly used for coating and holding a garnish in position, and is also used (chopped) to garnish a cold dish. You can make the jelly from a reduced clear stock, produced from ingredients rich in natural gelatin to ensure that it will set firmly. Should it not set, add some commercial gelatin.

The stock should be perfectly clarified. To add interest, pour in a little white wine or sherry, and add 15 ml (1 tablespoon) vinegar or lemon juice to add the right degree of sharpness. For coating purposes, allow the jelly to set to the consistency of unbeaten egg white, then place the item to be coated on a wire rack over a plate or tray. Spoon over the jelly until it is covered with an even layer. Leave until set, and repeat if necessary. Decorate by dipping pieces of garnish – tarragon, carrot or olives – in a little cool but liquid aspic before setting it in position with the point of a skewer. When it has set, glaze with more aspic. For chopped aspic, turn the jelly on to a piece of wet grease-proof paper and chop it up roughly (or into cubes) with a wet knife.

STOCK CUBES

If you need stock quickly and have none prepared, stock cubes make a convenient standby – but they give a slightly synthetic flavour and leave a persistent aftertaste (neither of these problems occur with home-made stock).

Meat or yeast extract and stock cubes are useful for strengthening the flavour of a home-made stock that you have not had time to reduce and concentrate by boiling. The extracts and stock cubes are among several additions you can make to a finished soup at the last minute if it lacks flavour.

SOUPS

Choose your soup to complement the rest of the meal. A hearty soup is welcome before a light main course, but not before a substantial casserole. Do not serve a fish soup before a main fish dish, or a tomato soup before a dish flavoured with tomatoes. Soups are usually classed as thin or thick.

THIN SOUPS

Among the variety of thin soups are some which are absolutely clear liquids: such a soup is now usually called a consommé. Chicken and beef are the ingredients most used. A clear soup should have a clean, sparkling quality, and should be free of fat. Its clean, pure flavour and lightness make it an excellent beginning to a rich or heavy meal.

The Japanese are particularly fond of thin, clear soups, served with the most delicate garnishes. Try a light fish stock with a single butterflied prawn and a few shavings of lemon rind for decoration.

To cook the prawn for the garnish, first remove the head and shell the prawn*, leaving the last tail section intact. Now butterfly the prawn by running a sharp knife down the middle (without cutting right through the flesh) and opening it out. Salt the prawn, dip it lightly in cornflour, then drop it into rapidly boiling water until just cooked. Dip into iced water and pat dry before adding the prawn to the soup.

Thin soups are not always clear. Even a consommé sometimes has a few spoons of cooked peas or carrot added to it. Others are broths in which the liquid is unthickened, but has pieces of vegetable or meat in it. Cock-a-leekie is this kind of soup, as is borsch, a filling soup based on beetroot, and onion soup – a thin, rich broth full of simmered onions. If you find this kind of soup is not thin enough when cooked, add clear stock or a little wine.

THICK SOUPS

There is a larger variety of thick soups than thin. Their satisfying and substantial nature gives them a broad appeal. Typical white soups include Jerusalem artichoke soup and creamy cauliflower soup. Oxtail soup is a typical brown soup.

Thickened broths, such as brisket and barley soup and Scotch broth, have pieces of vegetable and meat in a liquid thickened with flour or a grain such as pearl barley. Thick vegetable soups include those based on fresh vegetables, such as pumpkin soup, and those based on dried pulse vegetables, such as split pea soup.

Most thick soups need a thickening or binding agent; without it the solid ingredients would sink to the bottom.

The thickener is known as a liaison, from the French verb *lier* which means 'to bind'. Liaisons include:
Some form of starch, such as flour, cornflour, arrowroot, sago, pearl barley, semolina, oatmeal or potato.
Fat and flour in equal quantities heated gently together and mixed to a very thick, smooth paste called a roux.
Egg yolks mixed with cream, a little stock, or milk.

Cream, which is usually added to smooth, rich or white soups.

If flour or cornflour is the liaison, mix it first to a smooth, thin cream with a little of the soup liquid, or a little milk or water. Then stir it into the soup in the pan and continue to stir while cooking gently for at least 5 minutes.

A liaison of egg yolks should be added to the soup just before serving. Beat the yolks well in a cup or small basin, and stir in several spoons of liquid from the soup. Remove the soup from the heat while you stir in the egg mixture.

Return the soup to the heat to make sure that it is heated through for serving; stir it continuously and take great care not to let the soup boil again, or it will curdle.

Cold soups are popular during the hot summer months in South Africa. Usually they are made from raw ingredients, a case in point being gazpacho which is made from raw cucumbers, peppers, garlic and onions and tomato juice.

In addition to the many specific cold soups, many hot soups can quite successfully be served cold, though sometimes small modifications in preparation may be required. For example, when serving a cold purée it is often a good idea to add cream: this serves to enrich the purée and also helps to dilute it.

Fatty soups should not be served cold, however, since the fat congeals when the liquid cools.

Texture

Aim for an even texture in thick soups other than broths, but take care not to make the soup too smooth. An electric liquidizer will certainly save time in preparing the soup, but gives a rather bland, emulsified result. Rubbing through a sieve or passing through a food mill produces a more interesting, slightly grainy texture in the soup. If using a food processor, strain the soup, then process the vegetables to form a thick purée. Mix with the reserved liquid until smooth.

When you make a fish soup, do not overcook it, or the delicate texture of the fish will be spoiled.

Colour

Onion concentrate will enrich the colour and taste of a brown soup or broth. Meat glaze and tomato paste (used sparingly) also add colour. A pallid or muddy colour in a vegetable soup will not stimulate the appetite. Do not spoil green vegetables by overcooking them. If a green summer soup looks too pale, add a few drops of vegetable colouring.

Flavour

An appetising taste and aroma are a soup's most important features. The best guarantee of these is to start with a well-flavoured stock, but if your finished soup is a little short of flavour you can add some reduced stock or meat glaze, small amounts of herbs or spices, a relish such as tomato paste, or use concentrated onion.

Peel and slice an onion*, dust it with some flour and then fry it in a little butter until it is well browned. Rub it through a sieve and add it to the soup, a little at a time, until the flavour is correct.

Some soups benefit from the addition of soy sauce (either during the cooking time or swirled into each serving) or of a little sherry or other liquor. Experiment by removing a small amount of the soup from the pot and adding the flavouring to that, rather than ruin the entire pot with an ingredient that you find does not work.

Pistou can be served as a flavour-enhancing accompaniment to chunky, hot vegetable soup. Pound 4 fat cloves of garlic with 60 ml (¼ cup) basil leaves, 60 ml (¼ cup) tomato paste and 60 ml (¼ cup) grated Parmesan cheese to a paste. Gradually add 60-125 ml (¼ - ½ cup) olive oil. Add a spoonful or two to each serving at the table.

The flavour of fish soup can be enhanced by adding a spoonful of aïoli* to each serving. Or you can make a paste by pounding together ¼ tinned pimento or a cooked red pepper with a red chilli, 4 fat cloves of garlic (crushed) and a cooked potato. Once it forms a smooth, thick paste, gradually add 60 ml (¼ cup) olive oil and seasoning. Just before serving, thin the mixture down with a few spoonfuls of the hot fish soup. Add a spoonful or two to each serving at the table.

If you over-salt a soup by mistake, cook a peeled potato in it until tender (not broken), then lift it out: it will have absorbed much of the salt. If you make a soup which you wish to freeze, do not season it. Salt and pepper increase in strength when frozen, so instead add them when you re-heat the soup.

SERVING SOUPS

Serve a hot soup piping hot, because as it cools it loses flavour, and any fat in it floats to the top. Pour the soup into heated bowls for serving.

A cold soup, such as gazpacho, must be served really cold to achieve a refreshing effect. Chill the soup thoroughly in a refrigerator before serving, pour it into well-chilled bowls, and in hot weather add one or two ice-cubes before serving.

More seasoning is usually needed in a cold soup, as cold foods tend to have less flavour than hot foods. Add a little lemon juice to sharpen the taste.

Try a tablespoon of cream swirled on each serving and sprinkle with a pinch of cayenne pepper or paprika.

SOUP GARNISHES

Garnishes are added to soups either as an embellishment to improve the flavour or to provide a contrasting texture.

There is virtually no end to the type of ingredient one can use for garnishing. Some are integral to the recipe, but it is mostly a matter of personal taste.

Consommé julienne, for example, is garnished with julienne* strips of carrot, celery, leek and turnip. These strips are boiled until soft in lightly salted water, then rinsed in cold water and added to hot consommé just before serving.

Vegetable and fruit garnishes

Vegetable and fruit garnishes add colour to plain cream soups. Celery leaves, watercress and parsley should be trimmed and washed before floating them on top of the soup.

Cucumber may be cut into julienne* strips as a garnish for chilled soups. For hot soups, sauté cucumber strips or thin rounds of leeks in a little butter.

Thin slices of lemon or orange make an attractive garnish for clear soups and tomato soup.

A garnish of thinly sliced mushrooms lends additional texture and flavour to cream soups. Fry the sliced mushrooms in a little butter until soft, but not coloured. Drain thoroughly before spooning them over the soup.

Thin onion rings add more flavour to soups. They can be sautéed like cucumber strips and leek rounds; alternatively, coat them in milk and flour, and deep fry them until crisp and golden.

Add texture to a clear, home-made consommé by shredding lettuce or spinach and simmering in the soup for barely a minute to soften the vegetable slightly. Serve immediately.

Egg garnishes

Consommé royale is a garnish of firm savoury egg custard cut into tiny fancy shapes. Beat an egg with 15 ml (1 tablespoon) cleared stock and pour into a small bowl or dariole moulds. Bake the moulds in a pan of water for 20 minutes (or until firm), in the centre of a pre-heated oven at 180°C.

Another egg garnish for a clear consommé can be made as follows: beat an egg and pour it into a lightly oiled omelette pan. Cook until lightly browned, turn and lightly brown the other side. Roll the omelette up loosely and cut it into thin ribbons. Scatter them over the soup just before serving.

For a threadlike egg garnish in consommé, beat 1 or 2 eggs and pour into the boiling soup through a strainer. The egg threads will float when they are cooked. Do not overcook after the egg has been added.

Noodle garnishes

Pasta is used to garnish many thin soups. Macaroni, tagliatelle and spaghetti can be broken into short pieces and added to purée soups for the last 20 minutes of cooking. For hot consommés, cook the pasta separately so that the starch will not cloud the soup.

A traditional 'snysel' (noodle) soup is made by preparing dough with white flour and water and cutting it into long, thin strips before adding it to the soup.

Bread and cheese garnishes and accompaniments

Cheese makes a pleasant accompaniment to most vegetable soups. Choose a well-flavoured cheese, and serve it, grated, in a separate dish.

Bread croûtons are a classic garnish with thick soups. Remove the crusts from 1 cm thick slices of white bread; cut into 1 cm cubes and toast or fry in a little butter until crisp and golden. Serve in a separate dish or sprinkled over the soup.

Cheese toasts not only make a good garnish for a vegetable soup; they also turn it into an adequate meal in itself. Slice a French loaf and brush both sides of the slices with melted butter. Slowly toast the slices under the grill until golden. Sprinkle them with grated cheese and float the toasts on the soup. They can also be returned to the grill for a few minutes until the cheese melts.

For a fish soup, try hard-toasted French bread: slice a French loaf and bake the slices in a single layer at 160°C for 20-30 minutes until pale golden and dried out. You can drizzle the slices with olive oil half-way through the baking time. After baking, rub the slices with cut cloves of garlic.

For consommé, you could cut a few pancakes into thin shreds and add them to the simmering soup for a few minutes until they are heated through. If you like, add some chopped fresh herbs to the pancake batter.

Try fried pastry rounds as a garnish. Beat 2 eggs with 15 ml (1 tablespoon) water. Add 30 ml (2 tablespoons) sunflower oil. Sift 125 g flour with 2 ml (½ teaspoon) salt and 5 ml (1 teaspoon) baking powder. Mix the dry ingredients into the beaten egg mixture to form a soft dough. (Use more or less flour to achieve the right consistency.) Roll out the dough thinly and cut out tiny rounds. Deep-fry them in hot oil until golden. Drain very well and serve with hot soup.

Herb bread* makes a good accompaniment to many soups. Choose a herb that complements the flavour of the soup without overshadowing it.

Melba toast is made by toasting thin slices of white bread, splitting them through the middle, and toasting the uncooked surfaces under a hot grill. Alternatively, cut stale bread into thin slices, place them on a baking tray and dry them in the bottom of the oven until crisp and curling at the edges.

Dumplings

Dumplings are ideal for turning a meat or vegetable soup into a substantial family meal. 'Kluitjie' or dumpling soup is a traditional favourite among many South African families.

Mix 100 g self-raising flour with 50 g shredded suet and a sprinkling of salt and pepper. Bind the mixture with sufficient cold water to make a soft dough. Shape the dough into 16 balls and drop them into the simmering soup for the last 15-20 minutes of cooking.

For another simple dumpling soup, cream a little butter, beat in 1 or 2 eggs and add nutmeg, salt and a small quantity of breadcrumbs. Next, add just enough flour to bind the dough, which should have the consistency of pancake batter. Place the dumplings in the soup with a teaspoon (suitable for bean or pea soup).

The variety of dumplings is almost endless. Apart from the ones described here, there is a wider choice in the section on savoury sauces, stuffings and dumplings.

Liver dumplings

In Bavaria, West Germany, where the variety of dumplings exceeds even that of sausages, liver dumplings are, according to 19th century guidebooks, 'eaten at every opportunity'.

If you are feeling adventurous, this recipe is ideal for giving body to a soup.

PREPARATION TIME: 25 MINUTES
COOKING TIME: 10-15 MINUTES

INGREDIENTS FOR FOUR

225 g calf or chicken liver, minced
75 g fresh white breadcrumbs
275-300 ml chicken* or vegetable stock*
½ small onion, peeled* and grated
1 egg, beaten
Salt
Freshly ground black pepper

Pass the liver through the fine blade of a mincer twice. Place in a large bowl. Put the breadcrumbs into a small pan, add the stock and soak for 10 minutes.

Put the pan over a gentle heat and with a wooden spoon, or a pestle, pound the breadcrumbs and stock to a fine paste. Add more stock only if the mixture is too dry.

Remove from the heat and add the paste to the liver with the onion and beaten egg. Season well with salt and pepper and blend together.

Roll into small balls, about 4 cm in diameter.

Put the liver dumplings into a chicken or vegetable broth or a consommé for about the last 10 minutes of its cooking, keeping the pan covered.

The dumplings can be made very quickly and easily in a liquidizer. Use only 150 ml stock, or the dumplings may not hold.

Matzo dumplings

This Jewish speciality is associated with the Passover Seder or meal. Matzo dumplings, known as knaidlach, are served in chicken soup at the start of this festive meal.

PREPARATION TIME: 10 MINUTES
STANDING TIME: 3 HOURS
COOKING TIME: 20 MINUTES

INGREDIENTS TO YIELD 20
(4 CM DIAMETER) BALLS

3 eggs, separated
250 ml (1 cup) chicken stock*, cooled
45 ml (3 tablespoons) chicken fat (or a vegetable substitute)
Salt and white pepper
250 ml (1 cup) matzo meal

Whip the egg whites until stiff, then add the egg yolks and beat until thoroughly blended. Add the stock, chicken fat, salt and pepper. Stir in the matzo meal to make a soft mixture (it will stiffen as it stands).

Leave the mixture in the refrigerator for a few hours, or preferably overnight. Shape the mixture (using wet hands) into small balls and drop into boiling salted water. Cook for 20 minutes (covered) or until the dumplings are puffed and cooked through.

Avgolemono

AVGOLEMONO HAS played a vital role in Greek cuisine for centuries, possibly since lemons were brought from Byzantium 1 000 years ago. This dish, named after the Greek words for 'egg' and 'lemon', is eaten not only as a soup, but also as a flavouring for other soups and as a sauce for vegetable dishes.

PREPARATION TIME: 20 MINUTES
COOKING TIME: 25 MINUTES

INGREDIENTS FOR SIX

50 g rice
Juice of 1 lemon
3 eggs, beaten
1,5 litres hot chicken stock*
50 g cooked chicken meat, finely chopped
Salt and white pepper
30 ml (2 tablespoons) finely chopped parsley for garnish

Cook the rice in boiling, salted water for 10-15 minutes and drain well.

Meanwhile, add the lemon juice to the beaten egg and mix well. Add 150 ml of the hot stock, a little at a time, beating well with a wire whisk after each addition.

Bring the remaining stock to the boil, remove from the heat and mix in the cooked chicken and rice. Season lightly with salt and pepper. Whisk in the egg mixture and return to a low heat. Stir continuously without boiling for about 5 minutes, or until the soup is heated through and has a rich creamy texture. Adjust the seasoning and serve garnished with parsley.

Pea Soup with Mint

FRESH GARDEN PEAS make an exquisite soup. In hard times, even their pods have been used – they give a thinner, less well-flavoured dish, but still very palatable. This soup is a rich green velvet, thickened with cream and egg yolks and flavoured with fresh mint.

PREPARATION TIME: 20 MINUTES
COOKING TIME: 35 MINUTES

INGREDIENTS FOR SIX

50 g butter
1 small onion, peeled and finely chopped*
700 g shelled fresh peas
1 litre vegetable stock*
Salt and white pepper
1 ml (¼ teaspoon) castor sugar
2 sprigs of mint
2 egg yolks
150 ml cream

For the garnish:
125 g shelled and boiled young peas
15 ml (1 tablespoon) finely chopped mint

Heat the butter in a heavy-based medium saucepan, put in the onion and cook it over a low heat for 10-15 minutes, or until soft and transparent. Add the peas and continue to cook over a low heat until the butter has been absorbed.

Stir in the stock, season with salt and pepper, and add the sugar and sprigs of mint. Bring to the boil, cover and simmer gently for about 10 minutes, or until the peas are tender. Pass the soup through a fine sieve or food mill and return the purée to a clean pan.

Beat the egg yolks with the cream until smooth, and add to the soup. Heat through, stirring all the time until the soup has thickened. Do not let it boil, or the soup will curdle. Check the seasoning. Serve garnished with the peas and mint.

AVGOLEMONO *This traditional Greek soup is flavoured with egg and lemon.*

Scotch Broth

DR SAMUEL JOHNSON, the acerbic 18th century writer and critic, was introduced to this soup while travelling in Scotland. Asked whether he had tried the dish before, Johnson replied: 'No, sir; but I don't care how soon I eat it again.'

Like all good country soups, this can be made with whatever is in season. A little meat, barley and vegetables are the only essentials.

SOAKING TIME: OVERNIGHT
PREPARATION TIME: 20 MINUTES
COOKING TIME: 3½-4 HOURS

INGREDIENTS FOR SIX

1 kg scrag-end of lamb or mutton, with all excess fat trimmed off
5 litres water
125 g pearl barley
125 g dried peas, soaked in water overnight
Bouquet garni*
Salt and freshly ground black pepper
1 large leek, washed and sliced
1 medium onion, peeled and finely chopped*
1 small turnip, peeled and diced
2 large carrots, peeled and diced
100-125 g cabbage, shredded
15 ml (1 tablespoon) finely chopped parsley for garnish

Place the meat in a large, heavy-based saucepan and add the water, barley, drained soaked peas and bouquet garni. Season with salt and freshly ground black pepper.

Bring the pan slowly to the boil, skim any white scum from the surface, cover and simmer for 2 hours.

Add the leek, onion, turnip and carrots to the soup, and continue to simmer for 1 hour, occasionally skimming off any fat that rises to the surface.

Remove the meat from the soup with a slotted spoon and leave it to stand until it is cool enough to handle. Strip all of the meat from the bones and cut it into small pieces.

Return the meat to the soup and add the cabbage. Adjust the seasoning and continue to simmer for another 30 minutes. Garnish each serving with a sprinkling of parsley.

SOUPS

BRISKET AND BARLEY SOUP

Suitable for a cold winter night or a hearty Sunday lunch, this popular and easily prepared soup needs little time for preparation. You must, however, allow it to simmer for a long time to allow the flavours to mingle.

Preparation Time: 20 minutes
Cooking Time: 3 hours

INGREDIENTS FOR EIGHT
500 g lean brisket on the bone, cut into small pieces
2,5 litres water
6 carrots, sliced
1 onion, chopped*
125 ml (½ cup) chopped celery
3 potatoes, peeled and quartered
250 g pearl barley
15 ml (1 tablespoon) salt
2 ml (½ teaspoon) white pepper
2 beef stock cubes

Put the water in a large pot and place the brisket in it. Bring it to the boil, then remove the scum. Add the carrots, onion, celery, potatoes, barley, salt and pepper. Reduce the heat, cover with a lid and simmer gently for about 3 hours. Stir in the stock cubes and taste for seasoning.

SERVING SUGGESTION Serve with thick slices of rye bread* and butter.

BRISKET AND BARLEY SOUP *Slow simmering enhances its wholesome flavour.*

WON TON SOUP

This popular Chinese recipe combines a thin but tasty chicken soup with traditional Chinese won tons (wrappers) that are filled with minced pork and chopped spinach.

Preparation Time: 45 minutes
Standing Time: 30 minutes
Cooking Time: 20 minutes

INGREDIENTS FOR FOUR
For the won ton wrappers:
200 g flour
2 ml (½ teaspoon) salt
1 egg
45 ml (3 tablespoons) water

For the filling:
200 g lean pork, finely minced
175 g cooked, well-drained, finely chopped spinach
A small piece of fresh green ginger, finely chopped
5 ml (1 teaspoon) soy sauce
2 ml (½ teaspoon) salt

For the soup:
1 litre Chinese chicken stock*
5 ml (1 teaspoon) soy sauce
5 ml (1 teaspoon) salt
A pinch of pepper
Watercress or spinach leaves, finely chopped for garnish

To make the won ton dough, sift the flour and salt into a bowl. Beat the egg with the cold water, then pour the mixture into the centre of the flour and knead well together to form a smooth, stiff dough.

If necessary, add a little more flour or water to get the right consistency. Cover the dough with a damp cloth and leave for 30 minutes.

Prepare the wrappers in the manner described on the right and fill them with a mixture of the minced pork, finely chopped spinach, ginger, soy sauce and salt, all well pounded together.

Drop the prepared won tons into a large saucepan of boiling water. Reduce the heat slightly and cook uncovered for 10 minutes, or until tender. Drain and re-heat them in the chicken stock, which has been brought to the boil. Season with the soy sauce, salt and pepper, sprinkle with the leaves, and serve.

HOW TO MAKE WON TONS

Divide the dough into four and place on a lightly floured board. Then roll out the pieces, one at a time, into rectangles about 20 cm x 30 cm.

Dust each sheet of dough lightly with flour. Cut the rectangles to make six 10 cm square wrappers. Otherwise, use a pasta machine to roll out the dough.

Place 5 ml (1 teaspoon) of the filling in the centre of each individual square of dough. Bring the diagonally opposite corners together, and seal the parcels by pinching the top edges firmly together (moisten the edges of necessary).

Fold the other two corners together and seal. Keep the prepared won tons covered with a dry tea towel.

CHILLED CARROT VICHYSSOISE WITH MINT

THIS SOUP IS A delicious variation on a well-loved theme. It has a lovely colour and a light and delightful flavour, and is perfect for a summer lunch or as a starter before fish or poultry. It improves by being made ahead of time, and is equally good served hot.

PREPARATION TIME: 1 HOUR
CHILLING TIME: 4 HOURS

INGREDIENTS FOR SIX
1 medium onion, chopped*
2-3 leeks, well washed and chopped (include 5 cm of the green tops)
25 g butter
2 large potatoes, peeled and cut into small dice
4 carrots, scraped and sliced
50 ml chopped fresh mint
5 ml (1 teaspoon) dried origanum
250 ml (1 cup) water
250 ml (1 cup) milk
250 ml (1 cup) chicken stock*
Salt and freshly ground white pepper
125 ml (½ cup) sour cream (smetana)

For the garnish:
2 medium carrots, finely grated
30 ml (2 tablespoons) finely chopped fresh mint leaves

In a large saucepan, sauté the onion and leeks in butter until soft and golden. Add the potatoes, carrots, mint, origanum and water. Bring to the boil, turn down the heat and simmer (covered) for about 45 minutes – until all the vegetables are soft. Add the milk and stock, re-heat and season to taste.

Blend the soup to a fine purée in a blender or food processor, then sieve into a bowl. Stir in the sour cream, cover, and chill for at least 4 hours.

Check the seasoning again before serving and give the soup a good stir. Serve in pretty bowls, garnishing with grated carrot and chopped mint.

CHILLED CARROT VICHYSSOISE WITH MINT *A variation of an old favourite.*

COCK-A-LEEKIE SOUP

SLIVERS OF CHICKEN and rings of leek in good stock – this is cock-a-leekie, a broth that is substantial enough to make a meal on its own.

The cock of the title may have been the old farmyard rooster, or the loser in a vicious cock-fight. Such tough fowl needed long simmering – but the stock was all the better for this.

PREPARATION TIME: 30 MINUTES
COOKING TIME: 2½ HOURS
CHILLING TIME FOR STOCK: ABOUT 4 HOURS

INGREDIENTS FOR FOUR TO SIX
1 small chicken with giblets, cleaned
1 onion, unpeeled, washed and quartered
2 carrots, unpeeled, washed and chopped
Bouquet garni*
8 peppercorns
5 ml (1 teaspoon) salt
2 litres water
25 g butter
6 leeks, trimmed and thinly sliced
2 spring onions, trimmed and thinly sliced
Salt and pepper
30 ml (2 tablespoons) finely chopped parsley

Place the chicken with its giblets in a large, heavy-based saucepan. Add the onion, carrots, bouquet garni, peppercorns and salt to the pan and cover with the water.

Bring the pan very slowly to the boil, skim off any white scum and then simmer for about 1¼ hours until the chicken is tender. Strain off the stock into a large bowl, leave it to cool and then chill it in a refrigerator until the fat has hardened on the surface. Lift off the fat carefully with a slotted spoon.

Discard the vegetables, chicken neck and heart, bouquet garni and peppercorns. When the chicken is cool enough to handle, remove the skin from it and cut the flesh and the gizzard into thin strips.

Heat the butter in a large, heavy-based saucepan, add the leeks and spring onions and cook over a low heat for about 15 minutes until they are soft and transparent, and the butter has been absorbed. Add the stock (from which the fat has been removed), bring to the boil and add salt and pepper to taste.

Simmer the soup for about 15 minutes, or until the leeks and onions are tender. Add the chicken strips and simmer for a further 10 minutes. Mix in the chopped parsley and then serve.

VARIATIONS You can either put all the meat in the broth or, if you prefer, put in only the wing meat and serve the chicken separately with vegetables.

Some cooks choose to simmer a few prunes in the soup.

MURGH AUR KHADDU HALEEM

INDIAN SOUPS (known as haleems) are substantial and nutritious, and in some cases they are regarded as a main dish. Eastern spices are used for more than just their flavour and aroma, they are also highly valued for their health-giving properties.

Chicken and pumpkin soup makes a heartening dish on cold days. The pumpkin turns the soup into a golden orange colour, which makes it pleasing to the eye and tempting for children.

PREPARATION TIME: 1 HOUR
STANDING TIME: 30 MINUTES

INGREDIENTS FOR EIGHT
1,5 kg chicken, cut into pieces
7 ml (1½ teaspoons) salt
45 ml (3 tablespoons) melted butter or ghee*
2 onions, chopped*
8 cardamom pods
5 cm fresh green ginger, scraped and pounded with a little water to a paste
200 g pumpkin, diced
2 ml (½ teaspoon) turmeric
5 ml (1 teaspoon) pepper
2 ml (½ teaspoon) chilli powder or paprika
2 tomatoes, chopped
1 litre warm water

For the garnish:
30 ml (2 tablespoons) chopped mint or coriander leaves (known as dhania) or parsley

Wash the chicken pieces and pat them dry. Sprinkle salt over the pieces and leave them

SOUPS

to stand for 30 minutes. Heat the butter in a deep saucepan, add the onions and sauté for 2 minutes (or until soft).

Place the chicken and remaining ingredients (except the garnish) in the saucepan, cover with the lid and simmer gently for an hour or until the chicken is tender. Remove the chicken pieces from the soup, cut the meat from the bones, chop them finely and return to the soup.

SERVING SUGGESTIONS Serve hot in individual bowls and garnish with chopped herbs. Grilled bread and hot toast make good accompaniments.

VARIATIONS As a variation, try serving a heap of steaming rice with the soup. If a smooth soup is preferred, reduce it to a purée in a food processor. Ready-cut chicken pieces may be used, but some of the flavour may be lost.

BORSCH

THOUGH NOW REGARDED as something of a delicacy, this thick beetroot soup was for centuries the staple diet of the pre-Revolution Russian peasantry and the basis of their main daily meal. Borsch without doubt ranks among the best of the world's classic soups.

PREPARATION TIME: 25 MINUTES
COOKING TIME: 1 HOUR

INGREDIENTS FOR SIX

350 g whole, uncooked beetroot with leaves intact
2 large carrots, peeled
15 ml (1 tablespoon) sunflower oil
100-125 g (half a packet) streaky bacon, without rinds and cut into small pieces (optional)
1 large onion, peeled and finely chopped*
3 sticks celery, trimmed and cut into matchstick strips
1,5 litres chicken stock*
15 ml (1 tablespoon) vinegar
Salt and freshly ground black pepper
250 g tomatoes, skinned*, cored and seeded*
125 ml (½ cup) sour cream for garnish

Wash the beetroot and leaves well. Break off the leaves and separate them from their stalks and ribs. Cut the leaves into fine shreds and chop the stalks and ribs finely. Peel the beetroot and cut the flesh into thin strips. Slice the carrots thinly lengthways and cut the slices into fine strips.

Heat the oil in a large, heavy-based saucepan and fry the bacon (if used) over a low heat until the fat runs. Add the beetroot flesh, carrots, onion and celery to the pan and stir over a low heat until the fat has been absorbed.

Add the stock and vinegar, stir well and season with salt and pepper. Bring to the boil and simmer (covered) for 30 minutes. Pass the tomato flesh through a fine sieve or food mill to make a purée. Add it to the soup with the beetroot leaves and stalks. Continue to simmer for a further 15 minutes, or until the beetroot is tender.

BORSCH *The sliced beetroot in this soup gives it a deep, rich colour.*

Serve very hot with a swirl of sour cream in each serving.

VARIATIONS The classic borsch is always thick with vegetables, but if you prefer a less robust soup, strain it after cooking and serve it as a clear liquid, either hot or cold, with a spoonful of sour cream added to each bowl.

Try adding cucumber, pickled in dill-flavoured vinegar and chopped finely, to the soup or the sour cream.

JERUSALEM ARTICHOKE SOUP

DESPITE ITS NAME, the Jerusalem artichoke is in no way connected with the Israeli city; nor is it even an artichoke (it is a species of sunflower).

Jerusalem artichokes are available in South Africa between April and June – usually only in speciality shops. If bought fresh, they will keep in the refrigerator for four to five days. The soup has a very delicate flavour, and even though the Jerusalem artichoke is available for such a short season, it is well worth waiting for.

PREPARATION TIME: 20 MINUTES
COOKING TIME: ABOUT 1 HOUR

INGREDIENTS FOR FOUR TO SIX

500 g Jerusalem artichokes
15 ml (1 tablespoon) vinegar
30 g butter
2 medium onions, sliced*
2 stalks celery with green tops, sliced
Salt and white pepper
A pinch of sugar
3 ml (¾ teaspoon) marjoram
1 litre hot water
500 ml (2 cups) milk

Wash the artichokes well in water to which the vinegar has been added. Peel and slice them thinly. Heat the butter in a large saucepan and sauté the onions, celery and artichokes until they are glazed (do not let the vegetables brown). Season to taste and cook for about 10 minutes.

Add the sugar, marjoram and hot water and simmer gently (covered) until the vegetables are soft. Press them through a sieve or purée in a blender and then put through a sieve to catch the fibres from the celery. Return the purée to a saucepan. Add the milk, adjust the seasoning, bring to the boil and serve.

SERVING SUGGESTIONS Sprinkle with chopped parsley or spring onion tops.

For an unusual touch, sauté a few thinly sliced mushrooms and scatter them on each serving.

It is also delicious served cold.

VARIATION To make a richer soup, substitute a good, rich chicken stock* for the water and use 250 ml (1 cup) milk and 250 ml (1 cup) cream.

GAZPACHO

THIS LIGHT VERSION of the famous Andalusian soup, traditionally made in an earthenware pot from ingredients pounded together with pestle and mortar, is in many ways a liquid salad. It is certainly a cool and refreshing antidote to the heat of our South African summers.

PREPARATION TIME: 30 MINUTES
CHILLING TIME: 1 HOUR

INGREDIENTS FOR SIX
700 g ripe tomatoes
225 g fresh breadcrumbs
75 ml (5 tablespoons) olive oil
1 cucumber, peeled and chopped
2 green peppers, with cores and seeds removed, chopped
2 large cloves garlic, peeled
60 ml (¼ cup) red wine vinegar
600 ml water
15 ml (1 tablespoon) tomato paste
Salt and freshly ground black pepper
12 ice cubes

For the accompaniments:
2 slices white bread, prepared as croûtons*
2 hard-boiled eggs*, shelled and chopped
6 spring onions, trimmed and finely sliced
½ small cucumber, peeled and finely diced
1 small red pepper, finely chopped after core and seeds have been removed

GAZPACHO *A light, chilled soup, it is the perfect antidote to the heat of summer.*

Skin the tomatoes*, remove the cores and seeds, and chop the flesh. Place the breadcrumbs in a liquidizer, switch it on and gradually pour in the olive oil. Continue blending for about 1 minute, or until all the oil has been absorbed by the bread. Add the tomatoes and continue liquidizing until the mixture is reduced to a smooth paste, then transfer to a bowl.

Place the cucumber, green peppers and garlic in the liquidizer and blend for about 1 minute, or until they have been reduced to a smooth purée. Combine with the puréed tomatoes and stir in the vinegar, water and tomato paste. Taste and add salt and pepper if necessary. Cover the bowl and chill the soup in a refrigerator for at least 1 hour. Serve cold in shallow soup bowls, with two ice cubes added to each. Serve the accompaniments in separate bowls.

VARIATION To make a creamy soup, add mayonnaise*.

AVOCADO SOUP

A SATINY-SMOOTH SOUP which retains all the rich flavour of the ever-popular avocado. It is usually served well-chilled, but since avocados can be found in winter, a hot version is ideal for cooler nights. Whether served hot or cold, this is a particularly delicious soup.

PREPARATION TIME: 10 MINUTES
COOKING TIME: 25 MINUTES
CHILLING TIME: 2 HOURS

INGREDIENTS FOR SIX
30 g butter
1 small onion, finely chopped*
1 green pepper, seeded and finely chopped (optional)
30 ml (2 tablespoons) flour
250 ml (1 cup) warm milk
750 ml (3 cups) chicken stock*
2 ripe avocados, mashed
Salt and freshly ground black pepper
Chopped chives for garnish

Melt the butter in a medium-sized saucepan and gently sauté the onion and green pepper until soft. Remove from the heat, stir in the flour and gradually stir in the milk. Return to heat and bring to the boil. Add the chicken stock, cover and simmer for 20 minutes. Blend a little of the hot soup with the mashed avocado. Stir in the remaining soup and season to taste.

Liquidize and chill, and sprinkle with the chopped chives before serving.

VARIATION Serve hot, garnished with thinly sliced avocado first marinated in lemon juice, and a spoonful of sour cream. Remove from the stove as soon as it is hot enough, as overheating causes the avocado to taste bitter.

Cream of Asparagus Soup

This is a delicate, creamy soup which is Continental in origin. It is best made with fresh asparagus, but when it is not in season, the tinned variety makes a very acceptable substitute.

Preparation Time: 30 minutes
Cooking Time: 40 minutes

Ingredients for Six
1 kg fresh asparagus spears
1 small onion, chopped*
1 litre chicken or vegetable stock*
Salt and freshly ground white pepper
30 g butter
30 ml (2 tablespoons) flour
250 ml (1 cup) cream
2 egg yolks
Finely chopped parsley for garnish

Wash and peel the asparagus, then chop it – reserving some of the tips to use as a garnish. Simmer these separately, very gently, until just tender. Cook the rest of the asparagus with the onion, stock, salt and pepper (partly covered) for about 25 minutes, or until tender.

Purée the asparagus in a blender or food processor, then press through a sieve. Melt the butter, stir in the flour and cook for 1 minute. Gradually add the puréed soup, stirring all the time, until the mixture boils.

Beat the cream with the egg yolks, add a little of the hot soup, and pour into the remaining soup. Heat the soup gently while stirring, but do not allow it to boil. Add the cooked tips, check the seasoning. Serve hot, sprinkled with chopped parsley.

Serving Suggestion Pass around small crusty rolls and butter.

Variations Chill the soup, if necessary diluting it with plain drinking yoghurt.

Garnish with a rosette of whipped cream and a sprinkling of finely chopped chives or toasted flaked almonds.

Use two 410 g tins of asparagus pieces. Drain, but use the liquid as part of the litre of stock required. It is not necessary to cook the asparagus.

Add a grating of nutmeg to the prepared soup and serve hot with a sprinkling of grated Gruyère cheese and chopped parsley.

Chilled Cucumber Soup

This is a refreshing soup that is very nutritious owing to the vitamins B and C in the cucumbers.

Preparation Time: 10 minutes
Standing Time: 30 minutes
Chilling Time: 2 hours

Ingredients for Six
1 large (500 g) English cucumber
Salt and pepper
250 ml (1 cup) natural yoghurt*
125 ml (½ cup) cream
1 clove garlic, crushed
30 ml (2 tablespoons) olive or sunflower oil
30 ml (2 tablespoons) white wine vinegar
50 g walnuts, chopped

Peel the cucumber and dice into tiny cubes. Put these on a flat dish, sprinkle lightly with salt and leave standing for 30 minutes. Rinse the cucumber cubes in a colander under cold running water and then drain thoroughly.

In a bowl, blend the yoghurt with the cream, the crushed garlic, the oil and the vinegar, and season to taste with salt and pepper.

Fold in the cucumber and just over half the chopped walnuts: blend thoroughly and then chill in the refrigerator for about 2 hours.

Spoon the chilled soup into individual bowls, sprinkle the remaining chopped walnuts on top, and serve.

Serving Suggestions Serve with thin slices of crisp Melba toast* or wedges of pitta bread*.

Chilled Cucumber Soup *Chopped walnuts add an interesting dimension.*

Cauliflower Soup

The traditional cauliflower soup or crème du Barry, named after the French Comtesse du Barry (murdered in the French Revolution), is a rich and creamy concoction. For a lighter version more suited to our warmer climate, try this delicious adaptation.

Preparation Time: 10 minutes
Cooking Time: 20 minutes

Ingredients for Six
1 medium-sized, very firm cauliflower
500 ml (2 cups) chicken stock*
50 g butter
45 ml (3 tablespoons) flour
500 ml (2 cups) milk
Salt and pepper
Grated nutmeg

Trim the stalk from the cauliflower, cut the florets into small (fingertip-sized) pieces and simmer them gently in the stock in a medium-sized saucepan for about 5 minutes: they should be just cooked but still firm (do not overcook cauliflower, as it loses its delicate flavour and develops a musty bitterness). Drain off and reserve the stock, and turn out the cauliflower into a dish.

Clean the saucepan, add the butter and melt it over a gentle heat. Stir in the flour and cook for 1-2 minutes without browning. Gradually whisk in the stock and milk to make a smooth sauce. Bring to the boil, stirring continually, and simmer for 5 minutes. Add the cauliflower and re-heat gently. Season to taste with salt, pepper and nutmeg.

Serving Suggestions Sprinkle with crumbled, crisply fried bacon.

To turn this simple soup into an impromptu meal, serve it with garlic bread or piping hot fingers of buttered toast sprinkled with caraway seeds.

Variations For a smooth soup, add poached cauliflower florets to a milk base, season and continue to cook gently for a further 5-7 minutes, until the cauliflower is really tender. Sieve or purée the soup and re-heat it with 125 ml (½ cup) cream.

Broccoli makes a delicious alternative to cauliflower, and is good when flavoured with cumin rather than nutmeg.

SOUPS

Minestrone

THIS MUCH-LOVED vegetable soup forms the basis for many other Italian soups. Originally it was more like a stew; hence many different versions of this recipe are stews rather than soups.

It is important that the vegetables should not be overcooked, or they will lose the colour that makes this soup especially pleasing to the eye. Minestrone is quite a filling dish and is often served as a meal on its own.

PREPARATION TIME: 30 MINUTES
COOKING TIME: 1½ HOURS

INGREDIENTS FOR EIGHT
45 ml (3 tablespoons) sunflower oil
12 ml (2½ teaspoons) salt
3 cloves garlic, crushed
2 large onions, chopped*
2 potatoes, diced
2 fresh young carrots, diced
2 leeks, sliced
2 turnips, diced
4 sticks celery, chopped
2 florets cauliflower, divided into sprigs
100 g green beans, sliced
2 litres boiling water
300 g red sugar beans or haricot beans, cooked
3 medium-sized ripe tomatoes (unskinned), chopped
30 ml (2 tablespoons) chopped fresh basil leaves or 15 ml (1 tablespoon) dried
Salt and freshly ground black pepper
125 ml (½ cup) pasta shells
Parmesan cheese

Pour the oil into a heavy-bottomed pot and heat. Add the salt, garlic and all the vegetables except the cooked beans and tomatoes. Allow the vegetables to cook until they become transparent (do not allow them to brown).

Gradually add the boiling water to the saucepan, then add the cooked beans and tomatoes, basil and pepper. Cover and cook for 45 minutes.

Add the pasta shells to the simmering soup about 20 minutes before serving the minestrone. Check the seasoning and then serve with a sprinkling of freshly grated Parmesan cheese in each bowl.

Spinach Soup

FOR MANY YEARS spinach soup was eaten by unwilling children because their parents appreciated the nutritional value of spinach. Vitamins and iron are abundant in this vegetable. This soup is regaining popularity.

PREPARATION TIME: 30 MINUTES
COOKING TIME: 20 MINUTES

INGREDIENTS FOR SIX
1,5 kg fresh spinach (or 500 g frozen spinach)
25 g butter
500 ml (2 cups) chicken stock*
250 ml (1 cup) cream
250 ml (1 cup) milk
3-4 ml salt and a pinch of coarsely ground pepper
5 ml (1 teaspoon) lemon juice

If using fresh spinach, wash it well under cold running water and pat it dry. (If using frozen spinach, it is not necessary to thaw it before cooking.) Place the spinach in a large saucepan with the butter and simmer gently, stirring from time to time, until it is just tender. Allow to cool slightly, then liquidize or press the spinach through a sieve. Return it to the saucepan, add the chicken stock, cream and milk, and bring it to the boil. Flavour with salt, pepper and lemon juice, and serve.

SERVING SUGGESTIONS Serve with a drizzle of cream or a sprinkling of Gruyère, accompanied by fingers of hot wholewheat toast.

MINESTRONE, *a hearty Italian soup, has become a worldwide favourite.*

Onion Soup

FOR MANY YEARS, porters at the Paris market of Les Halles kept out the early morning cold by drinking large mugs of thick onion soup laced with cheese. It became such an attraction that late-night revellers made Les Halles a fashionable spot to end a wild evening. The market has long since disappeared, but the association still lingers.

PREPARATION TIME: 10 MINUTES
COOKING TIME: 45 MINUTES

INGREDIENTS FOR FOUR
500 g (4 medium) onions
50 g butter
30 ml (2 tablespoons) flour
125 ml (½ cup) dry white wine
625 ml (2½ cups) beef basic or chicken stock*
Salt and freshly ground black pepper
Butter for spreading
4 slices French bread (1 cm thick)
150 g Gruyère or Emmenthal cheese, grated

Peel and slice the onions* thinly into rings. Cook them in the 50 g butter over a medium heat until soft and lightly golden, stirring them often. Do not let them burn, or they will impart a bitter taste to the soup. Instead, a gentle caramelising gives the soup its rich colour.

Stir in the flour and cook for 1 minute. Add the wine, stock and seasoning and simmer for 25-30 minutes, until the onions are meltingly soft. Check the seasoning. Meanwhile, butter both sides of each slice of bread. Grill on both sides until golden and crisp. Sprinkle over half the cheese and continue to grill until the cheese has melted. Spoon the remaining cheese into the bottom of four individual soup bowls. Ladle over soup and float the cheese toast on top. Serve the soup at once.

SERVING SUGGESTIONS Add a dash of sherry to each bowl of soup. For a really traditional 'soupe gratinée', float a slice of toasted French bread in each oven-proof bowl. Then sprinkle the slices with cheese and place the bowls under the grill for a few minutes to melt the cheese slightly.

VARIATIONS To make a creamy soup, whisk together 2 egg yolks and 125 ml (½ cup) cream. Stir or whisk this mixture into the soup just before serving (re-heat it gently).

The soup can be sieved or puréed, but in this case omit the bread and cheese and stir in 125 ml (½ cup) cream (with or without egg yolks).

You can make leek soup in the same way, but without the cheese and bread. Sieve or purée half of the soup and combine the two halves with 125 ml (½ cup) cream or 125 ml (½ cup) grated cheese to make a hearty soup with character and an interesting texture.

Pumpkin Soup

Pumpkins and butternuts belong to the same, sadly neglected family. Both vegetables make a rich, creamy, golden soup that is delicious served as a starter but is also sufficiently hearty to eat as a meal-in-one with toasted rye bread and a topping of grated Cheddar cheese.

Preparation Time: 20 minutes
Cooking Time: 45 minutes

Ingredients for Six

45 g butter
750 g pumpkin or butternut, peeled and diced
1 large onion, chopped*
Finely grated rind of 1 orange
750 ml (3 cups) chicken stock*
Salt and freshly ground black pepper
15 ml (1 tablespoon) cornflour
250 ml (1 cup) milk
125 ml (½ cup) cream
30 ml (2 tablespoons) finely chopped parsley for garnish

Melt the butter in a large saucepan. Add the pumpkin, onion and orange rind, and cook over a very gentle heat until the onion is soft; this should take about 5 minutes. Add the stock and seasonings and then bring to the boil.

Reduce the heat and simmer gently (covered) for about 30 minutes, or until the pumpkin is tender. Sieve or purée the soup in a liquidizer or food processor. Return the purée to a cleaned saucepan. Mix the cornflour to a smooth paste with 45 ml (3 tablespoons) of the cold milk. Add this to the soup together with the remaining milk and bring slowly to the boil, stirring constantly. Reduce the heat and simmer for 5 minutes. Check the seasoning, pour into a pre-heated tureen, stir in the cream and sprinkle with parsley. Serve immediately.

Serving Suggestions Sour cream or yoghurt can be substituted for the cream.

For extra body, beat in an egg yolk.

Decorate with small golden croûtons*, and sprinkle the soup with paprika instead of parsley.

Variations Simplest of all is the classic soup – a golden purée, with or without cheese, using a whole pumpkin. For a sensational presentation, there is nothing to beat the recipe for traditional American baked pumpkin soup, in which pumpkins are wrapped in cabbage leaves and baked in the fire.

To make a similar version, cut a 'lid' from the stalk end of a 20 cm diameter pumpkin. Scoop out the seeds and fibres, and smear the inside with 30-45 g softened butter. Season with salt and pepper. Stand the pumpkin in an oven-proof dish, add 1 thinly sliced pickling sized onion, 15-20 g rice and 250 ml (1 cup) hot chicken stock*. Replace the lid and bake at 190°C for 1½-2 hours, or until the flesh is soft. Scrape some of the pumpkin flesh carefully into the soup and correct the seasoning. Stir in a good pinch of ground nutmeg. When serving, scrape more of the pumpkin flesh into each bowl.

Pumpkin Soup *uses an often neglected vegetable in a rich, creamy preparation that makes a good starter or light meal.*

How to Skin and Seed Tomatoes

Many recipes require the addition of skinned tomatoes, and sometimes they also need to be seeded. The following method is quick and simple.

Place the tomatoes in a bowl and cover with boiling water, allowing them to stand for 30-60 seconds.

Drain the tomatoes and rinse under cold running water (this saves you from burning your fingers).

Peel off the skin (with some types of tomatoes, the skin comes off more easily if it is peeled while still hot).

To seed the tomatoes, cut them in half crosswise and squeeze them over a bowl with the palm of your hand.

Tomato and Carrot Soup

Many years ago, the tomato was known as the love apple – a fruit thought capable of arousing dangerous passions, and therefore to be treated with suspicion.

In this recipe the carrot and apple combine beautifully with the flavour of the tomatoes to create a subtle and unusual tasting soup.

PREPARATION TIME: 15 MINUTES
COOKING TIME: 1¼ HOURS

INGREDIENTS FOR FOUR

15 g butter
10 ml (2 teaspoons) sunflower oil
1 onion, peeled and finely chopped*
2 cloves garlic, peeled and finely chopped
2 medium carrots, peeled and finely chopped
500 g tomatoes, skinned* and roughly chopped
1 apple, peeled, cored and chopped
Bouquet garni* of thyme, marjoram and 1 bay leaf
1 litre vegetable or chicken stock*
Salt and freshly ground black pepper

For the garnish:
60 ml (¼ cup) cream
60 ml (¼ cup) croûtons*

Heat the butter with the oil in a large, heavy-based saucepan. Put in the onion and garlic, and cook over a low heat for 10-15 minutes until the onion is soft and transparent. Add the carrots and stir over a low heat until all the fat has been absorbed. Add the tomatoes, apple, bouquet garni and stock, season with salt and pepper and bring to the boil. Cover and simmer for 45 minutes.

Remove and discard the bouquet garni and pass the soup through a fine sieve or a blender. Return it to a clean pan, heat through and adjust the seasoning.

Pour the soup into warm bowls and garnish with a spoonful of cream and croûtons.

SERVING SUGGESTION A particularly attractive garnish for this soup is a spoonful of whipped cream in each bowl, with a sprinkling of marigold petals or chives.

TOMATO AND CARROT SOUP *A garnish of marigold petals adds to its visual appeal.*

Split Pea Soup

This dish of dried peas and cured pork was first made in England in the Middle Ages. Today it is popular throughout South Africa, particularly since it is very economical to make.

PREPARATION TIME: 15 MINUTES
COOKING TIME: 2¼ HOURS

INGREDIENTS FOR SIX

3 rashers streaky bacon with rinds removed, diced
1 large onion, peeled and chopped*
2 medium carrots, peeled and chopped
500 g dried split peas
2,5 litres vegetable or chicken stock*
Salt and pepper
5 ml (1 teaspoon) Worcestershire sauce
Croûtons* as garnish for each soup bowl

Put the bacon in a large, heavy-based saucepan and cook over gentle heat until the fat runs out. Add the onion and carrots and cook gently until the fat has been absorbed.

Add the peas to the pan with the stock. Bring to the boil, season lightly with salt and pepper, cover and allow to simmer for about 2 hours, or until the peas are sufficiently mushy.

Pass through a sieve or food processor, taste and adjust the seasoning. Add the Worcestershire sauce and re-heat. Serve topped with croûtons.

Vegetable Soup

This soup makes a welcoming start to any meal, offering vegetable combinations which can vary according to the season. It can be made into a more hearty soup with the addition of starches and pulses.

Preparation Time: 30 minutes
Cooking Time: 45 minutes

Ingredients for Eight
1 large onion, peeled and chopped*
2 cloves garlic, crushed
4 sticks table celery, finely sliced
60 ml (¼ cup) sunflower oil
30 ml (2 tablespoons) tomato paste
1,5 litres chicken or vegetable stock*
750 g chopped carrot, baby marrow, green beans, potato, green pepper, turnip, cabbage, cauliflower, peas, corn, mushrooms, butternut
Salt and freshly ground black pepper
Chopped parsley for garnish

Sauté the onion, garlic and celery in the oil until tender. Add the tomato paste and stock, and simmer gently while you prepare the vegetables.

Cook the chopped vegetables until they are just tender (in a little water). Combine the vegetables and the cooking water with the soup 10 minutes before serving, season and bring to the boil. Simmer the soup for 3–4 minutes, correcting the seasoning. Garnish with chopped parsley and serve.

Serving Suggestion Add a few sprouts to each bowl when serving.

Variations For a herb flavour, add 5 ml (1 teaspoon) origanum, 10 ml (2 teaspoons) basil and 2 ml (½ teaspoon) rosemary.

To make a thicker soup, add 75 g cooked barley, cooked rice, cooked lentils or cooked soya beans.

Any left-over soup may be liquidized and served with firm pieces of vegetables.

Meal-in-one Fish Soup

This hearty and wholesome soup has a variety of flavours, and may be adapted in many ways to suit available ingredients.

Preparation Time: 1 hour
Cooking Time: 1¾ hours

Ingredients for Eight
1,5 kg line fish, skinned and filleted
45 ml (3 tablespoons) olive oil
3 ml (¾ teaspoon) curry powder
1 onion, sliced*
2 carrots, sliced
2 leeks, sliced
3 ripe tomatoes, skinned, seeded* and chopped
3 litres fish stock*
250 ml (1 cup) dry white wine
3 cloves garlic
2 strips orange rind
A good pinch of saffron (optional)
Salt and freshly ground black pepper
6 small potatoes, peeled

For the garnish:
8 slices French bread
Garlic mayonnaise (aïoli*)
50 g grated Gruyère cheese
45 ml (3 tablespoons) chopped parsley

Put the olive oil, curry powder and onion in a large saucepan and fry until the onion is translucent. Add the carrots and leeks. Heat until they are soft, then add the tomatoes, stock, white wine, garlic, orange rind, saffron (if used), salt and pepper. Cover the saucepan and simmer gently for 1 hour, then add the potatoes and fish.

Bring to the boil, then reduce the heat and simmer for about 10 minutes. Remove most of the fish fillets and place on a platter. Cover them with foil and keep warm. Allow the potatoes to cook for another 15 minutes. Remove the potatoes and set aside with the fish on the platter. Cool the soup, discard the orange rind and liquidize. Return the potatoes and fish.

Re-heat and taste to correct the seasoning. Place a slice of crusty French bread in each soup bowl and top with a dollop of garlic mayonnaise and a spoonful of grated Gruyère cheese. Ladle the soup on to the bread, add a slice of fish, and sprinkle with parsley.

Meal-in-one Fish Soup *Liven up the catch of the day with this interesting blend of vegetables and flavourings.*

SOUPS

Bean Soup

THIS POPULAR DISH is thought to have originated in northern Germany, from where it spread to Holland and beyond. Because the German and Dutch housewives had to cater for relatively large appetites, they learned to appreciate the value of good, filling soups such as the bean soup described here.

SOAKING TIME: 12 HOURS
PREPARATION TIME: 15 MINUTES
COOKING TIME: 2¼ HOURS

INGREDIENTS FOR EIGHT
150 g dried brown or sugar beans
3 litres cold water
100 g pork fat with rind, or bacon with rind
450 g shin of beef
1 onion, finely sliced*
5 ml (1 teaspoon) salt
1 ml (¼ teaspoon) pepper
125 ml (½ cup) chopped parsley
1 blade mace
15 ml (1 tablespoon) flour
15 ml (1 tablespoon) melted butter
250 ml (1 cup) milk
15 ml (1 tablespoon) lemon juice

Soak the beans in water for 12 hours (or overnight), then wash them. Drain the beans and place them in a large saucepan with the cold water.

Add the pork fat (or bacon) and shin, and cook for an hour. Add the sliced onion, salt, pepper, chopped parsley and mace, and cook for another hour.

Put the soup through a sieve, mash the beans and remove the shin bones. Re-heat the soup to boiling point. Meanwhile, combine the flour and melted butter, add the milk as for a white sauce* and stir it over a low heat until it thickens; add the mixture to the soup. Cook and stir for another 10 minutes, adding the lemon juice just before serving.

SERVING SUGGESTION Serve with an accompaniment of croûtons*.

VARIATION If you are not able to soak the beans overnight, cover with water and bring to the boil. Remove from the heat and allow to stand covered for an hour.

Oyster Soup

THERE IS A SCENE in the Dickens classic *Pickwick Papers* in which a character named Sam Weller said: 'It's a wery [sic] remarkable circumstance sir, that poverty and oysters always seem to go together.' These days, however, oysters are a relatively rare treat. Although usually served on the half shell, oysters also make a very tasty soup.

PREPARATION TIME: 20 MINUTES
COOKING TIME: 45 MINUTES

INGREDIENTS FOR SIX
24 fresh oysters
50 g butter
30 ml (2 tablespoons) flour
450 ml hot milk or veal basic stock*
125 ml (½ cup) dry white wine
3 ml (¾ teaspoon) anchovy essence (optional)
2 ml (½ teaspoon) nutmeg, freshly grated
Cayenne pepper
125 ml (½ cup) cream
Salt and freshly ground black pepper
5 ml (1 teaspoon) lemon juice
6 ml (1½ teaspoons) chopped parsley for garnish

Open the oysters* and discard the upper shells. Loosen the oysters left in the deep shells, leaving the liquid intact, and spoon both oysters and their juice into a bowl.

Melt the butter in a large saucepan and stir in the flour. Cook gently for 2-3 minutes (without browning) and add the milk or stock gradually, beating it well to make a smooth soup. Add the wine, season with the anchovy essence, nutmeg and cayenne pepper. Stir in the cream and simmer gently for 15-20 minutes.

Just before serving, add the oysters and their liquid to the soup and heat through for 1-2 minutes. Do not overcook: the oysters are ready when they begin to curl at the edges. Correct the seasoning, sharpen the flavour with lemon juice and serve the soup immediately, each serving garnished with 1 ml (¼ teaspoon) parsley.

VARIATIONS For a heartier soup, simmer 250 g chopped white leek stems and 125 g diced potato in 750 ml (3 cups) fish stock* until tender. Purée, season and re-heat it (do not boil) with cream and oysters.

Alternatively, substitute two 225 g tins of drained oysters, mussels or clams.

Frozen oysters can also be used.

OYSTER SOUP *is a tasty combination of interesting spices, a hint of anchovy and cream with lightly cooked oysters.*

Oxtail Soup

OXTAIL, A LONG-TIME favourite among cooks, produces an incomparable brown broth. During its long simmering, the dish gives off an appetising aroma – a prelude to the unique soup with its richly concentrated beefy taste.

PREPARATION TIME: 30 MINUTES
SOAKING TIME: AT LEAST 4 HOURS
COOLING TIME FOR STOCK: 5 HOURS
COOKING TIME: 4 HOURS

INGREDIENTS FOR FOUR TO SIX
1 meaty oxtail, divided into joints
5 ml (1 teaspoon) vinegar
30 ml (2 tablespoons) dripping*
2 onions, peeled and chopped*
2 large carrots, peeled and chopped
3 sticks celery, trimmed and chopped
1 rasher bacon, roughly chopped
2 litres basic beef stock*
Bouquet garni*
3 bay leaves
Salt and freshly ground black pepper
30 ml (2 tablespoons) flour
1 ml (¼ teaspoon) grated nutmeg
2 ml (½ teaspoon) lemon juice
60 ml (¼ cup) sherry

For the garnish:
1 carrot, peeled and cut in rounds
1 small onion, peeled and sliced*

OXTAIL SOUP *Preparation and cooking takes a long time, but its deliciously rich, beefy flavour is ample reward.*

Soak the oxtail in enough cold water to cover, together with the vinegar, for at least 4 hours. Drain and wipe dry. Heat half the dripping in a large, heavy-based saucepan. Add the oxtail pieces and cook over a high heat, shaking the pan frequently, until browned on all sides. Remove the oxtail with a slotted spoon.

Add the chopped onions, carrots, celery and bacon to the juices in the pan and cook over a medium heat, stirring occasionally, until the onions are golden-brown. Return the oxtail to the pan, add the stock, bouquet garni and bay leaves, season with salt and pepper, and bring to the boil. Skim off any white scum that rises to the top, then simmer the soup for 3 hours, or until the meat falls off the bones.

Strain off the stock into a large bowl and discard the vegetables, bacon, bouquet garni and bay leaves. Leave the stock to cool for 1 hour, then place in the refrigerator for about 4 hours to allow the fat to harden on the surface. Discard the fat.

Boil 500 ml (2 cups) of the stock in a small pan, add the carrot and onion rings, and simmer for 15 minutes. Strain off and keep the stock, reserving the vegetables.

Remove the meat from the bones and chop finely. Heat the remaining dripping in the cleaned saucepan. Add the flour and stir over a medium heat until the flour turns the colour of a hazelnut. Gradually add all the stock, stirring continuously until the soup comes to the boil and is thick and smooth. Simmer for 3 minutes, then add the meat, nutmeg and lemon juice. Taste and adjust the seasoning if necessary, and stir in the sherry. Garnish with a portion of the cooked carrot and onion rings.

Vichyssoise

THIS DELICIOUS SOUP was originally made by French peasants, who grew potatoes and leeks. Today we use the same ingredients, but the soup has a finer texture than in the past.

It can be served hot or well chilled, but the latter way is preferred if the true flavour of the leeks is to be retained.

PREPARATION TIME: 20 MINUTES
COOKING TIME: 25 MINUTES
CHILLING TIME: 4 HOURS

INGREDIENTS FOR EIGHT
3 leeks, finely chopped
1 medium onion, finely chopped*
30 g butter
4 medium potatoes, thinly sliced
1 litre chicken stock*
250 ml (1 cup) cream
Salt and pepper
Chopped chives for garnish

Sauté the leeks and onion in the heated butter in a medium-sized pan until soft, stirring constantly.

Add the potatoes and stock, then simmer (covered) for 15 minutes, or until tender. Push the mixture through a sieve, or liquidize, then add the cream and salt and pepper to taste.

Serve the vichyssoise well chilled, sprinkled with chopped chives.

VARIATIONS Serve the vichyssoise hot.
Substitute yoghurt* for the cream.

Fish

SOUTH AFRICANS are very fortunate in having access to a large variety of fish and shellfish – among the most delicious and nutritious of foods. Fish is at its best fresh from the water, when the simplest preparation turns it into a dish fit for a king. But there is no end to the ways in which fish can be prepared, from the family standby of fish and chips to something more exotic such as yellowtail with avocado sauce.

Before the advent of modern freezing techniques and refrigerated transport – which has brought seafood to the dinner tables of those who do not live close to the coast – smoking and drying were common methods of preserving fish in South Africa. The popularity of smoked fish has survived, particularly that of smoked snoek, which is still often prepared as the traditional gesmoorde snoek.

It is not, of course, only in South Africa that fish is so popular, and we have garnered many recipes from other cultures. Try a Spanish paella, which combines a variety of seafoods in a colourful rice dish, Chinese steamed sweet and sour fish, a spicy prawn curry from India, or a Hungarian fish dish with paprika cream sauce.

Fish is the perfect slimmer's food – as long as you choose the simpler methods of cooking such as grilling, poaching or steaming, and steer clear of recipes with rich, cream sauces. But you need not keep it entirely plain: you can often avoid the kilojoules by substituting yoghurt for cream.

PREPARING FISH AND SHELLFISH · *PAGE 54*

FISH RECIPES · *PAGE 60*

SPECIAL FEATURES

SIMPLE STEPS TO A SMOKY FLAVOUR · *PAGE 68*
MEAL-IN-ONE DISHES · SIX SEAFOOD TREATS · *PAGE 78*

PREPARING FISH AND SHELLFISH

Gram for gram, fish offers more goodness and less wastage than meat. It is an excellent and still relatively inexpensive food.

Health-conscious people like fish because it is easily digested, and rich in high-grade protein, vitamins and minerals. Fatty fish, such as mackerel and harder, are rich in polyunsaturates, which inhibit cholesterol formation.

Most of the fish eaten in South Africa is of three main groups: small oily fish such as pilchards, anchovies and harders; large oily fish such as snoek and tuna; and line fish such as hake, Cape salmon, kingklip and galjoen.

Fish is mostly sold frozen – only in the coastal areas can it usually be bought on the day it is caught.

BUYING FRESH FISH

There is no mistaking the plumpness and firmness of really fresh fish. Scaly fish should have a sequin-like iridescence, and the eyes should be clear, bright and bulging. As a general rule, fresh fish are bright, with firm, springy flesh and tight skin. Stale fish – no matter how often they are hosed down – look grey, dull and limp, with blurred eyes, flabby flesh and often a tell-tale smell.

These guidelines are easy to apply to whole fish, but because much of the fish we buy is already cut up or filleted, look for firm flesh and no more than a 'seaweedy' smell (a stronger smell means that the fish is past its prime).

Smoked fish should be plump and moist, with a glossy skin. There should be no unpleasant smell or traces of mould or mildew in the pack.

Shellfish are best bought alive, but as this is often impractical you should buy only from a reliable source. Choose crayfish and crabs that feel heavy and firm for their size. To check the freshness of a crayfish, ensure that the tail springs back sharply when flexed.

Oysters and mussels should always be tightly closed – a sign that they are alive. Never be tempted to buy oysters or mussels with half-open shells, and avoid shellfish with heavily encrusted shells (this is usually a sign of old age).

Frozen fish should be clean, neatly prepared and sealed into dry, 'frost-free' packets. Do not buy packets that are partly thawed.

PREPARING FISH

All fish, with the exception of anchovies and other very small fish, should be gutted and cleaned (most fishmongers will happily do this for you).

If you can buy fresh fish straight from a boat (or catch it yourself), gut it yourself at home: it is not at all difficult to do.

Cut off the spiky fins and, if the fish has scales, lay it on a few sheets of newspaper on a work-surface. Then, holding it by the tail with one hand, scrape away the scales with a short, blunt knife (working from the tail towards the head). Rinse the fish well under cold water.

If you prefer to do it the easy way, cook the fish with scales and skin intact, and carefully remove the skin before serving the fish.

The next step is to gut the fish. In a round fish, the entrails are in the belly, but in flat fish they lie in a cavity behind the head.

To gut a round fish, such as mackerel, pilchard or snoek, slit the fish (with a sharp knife) along the belly from behind the gills to just above the tail. Scrape out the entrails.

Rinse the fish in cold water and scrape away any traces of blood with a small, sharp knife. Cut off the head and tail (optional).

Flat fish, such as sole, are gutted by making a semi-circular slit just behind the head on the dark skin side. Scrape out the entrails, then cut off the fins and skin, or fillet (see Boning and filleting*) before cooking.

Skinning

Round fish are best cooked with the skin left intact: this keeps the flesh moist and tender (the fish are skinned and garnished before serving).

Alternatively, you can fillet the fish and, with the skin side of the fillet down, hold the tail end in one hand while easing the flesh carefully from the skin with a small, sharp knife (starting at the tail end).

A flat fish is also skinned from tail to head, but with the dark skin facing up. Make a slit just above the tail, then hold the tail while pulling the skin off (towards the head).

If necessary, use a small, sharp knife and scrape the skin off the flesh. Turn the fish over and skin the other side in the same way.

If the fish or skin is slippery, hold with a rough cloth, or dip your fingertips in salt.

Boning and filleting

A fish cannot be completely boned without first being divided into fillets. Filleted round fish have become as popular as fillets of flat fish, as they are easy to serve, and the portions look attractive on a plate.

The technique for boning and filleting fish is not difficult and you will need only a suitable knife with a thin, flexible blade (preferably a special fish-filleting knife). Follow the step-by-step directions on page 58 for the three methods of boning and filleting fish.

FREEZING

After being thoroughly cleaned and dried, really fresh fish can be frozen whole, or in cutlets and fillets (crumbed or minced). Wrap servings in individual sheets of freezer wrap, then overwrap in two plastic bags to prevent the fishy smell from spreading through the rest of your freezing compartment. See Freezing fish*.

COOKING METHODS FOR FISH

Shallow-frying

Choose a small whole fish or part of a fish for this cooking method and fry in a mixture of half sunflower oil and half butter. There should be about 5 mm of fat in the pan; make sure that it is really hot before adding the fish.

It is best to thaw frozen fish before frying (unless cooked in crumbs or batter).

Uncoated fish tends to make the fat spatter, and reduces the temperature of the oil so much that the final product can be soggy and greasy instead of crisp and delicious.

To prevent fish from becoming soggy when fried, first dip in a light coating of seasoned flour, oatmeal, batter, or egg and crumbs. Allow about 2 minutes' frying for each side, or fry until the fish is golden outside and opaque all the way through.

Deep-frying

Before adding the fish, test the oil by cooking a small cube of bread in it for 1 minute. The bread should turn golden-brown in this time. However, if it burns, the oil is too hot; if it becomes soggy, the oil is not hot enough.

The fryer should be only one-third full of oil. The fish should be at room temperature before frying; if colder, it will reduce the oil temperature too much.

Coat the fish portions with batter or egg and crumbs, and cook until golden. Before serving, lift out and drain well on crumpled paper towels or newspaper.

Grilling

Line the grill pan with aluminium foil to prevent the fishy flavour from clinging to the pan. Pre-heat the grill before starting.

Small, whole fish of about 250 g are best slashed 2-3 times on each side, then brushed with butter or sunflower oil and grilled for about 7 minutes on each side.

Whole sole and fillets should be brushed with butter, sprinkled with lemon juice and grilled for 2-6 minutes on each side.

Fish steaks of about 250 g should be buttered and grilled for 5-6 minutes on each side, basting once.

Left-over grill pan juices can be stirred with a little extra butter and a small glass of dry white wine or cream to make a delicious sauce.

For a more exotic flavour, sprinkle the fish with herbs before grilling and baste with brandy.

Poaching

Poaching means slowly simmering the fish in just enough liquid to cover it.

To make a basic cooking liquid (known as a court-bouillon), add the following peeled and chopped vegetables to a mixture of 250 ml (1 cup) dry white wine and 750 ml (3 cups) water: 2 carrots, 1 onion and 2 sticks celery. Add 3 parsley stalks, 2 sprigs thyme, 30 ml (2 tablespoons) lemon juice or vinegar, a bay leaf, salt and black pepper.

Bring the court-bouillon to the boil, cover and simmer over a low heat for about 15 minutes. Leave to cool slightly and strain before using as a poaching liquid for the fish.

Alternatively, poach the fish in milk and water. Place the fish in a large saucepan or special fish kettle and cover completely with the poaching liquid. Bring to the boil over moderate heat, then cover the pan or kettle, lower the heat and simmer until done. The fish is ready as soon as it becomes opaque and flakes away easily from the bone.

To eat hot, drain and serve immediately with herb butter*. For cold dishes, cool the fish completely in the poaching liquid before removing and garnishing.

Steaming

Sprinkle the fish with lemon juice and wrap loosely in aluminium foil before lowering into a steamer. Alternatively, arrange the fish on a buttered dish set over a saucepan of boiling water, cover loosely and steam for 10-15 minutes – depending on the thickness of the fish.

Check the fish to make sure it is cooked properly before serving.

If you regard steamed fish as too bland, follow the Chinese method and add chopped ginger, spring onion and a sprinkling of soy sauce before steaming.

Baking

To bake a whole fish, stuff the gutted fish with sliced tomato, fresh herbs, lemon juice and a few breadcrumbs (optional). Brush well with butter and bake at 190°C for about 30 minutes (cooking time depends on the size of the fish – allow less time for smaller, unstuffed fish).

For even better results, make a bed of finely sliced vegetables and herbs under the fish (only non-oily fish) and pour round a glass of dry white wine or fish stock*. Brush the fish with sunflower oil and bake or braise, covering the baking dish with a dome of foil.

Cooking in parcels

Fish cooked in aluminium foil retains its own juices and gives maximum flavour. Season well, dab with butter, wrap loosely in buttered foil and bake at 220°C for 15-40 minutes, depending on the size and thickness of the fish.

Try adding sliced tomatoes, mushrooms, onions and/or freshly chopped herbs to the foil parcels before cooking.

You can also cook fish in oiled grease-proof paper parcels. This is best done with cutlets or smaller fillets. Before wrapping, season the fish, sprinkle with lemon juice and herbs, and top with a spoonful of cream. Bake at 180°C for about 15 minutes, or until the fish is cooked but firm.

To serve, snip open the parcels with scissors and slide the fish on to a serving plate, pouring over any juices from the parcels.

Braaing

Nothing quite matches the flavour of fresh fish braaied over an open fire. There are various ways of preparing it, but the easiest is to wrap the seasoned fish in buttered aluminium foil and braai until firm and cooked, turning it carefully.

A similar flavour is achieved by cooking the fish on a solid plate or plough disc with a dab of butter, crushed garlic, chopped herbs and seasoning. The plough disc is set over the open fire and absorbs the heat, cooking the fish.

Best of all, however, is the following method (only for firm fish – filleted, or split open along the backbone). Oil the fish and the hinged grill rack. Heat the rack over the coals, then arrange the fish in it and braai over a fire. Sprinkle fresh herbs such as fennel, dill or thyme over the fish. Cook skin side down over a moderate heat, then turn the rack and cook the flesh side lightly to prevent it from drying out. Season the fish after it is cooked.

Many shellfish – such as mussels, prawns and perlemoen – are suitable for braaing. For extra ideas for braaing fish and shellfish see Braaivleis*.

A GUIDE TO COMMON SEA FISH IN SOUTH AFRICA

Angel fish

This much-prized table fish is also known as a bulleye or pomfret. (The smaller, brightly coloured, inedible 'angel fish' often displayed in aquaria belong to a different family.)

The edible fish is found at great depths – usually from Walvis Bay to Algoa Bay – and is normally caught only by trawler.

Angel fish are dusky brown, turning greyish after being caught. They grow to about 70 cm in length. They are bony fish, which are best filleted before you cook them.

Angel fish can be fried, baked (and served with a cream sauce*), braaied or smoked*. The flesh is firm, dry and rather rich.

Blacktail

More often called dassie or sometimes kolstert, this small, very vigorous surf and rock fish is found all along the South African coastline.

Although blacktail are predominantly silver, they have fine, dark vertical bars on their short, high and somewhat rounded bodies and a black spot just in front of their black tail.

Young fish, filleted and skinned, make excellent eating – deep-fried, baked, braaied or smoked*. Older fish develop tough, rather coarse flesh which is best smoked*.

Cape salmon

Called salmon or geelbek in the Cape, this highly prized line fish is found along the coast from the Cape to Natal, and more rarely in the colder waters of the west coast.

It is a striking fish that grows to about 60 cm in length and achieves a mass of 2-6 kg. It is distinguished by the bright yellow colour inside the mouth. The fish has an elongated, silver-grey body with an unmistakable salmon-shaped tail.

Cape salmon has firm white flesh that can be poached, fried, pickled, grilled, baked or braaied with very successful results. Southern Cape fishermen make a biltong (known as 'toutjies') from this fish.

Eel

Edible eels, including congers and morays, are found in many rivers as well as in the sea itself. They are aggressive and therefore dangerous, and difficult to kill unless you know how (experienced fishermen usually hit the eel hard on the back of the head).

Once you are sure it is dead, make a slit around the neck and, holding the head, peel off the skin in the direction of the tail. Salt the eel, allow to stand for some hours, then slit open and clean well. Remove the backbone and fry, bake or smoke* the eel.

Elf

Often called shad, or green or blue elf, this fish is caught in Natal throughout the year, but only in the summer in the Cape.

FISH

It is famous in Natal for the 'shad' run, when huge shoals chase pilchards (known locally as 'sardines').

Elf is slim, olive-green or blue on top, with a silver-grey belly. It is very energetic, and a fierce fighter, but bruises easily. For this reason, cook it as soon as possible after catching.

For the best results, fry, grill, braai or smoke* elf.

Galjoen

Considered a national fish by South African anglers, it is also known as black bream, damba, blackfish and highwater.

Galjoen are definitely tastier if caught in winter. The black-marbled flesh has a distinctive flavour. The fish is usually best if bled after being caught, then rinsed well (this gets rid of the marbling veins).

Galjoen can be grilled, braaied, fried, baked or pickled.

Hake

Hake, stockfish, Cape whiting, haddock or cod are different names for what is generally thought of as a commercial, not an angling, fish.

Found in the deeper waters around the coast, it grows to about 1 m in length and is coloured silver-grey.

When fresh, it is firm, delicately flavoured and ideal for frying (with some form of coating). Hake can also be grilled, baked, poached or smoked*.

Harder

Many species of harder (also known as mullet or springer) are found around the coast of South Africa from Cape Town to Durban.

Harders have long, rounded bodies with two small dorsal fins, a small mouth and almost invisible teeth.

Although very bony, they do have well-flavoured, firm flesh that is ideal for baking, frying, poaching, sousing, smoking*, salting or braaing.

Hottentot

From Walvis Bay to False Bay this fish is called Hottentot, but up the coast (Port Elizabeth onwards) it is known by the names bronze bream or copper bream. Another name for it is hangberger.

The Hottentot varies in colour from dark brown or black (on the west coast) to silver, grey and black (in the Mossel Bay area). It can have a mass of anything from 500 g to 2,5 kg.

Hottentot has a delicious flavour, with a soft, moist white flesh.

Smaller fish are usually very bony, but are good when baked with a robust sauce or poached in a court-bouillon*.

Kabeljou

Kabeljou (also known as kob, salmon, salmon bass, rietbul or boerkabeljou) is one of our best-known and most versatile table fishes. It is found all around the coast, virtually throughout the year.

Kabeljou has a sleek, scaly, mainly silver body, with a wide convex tail. It can grow to a length of 2 m and can have a mass of up to 70 kg.

All but the largest have a delicate, tasty flesh which can be fried, poached, baked, grilled, braaied, pickled or smoked*.

Kingklip

This is not an attractive-looking fish, with its elongated, eel-like body and mottled pink and brown colouring. However, it is prized for its firm, moist and delicious flesh.

Kingklip is trawled in deeper waters, from Walvis Bay to Algoa Bay. It can grow to about 1,5 m in length, but most catches are much smaller.

Kingklip is excellent fried, grilled, baked in aluminium foil or poached. It should be cooked until it just flakes; overcooking, a common fault, makes it dry and tasteless.

Mackerel

Of the same family as the tuna, mackerel travel in shoals along the south-east coast and are netted in vast hauls from Table Bay to Mossel Bay. Fresh mackerel have a metallic shine; the body is fleshy and elongated, with a tail shaped rather like a butterfly's wing.

The firm flesh goes soft rapidly. To cook mackerel, fry it in a mixture of butter and sunflower oil, grill or braai, poach, bake with herbs, souse, smoke* or pickle.

Monkfish

Monkfish (also known as anglerfish) is found on the sea bed off the coast of the Eastern Cape and Natal. It is an ugly fish, about 1 m long, a brownish colour with paler spots that provide excellent camouflage while the monkfish waits to trap smaller fish in its wide jaws.

Despite its looks, it has a good flavour. The firm flesh is sometimes substituted for crayfish, and is often served in restaurants as a starter. Monkfish may be poached, then served with a sauce, or it can be fried, or baked *au gratin*.

Musselcracker

Among the many common names of the two types of musselcracker found in South African waters are black steenbras, silver steenbras, musselcrusher, biskop, brusher, blue stompkop and poenskop. It is found in clear, deep waters from False Bay to northern Natal, as well as closer inshore.

Small musselcrackers are mottled in colour; fully grown ones are gun-metal grey, blue-black or a dull brown. They have very powerful jaws, and are considered fine angling fish. Young musselcracker is best for eating; it can be fried, baked, braaied, poached, smoked* or pickled.

Pilchard

Pilchards (also known as sardines, pelser, whitebait and anchovies) are found mainly in the cooler sea currents along the west coast, but in the winter some migrate east as far as Natal.

The pilchard is a silvery, cylindrical fish growing to 30 cm in length. It has a rich, oily flesh. Though bony, small pilchards may be eaten whole; they are very good dipped in flour and fried or braaied; larger fish can be fried, grilled, baked, smoked*, pickled or soused.

Red roman

A fine line fish found all the year round (but more plentiful in summer) in the seas from the Cape to Natal, red roman is bright orange-red, with a blue band over the eyes and a white band near the middle of the body.

Like many other fish, it changes colour to suit its surroundings – which explains why astonished fishermen have at times caught light yellow and 'blue' roman.

Red roman has a big mouth and powerful jaws studded with sharp teeth which can inflict a nasty bite. It has a mass of up to 5 kg, but is usually caught when much smaller.

Red roman has firm white flesh and is good baked (preferably stuffed) and served with a sauce. The fish can also be marinated, then braaied or grilled.

Red steenbras

This fish, also known as yellow steenbras, is found in the waters from False Bay to Natal and is popular both as a game fish and a table fish. It is a reddish to bronze colour and some have yellow undersides. The fish has strong jaws and sharp teeth which can inflict deep wounds.

The liver of this fish should not be eaten as it contains poisonous levels of vitamin A.

The juicy flesh is delicious filleted and fried, or baked, grilled, braaied, poached, pickled or smoked*.

Silverfish

This fish, also known as doppie, rooitjie, Karpenter or Kapenaar, is caught by trawlers and anglers from Cape Town to Natal. It is usually found in deeper waters, but sometimes swims close to rocky coastlines.

It is a shiny, silvery-pink fish that grows up to 1 m in length and can have a mass of more than 3 kg when fully mature. The flesh falls apart easily once cooked, so it should be baked or fried whole or made into fish cakes.

Skate

Skates (also called rays) are caught mainly in December and January by trawlers. They live on the sea bed and propel themselves on their enlarged pectoral fins like wings.

Skates belong to the same family as sharks. They have a skeleton of cartilage, no bone, and a slender tail that is long and whip-like in most species. The eyes are set on top of the flattened head and behind each one is a breathing aperture.

Most skates are grey or brown, but some are patterned with blurry spots.

FISH

The skate continues to form a sticky coating over its skin for up to 10 hours after being caught, so by wiping this away and watching it re-form you can soon tell if it is fresh.

In other countries skate is considered a delicacy, and although not very popular here it is worth trying the skinned fins fried in butter, and served with a sauce made of melted butter and lemon juice.

Snoek

Found in our cooler seas, snoek is caught in the Cape from April to July and in the Walvis Bay area from November to January. The snoek is a vicious fish with razor-sharp teeth which can cause profuse bleeding.

The adult is large and silver-coloured and grows to a length of 1-2 m. It is famed as a first-class eating fish, particularly in the Cape, where enormous quantities are sold (fresh, smoked or dried).

Fresh snoek flesh should be firm and tinged with pink. Some people soak snoek fillets in salted lukewarm water for several hours to rid it of excess oil before cooking. Dry well before frying, grilling, braaing, pickling or smoking*.

Sole

Also known as tongvis, flounder or flatfish, sole is found on the east coast from False Bay to Natal and on the west coast from Cape Town to Walvis Bay. East coast soles grow to about 60 cm in length, whereas west coast soles can be as long as 80 cm.

Soles are generally found on the sea bed, the darker side facing up. If disturbed, they can change colour to match their surroundings. They are flat fish, with both eyes on one side of the head.

Sole is very popular because of its delicate flavour. It can be cooked whole or filleted, and may be served with a pat of butter, or in more complicated classical dishes. For a simple and delicious dish, fry or grill sole and serve with lemon butter*.

Stumpnose

Although both white stumpnose and red stumpnose are found in the seas from Cape Point to Natal, the latter is probably the more common – particularly in False Bay in autumn.

Red stumpnose is an ugly fish with a large bossed forehead which, in the mature male, protrudes even further into a large white hump.

The brilliant colouring of the red stumpnose, with its red and silver body, banded irregularly with black markings on the sides, is quite unmistakable. The average mass of the fish is 3-5 kg but larger specimens (up to 8 kg) have been caught.

The flesh is delicious and strongly flavoured, and should ideally be baked whole or grilled.

Tuna

Tuna (or tunny, as it is sometimes called) is found in great numbers around the southern African coast from Angola to the Cape and further north to Natal – particularly during the early part of the year.

More species visit South African waters than anywhere else in the world; they include bluefin, big eye, yellowfin and longfin, as well as many smaller varieties.

The tuna has a powerful, torpedo-shaped body, mostly metallic blue-green in colour, but often spotted with silver on its sides. Large tuna, such as the bluefin, grow to more than 4 m long, while smaller specimens average 2-2,2 m.

Tuna flesh is firm, rich, oily and very tasty, but is inclined to be dry, so you should marinate it before grilling or braaing. Baste well during cooking. Tuna can also be roasted, baked or braised in white wine with onions, tomatoes and garlic.

Yellowtail

Yellowtail, known as geelstert, albacore or halfkoord in different parts of the country, is found in Cape waters from late spring to autumn. It occurs off the coast between Cape Town and Natal from June to April. It rarely comes close enough inshore to be caught by anglers, and is usually netted by commercial trawlers.

Yellowtail is a fine game fish with a blue body, yellow fins and a golden stripe streaking the body from head to tail. Its flesh is very firm and tasty, but is inclined to be coarse.

Overcooking or cooking at too high a heat tends to make the fish dry, so you should cook it carefully (skin the fish before cooking). Yellowtail is delicious grilled, braaied, fried, pickled or smoked*.

SHELLFISH AND OTHER SEAFOOD

Alikreukel

These tasty shellfish, also known as ollycrock, are found clinging to rocks, and are particularly common on the west coast. They resemble outsize snails.

Before being cooked, alikreukels must be washed well and rinsed 3-4 times to clean them completely. Cook them in salted boiling water (in their shells) for about 15 minutes, or until the 'trap door' on each alikreukel comes off easily.

Remove from the shells, cut off the hard 'trap door' and stomach, and serve in garlic butter* or a curry sauce*.

Calamari see Squid.

Crab

Crabs are usually caught with baited traps or lines, but some are pulled out in trawlers' nets. Most people buy only frozen or tinned crab, but if you are lucky enough to buy or catch fresh crab, prepare them as follows: suffocate the crabs by leaving them in fresh water for a few hours, then plunge them into heavily salted boiling water. Cover and simmer for 10 minutes, then drain (right side up).

Pull off the legs, remove the abdomen flap and pull off the upper shell. Remove the gills and intestines. Scoop the soft yellow-brown meat from the shell into a basin. Crack the claws and put the pinkish-white meat into a second basin.

TIPS FOR COOKING FISH

1 To eat fish at its best, cook it the day you buy it. If this is not possible, sprinkle it with coarse salt and refrigerate to ensure it remains firm. Before cooking fish, rinse it quickly and wipe all surfaces with a damp cloth.
2 Never overcook fish – it will toughen the flesh and destroy the flavour. Short, gentle cooking over a low heat gives the best results.
3 Test for readiness by inserting a skewer. The fish is cooked when the flesh separates easily from the bone, or, if boned, when a soft white liquid similar to curd oozes out.
4 If you need to re-heat fish that has already been cooked, it must be thoroughly heated through – to a temperature of 80°C. Finely slice, chop or mince the fish to allow the heat to penetrate. Re-heat only once.
5 Line the grill pan with aluminium foil when grilling fish. This prevents fishy smells from clinging to the pan.
6 When grilling fish whole, make two or three deep cuts on each side to help the heat penetrate.
7 To prevent fish from sticking to the grill rack, brush with melted fat, butter or sunflower oil on both sides before cooking.
8 Fish for frying should be crisp and dry, and free from grease. To prevent the fat from soaking into the fish, sprinkle it with a little salt or coat with seasoned flour, oatmeal, beaten egg and breadcrumbs or – for deep-frying – batter.
9 Do not overfill the pan when frying fish. The cold fish reduces the temperature of the cooking oil.
10 When baking fish without foil, use moderate heat and baste occasionally to prevent it from drying out.
11 Roll stuffed fillets of flat fish from head to tail with the skin side innermost before you bake them. This prevents the flesh from breaking.
12 Jugged kippers* or kippers baked in foil* are more digestible than when fried or grilled, and as a bonus the house does not reek of kippers.
13 Sprinkle a few drops of lemon juice on white fish before steaming. This prevents discoloration. Serve the fish with a colourful garnish, such as chopped parsley, fennel or watercress, or sieve hard-boiled* egg yolk over it.
14 Simmer fish gently when poaching. Cooking too rapidly will break the skin before the flesh near the bone is properly cooked.

FISH

A Guide to Boning and Filleting Fish

When boning and filleting fish, it is advisable to use a special fish-filleting knife with a thin flexible blade. In the case of a round fish, you should start by scaling the fish, cutting off the fins, and removing the entrails. When boning and filleting a flat fish, scaling is unnecessary.

Round Fish

To fillet a round fish, hold the knife horizontal and slice down the backbone, from head to tail, so that the backbone is exposed. To remove the upper fillet, slice it just behind the gills, then, using stroking motions, cut the fillet carefully away from the ribs. Turn the fish over and repeat this process for the bottom fillet. If the fillets contain small bones near the centre, remove them with tweezers. Trim away any discoloured flesh and, if desired, skin the fillet.

To fillet a firm-fleshed round fish after cooking, place it on a serving board or platter and strip off the skin from just below the head to just above the tail. Using a pair of kitchen scissors, snip the backbone just behind the head and above the tail. With a sharp knife separate the flesh from the backbone, and carefully ease out the bone without damaging the shape of the fish.

Flat Fish

To fillet a flat fish – sole is the most common flat fish available in South Africa – lay the fish (dark side up) on a board and cut a slit just above the tail. Carefully prise a flap of skin away from the flesh with a knife and pull the whole skin firmly away from the flesh all the way up to the head. Pull the skin over the head and then cut through the exposed flesh and bone, just behind the head, so that the head comes away but remains fully attached to the skin on the other side. Turn the fish over, and holding the head, continue pulling away the skin until you reach the tail.

Lay the skinned fish on a board and, holding the knife almost flat, cut down both sides of the backbone. With a stroking motion cut away the fillets on both sides of the backbone keeping the knife in contact with the bone. Turn the fish over and repeat the process. Remove any small bones.

To serve, mix the brown meat with a small quantity of fine fresh breadcrumbs and salt and pepper, then pack into the sides of the cleaned shell. Flake the white flesh and pile into the centre of the shell.

Alternatively, use the crab meat in soups or salads, or stir into a creamy sauce, sprinkle with grated cheese and grill until bubbly.

Crayfish

Crayfish (rock lobsters) are found all year round at the Cape and along the west coast, but the season is restricted. They are usually caught in nets, though divers (with permits) also take out limited numbers.

Most of us think of crayfish as orangey-red in colour, whereas the live crayfish is a much darker reddish-brown colour better suited to its natural habitat.

Unlike true lobsters, crayfish do not have large front claws – and most of the meat is in the tail.

If in doubt about the freshness of a crayfish, stretch out the tail: if it flips back smartly into place, the crayfish is still fresh.

As with crab, it is kinder (though not traditional) to drown crayfish in fresh water before cooking. Weigh and put into a large saucepan of boiling water or court-bouillon*, then simmer – allowing 6 minutes for every 500 g.

Cut in half right along the body, remove and discard the alimentary canal, and serve in the shell. Alternatively, peel away the shell, remove the entrails, chop the flesh and fold into a suitable crayfish sauce. See also Preparing crayfish*.

Langoustine see Prawn.

Limpet

Limpets (also known as barnacles or klipmossels) have ridged conical shells. They cling tightly to the rocks all around the coastline. You may collect only a limited number.

Steam the limpets out of their shells (using a little water or wine) and serve with garlic butter* or vinaigrette*. They can also be grilled or braaied in their shells.

Mussel

Black mussels and white mussels can be found all along the South African coast. Black mussels are more succulent, less chewy and generally more popular than the white variety.

Although they cling to the rocks, they can be picked quite easily at low tide. Remember that local laws limit the number that may be collected.

There is no 'safe season' for collecting and eating mussels – seek advice from local fishery offices. Never pick mussels from polluted areas, or after a red tide* (such tides are not always toxic, but it is best not to take the risk).

Mussel shells should be tightly closed once tapped, and as smooth and barnacle-free as possible.

To keep a catch of mussels overnight, either cover with seawater and leave in a cool place, or cook quickly and refrigerate. (See Cleaning and opening mussels*.)

Mussels are excellent in stews and curries, or grilled or braaied. Black mussels are available tinned.

Octopus

The octopus (or sea-cat or catfish) lives in and around rocky gullies near the shore, and is shy by nature. It can change colour to match its surroundings.

Like calamari, octopus has a sac of ink-like liquid that it can use to cloud the water if attacked.

The traditional method of preparing octopus (once it has been enticed from its home and killed with a blow against the rocks) is to beat it 99 times to tenderise it. However, stop well before the flesh disintegrates.

Before cooking octopus, it must be cleaned of bag, entrails and beak. Bake or simmer (do not add liquid) for 15-30 minutes, or until tender. Drain, cut up and fry, or use as an ingredient of any number of seafood dishes.

Oyster

Coastal oysters are in great demand when in season (from December to February), for, although they are not as 'meaty' as the cultivated kind, they have a really special flavour.

Cultivated oysters, on the other hand, are more easily available as they travel and keep better.

To keep oysters alive, chill or refrigerate them, and they will remain perfectly fresh for up to 7 days. To check for freshness, ensure that the shells are tightly shut, or that they close immediately when tapped.

To open oysters, wrap your left hand in a towel, and then, with the right hand holding an oyster knife or wide-bladed kitchen knife, prise the shell open at the hinged end. Carefully ease the knife right around, forcing the shells apart. (See also Cleaning and serving oysters*.)

Serve oysters in the deep half-shell with lemon juice, Tabasco (chilli sauce) and cayenne pepper. Alternatively, set them on a bed of coarse salt, then grill.

Periwinkle

Often called winkles, these shellfish are rather like miniature alikreukels or snails. They are eaten raw in many parts of the world, but are more appealing when lightly cooked.

Soak periwinkles in fresh water for 30 minutes, then rinse well and poach for about 5 minutes in salted boiling water or dry white wine. Drain, cool and pick out of the shells with a pin.

Pull off the 'trap door' and soft stomach and eat with brown bread* and butter, or toss in garlic butter* or tomato and onion sauce*.

Perlemoen

Abalone, klipkous or Venus ear – as perlemoen is also known – is readily available around the coast between St Helena Bay and East London. It has a beautiful 'ear-shaped' shell which is best removed while the fish is still alive.

Strike the perlemoen on the 'mouth' with a blunt stone or heavy boot to stun it, then quickly cut the fish out of the shell. To prepare it for cooking, scrub off the black slime with a hard brush, trim off the skirt and cut out the mouth. (See also Cleaning perlemoen*.)

Slice into thin rounds, then beat these 'steaks' well to make them tender. Marinate the steaks (optional) in sunflower oil and white wine with chopped herbs, then dry and fry in butter, or dip in egg and breadcrumbs or batter and fry quickly.

Prawn

Prawns, shrimps and langoustine are so similar in everything but size that they have been grouped together.

All three are found in the bays and river estuaries on the east coast of South Africa – most commonly on the Natal coast (though some appear as far south as the southern Cape coast).

They are sold fresh or frozen. To cook, deep-fry, grill or simmer in a tightly covered saucepan with 250 ml (1 cup) water or wine, shaking the pan from time to time, until the prawns change colour from muddy brown to pink (about 3 minutes). Cool, peel and remove the vein down the back. (See Shelling and de-veining prawns*.)

Use in salads, seafood dishes, kebabs, grills or soups.

Sea urchin

Found all along the coast in rock pools at low tide, they have to be snipped off the rocks with a sharp pair of scissors. Wear gloves to protect your hands.

Sea urchins are seasonal, and they are best collected during a spring tide. The deeper under the water they live, the better they taste – and they must be eaten fresh. If you are in doubt, sprinkle salt into the hollow mouth; if it starts moving, the sea urchin is fresh.

To prepare, cut around the shell and discard the prickly outer section. Turn upside down, rinse in sea water and you will find a bright red portion of what looks like caviar inside. Season, scoop out and eat raw.

If the inside of the sea urchin is black and mushy, do not eat it.

Shrimp see Prawn.

Squid

All the varieties of squid (also known as calamari, chokka, cuttlefish or ink fish) are found either in deep waters, where they are caught by trawlers, or in warmer waters closer to shore.

The squid has ten tentacles, while the octopus has only eight. Some species have noticeable fins, and these are edible as well as the tentacles.

To prepare the squid for cooking, first clean it carefully. Remove the ink sac, beak and entrails, and ease off the skin (see Preparing calamari*).

Wash well, dry thoroughly, then fry in butter with garlic and lemon, or coat with batter and deep-fry until golden. Do not overcook, or the squid will toughen.

FRESHWATER FISH

Provincial authorities limit the number and size of fish which may be caught in fresh water, and also issue further regulations that govern the sport.

All anglers older than 16 years must possess an angling licence, and a special licence is required for trout fishing. Check with the provincial administration office near you or local piscatorial society before you set out.

Barbel

These scale-less, eel-like fish, also known as catfish, have either six or eight barbels (or 'whiskers') around their mouths, depending on the type of barbel.

The barbel should be cleaned (taking care to avoid the barbs on its back) and filleted, then soaked for about 4 hours in lightly salted water (to rid it of its muddy flavour) before cooking.

Barbel has coarse-textured flesh, which is best fried. It can also be baked, poached, steamed or braised.

Bass

Three types of bass – the small-mouth, large-mouth and spotted bass – have been introduced as angling fish to South African waters.

Bass is prized as an eating fish. It should be scaled if you intend braising, grilling, baking, braaing or frying it, but need not be scaled if you wish to poach it. Bass is delicious smoked*.

Carp

Several species of carp – mirror, king (or full-scale) and leather carp – were introduced to dams in South Africa, from where they have escaped to rivers. They are now found in most rivers and dams throughout the country.

Scale and clean carp, and remove the gallstone at the back of the head, before soaking it in the same way as you would barbel to get rid of the muddy taste. The fish is suitable for baking, poaching, frying, steaming or braising.

Kurper

This Afrikaans name has been adopted for several species of bream and other fish that resemble bream.

The most popular angling and eating fish among the kurpers is the blue bream, which is found in warm vleis and dams and east coast estuaries, and the red-breasted bream, which has the same shape but often has a pink chest. Also included in this family are the olive-yellow canary kurper, the vlei kurper and the Cape kurper (or rocky).

Kurpers are regarded as good eating fish. Prepare and soak them in the same way as you would carp. They are best filleted before cooking.

Tiger fish

This prized sporting fish with its ferocious teeth is found only in rivers flowing from west to east.

The flesh is fatty, making it a good fish for grilling (there is no need to add extra fat). It can also be minced and used in fish cakes.

Trout

The trout is one of the most popular freshwater angling and eating fish. Four types have been introduced to South African waters – brown, tiger, golden and rainbow trout – and the fish is also exploited commercially.

Trout is best when it is simply wiped with a damp cloth, rather than being washed, and then prepared whole: smoked, poached, grilled, braaied, baked or sautéed.

Yellowfish

Yellowfish, scalie, kalwerkop, whitefish, silverfish, Clanwilliam yellowfish, large- and small-mouth yellowfish, and paper-mouth (the young silverfish) are all names which refer to South African freshwater fish of the same family and group. Some of them are regarded as good sporting fish but not good table fish.

Prepare and soak yellowfish in the same way as you would carp.

FISH

FISH AND CHIPS *This crisp and golden fish dish is one of the most traditional and popular family recipes.*

FISH AND CHIPS

TRADITIONAL FISH AND CHIPS can be made quite easily at home. The secret of making crisp, firm chips is to ensure that the cooking oil is hot enough; otherwise they will be limp and soggy.

PREPARATION TIME: 50 MINUTES
STANDING TIME: 30 MINUTES
COOKING TIME: 25 MINUTES
PRE-HEAT OVEN TO 140°C

INGREDIENTS FOR FOUR
4 fish fillets (with the skin left on, if preferred)
3 large potatoes, peeled
575-600 ml sunflower oil
Lemon slices for garnish

For the batter:
200 g self-raising flour
2 ml (½ teaspoon) baking powder
5 ml (1 teaspoon) salt
Water

First make the batter: mix the flour, baking powder and salt in a bowl. Add the water, beating in a very little at a time, until the mixture is of pouring consistency. Leave the batter to stand for about 30 minutes before using it.

Cut the potatoes lengthways into chips about 1,5 cm wide. Pat them dry with paper towels. Do not wash them, as this will make the chips too brittle.

Pour the oil into a deep pan. For a pan about 15 cm deep you will need about 8 cm of oil. Heat the oil to about 170°C. It will be at the right temperature when a cube of day-old bread turns golden brown in 1¼ minutes.

Fry the chips in small batches so that they can move about in the pan freely. As soon as they start to brown, lift them out of the pan with a slotted spoon and drain on a thick layer of paper towels. A wire chip-basket makes draining easier.

Put the chips into the pre-heated oven in a dish lined with paper towels while you cook the fish. Heat the oil to 190°C – a bread cube should brown in about 1 minute.

Dip the fish in the batter, turning it over so that it is well coated. Lower the fish into the oil, skin side down, in order to stop it curling.

When the fish starts to turn golden (about 4 minutes), turn the pieces over and fry them for the same amount of time on the other side.

Serve with the chips, garnished with lemon slices.

VARIATIONS For crisper chips, heat the oil up to 190°C – a bread cube dropped into the oil should brown in about 1 minute – and put the chips back in the pan for a minute.

You can make a simpler batter by dipping the salted slices of fish in beaten egg and then in flour. Fry the fish in hot oil over a medium heat until golden brown on both sides.

OVEN-FRIED FISH AND CHIPS

FOR SOME COOKS, this way of preparing fish – a method which leaves it crispy and delicious – is infinitely preferable to frying it over a hot stove. Try and avoid over-cooking the fish, or you will spoil the texture.

PREPARATION TIME: 25 MINUTES
BAKING TIME: 50 MINUTES
PRE-HEAT OVEN TO 250°C

INGREDIENTS FOR SIX
For the chips:
6 large potatoes
80 ml (⅓ cup) sunflower oil or melted butter
Salt and vinegar

For the fish:
1 kg firm fish fillets, sliced
Salt and freshly ground black pepper
Milk for dipping
Cornflake crumbs or dry breadcrumbs for coating the fish
30 ml (2 tablespoons) sunflower oil

Peel and wash the potatoes. Slice them up into chip shapes and soak for about 15 minutes in iced water. Drain and pat dry very thoroughly with paper towels, then arrange them in a single layer in a large baking tin.

Pour over the oil or butter and turn the chips around until they are well coated. Bake for about 40 minutes, or until browned and tender. Place in the warming oven.

Wash and dry the fish and season with salt and pepper. Dip the fish in milk and roll it in the crumbs. (The crumbed fish may be placed in the refrigerator for 15 minutes before baking to allow the crumbs to adhere better.)

Arrange the fish in a well oiled, shallow, oven-proof dish or baking tin. Drizzle with the cooking oil and bake for 10 minutes at 230°C without turning or basting. Serve immediately.

SERVING SUGGESTIONS Season the chips with salt and vinegar just before serving.

Provide lemon wedges for squeezing over each serving.

Baked Fish with Tomato and Onion Sauce

FRESH FISH TASTES WONDERFUL when baked in a tomato and onion sauce. The sauce is first made on top of the stove, then poured over the prepared fish slices and baked until just tender.

PREPARATION TIME: 30 MINUTES
COOKING TIME: 30 MINUTES
PRE-HEAT OVEN TO 200°C

INGREDIENTS FOR SIX
1 kg skinned and filleted* fresh fish
Salt and freshly ground black pepper
500 ml (2 cups) home-made tomato and onion sauce*
A small bunch of fresh parsley, fennel or origanum for garnish

Cut the fish into six portions and season lightly. Arrange in an oiled baking dish, pour over the home-made tomato and onion sauce, and bake for 25 – 30 minutes (or until the fish is firm and just cooked through).

When the dish is cooked, garnish it by placing the bunch of fresh herbs to one side, or chop the herbs and sprinkle over the top.

SERVING SUGGESTION Serve the fish fillets with baked potatoes* and a mixed green salad*.

VARIATIONS Add a layer of sliced cooked potatoes to the bottom of the baking dish.

Top each slice of fish with crumbled feta cheese before baking. Drizzle with sunflower oil and sprinkle with dried origanum.

Sprinkle with grated Cheddar cheese and breadcrumbs after baking. Dot with butter and slide under a hot grill until the cheese is just melted.

Curried Pickled Fish

THIS TANGY DISH provides an appetising meal and also offers an appropriate way of using up surplus fresh fish – once pickled it will keep for up to a month in a refrigerator.

Kabeljou, Cape salmon, kingklip or yellowtail are most suitable for this recipe.

PREPARATION TIME: 45 MINUTES
COOKING TIME: 40 MINUTES
STANDING TIME: 2-3 DAYS
PRE-HEAT OVEN TO 165°C

INGREDIENTS FOR EIGHT TO TEN
2 kg dry-fleshed white fish
Salt and pepper
Sunflower oil
250 ml (1 cup) sugar
45 ml (3 tablespoons) medium-strength curry powder
15 ml (1 tablespoon) turmeric
2 ml (½ teaspoon) cayenne pepper (optional)
750 ml (3 cups) malt vinegar
500 ml (2 cups) water
8 medium-sized onions, peeled and sliced* into 5 mm thick rings
8 lemon leaves
15 ml (1 tablespoon) whole allspice
30-45 ml (2-3 tablespoons) flour

Clean and fillet* the fish (yellowtail's leathery skin must be removed). Pack the fish pieces, cut into oblongs about 4 cm x 6 cm, into a deep, oiled oven pan. Sprinkle the fish with salt and pepper, brush it over with a little sunflower oil and then bake it in the oven until it is cooked, about 30 minutes.

Mix the sugar, curry powder, turmeric, 20 ml (4 teaspoons) salt, cayenne pepper, vinegar and water in a large flat-bottomed saucepan.

Add the onion rings, lemon leaves and allspice and cook these ingredients for 20-30 minutes – the onion rings must remain crisp and not be allowed to become mushy.

Just before removing the saucepan from the stove add the flour, mixed to a smooth paste with a little water. While stirring, bring this sauce to the boil, then simmer for 5 minutes to cook the flour.

Place the fillets of baked fish in layers in a dish and cover each layer completely with the warm curry sauce. Pour over the remaining sauce and allow it to cool. Cover the dish and keep it in a cool place for 2-3 days.

VARIATION Stockfish (hake) can also be used. Slice and sprinkle with salt, then refrigerate it overnight before using. Bake it carefully to ensure that the fish does not disintegrate.

Chinese Steamed Sweet and Sour Fish

THE CHINESE PREFER to cook fish whole – they feel that a fish without a head and tail is incomplete. For this purpose they use steamer dishes made of bamboo. Chinese bamboo steamers come in many sizes and stack on top of each other so that as many as four to five dishes can be steamed over one wok of boiling water.

PREPARATION TIME: 15 MINUTES
STANDING TIME: 30 MINUTES
COOKING TIME: 20 MINUTES

INGREDIENTS FOR SIX
A 1,5 kg whole fish, cleaned
10 ml (2 teaspoons) salt
45 ml (3 tablespoons) sunflower oil
1 chilli, seeded and shredded
6 spring onions, cut in 5 cm pieces
6 slices fresh green ginger, shredded
1 red pepper, seeded and sliced
1 tin bamboo shoots (230g), finely sliced
45 ml (3 tablespoons) soy sauce
45 ml (3 tablespoons) vinegar
25 ml (5 teaspoons) sugar
25 ml (5 teaspoons) tomato paste
45 ml (3 tablespoons) orange juice
10 ml (2 teaspoons) cornflour dissolved in 75 ml chicken stock*

Rub the fish inside and out with the salt and 15 ml (1 tablespoon) of the oil, and allow to stand for 30 minutes. Place the fish in an oval oven-proof dish which can be used at the table. Put the dish in a steamer and steam it over vigorously boiling water for 10 minutes, then turn and steam for a further 10 minutes.

Heat the remaining oil over moderate heat. Add the chilli and stir-fry for a minute. Add the rest of the ingredients, except the cornflour paste, and stir-fry these for half a minute. Add the cornflour paste and stir it until the sauce thickens. Remove the dish of fish from the steamer, pour the sauce over the fish and serve.

SERVING SUGGESTION Serve this dish with steamed rice*.

VARIATION Instead of using a whole fish you may use 500 g fish fillets.

Grilled Fish

GRILLING IS THE BEST WAY of bringing out the true flavour of fresh fish, and there are many methods – using a gas or electric grill, charcoal or a wood fire.

Generally speaking, the fattier the fish (for example, galjoen, snoek, elf and mackerel), the less chance it has of becoming dry during cooking. The firm-fleshed, leaner fish (such as steenbras, red stumpnose, white stumpnose, yellowtail, Cape salmon and tuna) should be basted with melted butter or oil and lemon juice during cooking. Instead of using a brush for basting, try using a bunch of fresh herbs – they impart a delicate herb taste.

PREPARATION TIME: 15 MINUTES
MARINATING TIME: 1 HOUR
COOKING TIME: VARIES DEPENDING ON THICKNESS OF FISH

INGREDIENTS FOR FOUR
A 1,5 kg whole fresh fish
Salt and freshly ground black pepper
125 ml (½ cup) chopped dill, fennel or parsley (optional)
Juice of 1 large lemon
60 ml (¼ cup) sunflower oil or melted butter

Clean and trim the fish. Cut three diagonal slits on each side of the skin. Rub the inside and outside of the fish with salt and pepper, then rub the herbs (if used) into the diagonal slits and into the body cavity.

Pour over the lemon juice and oil or butter, and allow to marinate in the refrigerator for at least 1 hour before grilling.

Place the fish on an oiled baking tin or oven-proof dish, and grill for about 8 minutes on either side. The fish is cooked when it flakes easily (test it with a fork).

SERVING SUGGESTION Serve with baked onions* and potatoes*, a large mixed salad and garlic bread*.

VARIATIONS For a different flavour, marinate the fish for 1 hour in a mixture of 125 ml (½ cup) olive or sunflower oil, 125 ml (½ cup) lemon juice, 1 clove garlic (crushed), 5 ml (1 teaspoon) dried basil, tarragon or thyme, salt and pepper.

Fish fillets can be marinated in the same way as whole fish. They require much less cooking, however.

WHOLE BAKED FISH

AN INCREASINGLY POPULAR way of serving Cape salmon, steenbras or yellowtail is to bake these fish whole. These deliciously flavoured fish can be served both hot or cold, and are ideal party fare.

PREPARATION TIME: 10 MINUTES
COOKING TIME: 30-40 MINUTES
PRE-HEAT OVEN TO 180°C

INGREDIENTS FOR SIX

A 1,5 kg whole fish, cleaned and prepared (with head and tail intact)
Salt and pepper
Juice of 1½ lemons
60 ml (¼ cup) clarified butter*

Clean the fish* and season the body cavity with salt and pepper. Sprinkle with lemon juice and brush with butter, then butter a dish large enough to hold the fish, or wrap it in buttered aluminium foil.

Place the fish in the oven and cook for 30-40 minutes (basting frequently if not wrapped in foil). Test to see if the fish is cooked by inserting a thin sharp knife into the flesh near the bone. If it comes away easily, and the juice runs clear, then the fish is cooked.

SERVING SUGGESTIONS Serve the fish with a Napolitana* or caper* sauce, accompanied by boiled new potatoes (with parsley) and peas.

VARIATIONS Sprinkle the body cavity and skin with any herbs of your choice. Use olive oil instead of butter, and serve with Napolitana sauce*.

Allow the fish to get cold, then decorate it with slices of pickling cucumber, overlapping them to achieve the effect of fish scales. Place stuffed olives in the eye cavities and arrange bunches of asparagus tips (bound by strips of tinned red pimento) along the sides. Serve with herb mayonnaise* and a salad.

WHOLE BAKED FISH *A recipe suitable for a number of different types of fish.*

FISH MEUNIÈRE

MEUNIÈRE IS A FRENCH TERM meaning 'in the style of the miller's wife.' In cooking parlance it refers to fish coated with flour, cooked in butter, and served with parsley and lemon juice.

PREPARATION TIME: 15 MINUTES
COOKING TIME: 20 MINUTES

INGREDIENTS FOR FOUR

800 g fish fillets
30 g flour
A pinch of salt
White pepper
Juice of 1 lemon
15 ml (1 tablespoon) chopped parsley
10 ml (2 teaspoons) chopped fresh chives or tarragon
50 g butter
15 ml (1 tablespoon) sunflower oil

Wipe the fillets and pat them dry. Mix the flour with a little salt and pepper and use it to coat the fish: shake off the excess. Combine the lemon juice and herbs with salt and pepper.

In a large frying pan, heat 20 g of the butter and the oil until it foams. Add a single layer of fish and cook over a medium-high heat for 1-3 minutes, until the fillets turn golden-brown (do not over-cook, or they will fall apart). Turn the fish and brown the other side. Transfer the fish to a serving dish and keep it warm while you fry the remaining fillets.

To make the sauce, wipe out the frying pan, put in the remaining butter and heat it until it turns nut-brown. Add the lemon juice mixture, stirring to blend properly, and pour the foaming mixture over the fish. Serve at once.

SERVING SUGGESTIONS Scatter a handful of finely chopped parsley over the fish and serve with new potatoes, crisp sautéed potatoes, or shoestring chips.

VARIATION Lay the fillets side by side in a buttered oven-proof dish, dot with butter, and bake at 220°C, basting with butter every 5 minutes: they should be cooked in about 18 minutes. Add 30 ml (2 tablespoons) of almond flakes to the butter in the pan, and brown slightly before adding the lemon juice. Sprinkle over the fish.

FISH IN CURRY SAUCE

THIS TASTY DISH can be prepared quickly and easily, using ingredients that most cooks will have readily in stock. The strength of the curry sauce can be altered simply by adding more or less chilli powder, according to one's taste.

PREPARATION TIME: 45 MINUTES
COOKING TIME: 1 HOUR

INGREDIENTS FOR FOUR TO SIX

1 kg white line fish fillets, skinned*
75 ml sunflower oil
15 ml (1 tablespoon) crushed coriander seeds
2 ml (½ teaspoon) turmeric
5 ml (1 teaspoon) ground cumin
5 ml (1 teaspoon) chilli powder
2 cloves garlic, crushed
1 large onion, peeled and finely chopped*
Salt
1 tin tomatoes (410 g), chopped
15 ml (1 tablespoon) desiccated coconut (optional)
175 ml fish stock* or water
A pinch of sugar
125 ml (½ cup) cream or sour cream (smetana)

Dry the fish thoroughly and cut into 3 cm pieces. Heat 60 ml (¼ cup) of the oil and gently fry the fish until lightly browned, being careful not to over-cook. Drain and set aside.

Mix the spices with the garlic and a little water to make a stiff paste. Fry the onion in the remaining oil until lightly browned. Add the spice paste and cook for 1-2 minutes, stirring in another 15 ml (1 tablespoon) of water if necessary.

Add all the remaining ingredients (except the cream or sour cream) and simmer gently until the sauce is thick – about 15 minutes. Gently immerse the fried fish in the sauce and cook for 4-5 minutes until it is tender and has fully absorbed the flavour. Check the seasoning and stir in the cream.

SERVING SUGGESTION Sprinkle the fish with freshly chopped parsley and eat it with cooked rice*, fresh chutney and a selection of sambals*.

FISH

FISH WITH PAPRIKA CREAM SAUCE *A Hungarian dish with a tangy pink sauce.*

FISH WITH PAPRIKA CREAM SAUCE

HUNGARY HAS NO COASTLINE, so freshwater fish, such as carp, sturgeon and wels (similar to the catfish) tend to figure prominently in its cuisine. In this Hungarian recipe, however, the more readily obtainable ocean fish such as kingklip or monkfish may be substituted without really altering the character of the dish.

It is the paprika – a fine, subtle spice with a distinctive red colour – that adds the true Hungarian quality.

PREPARATION TIME: 10 MINUTES
STANDING TIME: 30 MINUTES
COOKING TIME: 30 MINUTES

INGREDIENTS FOR SIX
900 g firm white fish fillets
Salt
50 g butter
1 large onion, peeled and finely chopped*
10 ml (2 teaspoons) paprika
150 ml sour cream (smetana)
1 red pepper, seeded and finely chopped
1 tomato, skinned* and finely chopped

Cut the fish into cubes, about 2,5 cm square, and sprinkle them with salt. Set aside for 30 minutes.

Melt the butter in a saucepan and fry the onion gently until transparent.

Remove from the heat, sprinkle on the paprika and stir in the sour cream. Return to the heat and add the fish pieces. Turn the fish gently in the pan and then add the chopped pepper and tomato. Cover, and cook over a very low heat for 20-25 minutes.

SERVING SUGGESTIONS Serve with parsley dumplings* or noodles. Toss the noodles in butter and poppy seeds.

SOUTH INDIAN FISH CURRY

SOUR TAMARIND and curry leaves are typical flavourings used in the south of India. This fresh fish in a thick tomato gravy has a sharp and hot taste, with aniseed, coriander and garlic flavouring. A firm fish – kabeljou, red roman, yellowtail or snoek – is best for this dish.

You can make the fish curry a day ahead, giving it time to absorb the flavours, or you can freeze it for later use.

PREPARATION TIME: 45 MINUTES
MARINATING TIME: 3-4 HOURS
COOKING TIME: 45 MINUTES

INGREDIENTS FOR SIX
1 kg fresh fish, sliced
60 ml (¼ cup) sunflower oil
10 ml (2 teaspoons) salt
5 ml (1 teaspoon) turmeric
5 ml (1 teaspoon) chilli powder
5 ml (1 teaspoon) aniseed, crushed
10 ml (2 teaspoons) coriander seeds, crushed
30 ml (2 tablespoons) flour
30 g tamarind
10 curry leaves
1 green chilli, sliced lengthways
6 cloves garlic, finely crushed
1 onion, grated or finely chopped*
6 ripe tomatoes, pulped
10 ml (2 teaspoons) sugar
4 sprigs fresh coriander (dhania) leaves, chopped, for garnish

Wash the fish, pat it dry and put on one side. Make a paste by mixing 15 ml (1 tablespoon) of the oil with the salt, turmeric, chilli powder, aniseed and coriander seeds. Rub the paste well over the fish slices and leave them to stand for 3-4 hours.

Mix the flour with 30 ml (2 tablespoons) water, then dissolve the flour paste in 190 ml (¾ cup) water.

Soak the tamarind in 125 ml (½ cup) water for 10 minutes, then remove the pips by straining, and reserve the purée.

Heat the remaining oil in a saucepan, then add the curry leaves, green chilli and garlic. Brown for about 10 seconds, then add the onion and stir-fry for about 30 seconds. Add the tomatoes, flour paste, tamarind purée and sugar. Stir, cover the saucepan, and simmer for 20 minutes.

Add the fish and marinade to the gravy, cover the saucepan and cook for 12-15 minutes, or until the fish is tender. Garnish with the coriander leaves.

SERVING SUGGESTION Serve with a helping of rice and crisp salads topped with mint dressing*.

FISH MAURITIAN

A SPICY, CREOLE-INFLUENCED DISH from the tropical island of Mauritius, this tasty pickled fish is gaining popularity as more and more South Africans sample Mauritian cuisine on holiday.

PREPARATION TIME: 15 MINUTES
COOKING TIME: 30 MINUTES
MARINATING TIME: 3 DAYS

INGREDIENTS FOR SIX
6-8 fillets or steaks of white line fish (about 200 g each)
Salt and freshly ground black pepper
250 ml (1 cup) sunflower oil
200 g pickling onions, or 2 medium-sized onions, peeled and sliced* in rings
4 cloves garlic, chopped
15 ml (1 tablespoon) chopped fresh green ginger
45 ml (3 tablespoons) turmeric
300 ml red wine vinegar
125 ml (½ cup) water

Sprinkle the fish pieces with salt and pepper and fry them in half the oil for 3-4 minutes until half cooked. Remove the fish and arrange the pieces (in a single layer) in a large, shallow dish. Blanch the onions in boiling salted water for 5 minutes. Drain and dry. Fry them in the left-over oil until golden. Add the onions to the fish.

Wipe out the frying pan, add the remaining oil and heat gently. Fry the garlic and ginger until the garlic is soft. Mix the turmeric, vinegar and water and add to the garlic mixture. Boil these ingredients gently for 3 minutes, then pour over the fish. Cover and marinate in the refrigerator for 3 days, or longer. Serve cold.

SERVING SUGGESTIONS This dish makes a good starter (sprinkle it with chopped spring onion stems), as it can be prepared well in advance.

Fish Bobotie

FULLY A HUNDRED YEARS AGO Mr Henry Cloete, the owner of the historic Alphen estate situated in the Constantia Valley, decided that he was tired of bobotie made from minced left-over leg of mutton – then a favourite in South African homes for Sunday midday dinner. So he suggested a fish bobotie instead – a gourmet brainwave.

Stockfish or alternatively any other sort of white fish is considered suitable for this tasty dish.

PREPARATION TIME: 45 MINUTES
COOKING TIME: 40 MINUTES
PRE-HEAT OVEN TO 140°C

INGREDIENTS FOR SIX
1 kg white fish
Salt and freshly ground black pepper
30 ml (6 teaspoons) lemon juice or white vinegar
15 ml (1 tablespoon) fat-free milk powder
1 slice of white bread, 2 cm thick (with crust)
1 medium-sized onion, peeled and finely chopped*
10 ml (2 teaspoons) butter
20 ml (4 teaspoons) fish masala
10 ml (2 teaspoons) sugar
2 large eggs
12 blanched almonds*
Fresh lemon leaves (do not substitute bay leaves)
125 ml (½ cup) whole milk

Poach the fish in a small quantity of seasoned water to which 10 ml (2 teaspoons) of the lemon juice or vinegar has been added. Remove the fish from this stock, cool it and flake it. Enrich 250 ml (1 cup) of the stock with the milk powder and soak the bread in it.

Using a covered pan, sauté the onion in the butter until it is just transparent. Add the masala, sugar and the remaining lemon juice, and simmer, covered, for 5 minutes. Add this sauce to the flaked fish.

Remove the bread from the stock, squeeze out the stock (all of which should be kept for the custard), mash and add to the fish and the sauce.

When the fish mixture has cooled, add one lightly whisked egg. Mix well and spoon the mixture into a buttered dish, smoothing it down well.

Stick the almonds at intervals into the surface, leaving the round ends protruding. Cut off the stems of the lemon leaves and twist the leaves into little cones. Insert them into the fish mixture at regular intervals, so that each serving has a leaf.

Whisk the remaining egg with the whole milk and the strained residue of liquid in which the bread was soaked. Pour this over a spoon on to the fish mixture so that the lemon leaves and almonds are not disturbed.

Place the baking dish in a pan of boiling water on the lower shelf of the oven. Bake until the custard is set – about 40 minutes.

SERVING SUGGESTIONS Serve the dish with steamed white rice*, apricot blatjang* and cucumber sambal*.

Cape Salmon in Aspic with Malay Dressing

IN THIS RECIPE the main ingredient is a whole line fish which is poached, skinned and coated with a cream curry sauce. The fish stock is made into clear fish aspic, which is used to coat the fish and garnish the completed dish. This dish takes time to prepare but the end result is a winner and well worth the effort.

PREPARATION TIME: 1 HOUR
COOKING TIME: 45 MINUTES
STANDING TIME: 45 MINUTES

INGREDIENTS FOR FOUR
A 1,5 kg Cape salmon
3 litres water
300 ml dry white wine
2 carrots, scraped and cut into 2,5 cm lengths
2 celery stalks, coarsely chopped
2 medium-sized onions, peeled and thickly sliced*
8 ml (1¾ teaspoons) salt
Black peppercorns
Bouquet garni*
3 slices of lemon
30 ml (2 tablespoons) gelatin dissolved in 30 ml (2 tablespoons) hot water
2 egg whites
2 egg shells
100 ml dry sherry

For the Malay dressing:
220 ml cream, sour cream (smetena) or natural yoghurt*
10 ml (2 teaspoons) medium-strength curry powder
5 ml (1 teaspoon) salt
3 ml (¾ teaspoon) dry mustard
25 ml (5 teaspoons) smooth apricot jam*, thinned slightly with warm water
30 ml (2 tablespoons) flour
1 egg, beaten
45 ml (3 tablespoons) lemon juice

Wash the fish and pat it dry. Place the water, wine, carrots, celery, onions, salt, peppercorns, bouquet garni and lemon slices in a fish kettle. Place the fish on to a rack and lower it into the kettle. Bring to the boil and simmer for 15 minutes. Then remove the kettle from the heat and allow it to cool. Lift the cold fish on to a working surface and carefully remove the skin. Strain the liquid in the kettle and discard the contents of the strainer.

To make the aspic, use 625 ml (2½ cups) of the liquid and stir in the dissolved gelatin. Whisk the egg whites and shells into the liquid and place in a pan over a high heat, whisking until it comes to the boil. Stop whisking and simmer the stock for 3 minutes. Cool it for 15 minutes, then strain it through muslin 2 or 3 times until it is clear. Stir in the sherry, cool and chill the mixture until it is almost set.

To make the Malay dressing, mix the cream with the curry powder, salt, mustard, apricot jam and flour to form a paste. Place a bowl over hot water and add the paste to the beaten egg. Beat until it starts to thicken, then add the lemon juice. Continue beating until it is the consistency of thick mayonnaise and does not have a starchy taste. Then cool it and spread liberally over the fish.

Spread the fish with some of the aspic and chill it until the aspic is set. Spread the remaining aspic on to a baking sheet and set completely, then cut it into cubes. Garnish the fish with these cubes.

SERVING SUGGESTION Serve with cold yellow rice and raisins served in tomato halves. Garnish with coriander leaves or celery.

VARIATIONS The fish may be baked at 180°C for 45 minutes before being skinned. In this case, make 625 ml (2½ cups) fish stock* for the aspic.

FISH BOBOTIE *A culinary innovation of a century ago still pleases today.*

WHOLE BAKED STUFFED FISH

BAKING KEEPS FISH MOIST – particularly if the head and tail are left intact. The fish will taste even better when stuffed. To do this, you will need to ask your fishmonger to gut and scale the fish and remove the fins.

Good choices for stuffed fish are fresh snoek, yellowtail, Cape salmon, red roman, hake, kabeljou and red steenbras.

Temperatures and times for baking fish differ from recipe to recipe, but as a general rule, you should cook a fish of 2 kg or more at 180°C for 12-15 minutes per 500 g. Cook smaller fish at 200°C, allowing 8-10 minutes per 500 g.

PREPARATION TIME: 30 MINUTES
COOKING TIME: 45 MINUTES
PRE-HEAT OVEN TO 180°C

INGREDIENTS FOR SIX TO EIGHT
A 2 kg whole fish
2 medium-sized onions, thinly sliced* and blanched* in boiling water
4-5 ripe tomatoes, sliced
30 ml (2 tablespoons) lemon juice
60 ml (¼ cup) chopped parsley
Salt and pepper
30-45 g butter
100 ml dry white wine or fish stock*

For the garnish:
Lemon wedges or slices
A few sprigs of watercress

Line a baking dish or roasting tin (large enough to hold the whole fish) with a double layer of aluminium foil and butter the foil well. Wipe and dry the fish and stuff the inside with alternate layers of onion and tomato, sprinkling each layer with lemon juice, parsley, salt and pepper and dotting it with flakes of butter.

Put the fish into the roasting dish, smear the outer skin of the fish with the remaining butter, and season. Pour in the wine or stock. Fold the aluminium foil around the fish to make a loose parcel and bake for 45 minutes to 1 hour.

Test the flesh after 45 minutes, using a fork or toothpick: the fish is done when the flesh flakes. Unwrap the fish and transfer it to a hot platter. Decorate with lemon wedges or slices, and sprigs of watercress.

SERVING SUGGESTIONS Serve the fish skinned* or unskinned with the juices poured over it, or with a cream sauce*.

VARIATIONS Try different stuffings based on breadcrumbs. Add sliced sautéed mushrooms and onion with lemon and seasoning, or chopped herbs, cooked onion and shellfish.

Make a quick topping of fresh white breadcrumbs mixed with chopped parsley, crushed garlic, seasoning and flakes of butter. Stir well and pat firmly over the fish before baking. Undo the aluminium foil halfway through the cooking process to allow the topping to brown.

GESMOORDE SNOEK

THIS FISH DISH may be made from the drier part (around the backbone) of fresh snoek, but it is traditionally made with dried snoek.

PREPARATION TIME: 1 HOUR
STANDING TIME: 6-8 HOURS
COOKING TIME: 1 HOUR

INGREDIENTS FOR FOUR TO SIX
1 kg dried, salted snoek
3 medium-sized onions, peeled and sliced* in half rings
70 g butter
3 medium-sized potatoes, peeled and diced
250 ml (1 cup) milk
Salt and freshly ground pepper
Cayenne pepper (optional)

Soak the fish for 6-8 hours in cold water, changing the water after about 3 hours. Drain and boil the fish in fresh water until it is tender (about 20 minutes). Drain the cooked fish and pull off the skin. Using two forks, take the flesh from the main spine and take out all the bones, if possible.

Sauté the onions in the butter, add the potatoes, the milk and lastly the flaked snoek. Cover the dish tightly and turn the heat to low, so that everything is cooked in the steam.

Season the mixture to taste with salt, pepper and a touch of cayenne pepper, if desired. If necessary, an extra piece of butter may be added during the cooking time.

VARIATION Use skinned* and chopped tomatoes instead of milk.

SANDVELD SNOEK *is a particularly succulent way of enjoying fresh snoek.*

SANDVELD SNOEK

WHEN GOOD FRESH SNOEK is available, use the belly and sides of the fish for grilling as the fishermen themselves do, namely wrapped in brown paper. This 'brown paper' method is also very suitable for braaing snoek.

PREPARATION TIME: 30 MINUTES
COOKING TIME: 50 MINUTES

INGREDIENTS FOR SIX
1 kg fresh snoek, cut into 6 portions
100 g butter or margarine cut into 6 pats
Salt and pepper
50 ml lemon juice
6 squares of grease-proof paper
12 squares of brown paper

Wrap each piece of fish, with a pat of butter, and seasoning and lemon juice, in grease-proof paper, tucking under the ends. Place these wrapped pieces on double thicknesses of brown paper (newspaper is sometimes used in the veld) and make a flat parcel of each, tucking the ends underneath.

Place the parcels on a grid about 20 cm below the grill – just far enough for the paper not to catch fire (the outer layer will become scorched). Cook for about 50 minutes, turning the parcels carefully.

Bring the parcels of fish to the table, and have kitchen scissors on hand to cut open the parcels to reveal the succulent portion of snoek in each little pool of savoury sauce.

SERVING SUGGESTIONS Serve this dish with slices of fresh brown bread* or baked potatoes*.

FISH

Smoked Snoek and Potato Bake

SMOKED SNOEK is a very well known and much enjoyed South African delicacy – especially along the Cape coast where this fish is usually to be found. It can be prepared in a number of ways – this simple dish uses few ingredients and makes a rich, flavourful family meal.

PREPARATION TIME: 45 MINUTES
COOKING TIME: 40 MINUTES
PRE-HEAT OVEN TO 190°C

INGREDIENTS FOR FOUR
350 g smoked snoek
7-8 medium-sized potatoes
3 onions, thinly peeled and sliced*
30 g butter
15 ml (1 tablespoon) sunflower oil
Salt and freshly ground black pepper
125 ml (½ cup) sour cream (smetana)
125 ml (½ cup) fresh cream
Fine dry breadcrumbs

Remove the skin and bones from the snoek and flake the flesh into fairly large pieces. Scrub and cook the potatoes until they are just tender, then skin and slice them when cool enough to handle.

Sauté the onions in the hot butter and oil, stirring them often, until they are soft and golden (if necessary, you can add more butter).

Using a well-buttered, oven-proof dish, layer the fish, onion and potato, starting and ending with a layer of potatoes. Season each layer with pepper, and be sparing with the salt if the fish is salty. Mix the creams together and pour into the prepared dish.

Sprinkle lightly with fine, dry breadcrumbs and bake for 30-40 minutes (or until golden-brown and piping hot).

SERVING SUGGESTION This dish is most enjoyable served with a tomato and onion salad*.

VARIATION If you are unable to obtain smoked snoek, use a tin of anchovies instead. In this case it will not be necessary to add any salt to the dish, as the anchovies are very salty.

SOLE VÉRONIQUE *A delicately flavoured and sophisticated dish – ideal for summertime entertainment.*

Sole Véronique

THIS IS A SUMMER CLASSIC that never fails to please. Delicately poached sole fillets are topped with a rich, creamy sauce containing pale green grapes which impart a subtle, fruity flavour to the sauce and provide a particularly interesting contrast in textures.

PREPARATION TIME: 1½ HOURS
(INCLUDING PEELING THE GRAPES)
COOKING TIME: 30 MINUTES

INGREDIENTS FOR FOUR TO SIX
10-12 fillets of sole
1 small onion, peeled and finely chopped*
50 g butter
125 ml (½ cup) white wine
200 ml fish stock*
5 ml (1 teaspoon) dried tarragon
Salt and freshly ground white pepper
1 egg yolk
125 ml (½ cup) thick béchamel sauce*
60 ml (¼ cup) cream
250 ml (1 cup) peeled and seeded green grapes
Boiling water

Sauté the onion in the butter (in a large pan) until soft and golden. Add the wine, stock and tarragon, simmer for 10 minutes, then strain. Meanwhile, season the fillets of sole lightly with salt and pepper, roll them up and fasten with a toothpick. Butter the cleaned pan lightly and arrange the fish rolls in the pan.

Pour over the strained stock, cover and poach the fish gently for 12-15 minutes, basting from time to time. Remove the toothpicks and arrange the soles carefully on a heated platter. Spoon a little of the stock over the fish, cover and keep warm.

Now reduce the fish stock to about a quarter, remove it from the heat, and strain. Beat the egg yolk into the béchamel sauce with the cream and add the reduced stock. Return to the heat to warm through (but not boil) and correct the seasoning if necessary.

While the sauce is heating, warm the grapes in a little boiling water, drain and distribute around the fish. Pour over the cream sauce.

SERVING SUGGESTIONS Serve garnished with small clusters of grapes. The sauce can make this dish look a little bland and uninteresting, so a pretty floral or pale green platter provides a pleasant foil to the lemon-coloured sauce. Fresh tarragon makes an attractive garnish if you have some.

A rosti* or potato croquette* is a delicious accompaniment, but plain rice also complements the creamy sauce. It is best not to serve a great variety of vegetables with this dish, as the flavour is lost with too many distractions. A simple salad to follow is quite adequate.

VARIATIONS Kingklip or even hake fillets make good alternatives to sole.

Although it is not strictly 'Véronique', a sliced crayfish tail or some prawns added to the sauce while warming is delicious.

Tinned sultana grapes can be used when grapes are not in season, and these need no peeling. They are considerably sweeter than fresh grapes.

Poached Sole with Mushrooms

This relatively quick and easily prepared dish will delight your family or friends. The delicate flavour of the soles is enhanced rather than overpowered by the mushrooms and wine, and the basic recipe allows for a number of equally tasty variations.

Preparation Time: 30 minutes
Cooking Time: 30 minutes
Pre-Heat Oven to 180°C

Ingredients for Four
6 soles, each 300g, filleted*
60 ml (¼ cup) finely chopped parsley
10 ml (2 teaspoons) lemon juice
Salt and freshly ground black pepper
250g button mushrooms, sliced
125g butter
250 ml (1 cup) dry white wine
15 ml (1 tablespoon) flour
125 ml (½ cup) cream
1 egg yolk
Sliced lemon for garnish

Lay the soles skin side up on a board, and sprinkle with parsley, lemon juice and seasoning. Fold the fillets in half and arrange them side by side in a buttered ovenproof dish large enough to accommodate all the fish in one layer.

Cook the mushrooms in 25 g of the butter, then sprinkle them on top of the fish. Pour over the wine and just enough water to cover the fish. Cover the dish with aluminium foil, bring it to simmering point on top of the stove, then place it in the oven and bake for 15-20 minutes (until the fish flakes easily).

Transfer the fish to a serving dish, spoon over the mushrooms, and keep the dish warm. Reduce the wine mixture to about half by boiling it rapidly. Mash 15 g of the butter and the flour together in a bowl. Stir in 30 ml (2 tablespoons) of the reduced wine and stir until smooth. Pour the mixture back into the pan, bring to the boil (stirring constantly), and simmer for 2-3 minutes. Remove from the stove. Whisk together the cream, egg yolk and remaining butter (cut into flakes) and add to the sauce. Check the seasoning. If the mixture is too stiff, add a little more wine, water or cream. Pour the sauce over the fish, garnish with sliced lemon, and serve.

Serving Suggestion Small boiled potatoes and green beans make very good accompaniments.

Variations Add toasted almond flakes, seedless grapes, chopped parsley or cooked shellfish to the sauce.

Try garnishing the finished dish with small diamonds or crescents of baked puff pastry*.

Grilled Sole

West coast soles, known as 'Agulhas' soles (after the current), and east coast soles are both available throughout the year. The west coast variety has a pale grey skin and is firmer and better-flavoured than the black-skinned sole.

Soles vary in size from small 'slippers' (about 200 g) to really large fish, but for most cooks a medium (300 g) fish is ideal: it fits easily into an average-sized frying pan and feeds one person adequately.

Preparation Time: 30 minutes
Cooking Time: 10 minutes

Ingredients for Four
4 soles, each 300 g
Salt
60 ml (¼ cup) clarified butter*
Savoury butter*
1 lemon, thinly sliced or quartered

Skin* each sole on both sides, leaving the head intact.

Brush the fish with clarified butter and grill for about 5 minutes a side. The cooking time depends on the thickness of the sole rather than its weight. Sprinkle lightly with salt and serve topped with 2-3 pats of savoury butter. Garnish with the lemon.

Serving Suggestions Serve with fresh mixed herb butter*, lemon* or anchovy butter*.

Egg and Lemon Fish

This delicious dish is best eaten the day after it is made (though it will keep for three or four days). It is very popular in England, and adapts well to both the warm climate and the wonderful quality of the line fish available in South Africa.

Preparation Time: 35 minutes
Cooking Time: 35 minutes
Standing Time: 4 hours

Ingredients for Six
750 g steenbras, sliced, with bones intact
1 large onion, peeled and thinly sliced*
60 g sugar
10 ml (2 teaspoons) salt
3 ml (¾ teaspoon) white pepper
Water to cover

For the sauce:
2 extra-large eggs
75 ml lemon juice
Sugar
5 ml (1 teaspoon) cornflour

In a saucepan large enough to hold the fish in one layer, place the onion, sugar, seasoning and enough water to cover the fish. Bring to the boil. Add the cleaned and seasoned fish and bring the mixture back to the boil.

Lower the heat, partially cover the saucepan and simmer gently for about 20 minutes, or until the fish flakes when tested. Using a slotted spoon, lift out the fish and place it in a serving dish.

Pour any stock that accumulates in the dish back into the saucepan with the rest of the fish stock. Boil this until the liquid has reduced to 200 ml, then strain.

To make the sauce, beat the eggs well, and add the strained fish stock, lemon juice, sugar and cornflour (which has been mixed to a paste with a little cold water).

Return to the saucepan and cook over a gentle heat, stirring all the time, until the sauce has the consistency of pouring custard. Do not allow the sauce to boil, or it will curdle. Taste, and add more lemon juice or sugar if required. Pour the sauce over the fish, allow to cool, and place in the refrigerator for at least 4 hours.

Serving Suggestion Serve garnished with lemon slices and parsley.

Tuna Baked with Anchovies and Garlic

This unusual tuna dish was originally devised in France during the 19th century. Although the recipe has subsequently been adapted to suit our conditions, it has lost none of its original appeal. Tuna, both fresh and frozen, is readily available in South Africa.

Preparation Time: 45 minutes
Cooking Time: 1 hour
Pre-Heat Oven to 170°C

Ingredients for Four
1 kg tuna steaks
1 tin flat anchovy fillets (55 g), soaked in cold water for 30 minutes
5 ml (1 teaspoon) basil
A little olive oil
2 bunches young spinach, well washed and trimmed
150 g tomatoes, skinned,* seeded and sliced
6 cloves garlic, crushed
2 onions, peeled and finely sliced*
1 large lemon, rind removed, and sliced
Salt and coarsely ground black pepper
250 ml (1 cup) dry white wine

Blanch the tuna by pouring boiling water over it, then pat dry with paper towels. 'Lard' the fish by making incisions in the flesh at 3 cm intervals and filling them with the anchovy fillets (on only one side of the steak). Sprinkle both sides of the fish with dried basil.

Pour a little olive oil into the base of a casserole that is just large enough to accommodate the fish.

Line the bottom with half the spinach leaves, then layers of tomatoes (sprinkled with garlic), onions and lemon slices. Layer the fish and add salt and pepper. Add a layer of shredded spinach and moisten with a little olive oil. Cover with another layer of tomatoes (again sprinkled with garlic), onions, lemon and shredded spinach.

Pour over the wine, sprinkle with oil, and cover with aluminium foil or a lid. Cook at 170°C for 1 hour. Remove the top layer of spinach leaves and serve the contents hot from the dish.

~ Simple Steps to a Smoky Flavour ~

Smoke roasting is an ingenious method of imparting a superb flavour to everyday foods, with very little effort. No expensive equipment is required: you will probably find most of the things you need in your kitchen cupboard.

Guidelines for Smoke Roasting

Smoke roasting must not be confused with the traditional methods of smoking, or commercial methods, whereby the meat is always cured in brine before being smoked.

Use an old saucepan with a heavy base (a cast-iron pot is ideal); it must have a really tight-fitting lid to prevent the smoke from escaping. If the lid does not provide a proper seal, place a sheet of aluminium foil over the pot and jam the lid on over the foil. You can also use a pressure cooker for smoke roasting.

You will need oak shavings – available at most hardware stores and some sports shops. A word of warning: use only 30 ml (2 tablespoons) shavings, thinly sprinkled over the base of the saucepan (if you use too much, the meat or fish will be bitter).

After the smoking process has been completed, discard the residue of fine black ash in the saucepan.

A small metal pot-stand or old iron stand, or even the metal ring from a fruit-preserve jar, is needed to keep the base of the food container above the shavings, thus allowing free circulation of the smoke.

Use a metal container for the food. It should fit comfortably into the saucepan, but not so tightly that it prevents the circulation of the smoke. You may use an aluminium foil dish, or an old layer cake tin. Pan drippings can be used to make gravies and sauces.

The smoking is done in two stages: a hot ('high') stage and a cooler ('low') stage.
High Place the saucepan containing the prepared food on the biggest plate of your stove, ensure that the pan is properly sealed, and switch on to the highest temperature. Heat the saucepan for 10-15 minutes.
Low Switch the stove to its lowest setting and continue cooking for the rest of the specified time. Do not open the lid at any time, or the smoke will be lost.

A 24-hour curing period, during which the food is wrapped and stored in a refrigerator, intensifies the smoked flavour, but some foods are delicious when served immediately after smoking.

The one food that should always be served cold is smoked beef; it is delicious the next day on wholewheat bread*.

Fish

Standing Time: 1 hour
Smoking Time: 25-30 minutes

Ingredients for Four to Six
1,5 kg whole mackerel or trout, or pieces of snoek
Salt

Season the fleshy side of the fish very well with the salt. Place in the refrigerator for 1 hour to firm.

Smoke the fish for 15 minutes on high and 10-20 minutes on low, depending on the size and thickness of the fish.

Serving Suggestions Serve cold with wholewheat bread*, cheese, spring onions and a few tomatoes.

Smoked trout is a real gourmet's delight: arrange each trout on a plate and serve with thick cream flavoured with horseradish root, sugar, salt and lemon juice.

For a French variation to the sauce, add 75 g walnuts, shelled and chopped, and 5 ml (1 teaspoon) breadcrumbs to the thick cream.

Chicken

Smoking Time: 1¼ hours

Ingredients for Four
1,5 kg chicken (whole or pieces)
10 ml (2 teaspoons) salt
2 ml (½ teaspoon) pepper
15 ml (1 tablespoon) flour
5 ml (1 teaspoon) chicken stock powder
2 ml (½ teaspoon) sugar

Season the chicken with a mixture of the remaining ingredients. Smoke for 15 minutes on high and 1 hour on low.

Serving Suggestions Serve hot with a gravy* made from the pan drippings. Accompany with parsley, potatoes and a green vegetable. Alternatively, serve cold on a bed of lettuce, with tomato wedges and black olives.

BEEF

SMOKING TIME: 1-1½ HOURS
CURING TIME: 24 HOURS

INGREDIENTS FOR FOUR TO SIX
1 kg beef fillet
30 ml (2 tablespoons) sunflower oil
10 ml (2 teaspoons) salt
2 ml (½ teaspoon) sugar
10 ml (2 teaspoons) black pepper
2 ml (½ teaspoon) paprika

Brush the meat lightly with the oil, then season with a mixture of the remaining ingredients. Smoke for 15 minutes on high, then 45 minutes on low for rare, and 1 hour 15 minutes on low for medium to well-done.

Wrap the meat in aluminium foil and, when cooled, place it in the refrigerator for 24 hours to cure.

SERVING SUGGESTION Smoked beef is superb served cold (after 24 hours' curing). Slice it thinly for a cold buffet and for use in sandwiches.

VARIATION Other cuts of beef may be used in place of the fillet, in which case the smoking time on low should be increased by 15 minutes.

PORK AND LAMB

SMOKING TIME: 1¼ HOURS

INGREDIENTS FOR FOUR
1,5 kg pork belly strips or lamb ribs
5 ml (1 teaspoon) salt
2 ml (½ teaspoon) sugar
2 ml (½ teaspoon) garlic salt
2 ml (½ teaspoon) celery salt
2 ml (½ teaspoon) onion salt
5 ml (1 teaspoon) paprika
2 ml (½ teaspoon) black pepper

Season the pork or lamb with a mixture of the other ingredients. Smoke for 15 minutes on high and 1 hour on low.

SERVING SUGGESTIONS Serve hot with savoury rice* and a tossed salad, or serve cold for a picnic or light lunch with crisp rolls and pickled cucumber*.

BOEREWORS AND BEEF SAUSAGE

SMOKING TIME: 30 MINUTES

INGREDIENTS FOR FOUR
1 kg boerewors or beef sausage

The sausage should be smoked for 15 minutes on high and then for 15 minutes on low.

SERVING SUGGESTIONS Serve the sausage hot with mashed potatoes* (or garlic bread*) and a tossed green salad*. Alternatively, you can serve it cold with sliced wholewheat bread*, pickled onions* and tomato wedges.

EGGS

PREPARATION TIME: 15 MINUTES
SMOKING TIME: 10 MINUTES

INGREDIENTS FOR FOUR TO SIX
6 eggs
Salt and freshly ground black pepper

Boil the eggs for 10-12 minutes, then remove the shells and season well with salt and pepper. Smoke the eggs for 10 minutes on high only.

SERVING SUGGESTION Serve the eggs cold, mashed together with chopped chives, mayonnaise* and black pepper, on wholewheat sandwiches.

SMOKING TROUT

FISH

YELLOWTAIL WITH AVOCADO SAUCE

THE SEASON FOR YELLOWTAIL usually coincides with the time when avocados are cheap and fresh herbs plentiful, so this dish is economical as well as tasty and stylish. It is also a boon to the busy cook, since it requires very little preparation and cooking time.

PREPARATION TIME: 30 MINUTES
COOKING TIME: 25 MINUTES
PRE-HEAT OVEN TO 180°C

INGREDIENTS FOR SIX TO EIGHT
1,5 kg yellowtail, filleted and skinned*
50 g butter
30 ml (2 tablespoons) fresh chopped fennel
30 ml (2 tablespoons) fresh chopped parsley
30 ml (2 tablespoons) fresh chopped basil
30 ml (2 tablespoons) fresh chopped marjoram
Salt and freshly ground black pepper
150 ml fish stock*
100 ml white wine
50 ml lemon juice
375 ml (1½ cups) avocado sauce*

Cut the prepared yellowtail into serving-sized pieces. Butter a large baking dish and arrange the fish pieces in a single layer. Sprinkle on the fennel, parsley, basil, marjoram, salt and black pepper, and then add the stock, wine and lemon juice.

Dot with the rest of the butter and cover with aluminium foil. Bake the fish for 20-25 minutes (it should flake easily when tested with a fork). Be careful not to over-cook.

While the fish is cooking, proceed with making the avocado sauce. Serve the sauce in a separate bowl for spooning over the fish when serving.

SERVING SUGGESTIONS If you find that you end up with too much stock, transfer the fish slices to a heated serving platter, reduce the stock and spoon a little over the fish pieces before serving. Garnish the yellowtail with sprigs of fresh herbs or wedges of lemon, or alternatively with small crescents of avocado.

New potatoes cooked in their jackets and crisply cooked snow peas both make good accompaniments. The dish is also excellent served with a helping of hot, white rice.

VARIATION Any well-flavoured, firm-fleshed fish is good when served in this manner. A number of local fish would be suitable, such as kingklip, tuna or even swordfish.

YELLOWTAIL WITH AVOCADO SAUCE *Quick and easy to prepare, this is an ideal recipe for entertaining at short notice.*

POACHED TROUT

SINCE THE ADVENT of trout farming, fresh and frozen trout are freely available almost anywhere in the country, and these make a relatively cheap and elegant addition to the menu. The flavour is inclined to be bland, so the fish needs to be poached in a well-flavoured stock.

PREPARATION TIME: 15 MINUTES
COOKING TIME: 30 MINUTES

INGREDIENTS FOR FOUR TO SIX
6 trout of even size
60 g butter
2 onions, peeled and thinly sliced*
250 ml (1 cup) fish stock*
250 ml (1 cup) water
250 ml (1 cup) white wine
1 bay leaf
4 sprigs parsley
1 sprig thyme, or 3 ml (¾ teaspoon) dried thyme
4 cloves
Salt and freshly ground black pepper

Clean the trout, remove the fins and set aside. Melt the butter in a large pan, and sauté the onion until soft. Add the stock, water, wine, herbs and spices, season lightly with salt and pepper, and bring to the boil.

Boil these ingredients for 10 minutes, then place the trout carefully in the liquid. Turn down the heat and simmer, basting often, for 12-15 minutes (or until the fish are cooked).

Transfer the fish carefully to a heated serving platter and spoon a little of the cooking liquid over each fish.

SERVING SUGGESTIONS Whole fish always look attractive when arranged at an angle on a large oval or fish-shaped platter. Garnish with fresh sprigs of parsley, thyme or bay leaves and thin slices of lemon.

Serve with a Hollandaise sauce* if you have garnished the fish with lemon.

Otherwise, sauté 125 ml (½ cup) of fine white breadcrumbs in 100 ml of melted butter until golden and pour this crunchy butter sauce over the fish just before serving.

VARIATION Poached trout can also be served cold. Remove the skin carefully from

FISH

the top side, leaving the head and tail intact. Coat with a thin layer of cold (but not set) aspic*.

Decorate with blanched herbs*, vegetable or egg cut-outs or simply with thin slices of lemon and cucumber. Coat with several more layers of aspic and serve with an egg and lemon sauce*.

TROUT WITH ALMONDS

THIS TRADITIONAL FRENCH DISH has gained popularity throughout the world, and is regarded as a culinary delight wherever trout is eaten. When cleaning the trout, take care not to tear the skin, or you will spoil the effect.

PREPARATION TIME: 12 MINUTES
COOKING TIME: 30 MINUTES
PRE-HEAT OVEN TO 180°C

INGREDIENTS FOR SIX
6 trout, each 180-200 g
Salt and freshly ground pepper
100 g flaked almonds
Flour for dredging
190 ml (¾ cup) clarified butter*
60 ml (¼ cup) sunflower oil
Juice of 1 lemon

Clean the trout through the gills and wash them thoroughly. Sprinkle with salt and pepper and put aside. Spread the almonds on an oven pan and place them in the pre-heated oven. Roast until golden-brown, turning from time to time (about 25 minutes), and put aside.

Meanwhile, dredge the fish with flour and shake off any surplus flour. Melt half the butter in a large frying pan and add half the oil. Fry 3 trout over a medium heat for 6 minutes on each side. Place on a heated serving dish and scatter with the roasted almonds. Keep warm while frying the remaining trout (using the rest of the butter and oil). Scatter these with almonds and sprinkle lemon juice over all 6 trout.

SERVING SUGGESTION Place the trout on a large platter, garnish with lemon wedges and parsley sprigs and serve with new potatoes or potato croquettes* and petit pois.

VARIATION Bake the trout in a well-greased pan at 200°C for 15-20 minutes. Baste with melted butter and lemon juice, and sprinkle with browned almonds when cooked.

MOULES MARINIÈRE

THIS WONDERFUL COMBINATION of shellfish, herbs and wine has the fresh taste of the sea. Cooks living at the coast are particularly fortunate, since there are many mussel beds within easy reach. Be cautious, however: do not exceed your quota, do not collect during or soon after a 'red tide'*, and make sure the mussels are alive. When fresh mussels are not available, or if you are short of time, you can use tinned mussels.

PREPARATION TIME: 2 HOURS
COOKING TIME: 20 MINUTES

INGREDIENTS FOR FOUR
48-60 black mussels, or 2 tins (900 g each) mussels in shells
70 g butter
1 large onion, peeled and finely chopped*
300 ml dry white wine
60 ml (¼ cup) dry red wine
5 ml (1 teaspoon) dried thyme
30 ml (2 tablespoons) chopped parsley
1 bay leaf
5 ml (1 teaspoon) salt
Freshly ground black pepper
10 ml (2 teaspoons) flour (optional)

Clean the mussels well*. Melt 60 g of the butter and fry the onion until soft. Add the wines, thyme, 1½ tablespoons of the parsley, the bay leaf, salt and a good twist of black pepper. Cover and simmer for 8 minutes, then strain the liquid. Drain the mussels, add them to the liquid in the saucepan, and cook gently until the shells open (5-10 minutes). Remove the mussels with a slotted spoon and keep warm.

Cook the liquid until slightly reduced. Melt the remaining butter in a pan, remove from the heat and stir in the flour if used. Return to the heat and gradually stir in the reduced liquid. When this soup thickens, pour over the mussels and sprinkle with left-over parsley.

SERVING SUGGESTION Serve with warm crusty French bread.

VARIATION If there are mussels left over, remove them from their shells, place them in a glass jar or bowl and marinate in a vinaigrette*. They will keep (if well chilled) for about 2 weeks.

MUSSEL RAGOUT

THIS RECIPE is a version of the French mussel stews *mouclade* and *moules marinière*. If you add water or stock to the ragout (from the French, meaning 'stew') as well as mussel liquid, you can turn the dish into a soup.

PREPARATION TIME: 20 MINUTES
COOKING TIME: 20 MINUTES

INGREDIENTS FOR FOUR
1,5-2 kg mussels
75 g butter
175 g mushrooms, roughly chopped
20 ml (4 teaspoons) flour
175-275 ml whipping cream
Salt and pepper
A pinch of nutmeg
10 ml (2 teaspoons) lemon juice
15 ml (1 tablespoon) chopped parsley

Scrub, scrape and check the mussels*. Discard any that are broken or open. Put a double layer of mussels in a heavy pan and put on the lid.

Cook the mussels for about 3 minutes over the highest possible heat, shaking the pan occasionally. Take the pan off the heat and leave the mussels in it for 3 minutes. Remove the open mussels, leaving the closed ones a minute or two longer.

Repeat this process with the rest of the mussels. Cooking them in batches makes them more tender than cooking them all at once for a longer period.

Remove the mussels from their shells (these can be thrown away). Strain the mussel juice carefully and reserve it for the sauce. Throw away any mussels that have not opened.

Melt the butter in a frying pan and turn the mussels in it until they are lightly coated. Remove them with a slotted spoon.

Add the chopped mushrooms to the pan, cook for about 3 minutes and, when they are soft, stir in the flour. Cook for a further 2 minutes, then add the mussel liquid and the cream.

A thick sauce will take 275 ml cream but if you prefer a lighter sauce use 175 ml.

Continue to cook the sauce for about 3 minutes, then stir in the salt, pepper, nutmeg and enough lemon juice to sharpen it slightly. Add the parsley and the mussels.

CLEANING AND OPENING MUSSELS

Discard mussels with slightly open or gaping shells, or any that do not close when lightly tapped.

With a stiff brush, thoroughly scrub and clean the shells under the cold tap. Scrape away the black weed, or beard, from the outside of the shells.

Shells open during cooking. Follow the recipe, or place in a heavy-based pan with 1,5 cm of water or white wine and chopped parsley and onions. Cook with the lid on for about 5 minutes over a low heat (until the shells open). Discard any mussels that remain closed.

Bring the mixture to just below boiling point to heat the mussels through, then divide the mussels among little pots.

SERVING SUGGESTION Serve with wholewheat bread* and fresh green salad*.

VARIATION The creamy sauce is also good if you substitute 750 g shelled and deveined* prawns or shrimps for the mussels. Simmer them gently for about 3 minutes in 250 ml (1 cup) water or court-bouillon*, then proceed as for the main recipe.

Cleaning Perlemoen

Once perlemoen (abalone) was an abundant shellfish but, since the lucrative export market to the Far East was developed, it has become a much sought-after and protected fish. Only fresh perlemoen can be fried – the tinned variety must be minced or finely chopped before being prepared with a cream sauce.

Give the perlemoen a sharp blow with a blunt instrument on the 'mouth'. Slip a sharp knife under the shell and lever out the flesh, working from the end opposite to the row of small holes.

Remove and discard the entrails, which are now visible on the underside of the perlemoen, and rinse under cold water.

Trim off the fringe or 'beard' and scrub the dark, flat side with a hard brush or non-metal pot scourer.

Slice the perlemoen horizontally into five or more steaks and pound each of these steaks with a metal mallet until limp (but not necessarily paper-thin). The perlemoen is now ready to cook.

Coastal Indian-Style Mussels

This spicy mussel dish, lightly cooked in a coconut-flavoured sauce, was inspired by one of the many Indian regional cooking styles.

Preparation Time: 30 minutes
Cooking Time: 30-40 minutes

Ingredients for Four
36-48 medium-sized mussels
375 ml (1½ cups) water
60 ml (¼ cup) sunflower oil
2 onions, peeled and finely chopped*
2 ml (½ teaspoon) chilli powder
7 ml (1½ teaspoons) crushed garlic
2 ml (½ teaspoon) turmeric
10 ml (2 teaspoons) cumin, crushed
30 ml (2 tablespoons) chopped coriander (dhania) leaves
5 ml (1 teaspoon) salt
30 ml (2 tablespoons) desiccated coconut, soaked in 125 ml (½ cup) hot water

Clean the mussels*, place them in a large saucepan and pour in the water. Cover with a lid and bring to the boil. Remove from the heat when the mussels have all opened, and drain.

Heat the oil in a large saucepan. Add the onions, chilli powder and garlic, and fry until the onions are soft. Add the turmeric, cumin, coriander leaves, salt and coconut water; cover the saucepan and simmer for 7 minutes.

Remove the lid and stir in the cooked mussels. Mix well and simmer for 5-10 minutes on a low heat.

Serving Suggestion Serve hot with saffron rice*.

Fried Perlemoen

The golden rule for this dish is never to touch perlemoen with salt or hot water until it is cooked, otherwise it becomes leathery.

Preparation Time: 45 minutes-1 hour
Standing Time: 20 minutes
Cooking Time: 15 minutes

Ingredients for Four
2 whole perlemoen
Freshly ground pepper
1 large egg, beaten
70 g fine biscuit crumbs
Sunflower oil for frying
Lemon slices for garnish
Salt

Remove the perlemoen from its shell and clean it*.

Holding the perlemoen flat, cut each into three flat steaks. If any are more than 5 mm thick, slice them again.

Pound these steaks very well on a board, using a wooden mallet, until they are limp. Then sprinkle a little freshly ground pepper over them.

Dip the perlemoen in the egg, then in the crumbs and place in the refrigerator for 20 minutes. Fry in hot oil for a minute on either side and then serve it immediately with slices of lemon and a little salt.

Creamed Perlemoen

As a tasty variation from fried perlemoen, try this subtly flavoured creamed recipe. It is suitable for frozen or fresh perlemoen.

Preparation Time: 45 minutes
Cooking Time: 20 minutes

Ingredients for Six
1 kg perlemoen, cleaned and pounded*
500 ml (2 cups) dry white wine
Juice of 1 lemon
Salt
125 ml (½ cup) fine fresh or toasted breadcrumbs
30 ml (2 tablespoons) butter
3 ml (¾ teaspoon) ground nutmeg
15 ml (1 tablespoon) cornflour
125 ml (½ cup) milk

Having cleaned and pounded the perlemoen – the slices must feel limp – proceed as follows: add the wine and lemon juice to a pressure cooker and bring it to pressure. Cook the perlemoen at high pressure for 5 minutes. Cool it down quickly and remove the fish, reserving the liquid that is left.

Coarsely mince the pieces of perlemoen and replace them in the cooker. Taste and add salt if needed. Then add the breadcrumbs, butter and nutmeg, and simmer the mixture gently to blend the flavours. Finally, add the cornflour, mixed into the milk. Simmer all these ingredients until the sauce is smooth.

Serving Suggestion Serve the dish on steamed rice* with a garnish of lemon slices. Pass around cayenne pepper.

Variation If you do not have a pressure cooker, first mince the perlemoen, then simmer it in a heavy-based saucepan with the wine and lemon juice very slowly until tender. Then add the breadcrumbs, butter and nutmeg, and continue as described in the recipe.

Baked Prawns with Garlic Butter

Prawns have long been considered a rather extravagant dish in this country. They are generally fried or grilled, but this particular recipe – which calls for baked prawns – yields results which should please the most demanding gastronome. The garlic flavour is strong but without being overpowering.

Preparation Time: 20 minutes
Cooking Time: 15 minutes
Pre-heat Oven To 200°C

Ingredients for Four
750 g large prawns (or 1 kg if heads are intact)
250 g butter
6 cloves garlic, crushed

Discard the heads, de-vein* but do not shell the prawns. Melt the butter in a large oven-proof dish, add the prawns, and turn to coat them with the butter.

Arrange in a single layer, being careful not to let the prawns overlap. Bake for 5 minutes, then turn and mix in the garlic. Return the prawns to the oven and bake for another 5-10 minutes (or until pink and curled, and firm to the touch).

Serving Suggestion The baked prawns can be served with herbed rice and a green salad*.

Alternatively bake the prawns in six individual dishes to serve as a starter along with crusty bread to soak up the delicious garlicky butter sauce.

PERI-PERI PRAWNS

PRAWNS FRIED in peri-peri sauce have long been popular in South Africa. The sauce in this recipe is quite strong: for a milder effect, halve the quantity of peri-peri spice.

This dish can be served on its own as a starter or on a bed of rice as a main course.

PREPARATION TIME: 20 MINUTES
COOKING TIME: 25 MINUTES

INGREDIENTS FOR SIX
36 large or 60 small prawns, fresh or frozen
250 g butter
125 ml (½ cup) sunflower oil
4 cloves garlic, peeled and crushed
10 ml (2 teaspoons) peri-peri powder
Salt

Defrost the prawns if they are frozen, then de-vein* them (leaving them in their shells with the heads and tails intact). Rinse the prawns and pat them dry with paper towels. Melt the butter with the oil in a large pan and then add the garlic and peri-peri powder. Swirl the ingredients around in order to mix well.

Fry the prawns (a few at a time) for 3 minutes and then place them in a serving dish in the oven warmer. Add salt to the remaining liquid (to taste) and then pour some of this sauce over the prawns just before serving.

SERVING SUGGESTIONS Serve the fried prawns on a bed of hot rice and pass around any remaining peri-peri sauce. Have individual finger bowls of warm water with slices of lemon in them next to each place. A green salad* is a good accompaniment to the prawns.

VARIATION Serve chunks of French bread instead of rice, and use to mop up the sauce.

PRAWN CURRY

SEAFOODS ARE POPULAR along India's coastal areas, where prawns are flavoured with garlic and cooked in many ways. In this recipe, prawns are simmered gently in a thick tomato gravy and flavoured with aniseed. The prawn curry can be frozen for a month or more without losing its flavour.

PREPARATION TIME: 20 MINUTES
COOKING TIME: 35 MINUTES

INGREDIENTS FOR FOUR
800 g prawns, shelled*
5 ml (1 teaspoon) salt
4 cloves garlic
A 2 cm piece of fresh green ginger
60 ml (¼ cup) sunflower oil
6 curry leaves
2 green chillies, sliced lengthways
2 medium-sized onions, peeled and chopped*
2 ml (½ teaspoon) chilli powder
2 ml (½ teaspoon) turmeric
5 ml (1 teaspoon) aniseed, crushed
2 ml (½ teaspoon) coriander seeds, crushed
5 ripe tomatoes, skinned*
4 sprigs fresh coriander (dhania) leaves, chopped, for garnish

De-vein* and wash the prawns, patting them dry with paper towels. Sprinkle them with salt and then leave aside for 15 minutes. Meanwhile, peel and crush the garlic and ginger.

Heat the oil in a saucepan, add the curry leaves and green chillies, and allow to brown for 10 seconds. Add the onions and fry until translucent, then stir in the garlic and ginger.

Place the chilli powder, turmeric, aniseed and crushed coriander seeds in the saucepan and fry for 2 minutes.

Cut the tomatoes in half and add to the saucepan. Cover and simmer for 15 minutes on a medium heat. Place the prawns in the saucepan, stir and simmer gently for a further 15 minutes.

Garnish with the fresh coriander leaves and serve.

SERVING SUGGESTION Prawn curry is excellent served with rice and a kachoomer salad*.

CRAYFISH NEWBURG

THIS RECIPE IS A LOCAL VERSION of the famous international favourite, Lobster Newburg. Another name for the delicious dish described here is Crayfish sauté a la crème.

In this recipe the flesh of the crayfish is removed from the shell after being poached, but it can, if desired, be put back into the shells before serving. If you wish to do this, take care not to damage the shells when you are initially removing the meat.

PREPARATION TIME: 15 MINUTES
COOKING TIME: 30 MINUTES

INGREDIENTS FOR TWO
2 raw crayfish (about 400-500 g each)
Court-bouillon*
60 g butter
80 ml (⅓ cup) brandy
4 egg yolks
500 ml (2 cups) thin cream
Salt and freshly ground black pepper

Prepare the crayfish*, using the first method described. Poach the crayfish in court-bouillon for 12-15 minutes, then drain and cool.

Using a sharp knife or a pair of scissors, carefully cut out all the tail meat, then crack the shell around the claws and remove the flesh. Cut up the flesh from the tail into fairly thin slices.

Melt all the butter in a deep frying pan and place the individual pieces of crayfish on the bottom. Heat the pan slowly, pour over the brandy and ignite. Remove from the heat.

Next, mix the egg yolks and cream together and pour into the pan, shaking and moving the pan gently to blend the ingredients.

Replace the pan on the stove over low heat and continue to move the pan until the sauce becomes creamy. Add salt and pepper to taste.

SERVING SUGGESTIONS Serve on a bed of rice, sprinkle with paprika and accompany with a green salad*.

You can also pile the sauce-covered flesh back into the crayfish shells and serve the rice around the shell.

DE-VEINING AND SHELLING PRAWNS

Prawns are one of the world's great delicacies. Although once considered a luxury item, they are finding wider acceptance in South African homes. Like all shellfish, they are low in kilojoules. If using frozen prawns, thaw them completely before de-veining.

If the head is attached, use a sharp knife to slit the prawn from head to tail. If the head is not attached, use a pair of scissors.

Lift the vein with a toothpick and pull it out with your fingers.

To shell the prawn, pull off the tail shell, twist off the head, then peel off the body shell.

Preparing Crayfish

The least 'traumatic' method of killing a crayfish is to immerse it in a bucket of fresh water for about half an hour, or until it is dead. Another way is to place the live crayfish in boiling water, having first stunned it on the back of the head. Ideally, it should be cooked in seawater. Two methods of cleaning crayfish are given below – the first is the easiest, but involves breaking the shell; the second preserves the shell for serving.

Method 1: Place the dead crayfish on its belly and use a very sharp knife with a large blade to cut through the middle, working from head to tail. If the crayfish is for one person, leave the last segment of the tail intact.

Method 2: Place the crayfish on its back and stretch out the tail. With a sharp knife or pair of scissors, cut from the vent at the end of the tail along the centre of the soft shell and flesh without cutting the back shell.

Gut the crayfish by removing the small sac in the head area with a teaspoon.

Cut up the centre (between the legs). Prise open the head and remove yellow sacs.

Remove the alimentary canal – it resembles a piece of cord running the length of the body. Do not remove the liver or the pink coral (in the female crayfish). Rinse under running water and pat dry.

Cut away and remove the soft shell of the tail. Gut the crayfish, rinse it and pat dry with paper towels.

Crayfish Thermidor

For the best results, this classic dish should be made with fresh, raw crayfish – but frozen crayfish may be used too. The successful preparation of crayfish thermidor is largely dependent upon gentle cooking. Add the ingredients in the order specified, and avoid over-seasoning the sauce.

Preparation Time: 1 hour
Cooking Time: 50 minutes

Ingredients for Two

2 fresh crayfish (about 400 g each)
30 ml (2 tablespoons) sunflower oil
1 medium-sized onion, peeled and finely chopped*
90 g butter
60 g mushrooms, finely sliced
180 ml dry white wine
5 ml (1 teaspoon) chopped parsley
300 ml béchamel sauce*
45 ml (3 tablespoons) cream
1 ml (¼ teaspoon) paprika
2 ml (½ teaspoon) dry mustard
1 ml (¼ teaspoon) cayenne pepper
15 ml (1 tablespoon) dry sherry
75 g grated Gruyère, Parmesan or Cheddar cheese
Salt and pepper
50 g breadcrumbs

Prepare the crayfish*, using the second method described to preserve the shell. Crack the large claws.

Heat the oil in a large, deep frying pan and place the crayfish (shell side up) in the pan. Cook for 3-4 minutes, then turn and cook (covered) for 12-15 minutes. The shell will turn bright orange. Remove the flesh from the tails and claws, taking care not to damage the shells. Place both shells and flesh in the pan in the warming oven.

Using a smaller saucepan, sauté the onion in 60 g of the butter until transparent, then add the mushrooms and cook for 3-4 minutes. Add the wine and parsley and cook (uncovered) until the liquid is reduced to half.

Remove from the heat and stir in the béchamel sauce and cream – a little at a time. Add the paprika, mustard, cayenne pepper, sherry and the strained juices from the crayfish pan.

Return to the stove, add the cheese and seasoning and cook gently until everything is well mixed and the cheese is melted. Remove from the stove. Cut the crayfish meat from the tails and claws into chunky pieces and stir it into the sauce, some of which has been used to coat the inside of the shells. Pile the sauce-coated crayfish into the shells, dot with the remaining butter and sprinkle with breadcrumbs. Place under the grill to brown, and serve immediately.

Serving Suggestions Serve on a bed of rice. A green salad* makes a good accompaniment.

Variations Add 1 ml (¼ teaspoon) tarragon together with the wine and parsley.

Try a mixture of Parmesan and Gruyère cheese.

Grilled Crayfish

This recipe is preferred by those cooks who believe that a sauce tends to obscure or spoil the very delicate flavour of crayfish.

There are, however, a few ways (see the variations at the end) in which you can add interest to this simple crayfish dish without offending the gastronomic sensibilities of the purists.

Preparation Time: 10 minutes
Cooking Time: 20 minutes
Pre-heat Oven to 200°C

Ingredients for Two

2 raw crayfish, prepared and cleaned*
60 ml (¼ cup) clarified butter*
Salt and freshly ground black pepper
60 ml (¼ cup) melted butter
Juice of 1 lemon

Brush the 2 raw crayfish with the clarified butter and then place, cut side up, on the oiled grid of your oven. Turn on the grill, positioning the grid about 10 cm from the grill in order to avoid charring the flesh of the crayfish.

Grill, brushing frequently with clarified butter, for 10-20 minutes, or until the flesh is white and opaque.

Season and serve at once with a sauce made from the melted butter mixed with the lemon juice.

SERVING SUGGESTION Sprinkle the crayfish with chopped parsley and serve with rice or garlic bread* and a green salad*.

VARIATION Before grilling, sprinkle lightly with any herbs of your choice, or with crushed garlic.

When cooked, cover the crayfish with grated cheese and place under the grill to melt.

GRILLED CALAMARI

THE SECRET OF GRILLING calamari successfully is to select a very young one. Older calamari may become tough and rubbery. If you are using a frozen calamari, allow it to thaw completely before cooking.

PREPARATION TIME: 20 MINUTES
COOKING TIME: 5 MINUTES
PRE-HEAT OVEN TO 200°C

INGREDIENTS FOR SIX
800 g fresh calamari, or 600 g frozen calamari
80 ml (⅓ cup) clarified butter*
Juice of 1 lemon
Salt and freshly ground black pepper

Clean the calamari* and slice the body into 1 cm rings. Cut the tentacles and fins into bite-sized pieces. Brush well with a mixture of the clarified butter and lemon juice.

Turn on the grill in the pre-heated oven and place the calamari on a well-oiled grid. Grill until the calamari turns white and singes slightly (about 5 minutes). Sprinkle with salt and pepper, and serve.

SERVING SUGGESTION Serve with wedges of lemon on a bed of rice, with a green salad*.

Savoury rice goes well with calamari.

VARIATIONS Add peri-peri spice to the lemon butter mixture, and use olive oil in the place of butter.

STEWED CALAMARI

FOR EASE OF PREPARATION, buy frozen calamari that has already been cleaned: this is now readily available in most of the larger supermarkets.

If you buy the calamari whole, use a sharp knife to slice the body into a series of neat rings.

PREPARATION TIME: 10 MINUTES
COOKING TIME: ABOUT 1 HOUR

INGREDIENTS FOR FOUR
600 g calamari
25 g butter
30 ml (2 tablespoons) sunflower oil
1 large onion, peeled and chopped*
2 ml (½ teaspoon) dried tarragon
30 ml (2 tablespoons) whisky, warmed
3 medium-sized tomatoes, skinned* and chopped
30 ml (2 tablespoons) dry white wine
Salt and freshly ground black pepper
2 ml (½ teaspoon) sugar
2 bay leaves
30 ml (2 tablespoons) cornflour
100 ml cream

Thaw the calamari if frozen, then rinse, dry and set aside. Heat the butter and oil in a heavy frying pan. Add the onion and tarragon and cook until the onion softens. Add the calamari and stir until the mixture is hot and the calamari has stiffened, then stand well back and flame with the warmed whisky.

Reduce the heat and add the tomatoes, wine, seasoning, sugar and bay leaves.

Bring the mixture back to the boil, then cover it and simmer very gently, stirring occasionally to mash the tomatoes, until the calamari is tender – about 45 minutes.

Remove the bay leaves. Slake the cornflour with the cream, add the mixture to the calamari and allow it to thicken (uncovered), stirring slowly all the time. Taste for seasoning, then serve at once.

SERVING SUGGESTION Ladle the hot calamari stew over portions of rice, and accompany this fish dish with a simple lettuce and avocado salad.

VARIATIONS Substitute sour cream (smetena) for the fresh cream.

One or two egg yolks can be used as a replacement for the cornflour as a thickening agent, but in this case take care that the mixture does not boil.

FRIED CALAMARI

TENDER RINGS OF CALAMARI, crisply coated in breadcrumbs and deep-fried in oil, are among South Africa's seafood favourites.

If you are using frozen calamari, make sure it is completely thawed before you slice and fry it.

PREPARATION TIME: 15 MINUTES
STANDING TIME: 45 MINUTES
COOKING TIME: 10 MINUTES

INGREDIENTS FOR SIX
800 g calamari
60 ml (¼ cup) lemon juice
80 ml (⅓ cup) flour
80 ml (⅓ cup) fine breadcrumbs
2 eggs
Sunflower oil for deep-frying
Salt and freshly ground pepper

Clean the calamari* and slice into 1 cm rings. Cut the tentacles and fins into bite-sized pieces. Marinate the calamari in lemon juice for 30 minutes.

Put the flour and breadcrumbs in a paper bag and shake well. Beat the eggs and 30 ml (2 tablespoons) oil in a wide soup plate. Place the flour mixture in a wide, shallow dish.

Drop the calamari into the egg and oil mixture, a few rings at a time, and then toss in the flour and breadcrumb mixture. Set aside in a single layer on a tray for 15 minutes to settle.

Heat oil for frying to 200°C in a deep saucepan fitted with a basket. Fill the basket a quarter of the way up with calamari and deep fry for about 16 seconds (if fried for too long, the calamari will toughen).

Drain on paper towels and sprinkle with salt and pepper. Fry the remaining calamari in the same way.

SERVING SUGGESTIONS Serve on a bed of hot rice with tartar sauce*, wedges of lemon and a French salad.

PREPARING CALAMARI

Calamari, or squid, has long been popular with Mediterranean cooks, but made an impression in this country relatively recently. It can be bought frozen (cleaned, sliced and cut into rings) or fresh. If frozen, calamari must be thawed out thoroughly before cooking.

To clean calamari, hold the body in one hand and the head section in the other, and gently pull apart. Skin and remove fins.

Using a sharp knife, cut the tentacles and arms off just below the eyes. Lift out the silver-grey ink sac: this will come away with the head section. If the calamari is very young, however, the sac may not be present.

Dislodge the small 'beak' with your fingers. Pull the long piece of plastic-like material out of the body, and discard. Thoroughly rinse the inside of the body – it may in fact be possible to turn it inside out for this purpose.

The body can now be sliced into 1 cm rings for frying or freezing. The fins, tentacles and arms are ideal (chopped) for stuffing.

Seafood Salad with Melon and Lemon Cream Sauce

THIS WHITE, GREEN AND PINK SALAD looks most appetising and attractive with its pale, lemon-coloured sauce. Be generous when ladling the sauce under the salad, as the dish looks better when not coated with sauce.

PREPARATION TIME: 1 HOUR
COOKING TIME: 45 MINUTES
COOLING TIME: 2 HOURS

INGREDIENTS FOR SIX TO EIGHT
500 g monkfish, filleted, skinned* and cut into 1 cm x 3 cm slices
500 ml (2 cups) well-flavoured fish stock*
250 g calamari, cleaned* and cut into 6 mm-wide slices
100 ml semi-sweet white wine
30 ml (2 tablespoons) lemon juice
30 g beurre manié*
Salt and freshly ground pepper
125 ml (½ cup) cream
5 ml (1 teaspoon) grated lemon rind
Watercress or shredded lettuce for garnish
1 tin (about 350-400g) prawns in brine (drained)
250 g green honeydew melon balls, chilled, or 250 g kiwi fruit, sliced and chilled
75 g pecan nuts, coarsely chopped
125 ml (½ cup) bean sprouts*, washed and picked over

Place the monkfish slices in a large saucepan and cover with the hot stock. Simmer over a gentle heat for 10 minutes (they must be done but not overcooked). Use a slotted spoon to transfer them to a dish, and leave to cool.

Cook the calamari rings in the same stock for about 3-5 minutes (until they turn opaque). Do not over-cook, or they will toughen. Remove the calamari from the stock with a slotted spoon and leave to cool.

Now pour the wine into the stock, add the lemon juice, and reduce by half.

Thicken the boiling stock very slightly by gently adding the *beurre manié*.

Remove the sauce from the heat, strain it through muslin, and chill. When properly chilled, season to taste. Whip the cream lightly and stir it into the sauce with the lemon rind. Correct the seasoning if necessary. Cover and chill while you arrange your salad platter.

Make a bed of well-washed fresh watercress or shredded lettuce on a large, preferably fish-shaped, platter (white and green are suitable colours). Arrange the monkfish, calamari, prawns, melon balls or kiwi fruit, nuts and bean sprouts on the greens, cover with plastic wrap, and chill. Serve cold but not icy (cellar temperature describes it well) with the lemon sauce.

If *you* are serving, ladle some of the sauce on to a plate and serve the salad on top of the sauce, garnished with watercress.

Alternatively, make up servings ahead of time with the salad arranged attractively on individual platters, and serve the rest of the sauce in a sauceboat.

SERVING SUGGESTIONS This salad is very good as a separate fish course after a light soup, as a starter, or as a light lunch dish served with fresh French bread.

VARIATIONS Almost any well-flavoured, fairly firm-textured fish (crayfish, kingklip, yellowtail, Cape salmon) can be used as a substitute for monkfish.

Cherry tomatoes or sliced celery can replace the melon balls – but in this case the colour scheme will be different, and not quite as appealing. Watermelon is too sweet, and the flavour of spanspek is not suitable for the dish.

Seafood Stew

THIS DELICIOUS STEW makes use of locally available ingredients for a dish with a distinctly Mediterranean flavour. The anchovy and garlic paste adds tremendous flavour to this rich and filling dish. Do not be tempted to omit any ingredients – each adds its own distinctive flavour.

PREPARATION TIME: 45 MINUTES
COOKING TIME: 35 MINUTES

INGREDIENTS FOR FOUR TO SIX
45 ml (3 tablespoons) sunflower oil
1 large onion, peeled and finely chopped*
1 clove garlic, crushed
250 ml (1 cup) dry white wine
1 large tin tomatoes (about 800g)
1 small tin tomato paste
A pinch of sugar
1 bay leaf
10 ml (2 teaspoons) dried origanum
Salt and freshly ground black pepper
500 g filleted firm white fish, cubed
500 g shrimps or prawns, shelled*
1 crayfish tail, cut into 6 pieces
18 fresh mussels, cleaned* (or a small tin of mussels with shells)
500 g cleaned calamari*, sliced

For the anchovy and garlic paste:
60 ml (¼ cup) finely chopped parsley
4 cloves garlic, finely chopped
4 anchovy fillets, finely chopped
Finely grated rind of 1 lemon

For the garnish:
Parmesan cheese, grated
A few unshelled prawns

Heat the oil in a heavy casserole. Add the chopped onion and cook gently until softened. Stir in the clove of crushed garlic, then the wine, and reduce over a high heat. Add the (finely chopped) tomatoes, plus the juice from the tin, the tomato paste, sugar, bay leaf and 5 ml (one teaspoon) of the origanum and seasoning.

Reduce the heat and simmer, half-covered, for 10 minutes. Add the white fish and cook for 5 minutes. Stir in the shrimps or prawns, crayfish and mussels, and cook (covered) for about 5 minutes (discarding any mussels that have not opened). Uncover the casserole and add the calamari. Cook for a minute or two until the calamari is opaque and tender. Add the remaining teaspoon of origanum and check the seasoning.

To make the anchovy and garlic paste: Mix together the chopped parsley, garlic, anchovy fillets and lemon rind to form a paste. Serve the paste in a separate bowl.

SERVING SUGGESTION Serve with freshly cooked spaghettini (500g should be enough). Toss the well-drained hot pasta in 60 ml (¼ cup) heated olive oil and a clove of crushed garlic. Turn on to a heated platter and pile the seafood stew on top. Pass around a bowl of Parmesan cheese with the anchovy and garlic paste.

Gefilte Fish

IF ONE WERE ASKED to name a traditional Jewish dish, almost certainly the first to come to mind would be gefilte fish. This dish originated in eastern Europe, where Jewish cooks made use of freshwater lake fish such as carp and bream.

The fish was finely chopped and seasoned before being stuffed into the skin of a carp and poached in a jellied fish stock.

These days, however, cooks generally use ready minced fish, avoiding the arduous process of stuffing the skin. The most suitable local fish are hake, silverfish, steenbras, red roman and stumpnose. Use at least three different types for the best results.

PREPARATION TIME: 35-45 MINUTES
COOKING TIME: 35-40 MINUTES
COOLING TIME: 2 HOURS

INGREDIENTS FOR SIX
1 kg fish, skinned and filleted* (preferably at least 3 types)
2 medium-sized carrots
1 medium-sized onion, peeled and chopped*
30 ml (2 tablespoons) matzo meal, or a 10 cm slice of white bread, crusts removed and soaked in water
2 eggs
7 ml (1½ teaspoons) salt
2 ml (½ teaspoon) white pepper
15 ml (1 tablespoon) sugar
60-125 ml (¼-½ cup) water
500 ml (2 cups) fish stock*

Mince together the fish, 1 carrot (grated), the onion, matzo meal or soaked bread, eggs, salt and pepper, sugar and water. With wet hands, form the mixture into balls about the size of small apples.

Place the balls and the remaining carrot (sliced) into the boiling fish stock, and cook gently for 35-40 minutes.

Place the balls in a large deep serving dish, place a slice of the carrot on top of each ball and pour the stock over. Allow to cool and place in the refrigerator until you are ready to serve them.

VARIATIONS For a simple, everyday version, use hake only.

The onion can be fried in 15 ml (1 tablespoon) sunflower oil before being added to the fish.

FISH

PAELLA *is a delicious marriage of a wide assortment of seafoods, meats, spices and vegetables.*

PAELLA

THIS IS ARGUABLY the best-known Spanish dish outside Spain. It is prepared all over Spain with slight variations, but is at its best along the Valencian coast. Paella is a combination of many different ingredients, resulting in a wonderful taste sensation.

PREPARATION TIME: 45 MINUTES
COOKING TIME: 1 HOUR

INGREDIENTS FOR EIGHT

250 g spicy Polish, Spanish or Russian sausages, cut into big slices
45 ml (3 tablespoons) olive oil
8 portions chicken (legs and thighs)
250 g chicken livers
3 cloves garlic, crushed
*1 large onion, peeled and chopped**
1 green pepper, cut into strips
300 g rice
*750 ml (3 cups) chicken stock**
2 ml (½ teaspoon) cayenne pepper
A good pinch of saffron
4 ripe tomatoes, skinned, seeded and thinly sliced*
6 large prawns or 2 small (cooked) crayfish, cut into pieces
12 black mussels (preferably fresh)
1 small tin red pimento, cut into strips
White wine for moistening
100 g green peas (frozen or fresh), cooked

For the garnish:
12 black olives
Lemon wedges

Heat the paella pan on the coals (or use an electric frying pan set on high). Fry the sausages until brown on both sides. Remove and put aside. Add oil to the pan and fry the chicken pieces until golden in colour; then remove from the heat.

Add the chicken livers and two cloves of crushed garlic, and lightly brown; then set aside. Add the onion and green pepper, and fry until golden. Stir in the rice and cook until pale gold in colour. Pour in half of the chicken stock, add the cayenne pepper, saffron, tomatoes and the remaining garlic. Return the sausages, chicken and liver to the pan, then the prawns or crayfish, mussels and pimento.

Cook carefully, stirring frequently. Add the remaining stock and, if necessary, some wine. Cook for about 30 minutes (or until the rice is tender). Stir in the green peas, taste and correct the seasoning. Garnish with the olives and lemon wedges.

FISH STEW WITH RED WINE

THIS SAFFRON-COLOURED DISH is midway between a stew and a soup, and has an interesting texture and a delicious taste. It could be rather expensive, but the cost is offset by the spectacular results. Be careful not to over-cook the fish, or its texture will be spoilt. Steenbras, kabeljou, Cape salmon and yellowtail are recommended.

PREPARATION TIME: 30 MINUTES
COOKING TIME: 1 HOUR

INGREDIENTS FOR FOUR

1 kg assorted firm fish
*250 g prawns, shelled**
45 ml (3 tablespoons) olive oil
*1 large onion, peeled and sliced**
2 carrots, sliced
1 leek, sliced
2 large tomatoes, skinned and chopped*
*3 litres fish stock**
250 ml (1 cup) dry red wine
3 ml (¾ teaspoon) dried thyme
3 cloves garlic, halved
2 strips of orange rind
A good pinch of saffron
Salt and freshly ground black pepper

For the garnish:
Chopped parsley
A few unshelled prawns

Wash the fish thoroughly, then skin and fillet. Shell the prawns and then put aside while you prepare the stock.

Heat the oil in a heavy-bottomed saucepan. Add the onion, carrots and leek. Sweat slowly in the hot oil until the onion turns golden, then add the tomatoes, fish stock, wine, thyme, garlic, orange rind, saffron, salt and pepper.

Simmer on a low heat for about 40 minutes. Next, cut the fish into large chunks and add to the liquid. Continue cooking slowly (adding the prawns after 5 minutes) until the fish is just done (about 10 minutes). Correct the seasoning, sprinkle with chopped parsley and decorate with the unshelled prawns.

SERVING SUGGESTION Serve in soup bowls with crusty French bread and aïoli* (place a slice of French bread in each bowl and top with a good dollop of aïoli, then ladle on the fish stew).

Six Seafood Treats

Here is a varied selection of delicious fish dishes that will satisfy even the heartiest appetites.

Fish Boulangère

IN THIS RECIPE a bed of sliced onions and potatoes is baked until crisp on top but meltingly tender underneath, then covered with cubes of filleted fish, crushed garlic, parsley and anchovy, and baked again until the fish is ready. Ring the changes by varying the type of fish used.

PREPARATION TIME: 30 MINUTES
COOKING TIME: 1 HOUR
PRE-HEAT OVEN TO 180°C

INGREDIENTS FOR SIX
1 kg white fish, filleted*
6 medium-sized potatoes, peeled
2 onions, peeled and thinly sliced*
250 ml (1 cup) freshly chopped parsley
2 cloves garlic, crushed
Finely grated rind of 1 or 2 lemons
1 tin (55 g) anchovy fillets
Salt and freshly ground black pepper
250 ml (1 cup) milk
60 g butter

Cut the boned fish into 2 cm cubes and set it aside. Slice the potatoes as thinly as possible and arrange one-third of them in a well-buttered 2-litre shallow oven-proof dish. Sprinkle the potatoes with half the onion slices.

Mix the parsley, garlic, lemon rind and finely chopped anchovy fillets together and sprinkle one-third of this mixture over the onion. Add another layer of potato, then onion, and then more of the parsley mixture. Finish with the remaining layer of potato slices.

Season the milk and bring it to the boil. Pour over the potatoes, dot them with two-thirds of the butter and bake this mixture, uncovered, for 40 minutes.

By this time the potatoes will be crisp on top but tender inside. Lay the cubed fish on top of the vegetable layers, sprinkle it with the remaining parsley mixture and dot with the rest of the butter. Continue to bake it for a further 15 minutes or until the fish flakes easily.

VARIATION Cook the potato and onion with two-thirds of the parsley mixture in the milk over a gentle heat until the ingredients are tender. Turn the mixture into an oven-proof dish, dot with butter, 50 ml dried breadcrumbs and 125 ml (½ cup) grated cheese, and grill until the cheese melts. Cover it with the fish, sprinkle on the rest of the parsley mixture, dot with butter and grill until the fish is cooked.

Baked Fish with Vegetables

THIS IS AN UNUSUAL but excellent way of preparing a large piece of fish (a centre cut of yellowtail or tuna is best). It makes a more than adequate Sunday meal.

PREPARATION TIME: 35 MINUTES
COOKING TIME: 1½ HOURS
PRE-HEAT OVEN TO 190°C

INGREDIENTS FOR SIX
2 kg piece of thick fish
125 g butter, melted
Juice of 1 lemon
2 cloves garlic, crushed
6 potatoes, peeled
6 large carrots, thickly sliced
3 large onions, peeled* and quartered
1 sprig rosemary
Salt and freshly ground black pepper

Score the fish lightly and place in an oven-proof dish. Mix the melted butter, lemon juice and garlic, and pour over the fish. Place the potatoes and carrots in cold salted water and bring to the boil for 10-15 minutes to partially cook them. Arrange the vegetables and onions around the fish and tuck the rosemary underneath.

Season with salt and pepper, and roast, turning the vegetables and basting the fish now and again, for about 1½ hours, or until the fish feels firm when pressed and the vegetables are tender.

Fish Pie

THIS LARGE GOLDEN PIE made with a fish, egg and parsley sauce makes a delicious and filling meal. The choice of fish allows you to vary the taste according to what is available.

PREPARATION TIME: 30 MINUTES
COOKING TIME: 1 HOUR
PRE-HEAT OVEN TO 180°C

INGREDIENTS FOR FOUR
750 g white fish or smoked haddock
2 ml (½ teaspoon) dill or fennel seeds
Salt and freshly ground black pepper
375 ml (1½ cups) milk
1 small onion, stuck with 4 cloves
75 g butter
50 g flour
3 hard-boiled eggs*, sliced
15 ml (1 tablespoon) parsley

For the topping:
9 medium-sized potatoes, peeled and halved
125 ml (½ cup) sour cream (smetana) or milk
50 g butter
Nutmeg, freshly grated
Salt and pepper
50 g Cheddar cheese, grated

Wipe the fish and place in a large saucepan or oven-proof casserole. Sprinkle with dill or fennel seeds, salt and pepper. Pour over the milk and then add the onion stuck with cloves. Cover and simmer or bake at 180°C for 10-15 minutes, or until the fish flakes easily. Increase the oven temperature to 200°C.

Meanwhile, drain off and keep the milk. Cool the fish, discard the skin and bones, and flake it into a shallow litre-sized pie or gratin dish.

Rinse out the saucepan and melt the butter, then stir in the flour and cook for 1 minute without browning. Slowly add the strained milk, stirring continually to make a smooth sauce.

Season well, and if the sauce is too thick, add a little more milk to give it a coating consistency. Pour it over the fish. Top with the sliced eggs and parsley.

To make the topping, boil the potatoes for 20-25 minutes, or until they are really tender. Mash and beat them with the cream or milk, half of the butter, nutmeg and seasoning.

Spread the mashed potato evenly over the fish mixture. Mark the top with the prongs of a fork to form a neat pattern. Dot with the remaining butter and sprinkle with the grated cheese. Bake at 200°C for 20 minutes, or brown under the grill.

VARIATIONS Top with puff pastry* instead of potato, for a less filling version, and bake until golden and puffy.

For a special meal, add 125-200 g cooked prawns and/or 200 g sliced, sautéed mushrooms to the fish.

For a more colourful dish, add a 410 g tin of chopped, drained tomatoes to the fish.

Fish in Pastry

JUICY FILLETS of buttery fish (kabeljou, kingklip or stockfish) topped with a nutritious mixture of sautéed vegetables and wrapped in a crisp, golden-brown pastry give you a perfectly balanced meal-in-one.

Use your favourite pastry recipe, frozen puff pastry, or try the recipe with sour cream flaky pastry.

PREPARATION TIME: 45-60 MINUTES
COOKING TIME: 30 MINUTES
PRE-HEAT OVEN TO 220°C

INGREDIENTS FOR FOUR
Sour cream flaky pastry* using 220 g flour
600 g white fish, filleted and skinned*
Coarse salt
15 ml (1 tablespoon) cornflour
50 g butter
Pepper

1 medium-sized leek, chopped or
1 medium-sized onion, peeled
and chopped*
45 ml (3 tablespoons) chopped
parsley
2 medium-sized sticks celery,
chopped
1 medium-sized or large carrot,
grated
10 ml (2 teaspoons) lemon juice
5 ml (1 teaspoon) sugar
Milk or egg for glazing

First, make the sour cream flaky pastry. Salt the fish well with coarse salt and allow it to firm in the refrigerator for 10 minutes. Roll out one-third of the pastry into an oblong and place the dough on a baking sheet. Bake the pastry blind* for about 10 minutes at 220°C.

Allow the pastry to cool, then sprinkle it lightly with the cornflour to prevent it from becoming soggy when the fish is placed on it.

Heat the butter in a heavy-based frying pan until it foams and starts to discolour. Sear the fish lightly in the butter on both sides to seal in the juices and develop the flavour.

Remove the fillets with an egg lifter and allow to cool on a plate. Season lightly with pepper.

Sauté the leek or onion, parsley, celery and carrot in the remaining butter, then add the lemon juice and sugar.

Place the fish fillets on the baked pastry, top with the glazed vegetables, and allow to cool.

Season the dish lightly with salt and pepper and then roll out the remaining two-thirds of the prepared pastry. Cover the fish fillets and base, and tuck the ends under the baked base.

Brush the pastry lightly with a little milk or egg to provide a glaze, and bake at 220°C for 15 minutes. Reduce the oven temperature to 190°C and bake for a further 15 minutes.

VARIATIONS Use chicken breasts instead of the fish.

Add 200 g sliced button mushrooms to the vegetable mixture to make it more 'luxurious'.

Add sliced or chopped tomato to the dish in order to make it go further, at the same time providing an interesting colour contrast.

FISH AND POTATOES WITH CHEESE TOPPING

BITE INTO a fluffy cheese soufflé to discover the flavour of fish and potato underneath. The dish can be prepared (up to the point before the topping is made) ahead of time, refrigerated until needed, then topped and baked.

PREPARATION TIME: 40 MINUTES
COOKING TIME: 25 MINUTES
PRE-HEAT OVEN TO 200°C

INGREDIENTS FOR FOUR
600 g white fish, filleted and skinned*
5 medium-sized potatoes, peeled and sliced
5 ml (1 teaspoon) salt
15 ml (1 tablespoon) flour
5 ml (1 teaspoon) brown sugar
A pinch of pepper
45 ml (3 tablespoons) melted butter

For the cheese topping:
45 ml (3 tablespoons) thick mayonnaise*
45 g mature Cheddar cheese, grated
3 ml (¾ teaspoon) dry mustard
A pinch of cayenne pepper
1 egg, separated

Divide the fish into suitable portions and put to one side. Steam the sliced potatoes or cook in a little salted boiling water until tender. Line a medium-sized oven-proof serving dish with the cooked potatoes.

Mix the salt, flour, sugar and pepper on a chopping board. Dip the fish portions into the seasoned flour, and then into the melted butter. Place the fish on the bed of potatoes and bake for 10 minutes while you prepare the topping.

Mix together the mayonnaise, grated cheese, mustard, cayenne pepper and egg yolk. Beat the egg white until fluffy and fold it into the mixture with a metal spoon.

FISH AND POTATOES WITH CHEESE TOPPING *is a fluffy and flavourful dish.*

Remove the dish from the oven and spread the cheese topping evenly over the fish portions to cover them completely. Bake for a further 15 minutes: the soufflé topping should be puffed up and golden-brown in colour.

VARIATION Turn this into a vegetarian main course – omit the fish and substitute buttered mixed vegetables.

FISH AND NOODLE CASSEROLE

THE NOODLES and cheese used in this fish dish make this a very satisfying and filling meal.

PREPARATION TIME: 30 MINUTES
COOKING TIME: 30 MINUTES
PRE-HEAT OVEN TO 180°C

INGREDIENTS FOR FOUR
500 g fish, skinned and filleted*
1 large onion, peeled and finely chopped*
50 g butter
30 ml (2 tablespoons) sunflower oil
2 carrots, finely chopped
125 ml (½ cup) water
45 ml (3 tablespoons) finely chopped parsley
Salt and pepper
250 g broad noodles, cooked*
1 egg yolk
250 ml (1 cup) sour cream (smetena)
125 ml (½ cup) Cheddar cheese, grated

Rinse the fish and pat it quite dry, then cut it into strips. Soften the onion in the hot butter and oil. Add the carrots and cook gently until they soften. Stir in the fish, adding more oil or butter if necessary.

Add the water, 15 ml (1 tablespoon) of the chopped parsley and some seasoning. Simmer gently for 10 minutes or until the fish is just cooked through.

Butter an oven-proof dish and arrange half the cooked noodles in it. Cover with a layer of the fish and then the remaining noodles. Pour over the egg yolk and cream, beaten together until just blended.

Sprinkle the dish with the cheese. Bake for 30 minutes, or until it is lightly browned. Garnish it with the rest of the parsley.

Meat

For centuries the plains of South Africa teemed with game, and it is probably because of the early abundance of cheap meat that this protein-rich food plays such an important role in the country's culinary tradition.

Few South Africans still hunt for the pot, and meat is now possibly the most expensive item on our grocery lists. Since it is likely to be the centrepiece of the meal, be sure that it is not ruined by overcooking or by using the incorrect cooking method for a particular cut.

Because of the high profile of meat in the South African cuisine, it is in this section that we find the strongest evidence of our rich and diverse cultural heritage. Every settler community contributed a national favourite: we find a recipe for denning vleis, brought here by Muslims from Java; kassler rib chops with mustard sauce from Germany; Greek lamb with yoghurt; an Indian biriani; traditional Jewish brisket with prunes; Chinese stir-fried beef with oyster-flavoured sauce; hearty roast beef with Yorkshire pudding; and many more.

There are also uniquely South African meat preparations such as Cape lamb pie and several ways to cook venison (which, thanks to game farms, has not disappeared from the scene altogether).

But one of the greatest pleasures of cooking with meat is that it lends itself so well to innovation. For a delicious change from family favourites, try stuffed leg of mutton, lamb casserole with orange, vitello tonnato (an Italian veal dish with a tuna sauce) or fillet steak caramel.

Tips on Choosing and Preparing Meat · *Page 82*

Meat Recipes · *Page 88*

Special Features

Bredies – A Tasty Malay Tradition · *Page 94*
Informal Fun with Fondues · *Page 104*
Meat Baked in Golden Pastry Parcels · *Page 112*
Meal-in-One Dishes · Hearty Stews for Healthy Appetites · *Page 120*

Tips on Choosing and Preparing Meat

Meat is the food richest in body-building proteins. The proteins are in the lean part of the meat – the muscle fibre and tissues of the animal. The fat in meat provides energy, while offal (the internal organs), particularly liver, is rich in vitamins.

The grade of meat does not affect its nutritional value, only its relative tenderness. The less tender parts of the carcass – the coarse-fibred meat – take longer to cook. Meat from older slaughter animals also tends to be tougher, but generally has better flavour.

Fat provides both juiciness and flavour, but too much fat does not improve either quality. Lean meat has a protective layer of fat around it, and in mature animals the fat is distributed among the muscle fibres, giving a flecked appearance known as marbling.

Beef, lamb and mutton are best if allowed to ripen before being eaten. This allows the fibres in the meat to soften, making it more tender. If your butcher has not hung the meat, you can ripen it yourself in the refrigerator for 5-10 days for beef, 2-5 days for lamb and 5-7 days for mutton. Pork and veal are never ripened.

Hints on Buying Meat

If you live in an urban area, the meat you buy will have been graded for quality at the abattoir.

The grading is done on the basis of the animal's age, fat on the carcass and general appearance. The carcass is then roller-marked with a harmless vegetable ink with the colour-coded grading.

The most tender grades of meat are from young animals, the tastiest from mature ones.

A medium amount of fat is generally considered best, but this varies with personal preference.

If you live outside the areas where graded meat is available, follow this guide to quality:

Good beef is cherry red, lamb and mutton lighter red, and pork greyish-pink. The fat should be firm to the touch and creamy-white. Bone surfaces should be red and porous where they have been sawn, and rib bones should have red flecks. The cartilage between the vertebrae should be white, soft and elastic.

Meat is sold on or off the bone. If you want your butcher to prepare a special cut for a dinner party, such as a crown roast or saddle of lamb, give him a few days' notice.

If you have to keep meat without a refrigerator for a day or two, dust it lightly with flour and pepper, cover it with muslin and hang it in a well-ventilated pantry.

See The Practical Cook* for hints on storing or freezing meat.

Beef

The best beef is from slaughter animals at least 18 months old.

When buying beef, allow about 250-350 g per person if it contains bone, about 200-250 g boned joints, and 150-200 g steak.

Follow the chart on Uses for cuts of meat* as a guideline on using the different cuts of beef generally available from butchers.

Steaks

Steaks are small portions of the rump and sirloin of beef. They are tasty and tender, and suitable for grilling, braaing or frying. Steaks are among the more expensive cuts.

Chateaubriand About 3 cm thick, cut from the centre of the fillet or undercut of the sirloin.

Filet mignon Small, triangular pieces cut from the end of the fillet.

Fillet Slices from the fillet or undercut of the sirloin.

Minute steak Thin cuts of tenderised steak for pan frying.

Porterhouse About 2-2,5 cm thick slice from the sirloin, containing some fillet.

Rump Most people regard this as the most tasty steak. It is a cut, up to 3 cm thick, from the rump.

Sirloin or entrecôte About 2,5 cm thick slice from the upper part of the sirloin.

T-bone This steak takes its name from the small, T-shaped piece of bone in the cut, which is from the fillet end of the sirloin.

Tenderising steak

To tenderise steak before grilling or braaing, place it between two sheets of wax paper and pound it with a wooden hammer for about a minute on each side. This breaks down the tissue.

Alternative methods are marinating* or brushing the steak with lemon juice or vinegar.

Veal

Veal is the meat from young calves. Because of the youth of the slaughter animal, the meat contains little fat, and the proportion of bone to meat is high. Veal bones are ideal for aspics, as they contain large amounts of gelatinous matter.

The flavour of veal is bland, and it needs long cooking to make it tender. Milk-fed veal, which is more tender, is popular in restaurants in Europe, but is not available commercially from South African butchers.

Allow about 250 g veal per person if it contains bone, or 175 g if it is off the bone.

Cook the meat as soon as possible after you buy it, as it does not keep well.

Lamb and Mutton

Lamb is the meat of a sheep 3-12 months old; mutton comes from older sheep. Lamb, the more tender, is also the more expensive. Mutton, which is slightly less readily available, has more flavour.

Buy 350 g lamb or mutton per person if it contains bones, or 200-250 g if it is boned.

Follow the chart on Uses for cuts of meat* as a guideline on using lamb and mutton.

Pork

Pork is the meat of young pigs. It has more fat than other meats and does not keep well. Pork should be cooked thoroughly, otherwise it can be dangerous to health.

Pork is tender, and is therefore graded into fewer grades than other meats. Ask your butcher to trim the fat layer to your preference and to score the fat (make cuts that penetrate it) of joints for roasting.

Allow 225-350 g per person of pork on the bone, 175 g if it is boned.

See the chart on Uses for cuts of meat* for the best ways to use pork.

Bacon, Gammon and Ham

Bacon pigs are larger than pork pigs and have less fat. Gammon and ham both come from the hindquarters of the bacon carcass.

Bacon is made by curing the meat in brine. Various methods can be used – salting the carcass, laying the meat in a brine bath, or injecting the meat with the brine. After brining, the meat is a greyish colour.

The bacon can then be heat-treated at 50°C to develop a pink colour without cooking the meat. This unsmoked bacon is known as 'green bacon'. The meat may also be smoked, which gives it a darker colour and stronger flavour.

Gammon is cured and smoked in much the same way as bacon. Follow the cooking instructions that come with the gammon, as preparation depends on the method of curing used.

Ham is also cured in a similar way. Commercial curers massage or tumble the meat in a drum to enhance its absorption of brine. Cooked and smoked ham is sold pre-packaged.

SAUSAGES

Sausages are made from minced beef, mutton or pork, mixed with fat, cereal, herbs and flavourings. The recipes for the meat mixtures vary considerably from butcher to butcher.

The sausage meat is encased in animal intestines or casings made from synthetic material.

Some butchers will sell you sausage casings so that you can make your own sausages. Wash them carefully before you stuff them.

Sausage mixtures can also be formed into patties or meatballs and cooked without a skin.

Allow 125-150 g per person.

OFFAL

Offal refers to the internal organs of animals – the liver and kidneys, for example – which are rich in nutrients. Other parts, such as the head, tail and feet, are also often sold as offal. It is usually cheap compared to other meat.

Avoid buying discoloured offal, and use the meat on the day you buy it, since it does not keep well.

If you have frozen offal make sure it is thoroughly thawed before you cook it.

Using offal

Liver Buy 100-175 g per person. Cut away any fat, gristle and tubes before cooking; clean with a damp cloth and dry. To reduce the strong flavour of ox liver, soak it in milk for 20-30 minutes. Liver is best fried, except ox liver, which can be braised or stewed.

Kidney Buy two per person, except for ox kidney (allow 100-175 g per person). Peel off the outer skin of the kidney before cooking. Cut the kidney in half lengthways and remove the white core. Drop the kidney halves in hot water for 2 minutes, then cold water for 30 seconds to prevent them from curling during cooking.

Ox and calf kidneys may be soaked in milk or water for 2 hours before cooking if you wish to reduce the strong flavour.

Lamb kidney is best for frying or grilling. Grill, fry or stew calf and pig kidney. Stew ox kidney, or use it in pies.

Heart Lamb heart is the most tender. Buy one heart per person, except for calf and ox (allow 100-175 g per person).

Wash the heart thoroughly under cold water to remove all blood before cooking. Cut away the gristle, fat and membranes from the cavity with a sharp knife. Trim away the ends of arteries and tendons with scissors. Soak in cold water for 30 minutes-1 hour.

Stuff and pot-roast lamb or pig heart; stew or braise ox or calf heart.

Sweetbreads (throat and chest glands from lamb or calf) Lamb sweetbreads have the most flavour. Allow 500 g for three to four people.

Soak in warm salted water for 30 minutes to remove any blood. Remove the sweetbreads from the rinsing water and drop them into fast-boiling salted water for 2 minutes.

Rinse the sweetbreads under cold running water and remove the thin outer membrane and the black veins running through.

Brain (lamb or calf) Allow one lamb brain per person, two calf brains for three people.

Soak the brains in cold water for about 2 hours before cooking in order to remove any blood. Snip off any fibrous tissue and bone.

Poach gently in stock, or boil, cool and gently fry.

Tripe (ox stomach lining) Allow 500 g to serve four.

Buy cleaned tripe, but blanch again at home before cooking. Some butchers sell cooked tripe. Tripe should be firm and white – if slimy and greyish it is stale.

Boil with onions and serve, or boil with onions, then cut into strips and fry.

Tongue One ox tongue serves six. Allow one lamb tongue per person.

Soak tongue for 1-2 hours in cold water; soak salted tongue overnight. To boil tongue, follow the chart on Cooking times for meat*.

To remove the skin after boiling, plunge the tongue into cold water, then slit the skin at the tip with a sharp knife and peel. Remove any bones or gristle at the root, and trim.

Serve tongue hot with sauce, or press* and serve cold in slices.

Feet or trotters (usually pig) Allow one pair per person.

Boil, stew or use in pies. Cow heel or calf foot is good for jellied stock or savoury jellies.

Oxtail Sold ready skinned and cut in portions. One tail serves three to four. Braise, stew or make into soup.

Marrow bones The marrow contained in the large thigh and shoulder bones of the ox is regarded as a delicacy by many. Ask your butcher to saw the bones into manageable lengths.

USES FOR CUTS OF MEAT

	Soup	Mince	Oven-roasting, grilling or frying	Pot-roasting	Stewing, braising and casseroling
Beef	Shin, Neck	Thick flank, Topside, Thin flank, Neck, Chuck, Bolo	Silverside, Sirloin, Rump, Wing rib, Prime rib	Silverside, Aitchbone, Thick flank, Flat rib, Brisket, Prime rib, Chuck, Hump, Bolo	Thick flank, Topside, Thin flank, Flat rib, Brisket, Neck, Prime rib, Chuck, Bolo
Veal	Fore shank, Hind shank	Neck	Topside, Breast, Shoulder, Loin, Loin chops, Rib, Rib chops, Thick rib, Chump, Chump chops, Fillet, Schnitzels (from Silverside, Topside or Thick flank)	Silverside, Topside, Thick flank	Breast, Shoulder, Silverside, Topside, Neck, Thick rib, Thick flank, Shank
Lamb and mutton	Neck	Thick rib, Flank, Neck	Leg, Loin, Loin chop, Chump chop, Rib, Rib chop, Thick rib, Thick rib chop, Raised shoulder	Flank, Breast and shank, Raised shoulder	Thick rib, Thick rib chop, Flank, Breast and shank, Neck, Raised shoulder
Pork	Shank and trotter	Thick rib, Breast	Leg (fillet end), Leg (shank end), Belly, Chump chop, Loin, Loin chop, Rib, Rib chop, Thick rib, Thick rib chop	Breast	Belly, Thick rib, Thick rib chop, Shank and trotter, Breast

Scrape and wash the bones, then seal the ends with a paste of flour and water. Tie each bone in cheesecloth or muslin and simmer gently in court-bouillon* for 1½-2 hours. Drain, extract the marrow, and spread it on toast.

Tripe and Trotters

PREPARATION TIME: 45 MINUTES
STANDING TIME: 30 MINUTES-1 HOUR
COOKING TIME: 5½ HOURS

INGREDIENTS FOR FOUR
1 kg tripe
4 sheep trotters
5 ml (1 teaspoon) salt
50 ml vinegar
10 ml (2 teaspoons) sugar
2 cloves
12 peppercorns
5 ml (1 teaspoon) whole coriander
5 whole allspice
1 bay leaf
1 medium-sized onion, peeled and chopped*
8 small potatoes, cooked (optional)
25 ml (5 teaspoons) melted butter
25 ml (5 teaspoons) flour

Clean the tripe thoroughly, washing it well. Clean the trotters and cut into the cleft of the trotters up to the first joint, removing the glands and hard covering over the toes. Scrape the trotters well.

Soak the tripe and trotters in salted water for 30 minutes-1 hour.

Place the tripe and trotters in separate saucepans, cover with fresh cold water, and simmer gently until tender and the meat is easily removed from the bones (3½-4 hours). Drain the tripe and trotters, reserving the cooking liquid from the trotters.

Cut the tripe and the meat from the trotters into small cubes, and place in a saucepan with the trotter liquid, vinegar and sugar. Tie the cloves, peppercorns, coriander, allspice and bay leaf into a muslin bag, and place in the saucepan. Add the chopped onion and simmer gently for 45 minutes. Add the potatoes (if used) and simmer for a further 15 minutes.

Mix the melted butter and flour to a smooth paste and add to the saucepan, cooking for a few minutes longer until the gravy thickens.

SERVING SUGGESTION Serve this dish with boiled rice*.

VENISON

Venison is the meat of deer and buck. It is sold at some butchers in joints – the leg or saddle is popular for roasting. It can also be used for casseroles, braising and in pies. Various types of venison are often made into biltong.

The meat is dry and inclined to be tough. It is hung for at least 7 days, and usually marinated* to tenderise it. Lard and strips of bacon are added when roasting to keep the meat moist.

Allow 250 g per person.

RABBIT AND HARE

Rabbits and hares are sometimes available at butchers or supermarkets, either whole or jointed, and some people still hunt them out in the country areas.

The meat should be hung before it is eaten – hare for 7-10 days, rabbit for up to 24 hours. When you are buying the meat check how long it has already been hung. Allow about 250 g meat per person.

To joint rabbit or hare, cut away the skin flaps below the rib cage with a sharp knife and discard. Slice the carcass in half lengthways, cutting down the backbone. Cut off the hind legs at the thigh, slicing through the joint. Remove the forelegs, cutting through the shoulder joints.

Divide the carcass in half along the backbone and cut each half into 2 serving portions.

If you intend to use the saddle for roasting, joint as above but leave the backbone complete.

Rabbits should be fresh, with firm, plump flesh. Wild rabbits are smaller than domesticated animals, but have a better flavour. Roast young rabbit, or use it in a fricassee, stew or pie.

Young hares are good for filling with stuffing and then roasting whole.

Alternatively, you can roast the saddle or use the hare jointed in a casserole. An old hare is better marinated before it is cooked.

GOAT

Kid's meat comes from a goat 6-16 months old, goat's meat from older animals.

Goat has a thinner outer layer of fat than lamb or mutton, and the meat has a coarser texture. The strong odour sometimes associated with goat's meat is present only in male animals, and then noticeable only rarely. Choose the meat carefully to avoid this.

The meat has much the same light red colour as lamb or mutton – dark, almost plum-coloured meat is a sign of age and of meat derived from male animals.

Kid should be cooked in the same way as lamb – roast, grill or fry the meat. Use goat for stews or pot-roasts.

Allow 175-250 g per person.

COOKING MEAT

There are several methods of cooking meat: some concentrate flavour, others ensure tender results with a tough cut of meat. It is important to use the correct method for the meat you have bought, otherwise you could ruin what is probably the most expensive item on the menu.

Follow the chart on Uses for cuts of meat* to get the best results.

Meat may be marinated* for 3-4 hours before cooking to make it more tender or to give it a variety of flavours.

Roasting

Roasting is cooking by radiant heat. The meat shrinks in the heat, which brings the juices to the surface. The juices dry out, sealing the meat and concentrating the flavour. Roasting should be used only for tender cuts of meat, otherwise the result will be tough and dry. The meat can be basted with the cooking juices or, if it has been marinated, with heated marinade.

Some cooks salt joints before roasting, while others say one should not do so since, they believe, this draws out the juices, which may be lost before the surface of the joint is hot enough to seal them in.

Roast meat with the fat side uppermost, and always roast pork with the rind uppermost to produce crisp crackling. You may also rub pork rind with olive or sunflower oil and coarse salt before roasting, to ensure the crackling is crisp.

Cover very lean meat, such as veal or venison, with strips of pork or similar fat during cooking (this is known as barding) to give a moister result.

When roasting boned and rolled meat, place the bones in the roasting tin with the meat to add flavour to the basting juices and gravy. The bones can later be used for making basic stock*.

When roasting in aluminium foil, wrap the meat with the shiny side inside. Since foil reflects heat, use a higher roasting temperature than you would otherwise use. If you use a cooking bag, pierce the bag a few times on top.

Tie aluminium foil around the tip of each rib of a crown roast to prevent them from burning. You may also decorate the individual ribs with bought paper frills before serving.

Always rest roasts for 15 minutes after cooking for juicier results and easier carving. Follow the chart on Cooking times for meat* as a guide to temperatures and cooking times.

To check whether roasted meat is done, stick a skewer into it (near the bone if there is one). The juice should be pink for underdone, clear for more thoroughly cooked meat.

Grilling and frying

Both methods of cooking should be used only for tender cuts of meat. Grilling – pan grilling, oven grilling or over the coals – is cooking by radiant heat, similar to roasting. Frying – fast cooking in hot fat – is suitable only for small, tender cuts.

Leave some fat on the meat when grilling to keep it moist. Slash any borders of fat on steak or chops to prevent curling during cooking.

Before grilling the meat, brush the rack or pan with sunflower oil or melted butter to prevent the meat from sticking to it. You may also brush the meat lightly with sunflower oil if desired.

The pan, grill or coals should be very hot before you begin. Sear the meat quickly on both sides to seal in the juices, then cook according to your preference at a slightly lower temperature. (This can be achieved by turning down the heat or moving the meat further from the source of heat.)

For frying, a vegetable oil such as sunflower or peanut oil is most suitable, since it can reach a high temperature without burning. Other fats may burn and spoil the results. Cook small amounts at a time so that the temperature of the fat is not lowered too much. Meat will become greasy in an over-crowded pan.

Fry liver slices quickly to prevent toughness. To test whether the liver is cooked, pierce with a skewer – the juice should be slightly pink.

Mixed grill

To make a mixed grill for four people, heat 2 large frying pans. Fry 4 rashers of rindless streaky bacon in the one hot pan and melt 50 g butter in the other. Fry 4 peeled and sliced onions* gently in the butter, stirring occasionally.

As soon as the bacon rashers begin to crisp, remove them from the pan and keep hot on a large platter.

Dip 4 lamb cutlets, 4 thin slices calf liver and 4 skinned and cored lamb kidneys in seasoned flour*. Fry them all gently in a little hot sunflower oil in the bacon pan until cooked through (turning once to brown both sides).

Place the cooked meat on the heated platter.

Push the onions to one side, then add tomato halves and 200 g sliced mushrooms, and fry, adding a little more butter if necessary. Add to the cooked meats and keep hot.

Next, trim the crusts from two large slices of white bread and cut across diagonally. Quickly fry in hot fat or oil until crisp and golden on both sides. Drain briefly on paper towels and arrange around the platter. Serve immediately.

Braising, pot-roasting and boiling

These methods use low, moist heat to soften the fibres of the meat, and are ideal for tenderising lower grades of meat.

Pot-roasting and braising are done mostly in steam in a covered pan with a tightly fitting lid. The meat is browned first in hot fat to seal in the juices. Basic stock*, wine, beer, vinegar or fruit juice are all good sources of liquid, since they also impart additional flavour to the dish.

In pot-roasting, the base of the pan is covered with liquid and the meat raised above it on a rack.

Braised meat is cooked on top of a bed of lightly fried vegetables with enough liquid to cover them. Make sure the pot is large enough so that the meat does not touch the edge, which may cause scorching.

Boiled meat is either cooked in water or stock. Bring the liquid just to the boil, then reduce the heat to keep it simmering (constant boiling at high heat should be avoided as it toughens the meat).

Parboiling ham before roasting helps to keep it moist. To get rid of excess salt, soak a whole ham for 12-24 hours, changing the water twice.

Alternatively, cover the ham with cold water and bring it to the boil, then drain and replace the water before cooking the meat.

Pot-roast of beef

For pot-roast of beef for four to six people, brown a 1-1,5 kg topside or silverside on all sides in 50 g butter, melted, then set it aside.

Lightly fry 2 large peeled* and quartered onions, 2 large scraped and sliced carrots and 1 medium-sized peeled and sliced turnip or swede in the butter until they just begin to brown, then put them into a large casserole.

Place the meat on a rack over the vegetables, sprinkle it with 5 ml (1 teaspoon) fresh thyme or 1 ml (¼ teaspoon) dried thyme and 1 clove crushed garlic, and salt and pepper.

Pour in 300 ml basic stock* and 125 ml (½ cup) red wine, and cover the casserole tightly. Place in an oven pre-heated to 180°C for at least 1½ hours, or until tender, removing the lid for the last 20 minutes to brown the meat.

COOKING TIMES FOR MEAT

As ovens vary in accuracy, refer to this chart as a guideline, adjusting roasting times to your oven. Always rest roast meats for 15 minutes in the warming oven for juicier results and easier carving.

	Roasting	Boiling	Grilling or frying
Beef	*High-heat roasting* On the bone: 10 minutes at 220°C, then 15 minutes per 500 g for rare, 18-20 minutes for medium, 25 minutes for well-done. Off the bone: 10 minutes at 220°C; then 12 minutes per 500 g at 180°C for rare, 15 minutes for medium, 20 minutes for well-done. *Slow-roasting* On or off the bone: 20-25 minutes at 160°C per 500 g for medium, 30-35 minutes for well-done. *Stuffed joints* Add 5-10 minutes per 500 g. *Whole fillet* 8 minutes at 230°C per 500 g for rare, 10 minutes for medium.	*Unsalted* 20 minutes plus 20 minutes per 500 g. *Salt beef* 25 minutes plus 25 minutes per 500 g.	*Steaks* (2,5 cm thick) Sear the steaks for 1 minute on each side at high heat, then cook for 2-3 minutes each side for rare, 3-4 minutes a side for medium, 5 minutes a side for well-done. *Sausages* 5-8 minutes each side.
Veal	Roast veal must be fully cooked but still juicy. 15 minutes at 190°C, then 25-30 minutes at 180°C per 500 g. *Stuffed joints* Add 5-10 minutes per 500 g.	20 minutes plus 20 minutes per 500 g.	*Chops* 6-8 minutes each side. *Schnitzels* 2-3 minutes each side. *Calf liver* 2-4 minutes each side.
Lamb and mutton	*High-heat roasting* 10 minutes at 230°C, then 10 minutes at 180°C per 500 g for pink meat, 15 minutes for medium, 20 minutes for well-done. *Slow-roasting* 25 minutes at 160°C, then 25 minutes per 500 g. *Stuffed joints* Add 5-10 minutes per 500 g.	*Mutton* 20 minutes plus 20 minutes per 500 g.	*Chops* Sear chops for 1 minute each side at high heat, then cook 2-3 minutes a side for 1 cm thick chops, 5-7 minutes for 2,5 cm thick. *Liver* 2-4 minutes each side. *Sausages* 5-8 minutes each side.
Pork	30 minutes at 190°C, then 30 minutes per 500 g. *Stuffed joints* Add 5-10 minutes per 500 g.	20 minutes plus 20 minutes per 500 g. *Cured bacon and ham* 25 minutes plus 25 minutes per 500 g (mass after soaking).	*Chops* 8-10 minutes each side. *Sausages* 5-8 minutes each side. *Bacon* 3-5 minutes each side. *Gammon steaks* 5-8 minutes each side. *Kassler rib chops* 5-7 minutes each side.

Boiled mutton

To boil mutton for four to six people, trim excess fat from a 1,5-2 kg leg of mutton, and put the meat in a large pan with 2 peeled* whole onions, 2 peeled and quartered carrots, 1 peeled and quartered turnip and a bouquet garni*.

Cover with warm water and bring to the boil for about 5 minutes. Remove the scum as it rises to the surface.

Reduce the heat, add a generous seasoning of salt and pepper, and simmer the mutton, covered, until cooked. Use the chart on Cooking times for meat* to judge when the meat is cooked.

Serve with caper sauce* made with the strained stock from the boiled meat.

Pot-au-feu

To make the French dish pot-au-feu for four people, tie a 1 kg topside of beef with string (so that it keeps its shape during cooking). Place it in a large pan with 3 litres cold brown stock*, bring slowly to the boil, covered, then remove any scum.

Add 2 large scraped and sliced carrots, 2 large peeled and coarsely chopped* onions, 2-3 cleaned and sliced leeks, 1 peeled and chopped turnip and 1 chopped stick of celery, and simmer gently for 1½ hours.

Add a set of cleaned chicken giblets and cook for a further 30 minutes.

Add 1 small washed and quartered cabbage, and cook until the cabbage is tender (about 15-20 minutes).

Lift out the meat, slice it and serve with the drained vegetables. The cooking liquid makes an excellent soup.

Stews and hotpots

Stews (or casseroles) are made from small pieces of meat cooked slowly in liquid that forms part of the final dish. They are usually flavoured with onions and diced vegetables, and thickened with flour or pearl barley.

Hotpots are similar to stews, but traditionally have potato toppings.

Brown stews are usually made with beef, mutton, lamb or rabbit; white stews with veal, chicken or rabbit. Any meat is suitable, but the long, slow cooking is best for tougher cuts, such as shin of beef.

Very tough meat may need up to 4 hours' cooking, but generally beef stews should be cooked for 2½-3 hours, mutton about 2 hours and lamb and veal 1-1½ hours.

Cook stews and hotpots in a tightly covered oven-proof dish on top of the stove or in the oven. For hotpots, remove the lid for the last 30 minutes and brown the potatoes.

The flavour of most stews is better the day after cooking – simply re-heat to just boiling point.

To make a stew, trim the fat from the meat and marinate*, if you prefer, for 4-12 hours. Cut the meat into bite-sized pieces, and fry better quality meat on all sides to brown.

For brown stews, fry the vegetables lightly to improve the colour. Remove the vegetables, then add flour (if used) and cook it gently until it is light brown. Use 25 g flour per 500 g meat.

Add cold liquid – stock, water, fruit juice, beer or wine – to the meat (350-500 ml per 500 g meat), and increase the heat gently to boiling point.

As soon as the boiling point is reached, reduce the heat until the stew is just simmering.

Add the vegetables and any other flavourings to the stew as directed in the recipe. Skim off excess fat while the stew is simmering.

For a white stew, drain off the stock after the meat has cooked, and use it to make a white sauce*. Pour the sauce back on to the meat, and re-heat.

RE-HEATING MEAT

When re-heating cooked meat, care should be taken that it is done properly to avoid a potential health hazard. The meat should be heated at a temperature of at least 77°C; or, if it is covered by sauce, cook until the sauce bubbles.

MAKING GRAVY

Gravy is best made from the meat juices left in the pan after roasting. It can be thickened, if you like, by adding flour or cornflour.

To make a thin gravy, spoon off the fat from the roasting pan, leaving only the meat juices.

For thick gravy, leave about 15 ml (1 tablespoon) of the fat in the juices, and stir in 15 ml (1 tablespoon) flour (or cornflour for a smoother result) over a gentle heat. Stir until the flour has become golden-brown.

Add 275-300 ml hot stock* or boiling water to both types of gravy, stir in any meaty residue from the bottom of the pan, and concentrate the flavour by boiling – 2-3 minutes for thin gravy, 3-4 minutes for thick gravy.

Stir thick gravy constantly to prevent lumps forming. (If it does become lumpy, pass the gravy through a sieve or beat it for a few seconds with a whisk.)

Draw a paper towel across the surface of the gravy to remove excess fat, then season to taste.

If you prefer a dark gravy, add a little gravy browning or meat extract. A little yeast or meat extract will improve a flavourless gravy.

For gravies that contain alcohol, follow the recipe instructions.

DRIPPING

Dripping is made from left-over fat which is rendered down.

The fat that has dripped from roast meat can be used, or you can make dripping from fat trimmed from raw meat.

Mince or chop the fat finely and place it in a heavy saucepan. Cover and place the saucepan over low heat, shaking the pan from time to time until the fat has melted well. Be careful to prevent the fat from burning.

When the fat has melted completely, strain carefully, add salt to taste and allow the dripping to cool slightly. Pour into glass jars and store in the refrigerator or a cool place.

CARVING MEAT

For the most tender results when carving a joint, it is best to slice across the grain of the meat. The exception is leg of lamb, which may be carved either at a 90 degree angle to the bone or almost parallel to the bone.

Carving a boned and rolled joint presents no problem – simply secure the meat with the carving fork and cut downwards across the grain.

When it comes to a joint which contains bone, however, it helps to know the shape and position of the bone. The meat charts displayed at most butchers will be of great help in this regard when you are buying a cut with which you are unfamiliar.

The thickness of carved slices is largely a matter of personal preference, but roast beef and ham are usually sliced very thinly, pork slightly thicker, and veal and lamb fairly thickly.

PRESSED MEAT AND BRAWN

Pressed meat is seasoned and simmered for several hours, strained, then pressed under a weight. The cooking liquid can be boiled to concentrate it, then poured over the meat and left to set as a jelly (or aspic) round it.

Tongue and the cheaper cuts of beef, such as brisket, are often made into pressed meat. Coarse-fibred cuts can be carved in thinner slices when they are cold and pressed than when they are hot.

Brawn is made from chopped meat placed in a pudding bowl or mould, covered with the liquid in which the meat was simmered, and left to set. When cold it can be turned out and sliced.

If you make brawn with a selection of meats or meat scraps, cook some bones with the meat, otherwise gelatin will have to be added to the liquid to ensure setting.

Pressed meat and brawn will keep for about a week in a refrigerator. It is not advisable to freeze brawn or pressed meat that includes jelly, as the freezing will tend to spoil the texture of the jellied stock.

Before cooking whole pieces of meat for pressing, tie them with fine string to keep them in shape while cooking. Remove the string after pressing.

Most brisket is bought boned. If it is not, remove the bones after cooking and before pressing.

Place the cooked meat, in whole pieces or chunks, in a special meat press or a cake tin. If using a meat press, follow the manufacturer's instructions. If using a cake tin, cover the meat with a plate and place a 1-2 kg weight on top. Leave the meat until cool.

If the cooking liquid is to be poured over the meat during pressing, follow the recipe instructions.

MEAT

BASIC GUIDELINES FOR CARVING MEAT

Considering the amount of time and trouble that goes into preparing large cuts of meat, it is a pity to detract from the final result by serving up torn, ragged slices. Carving meat is a skill that one develops with experience, however it is important to keep in mind the following basic guidelines.

STANDING RIB ROAST OF BEEF

Lay the joint rib side down on a cutting board and, inserting the sharp point of the knife horizontally between the ribs and meat, loosen the meat from the narrow ribs.

Carve the meat in thin downward slices up to the horizontal incision. If necessary insert the knife point again between ribs and meat to separate the slices from the full length of the bone.

RAISED SHOULDER OF LAMB

Place the joint meaty side up. Holding the shank end, cut a 2 mm thick slice from the centre, beginning as far back as the bone will allow.

Cut thick slices, fanning out from the centre cut. Loosen the meat from the horizontal blade bone.

Slice the remaining meat from the top of the joint horizontally, then turn it over and carve small slices across the grain from the other side.

ROAST LEG OF LAMB

Place the leg of lamb meaty side up. Holding the meat with a fork and the carving knife almost horizontal, cut a 2 mm thick slice from a third of the way along the leg, across to the shank end.

Next slice the meat thinly almost parallel to the bone, lengthening the slices towards the thick end of the joint. When you reach the bone, turn the joint and carve thin slices from the remaining meat.

WHOLE JOINT OF HAM

Place the joint fat side up with the shank bone to your right. Holding the meat with a fork, cut a few slices from the less meaty side, making a flat surface on which to rest the meat.

Turn the meat on to the cut surface and slice a wedge out of the meat at the shank end. Beginning from this cut at the shank end, slice the meat down to the bone in 4 mm thick slices. To cut the slices from the bone, hold the knife horizontally and slice from the shank end towards the carving fork against the bone. Turn the joint over to cut slices from the other side.

Pot-Roast Brisket with Prunes

This traditional Jewish dish is reminiscent of some of the old Cape dishes, combining as it does the sweetness of dried fruits with a slowly cooked, tender joint of meat.

Soaking Time: overnight
Preparation Time: 45 minutes
Cooking Time: 4 hours

Ingredients for Eight

1,5 kg boneless brisket
125 g prunes
30 ml (2 tablespooons) flour
3 ml (¾ teaspoon) salt
2 ml (½ teaspoon) pepper
5 ml (1 teaspoon) ground ginger
30 ml (2 tablespoons) chicken fat or sunflower oil
1 onion, peeled and thinly sliced*
3 allspice
1 stick cinnamon, whole
1 bay leaf, whole
2 potatoes, peeled and quartered
2 sweet potatoes, peeled and quartered
6 medium-sized carrots, scraped and sliced
1 parsnip, peeled and sliced
30 ml (2 tablespoons) honey

Soak the prunes overnight in cold water, or for about half an hour in boiling water. Trim any excess fat from the meat and roll the joint in the flour. Season with salt, pepper and ground ginger.

Gently heat the fat in a heavy oven-proof casserole. Add the meat and onion and allow to brown slowly (covered). When the meat has a good colour all over, add the water in which the prunes were soaked, plus enough water to half cover the meat. Add the spices and bay leaf, and cover the casserole tightly.

Simmer gently, turning the meat around from time to time. Cook for about 1½ hours, or until the meat starts to become tender.

Now add the vegetables, prunes and honey. Cover again and continue to cook gently for another hour, or until both the meat and the vegetables are very tender.

Check the seasoning before serving and remove the whole bay leaf and stick cinnamon.

Roast Beef and Yorkshire Pudding *A traditional English recipe that is widely enjoyed in South Africa.*

Roast Beef and Yorkshire Pudding

This tasty dish has long been popular in South Africa. In Yorkshire it was (and in some places still is) the custom to serve the pudding with gravy as a first course to help blunt hearty appetites. Other cooks serve it with the meat.

Preparation Time: 20 minutes
Cooking Time: 1¾-2¼ hours
Pre-heat Oven to 220°C

Ingredients for Six

1,5-2 kg joint of roasting beef
30 ml (2 tablespoons) dripping*

For the Yorkshire pudding:
125 g flour
2 ml (½ teaspoon) salt
2 large eggs
200 ml milk
30 ml (2 tablespoons) cold water

For the gravy:
15 ml (1 tablespoon) flour
300 ml beef basic stock*

Wipe the joint and put it in a roasting pan with the dripping. Roast for 15 minutes, then reduce the oven temperature to 190°C. Continue roasting the meat for a further 15 minutes per 500 g for rare beef, and 20 minutes per 500 g for medium-rare.

To make the Yorkshire pudding, sieve the flour and salt into a large basin and make a well in the centre. Break the eggs into the well and add a little of the milk. With a wooden spoon gradually draw in the flour, and mix the ingredients together, adding milk a little at a time until you have a thick batter. Beat with the wooden spoon until the batter is smooth, then stir in the remaining milk. Leave the mixture to stand for about 1 hour, or until the meat is cooked. Remove the joint from the oven and keep it hot.

Increase the oven temperature to 230°C. Cover the bottom of a baking tin with a thin layer of fat from the roast, and put it in the oven until the fat is smoking hot. Quickly stir the batter, mix in the cold water and pour it into the tin. Bake on the top shelf of the oven for 25 minutes, until risen, crisp and golden-brown.

While the Yorkshire pudding is cooking, make the gravy in the roasting tin. Pour off almost all the fat from the tin, but retain the brown juices. Mix the flour into the juices until smooth, then gradually add the stock, stirring continuously to loosen any meaty residue. Place the tin over a gentle heat and continue stirring until the gravy thickens and comes to the boil.

As soon as the Yorkshire pudding is cooked, cut it into squares.

Serving Suggestions Roast potatoes and a green vegetable are excellent accompaniments to roast beef.

Variations If you like, you can make small puddings in a bun tray instead of one large pudding. Put 5 ml (1 teaspoon) fat from the roasting tin into each section and put the tray in the top of the oven until the fat is smoking hot. Put 30 ml (2 tablespoons) batter into each tin and bake for 15 minutes.

For a thinner gravy, omit the flour and strengthen the gravy by reducing over a high heat. Use half dry red wine instead of all stock.

Fillet Steak Caramel

THE PREPARATION AND GRILLING of fillet steak has provoked many arguments, some people claiming it should be seared for a matter of seconds and served immediately, and others maintaining that it should be 'properly' cooked to enjoy the true flavour. Whatever your choice, avoid over-cooking the meat.

PREPARATION TIME: 30 MINUTES
COOKING TIME: 5-10 MINUTES
PRE-HEAT OVEN TO 75°C

INGREDIENTS FOR SIX
6 pieces of fillet steak, cut 4 cm thick
Freshly ground black pepper
30 ml (2 tablespoons) sugar
30 g butter
Coarse salt

Pre-heat a plate in the oven. Gently pound the steaks with a wooden mallet, reducing their thickness by a third. Grind pepper over both sides and allow to stand while you prepare the caramel.

Heat a heavy frying pan until it is extremely hot. Test the heat by dropping a few grains of sugar on to the pan: if the grains go up in smoke, the pan is ready.

Scatter 15 ml (1 tablespoon) of the sugar in the pan. When it blackens (after a few seconds), drop 15 g of the butter into the pan: it will caramelise immediately. Place 3 of the steaks in the pan and allow them to sizzle for a minute, then turn and sizzle for another minute.

If you prefer your steaks rare, remove them from the pan at this stage, transfer to the pre-heated plate in the oven and leave to stand for 5 minutes. Re-heat the pan, and repeat the process for the other 3 steaks. While this is being done, sprinkle a little salt over the steaks in the oven: they will 'relax' and release a small amount of delicious gravy.

For those who prefer their steak well done, the cooking time may be doubled (turn the meat often).

Beef Stroganoff

THIS IS ONE of the best-known Russian recipes, created during the 19th century. The dish is made from slender strips of beef fillet, cut across the grain. They are sautéed very quickly in butter and oil so that they are brown on the outside but still rare inside. The meat strips are then mixed into a delicious sour cream and mushroom sauce.

PREPARATION TIME: 45 MINUTES
COOKING TIME: 20 MINUTES

INGREDIENTS FOR FOUR
750 g fillet of beef
2-3 onions, peeled and thinly sliced*
30 g butter
200 g mushrooms, sliced
Salt and freshly ground pepper
250 ml (1 cup) sour cream, or fresh cream soured with juice of ½ lemon

Cut the fillet into strips across the grain (they should be about the size of your little finger).

Slowly fry the onion in butter until golden-brown, then remove and keep warm. Fry the mushrooms in the same pan and add to the onion.

Increase the heat and quickly fry half of the beef in the very hot frying pan (3-4 minutes on each side) so that the juices are firmly sealed in and the meat is lightly browned outside and rare inside.

Lift the first batch of meat out and set it aside while frying the second batch in the really hot pan. Return all the meat to the pan, season well, add the onion and mushrooms, and stir together for 1 or 2 minutes.

Pour in the cream, bring quickly to the boil, and serve immediately.

SERVING SUGGESTION Spoon over boiled rice* or buttered noodles.

VARIATIONS Add 15 ml (1 tablespoon) brandy or 15 ml (1 tablespoon) tomato paste to the cream sauce.

For a slightly different dish, sauté 1 cm thick slices of beef fillet in butter to seal, and add 30 ml (2 tablespoons) brandy, sour cream, seasoning and lemon juice. Serve with buttered baby potatoes and green beans or mushrooms.

Beef Loaf

TO MAKE A successful beef loaf, you should buy lean stewing beef or topside and mince it finely; ready-minced beef is too coarse and fatty for this recipe.

PREPARATION TIME: 20 MINUTES
COOKING TIME: 1½ HOURS
PRE-HEAT OVEN TO 150°C

INGREDIENTS FOR FOUR TO SIX
750 g stewing steak or topside of beef, finely minced
1 onion, peeled* and minced
50 g fine white breadcrumbs
2 ml (½ teaspoon) dried thyme
2 ml (½ teaspoon) dried origanum or marjoram
1 clove garlic, crushed
2 ml (½ teaspoon) salt
1 ml (¼ teaspoon) freshly ground black pepper
2 eggs, beaten
450 ml brown stock* reduced to 150 ml by fast boiling
15 g soft butter
Boiling water

Mix all the ingredients – except the boiling water – very well together and mould into a roughly oblong shape. Butter an oblong loaf tin, 20 cm long, and press the mixture into it until almost full.

Stand the loaf tin in a shallow roasting tin with enough boiling water to come halfway up the side of the loaf tin. This prevents the loaf from sticking at the base. Bake uncovered in the centre of the pre-heated oven for 1½ hours. If necessary, add more boiling water to maintain the level.

Turn out the loaf from the tin on to a warmed serving plate.

SERVING SUGGESTION Serve hot with fresh tomato and onion sauce*.

Preserving Meat in Brine

Brining is a very old process designed to preserve meat and give it a distinctive flavour. The cuts of meat most often salted in brine are brisket and silverside of beef, belly of pork, and tongue.

Corning is the old term for salting. What we know as corned beef is simply beef soaked in brine.

Another popular dish is pickled pork, which is cured in brine (with sugar added). Pork prepared in this way may need soaking before it is simmered.

The basic ingredients for brine are salt, saltpetre, brown sugar and bicarbonate of soda. The saltpetre may be omitted, but it gives the meat a nice pink colour.

Apart from these ingredients, spices can be added according to taste. The sugar is used to counteract the hardening effect of the saltpetre, and also adds a lovely flavour.

To preserve a 2 kg cut of beef or pork belly, boil 1,5 litres water, then add 250 g salt, 20 g saltpetre, 100 g brown sugar, 30 g bicarbonate of soda, 4 bay leaves, 3 cloves garlic, 5 peppercorns, 1 stick cinnamon and 10 whole allspice, and boil for 5 minutes.

Allow the brine to cool, then transfer it to a large container (use only a plastic, wood, earthenware or glass container). Place the meat in the brine, making sure it is completely covered. Press the meat down with a heavy object and leave it for 5 to 7 days.

Pierce with a skewer or sharp knife to see if it is pink all the way through. (If there is any sign of mould or scum, scrub the meat and place it in fresh brine.)

To shorten the curing time, the brine mixture may be injected into the meat with a brining needle. Inject the meat with about a quarter of the brine, and leave it in the rest of the mixture for 3-4 days.

Cooking salted meat To cook salted beef, place it in tepid water to cover, then gradually heat the water, removing any scum as it appears. When there is no more scum, add 5 carrots, cut into two or three pieces, 2 turnips, cut into slices, 2 large, whole onions, 10 peppercorns and a bouquet garni*.

Simmer gently, allowing 25 minutes for each 500 g, plus an extra 25 minutes. When the beef is done, serve with dumplings and a thick tomato and onion sauce*. Reserve the liquid for use as a soup stock. If the beef is very salty to begin with, place it in *cold* water, then heat slowly and continue as above.

To cook pickled pork, first soak it in a bowl of water for an hour. Place it in a large saucepan and add a sliced carrot, a swede and a turnip, a whole onion (studded with a few cloves), a sliced orange and 10 peppercorns. Pour over enough water to cover, heat gently and simmer, allowing 20 minutes per 500 g plus an extra 20 minutes, until tender.

MEAT

PEPPER STEAK

THE CLASSIC PEPPER STEAK is a great favourite among South Africans. Fillet, entrecôte or rump steaks are all suitable for this dish, though the last two cuts – despite their appealing flavour – require slight tenderising before frying.

PREPARATION TIME: 20 MINUTES
COOKING TIME: 5 MINUTES FOR RARE STEAKS;
8-10 MINUTES FOR MEDIUM-RARE STEAKS;
12 MINUTES FOR WELL-DONE STEAKS

INGREDIENTS FOR SIX
6 steaks (fillet, entrecôte or rump), about 1,5 cm thick
45 ml (3 tablespoons) black peppercorns
50 g butter
30 ml (2 tablespoons) olive or sunflower oil
Salt
30 ml (2 tablespoons) brandy
125 ml (½ cup) thick cream

Trim any gristle, untidy bits and excess fat from the steaks (though a little fat left on entrecôte and rump steaks helps to keep the meat succulent). You can tenderise entrecôte and rump steaks by placing them between 2 sheets of wax paper and pounding them on both sides with a wooden hammer before frying.

Crush the peppercorns coarsely in a mortar, or use a rolling pin on a wooden board. Press the ground pepper into the surface of the meat on both sides.

Heat half the butter with the olive or sunflower oil in a heavy frying pan until it is smoking hot, and cook the steaks over a high heat for 2 minutes, sealing and browning both sides.

Turn down the heat and cook for a further 3-10 minutes, according to taste. Do not cook too many steaks at one time, or the temperature of the pan will be too low to seal the meat properly. Transfer the steaks to a heated platter with a slotted spoon and salt them lightly. Keep them warm while you make the sauce.

Add the brandy to the pan juices, scrape in all the crusty brown left-overs, and bring to the boil. Add the remaining butter and slowly stir in the cream. Simmer to thicken the sauce and season lightly to taste. Pour the sauce over the steaks and serve immediately.

SERVING SUGGESTIONS Pepper steaks are best served with simple accompaniments, so that the sauce flavour is not overwhelmed. Boiled and peeled new potatoes, rolled lightly in parsley butter*, and green beans, topped and tailed and cooked with carrot strips until still firm, are suitable. Or serve with rosti* and a green salad*.

VARIATIONS A milder but equally delicious sauce can be made for the steaks using soft, green peppercorns. These are usually tinned, and are sometimes known as Madagascar green peppercorns. For this recipe, skip the coarsely ground pepper, but cook the steaks as in the main recipe. Add 30-45 ml (2-3 tablespoons) drained, soft green peppercorns to the sauce with the cream, and serve as above.

If you prefer a sauce which does not incorporate cream, add 75 ml dry white wine and 75 ml vegetable* or basic stock* to the pan, heat it to boiling point and scrape in all the brown bits. Then add 60 ml (¼ cup) brandy, boil briskly for a minute or so, and season to taste. Pour the sauce over the steaks and serve immediately. You can use either black or green peppercorns for this sauce.

BEEF OR VEAL OLIVES

BEEF OR VEAL OLIVES made their earliest appearances in the Middle Ages, alongside such delicacies as pudding of porpoise and morsels of whale. The 'olives' consist of meat slices wrapped around herb stuffing and baked.

PREPARATION TIME: 30 MINUTES
COOKING TIME: 40 MINUTES
PRE-HEAT OVEN TO 170°C

INGREDIENTS FOR FOUR
6 thin frying beef steaks, or 6 large veal schnitzels
600 ml brown stock*
25 g butter
25 g flour
45 ml (3 tablespoons) sherry

For the stuffing:
125 g fine white breadcrumbs
2 anchovy fillets, mashed and pounded in a mortar or with a wooden spoon in a small bowl
5 ml (1 teaspoon) dried thyme
2 ml (½ teaspoon) dried sage
1 small onion, peeled and very finely chopped*
1 egg, well beaten
Salt and pepper

First make the stuffing by mixing all the ingredients in a bowl. Form the mixture into 12 small balls.

Pound the steaks or schnitzels with the back of a heavy knife to flatten them. Trim off any fat and cut each piece in two lengthways. You should have 12 pieces, each about 6 cm x 12 cm.

Place a ball of stuffing on each, and roll the meat tightly around it. Tie each olive round the middle with thread or string.

BEEF OLIVES *'Parcels' of herb stuffing wrapped in beef.*

Lightly grease a shallow oven-proof dish and lay the olives in it so that they touch each other (this helps them to stay in shape). Pour the stock over the olives, cover the dish closely with foil, and cook in the pre-heated oven for 40 minutes.

Lift the olives very carefully on to a warm serving dish, reserving the stock. Snip the strings with scissors and pull them away. Keep the olives warm and covered while you prepare the gravy.

Make a roux* with the butter and flour, stir in the stock and bring to the boil. Add the sherry and check the seasoning. Pour the gravy over the olives and serve immediately.

MEAT

Beef and Tomato Pie

The appetising mixture of meat and tomatoes is very popular in South Africa. For this recipe you will need tomatoes which are firm and just ripe enough to blanch and peel.

Preparation Time: 30 minutes
Cooking Time: 2 hours
Pre-heat Oven to 180°C

Ingredients for Six

750 g best stewing steak, cut into 2,5 cm cubes
50 g seasoned flour*
2 medium-sized onions, peeled and sliced*
75 g butter
6 medium-sized tomatoes
5 ml (1 teaspoon) sugar
Freshly ground black pepper
5 ml (1 teaspoon) dried basil
Shortcrust pastry* using 225 g flour

Remove all the fat and skin from the steak cubes and dip them in the seasoned flour. Fry the onions gently in 50 g of the butter until soft. Put the onions in the bottom of a very large pie dish. Add the rest of the butter to the pan and fry the beef.

When the beef is lightly browned, arrange it in the dish on top of the onions and add just enough water to cover the meat. Cover the top of the dish with aluminium foil and cook it in the pre-heated oven for 1½ hours, or until tender.

Meanwhile, blanch and skin the tomatoes* and cut them into quarters, preserving all the juice. Sprinkle them with the sugar, black pepper and basil. Set aside the tomatoes while you roll out the pastry.

When the meat is tender, remove it from the oven. Place the tomatoes on top so that they form a cool layer on the hot meat – this prevents the meat from steaming the inside of the pastry lid and making it heavy.

Roll out the pastry fairly thinly, cut out a lid and put it on top of the pie dish. Use any left-over pastry to decorate* the pie with pastry leaves, if you like. Bake the pie near the top of the oven, still at the same temperature, for 30 minutes, or until the crust is golden-brown.

Serving Suggestions Serve the pie with a simple green salad*, or with buttered new potatoes and steamed green beans.

Stir-Fried Beef with Oyster-Flavoured Sauce

The taste of rich, dark brown oyster-flavoured sauce predominates in this dish. Oyster-flavoured sauce is used in stir-fried dishes in place of soy sauce, or may complement it. In Chinese recipes, beef is generally cut into very fine slices. Put the meat in the freezer for 30 minutes beforehand to make slicing easier.

Preparation Time: 30 minutes
Cooking Time: 15 minutes

Ingredients for Six

750 g boneless lean beef
3 spring onions, thinly sliced
45 ml (3 tablespoons) soy sauce
45 ml (3 tablespoons) water
25 ml (5 teaspoons) cornflour
25 ml (5 teaspoons) dry sherry
2 ml (½ teaspoon) salt
45 ml (3 tablespoons) sunflower oil
45 ml (3 tablespoons) oyster-flavoured sauce
7 ml (1½ teaspoons) sugar

Cut the meat (with the grain) into 3,5 cm strips. Cut each strip across the grain into 5 mm-thick slices. Combine the spring onions, soy sauce, water, cornflour, sherry and salt with the beef, mixing to coat it well. Allow to marinate for 15 minutes.

Place a wok or heavy frying pan over a high heat and add half the oil. When the oil is hot enough to ripple when the wok or pan is tilted from side to side, add half the meat mixture and stir-fry until browned. Remove from the wok or pan. Repeat using the remaining oil and the other half of the meat mixture.

Return all the cooked meat to the wok or frying pan, add the oyster-flavoured sauce and sugar, and stir-fry for 1 minute. Serve on a heated platter.

Variation Substitute boned, skinned, sliced chicken breasts for the beef. Stir-fry until just cooked through.

Stir-Fried Beef with Oyster-Flavoured Sauce *Beef cooked in the Oriental way.*

Cornish Pasties

In the English county of Devonshire, they say that if the Devil crossed the Tamar – the river dividing Devon from Cornwall – the Cornish would make him into a pasty. Perhaps this is a reference to the 'horns' of the Cornish pasty.

The pastry for a pasty used to be cut over a dinner plate, so it was quite a hefty size. It was the custom to mark one corner with an initial so that the half-eaten pasty could be claimed later.

Preparation Time: 30 minutes
Cooking Time: 40 minutes
Pre-heat Oven to 220°C

Ingredients for 4 Pasties

350 g chuck steak, diced
Shortcrust pastry* using 450 g flour
4 medium-sized potatoes, peeled
1 medium-sized onion, peeled* and diced
125 g swede, peeled and diced
Parsley, roughly chopped (optional)
50 g butter
Salt and pepper
1 egg, beaten, for glazing

Roll out the pastry to about 5 mm thick and cut out four 15 cm rounds.

Cut the potatoes by 'shripping' them, that is, cutting them into very fine wafers by constantly turning them to 'shrip' off the corners. Put a few pieces of potato in the centre of each pastry round.

Cover this with some diced onion and diced swede, and then some of the diced meat. If using parsley, add it now. Dot with the butter. Season well and cover with more potato slices to prevent it from drying.

Dampen the edges of the pastry and fold each round over to make a half-moon shape. Turn the edges round a little to make 'horns'.

Pinch and crimp the pastry edges into ridges to give a rope-like effect. Glaze with beaten egg and put the pasties on a greased baking sheet.

Bake in the pre-heated oven for 10 minutes. Lower the heat to 180°C, and continue cooking for 30 minutes.

The pasties are delicious hot or cold. They will stay warm for an hour or two if you wrap them up in a tea towel.

MEAT

VITELLO TONNATO *is a veal-based Italian speciality that makes a perfect dish for a summer's day.*

VITELLO TONNATO

ITALIANS CONSIDER vitello tonnato to be something of a luxury dish, and it is certainly a culinary delight – a classic cold dish that is especially suitable for an elegant buffet*. It combines veal with a delicious tuna sauce.

PREPARATION TIME: 25 MINUTES
COOKING TIME: 1½-2 HOURS

INGREDIENTS FOR EIGHT

1,5 kg veal (fillet end of leg rump)
1 tin (55 g) flat anchovy fillets, drained
1 large clove garlic
2 carrots, peeled and chopped
3 sticks celery, chopped
2 onions, peeled and chopped*
1,25 litres (5 cups) water
2 chicken stock cubes
375 ml (1½ cups) dry white wine
6 sprigs parsley

For the tuna sauce:
20 ml (4 teaspoons) capers
180 ml sunflower oil
1 egg yolk
1 tin (200 g) plain white-meat tuna
30 ml (2 tablespoons) lemon juice
Salt and pepper

For the garnish:
Salad greens
Black olives
Lemon wedges

Using the tip of a sharp knife, make small cuts along the length of the veal. Cut 4 anchovy fillets into 1 cm pieces, then insert these into the veal with garlic slivers.

Place the veal in a saucepan, cover with cold water, bring to the boil and boil (uncovered) for 1 minute. Pour off the water and rinse the veal under cold water.

Place the carrots, celery and onions in a saucepan with the veal, 1,25 litres water, crumbled stock cubes, wine and parsley. Bring to the boil, reduce the heat and simmer (partly covered) for 1½-2 hours, or until the veal is tender. Remove the veal from the stock and leave it to cool. Reserve about 60 ml (¼ cup) stock for the sauce.

To make the sauce, allow the reserved stock to cool, then blend it in a liquidizer together with the sauce ingredients.

Cut the cooled veal into thin slices. Dip the slices in the sauce and arrange in overlapping slices around a platter. Spoon on extra sauce. Before serving, garnish the centre of the platter with salad greens, black olives and lemon wedges.

BLANQUETTE DE VEAU

BLANQUETTE IS the traditional name for white stews made from white meats and coated with a smooth white sauce. This recipe is for breast of veal with a creamy mushroom sauce.

PREPARATION TIME: 30 MINUTES
COOKING TIME: 1½ HOURS

INGREDIENTS FOR FOUR

1 kg breast of veal, cut into 2 cm strips
200 g button mushrooms, washed
15-30 ml (1-2 tablespoons) lemon juice
60 ml (¼ cup) water
45 g butter
Salt and freshly ground black pepper
3 medium-sized carrots, scraped and cut into 2 cm lengths
2 medium-sized onions, peeled*
4 cloves
A pinch of mixed herbs
1 bouquet garni*
1 bay leaf
15 ml (1 tablespoon) flour
80 ml (⅓ cup) cream
2 egg yolks
Freshly grated nutmeg
Chopped parsley

Cut the meat into 2 cm strips and set aside. Mix the mushrooms with most of the lemon juice, the water, 15 g of the butter and seasoning in a small saucepan. Cover and boil for 1 minute.

Arrange the meat in a heavy-based saucepan and strain the mushroom liquor over it with enough cold water to cover the meat by 2 cm. Add salt and bring to the boil. Skim the top 2 or 3 times, taking off any foam and adding a little extra water if necessary.

Add the carrots, the onions studded with the cloves, the mixed herbs, bouquet garni and bay leaf, making sure all are completely under water.

Simmer very gently for about 1 hour, or until the meat is tender. Strain the liquid through a sieve and reserve. Pick out the onions, cloves, bouquet garni and carrots. Put the carrots on one side.

Melt the remaining butter in a clean saucepan, stir in the flour and cook for 1 minute without browning.

Slowly add the meat liquid and bring to the boil, stirring continually to make a smooth sauce. Simmer for 10 minutes or until the sauce is thick enough to lightly coat the meat.

Meanwhile, mix together the cream and egg yolks with pepper and nutmeg, and carefully stir in 30 ml (2 tablespoons) of the sauce. Remove the sauce from the heat and whisk the egg mixture into it. Re-heat it gently, check the seasoning, add the meat and mushrooms (and chopped carrots if liked) and stir well. Sprinkle with parsley and serve.

SERVING SUGGESTION This dish is best served with something simple such as rice or buttered noodles with a sprinkling of poppy seeds.

VARIATION Give left-over roast chicken the *blanquette* treatment by coating with the same sauce, but using chicken stock instead of the meat liquid. Serve sprinkled with grated Parmesan cheese.

SALTIMBOCCA ALLA ROMANA

THIS POPULAR AND TASTY Italian dish can be prepared using either thin veal schnitzels or beef steaks. Ask your butcher to pound them as thinly as possible.

PREPARATION TIME: 15 MINUTES
COOKING TIME: 10 MINUTES

INGREDIENTS FOR SIX
8 veal schnitzels or beef steaks, pounded thinly
90 g butter
150 g mushrooms, sliced
8 thin slices ham
4 slices mozzarella cheese, halved
60 ml (¼ cup) grated Parmesan or Cheddar cheese
Salt and freshly ground black pepper
2 large cloves garlic, crushed
2 ml (½ teaspoon) dried sage
60 ml (¼ cup) sunflower oil

Pat the schnitzels or steaks dry with paper towels. Melt 30 g of the butter in a saucepan and add the mushrooms. Cook gently until tender, then drain and discard the pan juices from the mushrooms.

Place a slice of ham and mozzarella on each schnitzel or steak. Divide the cooked mushrooms into 8 portions and arrange on top of the mozzarella.

Sprinkle Parmesan or Cheddar, salt, black pepper, crushed garlic and dried sage on each schnitzel, then roll them up and secure with toothpicks or metal skewers.

Heat the oil and remaining butter and fry (on a medium heat) for 4 minutes. Serve immediately.

SERVING SUGGESTIONS Serve with pasta or rice steamed with wine, chicken stock and herbs, and whole spinach leaves stir-fried with a little olive oil and garlic.

VEAL AND HAM PIE

THIS TASTY pie is encased in rough puff or flaky pastry. Serve it as a hot supper dish with steamed vegetables.

PREPARATION TIME: 1¼ HOURS
COOKING TIME: 35 MINUTES
PRE-HEAT OVEN TO 200°C

INGREDIENTS FOR FOUR
500 g fillet of veal, or stewing veal
1 large onion, peeled* and studded with 10 cloves
5 ml (1 teaspoon) chopped parsley
Grated rind of ½ lemon
2 ml (½ teaspoon) mixed dried herbs
Salt and pepper
100-125 g lean, home-cured, cooked ham*, or baked ham
2 hard-boiled eggs*, sliced
Rough puff* or flaky pastry* using 350 g flour

If you are using stewing veal, trim it very carefully and remove all the skin and fat. Put the veal and the onion studded with cloves in a saucepan with enough water just to cover the meat. Cook over a low heat for 40 minutes, or until tender. Remove the meat and onion, reserving the stock.

When the veal is cold, use a sharp knife to cut it into very thin slices. Put a little parsley, lemon rind, herbs, salt and pepper on each slice, and roll the slice of meat up carefully. Put a layer of the veal rolls inside a litre-sized pie dish.

Cut the thick ham slices into short strips. Arrange a layer of ham strips and sliced egg on top of the veal rolls. Put another layer of veal rolls on top.

Reduce the stock by fast boiling to about half its original quantity, then season well and pour into the pie dish. Allow to cool. Roll out the pastry to about 5 mm thick, cut out a lid and cover the pie dish with it.

Bake at the top of the oven for 25 minutes, or until the pastry is crisp and golden-brown. Cover the crust lightly with aluminium foil, move the pie to a lower shelf and cook for a further 10 minutes.

SERVING SUGGESTIONS Serve with a green vegetable or follow with a green salad*.

VEAL CUTLETS IN WHITE WINE

FOR CENTURIES veal was considered suitable only for invalids and the effete. Needless to say, this bias has happily disappeared, since this is one of the most delicious of meats. In this recipe, pork cutlets can be substituted for veal.

PREPARATION TIME: 30 MINUTES
COOKING TIME: 30 MINUTES
PRE-HEAT OVEN TO 190°C

INGREDIENTS FOR FOUR
4 veal or pork cutlets
50 g butter
2 large onions, peeled and finely chopped*
150 ml dry white wine
150 ml brown stock*
25 g breadcrumbs
25 g grated Parmesan cheese

Trim any excess fat off the cutlets. Melt the butter in a frying pan, add the onions and fry them gently until they are soft and golden. Stir in the wine and the brown stock, and set aside.

Combine the breadcrumbs and the Parmesan cheese. Coat the cutlets with the mixture, and place flat in an oven-proof dish large enough to hold them without overlapping. Carefully pour the onions and stock around the cutlets and cook (uncovered) in the pre-heated oven for 30 minutes, or until the meat begins to come away from the bone very slightly. If the liquid should reduce too much, add more wine and stock in equal quantities.

SERVING SUGGESTION Serve the cutlets straight from the dish, with mashed potatoes* and a fresh green vegetable or a green salad*.

WIENER SCHNITZEL

THESE QUICK AND EASY veal treats – and their equally delicious variations – have long been popular items on South African restaurant menus. The secret to making successful schnitzels lies in chilling them to ensure that the crumbs adhere well.

PREPARATION TIME: 15 MINUTES
CHILLING TIME: 1 HOUR
COOKING TIME: 10 MINUTES

INGREDIENTS FOR FOUR
8 thin slices leg of veal
Salt and freshly ground pepper
Flour for coating
2 eggs, beaten
Fine dried breadcrumbs for coating
Sunflower oil or clarified butter*
8 lemon wedges or slices

Pound the veal slices to flatten them evenly. Season with salt and pepper. Dip in the flour and shake off the surplus, then dip in the egg followed by the breadcrumbs. Dip again into egg and breadcrumbs to ensure an all-over coating. Chill in the refrigerator for at least an hour so that the crumb coating adheres during frying.

Fry in hot oil or clarified butter over a medium heat until golden-brown on both sides. Drain on paper towels and serve with the lemon.

SERVING SUGGESTIONS Sautéed potatoes, buttered green beans or young peas, make good accompaniments.

VARIATIONS Use skinned and filleted chicken breast instead of the veal.

To make veal cordon bleu, sandwich a slice of baked ham and Gruyère cheese between 2 pounded schnitzels, then dip in the prepared coating.

Cover each fried schnitzel with a slice of ham and a slice of mozzarella cheese. Place in a hot oven at 220°C for a few minutes until the cheese melts.

Bredies – A Tasty Malay Tradition

The bredie, a subtly flavoured meat and vegetable stew, was introduced to South African cuisine by the Cape Muslims, who eat particular bredies at religious and social occasions. The secret of a successful bredie lies in blending and integrating the various constituents so that no one flavour dominates.

The Bredie – The Basic Approach

Although there are many types of bredie, the basic method of preparation remains the same. The following guidelines apply to all the recipes on these two pages.

———•———

Fat mutton rib is the traditional meat to use for bredies, the meat being cut into 6 cm squares. However, neck or best-end-of-neck chops are equally acceptable, and the ratio of meat to bone is greater. Lamb can also be used (it must be fairly fat), but the essence of making a tasty bredie is long, slow cooking and a complete marriage of flavours – so with lamb there is the obvious danger of the meat overcooking and losing texture. Of course, careful timing and testing of the bredie can prevent this.

———•———

The fat that is required to braise both the meat and onions can be trimmed from the meat, finely chopped and rendered in the pot before being used. Alternatively, butter or mutton dripping* may be used.

———•———

A lidded, cast-iron pot is ideal for bredie making. A bredie is often served in the pot in which it was cooked.

———•———

The flavouring of a bredie should always be subtle, with no ingredient dominating. Chillies are traditionally used but they can be omitted. Wild sorrel is also a traditional ingredient, its slightly sour, citrony flavour being ideal. The whole sorrel plant – namely, its yellow flowers, clover-like leaves and some of the stem – can be used. However, wine, vinegar or lemon juice can be used as a substitute. A little sugar added with vegetables such as pumpkin, carrot, parsnip and peas gives the pleasant sweet-sour taste that is traditional to many bredies.

———•———

Very little additional liquid is used in a bredie, the flavour deriving from the meat and vegetable juices. For this reason it is essential to shake or gently stir the bredie while cooking. The 200 ml water (or water and wine mixture) listed among the ingredients should be used sparingly and with discretion *throughout* the cooking – remember, it is used only to prevent the bredie from sticking to the pot. If the vegetables give out sufficient liquid of their own, additional liquid should be omitted altogether. A small glass of wine, or a little lemon juice, added to the bredie at the end of cooking is all that is needed to moisten it. There should be no actual gravy.

———•———

Although bredies are made with fat mutton, they should never be greasy or contain lumps of fat. Excess fat can be skimmed off during cooking and especially at the end of cooking just before adding the wine or lemon juice.

———•———

Bredies are virtually meals in themselves, and need little more than a dish of white rice as accompaniment. Malay bredies are often served with salads, or sambals* and chutneys, but too many extras eclipse the flavour.

———•———

Potatoes are often added to the bredie to absorb some of the delicious flavours and add bulk to the dish. They should never predominate over the vegetable used, though a plain potato bredie is very good.

Pumpkin Bredie

PREPARATION TIME: 45 MINUTES
COOKING TIME: 2-2½ HOURS

INGREDIENTS FOR FOUR

1 kg dry pumpkin
50 g butter or mutton fat
700 g fat mutton, cut into neat pieces
2 medium-sized onions, peeled and sliced*
A 1 cm piece of fresh green ginger, scraped and chopped
½ chilli, seeded and chopped
1 clove garlic, crushed
2 cardamom seeds, pounded
2 coriander seeds, pounded
150-200 ml water, or half water and half white wine
15 ml (1 tablespoon) brown sugar
A 2,5 cm cinnamon stick
Salt and freshly ground white pepper
15 ml (1 tablespoon) lemon juice or white wine

Peel the pumpkin and cut into 5 cm cubes. Heat the butter or fat and brown the meat in the pot with the onions, ginger, chilli, garlic, cardamom and coriander. Pour on a little of the water, or water and wine mixture, and cover. Simmer on a very low heat for 1½ hours, shaking from time to time and adding liquid when necessary.

Add the pumpkin, sugar, cinnamon stick, salt, pepper and a little extra liquid (some pumpkins contain a lot of water). Cover and simmer slowly, stirring carefully, or shaking from time to time, until the pumpkin is soft and the meat is tender (about 30 minutes). There should be very little liquid, so watch the pot carefully and remove the cover to evaporate excess moisture if necessary.

Skim off any excess fat and add the lemon juice or white wine. Correct the seasoning to taste.

Green Bean Bredie

PREPARATION TIME: 1 HOUR
COOKING TIME: 2-2½ HOURS

INGREDIENTS FOR FOUR

700 g fat mutton
300 g green beans
50 g butter or mutton fat
2 medium-sized onions, peeled and thinly sliced*
1 clove garlic, crushed
½ chilli, seeded and chopped
5 ml (1 teaspoon) dried basil, or a handful of fresh chopped basil
1 ml (¼ teaspoon) grated nutmeg
200 ml water, or basic stock*, or half water and half wine
1 large or 2 medium-sized potatoes, peeled and quartered
5 ml (1 teaspoon) sugar (optional)
Salt and freshly ground pepper
15 ml (1 tablespoon) lemon juice

Cut the mutton into neat pieces, and trim and cut the beans in slanting pieces about 4 cm long.

Heat the butter or fat and brown the meat a few pieces at a time, then set aside. Brown the onions and then return all the meat to the pot with the garlic, chilli, basil and nutmeg. Add a little of the water, stock, or water and wine mixture.

Cover and simmer very slowly (shaking occasionally) for 1½ hours until the meat is tender. Then add the beans, potatoes, sugar (if used), salt, pepper and a little more liquid, stirring the vegetables into the bredie. Cover and cook for 30 minutes.

Remove the lid and cook until the bredie is sufficiently dry, and the meat and vegetables are tender. Be careful when adding liquid after the beans have been added as they sometimes give off a lot of liquid themselves.

When the bredie is done, skim off any excess fat, add the lemon juice and correct the seasoning.

TOMATO BREDIE

PREPARATION TIME: 1 HOUR
COOKING TIME: 2½-3 HOURS

INGREDIENTS FOR FOUR

700 g fat mutton, cut into neat pieces
30 g flour
50 g butter or mutton fat
2 medium-sized onions, peeled and sliced*
1 leek, trimmed and sliced 1 cm thick
1 clove garlic, crushed
A 1 cm piece of fresh green ginger, peeled and chopped
1 cardamom seed
2 coriander seeds
3 peppercorns
2 ml (½ teaspoon) fennel seeds
5 ml (1 teaspoon) fresh, crushed thyme, or 2 ml (½ teaspoon) dried thyme
2 ml (½ teaspoon) fresh chopped marjoram, or 1 ml (¼ teaspoon) dried marjoram
½ green or red chilli, seeded and chopped
700 g (about 4 large) ripe tomatoes, skinned* and quartered
Salt and freshly ground pepper
5 ml (1 teaspoon) chutney
5 ml (1 teaspoon) brown sugar
1 large potato, peeled and quartered (optional)
100 ml white wine

Dust the meat with the flour. Heat the butter or fat and brown the pieces of meat, a few at a time. Then return all the meat to the pot and add the onions, leek and garlic. Stir until the onion is lightly browned, then add the ginger, cardamom, coriander, peppercorns, fennel, thyme, marjoram, chilli and tomatoes.

Cover and cook on a very low heat (shaking frequently to prevent the meat from sticking) for 1½-2 hours. Season with the salt and pepper, and add the chutney and brown sugar.

Simmer, uncovered, until the tomato sauce has thickened and the meat is tender (about 1 hour, depending on the water content of the tomatoes and the quality of the meat). Forty-five minutes before the dish is ready, add the potato quarters (if used), pressing them under the surface.

Before serving, skim off the fat. Alternatively, make the dish ahead, and then cool and chill – the fat can then be easily removed before re-heating. Add the wine just before serving.

VARIATIONS A simpler tomato bredie can be made without the herbs and spices, though chilli, onion, a little sugar, salt and pepper are essential.

The bredie should always be subtly flavoured, no spice or herb being too dominant. Should you like a really hot tomato bredie, add the chilli seeds and plenty of black pepper.

TOMATO BREDIE

WATERBLOMMETJIE BREDIE

PREPARATION TIME: 45 MINUTES
SOAKING TIME: 2-3 HOURS
COOKING TIME: 2-2½ HOURS

INGREDIENTS FOR FOUR

1-2 bunches of waterblommetjie buds or open flowers
Salt and freshly ground pepper
50 g butter or mutton fat
700 g fat mutton, cut into neat pieces
2 medium-sized onions, peeled and sliced*
1 clove garlic, crushed
½ green chilli, seeded and finely chopped
3 stalks wild sorrel, well-washed and finely chopped, or 20 ml (4 teaspoons) lemon juice
1 ml (¼ teaspoon) grated nutmeg
200 ml white wine, or half basic stock* and half wine

Trim the stalks from the waterblommetjie buds or flowers and wash well. Rinse and put into a bowl of water to which 15 ml (1 tablespoon) salt has been added. Leave to soak for 2-3 hours (or overnight).

Heat the butter or fat and brown the meat a few pieces at a time. Return all the meat to the pot and add the onions, garlic and chopped chilli. Stir until the onion is soft and brown.

Drain and rinse the waterblommetjie buds or flowers, and add to the meat with the chopped sorrel or lemon juice, and the nutmeg. Add 100 ml or so of the wine, or wine mixture, then cover and cook gently for 1½-2 hours, or until the meat is tender. Periodically add more liquid and shake the pot to prevent the meat from sticking to the bottom. Avoid stirring the bredie, as this can break up the flowers.

After 1½-2 hours, season the bredie. If there is too much moisture, cook uncovered until the consistency is right. Skim off any excess fat before serving.

OSSO BUCCO

THIS DISH is a well-loved speciality of Milan, Italy: the name means 'hollow bones'. Veal, the main ingredient, is easily Italy's favourite meat. Ask your butcher to cut the meat into pieces for you.

PREPARATION TIME: 20 MINUTES
COOKING TIME: 1½-2 HOURS
PRE-HEAT OVEN TO 180°C

INGREDIENTS FOR SIX
2 kg veal shanks or knuckles (cut into 6 cm pieces by your butcher)
Flour for dusting
Salt and freshly ground black pepper
90 g butter
2 carrots, peeled and coarsely chopped
3 sticks celery, sliced
2 large onions, peeled and coarsely chopped*
4 cloves garlic, crushed
60 ml (¼ cup) sunflower oil
2 tins (each 410 g) tomatoes
500 ml (2 cups) beef basic stock*
125 ml (½ cup) dry white wine
5 ml (1 teaspoon) basil
5 ml (1 teaspoon) thyme
1 bay leaf
A 2,5 cm strip of lemon rind

For the garnish:
5 ml (1 teaspoon) grated lemon rind
45 ml (3 tablespoons) freshly chopped parsley
4 cloves garlic, chopped

Dust the meat with flour and season with salt and black pepper.

Heat 30 g of the butter in a pan. Add the carrots, celery, onions and garlic, and cook gently until the onions turn golden. Transfer to a large oven-proof dish.

Heat the remaining butter and oil in a large frying pan, add the veal and lightly brown it on all sides. Carefully pack the veal on top of the vegetables in the oven-proof dish (stand shanks upright to retain the marrow in the bones).

Pour away all the fat from the pan in which the meat was cooked. Pour in the tinned tomatoes (and their juice). Add the stock, wine, basil, thyme, bay leaf and lemon rind. Season and bring to the boil.

Pour the sauce over the veal and vegetables, cover the casserole and bake in the pre-heated oven (stirring occasionally) for 1½ hours – or until the veal is very tender.

Before serving, mix together the garnish ingredients, which constitute 'gremolata', the classic Italian seasoning, and sprinkle over the dish.

ROAST SADDLE OF LAMB

FOR THIS RECIPE buy a short saddle of lamb which includes: a pair of loins (one on either side of the backbone), the tender strips of fillet underneath the backbone, and the aprons – the flaps of meat attached to each eye of the loin. These are tucked underneath to protect the fillets from over-cooking. A long saddle includes the chump chops as well as the loin, making it difficult to carve.

PREPARATION TIME: 15 MINUTES
COOKING TIME: 1 HOUR
PRE-HEAT OVEN TO 200°C

INGREDIENTS FOR FOUR
1,5 kg short saddle of lamb
15 ml (1 tablespoon) sunflower oil
5 ml (1 teaspoon) dry mustard
Salt
Coarsely crushed black peppercorns
1 or 2 sprigs fresh rosemary
125 ml (½ cup) dry red wine

Trim the outer layer of fat from the meat and any other excess fat. Rub the meat with the oil, mustard, salt and pepper. Place in a roasting pan just large enough to accommodate it. Tuck the rosemary underneath and roll the aprons under the lamb so that they touch.

Roast for 45 minutes, then allow the roast to stand in the warming oven for 15 minutes (this makes for easier carving). Skim the fat from the roasting pan by patting with paper towels. Pour in the wine and reduce on top of the stove over a high heat. Check the seasoning.

To carve, slice each section separately, sharing the slices equally. Slice the eye of the loin lengthways into long strips. Carve each fillet and each apron across.

SERVING SUGGESTION Serve with a vegetable in season and sautéed potatoes.

ROAST STUFFED SHOULDER OF LAMB

A SHOULDER OF LAMB is a particularly flavoursome and juicy cut of meat, with a good proportion of fat to lean. It is equally delicious roasted plain, or boned and stuffed.

PREPARATION TIME: 45 MINUTES
SOAKING TIME: OVERNIGHT
COOKING TIME: 2½ HOURS
PRE-HEAT OVEN TO 160°C

INGREDIENTS FOR SIX
2 kg shoulder of lamb, boned
Salt and freshly ground black pepper
Sunflower oil

For the stuffing:
125 g dried apricots, soaked overnight
125 g fresh breadcrumbs
15 ml (1 tablespoon) chopped fresh parsley
50 g butter, melted
50 g walnuts, roughly chopped
1 large egg, lightly beaten

Open out the shoulder. To make the stuffing, drain and chop the apricots, mix with the other ingredients, and stuff the mixture into the cavity of the shoulder. Close it up into the original shape and hold it together with a skewer (or sew it together with string). Season, and rub with a little oil.

Set the lamb in a roasting tin and roast (allow 25-30 minutes per 500 g), basting with oil from time to time.

Transfer to a warm serving dish and leave the lamb to stand in a warming drawer for 10-15 minutes before taking out the skewer or cutting away the string. Carve it into thin slices and spoon over re-heated pan juices.

SERVING SUGGESTION Roast meat is traditionally served with roast potatoes, but boiled new potatoes are equally delicious.

VARIATIONS Stuff the lamb with 250 ml (1 cup) cooked rice mixed with 125 ml (½ cup) plumped seedless raisins, 50 g almonds, chopped, 15 ml (1 tablespoon) chopped parsley, 5 ml (1 teaspoon) cinnamon, salt and pepper.

Alternatively, stuff it with breadcrumbs, chopped onion*, parsley, thyme, grated lemon rind, seasoning and beaten egg.

DEVILLED SHOULDER OF LAMB

BEFORE REFRIGERATION revolutionised the keeping of meat, devilling was a popular method of treating joints, pieces of poultry and game, and even left-overs.

There were 'wet' devils and 'dry' devils. In both cases, the meat was treated with a mixture of hot spices. For a dry devil, the spiced meat was broiled under a grill or roasted, as in this 18th century recipe. In a wet devil, the meat was cooked or heated in a sauce.

PREPARATION TIME: 10 MINUTES
COOKING TIME: 1½ HOURS
PRE-HEAT OVEN TO 160°C

INGREDIENTS FOR SIX
1,5-2 kg shoulder of lamb
30 ml (2 tablespoons) seasoned flour*

For the devil mixture:
15 ml (1 tablespoon) French mustard
2 ml (½ teaspoon) paprika
1 ml (¼ teaspoon) cayenne pepper
1 ml (¼ teaspoon) white pepper
1 ml (¼ teaspoon) salt
2 ml (½ teaspoon) turmeric
2 ml (½ teaspoon) ground mace or nutmeg
75 g butter or cooking fat
10 ml (2 teaspoons) lemon juice

Rub the shoulder of lamb with half the seasoned flour and roast in a baking tin in the oven for 40 minutes.

While the lamb is roasting, make the devil mixture. Beginning with the mustard, combine all the ingredients in a small bowl. Put in the lemon juice last, and mix well.

After 40 minutes, remove the joint from the oven and make four deep crossways slashes in it. Spread the prepared devil mixture in the slashes. Baste with the juices which have run out from the slashes. Sprinkle again with the remaining seasoned flour and return to the oven for 40 minutes.

Keep the lamb hot on a serving dish while you make gravy* in the pan.

SERVING SUGGESTION Serve with rice or mashed potatoes*, accompanied by apple or redcurrant jelly.

CROWN ROAST OF LAMB *This elegant-looking dish is one of the most delicious ways of eating lamb cutlets.*

CROWN ROAST OF LAMB

IN EDWARDIAN TIMES, the elegant 'crown roast' of lamb was particularly fashionable at small country-house dinners. You may find you have to order the crown from your butcher in advance.

PREPARATION TIME: 30 MINUTES
COOKING TIME: 1½ HOURS
PRE-HEAT OVEN TO 200°C

INGREDIENTS FOR FOUR
Crown of 12 best-end-of-neck lamb cutlets
75 g butter

For the filling:
500 g stuffing* of your choice, or 500 g hot mixed vegetables simmered together in salted water until tender – this can be any mixture of your choice, such as green peas, diced carrots, diced turnips, sliced celery, sliced baby marrows, tiny new potatoes, tiny onions and florets of cauliflower

For the sauce:
300 ml gravy*
10 ml (2 teaspoons) redcurrant jelly
30 ml (2 tablespoons) sherry

Place the butter in small pieces in a roasting tin large enough to hold the roast and stand the crown upright in the tin. If you are using stuffing for the filling, spoon the mixture into the centre of the crown before roasting. If using vegetables, cook the meat without the filling.

Place the roast in the pre-heated oven for 15 minutes. Reduce the heat to 180°C and roast for another hour. While the crown is cooking, baste the top of the stuffing twice with the dripping from the pan, or prepare the alternative filling.

To make the sauce, heat the gravy thoroughly in a small pan and stir in the redcurrant jelly and sherry.

Lift the cooked crown carefully on to a hot serving dish and, if not filled with stuffing, spoon the very hot mixed-vegetable filling into the centre.

If the crown is filled with stuffing, you can put small heaps of vegetables (as suggested for the filling) around it. Serve the sauce separately.

SERVING SUGGESTION For a dinner party, top each rib bone with a paper frill.

HONEYED LAMB

THE MARRIAGE of lamb and honey is a particularly successful one, especially with a few herbs added to heighten the subtle flavour of the dish.

PREPARATION TIME: 10 MINUTES
COOKING TIME: 1¾ HOURS
PRE-HEAT OVEN TO 230°C

INGREDIENTS FOR SIX
1,5-2 kg shoulder of lamb
1 clove garlic
Salt and freshly ground black pepper
100-125 g honey
450-500 ml cider
5 ml (1 teaspoon) chopped fresh mint
7 ml (1½ teaspoons) chopped fresh thyme
15 ml (1 tablespoon) flour
5 ml (1 teaspoon) lemon juice

Line a roasting tin with a piece of aluminium foil large enough to wrap over the top of the joint. Rub the meat all over with the clove of garlic. Place the joint in the tin and season well with salt and pepper.

Mix the honey with 300 ml of the cider, and pour the mixture over the joint. Sprinkle the top with the chopped mint and thyme. Fold the foil loosely over the joint and cook in the pre-heated oven for 30 minutes. Open the foil and baste with the remaining cider.

Close up the foil again, reduce the oven temperature to 180°C and cook for a further hour, folding back the foil to brown the meat after 30 minutes.

Remove the meat from the oven, place in a serving dish, and keep hot.

To make the gravy, pour the juices from the roasting tin into a small saucepan, leave to stand for 5 minutes, then skim off the fat from the surface. Blend the flour in a basin with 60 ml (¼ cup) of the juices, then stir back into the saucepan.

Bring to the boil, stirring constantly until smooth and thickened. Season with salt and pepper, and stir in the lemon juice. Serve the gravy piping hot in a sauceboat with the joint.

SERVING SUGGESTION Baked onions* and boiled new potatoes sprinkled with mint are excellent accompaniments for honeyed lamb.

MEAT

Greek Lamb with Yoghurt This is an ideal dish for those with a palate for herbs and garlic-flavoured meat.

Greek Lamb with Yoghurt

THIS RECIPE should be in every cook's repertoire. Its preparation is easy: a strongly garlic-flavoured joint of lamb is smeared with herb butter before baking and served with rich gravy and a delicious yoghurt sauce.

PREPARATION TIME: 20 MINUTES
COOKING TIME: 1 HOUR 40 MINUTES
PRE-HEAT OVEN TO 180°C

INGREDIENTS FOR SIX TO EIGHT
1,5-2 kg leg of lamb
3-4 cloves garlic
50 g butter, softened
15 ml (1 tablespoon) chopped rosemary
15 ml (1 tablespoon) chopped thyme
Salt and freshly ground black pepper
Juice of 1 lemon

For the gravy:
10 ml (2 teaspoons) flour
250 ml (1 cup) vegetable* or basic stock*, or wine
Salt and freshly ground black pepper

For the sauce:
200 ml natural yoghurt*
2 cloves garlic, crushed
10 ml (2 teaspoons) chopped chives
10 ml (2 teaspoons) chopped mint
Salt and freshly ground black pepper

Make little knife slits all over the outer skin of the lamb and press in the garlic, cut into slivers. Beat the softened butter with rosemary, thyme and seasoning, and spread it all over the meat. Pour over the lemon juice.

Roast the meat on a rack over a roasting tin, allowing 20-25 minutes for each 500 g, basting from time to time. Transfer the meat to a serving dish and leave to 'set' in a warming drawer or warm oven for 15-20 minutes.

To make the gravy, pour off excess fat from the roasting tin and stir in the flour to mop up the remaining fat.

Cook for 1 minute, then add the stock or wine, and season with salt and freshly ground black pepper.

Bring to the boil, strain and keep hot. To make the sauce, mix all the ingredients together and season well. Serve slices of meat topped with a spoonful of gravy and a dollop of yoghurt sauce.

SERVING SUGGESTIONS This dish is perfect with rice or baked potatoes*, green beans or broccoli, or a Greek salad*.

VARIATION Spread the lamb with fresh white breadcrumbs (from 2 slices of bread) mixed with 5 ml (1 teaspoon) mixed herbs, grated rind of 1 lemon, 50 g butter, 8 chopped olives, 3 ml (¾ teaspoon) salt and a dash of pepper. Roast without basting the joint so that the breadcrumbs form a crisp, golden crust.

Stuffed Leg of Mutton

THIS RECIPE will provide a large, trouble-free meal. The filling adds a wonderful flavour to the mutton, as does the rich gravy. The stuffed leg of mutton is equally delicious served again as a cold dish.

PREPARATION TIME: 1 HOUR
COOKING TIME: 2 HOURS

INGREDIENTS FOR SIX
2 kg leg of mutton
125 ml (½ cup) vinegar
Salt and freshly ground black pepper
5 ml (1 teaspoon) ground ginger
5 ml (1 teaspoon) ground coriander
15-30 ml (1-2 tablespoons) fat or dripping*
125-250 ml (½-1 cup) water
10 ml (2 teaspoons) flour

For the stuffing:
40 g fresh breadcrumbs
200 g minced mutton or veal
2 rashers of bacon or ham, rinds removed and finely chopped
30 ml (2 tablespoons) lemon juice
30 ml (2 tablespoons) fruit chutney
A few cloves
1 small onion, grated, with juice
Salt
1 egg, beaten

Bone the leg, leaving a cavity for the stuffing. Wipe inside and outside with a damp cloth dipped in the vinegar, then rub the meat with salt and pepper.

Mix the ginger and coriander and rub the mixture into the meat, both outside and in the cavity.

To prepare the stuffing, combine all the ingredients with the egg. Press the mixture into the cavity and use a long darning needle and thick cotton to sew shut the cavity at both ends so that none of the stuffing oozes out.

Put the prepared leg in a saucepan with the hot fat or dripping and brown on both sides. Add a little of the water and reduce the heat. Cover the saucepan and cook until tender (about 2 hours), adding a little water from time to time. Turn the meat during cooking to brown evenly on both sides. Remove the meat from the saucepan and place it in a warming drawer to set.

Thicken the gravy by adding the flour mixed with a little water to make a paste. Pour on the pan drippings and stir until cooked to a nice gravy consistency. Remove the thread carefully, without tearing the meat, and serve.

SERVING SUGGESTIONS Slice the meat into thin slices and serve warm with gravy, cooked vegetables, roast potatoes or rice.

The left-overs are ideal for bobotie* or hashed lamb with tomatoes*.

IRISH STEW

THE ORIGINAL IRISH STEW was made with the meat of a young male goat. It was cooked, suspended over a peat fire, in a bastable oven – an all-purpose iron pot used for boiling, roasting and even for baking bread. To keep in the fragrance, the pot was sealed with a paste of flour and water, which was thrown to the hens when the stew was ready.

PREPARATION TIME: 20 MINUTES
COOKING TIME: 2 HOURS
PRE-HEAT GRILL TO HOT

INGREDIENTS FOR FOUR TO SIX
1 kg lamb cutlets, trimmed of skin and fat
Salt and freshly ground black pepper
4 large onions, peeled* and quartered
10 large potatoes, peeled and thickly sliced
850 ml cold water

Lay half the cutlets in the bottom of a large oven-proof casserole and season with a little salt and pepper.

Cover the meat with half of the onions, season, cover with half the potatoes and season again. Repeat the layers, ending with a layer of potatoes.

Pour in the water and bring slowly to the boil. Remove any white scum, then lower the heat, cover and simmer very gently for 2 hours.

A few minutes before serving, remove the lid and place the pan under a hot grill or in a hot oven to brown the top layer of potato slices.

VARIATION Irish stew can also be cooked in a moderate oven at 180°C for 2 hours.

LAMB CASSEROLE WITH ORANGE

THIS IS A MAGNIFICENT RECIPE to try when navel oranges are at their sweetest and best. It is not a spur-of-the-moment dish – take your time in preparing and cooking it, and the results will exceed your highest expectations.

PREPARATION TIME: 45 MINUTES
COOKING TIME: 3 HOURS

INGREDIENTS FOR SIX
2,5 kg lamb shoulder, boned and cut into 3 cm cubes
25 ml (5 teaspoons) flour
60 ml (¼ cup) olive or sunflower oil
3 carrots, scraped and cut into 2 cm pieces
3 leeks, well-washed, trimmed and coarsely chopped
3 sticks celery, washed, trimmed and coarsely chopped
3 cloves garlic, peeled and crushed
375 ml (1½ cups) dry white wine
375 ml (1½ cups) orange juice
4 sprigs parsley
2 bay leaves
Rind of ½ orange, cut into julienne* strips
30 ml (2 tablespoons) white sugar
Salt and freshly ground pepper
3 large navel oranges, peeled and segmented, with pith and membrane removed

Dredge the meat with the flour, shaking off the excess, and put it on one side. Heat the oil in a large oven-proof casserole and gently sauté the carrots, leeks, celery and garlic until soft and golden. With a slotted spoon, transfer the vegetables to a dish, then turn up the heat.

Sear the lamb cubes in batches in the casserole, adding a little more oil if necessary, for about 2 minutes (until they are well browned).

Return all the meat cubes to the casserole, adding the wine and the orange juice. Bring the liquid slowly to the boil before adding the sautéed vegetables.

Tie the parsley, bay leaves and julienne strips of orange rind in a piece of clean muslin and add to the casserole. Turn the heat to very low and simmer the dish (covered) for 1 hour.

Next, heat the sugar in a small saucepan until it melts and caramelises, and carefully add 125 ml (½ cup) of the stew juices to the caramel. Stir it until smooth, add to the casserole, and season with salt and pepper. Cook for another hour, or until the lamb is tender.

Using a slotted spoon, transfer the lamb to a dish. Cover the lamb and keep it warm while you make the sauce.

Discard the muslin bag and strain the cooking liquid into a saucepan, pressing the vegetables through a sieve.

Boil the cooking liquid for 10 minutes to reduce it and skim off as much of the fat as you can.

Return the meat and sauce to the casserole and add the orange segments. Bring to the boil, correct the seasoning if necessary, and serve.

SERVING SUGGESTIONS Garnish with any of the following: 30 ml (2 tablespoons) finely chopped parsley; 15 ml (1 tablespoon) grated orange rind; or 2 cloves of garlic, peeled and finely chopped. Try serving the casserole with crusty bread and a salad of spinach with bacon, sprouts* and orange segments.

VARIATION For a summer version, leave out the orange juice, rind and orange segments and substitute chicken stock* mixed in equal proportions with apple juice. Add baby beans (cooked until still firm) and fresh litchis, peeled and pipped, towards the end of cooking. Garnish with coarsely chopped celery and decorate with celery leaves. Serve with peeled new potatoes (in lemon butter*) and carrots garnished with chopped, fresh basil.

LAMB CASSEROLE WITH ORANGE *effectively marries a variety of flavours.*

MEAT

Portmanteau'd Lamb Chops

THIS TASTY DISH derives its name from the rather heavy leather case called a portmanteau, favoured by Victorian ladies and gentlemen for train travel. It opened along the top and part of the way down each end, allowing clothes and toilet articles to be shut safely away. In a similar way, the filling of chicken livers and mushrooms is sewn into lamb chops.

Preparation Time: 40 minutes
Cooking Time: 15 minutes
Pre-heat Oven to 200°C

Ingredients for Six
6 large lamb loin chops, 4-5 cm thick
4 chicken livers, about 50 g
8 medium-sized mushrooms
Salt and pepper
100-125 g butter
2 eggs, beaten
250 g white breadcrumbs

Remove the skin and trim some of the fat from each chop. With a very sharp knife, slit the lean eye of the chop, cutting inwards to the bone.

Finely chop the livers and mushrooms, and season with salt and pepper. Melt 50 g of the butter in a small frying pan, add the mushrooms and liver, and cook gently for about 5 minutes without browning. Allow to cool, then stuff the mixture into the incisions made in the chops. Sew up the chops, using a darning needle and heavy cotton thread.

Dip the stuffed chops in the beaten eggs and coat generously with breadcrumbs. Place the chops in a roasting tray. Melt the remaining butter and pour a little over each of the chops.

Bake in the pre-heated oven for 6 minutes, then turn and bake for another 6 minutes. Cook the chops for longer if you like them well done. Be sure to remove the stitches before serving.

Serving Suggestion You can turn this recipe into a dish for a dinner party by serving it with savoury butter*, new potatoes and peas with mint.

Variations Leave out the egg and crumb coating, and gently braise the chops until they are tender.

Alternatively, shallow-fry the chops in 15 g butter and 15 ml (1 tablespoon) sunflower oil.

Portmanteau'd Lamb Chops *A novel way of turning chops into a tasty treat.*

Spicy Red Lamb Ribs

THESE RICHLY COLOURED, flavourful titbits make a delicious and easy course for a Chinese meal. They are doubly appealing to the busy hostess because they require no last-minute attention. Spicy red lamb ribs can also be cooked and frozen – in this case, defrost them before re-heating in a cool oven. Ask your butcher to chop the lamb ribs in half.

Preparation Time: 45 minutes
Marinating Time: 2-3 hours
Cooking Time: 40 minutes
Pre-heat Oven to 200°C

Ingredients for Six
1,5 kg lamb ribs, chopped in half by your butcher
15 ml (1 tablespoon) tomato sauce*
30 ml (2 tablespoons) dark soy sauce
3 ml (¾ teaspoon) finely chopped fresh green ginger
20 ml (4 teaspoons) soft brown sugar
15 ml (1 tablespoon) dry sherry
15 ml (1 tablespoon) water
30 ml (2 tablespoons) brown vinegar
10 ml (2 teaspoons) Tabasco (chilli sauce)
2 ml (½ teaspoon) five spice powder (optional)
15 ml (1 tablespoon) Hoisin sauce
Salt and freshly ground black pepper

Steam the ribs (covered, preferably in a Chinese steamer) until they are tender – this removes some of the fat from the meat. Drain and place the ribs side by side in a shallow oven-proof dish. Combine the remaining ingredients and pour over the ribs. Marinate for 2-3 hours (or overnight) in the refrigerator, turning once.

Bake fairly high up in the oven for 20 minutes. Turn the ribs over and baste with the sauce, then bake for a further 20 minutes. This dish can be prepared ahead of time and frozen. To serve, defrost, cover the meat with aluminium foil and re-heat at 130°C until piping hot.

Serving Suggestion Provide side plates for the bones and warm, damp, perfumed napkins for wiping the hands.

Variations You may use pork spare ribs instead of lamb.

Chicken legs and wings are also delicious prepared in this way, and do not need to be steamed first.

Denning Vleis

TO SOME MUSLIMS in the Cape, denning vleis means meat flavoured with tamarind and bay leaves. Others, however, prefer white vinegar or lemon juice to tamarind, which they say makes the meat too dark.

The origin of 'denning' meat is the Javanese dish 'dendeng', made from the meat of the water-buffalo, cut into small pieces, treated with salt and spices, dried in the sun and then fried in coconut milk or coconut oil.

Preparation Time: 30 minutes
Cooking Time: 1-1½ hours

Ingredients for Six
1,5 kg fat mutton
30 ml (2 tablespoons) mutton dripping*
3 cloves garlic, thinly sliced
4 large onions, peeled and thinly sliced*
4 allspice
4 cloves
2 bay leaves
3 ml (¾ teaspoon) grated nutmeg
Salt and pepper
2 chillies, seeded and sliced
250 ml (1 cup) water
A piece of tamarind the size of a date

Wash the mutton thoroughly. Cube it and set aside. Heat the dripping in a saucepan, then add the meat. Add the garlic and onion to the meat, together with the spices, seasoning and chillies.

Brown the mutton slowly over a low heat: the meat must not be dry. Add half the water and allow to braise.

Meanwhile, heat the rest of the water and dissolve the tamarind in it, then strain and add the tamarind water to the meat, allowing its flavour to permeate the meat while it braises slowly for 1-1½ hours, or until tender.

Serving Suggestion Serve with potatoes, vegetables and rice.

HARICOT OF MUTTON

THE WORD HARICOT at first meant a stew of mutton and turnips. The beans were included later, possibly as a result of confusion over their name, which is derived from the old Norman word *halicot* ('chopped up').

PREPARATION TIME: 30 MINUTES
SOAKING TIME: OVERNIGHT
COOKING TIME: 2 HOURS
PRE-HEAT OVEN TO 180°C

INGREDIENTS FOR FOUR

500 g lean lamb from the leg, cut into 2,5 cm cubes
180 g dried haricot beans
25 g seasoned flour*
75 g butter
2 medium-sized onions, peeled and sliced*
4-5 medium-sized carrots, scraped and sliced
1 turnip, peeled and cut into 1,5 cm cubes
1 leek, cleaned and cut into 2,5 cm lengths
5 ml (1 teaspoon) dried thyme
1 clove garlic, crushed
Salt and pepper
850 ml vegetable* or basic stock*
15 ml (1 tablespoon) finely chopped parsley

Wash and drain the beans. Pour cold water over them and soak overnight.

Dip the pieces of lamb in the seasoned flour. Melt 50 g of the butter in a large frying pan and lightly fry the lamb. Turn two or three times to brown evenly. Lift the meat on to a plate, and keep warm while you prepare the vegetables.

In the same pan, fry the onions, carrots, turnip and leek until they begin to brown. Turn the vegetables into a deep casserole and place the meat on top. Add the thyme, garlic, salt and pepper. Pour in the stock and add the drained beans, which should be just covered by the stock.

Cook the casserole, uncovered, for 2 hours. As the beans soften they will form a crust over the meat and vegetables. After 1 hour, remove the casserole from the oven, dot the beans with the remaining butter and return to the oven.

When the dish is ready to serve, sprinkle the top with the parsley.

MUTTON BIRIANI

BIRIANI FOUND ITS WAY into South African cuisine via the Cape Muslims. This mutton biriani will appeal to those with an adventurous palate and a penchant for spicy food.

PREPARATION TIME: 1 HOUR
COOKING TIME: 2½ HOURS

INGREDIENTS FOR SIX

1,5 kg mutton
4 medium-sized onions, peeled and sliced*
125 ml (½ cup) sunflower oil
A 2,5 cm piece of fresh green ginger
3 cloves garlic
6 cinnamon sticks
4 cardamom seeds
6 cloves
6 allspice
3 chillies, seeded and sliced
10 ml (2 teaspoons) ground coriander
10 ml (2 teaspoons) garam masala
5 medium-sized potatoes, peeled and sliced
250 g rice
Salt
100 g brown lentils
6 eggs, hard-boiled*
125 g butter
5 ml (1 teaspoon) saffron

Wash the mutton and cut into cubes. Sauté the onions in half the oil, together with pounded ginger and garlic, cinnamon, cardamom, cloves, allspice and chillies. Cook until the onions are golden. Add the meat, coriander and masala.

Fry the potato slices in the remaining oil. Boil the rice in salted water (uncovered) until nearly soft, then strain and steam the rice in a colander. If preferred, you can add the rice to the meat at this stage.

Boil the lentils until soft, and slice the eggs. Spoon a layer of rice into a large saucepan and then, in sequence, the potatoes, meat mixture, eggs and lentils. Repeat, ending with a layer of rice mixed with the butter and saffron. Cover with a tight-fitting lid and place over a very low heat. Allow the biriani to steam or simmer very slowly for 1 hour. Do not remove the lid until you are ready to serve.

ACCOMPANIMENTS TO MALAY DISHES

A Cape Muslim culinary tradition is to grate vegetables such as carrots and cucumbers, or fruit such as apples and quinces, then season them with salt, vinegar and chillies to make a relish known as a sambal. These are then served with curries or with meat or fish dishes. The following four sambal recipes are particularly popular. As a general rule, people help themselves to 1-2 spoonfuls of each sambal. When catering, allow 15-30 ml (1-2 tablespoons) of each sambal per person.

APPLE SAMBAL

PREPARATION TIME: 20 MINUTES
STANDING TIME: AT LEAST 30 MINUTES

INGREDIENTS TO YIELD 500 ML (2 CUPS)

3 firm sour apples (not floury in texture), coarsely grated
5 ml (1 teaspoon) salt
2 cloves garlic, crushed
2 green chillies, seeded and sliced

Sprinkle the grated apples with the salt and leave the fruit to stand for at least 30 minutes to draw out some of the water, then drain thoroughly. (Sometimes, if the apples are particularly sour, a little boiling water is added to the apples after salting.) Add the garlic and chillies.

SERVING SUGGESTIONS Use as an accompaniment to meat dishes or curry.

CARROT SAMBAL

PREPARATION TIME: 15 MINUTES
STANDING TIME: AT LEAST 30 MINUTES

INGREDIENTS TO YIELD 375 ML (1½ CUPS)

3 medium-sized carrots, coarsely grated
5 ml (1 teaspoon) salt
1 small onion, peeled* and grated
1 clove garlic, crushed
1 green chilli, seeded and chopped
5 ml (1 teaspoon) sugar
25 ml (5 teaspoons) vinegar or lemon juice

Sprinkle the grated carrots with the salt and allow to stand for at least 30 minutes to draw out some of the water, then drain. Add the onion, garlic and chopped chilli. Add the lightly mixed sugar and vinegar or lemon juice. It is important that the sambal is not too mushy.

SERVING SUGGESTIONS Serve with meat or curry dishes.

ONION SAMBAL

PREPARATION TIME: 10 MINUTES
STANDING TIME: 5 MINUTES

INGREDIENTS TO YIELD 125 ML (½ CUP)

3 medium-sized onions, peeled* and coarsely grated
3 ml (¾ teaspoon) salt
Boiling water
25 ml (5 teaspoons) vinegar
5 ml (1 teaspoon) sugar
3 green chillies, seeded and chopped

Sprinkle the grated onions with salt, pour boiling water over and leave for 5 minutes. Drain and rinse the onions under cold water in a sieve or colander. Press out all the surplus water.

Arrange the dried onion in a salad bowl. Add the mixed vinegar and sugar, and the chillies, and then mix these ingredients together.

SERVING SUGGESTIONS This sambal is usually served with a variety of curried dishes or fried fish.

CUCUMBER SAMBAL

PREPARATION TIME: 15 MINUTES
STANDING TIME: AT LEAST 30 MINUTES

INGREDIENTS TO YIELD 500 ML (2 CUPS)

2 fresh cucumbers, peeled and coarsely grated
10 ml (2 teaspoons) salt
2 green chillies, seeded and sliced
1 clove garlic, crushed
5 ml (1 teaspoon) sugar
20 ml (4 teaspoons) vinegar

Sprinkle the grated cucumber with salt and allow to stand for at least 30 minutes to draw out the water.

Squeeze out all the water. Add the chillies, garlic and the mixed sugar and vinegar.

SERVING SUGGESTIONS Serve with meat dishes or curry.

PARSI DHANSAK

DHANSAK IS THE FAVOURITE Sunday food of many Parsees, the religious community which settled in India after fleeing Persia more than a thousand years ago. In time, they created a distinct Parsee cuisine, combining something of both lands.

The dish is a rich mutton curry with a thick, golden-brown gravy. Dhansak can be frozen for up to two months.

PREPARATION TIME: 30 MINUTES
COOKING TIME: 1½-2 HOURS

INGREDIENTS FOR FOUR TO SIX

1 kg mutton
250 g red lentils
1,5 litres (6 cups) warm water
100 g pumpkin, peeled and cubed
100 g brinjals, peeled and cubed
45 ml (3 tablespoons) chopped parsley
5 ml (1 teaspoon) turmeric
10 ml (2 teaspoons) salt
60 ml (¼ cup) sunflower oil
2 medium-sized onions, peeled and sliced*
A 4 cm piece of fresh green ginger, scraped and pounded to a paste with a little water
10 cloves garlic, peeled and crushed to a paste
15 ml (1 tablespoon) red chilli powder
1 whole green chilli, sliced lengthways
15 ml (1 tablespoon) cumin seeds, roasted in a dry saucepan for 2 minutes, then coarsely crushed
15 ml (1 tablespoon) crushed coriander seeds (roasted as above)
2 tomatoes, chopped
30 ml (2 tablespoons) finely chopped coriander (dhania) leaves

Cut the mutton into convenient-sized pieces and wash. Wash the lentils and set aside. Pour the warm water into a large saucepan. Add the mutton, lentils, pumpkin, brinjals, parsley, turmeric and salt.

Cover the saucepan and cook on a medium heat for an hour, or until the mutton pieces are soft (stir occasionally). Extra water may be added to keep the gravy to a pouring consistency. Remove from the heat and stir well. The vegetables and lentils should blend into a smooth, thick gravy.

Heat the oil in a smaller saucepan. Add the sliced onions and allow to cook to a golden colour. Add the ginger and garlic to the onions and fry for 1 minute, then add the chilli powder, green chilli, cumin, coriander seeds and tomatoes.

Fry on a medium heat until soft and well blended with the spices. Pour the tomato and onion gravy on to the cooked meat, stir well together and simmer on a medium heat for 15 minutes.

Garnish with the chopped coriander leaves, and serve.

SERVING SUGGESTION Serve with piping hot rice, lemon wedges and kachoomer*.

PARSI DHANSAK *A rich mutton dish with a spicy flavour.*

MUTTON CURRY

MUTTON CURRY is a favourite Cape Malay dish that has firmly established itself in South African cuisine. Piquant, but not too hot, this dish is best served in the traditional way, namely with rice or roti* and salad.

PREPARATION TIME: 30 MINUTES
COOKING TIME: 2 HOURS

INGREDIENTS FOR FOUR TO SIX

1 kg mutton
A pinch of thyme
5 ml (1 teaspoon) cumin seeds, pounded to a powder
3 ml (¾ teaspoon) cayenne pepper
5 ml (1 teaspoon) garam masala
2 ml (½ teaspoon) turmeric
A 2-2,5 cm piece of fresh green ginger
3 cloves garlic
30 ml (2 tablespoons) sunflower oil
2 medium-sized onions, peeled and sliced or chopped*
4 medium-sized potatoes, peeled and diced
2 medium-sized tomatoes, chopped
250 ml (1 cup) water
Salt
15 ml (1 tablespoon) chopped fresh coriander (dhania) leaves

Cube and wash the meat thoroughly. Blend the thyme and spices. Pound the ginger and garlic together in a mortar and mix with the spices and meat cubes. Leave to stand for a few minutes.

Heat the oil in a saucepan and sauté the onions. Add the potatoes and tomatoes to the onion. Simmer for 5 minutes. Add the meat and braise slowly until the meat begins to dry, then add water – little by little – until the meat is done. Add the salt and coriander leaves when the curry is cooked.

GIEMA CURRY

GIEMA CURRY is a Malay dish made of minced meat. As any convert to spicy foods will tell you, Malay curry made at home – with fresh ingredients – has a rich flavour all its own.

PREPARATION TIME: 30 MINUTES
COOKING TIME: 1¼ HOURS

INGREDIENTS FOR SIX

1 kg minced mutton or beef
2 large onions, peeled and chopped*
30 ml (2 tablespoons) sunflower oil
2 cloves garlic
A 2-2,5 cm piece of fresh green ginger
A few cinnamon sticks
A few cardamom seeds
A few cloves
A few allspice
10 ml (2 teaspoons) turmeric
15 ml (1 tablespoon) red leaf masala

- 5 ml (1 teaspoon) ground fennel
- 5 ml (1 teaspoon) ground cumin seeds
- 5 ml (1 teaspoon) ground coriander
- 2 large tomatoes, skinned* and mashed
- 2 chillies, chopped
- 3 large potatoes, peeled and sliced
- Salt
- 450 g peas, fresh or frozen (optional)

Cook the onions in a saucepan with the oil and pounded garlic and ginger, and add the cinnamon, cardamom, cloves and allspice. Allow the mixture to brown.

Add the meat to the onion mixture, stir and cook (uncovered) for 30 minutes, or until tender. Mix the rest of the spices with the tomato pulp and chillies, then add to the meat, together with the potatoes. Simmer slowly for about 25 minutes until the potatoes are soft, and season with salt.

Add the peas (if used) at this stage and continue simmering the dish until done (5-10 minutes).

Cape Lamb Pie

THIS PIE TYPIFIES all the best of local traditional cooking. Robust, with an aromatic flavour, it is the kind of food South Africans cannot resist.

This is a family recipe which has been refined and perfected, and is easy for the inexperienced hostess if she uses bought flaky pastry instead of the sour cream pastry.

PREPARATION TIME: 3 HOURS
COOKING TIME: 45 MINUTES
PRE-HEAT OVEN TO 220°C

INGREDIENTS FOR SIX TO EIGHT
- Sour cream flaky pastry* using 440 g flour
- 1 egg white, beaten with 3 ml (¾ teaspoon) salt (optional)

For the filling:
- 1 kg lamb (use shoulder, neck or other stewing meat)
- 250 ml (1 cup) water
- 1 whole onion, peeled*
- 1 bay leaf
- 3 cloves
- 5 peppercorns

For the seasoning:
- 1 large onion, spiked with a few cloves
- 3 ml (¾ teaspoon) crushed coriander
- 2 cloves garlic, crushed
- 3 ml (¾ teaspoon) dried chillies
- 5 ml (1 teaspoon) dry mustard, mixed with 30 ml (2 tablespoons) sugar, 30 ml (2 tablespoons) vinegar, 5 ml (1 teaspoon) salt and 3 ml (¾ teaspoon) freshly ground black pepper

First, make the sour cream flaky pastry. Place it in the refrigerator and chill for at least 30 minutes.

Place the lamb in the water with the onion and the bay leaf, cloves and peppercorns tied together in a clean cloth, and simmer very slowly until the meat is tender enough to start falling away from the bones (about 2 hours).

When it is ready, allow it to cool slightly before removing all bones, fat, gristle and spices. Flake the meat lightly and return it to the stock, together with all the remaining seasoning ingredients.

Re-heat all the ingredients together, then taste and adjust the seasoning. Add a little more water if too dry, or thicken the sauce with a little cornflour if too watery. Transfer to a large pie dish, placing the onion in the middle to help support the pastry lid.

Allow the filling to cool, then cover* with the prepared pastry (you can freeze the pie at this stage). Bake for 25 minutes at 220°C and another 20 minutes at 190°C until the pie is golden-brown and cooked. The pastry may be glazed just before baking with an egg white lightly beaten with 3 ml (¾ teaspoon) salt.

SERVING SUGGESTION Serve with steamed or boiled green beans, and pumpkin baked with butter, honey or brown sugar and cinnamon. Serve a tossed salad afterwards to refresh the palate.

Remember when defrosting a frozen pie that the pastry must not be covered with aluminium foil or plastic wrap, or the condensation during defrosting will make it soggy. When cooking the pie in its frozen state, 20-30 minutes must be added to the cooking time to allow for defrosting in the oven.

Kheema Kebabs

KEBABS ARE AMONG India's classic meat preparations. The combination of spices in these kheema kebabs is perfectly balanced to give the beef or lamb meatballs an outstanding flavour.

Kheema kebabs can also be placed on skewers and baked in the traditional tandoor clay oven. The kebabs may be frozen (after cooking) for up to 4 weeks.

PREPARATION TIME: 20 MINUTES
COOKING TIME: 30 MINUTES

INGREDIENTS FOR FOUR
- 500 g beef or lamb mince
- 1 medium-sized onion, finely chopped*
- 5 ml (1 teaspoon) salt
- 5 ml (1 teaspoon) turmeric
- 7 ml (1½ teaspoons) ground ginger
- 4 small cloves garlic, crushed
- 5 ml (1 teaspoon) crushed cumin seeds
- 5 ml (1 teaspoon) crushed coriander seeds
- 2 green chillies, chopped
- 30 ml (2 tablespoons) chopped coriander (dhania) leaves
- 45 ml (3 tablespoons) ghee*
- 2 tomatoes, cut in half and coarsely grated

Place the mince in a large mixing bowl and break it up with your fingers. Squeeze the juice from the onion, then add the flesh with the salt, turmeric, ginger, garlic, cumin, coriander seeds, chillies and coriander leaves to the meat. Mix well and form into balls the size of walnuts.

Heat the ghee in a saucepan. Place the mince balls in the saucepan and fry them gently for 10 minutes.

Add the grated tomato, cover the saucepan and simmer for a further 20 minutes over a low heat.

SERVING SUGGESTION Serve with dhania phoodini chatni*, wedges of lemon and roti*.

KHEEMA KEBABS *Spicy meatballs prepared in the classic Indian way.*

~ Informal Fun with Fondues ~

Most dinner parties tend to place a strain on the host and hostess, who generally share the responsibility of welcoming guests and preparing the food. However, fondues allow much more freedom: guests enjoy the informality of choosing and cooking their own food, dipping morsels into a variety of delicious sauces.

The ideal setting is a round table large enough to seat all those present comfortably. Each guest is given a long fondue fork for cooking and dipping, a table fork for eating, a plate and a napkin.

It is a simple matter to work out the quantities required: allow 200-250 g meat or fish per person as a main course. Cut it into bite-sized pieces about 1 hour before the meal and leave, covered, at room temperature. (If the cubed pieces are too cold, they reduce the temperature of the oil, and take too long to cook.)

Choose a good-quality, clean oil for frying. If you like a buttery flavour for meat or fish fondues, fry in a mixture of 1 part clarified butter* to 3 parts oil.

It is easiest to heat the oil or other cooking liquid for the fondue on the stove and, when ready, to carry it to the fondue heater. For a meat fondue, oil should be hot enough to colour a day-old cube of bread to a golden-brown almost instantly (a temperature of about 220°C). Most other fondues cooked in oil need more gentle heat: the bread cube should turn golden in 1 minute (the oil temperature will be about 190°C).

Beef Fondue Bourguignonne

Allow 200-250 g fillet of beef per person. Remove all sinew and fat, and cut the meat into 2 cm cubes. Pour oil into the fondue pot until it is a third to half full. Heat until very hot (a cube of day-old bread should brown in a few seconds), then regulate the burner to maintain this heat. Add a bay leaf for extra flavour (optional).

Guests skewer cubes of meat on to their fondue forks and cook them for a few moments in the hot oil before dipping them into accompanying sauces such as mustard*, creamed horseradish*, tomato*, Béarnaise* or mayonnaise*.

Sausage and Bacon Fondue

Wrap cocktail sausages in thin rashers of streaky bacon and cook in oil as for beef fondue Bourguignonne* until the bacon is crisp.

Alternatively (for four people), blend 500 g sausage meat with 1 finely chopped onion*, 25 g soft white breadcrumbs, 30 ml (2 tablespoons) freshly chopped parsley, 5 ml (1 teaspoon) prepared mustard, 100 g cream cheese, salt and freshly ground black pepper, and 1 beaten egg. Shape the mixture into 1-2 cm balls, coat them with flour, then dip in beaten egg and finally roll in breadcrumbs. Cook in hot oil until golden. Serve with mustard*, tomato* or curry sauce*.

Mongolian Fire Pot

For four people, slice 400 g boned chicken breast into thin strips and arrange them neatly on individual plates. Add 400 g sirloin steak (cut into thin strips) and 400 g pork fillet (in strips). Slice 250 g firm kingklip into strips and arrange next to the meat.

Next, slice 400 g raw spinach, 1 crisp lettuce, 2 bunches watercress and 1 bunch spring onions into 5 cm pieces. Distribute among the plates. Pour boiling chicken stock* into the fondue pot: guests cook individual ingredients in the stock until just tender, then lift them out and dip them in soy sauce or sweet and sour sauce*. After the food has been eaten, ladle the stock into small bowls and serve as a soup.

Turkish Lamb Fondue

For four people, mix 500 g minced lamb with 30 ml (2 tablespoons) fine dry breadcrumbs, 10 ml (2 teaspoons) finely chopped onion*, 5 ml (1 teaspoon) turmeric, 10 ml (2 teaspoons) ground cumin, and salt and pepper. Stir in 30 ml (2 tablespoons) finely chopped parsley, the finely grated rind of 1 lemon, 2 cloves crushed garlic and 1 large beaten egg.

Shape teaspoonfuls of the mixture into balls and fry them in oil in the fondue pot for about 2 minutes, or until golden. Serve with sour cream and chopped mint, aïoli*, tartar* or tomato sauce*.

Seafood Fondue

Allow 200-250 g firm, raw white fish or shellfish per person. Cut the fish into bite-sized pieces, season well and cook as for beef fondue Bourguignonne*.

Dip in tartar* or mushroom sauce*, or lemon-flavoured melted butter*. Some fish – such as crab, oysters and scallops – are unsuitable for a fondue, but prawns, mussels, line fish and fish croquettes* are excellent.

Vegetable Fondue

For six people, cut 1 large brinjal into thin rounds. Sprinkle with salt, leave for at least 30 minutes, then pat dry.

Boil 3 large peeled potatoes until really tender. Drain, purée and mash them to a stiff cream with butter, seasoning and a little milk or cream. Stir in 15-30 ml (1-2 tablespoons) flour, chill, then shape into 2 cm balls.

Wipe 300 g large button mushrooms and set aside. Cut a medium-sized cauliflower into florets and blanch* them in salted boiling water for 2 minutes.

Dip all the prepared vegetables in beaten egg, then in dried breadcrumbs. Chill for about 30 minutes in the refrigerator to help the crumbs adhere. (The potato balls will hold their shape better during cooking if they are kept cold at the table over a bowl of crushed ice.) Fry in hot oil until the vegetables are crisp on the outside and just cooked inside. Dip in lemon-flavoured melted butter* or aïoli*.

HORSERADISH SAUCE

BEEF FONDUE BOURGUIGNONNE

CHEDDAR FONDUE

For four people, warm 125 ml (½ cup) cream with half a crumbled chicken or vegetable stock cube, stirring well. Sauté 1 finely chopped onion* in 15 g butter until soft. Add a further 15 g butter, then stir in 25 ml (5 teaspoons) flour and cook for 2 minutes over a gentle heat.

Slowly stir in 200 ml milk to make a smooth sauce. Whisk in the cream mixture, then stir in 200 g grated mature Cheddar cheese. Once this has melted, add 45 ml (3 tablespoons) dry sherry and bring to the boil, whisking constantly. Serve with crisp bread or raw vegetable dips.

SWISS CHEESE FONDUE

For four people, toss 350 g coarsely grated Gruyère cheese with 350 g coarsely grated Emmenthal or Jarlsberg cheese and 7 ml (1½ teaspoons) cornflour. Rub the inside of an earthenware casserole or fondue pot with the cut surface of a clove of garlic. Pour in 250-375 ml (1-1½ cups) dry white wine, and heat over a very low heat until the wine starts to bubble.

Gradually stir in the cheese until it is well blended. When smooth, add 30-45 ml (2-3 tablespoons) Kirsch, a sprinkling of grated nutmeg, and salt and freshly ground black pepper to taste. Keep warm (but not too hot), and if the mixture becomes too thick, add a little more wine. Dip cubes of bread and serve with a green salad*.

CHOCOLATE FONDUE

For four people, chop or break 250 g milk or dark chocolate into a bowl standing in a saucepan of hot water. Leave until the chocolate has melted, then stir in 250 ml (1 cup) cream and a knob of butter.

Add 30 ml (2 tablespoons) Kirsch, brandy or orange liqueur, then blend well. Turn into a small fondue pot and serve with cubes of fresh banana, peach, apricot, pineapple, whole strawberries, marshmallows or sponge fingers.

FRENCH CANADIAN FONDUE

For six people, cut a French loaf into bite-sized pieces. Beat 2 eggs with 60 ml (¼ cup) milk. Pour oil into the fondue pot until 5 cm deep, and heat. Spear the sliced bread through the crust, dip it into the egg mixture and fry until golden. Dip in a bowl of maple syrup and then in whipped cream – use 250 ml (1 cup) of each.

ACCOMPANIMENTS TO FONDUES

Side dishes and dips are an integral part of a successful fondue. Most fondues go well with a fresh salad, crusty French bread and small baked potatoes*, along with a selection of complementary sauces for dipping.

Most mayonnaise-based sauces described in this book can be used as dips, as can the special recipes for dips*.

Olive Sauce Blend 250 ml (1 cup) mayonnaise* with 1 finely chopped hard-boiled egg*, 45 ml (3 tablespoons) finely chopped stuffed olives, 30 ml (2 tablespoons) tomato sauce*, 30 ml (2 tablespoons) finely chopped onion* and 30 ml (2 tablespoons) finely chopped parsley. Season and stir in 30 ml (2 tablespoons) sour cream (smetana).

Creamed Horseradish Sauce Mix 250 ml (1 cup) sour cream (smetana) with 45-60 ml (3-4 tablespoons) bottled creamed horseradish sauce, salt and freshly ground black pepper.

Curry Sauce Fry 1 finely chopped onion* in a little butter or oil until soft. Add 10-15 ml (2-3 teaspoons) curry powder and cook gently for a further 5 minutes, adding a little more butter or oil if necessary. Cool slightly and stir in 15 ml (1 tablespoon) smooth apricot jam*. Mix with 200 ml mayonnaise* or smooth cottage cheese and 30 ml (2 tablespoons) whipped cream.

Mustard Sauce Add 15 ml (1 tablespoon) French mustard to each 175 ml mayonnaise* or sour cream (smetana).

Green Herb Sauce Place 30 g dry (raw) spinach in a food processor or liquidizer with 200 ml mayonnaise*, and blend to make a purée. Add 15 ml (1 tablespoon) finely chopped fresh tarragon, 15 ml (1 tablespoon) finely chopped parsley, 10 ml (2 teaspoons) lemon juice, grated rind of 1 lemon, and salt and pepper to taste.

Mushroom Sauce Chop one small onion* and fry until soft in 15 ml (1 tablespoon) sunflower oil. Add 200 g thinly sliced mushrooms. Stir-fry for 1-2 minutes then pour in 15 ml (1 tablespoon) brandy and simmer for 1 minute. Season well, cool and stir into 250 ml (1 cup) sour cream (smetana).

MAYONNAISE

TOMATO SAUCE

MARINATED PORK SPARE RIBS

YOU NEED NOT GO to an expensive restaurant to taste the unique flavour of marinated pork spare ribs. This recipe will give very good results, and can be prepared at a fraction of the price you would pay in a restaurant.

PREPARATION TIME: 1 HOUR
MARINATING TIME: AT LEAST 24 HOURS
COOKING TIME: 45 MINUTES

INGREDIENTS FOR FOUR

2 kg spare ribs of pork

For the marinade:
250 ml (1 cup) tomato sauce*
250 ml (1 cup) water
2 medium-sized onions, peeled and chopped*
1 clove garlic, chopped
3 ml (¾ teaspoon) Tabasco (chilli sauce)
30 ml (2 tablespoons) chopped parsley
30 ml (2 tablespoons) soft brown sugar
15 ml (1 tablespoon) brown vinegar
5 ml (1 teaspoon) coarse salt
3 ml (¾ teaspoon) freshly ground black pepper
3 ml (¾ teaspoon) ground allspice
15 ml (1 tablespoon) soy sauce
125 ml (½ cup) sweet sherry

Make cuts between the ribs and set the meat aside while you prepare the marinade. Mix all the ingredients for the marinade (except the sherry) and boil together for 5 minutes to a creamy consistency. Remove from the stove. Add the sherry and allow the mixture to cool.

Arrange the spare ribs in a flat enamel pan or plastic container. Cover with the sauce and marinate for at least 24 hours.

Grill for 30-45 minutes under a medium heat and spoon the marinade over the ribs frequently. The meat goes very dark and care should be taken to avoid burning.

SERVING SUGGESTIONS Serve with baked potatoes* and a crunchy coleslaw*.

VARIATION Instead of grilling, bake the ribs at 180°C (uncovered) for 1¼ hours, or until dark and sticky and very tender.

PAPERED FILLETS OF PORK *Grease-proof paper seals in the succulence.*

PAPERED FILLETS OF PORK

THE 'PAPERING' of spit-roasted meat, as a means of preventing the outside from becoming too hard, succeeded the earlier method of dredging the meat with herb-flavoured breadcrumbs about the beginning of the last century.

The following method of 'parcelling', primarily designed to seal in the flavours, belongs to the kitchen-range-and-oven era of 100 years later.

You can wrap the fillets in aluminium foil instead of paper, but allow 10 minutes' extra cooking time, since foil reflects heat.

PREPARATION TIME: 20 MINUTES
COOKING TIME: 35 MINUTES
PRE-HEAT OVEN TO 180°C

INGREDIENTS FOR FOUR

2 pork tenderloins
15 g butter
15 ml (1 tablespoon) finely chopped onion*
75 g fresh breadcrumbs
15 ml (1 tablespoon) finely chopped parsley
5 ml (1 teaspoon) dried, or very finely chopped fresh, rosemary
Salt and pepper
100-125 g softened butter
1 ml (¼ teaspoon) ground mace
15 ml (1 tablespoon) flour

Cut each tenderloin in half and make a slit lengthways in each half without cutting right through, as the back should still be joined. Set the 4 fillets aside while you prepare the stuffing and the papers.

Heat the 15 g butter in a small saucepan and cook the onion in it very gently until just soft but not coloured. Mix the breadcrumbs, parsley and rosemary into the onions, and season lightly.

Cut 4 ovals of grease-proof paper about 25 cm long and 15 cm wide. Spread the softened butter thickly over the centre of each paper. Sprinkle with salt, pepper and the mace.

Fill the slit in each fillet with a quarter of the stuffing. Spread and firm it in place with the blade of a knife. Rub the stuffed fillets with flour.

Place each fillet on a prepared piece of grease-proof paper. Fold the longer sides loosely over the meat, leaving some space round the fillet, and twist the ends tightly. Place in a large baking dish, and cook in the centre of the oven for 35 minutes.

Serve the pork fillets in their parcels so that your guests can unwrap their own and enjoy the full aroma.

POT-ROAST CUSHION OF PORK WITH APPLE AND PRUNE STUFFING

THIS IS A RICHLY FLAVOURED dish which combines pork, apples and prunes with such success that the individual flavours are easily identified yet complement each other to produce a memorable taste sensation.

PREPARATION TIME: 45 MINUTES
SOAKING TIME FOR PRUNES: OVERNIGHT
COOKING TIME: 2 HOURS

INGREDIENTS FOR SIX

2 kg boned thick rib of pork
Salt and freshly ground black pepper
4 fresh sage leaves or 5 ml (1 teaspoon) dried sage
A little grated fresh green ginger
30 ml (2 tablespoons) sunflower oil
30 g butter
250 ml (1 cup) apple juice
60 ml (¼ cup) cider vinegar

For the filling:
6 prunes, soaked overnight in 60 ml (¼ cup) gin
30 (2 tablespoons) sugar
3 apples, peeled, cored and sliced
60 g butter

For the sauce:
Grated rind and juice of 1 orange
125 ml (½ cup) dry white wine

Season the meat inside and out with salt and pepper, sage and ginger.

To make the filling, stone the prunes, then sprinkle the sugar over the apples. Heat the butter and fry the apples until

golden-brown. Add the prunes and gin, and cook until all the liquid has evaporated. Leave to cool, then fill the meat. Sew up with a needle and thread.

Next, heat the oil and butter, and brown the meat all the way around. Heat the apple juice and vinegar, and add it to the meat. Cover and simmer for 1½-2 hours, until the meat is tender. Remove the meat and let it stand for 10-15 minutes. Slice and arrange the slices of meat on a serving platter. Cover and keep warm.

Add the orange rind, juice and white wine to the pan juices, and heat to boiling point. Taste and adjust the seasoning if necessary. Reduce by half and spoon over the meat.

SERVING SUGGESTIONS Serve with buttered new potatoes and red cabbage. Potato croquettes* and broccoli cooked until still firm and served with cheese sauce* also make delicious accompaniments.

VARIATIONS Instead of white wine, use meat basic stock* for the sauce.

Try soaking the prunes in rooibos tea.

KASSLER RIB CHOPS WITH MUSTARD SAUCE

KASSLER RIB CHOPS can be rather dry and tough if not cooked carefully. Simmered with wine and rosemary, they become superbly succulent, and the sauce made with the pan juices is the perfect accompaniment.

PREPARATION TIME: 15 MINUTES
COOKING TIME: 3 HOURS

INGREDIENTS FOR SIX
6-8 kassler rib chops, about 1 cm thick
50 g dripping*
2 onions, peeled and sliced*
5-10 ml (1-2 teaspoons) dried rosemary
1 clove garlic, peeled and crushed
Pepper
250 ml (1 cup) white wine
250 ml (1 cup) water

For the sauce:
30 ml (2 tablespoons) flour
125 ml (½ cup) white wine
125 ml (½ cup) water
125 ml (½ cup) milk
15 ml (1 tablespoon) dry mustard
10 ml (2 teaspoons) brown sugar
3 ml (¾ teaspoon) rosemary
Salt and freshly ground black pepper

Melt the dripping in a large frying pan or electric frying pan and sauté the onion until soft. Remove the onion from the pan with a slotted spoon, and set aside. Brown the chops lightly on either side, doing two or three chops at a time.

Pour the fat out of the pan and return the chops, with the onion, rosemary and garlic. Season them lightly with pepper and pour over the wine. Cover the pan and simmer, turning the chops from time to time, until all the liquid has been absorbed (about 1½ hours).

Now add the water, a little at a time, and braise until the chops are tender – adding water as it is needed. When they are done, use a slotted spoon to transfer the chops to a heated platter. Cover them with foil and keep warm: you should now have a nice brown pan with a little bit of pan juice. To make the sauce, stir in the flour to make a smooth paste, add the 125 ml wine and 125 ml water (stirring until the mixture thickens), and then the milk. Stir to make a smooth, glossy sauce.

Mix the mustard and sugar together with a little wine and stir it into the sauce. Add the 3 ml rosemary and correct the seasoning. Spoon some of the sauce over the chops and serve the remaining sauce in a heated sauceboat.

SERVING SUGGESTIONS This dish is good with rice or baked potatoes* and green vegetables such as broccoli or baby marrows cooked until they are still firm.

VARIATION Instead of the mustard sauce, try the cooked chops layered in a casserole dish with a small tin of sauerkraut (well rinsed) which you have sautéed in 15 ml (1 tablespoon) butter with a finely chopped*, medium-sized onion, a small grated Granny Smith apple and 50 ml quince jelly*. Pour over the pan juices (mixed with wine and water) and bake, covered, at 150°C for 30-35 minutes.

CURED HAM IN CIDER

THE MAIN INGREDIENT for this succulent recipe is a 6,5 kg cured ham. It can be bought from your butcher, or alternatively you can do the curing yourself by following the method described in the panel alongside.

If you are going to cure the ham yourself, you need to plan the meal well in advance, since the curing process takes almost two weeks.

PREPARATION TIME: 30 MINUTES
SOAKING TIME: 2-3 HOURS
COOKING TIME: 3-4 HOURS
COOLING TIME: 2-3 HOURS
PRE-HEAT OVEN TO 230°C

INGREDIENTS FOR THIRTY
A 6,5 kg cured ham*
275-300 ml cider
225 g brown sugar
100-125 g fine breadcrumbs or 100-125 g brown sugar and 24 cloves

Soak the cured ham in cold water for 2-3 hours. Put the soaked ham into a very large fish kettle or preserving pan and cover with fresh water. Add the cider and brown sugar. Bring to the boil, cover, and simmer for 3-4 hours. Leave, covered, in the liquid until cold.

Pre-heat the oven to 230°C. Lift out the ham, wipe it dry and trim off all the skin. If you are using breadcrumbs, cover the ham with the breadcrumbs and brown in the oven for 10 minutes.

Instead of coating the ham with crumbs, you can stick cloves in it at 4 cm intervals and sprinkle thickly with brown sugar. Put in the pre-heated oven for 5-10 minutes to set and crisp the sugar.

SERVING SUGGESTION Serve the ham cold, sliced, with a good selection of salads for a summer buffet*.

VARIATION After simmering the ham, finish it off with a lemon glaze. First remove the rind and part of the layer of fat. If you like, score the fat into diamond patterns, studding with cloves at the intersections. Place in a roasting pan, tucking a sprig of fresh rosemary underneath. Pour over 250 ml (1 cup) port and bake in the oven at 180°C for 15 minutes. Mix together 100 g brown sugar, 125 ml (½ cup) lemon juice and 45 ml (3 tablespoons) brandy, stirring until the sugar is dissolved. Pour the mixture over the ham and baste frequently while baking for another 45 minutes (or until the glaze is syrupy and the ham shiny). If necessary, brown it a little more under the grill, watching it carefully to avoid burning. Transfer to a platter and pour any remaining glaze into a small bowl. Allow the glaze to get quite cool before refrigerating. Before serving, remove the fat from the glaze and pour it over the ham. Garnish with fresh rosemary and, if you like, add a ham frill.

CURING A HAM

Although most hams today are factory-cured, there is no doubt that a ham tastes much better if it is cured at home. Your butcher will get a fresh one for you if you give him enough notice.

The following ingredients will be necessary for pickling a 6,5 kg fresh ham:

1,6 kg table salt
450 g sea-salt crystals
40 g allspice
75 g ground black peppercorns
350 g golden syrup
225 g clear honey
5 litres cold water

Lay the ham on a very large, flat dish or a marble slab and rub 900 g of the table salt into it. Cover with another 450 g of the salt and leave to stand for 24 hours.

A good deal of salty liquid will run from the ham. Rub this back into the ham twice during the 24 hours.

To prepare the pickling brine, put the rough sea-salt crystals, allspice, pepper, syrup and honey in a large fish kettle or preserving pan and add 5 litres of cold water. Bring the brine to the boil, remove it from the heat, then cover and leave it to get cold.

When the ham has been salted for 24 hours, place it in the pickling brine, cover and leave in a cool place for 12 hours. Remove the ham from the brine and cover with the remaining 250 g of table salt. Leave to stand for 12 hours.

Boil up the brine again and allow it to become cold before putting the ham back into it. Leave to stand in a cool place for 10 days, turning the ham from time to time.

After curing you can store the uncooked ham in a refrigerator for about a week.

Moulding Hot-Water Pastry

Wrap aluminium foil around a jar or tin with a 15 cm diameter.

Mould the dough over the aluminium foil to a depth of about 7 cm and cut a neat, clean edge. Leave the pastry case to cool on the foil-wrapped jar.

Wrap another protective band of aluminium foil around the outside of the case to prevent it from collapsing during baking. Ease the jar out of the case – leaving the foil on the inside and outside.

After baking blind and filling, damp the top edges of the pie with a little milk, press on the lid and firmly crimp the edges all round to make a raised ridge, being careful not to break the case. Decorate the lid with pastry leaves, leaving 2 cm clear in the centre to allow for the hole.

Melton Mowbray Pie

The most famous English pie is the Melton Mowbray or pork pie, originally designed to satisfy appetites sharpened by hunting. The earliest recipe dates back to the 14th century. The pie should be served cold – making it an ideal picnic treat or addition to a buffet*.

Preparation Time: 1¼ hours
Cooking Time: 4½ hours
(including making the stock)
Cooling Time: 3 hours
Pre-heat Oven to 190°C

Ingredients for Four to Six

For the stock:
Pork or veal bones
575-600 ml water
*1 onion, peeled**
1 sage leaf
1 bay leaf
A sprig of marjoram
A sprig of thyme
Salt and pepper

For the filling:
450 g pork from leg or shoulder (300 g lean and 150 g fat)
2 ml (½ teaspoon) salt
1 ml (¼ teaspoon) pepper
1 sage leaf, finely chopped
A few drops of anchovy essence (optional)

For the hot-water pastry:
340 g flour
5 ml (1 teaspoon) salt
75 g lard
200 ml liquid (equal quantities of milk and water)
A little extra milk
1 egg, beaten
Boiling water

First make the stock. Place any bones from the pork, plus a few extra, into a pot with the water, onion, herbs, salt and pepper. Partially cover and boil for 2 hours – adding more water if necessary – to reduce the stock to about 275-300 ml. Let it cool, then skim off all the fat, and taste to check the seasoning. The stock should begin to jell as it cools.

Meanwhile, prepare the filling. Dice the pork in very small pieces, about 5 mm square. Do not mince it, as the texture will be spoilt. Remove any skin or gristle. Combine the pork, salt, pepper, sage and anchovy essence (if used).

Prepare the crust pastry. Warm the pastry board, bowl, wooden spoon and a jar or tin with a 15 cm diameter suitable for moulding the case.

Sieve the flour and salt into the warmed bowl and make a well in the middle of the flour. Bring the fat and liquid to the boil in a saucepan, then pour at once into the flour well.

Mix rapidly with the warm wooden spoon to a soft, elastic dough. Turn it out on to a floured board and knead until smooth. If the pastry is too dry, add a few drops of boiling water.

Cut off one-third of the pastry to make the lid, and keep it warm and moist by placing it in a container over a bowl of hot water while you are moulding the case.

Mould the pastry into the required shape while it is still warm, otherwise it will become too hard and difficult to handle. Follow the instructions alongside for moulding the pastry case, or use an 18 cm special hinged pie tin with detachable base, working the dough up the sides of the tin with your knuckles and fist. Allow the dough to cool.

If you are using a special hinged pie tin, the next step is to bake the pastry in the pre-heated oven for 20 minutes, or until the pastry is set and beginning to brown. If you have moulded the pastry over a tin or jar, bake the pastry for 10 minutes, then carefully remove the aluminium foil on the

Melton Mowbray Pie *An English recipe needing a modicum of pastry skill.*

inside of the crust (leave the outer aluminium foil), and bake for a further 10-15 minutes.

Remove the aluminium foil or pie tin, stand the pie case on a baking tray and put in the pork filling.

Roll out the rest of the pastry to make a lid and decorate as shown alongside. Cut a hole in the centre of the lid to let the steam out during cooking.

Lower the oven temperature to 180°C and bake the pie for a further 1¾ hours, covering the top lightly with foil if it begins to brown too quickly.

To glaze the pie, remove it from the oven 10 minutes before it should be cooked, brush the top with beaten egg and return it to the oven.

When the pie is cooked, take it out of the oven and allow it to stand for 15 minutes. Meanwhile, re-heat the jellied stock until it has just melted. When it is fairly cool but still liquid, pour as much of the stock as the pie will hold through the hole in the top of the crust, using a small funnel if you have one.

Refrigerate for 2½ hours to allow the stock to set to jelly around the meat.

CHOP SUEY

ALTHOUGH MOST Westerners consider chop suey to be typically Chinese, it actually originated in America, and is unknown in China. There are many variations in the preparation of chop suey, and ingredients may be substituted or added according to availability.

PREPARATION TIME: 25 MINUTES
COOKING TIME: 30 MINUTES

INGREDIENTS FOR SIX
2 boned, skinned chicken breasts
1 large carrot
1 tin (about 230g) bamboo shoots
250 ml (1 cup) water
10 ml (2 teaspoons) cornflour
1 chicken stock cube
15 ml (1 tablespoon) soy sauce
30 ml (2 tablespoons) sunflower oil
250 g pork, minced
½ Chinese or ordinary cabbage, shredded
125 g green beans, sliced diagonally
4 spring onions, sliced
3 sticks celery, sliced diagonally
250 g prawns, shelled and de-veined*

Steam the chicken breasts until tender, then cool and cut into cubes. Clean the carrot and cut it into julienne* strips, then drain and rinse the bamboo shoots and slice them into strips.

Combine the water, cornflour, crumbled stock cube and soy sauce and set aside.

Heat the oil in a wok or a heavy frying pan and add the minced pork. Stir-fry until well browned before adding the cabbage, beans, carrots, spring onions and celery. Combine well and stir-fry over a high heat for 2 minutes.

Make a well in the centre of the wok, add the cornflour mixture and stir until the sauce boils and thickens. Add the chicken, prawns and bamboo shoots and cook the mixture for a further 3 minutes (or until the prawns are done).

SERVING SUGGESTIONS Serve in a heated shallow bowl surrounded by crisp Chinese prawn chips.

As an accompaniment, serve fried rice*.

VARIATIONS Use lamb instead of pork.

Alternatively, leave out the meat and use only seafood and chicken, or only seafood.

VENISON CASSEROLE WITH SOUR CREAM

VENISON NECK, shoulder and ribs are best stewed. This deliciously aromatic casserole can be made from either marinated meat (using the marinade described for saddle of venison) or unmarinated.

PREPARATION TIME: 30 MINUTES
COOKING TIME: 2 HOURS

INGREDIENTS FOR EIGHT
1,5 kg venison, cut into 2,5 cm cubes with gristle removed
50 ml seasoned flour*
6 rashers bacon, trimmed and cut in squares
30 ml (2 tablespoons) sunflower oil
12-15 pickling onions
200 g button mushrooms
4 carrots, scraped and cut into 1 cm pieces
2 sticks celery, trimmed and cut into 1 cm pieces
1 clove garlic, crushed
30 ml (2 tablespoons) chopped parsley
1 bay leaf
3 ml (¾ teaspoon) dried thyme
3 ml (¾ teaspoon) grated nutmeg
4 cloves
1 cinnamon stick
3 ml (¾ teaspoon) cayenne pepper
500 ml (2 cups) red wine or basic stock*, or a mixture of both
30 ml (2 tablespoons) port
Salt and freshly ground pepper
Beurre manié* or cornflour (optional)
125 ml (½ cup) sour cream (smetana)
45 ml (3 tablespoons) finely chopped parsley for garnish

Dredge the meat with the seasoned flour, shaking off the excess. Fry the bacon in the oil in an oven-proof casserole until it is soft and starting to brown, then remove it with a slotted spoon and set aside. Lightly sauté the onions and mushrooms for 5 minutes, remove them with a slotted spoon, and set aside with the bacon.

Brown the meat, cooking a single layer at a time. When all the meat has been browned, return it to the casserole and add the carrots, celery, garlic, herbs and spices. Pour over the red wine (or wine and stock), cover the casserole and bring it to the boil.

Turn down the heat very low and cook on top of the stove until tender (about 1 hour). Stir from time to time to prevent sticking. Add the onions, bacon and mushrooms, and cook for 20 minutes.

Add the port, correct the seasoning and thicken if necessary with a little *beurre manié* (or cornflour mixed with water to a smooth paste). Remove the cinnamon and swirl in sour cream just before serving. Garnish with the parsley.

SERVING SUGGESTION This substantial stew needs very little in the way of vegetable accompaniment, though mashed potatoes*, chopped spinach (mixed with lemon-flavoured sorrel if you have some) or young green beans go well with the dish.

VARIATION Instead of cooking the casserole on top of the stove, bake it in the oven at 150°C until tender (about 1 hour).

COOKING WITH WINE

Do experiment with wine in cooking. Wine adds relish to the simplest recipe and, when properly used, can turn a meal into a feast. It need not be an expensive wine either.

All the alcohol evaporates from the wine during the cooking process, leaving a delicate flavour that will enhance a large variety of dishes. Never drown a dish in wine.

When cooking fish, veal, chicken, sweetbreads and similar delicate foods, use a medium dry white wine, such as riesling.

Red meats, such as lamb, beef and game, are prepared with red wines. However, certain classic poultry dishes, such as coq au vin, should also be prepared with red wine.

Apart from adding flavour to food, wine can be used to make it moist and tender. Fish marinated in white wine, or meat steeped in red wine, are enhanced in both texture and taste. Fish need not be marinated for more than an hour; but dry meats, such as venison or beef, may be left for up to four days. A useful marinade consists of 1 part olive oil to 3 parts dry red or white wine (depending on the use), to which a bouquet garni*, grated onion and garlic are added.

Wine left over after a meal can be kept for use in cooking or as a marinade. Pour the wine into a small bottle, cork it to keep out the air and store in the refrigerator. You can, if you wish, seal the left-over wine with a film of oil; or alternatively freeze the wine in ice trays – then take out as many iced wine cubes as needed. Boxed wine is useful for cooking since small quantities can be used at a time without exposing the wine to the air.

Fortified and dessert wines, such as Marsala, port, sherry and vermouth, can be used to enhance simple dishes. Marsala is an ingredient of the Italian dessert zabaglione, and sherry is added to trifles.

Wine is not the only alcoholic drink that improves a dish. Beer and cider can also be used in cooking, although they do not have as many uses as wine. Beer is an essential ingredient of certain classic dishes, and also makes an excellent marinade.

Spirits, such as brandy, whisky or gin, can be used to flame shellfish, steaks, veal escalopes, and other dishes which do not require long cooking. Before flaming a dish, warm the spirit slightly in a ladle. Then set it alight with a match and pour it over the hot food. Spirits can also be used to flavour dishes.

ROAST SADDLE OF VENISON

SOUTH AFRICANS are very lucky in having a plentiful supply of relatively cheap venison of many kinds. Springbok has a fine texture and a very good flavour. It seldom needs marinating except to give the meat a more gamey flavour. Gemsbok tastes very much like beef, and has a relatively fine texture, but kudu can be tough and almost always needs marinating.

PREPARATION TIME: 30 MINUTES
MARINATING TIME: 2 DAYS
COOKING TIME: 1½ HOURS
PRE-HEAT OVEN TO 200°C

INGREDIENTS FOR TWELVE

1 saddle of venison
8 rashers streaky bacon
100-125 ml port (optional)
Beurre manié* (optional)

For the marinade:
275-300 ml red wine
275-300 ml red wine vinegar
275-300 ml water
1 sprig of thyme
6 juniper berries, crushed
2 bay leaves, crumbled
1 blade of mace, crumbled
1 piece of orange peel, dried or fresh, with pith removed (about 2,5 cm square)

Using a very sharp knife, trim any hard skin from the meat, taking care not to tear the flesh. Put the meat in a dish that almost completely encloses it.

Combine all the ingredients for the marinade, and pour the mixture over the meat. If necessary, add more water to cover the saddle. Leave in a cool place for 2 days. Do not put a lid on the dish, but rather cover it with a net or a piece of loosely woven material to keep off flies and dust. Turn the meat from time to time.

At the end of the marinating time, drain the joint and pat it dry with paper towels. Lay the bacon rashers across the top of the saddle and tie them in place with string. Then place the saddle in a roasting tin, cover with a sheet of aluminium foil and cook in the pre-heated oven for 30 minutes to seal the meat.

Reduce the temperature to 180°C and continue cooking for another 45 minutes-1 hour. During this time, lift the aluminium foil and baste the saddle with the marinade every 15 minutes, or as often as necessary to keep the meat from drying out. If you like, you can pour the port into the roasting tin when you reduce the oven temperature, and incorporate it with the basting mixture.

Ten minutes before the meat is done, lift the foil and remove the bacon rashers, reserving them for a garnish. Raise the oven temperature to 200°C and return the saddle to the oven for 10 minutes to brown the outside of the meat.

Remove the venison from the oven and keep it warm while you make the sauce. Add enough boiling water to the meat juices in the roasting tin to make 275-300 ml of liquid. Stir over a high heat to blend and, if you like, thicken with *beurre manié*. Strain the sauce before serving.

SERVING SUGGESTIONS Serve the sauce separately with redcurrant or quince jelly* and game chips*.

VARIATIONS Make little slits in the flesh and stuff with fresh thyme or rosemary and slivers of garlic.

Cover with rashers of streaky bacon, pour over 250 ml (1 cup) red wine (or the marinade) and roast, uncovered, at 220°C for 1 hour. Remove the bacon and allow the meat to brown, roasting for another 20-30 minutes. Place the meat in the warmer drawer for 30 minutes while you make a gravy from the pan juices, adding red wine, port, garlic and herbs to taste.

You can make left-over roast venison into a delicious pie. Cut all the meat off the bone, cube it and combine with 150 g mushrooms, 12 baby onions and 1 large brinjal, sliced and lightly sautéed in butter. Pour over the left-over gravy. If you need to increase the volume, add stock, port and red wine to taste. If necessary, thicken with *beurre manié*. The meat should not 'swim' in the sauce; there should be just enough to moisten it well. Top with shortcrust* or puff pastry* and bake at 200°C until the pastry is well browned and the pie heated through. You can freeze the pie before or after baking.

ROAST SADDLE OF VENISON *not only looks sumptuous — it is also a delicious way of eating game.*

Rabbit with Mustard

During the Middle Ages, rabbit was esteemed above hare in England by both cottage and castle. Consequently, English rabbit recipes tended to be the more imaginative, making plentiful use of herbs. The following recipe is given a sharp piquancy through the addition of a generous portion of French mustard.

Preparation Time: 15 minutes
Cooking Time: 1½ hours

Ingredients for Four

1 large rabbit, jointed*
25 g butter
30 ml (2 tablespoons) sunflower oil
2 rashers rindless streaky bacon, diced
2 large onions, peeled and roughly chopped*
60 ml (¼ cup) French mustard
1 ml (¼ teaspoon) thyme
175 ml dry white wine
Salt and freshly ground black pepper

Heat the butter and oil together in a frying pan, and gently fry the bacon in it until the fat runs. Remove the bacon pieces to a large, heavy-based saucepan with a well-fitting lid. Put the pieces of rabbit in the frying pan and cook them over a high heat until browned on all sides. Add them to the bacon and keep warm.

Cook the onions gently in the fat that is left in the frying pan for about 10 minutes, then lift out with a slotted spoon, letting as much fat as possible drain off, and put in the saucepan with the rabbit and bacon. Add the mustard, thyme and wine. Season with salt and pepper, cover and bring to the boil. Turn down to the lowest heat and simmer for 1 hour.

Serving Suggestion Serve the rabbit with glazed carrots* or braised leeks and boiled or mashed potatoes* followed by a green salad*.

Variation You can cook the rabbit in an oven, pre-heated to 240°C. In this case, transfer the browned ingredients to a casserole and bring the wine almost to the boil before adding it. After 10 minutes, reduce the oven temperature to 190°C and cook, covered, for 1½ hours, or until tender.

Fried Young Rabbit *A tasty treat to delight family or friends.*

Fried Young Rabbit

Historically, the term 'young rabbit' is something of a misnomer. Until the 18th century at least, the word 'rabbit' meant the animal up to a year old; after that age it was called a 'coney'.

The following recipe makes a tasty family supper or can be served at a small informal dinner party.

Preparation Time: 1¼ hours
(including making the stock)
Cooking Time: 30 minutes

Ingredients for Four

2 young rabbits, jointed*
50-75 g butter
30 ml (2 tablespoons) sunflower oil
250 g spinach, washed and drained, or young cabbage leaves, finely chopped
Salt and pepper

For the stock:
Trimmings from the rabbits
1 carrot, roughly cut
1 turnip, roughly cut
1 onion, peeled and roughly chopped*
Salt and pepper

Ask the butcher to joint the rabbits, or do it yourself*. Use only the back and thighs for the dish.

To make the stock, place the rabbit trimmings in a saucepan with the carrot, turnip, onion and seasoning. Add just enough water to cover, then simmer, covered, for 1 hour. Strain and set aside the stock while you fry the rabbit pieces.

Heat 25 g of the butter and the oil together in a large frying pan with a well-fitting lid, and fry the rabbit pieces on both sides over a medium heat for 5 minutes, turning occasionally. Remove the back pieces and keep them warm in a covered dish, leaving the thighs to continue cooking for a further 5 minutes.

Return the back pieces to the pan, with the spinach or cabbage, 150 ml of the stock, and salt and pepper. Cover with the lid, and simmer for 10 minutes.

Remove the spinach or cabbage from the pan and put it on a hot serving dish. Arrange the rabbit pieces over the vegetable and keep warm.

Quickly make a sauce by breaking the rest of the butter in small pieces, then stirring them into the remaining liquid in the frying pan. Season to taste with salt and pepper, pour the sauce over the rabbit and vegetables, and serve.

Moussaka

Moussaka, it seems, was an Arab dish that Turkish invaders introduced to Europe. But Greece has made the dish especially its own.

Preparation Time: 45 minutes
Soaking Time: 30 minutes
Cooking Time: 1 hour
Pre-heat Oven to 150°C

Ingredients for Six

750 g lean raw lamb or beef, minced
900 g brinjals
60 ml (¼ cup) olive oil
25 g butter
1 large onion, peeled and finely chopped*
2 cloves garlic, crushed
7-8 medium-sized tomatoes, skinned* and quartered
5 ml (1 teaspoon) dried thyme
5 ml (1 teaspoon) dried rosemary
Salt and pepper
450 ml cheese sauce*
2 egg yolks, well beaten
50 g Parmesan cheese, grated

Slice the unpeeled brinjals thinly and soak them in salted water for 30 minutes. Drain well and pat dry with paper towels.

Heat half the oil in a large frying pan, and put in a layer of brinjal slices. Fry gently for 1 minute, then fry the other side for 2 minutes. Turn again and fry the first side for another minute. Transfer to a plate and fry the rest of the slices, adding more oil if needed. Set the slices aside.

Heat the butter in a large saucepan and fry the onion. After 3-4 minutes, add the garlic and minced meat. Fry, stirring all the time, for about 3 minutes, to brown the mince a little. Stir in the tomatoes, thyme and rosemary, and season well. Simmer for 15-20 minutes, stirring occasionally.

Meanwhile, make the cheese sauce. Cool for 5 minutes and stir in the egg yolks.

Butter a deep, oblong, oven-proof dish or a bread tin and place a layer of brinjal slices in the bottom. Cover with a layer of mince about 2 cm deep. Put in another layer of brinjals and another layer of mince, and finish with a layer of brinjals. Cover with the cheese sauce and sprinkle the Parmesan cheese over the top. Bake for 1 hour, or until the top is crisp and well browned.

Meat Baked in Golden Pastry Parcels

Meats, roasted or sautéed, can be even more delectable when wrapped in a good pastry and baked to a deep golden-brown. An advantage to the hostess catering for a special occasion is that this dish may be prepared beforehand and requires minimum supervision during cooking.

Fillet of Beef in Brioche

Preparation Time: 15 minutes
Cooking Time: 45 minutes
Pre-heat Oven to 220°C

Ingredients for Six to Eight

1 kg thick piece of fillet of beef
30 ml (2 tablespoons) sunflower oil
Brioche pastry* using 450 g flour
250 g chicken liver pâté*
1 egg, beaten

Trim the beef and pat it dry. Brown the meat on top of the stove in the heated oil.

Roll out the brioche pastry so that it is fairly thin (about 7 mm), and cut out a rectangle large enough to enclose the fillet, reserving offcuts for decoration (any remaining pastry may be stored in the refrigerator for a day or two for making brioches). Spread the pâté all over the meat, and place the meat in the centre of the pastry. Wrap the pastry around the beef so that it is completely enclosed, pinching the joins well together.

Place, seam-side down, on a baking sheet that has been greased or coated with a non-stick cooking spray. Brush generously with the beaten egg and make a few slashes across the top. Cut out some leaves from the pastry offcuts and arrange them on top, brushing them with egg.

Bake for 15 minutes, then reduce the heat to 180°C and bake for a further 30 minutes, or until well browned and shiny.

Serving Suggestions Serve with a mushroom sauce* or make a gravy* in the pan in which the beef was browned, adding 15 ml (1 tablespoon) port together with the stock. Cut the beef across into thick slices. A fresh green vegetable, lightly steamed and buttered, and crisp sautéed potatoes make good accompaniments.

Variations Use a puff* or sour cream flaky pastry* instead of the brioche pastry.
Use a well-hung piece of Scotch fillet.

Lamb Chops in Phyllo

Preparation Time: 20 minutes
Cooking Time: 20 minutes
Pre-heat Oven to 200°C

Ingredients for Six

6 thick loin lamb chops
30 ml (2 tablespoons) sunflower oil
Salt and freshly ground black pepper
6 squares of feta cheese (about 100g)
5 ml (1 teaspoon) dried origanum
6 sheets phyllo pastry*
60 ml (¼ cup) melted butter

Trim all the fat from the chops. Brown the chops on both sides in the hot oil and season. Slit each chop across and push in a square of feta cheese. Sprinkle with origanum.

Brush each phyllo pastry sheet with melted butter and wrap around a chop. Brush with more butter and bake for 15-20 minutes, or until crisp and golden.

Serving Suggestions Serve with a homemade tomato and onion sauce*, buttered green beans or baby marrows and steamed new potatoes.

Variation Use puff pastry*.

Steak in Puff Pastry

Preparation Time: 40 minutes
Cooking Time: 20 minutes
Pre-heat Oven to 220°C

Ingredients for Six

6 small, thick slices of fillet of beef (about 850g)
105 g butter
15 ml (1 tablespoon) sunflower oil
6 large mushrooms
Salt and freshly ground black pepper
25 ml (5 teaspoons) French mustard
15 ml (1 tablespoon) chopped parsley
15 ml (1 tablespoon) snipped chives
1 clove garlic, crushed
2 ml (½ teaspoon) lemon juice
Puff pastry* using 335 g flour, or 750 g bought pastry
1 egg, beaten

Quickly seal the steaks on both sides in 10 g of the butter heated with the oil. Remove the steaks and allow to cool. Pour off the fat. Sear the mushrooms in 40 g of the remaining butter. Allow to cool for about 10 minutes and season.

Spread the steaks with the mustard. Make a garlic and herb butter by creaming the rest of the butter with the parsley, chives, garlic and lemon juice. Sandwich the mushrooms and steaks together with the garlic butter.

Roll out the pastry thinly and cut out 12 rounds. Place a steak and mushroom sandwich in the centre of 6 of the pastry rounds. Dampen the edges with water. Cover with the remaining rounds of pastry. Crimp and seal the edges. Make 1 or 2 slits on top of each. Brush with beaten egg and bake for 20 minutes, or until puffed and golden.

Serving Suggestion Serve with sautéed potatoes and creamed spinach*.

Leg of Lamb in Phyllo

Preparation Time: 1 hour
Cooling Time: 45 minutes-1 hour
Cooking time: 2 hours
Pre-heat Oven to 180°C

Ingredients for Six to Eight

2 kg leg of lamb, boned but with shank bone intact
125 ml (½ cup) chopped parsley
5 ml (1 teaspoon) origanum
2 ml (½ teaspoon) thyme
2 onions
2 cloves garlic, crushed
Salt and freshly ground black pepper
Sunflower oil for browning
2 carrots, sliced
500 ml (2 cups) dry red wine
625 ml (2½ cups) beef basic stock*
3 sprigs parsley
1 bay leaf
1 sprig rosemary
30 ml (2 tablespoons) tomato paste
6 sheets phyllo pastry*
60 ml (¼ cup) melted butter for brushing
15 ml (1 tablespoon) cornflour
15 ml (1 tablespoon) port

Ask the butcher to bone the lamb but to leave on the shank bone to give the meat a good shape for baking. Take home the bones to give flavour to the sauce.

Mix together the chopped parsley, origanum, thyme, one of the onions, peeled and chopped*, one garlic clove, 5 ml (1 teaspoon) salt and a grinding of pepper.

Wipe the lamb all over with paper towels and season it lightly. Spread the herb mixture inside the lamb and tie the joint up with string. Brown the lamb and the washed, well-dried bones in a little hot oil in an oven-proof casserole. Remove and set aside.

Brown the carrots and the remaining onion, peeled and sliced*, in the same casserole. Add the wine and bring to the boil while stirring. Allow to reduce to half the quantity. Return the lamb and bones to the casserole and add the stock, parsley, bay leaf, rosemary, remaining garlic clove and the tomato paste. Bring to a simmer on top of the stove. Cover the casserole with aluminium foil and then with the lid.

Bake in the oven for 1½ hours, or until the meat is quite tender. Remove the lamb from the casserole. Strain the stock and leave both the stock and the lamb to cool (45 minutes-1 hour).

Increase the oven temperature to 220°C. Now, brush each sheet of phyllo pastry with melted butter until well moistened, then stack them together. Remove the string from the lamb and wrap the leg in the stacked sheets of pastry, brushing them with more melted butter as you wrap. See that the joins are well sealed with melted butter. Have the bulk of the pastry on top so that it can brown and crisp in the oven. Bake for 30 minutes, or until golden-brown.

To complete the sauce, remove the fat from the cooled stock. Allow the stock to reduce on top of the stove on a high heat until slightly thickened. Thicken further with the cornflour slaked with the port. Stir into the simmering sauce and keep stirring until it boils for 1-2 minutes, then check the seasoning. The sauce may be made ahead of time and re-heated, while stirring, when needed.

Serving Suggestions Serve the lamb thinly sliced, moistened with the hot sauce. Spanakoriso* (spinach rice) makes a perfect accompaniment.

Variations Use puff pastry* or sour cream flaky pastry*, thinly rolled, instead of the stacked sheets of phyllo pastry.

Gammon Steaks in Puff Pastry

Preparation Time: 20 minutes
Cooking Time: 45 minutes
Cooling Time: 1 hour
Pre-heat Oven to 160°C

Ingredients for Six

6 gammon steaks (about 750 g)
30 ml (2 tablespoons) sunflower oil
30 g butter
15 ml (1 tablespoon) brown sugar
15 ml (1 tablespoon) French mustard
60 ml (¼ cup) dry sherry
Freshly ground black pepper
Puff pastry* using 225 g flour, or 500 g bought pastry
1 egg, beaten

Trim the fat off the steaks, then sear the steaks on both sides in the hot oil. Remove and place in an oven-proof dish.

Pour off the oil from the pan and add the butter. Allow it to melt, then stir in the sugar, mustard and sherry, stirring until smooth. Pour the mixture over the steaks, add a grinding of pepper and bake, covered, for 20-30 minutes, or until tender. Allow the steaks to cool in the sauce for about 1 hour, then remove them with a slotted spoon. Reserve the sauce.

Roll out the pastry thinly. Cut out 6 pieces of pastry, slightly larger than the steaks. Place the steaks in the middle. Lift on to baking sheets. Cut strips from the remaining pastry about 1 cm wide and place on top of the steaks, weaving them into a lattice pattern and tucking the ends underneath. Brush with beaten egg. Chill while increasing the oven temperature to 220°C. Bake for 15 minutes, or until puffed and golden.

Reduce the reserved sauce in a pan over high heat, while stirring, until slightly thickened. Spoon a little of the sauce over each pie before serving.

SAUTÉED POTATOES

FILLET OF BEEF IN BRIOCHE

BOBOTIE

BOBOTIE IS ONE of the best-known South African dishes, and like sosaties, chutney, sambals and some preserves it was brought here by Muslim slaves in the late 17th century. It was traditionally made from left-over meat (the roast leg of mutton from the Sunday meal was served as bobotie on Monday). When made from minced left-over meat – be it mutton, beef or venison – the bobotie will have a much finer texture than when made from fresh meat. The same ingredients are used, with a slight change in cooking times.

PREPARATION TIME: 40 MINUTES
COOKING TIME: 2 HOURS
PRE-HEAT OVEN TO 180°C

INGREDIENTS FOR SIX

1 kg minced mutton or beef
2 medium-sized onions, peeled and thinly sliced*
30 ml (2 tablespoons) sunflower oil
15 ml (1 tablespoon) medium-strength curry powder
5 ml (1 teaspoon) turmeric
30 ml (2 tablespoons) white vinegar or lemon juice
15 ml (1 tablespoon) sugar
5 ml (1 teaspoon) salt
2 ml (½ teaspoon) black pepper
1 slice white bread (3 cm thick)
250 ml (1 cup) milk
2 large eggs
75 g seedless raisins
45 ml (3 tablespoons) fruit chutney
Grated rind of 1 lemon (optional)
2 bay leaves
6-12 almonds, blanched* and quartered
6 lemon leaves

Parboil the onions in a little water until just opaque, then drain (reserving the water), chop and fry in the oil until just golden. Add the curry powder and turmeric. Fry for 2 minutes, stirring all the time, then add the vinegar or lemon juice, sugar, salt and pepper.

In the meantime, soak the bread in the milk, then squeeze dry, strain the milk and set aside. Crumble the minced raw meat into a pan with the onion water and a little boiling water. Cook for 5 minutes.

Next, lightly mix the meat, soaked bread, onion mixture, 1 egg, raisins, chutney and lemon rind (if used). Pack into a buttered casserole, add the bay leaves, cover and cook in the oven for 1½ hours.

Remove from the oven and stick the almonds and lemon leaves (turned into little cones) into the meat. Whip up the remaining egg with the milk – add about ½ cup more to make a full 250 ml (1 cup) – and carefully pour on to the meat (over the back of a spoon) to make a smooth layer. Return the casserole to the oven, turning the heat down to 150°C, and bake (uncovered) for a further 30 minutes, or until the custard has set.

SERVING SUGGESTIONS Serve bobotie with fluffy white rice rather than yellow rice, and apricot blatjang*, cucumber or apple sambal*, or a mixed salad.

VARIATIONS If you decide to use cooked (left-over) meat instead, smooth the mixture down in a buttered dish. Place the lemon leaf cones and (whole) almonds on top of the meat and pour over the remaining whipped egg and milk. Place a flat pan of water on the bottom shelf of the oven. When it begins to bubble, place the bobotie dish in the water and bake for 45 minutes, or until the custard has set.

Cook bobotie in the Argentinian way by cutting off the top of a pumpkin big enough to hold the bobotie mixture. (If you cannot find one pumpkin big enough, use two.) Scrape out all the pips, brush melted butter over the inner surface, lightly roll a little sugar inside the pumpkin and tip out the surplus sugar. Wipe the outside of the pumpkin with a damp cloth, rub a little sunflower oil over the surface and fill with the bobotie mixture. Replace the lid and bake at 180°C (standing in a shallow baking tin) for 1½ hours, or until a skewer can just pierce the pumpkin shell (it must not be mushy).

BOBOTIE *One of our most famous dishes – a must for every cook's repertoire.*

FRIKKADELS

MINCED MEAT is a versatile standby for the imaginative cook; these frikkadels (savoury rissoles) are among the many tasty dishes you can prepare from mince. The early South African diarist and cookery writer Hildagonda Duckitt used only mutton for her 'frikkadels', but most cooks today opt for a combination of meats. Minced beef on its own, although more coarsely textured, is also acceptable.

PREPARATION TIME: 20 MINUTES
STANDING TIME: 30 MINUTES
COOKING TIME: 40 MINUTES

INGREDIENTS FOR FOUR

250 g minced topside
250 g minced lamb or mutton (not too fat)
1 slice white bread, 4 cm thick
125 ml (½ cup) milk
1 extra-large egg
1 medium-sized onion, peeled* and grated
5 ml (1 teaspoon) ground coriander or 5 ml (1 teaspoon) grated nutmeg
5-10 ml (1-2 teaspoons) salt
3 ml (¾ teaspoon) freshly ground black pepper
Fine dried breadcrumbs
Sunflower oil for frying
3 ripe, firm tomatoes
125 ml (½ cup) boiling water

Mix the meats with a fork. Soak the bread in the milk and mash it, then mix well with all the other ingredients except the breadcrumbs, oil, tomatoes and water.

When well mixed, leave to stand for at least 30 minutes to let the flavours mingle. Remove small quantities of the mixture and lightly roll into 6 cm balls.

Roll these in breadcrumbs, shake off the surplus and place the coated meatballs on a board. Meanwhile, heat a little oil in a saucepan and lift the balls into the saucepan with a spatula. The frikkadels must not be deep-fried – there should be just sufficient oil to sear their bases.

Cut two of the tomatoes into 1 cm slices and place a slice of tomato on each frikkadel and lightly dust it with breadcrumbs. Skin* the remaining tomato, cut it into small pieces and drop the pieces into the saucepan between the frikkadels: they provide moisture for cooking. Add the boiling water, cover, and allow to simmer for 30-40 minutes.

To serve, lift the frikkadels on to a platter and pour over the gravy.

VARIATIONS If you like, flavour the gravy with chopped, pre-cooked mushrooms or freshly chopped parsley and dry sherry.

To make delicious cocktail snacks, add half a medium-sized Granny Smith apple, finely grated, to the meat mixture, roll small (3 cm) balls of meat in fine breadcrumbs and shallow-fry in oil for 5 minutes, or until done. Serve with a bowl of tomato sauce*.

Large frikkadels can be dipped in beaten egg, rolled in crumbs, packed into a greased oven-proof dish and topped with small pats of butter. Add 125 ml (½ cup) boiling water and bake (uncovered) at 180°C for 30-45 minutes. Baste the frikkadels from time to time and add a little more boiling water if necessary.

Flat frikkadels also make satisfactory hamburgers.

COTTAGE PIE

NOT SO LONG AGO a cottage pie was traditionally a tasty way of using up left-overs. Today it is regarded as a satisfying meal in its own right, with many variations – some cottage pies are bland, while others are livened up with Worcestershire sauce or cayenne pepper.

PREPARATION TIME: 30-40 MINUTES
COOKING TIME: ABOUT 1 HOUR
PRE-HEAT OVEN TO 180°C

INGREDIENTS FOR FOUR

500 g minced lamb, mutton, beef or pork, either cooked or raw
6 medium-sized potatoes, peeled and halved
75 g butter
1 medium-sized onion, peeled and finely chopped*
300 ml basic stock*
Salt and pepper
15 ml (1 tablespoon) cornflour
150 ml milk

Place the potatoes in a saucepan with salted water to cover. Cook until tender, and drain immediately. Prepare the mince while the potatoes are cooking.

If the mince is raw, use the following method. Melt 25 g of the butter in a frying pan and fry the onion lightly in it. Add the mince and stir until lightly browned. Add the stock and simmer gently for 30 minutes. Allow to stand for a few minutes, then skim off as much fat as possible. Season highly with the salt and pepper.

Thicken the liquid a little by stirring in the cornflour, mixed to a paste with a little water. Boil for 3 minutes, stirring constantly to prevent sticking. Turn into an oven-proof dish in which the pie will be served. The meat must cool enough to form a skin before the potato is put on to it.

If you use meat already cooked, fry the onion as above and stir it into the mince. Season well and add a little thickened stock until the meat has a soft, moist consistency. Set aside to form a skin.

Mash the cooked potatoes with at least 25 g butter and enough milk to make it creamy. Season well. When the mince has a skin, spread the mashed potato on top carefully, so that it does not sink into the mince. The potato layer should be about 2,5-4 cm thick. Mark the top with a fork, and dot with the remaining butter. Bake for 30 minutes near the top of the oven so that the potato is well browned.

VARIATIONS Add 15 ml (1 tablespoon) tomato paste to the mince with the stock, or sprinkle the potato topping with grated Cheddar cheese before baking.

Add peas and carrots – this will in effect make it a traditional shepherd's pie.

STEAK AND KIDNEY PIE

THIS MUST RANK as one of the most popular pie dishes. This recipe calls for a lid of light, rich puff pastry. If the filling is cooked the day before and the pastry is ready to roll out, you can complete the pie in very little time.

PREPARATION TIME: 50 MINUTES
STANDING TIME: (FOR PASTRY) 1 HOUR
COOKING TIME: 2 HOURS 5 MINUTES
COOLING TIME: SEVERAL HOURS
PRE-HEAT OVEN TO 150°C

INGREDIENTS FOR FOUR

500 g rump or stewing steak, cut in 2 cm cubes
350 g ox kidney

STEAK AND KIDNEY PIE *is a popular dish among young and old alike.*

Puff pastry* using 350 g flour
50 g butter
1 large onion, peeled and sliced*
30 ml (2 tablespoons) seasoned flour*
250 g mushrooms, sliced
Salt and pepper
15 ml (1 tablespoon) flour
About 300 ml brown stock*
2 hard-boiled eggs* (optional)
1 egg, beaten

Prepare the puff pastry and allow to stand for an hour before folding it over the pie. Heat the butter in a frying pan and cook the onion in it until soft. Use a slotted spoon to transfer the onion to a warmed plate.

Remove any fat from the cubes of steak and dip them in the seasoned flour. Then brown the cubes in the pan in which the onion was cooked, adding a little more butter if necessary. Remove from the pan.

Chop the kidney thinly, remove all skin and fat, and dip the kidney in the seasoned flour. Lightly brown it in the same pan.

Arrange the steak, kidney, sliced mushrooms and onion in layers in a large pie dish, lightly seasoning each layer.

Use a wooden spoon to stir the flour into the pan in which the meat and onion were browned, and add the stock. Cook together for a few minutes, stirring all the time, until the stock has slightly thickened.

Pour enough stock into the dish to almost cover the meat. Cover the dish tightly with aluminium foil and cook in the pre-heated oven for 1½ hours, adding more stock during cooking if the meat becomes dry. Remove from the oven and allow to cool completely (this may be done the day before you want to eat the pie).

Increase the oven temperature to 230°C. When the meat is cold, cut the hard-boiled eggs into quarters, if you are using them, and add them to the pie dish.

Roll out the pastry to make a lid for the pie. Lay it over the filling, decorate* the top, and glaze with the beaten egg. Bake in the pre-heated oven for 10 minutes. Reduce the heat to 180°C and cook for a further 25 minutes, or until the pastry is crisp and golden-brown.

SERVING SUGGESTION Serve with mashed potatoes* and carrots.

BRAWN

BRAWN IS A LONG-STANDING favourite with South Africans. Although sliced brawn is available commercially, it does not have the same appeal as the home-made variety. Allow yourself plenty of time for preparing this dish.

Ask the butcher to clean the trotters and saw the shin into smaller pieces.

PREPARATION TIME: 45 MINUTES
SOAKING TIME: 1 HOUR
COOKING TIME: 3½-4 HOURS
SETTING TIME: 6-8 HOURS

INGREDIENTS FOR EIGHT TO TEN
2 pig or calf trotters, cleaned
1,5 kg sawn beef shin
500 ml (2 cups) water and 60 ml (¼ cup) vinegar, mixed
15 ml (1 tablespoon) whole coriander
4 cloves
12 allspice
12 peppercorns
2 medium-sized onions, peeled and chopped*
15 ml (1 tablespoon) salt
5 ml (1 teaspoon) pepper
1 bay leaf

For the garnish:
Hard-boiled eggs*
Gherkins

Soak the trotters and shin in vinegar water for 1 hour.

Cover the prepared trotters and shin with water, and simmer until tender and the meat comes away from the bone (about 3½ hours). Remove all skin and bones, and cut the meat into smaller pieces.

Add the spices (tied up in a clean piece of cheesecloth) and the onions, salt, pepper and bay leaf, and boil down, uncovered, until reduced and thickened (about 25 minutes). Remove the spices and bay leaf, and skim off the fat.

Decorate a mould with slices of gherkin and hard-boiled egg: simply dip the slices in the cooled brown gravy and 'glue' to the inside of the mould. When quite set, spoon in the brawn and then allow the completed dish to stand in a refrigerator for about 6-8 hours to set.

SERVING SUGGESTION Unmould and serve with sliced cold meats and salads.

OXTAIL STEW *Mouthwatering in appearance, this filling dish is a good choice for hungry friends or family.*

OXTAIL STEW

OXTAIL IS A relatively inexpensive, nourishing but fatty meat. It requires a great deal of cooking, but the end result is well worth it. It is quite a rich dish, best served with rice or mashed potato*.

PREPARATION TIME: 25 MINUTES
COOKING TIME: 3-4 HOURS
PRE-HEAT OVEN TO 150°C

INGREDIENTS FOR FOUR
1 kg oxtail, jointed
30 ml (2 tablespoons) sunflower oil
2 medium-sized onions, peeled and finely sliced*
2 leeks, trimmed and sliced
8-10 medium-sized carrots, cut in rounds
2 sticks celery, sliced
30 ml (2 tablespoons) seasoned flour*
2 bay leaves
2 ml (½ teaspoon) thyme
6 cloves
12 peppercorns
1 clove garlic, crushed
1 litre (4 cups) boiling water, or half water and half red wine (or cider)
2-3 medium-sized tomatoes, skinned* and quartered
15 ml (1 tablespoon) cornflour (optional)
15 ml (1 tablespoon) finely chopped parsley for garnish

Heat the oil in a heavy-based frying pan and fry the oxtail for 5 minutes, turning frequently. Lift the pieces on to a dish.

Fry the onions, leeks, carrots and celery in the fat until they begin to brown, then place them in a large, deep casserole. Rub the cooled oxtail pieces with the seasoned flour and put them in the casserole. Add the bay leaves, thyme, cloves, peppercorns and garlic, and cover with the water, or the wine or cider mixture.

Cover the casserole tightly and place it in the pre-heated oven for 2½-3½ hours, or until the meat is tender. Add the quartered tomatoes and cook the dish for a further 30 minutes.

Check the seasoning. If the gravy seems too thin, thicken it by mixing the cornflour with a little water and pour a cup of the hot gravy on to it, stirring all the time. Stir the mixture back into the casserole and place in the oven for a further 5 minutes. Garnish with parsley.

MEAT

Devilled Lamb Kidneys

LAMB KIDNEYS were traditionally prepared in some parts of the country by covering them with 'netvet' (caul) and then braaing them on the coals. This recipe for devilled kidneys can be served as a supper or luncheon dish, but is equally suitable for a hearty breakfast.

PREPARATION TIME: 10 MINUTES
COOKING TIME: 5 MINUTES

INGREDIENTS FOR SIX
12 lamb kidneys, trimmed
50 ml beef basic stock*
75 ml red wine
50 ml cornflour
Salt and freshly ground black pepper
60 g butter
10 ml (2 teaspoons) sunflower oil
1 clove garlic, crushed
2 red chillies, seeded and finely chopped, or a pinch of cayenne pepper

Remove the surrounding fat from the kidneys before peeling the skin off with your fingers. Slice the kidneys almost through so that the two halves can be opened out flat, and remove the white core. Wash the kidneys well in salted cold water, dry and set aside.

Mix the stock and wine, and slake the cornflour with a little of the mixture. Add the remaining mixture until smooth, and season with salt and pepper.

Heat the butter and oil, and quickly fry the kidneys (3-5 minutes). Transfer to a warm dish with a slotted spoon. Season with salt and pepper.

Add the garlic and chillies or cayenne pepper, and stir-fry quickly. Add the cornflour mixture and cook over high heat until clear. Adjust the seasoning, add the kidneys and transfer immediately to a warmed serving dish.

SERVING SUGGESTION Serve with buttered noodles sprinkled with parsley.

VARIATIONS Add one or two seeded and finely chopped sweet peppers when frying the chillies.

Chopped onion* can also be added, and a good sprinkling of chopped parsley added afterwards gives a pleasant colour to the dish.

Calf Liver with Onions

WHEN PROPERLY PREPARED, liver makes a delicious dish. To achieve the tastiest results, always choose calf rather than ox liver. The Italians combine it with sage for an excellent marriage of flavours: use fresh sage, if possible, and be sparing when using the dried variety.

PREPARATION TIME: 15 MINUTES
COOKING TIME: 25 MINUTES

INGREDIENTS FOR SIX
750 g calf liver, thinly sliced
Salt and freshly ground black pepper
Flour for coating
60 ml (¼ cup) sunflower oil
60 g butter
3 medium-sized onions, peeled and thinly sliced*
Juice of 1 lemon
60 ml (¼ cup) dry white wine
15 ml (1 tablespoon) chopped fresh sage leaves, or 2 ml (½ teaspoon) dried sage
Finely chopped parsley for garnish

Pat the liver slices quite dry with paper towels. Season and coat them lightly with flour. Heat half the oil and half the butter in a frying pan and add the onions. Cook very gently for 15-20 minutes, or until soft and pale golden in colour, then season lightly and keep warm in a separate dish.

Heat the rest of the oil and butter in the same pan. Add the liver and sauté quickly until brown outside but still pink inside. Place on top of the onions. Add the lemon juice and wine to the pan. Stir in the sage and bring to the boil, stirring all the time. Pour over the hot liver and onions, sprinkle with parsley and serve immediately.

SERVING SUGGESTION Serve with golden sautéed potatoes and buttered spinach.

VARIATIONS After frying the onions, add 15 ml (1 tablespoon) butter to the pan and cook 250 g sliced mushrooms. Remove from the pan, and keep warm while cooking the liver.

Add a thinly sliced small avocado when heating up the lemon juice and wine sauce (be careful not to overheat the avocado, as it will become bitter).

Brains

ALTHOUGH EATING brains does not appeal to everyone, it is a very tasty food with a flavour similar to that of bone marrow. In this recipe, the brains are gently simmered, then coated in breadcrumbs and lightly fried.

PREPARATION TIME: 15 MINUTES
STANDING TIME: 30 MINUTES
COOKING TIME: 10 MINUTES

INGREDIENTS FOR SIX
6 sets of sheep brains
Salt and freshly ground black pepper
15 ml (1 tablespoon) vinegar or lemon juice
15 ml (1 tablespoon) flour
1 egg, beaten
50 g dried breadcrumbs
2 cloves garlic, crushed
25 g butter
15 ml (1 tablespoon) sunflower oil
30 ml (2 tablespoons) chopped parsley

Wash and soak* the brains well, then cover with salted water, add the vinegar or lemon juice (to keep the brains white) and simmer gently for 15 minutes.

Drain and season with salt and pepper, then dust the flour over the brains. Roll them in the lightly beaten egg and then in the breadcrumbs.

Allow the brains to stand for 30 minutes in the refrigerator.

Heat the garlic, butter and oil, and fry the brains for 8-10 minutes. Transfer to a serving dish and sprinkle with the chopped parsley. Spoon the butter from the frying pan over the brains, and serve.

VARIATION Pre-cook the brains in a strong meat basic stock*, cut into thin slices and fry (without the crumbs) in butter, oil and garlic as specified above. Add a few tablespoons of the meat stock to the butter in the pan, reduce slightly and pour this gravy over the brains.

Ox Tongue

TONGUE IS DELICIOUS, whether served hot or cold. Mustard sauce* is the traditional accompaniment, but this recipe gives some equally delicious alternatives.

PREPARATION TIME: 20 MINUTES
SOAKING TIME: 1-2 HOURS
COOKING TIME: 3¼ HOURS

INGREDIENTS FOR EIGHT TO TEN
1 ox tongue (about 1,5-2 kg)
2 medium-sized carrots, scraped
2 medium-sized onions, peeled* and quartered
1 medium-sized turnip, peeled and quartered
12 peppercorns
Bouquet garni*

Wash the tongue thoroughly and soak it in cold water for 1-2 hours. Drain, place in a very large saucepan and cover with water heated until tepid. Bring slowly to the boil and remove the scum.

Add the carrots, onions, turnip, peppercorns and the bouquet garni to the saucepan. Cover and boil gently for about 3 hours.

Lift the tongue on to a board and carefully remove the skin and any small bones. Discard the stock, which tends to be greasy and tasteless. If the tongue is to be served hot, place it in its natural shape on a large serving dish.

SERVING SUGGESTION Serve with a homemade Cumberland sauce*, tomato and onion sauce* or Marsala sauce*. Pour a little of the sauce over the meat and serve the rest separately in a sauceboat.

VARIATION If the tongue is to be served cold, curl the boned and skinned tongue in a large, round cake tin or soufflé dish. Dissolve 15 g gelatin in 575-600 ml beef basic* or chicken stock*, and pour into the tin or dish until it is just level with the top of the tongue. Cover with aluminium foil and place a heavy weight on the meat. Leave in the refrigerator overnight. The next day, turn out the pressed tongue and carve it horizontally in thin, round slices. Serve cold ox tongue with salads.

Alternatively, you can use a meat press to press the cold tongue.

MEAT

TRIPE VENETIAN STYLE *An unusual yet inexpensive dish of Italian origin.*

TRIPE VENETIAN STYLE

ALTHOUGH TRIPE HAS long been associated with 'budget' meals, many cooks do not realise its potential for dishes of interesting flavour and texture. This dish is both tasty and economical. The knack of cooking tripe successfully lies essentially in the cutting technique.

PREPARATION TIME: 20 MINUTES
COOKING TIME: 2½ HOURS

INGREDIENTS FOR SIX

1 kg white tripe, cleaned
Salt and freshly ground black pepper
1 onion, peeled and sliced*
1 stick celery, sliced
1 carrot, sliced
30 ml (2 tablespoons) olive or sunflower oil
1 large tomato (red and ripe)
125 ml (½ cup) dry white wine
125 ml (½ cup) clear stock*
60 ml (¼ cup) brandy
1 tin (410g) butter beans, heated and drained

Wash the tripe several times in cold water. Drain, then cut it into very fine strips with a sharp knife. Season the onion, celery and carrot, and fry in the heated oil in a pan until slightly golden (stir to keep moist).

Add the seasoned tripe strips and fry for a few minutes. Add the well-chopped and seasoned tomato with the wine. Stir and allow to cook together briefly.

As soon as it starts to boil, reduce the heat, cover the saucepan and cook for 2 hours over a low heat, adding the clear stock a little at a time.

When the tripe is tender, check the seasoning and pour in the brandy. Arrange the tripe on a serving dish and surround it with the hot, cooked beans.

TRIPE AND ONIONS

TRIPE ROASTED OR CURRIED, stuffed, fried or fricasseed is enjoyed in many parts of the world.

Tripe and onions is the delicious result of many generations of experimenting in homely cooking.

PREPARATION TIME: 30 MINUTES
COOKING TIME: 3¼ HOURS

INGREDIENTS FOR SIX

700 g tripe, dressed by the butcher
750 ml (3 cups) milk
275-300 ml water
3 large onions, peeled and finely sliced*
Salt and pepper

For the sauce:
15 ml (1 tablespoon) flour
50 ml milk
15 g butter
Salt and pepper

Cut the dressed tripe into 8 cm squares. Place the pieces in a saucepan and cover with cold water. Bring to the boil over high heat and then discard the water, leaving the tripe in the saucepan.

Add the milk, 275-300 ml water, onions, salt and pepper to the tripe, and simmer for 3 hours.

To make the sauce, mix the flour and milk, and strain into the saucepan away from the heat. Return to the heat, add the butter and stir until the liquid boils and thickens. Add salt and pepper to taste.

SERVING SUGGESTION Serve the tripe and its sauce very hot with slices of dry toast.

PORK SAUSAGES

MOST SOUTH AFRICANS have a favourite brand of sausage which remains fixed in the mind as the finest ever created. A typical attitude to the sausages of long ago was that of the writer James Joyce who, when he was exiled in Paris, used to beseech visiting pilgrims to bring a pound of Dublin sausages and a bottle of whiskey.

Sausage skins are not always easy to find, though many butchers will order them for you. The same mixture can, of course, be made skinless. Simply roll it, cut it into lengths, flour lightly and fry.

PREPARATION TIME: 30 MINUTES
STANDING TIME: 1 HOUR

INGREDIENTS TO YIELD ABOUT 20 FULL-SIZE OR 40 CHIPOLATA SAUSAGES

1 kg very lean pork, finely minced
350 g shredded suet, preferably pork
250 g fresh white breadcrumbs
1 ml (¼ teaspoon) grated nutmeg
5 ml (1 teaspoon) powdered sage
2 ml (½ teaspoon) powdered thyme
2 ml (½ teaspoon) powdered marjoram
7 ml (1½ teaspoons) salt
2 ml (½ teaspoon) freshly ground black pepper
25 g sausage skins

Mix all the ingredients (except the skins) thoroughly together, ensuring that seasonings are evenly distributed.

To put the mixture into the skins, use a forcing bag with a long, wide nozzle. Knot one end of a length of skin about 90 cm long. Place the other end over the nozzle and push the rest of the length on until the knot is as near the nozzle as possible.

Force the meat in, drawing the filled skin back from the nozzle. Do not overstuff. Knot the open end and twist the filled skin at 8 cm intervals. Let the twisted sausages lie in a cool place for up to an hour to set before cooking or storing.

BOEREWORS

THERE APPEAR TO BE as many recipes for boerewors as there are farming districts in South Africa: beef and pork are used in the beef farming districts, while in the Karoo beef, mutton and pork are used. In the north-western districts of Calvinia and Namaqualand only mutton is used.

The recipe also includes sheep tail fat, cut by hand into tiny pieces. Boerewors must have fat which can be grilled out. If it is to be dried (and therefore eaten raw), no pork at all should be used.

PREPARATION TIME: 2-3 HOURS
STANDING TIME: 3 HOURS
MATURING TIME: AT LEAST 2 DAYS

INGREDIENTS TO YIELD 7 KG

3 kg boneless beef (preferably topside)

MEAT

3 kg boneless mutton (preferably leg – do not use lamb)
1 kg sheep tail fat
30-45 ml (2-3 tablespoons) cooking salt
10 ml (2 teaspoons) freshly ground black pepper
5 ml (1 teaspoon) finely ground allspice
60 ml (¼ cup) ground coriander
100 g sausage casings, soaked in salted water and rinsed

The meats must be well ground, but not too finely, or the sausage will have too firm a texture. Dice the tail fat into 5 mm cubes. Mix the salt, pepper and spices well together. Mix the minced meats, and toss the fat pieces into the meat with a fork. Do not handle too much.

Pack the meat in layers in a basin, seasoning each layer with the spices, and leave to stand for 3 hours.

Mix thoroughly with a fork and take out a small lump and fry to test for flavour, adding salt and pepper if required.

Stuff the mixture into the casings, using a forcing bag with a long, wide nozzle. Knot one end of a length of sausage casing (about 90 cm long). Place the other end over the nozzle and push the length of skin on to the nozzle until the knot is as close as possible to the nozzle.

Force the meat in, drawing the filled skin away from the nozzle. Stuff fairly loosely, and, if preferred, make twists for individual sausages every 20 cm.

Allow the boerewors to mature for at least 2 days before using.

This sausage must not be overcooked; it is delicious if slightly underdone.

VARIATION To make dried sausage, use less of the sheep tail fat – 200 g instead of 1 kg. Add 60 ml (¼ cup) vinegar to the mixture, sprinkling it over the meat together with the spices. Roast the coriander before grinding, and add 5 ml (1 teaspoon) ground cloves and 5 ml (1 teaspoon) finely grated nutmeg. You need not twist the sausage casings, but knot the ends of each length. To dry the sausages, hang them in a cool draught, well above the floor, for at least a week. Butchers use a wind tunnel, while farmers select a shady, fly-screened corner of the verandah. As 60 per cent of the mass is lost when drying, this variation will yield just over 3 kg.

TOAD-IN-THE-HOLE

TOAD-IN-THE-HOLE has changed its ingredients over the centuries. Apparently it originated when 18th century cooks first wrapped a small piece of mutton in a large suet crust to make the meat go further. This dish was thought to resemble a toad in a hole. But for most people then, as now, a 'toad' is a sausage and the batter a Yorkshire pudding.

PREPARATION TIME: 15 MINUTES
COOKING TIME: 25-30 MINUTES
PRE-HEAT OVEN TO 220°C

INGREDIENTS FOR SIX
450 g pork sausages*
30 ml (2 tablespoons) dripping*

For the batter:
125 g flour
2 ml (½ teaspoon) salt
2 eggs
200 ml milk

To make the batter, sift together the flour and the salt in a mixing bowl, and break the eggs into the middle. Stir well with a wooden spoon and add the milk, a little at a time, beating hard until the batter is smooth and has the consistency of thin cream. Leave it to stand while you prepare the sausages.

Cut the sausages in two. Heat half the dripping in a heavy frying pan and fry the sausage halves gently until they are golden-brown.

Put the rest of the dripping in a baking tin or shallow oven-proof dish. Place it in the pre-heated oven for a few minutes until it is very hot.

Arrange the sausages in the dish and pour the Yorkshire pudding batter gently around them. Return the baking tin to the oven for 25-30 minutes, until the batter has set and risen.

SERVING SUGGESTION If you like, serve with a basic brown sauce*.

TOAD-IN-THE-HOLE *may sound exotic, but the ingredients are very simple.*

BILTONG

BILTONG IN ITS many forms is as South African as the song Sarie Marais. There are seemingly endless theories as to how it is best prepared, and at what stage of dryness it should be eaten.

When making biltong, choose good cuts of meat, and make a substantial quantity: it will be eaten faster than you would have believed possible!

PREPARATION TIME: 3 DAYS
HANGING TIME: UNTIL DRY

INGREDIENTS TO YIELD 4,25 KG
10 kg meat (game, beef or ostrich)
625 ml (2½ cups) brown vinegar
75 g brown sugar
8 ml (1¾ teaspoons) ground saltpetre
8 ml (1¾ teaspoons) bicarbonate of soda
10 ml (2 teaspoons) pepper
45 ml (3 tablespoons) whole coriander seeds
275 g salt

Cut the meat into suitable-sized strips and rub thoroughly with vinegar, ensuring that all the meat is coated. Next, mix the sugar, saltpetre, bicarbonate of soda and pepper, and set aside. Roast the coriander in a pan over a medium heat, remove and mince (or pound in a mortar) until fine. Combine with the sugar mixture.

Place the thicker biltong strips at the bottom of an enamel container, cover with a layer of salt and then a layer of the spice mixture. Repeat the layers until the thin strips are on top, and add a final dressing of salt. Leave for 12 hours. Remove the thinner strips at the top and dip them quickly in hot water.

Dry the strips very well, then hang on S-shaped wire hooks. Take care to hang the pieces of biltong well apart so that air can circulate between them. After another 12 hours, remove the medium-sized biltong, treat exactly as before, and hang. After 36 hours, the thick portions may be removed, treated and hung.

The drying time depends on factors such as temperature, air circulation and personal preference.

SERVING SUGGESTION Cut the biltong into slices, and serve as a snack, or eat in sandwiches.

MEAL-IN-ONE DISHES

HEARTY STEWS FOR HEALTHY APPETITES

Delicious stews using more economical cuts of meat are slow-cooked to develop tenderness and a rich, meaty flavour.

HASHED BEEF OR LAMB WITH TOMATOES

THIS RECIPE combines left-over cooked meat with beans, tomatoes, mushrooms and herbs to make a tasty, nourishing and filling dish.

PREPARATION TIME: 1¼ HOURS
SOAKING TIME: OVERNIGHT
COOKING TIME: 30-40 MINUTES
PRE-HEAT OVEN TO 180°C

INGREDIENTS FOR FOUR
225 g dried beans: haricot, butter, sugar beans or others as available
50 g butter
2 large onions, peeled* and quartered
125 g mushrooms, sliced
8-12 slices cooked beef or lamb, trimmed of fat
Salt and freshly ground black pepper
25 g flour
600 ml brown stock*
5 ml (1 teaspoon) dried thyme
1 ml (¼ teaspoon) dried basil
3-4 ripe tomatoes, blanched, skinned* and quartered
5 ml (1 teaspoon) sugar

Pour cold water over the beans, and leave to soak overnight. The next day, drain and put them in a saucepan with fresh water. Boil gently for about 1 hour (or until tender but not mushy) while preparing the other vegetables.

Melt half the butter and gently fry the onions in it until soft and transparent, but not brown. Lift them out with a slotted spoon and place in a shallow casserole. Use the butter in the pan to fry the mushrooms lightly. Place them on the onions and lay the slices of meat on top. Season with salt and pepper.

Melt the remaining butter in the pan in which the vegetables were cooked, and stir in the flour. Add the stock a little at a time, stirring continuously, and cook over a medium heat until a thin, smooth sauce is formed.

Drain the cooked beans and put them in a layer over the meat. Sprinkle with the thyme and basil. Pour in the sauce and put the tomatoes on top. Season with salt and pepper, and sprinkle the sugar over the tomatoes. Cook the casserole, uncovered, in the centre of the pre-heated oven for 30-40 minutes.

LANCASHIRE HOTPOT

LANCASHIRE HOTPOT was traditionally cooked in the farmhouse bread oven at the end of a busy baking day. This typically English meat dish transplanted well to South Africa, where mutton and lamb are so extensively reared.

PREPARATION TIME: 30 MINUTES
COOKING TIME: 3 HOURS
PRE-HEAT OVEN TO 180°C

INGREDIENTS FOR SIX
1,5 kg best end of the neck of lamb, divided into chops
Salt and pepper
4 large onions, peeled and sliced*
875 ml (3½ cups) basic stock*
225 g mushrooms
9 medium-sized potatoes, peeled and thickly sliced
25 g butter, in small pieces

Place a layer of lamb chops, lying head to tail, in a large casserole with a lid or in a large, deep pie dish. Sprinkle the meat with salt and pepper.

Cover this first layer of chops with a layer of onions and season again. Repeat with the rest of the chops, covering each layer with sliced onions and seasoning with salt and pepper. Pour in the stock until it almost covers the meat.

Place the mushrooms over the chops and onions, and cover thickly with overlapping potato slices. Dot with half the butter pieces, cover tightly and then cook in the pre-heated oven for 2 hours. Remove the cover, dot with the remaining butter and cook for a further hour in order to brown the potatoes.

BRAISED LAMB WITH SPINACH

THIS SIMPLE RECIPE describes how to make a deliciously filling dish of braised lamb chops cooked with onions, carrots, potatoes and chopped spinach.

PREPARATION TIME: 20 MINUTES
COOKING TIME: 1 HOUR

INGREDIENTS FOR FOUR
8 large lamb chops (use thick rib or leg chops)
15 ml (1 tablespoon) sunflower oil
2 onions, peeled and thinly sliced*
1 cinnamon stick
2 cloves garlic, crushed
5 ml (1 teaspoon) dried origanum
Juice of 1 lemon
Salt and freshly ground black pepper
4 carrots, peeled and grated
250 ml (1 cup) beef basic stock*
4 medium-sized potatoes, peeled and quartered
300 g spinach leaves, well washed and chopped

Trim any excess fat from the chops. Brown them in a heavy-based saucepan with a tight-fitting lid in the heated oil, adding a little more oil if necessary.

Add the onions, cinnamon, garlic, origanum and lemon juice, and season with salt and pepper to taste.

When the onions have a good colour, stir in the grated carrots and stock. Bring slowly to the boil and add the potatoes and a little more seasoning. Add more stock only if necessary.

When the meat and potatoes are almost tender (cooked with the lid on for about 45 minutes), stir in the chopped spinach leaves.

Allow the contents to simmer gently on the stove until the meat and vegetables are quite tender. Check the seasoning again and then serve.

PORK AND BAKED BEANS

LONG BEFORE the economical version of this recipe was commercially tinned, pork and baked beans were a poor man's staple all over Britain.

While its popularity in South Africa is more recent, it is a widely used standby meal. This is an inexpensive dish for feeding large numbers of people.

PREPARATION TIME: 20 MINUTES
SOAKING TIME: OVERNIGHT
COOKING TIME: AT LEAST 4 HOURS
PRE-HEAT OVEN TO 150°C

INGREDIENTS FOR SIX
50 g butter
500 g lean pork, cut into 1,5 cm cubes
2 rashers rindless streaky bacon, cut into strips
500 g dried haricot beans, soaked overnight and parboiled for 10 minutes
3-4 tomatoes, blanched and skinned*
5 ml (1 teaspoon) salt
2 ml (½ teaspoon) freshly ground pepper
1 ml (¼ teaspoon) dried basil
1 ml (¼ teaspoon) dried thyme
10 ml (2 teaspoons) sugar
600 ml basic stock*, heated through

Heat 40 g of the butter in a heavy frying pan and fry the pork cubes, turning until lightly browned all over.

Grease a deep casserole with the remaining butter and put the strips of bacon at the bottom. Drain the parboiled beans and put half of them in the casserole. Put the pork cubes on top and then cover with the rest of the beans.

Purée the tomatoes, season with salt and pepper, and add the basil, thyme and sugar. Add the stock to the purée, stir well and pour over the beans and meat.

Cover the casserole closely with a lid or foil and cook in the pre-heated oven for at least 4 hours. The dish can be made in advance, but should then be re-heated thoroughly before serving.

Beef and Noodles

This inexpensive dish is ideal for the sort of evening on which you would like to relax and not exhaust too much time and energy making supper.

Preparation Time: 30 minutes
Cooking Time: 2 hours

Ingredients for Four to Six
4 thick slices beef shin (about 1 kg)
45 ml (3 tablespoons) sunflower oil
Salt and freshly ground black pepper
1 large onion, peeled and chopped*
1 clove garlic, crushed
1 onion, peeled* and grated
6 carrots, scraped and grated
30 ml (2 tablespoons) tomato paste
5 ml (1 teaspoon) dried thyme
1 bay leaf
Strip of dried naartjie or orange peel
500 ml (2 cups) beef basic stock*
500 g small shell noodles

Remove the meat from the bone and cut it into small cubes. Brown the meat in 30 ml (2 tablespoons) of the heated oil. Remove and season with salt and pepper.

Heat the rest of the oil in the same pot and add the chopped onion. Sauté gently, stirring now and again, until the onion turns golden. Add the crushed garlic and cook for a further minute.

Return the meat to the pot and add the grated onion, carrots, tomato paste, thyme, bay leaf and dried peel. Stir everything around and then add the hot beef stock. Place the (very well-washed) marrow bones on top.

Bring the pot to the boil, then reduce the heat. Cover and simmer very gently for 2 hours (or longer) until the meat is very tender.

Meanwhile, cook the noodles in plenty of salted boiling water and drain well. Stir the noodles into the meat and sauce, and season to taste.

Serving Suggestions Eat the marrow first on hot toast, then enjoy the beef and noodles. If you like, sprinkle grated cheese over each serving.

Beef Stew with Parsley Dumplings

Parsley dumplings make excellent companions to set off this cider-flavoured stew.

Preparation Time: 20 minutes
Cooking Time: 2½ hours

Ingredients for Four to Six
900 g beef shin
40 g well-seasoned flour*
50 g beef dripping* or butter
2 large onions, peeled and sliced*
600 ml brown stock*
300 ml cider
Salt and freshly ground black pepper
3 carrots, peeled and diced
3 turnips, peeled and diced
2 sticks celery, cleaned and diced
Parsley dumplings*

Cut the meat into 2,5 cm cubes and toss them in the seasoned flour. Heat the dripping in a heavy-based pan or oven-proof casserole and cook the onions in it gently until transparent. Add the meat and fry until brown.

Stir in the stock and cider, scraping up any bits sticking to the pan, and season with salt and pepper. Bring the contents to the boil, and remove any white scum from the surface.

Add the carrots, turnips and celery. Reduce the heat, cover the pan with a lid, and simmer the stew for about 2½ hours, or until the meat is tender.

Make the dumplings and place them on top of the stew for the last 15-20 minutes of cooking.

Serving Suggestion Ladle the stew and vegetables into a deep dish and surround with the dumplings. Serve immediately with hunks of crusty bread.

Beef Stew with Parsley Dumplings *Visually appealing and delicious.*

Braised Beefburgers with Vegetables

This combination of beefburgers and fresh vegetables makes a nourishing meal with an interesting variety of flavours.

Preparation Time: 45 minutes
Cooking Time: 1 hour

Ingredients for Four
1 kg lean beef mince
1 egg, beaten
250 ml (1 cup) finely chopped celery leaves
1 onion, peeled* and grated
5 ml (1 teaspoon) Worcestershire sauce
15 ml (1 tablespoon) tomato sauce*
15 ml (1 tablespoon) chutney
5 ml (1 teaspoon) dried thyme
5 ml (1 teaspoon) salt
Freshly ground black pepper
1 thick slice wholewheat bread*, crumbled
125 ml (½ cup) water
30 ml (2 tablespoons) sunflower oil
1 onion, peeled and thinly sliced*
6 medium-sized carrots, scraped and sliced
3 or 4 turnips, peeled and diced
4 parsnips, peeled and diced
4 potatoes, peeled and quartered
250 ml (1 cup) beef basic stock*
Beurre manié*
Finely chopped parsley for garnish

Mix the beef mince with the egg, celery, grated onion, sauces, chutney, thyme, salt and pepper. Soak the crumbled bread in the water and add to the meat mixture.

Form the mixture into 12-16 patties and fry in a casserole or heavy saucepan in the hot oil (6-8 at a time) until they are lightly browned on both sides. Return all the patties to the casserole or saucepan and add the remaining vegetables with a little more seasoning.

Pour in the beef stock. Cover tightly and simmer for about 40 minutes, adding a little more stock only if necessary. Once everything is tender, thicken the sauce with beurre manié, then check the seasoning. Sprinkle generously with chopped parsley and serve.

Poultry

*S*AY 'POULTRY' and most people think immediately of chicken. The category of poultry covers a wide range of edible birds, however, including duck, turkey, guinea fowl, goose, pigeon and South Africa's big game bird, the ostrich.

Poultry has traditionally been a festive dish – particularly in the form of roast turkey at Christmas. In fact, roasting is probably the most popular way to cook all poultry – whether with a choice of the endless selection of delectable stuffings available, glazed with a fruit syrup, or simply flavoured and accompanied by crispy roast potatoes.

Many other cooking methods are suitable for poultry: it is superb curried, casseroled with vegetables and herbs, pot-roasted or fricasseed. It lends itself well to being cooked in wine, or with many other liquors, as in the recipe for roast duck with orange and Van der Hum liqueur.

New ideas for preparing chicken are constantly being introduced as South Africans realise the enormous potential of this nutritious and tasty food. Almost as rich in body-building proteins as red meat, poultry was expensive until fairly recently, when battery-rearing turned chicken into a popular budget food.

The heat of South African summers has induced local cooks to exploit the full value of chicken and turkey in light salads, while Eastern-inspired dishes – such as chicken biriani, Malay braised chicken, sooki murghi and stir-fried chicken and vegetables – have further enriched our daily diet.

Although other types of fowl are less freely available, they sometimes appear in speciality food stores and make a delightful change for family or guests. Surprise them with a dish of stewed pigeons, casseroled guinea fowl or ostrich fillet steak.

BUYING AND PREPARING POULTRY AND
GAME BIRDS · *PAGE 124*

POULTRY RECIPES · *PAGE 126*

SPECIAL FEATURES

ADD ZEST WITH SPICES AND SEASONINGS · *PAGE 130*
PUTTING CHINA ON THE TABLE · *PAGE 138*
MEAL-IN-ONE DISHES · WINNING WAYS WITH
ECONOMICAL CHICKEN · *PAGE 146*

BUYING AND PREPARING POULTRY AND GAME BIRDS

POULTRY

The place that chicken occupies in South African cookery has changed dramatically during the past 20 years. From being a once-a-week special treat it has now become part of our staple diet. This is the result of mass chicken-rearing, the lack of ethnic or cultural restrictions on its consumption, and the fact that poultry is considered to be a healthy food, with low levels of cholesterol and high levels of protein. Chicken is also a versatile meat that lends itself to a multitude of preparations and presentations.

Other forms of poultry such as duck, goose and turkey are, however, far less popular in South Africa.

CHOOSING POULTRY

Most chicken is slaughtered and packaged in processing plants under the supervision of the Department of Veterinary Services and is marketed in various oven-ready forms.

Fresh chicken is usually marketed with a 'sell-by' date on the price ticket. The practice is to allow up to two days for the processing of poultry and three days in the retail store. A further margin of two to five days for the purchaser is allowed.

This time factor is called the 'life' of a chicken. Poor storage conditions (mainly high temperatures) at wholesale, retail or customer level can greatly shorten its 'life'.

PREPARING POULTRY

Almost all poultry is now sold oven-ready. If you are offered a bird in feather or one that has been rough-plucked, it will need to be hung, plucked and drawn before you prepare it for the oven.

To prepare frozen chicken for cooking, allow the chicken to thaw out overnight in the main compartment of your refrigerator and remove the package of giblets before cooking. Incomplete thawing of poultry can lead to uneven cooking.

Hanging

Poultry, like other meats, should be hung to tenderise it. If bought in feather, ask how long the bird has already been hanging.

Hang fresh chicken for 24 hours after killing; duck or goose for up to 48 hours; turkey for 3-5 days.

Hang the bird by the feet in a cool, dry, well-ventilated place, free from flies. Check its condition occasionally, as the hanging time will vary a little according to weather conditions. In hot weather, a bird will tend to decompose rather more rapidly.

Plucking

Hold the bird firmly on a large sheet of paper, in a draught-free space. Have a large bag handy for the feathers as you pluck them.

Start with the legs and wings, drawing the feathers out with a slight, backward pull against the lie of the feathers.

Pluck the breast last. Do not try to pluck too many feathers at one time, and take care not to tear the skin.

After plucking, get rid of remaining down and hairs by singeing. Use a lighted taper, or pour a little methylated spirit into a dish, set alight and turn the bird over the flame. Be careful not to scorch the skin.

Wipe the bird thoroughly with a clean cloth. If any long hairs or quills still need to be removed, you can pluck them out with a pair of tweezers.

Drawing

Cut off the head, leaving about 8 cm of neck. Slit the skin on the underside of the neck and pull it towards the body. Cut the neck again close to the body. (Set the neck aside to use for giblet stock*.)

Put your hand, knuckles upwards, into the neck cavity. Remove the crop, windpipe and any fat present. Keeping your hand high under the breastbone, gently loosen and dislodge the entrails.

Turn the bird on its back. Make a slit with a sharp knife to enlarge the vent at the tail end. Loosen the fat and the skin, then, holding the bird firmly with one hand, put the other hand inside and gently draw out the entrails.

Clean the giblets and cut the bitter, green gall bladder away from the liver. Put the liver, heart and gizzard (the bird's second stomach) with the neck to make stock.

Wipe the bird thoroughly, inside and out, with a damp, clean cloth.

Break the legs at the lower joint, at the base of each drumstick, to expose the tendons. Use a skewer to pull out one tendon at a time, taking care not to tear the flesh. Bend the joint backwards, then twist and break the bone. Cut through the skin. Scald and scrub the feet and remove the scales. Put the feet with the giblets to make stock.

Stuffing

As a general rule, use 100-125 g, or 190-250 ml (¾-1 cup), stuffing for each 500 g of bird.

Most poultry and game birds are stuffed from the crop (neck) cavity. Do not fill too tightly: the stuffing needs room to expand. Duck and goose are commonly stuffed from the body (tail) end. Turkey traditionally has two stuffings: a bread-and-herb one spooned into the neck, and sausage meat filling for the body.

Trussing

Place the bird, breast down, on a table or chopping block. Close the neck cavity by folding the loose skin over the back. Fold back the wings, and hold the skin in place with a poultry skewer or with a trussing needle and fine string.

Turn the bird over. Make a horizontal slit in the skin above the tail vent, and push the parson's nose (tail) through it.

Draw the thighs close to the body and cross the legs over the tail end. Loop the string around the legs and parson's nose, and tie securely.

Boning

See Boning chicken* in the recipe section.

Jointing

Pull the bird's leg away from the body and, using a sharp knife, slice down to the thigh joint. Break at the joint and cut away the whole leg. Repeat with the other leg.

Slice through the outer breast meat towards the wing joint. Sever the wing from the body. Fold the breast meat over the wing joint. Repeat with the other wing.

There is a natural division in the rib cage. Slice along it to separate the breast from the lower carcass.

Cut the breast meat into serving portions. If jointing a large bird, separate the drumstick (the lower leg joint) from the thigh.

Use what is left of the carcass to make poultry stock*.

Larding

Larding is a method of adding fat to poultry, game and meat which has no fat and would be dry when cooked. It is done by threading strips of fat (lardons) through the flesh.

To make lardons, take a piece of firm, fat bacon and place it, rind down, on a chopping block. Using a sharp knife, cut the bacon into lardons about 5 cm long and 5 mm wide. Put the lardons in a refrigerator for about 30 minutes to cool and become firm.

Place a lardon in the split end of a larding needle and draw it through the bird or meat, leaving roughly equal projecting ends. Arrange lardons roughly 2 cm apart. Insert them on either side of the breastbone and at right angles to it.

COOKING POULTRY

Poussin A chicken 3-4 weeks old weighing up to 575 g. Roast, spit-roast or grill. If roasting, place a nut of butter inside the bird. If spit-roasting, first brush all over with melted fat or sunflower oil.

Roasting chicken or broiler The most widely sold bird, 6-8 weeks old, weighing on average 1,5 kg. Roast, spit-roast, grill or fry.

Boiling fowl Usually 12 months old or more. It can weigh up to 3,2 kg and is well flavoured and meaty, but tougher than a roasting bird. Boil, casserole or steam it – or use it to make soup. A pressure cooker speeds up cooking.

Turkey Choose a turkey of medium size (4,5-5,5 kg). The best choice is a hen bird 6-8 months old. Turkey is usually dry, so bard it (lay bacon rashers across the top) or lard* it and cover with aluminium foil or grease-proof paper for most of the cooking time.

Duck Oven-ready ducks on sale usually weigh 1,75-2,75 kg. The proportion of meat to bone is less generous than in chicken – a 1,75 kg duck will serve no more than four people.

A duck is fatty: prick the skin before cooking in order to allow some of the fat to escape.

Goose A fresh bird, at its best from May to August, will have yellow, soft, pliable feet. Roast or braise. Goose can be bought all the year round, but it is sensible to order well in advance of requirements. The average mass is 2,75-5,5 kg, but the proportion of meat per kilogram is less than for chicken.

Testing whether poultry is cooked

Never serve poultry undercooked. To see if a roasted bird is ready, push a skewer into the thickest part of the thigh. If clear juices run out, the bird is ready; if the juices are pink, it needs longer cooking.

A bird which is being boiled or casseroled will be ready when a skewer penetrates the thigh easily.

Carving poultry

First, cut off both legs. Hold the leg in position with a fork while you use a sharp knife to sever the thigh joint. Remove both wings. Carve the meat from the breast downwards, in thin or thick slices as you prefer.

GAME BIRDS

Game birds are generally available only to the families and friends of hunters, but are sometimes to be found in butchers and speciality shops.

Specialist farming with game birds, such as guinea fowl, pheasant, partridge and quail, has met with little success in South Africa.

The season for guinea fowl, pheasant and partridge is from May to August; the quail season varies from one area to another; pigeon are in season throughout the year but are in prime condition from April to June; the season for wild duck is May.

Choosing and preparing game birds

Look for smooth, pliant legs, with rounded or short spurs on the male.

If unplucked, turn the feathers back to see if the breast is plump and firm.

The plumage of a young bird will not be as bright as that of an older bird.

Be careful with a bird that shows signs of having been badly shot (its skin will be 'peppered' with shot marks). Some parts will be decomposing before the rest is tender.

Hanging

Hang by the neck, unplucked and undrawn, in an airy, cool larder or pantry. Do not hang two or three together: there should be a free circulation of air around each bird.

If flies are a nuisance, dredge the birds with pepper or enclose in a loose muslin bag.

Small birds should be hung for 24 hours, and large ones for 3-4 days. But hanging time depends on age, condition, and the weather. If the weather is warm and humid, the bird will decompose faster.

Plucking and drawing

Follow the instructions for plucking and drawing poultry.

Roast game birds are often served with the feet still on. If you decide to serve a bird like this, scald the feet in boiling water, after the bird has been plucked, and scrub clean.

COOKING

Young birds are best roasted. Lay bacon rashers across the breast to keep the flesh moist. If you have an older, tougher bird, braise or casserole it.

In general, small birds such as quail and pigeon provide a meal for one person. After roasting they are often served on a slice of crustless fried bread or hot buttered toast.

If you do not make a stuffing when roasting, you can put one or two small pieces of butter in the body, or a few pieces of juicy steak, a peeled, cored apple or a whole, peeled* onion to give moisture.

About 10 minutes before a roast bird is served, remove the strips of bacon covering the breast. Baste well with butter and pan juices, dredge with seasoned flour, baste again and return to the oven. This gives a good, golden-brown, crispy finish.

To give a distinctive flavour to game birds and counteract any fattiness, flame them with brandy when almost cooked. Heat 15-30 ml (1-2 tablespoons) in a ladle, light it and pour over the bird.

A GENERAL GUIDE TO ROASTING POULTRY AND GAME BIRDS

Type of bird	Mass	Time	Servings
Chicken	500 g-3,5 kg	30 minutes at 220°C + 10 minutes per 500 g at 180°C	1 kg serves 4 people
Duck	1,5-3 kg	30 minutes at 220°C + 15 minutes per 500 g at 180°C	2 kg serves 4 people
Goose	2,5-4,5 kg	45 minutes at 220°C + 15 minutes per 500 g at 160°C	4,5 kg serves 6-8 people
Guinea fowl	500 g-2 kg	20 minutes per 500 g at 220°C	1 kg serves 4 people
Turkey	2,5-8 kg	50 minutes at 220°C + 12 minutes per 500 g at 180°C	4 kg serves 8-10 people
Partridge		30-45 minutes at 190°C	1 young bird serves 1 person
Pheasant (hen)		45 minutes-1 hour at 190°C	1 bird serves 2 people
Pheasant (cock)		1-1½ hours at 190°C	1 bird serves 3-4 people
Quail, pigeon and poussin		20 minutes per 500 g at 220°C	1 bird serves 1 person

For stuffed poultry and game, allow an extra 15-20 minutes for birds of up to 1,7 kg; 30-45 minutes for 1,8-4,5 kg birds.

These are general guidelines only: see individual recipes for specific cooking times.

Egged, Breaded and Roasted Chicken

THE NOTION of dredging spit-roast meat with fine white breadcrumbs or oatmeal to prevent it drying out in the heat of the fire probably goes back to the early days, when thrifty housewives used to gather up and store crumbs for a number of purposes.

This recipe is a delicious method of sealing in all the succulence and flavour of a roasting chicken.

PREPARATION TIME: 30 MINUTES WITHOUT STUFFING; 50 MINUTES WITH STUFFING
COOKING TIME: ABOUT 1½ HOURS WITHOUT STUFFING; ABOUT 2 HOURS WITH STUFFING
PRE-HEAT OVEN TO 200°C

INGREDIENTS FOR SIX
1 roasting chicken, about 1,5 kg
Herb stuffing* (optional)
125 g butter
180 g fresh white breadcrumbs
Salt and pepper
1 egg, separated
Finely grated rind of 1 lemon
2 ml (½ teaspoon) ground cinnamon
15 ml (1 tablespoon) mixed and chopped tarragon, parsley (and lemon thyme, if available)

Wipe the chicken clean and remove the giblets. If using a stuffing, fill the bird loosely from the neck cavity. Secure with a skewer, or truss* the chicken.

Rub 30 ml (2 tablespoons) of the butter over the breast and legs of the chicken, put it in a roasting pan and cook in the centre of the pre-heated oven for 35 minutes (allow an extra 30-45 minutes if the bird has been stuffed).

Meanwhile, gently melt the rest of the butter. Season half the breadcrumbs with salt and pepper, and stir in the yolk from the separated egg.

Remove the bird from the oven and spoon about half of the melted butter over it, then sprinkle on the egged breadcrumbs, pressing them down slightly.

Put the chicken back in the oven to cook for another 20 minutes.

Meanwhile, add the grated lemon rind, cinnamon and herbs to the remaining crumbs, season and mix well together. Whisk the egg white lightly and fold it gently into the breadcrumb mixture (using a metal spoon).

Remove the chicken from the oven, and spread the second mixture of breadcrumbs over the first. Dribble the remaining butter over the top. Baste, but take care not to dislodge the crust.

Cook for a further 30 minutes.

Roast Stuffed Chicken

ROAST CHICKEN has long met with universal approval. In South Africa, roast chicken was once a Sunday lunch time treat – until the cost of this meat plunged with the advent of battery farming. One of the big advantages of a roast chicken is that any left-overs can be eaten cold during the following few days or used in a hot pie or fricassee.

PREPARATION TIME: 30-40 MINUTES
COOKING TIME: 1½ HOURS
PRE-HEAT OVEN TO 200°C

INGREDIENTS FOR SIX
1 large roasting chicken (1,5-2 kg)
30 ml (2 tablespoons) butter or chicken dripping

For the stuffing:
4 slices stale bread with crusts removed, or 100-125 g fresh breadcrumbs
150 ml milk or chicken stock*
Chicken liver
15 ml (1 tablespoon) fresh parsley, thyme and chives, mixed and chopped, or 7 ml (1½ teaspoons) dried mixed herbs
Grated rind and juice of 1 lemon
1 small onion, chopped*
15 ml (1 tablespoon) shredded chicken fat, or 30 g butter
15 ml (1 tablespoon) ground almonds
Salt and pepper

For the gravy:
275-300 ml chicken stock*, or cider
10 ml (2 teaspoons) cornflour (optional)

Wipe the chicken, remove the giblets and set aside the liver. To make the stuffing, soak the bread in the milk. If you are using breadcrumbs, add the milk or stock gradually (do not oversaturate). Leave for 20 minutes or until all the moisture has been fully absorbed.

Add the chopped chicken liver, herbs, lemon rind and juice, onion, chicken fat or butter and ground almonds. Mix together well and then season with salt and pepper to taste.

Spoon the stuffing into the neck cavity of the chicken until the breast is plump, but be careful not to pack too tightly; the stuffing will swell a little during the cooking. Secure with a skewer or with a trussing needle and string.

Use the remainder of the stuffing to fill the body of the bird from the tail end, or shape into small stuffing-balls (to be added to the pan juices for the last 30 minutes of cooking).

Lightly grease a roasting tin. Rub the breast and legs of the chicken with the butter or dripping and sprinkle with salt and pepper. Put in the roasting tin and cover loosely with grease-proof paper or aluminium foil.

Roast in the centre of pre-heated oven for 1 hour. Then reduce the oven temperature to 180°C, remove the grease-proof paper or foil, baste well and cook for a further 30 minutes (or until golden-brown on top). Keep warm.

To make the gravy, pour off the fat from the roasting pan. Add the strained chicken stock or cider. Stir well and boil rapidly on top of the stove for a few minutes. Season to taste. To make a thicker gravy, add the cornflour to the cold stock and stir as you bring it to the boil.

EGGED, BREADED AND ROASTED CHICKEN *Sealed-in succulence and flavour.*

Roast Baby Chickens with Rice and Raisin Stuffing

THIS RECIPE is for really small chickens (about 250-300 g), serving one person each. Cooking in stock makes the flesh delightfully moist and succulent (even when cooking a tiny bird).

The skin is crisped only during the last minutes of cooking. The aromatic herbed rice stuffing makes a delicious accompaniment, the raisins adding a slight sweetness which blends well with the tarragon.

PREPARATION TIME: 1 HOUR
COOKING TIME: 1 HOUR
PRE-HEAT OVEN TO 180°C

INGREDIENTS FOR SIX
6 baby chickens (about 250-300 g each)
Salt and freshly ground black pepper
250 ml (1 cup) chicken stock*
100 ml white wine
30 ml (2 tablespoons) lemon juice
10 ml (2 teaspoons) dried tarragon
45 ml (3 tablespoons) butter

For the stuffing:
45 ml (3 tablespoons) butter
1 onion, finely chopped*
125 g rice
500 ml (2 cups) chicken stock*
45 ml (3 tablespoons) seedless raisins
30 ml (2 tablespoons) finely chopped parsley
5 ml (1 teaspoon) dried tarragon
30 ml (2 tablespoons) lemon juice
30 ml (2 tablespoons) melted butter

For the gravy:
25 ml (5 teaspoons) flour
500 ml (2 cups) chicken* or vegetable stock* or water

ROAST BABY CHICKENS WITH RICE AND RAISIN STUFFING *Topped with lemon and parsley, this makes an attractive dish.*

Remove the chicken giblets (retain for use in the stock) and wipe the chickens inside and out with a damp cloth. Season the insides lightly with salt and pepper.

To make the stuffing, melt the butter in a saucepan and sauté the onion on a low heat until soft. Add the rice and stir with the butter until it turns golden, then add the stock. Cook until the rice is done (but still firm in the centre). Drain if necessary and mix the rice with the raisins, parsley, tarragon and lemon juice. Season to taste and add the melted butter.

Stuff the chickens lightly and truss* them. Place in a roasting pan which is large enough to contain the chickens neatly, but not too closely. Pour over the stock, wine and lemon juice, add a sprinkle of tarragon and dot the chickens with butter. Cover loosely with wax paper, tucking it in at the sides to contain the moisture.

Roast the chickens, basting frequently, for 30-45 minutes – until the juice from the thigh runs clear (the birds will have browned lightly through the paper). Now remove the paper and turn the heat up to 220°C. Quickly complete browning the chickens, basting with the pan juices, which should have reduced considerably.

When they are nicely browned, transfer them carefully to a heated serving platter. To make the gravy, stir the flour into the pan juices to make a smooth paste. Stir in the hot stock or water, seasoning to taste. Serve the gravy separately in a heated sauceboat.

SERVING SUGGESTIONS Arrange the chickens on a large platter and garnish with lemon and fresh parsley. Green beans, cooked whole and then mixed with sautéed mushrooms, spring onions and round 'game' chips* make a good accompaniment to this dish.

Any excess stuffing can be used as a bed on which to serve the chickens.

VARIATION Sprinkle the insides with seasoning and tarragon, adding a nut of butter and a quarter of lemon. Roast in the way described in the original recipe and serve with a spoonful of the reduced pan juices poured over the chickens just before serving. Serve with baked potatoes* and a sour cream dressing*, and a substantial salad containing mushrooms, lettuce, tomatoes and cucumbers doused with a good, garlicky vinaigrette*.

Boning a Chicken

To bone a chicken effectively, you need a short, flexible knife. Keep it as close to the bone as possible, scraping and easing the flesh away rather than cutting. If you intend roasting the boned chicken, leave the wings intact to give shape to the bird. For a chicken roll or galantine, however, cut off the wing tips and middle section, and remove the largest wing bone at the same time as the leg bone.

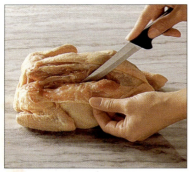
Hold the bird breast side down and slit through the skin along the backbone, scraping and easing the flesh away on either side and gradually exposing the rib cage.

When you get to the wings and legs, cut through the tendons close to the carcass at the joints, leaving the wings and legs attached to the skin (not the carcass).

Work round the bird, taking care not to puncture the skin – especially at the breastbone, which is close to the surface.

To bone the legs work from the thicker end of the joint and ease out the bones, scraping off the flesh as you pull carefully.

Spread the boned chicken on the work surface, skin side down, and lay stuffing down the middle.

Sew up the chicken along the back so as to enclose the stuffing completely. The final step is to truss* the bird.

Stuffed Boned Chicken

MANY BONED DISHES have a long history, some dating from the days when help in the kitchen was cheap and cooks had more time to spend on complicated preparation.

Stuffed boned chicken is worth mastering. It not only gives a neatly shaped piece of meat that cooks evenly and is more moist than usual, but is also easier to carve and a wonderful way of impressing guests.

PREPARATION TIME: 30 MINUTES
COOKING TIME: 1½ HOURS
PRE-HEAT OVEN TO 190°C

INGREDIENTS FOR SIX
1 chicken (1,5-2 kg), boned*
Sunflower oil
5 ml (1 teaspoon) butter
1 small onion, peeled and finely chopped*
1 carrot, finely chopped
1 bay leaf
400 ml chicken stock*, made from the bones
Salt and pepper

For the stuffing:
15 ml (1 tablespoon) butter
1 small onion, peeled and finely chopped*
250 g pork sausage meat
30 ml (2 tablespoons) fresh white breadcrumbs
1 small apple, peeled and chopped
5 ml (1 teaspoon) fresh sage, chopped
1 large egg
Salt and freshly ground black pepper

To make the stuffing, melt the butter and fry the onion in it until soft. Mix with the remaining stuffing ingredients and season well. Spread the boned chicken on to a work surface (skin side down) and lay the stuffing down the middle.

Bring up the sides to enclose it and sew or tie them together with cotton or fine string to make a neat parcel. Heat a little oil in a large casserole, and add butter: when it begins to foam, put in the chicken and brown it. Remove the bird and reduce the heat.

Add the onion and carrot, return the chicken to the casserole and add the bay leaf, stock and seasoning. Cover and bake at 190°C for 1½ hours. Transfer the chicken to a serving plate and then remove the string or cotton.

To make the sauce, skim the fat from the cooking juices and liquidize or sieve the vegetables and remaining liquid. Return to a clean saucepan and boil rapidly until the mixture thickens. Serve with the chicken.

SERVING SUGGESTION Garnish the dish with watercress. Try serving the chicken cold (sliced), together with a tossed green salad*.

VARIATIONS For a thinner, more delicate sauce, strain the cooking juices into a clean saucepan and discard the vegetables. Reduce the sauce to a syrup and enrich it with cream.

Beef sausage meat could be used as an alternative to pork.

Wholewheat breadcrumbs are a tasty variation to white breadcrumbs.

Pot-Roasted Chicken

A POT-ROASTED CHICKEN, cooked in a heavy black iron pot, has long been traditional Sunday fare on many South African farms.

PREPARATION TIME: 15 MINUTES
COOKING TIME: 2 HOURS

INGREDIENTS FOR SIX
1 chicken (1,5-2 kg)
Salt and white pepper
2 cloves
5-10 ml (1-2 teaspoons) flour
30 ml (2 tablespoons) sunflower oil
15 ml (1 tablespoon) butter
2 small onions, peeled*
500 ml (2 cups) boiling water
125 ml (½ cup) sweet wine, port or brown sherry
Beurre manié* (optional)

Cut away all surplus fat from the chicken, carefully cut out the oil gland on top of the 'parson's nose', and discard. The gizzard, heart and neck (which has been pulled out of its skin) can be cooked with a little seasoned water, and the strained liquid later added to the pot gravy. Wash and dry the chicken (inside and out). Lightly rub the inside of the carcass with salt and pepper and insert cloves. Truss* the chicken, making sure that no small feather pins or fluff remains.

The skin of the neck is folded under when trussing, and browns beautifully. Rub the bird all over with a mixture of 2 ml (½ teaspoon) salt, 1 ml (¼ teaspoon) pepper and the flour.

Mix the oil and butter, and heat in a pot to just under smoking point. Brown the whole onions lightly and remove from the pot (they are later chopped finely and added to the gravy).

Place the chicken in the open pot and brown the breast, sides and back. Turn it breast side up, add one quarter of the boiling water, bring to the boil and simmer, uncovered, for 30 minutes.

Turn the bird to cook each side, adding a little more boiling water if necessary. Finally, turn it breast side down and brown further in the gravy. Test with a skewer, add the wine, turn up the heat and spoon over the gravy until the surface has developed a slight glaze.

Remove from the pot and keep warm. Add the onions, the strained liquid from the gizzard, heart and neck, and a little *beurre manié* (if used) to the gravy. Simmer with the lid on for a few minutes: this will dislodge the tasty deposits from the sides of the pot. Serve separately in a heated gravy boat.

SERVING SUGGESTION Serve with white or yellow rice* and a mixed green salad*.

VARIATION Add chopped mushrooms to the gravy.

CHICKEN FRICASSEE WITH SHERRY

FRICASSEE IS AN OLD French word for a stew served with white sauce. The secret of a good fricassee is to cook the chicken slowly at a low temperature, to produce a succulent and tender dish. The ideal bird to use in this recipe would be an older boiling fowl – if you can get one.

PREPARATION TIME: 30 MINUTES
COOKING TIME: 1½ HOURS

INGREDIENTS FOR SIX
1 whole chicken, (2 kg)
750 ml (3 cups) water
250 ml (1 cup) white wine (or water)
1 carrot, scraped and sliced
1 onion, peeled* and studded with 4 cloves
1 bay leaf
Salt and freshly ground black pepper

For the sauce:
45 ml (3 tablespoons) butter
30 ml (2 tablespoons) flour
1 ml (¼ teaspoon) cayenne pepper
5 ml (1 teaspoon) sugar
125 ml (½ cup) medium sherry
250 ml (1 cup) cooked peas
5 medium-sized carrots, scraped, sliced and cooked
4 sticks celery, sliced and cooked

Place the chicken in a large pot or pressure cooker, add the water, wine, carrot, onion, bay leaf and salt and pepper. Bring to the boil, then turn down the heat and simmer gently (covered) until the meat is tender.

Remove the chicken from the stock and cut it into serving-sized pieces, removing the skin, breastbones and backbones and wing tips. Arrange the chicken pieces in a large, fairly deep, heated casserole dish and moisten it lightly with a few spoons of stock. Cover it tightly and keep warm.

Return the skin and bones to the stockpot and reduce the stock down to about half the original quantity.

Melt the butter in a saucepan and stir in the flour to make a smooth paste. Strain the stock and add it slowly (stirring constantly) to form a thickish sauce, leaving the sauce to bubble gently for a minute or so. Add the cayenne pepper, sugar, sherry and cooked vegetables and heat through. Pour the sauce over the chicken pieces and serve immediately.

SERVING SUGGESTION Buttered brown rice and a good green salad* make ideal companions for this simple, hearty dish.

VARIATION Try adding cream (about 75 ml) to the sauce, and instead of butter and flour, use 2 egg yolks to thicken the sauce.

DEVILLED CHICKEN *for those with a hankering for spicy foods.*

DEVILLED CHICKEN

DR KITCHINER, in his *Cook's Oracle* (1817), introduces Devil Sauces with fine Regency aplomb: 'Every man must have experienced that when he has got deep into his third bottle . . . his stomach is seized with a certain craving which seems to demand a stimulant. The provocatives used on such an occasion an ungrateful world has combined to term devils.'

Throughout the 19th century, devilling – flavouring to give a hot, sharp taste – was a popular and lively means of returning the remains of the previous day's joint or fowl to the table.

PREPARATION TIME: 20 MINUTES
COOKING TIME: 10-15 MINUTES

INGREDIENTS FOR FOUR
6-8 meaty poultry joints, such as chicken or turkey, cooked or freshly part-cooked

For the sauce:
100 g butter
15 ml (1 tablespoon) dry mustard
30 ml (2 tablespoons) stale breadcrumbs
15 ml (1 tablespoon) Worcestershire sauce
15 ml (1 tablespoon) mango atjar* or fruit chutney
Salt and cayenne pepper

Place the chicken joints in a grill pan lined with a sheet of aluminium foil and lightly greased with butter or sunflower oil.

To make the sauce, put the butter, mustard, breadcrumbs, Worcestershire sauce and chutney in a bowl and blend together with a fork or the back of a spoon. Break up any pieces of fruit or vegetable in the chutney and then season with salt and cayenne pepper.

Spread the sauce over the chicken joints and grill gently so that the meat heats through, or completes cooking as the sauce browns. Serve on warmed plates.

SERVING SUGGESTION Serve it with a variety of salads such as potato*, coleslaw* or a watercress salad*.

Add any sauce left to a little giblet or game basic stock*. Heat thoroughly and pour it around the devilled joints.

~ Add Zest with Spices and Seasonings ~

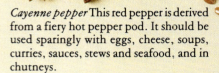

Spices have been prized in various parts of the world for thousands of years – for their qualities as preservatives as well as for their appetising flavour.

South Africa's position on the old spice route between Europe and the East gave local cooks access to spices from the earliest times of our colonial history. A taste for spices was introduced to the country mostly by slaves and freemen from the East, although the Dutch and English had already had contact with many spices through their colonial acquisitions.

Today, spices are an integral part of the South African cooking scene, reflected in the wide popularity of Indian and Malay dishes, and the presence of spices and seasonings in so much of what we eat.

Spices in Cooking

Spices consist mainly of the fruits, seeds, bark or roots of a wide variety of plants. These are used fresh or dried for their sharp or fragrant flavours. They are best bought in small quantities and preferably whole, as they tend to lose their flavour once they are ground or powdered. Spices should be stored in small, airtight containers in a cool, dry place.

The following is a list of the most commonly used spices and seasonings. Some spices are available only through speciality shops, where they are often sold under Indian or Malay names. Alternative names are provided in brackets after the common English names.

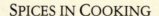

Allspice (pimento) The small, unripe berries of the tropical allspice or pimento tree are sun-dried and used in many spice mixtures. Allspice derives its name from its versatile nature and taste, which is like a mixture of cinnamon, cloves and nutmeg. It is used in baking and pickling, and to flavour sauces, fish, meat, vegetables and desserts.

Aniseed (anise) The liquorice-flavoured seed of the anise plant (not to be confused with star anise) is used mostly in cakes, biscuits and confectionery. It is also used to flavour liqueurs.

Asafoetida (hing) This spice is obtained from the milky sap of a type of fennel. The sap dries to a resin, which is then powdered for use in Indian dishes, especially vegetables, dhal and fish preparations. It is best to buy the spice in powdered form, since the resin is very hard.

Caraway seeds The seed-like fruits of a plant similar to parsley are used to flavour bread, cakes, cheeses, pork dishes and stews. They are also used to flavour liqueurs.

Cardamom (caramong, caramonk, elaichi, illaichi) The straw-coloured or pale green cardamom pod, which contains several tiny black seeds, is the most expensive spice in the world after saffron. The pungent flavour is particularly suitable for curries, and the spice is also used to flavour soups, eggs, meat, stewed fruit and such traditional Malay drinks as boeboer and Gedat milk.

Cassia This reddish-brown bark of a type of cassia tree is often confused with cinnamon, which it closely resembles. Its pungently sweet taste is suitable for curries, meat and rice dishes.

Cayenne pepper This red pepper is derived from a fiery hot pepper pod. It should be used sparingly with eggs, cheese, soups, curries, sauces, stews and seafood, and in chutneys.

Celery seeds The tiny seeds of the annual celery plant have a bitter flavour. They are used in soups, stews, vegetables or curries. The seeds are also crushed and added to salt to make celery salt.

Chilli powder Made from ground, dried chillies, it can be as mild or hot as the chillies from which it is made, and is one of the basic ingredients of curry.

Cinnamon (dalchini) A pungent, sweet spice sold in sticks of curled bark from the cinnamon tree or in ground form. It is a popular flavouring for sugar, cakes, biscuits, soups, meat, stewed fruit, vegetables, sauces, drinks, relishes, chutneys and rice.

Cloves The dried, unopened flower buds of a tropical tree, cloves have a pungent, aromatic flavour. The oil is used for relieving toothache, and the spice (whole or ground) is used to flavour apples, and in bread sauce, ham, pickles and winter punches.

Coriander (dhania, dhunia) This hardy annual, cultivated widely for both its leaves and aromatic seeds, is related to the carrot. The leaves and seeds taste totally different, but both are very popular curry ingredients. The seeds are also useful for flavouring soups, eggs, fish, meat, marinades, vegetables, pickles and chutneys, and are a basic ingredient in many curry pastes and powders.

Cumin (gira, jeera, zeera) The small, aromatic, seed-like fruit of an Indian and North African plant, this spice is available whole or ground, and tastes and looks like caraway. It is used in Mexican and Indian dishes, and also as a flavouring for meat, poultry, rice, eggs, cheese and pickles.

Curry leaves The leaves of the curry bush (a relative of the lemon tree) give a pungent flavour to various Indian dishes. They are available dried from speciality spice shops.

Dill seeds The seed-like fruits of the dill plant, with their mild aniseed flavour, are used particularly for pickling cucumbers. The fresh or dried leaves of the plant are also used as a herb. Use the spice to flavour soups, sauces and salad dressings.

Fennel seeds (berishap, barishap, sonf) These seeds, with their slight aniseed taste, are used in Malay and Indian curries, in fish or egg dishes, and in liver, pork or lamb stews. The seeds can also be used to stud bread or rolls, or be added to spice beets, cabbage, lentils, rice or squash.

Fenugreek (methi, methre) This is the pod of an annual, heavily scented legume. The seed is mixed with flour for bread, and used in curry powder. Fenugreek is also used to make vanilla essence.

Ginger (adrak) The rhizome or rootstock of a tropical plant, ginger is frequently used fresh (peeled) in curried and spiced dishes. It is also preserved in syrup or crystallised, or dried and sold whole or ground. It is prevalent in many Oriental dishes, and in cakes, biscuits, puddings, preserves and pickles.

Horseradish The thick, pungent, white root of this plant is ground or grated and made into a popular relish for serving with roast beef.

Mace see Nutmeg.

Mustard The whole seeds, called rai in India, are used in pickles, soused herring and salted meat. They can also be sprouted* for use in salads and sandwiches. Prepared mustards add zest to a large range of dishes (which are often referred to as 'devilled'). American mustard is mild and yellowish; French mustards are stronger and sometimes have whole seeds and other spices added; and English mustard is very hot.

Naartjie peel This traditional flavouring in Malay food is made by drying the peel of naartjies in the oven or sun for later use (whole or ground). It is used mostly in sweet dishes such as cakes and puddings, but also in meat and vegetable dishes.

Nutmeg and mace Mace is the amber, fibrous network surrounding the brown nutmeg, the fruit of a tropical tree. Both have a sweet, delicate taste, but mace is traditionally used for savoury food and nutmeg for sweet.

Paprika This spice, which is ground into a bright red powder, comes from the same family as cayenne. Its flavour is, however, sweet and mild, while cayenne is hot. Paprika is used to flavour goulashes, soups, white sauces, eggs, cheese, rice, chicken, meat and fish dishes.

Pepper The dried berries from a tropical vine provide the most widely used seasonings of all. When the berries are picked just before they are ripe, we get black pepper, which is aromatic. If they are left to ripen and then dried, we get white pepper, which has a hotter flavour. Both retain their flavour better if stored whole.

Poppy seeds The small grey seeds of one of the poppy types are used in baking breads and cakes.

Saffron (zaafraan) This spice, made from the stigmas of the purple-flowering saffron crocus, takes its name from the Arabic for yellow (za'faran). It is the most expensive spice in the world, and is used to colour and flavour soups, cakes and savoury rice dishes. Because of the price, many people substitute turmeric in recipes calling for saffron.

Salt This white crystalline powder, consisting mostly of sodium chloride, is the most prevalent seasoning in both savoury and sweet dishes. It is also used extensively for preserving and pickling in brine. Flavoured salts, such as garlic salt and celery salt, are also available commercially.

Sesame seeds These seeds of a tropical plant are a popular source of oil in some parts of the world. The seeds themselves are used in cakes, biscuits, sweets and bread.

Tamarind (imli) The acid fruit of the tropical tamarind tree is sold dried for use particularly in Indian and Malay cooking. It is soaked in boiling water, then strained to produce tamarind water.

Turmeric (haldi) A dried, ground root of a plant of the ginger family, it is aromatic and mild. The bright yellow powder is inexpensive and frequently used in place of saffron for this reason. It should be used sparingly, however, as it has a bitter taste. Turmeric is used to flavour and colour curries, pickles, sauces and rice, and is an ingredient in curry powders.

Vanilla The pod or bean of a tropical climbing orchid, it is used in confectionery, baked goods and ice cream. Vanilla essence is more commonly used in the kitchen.

SPICE MIXTURES

Curry powder The word curry comes from the Tamil *kari*, meaning sauce or relish. While commercial curry powders have introduced the joys of Oriental spiced food to many Western palates, they are no substitute for mixing your own fresh spices for individual dishes. It is best to crush the spice seeds yourself, as whole spices retain their flavour better. Speciality spice shops will also sell you freshly blended spices, sometimes known as masala, for curries.

The spices most often used in curry powders are cayenne pepper, coriander, cumin, fenugreek, turmeric, cinnamon, cloves, fennel, ginger, mace, mustard and pepper.

Garam masala is a collective term for a hot spice mixture containing black pepper, cardamom, cloves, cumin, cinnamon, nutmeg and bay leaves.

Five spice powder This Chinese spice mixture can be bought ready mixed for use in meat and poultry dishes. It contains star anise, anise pepper (Szechuan peppercorns), fennel, cloves and cinnamon (or cassia). The mixture is very pungent and should be used sparingly.

Mixed spice A commercial blend of spices is sold under this name for use in breads, cakes, puddings and biscuits.

Peri-peri This flavouring is made of a mixture of some of the hot varieties of chilli peppers, sometimes with origanum added. Available in a powder or sauce, it is used to flavour seafood, poultry and meat.

Pickling spices Most supermarkets sell a pickling spice mixture. You can also make up your own mixture – see Making spiced vinegar*.

CURRY LEAVES

BAY LEAVES

TURMERIC

SAFFRON

FRESH GREEN GINGER

FENNEL SEEDS

CINNAMON STICKS

VANILLA POD

SESAME SEEDS

FENUGREEK

ALLSPICE

CHICKEN CASSEROLE WITH 20 CLOVES OF GARLIC

THIS IS A DELICIOUS DISH, with a rich, creamy sauce and good flavour – just the thing for a winter dinner. Strangely enough, it does not have an excessively garlicky flavour, as the cloves of garlic are blanched before cooking.

PREPARATION TIME: 30 MINUTES
COOKING TIME: 1½ HOURS
PRE-HEAT OVEN TO 160°C

INGREDIENTS FOR SIX
8-12 chicken thighs
50g butter
50ml sunflower oil
300ml white wine
20 cloves garlic, peeled and blanched*
Salt and freshly ground black pepper
250ml (1 cup) cream

Melt the butter with the oil in an oven-proof, lidded casserole and brown the chicken pieces (two or three at a time) on both sides. When they are done, return all the chicken pieces to the casserole, add the wine and garlic, and then season lightly with salt and pepper.

Seal the casserole lid tightly with at least four layers of wax paper (folded under the lid) and bake at 160°C for about 1 hour, or until tender. Then pour over the cream and bake for another 30 minutes or so, (uncovered) until the sauce has reduced and thickened (you can also do this on top of the stove). Correct the seasoning and serve.

SERVING SUGGESTION The dish can be served in the casserole in which it was cooked, and needs little more than fluffy rice and snow peas cooked till they are still firm as accompaniment. Follow with an interesting and tasty salad of parsley sprigs with blanched almonds* and spring onions, drenched in vinaigrette*.

GREEK CHICKEN *offers a delectable combination of appetising flavours.*

GREEK CHICKEN

THIS DISH CONSISTS essentially of chicken flavoured with cinnamon and baked with black olives. Its taste is piquant and, to the converted, quite irresistible.

PREPARATION TIME: 15 MINUTES
COOKING TIME: 1 HOUR
PRE-HEAT OVEN TO 190°C

INGREDIENTS FOR SIX
6 large portions of chicken
2 cloves garlic, crushed
Salt and freshly ground black pepper
30ml (2 tablespoons) olive oil
6 cinnamon sticks
4 tomatoes, skinned* and sliced
150g black olives, stoned and halved
6 slices lemon
125ml (½ cup) dry white wine
60ml (¼ cup) orange juice

Arrange the chicken pieces side by side in a shallow oven-proof dish. Smear them all over with crushed garlic and then sprinkle with the salt, pepper and olive oil. Place the cinnamon sticks under and around the chicken.

Arrange slices of tomato and halved olives around the chicken pieces, with slices of lemon on top. Pour over the wine and orange juice, and cover with aluminium foil.

Put in the oven and bake at 190°C for about 1 hour, remove the cinnamon sticks, and serve.

SERVING SUGGESTION This chicken dish will taste very good served with either buttered noodles or rice and a simple traditional Greek salad consisting of lettuce, cucumber and feta cheese.

VARIATION Add chopped or crushed fresh ginger or a mixture of both in the place of cinnamon.

STIR-FRIED CHICKEN AND VEGETABLES

FRESHNESS IS A MOST IMPORTANT quality for vegetables in all Chinese cooking. Several vegetables (with varying textures) are usually combined – those with the firmest textures being placed in the pan first. Factors such as the way a vegetable is cut, its freshness, the size of the pan and the degree of heat all affect the cooking time. Small quantities of meat and poultry can be stretched by cooking with this method.

PREPARATION TIME: 45 MINUTES
COOKING TIME: 10 MINUTES

INGREDIENTS FOR FOUR
375g chicken meat, cubed
45ml (3 tablespoons) sunflower oil
2 teaspoons (10ml) grated fresh green ginger
1 clove garlic, crushed
2 onions, peeled* and cut into wedges, then separated
2 sticks celery, sliced diagonally into 1cm lengths
250g broccoli, stems sliced diagonally, heads separated into small florets
4-5 dried Chinese mushrooms, soaked in boiling water for 30 minutes, then squeezed dry and sliced, or 50g button mushrooms
125g young green beans, trimmed
6 spring onions, sliced diagonally into 1cm lengths
20ml (4 teaspoons) cornflour
250ml (1 cup) water
40ml dry sherry
20ml (4 teaspoons) soy sauce
10ml (2 teaspoons) instant chicken stock powder
1 small tin baby corn, drained

Heat the oil to a high heat in a wok or pan, add the ginger and garlic, then the cubed chicken, and stir-fry for 1 minute. Add the onions, celery and broccoli stalks, stir-fry for 1 minute, then add the mushrooms, beans and spring onions and stir-fry for about 1 minute before adding the broccoli florets.

Mix the cornflour with a few drops of the water, then add the rest of the water, sherry, soy sauce and chicken stock powder.

Pour the mixture into the pan and bring to the boil. Add the baby corn, simmer for 4 minutes and serve.

Serving Suggestion Serve on a bed of steamed rice* or noodles*.

Variations You may leave out any vegetables that are not available, or substitute others. Snow peas are very good in place of the beans.

You may also add sliced Chinese cabbage to the dish.

Instead of chicken, use shrimps or prawns, or use vegetables alone.

Paper Wrapped Chicken

This interesting dish is fairly simple to prepare. The rice paper wrapping fries to a light crisp coating, keeping the chicken filling moist and tasty with the familiar Chinese taste of ginger, garlic and spring onion. Make it a Western-style main course accompanied by a medley of stir-fried vegetables, or to start a Chinese meal – hot off the pan.

Preparation Time: 30 minutes
Marinating Time: 1 hour
Cooking Time: 15 minutes

Ingredients for Four (24 parcels)
500 g chicken breasts, filleted and skinned
5 ml (1 teaspoon) soy sauce
10 ml (2 teaspoons) oyster sauce
5 ml (1 teaspoon) sesame oil
15 ml (1 tablespoon) dry sherry
5 ml (1 teaspoon) sugar
1 ml (¼ teaspoon) salt
15 ml (1 tablespoon) finely chopped ginger
4 spring onions, finely chopped
1 clove garlic, finely chopped
12 sheets rice paper

Slice the chicken into thin strips. Marinate with the rest of the ingredients (except the rice paper) for an hour or longer.

Cut the sheets of rice paper in half to form squares, fill each square with about 15 ml (1 tablespoon) of the chicken mixture and wrap up to encase the filling. Deep fry the flat, square parcels in hot oil for a few minutes, or until golden-brown and crisp. Remove with a slotted spoon and drain well on paper towels. Serve immediately.

Chicken with Cashew Nuts

Sliced chicken breasts, pineapple chunks and other ingredients are cooked quickly in a wok and served immediately to provide a very tasty meal. This Oriental dish tastes good even when cold and re-heats very successfully.

Preparation Time: 10 minutes
Freezing Time: 30 minutes-1 hour
Cooking Time: 10 minutes

Ingredients for Six
6 chicken breasts
7 ml (1½ teaspoons) salt
Pepper
22 ml (1½ tablespoons) cornflour
1 tin (410 g) pineapple chunks
15 ml (1 tablespoon) sugar
15 ml (1 tablespoon) light soy sauce
15 ml (1 tablespoon) vinegar
30 ml (2 tablespoons) dry sherry
15 ml (1 tablespoon) Hoisin sauce
60 ml (¼ cup) sunflower oil
100 g unsalted cashew nuts, split into halves
1 clove garlic, crushed
5 ml (1 teaspoon) crushed fresh green ginger

Freeze the chicken breasts until they are firm enough to slice thinly. Combine the salt, a sprinkling of pepper and 15 ml (1 tablespoon) of the cornflour and then dredge the sliced chicken in the mixture. Drain the tinned pineapple chunks, reserving the juice.

Mix the remaining cornflour with the pineapple juice, sugar, soy sauce, vinegar, sherry and Hoisin sauce.

Heat half the sunflower oil in a wok or pan, then add the cashew nuts and stir-fry them until golden. Turn out into paper towels and reserve.

Heat the remaining oil in the same pan, add the garlic and ginger and stir-fry for half a minute. Add the chicken and stir-fry for 2 minutes. Remove the chicken from the wok and add the pineapple.

Turn the pineapple pieces over in the pan, add the sauce and cook until it thickens, then add the chicken and cashew nuts and stir-fry for 1 minute.

If you do not intend to serve immediately, do not stir-fry after adding the chicken and nuts. Allow to cool and then refrigerate. To re-heat, stir-fry very quickly in 15 ml (1 tablespoon) hot oil (just until it is heated through).

Serving Suggestions Spoon the mixture on to a warm oval platter and surround with deep-fried Chinese vermicelli or deep-fried egg noodles, or alternatively serve with steamed rice*.

Variation Substitute fried almonds for the cashew nuts.

Chicken with Cashew Nuts *is a quick and easy dish to prepare and can be eaten either hot or cold.*

POULTRY

CHICKEN KIEV

THIS IS A CLASSIC Ukranian speciality of boned chicken breasts rolled around a finger of butter, coated with crumbs and fried just long enough to cook the chicken without losing the butter inside until they are cut. Traditionally, chicken suprêmes (the whole of the white breast meat, including wing bone) should be used, but boned breasts are just as successful.

PREPARATION TIME: 45 MINUTES
CHILLING TIME: AT LEAST 3 HOURS
COOKING TIME: 30 MINUTES

INGREDIENTS FOR FOUR
4 large boned chicken breasts
Sunflower oil for deep-frying

For the herb butter:
100 g butter
Grated rind and juice of 1 lemon
15 ml (1 tablespoon) freshly chopped parsley
5 ml (1 teaspoon) chopped tarragon
5 ml (1 teaspoon) chopped chives
2 cloves garlic, very finely chopped (optional)
Salt and freshly ground black pepper

For the coating:
50 g flour, seasoned with salt and pepper
1 extra-large egg, beaten with 5 ml (1 teaspoon) sunflower oil and 5 ml (1 teaspoon) water
75 g dry white breadcrumbs

Trim any skin or gristle from the chicken breasts and place them 3-4 cm apart between two large sheets of grease-proof paper. Beat them with a meat pounder or wooden rolling pin until flat and large enough to hold a stick of butter about the diameter of your little finger (do not puncture the chicken meat).

To make the herb butter, blend the butter, lemon rind, juice, herbs and garlic (if used) with plenty of seasoning. Shape into a 6 cm-square cake on a sheet of grease-proof paper. Cover and chill or freeze until very firm, then cut into 4 long sticks.

Place one stick in the centre of each piece of flattened chicken (the inner surface) and roll the chicken up around it, tucking in the ends to make a neat, sausage-shaped package that completely seals in the butter. Roll the chicken packages in seasoned flour, brush or dip them in the beaten egg mixture, and roll them in crumbs – pressing them firmly on to the chicken.

Chill (uncovered) for at least 3 hours or overnight. You could also freeze them, but in this case you should allow them to thaw for about 6-7 hours in the refrigerator before cooking.

Heat the oil in a deep-fryer to 180°C (a cube of day-old bread should turn golden-brown in 1-1¼ minutes) and fry the chicken breasts, two at a time, until golden-brown (about 5 minutes). Drain on paper towels and keep hot in an oven (with the door ajar) for 5-10 minutes while frying the remaining chicken.

Arrange the pieces side by side on a serving dish, and serve immediately.

SERVING SUGGESTIONS Decorate with parsley sprigs and lemon wedges or watercress. New potatoes and baby marrows or asparagus make good accompaniments.

Baked potatoes* with sour cream, together with a salad, also go very well with this dish.

MALAY BRAISED CHICKEN

THE DISTINCT MALAY FLAVOUR of this simple chicken dish is provided by the addition of ginger, cardamom and other spices. Wherever possible, try to use fresh ingredients to ensure the best flavour.

PREPARATION TIME: 30-40 MINUTES
COOKING TIME: 1 HOUR

INGREDIENTS FOR FOUR TO SIX
1 chicken (about 1 kg), cut into small portions
150 ml sunflower oil
2 onions, finely chopped*
2 potatoes, peeled and diced*
4 cloves garlic, chopped
A 4 cm piece of fresh green ginger (pounded), or 1 ml (¼ teaspoon) ground ginger
2 ml (½ teaspoon) cumin seeds
4 cardamom seeds or 1 cardamom pod, bruised
1 green chilli, seeded and chopped
A pinch of ground cloves
45 ml (3 tablespoons) lemon juice
250 ml (1 cup) water

Wash the chicken portions. Heat the oil in a saucepan and sauté the onions until golden-brown, then remove the onions from the saucepan and reserve. Add the potatoes to the oil and brown slightly. Add the chicken portions and then brown on both sides.

Stir in the garlic, ginger and sautéed onions (when using ground ginger, it is advisable to mix it with the other spices). Mix the cumin seeds, cardamom, chilli and cloves; add to the juice and water, stir and add the mixture to the contents of the saucepan. Simmer slowly until the chicken pieces are attractively browned and properly cooked.

Remove the cardamom seeds or pod before serving.

SERVING SUGGESTION Serve with boiled rice* and a green salad*.

OVEN-FRIED CRUMBED CHICKEN

AN EASY WAY to prepare chicken pieces. They are nice to take on a picnic or include in a lunch box. Children particularly like drumsticks, which work very well with this recipe.

PREPARATION TIME: 15 MINUTES
CHILLING TIME: 30 MINUTES
COOKING TIME: 45 MINUTES
PRE-HEAT OVEN TO 180°C

INGREDIENTS FOR FOUR TO SIX
8 chicken pieces
125 ml (½ cup) mayonnaise*

CHICKEN KIEV *A deep-fried and delicious way of preparing poultry.*

10 ml (2 teaspoons) mild mustard
5 ml (1 teaspoon) Worcestershire sauce
1 clove garlic, crushed (optional)
75 ml (5 tablespoons) cornflake crumbs
2 ml (½ teaspoon) salt
1 ml (¼ teaspoon) pepper
30 ml (2 tablespoons) sunflower oil or melted butter

Wipe the pieces of chicken and set aside. Mix together the mayonnaise, mustard, Worcestershire sauce and garlic (if used). Coat the chicken pieces with this mixture, then dip into crumbs mixed with the seasoning, making sure that the pieces are well coated. Refrigerate for at least half an hour to allow the crumbs to set.

Arrange the chicken skin-side up in a baking tin lined with a sheet of oiled aluminium foil. Drizzle with the oil or butter and bake (uncovered) for 45 minutes without turning. Baste occasionally.

SERVING SUGGESTIONS Serve the chicken Southern American style, with sweet corn fritters* and fried bananas.

Alternatively, you can serve with baked potatoes* and a crunchy coleslaw*.

CHICKEN STEW WITH ORANGE AND TOMATO

THE COMBINATION of orange and tomato, though it may sound illogical, is actually quite delicious. Sweet basil and caraway seeds add a very compatible piquancy to a dish which, although inexpensive, is stylish enough for a dinner party.

PREPARATION TIME: 20 MINUTES
COOKING TIME: 2 HOURS
INGREDIENTS FOR SIX

2 kg chicken thighs or 1 large chicken, cut into serving-sized portions
2 onions, peeled and sliced*
50 ml sunflower oil
3 cloves garlic, crushed
10 ml (2 teaspoons) sweet basil
1 tin (390-410 g) skinned tomatoes or 500 g fresh tomatoes, skinned*
30 ml (2 tablespoons) tomato paste
250 ml (1 cup) orange juice
Rind of 1 orange, grated
100 ml white wine

CHICKEN STEW WITH ORANGE AND TOMATO *A piquant and unusual dish.*

Salt and freshly ground black pepper
2 ml (½ teaspoon) caraway seeds
30 ml (2 tablespoons) cornflour mixed to a paste with water

For the garnish:
Chopped parsley
Parmesan cheese

Wipe the chicken pieces and set aside. In a heavy-based saucepan, brown the sliced onion in oil, remove with a slotted spoon, and brown the chicken pieces. Pour off the fat and return the chicken to the pot.

Add the onion, garlic, basil, tomatoes, tomato paste, orange juice, orange rind and wine. Cover and simmer on a low heat until tender (1½-2 hours). Season to taste and add the caraway seeds. Thicken the sauce with the cornflour paste, and bring to the boil once again.

SERVING SUGGESTIONS Serve the stew on a large, heated platter, surrounded by peeled new potatoes rolled in parsley butter* or herb butter*. Garnish with chopped parsley and Parmesan cheese.

This dish is also very good served with fettucine or vermicelli, in which case it is best to bone* the chicken pieces (before or after cooking).

Fresh greens, crisply and simply cooked, are also good with this rich, tasty dish. Baby marrows, green beans, spinach or cabbage are all compatible, as are small, young gem squashes (cooked and served whole).

VARIATIONS The aniseed flavour of caraway is not to everyone's taste, and can be omitted without detracting too much from the overall flavour.

Substitute chicken stock* or water for the wine (as you could in most casserole dishes). This is a good recipe to make with cheap frozen chickens, since the stew freezes well. It can also be made a few days ahead and refrigerated (it is best to thicken the stew on re-heating).

CHICKEN PERI-PERI

A SPICY DISH of Portuguese origin, this is probably among the best-known of the 'hot' chicken dishes. For those with sensitive tastebuds, simply reduce the chilli content.

PREPARATION TIME: 20 MINUTES
MARINATING TIME: 2 HOURS
COOKING TIME: 15 MINUTES

INGREDIENTS FOR FOUR
8 small portions chicken, or 1 chicken cut into 8 small portions
30 ml (2 tablespoons) coarsely crumbled dried hot chillies
3 large cloves garlic, crushed
5 ml (1 teaspoon) salt
250 ml (1 cup) sunflower oil

For the sauce:
70 g butter
60 ml (¼ cup) lemon juice

Wipe the chicken portions and set aside. Combine the chillies, garlic, salt and 125 ml (½ cup) of the oil in a liquidizer and blend thoroughly. Pour the mixture into a deep bowl and stir in the remaining oil (if you wish to make the sauce by hand, pound the chillies and garlic to a paste in a small bowl and stir in the oil and salt).

Add the chicken pieces to the chilli mixture and coat them evenly. Marinate at room temperature for about 2 hours, then place the chicken on a grill pan or baking sheet, and grill about 5 cm from the heat for about 7-8 minutes on each side (until cooked through).

Keep the chicken warm while making the sauce as follows: melt the butter gently, stir in the lemon juice, and pour the sauce over the chicken.

SERVING SUGGESTION A spicy dish such as this is best served with plain boiled rice*.

VARIATION Prawns or fish can be marinated in the same mixture and grilled for 2-3 minutes.

ACCOMPANIMENTS TO INDIAN DISHES

One of the most enjoyable aspects of eating Indian foods is the wide assortment of accompaniments that are traditionally used. Some are hot and spicy, while others serve to cool one's palate.

CHAPATI

PREPARATION TIME: 10 MINUTES
STANDING TIME: 30 MINUTES
COOKING TIME: 30 MINUTES

INGREDIENTS FOR 12 CHAPATI
250 g wholewheat flour
2 ml (½ teaspoon) salt
100 ml water

Mix the flour and salt in a bowl, then add the water to make a dough. Knead thoroughly until smooth and place in a bowl. Cover with a damp cloth and leave the dough for 30 minutes.
Meanwhile, heat a large, heavy frying pan over a medium heat. Cut the dough into 12 pieces, shape them into balls, and roll each one out very thinly, using plenty of flour. Put 2-3 chapati into the frying pan at a time and cook them until the edges start to curl, then turn and cook the other side. Wrap in a napkin and serve.

POPPADUMS

Buy the wafer-thin pancakes and fry in oil until crisp and golden (be careful not to burn them; the process takes only a few seconds). Drain and serve with curry.

KHAJOOR NI CHATNI

PREPARATION TIME: 20 MINUTES

INGREDIENTS TO YIELD 250 ML (1 CUP)
40 g tamarind (available at specialist Indian grocers)
80 ml (⅓ cup) water
12 dates, pitted
A 2,5 cm piece of fresh green ginger, scraped
1 small onion, peeled*
5 ml (1 teaspoon) ground cumin
5 ml (1 teaspoon) ground coriander
3 ml (¾ teaspoon) salt
3 ml (¾ teaspoon) chilli powder

Soak the tamarind in 80 ml (⅓ cup) water for 10 minutes. Remove the bits and strain, retaining the water. Blend the remaining ingredients in a liquidizer with the tamarind water to a smooth pulp.

DHANIA PHOODINI CHATNI

PREPARATION TIME: 20 MINUTES

INGREDIENTS TO YIELD 250 ML (1 CUP)
100 g (1 bunch) fresh coriander
125 ml (½ cup) fresh mint leaves
½ ripe tomato
10 ml (2 teaspoons) cumin seeds
7 ml (1½ teaspoons) salt
1-2 green chillies, cut into 2,5 cm pieces
4 cloves garlic, peeled
30 ml (2 tablespoons) lemon juice
15 ml (1 tablespoon) malt vinegar

Remove the coriander roots and wash several times. Wash the mint and drain, then cut the tomato into wedges. Place all the ingredients in a blender and reduce to a thick, smooth pulp. Transfer the chutney to a small bowl and serve.

CUCUMBER RAITA

PREPARATION TIME: 5-10 MINUTES
STANDING TIME: 1 HOUR
CHILLING TIME: 30 MINUTES

INGREDIENTS FOR FOUR TO SIX
1 English cucumber
15 ml (1 tablespoon) salt
1 clove garlic, peeled and crushed
150 ml natural yoghurt*
30 ml (2 tablespoons) freshly chopped mint
30 ml (2 tablespoons) lemon juice
A pinch of cayenne pepper

Peel the cucumber and slice it thinly. Arrange the slices on a flat dish and sprinkle them with salt, leaving them to stand for 1 hour to extract the moisture. Drain the cucumber and pat dry with a paper towel.
Stir the crushed garlic into the yoghurt with the mint, lemon juice and a pinch of cayenne pepper. Pour the mixture over the cucumber, mix together well and chill for about 30 minutes.

KESAR MASALA MURGHI

THIS POPULAR DISH, chicken in saffron gravy, improves on standing, and can be prepared well ahead of the serving time – in fact it tastes better if you do so. Spiced chicken pieces are browned, braised with onions, then cooked slowly until done. The cooked chicken can be frozen for up to 2 months.

PREPARATION TIME: 20 MINUTES
COOKING TIME: 1 HOUR

INGREDIENTS FOR SIX
1 chicken (1,5 kg), cut into small pieces
10 ml (2 teaspoons) chilli powder
5 ml (1 teaspoon) turmeric
20 g garlic (about 10 cloves), peeled and crushed finely
30 g fresh green ginger, scraped and pounded to a paste with a little water
7 ml (1½ teaspoons) salt
2 ml (½ teaspoon) saffron
250 ml (1 cup) milk
60 ml (¼ cup) sunflower oil
2 cinnamon sticks
6 cloves
6 cardamom pods
1 onion, peeled and sliced*
125 ml (½ cup) natural yoghurt*
250 ml (1 cup) hot water
2 tomatoes, cut in half and grated
15 ml (1 tablespoon) chopped coriander leaves

Wash the chicken pieces and drain. In a bowl, mix the chilli powder, turmeric, garlic, ginger and salt and rub over the chicken pieces. Place the saffron in the milk and set aside.
Using a large saucepan, heat the oil, then add the cinnamon, cloves and cardamom and brown for 10 seconds. Add the sliced onion and brown lightly. Add the chicken pieces to the pot and braise with the onion for 10 minutes. Pour the yoghurt, saffron milk and hot water over the chicken, then add the grated tomatoes. Stir, cover the saucepan and cook on a medium heat for 45 minutes. Garnish with chopped coriander.

SERVING SUGGESTIONS Prepare 500 g white or basmati rice to serve with the saffron gravy.
Alternatively, serve with a flaky roti*.

SOOKI MURGHI

IN THE NORTH OF INDIA, meat dishes are generally made with very little gravy, or none at all. In this popular recipe the chicken remains succulent and tasty, as it absorbs the spicy aroma of the cinnamon and cloves.

PREPARATION TIME: 15 MINUTES
STANDING TIME: 2 HOURS
COOKING TIME: 1 HOUR

INGREDIENTS FOR FOUR TO SIX
1 chicken (about 1-1,5 kg)
20 g garlic (about 10 cloves), peeled and crushed to a paste
40 g fresh green ginger, scraped and pounded to a paste with a little water
2 green chillies, chopped
7 ml (1½ teaspoons) salt
2 ml (½ teaspoon) turmeric
15 ml (1 tablespoon) sunflower oil
2 cinnamon sticks
6 cloves
375 ml (1½ cups) warm water
2 eggs
30 ml (2 tablespoons) chopped coriander leaves
125 ml (½ cup) ghee*

Wash the chicken and pat it dry, then truss* very securely.
Make a paste with the crushed garlic, pounded green ginger, chopped green chillies, salt, turmeric and sunflower oil. Rub over the chicken and allow to stand for 2 hours. Place the chicken in a saucepan, add the cinnamon sticks and the cloves and cover with the warm water.
Cover the saucepan and cook gently for 45 minutes, or until the chicken is tender: all the water should evaporate. Beat the eggs and coriander leaves, and brush this over the chicken.
Heat the ghee in a pan and place the chicken in it. Fry each side until the whole chicken is coated with a crispy layer.

SERVING SUGGESTIONS Serve with a helping of mushroom pilaff* and red tomato chutney*.
Serve with any vegetables that are in season.
Green beans, peas and brinjals (Indian style) would complement the chicken superbly.
For a salad, serve kachoomer*.

CHICKEN BIRIANI

BIRIANI IS A SAVOURY DISH of meat or fish, rice, usually lentils and eggs. Indian people regard it as food fit for a king, and it is a favourite with the Cape Muslims.

PREPARATION TIME: 30 MINUTES
COOKING TIME: 2 HOURS

INGREDIENTS FOR SIX
1 chicken (1,5 kg)
Salt
90 ml sunflower oil or ghee*
1 large onion, chopped or sliced into rings*
2 cm piece fresh green ginger
2 cloves garlic
2 ml (½ teaspoon) cumin seeds
5 ml (1 teaspoon) coriander
1 ml (¼ teaspoon) cayenne pepper
A few fresh coriander or bay leaves
1 large tomato, skinned* and grated
80 ml (⅓ cup) sour milk
4 small potatoes, cut into quarters
250 g rice
A few cardamom seeds
2 cloves
A pinch of saffron
250 ml (1 cup) boiling water

Cut the chicken into small pieces, salt and put aside. Heat 60 ml (¼ cup) of the oil or ghee and sauté the onion in it until golden. Pound the ginger, garlic, cumin seeds, coriander, cayenne pepper and leaves in a mortar, add to the onions and cook for 4 minutes over a very low heat.

Add the chicken and cook for another 7 minutes. Next, add the tomato and sour milk, and let the chicken simmer slowly for 30 minutes. Fry the potatoes in the remaining 30 ml (2 tablespoons) hot oil and add them to the chicken mixture. In the meantime, cook the rice* with salt, cardamom and cloves until almost cooked; then strain.

Spoon a layer of rice into a large, heavy-bottomed saucepan, followed by a layer of the chicken mixture. Repeat, ending with a layer of rice.

Dissolve the saffron in the boiling water and pour over the rice. Cover the saucepan with a tight-fitting lid and cook over a very low heat until the rice is done. Do not remove the lid until you are ready to serve.

CHICKEN PIE

THE OLD FASHIONED *hoenderpastei* made with free range farm chickens is one of our culinary gems. However, the pie described here is just as good to eat, and is infinitely easier to make. The wine and chicken stock powder which is used in cooking the chicken give all the flavour that supermarket chickens may otherwise lack. This is a meaty pie, bound with a rich creamy sauce.

PREPARATION TIME: 40 MINUTES
COOKING TIME: 2½ HOURS
PRE-HEAT OVEN TO 180°C

INGREDIENTS FOR EIGHT
2 chickens
5 ml (1 teaspoon) salt
2 ml (½ teaspoon) pepper
10 ml (2 teaspoons) chicken stock powder
500 ml (2 cups) dry white wine
2 onions, peeled* and quartered
250 ml (1 cup) water
Sour cream flaky pastry* (using 500 g flour)
1 egg white, beaten with 2 ml (½ teaspoon) salt

For the sauce;
125 g butter
60 g flour
250 ml (1 cup) stock from cooked chickens
750 ml (3 cups) milk
200 g cooked ham, sliced and diced
5 ml (1 teaspoon) dry mustard
60 ml (¼ cup) chopped parsley
A little fresh cream

Place the chickens in a roasting pan and season with salt, pepper and chicken stock powder. Carefully pour in the wine on the side of the pan and scatter the onions around and between the chickens. Cover the pan with aluminium foil (shiny side facing inwards) and bake at 180°C for 1¼ hours. Remove from the oven and increase the heat to 220°C.

Allow to cool, remove the skin and bones, and break the chickens into smaller pieces. Arrange the pieces in a big pie dish.

Put the skin and bones that have been removed back into the pan in which the chickens were roasted, add the water, and then bring to the boil to de-glaze the pan and extract all the flavour from the skin and bones.

Strain the liquid and keep it for the sauce. Make a white sauce* with the butter, flour, chicken liquid and milk. Add the ham, mustard, parsley and cream.

Taste, season if necessary, and pour over the chicken. Allow to cool before covering* loosely with sour cream flaky pastry (rolled out to a thickness of 3 mm).

Fold the edges back and place an extra strip of pastry – about 2 cm wide – right around the outer edge of the pie dish. Damp it down with a little water. Fold the large pastry covering back over the edge strip, push it down lightly with your fingertips, and trim the pastry to fit the dish. This will give the illusion of a thick pastry edge and will be easier to scallop.

Cut a few vent holes and decorate the pie with pastry leaves*. Glaze the pastry just before baking with the egg white.

Bake for 20 minutes at 220°C, then reduce the heat to 190°C and cook for a further 20 minutes (or alternatively until golden-brown and cooked).

SERVING SUGGESTION Serve with fresh green vegetables, onions in a vinegar sauce, and yellow rice* with raisins.

CHICKEN PIE *contains a creamy sauce and is topped with crisp pastry.*

~ Putting China on the Table ~

Cooking is an important part of Chinese culture, an art that has evolved over many centuries. The selection and quantity of ingredients in Chinese dishes are crucial, as in most recipes, but where Chinese cookery excels is in the preservation of individual flavours and textures.

M ANY SOUTH AFRICANS are discovering that Chinese-style food is both fun to prepare and delicious to eat.

No exotic utensils are needed – except perhaps a wok. Special ingredients, such as bean curd (or tofu), dried Chinese mushrooms and jasmine tea can be obtained at some speciality food stores or health food outlets, but because they are not always readily available, local equivalents are also given.

The menu that follows is a tasty selection of dishes that together make up a memorable Chinese meal.

Hot and Sour Soup

•

Whole Marinated Red Roman

•

Peking Duck

•

Spicy Red Lamb Ribs*

•

Chinese Stir-fried Vegetables*

•

Fried Rice*

•

Fried Ice Cream Balls

•

Jasmine Tea

HOT AND SOUR SOUP

PREPARATION TIME: 25 MINUTES
SOAKING TIME: 20-30 MINUTES
COOKING TIME: 25 MINUTES

INGREDIENTS FOR SIX

4 large dried Chinese mushrooms (or fresh giant black mushrooms)
1 litre (4 cups) Chinese chicken stock*
80 ml (⅓ cup) tinned bamboo shoots, drained and cut into matchsticks
100 g pork fillet, finely shredded
15 ml (1 tablespoon) dry sherry
15 ml (1 tablespoon) wine vinegar
15 ml (1 tablespoon) soy sauce
1 cake bean curd, cut into strips (optional)
White pepper
15 ml (1 tablespoon) cornflour
30 ml (2 tablespoons) cold water
1 egg, beaten
A few drops of sesame seed oil (optional)
1 spring onion, finely chopped
Salt

If using dried mushrooms, first soak them in warm water for 20-30 minutes, then drain well before slicing them.

Bring the stock to the boil and add the mushrooms, bamboo shoots and shredded pork. Reduce the heat to low, cover the pot and simmer for a few minutes. Add the sherry, vinegar, soy sauce, bean curd (if used) and a good pinch of pepper.

Slake the cornflour with the cold water and add it to the soup. Allow the soup to return to the boil, stirring until it thickens slightly. Slowly stir in the beaten egg.

Remove from the heat, add a few drops of sesame seed oil (if used) and the chopped spring onion. Check the seasoning and serve immediately.

HOT AND SOUR SOUP

WHOLE MARINATED RED ROMAN

PREPARATION TIME: 15 MINUTES
MARINATING TIME: AT LEAST 1 HOUR
COOKING TIME: 20 MINUTES
PRE-HEAT OVEN TO 220°C

INGREDIENTS FOR SIX

A 1-1,5 kg red roman
3 carrots, cut in thin rounds
6 spring onions, finely chopped
275-300 ml chicken stock*

For the marinade:
A 1,5 cm piece of fresh green ginger, peeled and chopped; or 10 ml (2 teaspoons) ground ginger
15 ml (1 tablespoon) soy sauce
10 ml (2 teaspoons) brown sugar
1 clove garlic, crushed
Juice of ½ lemon

To make the marinade, combine the ginger, soy sauce, sugar, garlic and lemon juice in a large dish. Add the fish and leave for at least 1 hour, turning the fish from time to time to soak it completely.

Lightly grease a roasting dish and put in the sliced carrots and spring onions. Arrange the fish on top. In a small saucepan mix the marinade liquid with the chicken stock and quickly bring it to the boil. Pour the mixture over the fish and cover the dish closely with a double sheet of aluminium foil.

Bake for 5 minutes, then reduce the heat to 190°C. Cook for another 8-10 minutes, then transfer the fish to a warmed, deep-sided serving dish. Lift the vegetables from the dish with a slotted spoon and arrange them around the fish. Pour the liquid into a saucepan and boil it, stirring all the time, until reduced and thickened. Pour it over the fish or serve it separately.

PEKING DUCK

Peking Duck

Preparation Time: 2 hours
Hanging Time: 3-4 hours, or overnight
Cooking Time: 1½ hours
Pre-heat Oven to 200°C

Ingredients for Six
1 large duck (about 2,5 kg)
30 ml (2 tablespoons) brandy, vodka or gin (optional)
18 spring onions

For the pancakes:
450 g flour
600 ml boiling water
30 ml (2 tablespoons) sesame oil

For the table sauce:
125 ml (½ cup) Hoisin (or plum) sauce
20 ml (4 teaspoons) sugar
20 ml (4 teaspoons) sesame oil
20 ml (4 teaspoons) cold water

For the basting sauce:
45 ml (3 tablespoons) soy sauce
20 ml (4 teaspoons) castor sugar
150 ml cold water

The essence of Peking duck is its crisp skin, which is stripped off the cooked duck and served separately. To obtain this, the skin of the uncooked duck should be thoroughly dried. Wipe and dry the duck and pass a length of string under the wings so that it can be suspended from a rod or broom handle placed across the seats of two chairs. Set a plate under the duck to catch any drips.

Rubbing the skin with the brandy, vodka or gin aids the drying process. Direct a blast of cold air on to the duck from an electric fan and leave it for at least 3-4 hours. Alternatively, hang the duck overnight in a draughty place.

Remove any bits of roots and blemished leaves from the spring onions – trimming the onions to a length of 7-10 cm. Wash them thoroughly. Use a sharp knife to make two vertical cuts, 1-2 cm long, at the bulb end of each onion, then make two similar cuts at right angles to the first cuts. Put the onions in a large bowl of iced water and leave in the refrigerator until required. The cut end will fan out to resemble a brush.

To make the pancakes, sift the flour into a bowl and, mixing all the time, add about 600 ml boiling water to make a soft dough that leaves the sides of the bowl clean. Knead the dough for 10 minutes on a lightly floured surface until it becomes rubbery. Cover with a cloth and leave for 20 minutes.

Roll the dough out, 5 mm thick, and cut it into rounds with a plain 5 cm scone cutter. Brush the top of half the rounds with sesame seed oil and place an unbrushed round on top. Roll out each pair of pancakes (about 14) as thinly as possible, to a diameter of about 15 cm.

Heat an ungreased griddle or heavy frying pan for 30 seconds, then lower the heat. Put in the first pancake, turning it when bubbles appear on the surface and the underside is flecked with brown and looks floury.

Cook all the pancakes in this way (they may puff up into balloons), and allow them to cool. Wrap the cooked pancakes in aluminium foil parcels and store them in the refrigerator until needed.

Mix the table sauce ingredients together in a small pan, and bring the sauce to the boil; stir over a low heat for 2-3 minutes. Pour the sauce into a serving bowl.

Mix the ingredients for the basting sauce, and brush the sauce all over the duck. Place the duck, breast upwards, on an open grid or wire rack in a roasting pan. Pour in enough boiling water to reach 6 mm up the sides of the pan. Roast the duck in the lower part of the pre-heated oven for 1¼ hours. Brush with the basting sauce every 15 or 20 minutes. After 45 minutes, turn up the heat to 230°C. Put the parcels of prepared pancakes into the oven to re-heat.

To assemble the final dish, cut the duck skin with scissors or a sharp knife in 3-5 cm squares; place on a serving dish and keep warm. Carve the meat into long, thin slivers and arrange on another dish to keep warm. Pile the pancakes on a hot dish and cover with a napkin or folded cloth to keep them warm. Put the onion brushes in a bowl or dish and arrange all these dishes, with the table sauce, on the table.

To eat the dish, carefully pull the two halves of a pancake apart, starting where the join can be seen quite clearly. Dip an onion brush in the sauce and brush it liberally on to the soft moist side of the open pancake. Top with pieces of duck skin and slivers of meat; fold and roll up the pancake.

Fried Ice Cream Balls

Preparation Time: 1 hour
Cooking Time: 10 minutes for the ice cream balls; 5 minutes for the caramel sauce

Ingredients for Six
2 litres vanilla ice cream*
120 g flour
2 eggs
60 ml (¼ cup) milk
1 packet Marie biscuits
Sunflower oil for deep-frying

For the caramel sauce:
60 g butter
80 ml (⅓ cup) water
45 ml (3 tablespoons) brandy
125 ml (½ cup) cream
150 g brown sugar
15 ml (1 tablespoon) cornflour

Place a baking tray in the freezer for a few minutes to chill it. Form ice cream balls with a scoop and drop them on to the ice-cold baking tray.

Replace the ice cream balls in the freezer immediately. Next, put the flour in a small deep bowl. Toss the balls in the flour, then replace in the freezer.

Beat the eggs together with the milk and pour into a small, deep bowl. Break up the biscuits and process in a food processor or liquidizer until very fine (or crush them with a rolling pin). Toss the balls (one by one) in the egg mixture and then in the fine crumbs. Return them once again to the freezer to harden.

Repeat the process of coating the ice cream balls with egg and crumbs. Keep in the freezer, well sealed, until ready to serve.

Next, make the caramel sauce by combining all the sauce ingredients and simmering in a pan. Keep the sauce warm.

Heat the oil in a pan until very hot. Quickly deep-fry the ice cream balls, a few at a time, on both sides. Drain on paper towels and serve immediately with the warm caramel sauce.

CHINESE STIR-FRIED VEGETABLES

FRIED RICE

Grilled Chicken with Lemon and Herb Marinade

This is a fairly quick chicken dish requiring few ingredients. The marinade adds an unusual and very appealing flavour. Chicken cooked this way is crisp, attractive and delicious.

Preparation Time: 10 minutes
Marinating Time: about 3 hours
Cooking Time: 45 minutes
Pre-heat Oven to 180°C

Ingredients for Four
1 chicken (1 kg), split in two or quartered
90 g soft butter

For the marinade:
Juice of 2 lemons (about 120 ml)
Grated rind of 1 lemon
1 clove garlic, crushed
15 ml (1 tablespoon) fresh thyme
Salt and freshly ground black pepper
30 ml (2 tablespoons) sunflower oil

Wash and dry the chicken pieces. To make the marinade, combine the lemon juice, rind, garlic, thyme, salt and pepper. Add the sunflower oil and then stir until all the ingredients are thoroughly blended. Pour this mixture over the chicken pieces and allow to marinate for a few hours in the refrigerator.

Place the chicken pieces on a rack in a grill pan (skin side down). Smear with half the butter and place in the oven.

Cook for 20 minutes, basting from time to time with the marinade. Turn the chicken pieces, smear the skin with the remaining butter, and repeat the procedure.

Test to see whether the chicken is done by piercing the meat with a sharp-pointed knife. If the juices are clear (not pink), the chicken is ready to serve.

Serving Suggestion Serve the chicken with chips or baked potatoes* and a butter lettuce salad.

Variation After marinating the chicken pieces, make a paste from 40 g butter, 2 ml (½ teaspoon) dried thyme and 1 clove of garlic, crushed, and smear this under and over the skin before grilling.

Chicken Salad

This fresh, rich salad goes well with virtually anything, and is also a meal in itself. For the best results make sure all the greens are fresh and crisp.

Preparation Time: 15 minutes

Ingredients for Four to Six
1 cooked chicken, skinned and cut into cubes
4 sticks celery, sliced
6 spring onions, finely sliced
1 green apple, core removed and thinly sliced
1 green pepper, thinly sliced or chopped
125 ml (½ cup) mayonnaise*
60 ml (¼ cup) thick cream
Salt and freshly ground black pepper
Large lettuce leaves
1 ripe avocado, sliced and brushed with lemon juice

For the garnish:
10 ml (2 teaspoons) chopped fresh tarragon or parsley

Combine the chicken, celery, spring onions, apple, green pepper, mayonnaise, cream, salt and pepper. Toss the ingredients together and taste to correct the seasoning.

Arrange the lettuce leaves on a flat serving platter, place the avocado on the lettuce leaves and spoon over the chicken mixture. Garnish the salad with the chopped tarragon or parsley.

Serving Suggestion Try serving with home-baked brown bread* and butter and a bottle of (well-chilled) white wine.

Variations Add 5 ml (1 teaspoon) curry powder to the cream and mayonnaise to make a curried chicken salad.

Instead of the mayonnaise and cream, mix together 30 g Roquefort cheese, 45 ml (3 tablespoons) wine vinegar and 90 ml sunflower oil, and blend with the other ingredients as directed.

Chicken Breasts with Apricots and Almonds

Apricots, almonds and slices of ham add an exotic touch to this quick-and-easy dish. Fresh apricots (with apricot nectar) can be used in season, but tinned apricots also serve the purpose (though the flavour is a little sweeter).

Preparation Time: 15 minutes
Cooking Time: 45 minutes

Ingredients for Six
6 chicken breasts, filleted and skinned
125 ml (½ cup) seasoned flour*
75 g butter
60 ml (¼ cup) oil
12 slices ham (optional)
50 g halved, blanched almonds*
60 ml (¼ cup) brandy, warmed (optional)
125 ml (½ cup) apricot nectar (or juice from the tin)
125 ml (½ cup) white wine or water
12 whole apricots, pitted, or 24 tinned apricot halves (410 g tin)
2 ml (½ teaspoon) powdered chicken stock
30 ml (2 tablespoons) butter
Salt and freshly ground pepper

Coat the chicken breasts in seasoned flour, shake off the excess and place on a rack. Heat 75 g butter and oil in a large frying pan and quickly sauté the ham slices (if used) on either side. Remove from the pan with a slotted spoon, arrange in a heated serving dish, cover and keep warm.

Sauté the chicken breasts, two or three at a time, until they are nicely browned on both sides. Do not overcook, or they will become dry and tough. Depending on their size, 10-15 minutes for each batch should be sufficient. Remove the cooked chicken breasts with a slotted spoon and arrange them on the ham slices. Cover tightly and keep warm.

Lightly brown the almonds in the fat and sprinkle them around the chicken breasts. Pour warmed brandy (if used) into the pan and ignite: when the flame dies down, pour in the apricot juice and wine or water. Bring to the boil and add the apricots. Heat through (this should take about 30 seconds) and arrange the apricot halves around the chicken pieces.

Add the chicken stock powder and 30 ml butter to the pan juices and stir until the butter is melted. Season lightly with pepper and a little salt if required (remember that both the ham and stock powder are salted).

Pour the sauce over the chicken pieces and serve immediately.

Serving Suggestions Plain rice* or a rice pilaff* and a salad of cucumber and natural yoghurt* are all good served with this dish.

Potato croquettes* and baby marrows, herbed and cooked in cream, make a delicious alternative.

Variations You can omit both the brandy and wine from the recipe, and replace with plain apricot nectar or the juice from the tin (however, this could be a little sweet for some tastes).

Pine nuts can be satisfactorily substituted for the almonds, and an interesting variation on this theme is to use peeled and sliced fresh, white peaches, peach nectar and pine nuts.

Roast Duck with Grapefruit

The tartness of grapefruit combines perfectly with the richness of the duck, making this a particularly piquant and tasty way of preparing this bird.

Preparation Time: 40 minutes
Cooking Time: 2 hours
Pre-heat Oven to 220°C

Ingredients for Six to Eight
2 ducks (each about 2 kg)
Salt and freshly ground black pepper
1 onion, peeled and sliced*
A few sprigs parsley
A few celery leaves
2 sprigs rosemary
2 garlic cloves, split
15 ml (1 tablespoon) clear honey

For the sauce:
4 grapefruit
125 ml (½ cup) water
50 g sugar

45 ml (3 tablespoons) white wine vinegar
375 ml (1½ cups) poultry stock*
125 ml (½ cup) port
15 ml (1 tablespoon) cornflour
30 ml (2 tablespoons) brandy

Prick the cleaned ducks all over and remove the excess fat. Season inside and out with salt and black pepper and stuff the ducks with the sliced onion, herbs and garlic.

Place them breast side up on the rack of a grill pan, pour some water into the bottom of the pan to prevent smoking, and roast at 220°C for 30 minutes.

Reduce the heat to 180°C. Turn the ducks, pricking them again, and roast for an hour. Remove them from the oven and set aside. Pour off the water and accumulated fat (you can do this ahead of time and complete roasting the ducks 30 minutes before serving). Cut the ducks into quarters and place them (skin side up) in the bottom of the roasting pan.

To make the sauce, remove the rind (it should be free of the bitter pith) from one of the grapefruit and cut it into thin strips. Simmer in the water for about 15 minutes (or until tender) and drain. Boil the sugar and vinegar together with the rind (without stirring) until the mixture turns the colour of caramel.

Remove from the heat and add the stock very slowly. Return to the stove to dissolve any remaining caramel, then remove from the heat and stir in the port and the juice of 2 grapefruit. Slake the cornflour with the brandy and stir it into the warmed sauce. Bring to the boil and stir until the sauce has slightly thickened. Check the seasoning and pour over the ducks.

Peel the remaining 2 grapefruit, removing all the pith. Slice them into neat sections and set aside. To complete cooking the ducks, roast them at 220°C (one shelf below the middle of the oven) until tender, golden-brown and crisp (about 20 minutes).

Brush with the honey and cook for a further 5 minutes, or until nicely glazed. Garnish with grapefruit sections.

SERVING SUGGESTION Roast potatoes and puréed spinach heated with cream and garlic make a good accompaniment.

VARIATION The duck livers can be browned and mashed, and added to the sauce to enhance the flavour.

ROAST DUCK WITH ORANGE AND VAN DER HUM

THIS RECIPE DESCRIBES a wonderfully rich dish which is well worth the time and trouble spent in preparing it. The duck and its accompaniments make up a substantial menu.

PREPARATION TIME: 30-45 MINUTES
COOKING TIME: 2 HOURS
PRE-HEAT OVEN TO 210°C

INGREDIENTS FOR FOUR

1 duck (about 2 kg), cleaned and patted dry
5 ml (1 teaspoon) salt
1 clove garlic, crushed
4 black peppercorns
2 oranges, quartered (unpeeled)
2 sticks celery, sliced
1 onion, peeled* and quartered
60 ml (¼ cup) Van der Hum liqueur*
60 ml (¼ cup) orange marmalade*

For the orange sauce:
2 oranges
45 ml (3 tablespoons) butter
Duck liver
45 ml (3 tablespoons) brandy
1 clove garlic, crushed
30 ml (2 tablespoons) flour
10 ml (2 teaspoons) tomato sauce*
7 ml (1½ teaspoons) beef extract
A dash of white pepper
250 ml (1 cup) chicken stock*
60 ml (¼ cup) Van der Hum liqueur*
60 ml (¼ cup) orange marmalade*

For the garnish:
2 oranges, peeled and divided into segments
Fresh watercress

Sprinkle the inside of the duck with salt and rub with the crushed garlic. Stuff the duck with the peppercorns, oranges, celery and onion, and pour in the Van der Hum. Place the duck breast side up on the rack of the grilling pan and roast at 210°C for 30 minutes, pricking the flesh from time to time to release the fat. Discard the fat in the pan and place the duck in a roasting dish with 125 ml (½ cup) water under the grill rack. Reduce the oven temperature to 185°C. Spread the duck with the marmalade and roast for 1½ hours.

While the duck is roasting, make the orange sauce. Peel the rind of one orange and cut it into fine slivers. Squeeze the juice from both oranges and put on one side. Melt 30 ml (2 tablespoons) of butter and gently fry the duck liver until brown on both sides and pink inside. Remove from the heat.

In a small saucepan, heat the brandy and ignite. Pour the flaming brandy over the liver: when the flame subsides, remove the liver and add the remaining 15 ml (1 tablespoon) butter, orange peel and garlic.

ROAST DUCK WITH ORANGE AND VAN DER HUM *Rich, delicious and attractive.*

Cook for 3 minutes, then remove from the heat and stir in the flour, tomato sauce, beef extract and pepper until well mixed.

Gradually stir in the chicken stock, Van der Hum, marmalade and orange juice. Bring to the boil, then reduce the heat and simmer for 15 minutes. Chop the liver and add to the sauce. Pour the hot orange sauce into a heated gravy boat.

SERVING SUGGESTION Place the duck on a heated serving platter and decorate with orange segments and watercress. Serve the roast duck with crisp roast potatoes and minted peas.

Turkey with Two Stuffings

TURKEY AS THE TRADITIONAL Christmas treat has retained its popularity in this country regardless of the fact that our summer climate is not conducive to the consumption of large meals at midday.

This recipe ensures that the bird remains succulent and tastes good whether served hot, warm, or at room temperature. The neck stuffing serves to keep the breast marvellously moist as well as giving it a distinctive flavour.

PREPARATION TIME: 2 HOURS
COOKING TIME: 3½ HOURS
PRE-HEAT OVEN TO 150°C

INGREDIENTS FOR TEN TO TWELVE
1 turkey (4-5 kg)
250g butter
Salt and freshly ground black pepper
8 rashers streaky bacon, trimmed
500 ml (2 cups) chicken stock*
250 ml (1 cup) red wine

For the neck stuffing:
90g butter
250g fresh mushrooms
6 rashers rindless streaky bacon, coarsely chopped
200g cooked pork, minced
125g chicken livers
1 large onion, peeled* and quartered
1 clove garlic, peeled and sliced
4 anchovy fillets
125g liver pâté
Grated rind of 1 lemon
30 ml (2 tablespoons) chopped parsley
2 ml (½ teaspoon) dried thyme
2 ml (½ teaspoon) dried marjoram
15 ml (1 tablespoon) brandy
Freshly ground black pepper

For the body stuffing:
500 ml (2 cups) fresh white breadcrumbs
6 pork sausages, pressed out of their skins
1 onion, peeled* and grated
Grated rind of 2 lemons
5 ml (1 teaspoon) dried sage
5 ml (1 teaspoon) dried mixed herbs
45 ml (3 tablespoons) chopped parsley
1 egg
125 ml (½ cup) sour cream (smetana)
Salt and freshly ground black pepper

For the giblet gravy:
Turkey giblets (gizzard, heart and liver)
1 clove
2 onions, peeled*
2 sprigs parsley
1 bay leaf
Salt and fresly ground black pepper
1 litre (4 cups) water
90g flour
125 ml (½ cup) red wine
30 ml (2 tablespoons) cranberry jelly

Wipe the turkey clean and remove the giblets, reserving them for the stock. Now make the neck stuffing: melt 30g of the butter and sauté the mushrooms until they just start to soften. Combine all the stuffing ingredients except the remaining butter and pepper, and mince together.

Melt the rest of the butter and stir it into the stuffing, mixing well. Season with pepper. Starting at the neck, work your fingers carefully under the skin to about halfway down the breast, being careful not to pierce the skin with your nails. Stuff the neck cavity and insert the stuffing under the skin on the breast, pressing it well into the breast meat and arranging it evenly to give the bird a well-rounded appearance.

Tuck the loose neck skin under a wing and skewer it into place, or truss* it to ensure that there will be no danger of the stuffing oozing out during cooking.

Next, make the stuffing for the body cavity. Mix all the ingredients together, adding extra breadcrumbs if the stuffing is too moist. Stuff the body cavity, sew it up, and truss the legs.

TURKEY WITH TWO STUFFINGS *is a succulent treat, served hot or cold.*

Rub the turkey all over with butter, sprinkle with salt and pepper and place it (breast side up) in a roasting pan. Cover the breast with rashers of bacon. Combine the chicken stock and wine and pour the liquid over the bird. Cover with buttered wax paper and roast for 3 hours, basting from time to time.

While the turkey is cooking, make a stock with the giblets, clove, onions, parsley, bay leaf, salt, pepper and water. Simmer for an hour, then strain.

Remove the wax paper and bacon from the turkey when the 3 hours are up and then leave it to brown for about 30 minutes at a temperature of 200°C.

When it is cooked, transfer the turkey to a warmed serving platter.

To make the gravy stir the flour into the pan juices to make a smooth paste, scraping all the crisp, tasty bits from the sides of the pan. Add the red wine and the prepared giblet stock and simmer, stirring, until the mixture starts to thicken.

Add the jelly, and as soon as the gravy comes to the boil, turn down the heat and simmer for 2 minutes. Season to taste and strain into a heated sauceboat.

SERVING SUGGESTIONS Turkey is traditionally served with bread sauce* and cranberry jelly, roast potatoes, onions and Brussels sprouts.

As we have a far wider choice of summer vegetables than in the northern hemisphere, you could replace or supplement the Brussels sprouts with minted peas, cauliflower, baby marrows or broccoli.

VARIATIONS For alternative stuffings, see the chapter on Savoury Sauces, Stuffings and Dumplings. Cranberry jelly is not always available in this country but you could, however, try quince*, apple or guava jelly.

As turkeys are quite large, there is often quite a bit of the bird left after a meal. To save space in the refrigerator, cut all the meat from the bone, cover and refrigerate for use later in pies, hash, croquettes or salad.

The stuffings can be pressed into a bowl and served as pâtés with hot toast or crusty bread.

Otherwise, slice them and serve in a salad or on a cold meat platter, or layered with turkey meat to make a tasty pie.

POULTRY

TURKEY SALAD WITH CHEESE AND SESAME SEEDS *is a perfect way of using left-over meat to make a light, tasty dish.*

TURKEY SALAD WITH CHEESE AND SESAME SEEDS

LEFT-OVER TURKEY lends itself to the creation of many interesting salad dishes. Water chestnuts and diced celery give this particular salad a nice crunchy texture, contrasting well with the Gruyère. The dressing serves to flavour the meat, keeping it moist.

PREPARATION TIME: 45 MINUTES
COOKING TIME: 5-10 MINUTES
CHILLING TIME: 3 HOURS

INGREDIENTS FOR FOUR
750 ml (3 cups) diced cooked turkey meat or smoked breast of turkey
250 ml (1 cup) sliced celery
1 tin (230 g) diced water chestnuts
125 ml (½ cup) thinly sliced spring onions
125 ml (½ cup) thinly sliced strips of Gruyère cheese

For the dressing:
15 ml (1 tablespoon) sesame seeds
125 ml (½ cup) olive oil or sesame oil
60 ml (¼ cup) white vinegar
60 ml (¼ cup) lemon juice
5 ml (1 teaspoon) mild (prepared) mustard
Salt and freshly ground black pepper

Combine all the salad ingredients in a bowl. Sauté the sesame seeds in the olive oil or sesame oil until lightly browned, then remove from the heat and leave to cool.

When the sautéed sesame seeds have cooled, mix together the vinegar, lemon juice and mustard and then pour on the oil, with the sesame seeds, in a thin stream, whisking the mixture as you pour.

Season to taste and pour over the turkey salad. Toss the salad to coat it well with the dressing, cover, and refrigerate for 3 hours.

SERVING SUGGESTIONS Serve the turkey salad on a bed of shredded lettuce garnished with egg and tomato wedges, and serve with crispy rolls or French bread.

This turkey salad makes an ideal light supper dish or lunch dish and is particularly recommended as a summer meal or even as an hors d'oeuvre.

VARIATIONS Julienned* strips of thinly sliced Emmenthal cheese make a good substitute for the Gruyère.

Slices of fresh or tinned pineapple are delicious in place of the egg and tomato garnish.

TURKEY PUFF

NO MATTER HOW generous the servings, there is usually a considerable amount of turkey left over after a meal. This recipe is for a quick and easy dish made with turkey left-overs. It is ideal for a light supper or lunch. For the best results, serve straight from the oven.

PREPARATION TIME: 55 MINUTES
COOKING TIME: 35 MINUTES
PRE-HEAT OVEN TO 190°C

INGREDIENTS FOR FOUR
250-300 ml stuffing* of your choice
500 ml (2 cups) diced, cooked turkey
45 ml (3 tablespoons) butter
375 ml (1½ cups) béchamel sauce*, made with half poultry stock*
60 ml (¼ cup) grated Parmesan cheese
2 eggs, separated
2 ml (½ teaspoon) nutmeg
Salt and freshly ground black pepper

Butter a gratin dish and place a layer of stuffing (about 1 cm deep) on the bottom, smoothing it evenly. Top it with the diced turkey, spread this layer evenly, and dot with butter.

Cover with aluminium foil and bake for 10 minutes.

Meanwhile, mix the béchamel sauce with the Parmesan cheese and lightly beaten egg yolks. Season with nutmeg, salt and pepper.

Whisk the egg whites with a pinch of salt until they have become stiff, then stir about a quarter of the whites into the béchamel sauce.

Next, gently fold the sauce mixture into the rest of the egg whites, and spoon the mixture over the turkey. Bake (uncovered) until the dish is well-puffed and browned (about 25 minutes).

SERVING SUGGESTIONS Serve immediately, with a green salad*.

VARIATIONS Chopped, cooked bacon or chipolatas can be added to the turkey meat.

Alternatively, add lightly sautéed button mushrooms or left-over cooked peas to make an interesting variation.

Casseroled Guinea Fowl

CASSEROLING, THE PROCESS of sealing meat or poultry in a pot with herbs and vegetables, and permitting it to cook slowly in the natural juices, is a method particularly well suited to fowl or game birds that have passed the first flush of youth.

The older and tougher they are, the longer they should be cooked. Indeed, to re-heat the pot after allowing it to stand and cool overnight will add even greater distinction to both the flavour and the texture. Guinea fowl is particularly good cooked in this way.

PREPARATION TIME: 30 MINUTES
COOKING TIME: 1½ HOURS
PRE-HEAT OVEN TO 180°C

INGREDIENTS FOR FOUR
1 guinea fowl (about 1 kg), with giblets
1 large onion, peeled and sliced*
2 carrots, scrubbed and sliced
2 leeks, trimmed, washed and sliced
Bunch of mixed fresh herbs or 5 ml (1 teaspoon) dried mixed herbs
Salt and pepper
8 thin rashers streaky bacon, with rinds removed

For the sauce:
275-300 ml stock* made from giblets
15 ml (1 tablespoon) butter
15 ml (1 tablespoon) flour
60 ml (¼ cup) thin cream
15 ml (1 tablespoon) chopped parsley

Clean the bird and remove the giblets. Truss* it and place in a deep casserole with the vegetables, herbs, salt and pepper to taste, and just enough water to cover. Bring to the boil, then place, tightly covered, in the pre-heated oven for 1 hour (or until the bird is tender). During this time, prepare the giblet stock.

Take the casserole from the oven and strain off 275-300 ml cooking liquid. Lower the oven heat to 130°C and put the casserole back. Strain the prepared stock into the cooking liquid and boil rapidly to reduce to about 275-300 ml.

Roll up the bacon rashers and thread on skewers. Grill for about 5 minutes, turning, until they are crisp. Keep warm.

To make the sauce, heat the butter, stir in the flour and cook gently for 2-3 minutes. Pour on the hot stock, stirring all the time, until smooth and thickened. Taste for seasoning, then add the cream and parsley. Warm the sauce well.

Carve into serving portions. Place on a warmed serving dish, pour on the sauce and arrange the bacon rolls around it.

SERVING SUGGESTIONS Serve the casserole with plain boiled new or mashed potatoes* and a crisp green salad*.

Alternatively, you can serve with glazed carrots*, boiled rice* and a watercress salad*.

Braised Guinea Fowl

THIS RECIPE IS FOR GUINEA FOWL cooked in a rich sauce. When choosing your birds, try to obtain them well matured. Otherwise hang them in a cool place for 5-7 days – depending on the climate – to achieve the best results.

PREPARATION TIME: 15 MINUTES
COOKING TIME: 1¼ HOURS

INGREDIENTS FOR SIX TO EIGHT
2 guinea fowl
30 ml (2 tablespoons) butter
30 ml (2 tablespoons) sunflower oil
Salt and freshly ground black pepper
300 g (4-5) pickling onions, peeled*
30 ml (2 tablespoons) flour
500 ml (2 cups) chicken stock*
Grated rind and juice of 1 large orange
15 ml (1 tablespoon) apple jelly
15 ml (1 tablespoon) brown vinegar

Brown the guinea fowl in the butter and oil (using a deep frying pan). Remove from the frying pan and place in an oven-proof dish. Season with salt and black pepper, then brown the onions in the frying pan and reserve.

Add the flour to the pan juices, stir and cook for 2 minutes. Slowly add the stock, whisk until the sauce is smooth and add it to the guinea fowl. Mix the orange rind, orange juice, jelly and vinegar, and pour over the guinea fowl. Cover and simmer for one hour.

Remove the lid, add the browned onions, and simmer until the sauce has been reduced and the meat is soft. Taste, adjust the seasoning if necessary, and serve at once.

SERVING SUGGESTION Boiled rice* or boiled potatoes make suitable accompaniments to this dish.

VARIATIONS Replace the stock with dry white wine and whisk 125 ml (½ cup) crème fraîche* into the sauce just before adding the onions.

The pickling onions can be replaced with leeks, which should be cut into 2,5 cm lengths.

CASSEROLED GUINEA FOWL *is particularly recommended when the bird is fully grown and on the tough side.*

Roast Goose with Rum-soaked Apples

IN THE LATE 18TH CENTURY, onion, sage and apples were considered the ideal stuffing for roast goose. The ingredients and the goose complement one another, while the apple also does much to counteract any greasiness.

PREPARATION TIME: 30 MINUTES
SOAKING TIME: 4 HOURS
COOKING TIME: 4 HOURS
PRE-HEAT OVEN TO 180°C

INGREDIENTS FOR SIX
1 goose (about 4,5 kg)
Salt and freshly ground black pepper
45 ml (3 tablespoons) sunflower oil or dripping
850 ml poultry stock*
100-125 ml dark rum

For the stuffing:
6 large eating apples, peeled, cored, chopped and soaked in rum for 4 hours
1 large onion, peeled and chopped* and softened with 30 ml (2 tablespoons) butter in a frying pan
3 finely chopped sage leaves or 1 ml (¼ teaspoon) ground sage
1 ml (¼ teaspoon) ground mace
350 g freshly made breadcrumbs

Remove the giblets and wipe the goose clean, inside and out.

Mix the stuffing ingredients together and spoon into the body of the bird. If there is any left, put it into the neck cavity.

Rub salt and pepper into the skin and then prick it all over. Place the goose on a rack in a baking tin and smear the legs and wings with the oil or dripping. Cover the breast with a large piece of aluminium foil or grease-proof paper. Place in the centre of the pre-heated oven.

Roast for 30 minutes, then spoon off any excess fat and baste well with the warm poultry stock: do this every 30 minutes. After 2½ hours' cooking, remove the foil or grease-proof paper so that the breast can crisp and brown for the last 1½ hours.

Place the goose on a warmed serving dish and keep warm. Strain off excess fat from the pan juices and boil rapidly to reduce and make gravy.

Heat the rum in a ladle or small pan and pour over the bird, then set it alight.

SERVING SUGGESTIONS Serve immediately with mashed celeriac and potatoes or a purée of turnips, parsnips or Jerusalem artichokes, and a salad.

Stewed Pigeons

PIGEONS ARE AN OLD favourite in South Africa. One of the famous traditional Cape dishes is pigeon pie, which is prepared more or less like chicken pie.

Pigeon liver contains no gall, so it is not removed before stewing. The younger the bird, the shorter the stewing time. Normally it takes about 1½ hours to stew a pigeon.

PREPARATION TIME: 10 MINUTES
COOKING TIME: 1½ HOURS

INGREDIENTS FOR FOUR
8 pigeons
Salt and pepper
16 rashers of rindless bacon
4 onions, peeled and sliced*
1 clove
Sprinkling of grated nutmeg
60 ml (¼ cup) water

If there are any feathers remaining on the pigeons, singe them over a candle flame. Trim the neck away. Season the pigeons with salt and pepper and wrap 2 rashers of bacon around each pigeon. Arrange the onion slices in a large casserole. Place the pigeons on top of the onions, season again and add the clove. Grate a little nutmeg over the pigeons, add the water, cover and simmer until the pigeons are tender. Remove the lid and brown them lightly under the grill.

SERVING SUGGESTIONS Serve with sour apples stewed in white wine, new potatoes in their jackets, mashed potato*, rice or buttered noodles.

OSTRICH FILLET STEAKS *Much like beef fillet in taste and appearance.*

Ostrich Fillet Steaks

THERE ARE TWO WAYS to prepare ostrich fillet steaks. The first and most obvious is to follow the rules applicable when grilling a beef steak.

The second method is to prepare the meat as for an escalope: cut it into thin slices and beat it as thin as possible with a meat hammer before pan-grilling it.

PREPARATION TIME: 10 MINUTES
COOKING TIME: 5 MINUTES

INGREDIENTS FOR FOUR
350 g ostrich fillet escalopes or steaks
20 ml (4 teaspoons) butter
10 ml (2 teaspoons) sunflower oil
Salt and pepper
60 ml (¼ cup) cream
2 ml (½ teaspoon) green Madagascar peppercorns, crushed
2 ml (½ teaspoon) dry mustard

Heat a heavy cast-iron pan or, preferably, grid (with grooves to allow air circulation) until quite hot. Heat the butter and oil and fry the escalopes in batches for 30-45 seconds on each side. Remove and place on a warmed serving plate. Season with salt and pepper.

Allow the pan to cool slightly, then add the remaining ingredients (if you have used a grid, heat the sauce in a clean pan, scraping any meaty residue from the grid into the pan). Season and stir, then pour over the escalopes. Serve immediately.

WINNING WAYS WITH ECONOMICAL CHICKEN

These seven imaginative dishes show off the versatility of chicken in a variety of tasty ways.

SPANISH CHICKEN WITH RICE

THIS IS A VERSION of the traditional Spanish dish known as *arroz con pollo*. It makes use of ingredients such as onions, tomatoes, sweet red peppers and saffron. The rice is cooked in the same pot as the chicken, making it a simple meal-in-one dish that is easy to prepare.

PREPARATION TIME: 20 MINUTES
COOKING TIME: 1 HOUR

INGREDIENTS FOR FOUR TO SIX
8 chicken pieces
45 ml (3 tablespoons) olive or sunflower oil
1 large onion, peeled and thinly sliced*
1 large clove garlic, crushed
1 large sweet red pepper, thinly sliced
4 ripe red tomatoes, skinned, seeded* and roughly chopped
A good pinch of saffron
Salt and freshly ground black pepper
400 g rice
500 ml (2 cups) hot chicken stock*
12 black olives, stoned
15 ml (1 tablespoon) capers (optional)
125 g frozen peas

Choose a heavy-based or non-stick pan (with a tight-fitting lid) and fry the cleaned and well-dried chicken pieces in the oil until lightly browned on both sides. Remove from the pan and set aside.

Add the onion to the pan and fry gently for 5-10 minutes (or until soft). Add the garlic and sliced red pepper and cook gently for another 5-10 minutes.

Stir in the chopped tomatoes and saffron, and cook for another 10 minutes, then add the chicken pieces. Season and cook (tightly covered) for 15 minutes.

Stir in the rice and half the chicken stock and simmer for 15 minutes. Stir in the rest of the stock, adding the olives, capers (if used) and peas, and cook for another 15 minutes (or until the rice is tender and the liquid has been absorbed). Stir the pot now and again while cooking. If necessary, add a little extra stock to complete cooking the rice. Check the seasoning and serve.

VARIATION Stir in 4 tinned artichoke hearts (quartered) along with the peas.

BAKED CHICKEN AND POTATOES

ALTHOUGH VERY SIMPLE, this dish of chicken and potatoes makes a thoroughly satisfying meal-in-one with a minimum of preparation.

PREPARATION TIME: 15 MINUTES
COOKING TIME: 1 HOUR
PRE-HEAT OVEN TO 190°C

INGREDIENTS FOR FOUR
8 chicken pieces
5 ml (1 teaspoon) paprika
5 ml (1 teaspoon) prepared mustard
1 large clove garlic, crushed
Salt and freshly ground pepper
1 large onion, peeled and very thinly sliced*
2 or 3 sprigs fresh rosemary, or 10 ml (2 teaspoons) dried origanum
4 medium-sized potatoes, peeled and halved
Juice of 1 lemon
125 ml (½ cup) chicken stock*
15 ml (1 tablespoon) sunflower oil

Arrange the chicken pieces in a single layer in a baking pan or oven-proof dish. Flavour with the paprika, mustard, garlic and seasoning.

Tuck the sliced onion and rosemary underneath (or sprinkle over the origanum) and then arrange the potatoes around the chicken.

Pour over the lemon juice and stock, and drizzle with the oil. Bake for about 1 hour, or until the chicken is tender and nicely browned.

OPEN ROAST CHICKEN WITH ORANGE JUICE AND APPLES

IN THIS RECIPE, the combination of orange and apple adds a very appealing flavour, and the resulting dish should become a family favourite.

PREPARATION TIME: 30 MINUTES
COOKING TIME: 1 HOUR
PRE-HEAT OVEN TO 200°C

INGREDIENTS FOR FOUR
1 chicken (1 kg)
4 medium-sized potatoes, peeled and very thinly sliced
2 large green apples, peeled and sliced into wedges
1 large onion, peeled and very thinly sliced*
1 small bay leaf
A few sprigs of parsley
1 stick celery, thinly sliced
Grated rind of 1 orange
A pinch of ground cloves
3 ml (¾ teaspoon) ground cinnamon
1 ml (¼ teaspoon) ground allspice
Salt and freshly ground black pepper
250 ml (1 cup) fresh orange juice
15 ml (1 tablespoon) fine dry breadcrumbs
15 ml (1 tablespoon) sunflower oil

Cut the chicken down the back and open it out so that all the skin is crisped during the roasting period.

Wash and dry the chicken. Arrange the sliced potatoes, apples and onion in an oiled baking dish with the bay leaf, parsley, celery and orange rind. Sprinkle over the ground cloves, cinnamon and allspice, and season with salt and pepper. Season the chicken and place it skin-side up in the centre of the dish. Pour over the orange juice and sprinkle with the crumbs and oil. Bake for at least 1 hour, until the chicken is crisp, brown and tender.

CHICKEN, BRINJAL AND NOODLE CASSEROLE

AS IN ANY CASSEROLE this combination of chicken pieces, brinjals and rice noodles should be cooked just long enough to ensure that the chicken is tender and the flavours have mingled. Over-cooking will ruin the texture.

PREPARATION TIME: 30 MINUTES
STANDING TIME: 1 HOUR
COOKING TIME: 1¼ HOURS
PRE-HEAT OVEN TO 180°C

INGREDIENTS FOR FOUR TO SIX
3 medium-sized brinjals (500g), cubed
Salt and freshly ground black pepper
8 chicken pieces
30 ml (2 tablespoons) sunflower oil
1 large onion, peeled and thinly sliced*
2 cloves garlic, crushed
375 ml (1½ cups) chicken stock*
125 ml (½ cup) dry white wine
45 ml (3 tablespoons) tomato paste
5 ml (1 teaspoon) dried origanum
1 bay leaf
2 sticks cinnamon
250 g rice noodles, or rice, cooked*

For the garnish:
Finely chopped parsley
Grated Parmesan cheese (optional)

Place the brinjal cubes in a colander. Salt them and leave them weighted down with a plate for about an hour to drain off excess moisture. Rinse off and pat dry.

Brown the chicken pieces in the hot oil in a casserole on top of the stove. Remove the chicken and add the onion. Gently sauté the onion until it has softened. Add the garlic, then the brinjal cubes. Cook for about 10 minutes, stirring often, adding a little more oil if necessary.

Return the chicken to the casserole and season lightly. Add the stock, wine and tomato paste. Bring this mixture to the boil. Add the origanum, bay leaf and cinnamon. Cover tightly and bake in the oven for about 30 minutes.

Stir the drained, cooked noodles or rice into the casserole, together with a little more seasoning. Return to the oven for another 15 minutes, or until the chicken is tender and everything is piping hot.

Check the seasoning, sprinkle the casserole with finely chopped parsley, and serve. Pass around grated Parmesan cheese (optional).

CHICKEN WITH MUSHROOMS AND BARLEY

IN THIS QUICK CASSEROLE, chicken pieces, barley and mushrooms are cooked in a rich stock until tender, then served with a garnish of chopped parsley.

PREPARATION TIME: 25 MINUTES
COOKING TIME: 1 HOUR
PRE-HEAT OVEN TO 190°C

INGREDIENTS FOR FOUR
8 chicken pieces
30 ml (2 tablespoons) sunflower oil
30 g butter
Salt and freshly ground black pepper
1 large onion, peeled and finely chopped*
200 g mushrooms, sliced (or left whole, if small)
250 ml (1 cup) pearl barley
500 ml (2 cups) chicken stock*
Chopped parsley for garnish

Heat half the oil and half the butter in a heavy oven-proof casserole and brown the chicken pieces. Remove the chicken with a slotted spoon and season. Stir the onion into the fat in the casserole, then reduce the heat and cook gently until softened.

Add the rest of the butter and oil, and increase the heat. Stir-fry the mushrooms for a few minutes. Stir in the barley, then pour in the chicken stock and add some seasoning.

Return the chicken to the casserole. Bake for 1 hour, tightly covered, or until the chicken and barley are quite tender.

If necessary, pour a little more stock into the casserole while baking. Check the seasoning and serve, sprinkled generously with parsley.

BRAISED CHICKEN WITH SWEET POTATO AND PUMPKIN

THE DISTINCTIVE FLAVOURS of sweet potato and pumpkin are retained in this quick family meal. For the best results, serve as soon as the food is cooked.

PREPARATION TIME: 30 MINUTES
COOKING TIME: 1 HOUR

INGREDIENTS FOR FOUR TO SIX
8 chicken portions
15 ml (1 tablespoon) sunflower oil
1 large onion, peeled and thinly sliced*
2 sticks cinnamon
Salt and freshly ground black pepper
1 clove garlic, crushed
500 g sweet potato, peeled and cubed
500 g pumpkin, peeled and cubed
250 ml (1 cup) chicken stock*
125 g prunes

Pat the chicken quite dry, then brown in the hot oil. Add the onion, cinnamon and a little seasoning. Cook gently until golden.

Add the garlic, sweet potato and pumpkin and a little more seasoning, then pour in the stock and bring to the boil. Cover and reduce the heat, cooking gently for 40 minutes (or until everything is quite tender).

Add the prunes and allow them to heat through until they are plump and soft.

If there appears to be too much liquid, remove the chicken and vegetables with a slotted spoon and keep warm on a suitable platter while you reduce the stock over a brisk heat (uncovered). Check the seasoning and pour the stock over the hot chicken and vegetables.

VARIATION Use butternut instead of pumpkin.

BRAISED CHICKEN WITH SWEET POTATO AND PUMPKIN *Filling and nutritious.*

CASSEROLE OF CHICKEN WITH SPRING VEGETABLES

THIS DELICIOUS chicken casserole relies on fresh vegetables for optimum flavour and texture.

PREPARATION TIME: 1 HOUR
COOKING TIME: 2½ HOURS

INGREDIENTS FOR SIX
1 chicken (1,5-2 kg), cut into serving-sized portions
4 rashers streaky bacon, trimmed
40 g butter
1 bunch spring onions, peeled and cut into 2,5 cm pieces
5 medium-sized carrots, scraped and quartered
100 g (2 medium-sized) cauliflower florets, blanched*
2 sticks celery, cleaned and cut into 2,5 cm pieces
5 baby marrows, wiped and sliced
125 ml (½ cup) shelled fresh green peas
200 g (12-15) button mushrooms
15 ml (1 tablespoon) fresh chopped origanum leaves
15 ml (1 tablespoon) fresh chopped parsley
10 ml (2 teaspoons) fresh chopped marjoram
Salt and freshly ground pepper
100 ml white wine

Lightly brown the bacon in a large oven-proof casserole or saucepan. Transfer it to a dish. Add the butter to the casserole and lightly sauté the vegetables in batches, transferring them to separate dishes as soon as they are well-coated in fat and lightly browned.

Brown the chicken pieces, pour off the excess fat and add the herbs and a light seasoning of salt and pepper. Pour over the wine and add enough water to cover. Cover and cook the chicken on a low heat for about 1 hour. Add the bacon followed by the 'harder' vegetables, and then the others. Cook until all the vegetables are still firm, then transfer the chicken pieces to a heated serving platter.

Arrange the vegetables around the chicken. Reduce the pan juices by half over a high heat until you have a well-flavoured stock: pour this over the chicken and vegetables, and serve.

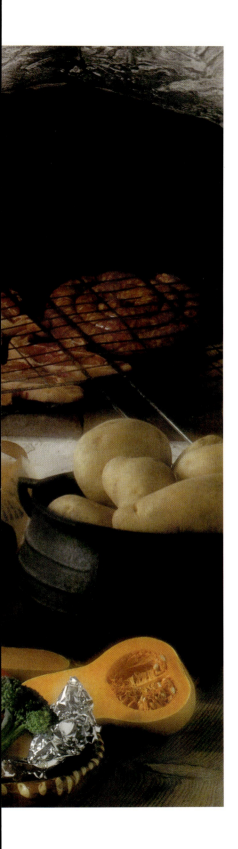

Braaivleis

*A*NY TRUE South African knows that a braaivleis is more than just a matter of making a fire and grilling meat on top. There is a whole art to the procedure, and woe betide the newcomer who barges in on the preserve of the dedicated braaier without a thought for the niceties of that art!

A successful braai is one that has been thoughtfully planned and skilfully executed. You do not need to spend a fortune on equipment, though it is certainly possible to do so.

When choosing meat it helps to buy from a congenial butcher who can advise you as to quantity and quality. And remember that fish can be cooked over an open fire too, as a succulent alternative to the standard braai fare of chops, boerewors and kebabs (or sosaties). Crayfish can be cooked in their shells, and mussels removed from their shells and then braaied on skewers. Small fish may be wrapped, well buttered and seasoned, in aluminium foil parcels.

Marinades and sauces are among the extras that can transform a conventional picnic braai into something more in the gourmet class. They help to tenderise the meat and add flavour. Fresh herbs are another must: tuck a branch of rosemary under the roasting lamb, or tie together a varied bunch of herbs and use as a brush with which to baste fish.

Potatoes and onions, wrapped in foil and thrust into the embers, are traditional braai accompaniments. Vary the menu by submitting mealies or butternut squash, or a selection of mixed vegetables, to the same treatment. And for dessert there's nothing to beat bananas, baked in the protective wrapping of their own thick skins, and then served with cream or ice cream, and maple syrup.

To the imaginative cook a braai presents an impressive range of stimulating possibilities.

A STEP-BY-STEP GUIDE TO BRAAIING · *PAGE 150*

BRAAIVLEIS RECIPES · *PAGE 154*

SPECIAL FEATURE

KEBABS – A SUCCULENT MEAL ON A STICK · *PAGE 158*

A Step-by-Step Guide to Braaing

The braaivleis or braai – the South African version of a barbecue – holds a prominent place in the food culture of the country. It is a relaxed, informal occasion taking place around an open fire on which the meal is cooked.

Customs at braais are often strongly distinctive of a particular area of South Africa. For instance, people living on the southern Cape coast are past masters at braaing tasty Cape fish such as snoek, galjoen, steenbras and Cape salmon. They pride themselves on their braaied side dishes of home-baked bread with delectable fillings. Sweet potatoes baked in the coals are a favourite – especially when eaten with snoek. The delicate flavour of snoek is often further enhanced by a sweet addition such as 'moskonfyt' (syrup cooked from must during wine making) or hanepoot grape jam (called 'korrelkonfyt' by the locals).

Further north, Karoo dwellers usually serve mutton and lamb at a braai. The meat has a distinct herb flavour imparted by the plants on which the animals graze. Delicacies such as lamb tongues, 'Karoo prawns' (lamb testicles), 'tortoise' (chopped liver and onions in fat from the intestinal colon) and butterflied leg of lamb are accompanied by baked quinces, crushed wheat salad and 'roosterkoek' (bread baked on the grill), the latter being a traditional food of the indigenous people of the area.

In the Orange Free State, entertaining is done with considerable flair, the spit-braaing of a whole lamb being very popular. Special spits are turned either mechanically or by hand; continuous slow cooking and skilled basting give succulent, mouthwatering results. A traditional side dish is green mealies cooked in a very special way: the outer leaves enclosing the cob are retained and the fresh cobs are buried in the coals. A lovely, toasted product with a very tempting aroma is the result.

Game farms have the advantage of being able to serve exotic meats not readily available to the public. Wild boar steaks with a crisp crackling, or marinated kudu steaks, are connoisseur dishes prepared at a braai. After the hunt, the liver of the buck is the first delicacy to be served from the grid. Three-legged pots are often used to produce delectable impala stews or blesbok 'potjiekos' (literally 'pot food'), simmered for hours over an open fire. Sausages made from various kinds of antelope are interesting extras. 'Vetkoek' (leavened bread dough fried in oil) is served as a side dish which, together with a jar of marula jelly, tones down the strong flavour of game.

Natal is known for barracuda and yellowtail braais at which the fish is wrapped and cooked in banana leaves. Typical Zulu dishes are served, such as green mealie fritters or steamed green mealie bread. The 'putu' porridge of the Zulus has been imported to the Transvaal, and porridge with tomato and onion topping complements beef steaks, lamb chops and sausage at many home braais in the Transvaal.

The influence of indigenous people is also noticeable at traditional Namaqualand picnics and braais. Food from the veld is often collected to prepare a braai of unique quality. Tortoise, cooked in the embers, used to be popular, but it is now a protected species in the Cape. Other veld favourites are wild veld cabbage and 'bloublommetjie-uintjies', which are boiled in water and served as a side dish. Numerous kinds of wild berries are also collected as additional snacks.

The succulent lamb of Namaqualand has given rise to traditional braai favourites such as 'pofadder' (chopped liver in caul fat), fried fat lamb tails (during shearing) and 'soutribbetjie' (salt ribs). The area's rich coastal waters provide additional variety for the braai: 'bokkems' (dried harders), snoek roe and crayfish are special favourites. Various types of bread such as 'askoek' (ash bread) and 'skuinskoek' (bread dough rolled and cut into angled pieces) are baked on the coals.

The traditional braai of the black peoples of South Africa is usually attended only by men. Pieces of meat are grilled on the open flame and held by hand on a long skewer. The outside is sealed but the meat remains very underdone on the inside. It is enjoyed with the accompaniment of traditional sorghum beer.

Building and Lighting the Fire

Although an open fire has been the basic mode of cooking since early man managed to kindle fire with flint or fire sticks, the art of open fire cooking has largely been lost with the advent of modern electric or gas stoves.

The success of any braai depends on the skill with which the fire is managed. Experts choose their wood with care. In the southern Cape, for example, vine cuttings are the favourite, while 'waboom' (from the protea family), 'hardekool' (leadwood), 'kameeldoring' (camelthorn), sickle bush, sand apple and wild sage are the preferred fuels in the areas where they are found. In the maize-growing areas, mealie cobs are used for the braai fire. Whatever material is used, it should not be rotten, crumbling or damp.

The fire is started with paper, twigs, leaves, pieces of bark or wood shavings, and larger twigs are gradually added. Commercial firelighters work wonders when starting a charcoal fire, but should be used sparingly to avoid tainting the food. Avoid using petrol, liquid paraffin or grease to kindle the fire.

As the fire becomes established, larger logs are added. Braaing can begin after the flames have subsided and when only a bed of glowing coals remains.

Branches of aromatic woods, shrubs and herbs may be added during cooking to enhance the flavour of the cooked food. Avoid resinous woods or shrubs such as eucalyptus, as these impart strong medicinal flavours to food.

Charcoal, available in lump or briquette form, is a popular fuel but remember that it burns from the bottom to the top and needs bottom ventilation.

Remember to braai over heat, not flames, and to avoid thick smoke.

The coals should be radiant and they should be maintained at the same temperature throughout the time that you braai the food.

The heat of the fire should be stabilised by adding fuel to the edge of the fire, not on top.

Should the fire become very hot, it can be cooled down by the addition of old cinders from a previous braai, or alternatively by sprinkling a small amount of water over it.

The heat should be even and glowing. Spread out the coals to obtain a lower heat, while a greater heat can be activated by flicking the white ash off the top of the charcoal or coals.

A rule of thumb by which to judge the heat of the fire is as follows: hold the palm of your hand towards the heat at the same distance as the food will be cooked. Count slowly until the heat forces your hand away. The coals are hot at a count of 'one', medium at 'three' and low at 'five'.

The braaing time will depend on the heat of the fire, the distance between fire and food, and the temperature of the food when the braaing begins. (Ideally the food should be at room temperature.)

Choosing Braai Equipment

Constructing braai facilities can be very simple. A few large stones placed in a circle, or a hole in the ground, can serve for basic braaing. Two bricks will do as supports for the grill, which may be placed at different levels simply by moving the bricks while the grill is supported on a long stick.

You can also use a large terracotta or concrete flower pot as a fire holder, with a circular cake rack or double-thickness chicken wire for a grill. Raise the flowerpot on bricks to ensure a good draught for the fire.

Alternatively, put some large stones into a metal wheelbarrow to even up the bottom of the barrow; light the fire on these, and top with a grill rack which extends over the sides of the wheelbarrow. Avoid this method if the rubber tyre of the wheelbarrow is particularly close to the container section, otherwise it will melt.

The only critical dimension is the distance between the top of the coals and the grill, which should be adjustable from about 5 cm for fast searing to about 15 cm for slow braaing.

A permanent outdoor braai is very useful, and, if well designed, can be an attractive feature of a house. The following points should be remembered when designing one:
Choose a site with the garden layout in mind – the site should be sheltered and within easy reach of the kitchen;
The height of the grill should be convenient, and an adjustable grill level should allow 15 cm clearance over a charcoal fire and 35 cm over a wood fire;
Include a special area where the wood or charcoal can be stored.

A permanent indoor braai allows braaing whatever the weather. It can be built as part of the kitchen range or fireplace, but the following points should be kept in mind:
It must be erected on sound and fireproof foundations;
Bricks or stones liable to become hot during braaing should be insulated from the existing structure;
A canopy and an exhaust fan to extract smoke and dangerous carbon monoxide gas may be necessary.

A large variety of portable braais is available, allowing the site of the braai to be changed according to the weather; the equipment can also be dismantled and packed into the car for a picnic or camping trip.

Always locate the portable braai at a safe distance from shrubs, trees and dry grass, and in a spot where the breeze will not carry the smoke towards the seating area.

Portable braais range from the very simple, like the disposable kind with its own fuel, to very sophisticated devices fitted with battery-operated rotating spits. These braais usually have adjustable grills and burn either charcoal or firewood.

The hibachi (literally 'fire ball') from Japan is a portable brazier which allows you to regulate the heat by controlling the draught: you start the fire with an open air vent, and closing the vent reduces the heat.

Gas-operated braais either have an open flame directly under the adjustable grate or a plough disc suitable for frying sausages, chops, frikkadels and chicken.

Electrically operated braais have become increasingly popular, particularly among flat dwellers with a large veranda. An electric element heats chips of volcanic rock, which in turn cooks the food. A drip pan collects unwanted fat.

Electric and coal smokers are gaining in popularity too. They are available in different sizes and are suitable for preparing meats, fish and chicken. The principle of smoke-cooking is that, while the heat does the cooking, wood chips, sawdust, herbs or leaves are added to impart their aroma to the food.

Braai accessories

Very few braai accessories are essential, although certain items do make life easier. When choosing these items, remember that a sturdy design is necessary to withstand rough outdoor treatment.

A pair of thick oven gloves to protect your hands from splashing hot fat, a pair of long-handled, insulated tongs and an apron to protect clothing can be useful. Apron pockets are convenient for holding a cloth to wipe your hands.

Long-handled wooden spoons for stirring sauces and marinades, sharp knives, a cutting board, a seasoning sprinkler and a bottle of water for controlling the fire are essential. Marinades, oil and melted butter can be kept in fireproof pots next to the braai fire.

Bristle brushes are used for basting food: small paintbrushes are ideal, but avoid the plastic or nylon varieties. Cooking pots and pans should be thick and heavy to cope with the intense heat of a braai. Iron containers are suitable for this purpose.

Plates, cutlery, glassware and table coverings should be hardy and easy to clean. Plastic or disposable tableware is convenient for large groups. Colourful paper table napkins and decorative paper plates contribute to a gay atmosphere.

An important item often overlooked at the braai site is a first aid kit. A motorist's or small household kit is suitable for the small cuts and burns that may occur at a braai.

Building a Smoking Oven

With the current interest in smoke-cooking or curing food, it might be a good idea to build a combined braai and smoking oven.

The essential thing in smoking is to have a wide chimney, not only to allow plenty of space for the food but to make possible a slow passage of heat and smoke. A tapered chimney generating a strong up-draught and a roaring fire is to be avoided.

The fire area should have a cover in front of it to create a poor draught so that the wood fire burns slowly. As a result, the heat and smoke stay in the chimney for a maximum period, the smoke escaping through tiny vent holes in the chimney cover.

The metal parts required for a smoking oven are a fire grate made of cast iron or steel, a rectangular chimney cover of sheet metal with vent holes, and a metal panel to cover the front opening of the fire chamber.

In addition, several steel rods with hooks from which to suspend the food should be positioned in the chimney at convenient intervals.

Choosing the Meat for a Braai

Only the best quality, tender cuts of meat should be bought for a braai. Choose well-marbled meat and avoid that which has yellow fat. A reliable butcher is a useful ally in making your choice.

One of the most effective ways of tenderising meat is simply to let it ripen. If you buy meat from a butcher, he will usually be able to tell you how long his meat has been ripening – and if necessary, you can let it mature further. When buying meat from supermarkets, obtaining this information is more difficult.

Beef should ideally be allowed to ripen for 5-10 days, lamb for 2-5 days and mutton about 5-7 days. Pork and veal should not be ripened.

Meat can be matured in a household refrigerator (not the freezer) at 0-4°C. Ripen a large cut of meat before cutting it into steaks or chops, to prevent drying out. Wipe the meat with a damp vinegar cloth to retard bacterial growth and place the uncovered meat on a wire grid to ensure a good circulation of air.

Frozen meat can be used for braaing, but it should thaw very slowly in the refrigerator for about 12 hours. Slow thawing ensures succulent meat because less juice is lost.

Suitable cuts for a braai

Beef The best cuts from the forequarter are flat rib, cut into strips across the rib bone, and prime rib steaks. From the hindquarters, use club steaks from the wing rib, T-bone steaks, fillet steaks, rump steaks or porterhouse steaks.

All steaks should be cut about 2,5 cm thick, except porterhouse steaks, which should be much thicker – about 5,5 cm.

Mutton Rib, loin or leg, whole or cut into chops, are all suitable. Mutton slices should be about 2 cm thick.

Pork Pork is tasty and tender, and therefore excellent for a braai. It tends to be dry, however, so a marinade is desirable. Most cuts are suitable for a braai – thick rib, loin, rib and chump, as well as the traditional spare ribs.

Remove the rind and cut the pork into 2-2,5 cm thick chops. Pork *must* be well cooked, especially in the hot South African climate.

Sausages Boerewors, mutton sausages and most other varieties of sausages are suitable for braaing. The sausage casings should not be filled too tightly, otherwise they may burst during cooking. It is important to know the quality of the product – again, a reliable butcher is the best way to obtain good sausages unless you make your own. Sausages should be a day old before braaing to ensure a well-flavoured product.

Sosaties This traditional South African dish of Malayan origin needs special mention because it is frequently served at braais. Sosaties are normally made from lamb or mutton cubes cut from the leg and marinated in a mixture of spices and onions. The pieces are strung on bamboo, wood or metal skewers and interspersed with pieces of lard and sometimes apricots.

A kebab, on the other hand, may be any one of a number of preparations in which meat, fish, chicken, vegetables and/or fruit are cooked on skewers. Kebabs, like sosaties, may be marinated before cooking.

Poultry Poultry is seldom tough, making it an ideal choice for a braai. Chicken is best – use portions of similar size in order to synchronise the braaing time.

BRAAING MEAT AND POULTRY

Grease the grid with oil or margarine to prevent the meat from sticking to it. When the coals are ready, pack the meat on the hot grid.

Meat and poultry should be cooked on both sides; the time you allow will depend on the heat of the coals, the thickness of the meat and the taste preferences of the guests.

Braaing experts differ in their methods. Some believe in searing the meat before slow-braaing it; some like to turn it frequently, others turn it only once or twice. The most common method is to braai meat for 4-5 minutes before turning it over.

Some people also believe meat should not be salted before braaing – salt extracts the meat juices – but rather during or after braaing.

FISH BRAAING

Braaing fish requires skill and patience, but with a little practice it is easy enough for anyone to master the art.

Whole fish, fish steaks, fillets of fish, kebabs and shellfish are delicious when prepared on a braai, especially when the fish is freshly caught.

Fish has a delicate texture and should be treated with care when grilled directly on the open grid. It should not be scaled and should be turned only once on the grid to prevent it from breaking up.

Fish braaied on the grid has a crisp, brown skin, but the grid should be well greased with sunflower oil to prevent the fish from sticking to it.

The fish should be cooked not more than 20 cm from the coals.

Dry fish needs frequent basting. Oily fish requires no basting, but should be brushed with butter and lemon juice when ready to serve. Whole fish can be braaied in a well-greased wire basket to ease turning.

Fish cooked in aluminium foil is moist and will retain its juices. The foil should be greased and sealed, but the foil wrapping can be opened during the last 5 minutes of cooking to allow the fish to develop a smoked flavour. Fish wrapped in foil will take slightly longer to cook.

Small, freshly caught fish, or fish pieces, are often threaded on skewers and braaied directly over the open fire.

Fish can be considered properly cooked when the translucent flesh has turned opaque and flakes readily (use a fork or skewer to test it).

Shellfish has a firmer texture and lends itself better to braaing. Either braai it directly over coals or cook it in a heavy saucepan over an open fire.

Crack the shell of crayfish lengthways to prevent it from curling when braaing. Braai the fleshy side first, turn it over, and baste with butter. Continue braaing the crayfish until properly done, that is, when the flesh has turned opaque.

Prawns should be closely threaded on a skewer and braaied over warm coals for about 10 minutes. The prawns should be basted and turned throughout the braaing period.

BRAAING IN FOIL

Aluminium foil is extremely versatile in its uses at a braai. Meat, poultry, fish, bread, fruit and vegetables cooked in foil retain their flavour, nutritional value and natural juices.

The term 'braaing in foil' is, however, erroneous – the process is actually one of cooking in foil over a fire.

Use heavy-duty foil for extra strength and, if dry foods are to be wrapped, grease the inside of the foil with butter, margarine, oil or fat. Season the food before wrapping.

To wrap food in foil, use enough to cover the food completely and use the dull side outwards to prevent heat reflection. The purpose is to retain moisture, so juices should not be allowed to escape.

Loose wrapping, as described in the following two methods, ensures the circulation of air around the food.

Food can be wrapped in a loose tent wrap. This is done by placing the food in the centre of the foil and then folding the two opposite edges loosely across the top. The edges are then sealed with a triple fold.

For a bag wrap, put the food in the centre of the foil and bring all sides of the foil up around the food, sealing it in a twist at the top. Bag wrapping is suitable only when the 'food parcels' are not to be turned frequently.

Food can, of course, also be wrapped tightly in foil.

HINTS FOR BRAAING MEAT AND POULTRY

1 Do not pierce meat when turning it. This causes loss of juices and dry, flavourless meat.
2 Over-grilling leads to a dry, tough, unattractive product with a nasty taste.
3 Braaied meat should be served immediately and not left in a covered dish, because juices are lost and the meat turns tough and dry.
4 Cut slashes in the fat of steaks and chops to prevent the meat from curling.
5 Seasoning and marinades help considerably to make the meat tasty and enjoyable, but they must be used sparingly so as not to overpower the delicate flavour of the meat. Top-grade, well-ripened meat does not require marinating and should be prepared without any additions so that its quality can be enjoyed to the full.
6 Sausages should be braaied slowly and not pierced with a fork, since this causes loss of juices and a dry end product.
7 Sosaties should be braaied slowly on the side of the braai to prevent the strong flavour from contaminating other meat.
8 Undercooked poultry tends to be tasteless, while overcooking dries it out.
9 Poultry is often marinated. The portions should be brushed with sunflower oil, melted butter, mayonnaise or a basting sauce during the braai. Sauce containing sugar (such as a chutney) should be used only at the end of the braai, to prevent a burnt taste.
10 Remember that the cooking period for chicken is considerably longer and the cooking process much slower than for other meats. Chicken is braaied for about 10-15 minutes on each side, depending on the thickness of the pieces.
11 Chicken should be cooked over medium-hot coals and done right to the bone (any pink or reddish tints should be from the marinade and not from the meat itself).
12 For a big party, a rotating spit with a number of chickens is ideal. Chickens braaied in this way should be basted frequently, with oil or marinade, for a tasty, moist result.
13 A useful tip is to partly oven-cook chicken beforehand. This shortens the braai period considerably, but ensures a lovely smoky braai taste. It is not necessary to pre-cook chicken kebabs because the pieces are small and cook in a short time.

Food wrapped in foil may be placed directly on coals or on a grill above the coals. One of the advantages of cooking food in foil is that it does not dry out when kept warm on the side of the fire.

MARINADES

The original use of a marinade was to prevent meat from going bad. Nowadays marinades are used simply to enhance the flavour of the dish. Strong-flavoured marinades are ideal for red meats and game, while mild-flavoured marinades are more suited to poultry and fish.

An equal quantity of dry red wine and sunflower or olive oil can be used as a basic tenderising marinade for red meat. Flavourings such as freshly crushed garlic, chopped or minced onion, peppercorns, bay leaves, tomato sauce or a dash of Tabasco (chilli sauce) can be added to this marinade according to taste. A tenderising marinade should always contain wine, vinegar or lemon juice.

Place the meat in a glass or porcelain dish, pour the marinade over and leave in the refrigerator to marinate. (Cover the marinating dish to prevent the strong flavour of the marinade from spreading to other foods in the refrigerator.) Small pieces of meat need to be marinated for a few hours only, but large pieces should be marinated overnight.

Meats in a marinade can be left outside the refrigerator for a few hours to speed up the process, but take care that bacterial growth is not encouraged by too high a room temperature.

Meat should be turned a few times to expose all sides to the marinade. If they do not contain sugar, marinades can also be used for basting while braaing, and they can be served, heated, with the cooked meat.

A small paintbrush can be used for basting, or use a bouquet of fresh herbs as a 'brush', to add extra flavour.

Apart from the flavour that marinades impart to meat or fish, they also add an attractive glazed appearance if the food is basted throughout the cooking period.

Many people prefer not to add salt to a marinade, as it extracts the juices from the meat or fish. Marinades should never be over-spiced, as this will blanket the taste of the meat or fish.

To dry food that has been marinated, roll it on a paper towel before transferring it to the grid.

Marinades containing fruit and wine are popular in South Africa for meat, poultry, fish and game braaing.

Marinades may be made from either cooked or uncooked ingredients. A basic mixture for an uncooked marinade consists of sunflower or olive oil, onion rings, parsley, peppercorns, bay leaves and garlic.

As a variation, add a mixture of tomato juice, Worcestershire sauce, fruit chutney, brown vinegar, brown sugar and whole cloves.

For a more delicate marinade, add pineapple juice and ginger. If an alcoholic flavour is required, add red or white wine or beer. If a creamy marinade is required, use sour cream or yoghurt flavoured with lemon juice and a pinch of paprika.

Basic ingredients for a cooked marinade are sunflower or olive oil, onion, celery, carrots, parsley, garlic, bay leaves, thyme, rosemary, peppercorns, cloves, juniper berries and apple cider vinegar. To add an alcoholic flavour, replace the vinegar with wine or beer.

Additional special marinade recipes for braais are available in the recipe section following.

TRADITIONAL POT COOKING

Our great-grandmothers probably had two pots without which they would have been lost.

The first one was the round-bellied, three-legged iron pot. This often had the legs sawn down so that it could be used on a black coal stove – one of the stove plates was removed and the pot fitted comfortably in this 'nest'. Soups, stews and meal-in-one dishes ('potjiekos') were cooked to perfection. The rounded shape of the base (almost like a Chinese wok) ensured that all the juices accumulated at the base of the pot near the heat.

The second standard pot was a flat, shallow, casserole-shaped iron pot, which was used almost as a miniature oven, to make pot-roasts, especially pot-roasted leg of lamb, and to bake bread. This is how pot bread originated.

Today iron pots are still popular for outdoor cooking over an open fire, particularly for slow-simmering venison 'potjiekos' or other meat stews.

To make pot bread, prepare a yeast bread dough in the usual way and shape into a flat round with the sides neatly tucked under. Leave to double in size in a cosy corner and then bake in the well-greased heavy iron pot, without opening the lid, for 45 minutes-1 hour, depending on the size of the bread and the heat of the fire. Hot coals are often placed on the lid of the pot to brown the top of the pot bread.

On baking day, because the dough was available, a king-size yeast dumpling was often placed over pot-roasted meat halfway through the cooking. The flavour of the meat, with its syrupy brown gravy glaze, combined with the yeasty taste of the bread is truly memorable.

Roosterkoek

Roosterkoek was traditionally made on the mornings of bread-baking days. A few 'pinches' of dough were nipped off, rolled into bun-shaped patties, and cooked over the breakfast fire. This recipe for a braai accompaniment is a bit richer than plain bread dough.

PREPARATION TIME: 15-20 MINUTES
STANDING TIME: 65 MINUTES
COOKING TIME: 15-20 MINUTES

INGREDIENTS FOR ABOUT 30 ROLLS
3 ml (¾ teaspoon) sugar
100 ml lukewarm water
10 ml (2 teaspoons) dried yeast, or 15 g fresh yeast
400 g flour
3 ml (¾ teaspoon) salt
60 g butter (room temperature)
2 eggs
Sunflower oil

Mix the sugar, water and yeast together, sprinkle 5 ml (1 teaspoon) of the flour on the top, and leave the mixture in a warm place for 10 minutes, or until frothy. Sieve the flour into a bowl, add the salt, and rub the butter into the flour with your fingertips.

Beat the eggs lightly with a fork and add them to the yeast mixture. Make a hollow in the sifted flour, add the yeast mixture and use your hands to form a soft, pliable dough. Knead it well.

Brush the dough with a little sunflower oil, cover it with plastic wrap and leave it in a warm place for about 40 minutes until it has doubled in bulk.

Knead the dough once more to distribute the yeast and develop the gluten. It is now ready to use.

Pinch off egg-sized balls of dough and shape them into round flat patties. Leave in a warm place until they are well risen – about 15 minutes.

Place the patties on a fine mesh grid over the coals and bake until they are brown on both sides and cooked inside.

SERVING SUGGESTIONS Serve for breakfast with coffee or as a braai accompaniment.

VARIATIONS Make a simpler dough for camping trips by omitting the butter and eggs, and adding a little more water.

To make stokbrood (stick bread), twist long, thin strips of the dough around 1 cm thick sticks and cook over the coals as you would roosterkoek. When cooked, remove the sticks and fill the hollows with butter and jam.

TOASTED SANDWICHES

A sweet or savoury sandwich, toasted on the fading embers of the braai, can be served with the main braai meal or with coffee as the dessert.

Cut white bread into slices 1,5 cm thick and butter one side only. Put the filling of your choice on the buttered sides and close the sandwiches.

Place them in a folding grid and toast slowly, turning them over when the undersides are golden-brown. (If you use a single grid, the sandwiches should be patted down before you turn them carefully with tongs.)

Delicious fillings to try on braaied sandwiches include:
Tomato and onion slices, seasoned with salt and pepper;
Cheddar cheese slices with sliced tomato and freshly ground black pepper;
Cheddar cheese with apricot jam* or fruit chutney;
Sliced or mashed bananas with a sprinkling of walnuts or pecan nuts.

SOSATIES

SOSATIES IS A TRADITIONAL Cape Malay dish that has become a firm favourite at braai occasions throughout the country. The 'hot' flavour of this recipe can be lessened by reducing the chillies used.

PREPARATION TIME: 45 MINUTES
MARINATING TIME: OVERNIGHT
COOKING TIME: 10-15 MINUTES

INGREDIENTS FOR SIX

1,5 kg leg of mutton, trimmed and cut into 2 cm cubes
250 g mutton fat (trimmed from the leg of mutton) cut into 1 cm cubes
A 1 cm piece of fresh green ginger, scraped and finely chopped
2 cloves garlic, peeled and finely chopped
30 g butter or dripping*
2 medium-sized onions, peeled and finely chopped*
100 ml pale dry sherry
50 ml water
100 ml white vinegar
15 ml (1 tablespoon) curry powder
15 ml (1 tablespoon) sugar
3 bay leaves, bruised
3 orange or lemon leaves, bruised
2 chillies, chopped
Salt

Put the meat and fat into a bowl with the ginger and garlic. Toss well so that all the meat pieces are coated with the ginger and garlic. Cover and set aside.

Heat the butter or dripping in a pot and add the onions. Stir-fry until soft and golden, then add the sherry, water, vinegar, curry powder and sugar. Bring to the boil and cook for 2 minutes. Leave until quite cold and then pour over the meat.

Add the bay leaves, orange or lemon leaves and chopped chillies and toss the meat well to coat evenly with the liquid. Cover and leave overnight in a cool place. Thread the cubes of meat on to 6-8 skewers, alternating pieces of meat with fat. A hot fire or grill is essential for cooking the meat, but care must be taken not to overcook or burn the sosaties. Grill for 10-15 minutes, basting from time to time with the marinade. Salt the sosaties after cooking.

SERVING SUGGESTION Sosaties are traditionally served with rice and a sauce made by heating the marinade.

VARIATIONS Dried apricots are often used for sosaties, either halved and threaded on to the skewers with the meat, or as a purée which is added to the marinade. To plump the dried apricots, add them to the marinade as it cools and then cut in half when cold. Do not marinate with the meat.

Pieces of onion, marinated or not, can also be threaded on to the skewers.

Traditionally, sosaties always had pieces of fat threaded on to the skewers to keep the meat moist and flavourful, but if you wish to omit the fat, add 60 ml (¼ cup) sunflower oil to the marinade and brush the sosaties with oil before grilling.

The same marinade can be used with cubes of a firm, meaty fish such as tuna or yellowtail. For these fish sosaties, sunflower oil should always be added to the marinade, and the apricot flavour is particularly compatible. Grill over hot coals for 10-15 minutes until the fish is opaque and just cooked through.

SALT RIBS

IN THE DAYS when meat had to be kept fresh without refrigeration, it made a lot of sense to salt and spice it well, and then allow it to get wind-dry.

Braai enthusiasts in South Africa have retained a taste for these crisp mutton spare ribs cooked over the coals.

PREPARATION TIME: 15 MINUTES
STANDING TIME: 24 HOURS
COOKING TIME: 1 HOUR

INGREDIENTS FOR TWO TO FOUR

2 sheets (about 1 kg) mutton spare ribs
20 ml (4 teaspoons) soft brown sugar
25 ml (5 teaspoons) coarse salt
10 ml (2 teaspoons) freshly ground coriander seeds
3 ml (¾ teaspoon) freshly grated nutmeg
5 ml (1 teaspoon) freshly ground black pepper
3 ml (¾ teaspoon) saltpetre (use only if meat has to last without refrigeration, such as on a camping trip)

Using a sharp knife, cut a diamond pattern into the fatty skin side of the meat.

Mix the remaining ingredients together. Rub well into the meat. Leave in a dish for 24 hours, turning occasionally.

The meat can now be cooked over the coals. Cook it slowly as the ribbetjie – spare rib – is a tough part of the carcass and needs long cooking to tenderise the inside and crisp the outside.

SERVING SUGGESTIONS Salt ribs are delicious with a slice of hot buttered mealie bread*, krummelpap* or baked potatoes*.

VARIATION If you have a particularly tough piece of meat parboil it for 45 minutes in very little water before grilling it over the coals.

AMERICAN BARBECUE LAMB CHOPS

PURISTS MAY SHUDDER at this recipe's American barbecue sauce, insisting that it masks the true flavour of the lamb. Nevertheless the sauce tastes good, and children will love it.

PREPARATION TIME: 45 MINUTES
MARINATING TIME: 3-4 HOURS, OR OVERNIGHT
COOKING TIME: 10-15 MINUTES

INGREDIENTS FOR SIX

12 thick lamb braai chops
1 medium-sized onion, peeled and sliced*
80 ml (⅓ cup) sunflower oil
2 cloves garlic, crushed
80 ml (⅓ cup) wine vinegar
80 ml (⅓ cup) water
80 ml (⅓ cup) dry red wine
15 ml (1 tablespoon) prepared mustard
15 ml (1 tablespoon) soy sauce
30 ml (2 tablespoons) brown sugar
15 ml (1 tablespoon) honey
1 small bay leaf
5 ml (1 teaspoon) salt
1 ml (¼ teaspoon) cayenne pepper
Freshly ground black pepper
160 ml tomato sauce*
30 ml (2 tablespoons) Worcestershire sauce
A few sprigs of fresh rosemary

Trim any excess fat from the chops. Place them in a single layer in a shallow ovenproof dish.

Fry the onion gently in the heated oil until softened, stir in the garlic, then add the vinegar, water, wine, mustard, soy sauce, sugar, honey, bay leaf, salt, cayenne pepper and black pepper.

Bring the sauce to the boil while stirring, then reduce the heat and simmer, uncovered, for about 20 minutes.

Remove the bay leaf and add the tomato and Worcestershire sauces. Bring barely to boiling point, then remove the pan from the stove.

Purée the sauce and pour it over the chops, adding a few sprigs of rosemary. Marinate the chops overnight (or for 3-4 hours) in the refrigerator.

Braai gently over medium-hot coals for about 5 minutes on each side until the meat is well-browned, but not burnt, and still pinkish inside.

SERVING SUGGESTIONS Serve with baked potatoes* and a crunchy coleslaw*.

VARIATIONS Should the weather turn bad, bake the chops, uncovered, in the oven at 180°C for 45 minutes, or until tender. Slide under a hot grill to crisp and brown the chops quickly on both sides.

Use the marinade over chicken pieces, braaing very gently for about 10 minutes on each side until crisply browned and cooked through but still succulent.

DEVILLED KIDNEY SKEWERS

THIS DISH of kidneys skewered with ham and bacon is a total departure from the fare one usually has at braais – and one that is sure to be a real winner. Avoid overcooking the kidneys, otherwise they will be tough and unappetising.

PREPARATION TIME: 45 MINUTES
MARINATING TIME: 45 MINUTES
COOKING TIME: 10-15 MINUTES

BRAAIVLEIS

INGREDIENTS FOR SIX
250 g bacon (4 mm thick)
250 g sliced, cooked ham (4 mm thick)
12 lamb kidneys, skinned, split and with fat and membrane removed
18 button mushrooms
6 small, ripe tomatoes, quartered

For the marinade:
250 ml (1 cup) olive oil or a mixture of olive and sunflower oil
60 ml (¼ cup) lemon juice
1 clove garlic, crushed
5 ml (1 teaspoon) grated onion
5 ml (1 teaspoon) dried tarragon
10 ml (2 teaspoons) chopped parsley
5 ml (1 teaspoon) dried chervil, or 10 ml (2 teaspoons) fresh chopped chervil (optional)
15 ml (1 tablespoon) prepared hot mustard
5 ml (1 teaspoon) Worcestershire sauce
2 ice cubes
Chopped parsley and sprigs of watercress for garnish

Trim the bacon and ham slices, and cut into pieces about 4 cm square. Carefully thread the skewers with a kidney half, a piece of bacon, a mushroom cap, a piece of tomato and a piece of ham. Repeat until 6 skewers are full, dividing the ingredients equally and ending with a kidney half.

To make the marinade, combine the oil, lemon juice, garlic, onion, herbs, mustard and Worcestershire sauce in a bowl, and beat with the ice cubes until thick. Remove the ice cubes.

Arrange the skewers in a shallow dish that contains them neatly and pour over the marinade. Turn to coat them well and marinate for 45 minutes, basting often.

Grill about 10 cm from the heat (or more if you like your kidneys fairly rare) for 10-15 minutes, or until the bacon is crisp and the other ingredients done to your taste.

Arrange the skewers on beds of watercress and sprinkle with parsley.

SERVING SUGGESTIONS Serve with triangles of hot buttered toast as a starter or lunch dish. The remaining marinade can be heated and served separately in a sauceboat with the kidneys.

BUTTERFLIED LEG OF LAMB *Boned lamb basted with a buttery garlic sauce makes a delightful party piece.*

BUTTERFLIED LEG OF LAMB

BONING THE LEG and opening it butterfly-style has two advantages: the thinner, flatter piece of meat will be easy to cook through and, because the bones have been removed, the carving is very straightforward. If the meat is sliced thinly, the leg will serve many more people. Use of the buttermilk marinade not only gives a subtle flavour to the meat, but will also tenderise it. Ask your butcher to bone the lamb for you.

PREPARATION TIME: 15 MINUTES
MARINATING TIME: 24 HOURS
COOKING TIME: ABOUT 1-1½ HOURS

INGREDIENTS FOR SIX TO EIGHT
1,5 kg leg of lamb, boned and opened up butterfly style
125 ml (½ cup) buttermilk
10 ml (2 teaspoons) coarse sea salt
3 ml (¾ teaspoon) freshly ground black pepper

For the basting sauce:
100 ml melted butter (do not substitute margarine)
2 cloves garlic, finely chopped or put through a garlic press
3 ml (¾ teaspoon) sugar
Juice of ½ lemon

Place the meat in a glass dish with the buttermilk and turn it a couple of times to coat every part of the meat with buttermilk. Leave to marinate for 24 hours in the refrigerator.

Next day, remove the meat from the buttermilk and dry it carefully with paper towels. Season it with the coarse sea salt and black pepper.

Make the basting sauce by mixing together the melted butter, garlic, sugar and lemon juice. Place the meat over moderately hot coals and cook for 15 minutes on one side until it is nicely browned, then turn it with a pair of tongs.

Baste the cooked side with the basting sauce. When the second side is nicely browned, turn the meat and baste this freshly cooked side. Do not overcook the meat – it must still be pink inside.

Cooking time varies from 1-1½ hours, depending on the thickness of the joint and the intensity of the heat. Carve the meat into thin slices and serve immediately on hot plates.

SERVING SUGGESTIONS Serve the lamb with baked potatoes*, or hot garlic bread* and salads of your own choice.

VARIATION Add fresh herbs such as rosemary or mint to the basting sauce, or use a 'brush' made of sprigs of herbs for basting.

T-Bone Steak

Braaing one thick T-bone steak produces more succulent meat than using individual steaks.

PREPARATION TIME: 5 MINUTES
COOKING TIME: 30 MINUTES

INGREDIENTS FOR FOUR
1 kg T-bone steak (well matured) in one piece, about 6 cm thick
15 ml (1 tablespoon) olive or sunflower oil
Freshly ground black pepper
A few sprigs of rosemary

Moisten the steak with the oil and season generously with ground black pepper. Place it on a grid with the rosemary tucked beneath and cook over hot coals on both sides until nicely browned on the outside. Then cook over a gentler heat (by moving the meat further from the coals) for not more than 15-20 minutes so that it is still rare inside. Cut out the bone and carve the meat into thin slices.

Whole Beef Fillet

This is an excellent choice for an elegant outdoor dinner. The fillet is stuffed with slivers of garlic, basted with an oil mixture, then grilled whole over the coals.

PREPARATION TIME: 10 MINUTES
COOKING TIME: 30 MINUTES

INGREDIENTS FOR SIX
1,5 kg whole fillet of beef
1 clove garlic
15 ml (1 tablespoon) soy sauce
15 ml (1 tablespoon) sunflower oil
5 ml (1 teaspoon) dry mustard
Freshly ground black pepper

See that the beef is neatly trimmed. Cut the garlic into small pieces and insert into the meat with the point of a sharp knife. Rub the beef with the soy sauce, oil and mustard. Season generously with pepper.

Brown the fillet well over hot coals, then reduce the heat (by moving the meat further away from the coals) and cook for another 20 minutes, turning it over every 5 minutes, until charcoal-brown outside and juicy rare inside. Serve the fillet thickly sliced.

Hamburgers

A mixture of mainly lean beef and some fatty beef makes a good combination for these hamburgers. The meat does not have to be minced too finely.

PREPARATION TIME: 20 MINUTES
COOKING TIME: 15-20 MINUTES

INGREDIENTS FOR FOUR TO SIX
1 kg minced beef
1 medium-sized onion, peeled and finely chopped*
1 slice wholewheat bread*
60 ml (¼ cup) natural yoghurt*, water or basic stock*
1 egg
15 ml (1 tablespoon) chopped parsley
5 ml (1 teaspoon) barbecue spice or dried origanum
15 ml (1 tablespoon) tomato sauce*
15 ml (1 tablespoon) chutney (optional)
5 ml (1 teaspoon) Worcestershire sauce
1 clove garlic, crushed
5 ml (1 teaspoon) salt
Freshly ground black pepper

Mix the mince and onion together so that the onion is evenly distributed. Trim the crusts from the bread and crumble it into the yoghurt or other liquid and lightly beaten egg to soften. Add to the mince with the rest of the ingredients.

Form the mixture into patties. (This may be done a day or two before the hamburgers are needed and the patties stored in a single layer in the refrigerator.)

Cook the burgers over hot coals to brown the outside, then cook more gently (further away from the coals) for 10-15 minutes until cooked but still pink inside.

SERVING SUGGESTIONS Serve on hot buttered rolls. Put out a plate of crisp lettuce leaves, sliced tomato and sliced onion* to add to the burgers. Offer a choice of tomato sauce*, mustard, Worcestershire sauce and relishes.

VARIATION To make cheese burgers, top each patty with a slice of Cheddar, Gruyère or mozzarella cheese for the last 5 minutes of cooking to allow the cheese to warm and melt slightly.

HERBED CHICKEN *Flavoured oil and lemon juice keep the chicken tender.*

Herbed Chicken

Chicken lends itself well to braaing, especially when marinated in this light, herbed oil and lemon juice mixture. It is also a less expensive dish for a braai than the more traditional red meat.

PREPARATION TIME: 10 MINUTES
MARINATING TIME: 3 HOURS
COOKING TIME: 20 MINUTES

INGREDIENTS FOR FOUR
8 chicken pieces
125 ml (½ cup) sunflower oil
Juice of 1 lemon
1 medium-sized onion, peeled* and grated
2 bay leaves, crumbled
10 ml (2 teaspoons) dried origanum
Salt and freshly ground black pepper

Pat the chicken pieces dry. Mix the remaining ingredients in a bowl and add the chicken pieces.

Leave to marinate for at least 3 hours, turning occasionally.

Place the chicken pieces in a hinged grid and cook gently over medium-hot coals for about 10 minutes, until crisply browned. Turn and cook the other side for 10 minutes, until the chicken is cooked through but still succulent.

SERVING SUGGESTIONS Serve with a bowl of natural yoghurt*, a Greek salad* and brown rice.

VARIATIONS Use chicken breasts only. Cut the chicken into cubes and thread them on to 8 wooden skewers, then marinate and braai for 8-10 minutes on each side, turning once only.

Use the same marinade over lamb chops or skewers of tender beef.

Barbecue Spare Ribs

JUICY, SUCCULENT spare ribs are marinated overnight in a tangy barbecue sauce, partially cooked in the oven, then braaied over the coals until crisp.

PREPARATION TIME: 10 MINUTES
MARINATING TIME: 24 HOURS
COOKING TIME: 45 MINUTES
PRE-HEAT OVEN TO 140°C

INGREDIENTS FOR FOUR
4 sheets (about 2 kg) lean pork spare ribs
2 cloves garlic, crushed
A 2 cm piece of fresh green ginger, peeled and crushed
125 ml (½ cup) honey
60 ml (¼ cup) orange juice
60 ml (¼ cup) apple cider vinegar
60 ml (¼ cup) soy sauce
125 ml (½ cup) tomato sauce*
30 ml (2 tablespoons) Worcestershire sauce
Freshly ground black pepper

Wipe the spare ribs and place them in a shallow dish. Mix the remaining ingredients together and pour over the ribs. Cover tightly and refrigerate for 24 hours, turning occasionally.

Place the spare ribs directly on the oven rack with a pan of water below to catch any drippings. Bake in the pre-heated oven for 30 minutes.

Brush the ribs with the reserved marinade and set aside until needed.

Gently cook the ribs over medium-hot coals, first the underside, then the meaty side, for about 8 minutes each side, or until brown and crisp.

Separate the sheets into individual ribs for serving.

SERVING SUGGESTIONS Serve with baked potatoes* and a crunchy cabbage and fresh sprout* salad. Alternatively, you can serve the spare ribs with noodle salad* and marinated broccoli.

The ribs also make a fun starter for an informal meal. Provide finger bowls of warm water with slices of lemon in them.

VARIATIONS Use lamb ribs.

If the weather turns bad, finish cooking the ribs indoors by crisping them under a hot grill.

Whole Marinated Fish

A GOOD WAY to prevent a whole fish from breaking apart as it is turned on the braai is to place it in a long, double-sided, folding grid which has been brushed beforehand with oil. The flavour and texture of most fish available in South Africa is improved by braaing.

PREPARATION TIME: 15 MINUTES
MARINATING TIME: 1 HOUR
COOKING TIME: 40 MINUTES

INGREDIENTS FOR SIX
A 2 kg whole fish, cleaned

For the marinade:
90 ml sunflower oil
Salt and pepper
125 ml (½ cup) lemon juice
60 ml (¼ cup) chopped parsley

Mix all the marinade ingredients together. Score the fish diagonally 3 times on each side, slitting the flesh almost to the bone. Rub the marinade all over the fish, pressing it into the slits.

Cover the fish and allow it to marinate for about 1 hour in the refrigerator.

Brush the wires of a long, double-sided, folding grid with sunflower oil, place the fish in the grid and close it.

WHOLE MARINATED FISH *is one of the best ways to enjoy fish.*

Grill the fish over medium-hot coals (about 15 cm from the heat) for about 20 minutes on each side, basting it often with the marinade. When the flesh flakes easily from the thickest part it is done.

SERVING SUGGESTIONS Transfer the fish to a long, warm serving dish and serve with wedges of lemon and melted butter.

VARIATION Place the fish on heavy foil in an oven-proof dish, and dot with pieces of butter. Pour over 80 ml (⅓ cup) of the marinade, close the foil securely and bake in a 180°C oven for about 40 minutes, or until the fish flakes easily.

Trout Parcels

TROUT IS A DELICIOUS FISH that is very versatile. This recipe for braaied trout enhances its exquisite flavour.

PREPARATION TIME: 30 MINUTES
COOKING TIME: 20 MINUTES

INGREDIENTS FOR SIX
6 trout, cleaned
90 g butter, softened
Salt and pepper
4 lemons
1 small onion, peeled* and cut lengthways into 6 pieces
Juice of 3 limes

Rub the trout all over with the butter, and sprinkle them with the salt and pepper. Cut one lemon lengthways into 6 pieces. Insert a piece of lemon and a piece of onion into the body cavity of each trout.

Place each fish on a separate piece of heavy-duty aluminium foil. Squeeze and strain the juice of the remaining three lemons, mix with the lime juice and sprinkle equally over all the fish.

Wrap the foil tightly around the trout and place on a grill rack over fairly hot coals. Braai the fish for 20 minutes. There is no need to turn them.

Serve the fish in their foil wrappers.

VARIATIONS For an extra garnish, add sliced mushrooms or almonds to the fish. In this case, turn the fish packages once while they are on the grill so that the mushrooms or nuts do not stick to the foil.

Harders or salmon trout are also very good prepared in this way.

Kebabs – A Succulent Meal on a Stick

Easy to make and quick to cook, kebabs consist of small pieces of meat skewered together, often with vegetable pieces threaded in between. Many kebabs are marinated, which means less expensive cuts of meat can be used, thus making the kebab a useful braai dish.

Hints on Making Kebabs

Most kebabs benefit from being marinated, but this is not essential.

The size and variety of the pieces of food dictate at which distance from the coals you cook them, and this is often a matter of individual taste. The coals or grill should always be hot, however. On average, larger pieces of meat or chicken should be cooked 6-10 cm from the heat for 10-15 minutes. Cook smaller pieces 6 cm from the coals for 7-10 minutes. Pre-cooked chicken need only be heated through and lightly browned. For rare skewered meat, the pieces should be pushed closely together, and for well-done kebabs the cubes should be far apart so that they will cook on all sides.

•

Almost any kind of skewer can be used – metal, bamboo, wood or even pieces of wire with one end bent over. Wood and bamboo skewers are best if pre-soaked to prevent them from burning. The advantage of wood and bamboo skewers is that the meat has a better grip and tends not to swivel around.

•

Basting during cooking is important as it prevents the meat from drying out. It also improves the flavour if a marinade is used for basting. Kebabs that have not been marinated should be brushed with sunflower oil or melted butter.

•

Kebabs can be served on a bed of fresh watercress, shredded lettuce or fresh herbs such as marjoram or origanum. They can also be served on a mound of rice, in a roll, or in pitta bread*.

Kofta Kebabs

PREPARATION TIME: 30 MINUTES
COOKING TIME: 10-15 MINUTES

INGREDIENTS FOR FOUR TO SIX

1 kg lamb mince
500 g beef mince
1 onion, peeled* and grated
2 cloves garlic, crushed
15 ml (1 tablespoon) finely chopped parsley
5 ml (1 teaspoon) ground cumin
3 ml (¾ teaspoon) ground coriander
5-10 ml (1-2 teaspoons) salt
Freshly ground black pepper
2 extra-large eggs
Sunflower oil

Combine the meat, onion, garlic, herbs, spices and seasoning, working with the hands until well mixed and of a rather dense texture. Add the eggs and knead again, mixing until light and smooth.

Form the mixture into 24-36 balls, then slide these on to 6-8 skewers and flatten slightly. Brush with the oil and grill about 6 cm from the heat for 10-15 minutes until crusty all round but still pink in the centre.

SERVING SUGGESTIONS Serve with pitta bread* and a moist green salad*, to which you have added tomato, spring onion and avocado, if available. You can spoon some of the salad into the pitta before serving, sliding the meatballs off the skewer on top of the salad.

KOFTA KEBABS

Pork Satay Kebabs and Peanut Sauce

PREPARATION TIME: 1 HOUR
MARINATING TIME: 2 HOURS
COOKING TIME: 10-15 MINUTES

INGREDIENTS FOR FOUR TO SIX

1 kg lean pork, cut into 2 cm cubes

For the marinade:
2 chillies, seeded (or unseeded if a really hot marinade is required)
1 medium-sized onion, peeled and chopped*
A 7 cm piece of fresh green ginger, scraped and chopped
350 ml orange juice
Juice of 1 lemon
2 cloves garlic, crushed
30 ml (2 tablespoons) coriander seeds, pounded
6 Brazil-nuts, grated
125 ml (½ cup) soy sauce
30 ml (2 tablespoons) peanut or sesame oil
30 ml (2 tablespoons) molasses or molasses-flavoured syrup

For the peanut sauce:
25 g butter
30 ml (2 tablespoons) peanut butter
15 ml (1 tablespoon) soy sauce
5 ml (1 teaspoon) lemon juice
3 ml (¾ teaspoon) chilli powder, or a few drops Tabasco (chilli sauce)
60 ml (¼ cup) cream

To make the marinade, combine the chillies, onion, ginger, orange juice, lemon juice, garlic and coriander seeds in a blender and purée until smooth. Stir in the nuts, soy sauce, oil and molasses (or syrup).

Toss the pork cubes in the mixture until well coated, cover and chill for 2 hours.

To make the peanut sauce, combine the butter, peanut butter, soy sauce, lemon juice and chilli powder or Tabasco in a saucepan and heat, stirring well, over a low heat until well mixed (about 15 minutes). Then stir in the cream and beat until well mixed, smooth and warmed through.

Thread the meat on to 6-8 skewers. Grill, basting from time to time with the marinade, over hot coals or 5 cm under a hot grill, for 10-15 minutes until lightly browned, crisp at the edges and well done. Serve with the peanut sauce.

VARIATION These satay kebabs are frequently threaded on to small skewers and served as a snack with drinks.

Chicken can be substituted for the pork, but cook for 6-8 minutes only.

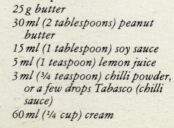

PITTA BREAD

HUSAINI KEBABS AND SAS SAUCE

PREPARATION TIME: 1 HOUR
MARINATING TIME: 3-6 HOURS
COOKING TIME: 20 MINUTES FOR THE SAUCE;
10-20 MINUTES FOR THE KEBABS

INGREDIENTS FOR SIX

1 kg leg of lamb, cut into 3 cm cubes off the bone and trimmed of excess fat
1 small onion, peeled and finely chopped*
5 ml (1 teaspoon) ground cumin
3 ml (¾ teaspoon) ground coriander
3 ml (¾ teaspoon) ground cinnamon
3 cardamom pods, pounded
3 ml (¾ teaspoon) ground cloves
5 ml (1 teaspoon) turmeric
2 ml (½ teaspoon) freshly ground black pepper
30 ml (2 tablespoons) finely chopped coriander (dhania) leaves or parsley
A 2 cm piece of fresh green ginger, scraped and grated
2 cloves garlic, crushed
45 ml (3 tablespoons) natural yoghurt*

For the sas sauce:
75 g ground almonds
Seeds of 4 cardamom pods
125 ml (½ cup) milk
30 g butter
250 ml (1 cup) cream
5 ml (1 teaspoon) salt
1 pinch saffron threads steeped in 10 ml (2 teaspoons) boiling water for 5 minutes, or 3 ml (¾ teaspoon) turmeric

Put the meat into a bowl, add the onion and sprinkle on the cumin, ground coriander, cinnamon, cardamom, cloves and turmeric, turning the meat to coat evenly. Then add the pepper, coriander leaves or parsley, ginger, garlic and yoghurt, and toss together until well mixed and evenly coated. Cover and marinate in the refrigerator for 6 hours or at room temperature for 3 hours.

To make the sas sauce, blend the almonds, cardamom seeds and milk at high speed in a blender or food processor for 30 seconds. Scrape the sides of the bowl and then blend again to a smooth purée.

Melt the butter in a small saucepan, then add the nut mixture and half the cream. Bring to the boil, stirring all the time, and then add the rest of the cream, salt and saffron or turmeric.

Stir until the sauce thickens enough to coat a wooden spoon. Remove from the heat, cover and set aside for 20 minutes before serving.

Thread the meat on to 6 skewers and grill about 8 cm from the heat for 10-20 minutes, turning from time to time until browned.

SERVING SUGGESTION To serve, slide the lamb off the skewers and serve with chapati* or puri* and the sas sauce.

HUSAINI KEBABS

SAS SAUCE

INDONESIAN LAMB KEBABS WITH YOGHURT SAUCE

PREPARATION TIME: 45 MINUTES
MARINATING TIME: OVERNIGHT
COOKING TIME: 15 MINUTES

INGREDIENTS FOR SIX

1,5 kg shoulder of lamb, cut into 2 cm pieces
2 green peppers, seeded, washed and cut into 2 cm pieces
24 cherry tomatoes
50 ml sunflower oil

For the marinade:
100 ml lemon juice
100 ml sunflower oil
2 cloves garlic, crushed
10 ml (2 teaspoons) ground cumin
5 ml (1 teaspoon) paprika
5 ml (1 teaspoon) cayenne pepper

For the yoghurt sauce:
500 ml (2 cups) natural yoghurt*
30 ml (2 tablespoons) lemon juice
60-125 ml (¼-½ cup) coriander (dhania) leaves or parsley, well washed and chopped
3 ml (¾ teaspoon) salt

Mix together the marinade ingredients in a blender or food processor until smooth. Pour the marinade over the meat pieces and mix well to coat evenly. Marinate, covered, overnight in the refrigerator.

Make the sauce by whisking together the yoghurt, lemon juice, coriander (or parsley) and salt. Chill, covered, overnight.

Divide the meat, green pepper pieces and tomatoes among 6 skewers, alternating the meat and vegetables. Brush lightly with oil.

Grill over hot coals or under a hot grill for 15 minutes, or until the lamb is firm and browned.

SERVING SUGGESTION Serve with rice and the yoghurt sauce. Brown rice is very good with these kebabs, especially if you add a little chopped spring onion and pine nuts.

SPICY CHICKEN KEBABS

PREPARATION TIME: 45 MINUTES
COOKING TIME: 25 MINUTES

INGREDIENTS FOR FOUR TO SIX

1 small onion, peeled and chopped*
1 medium-sized carrot, scraped and sliced
1 stick celery, sliced (or a few leaves)
250 ml (1 cup) water or chicken stock*
125 ml (½ cup) white wine
1 kg boned chicken*, cut in 5 cm cubes
Sunflower oil

For the coating:
10 ml (2 teaspoon) black peppercorns
30 ml (2 tablespoons) brown sugar
15 ml (1 tablespoon) sesame seeds
15 ml (1 tablespoon) poppy seeds

Combine the vegetables, water (or stock) and wine in a saucepan and bring to the boil. Cook for 5 minutes and then add the chicken pieces. Cover and remove from the heat. Leave until the stock has cooled slightly (about 20 minutes).

Meanwhile, pound the peppercorns with the sugar in a mortar, or crush them with a rolling pin (not too finely), and mix with the sesame and poppy seeds.

Drain and dry the chicken pieces and thread on to 6-8 skewers, dividing them equally. Brush them with the sunflower oil and press the spice and seed mixture thickly on to one side of the kebabs.

Grill the side with the seeds over hot coals (or under a hot grill) until the coating is brown. Turn carefully, coating and grilling each side in turn. Do not allow the coating to burn.

SERVING SUGGESTION New potatoes with parsley butter* and a crisp green vegetable such as green beans, baby marrows or broccoli go well with these kebabs.

SPICY CHICKEN KEBABS

BRAAIVLEIS

YELLOWTAIL CUBES WITH CITRUS MARINADE *The sauce is delicate enough not to overpower the fish flavour.*

YELLOWTAIL CUBES WITH CITRUS MARINADE

THE FIRM FLESH of yellowtail is particularly suitable for this method of grilling fish. The orange and lemon juice give the fish a delicious citrus tang.

PREPARATION TIME: 30 MINUTES
MARINATING TIME: 3 HOURS
COOKING TIME: 7-10 MINUTES

INGREDIENTS FOR FOUR TO SIX
1,5 kg yellowtail, trimmed, filleted and cut in 4 cm cubes
Salt and freshly ground pepper

For the marinade:
100 ml sunflower or olive oil
250 ml (1 cup) orange juice
30 ml (2 tablespoons) lemon juice
15 ml (1 tablespoon) grated orange rind
5 ml (1 teaspoon) dried origanum
5 ml (1 teaspoon) dried basil
15 ml (1 tablespoon) chopped parsley
2 cloves garlic, crushed

Combine all the marinade ingredients well in a medium-sized bowl. Put the fish cubes into a large shallow dish and pour over the marinade. Toss the cubes to coat evenly. Cover and chill for 3 hours.

Thread the fish on to 6-8 wood skewers and grill for 7-10 minutes until the pieces are lightly browned and the flesh turns opaque. Baste frequently with the marinade. Season when done.

SERVING SUGGESTIONS Reduce the marinade by one-third by boiling briskly. Serve with peeled new potatoes or triangles of toast, with the marinade in a separate sauceboat.

The marinade may also be used for larger pieces of filleted fish, which may be grilled in the oven.

FISH IN NEWSPAPER

BRAAING FISH in newspaper gives superbly succulent results. When the fish parcels are opened, the skin comes away with the paper – leaving only the white flesh behind. Use very fresh good quality fish for best results. Any large-size white fish will do, but kabeljou is especially good cooked in this way.

PREPARATION TIME: 30 MINUTES
COOKING TIME: 1 HOUR

INGREDIENTS FOR EIGHT TO TEN
A 2-3 kg whole kabeljou
Salt
Juice of ½ lemon
90 g butter
2-3 cloves garlic, sliced
2-3 very ripe red tomatoes, sliced
Freshly ground black pepper
A pinch of sugar
5 ml (1 teaspoon) mixed dried herbs
2 small or medium-sized onions, peeled and sliced*
100 ml chopped parsley

Remove the scales, then 'vlek' the fish – that is, cut it open along the backbone and through the head, leaving the spine attached to one side, so that the fish opens like a book. Remove the big centre bone but leave the head, tail and skin on.

Salt the fleshy side of the fish. Squeeze the lemon juice over the fish. Spread with butter and dot with the garlic slices.

Place the sliced tomatoes on one side, and season the tomatoes with salt, pepper, sugar and herbs. Layer the onions over the tomatoes and sprinkle them with chopped parsley. Fold the fish back into its original shape.

Wrap the fish in grease-proof paper. Overwrap it in 3 layers of newspaper and roll it up in a tight parcel. Wet the paper under a cold-water tap. (The fish may be kept in the wet paper in a cool place for a few hours before cooking if necessary.)

Bury the parcel under the hot coals. Allow it to bake slowly for about 1 hour. The fish will be cooked when the paper looks charred.

Remove the fish parcel carefully from the bed of hot coals, place it on clean newspaper and open it carefully. The skin of the fish will adhere to the inner lining of grease-proof paper and the fish flesh will be soft, juicy and succulent.

SERVING SUGGESTION Serve the fish with a risotto Milanese* and a crisp green salad*.

VARIATION Use leeks instead of onions in the filling and add thin slices of bulb fennel if this is available.

MUSSELS ON SKEWERS

FRESH MUSSELS add a special touch to any braai. Avoid cooking them for too long over the coals, otherwise they will toughen and shrivel.

PREPARATION TIME: 1¼ HOURS
COOKING TIME: 5 MINUTES

INGREDIENTS FOR SIX
60 mussels, cleaned*
90 ml white wine

4 spring onions, chopped
White pepper
45 g butter
A pinch of salt
20 button mushrooms, cut into 60 thin slices
60 thin rashers streaky bacon
30 ml (2 tablespoons) flour, sifted
70 g fine white breadcrumbs
3 eggs, well beaten
60 ml (¼ cup) oil
Parsley sprigs for garnish

Place the mussels, wine, spring onions and a little pepper in a saucepan. Cover and shake over a brisk heat for 4-6 minutes, or until the mussels have opened. Do not overcook the mussels. Shell the mussels and throw away any that have not opened.

Melt the butter and then add the mussels briefly, shaking the pan. Season with salt and remove from the heat.

Wrap a mussel and mushroom slice in each rasher of bacon and assemble on 6 skewers.

Place the flour on a flat plate, the breadcrumbs on another flat plate and the beaten eggs in a shallow dish. Gently dip each skewerful of mussels first in the flour, then into the beaten eggs and finally into the breadcrumbs. Brush very gently with oil or drizzle the oil over the mussels.

Grill over coals for about 5 minutes, basting with oil and turning frequently, until the bacon is crisp and brown on all sides. Serve garnished with the parsley.

BRAAIED CRAYFISH

Fresh crayfish is delicious prepared over the coals. Braaing it in the shell keeps the crayfish meat succulent.

PREPARATION TIME: 30 MINUTES
COOKING TIME: 10 MINUTES

INGREDIENTS FOR SIX
3 live crayfish
2 litres (8 cups) water
200 g salt
450 g butter
A pinch each of salt, pepper and paprika
3 lemons, cut in wedges

Place the crayfish in a sinkful of fresh cold water for a few minutes. In a large pot, boil the water with the salt. Plunge the crayfish, one at a time, into the boiling water, and time them from when the water returns to the boil. Boil for about 6 minutes. Cool slightly, split lengthways and remove the intestinal vein.

Mix together 90 g of the butter, the salt, pepper and paprika. Spread half of this mixture on the flesh side of the crayfish halves and, with the flesh side down, grill over a medium heat for 5 minutes. Turn the halves over, spread the rest of the butter mixture on the flesh, and grill for about 5 minutes more.

Place the crayfish halves on a large heated platter or on individual plates and garnish with the lemon wedges. Serve at once with the remaining butter, melted.

PRAWNS TERIYAKI

Prawns marinated in this Japanese-style sauce are delicious braaied. The recipe is also suited to thinly sliced rump steak, venison, pork or chicken breasts.

PREPARATION TIME: 30 MINUTES
MARINATING TIME: 3 HOURS
COOKING TIME: 4-8 MINUTES

INGREDIENTS FOR FOUR TO SIX
36 prawns, de-veined* but still in the shells

For the marinade:
125 ml (½ cup) soy sauce
60 ml (¼ cup) olive or sunflower oil
3 cloves garlic, crushed
60 ml (¼ cup) dry sherry
10 ml (2 teaspoons) brown sugar
45 ml (3 tablespoons) grated fresh green ginger
A 2 cm piece of orange or naartjie rind, finely shredded

Mix the marinade ingredients well and pour over the prawns in a bowl. Turn the prawns to coat them evenly, then cover and leave to marinate in a cool place for 3 hours.

Thread the prawns on 6 skewers and grill, shell side down for 3-5 minutes and flesh side down for 1-3 minutes. (If you are cooking them under a grill, reverse the procedure.) Brush from time to time with the marinade.

SERVING SUGGESTION Serve with fluffy white rice and a cucumber salad*.

BUTTERNUT SQUASH

Butternuts are rubbed with oil, then foil-wrapped or cooked open over the coals to make a delicious accompaniment to a braaied meal.

PREPARATION TIME: 10 MINUTES
COOKING TIME: 45 MINUTES – 1 HOUR

INGREDIENTS FOR SIX
3 medium-sized butternuts or 6 small butternuts
Sunflower oil
Salt and freshly ground black pepper

If using small butternuts, oil well, wrap in aluminium foil and place on the grill, turning every 15 minutes.

If using medium-sized butternuts, slice in half lengthways, leaving the pips intact. Score diagonally to make diamond-shaped markings. Brush well with oil, and sprinkle with salt and pepper. Place flesh downwards on the grill to brown and cook, and then turn.

SERVING SUGGESTIONS Scoop out the pips and fill the hollows with peas that have been cooked with fresh mint. Alternatively, place a dollop of herbed butter* into the hollow.

A sprinkling of brown sugar and cinnamon is also an agreeable addition.

Any left-over savoury rice* topped with chopped parsley or grated cheese, will serve as a filling.

MUSHROOMS ON SKEWERS

Braaied mushrooms are flavoured with lemon juice and thyme to provide a delicious appetiser or accompaniment to a braaied meat or fish dish.

PREPARATION TIME: 45 MINUTES
COOKING TIME: 10 MINUTES

INGREDIENTS FOR SIX
36 fresh button mushrooms (about 1 kg)
90 ml melted butter
10 ml (2 teaspoons) olive oil
15 ml (1 tablespoon) lemon juice
5 ml (1 teaspoon) dried thyme
Salt and freshly ground black pepper

Clean the mushrooms, remove the stems (save them for another use) and place 6 mushroom caps on each of 6 metal skewers.

Combine the melted butter and olive oil, and flavour with the lemon juice, thyme, salt and pepper.

Brush the mushrooms with this mixture. Grill them over coals, turning so as to brown them on all sides and basting from time to time with the sauce.

VARIATIONS Pieces of onion, tomato and green pepper may be sandwiched between the mushrooms, and garlic and rosemary may be used for an alternative flavour.

Whole large mushrooms, with their stems pared to ensure that they sit evenly on the grill, should be brushed with sunflower oil and placed with the cut side on the hot grill to sear them, and then turned over to continue cooking over a moderate heat. Baste them occasionally with a brush dipped in oil.

ONIONS BAKED IN COALS

Onions cooked in their skins and flavoured with ground cloves provide a tasty side dish.

PREPARATION TIME: 10 MINUTES
COOKING TIME: 45 MINUTES-1 HOUR

INGREDIENTS FOR SIX
6 large onions
Salt
Freshly ground black pepper
1 ml (¼ teaspoon) ground cloves (optional)
60 ml (¼ cup) melted butter

Leaving the skins on the onions, wash them well and wrap them in aluminium foil.

Place the onions in the embers and cook until they are soft. Test for softness by piercing them with the sharp point of a knife.

Open up the foil, and peel back the onion skins. Sprinkle the onions with salt, pepper and ground cloves (if used). Brush them with melted butter.

VARIATIONS Nutmeg may be substituted for cloves, or herb butter* may be used instead of plain butter.

Grated cheese may be piled on to the onions. The heat of the onions will melt the cheese slightly.

Potatoes Baked in Coals

A BRAAI MENU would hardly seem complete without potatoes baked in the coals. This standby staple lends itself to several delicious variations.

PREPARATION TIME: 10 MINUTES
COOKING TIME: 1 HOUR

INGREDIENTS FOR SIX
6 large potatoes
50 g softened butter, or 50 ml olive oil
30-60 ml (2-4 tablespoons) coarsely chopped chives
300 ml sour cream (smetana)
Salt and freshly ground black pepper
Chopped chives for sprinkling

Scrub the potatoes thoroughly and dry them. Rub them with the softened butter or olive oil. Wrap each potato in aluminium foil and bury in the embers of the braai. Pierce the potatoes with a sharp pointed knife to test whether they are cooked.

Fold the chives into the sour cream and season with salt and pepper. Fold back the foil from the potatoes so as to make cups for them, or remove the foil.

Make 2 deep incisions crossing on top of each cooked potato and then squeeze the base of the potato gently to force the cooked potato inside to emerge. Top each potato with the sour cream and chive dressing. Add a sprinkling of chopped chives and serve.

SERVING SUGGESTIONS These potatoes served with a green salad* or any other salad make a good light luncheon dish.

VARIATIONS Bury a good dollop of garlic butter* or herb butter* in the potato and then top it with grated Cheddar or Emmenthal cheese. A tin of mushroom/celery/asparagus soup heated and thinned with a little cream makes a good sauce. Sprinkle with paprika, cayenne pepper or nutmeg.

Hollow out the potato with a melon ball scoop before cooking, and stuff it with sliced mushrooms that have been slightly softened in a little water. A Napolitana sauce* may be spooned over the potato – sprinkle with parsley or chopped mint.

Sweet potatoes are also delicious braaied in this way.

Whole Mealies or Sweet Corn

MEALIES OR SWEEET CORN on the cob can provide an easy and appetising addition to your family braai.

PREPARATION TIME: 20 MINUTES-1 HOUR
COOKING TIME: 30 MINUTES

INGREDIENTS FOR SIX
For mealies:
6 mealies
30 ml (2 tablespoons) melted butter or oil for brushing
For sweet corn:
6 sweet corn cobs (or 12 if they are very small), with husks intact

To braai mealies, husk them and simmer in unsalted water for 15 minutes. Brush with melted butter or oil, then place on the grill. Turn regularly until the mealies are slightly charred, by which time they will be ready to eat.

To braai sweet corn, peel back the husks and remove the silk. Using kitchen string, tie the husks back on to form a protective sheath around the ears.

Soak in cold water for 30 minutes. (This will help to keep the corn soft.) Shake off the excess water.

Start cooking on a very hot grill, turning the sweet corn to sear it quickly on all sides. After a few minutes, move the sweet corn cobs away from the hot side of the grill, and then continue cooking and turning them until they can be easily pierced with the tip of a sharp knife (this will be after about 30 minutes).

The sweet corn can be moistened with water from time to time to prevent them from drying out.

WHOLE SWEET CORN *Tuck into the nutty flavour of this braaied vegetable.*

Mixed Vegetables in Foil

PARCELLED IN ALUMINIUM FOIL, various vegetables may be cooked successfully on a fire, thus helping to round off and balance the braaied meal.

PREPARATION TIME: 25 MINUTES
COOKING TIME: 35 MINUTES

INGREDIENTS FOR SIX
600 g broccoli or cauliflower, cut into florets
3 small butternuts, peeled, quartered and seeded
24 green beans, topped and tailed
12 small new potatoes
2 medium-sized onions, peeled and sliced*
2 medium-sized ripe tomatoes, sliced
5 ml (1 teaspoon) sunflower oil
5 ml (1 teaspoon) dried thyme
5 ml (1 teaspoon) lemon juice
Salt and freshly ground black pepper

Wash the vegetables but do not dry them. Divide them into 6 equal portions and place these portions on 6 pieces of oiled aluminium foil big enough to make into parcels.

Sprinkle the portions with oil, thyme and lemon juice, then season with salt and pepper.

Close up the foil tightly so that no juices can escape, and place the parcels on a medium-hot grill or on the coal embers. Turn them over after 20 minutes.

SERVING SUGGESTIONS Place a foil parcel on each plate (to be opened individually).

Alternatively, open the foil parcels and tip the braaied vegetables on to a bed of rice or pasta and sprinkle with a little grated Parmesan cheese.

VARIATIONS A combination of brinjals, tomatoes, onions, potatoes and rosemary may be used.

Alternatively, try custard marrows, baby carrots, onions, tomatoes, peas and chopped mint.

Baby marrows, mushrooms, onions, baby potatoes and celery make another good combination.

All these combinations can be sprinkled with chopped parsley when cooked.

Bananas in Their Skins

Bananas are ideal fruit for braaing since they come ready-wrapped in thick, protective skins, and need not be covered with aluminium foil.

Preparation Time: 10 minutes
Cooking Time: 20-30 minutes

Ingredients for Six
6 large bananas
45 ml (3 tablespoons) melted butter
30 ml (2 tablespoons) lemon juice
15 ml (1 tablespoon) brown sugar

Slice the bananas in half lengthways and brush the sliced surfaces with butter. Sprinkle with the lemon juice and sugar.

Place the bananas, cut side down, on a hot part of the grill to sear. Then turn the bananas over and move them to a cooler side of the grill. Bake until soft, then remove from their skins.

Serving Suggestions Serve hot with ice cream (or cream) and maple syrup.

Variations Cinnamon may be sprinkled on the bananas, which may be left in, and eaten from, their skins.

The bananas may be left whole on a cool side of the grill for 20-30 minutes. With this method it is difficult to know when they are cooked, but at any rate they cannot be overcooked if left on the grill for a little longer than 30 minutes.

Pineapple also lends itself well to this treatment. For four people, slice the tops off 2 medium-sized pineapples and scoop out the flesh, being careful not to pierce the skin. Cut the fruit into bite-sized cubes and marinate for 2 hours in 125 ml (½ cup) orange juice. Mix in 20 ml (4 teaspoons) brown sugar and 40 ml (8 teaspoons) light rum, and pile half the fruit into the pineapple shells. Place a knob of butter in each, then pile in the remaining fruit, topped with another knob of butter. Pour in as much of the orange juice as the shells will hold, then replace the tops, wrap in double layers of foil and bake in the coals for 30 minutes.

Ambrosia Skewers *An appealing array of fruit makes a braaied dessert with a honeyed wine sauce.*

Ambrosia Skewers

Summer fruits skewered together in an attractive colour sequence make a braai dessert which is appealing to the eye as well as the palate. The fruit used on these skewers is soaked beforehand in a heady spiced marinade.

Preparation Time: 35 minutes
Marinating Time: 3 hours
Cooking Time: 15 minutes

Ingredients for Six
2 firm, ripe peaches
1 firm, ripe pear
3 kiwi fruit
½ pineapple
2 bananas
3 apricots
12 cherries (glacé, maraschino or fresh)

For the marinade:
125 ml (½ cup) orange juice or any fruit juice of your choice
125 ml (½ cup) semi-sweet wine
60 ml (¼ cup) honey
45 ml (3 tablespoons) brandy or any fruit-based liqueur
2 cloves
1 small cinnamon stick
3 ml (¾ teaspoon) almond essence
10 ml (2 teaspoons) vanilla essence

To make the marinade heat the juice, wine, honey, brandy (or liqueur), cloves and cinnamon until the honey has melted completely. Leave to cool and then add the almond and vanilla essence.

Peel the peaches, pear, kiwi fruit, pineapple and bananas, and cut into 2 cm pieces of even size. Halve and stone the apricots, and stone the cherries if necessary.

Thread the fruit on to 6 wood skewers in an attractive colour sequence, dividing the fruit equally among the skewers. Arrange the skewers in a shallow dish and pour over the strained marinade. Cover and chill for 3 hours, turning from time to time.

Cut 6 pieces of heavy-duty aluminium foil large enough for each to contain 1 skewer completely. Place the skewers in the centres of the foil pieces and spoon over marinade. Seal the foil well.

Grill in a clamp grid until heated through (about 15 minutes), turning once. If you do not have a clamp grid, carefully turn the foil packages with tongs, making sure not to pierce them.

Serving Suggestion To serve, open the foil packets over individual plates so that none of the marinade sauce is lost. Sprinkle with grated coconut or flaked almonds and serve with cream or ice cream.

Savoury Sauces, Stuffings and Dumplings

THE CHOICE OF SAUCE, stuffing or dumpling can do much to transform even the most everyday dish into something quite special. A plain roast becomes a sumptuous meal with the right sauce and a tasty stuffing, while a simple, wholesome stew or soup gets a fillip from the addition of dumplings.

It is quite fitting that the English word 'sauce' should have its origin in an old French word, since the chefs of France have probably perfected the art of making sauces. The French, in turn, derived the word from the Latin for 'salted', and many people regard salt as the ultimate flavour-enhancer.

Sauces are often an integral part of dishes, as in avocado vinaigrette, eggs Benedict and steak chasseur. Others have become such a part of culinary tradition that some people would not think of serving, say, roast pork without apple sauce or the Christmas turkey without bread sauce.

The richer, more flavourful sauces are useful in perking up otherwise bland foods such as stockfish or for ringing the changes with often-used budget foods such as chicken. As a rule, one uses a simpler sauce as an accompaniment to a tender, top-grade cut of meat such as a juicy fillet steak, although this kind of decision is entirely up to personal choice.

Many people already have their favourite stuffing. But why not also try something a little more out of the ordinary, such as prune stuffing or celery, mushroom and walnut stuffing?

Whether you stick to traditions or experiment with something entirely new, these recipes can help you make magic in your kitchen.

TECHNIQUES FOR MAKING SAVOURY SAUCES, STUFFINGS AND DUMPLINGS · *PAGE 166*

SAVOURY SAUCES, STUFFINGS AND DUMPLINGS RECIPES · *PAGE 170*

Techniques for Making Savoury Sauces, Stuffings and Dumplings

Savoury Sauces

Sauces have been used for many centuries – although the reasons for their use have changed through the ages. In the past rich sauces were often employed to disguise the flavour of meat or fish that was less than fresh.

Some sauces are traditionally served with certain dishes because it has been discovered that the interaction of flavours and textures is hard to improve. The sauce is an integral part of the dish.

A sauce can act as a foil to a dish: apple sauce tempers the sweetness of pork; gooseberry sauce counters the oiliness of mackerel; bread sauce gives moisture to a turkey.

For some dishes, a sauce is a foundation; it binds croquettes or rissoles, for example.

The most common sauces are those thickened with a roux – a blend of fat and flour. The word 'roux' is taken from the French for 'reddish brown'. Roux-based sauces can be given many flavourings.

Some sauces are thickened in other ways – with other starches such as cornflour or arrowroot, or with eggs, butter or oil, or by reduction.

Sauces should be carefully flavoured so that they do not overpower the individual taste of the dish and at the same time do not lose their own distinctive taste. They should be smooth, light and attractively glossy to the eye.

Contrary to what is often supposed, sauces are easy to make and mistakes can be remedied; but do follow the instructions carefully.

The equipment you need
Heavy-based saucepan
Double boiler or a large, heavy-based saucepan with a bowl to fit over it
Wooden spoon or spatula
Balloon whisk
Sieve
Sharp knife
Liquidizer or food processor (optional)
Grease-proof paper

Sauces Thickened with a Roux

A roux consists of equal quantites of fat and flour, blended together and cooked for a few minutes over a gentle heat. The length of cooking depends on whether you want a white or brown sauce.

The proportion of fat and flour to liquid varies according to the consistency required – thin enough for pouring or thicker for coating and binding.

The recipes for basic brown, Espagnole, white and béchamel sauces are for pouring sauces.

Basic Brown Sauce

A basic brown sauce is used to accompany many dishes. Gravy can also be made in this way.

Ingredients to Yield 600 ml
40 g butter
40 g flour
600 ml brown stock*

Melt the butter in a heavy-based saucepan, then draw the pan off the heat and mix in the flour smoothly with a wooden spoon or spatula.

Stir continuously over a gentle heat for 2-3 minutes until you have a thick paste. Cook for a further 3-4 minutes to a light chestnut-brown.

Remove the pan from the heat and add the warm, strained stock, stirring all the time. When the mixture is thoroughly blended, return the saucepan to the heat and bring to boiling point, stirring continuously.

Cook gently for 5-7 minutes, stirring from time to time, until the sauce is smooth.

Espagnole Sauce

This rich, brown sauce is the basis of many other sauces to accompany meat. Different versions can include mushrooms, onions, red wine, Marsala, tomatoes, brandy or jellied veal stock.

Ingredients to Yield 500 ml (2 cups)
1 rasher bacon, diced
15 ml (1 tablespoon) sunflower oil
1 small onion, peeled and finely chopped*
1 carrot, scraped and diced
1 stick celery, diced
10 ml (2 teaspoons) flour
5 ml (1 teaspoon) tomato paste
500 ml (2 cups) brown stock*
1 bouquet garni*, or 2 ml (½ teaspoon) dried mixed herbs
Salt and pepper

Gently fry the diced bacon in the oil. Add the onion, carrot and celery. Stir in the flour and cook the mixture for 6-8 minutes, or until golden-brown.

Remove from the heat and stir in the tomato paste and stock. Bring to the boil, add the bouquet garni and season to taste. Reduce the heat to a simmer and cook, covered, for 15-20 minutes. Strain and skim off any fat.

Demi-glace Sauce

Mix 500 ml (2 cups) Espagnole sauce* and 125 ml (½ cup) jellied brown stock*, and bring to the boil. Simmer until the sauce has a shiny consistency and will coat the back of a wooden spoon.

Red-wine Sauce

This Espagnole-based sauce is made by frying a small peeled and chopped onion* in 15 g butter until translucent. Add 250 ml (1 cup) red wine and a bouquet garni*, and boil until the wine has reduced by half. Strain and add it to 250 ml (1 cup) Espagnole sauce*. Simmer until the liquid has reduced to about 250 ml (1 cup). Stir in 15 g butter and serve. (If making the sauce in advance, do not add the butter until you are re-heating the sauce for serving).

White Sauce

This basic recipe can be used with various flavourings to make sauces for vegetables, poultry, fish or egg dishes.

Ingredients to Yield 600 ml
40 g butter
40 g flour
600 ml warm milk, or white* or chicken stock*

Melt the butter in a heavy-based saucepan, then draw the pan off the heat and mix in the flour smoothly with a wooden spoon or spatula. Stir continuously over a gentle heat for 2-3 minutes until it becomes a thick paste. Do not allow the roux to brown.

Remove the pan from the heat again and add the warm, strained liquid, stirring all the time. When the mixture is thoroughly blended, return the saucepan to the heat and bring it to boiling point, stirring continuously. Cook gently for 5-7 minutes, stirring from time to time, until the sauce is smooth and creamy.

Béchamel Sauce

When making the basic white sauce*, put a small, peeled onion*, a bay leaf, 2-3 cloves and peppercorns and a blade of mace in the saucepan with the milk or other cooking liquid. Heat gently, put the lid on the pan and leave to infuse for 5-10 minutes. Strain before using.

Alternatively, add a little cream, an egg yolk or a few drops of lemon juice to a white sauce*. Always add these ingredients off the heat, just before serving, so that the sauce will not curdle. Soured cream (smetena) curdles very easily.

Another method is to add up to 5 ml (1 teaspoon) French mustard.

Whisk in a nut of butter to give a glossy finish.

Cream Sauce

Make a basic béchamel* or white sauce*, replacing part of the milk with cream. Alternatively, enrich a velouté sauce* with cream.

Another method is to use the pan in which you have sautéed meat or fish. Add cream and stock or wine (off the heat), then reduce over a high heat until slightly thickened.

Binding Sauce

A binding sauce, also referred to as a panada, is used to bind meat, fish or poultry into croquettes. It is also the basis of many hot soufflés. Make a binding sauce in the same way as you would a white sauce*, using 100-125 g fat and 100-125 g flour to 575-600 ml milk, or white* or chicken stock*.

Velouté Sauce

INGREDIENTS TO YIELD 150 ML

25 g butter
25 g flour
300 ml white stock*
Salt and freshly ground black pepper
15-30 ml (1-2 tablespoons) thin or thick cream (optional)

Melt the butter in a heavy-based saucepan, then draw the pan off the heat and mix in the flour smoothly with a wooden spoon or spatula. Stir continuously over a gentle heat for 2-3 minutes until it becomes a thick paste. Do not allow the roux to develop any colour.

Remove the saucepan from the heat once again and gradually stir in the hot stock until the sauce has become quite smooth. When the mixture is thoroughly blended, return the saucepan to the heat and bring it up to boiling point, stirring continuously. Lower the heat, and allow the sauce to simmer gently for about 1 hour (or until it has reduced by half).

Stir the sauce occasionally. Strain through a sieve, season to taste, and stir in the cream (if used).

Suprême Sauce

This rich sauce is made by adding eggs and cream to 300 ml velouté sauce*. Beat 2 egg yolks with 30 ml (2 tablespoons) thick cream. Add a little of the warm velouté sauce to the egg mixture, then add this blend to the remaining velouté sauce (off the heat). Stir in 25 g butter, cut into pieces, and serve immediately.

Coating Sauce

To make a coating sauce for dishes such as cauliflower cheese, use 50 g fat and 50 g flour to 575-600 ml milk, or white* or chicken stock*. Make in the same way as white sauce*.

To coat cold poultry, game or fish, add a little home-made aspic* to the sauce (or aspic made from gelatin dissolved in water).

Chaud-Froid Sauce

This classic French sauce is actually an integral part of the recipe 'cold chicken in a jellied velouté sauce'. The chaud-froid (or jellied velouté) sauce is prepared from the jelly or aspic that is produced when the chicken is poached in a court-bouillon*.

The completed sauce is poured over the cold chicken and then left to set. The finished dish is then glazed with more of the aspic for a shiny appearance.

INGREDIENTS TO YIELD ABOUT 1,5 LITRES (6 CUPS)

1 litre (4 cups) aspic*
125 g butter
60 g flour
450 ml thick cream
Salt and pepper

Heat the aspic until it is just warm.

In the meantime, melt the butter in a saucepan and add the flour. Stir this mixture well and cook it for 2 minutes, or until the roux begins to foam.

Add the warmed aspic to the roux while beating all the time. Simmer the sauce over low heat for 8 more minutes, then pour in the thick cream while beating continuously. Cook for a further minute only. Strain the sauce and season it with salt and pepper. Allow to cool before using to coat the chicken.

Note: Some chefs prefer to add an egg yolk or two to the sauce (at the same time as the cream).

Rescuing a roux-based sauce that has gone wrong

Too thick Dilute with a little milk, water or stock*. Bring to the boil, stirring or whisking continuously, then remove from the heat.

Too thin Reduce by cooking rapidly, uncovered, for a few minutes. Stir or whisk continuously until the consistency is correct, then remove the pan from the heat.

Lumpy Remove the pan from the heat and beat the sauce vigorously with a whisk for a few seconds. Alternatively, rub the sauce through a sieve or else liquidize it.

OTHER THICKENING FOR SAUCES

Sauces thickened with cornflour

Like flour, this is a reliable thickener. Use in small quantities and cook well so that the sauce is not dominated by a starchy taste. Add 5 ml (1 teaspoon) to 30 ml (2 tablespoons) cold water for 275-300 ml liquid. Blend into a smooth paste and stir into the hot cooking liquid. Boil for 2-3 minutes, stirring all the time.

Follow the directions in individual recipes for quantities different from those above.

Sauces thickened with arrowroot

Arrowroot gives a clear thickness to a sauce. Use in the same way as cornflour, but after you bring the sauce to the boil, simmer for 2-3 minutes, remove from the heat and serve immediately. Arrowroot liquefies easily, and sauces and glazes incorporating it cannot be re-heated.

Sauces thickened with beurre manié* (kneaded butter)

This is a quick and easy way to thicken a sauce or soup. Use equal quantities of butter and flour – about 15 g of each to 275-300 ml liquid. Soften the butter, blend with the flour and, just before serving, add in small pieces to the cooking liquid, whisking continuously.

Sauces thickened with eggs, butter or oil

Eggs, butter or oil are used as thickeners for hot sauces such as Hollandaise* and cold sauces such as mayonnaise*. The ingredients are blended by whisking and beating.

TIPS FOR KEEPING AND RE-HEATING ROUX-BASED SAUCES

1 Remove the sauce from the heat as soon as it is cooked.
2 If the sauce is one that contains herbs, do not add them until the sauce is re-heated, or their distinctive flavour will be reduced or lost.
3 If a recipe specifies adding knobs of butter at the end of the cooking time, do this when re-heating the sauce.
4 A sauce which is being kept for re-heating a little later can remain in the saucepan with a circle of wet grease-proof paper on top to prevent a skin from forming on the surface. Cover the pan with a lid.
5 To re-heat, remove the paper and put the pan over a gentle heat, or put the sauce in the top of a double boiler or in a bowl placed over simmering water. Stir or whisk the sauce continuously as it is heating through, so that lumps do not form.
6 An alternative method of keeping a thick, roux-based sauce for a short time is to reserve about 50-100 ml of the liquid when making it. Once the sauce is cooked, carefully pour the reserved liquid on top of the sauce to prevent contact with air. When re-heating the sauce, simply stir well to blend.
7 White sauces may also be refrigerated or alternatively frozen in airtight containers or plastic bags. If the white sauce has been frozen, thaw it completely before re-heating gently in the top of a double boiler or in a bowl placed over simmering water. Stir continuously to prevent lumps from forming. If lumps do form, follow the tips for rescuing a roux-based sauce that has gone wrong*.

Have all the ingredients at room temperature before you start, or the sauce may curdle.

Should mayonnaise* curdle while you are adding the oil to the eggs, you may beat an egg yolk in a clean bowl, then beat the curdled mixture into the yolk, drop by drop.

When adding eggs or egg yolks to hot sauces – for example velouté or chaud-froid sauce – first lightly beat the eggs (with cream, if it is being added too) in a bowl. Add a little of the hot sauce to the egg to bring it to the same temperature as the sauce.

Remove the sauce from the heat and stir in the egg mixture with a wooden spoon. Return the sauce to the heat and heat gently over low heat until the sauce has thickened. Be careful not to boil or overcook the sauce, as the eggs will curdle.

Egg-based sauces should not be frozen, as they may separate when thawed. Most egg sauces – apart from mayonnaise – will not keep for longer than three days in the refrigerator.

Sauces thickened by reduction

There is no substitute for a well-made sauce for contributing flavour, texture and colour to a meal. The trend in nouvelle cuisine is to make sauces which depend on reduced liquids for concentrated flavour and thickening, rather than on the classic haute cuisine methods of using starchy thickeners such as flour.

Rich stocks and heavy cream are cooked until their flavours are concentrated and their consistency thickened.

Supplementary thickening from puréed vegetables, eggs, ground nuts or butter may also be used.

Crayfish Sauce

This sauce uses vegetables and crayfish shells to provide the basic flavour. The cooked crayfish flesh is then added and the sauce served hot on a tiny mould of fluffy steamed rice*.

INGREDIENTS FOR FOUR
2 whole crayfish, prepared* and cooked
125 g butter
2 large stalks celery, chopped
3 medium-sized carrots, scraped and chopped
2 medium-sized onions, peeled and chopped*
1 large tomato, chopped
5 ml (1 teaspoon) dried thyme
250 ml (1 cup) white wine
250 ml (1 cup) fish* or chicken stock*
250 ml (1 cup) cream
A pinch of nutmeg
A pinch of cayenne pepper
A pinch of sugar
A squeeze of lemon juice
Salt

Slice the 2 crayfish in half and remove all the edible flesh from the shell and claws. Break the shells into small pieces.

Melt 25 g of the butter in a large, flat, heavy-based saucepan. Add all the vegetables and the thyme, then stir-fry quickly over medium-high heat until the vegetables have become limp and glazed. Add the broken crayfish shells, white wine and fish or chicken stock, and allow to simmer for 20 minutes with the pan lid on. Strain the stock and discard all the solids.

Bring the strained stock to the boil in the same saucepan and boil it rapidly without a lid until the volume has been reduced by half. Add the cream and continue boiling rapidly – do not stir. A sea of tiny bubbles will form all over the sauce.

Dip a wooden spoon into the boiling sauce from time to time – when it is thick enough to form a coating on the spoon, it is time to add the remaining butter.

Switch off the stove but leave the saucepan on the stove plate. With a wire whisk, beat the cold butter into the sauce, bit by bit, until it has become thick and glazed.

Add the cooked crayfish to the sauce. Re-heat the sauce. Season it with the nutmeg, cayenne pepper, sugar and lemon juice. Taste it and adjust the seasoning.

Mint sauce

This sauce is the traditional accompaniment to roast lamb and keeps for four months or more.

INGREDIENTS TO YIELD 300 ML
300 ml distilled white vinegar
175 g sugar
75 g mint sprigs, washed and drained

Put the vinegar with the sugar in a heavy-based pan. Bring to the boil slowly, stirring continuously, until the sugar dissolves.

Boil for 1 minute, then remove the pan from the heat.

Strip the leaves from the mint, chop them and add to the pan. Return the pan to the heat and bring to the boil for about 1 minute.

Allow to cool, then bottle the mint sauce as you would a flavoured vinegar*.

VARIATION For an even longer-lasting version, chop the leaves finely, put them in a jar and cover with a layer of golden syrup. To use, take a spoonful of the mixture, stir with a little wine vinegar, and serve.

SALAD DRESSINGS

A good dressing is essential to a salad, but it must be varied to accord with the salad ingredients.

A sharp vinaigrette*, made from a blend of oil and vinegar, is probably best for a green salad*, but egg, fish, meat or vegetable salads would nearly always need additional flavours.

Other good bases for salad dressings include yoghurt, lemon juice, buttermilk or mayonnaise*, with herbs, spices and flavourings added.

FATS AND OILS

Fats and oils play an important part in cooking, as they contribute to or sometimes alter the flavour of food – particularly when frying.

Fats

These are derived from animal tissue (for example, from meat, dairy products or oily fish) and from nuts or vegetables.

Cooking fats that are commonly used include butter, blended fats, dripping*, lard, margarine and suet.

Butter Made from the fatty substances skimmed from full-cream milk. It is churned, then pressed to squeeze out water, and salt is often added.

Butter is used as the cooking medium for egg dishes, sautéed vegetables and shallow-frying, and in the baking of cakes and biscuits.

Melted butter This is usually served as a sauce with poached fish* or boiled vegetables. Heat the butter over low heat and season lightly with salt, freshly ground pepper and a few drops of lemon juice.

Beurre noisette (noisette butter) This is melted butter allowed to brown lightly before being seasoned. It is served with eggs, brains, poached skate, fish roe or boiled vegetables.

Beurre noir (brown butter) Melted butter in this instance is heated until it becomes nut-brown, but not black. Add 30 ml (2 tablespoons) finely chopped parsley, 15 ml (1 tablespoon) wine vinegar and 15 ml (1 tablespoon) chopped capers to every 100 g butter. Serve with the same types of food as you would *beurre noisette*.

Meunière butter This sauce is made from butter in which fish has been shallow-fried. Add a little extra butter to the pan juices and cook until lightly brown. Blend in a squeeze of lemon juice and a little chopped parsley (optional).

Savoury butters These are used to garnish meat, fish and vegetable dishes, or they may be added to sauces. Softened butter is flavoured with varying ingredients according to the dish it is meant to garnish. See the recipe section for suggested ingredients. On average, allow 25 g butter per person.

Soften the butter in a bowl, before blending in the flavouring ingredient. Herbs and vegetables must be finely chopped, pounded or thoroughly crushed. A mortar and pestle are ideal for this purpose. When all the ingredients are combined, roll the butter flat between two sheets of damp grease-proof paper. Chill thoroughly in the refrigerator before cutting the butter into small fancy shapes.

Ghee This form of clarified butter is sometimes used in Indian cooking. Since it can be heated to a high temperature, ghee makes frying less troublesome, as butter in its conventional form burns rapidly.

Another advantage is that it can be stored at room temperature for over six months; this is vital in India, where the heat can quickly cause spoilage.

Use 500 g butter; this will yield about 350-400 g ghee. Put the butter in a deep saucepan, place it on the stove and bring to a gentle boil. Keep at a medium to low temperature and boil the liquid butter slowly for 15-20 minutes. The butter will bubble audibly as the water evaporates (however, once all the water has evaporated, the sound will cease).

At this stage a layer of scum will rise to the surface, the salt will settle at the bottom, and the clarified butter will settle in the middle. Place a steel, enamel or glass container on a flat surface nearby. Remove the ghee from the heat and blow the scum to one side of the saucepan.

Pour the clarified butter into the container, leaving the salt at the bottom of the saucepan. The ghee should be crystal-clear. Cool and store.

Clarified fat or dripping Add water to fat or dripping – about one-third as much water as fat. For example, for 250 g fat, use 80 ml (⅓ cup) water. Bring the mixture to the boil, then strain it into a bowl and leave it to cool.

When cold and set, remove the cake of clarified fat and scrape any scum from the bottom.

Store in a dry bowl or jar. It will keep for up to three weeks in a refrigerator. Heat again to use for sealing.

Crème fraîche To make crème fraîche, beat 250 ml (1 cup) cream with 250 ml (1 cup) sour cream (smetena) in a bowl. Cover the mixture loosely with plastic wrap and leave it to stand overnight, or until it has thickened. Then refrigerate it for at least four hours to thicken it even further. The tart flavour of this sauce will intensify the longer it remains in the refrigerator.

Clarified butter This is sometimes used in recipes for frying or grilling, or for sealing potted food. It is an expensive cooking medium, as 250 g butter produces about 175 g clarified butter.

Put the butter in a saucepan and place the saucepan over a low heat to melt the butter completely. Skim off the foam as the butter heats.

The sediment will sink to the bottom. To make sure that it stays there, remove the pan from the heat and leave it to stand for 5 minutes. Then strain the butter through a double layer of scalded cheesecloth or fine cotton into a bowl.

If you are using the butter to seal potted meat or fish, allow to cool a little before pouring it over the surface.

Store clarified butter in pots marked with the date of preparation. It will keep 3-4 weeks in a refrigerator or up to six months in a freezer.

Oils

Oils, which are expressed from seeds, nuts, fruit and vegetables, are not only important components of sauces and salad dressings, but are widely used in the kitchen – for frying, glazing, baking, sweet-making, greasing cooking surfaces and as an ingredient in a wide range of foods.

There are several types of oil, differing in flavour and colour, and used for different purposes. Some commercial oils are blends sold as 'cooking oil' or 'salad oil'. The price varies considerably, depending on the demand and the cost of the refining process.

All-round oils, which can be used for cooking and salad dressings, are made from corn (maize), olives, peanuts (groundnuts), sesame seeds, soybeans or sunflower seeds.

Walnut and wheatgerm oil are particularly expensive. Both are used in small quantities in salad dressings for their distinctive flavours.

Sweet almond oil is used in sweet-making, particularly for coating the trays on which the sweets are set to cool.

Making herb oils

Herb oils are delicious for use in salad dressings. Use a good-quality oil – preferably olive oil. Place sprigs of fresh herbs in an attractive glass jar. Thyme, tarragon and marjoram work particularly well. Pour the oil into the container, seal and leave for at least two months before using.

STUFFINGS

A stuffing consists of a base to which fat, seasoning and flavouring are added. The base may consist of breadcrumbs, sausage meat, potatoes, rice, oatmeal or a similar bulk ingredient. The flavouring may include herbs, fruit, vegetables, nuts or any ingredients which complement the food with which the stuffing is to be served.

Stuffings are used to flavour and add bulk to meat, poultry or fish. They also keep the flesh moist as they steam during cooking.

All stuffed dishes need slightly longer cooking times, as the heat does not easily penetrate.

Stuffings can be made ahead of time and kept in the refrigerator or freezer. However, never put the stuffing inside the food and then freeze it, as it can easily turn sour.

Making stuffings

If the recipe calls for breadcrumbs, make them yourself from slightly stale (2-day-old) bread. Cut the crusts off the bread and rub through a grater or wire sieve, or use a liquidizer. Commercially dried breadcrumbs are not a suitable base for a stuffing.

If you use the liver of the bird, brown it lightly in fat before chopping it finely and adding it.

If you cannot buy good sausage meat, buy well-flavoured sausages instead and skin them. Those flavoured with herbs are especially good.

Use chopped, fresh herbs if you can. For dried herbs, halve the quantity.

Always taste the stuffing before you use it, to make sure that the balance of flavours is right.

Ensure that the texture is crumbly. If too wet, it will be sodden and heavy when cooked; if too dry, it will fall apart. Too much egg used in binding the mixture will make the stuffing hard and close-textured.

Using stuffing

Stuffing should be packed loosely in the body cavity of poultry to allow for expansion during cooking.

It may also be inserted in joints of meat that are to be roasted – stuff the mixture in the cavity formed by boning a leg, or make a special incision in other joints by inserting a long, thin knife through the meat and twisting it slightly to enlarge the cut.

It is not necessary to sew up the cavity of poultry after inserting the stuffing (except when the bird has been boned*). However, it is best to sew up the ends of incisions in meat joints to prevent the stuffing from falling out.

Boned meat – such as shoulder, breast or rib – is also ideal for stuffing and rolling. Spread out the meat, cover it with stuffing and roll it up. Secure the roll with string before roasting.

As a general rule, use about 125 g – or 190-250 ml (¾-1 cup) – stuffing to each 500 g bird or meat. If any stuffing is left over, use it to make stuffing balls that may be added to soups or stews.

Alternatively, bake any left-over stuffing in a greased baking tin, inserted in the oven for the last 30-45 minutes' cooking time for your roast. Baste the stuffing from time to time.

DUMPLINGS

Dumplings are small balls of dough, stuffing or potato mixture that are steamed or poached to serve with soups and stews.

Some dumplings are also suitable as a dessert when sprinkled with cinnamon sugar.

Make sure that the dumpling dough is moist, and the dumplings are quite small – the size of a large walnut.

The dumplings will swell during cooking, so allow room for them to expand in stocks and broths. If there are too many, cook half at a time, take them out with a slotted spoon and keep them warm while cooking the rest.

Cook dumplings gently, at simmering point or a gentle boil. Too vigorous cooking will make them crumble and break up.

When making potato dumplings, choose a floury potato. It will bind better than a waxy potato.

For further hints on making dumplings, see the section on basic stocks and soups, or follow the directions in specific recipes.

SAVOURY SAUCES, STUFFINGS AND DUMPLINGS

APPLE SAUCE

THE APPLE SAUCE that is so popular today with pork was already in existence by the 17th century. It is equally delicious with roast goose.

PREPARATION TIME: 15 MINUTES
COOKING TIME: 20-25 MINUTES

INGREDIENTS TO YIELD 500 ML (2 CUPS)
5 medium-sized cooking apples, peeled, cored and sliced
60-80 ml (¼-⅓ cup) water
40 g butter
30 ml (2 tablespoons) sugar
1 ml (¼ teaspoon) freshly grated nutmeg
1 ml (¼ teaspoon) salt

Put the sliced apples in a saucepan with the water. Bring to the boil, then simmer for 15-20 minutes, stirring from time to time with a wooden spoon, until the fruit is soft. Rub the pulp through a sieve to purée it, or liquidize it.

Melt the butter in the cleaned pan and add the apple purée, sugar, nutmeg and salt. Beat well and taste, adjusting the seasoning if necessary.

SERVING SUGGESTIONS The sharpness of apple sauce acts as a foil to the richness of pork, duck, game and mackerel. Serve hot or cold.

AVOCADO SAUCE

RIPE AVOCADOS make a smooth, rich sauce that is superb served with fish or salad, or as a dip.

PREPARATION TIME: 10 MINUTES

INGREDIENTS TO YIELD 375 ML (1½ CUPS)
1-2 ripe avocados, peeled and cubed
1-2 cloves garlic, peeled and crushed
30 ml (2 tablespoons) lemon juice
15 ml (1 tablespoon) olive or sunflower oil
Salt and freshly ground black pepper

Combine the avocados, garlic, lemon juice and oil in a food processor or blender, and blend to a smooth, thick sauce. Season to taste with salt and pepper.

BARBECUE SAUCE *A perfect complement to red meats and poultry.*

BARBECUE SAUCE

IT IS A GOOD IDEA to have an appetising barbecue sauce on hand ready for meals around the braai. Store the sauce in a glass jar in the refrigerator for up to three weeks, or freeze it for up to three months.

PREPARATION TIME: 20 MINUTES
COOKING TIME: 45 MINUTES

INGREDIENTS TO YIELD 750 ML (3 CUPS)
2 cloves garlic, peeled and crushed
1 onion, peeled* and grated
1 tin (410 g) peeled tomatoes, chopped
125 ml (½ cup) sunflower oil
125 ml (½ cup) white wine
Juice and grated rind of 1 orange
125 ml (½ cup) lemon juice
30 ml (2 tablespoons) Worcestershire sauce
100 g brown sugar
Salt and freshly ground black pepper
A dash of Tabasco (chilli sauce)

Combine all the ingredients, except the seasoning and Tabasco, in a saucepan and bring to the boil. Turn down the heat and simmer the mixture for 45 minutes until the tomato is completely cooked and the sauce has thickened. Season to taste with salt and pepper, and add 6-9 drops Tabasco to taste. Strain the sauce.

SERVING SUGGESTION Use this as a basting sauce for grilled beef, lamb or chicken.

VARIATION The sauce can be thickened with the addition of 30 ml (2 tablespoons) cornflour mixed to a smooth paste with water. This should be added to the sauce when it is done, and then the sauce should be brought to the boil again.

BEARNAISE SAUCE

THIS SAUCE is made in much the same way as Hollandaise sauce, except that it has a flavourful base of herbs and onion. It is a superb accompaniment to egg, fish, poultry or meat dishes.

PREPARATION TIME: 20 MINUTES

INGREDIENTS TO YIELD 250 ML (1 CUP)
30 ml (2 tablespoons) chopped spring onion
30 ml (2 tablespoons) chopped fresh tarragon, or 10 ml (2 teaspoons) dried tarragon
60 ml (¼ cup) tarragon vinegar
Salt and pepper
15 ml (1 tablespoon) cold water
3 egg yolks, lightly beaten
250 ml (1 cup) melted clarified butter*, cooled
Chopped parsley

Combine the spring onion, tarragon, vinegar and a little salt and pepper in a saucepan, and reduce them on the stove to 15 ml (1 tablespoon). Remove from the heat, then add the cold water and egg yolks.

Transfer to a bowl (not metal), whisk the mixture over boiling water until the sauce is thick and creamy, and then beat in the clarified butter, a little at a time, until the sauce is thick and firm. Season the sauce, and add chopped parsley to taste.

VARIATIONS A simpler version can be made using a base of Hollandaise sauce* prepared in a blender or food processor. Combine 30 ml (2 tablespoons) white vinegar, 15 ml (1 tablespoon) tarragon vinegar, 10 ml (2 teaspoons) minced spring onion, 5 ml (1 teaspoon) dried tarragon and a pinch of cayenne pepper. Reduce in a saucepan to about 10 ml (2 teaspoons). Blend into 250 ml (1 cup) Hollandaise sauce at high speed for 3 seconds.

Green peppercorn sauce can be made by adding 30 ml (2 tablespoons) tinned green peppercorns, well drained, to 250 ml (1 cup) Bearnaise sauce just before serving. You may also add 30 ml (2 tablespoons) cream with the peppercorns. Alternatively, heat 25 g butter in a pan until frothy, then add 30 ml (2 tablespoons) green peppercorns, well drained, and cook for 1 minute. Pour over 15 ml (1 tablespoon) warm brandy, ignite the brandy and stir in 250 ml (1 cup) Bearnaise sauce, beating well.

Bread Sauce

This milk-based sauce, first recorded in Scotland, is occasionally maligned because of the unfortunate practice of boiling the breadcrumbs for too long. To avoid this, serve the sauce immediately and do not re-boil.

Preparation Time: 15 minutes
Standing Time: 30 minutes

Ingredients to Yield 500 ml (2 cups)
1 medium-sized onion, peeled*
4 cloves
1 ml (¼ teaspoon) ground mace
4 peppercorns
500 ml (2 cups) milk
125 ml (½ cup) fresh white breadcrumbs
Salt and pepper
7 ml (1½ teaspoons) butter
30 ml (2 tablespoons) thin cream

Stud the onion with the cloves and put it in a pan with the mace, peppercorns and milk. Bring to the boil, then remove the pan from the heat immediately and leave it to infuse (covered) for about 30 minutes.

Strain the milk into another pan and stir in the breadcrumbs. Return to the heat, stirring continuously until the mixture boils and becomes quite thick.

Season to taste and stir in the butter and cream. Serve warm, but do not re-boil.

Serving Suggestion Serve the sauce with roast chicken, turkey or game.

Caper Sauce

This piquant and unusual sauce provides a tasty contrast when served with mutton and other meats.

Preparation Time: 10 minutes

Ingredients to Yield 500 ml (2 cups)
25 g butter
25 g flour
500 ml (2 cups) hot vegetable* or basic stock*
15 ml (1 tablespoon) capers
10 ml (2 teaspoons) finely chopped parsley
10 ml (2 teaspoons) lemon juice
Salt and pepper
15 ml (1 tablespoon) thin cream

Melt the butter in a pan over a gentle heat. Mix in the flour, and cook for 2-3 minutes, stirring continuously. Remove the pan from the heat and gradually add the hot stock, stirring until smooth and creamy.

Put the pan back on the heat and bring to the boil, stirring continuously, then simmer for a further 5 minutes, stirring from time to time. Add the capers, parsley and lemon juice. Season to taste and stir in the cream.

Serving Suggestion Serve with boiled mutton*.

Celery Sauce

This creamy celery sauce is particularly suitable as an accompaniment to poultry, ham or veal.

Preparation Time: 20 minutes
Cooking Time: 45 minutes

Ingredients to Yield 1 litre (4 cups)
1 large head of celery or 2 celery hearts, washed, drained and finely chopped
575-600 ml water, or chicken stock*
Salt and pepper
1 ml (¼ teaspoon) ground nutmeg
40 g butter
40 g flour
500 ml (2 cups) milk
30 ml (2 tablespoons) thin cream (optional)

Put the chopped celery in a pan with the water or stock. Bring it to the boil, then simmer (covered) until tender – about 20 minutes. Drain, reserving the cooking liquid, and rub the celery through a sieve or liquidize it. Season with salt, pepper and nutmeg.

Melt half of the butter and stir in half of the flour. Cook gently, stirring continuously with a wooden spoon, for 2-3 minutes.

Add the milk and 100 ml of the celery stock, stirring well to avoid lumps. Bring to the boil, then simmer for about 5 minutes. Stir in the puréed celery.

Blend the remaining butter with the remaining flour, and add to the sauce in small pieces, stirring well until the sauce is smooth and thick. Add the cream, if used. Serve hot.

Chasseur Sauce

This tasty tomato and mushroom sauce is easy to prepare. It is useful to make a fairly large quantity of basic brown sauce to freeze in 250 ml containers and have handy for recipes such as this.

Preparation Time: 15 minutes

Ingredients to Yield about 750 ml (3 cups)
125 g mushrooms, sliced
30 g butter
250 ml (1 cup) basic brown sauce*
125 ml (½ cup) white wine
30 ml (2 tablespoons) brandy
125 ml (½ cup) tomato purée
Salt and freshly ground pepper

Sauté the mushrooms in the butter, then add the rest of the ingredients and simmer for 5 minutes. Season the sauce to taste.

Serving Suggestions This popular steak sauce is also good with lamb chops.

Variations Crushed garlic can be added to taste, and a little sage combines well with the other flavours.

The success of the sauce depends on the quality of the brown sauce, but a very acceptable alternative can be made using gravy made with pan juices as a base.

Cheese Sauce

Cheese sauces are often made with Cheddar or Cheshire. Of the two, Cheddar gives a sharper tang to the sauce.

Experiment with other strong cheeses, if you like: you will find a variety of local and imported cheeses in your local supermarket or delicatessen. The character of the sauce will change, sometimes subtly, sometimes dramatically.

Preparation Time: 15 minutes
Cooking Time: 15 minutes

Ingredients to Yield 700 ml
575-600 ml milk
40 g butter
40 g flour
5 ml (1 teaspoon) dry mustard
100-125 g Cheddar or Cheshire cheese, grated
A pinch of cayenne pepper, or 1 ml (¼ teaspoon) ground nutmeg

Heat the milk through gently in a saucepan. Remove when warm, cover with the lid and set aside.

Melt the butter over the same gentle heat in another pan. Mix in the flour, using a wooden spoon, and continue to cook gently for 2-3 minutes, stirring all the time. Add the mustard.

Remove from the heat and add the warm milk, stirring continuously. Return the pan to the heat and bring the sauce up to the boil, still stirring, then simmer for about 5 minutes, stirring from time to time.

When the sauce is creamy, add the cheese, a little at a time, stirring. Season with the cayenne pepper or nutmeg.

Serving Suggestions This sauce is an excellent accompaniment to fish, eggs, vegetables, pasta, blintzes or pancakes.

Cumberland Sauce

Queen Victoria's uncle, the Duke of Cumberland, is said to be honoured in the name of this sauce, although no one seems to know how or when the Cumberland label became attached.

During the last years of Victoria's reign the sauce became an almost inseparable companion to any game dish.

Preparation Time: 20 minutes
Cooking Time: 1 hour

Ingredients to Yield 500 ml (2 cups)
450 g redcurrant jelly
375 ml (½ bottle) port
Grated rind and strained juice of 1 orange and 1 lemon
1 ml (¼ teaspoon) cayenne pepper
30 ml (2 tablespoons) Worcestershire sauce

Place the redcurrant jelly and port in a small saucepan, and bring to the boil, stirring from time to time. Cook over a gentle heat until reduced by about one-third and just runny. Leave to cool.

Stir in the grated orange and lemon rind and juice. Add the cayenne pepper and Worcestershire sauce, and mix well.

Serving Suggestions Serve Cumberland sauce cold with cold meats or game or hot dishes of ham or tongue. It will keep for about 2 months in the refrigerator.

Crayfish and Prawn Sauce

THIS IS A SPECIAL sauce to serve with poached fish or seafood soufflés. It is ideal to make when you have a pile of crayfish shells and legs left over. Alternatively, you can freeze crayfish shells until you have collected enough. Frozen, shelled crayfish leg meat is easily available and can be used in place of the tail meat.

PREPARATION TIME: 30 MINUTES
COOKING TIME: 1½ HOURS

INGREDIENTS TO YIELD 1 LITRE (4 CUPS)
3 cooked crayfish shells, chopped coarsely
500 ml (2 cups) fish stock*
70 g butter
45 ml (3 tablespoons) flour
250 ml (1 cup) cream
100 g cooked, shelled* prawns, diced
250 g cooked crayfish meat, diced
30 ml (2 tablespoons) brandy
Salt and freshly ground white pepper
Cayenne pepper (optional)

Simmer the chopped crayfish shells in the fish stock for 20 minutes, then strain. Melt 45 g of the butter in a saucepan and stir in the flour to make a smooth paste. Stir in the stock slowly and keep stirring until the sauce thickens and starts to bubble. Turn down the heat and simmer it gently for 20 minutes. Then add the cream and simmer (uncovered, stirring from time to time to prevent sticking or a skin forming) for about 10 minutes, or until the sauce has been reduced to about 500 ml (2 cups).

Melt the remaining butter and sauté the diced prawn and crayfish meat until it is heated through. Pour the brandy over the shellfish and set it alight when heated sufficiently. Add to the sauce and flavour it to taste with salt, pepper and a little cayenne pepper, if liked.

SERVING SUGGESTIONS Serve, as suggested, with poached fish* or soufflés, or combine with left-over flaked fish to make a tasty pie filling.

VARIATIONS A few sliced and sautéed mushrooms may be added to the sauce, if desired, and the sauce may also be lightly flavoured with garlic or herbs such as fennel, basil or tarragon.

The brandy may be left out of the sauce and, instead of being sautéed, the crayfish and prawns may be simmered in a little white wine.

Curry Sauce

THIS RECIPE is for quite a large quantity of curry sauce as it freezes very well and is useful to have on hand. It can be varied considerably by several delicious additions just before serving.

PREPARATION TIME: 15 MINUTES
COOKING TIME: 1 HOUR

INGREDIENTS TO YIELD 1,5 LITRES (6 CUPS)
50 ml sunflower oil
4 onions, peeled and finely sliced*
4 cloves garlic, crushed
4 apples, peeled and grated
75 ml (5 tablespoons) curry powder (hot or mild)
Juice of 1 lemon
1 litre (4 cups) chicken stock*
125 ml (½ cup) chutney
60 ml (¼ cup) smooth apricot jam*
15 ml (1 tablespoon) salt
30 ml (2 tablespoons) cornflour, mixed to a paste with water (optional)

Heat the oil in a large saucepan and sauté the onion, garlic and apple lightly. Add the curry powder, and cook this mixture for 3 minutes. Add the rest of the ingredients, except the cornflour, and simmer, uncovered, for 45 minutes, stirring from time to time. Thicken the sauce slightly with the cornflour if you wish, bringing it to the boil after adding the paste.

SERVING SUGGESTIONS This sauce has many uses. It can dress up poached fish*, halved hard-boiled eggs* or left-over chicken, or be combined with left-over lamb (diced) or mince to make pancake* fillings.

VARIATIONS Natural yoghurt* or cream, added just before serving, provide a richer curry sauce.

Or try 125 ml (½ cup) milk in which 30 ml (2 tablespoons) coconut has been infused.

Raisins, sultanas, almonds, cashew nuts or peanuts make interesting additions.

This curry sauce freezes very well. Cream, natural yoghurt or milk should be added to it on re-heating, and the sauce should also be thickened on re-heating.

Reduce the quantity of cornflour in proportion to meet these variations.

CRAYFISH AND PRAWN SAUCE *A delicious treat for those who like their sauces rich and creamy.*

EGG AND LEMON SAUCE

Originating in Greece, this sauce is especially suited to the more subtle flavours of poached chicken or fish dishes, although it is also enjoyable with roast chicken or even lamb.

PREPARATION TIME: 5 MINUTES
COOKING TIME: 45 MINUTES

INGREDIENTS TO YIELD 375 ML (1½ CUPS)
30 g butter
30 ml (2 tablespoons) flour
250 ml (1 cup) hot chicken stock*
3-4 egg yolks, or 2 eggs
Juice of 2 lemons, strained
30 ml (2 tablespoons) cold water
Salt and freshly ground white pepper

Melt the butter and stir in the flour to make a smooth paste. Do not allow the butter and flour to brown.

Add the hot stock slowly, stirring all the while, until the mixture is smooth and thick and starts to bubble. Turn down the heat and simmer the sauce, stirring all the time, for 5 minutes.

When cooked, keep the sauce hot while you beat the egg yolks or whole eggs until they are light and frothy. Add the lemon juice and cold water to the eggs, and stir together. Now remove the sauce from the heat and add one-quarter of the sauce to the egg mixture, 15 ml (1 tablespoon) at a time, beating as you go.

Then add the rest of the egg mixture slowly to the sauce, stirring well all the time. Correct the seasoning if necessary and re-heat the sauce, being careful not to bring the mixture to the boil or it will curdle.

SERVING SUGGESTIONS This sauce is very good with poached fish* or chicken dishes and is also served with roast lamb, chicken or vegetables. Do not freeze it.

HORSERADISH SAUCE

For centuries the main uses of horseradish were medicinal, and it is possible that the essentially English practice of serving grated horseradish with roast beef was introduced to aid digestion. In South Africa, too, many people consider horseradish a must with beef.

PREPARATION TIME: 30 MINUTES

INGREDIENTS TO YIELD 250 ML (1 CUP)
1 large horseradish root, to give 60 ml (¼ cup) when grated, or use 60 ml (¼ cup) bottled horseradish
15 ml (1 tablespoon) castor sugar
2 ml (½ teaspoon) dry mustard
30 ml (2 tablespoons) white wine vinegar
150 ml thick cream, lightly whipped

Wash and peel the horseradish root, then grate it finely into a bowl. If you are using bottled horseradish, drain it very well. Stir in the sugar, mustard and vinegar, and add the cream. Chill in the refrigerator.

SERVING SUGGESTIONS Serve with roast beef, smoked fish or salads.

VARIATIONS Horseradish gives out pungent fumes, so a more comfortable method of preparing the clean, peeled root is to chop it roughly and shred or mince it in a food processor with a little water. Drain, then add the other ingredients.

To make hot horseradish sauce, grate about 45 ml (3 tablespoons) of the root into 275-300 ml white sauce*. Simmer, stirring from time to time, for about 10 minutes. Hot horseradish sauce goes well with boiled salt beef and fish.

HOLLANDAISE SAUCE

The renowned French chef Auguste Escoffier listed Hollandaise sauce as one of five basic sauces which no cook should be without. This classic French sauce is, as its name suggests, of Dutch origin, and was originally made with the best butter on Dutch farms.

There are two basic methods of preparing the sauce: by whisking the ingredients or by using a food processor or blender. Both methods are described below.

PREPARATION TIME: 5 MINUTES
COOKING TIME: 10-15 MINUTES

INGREDIENTS TO YIELD 375 ML (1½ CUPS)
225 g butter
3 egg yolks
15 ml (1 tablespoon) water
15 ml (1 tablespoon) lemon juice
Salt and pepper

Whisking method Cut the butter into pieces and place all but about 25 g in a small, heavy-based pan. Put the pan on a very gentle heat and remove as soon as the butter has melted.

Half-fill a large pan with water. Bring to the boil, then remove from the heat. Put the egg yolks with the tablespoon of water in a bowl over the pan of hot water (do not use a metal bowl, as the eggs will discolour when you beat them), and whisk for 1-2 minutes.

Put the pan back over a low heat and add half the reserved cold butter to the bowl. Whisk again for 1 minute.

Whisk in the other half of the reserved butter, remove from the heat, but keep the bowl over the hot water. The mixture should look smooth and creamy.

Gradually add the melted butter, whisking it in until the sauce is thick. Then beat in the lemon juice and season with salt and pepper to taste.

If the sauce curdles during the cooking, remove it from the heat immediately. Put another egg yolk in a bowl and gradually beat the sauce into it. Then resume the cooking. If the sauce is too thick, add 5-10 ml (1-2 teaspoons) hot water.

Processor/blender method It is easier to make Hollandaise sauce using a food processor or blender. For this method, the ingredients are the same but the way they are combined varies slightly.

Melt the butter in a saucepan until it starts to bubble. Meanwhile, blend the egg yolks with the lemon juice, salt and pepper in a blender or food processor for 1 second – just long enough to mix but not froth them. When the butter is hot, switch the blender on to high and gradually pour in the hot butter in a very thin stream.

When all the butter has been incorporated, turn the machine off immediately. Pour this sauce into a small plastic or glass bowl and put it over hot (not boiling) water until it is required. If you find that your sauce is too thin after beating in the butter, this 'rest' on top of a bowl of warm water will often be enough to thicken it.

If you need to re-heat the sauce, beat it over hot water until it is warmed through and fluffy.

SERVING SUGGESTIONS Hollandaise sauce can be served warm with fish, asparagus, broccoli, baby marrows or artichokes.

VARIATIONS TO HOLLANDAISE SAUCE

Hollandaise sauce is the basis of many delicious sauces; for example, wine may be substituted for the lemon juice, or a little grated lemon rind and onion juice added with a few grains of cayenne pepper to vary the flavour.

Tomato purée or chopped fresh herbs such as parsley, chervil or chives may also be added to the cooked sauce.

Caper Sauce can be made by adding 30-45 ml (2-3 tablespoons) capers to 250 ml (1 cup) Hollandaise sauce.

Cucumber Hollandaise is made with the addition of half a peeled and grated cucumber (well squeezed in a dry cloth to remove excess moisture) and a pinch of cayenne pepper to 250 ml (1 cup) Hollandaise sauce. This is delicious with any poached* or grilled fish*.

Horseradish Hollandaise is good with rare roast beef. Add 60 ml (¼ cup) fresh grated horseradish (or used bottled horseradish, well drained) and 125 ml (½ cup) whipped cream to 500 ml (2 cups) Hollandaise sauce. If the sauce is too hot, add more whipped cream; if it is too mild, add more horseradish.

Maltaise Sauce is a classic accompaniment to asparagus and is also good with broccoli, baby marrows, artichokes, fish or chicken. Add 45 ml (3 tablespoons) orange juice and 5 ml (1 teaspoon) grated orange rind to 250 ml (1 cup) Hollandaise sauce.

Mousseline Sauce is another Hollandaise-based classic. Add 60 ml (¼ cup) whipped cream to 250 ml (1 cup) Hollandaise sauce and serve with poached eggs, fish or vegetables.

Try spreading a fairly thick layer of mousseline sauce over fresh asparagus or cooked chicken, and browning it swiftly under a hot grill before serving.

Mustard Hollandaise can be made by adding 20 ml (4 teaspoons) French mustard to 250 ml (1 cup) Hollandaise sauce.

Sauce Toulouse is made by adding 6 medium-sized mushrooms, sautéed and minced or very finely chopped, to 250 ml (1 cup) Hollandaise sauce that has been made with a white wine base.

SAVOURY SAUCES, STUFFINGS AND DUMPLINGS

MARSALA SAUCE

THIS APPETISING SAUCE, flavoured with Marsala, is simple to make and may be varied easily by substituting other fortified wines. It complements ham, tongue, mutton or veal.

PREPARATION TIME: 5 MINUTES

INGREDIENTS TO YIELD 350 ML
500 ml (2 cups) basic brown sauce*
100 ml Marsala wine

Reduce the brown sauce by rapid boiling to halve the quantity and then add the Marsala wine. Return the sauce to the heat, and heat it through but do not allow it to boil.

VARIATIONS Substitute muscadel or sweet sherry to vary the flavour.

Sauté 500 ml (2 cups) sliced mushrooms in 100 g butter until golden and then add them to the hot Marsala sauce with 15 ml (1 tablespoon) minced onion. Simmer the sauce for 5 minutes and serve with gammon steaks. Garnish with chopped parsley.

MINT AND PINEAPPLE SAUCE

THIS DELICIOUS variation of the traditional accompaniment to lamb is quick and simple to make. It is also good served with ham.

PREPARATION TIME: 5 MINUTES

INGREDIENTS TO YIELD 125 ML (½ CUP)
60 ml (¼ cup) orange juice
60 ml (¼ cup) lemon juice
15 ml (1 tablespoon) chopped fresh mint
15 ml (1 tablespoon) castor sugar
A little grated pineapple

Mix together all the ingredients and stir well to dissolve the sugar.

MUSHROOM SAUCE

MUSHROOM SAUCE can have either a white* or brown sauce* base, the white sauce being more suitable for chicken or fish dishes.

PREPARATION TIME: 20 MINUTES
COOKING TIME: 30 MINUTES

INGREDIENTS TO YIELD 750 ML-1 LITRE (3-4 CUPS)
125 g fresh button mushrooms, sliced
60 g butter
30 ml (2 tablespoons) flour
500 ml (2 cups) fish* or chicken stock*, or half cream and half stock
15 ml (1 tablespoon) grated onion, blanched* for 1-2 minutes
Salt and freshly ground white pepper
30 ml (2 tablespoons) medium cream sherry

Sauté the mushroom slices in the butter and remove them from the saucepan with a slotted spoon.

Stir the flour into the pan juices to make a smooth paste and then stir in the stock or stock/cream mixture to make a smooth sauce. Bring this to the boil, then turn down the heat and simmer the sauce for about 5 minutes.

Add the mushroom slices and onion to the mixture and simmer it for a further 10 minutes. Season the sauce to taste and add the sherry.

SERVING SUGGESTIONS Serve hot with chicken or fish, grilled, pan-fried or baked. Left-over chicken or fish can be combined with the sauce for a tasty pie filling, with more mushrooms, sliced spring onions and sliced pimento-stuffed olives added to the diced chicken or flaked fish to plump out the filling if necessary.

VARIATION Sautéed sliced mushrooms (tinned or fresh) can be added to béchamel sauce* with a little sherry for a quick mushroom sauce.

MUSTARD SAUCE

THE ROMANS THOUGHT that many things tasted better with mustard, and so took the seeds with them to the outermost parts of their empire. This attitude is reflected in the dishes brought to South Africa by settlers from northern Europe, where great play was made with home-grown spices such as mustard.

PREPARATION TIME: 5 MINUTES
COOKING TIME: 15 MINUTES

INGREDIENTS TO YIELD 600 ML
575-600 ml milk
40 g butter
25 g flour
15 ml (1 tablespoon) dry mustard
15 ml (1 tablespoon) vinegar
5 ml (1 teaspoon) sugar
Salt

Put the milk in a pan over a gentle heat. Remove when warm, put the lid on the pan and set aside.

Melt the butter over the same gentle heat in another pan. Mix in the flour with a wooden spoon until smooth, and continue to cook gently for 2-3 minutes, stirring all the time to avoid lumps.

Remove from the heat and add the warm milk, stirring continuously. Return to the heat and bring the sauce to the boil, stirring. Simmer for 5 minutes, stirring from time to time.

When the sauce is smooth and creamy, remove it from the heat and stir in the mustard, vinegar, sugar and salt.

SERVING SUGGESTIONS Serve hot with boiled tongue, or cold with beef or ham, or fondues.

If serving cold, cover the surface of the warm sauce with a circle of grease-proof paper dipped in cold water and placed wet side down. Cover with a lid. This prevents a skin from forming.

ONION SAUCE

SIR THOMAS ELYOT, British diplomat and author, wrote in 1539 that 'onyons beying eaten in great abundance with meate, they cause one to sleape soundly'. Today, however, it is gourmets and not insomniacs who favour the combination of meat and onion sauce.

PREPARATION TIME: 15 MINUTES
COOKING TIME: 30-40 MINUTES

INGREDIENTS TO YIELD 600 ML
50 g butter
4 large onions, peeled and thinly sliced*
575-600 ml milk or basic stock*
A pinch of ground mace
A pinch of ground nutmeg
Salt and freshly ground black pepper
25 g flour

Melt half the butter in a large pan and slowly fry the sliced onions, stirring from time to time, until soft (but not brown). Meanwhile, heat the milk or stock in another pan. Remove from the heat when hot.

Add the milk or stock. Season with the mace, nutmeg, salt and pepper. Simmer for 10-15 minutes, then strain; reserve the liquid and onion.

Melt the remaining butter in the cleaned pan. Add the flour, stirring with a wooden spoon, and cook gently for 2-3 minutes. Remove from the heat and gradually add the onion liquid, stirring all the time.

Chop the drained onions finely, or rub them through a sieve and add them to the sauce, stirring well. Heat through again.

SERVING SUGGESTIONS Serve hot with mutton, lamb or rabbit.

PARSLEY SAUCE

PARSLEY SAUCE, recommended by the famous Mrs Beeton in the 19th century, is the classic complement to broad beans and carrots. It is also good with fish, poultry or ham.

PREPARATION TIME: 10 MINUTES
COOKING TIME: 15-20 MINUTES

INGREDIENTS TO YIELD 600 ML
575-600 ml milk
40 g butter
40 g flour
60 ml (¼ cup) finely chopped parsley
Salt and white pepper

Heat the milk gently in a pan, remove from the heat, cover and set aside.

Melt the butter gently in a small saucepan. Add the flour, mixing with a wooden spoon, and cook for 2-3 minutes, stirring all the time.

Remove from the heat and add the warm milk, stirring continuously. Return the pan to the heat and bring to the boil, still stirring, then simmer for about 5 minutes more, stirring from time to time.

When the sauce is smooth and creamy, add the finely chopped parsley and season to taste. Do not cook further because the taste of the fresh parsley may be lost.

VARIATIONS Chives, tarragon or mixed fresh herbs can be used instead.

SAVOURY SAUCES, STUFFINGS AND DUMPLINGS

SWEET-SOUR SAUCE *This Chinese speciality adds a pleasant piquancy to a variety of meats.*

SWEET-SOUR SAUCE

SWEET-SOUR SAUCE is good with the traditional Chinese dish of pork, fish and chicken cubes fried in crispy batter. It also makes a delicious marinade or dipping sauce for fondue.

Here the recipe is for quite a large quantity of sauce, as it freezes well and may be kept for use when required.

PREPARATION TIME: 20 MINUTES
COOKING TIME: 30 MINUTES

INGREDIENTS TO YIELD 1 LITRE (4 CUPS)
100g butter
4 onions, peeled and finely sliced*
2 green peppers, wiped, seeded and cut into strips
250 ml (1 cup) chicken stock*
250 ml (1 cup) pineapple juice
250 ml (1 cup) pineapple pieces
60 ml (¼ cup) orange juice
125 ml (½ cup) vinegar
125 g sugar
60 ml (¼ cup) soy sauce
5 ml (1 teaspoon) ground ginger
Salt and freshly ground pepper
15 ml (1 tablespoon) cornflour mixed to a smooth paste with 30 ml (2 tablespoons) soy sauce

Heat the butter in a large saucepan and soften the onion slices and green pepper strips in it. Add the stock, pineapple juice and pieces, orange juice, vinegar, sugar, soy sauce, ginger and seasoning, and simmer for 20 minutes or so.

Thicken the sauce with the cornflour and soy sauce mixture and continue cooking for a further 1-2 minutes.

SERVING SUGGESTIONS The sauce can be used as a basting sauce for baby chickens or braaied chicken pieces. If using the sauce after freezing, it should be thickened on re-heating.

VARIATIONS You may wish to liquidize the pineapple pieces before you add them to the sauce.

This sauce is also very good with pork sausages or kassler rib chops. You should dispense with the soy sauce if the sausages or chops are very salty.

Pork or lamb spare ribs can be marinated in the sauce before you grill them over the coals or under a grill.

PERI-PERI SAUCE

THIS IS AN IDEAL basting sauce for chicken or prawns 'peri-peri'. The strength of the peri-peri flavour is determined by the number of times you anoint the food while grilling or braaing it. The sauce may also be used with pork sausages or fish.

PREPARATION TIME: 5 MINUTES
COOKING TIME: 5 MINUTES

INGREDIENTS TO YIELD 625 ML (2½ CUPS)
250g butter
125 ml (½ cup) olive or sunflower oil
125 ml (½ cup) lemon juice
10 ml (2 teaspoons) paprika
10 ml (2 teaspoons) peri-peri powder
4 cloves garlic, peeled and crushed or finely chopped
10 ml (2 teaspoons) salt

Combine the ingredients in a saucepan and stir together vigorously over medium heat until the butter has melted and all the ingredients are well mixed (if necessary, use an electric beater or balloon whisk to blend the ingredients thoroughly).

SERVING SUGGESTIONS Brush the mixture on to chicken pieces, fish or prawns before grilling over open coals or under an electric grill. Serve on a bed of rice, accompanied by a green salad*.

To ensure that thick chicken pieces (such as thighs) are cooked to the bone, simmer in a little wine or chicken stock* before basting and grilling.

Pork sausages are delicious with a light brushing of peri-peri sauce; serve with simple accompaniments such as boiled new potatoes (with a sour cream dressing*) and a simple green salad*.

Left-over peri-peri sauce can be stored in a glass jar in the refrigerator for about 2 weeks, or it may be frozen for up to a month. (The sauce will eat through plastic or aluminium foil.) Shake the jar well before using.

VARIATIONS If you require less sauce, simply halve the ingredients.

Try adding herbs such as sweet basil, rosemary or origanum.

For an even hotter sauce, seed 1 or 2 red chillies, chop them finely and add to the sauce ingredients.

SAVOURY SAUCES, STUFFINGS AND DUMPLINGS

NAPOLITANA SAUCE

IT IS DIFFICULT to imagine Italian cookery without fresh tomato sauce. Certainly Italy was the first European country to adopt the *pomodoro* or 'golden apple' without reservations.

This is one of the most widely used sauces – with fish, poultry, meat, vegetables, rice, pasta or eggs, or as a base for other sauces or composite dishes.

PREPARATION TIME: 15 MINUTES
COOKING TIME: 35-45 MINUTES

INGREDIENTS TO YIELD 500 ML (2 CUPS)
40 g butter, or 15 ml
   (1 tablespoon) olive oil
1 small onion, peeled and finely
   chopped*
1 kg ripe tomatoes, skinned* and
   quartered, or a large tin (825 g)
   of tomatoes
1 bay leaf
1 sprig thyme
30 ml (2 tablespoons) red wine
   (optional)
1 clove garlic, peeled and crushed
   or finely chopped
1 ml (¼ teaspoon) salt
1 ml (¼ teaspoon) sugar
1 ml (¼ teaspoon) freshly ground
   black pepper
10 ml (2 teaspoons) lemon juice
   or vinegar
2 ml (½ teaspoon) each finely
   chopped fresh basil and
   marjoram, or 1 ml (¼
   teaspoon) each dried basil and
   marjoram

Heat the butter or oil in a large, heavy-based pan. Add the onion and cook gently, stirring occasionally, until it is soft but not brown.

Put the tomatoes in the pan with the bay leaf, thyme, wine (if used), garlic and salt. Stir, cover and simmer until tender.

Rub through a sieve and return to the cleaned pan. Bring to the boil and cook for about 20 minutes until reduced to a purée.

Season the sauce with the sugar, pepper, lemon juice or vinegar and remaining herbs. Taste and adjust the seasoning.

SERVING SUGGESTION There are few more simple and satisfying summer dishes than this sauce served over a plate of pasta with a little grated cheese.

AÏOLI *A generous addition of garlic is the mainstay of this popular sauce.*

AÏOLI

ORIGINALLY FROM PROVENCE, this rich garlic sauce provides the flavouring for various delicious speciality dishes in that district and has been adopted and adapted widely in many lands.

PREPARATION TIME: 30 MINUTES

INGREDIENTS TO YIELD 300 ML
1 slice fresh white bread, about
   1,5 cm thick with crusts
   removed
45 ml (3 tablespoons) milk
3 cloves garlic, peeled and
   crushed
2 large egg yolks, lightly whisked
250 ml (1 cup) olive oil
30 ml (2 tablespoons) lemon juice
Salt and freshly ground white
   pepper

Soak the bread in the milk for 10 minutes, then crumble and squeeze out the excess milk. Put the bread into a blender with the garlic and process at high speed, adding the egg yolks fairly slowly.

Add the olive oil, still processing at speed, first drop by drop and then in a thin stream, processing until the mixture thickens. Add the lemon juice and season the mixture to taste. Thin the sauce, if necessary, with cream or water.

SERVING SUGGESTIONS Serve aïoli as a dip for crudités or fondues, with poached fish or asparagus, over hard-boiled eggs* or as a sauce with baked jacket potatoes*. It is also very good with boiled beef or mutton. Serve with fish soup or stew.

To make green beans Provencale, serve aïoli over topped and tailed, boiled green beans (hot or cold).

VARIATION If you add 60 ml (¼ cup) ground almonds, 60 ml (¼ cup) extra fresh white crumbs, 30 ml (2 tablespoons) chopped parsley and a little more lemon juice you can call the sauce *skordalia*. Serve it in the same way as aïoli.

BOILED SALAD DRESSING

THIS DRESSING is a useful substitute for mayonnaise, whether you use the main recipe or one of the variations. It is cheaper to make than mayonnaise, since it contains no oil and only one egg.

PREPARATION TIME: 10 MINUTES
COOKING TIME: 15-20 MINUTES

INGREDIENTS TO YIELD 250 ML (1 CUP)
5 ml (1 teaspoon) dry
   mustard
30 ml (2 tablespoons) sugar
3 ml (¾ teaspoon) salt
30 ml (2 tablespoons) flour
3 ml (¾ teaspoon) paprika
125 ml (½ cup) cold water
1 egg
60 ml (¼ cup) vinegar
55 g butter

Combine the mustard, sugar, salt, flour and paprika in a cup or small bowl, add the water and mix these ingredients to a smooth paste.

Beat the egg with the vinegar in the top of a double boiler and then beat in the dissolved mustard mixture.

Cook the sauce over boiling water until it is thick and smooth. Do not allow the boiling water to touch the base of the upper pot and be careful not to allow the lower pot to boil dry.

Flake in the butter and stir until all the butter has dissolved. Cool the sauce, cover and chill.

SERVING SUGGESTION Use the dressing in coleslaw*, potato salad* or wherever mayonnaise is indicated. Keep it refrigerated and do not freeze. The dressing can be thinned with sour cream or yoghurt, if necessary.

VARIATIONS A pinch of cayenne pepper can be added for a change in flavour.

You may add chopped fresh herbs or dried herbs to make a herb dressing.

Alternatively, give it a spicy flavour with celery, garlic or dill seeds.

Dahi

IN THIS INDIAN recipe, yoghurt is seasoned with chilli powder, pepper and fresh coriander to make a tasty dressing. It is best made a day ahead, and will store in the refrigerator for at least a week.

PREPARATION TIME: 10 MINUTES

INGREDIENTS TO YIELD 250 ML (1 CUP)
250 ml (1 cup) natural yoghurt*
7 ml (1½ teaspoons) sugar
3 ml (¾ teaspoon) salt
5 ml (1 teaspoon) lemon juice
1 ml (¼ teaspoon) freshly ground black pepper
15 ml (1 tablespoon) fresh coriander (dhania) leaves, chopped
1 ml (¼ teaspoon) chilli powder

Blend the yoghurt with the sugar, salt, lemon juice, pepper and coriander.

Place this mixture in a glass serving bowl. Sprinkle it with the chilli powder and allow it to cool in a refrigerator.

SERVING SUGGESTION Place the bowl in the centre of a large plate and arrange a salad around it. The dressing can be used as a dip for the salad.

Garlic Dressing

THE PUNGENT AROMA and flavour of garlic is unique, and while shallots are sometimes recommended as a substitute, the two flavours cannot be compared. Used with discretion, garlic gives heightened flavour to almost any savoury dish.

PREPARATION TIME: 5 MINUTES

INGREDIENTS TO YIELD 125 ML (½ CUP)
90 ml olive oil
45 ml (3 tablespoons) lemon juice
Salt and freshly ground black pepper
2-3 cloves garlic, crushed or finely chopped

Blend the oil and lemon juice, and season to taste with the salt, pepper and garlic. Shake together vigorously.

SERVING SUGGESTIONS Use to dress Greek salad*, green salad*, tomatoes, mixed vegetables or rice salad*.

Minted Yoghurt Sauce

THIS SAUCE has Middle Eastern origins and is very good with many Greek, Lebanese or Turkish dishes. It can also be used as a dip.

PREPARATION TIME: 15 MINUTES
STANDING TIME: 2 HOURS
CHILLING TIME: 2 HOURS OR OVERNIGHT

INGREDIENTS TO YIELD 750 ML (3 CUPS)
500 ml (2 cups) natural yoghurt*
10 ml (2 teaspoons) cumin seeds (optional)
250 ml (1 cup) sour cream (smetana)
1 clove garlic, peeled and crushed (optional)
60 ml (¼ cup) chopped fresh mint
5 ml (1 teaspoon) salt

Line a sieve with a single layer of damp paper towel and set it over a bowl. Pour the yoghurt into the sieve and leave it to drain for 2 hours.

Meanwhile, if you are using the cumin, heat a heavy-based pan and toast the seeds, shaking the pan continuously, for 1½ minutes, or until they are brown and begin to pop. Then pulverise the seeds with a pestle and mortar, or use the handle of a knife and a small, strong dish.

Blend the yoghurt with the sour cream, garlic (if used), mint, salt and half the cumin seeds until the mixture is smooth and pale green. Pour into a serving bowl, cover and chill for at least 2 hours or overnight. When the sauce is ready to serve, sprinkle on the remaining crushed cumin seeds (if used).

SERVING SUGGESTIONS Serve the sauce with crudités*, stir-fried mixed vegetables*, fish croquettes*, small chicken or lamb frikkadels*, or as a dressing for cucumber salad*. It may also be served as an accompaniment to roast lamb.

VARIATIONS Omit the mint and add grated cucumber to make a delicious sambal to serve with curry.

If you are short of time, the yoghurt need not be drained, but the sauce in this case will be thinner.

In place of the cumin seeds and chopped mint, use celery seeds and finely chopped fresh soup celery to flavour the yoghurt.

Mayonnaise

THE SECRET of making perfect mayonnaise lies in the 'unremitting beating of the olive oil into the egg yolks'. That was the pronouncement of Antonin Carême, the master chef generally regarded as the founder of classic French cookery.

It does not take a great deal of skill and patience to make this classic sauce, a rich and subtle complement to many cold dishes and salads. You can even whisk it in a liquidizer or food processor. Make sure all the ingredients are at room temperature before you start.

PREPARATION TIME: 20 MINUTES

INGREDIENTS TO YIELD ABOUT 275 ML
2 egg yolks
15 ml (1 tablespoon) lemon juice or wine vinegar
1 ml (¼ teaspoon) salt
1 ml (¼ teaspoon) dry mustard
275-300 ml olive or sunflower oil, or a mixture of both
15 ml (1 tablespoon) boiling water
1 ml (¼ teaspoon) freshly ground black pepper

Put the egg yolks in a mixing bowl (do not use a metal one) and whisk well for 1 minute. Add the lemon juice or vinegar, the salt and mustard, and beat the mixture for 1 minute more.

Add the oil, drop by drop, whisking continuously. After about a quarter of the oil has been added, the mayonnaise takes on the consistency of thin cream. The rest of the oil can be added more rapidly; beat well after each addition.

When all the oil is absorbed, whisk in the boiling water. This helps to ensure that the mayonnaise does not curdle (it will also keep better). If it does curdle, beat another egg yolk in a clean bowl, then beat the curdled mixture into it, drop by drop.

Taste, add a little more lemon juice and salt if necessary, and stir in the pepper. Store in a glass jar in the refrigerator.

VARIATION If you are making the mayonnaise in a food processor or blender, place all the ingredients except the oil and water in the container and blend for 4 seconds. Add the oil in a steady stream until the sauce is thick and creamy, then blend in the boiling water.

Sauces Based on Mayonnaise

Curry Mayonnaise To 250 ml (1 cup) mayonnaise add 10 ml (2 teaspoons) mild curry powder, 1 ml (¼ teaspoon) ground ginger, 5 ml (1 teaspoon) honey, 15 ml (1 tablespoon) chutney, 5 ml (1 teaspoon) lemon juice and 15 ml (1 tablespoon) slivered almonds. Serve this mayonnaise with chicken or fish salad.

Herb Mayonnaise To 250 ml (1 cup) mayonnaise add 30 ml (2 tablespoons) chopped marjoram, 30 ml (2 tablespoons) chopped parsley, 30 ml (2 tablespoons) chopped chives (or fennel, watercress, tarragon or chervil – or combine as you wish) and 5 ml (1 teaspoon) dried mixed herbs (optional). Serve herb mayonnaise with chicken, egg or seafood.

Seafood Mayonnaise To 250 ml (1 cup) mayonnaise add 60 ml (¼ cup) tomato purée, 10 ml (2 teaspoons) onion juice, 1 finely chopped anchovy fillet, 1 clove crushed garlic, 15 ml (1 tablespoon) chopped chives, 15 ml (1 tablespoon) lemon juice and a little sugar and Tabasco (chilli sauce) to taste.

Tartar Sauce To 300 ml mayonnaise add 3 small gherkins, chopped, 2 spring onions, trimmed and chopped, 1 hard-boiled egg*, finely chopped, 15 ml (1 tablespoon) capers, chopped, 5 ml (1 teaspoon) dried tarragon, 3 ml (¾ teaspoon) dry mustard, 5 ml (1 teaspoon) lemon juice, 5 ml (1 teaspoon) sugar, 15 ml (1 tablespoon) chopped chervil or parsley and seasoning. Serve with fried fish or chicken.

Thousand Island Dressing To 250 ml (1 cup) mayonnaise, add a dash of Tabasco (chilli sauce), 30 ml (2 tablespoons) chopped green pepper, 10 ml (2 teaspoons) minced pimento, 5 ml (1 teaspoon) chopped chives, 15 ml (1 tablespoon) tomato sauce*, 15 ml (1 tablespoon) vinegar and 2 ml (½ teaspoon) paprika. Cover and chill before use.

Horseradish Mayonnaise To 250 ml (1 cup) mayonnaise add 60 ml (¼ cup) freshly grated horseradish (or bottled horseradish, well drained), 10 ml (2 teaspoons) grated lemon rind and 60 ml (¼ cup) sour cream (smetana). Serve this mayonnaise with smoked mackerel, smoked salmon or any smoked meat or fish.

SAVOURY SAUCES, STUFFINGS AND DUMPLINGS

DRESSINGS BASED ON VINAIGRETTE

One of the easiest ways to vary the taste of vinaigrette is to use herb oils* as a base.

•

Avocado Dressing Put a peeled and chopped ripe avocado into a blender or food processor and process it until smooth. Slowly add 250 ml (1 cup) vinaigrette and blend until the mixture is smooth, then check for seasoning. This dressing is delicious with poached* kingklip or on sliced, peeled and chilled tomatoes.

•

Herbed Vinaigrette Add 15 ml (1 tablespoon) chopped fresh herbs (such as parsley, chives or tarragon) to 250 ml (1 cup) vinaigrette (made with lemon juice and vinegar).

•

Horseradish Vinaigrette Add 10-15 ml (2-3 teaspoons) grated horseradish to 250 ml (1 cup) vinaigrette.

•

Roquefort or Blue Cheese Dressing To 125 ml (½ cup) vinaigrette add 45 ml (3 tablespoons) crumbled Roquefort or other blue cheese and 45 ml (3 tablespoons) cream. Beat these ingredients well together. Serve the dressing over a mixed salad.

•

Ravigote Sauce To 250 ml (1 cup) vinaigrette add 125 ml (½ cup) finely chopped spring onion, 15 ml (1 tablespoon) finely chopped capers, 10 ml (2 teaspoons) finely chopped parsley and 3 ml (¾ teaspoon) finely chopped fresh tarragon (or a pinch of dried tarragon). Beat them well together and serve the sauce on a green salad* or with white meat or fish.

•

Sesame Dressing Before adding the oil in the basic vinaigrette, lightly brown 15 ml (1 tablespoon) sesame seeds in it. (You may use sesame oil if you prefer.) Allow the oil to cool before adding it with the seeds to the dressing.

•

Hot Vinaigrette with Egg Bring 250 ml (1 cup) vinaigrette to the boil in a saucepan, then add 2 hard-boiled eggs*, finely chopped, 15 ml (1 tablespoon) finely chopped parsley, 15 ml (1 tablespoon) finely chopped celery, 15 ml (1 tablespoon) finely chopped chives, 3 ml (¾ teaspoon) dry mustard and 3 ml (¾ teaspoon) Worcestershire sauce. Beat them well together. Serve this sauce with hot asparagus, over hot potato salad or with corned beef.

MUSTARD AND DILL DRESSING

Raw, smoked or pickled salmon is traditionally served with a strong mustard and dill dressing, which can also be served with smoked mackerel or trout.

PREPARATION TIME: 10 MINUTES

INGREDIENTS TO YIELD 150 ML

30 ml (2 tablespoons) French mustard
15 ml (1 tablespoon) sugar
1 egg yolk
90 ml olive oil
30 ml (2 tablespoons) white wine vinegar or dill vinegar
7 ml (1½ teaspoons) fresh, chopped dill
Salt and pepper

Beat the mustard with the sugar and egg yolk until smooth. Add the oil and vinegar, little by little, beating thoroughly after each addition.

Fold in the dill and season to taste with salt and pepper.

SAUCE VINAIGRETTE

This sauce is the classic French dressing for a salad, and is also excellent with hot cooked vegetables.

PREPARATION TIME: 5-10 MINUTES

INGREDIENTS TO YIELD 250 ML (1 CUP)

5 ml (1 teaspoon) dry or prepared mustard
5 ml (1 teaspoon) sugar (optional)
2 ml (½ teaspoon) salt
180 ml olive oil or good vegetable oil
80 ml (⅓ cup) wine or cider vinegar, or a mixture of both, or mixed vinegar and lemon juice
Freshly ground black pepper

Blend together the mustard, sugar (if used) and salt. Whisk in the oil, stir in the vinegar (or vinegar mixture) and add the freshly ground black pepper. Taste and adjust the seasoning.

VARIATIONS Vary the proportion of oil to vinegar to suit your taste.

If you like, blend in 1 clove of garlic, crushed, with the dry ingredients.

SOUR CREAM AND DILL DRESSING

This dressing, flavoured with onion and dill seeds, may be used as a substitute for mayonnaise to give a special tang to various vegetable salads.

PREPARATION TIME: 20 MINUTES

INGREDIENTS TO YIELD 250 ML (1 CUP)

250 ml (1 cup) sour cream (smetena)
5 ml (1 teaspoon) peeled* and grated onion
5 ml (1 teaspoon) dill seeds
30 ml (2 tablespoons) chopped pimento
Salt and freshly ground black pepper

Place the sour cream in a bowl and stir in the onion, dill seeds, pimento and seasoning until well blended. Cover the bowl with plastic wrap and chill in the refrigerator before serving.

SERVING SUGGESTIONS This dressing is delicious instead of mayonnaise on a salad of sliced, unpeeled new potatoes or with whole green beans, cooked until still firm and chilled. It also goes well with cucumber slices or small whole, skinned* and chilled tomatoes.

VARIATIONS To make your own cultured sour cream, mix 125 ml (½ cup) cream, 125 ml (½ cup) skim milk and 30 ml (2 tablespoons) buttermilk, and allow the mixture to stand at room temperature for 4-6 hours before refrigerating.

Add 5 ml (1 teaspoon) French mustard and 5 ml (1 teaspoon) sugar to the dressing.

Add a little Tabasco (chilli sauce) and chopped chives to the dressing and serve it with baked jacket potatoes* or as a dip for vegetable crudités*.

Omit the pimento and add chopped capers and about 60 ml (¼ cup) red lumpfish 'caviar' to make another delicious potato topping.

APPLE AND RAISIN STUFFING

This stuffing is moist and richly flavoured, and is particularly suitable for duck or goose. It is also suitable for stuffing game birds such as guinea fowl.

PREPARATION TIME: 30 MINUTES
COOKING TIME: 15 MINUTES
COOLING TIME: 1 HOUR

INGREDIENTS TO YIELD 7 CUPS

35 g seedless raisins
100 ml semi-sweet sherry
100 g butter
2 rashers bacon, trimmed and chopped
1 goose liver, or 150 g chicken livers
250 ml (1 cup) minced onions
1 large Granny Smith apple, peeled, cored and minced
250 ml (1 cup) minced celery stems
125 ml (½ cup) coarsely chopped pecan nuts
1 litre (4 cups) white bread cubes (1 cm), toasted lightly in the oven
10 ml (2 teaspoons) dried sage
Salt and freshly ground pepper

Put the raisins in a small saucepan and pour over the sherry. Cover and simmer over a medium heat for 2 minutes, or until the raisins are well-plumped. Remove from the heat and set on one side.

Melt the butter in a pan and sauté the bacon and chopped liver until lightly browned (the liver should still be slightly pink in the centre). Remove and set aside.

Now sauté the onion and apple until the onion is soft, then add the celery. Mix well together, then combine with the well-drained raisins, liver and bacon, pecans, bread cubes and sage. Season to taste, mixing well. Allow the stuffing to cool.

SERVING SUGGESTIONS Loosely stuff the body cavity of the bird. Sew up the cavity before roasting. Baste the bird with sherry and lemon juice while roasting.

VARIATION Substitute port and sultanas for the sherry and raisins, and substitute orange juice for the lemon juice when roasting duck (in this case, a garnish of orange segments simmered in a little port and butter would be delicious).

Apricot Stuffing

This is a good stuffing for turkey, goose or duck. The recipe yields enough stuffing for a fairly large bird, so you should reduce the ingredients (in proportion) if it is intended for a duck.

Preparation Time: 30 minutes
Standing Time: 1 hour
Ingredients to Yield 5 cups

250 g dried apricots, quartered
75 g seedless raisins
60 ml (¼ cup) apricot nectar
Boiling water or stock*
150 g white breadcrumbs
1 apple, peeled, cored and coarsely grated
100 g pine nuts
60 ml (¼ cup) chopped fresh parsley
30 ml (2 tablespoons) melted butter
3 ml (¾ teaspoon) ground cinnamon
3 ml (¾ teaspoon) ground cloves
Salt and freshly ground pepper

Place the apricots and raisins in a bowl and pour over the apricot nectar and enough boiling water or stock to cover. Leave to stand for 1 hour, then drain (reserving the liquid) and dry.

Combine the apricots, raisins and all the other stuffing ingredients and the reserved liquid in a large bowl, mixing thoroughly, and season to taste. Add a little more stock if the stuffing seems too dry.

Serving Suggestion Pack the body cavity of the bird with the stuffing and sew up. If using the stuffing for goose, make a gravy with stock (using all the giblets except the liver), then add some sour cream, brandy (flamed) and lightly sautéed slices of goose liver to the sauce just before serving.

Celery, Mushroom and Walnut Stuffing

This quick-and-easy stuffing is very good with roast chicken. The addition of crushed cream crackers creates an interesting texture.

Preparation Time: 20 minutes
Cooking Time: 15 minutes

Ingredients to Yield 4 cups

100 g butter
1 onion, peeled and chopped*
250 ml (1 cup) chopped celery (including the leaves)
125 g large black mushrooms, peeled and coarsely chopped
50 g walnuts, coarsely chopped
Cooked giblets
200 g cream crackers, crushed
1 egg, lightly beaten
60 ml (¼ cup) chopped parsley
5 ml (1 teaspoon) dried thyme
3 ml (¾ teaspoon) dried sage
Salt and freshly ground pepper

Melt the butter in a saucepan and sauté the onion, celery, mushrooms and walnuts for 5 minutes. Chop the giblets finely (not the neck) and add to the celery mixture. Combine this mixture with the cream cracker crumbs, egg, herbs and seasoning, and mix well. Leave to cool.

Serving Suggestion Stuff the body cavity of the chicken loosely (this allows for expansion) before roasting.

Chestnut Stuffing

Chestnuts give a deliciously nutty flavour to this simple stuffing, which is particularly suitable for turkey.

Preparation Time: 40-50 minutes

Ingredients to Yield 5 cups

700 g chestnuts
1 turkey liver, chopped
100-125 ml melted butter
Salt and pepper

Make a slit along the side of each chestnut, place in a large pan and cover with water. Bring to the boil, then simmer, covered, for about 20 minutes (or until tender). Remove from the heat and take the lid off the pan, but do not drain.

Take the chestnuts out of the hot cooking water, one at a time, and remove the shells and skins. Mash or chop about half, but leave the remainder whole. Put them all in a mixing bowl and stir in the chopped liver and melted butter, and season with salt and pepper to taste.

Variation Use 350 g chestnuts and 350 g sausage meat, adding 30 ml (2 tablespoons) chopped parsley and 1 beaten egg.

Savoury Butters

These are used to garnish meat, fish or vegetable dishes, or are added to sauces. Softened butter is flavoured with varying ingredients according to the dish it is to garnish. Allow 25 g butter per person.

Soften the butter in a bowl before blending in the flavouring ingredient. Herbs and vegetables must be finely chopped, pounded or thoroughly crushed. A mortar and pestle are ideal for this purpose.

When all the ingredients are combined, roll the savoury butter flat between two sheets of damp grease-proof paper. Chill thoroughly in the refrigerator before cutting the butter into small fancy shapes.

Anchovy Butter Rinse 6 anchovy fillets in cold water to remove the salt and oil. Dry, rub through a sieve and blend with 100 g butter. Serve with grilled meat or fish. Alternatively, add to a white sauce*.

Lemon Butter Blend the grated rind of half a lemon with 100 g butter. Season to taste with salt and black pepper.

Tomato Butter Blend 30 ml (2 tablespoons) tomato paste with 100 g butter. Serve with grilled meat or fish, or add to sauces and thick soups.

Chive Butter Blanch* and drain 125 ml (½ cup) chives, then chop finely and pound to a paste. Blend into 100 g butter. Serve with grilled meat or fish.

Maître d'Hôtel Butter Blend 15 ml (1 tablespoon) finely chopped parsley with 100 g butter and season to taste with salt, freshly ground black pepper and a few drops of lemon juice. Serve with grilled meat or fish, coated fried fish or boiled vegetables.

Tarragon Butter Blanch* 50 g fresh tarragon leaves in scalding hot water, then drain and dry. Pound to a paste and blend with 100 g butter.

Nut Butter Crush 50 g blanched* almonds, walnuts or pistachio nuts to a fine paste, adding a few drops of water to prevent it from becoming oily. Blend the paste with 100 g butter. Add to sauces and soups.

Sesame and Almond Butter Blend 150 ml ground almonds, 60 ml (¼ cup) toasted sesame seeds and 30 ml (2 tablespoons) chopped fresh parsley with 100 g butter.

Garlic Butter Peel and crush 4 cloves of garlic and blend with 100 g butter. Serve with grilled steaks or fish.

Green Butter Blanch* 100-125 g spinach, then drain and press out as much of the moisture as possible. Pound until smooth, then blend with 100 g butter. Add to white sauces.

Horseradish Butter Pound 60 ml (¼ cup) grated horseradish (or bottled, well-drained horseradish) in a mortar together with 100 g butter. Add to white sauces.

Mushroom Butter Chop 100-125 g button mushrooms finely, then cook them lightly in 25 g butter, and season to taste with salt and black pepper. Pound until smooth, then blend with 100 g butter. Add to white sauces.

Mustard Butter Blend 15 ml (1 tablespoon) dry mustard thoroughly with 100 g butter. Serve with grilled meat or fish.

Butter for Escargots Chop 15 ml (1 tablespoon) onion* and 5 ml (1 teaspoon) parsley. Peel and crush 2 fat cloves garlic, add to the chopped onion and parsley, and blend with 100 g butter, seasoning to taste with salt and black pepper. Serve stuffed into snail shells.

Roast Chicken with Herb Butter Stuffing Under the Skin

Prepare a chicken for roasting*. If you prefer, you can cut it down the back and open it out flat.

Make a herb butter by creaming together 125 g butter with two crushed cloves of garlic, 30 ml (2 tablespoons) chopped parsley, 15 ml (1 tablespoon) chopped chives, 15 ml (1 tablespoon) chopped fresh thyme or 5 ml (1 teaspoon) dried thyme, 15 ml (1 tablespoon) chopped fresh tarragon or 5 ml (1 teaspoon) dried, and a little seasoning. Mix this with the finely chopped chicken liver, 15 ml (1 tablespoon) brandy and 250 ml (1 cup) stale white breadcrumbs. Mix the ingredients well together with a wooden spoon or in a food processor or blender.

Gently loosen the skin of the chicken about the breast, drumsticks and thighs and push the stuffing underneath the loosened skin, being very careful not to pierce it.

Roast the chicken* until it is crisp and golden. The flesh of the chicken stays wonderfully moist and gains delicious flavour from the herby, garlicky stuffing.

SAVOURY SAUCES, STUFFINGS AND DUMPLINGS

BROWN RICE AND WATER CHESTNUT STUFFING

THIS IS A DIFFERENT and delicious stuffing to try with wildfowl, turkey or duck. The nuts and water chestnuts provide a pleasant crunchy texture, while the bacon and herbs give the flavour.

PREPARATION TIME: 15 MINUTES
COOKING TIME: 45 MINUTES

INGREDIENTS TO YIELD 5½ CUPS

250 ml (1 cup) brown rice
1 litre (4 cups) stock* (made with giblets)
100 g butter
Reserved giblets, chopped
3 rashers bacon, chopped
30 ml (2 tablespoons) chopped spring onion
125 g button mushrooms, chopped
100 g chopped mixed nuts (not peanuts or cashews)
5 ml (1 teaspoon) dried basil
5 ml (1 teaspoon) dried origanum
15 ml (1 tablespoon) chopped fresh parsley
125 ml (½ cup) water chestnuts, sliced (from a tin)
Salt and freshly ground black pepper

Cook the rice in the stock until nearly tender (about 30 minutes), then drain and rinse with hot water.

Melt the butter in a saucepan and sauté the giblets and bacon until they just start to brown, then add all the remaining ingredients, except the seasoning. Stir-fry for 5 minutes and add the rice. Mix well together and season to taste. Allow to cool before stuffing the bird.

SERVING SUGGESTIONS Double up on the quantity of stuffing and serve the remainder as a side dish to accompany the fowl. Tiny frozen peas with a savoury butter* and baby carrots make good accompaniments.

VARIATIONS Omit the bacon, and use chopped celery stalks in place of the water chestnuts (the juice of half a lemon adds an extra tang).

If you like, crush one or two cloves of garlic into the stuffing (omit if you are making the side dish).

HERBED PRUNE STUFFING *An exciting selection of interesting ingredients makes this a delectable treat.*

HERBED PRUNE STUFFING

HERE IS AN EXCELLENT stuffing for turkey. Any remaining stuffing can be baked separately in a soufflé dish to serve (sliced) on the side, or the next day as a paté. It is very tasty whether hot or cold.

PREPARATION TIME: 45 MINUTES
MARINATING TIME: 2 HOURS
COOKING TIME: 30 MINUTES
COOLING TIME: 1 HOUR

INGREDIENTS TO YIELD 10 CUPS

250 g prunes, pitted and coarsely chopped
125 ml (½ cup) semi-sweet sherry
Turkey stock* (made from turkey giblets)
125 g butter
500 ml (about 5 medium-sized) peeled and chopped onions*
500 ml (about 4 medium-sized) chopped celery stalks
1 Granny Smith apple, peeled, cored and chopped
750 g pork sausage meat
Cooked turkey liver, minced (from stock)
1 litre (4 cups) white bread cubes, lightly toasted in the oven
125 ml (½ cup) chopped fresh parsley
30 ml (2 tablespoons) finely chopped fresh sage
15 ml (1 tablespoon) finely chopped fresh thyme
3 ml (¾ teaspoon) ground allspice
3 ml (¾ teaspoon) ground nutmeg
Salt and freshly ground pepper

Put the chopped prunes in a glass or ceramic bowl, pour over the sherry and leave to soak for 2 hours. Meanwhile, make turkey stock* from the giblets (strain and reserve the giblets).

Melt the butter in a saucepan and sauté the onions until soft (but not brown), then add the celery and apple. Cook for 5 minutes, then use a slotted spoon to transfer the celery mixture to a large bowl. Cook the sausage meat in the remaining butter, breaking it up with a fork. Add the turkey liver and cook for 5 minutes, or until lightly browned.

Now combine the drained prunes, reserved sherry, celery mixture, sausage mixture, toasted bread cubes, herbs and spices in a large bowl, and mix well together. Season generously with salt and pepper, and add enough strained stock to the stuffing to moisten to your taste. Leave the stuffing to cool.

SERVING SUGGESTIONS Stuff the body and neck cavities of the turkey, packing the stuffing in loosely. Sew up the cavities before roasting the turkey.

Increase the liquid from the drained prunes to 250 ml (1 cup) and make a gravy using the pan juices, prune liquid, remaining stock and 125 ml (½ cup) cream. Scrape in all the tasty brown bits from the pan after roasting the turkey. Thicken with flour or cornflour and cook for a further 1-2 minutes.

COUNTRY HERB STUFFING

IT IS SOMETIMES difficult to tell whether our ancestors included particular herbs and spices in their food as flavourings or for their medicinal value. In bygone days a stuffing, for example, might well have included herbs that were somewhat less than pleasing to the palate.

This modern version of a country herb stuffing, however, can be enjoyed simply for its flavour with most roast poultry or meat. If the herbs also act as an aid to digestion, as herbalists have claimed for centuries, then so much the better.

PREPARATION TIME: 20 MINUTES

INGREDIENTS TO YIELD 4 CUPS

175 g fine white breadcrumbs
100-125 g shredded suet
50 g lean bacon, diced and fried until crisp
Grated rind of ½ lemon
15 ml (1 tablespoon) chopped, mixed parsley, thyme and marjoram
1 ml (¼ teaspoon) freshly grated nutmeg
Salt and pepper
1 egg, beaten

Combine the breadcrumbs with the shredded suet and bacon in a large bowl. Stir in the lemon rind, herbs and nutmeg, then season well with salt and pepper. Finally, work in the beaten egg to bind the mixture.

VARIATIONS In pork dishes, substitute sage for the thyme; in veal dishes, use chopped tarragon instead of thyme.

For a very smooth stuffing, blend all the ingredients in a liquidizer. Make small stuffing meatballs out of any left-over stuffing, and place around roasting poultry or meat for the last 30 minutes of cooking.

SAGE AND ONION STUFFING

THIS STUFFING is attributed to Sir Kenelm Digby, the English seaman, philosopher, diplomat and amateur man of science, who proposed that sage, onion and butter be worked into a mass before being stuffed into a wild duck and roasted. His invention proved so successful that it was soon used in the preparation of domestic duck, geese and pork – as it still is.

PREPARATION TIME: 20 MINUTES

INGREDIENTS TO YIELD 2 CUPS

2 large onions, peeled and roughly chopped*
60 ml (¼ cup) water
8 sage leaves, or 5 ml (1 teaspoon) dried and rubbed sage
100-125 g fresh white breadcrumbs
45 ml (3 tablespoons) melted butter
1 egg, beaten
Salt and freshly ground black pepper

Put the onions in a small pan with the water. Bring to the boil, then simmer, covered, for about 10 minutes before draining well.

If using fresh sage, blanch the leaves in boiling water for 1 minute, then drain and chop finely.

Chop the parboiled onions finely and put in a mixing bowl. Add the sage, breadcrumbs, melted butter and beaten egg. Season with salt and pepper, and stir well together so that all the ingredients are thoroughly mixed.

VARIATIONS Peel, core and chop 2 medium-sized cooking apples and cook them with the onion.

Alternatively, add the finely grated rind of half a lemon or orange and 10 ml (2 teaspoons) soft brown sugar.

SUET DUMPLINGS

THE FIRST DUMPLINGS were allegedly made in Norfolk – the British essayist Sir Richard Steele wrote in 1706 about a Norfolk squire who was reputed to eat 'two pounds' of dumplings at every meal.

Modern appetites will not cope with that quantity, but these dumplings, plain or flavoured with a little horseradish, should disappear fast on a cold day.

PREPARATION TIME: 10 MINUTES
COOKING TIME: 15 MINUTES

INGREDIENTS FOR FOUR

100-125 g self-raising flour
45 ml (3 tablespoons) shredded suet
Salt and pepper
Water to mix

Sieve the flour into a mixing bowl. Stir in the suet and a generous seasoning of salt and pepper. Carefully mix in just enough water to make a soft dough.

Turn on to a floured surface and, with lightly floured hands, shape into balls about the size of large walnuts.

If serving the dumplings with a meat dish – such as boiled beef – remove the meat when it is cooked and keep it warm. Bring the cooking liquid up to the boil in a very large pan which will allow enough room for the dumplings to swell during cooking.

Put in the dumplings and poach at a gentle boil, turning them over once. They will rise to the surface when they are cooked (after about 15 minutes).

Dumplings can also be cooked with a stew in a very large pan. Add them to cook for the last 15-20 minutes: they will lie on top and cook through in the steam without having to be turned over.

If the dumplings are to accompany a dish which is not cooked in its own stock, poach them in a large pan of boiling, salted water.

VARIATION To make horseradish dumplings, have ready about 10 ml (2 teaspoons) grated horseradish (or bottled, well-drained horseradish). Carefully roll the dough into walnut-sized balls, then make a hollow in each by pushing a finger into it. Put a portion of the horseradish into each hollow and squeeze the dough over it to seal it in tightly. Horseradish dumplings are very good with salt beef and carrots.

SEMOLINA DUMPLINGS

THESE SEMOLINA DUMPLINGS may be used as an accompaniment to meat dishes or sweetened and served as a dessert.

PREPARATION TIME: 45 MINUTES
COOKING TIME: 15 MINUTES

INGREDIENTS FOR SIX

1,5 litres (6 cups) milk
10 ml (2 teaspoons) butter
190 g semolina
3 eggs
5 ml (1 teaspoon) salt

Boil 500 ml (2 cups) of the milk, stir in the butter, then slowly add the semolina, stirring all the time on the heat until the mixture forms into quite a thick paste.

Remove from the heat and cool, then beat the eggs and add them, beating, a little bit at a time to the paste (use a food processor or blender to make the mixing easier). Season with salt.

Boil the remainder of the milk. With a teaspoon, take little balls of the dough, put them into the milk and boil them for 15 minutes (being careful not to allow the milk to burn).

SERVING SUGGESTION Serve these dumplings with meat.

VARIATION For a pudding, sweeten the dumplings by sprinkling cinnamon sugar* over them.

PARSLEY DUMPLINGS

THE GREEN of the chopped parsley contrasts attractively with the white of the basic dumpling in this dish. The dumplings are particularly good accompaniments to hearty beef stews.

PREPARATION TIME: 15 MINUTES
COOKING TIME: 15-20 MINUTES

INGREDIENTS FOR FOUR TO SIX

45 ml (3 tablespoons) self-raising flour
30 g fresh breadcrumbs
30 ml (2 tablespoons) shredded suet
15 ml (1 tablespoon) finely chopped parsley
10 ml (2 teaspoons) finely grated lemon rind
Salt and freshly ground pepper
1 egg, beaten

Put the flour, breadcrumbs, suet, parsley and grated lemon rind in a large bowl. Mix together well with a fork or wooden spoon. Season with salt and pepper, and blend in the beaten egg.

Use lightly floured hands to shape the mixture into balls the size of large walnuts.

Poach the dumplings in a large saucepan of boiling salted water. They will rise to the surface when they are cooked through (after about 15 minutes).

If the dumplings are to accompany meat cooked in its own stock, follow the cooking directions given for suet dumplings*.

VARIATION Substitute any other herb of your choice in place of parsley.

Vegetables and Salads

SELDOM HAS FOOD played such a major role in a country's history as the vegetable has in South Africa's. The earliest European settlers were lured to the southern tip of the continent essentially because of its potential to provide fresh produce for passing ships.

The Dutch East India Company established a settlement and vegetable garden at the Cape in 1652. Within a few years the garden had gained a worldwide reputation – and the settlement was the first step on the road to colonisation of South Africa.

Those 17th century Dutch traders and businessmen knew already that the nutrients in vegetables were essential to health and survival, and few people today need to be told how rich in healthy minerals and vitamins they are. In fact many people subsist on a purely vegetarian diet and claim enormous health benefits from doing so.

Needless to say, most vegetables are ideal fare for those watching their waistlines – particularly those vegetables that are high in fibre, such as squashes and leaf varieties.

Vegetables are equally useful as starters, main dishes and accompaniments, and can even be served for dessert, as in pumpkin fritters or carrot cake. They can be steamed or boiled, or cooked in a variety of other ways: stuffed and baked, casseroled, curried or *au gratin* (with breadcrumbs and/or melted cheese).

Whether you are serving a hearty meal with creamed spinach and glazed sweet potatoes, or a slimmers' meal-in-one salad, few meals are complete without vegetables.

A COMPREHENSIVE GUIDE TO PREPARING VEGETABLES · *PAGE 184*

VEGETABLE AND SALAD RECIPES · *PAGE 188*

SPECIAL FEATURES

HERBS FOR ALL SEASONS · *PAGE 198*
MEAL-IN-ONE DISHES · MAKING A MEAL OF VEGETABLES · *PAGE 210*

A Comprehensive Guide to Vegetables

Vegetables, both raw and cooked, form an indispensable part of our diet since they are a vital source of minerals and vitamins. A wide selection of vegetables is grown locally: some are available fresh all the year round, others only at particular times of the year. And of course many vegetables are obtainable frozen, dried or tinned throughout the year.

Storing Vegetables

Where large quantities of vegetables need to be stored for some time, it is important to consider the temperature and relative humidity of your storage space. The ideal storage temperature for most vegetables is 4°C. However, some – such as onions, potatoes, squashes and pumpkins – can tolerate room temperature storage.

The basic principle in vegetable storage is to limit moisture loss. The vegetables should be covered or stored in perforated plastic or paper bags, or individually wrapped in newspaper. This ensures that moisture loss is kept as low as possible. Few vegetables keep well for longer than about 10 days unless they are well wrapped and the humidity kept at a reasonable level.

Preparing Vegetables

Wash vegetables just before using. Most vegetables can be used with their skins. If stalks, leaves or skins need to be removed, do this with a sharp knife. Peel as thinly as possible or use a pot-scourer or brush to remove any undesirable outer layer.

Vegetables can be sliced, diced or chopped by hand on a chopping board with a knife. Many food processors, however, have fittings that regulate the size of the slice or dice and therefore ensure uniform shapes if used correctly.

Shredding and grating can also be done either manually or with the help of specialised equipment. Many food processors have shredding and grating attachments that are quite easy to use when large quantities have to be prepared.

Cooking Vegetables

Some vegetables are used raw or cooked, while others should be cooked but may be served either hot or cold. These two groups of vegetables are described in separate sections.

Most vegetables can be blanched, boiled, steamed, braised or stir-fried. Vegetables such as potatoes, sweet potatoes, onions and pumpkins can be baked on their own. Other vegetables usually require to be baked in combination, or to be baked with a sauce; they may be placed in a casserole or baking dish in the oven.

The following is a guide to the terms used in vegetable cooking:

Blanching

Vegetables are blanched by being dunked into boiling water for 2-3 minutes. This is usually done prior to freezing or if vegetables are tough and are to be used in salads, stir-fried or braised.

Boiling

This method of cooking is applied to roots, tubers and greens. Put cleaned roots and tubers into a saucepan, and add enough water to cover. Add salt to taste. Cover and boil until tender. Do not boil too long, as overcooked vegetables will lose their flavour.

Green vegetables are placed in a small amount of boiling water with salt – usually about 150 ml water per 500 g vegetables. Cover and boil for 5-10 minutes.

Steaming

Vegetables can be steamed over boiling water in a steamer or in a colander that fits on a saucepan and is covered with a lid. Steaming vegetables takes longer than boiling them.

Braising

Vegetables are braised by being lightly fried in butter, oil or fat. A liquid or stock is added and the vegetables are then cooked until tender. The juices may be reduced by rapid boiling. Braised vegetables are usually brownish in colour and cooked until soft.

Stir-frying

A wok, electric frying pan or heavy-based frying pan is used for stir-frying. Place a small amount of fat or oil in the pan, cut the vegetables into small pieces and toss them in the heated oil until lightly cooked and still crisp. (See Chinese stir-fried vegetables*.) If oil is not desired, use a small amount of white wine in the pan. Close firmly with a lid and leave the chopped vegetables to steam in the wine.

Vegetables Used Raw or Cooked

Avocado Available from spring to autumn. Green- and black-skinned varieties are obtainable. Store wrapped in newspaper to control ripening. Use halved, as a container for a filling such as shrimp mayonnaise. Avocado is often served simply on its own with lemon juice and black pepper. It is a popular ingredient in salads but can also be used in purée form as a cold soup* or sauce*, or for a salad mould.

Baby marrow (courgette, zucchini) Available in spring and summer. The baby marrow is harvested before the marrow has reached maturity. The larger ones can be stuffed and cooked like a fully grown marrow. Small, fresh baby marrows have a pleasant taste if sliced into a salad or used whole as a crudité. Boiled for a few minutes, they also make a delightful vegetable and can be mixed with onions, tomatoes and fresh mushrooms for ratatouille*.

Bamboo shoot Available fresh at Eastern markets, but elsewhere mostly as a tinned product. Use in Chinese dishes. Tender, fresh bamboo shoots can be pickled in vinegar or eaten raw. Their distinctive flavour does not appeal to everyone.

Broad bean Available fresh in winter. This highly nutritious bean is mostly bought dried, but can also be obtained fresh. There are many varieties, but generally the pods are long and pale green with large white seeds bulging through. The pods are removed and the white beans boiled in salted water for 15 minutes, or until tender. Broad beans may also be eaten raw when they are very young.

Broccoli Available fresh in autumn and early winter, or frozen all year round. Broccoli was enjoyed by the Romans, and still has an Italian connection: the word 'brocco' means 'sprout'. Broccoli is a good source of vitamin C. Serve boiled lightly in a little water, or braised, with a white* or cheese sauce*. It is often used, blanched, as a crudité with a cream cheese dip*.

Cabbage Different varieties of this vegetable can be bought in season throughout the year. Cabbages may be conical, semiglobular or round, with darker outer leaves and lighter centre leaves. They are a good source of vitamin C and calcium. Boil them shredded or boil the whole green leaves lightly in a little water, or braise with onion and/or meat and potatoes. Serve cabbage with a sauce, or stuff the leaves with a meat or vegetable filling and braise until lightly brown and tender.

VEGETABLES AND SALADS

Carrot Different seasonal varieties are available throughout the year. Young, tender carrots are best steamed lightly and served whole. Raw carrots can be grated and served in combination with orange, pineapple or apple as a salad. They can be boiled, braised, glazed* or served in stews with other vegetables such as parsnips, turnips, peas and potatoes.

Cauliflower Available from autumn to spring. Cauliflower can be braised with olives and tomatoes or served with a cheese sauce. It can be served *à la polonaise*, that is, covered with cooked egg yolks and buttered breadcrumbs. The florets, dipped in batter, can be deep-fried. Cauliflower can also be used raw – or very lightly cooked – in a salad, or on a crudité platter with a dip.

Celery Available in summer, celery is grown both as a herb and as a vegetable. There are two varieties: soup celery and table celery. Table celery has big, strong, ribbed stalks and can be used as a crudité. Both the leaves and stalks are good in soup or salads; the stalks, braised, may also be served as a vegetable.

Celeriac Available from autumn to spring. This is a variety of celery cultivated for its bulbous root like a turnip. The fibrous skin has to be peeled. Celeriac is excellent in purée form (used as a thickening agent) or in soup. It can be eaten raw; lightly cooked and marinated for serving as a salad; or blanched and then fried in butter with a little water or vegetable stock* added.

Chicory Available in spring. Confusingly, it is also sometimes referred to as French or Belgian endive. The firm heads are made up of white leaves with a yellow edge. These can be broken off and used as a crudité or as a salad. The whole head can be steamed or boiled and served with a cheese sauce*. It has a distinctly bitter taste which increases later in the season.

Chilli Available all year round, chillies are small green or red conical-shaped peppers. Chillies are essential in Indian and Mexican cooking. When handling chillies be careful not to touch your face or eyes, and wash your hands well afterwards. Work under cold running water – pull out the stems and split the chillies, removing the seeds if you intend discarding them. The seeds are the hottest parts of the chilli and may be included in the dish if you like a fiery taste.

Chinese cabbage Available in spring. This cabbage looks like a cos lettuce with large white midribs. It may be confused with Swiss chard or mustard greens if the variety is very green and leafy. Chinese cabbage is best served braised or with Chinese stir-fried vegetables*, or used to make a pickled cabbage or sauerkraut. It has a pleasant, sweet taste and can be eaten fresh as a salad.

Cucumber Abundant in spring and summer, and generally obtainable throughout the year, though scarce in winter. The tunnel or hybrid varieties are generally referred to as English cucumbers. Different varieties have either ribbed or smooth skins. Use fresh with or without the skin, cut in various sizes in salads. The gherkin types can be pickled* or bottled in brine.

Dandelion Available in spring and summer. This common garden weed should be eaten before it grows bitter. The leaves are used in salad or cooked like spinach, and are referred to as dandelion greens.

Endive Available from autumn to spring. The two main types are the broad-leaved and the curly-leaved. Endive is similar to lettuce and can be used judiciously in cold salad dishes as the leaves taste bitter. Like Chinese cabbage, it can also be used in the same way as spinach.

Fennel (Florence fennel) Available in spring. The bulbous root of cultivated garden fennel must not be confused with the wild fennel of which only the leaves, stalks and seeds are used. The bulb can be eaten raw in salad or cooked and served with a béchamel sauce*. The flavour is similar to aniseed.

Garlic Available all year. This member of the onion family grows in bulbs made up of a cluster of cloves. The cloves are used whole, crushed or chopped in meat dishes, with poultry, in salad dressings and with pickled fish*. If using a strong garlic crusher, there is no need to peel the cloves first. Garlic can also be used in all starchy dishes containing tomatoes and onions. Rub a clove of garlic inside a salad bowl before making a fresh green salad*. Whole bulbs of garlic roasted in the oven for about 1 hour at 200°C make a delicious accompaniment to roast lamb.

Green bean (snap bean, runner bean, French bean) Available in summer and autumn, or frozen all year round. The earlier in the season fresh green beans are bought, the more tender they will be. Young, fresh, whole beans can be served raw or blanched as a salad, vegetable or crudité. Later in the season it is preferable to slice the beans – either lengthways or across – before boiling or steaming.

Leek Available from autumn to spring. The leek is a member of the onion family and is quite mild. Because it is less potent than onion, it is more suitable for soups and stews, but can also be served raw in salad. Boiled leeks are good served with a white sauce* or baked in the oven with grated cheese.

Lettuce Available all year. There are four recognised classes of lettuce: leaf, cos or romaine, butterhead and crisphead. Butterhead lettuce hearts are not as tight as the crisphead varieties and the leaves are softer. Although lettuce may be braised and used in soups, it is more generally used as the major ingredient of green salad*.

Mushroom Available all year. The cultivated mushroom is now a basic part of our cuisine. Its size and openness depends on the stage at which it is picked. Mushrooms can be used raw, baked or sautéed, and make a valuable accompaniment to most meat dishes. They can also be used to make soup, or in casseroles or sauces.

Mustard and cress This is a short-season crop grown in shallow containers mainly by the home gardener. A combination of mustard and cress sprouts can be used in sandwiches and as a garnish.

Olive Available in autumn, and in tins all year. Green olives are the unripened form and black ones the fully ripened fruit. They can be cooked in savoury dishes, mixed in stuffings or used as an ingredient in the traditional Greek salad*.

Onion Available all year. The two onions grown most in South Africa are the bulbing and Welsh varieties. Onions, known as the king of vegetables, are extremely versatile – virtually no savoury dish is complete without them. Some onions are less pungent than others. Young, spring or green onions are not a particular variety, but have simply been picked when still immature. Onions can be fried, boiled, baked*, braised or used raw.

Pepper (capsicum) Available fresh throughout the year. The sweet, green pepper changes from green to red when it ripens. Some yellow varieties are also marketed. The sweet pepper is used raw in salads, as a vegetable crudité or in hors d'oeuvres; or cooked in stews, poultry or Italian dishes, or Chinese stir-fried vegetables*.

Radish Available early in spring and throughout summer. Small, round, scarlet types as well as a white or red turnip variety are available. Radishes are used raw in salads; they make an excellent garnish used whole with a bit of the leaf top.

Salsify Available from spring to autumn. This plant root is sometimes called the 'oyster plant' because of its slightly glutinous and glossy appearance when being cooked. Salsify should be peeled and cut into chunks, then dipped into cold water with lemon juice to prevent discoloration. It can then be boiled in court-bouillon* for about 2 hours, sautéed in butter and served with béchamel* or cream sauce*; or used in salads, soups, stews or purées. The stalks or tender shoots of salsify can be eaten raw in salads.

Shallot Available in spring and summer. This variety of onion is quite rare and is often grown only by the home gardener. Also known as 'potato onions', shallots multiply to produce clusters at the root end. Shallots are popular in French cooking and make the best pickled onions. They keep well and can be used fresh – whole or chopped – in a green salad*.

Sorrel Available in winter and spring. Use a leaf of sorrel when cooking lamb stews and especially waterblommetjie bredie*. Sorrel can be cooked with spinach or used in combination with lettuce and cress for a salad. It makes an excellent soup and can also be used for quiches* or in egg dishes.

Spinach Available from autumn to spring. The true spinach is not as widely grown as Swiss chard. Like sorrel, it has a pleasant, acidic taste and can be used in soups, quiches* or soufflés*. It has the advantage of freezing well.

Swiss chard (spinach beet) Available all year. This vegetable is related to beetroot, which it resembles. It has large, dark-green, curly leaves and clear white stems. Early in the season the leaves are young and tender, and the stems still green. Use the young leaves fresh for a salad and the older leaves as you would spinach.

Tomato Available all year. Probably the most popular and well-known 'fruit' vegetable. Numerous varieties are available, although the smaller varieties are less frequently seen. Tomatoes can be used raw or cooked, and form the basis of many well-known sauces and dishes. Often recipes recommend that tomatoes be skinned* and/or seeded*.

Turnip Available in spring and summer. Turnips vary in size, shape and colour, being round or cylindrical, and yellowish or with a purple ring at the top. Use fresh, young turnips in a salad or boiled whole. If the turnips have been kept for some time, use them as an ingredient for soups, mixed vegetable dishes or stews.

Watercress Available in spring. Watercress was originally gathered in the wild, where it grows in shallow streams. It is now commercially cultivated. It has a peppery taste that makes it an excellent accompaniment to egg dishes. It can also be used fresh in salads or as a purée in soups.

VEGETABLES THAT SHOULD BE COOKED

Amadumbe Available in spring and summer. This is a potato-like vegetable which takes 7-11 months to ripen. It is grown by farmers in Natal and is particularly well-liked by Zulus and Indians. The amadumbe keeps for up to 3 months. It can be prepared just like the potato – baked in its skin or peeled, sliced and boiled. Amadumbe has a sweet, nut-like taste and the texture of a sweet potato.

Artichoke (globe) Available in late spring and beginning of summer. Some globe artichokes are green and others have a purple tinge on the leafy, flower-like globe. Buy when the globe is still firm and has not opened – the leaves should be young and tender. Trim them before preparing and serving*.

Artichoke (Jerusalem) Available from late summer to early winter. This is a member of the sunflower family, and 'Jerusalem' is probably a corruption of the Italian 'girasole' meaning 'turning to the sun'. The edible portion – the tuber – has a distinct flavour which does not appeal to everyone. After peeling, place immediately in salt water to which lemon juice has been added to prevent discoloration. Serve fresh in a salad or use the purée for a soup*. The Jerusalem artichoke can be sliced and cooked in the same way as potato.

Asparagus Available in spring or tinned all year. The earliest fresh variety is usually the California, with thick, white spears, and the later ones are long, thin and green. Asparagus can be used in soup, in egg dishes and in a variety of savoury dishes, or prepared and served* as a vegetable side dish or hors d'oeuvre.

Beetroot Available all year. Beetroot must not be scrubbed with a brush, as it may start bleeding and the colour will be lost while boiling. Cooked beetroot is generally served cold as a salad but it can also be served hot. It can be pickled and bottled. Borsch*, the popular Russian soup, is made with beetroot.

Brinjal (eggplant, aubergine) Available from spring to autumn. It can be fried or braised, with or without its skin. It can also be baked whole or stuffed*. If the fruit is old, it tends to be bitter, in which case peel and sprinkle it with salt, and leave it for 30 minutes before preparation.

Brussels sprouts Available fresh in winter and frozen all year. This is a type of miniature cabbage which sprouts from a tall, woody stem. Many varieties are found on the market today. They can be used marinated as a salad, boiled as a vegetable (try them with chestnuts), baked in the oven with a cheese sauce*, or added to a cream soup.

Cho-cho (sou-sou, chayote) Available in summer. This is a ribbed, green, pear-shaped gourd that grows on a climbing vine. The flesh is creamy white with a small pip in the centre. Boil it sliced but unpeeled in salted water. Serve hot or cold.

Kale (borecole, boerenkool, winter greens) Available in winter. This is a type of non-heading cabbage that is not particularly well known. It used to be the 'peasant's cabbage' in the earliest days in Britain, the best-known variety being Scottish kale. When young, it is excellent, cooked for about 20 minutes in boiling water. When it is old, the flavour is far too strong to be enjoyed.

Kohlrabi Available in winter. One of the 'newer' vegetables, kohlrabi was first described 400 years ago in Germany. It is a variety of cabbage and can be cooked in the same manner as turnips. It can be sliced, steamed and served with the cooked leaves or in a macedoine* of vegetables.

Lima bean Available fresh in winter and frozen all year. Lima beans may be small- or large-seeded and, like broad beans, have to be taken from the pod before boiling. The seeds are pale green.

Marrow Available in summer. The marrow can be 40 cm or more in length, depending on the variety. Generally, it is pale yellow or green. Marrow is traditionally peeled, cut into cubes, boiled and then combined with bread cubes and sugar; cook together for an additional 15-20 minutes. This dish is known as 'boerpampoen'. Marrow can also be boiled, steamed, baked in slices or stuffed and baked.

Mealie (corn, sweet corn, maize) Available fresh in summer, and tinned and frozen all year. The 'indentata' variety, or 'field corn', is the most generally known and is used to make maize meal. In South Africa 'sweet corn' is the name for a garden variety ('saccharata') that has been developed, and is excellent as a fresh vegetable. It can be baked in its leaves, in the fire or the oven. Otherwise, mealies are boiled and served with butter and salt. Whole kernels can also be used to make mealie bread* or sweet corn fritters*.

Okra (lady's finger) Available in summer and autumn. A member of the mallow (hibiscus) family, it is cultivated mainly for the immature pod. It is a mucilaginous pod which becomes slimy when cooked, and as such it is not liked by all. It can be boiled or steamed and used with onions, tomatoes and meat in stews or Indian recipes.

Parsnip Available from autumn to spring. This long, sweetish root is similar to the carrot, but pale white or cream. Fresh, young parsnips need only be scraped, but older ones should be peeled. They can be boiled, braised, used in soups or stews, or pan-roasted with meat.

Pea Available fresh from early summer to autumn, or frozen, dried or tinned all year. There are many varieties, from the small *petit pois* to the large kind that is mostly preferred for drying. Peas are best boiled lightly and served with chopped fresh mint. They can also be used in soups and stews or as a purée for thickening.

Potato Available all year. Choose the right variety of potato for the cooking method required: a firm, glossy potato for chips, a soft 'mealie' potato for mash, and a firm, young potato for roasting. For crisp roast potatoes, peel and parboil, then toss in oil and seasoning. Bake at 220°C for 40 minutes, turning once. When mashing boiled potatoes, add hot milk, plenty of butter, seasoning and grated nutmeg to taste. To make sautéed potatoes, dice peeled raw (or boiled) potatoes and gently sauté in butter until golden and soft. Add seasoning and a sprinkling of chopped parsley. Store potatoes in a cool, dry place, but not in the refrigerator.

Pumpkin and squash
Flat boer (boerpampoen) and hubbard squash Available all year. The 'flat boer' or 'boerpampoen' has a white, smooth skin, and the hubbard can be dark green, bright orange or even purple-blue. Both kinds have firm, brightly coloured and highly nutritious flesh. Bake, with or without skin, and flavour with cinnamon, sugar or nutmeg. Use also for pumpkin fritters*.

Table queen and gem squash Available all year. The table queen has a fluted appearance and the gem squash a smooth round appearance. When young and fresh, the skins of both are also edible. These squashes are mostly boiled and the halves served with a filling such as peas, mushrooms, cheese or a bread stuffing.

Butternut squash Available in summer. It has a pear or calabash shape, with a small seed cavity and bright yellow flesh. Halve and bake in the oven, or slice and bake with cinnamon and sugar or cheese and herbs. Use the flesh to make pumpkin pie.

Swede (rutabaga, Swedish turnip) Available from spring to autumn. Swedes are larger and less watery than turnips, with yellow to orange flesh and coarse skin. They can be distinguished from turnips by the concentric rings round the top. Boil or prepare in a similar way to turnips.

Sweet potato Available from spring to autumn and also in dehydrated form. It comes in various sizes and shapes, and can be white or yellow inside and brown or reddish-brown outside. The yellow-fleshed variety is also known as 'borrie' sweet potato. Sweet potato can be baked whole, boiled, candied or mashed.

Waterblommetjie (Cape pond-weed, water onion, water hyacinth) This fresh-water aquatic plant traditionally flowers in spring. It can be frozen and is available tinned. The flower sections are used in waterblommetjie bredie*.

Vine leaves Available in early spring. Vine leaves are not marketed fresh, but they can be bought tinned in brine. They are used for stuffed vine leaves (dolmades*).

DRIED LEGUMES (PULSES)

Dried legumes, also known as pulses, include beans, lentils and peas. Legumes are a rich and economical protein source, forming the basis of many vegetarian diets.

Legumes – other than lentils – are generally soaked overnight in water before cooking. Some pre-boiled products are also on the market. Soaking in hot weather may result in fermentation and give an undesirable aftertaste when cooking. This can be avoided by allowing the legumes to soak in a bowl in the refrigerator.

Beans
Alfalfa This bean is generally used only for sprouting. The sprouts can be used in salads, in soups and as a garnish.

Broad bean (Windsor bean, Fava bean) Broad beans are generally eaten cooked (for about 1-1½ hours) and are sold whole, peeled and tinned. They make a good accompaniment to dishes with bacon or smoked sausages or as a base for a thick bean soup.

Butter bean (Lima bean, Madagascar bean) Butter beans are among the best-flavoured beans and can be served cooked, but cold, as an hors d'oeuvre. Generally these beans are quite tough and should be cooked for 1 hour or longer after soaking.

Haricot bean (kidney bean, Boston bean, common bean) There are white, red and black varieties which go under names such as the red kidney bean, black bean and large haricot or sugar bean.

Cook the beans slowly for 1-2 hours, or leave in a low oven overnight. The best way to cook them, however, is in a pressure cooker.

Wash the beans, put them in the pressure cooker without salt, cover with cold water, seal and bring to the boil for 5 minutes. Cool the cooker under cold water, then open and drain the beans. Add any flavourings desired, such as onion, cloves, bouquet garni*, garlic and salt. Cover and pressure-cook for another 40 minutes.

Mung bean Although the mung bean is almost always thought of as a sprouting* bean, it can also be cooked. It needs less cooking than the kidney bean – about 1 hour is enough.

Soya bean The soya bean is highly nutritious and many varieties of texturised soya bean protein products are available as meat substitutes. Soya beans in their natural form are inferior in flavour to the haricot or kidney bean.

Dried Peas
Many small-sized beans are referred to as peas. Dried peas form a staple in the diets of many Eastern cultures. In the split form these are sometimes referred to as 'dhal' or 'gram'.

Dried peas include whole marrowfat or 'blue' peas (which tend to have tough skins and a soft, floury texture) and the skinless split peas.

Split peas There are green and yellow split peas. Both have a sweet taste and make an excellent purée. Split peas are used in soups, baked dishes and salads – best known is the British 'pease pudding'.

Chick-peas Several varieties of this legume are generally available in health stores and used as a major salad ingredient or for sprouts*. Chick-peas are best if soaked in boiling water for 12 hours and then cooked in fresh water. Add chopped onion, garlic and herbs for flavour. Do not stir, as doing so will break the peas. Serve hot or cold.

Cowpeas Cowpea pods are about as thick as a pencil, up to 30 cm long and hang downwards from the plant. The young pods are used in curries or boiled as a vegetable. The seed of the ripe bean may be red, blue, brown, black, white or speckled. The black-eye cowpea is best known. The cowpea is available whole, split as 'dhal', or ground to a flour.

Lentils
There are many different varieties, usually identified by their colour, namely green, red, yellow, brown or black. Some are best known by their Indian names as various types of 'dhal'.

Lentils are extremely nutritious, containing protein, vitamin B and iron.

SEEDS FOR SPROUTING

Any of the pea, lentil or bean varieties can be used for sprouts*. Some – such as alfalfa, mung beans, chickpeas and lentils – sprout more easily than others. When seeds sprout, the nutrient concentration changes and they become a source of vitamin C. Only seeds that have the potential to germinate will sprout – if seeds have been heat-treated, they will not do so.

There are various sprouting methods. In general, the seeds need to be washed daily with tepid water and left in a cool moist atmosphere to germinate. This may take 3-4 days.

Sprouts can be kept in a sealed container or plastic bag in the refrigerator for up to three weeks.

Mung beans should be soaked continuously for 12-24 hours, until the skins just start to burst. Drain off and follow instructions for sprouting. Remove husks by hand after sprouts are long enough.

Soya beans are difficult to sprout and must be soaked well beforehand. The best temperature is 20-25°C and the beans must be continuously dunked in water to avoid mouldiness. It is best to tip them out once a day and to remove those going mouldy. In 3-4 days the sprouts should be long enough. Rinse and steam gently for a few minutes to remove the raw 'beany' taste.

Alfalfa produces fine 2 cm sprouts in 3-4 days. They have a delicate nut-like flavour.

Whole dried peas give sprouts 5 cm long that have a pleasant flavour of peas.

Lentils are delicious when the sprout is about 2 cm long.

Preparing and Serving Asparagus

Asparagus is grown very successfully in South Africa, the Free State being a big producer.

One of the most important criteria for selecting good fresh asparagus is the condition of the tip. The bud cluster should be tightly closed and not show any sign of wilting. Avoid packed asparagus that has gone mouldy in the wrapping, or asparagus with woody-looking root ends.

The best in locally grown asparagus will range in thickness from 5 mm to 1,5 cm. Choose asparagus of equal thickness for even cooking.

Two kinds are available, the slender, green spears grown above ground, or the soft, white spears grown underground to prevent chlorophyll development.

•

Preparing Wash the spears in cold water, then bunch them together on a chopping board – levelling all the heads. Cut off the dry centimetre or two of the root end and at the same time size them uniformly.

If you are using young, tender stalks, scraping and peeling is undesirable as you will lose flavour, texture and nutrition. Older stalks can be cleaned with a potato peeler exactly like scraping a carrot – but do not damage the tender tips in any way.

•

Cooking Steaming is the best way to cook fresh asparagus. Lay the spears neatly in a vegetable steamer basket, and cook in the steam from rapidly boiling water.

Alternatively, they can be tied together in a bunch with the tips pointing upwards, and cooked in a small pot of water. The pot should be small enough to ensure that the bunch does not fall on its side, and the water level should be about halfway up the stems. Cooking time varies from 8 to 15 minutes, depending on thickness. The green variety of asparagus should be a bright green colour. Take out one of the spears and bite it to test it. The spear should still be slightly resistant. Limp, mushy asparagus is overcooked.

•

Serving suggestions Melted butter or a Hollandaise sauce* make good accompaniments to hot asparagus. The cooked spears can also be used in the recipe for asparagus in cheese sauce*.

Cold asparagus may be served either with vinaigrette* or a smooth, lemon-flavoured mayonnaise*.

Asparagus in Cheese Sauce

Asparagus is a popular delicacy which always adds special interest to a meal. This recipe makes a tasty starter.

Preparation Time: 25 minutes
Cooking Time: 20 minutes
Pre-heat Oven to 180°C

Ingredients for Four
1 tin (410g) asparagus, or 400g cooked* fresh asparagus spears
125 ml (½ cup) asparagus liquid
70 g butter
45 ml (3 tablespoons) flour
125 ml (½ cup) cream
250 ml (1 cup) grated mature Cheddar cheese
Salt and pepper
A pinch of dry mustard
250 ml (1 cup) fresh white breadcrumbs

Drain the asparagus, reserving 125 ml (½ cup) of the liquid. Arrange the asparagus in a greased oven-proof dish.

Melt 40 g of the butter, add the flour and cook for about 1 minute, stirring all the time. Remove from the heat, and add the asparagus liquid. Return to the heat and cook, stirring constantly, until the sauce thickens.

Add the cream, 125 ml (½ cup) of the grated Cheddar cheese, salt, pepper and mustard. Pour this cheese sauce over the asparagus.

Melt the remaining butter. Toss the breadcrumbs and remaining cheese in the melted butter, and sprinkle this mixture over the asparagus. Bake for 20 minutes or until the sauce is golden-brown.

Variation Replace the breadcrumbs with crushed potato crisps.

Baby Marrow Salad

Baby marrows (known as zucchini in Italy and courgettes in France) are much enjoyed for their delicate flavour when cooked. However, the full nutritional benefit is derived only when they are eaten raw, as these vegetables have a high sodium content which is dissipated once they have been boiled.

Preparation Time: 15 minutes
Cooking Time: 5 minutes
Marinating Time: overnight

Ingredients for Four to Six
6 medium-sized baby marrows (300-350g), sliced into 2 cm rounds
Salt and freshly ground black pepper
5 ml (1 teaspoon) chopped fresh basil
5 ml (1 teaspoon) chopped fresh origanum
15 ml (1 tablespoon) chopped parsley
150 ml garlic dressing*
1 medium-sized tomato

Cook the baby marrows in a minimum of water for 3 minutes, or steam them. Drain, then add the seasoning and basil, origanum and parsley. Add the garlic dressing and marinate overnight. Chop the tomato and use as garnish.

Serving Suggestion Serve individual portions on a bed of lettuce or watercress accompanied by a baked potato*.

Variation Instead of the garlic dressing, dress with natural yoghurt* and scatter chopped mint over the top.

Baby Marrows in Cheese Sauce

This is a very useful vegetarian dish that can be made ahead of time, then baked before serving.

Preparation Time: 30 minutes
Cooking Time: 35 minutes
Pre-heat Oven to 180°C

Ingredients for Six
12 medium-sized baby marrows (600-700g)
30 g butter
30 ml (2 tablespoons) flour
250 ml (1 cup) milk
100 g feta or Cheddar cheese, grated
2 egg yolks
30 ml (2 tablespoons) cream
Salt and freshly ground black pepper
15 ml (1 tablespoon) finely grated Parmesan cheese for sprinkling

Cut the baby marrows in half lengthways. Drop them into a large saucepan of boiling, salted water. When the water has returned to the boil (about 5 minutes) remove the marrows and drain well.

Make a thick white sauce by melting the butter, stirring in the flour until smooth, then gradually adding the milk, stirring all the time, until the sauce is thick and smooth. Stir in the feta or Cheddar cheese. Beat the egg yolks with the cream and add the sauce gradually to this mixture. Add a grinding of pepper to the sauce, but add salt only if it is needed.

Place the baby marrows in an oiled, oven-proof dish, and pour over the cheese sauce. Sprinkle the surface lightly with the Parmesan, and bake the dish for 30-35 minutes until golden.

Spiced Brinjals

As brinjals originally came to South Africa from India, it is not surprising that some of the best recipes for them include spices which have become familiar to us in curries, such as asafoetida, a gum resin with a strong, oniony odour, relished as a condiment in India and Iran.

Preparation Time: 45 minutes
Standing Time: 40 minutes
Cooking Time: 35-40 minutes

Ingredients for Four to Six
2 medium-sized brinjals, cut into 1,5 cm slices
Salt
90 ml sunflower oil or ghee*
30 ml (2 tablespoons) sesame seeds
A pinch of asafoetida (optional)
A piece of fresh green ginger, about 2,5 cm, chopped
5 ml (1 teaspoon) paprika
1 ml (¼ teaspoon) freshly ground black pepper
Juice of 1½ lemons or 2 limes
30 ml (2 tablespoons) chopped coriander (dhania) leaves or parsley for garnish

Place the brinjal slices in a colander and sprinkle them with salt. Leave them to stand for 40 minutes to remove some of the excess moisture. Dry them thoroughly with paper towels.

Heat 60 ml (¼ cup) of the oil or ghee in a heavy frying pan, and add the brinjals. Fry the slices quickly on both sides. Remove from the pan and set aside.

Heat the remaining 30 ml (2 tablespoons) of the oil or ghee in the pan. Add the sesame seeds, asafoetida (if used), ginger, paprika and black pepper, and fry for 2-3 minutes.

Return the brinjals to the frying pan and stir in the lemon juice or lime juice. Cover and simmer over a very low heat for about 30 minutes.

Place the brinjals in a warmed serving dish, and sprinkle them with the chopped coriander or parsley.

SERVING SUGGESTION Serve this dish with grilled lamb or chicken.

STUFFED BRINJALS

BRINJALS, ALSO KNOWN as eggplants or aubergines, are a rich and nutritious vegetable (high in potassium). They are also very versatile, and can be eaten hot or cold, with or without accompaniments. This relatively simple recipe will produce delicious results.

PREPARATION TIME: 1 HOUR
COOKING TIME: 30 MINUTES
PRE-HEAT OVEN TO 180°C

INGREDIENTS FOR SIX
6 small brinjals, about 12 cm long
1 medium-sized onion, peeled and finely chopped*
2 cloves garlic, crushed
30 ml (2 tablespoons) sunflower oil
1 medium-sized tomato, skinned* and cubed
1 small green pepper, seeded and chopped
10 ml (2 teaspoons) chopped fresh basil
75 g cooked rice* or 75 g fresh breadcrumbs
45 ml (3 tablespoons) chopped parsley
Salt and freshly ground black pepper
75-100 g Cheddar or mozzarella cheese, grated
250 ml (1 cup) chicken* or vegetable stock*

Wash and trim the bud ends of the brinjals, and boil them in unsalted water for about 10 minutes, or until they begin to soften.

Halve the brinjals lengthways and, when they are cool, remove the pulp – leaving just enough to make the shells into 'boats' that will hold the stuffing without collapsing. Chop the flesh.

Sauté the onion and garlic in a little oil, add the tomato, green pepper, basil, rice or breadcrumbs, parsley and chopped brinjal pulp, and season.

Fill the brinjal skins with this mixture and arrange them close together in an oiled oven-proof dish.

Top with grated cheese, and carefully pour about 2 cm of chicken or vegetable stock into the dish. Bake, uncovered, for 30 minutes.

SERVING SUGGESTION Serve on a bed of rice to which some slivered almonds or pine kernels and currants have been added.

Accompany the stuffed brinjals with a tossed green salad*.

VARIATIONS Substitute 60 g chopped mushrooms for the green pepper.

If basil is not available, use thyme.

BRINJALS À LA GRECQUE

THIS VEGETABLE is usually cooked in oil to be served as an accompanying vegetable, or stuffed with a variety of fillings and baked.

Brinjals keep fresh for longer than most other vegetables, especially if they are stored in the salad basket of a refrigerator. The following recipe makes an unusual and appetising first course.

PREPARATION TIME: 10 MINUTES
COOKING TIME: 30 MINUTES
CHILLING TIME: 2 HOURS

INGREDIENTS FOR FOUR TO SIX
2 medium-sized brinjals, about 16 cm long
300 ml white wine
300 ml water
45 ml (3 tablespoons) sugar
45 ml (3 tablespoons) olive oil
6 coriander seeds
Juice of ½ lemon
1 small bay leaf
30 ml (2 tablespoons) tomato paste
1 bouquet garni*
Salt and freshly ground black pepper
Chopped basil for garnish

Peel the brinjals and dice them into 3 cm cubes. Put all the remaining ingredients (except the basil) into a saucepan, seasoning with the salt and freshly ground black pepper. Stir well, then bring this sauce to the boil, add the diced brinjals and bring back to the boil.

Simmer the brinjals for 15 minutes, or until they are tender but still intact. Lift them into a dish with a slotted spoon, and boil the sauce rapidly until it has reduced by a quarter.

Strain the sauce over the brinjals, allow to cool, then chill in the refrigerator for 2 hours. Sprinkle with basil before serving.

SERVING SUGGESTION Spoon the brinjals and the sauce into deep plates and serve as a first course.

Serve with crusty bread that can be used to mop up the dressing.

VARIATION Instead of brinjals use button mushrooms. Simmer them, whole, in the sauce, for not more than 10 minutes, when they will be tender.

PREPARING AND SERVING GLOBE ARTICHOKES

The Mediterranean-type climate at the Cape is ideal for growing globe artichokes. The thistle-like plants are hardy perennials, with silvery-grey leaves. The bushes grow to about a metre tall and require a minimum of water and attention.

Pick the artichokes when they are fist-sized and well formed, but the overlapping leaves must still hug each other closely. Once the leaves start opening, the artichokes are past their best.

Don't expect to get a large serving from each one; the only edible parts are the bottom, and the small fleshy segments at the base of the individual leaves.

How to prepare One can serve them either whole with the leaves trimmed or only the bottoms, fully trimmed of all the leaves.

Trimming whole artichokes With a sharp, strong knife cut off the top quarter of the head.

To remove the hairy core, stretch the middle leaves apart, reach into the centre and scoop out the fuzzy core (a grapefruit spoon works well).

Trim the base flat by cutting it level, removing the stem at the same time. The sharp points of the remaining leaves can then be snipped with kitchen scissors for cosmetic reasons.

To prevent excessive discoloration, the prepared artichokes can be kept in water to which lemon juice has been added.

Trimming artichoke bottoms With a sharp, strong knife, cut off two-thirds of the artichoke top.

Trim the base flat by cutting it level, removing the stem at the same time.

Peel off the outer leaves, using a sharp vegetable knife, starting at the base and turning the vegetable in your hand as if you were peeling an orange.

Remove the hairy core with a grapefruit spoon and soak the artichoke bottoms in lemon water.

How to cook Avoid using iron or aluminium cookware as this will cause severe discoloration.

Wash the artichoke and trim it as described. Allow it to simmer, submerged in water to which you have added lemon juice (to prevent discoloration), olive oil (to give richness, gloss and flavour), salt, pepper and garlic.

Cook for about 30 minutes. To test whether the artichoke is sufficiently cooked, pierce the base with a fork to check that it is tender.

Serving suggestion Serve one artichoke per guest as a starter, accompanied by melted butter.

Variations If you are serving just the artichoke bottoms, serve them filled with a seafood or cheese stuffing, hot or cold.

Alternatively, coat the artichoke bottoms with a thick, well-seasoned, white sauce*, and bake in the oven – then serve as an extra vegetable or a starter. The bottoms may also be served cold with garlic mayonnaise (aïoli*) or vinaigrette*, or served as part of a salad or vegetable platter.

VEGETABLES AND SALADS

MATAR AUR BAÏGAN SAKH

THIS SPICILY FLAVOURED dish incorporates beans, peas and brinjals (one of the most popular vegetables used in Indian cuisine). The Indian brinjal is a small, sweet variety with a thin skin. Brinjals are used primarily as a thickener.

PREPARATION TIME: 20 MINUTES
COOKING TIME: 30 MINUTES

INGREDIENTS FOR SIX

200 g fresh green beans, cut in 2,5 cm strips
400 g fresh unshelled peas or 200 g frozen peas
2 small brinjals, washed and cut into 2,5 cm cubes
1 large onion, peeled and chopped*
5 ml (1 teaspoon) turmeric
7 ml (1½ teaspoons) salt
A 5 cm piece of fresh green ginger, crushed to a paste
5 ml (1 teaspoon) red chilli powder
10 ml (2 teaspoons) coriander seeds, crushed
10 ml (2 teaspoons) cumin seeds, crushed
125 ml (½ cup) sunflower oil or ghee*
2 cinnamon sticks (each 7,5 cm long)
5 ml (1 teaspoon) lovage seeds (ajmo), or cumin
1 medium-sized ripe tomato, chopped
30 ml (2 tablespoons) chopped coriander (dhania) leaves for garnish

Mix together the beans, shelled peas, brinjals, onion, turmeric, salt, ginger, chilli powder, coriander and cumin in a bowl. Set aside.

Heat the oil or ghee in a saucepan, add the cinnamon sticks and lovage seeds (or cumin), and brown for a few seconds.

Add the mixture of spiced vegetables to the pot, stir and cover the saucepan. Simmer on a low heat for 20 minutes. Add the chopped tomato, and cook, covered, for a further 10 minutes.

Garnish with the chopped coriander leaves and serve.

SERVING SUGGESTIONS Serve as a main course together with warm chapati* and pickles.

This can also be served as a side dish with chicken, meat or fish.

BROAD BEANS WITH BUTTER

TO GET THE BEST from this dish, choose young beans, no thicker than your finger and about 7,5 cm long.

PREPARATION TIME: 10 MINUTES
COOKING TIME: 15 MINUTES

INGREDIENTS FOR SIX

500 g young broad beans
Salt and freshly ground pepper
75 g butter
Juice of ½ lemon
10 ml (2 teaspoons) chopped basil or parsley for garnish

Wash the beans, then top and tail them and place them in a pan of lightly salted, boiling water. Bring this back to the boil and cook, covered, until the beans are tender (10-15 minutes).

Drain the beans thoroughly, melt the butter in a pan and toss the beans in it until they are evenly coated. Sprinkle them with freshly ground pepper and lemon juice. Garnish with the basil or parsley.

VARIATIONS Arrange the hot beans in a dish and spoon a little soured cream over them.

Instead of tossing the beans in the butter, make a separate sauce by adding the lemon juice to the melted butter.

GREEN BEANS WITH HERBS

BEANS MIX WELL with a variety of herbs. The following light and tasty dish can be served either on its own or as an accompaniment to a meat dish.

PREPARATION TIME: 25 MINUTES
COOKING TIME: 35-40 MINUTES

INGREDIENTS FOR SIX

500 g green beans
45-60 ml (3-4 tablespoons) sunflower oil
1 medium-sized onion, peeled and finely chopped*
1 clove garlic, crushed
1 medium-sized carrot, chopped
30 ml (2 tablespoons) chicken* or vegetable stock*
10 ml (2 teaspoons) finely chopped parsley, tarragon or chives

MATAR AUR BAÏGAN SAKH *Condiments and spices flavour this vegetable casserole from India.*

VEGETABLES AND SALADS

10 ml (2 teaspoons) each finely chopped chervil and spring onions
5 ml (1 teaspoon) chopped marjoram
5 ml (1 teaspoon) salt
2 ml (½ teaspoon) sugar

Wash, top and tail the green beans, and cut them in half.

Heat the oil in a heavy-based pan and cook the onion, garlic and carrot for about 5 minutes, or until the onion has turned a golden colour.

Add the beans, stock and all the finely chopped herbs, mixing these thoroughly, then cover with a lid and simmer gently for about 25 minutes, or until the beans are tender. Stir occasionally, and add a little more stock if the mixture begins to dry out. Season to taste with salt and sugar.

SERVING SUGGESTION This makes a light dish on its own, served with small, new, buttered potatoes sprinkled with parsley or chives.

VARIATION For a more substantial version of this dish, simply add 250 g cooked, diced ham to the beans for the last 5 minutes of cooking.

SWEET AND SOUR BEETROOT WITH CITRUS SAUCE

BEETROOT REGULARLY APPEARS on our tables in the form of a salad. Serve it hot, with lemon and orange juice, and you have a vegetable dish with dramatic colour appeal and a clean, tart taste.

PREPARATION TIME: 15 MINUTES
COOKING TIME: BEETROOT 30 MINUTES; SAUCE 5 MINUTES

INGREDIENTS FOR FOUR TO SIX
6 small, even-sized beetroots (with 2 cm of stems intact)
25 g butter
30 ml (2 tablespoons) brown sugar
125 ml (½ cup) orange juice
60 ml (¼ cup) lemon juice
10 ml (2 teaspoons) cornflour
125 ml (½ cup) strong chicken stock*
A pinch of cinnamon
Salt and pepper
Chopped parsley for garnish

Boil the beetroots briskly in salted water (or steam) for 30 minutes, then skin them and dice them.

Place the butter, sugar, orange juice and lemon juice in a small saucepan and heat gently until the sugar is dissolved. Mix the cornflour with the stock and add to the sauce, stirring until slightly thickened. Add a pinch of cinnamon, season, and pour the sauce over the beetroot.

Sprinkle chopped parsley over the top just before serving.

SERVING SUGGESTION Serve with roast lamb or roast pork.

VARIATION Carrots are excellent prepared in this way.

BEETROOT SALAD

THIS PICKLED BEETROOT salad keeps remarkably well in the refrigerator. It makes a very good accompaniment to pickled meats or pickled fish when served together with hot boiled potatoes.

Though beetroots have a high protein content, they also have more than twice the average number of kilojoules to be found in other vegetables, so they are not for dedicated slimmers.

PREPARATION TIME: 10 MINUTES
COOKING TIME: BEETROOT 1 HOUR; MARINADE 5 MINUTES
COOLING TIME: 1 HOUR

INGREDIENTS FOR SIX
6 medium-sized beetroots (with 2 cm of stems intact)
1 large onion, peeled and thinly sliced*
125 ml (½ cup) vinegar
125 ml (½ cup) water
15 ml (1 tablespoon) sugar
1 bay leaf
6 peppercorns
2 cloves
2 ml (½ teaspoon) salt

Boil the beetroot in salted water for an hour, then skin and slice. Arrange the beetroot and onion slices in layers in a casserole dish or other heat-resistant bowl.

Bring the vinegar, water, sugar, bay leaf, peppercorns, cloves and salt to the boil and pour this sauce over the vegetables. Allow to cool, then chill in the refrigerator.

BROCCOLI ALLA PARMIGIANA

BROCCOLI IS A NATIVE of Southern Europe and it was first introduced to the cuisines of France and Britain at the start of the eighteenth century. In Italian the word *broccoli* means cabbage sprouts or flowers; but *broccoletti*, meaning little branches, is the name by which the vegetable is sold on the colourful market stalls of Italy.

'Alla Parmigiana' means that the dish contains Parmesan cheese. It also uses mozzarella cheese, and a tomato sauce that is fragrant with basil.

PREPARATION TIME: 45 MINUTES
COOKING TIME: 20 MINUTES
PRE-HEAT OVEN TO 200°C

INGREDIENTS FOR FOUR
1 large head of broccoli
30 ml (2 tablespoons) olive oil
1 medium-sized onion, peeled and finely chopped*
1 clove garlic, chopped
4 tomatoes, skinned*
15 ml (1 tablespoon) chopped fresh basil or 10 ml (2 teaspoons) dried basil
Salt and freshly ground black pepper
100-125 g mozzarella cheese, finely sliced
30 ml (2 tablespoons) grated Parmesan cheese
15 ml (1 tablespoon) dry white breadcrumbs

Wash the broccoli head and break it into even-sized spears.

Put the spears in a steamer (or else a colander), and place the steamer in a pan above boiling water. Cover the pan with a tightly fitting lid and steam for about 20 minutes until the broccoli is just tender but still crunchy.

Heat the oil in a heavy frying pan, add the onion and garlic, and fry gently for 5 minutes until soft. Add the tomatoes and basil and cook, stirring, until the mixture forms a thick sauce, moistening with a little water if necessary. Season with salt and freshly ground black pepper.

Arrange the steamed broccoli in an ovenproof dish and pour the tomato sauce over it. Arrange slices of mozzarella cheese on top. Sprinkle the dish with the grated Parmesan cheese, and then top with a sprinkling of breadcrumbs.

Bake the mixture, uncovered, in the pre-heated oven for about 20 minutes until browned and bubbling. Serve hot in the same dish.

SERVING SUGGESTIONS The dish makes a good first course to be followed by pasta.

It can also be served as an accompaniment to grilled fish, meat or chicken.

VARIATION Instead of broccoli use brinjals, cut up into slices.

GROWING AND USING SPROUTS

There is a simple technique for turning a dormant seed into a living plant packed with life-giving nutrients (especially rich in vitamin C).

Don't rush out to buy expensive equipment – you have all that you need ready to hand. Flat-dwellers can become farmers in miniature by growing their own sprouts in an empty mayonnaise bottle placed in the grocery cupboard. In terms of cost, this is the best vitamin bargain of the century.

Bean sprouts were traditionally used in Chinese dishes and more recently they have been used in salads. But why not let all the pulses which you would normally use in soups, stews and curries (such as dried peas, beans and lentils) germinate before you use them? (See Seeds for sprouting*.)

Not only will they cook more quickly, but you will find that the taste will be better and fresher, and the gain in nutritional value will be immense.

Prepare the sprouts by filling a large glass jar one-quarter full with dried peas, beans or lentils.

Cover the mouth of the jar with a clean piece of thin cloth, and fix the fabric in place with a rubber band.

Hold the jar under a tap and cover the seeds with cold water, then drain the water off immediately by turning the jar upside down.

Store the jar, with the damp seeds, on a shelf in a dark cupboard. Rinse the seeds once or twice a day.

Use them in stews, soups and curries when they first start to germinate after about 1½-2 days, or keep them for salads and Chinese dishes when more mature (after 4-5 days).

Broccoli with Almonds

A PARTICULARLY APPETISING WAY to serve broccoli is with almonds. This dish goes well with grilled fish or even on its own as a first course.

PREPARATION TIME: 5 MINUTES
COOKING TIME: 10 MINUTES

INGREDIENTS FOR SIX
500 g broccoli spears
Salt
50 g butter
50 g flaked almonds
Juice of ½ lemon

Trim the stalks of the broccoli spears and remove the leaves. Wash the spears in cold water.

Put the broccoli in a pan with a tightly fitting lid and add a small amount of boiling, lightly salted water. Bring the water back to the boil and simmer with the lid on for about 7 minutes, or until the broccoli is just tender. With overcooking, the florets easily disintegrate.

Meanwhile, melt the butter in a pan, add the flaked almonds, sprinkle them with salt and fry them over low heat until they are golden-brown. Keep stirring the almonds, as they tend to burn easily. Stir in the lemon juice.

Drain the broccoli thoroughly through a colander, arrange in a serving dish and pour over the browned butter and almonds.

SERVING SUGGESTION This makes an ideal vegetable dish with delicate meats such as veal.

VARIATION Cover the broccoli spears with a Hollandaise sauce*, and serve as a vegetable dish.

Stuffed Butternuts

BUTTERNUTS CAN BE COOKED in many different ways. You could peel and cube them, then cook by stewing or steaming, or slice and bake them. They are often teamed with spices such as ginger and cinnamon, and their nutty flavour also combines well with a touch of sweetness in the form of brown sugar or honey. In the following recipe, they are boiled until tender and stuffed with a crunchy rice mixture before being baked.

STUFFED BUTTERNUTS *have a crunchy rice and vegetable filling.*

PREPARATION TIME: 55 MINUTES
COOKING TIME: 25 MINUTES
PRE-HEAT OVEN TO 160°C

INGREDIENTS FOR FOUR TO SIX
2-3 butternuts (1,2 kg)
Salt
30 ml (2 tablespoons) sunflower oil
30 g butter
1 medium-sized onion, peeled and coarsely grated*
1 carrot, coarsely grated
1 stick celery, thinly sliced
*200 ml cooked brown rice**
50 g mixed nuts, chopped
15 ml (1 tablespoon) soy sauce
10 ml (2 teaspoons) honey

For the topping:
Butter
Cinnamon

Wash and halve the butternuts lengthways. Scoop out the seeds and boil the butternuts (cut side down) in salted water for about 30 minutes, or until tender. Take care that they do not break. If the butternuts are large, you will have to use two saucepans.

While they are boiling, prepare the stuffing. Heat the oil and butter in a frying pan, add the onion, carrot, celery, rice and nuts, and toss over a medium heat until tender-crisp. Spoon the rice mixture into a bowl.

Carefully remove the flesh from the cooked butternuts, leaving a firm shell. Mix the pulp thoroughly with the rice mixture, season with the soy sauce and add the honey.

Place the shells in a buttered oven-proof dish and fill with the stuffing. Dot with butter and sprinkle with cinnamon, then bake them in the oven for 25 minutes.

VARIATION Top the butternuts with buttered crumbs and paprika, and serve as part of a vegetarian meal (omit the cinnamon).

Creamed Cabbage

OVER THE YEARS, cabbage has become an everyday vegetable, often overcooked and served with insufficient seasoning. This recipe transforms it in flavour and appearance, making it an ideal accompaniment to grilled meat.

PREPARATION TIME: 10 MINUTES
COOKING TIME: 15 MINUTES

INGREDIENTS FOR FOUR
50 g butter
450 g cabbage, coarsely chopped
1 clove garlic, finely chopped (optional)
Salt and freshly ground black pepper
1 ml (¼ teaspoon) freshly grated nutmeg
80 ml (⅓ cup) thick cream

Melt the butter in a heavy frying pan. Add the cabbage and the garlic (if used). Fry gently, stirring frequently, for about 10 minutes, until the cabbage has softened a little but is still crunchy. Season with salt, pepper and nutmeg, and stir in the cream. Cook for 3-5 minutes, stirring. Remove from the heat and serve at once.

Bubble and Squeak

WHAT MOST PEOPLE think of as bubble and squeak derives from a 19th century dish of warmed left-overs. The title is a poetic interpretation of the noise the potato, cabbage and onion make while frying.

This recipe is an older and grander version that incorporates pieces of cold roast beef; these may be laid on top, or layered between slabs of the vegetables.

PREPARATION TIME: 10 MINUTES
COOKING TIME: 20 MINUTES

INGREDIENTS FOR FOUR
350 g cold roast beef
75 g beef dripping or butter*
*2 medium-sized onions, peeled and chopped**
Salt and freshly ground black pepper
*6 medium-sized potatoes, cooked and mashed**
175 g cooked green cabbage, well drained and chopped

Cut the roast beef into slices about 5 cm by 2,5 cm. Heat 25 g of the dripping or butter in a large, heavy-based frying pan and fry the onions in it over a gentle heat until they are a light golden-brown. Remove these from the pan and keep them hot.

In the same fat, fry the pieces of beef for 4-5 minutes, stirring or turning them over so that they brown on all sides. Sprinkle with salt and pepper, remove from the pan, cover and keep hot.

Melt half the remaining dripping or butter in the pan and put in the mashed potatoes. Mix in the cabbage, season the mixture with salt and pepper, and spread it out over the base of the pan to make a cake about 2,5 cm thick.

Cook this for 4 minutes, or until it is golden-brown underneath, shaking the pan to prevent the mixture from sticking. Put a large plate over the pan and turn the pan upside-down, so that the bubble and squeak is on the plate.

Heat the remaining dripping or butter in the frying pan and slide the cake back into the pan so that the underside will brown. Cook the cake for another 4 minutes. Turn it on to a plate as before, and slide it on to a warmed serving dish. Arrange the onions and beef on half of the cake and fold the other half over it. Serve very hot with a good brown sauce* or gravy*.

VARIATION Leave out the roast beef for a hearty vegetarian dish.

COLESLAW

WIDELY POPULAR as a salad, coleslaw combines the crisp freshness of cabbage with a variety of other appetising seasoning flavours.

PREPARATION TIME: 15 MINUTES

INGREDIENTS FOR SIX TO EIGHT
1 small cabbage
1 medium-sized green pepper, seeded and chopped
1 large carrot, coarsely grated
1 medium-sized onion, peeled and chopped*
200 ml mayonnaise*
60 ml (¼ cup) sour cream (smetena)
Salt and pepper

Shred the cabbage and crisp it in a bowl of iced water. Drain it well and then mix with all the remaining ingredients, seasoning to taste with salt and pepper.

SERVING SUGGESTIONS Present the coleslaw in a salad bowl, or arrange it on a bed of soft, young butter lettuce leaves on individual side plates.

Decorate with pecan nuts and alfalfa, sunflower, mung bean or other sprouts*.

VARIATION Add a grated green apple and finely sliced celery to the ingredients.

GLAZED CARROTS

THE SWEET TASTE of the carrot caused it to be referred to in early Celtic literature as 'honey underground'. Throughout the centuries, when sugar has been scarce or expensive, carrots have helped to replace it in puddings, pies and preserves.

In this simple recipe, however, sugar is added. It is used to give the carrots an appetising glaze.

PREPARATION TIME: 10 MINUTES
COOKING TIME: 20-30 MINUTES

INGREDIENTS FOR FOUR TO SIX
10 medium-sized carrots, peeled and sliced into 2,5 cm rounds
450 ml chicken* or vegetable stock*
30 ml (2 tablespoons) brown sugar
75 g butter, cut into small pieces
Freshly ground black pepper
Salt
30 ml (2 tablespoons) chopped parsley

Put the carrots in a saucepan with the stock, sugar and butter. Season the mixture with pepper. Cover the pan, bring it to the boil, and simmer for about 20 minutes until the carrots are tender and the liquid has reduced to a glaze.

If the liquid does not seem to be reducing fast enough, uncover it towards the end of the cooking time and increase the heat under the pan.

Place the glazed carrots on a warmed serving dish. Add salt to taste and sprinkle the top with parsley.

SERVING SUGGESTION Serve with roast beef, lamb, chicken, pork or game.

CARROT SALAD

ALTHOUGH CARROTS are known for their high vitamin A content, few people realise that they also contain other important vitamins. They are a boon to slimmers and popular among cooks because they can be prepared in a variety of ways to make delicious dishes.

PREPARATION TIME: 45 MINUTES

INGREDIENTS FOR FOUR TO SIX
5 medium-sized carrots, grated
1 medium-sized green pepper, seeded and finely chopped
1 stick celery, finely sliced
45 ml (3 tablespoons) finely chopped parsley
125 ml (½ cup) seedless raisins
Juice of 1 large orange
Juice of 1 lemon
30 ml (2 tablespoons) sunflower oil

Mix the carrots, green pepper, celery, parsley and raisins together and dress with the orange and lemon juices. Sprinkle the oil over the mixture and serve.

SERVING SUGGESTION Serve the carrot salad on a bed of lettuce with either cottage cheese or Ricotta cheese.

VARIATIONS Omit the celery and peppers and add 190 ml (¾ cup) sunflower seeds.

Alternatively, add 190 ml (¾ cup) chopped pineapple, grapefruit or green melon, and dress with natural yoghurt*. Sprinkle the salad with chopped parsley or with alfalfa sprouts.

CARROT SALAD *The colourful mixture is packed with vitamins.*

Spiced Cauliflower

Cauliflower is a popular vegetable with a delicate flavour that can, however, all too easily be lost in the cooking. For a change, try this spicy version to complement grilled fish, chicken or lamb chops.

Preparation Time: 15 minutes
Cooking Time: 25 minutes

Ingredients for Six
1 large cauliflower
60-90 ml (4-6 tablespoons) sunflower oil
2 medium-sized onions, peeled and finely chopped*
2 ml (½ teaspoon) mustard seeds
5 ml (1 teaspoon) ground ginger
5 ml (1 teaspoon) salt
7 ml (1½ teaspoons) turmeric
2 large tomatoes, skinned* and finely chopped
2 ml (½ teaspoon) cumin (optional)
30 ml (2 tablespoons) finely chopped parsley
5 ml (1 teaspoon) sugar

Trim the leaves and stalk from the cauliflower, divide into florets and wash thoroughly in water.

Heat the sunflower oil in a heavy-based pan, and cook the onions for a few minutes on medium heat until they are soft and transparent. Add the mustard seeds, ground ginger, salt and turmeric. Cook this mixture, stirring all the time to blend, for about 5 minutes.

Add the cauliflower florets to the pan, turning them until they are thoroughly coated with the spice mixture.

Stir the finely chopped tomatoes into the cauliflower mixture with the cumin, if used, and the chopped parsley. Add sugar to taste.

Cover the pan with a lid and continue cooking over a gentle heat for 10-15 minutes. Stir the mixture occasionally to prevent it from burning. Do not overcook or allow the mixture to become a mush.

Cauliflower Cheese

This delicious dish is much loved by South Africans. It consists essentially of florets of blanched cauliflower baked in a creamy cheese sauce, and it can be served either as a main course or as an accompaniment.

Preparation Time: 35 minutes
Cooking Time: 30 minutes
Pre-heat Oven to 200°C

Ingredients for Four to Six
1 medium-sized cauliflower
Salt
1 bay leaf
60 g butter
60 ml (¼ cup) flour
500 ml (2 cups) milk
Freshly ground black pepper
Freshly grated nutmeg
5 ml (1 teaspoon) prepared mustard
250 g mature Cheddar cheese, grated
50 g fresh breadcrumbs
15 ml (1 tablespoon) melted butter

Trim the leaves and stalk from the cauliflower, and break it into large, even-sized florets (or leave whole if preferred). Cook in salted boiling water with the bay leaf for 5-7 minutes, or until just tender. Drain thoroughly and place in a shallow oven-proof dish.

To make the sauce, melt the first measure of butter and stir in the flour. Cook for 1 minute without browning. Slowly stir in the milk and bring to the boil, stirring continually, to make a smooth sauce. Reduce the heat and simmer (stirring) for 2 minutes. Season to taste with salt, pepper and nutmeg. Add the mustard and half the grated cheese.

Pour the sauce over the cauliflower. Sprinkle with the remaining cheese mixed with the breadcrumbs and melted butter. Bake for 30 minutes, or grill until golden-brown.

Variations Add chopped, hard-boiled eggs*, diced ham or sautéed mushrooms to the sauce before spooning it over the cauliflower.

Alternatively top with grilled bacon rashers just before serving.

Cauliflower Cheese *This family favourite has a tangy cheese sauce seasoned with nutmeg and mustard.*

CHICORY AND ORANGE SALAD

AN UNUSUAL COMBINATION of ingredients helps to make this a memorable salad. The chicory leaves have a slightly bitter, though pleasant, flavour.

PREPARATION TIME: 30 MINUTES

INGREDIENTS FOR SIX
6 heads of chicory
3 medium-sized oranges, peeled and segmented (remove all the pith and membrane)
3 medium-sized carrots, scraped and shredded into fine julienne* strips
125 ml (½ cup) vinaigrette* flavoured with 3 ml (¾ teaspoon) grated orange rind and 3 ml (¾ teaspoon) basil

Trim the root end of each head of chicory, discard the outside leaves and remove the conical core formed by the inside leaves at the base. Wash well and wipe dry.

Slice into thick (about 2 cm) diagonal pieces and divide the pieces into rings. Mix with the prepared orange segments and shredded carrot and moisten with the flavoured vinaigrette.

SERVING SUGGESTION Serve with cold roast lamb or chicken.

VARIATION Substitute cooked and chilled cubes of beetroot for the carrot, and add thinly sliced circles of sweet onion.

CUCUMBER AND RADISH SALAD

THE PEPPERY, SOMEWHAT SHARP taste of the radishes in this simple and delicious salad is offset by the cool, relatively bland cucumber. Serve the salad as soon as possible after chilling.

PREPARATION TIME: 20 MINUTES
CHILLING TIME: 30 MINUTES

INGREDIENTS FOR SIX
1 small English cucumber, wiped and thinly sliced
1 bunch (about 125 g) radishes, well washed, trimmed and thinly sliced
60 ml (¼ cup) cream
60 ml (¼ cup) natural yoghurt*
30 ml (2 tablespoons) lemon juice
5 ml (1 teaspoon) sugar
Salt and freshly ground pepper
3 spring onions, washed, trimmed and thinly sliced (including half the green parts)

Combine the cucumber and radish slices in a salad bowl. Mix together the cream, yoghurt, lemon juice and sugar, and season. Pour over the salad and mix well. Sprinkle with sliced spring onions, cover and chill.

SERVING SUGGESTION Serve with grilled or baked fish.

FENNEL, TOMATO AND MUSHROOM SALAD

FENNEL SALAD is often served at the end of a meal in Italy. The distinctive taste of fennel, reminiscent of liquorice, complements the less powerful flavours of tomatoes and mushrooms. Fennel is a nutritious vegetable, too: the Romans even believed that it prolonged life.

PREPARATION TIME: 30 MINUTES
CHILLING TIME: 30 MINUTES

INGREDIENTS FOR SIX
2 medium to large heads of fennel
3 large, ripe and firm tomatoes, skinned*
100 g button mushrooms, trimmed and wiped
125 ml (½ cup) vinaigrette*, flavoured with a pinch of basil

Trim the base of the fennel and remove the stalks and leaves. Peel the outer layer from the stalks and bulbs, and slice thinly, then place in iced water for 30 minutes to crisp.

Next, slice the tomatoes and mushrooms. Arrange slices of fennel (drained and dried), tomato and mushroom on a platter and pour over the vinaigrette.

SERVING SUGGESTION This salad goes well with chicken or fish dishes.

VARIATIONS Substitute thin slices of peeled orange for the tomato, and add pitted olives to the salad.

Watercress is another suitable addition.

STUFFED GEM SQUASH

THE DELICATE FLAVOUR of gem squash is effectively complemented by adding a few readily available ingredients. In this recipe, cooked squash are halved and filled with a cheese soufflé mixture, then baked until puffy.

PREPARATION TIME: 1 HOUR
COOKING TIME: 25 MINUTES
PRE-HEAT OVEN TO 200°C

INGREDIENTS FOR FOUR TO SIX
4 large gem squash
Salt

For the filling:
30 g butter
30 ml (2 tablespoons) flour
200 ml milk
100 g mature Cheddar cheese, grated
Salt and freshly ground pepper
3 egg yolks
4 egg whites

With the tip of a sharp knife, score a line around the middle of each squash. Cook the squash in salted boiling water for 15-20 minutes, or until the flesh is tender. Drain, cool, halve the squash and remove the seeds.

Slice a thin segment from the base of each shell so that they stand straight. Scoop out most of the flesh into a bowl.

To make the filling, melt the butter, stir in the flour and cook for 1-2 minutes without browning. Add the milk and bring to the boil, stirring continually, to make a smooth sauce. Simmer for 2 minutes, then beat in the mashed or puréed flesh of the squash, together with the cheese and seasoning.

Remove from the heat and beat in the egg yolks one by one. Whisk the egg whites until stiff, fold into the mixture, and spoon into the hollowed squash shells. Place the squash on a baking sheet and cook for 20-25 minutes.

VARIATIONS Cook, halve and fill the squash with a mixture of the squash flesh and a savoury beef mince, or with a mixture of the squash, rice, minced lamb and parsley.

For a different effect, sprinkle with grated cheese and bake at 180°C for 30 minutes (or until the tops are golden).

BRAISED JERUSALEM ARTICHOKES

THE NAME 'JERUSALEM' has aroused much discussion, but it is generally accepted that it derives from the Italian word *girasole* – a species of sunflower of the same family as this type of artichoke. The globe artichoke, whose flavour it is said to resemble, is an entirely different vegetable.

Jerusalem artichokes can be cooked like potatoes: mashed, sautéed in butter, sliced and baked *au gratin* or stewed whole in stock. They can be served in a rich white sauce* or braised as below, their flavour sharpened with garlic and capers.

PREPARATION TIME: 15-20 MINUTES
COOKING TIME: 45 MINUTES

INGREDIENTS FOR FOUR
25 g butter
15 ml (1 tablespoon) oil, preferably olive oil
1 medium-sized onion, peeled and sliced*
1 clove garlic, crushed (optional)
15 ml (1 tablespoon) flour
250 ml (1 cup) dry cider or white wine
700 g Jerusalem artichokes, peeled
Salt and freshly ground black pepper
15 ml (1 tablespoon) capers (optional)
15 ml (1 tablespoon) chopped parsley

Heat the butter and oil in a heavy-based saucepan. Add the sliced onion and the crushed garlic (if used) and fry gently for 5 minutes until soft.

Stir in the flour and cook over a low heat for a few minutes, stirring to prevent it from burning. Add the cider or wine and bring to the boil. Put in the peeled artichokes and pour in enough water to just cover the vegetables. Season them with the salt and pepper.

Cover the pan and simmer the mixture gently for about 45 minutes until it is cooked, adding more water if necessary. Cooking time will vary according to the size of the artichokes.

Sprinkle the dish with capers (if used) and parsley, and serve.

SERVING SUGGESTION Serve with chicken, ham or game.

LEEKS VINAIGRETTE

TOO OFTEN RELEGATED to soups and stews, leeks, when fresh and young, make an unusual and economical starter with a delicate flavour. It is sometimes referred to as 'the poor man's asparagus'.

PREPARATION TIME: 30 MINUTES
COOKING TIME: 20 MINUTES
CHILLING TIME: 4 HOURS

INGREDIENTS FOR FOUR
500 ml (2 cups) water
2 ml (½ teaspoon) salt
1 bay leaf
3 sprigs fresh rosemary
16 leeks, washed and trimmed
Sliced black olives

For the dressing:
60 ml (¼ cup) sunflower or olive oil
30 ml (2 tablespoons) tarragon vinegar
½ clove garlic, crushed
1 ml (¼ teaspoon) salt
1 ml (¼ teaspoon) dry mustard
5 ml (1 teaspoon) sugar
5 ml (1 teaspoon) capers, chopped

For the garnish:
Chopped, hard-boiled egg* and/or chopped parsley

Mix the ingredients for the dressing and set it aside for the flavours to blend.

In a wide-based saucepan bring the water, salt, bay leaf and rosemary to the boil and simmer for 10 minutes. Add the leeks, laying them flat, then cover them and cook gently until they are tender (about 10 minutes). Drain the leeks, refresh them quickly under cold water, pat them dry on paper towels, and arrange them on a dish in a single layer.

Pour over as much of the dressing as is necessary to moisten the leeks thoroughly. Add the olives, then cover the dish and chill it. Garnish before serving.

SERVING SUGGESTIONS Serve on individual plates as a first course with fingers of buttered brown bread*, or as part of a cold buffet.

VARIATION Leeks are also delicious poached in stock until tender, left to cool in the poaching liquid, then drained and served with mayonnaise*.

VEGETABLES AND SALADS

CAESAR SALAD *is a delectable combination of crisp lettuce, anchovies, egg and croûtons.*

CAESAR SALAD

THIS IS AN UNUSUAL combination of crisp lettuce leaves mixed with anchovies and croûtons, and dressed with an oil and egg mixture. The recipe originated in California.

PREPARATION TIME: 20 MINUTES

INGREDIENTS FOR SIX TO EIGHT
Salt
1 clove garlic, peeled
5 ml (1 teaspoon) dry mustard
15 ml (1 tablespoon) lemon juice
5 ml (1 teaspoon) Worcestershire sauce
45 ml (3 tablespoons) fine olive oil
2 medium-sized lettuces, washed and dried
15 ml (1 tablespoon) finely grated Parmesan cheese
Coarsely ground black pepper
½ tin anchovies, drained and finely chopped
1 egg, coddled* for 1 minute
125 ml (½ cup) croûtons* (made with white bread)

Use a wooden salad bowl for the best results. Sprinkle the bowl with a little salt, then rub well with the garlic.

Add the dry mustard, lemon juice and Worcestershire sauce and stir the mixture with a wooden spoon until the salt has dissolved completely.

Gradually stir in the olive oil until all the ingredients are well blended. Tear the lettuce leaves into bite-sized pieces and add them to the salad bowl. Scatter with the grated Parmesan cheese and the black pepper, then add the anchovies, coddled egg and croûtons.

Gently toss so as to coat all the lettuce pieces with the dressing. Serve the salad immediately.

SERVING SUGGESTION Serve on its own as a crunchy starter.

VARIATION If you want a less salty dish, soak the anchovies in milk overnight.

STUFFED MARROW

THE CREAMY TEXTURE and delicate flavour of young marrow make it a good vegetable to cook on its own and serve with a white sauce*. When it is older it can be baked with this tasty meat, tomato and herb stuffing.

PREPARATION TIME: 25 MINUTES
COOKING TIME: 1 HOUR
PRE-HEAT OVEN TO 180°C

INGREDIENTS FOR FOUR
1 medium-sized marrow
50 g butter
1 medium-sized onion, peeled and finely chopped*
1 clove garlic, chopped
250 g minced beef
4 medium-sized tomatoes, skinned*, chopped and seeded
30 ml (2 tablespoons) fresh breadcrumbs
15 ml (1 tablespoon) chopped fresh basil or 7 ml (1½ teaspoons) dried basil
30 ml (2 tablespoons) chopped parsley
1 egg, beaten
Salt and freshly ground black pepper

Cut off the end of the marrow and scoop out the seeds with a spoon.

Melt half the butter in a frying pan, add the chopped onion and garlic, and fry gently for 5 minutes until it is soft. Add the minced beef and brown the meat for a few minutes, stirring occasionally to prevent it burning.

Put the onion, garlic and meat in a mixing bowl. Add the chopped tomato flesh, breadcrumbs, basil, parsley and egg. Season with salt and pepper and mix all the ingredients well together.

Stuff the marrow with this mixture and replace the end. Place the marrow in a greased, oven-proof dish and dot it with pieces of the remaining butter. Arrange a layer of aluminium foil loosely over the top, and bake the dish in the oven for 1 hour or until it is tender.

SERVING SUGGESTIONS Marrow stuffed with minced beef and herbs can be served with rice or potatoes as a main course.

For a delicious summertime supper, add a crisp, green salad* as well.

GLAZED MARROW

IN THIS SIMPLE but appealing recipe, cubes of marrow are tossed in butter and cooked for a short time until just tender. Remember that overcooking will ruin the texture of the marrow.

PREPARATION TIME: 15 MINUTES
COOKING TIME: 10 MINUTES

INGREDIENTS FOR FOUR TO SIX
1 medium-sized marrow
75 g butter
Salt and freshly ground black pepper

For the garnish:
30 ml (2 tablespoons) freshly chopped parsley, basil or tarragon

Peel the marrow, cut it in half lengthways and scoop out the seeds. Cut it into 3 cm cubes.

Melt the butter in a heavy-based saucepan, add the marrow and season with salt and pepper. Stir-fry over a gentle heat for 1 minute, cover, and continue to cook gently for 5-7 minutes (until the marrow is just tender). Sprinkle with herbs and serve immediately.

SERVING SUGGESTION Glazed marrow is best with roast or grilled meats.

SWEET CORN FRITTERS

THIS IS A CLASSIC accompaniment to fried chicken – crisp, golden fritters popping with whole-kernel sweet corn.

PREPARATION TIME: 10 MINUTES
COOKING TIME: 20 MINUTES

INGREDIENTS FOR SIX
2 extra-large eggs, separated
Salt and freshly ground black pepper
A pinch of sugar
1 tin (410 g) whole-kernel sweet corn (not creamed)
5 ml (1 teaspoon) baking powder
50-60 g fresh breadcrumbs
Sunflower oil for frying

Beat the egg yolks with salt and pepper, then add the sugar and the sweet corn drained of all its liquid. Whisk the egg whites until stiff and fold into the yolk mixture, together with the baking powder and crumbs.

Pour oil into a frying pan (to a depth of about 5 mm) and drop tablespoons of the mixture into the pan. Fry until golden-brown, then turn and fry the other side. Drain well and serve hot.

SERVING SUGGESTIONS Serve as a quick lunch, snack or 'brunch' dish, with fresh tomato and onion sauce* or mushroom sauce*, or with grilled bacon, sausages or cooked sliced ham.

VARIATIONS To make the fritters more substantial, add finely chopped onion*, diced ham or sliced cooked sausage to the basic mixture.

The fritters can also be made with flour, but this version is lighter and tastier.

CREAMED MUSHROOMS

OF THE NUMEROUS SPECIES of edible fungi that grow in South Africa, only two types are commonly available in the shops – small button mushrooms and the large flat ones that have a rather more distinctive flavour.

Cook them soon after buying or picking, as mushrooms become limp quickly and lose their flavour. Do not overcook them or the texture and taste will be spoiled.

This delicious recipe takes little time and is a versatile way of using either button mushrooms or the large, flat kind.

PREPARATION TIME: 10 MINUTES
COOKING TIME: 10-15 MINUTES

INGREDIENTS FOR FOUR
15 ml (1 tablespoon) olive oil
50 g butter
450 g mushrooms, cleaned and sliced
30 ml (2 tablespoons) peeled and finely chopped shallots or spring onions
150 ml thick cream
Salt and freshly ground black pepper
30-45 ml (2-3 tablespoons) Marsala or port (optional)
30 ml (2 tablespoons) softened butter
1 ml (¼ teaspoon) freshly grated nutmeg

Heat the oil and butter in a heavy frying pan. Add the mushrooms and shallots or spring onions. Cook over a moderate heat for about 3 minutes, stirring so that the vegetables do not stick to the pan.

Stir in the cream, and season with salt and pepper. Cook the mixture for a further 5 minutes, stirring it, until the sauce is reduced and thickened. Add the Marsala or port, if liked, bring the mixture to the boil, and cook for 1 minute.

Remove from the heat and stir in the softened butter. Add the nutmeg, check the seasoning and serve.

SERVING SUGGESTIONS These creamed mushrooms can come to the table as a savoury on toast, or with croûtons* of fried bread; as a filling for omelettes*, or under poached eggs* on toast.

They also go well with chicken, veal and sweetbreads.

A SIMPLE GREEN SALAD

Lettuce leaves tossed in a good dressing, fragrant with fresh herbs, make an excellent, simple salad. Chopped fresh parsley, chives, thyme, mint, chervil and dill are all good. To make the salad more interesting, use a mixture of lettuce leaves, the more usual crisp lettuce leaves mixed with soft butter lettuce and cos when in season.

For more texture, make use of any greenstuffs in season. Try leaves of chicory, the curly endive leaves, very young spinach leaves and watercress. Fresh sprouts* are nice to add too.

For a more substantial salad, add spring onions, chunks of table celery, thin slices of cucumber, avocado and green pepper.

Salad dressing Mix the following ingredients: 190 ml (¾ cup) sunflower oil; 60-80 ml (¼-⅓ cup) lemon juice. Use olive oil (or half olive and half sunflower oil) for a robust Mediterranean type dressing, with a crushed, fat clove of garlic and 5 ml (1 teaspoon) dried origanum.

Add 5 ml (1 teaspoon) mustard: the hot powder or a more gentle seed mustard. If the dressing seems too sharp, soften it with honey, or a pinch of sugar. Add 60 ml (¼ cup) natural yoghurt* for variety. Season with salt and freshly ground black pepper. Pour the dressing over just before serving. Do not drown the salad, add only enough dressing to ensure that the greens glisten.

Herbs for All Seasons

The judicious use of fresh and dried herbs is one of the most important of all the skills required in cooking. Culinary herbs consist of the leaves, stems, bulbs, flowers or seeds of a number of small aromatic plants. Some herbs are best used on their own, while others are preferable in combinations.

Drying

Herbs must be processed as soon as possible after picking. If necessary, wash them and then wipe them with a towel. Preferably dry the herbs as branches; if only the leaves are to be used, these can be stripped off after drying.

One of the easiest ways to dry herbs is to spread the leaves on a mesh rack in a very cool oven: heat the oven to the lowest temperature, then switch it off and wait for the temperature to drop to 40-50°C before inserting the herbs. Leave them in the oven overnight.

If the weather is warm, herbs can be left out to dry naturally. In an area where the room temperature reaches around 23°C herbs will dry within a day or two.

When substituting dried herbs for fresh ones in a recipe, take about half of the amount specified, since the flavour is more concentrated.

Freezing

Herbs that freeze especially well are marjoram, origanum, thyme, rosemary, savory, salad burnet, dill, lemon balm, mint and the delicate-tasting herbs that do not dry well – namely borage, tarragon, parsley and basil.

Herbs to be frozen should be gathered when the leaves and sprigs are young and small. However, be sure not to over-pick young plants. Before freezing, the herbs should be washed and patted dry with towels.

Herbs are best frozen in aluminium foil or plastic bags in which quantities of 15-20 g can easily be stored. Strip the leaves from the twigs or branches, or freeze whole sprigs. If the leaves are large, they may be washed and chopped as desired. Herbs frozen this way should be used within six weeks. If longer storage is required, blanch* for 45 seconds.

Sprigs of frozen herbs may be used whole or crumbled, without thawing, in dishes that require cooking. Frozen herbs added to fresh salads require pre-thawing – the thawing time will depend on the thickness of the frozen package and the room temperature.

Year Round

Bay leaves Use the leaves fresh or dried. They may be used alone or in a bouquet garni*. Add them to soups, chowders, fish, pickles, lamb, beef, mutton or game roasts, stews, bobotie and poultry stuffing, or use in custard instead of cinnamon.

Borage Use the leaves and flowers – fresh, dried or frozen. The foliage has the aroma and flavour of cucumber.

Chop the leaves into soups in place of parsley. Cook young leaves with green peas or beans. Use borage freshly cut up in a mixed green salad*, with or without other fresh herbs. Garnish fresh salad or fruit drinks with the blue flowers.

Fennel Wild fennel – use fresh stems and leaves, and dried seeds. Garden fennel – use seeds, stems and bulbous base.

The leaves can be used in salad or as a garnish. The stems can be used as a bed on which to grill fish, and the seeds used as a spice for fish, egg, meat or vegetable dishes. Use fennel bulbs as a vegetable – freshly cut up in salad, or boiled and served with a white* or cheese sauce*.

Marjoram Use the leaves – fresh, dried or frozen.

Add chopped marjoram to fresh avocados or mushrooms. Use for flavouring soups and pâtés. It is best used with beef, pork, veal or mutton pot-roast – place a few branches in the roasting pot. Chop the leaves for use in stews, egg dishes, poultry stuffings or with fish.

Origanum Use leaves – fresh, dried or frozen. Try a crushed leaf in a tomato cocktail*. It is a pungent herb, so take care when using it. Origanum is recommended with fish, stews or meat and is also good with Italian food or in stuffings. Use in a bouquet garni*.

Parsley Use leaves – fresh, dried or frozen. It is widely used as a garnish or salad base and is especially good in cheese sauces*, scrambled eggs*, omelettes*, stuffings, cheese muffins or herb breads*. Parsley makes a pleasant seasoning and garnish for most dishes.

Rosemary Use leaves – fresh, dried or frozen, also sprigs and fresh tops.

Use sprigs in casseroles or when roasting beef, mutton or game. Chop fresh leaves into salads. Bake with fish or sauté with fresh mushrooms or perlemoen.

Sage Use leaves – fresh or dried.

Add to a bouquet garni* or to cheese or savoury dips. Use it in pork sausage* or mutton stew. Sage adds to the flavour of poultry and is especially good with stuffings for goose or fish.

Salad burnet Use leaves – fresh or frozen.

Add the fresh chopped leaves to asparagus*, celery or mushroom soup. Its delicate cucumber aroma also goes well with poultry stuffing or salad dressing. Toss whole leaves into beets, cabbage, carrots, celery or a mixed salad.

Tarragon Use leaves and sprigs – fresh, dried or frozen.

It is best known in tarragon vinegar and is also added to salads, salad dressing and fish or poultry mousses. It has a delicate taste and is a good addition to chicken livers, consommés or chicken or turkey dishes.

CHIVES • SUMMER SAVORY • PARSLEY • SWEET BASIL • RED BASIL • SAGE

Thyme Leaves and the leafy flowering tops of both wild and garden thyme can be used fresh, dried or frozen. Use in a bouquet garni*. Sprinkle into soups and stews, or use in game pies or meat loaves. Add to poultry, carrots or boiled potatoes.

Winter savory Use leaves – fresh, dried or frozen.

Add sprigs to sautéed chicken livers and mincemeat dishes, or use in herb breads*. Boil with legumes such as lentils, kidney beans or chick-peas, or when preparing artichokes*, beets or green beans.

WINTER/SPRING

Celery Use fresh leaves and stalks of table or soup celery; also use dried seeds and leaves.

Use fresh in salad or with canapés. Serve table celery stalks as a crudité with dips. Add chopped fresh soup celery to soups, meat loaves, fish croquettes*, scrambled eggs or poultry dishes, or stir into savoury biscuits or herb bread*. Use seeds as a spice for boiled cauliflower, cabbage or stewed tomatoes.

Chervil Use leaves – fresh or dried; also whole sprigs.

Use in cooking or as a garnish for fresh asparagus or chicken. Its mild, parsley-like flavour mixes well with all sauces served with fish or vegetables. Chervil also blends well with veal, pork, chicken or lamb casseroles. Serve with potato salad* and cooked brinjals or in fresh green salads*.

Dill Use fresh leaves and stems; also use dried or frozen leaves, and dried seeds.

Add a twig or chopped leaves to avocado cocktail or cold soup. Dill goes well with fish or poultry. Leaves and seeds are excellent combined with cheese or eggs. A few seeds will improve the taste of cauliflower, cabbage or beets. Use for pickles and in small quantities in fresh salads.

Rocket Use fresh leaves.

Add it to salads or boil with vegetables such as cabbage, spinach, carrots or turnips. Rocket makes a delightful garnish for canapés and vegetable crudités. Chop and mix with cottage cheese for dips or as a sandwich spread.

SUMMER/AUTUMN

Applemint Use fresh, dried or frozen leaves.

Chop and serve it fresh with apple or pawpaw, or in fruit salad, or use it to make mint sauce*. It is refreshing when crushed into fruit drinks. Use it liberally in salad dressing for green salads*.

Basil Use leaves and leaf stems – fresh, dried whole or ground, or frozen.

Use fresh in salad or as a garnish, or arrange it on the table if there is enough. Basil makes a pungent addition to egg dishes, fish or shellfish, and is traditionally used in pastas and other Italian dishes. It is especially good in ratatouille* and with dishes where tomato is the main ingredient.

Bergamot Use fresh or dried leaves.

Also known as orange mint, it is less pungent than the other mints. The delicate flavour blends well with fruit drinks, fruit cocktails or fresh fruit salad.

Chive The grass-like leaves can be used whole or chopped, fresh, dried or frozen.

Add chives to soup, stews or omelettes* just before serving. The delicate flavour is lost if it is cooked for too long. Chives enhance the flavour of a cold vichyssoise*, seafood cocktail or vinaigrette*.

Lemon balm Use fresh or frozen leaves and young shoots, or dried whole or powdered leaves.

Crush the leaves or use them whole in fruit drinks or as a garnish for fruit cocktails. Use freshly chopped leaves in fruit salad, sorbet or with lemon desserts. Replace the cinnamon stick used in making an egg custard with a twig of lemon balm. It is also a good addition to fresh green salads*.

Lemon thyme Use fresh leaves and young branches.

It is especially good in fresh green salad*, with French chicory, sorrel or dandelion greens. Milder than that of ordinary garden thyme, the citron flavour of lemon thyme blends well with stews or fish.

Lovage Use fresh, dried or frozen leaves, and the fresh young stems and leafstalks.

It is an excellent accompaniment to fish soup or consommé. Lovage has a celery-like taste and can therefore be used as a flavouring where celery is omitted. Chop leaves and add to stews or soups, or use fresh in a green salad*.

Peppermint Use fresh, dried or frozen leaves.

Since it has a pungent, aromatic and strong flavour, it is best to make an extract by pouring boiling water over the leaves. Use the infusion as a base for fruit drinks, as a tea, or for ice cream, gelatin desserts, sweet sauces or mint sauce*.

Summer savory Use fresh, dried or frozen leaves.

It can be used freshly chopped in lamb, veal, mutton or pork stew. Boil with sugar or kidney beans for a bean soup or stew. It makes an interesting combination if stewed with pears or quinces.

Watermint Use fresh, dried or frozen leaves.

The chopped leaves are mostly used for mint sauce*, in salad dressing, with fruit drinks or in fruit salad.

BOUQUET GARNI

Bouquet garni is a term much used in French cooking. It refers to a sachet or piece of cheesecloth or muslin into which fresh sprigs of herbs have been tied. In this way, the herbs can be cooked with the stock or stew and then be easily removed when the dish is ready. Fresh or dried herbs or a combination of these may be used in a bouquet garni. If no cheesecloth or muslin is available, the sprigs of fresh herbs can be tied with string round the stems and removed at the end of the cooking process.

The traditional bouquet garni consists of the three common aromatic herbs, namely parsley, thyme and bay leaves. These can be compiled in varying ratios, with the bay leaves generally in the smallest quantity as they are the most overpowering. Other herbs, such as celery, garlic, rosemary, marjoram and savory, may also be added, but there is no hard-and-fast rule. Other ingredients that may be added are shallots or dried orange peel or naartjie peel.

STUFFED MUSHROOMS

In ancient Egypt, only the Pharaohs were allowed to eat mushrooms, ordinary mortals being considered unworthy of this exotic food. In ancient Rome, too, they were reserved solely for the Caesar and the aristocracy.

Happily for the rest of us, commercial production today enables mushrooms to be enjoyed by all, and they are available in South Africa throughout the year.

PREPARATION TIME: 25 MINUTES
COOKING TIME: 20 MINUTES
PRE-HEAT OVEN TO 180°C

INGREDIENTS FOR SIX
8-12 large black mushrooms (about 450g)
30 ml (2 tablespoons) sunflower oil
30 g butter
1 small onion, peeled and finely chopped*
1 clove garlic, crushed
5 ml (1 teaspoon) fresh rosemary needles, finely chopped
60 ml (¼ cup) fine, dry, brown breadcrumbs
15 ml (1 tablespoon) soy sauce
A pinch of sugar
60 g mozzarella cheese, coarsely grated
Salt and freshly ground black pepper

For the topping:
Flaked almonds
Paprika

Wipe the mushrooms with a damp cloth, cut off the stems of the mushrooms and, using a grapefruit knife, carefully enlarge the hollows of the caps. Chop the stems and other mushroom parings finely.

Heat the oil and butter in a frying pan, add the onion, garlic, rosemary and mushroom parings, and sauté until soft. Bind with the crumbs.

Remove from the heat and season the mixture with the soy sauce. Add the pinch of sugar and the coarsely grated mozzarella, and mix well.

Arrange the mushroom caps in a liberally buttered oven-proof dish and sprinkle lightly with salt and black pepper. Divide the stuffing equally between the caps, mounding them slightly.

Top each mushroom with flaked almonds, allowing about 5 ml (1 teaspoon) per cap. Sprinkle with paprika and bake (uncovered) in the pre-heated oven for 20 minutes.

SERVING SUGGESTIONS Serve the mushrooms with buttered wholewheat bread*.

This dish can be prepared and assembled beforehand, then covered and refrigerated, but in this case you should allow it to return to room temperature before baking it in the oven.

VARIATION Vary the flavour with different herbs (such as origanum, parsley, chives or thyme) and different cheeses (a mild Cheddar or Gruyère).

MUSHROOM SALAD

Mushrooms are wonderfully low in kilojoules; about 80 per cent of their content is water, with 8 per cent carbohydrate and 1 per cent fat.

This mushroom salad has a tangy and appealing flavour. Since the mushrooms are eaten raw, choose unblemished specimens and ensure that they are very fresh.

PREPARATION TIME: 15 MINUTES

INGREDIENTS FOR SIX
350 g mushrooms
60 ml (¼ cup) lemon juice
1 small onion, peeled and finely chopped*
30 ml (2 tablespoons) finely chopped parsley
Salt and freshly ground black pepper

Wipe the mushrooms clean with a damp cloth or paper towel. Slice them thickly, stems included.

Toss the mushrooms, lemon juice, chopped onion and parsley together, then season to taste with the salt and pepper.

SERVING SUGGESTIONS Serve as part of a salad buffet, or with cold meats, fish or poultry.

Alternatively, serve on a bed of crisp green lettuce leaves as a starter, with crusty bread to soak up the juice.

VARIATION Add 10 ml (2 teaspoons) sunflower oil to the ingredients and some freshly chopped herbs.

BAKED ONIONS *are a tasty accompaniment to meat or fish.*

BAKED ONIONS

Although the health-giving properties of onions may have been exaggerated in the past, they are undoubtedly beneficial. Onions are the basic ingredient in many traditional recipes.

PREPARATION TIME: 5 MINUTES
COOKING TIME: 2-3 HOURS
PRE-HEAT OVEN TO 170°C

INGREDIENTS FOR FOUR
8 medium-sized onions
Salt and freshly ground black pepper
50 g butter
30 ml (2 tablespoons) chopped parsley for garnish

Wash the onions in their skins, removing as much grit as possible. Dry them well.

Line a baking tin with aluminium foil to prevent the onions from sticking to the tin. Put in the onions and place the tin in the pre-heated oven. Bake for 2-3 hours until the onions are tender when pierced with a skewer.

Sprinkle them with salt and pepper and put a knob of butter on each.

Garnish the onions with the chopped parsley, and serve.

SERVING SUGGESTIONS Serve baked onions with grills, roast beef, lamb or chicken, or as an accompaniment to fish.

VARIATION If you like, you can flavour the butter with cinnamon and cayenne pepper.

Onion Salad

This is an ideal salad to go with meat or fried fish. It has a creamy texture and a piquant flavour.

Preparation Time: 1 hour
Cooking Time: 25 minutes

Ingredients for Six
1 kg pickling onions
Salt

For the dressing:
7 ml (1½ teaspoons) dry mustard
10 ml (2 teaspoons) cornflour
5 ml (1 teaspoon) salt
75 g sugar
Pepper
3 eggs
125 ml (½ cup) vinegar
350 ml milk
250 ml (1 cup) cream

Leaving the skins on, wash the onions and cook them in salted water. When they are tender but not broken, drain them and leave them to cool. Remove the skins, then place the onions in a salad bowl.

To make the dressing, mix the mustard, cornflour, salt, sugar and pepper, then beat the eggs until they are light and creamy. Add the beaten eggs to the dry ingredients. Beat this mixture thoroughly to blend it. Add the vinegar slowly, beating the mixture constantly.

Beat the milk and cream together and combine them slowly with the vinegar mixture, beating all the time to prevent curdling.

Pour this dressing mixture into a saucepan. Boil, stirring constantly, until thick and creamy. If it is too thick, thin it with more cream or milk.

Leave the dressing to cool and then pour over the onions.

Serving Suggestion Serve on a bed of lettuce.

Variation Season the dressing with chopped parsley or, for a stronger flavour, a sprinkling of dried sage.

Onions à la Monégasque

This recipe for sweet-sour onions originates in Monaco. The onions are delicious either on their own as a starter, or when accompanying a main course of meat. They can be kept in the refrigerator for some time after preparation.

Preparation Time: 30 minutes
Cooking Time: 30 minutes
Chilling Time: 1 hour

Ingredients for Six
500 g pickling onions
Boiling water
30 ml (2 tablespoons) olive oil
30 ml (2 tablespoons) brown sugar
250 ml (1 cup) white wine
60 ml (¼ cup) white vinegar
30 ml (2 tablespoons) tomato paste
3 ml (¾ teaspoon) dried thyme
75 g currants
Salt and freshly ground black pepper
Finely chopped parsley for garnish

Put the onions in an oven-proof bowl and pour over enough boiling water to cover; leave to stand for 5 minutes. Drain in a colander and rinse with cold water, then peel and pat dry.

Heat the olive oil in a saucepan and sauté the onions until they are very lightly browned. Sprinkle with the brown sugar, and stir-fry until the sugar has melted and slightly caramelised.

Carefully add the white wine, vinegar, tomato paste, dried thyme and currants, and season lightly with the salt and freshly ground pepper.

Bring the mixture to the boil, then turn down the heat and simmer for 10-15 minutes, or until the sauce has thickened and the onions are tender but still crisp in the centre.

Spoon the onion mixture into a serving dish, cover with plastic wrap and chill for at least 1 hour before serving.

Just before serving, sprinkle over the finely chopped parsley.

Serving Suggestions Serve, chilled, as an hors d'oeuvre, or as an accompaniment to roasted, herbed lamb or ham.

Creamed Button Onions

These little onions have a light, delicate flavour: when they are brought to the table, bathed in their creamy sauce, it is not difficult to believe that the word 'onion' comes from the Latin *unio* – meaning 'a large pearl'. Creamed onions go well with a variety of meat dishes.

Preparation Time: 30 minutes
Cooking Time: 40 minutes

Ingredients for Six
1 kg pickling onions
150 ml chicken stock* or dry white wine
50 g butter, softened
30 ml (2 tablespoons) flour
450 ml milk
150 ml thick cream
1 bay leaf
Salt and freshly ground black pepper
1 ml (¼ teaspoon) freshly grated nutmeg
15 ml (1 tablespoon) chopped parsley

Bring a large pan of water to the boil and drop in the onions. Boil them for a few minutes. Drain and, while still hot, slip off their skins.

Put the onions back in the clean saucepan and add the chicken stock or white wine. Cover and simmer on a low heat for about 30 minutes.

Meanwhile, melt 25 g of the butter in a small saucepan and add the flour. Cook over a low heat for 2 minutes, stirring all the time, but do not allow to brown. Add the milk and cream, and bring to the boil, still stirring. Add the bay leaf. Season with salt and pepper and simmer, stirring continuously, until the sauce has thickened.

Drain the onions, return them to the pan and pour the sauce over them. Place over a gentle heat and mix in the rest of the butter in small pieces.

Transfer to a warmed serving dish, sprinkle with nutmeg and parsley, and serve while still very hot.

Serving Suggestions Serve as an accompaniment to plain roast chicken or turkey, grilled chops, steak, or liver and bacon.

Variation Add 30 ml (2 tablespoons) sherry to the sauce.

Peeling, Slicing and Chopping Onions

The onion must surely be the cornerstone of aromatic cooking the world over. Originally a native of Asia, it has been cultivated since earliest times. Onions are readily available all the year round in South Africa, although the supply will vary during the year.

Because our onions are grown in a warm climate, they are milder in flavour than the European winter varieties.

Buy firm, well-shaped onions that feel heavy for their size. The protective dry papery skins should be smooth and shiny, never soft, dark spotted, stained or blotchy. The onions should have small tight necks. A sprouting, opened neck is a sign of over-maturity or incorrect storage.

Peeling One way to simplify the peeling of a large number of onions is to blanch them in boiling water first for 5-10 minutes. The skin will then slip off more easily and your eyes will suffer a little less.

Chopping onions Cut the onions in half lengthways from root end to neck end. Cut off a thin slice at both ends and slip off the skin. Place the onion, flat side down, on a chopping board. Grip the rounded sides with your four fingers on one side and your thumb on the other side. Slice thinly, starting on the side with four fingers and ending near your thumb. Your second series of cuts will be at right angles to the first one. Turn the onion through 90 degrees and slice in exactly the same way, but across the bulb this time. The closer the cuts the finer will be the chopped onion pieces.

Slicing onions Cut off a thin slice at both the root and neck ends. Make a shallow cut through the papery skin from the root to the neck and slip off the skin. Slice a very thin disc off one side to provide the onion with a flat surface on which to stand it. Grip the sides of the onion between your four fingers on one side and thumb on the other side and, starting at either the root or neck end, slice across in slices. The slices can then easily be broken apart to form onion rings, if required.

Minimising tears The various methods of counteracting onion vapours are usually more trouble than they are worth. Use a sharp knife, cut with quick clean movements and work near an open window.

VEGETABLES AND SALADS

PARSNIP BALLS

PARSNIP BALLS – crunchy on the outside, and soft inside – are delicious served hot with roasted or grilled meat.

PREPARATION TIME: 25 MINUTES
COOKING TIME: 20 MINUTES

INGREDIENTS FOR FOUR TO SIX
700 g parsnips, peeled and cut into 2,5 cm pieces
Salt
75 g butter
30 ml (2 tablespoons) thick cream
Freshly ground black pepper
1 ml (¼ teaspoon) freshly grated nutmeg
½ egg, beaten
125 ml (½ cup) dry breadcrumbs
Sunflower oil for deep-frying

Put the parsnips in a pan and cover them with cold water. Add salt and cover the pan. Bring this to the boil and cook for 15 minutes until the parsnips are tender. Drain them thoroughly.

Melt the butter in a small saucepan, and add it, with the cream, to the parsnips. Season the mixture with salt, pepper and nutmeg, and mash well.

Allow it to cool, then stir in the egg. Using your fingers, form the mixture into walnut-sized balls and roll them in breadcrumbs.

Put the oil in a deep pan and heat to 200°C – a cube of day-old bread should turn golden in about 45 seconds. In a frying basket, place as many balls as will fit without touching. Lower the basket carefully into the hot oil and fry the balls for 2-3 minutes until golden-brown. Repeat with more batches of the balls until they are all cooked.

SERVING SUGGESTIONS Serve them hot, and if desired, sprinkle with lemon juice and chopped parsley.

Alternatively, cover with cheese sauce* and brown under the grill.

PARSNIP BALLS *Rolled in breadcrumbs and fried until golden-brown.*

CREAMED PEAS

THIS DELICIOUS PEA DISH, flavoured with cream, nutmeg and cucumber, is an excellent accompaniment either to a roast or to grilled fish.

PREPARATION TIME: 15 MINUTES
COOKING TIME: 45 MINUTES

INGREDIENTS FOR SIX
1 small English cucumber, peeled, seeded and cut into 1 cm cubes
Salt
250 ml (1 cup) cream
1 ml (¼ teaspoon) ground nutmeg
Freshly ground pepper
250 g frozen peas
10 ml (2 teaspoons) lemon juice
15 ml (1 tablespoon) finely chopped parsley for garnish

Parboil the cucumber cubes in salted water for 2 minutes. Place the cream, nutmeg, cucumber and a light seasoning of salt and pepper in the top of a double boiler and cook, stirring occasionally, for 20 minutes.

Add the peas and cook for a further 25 minutes, then add the lemon juice and stir. Pour into a heated serving dish and sprinkle with the chopped parsley.

STUFFED PEPPERS

PEPPERS GO WELL with a great variety of fillings. In this recipe, they are stuffed with a ham, walnut and cottage cheese mixture, then baked until tender.

PREPARATION TIME: 45 MINUTES
COOKING TIME: 1 HOUR
PRE-HEAT OVEN TO 180°C

INGREDIENTS FOR SIX
6 large, even-sized sweet green, red or yellow peppers
1 large onion, peeled and finely chopped*
60 ml (¼ cup) sunflower oil
1 tin (410 g) tomatoes
5 ml (1 teaspoon) dried basil
2 cloves garlic, crushed
125 ml (½ cup) dry red wine
Salt and freshly ground black pepper
100 g ham, chopped
30 ml (2 tablespoons) walnuts, coarsely chopped
250 g chunky cottage cheese
60 ml (¼ cup) dry breadcrumbs
60 ml (¼ cup) water
30 g Parmesan cheese, grated

For the sauce:
125 ml (½ cup) cream or sour cream (smetena)
5 ml (1 teaspoon) French mustard
1 egg yolk
Chicken* or vegetable stock* or white wine

Cut a lid from the top of each pepper and carefully remove the stem, seeds and membranes.

Fry the chopped onions in the sunflower oil until soft. Add the tomatoes, basil, garlic and wine, season with the salt and pepper, and simmer until the mixture is fairly thick (10-15 minutes).

Stir in the ham, walnuts, cottage cheese and half the breadcrumbs. Check the seasoning, then fill the peppers with the mixture.

Arrange the peppers side by side in a shallow oven-proof dish and pour the water around them. Sprinkle the tops with the rest of the breadcrumbs mixed with the Parmesan cheese. Bake for about 1 hour (or until tender).

To make the sauce, mix together the cream (or sour cream), French mustard and egg yolk, and heat gently, stirring all the time, until the sauce thickens. Do not let it boil.

Stir in a little stock or white wine if the mixture seems too thick, season, and spoon the sauce over the peppers.

SERVING SUGGESTIONS For a nourishing family meal, serve the stuffed peppers in bowls of steaming hot tomato soup.

Serve on a bed of brown rice.

VARIATIONS Leave out the ham for a vegetarian dish.

Fill with cooked savoury minced beef and bake until tender. Serve with a home-made tomato and onion sauce*.

Pepper Salad

For the best results, choose smooth, sleek, glossy peppers. The ripe red and yellow varieties are sweeter and more mellow than the green type, and they make wonderful salads which are rich in vitamin C.

Preparation Time: 30 minutes
Cooking Time: 15 minutes
Cooling Time: 30 minutes
Standing Time: 1 hour

Ingredients for Four to Six
3 large red or yellow peppers

For the dressing:
1 clove garlic
Salt and freshly ground black pepper
15 ml (1 tablespoon) grape vinegar
60-75 ml (4-5 tablespoons) sunflower or olive oil
30 ml (2 tablespoons) freshly chopped parsley, basil or tarragon

Roast the whole peppers on a rack under a medium-high grill, turning them from time to time, until their skins are blistered and slightly charred all over. Remove and cover with a damp tea towel until cool.

Peel off the skins over a plate to catch the juice (reserve to use in the dressing). Next, cut open the peppers and pull out the seeds and stem (discard these). Arrange the peppers, peeled side up, on a serving dish.

To make the dressing, pound the garlic to a paste with salt and pepper. Stir in the vinegar and the reserved pepper juice, then blend in the oil and chopped herbs. Stir thoroughly and spoon the sauce over the peppers. If possible, leave the peppers to stand for 1 hour to allow the flavours to blend.

SERVING SUGGESTIONS This makes an excellent accompaniment to an *alfresco* lunch of pasta. It is also a suitable side dish for grilled or braaied meat.

VARIATIONS Combine with sliced, hard-boiled eggs*, sliced tomatoes and black olives. Add 125 g Gruyère cheese (diced) and pour over a salad dressing flavoured with French mustard and mixed with 30-45 ml (2-3 tablespoons) cream.

Add a little onion, chopped walnuts or tomatoes.

Potato Croquettes

In this simple recipe, creamed potato is bound with egg and rolled into even-sized sausage shapes, before being coated with egg and breadcrumbs, and fried until crisp and golden-brown.

Preparation Time: 30 minutes
Chilling Time: 1½ hours
Cooking Time: 35 minutes
Pre-heat Oven to 180°C

Ingredients for Six
10 medium-sized potatoes, boiled and mashed
2 egg yolks
Salt and freshly ground black pepper
Freshly grated nutmeg
1 large egg, beaten
100 g fine dry breadcrumbs
Sunflower oil for frying

Beat the mashed potato with the egg yolks. Season well with salt, pepper and nutmeg, then leave to cool.

Divide the mixture into 16 equal portions, rolling them into sausage-shaped croquettes. Dip these in beaten egg and then in breadcrumbs, patting the crumbs firmly into place.

Chill for 1½ hours, then fry the croquettes in batches in deep, hot oil (about 180°C) until golden-brown, turning them so that they colour evenly.

Drain each batch of croquettes on paper towels and keep them hot in the oven (with the door slightly ajar) while frying the remaining batches.

SERVING SUGGESTIONS The croquettes make a delicious accompaniment to game or roast beef. They are also very good with fish.

VARIATIONS For a vegetarian main meal or supper dish, make double the quantity, adding 6 chopped, hard-boiled eggs* and 75 g cheese, grated, to the potato and egg yolk mixture. Season, mould into 8 large croquettes, and finish as above.

Chopped ham and cheese, sautéed sliced mushrooms or flaked cooked fish can also be added to the basic mixture for an interesting change.

Although croquettes are traditionally fried, they can also be brushed with oil or melted butter, sprinkled with paprika, and grilled until crisp.

The Versatile Baked Potato

Crisp-skinned potatoes, with meltingly soft insides, offer a tasty and substantial side dish. With imaginative variations, they become meals in themselves.

Choose large, main crop potatoes (the following suggestions for fillings are for 4 potatoes). Scrub them well and use the point of a sharp knife to remove any eyes.

Prick the skin several times with a fork, sprinkle with salt (optional), and bake at 200°C for 1-1½ hours, or until the potatoes are crisp on the outside and soft inside. (Or first parboil them for 7-10 minutes, then bake until soft – about 40 minutes.)

Sour Cream and Chives Bake the potatoes, slash the tops in a crisscross fashion and squeeze the potatoes gently to force them open. Fill with butter, sprinkle with salt and pepper and top each potato with 30 ml (2 tablespoons) sour cream (smetena) mixed with 15 ml (1 tablespoon) chopped chives.

Soufflé Bake the potatoes, cut a thin lid from the top of each and scoop out the centres into a bowl, taking care not to break the skins. Mash the filling with a fork, beat in 50 g butter, 125 ml (½ cup) cream and 3 large egg yolks. Season, and fold in 3 stiffly whisked egg whites. Spoon into the potato shells and bake at 200°C for 15-20 minutes.

Garlic Bake the potatoes, then cut a thin lid off the top and scrape the insides into a bowl. Add 125 g cream cheese mixed with herbs, 1 clove crushed garlic, 50 g butter, salt and pepper. Beat until smooth, press the mixture back into the shells, sprinkle with grated Cheddar and grill until the cheese melts.

Bacon and Leek Bake the potatoes, cut a lid off the top, scoop out the centres, and reserve. Fry 8 rashers of chopped streaky bacon until just crisp. Remove from the pan and fry 3 sliced leeks, adding 50 g butter if necessary. Reduce the heat and simmer until tender. Add the bacon and leeks to the potato filling, with 50 g butter, 100 ml cream and seasoning. Mix well, pile into the potato shells, sprinkle with grated cheese and grill.

Egg Bake the potatoes, halve and scoop out the centres. Add butter and seasoning and mash until smooth. Pile the mixture back into the shells and make a hollow in the centre of each. Break an egg into each hollow and bake until the whites have set.

Smoked Fish Flake 100 g smoked, cooked fish with a pinch of cayenne pepper. Add this to the scooped-out baked potato, together with 15 ml (1 tablespoon) finely chopped parsley (and a little cream if it is too stiff). Spoon the mixture back into the potatoes, dot with butter and re-heat.

Mushroom and Ham Sauté 1 finely chopped onion in butter. Add 150 g sliced mushrooms and 100 g diced ham. Stir into the mashed potato filling and pile back into the shells. Dot with butter and bake until hot.

Caviar Bake the potatoes, split, and serve topped with sour cream (smetena), chopped chives and lumpfish roe (mock caviar).

Game Chips

These are the most aristocratic of chips – cut very thinly indeed, and cooked to a crisp golden-brown. Like bread sauce, redcurrant jelly and watercress, they are one of the customary accompaniments of game, but there is no reason why you should not serve them with other roast meats as well.

Preparation Time: 10 minutes
Soaking Time: 30 minutes
Cooking Time: 10 minutes

Ingredients for Four
500 g potatoes
Sunflower oil for deep-frying
Salt and freshly ground pepper

Peel the potatoes and slice them very thinly with a cheese parer. Soak the slices in cold water for 30 minutes to remove excess starch. Drain them well and pat them dry on paper towels.

Pour the oil into a deep pan to a depth of 5 cm or more depending on the size of the pan and heat it to 200°C – a cube of bread dropped in it should turn golden-brown in about 45 seconds.

Put half the potato slices into a frying basket and lower it carefully into the oil. Move the slices around so that they do not stick together. Remove them after about 5 minutes when they are golden-brown. Drain them on paper towels. Keep them warm, uncovered, under a moderate grill while you cook the rest of the slices.

Sprinkle with salt and pepper.

VEGETABLES AND SALADS

POTATO SALAD

THIS WELL-FLAVOURED potato salad should be made on the day of serving, and served at room temperature, rather than chilled from the refrigerator.

PREPARATION TIME: 15 MINUTES
COOKING TIME: 25 MINUTES

INGREDIENTS FOR SIX TO EIGHT
1 kg potatoes (use either large potatoes or tiny new ones)
60 ml (¼ cup) apple cider vinegar
1 medium-sized onion, peeled and finely chopped*
125 ml (½ cup) home-made mayonnaise*
125 ml (½ cup) sour cream (smetena)
Salt and freshly ground black pepper
Chopped parsley or paprika for garnish

Boil the potatoes in their jackets until tender. If you are using large potatoes, peel them as soon as they are cool enough to handle and slice. Leave baby new potatoes whole and unskinned.

Place the prepared potatoes in a salad bowl and moisten with the vinegar. Mix in the onion, then the mayonnaise and sour cream.

Using two spatulas, mix these ingredients together until the potatoes are well coated with the dressing.

Season and sprinkle the salad with paprika or a little finely chopped parsley.

SERVING SUGGESTIONS Serve with cold meats, or at a braaivleis.

VARIATIONS Use natural yoghurt* instead of the sour cream.

Use a bunch of chopped spring onions instead of the whole onion.

Garnish with 125 ml (½ cup) chopped pickled cucumber and two chopped hard-boiled eggs*.

For a more substantial salad, add thin slices of smoked sausage.

POTATO PANCAKES

PANCAKES ARE USUALLY MADE with a batter of eggs, milk and flour, but in this recipe potatoes and flour are bound together with milk, and no eggs, to form the batter.

Fried to a crispy golden-brown on both sides – preferably in bacon fat – they have a delicious flavour.

PREPARATION TIME: 15 MINUTES
COOKING TIME: 15 MINUTES

INGREDIENTS FOR FOUR TO SIX
450 g potatoes, peeled
100-125 g self-raising flour
80-125 ml (⅓ - ½ cup) milk
Salt and freshly ground black pepper
50 g butter

Grate the potatoes and put them in a colander. Cover with paper towels and press down to squeeze out the surplus starch. Alternatively, wring the grated potatoes in a clean tea towel.

Sieve the flour into a mixing bowl and stir in the milk. Mix in the grated potatoes and season the mixture with salt and pepper.

Heat the butter in a heavy-based frying pan until it foams. As soon as the foam begins to subside, drop in about 15 ml (1 tablespoon) of the potato batter to make each pancake. Cook the pancakes for 3-4 minutes, or until they are golden-brown, on each side.

Remove the pancakes with a fish slice, and keep them warm in an oven-proof dish under a moderate grill while you cook the rest of the pancakes in the same way.

Sprinkle them with salt, if you wish, before serving.

SERVING SUGGESTIONS Serve them with chops, roasts, liver and bacon, fried sausages and stews.

For a delicious light supper, serve the pancakes on their own, covered with tomato and onion sauce* and a sprinkling of chopped ham.

VARIATIONS These pancakes may also be flavoured with caraway seeds, sage or chopped onions. Stir in the flavouring with the salt and pepper and mix well.

Alternatively, they may be flavoured with meat, such as diced streaky bacon, flaked corned beef or finely chopped ham.

ROSTI *The golden potato crust hides a tender interior.*

ROSTI

THIS SWISS POTATO CAKE is deliciously crisp and golden on the outside but soft and tender inside. Rosti can be prepared and cooked in less than an hour – a boon to the busy cook.

PREPARATION TIME: 30 MINUTES
COOKING TIME: 25 MINUTES

INGREDIENTS FOR SIX
10 medium-sized boiling potatoes
75 g butter
Salt and freshly ground black pepper

Scrub the potatoes and place them in a saucepan of cold water. Cover and boil for 10-15 minutes, or until they are barely tender. Drain and leave to cool, then peel the potatoes and grate on a fairly coarse blade of the grater.

Melt the butter in a large, heavy-based frying pan. Add the grated potatoes and sprinkle with salt and pepper. Pat into a cake and fry over a medium heat for about 10 minutes until lightly browned. Then put a plate over the pan and invert the cake on to the plate.

Add more butter to the pan if necessary, and slide the rosti back into the pan to cook on the other side for about 10 minutes until lightly brown.

Loosen with a spatula and invert the potato cake on to a large, round serving plate. Serve immediately.

SERVING SUGGESTIONS Rosti is traditionally served with strips of veal cooked in a cream sauce*, but it also makes a pleasant accompaniment to, for example, grilled sausages, chops or bacon.

If you like, serve each portion of rosti topped with a fried egg.

VARIATIONS Finely sliced*, cooked onion, chopped ham or sausage can be added to the grated potato mixture before it is patted into a cake and fried.

Pommes Gratin Dauphinois

In this classic dish, named after the mountainous Dauphine area of France that borders on Switzerland, butter and cream are the rich local ingredients that combine with potatoes.

When cooked, the potatoes are brown on top and the sauce has thickened and tastes of cheese, even though in fact there is no cheese in the recipe.

Preparation Time: 15 minutes
Cooking Time: 1 hour
Pre-heat Oven to 180°C

Ingredients for Four
1 clove garlic
450 g potatoes, peeled and sliced very thinly
Salt and freshly ground black pepper
275-300 ml thick cream
40 g butter, cut into pieces

Grease an oven-proof dish with a little butter, and rub it well with the clove of garlic. Arrange a layer of potato slices in the dish and season them with salt and pepper. Add another layer, season it and continue in this way until all the potato slices have been used up.

Pour over the cream until it comes to within 2 cm of the top of the potatoes. Dot the potatoes with butter.

Place the dish in the pre-heated oven and bake for 1 hour until the top is nicely browned. If necessary, turn up the heat for the last 10 minutes to allow the top to brown completely.

Serve the potatoes hot.

Serving Suggestion This dish goes well with grilled meat, roast beef, pork, lamb or chicken, and cold meats.

Pumpkin Purée

This dish is simple to prepare and is a particularly enjoyable way of eating a very inexpensive vegetable. The pumpkin purée is served hot, usually as an accompaniment to a meat dish.

Preparation Time: 20 minutes
Cooking Time: 35 minutes

Ingredients for Six to Eight
1 kg pumpkin, peeled and cubed
300 ml water
60 g brown sugar
10 ml (2 teaspoons) honey
2 ml (½ teaspoon) ground cinnamon
15 ml (1 tablespoon) lemon juice
2 ml (½ teaspoon) salt
20 g butter

Put the pumpkin in a heavy-bottomed saucepan and add the water, sugar, honey, cinnamon, lemon juice and salt. Boil for 15 minutes, reduce heat and simmer for 20 minutes or until soft. Stir occasionally. Purée the pumpkin with the butter.

Pumpkin Fritters

Because they keep so well, lined up in a sunny place, pumpkins are an all-year-round standby. Make pumpkin fritters the way grandmother used to do and serve them piping hot.

Preparation Time: 25 minutes
Cooking Time: 20 minutes

Ingredients for Six
450 g peeled pumpkin
A pinch of salt and sugar
60 g flour
5 ml (1 teaspoon) baking powder
2 eggs
Milk (optional)
45 ml (3 tablespoons) sunflower oil
45 ml (3 tablespoons) butter
Lemon wedges for garnish

For the cinnamon sugar:
100 g sugar
5 ml (1 teaspoon) cinnamon

Steam the pumpkin over boiling water in a vegetable steamer with a little salt and sugar until it is just done.

Mix the pumpkin, flour, baking powder and eggs to form a batter of dropping consistency. Add a little milk if it is too stiff.

Fry spoonfuls in the mixed, heated oil and butter in a big heavy-based frying pan. Drain the fritters on brown paper.

Sprinkle them with cinnamon sugar and serve hot with wedges of lemon on the side.

Variation Substitute sweet potatoes.

Stewed Red Cabbage

Apples, onions and spices, together with wine and vinegar, are traditional ingredients to cook with red cabbage. The long, slow cooking allows the flavours to be absorbed, and gives the spicy, sweet-sour taste for which it is renowned.

The addition of the wine helps both colour and flavour, and prevents the cabbage from turning blue.

Preparation Time: 20-25 minutes
Cooking Time: 2½-3 hours
Pre-heat Oven to 150°C

Ingredients for Six
25 g butter
2 medium-sized onions, peeled and chopped*
3 carrots, peeled and chopped
4 rashers bacon, rinds removed, chopped
4 cooking apples, peeled, cored and chopped
1 kg red cabbage, finely chopped
1 clove garlic, finely chopped
Salt and freshly ground black pepper
2 ml (½ teaspoon) freshly grated nutmeg
1 bay leaf
2 cloves
30 ml (2 tablespoons) port
30 ml (2 tablespoons) red wine vinegar

Melt the butter in an oven-proof dish. Add the onions, carrots and bacon, and cook for 5 minutes until they are soft.

Remove them from the heat and add the chopped apples, cabbage and garlic. Season with salt, black pepper and nutmeg, and add the bay leaf and cloves. Mix all these ingredients well together, then stir in the port and the red wine vinegar.

Cover the dish and bake in the pre-heated oven for 2½ to 3 hours. Serve it hot or cold, as you wish.

Serving Suggestions Red cabbage goes well with duck, goose, venison and pork, and is also good with ham and sausages. It can be served cold or re-heated with a little cooked bacon added to it.

Stewed Red Cabbage *A truly appetising line-up of ingredients.*

Creamed Spinach

This is a wonderful way to serve fresh spinach. The basis of the recipe is roughly chopped (cooked) spinach mixed with a few spoonfuls of fresh or sour cream, a knob of butter, salt and black pepper. Even frozen spinach can be resuscitated by means of the same treatment.

Preparation Time: 20 minutes
Cooking Time: 15 minutes

Ingredients for Four
1 kg spinach
80 ml (⅓ cup) cream or sour cream (smetana)
50 g butter
Salt and freshly ground black pepper
Freshly grated nutmeg

Tear the spinach leaves from the stalks, discarding any brown leaves. Wash in 2 or 3 changes of water, making sure the leaves are really clean. Put them in a large, heavy-based saucepan, cover and set over a low heat (do not add water).

After 1 minute, stir with a wooden spoon. Raise the heat and cook for about 10 minutes, stirring from time to time to prevent the leaves from sticking to the pan. Then drain very thoroughly, pressing out all the moisture.

Just before serving, chop the spinach roughly and drain again. Return it to a clean saucepan, stir in the cream or sour cream and re-heat gently.

Add the butter, cut into flakes, and stir over a gentle heat until it has been absorbed into the creamed spinach. Season well with salt, pepper and nutmeg, and serve piping hot.

Serving Suggestions Turn the spinach into a dish and surround it with small triangles of fried bread.

Serve with boiled ham, roast beef, grilled steak or chops.

Alternatively, use the spinach as a filling for omelettes*, as a base for soft-boiled eggs*, or in shortcrust tartlet cases topped with a sprinkling of grated cheese and served with roast lamb.

Variation Final seasoning can include grated Parmesan cheese, a little lemon juice, crushed garlic and a teaspoonful of vegetable extract.

Glazed Sweet Potatoes

Try this traditional way to cook sweet potatoes to serve with a roast leg of mutton or other roast meat.

Preparation Time: 30 minutes
Cooking Time: 1 hour

Ingredients for Six
1 kg sweet potatoes (yellow type called 'borrie')
Salt
100 g butter
200 g soft brown sugar
30 ml (2 tablespoons) honey (optional)
A 5 cm piece of dried naartjie peel
2 cinnamon sticks, or a 5 cm piece of peeled, fresh green ginger
200 ml water

Wash, peel and slice the sweet potatoes, then wash in salted water. Place the sliced sweet potatoes in a heavy-based saucepan with the butter, sugar, honey (if used), naartjie peel, cinnamon or ginger and water.

Cook on medium-low heat until the water has disappeared. Shake the saucepan instead of stirring the ingredients to prevent the sweet potatoes from breaking.

Increase the heat and fry to a golden caramel colour, making sure that the potatoes do not burn.

Remove the naartjie peel and cinnamon or ginger before serving.

Tomato and Onion Salad

Low in kilojoules, this salad is good as an accompaniment to curries, cold meats, fish or poultry.

Preparation Time: 10 minutes

Ingredients for Four
4 medium-sized ripe tomatoes
*1 large onion, peeled and finely sliced**
30 ml (2 tablespoons) chopped parsley
30 ml (2 tablespoons) wine vinegar
Salt and freshly ground black pepper

Slice the tomatoes into rounds and arrange them on a flat platter. Arrange the onion slices on top of the tomato and sprinkle the salad with parsley. Add the vinegar, salt and pepper.

Variation Instead of using parsley, try fresh basil, chives, marjoram or celery.

Hot Vegetable Platter

This medley of vegetables makes a good vegetarian main course or a fine accompaniment to a simple roast.

Preparation Time: 45 minutes
Cooking Time: 25 minutes

Ingredients for Six
250 g shelled young peas, or 250 g young green beans, or 250 g slim baby marrows
250 g baby carrots, scraped
250 g young turnips, peeled and quartered, or 250 g baby potatoes, scrubbed and halved
½ small cauliflower, broken into florets, or 250 g slim broccoli stalks
60 g butter
200 g big black mushrooms, sliced
30 ml (2 tablespoons) flour
*250 ml (1 cup) milk or vegetable stock**
Salt and freshly ground black pepper

For the garnish:
Chopped parsley or chervil
125 ml (½ cup) grated Cheddar cheese (optional)

Set aside the mushrooms but cook the rest of the vegetables (separately) until they are just tender. Drain them well and arrange them attractively in groups on a deep platter. Keep the vegetables warm.

Melt the butter and add the mushrooms. Stir-fry for a few minutes, add flour, then gradually add the milk or stock, stirring all the time, until the sauce is thick and smooth. Season with salt and pepper, and spoon it over the hot vegetables.

Sprinkle the dish generously with the herbs and grated cheese, if used.

Variation Use a cheese sauce* or a Hollandaise sauce* instead of the mushroom sauce.

Watercress Salad

Watercress has a high vitamin content, and its fresh, slightly peppery taste makes it an excellent salad ingredient. In this adaptation of a Chinese recipe, water chestnuts and bean sprouts add their delicate flavour and distinctive crispness to a tangy, watercress salad, which is very good with cold duck.

Preparation Time: 15 minutes

Ingredients for Four to Six
2 bunches watercress
*250 g fresh bean sprouts**
1 tin (230 g) water chestnuts, drained
Salt

For the dressing:
20 ml (4 teaspoons) sesame seeds
50 ml sesame oil
60 ml (¼ cup) soy sauce
30 ml (2 tablespoons) lemon juice
1 small onion, peeled and grated*
1 ml (¼ teaspoon) sugar
Freshly ground black pepper

Wash the watercress and bean sprouts and pat them dry with paper towels. Slice the water chestnuts. In a salad bowl, mix together the watercress, bean sprouts and water chestnuts.

Toast the sesame seeds in a dry pan over a moderate heat. Put the seeds in a bowl and add the sesame oil, soy sauce, lemon juice, grated onion and sugar. Season this with pepper and stir all the ingredients together.

Pour the dressing over the salad and toss the salad. Check the seasoning and add salt if necessary.

Serve straight away, while crisp.

Serving Suggestion Serve with either cold duck or cold chicken.

Variation You can use orange juice instead of lemon juice in the dressing, and, if serving the salad with duck, garnish the duck with slices of orange.

Ratatouille

Colourful and richly flavoured, ratatouille is a blend of vegetables and herbs that has in it the authentic taste of the south of France. Onions, brinjals, baby marrows, peppers and tomatoes all intermingle their flavours as they stew slowly in olive oil.

Two rules must be observed when making ratatouille – always use olive oil and never add water.

Preparation Time: 40 minutes
Standing Time: 40 minutes
Cooking Time: 1 hour

Ingredients for Six

2 large brinjals, cut into
  1,5 cm slices
8 baby marrows, cut into 1,5 cm
  slices
Salt
30 ml (2 tablespoons) olive oil
2 large onions, peeled and sliced*
3 green peppers, seeded and
  sliced
2 cloves garlic, finely chopped
4-5 medium-sized tomatoes,
  skinned* and sliced
15 ml (1 tablespoon) crushed
  coriander seeds
Freshly ground black pepper

For the garnish:
15 ml (1 tablespoon) chopped
  basil
15 ml (1 tablespoon) chopped
  parsley

Put the sliced brinjals and baby marrows into a colander and sprinkle them with salt. Leave them for 40 minutes so that the salt has time to draw out some of the excess moisture. Dry the slices thoroughly with paper towels.

Heat the olive oil in a large frying pan. Add the sliced onions and green peppers, and cook these for 5 minutes until the onions are soft and transparent. Add the brinjals, baby marrows and garlic. Cover the frying pan and simmer this mixture over medium heat for 10 minutes.

Add the tomatoes and coriander seeds. Season with salt and pepper. Cover again and cook for 45 minutes over a gentle heat, checking occasionally to make sure the vegetables are not sticking to the bottom of the pan.

Check and if necessary adjust the seasoning, sprinkle the dish with the chopped basil and parsley, and serve.

Serving Suggestions Serve the ratatouille hot or cold with freshly baked bread as a first course and, if liked, top each portion with a fried egg.

Or serve it as an accompaniment to roast or grilled meat or chicken.

Stuffed Tomatoes

Stuffed tomatoes form an easily prepared dish that can be served as a first course, an accompaniment to a main course or on its own.

Preparation Time: 10 minutes
Cooking Time: 20 minutes
Pre-heat Oven to 180°C

Ingredients for Six

6 large tomatoes
25 g butter
1 medium-sized onion, peeled
  and chopped*
100-125 g mushrooms, washed
  and chopped
100-125 g fresh breadcrumbs
30 ml (2 tablespoons) chopped
  basil or parsley
Salt and freshly ground black
  pepper
30 ml (2 tablespoons) grated
  Parmesan cheese
2 ml (½ teaspoon) paprika

Slice the tops off the tomatoes and put the tops to one side. Scoop out the pulp and seeds from the tomatoes with a spoon, taking care not to break the skins. Put the pulp into a mixing bowl and put the skins aside.

Melt the butter in a frying pan over a gentle heat. Add the onion and fry this until it is soft and transparent. Add the mushrooms and cook them for a few minutes.

Put the onion and mushrooms into the bowl with the tomato pulp and add the breadcrumbs and herbs. Season the mixture with salt and pepper, and mix well.

Put spoonfuls of the mixture into the tomato skins, sprinkle with cheese and paprika and replace the tops.

Stand the stuffed tomatoes in a greased oven-proof dish and bake in the pre-heated oven for 15-20 minutes. Serve hot.

Chinese Stir-Fried Vegetables

Because of the unique shape of the wok, it is the perfect utensil to use for stir-frying. The oil and juices will constantly run back to the centre of the wok, basting and moisturising the ingredients while they are stirred around during the quick frying process. Many of our everyday vegetables, such as cabbage, green beans, broccoli and spinach, lend themselves to being cooked in this way.

How to prepare the vegetables
Cabbage Cut the cabbage head into even-sized wedges. Remove the hard stalk. Place the wedges, flat edge down, on a chopping board and shred very finely with a sharp knife (or use a food processor for shredding).
Green beans Top and tail the beans. Slice them diagonally in 1-2 cm long pieces.
Broccoli Slice the stems diagonally into neat slivers, cut the heads into miniature florets.
Spinach Wash the spinach very well in cold water. Remove the white stalks. Pile 5 or 6 leaves on top of each other and roll them into a tight roll. With a sharp knife, slice this across into fine shreds.
Spring onions or leeks Remove the root ends and any damaged tips of the green leaves, then slice the onions or leeks into diagonal slices.
Celery Use the thick, milder flavoured table celery. Remove any green leaves and slice the stalks into fine diagonal slices.

How to cook
Place 30-45 ml (2-3 tablespoons) sunflower oil with 1 or 2 peeled cloves of garlic in the wok. Heat until a blue haze appears, then remove the garlic. Start adding the vegetables in order of the length of cooking time required, that is, start with the beans, then the leeks, then the celery, then the broccoli, cabbage and lastly the spinach.

Lift and turn the vegetables with a flat spatula all the time during the cooking process. Shake the wok from time to time. Do not overcook the vegetables – they must be bright in colour and crisp in texture when served.

Sauce Mix 15 ml (1 tablespoon) cornflour in 125 ml (½ cup) water. Add a crumbled chicken or vegetable stock cube and 30 ml (2 tablespoons) soy sauce. Stir this into the vegetable mixture. Allow to cook and glaze before removing from the heat. Stir-fried vegetables must be served promptly after cooking for best results.

Other vegetables can be used:
Turnips or carrots may be used, cut into julienne* strips.
English cucumber should be sliced lengthways, seeded and sliced across in fine discs.
Red and green peppers – remove the inner membranes and seeds, cut in half lengthways and shred into fine strips.
Fresh green ginger may also be used. Peel the ginger root and slice it into fine discs or grate it on the coarse side of a grater.

VEGETABLES AND SALADS

KACHOOMER

THIS TASTY TRADITIONAL Indian salad is seasoned with chillies, cumin and vinegar before serving. Some cooks choose to wear gloves when working with chillies as their hot flavour can remain on one's fingers for hours.

PREPARATION TIME: 15 MINUTES

INGREDIENTS FOR FOUR TO SIX
2 onions, peeled*
2 medium-sized ripe tomatoes
1 green pepper, seeded
2 ml (½ teaspoon) salt
½ green chilli, finely chopped (optional)
2 ml (½ teaspoon) cumin, crushed
2 ml (½ teaspoon) sugar
30 ml (2 tablespoons) lemon juice
15 ml (1 tablespoon) vinegar
2 sprigs coriander for garnish

Dice the onions, tomatoes and green pepper. Season with the salt, chilli (if used), cumin, sugar, lemon juice and vinegar. Mix well and garnish with the sprigs of coriander. Serve cold.

SERVING SUGGESTION Kachoomer goes very well with meat, poultry or fish dishes.

SOUSBOONTJIES

THIS TRADITIONAL South African dish makes an interesting accompaniment to any sort of roast meat. One of its advantages is that it keeps well in the refrigerator.

PREPARATION TIME: 5 MINUTES
SOAKING TIME: OVERNIGHT
COOKING TIME: 1¼ HOURS

INGREDIENTS FOR TEN TO TWELVE
500 g butter or sugar beans
500 ml (2 cups) water
125 ml (½ cup) vinegar
60 g sugar
3 ml (¾ teaspoon) salt
15 g butter

Soak the beans overnight. Cook them very slowly in the 500 ml (2 cups) water until they are tender. Add the vinegar, sugar, salt and butter according to your own taste. Press a few of the beans to pulp stage to bind the sauce. Allow to cool.

BUTTER BEANS WITH TOMATO *The beans are slowly simmered, and garlic adds tang.*

BUTTER BEANS WITH TOMATO

THIS MAKES a very good vegetarian dish, perhaps topped with squares of feta. It is an ideal accompaniment to roast lamb.

PREPARATION TIME: 20 MINUTES
SOAKING TIME: OVERNIGHT
COOKING TIME: 2 HOURS

INGREDIENTS FOR SIX
350 g dried butter beans
2 medium-sized onions, peeled and thinly sliced*
1 medium-sized carrot, sliced
2 fat cloves garlic, crushed
1 bay leaf
1 sprig rosemary
60 ml (¼ cup) sunflower oil
4 medium-sized tomatoes, skinned* and chopped
Salt and freshly ground pepper
Chopped fresh basil or parsley

Soak the beans overnight in cold water – or cover with water, boil, take from the stove and leave covered for an hour.

Place the soaked beans plus the soaking liquid in a heavy saucepan (ensure that there is enough water to cover the beans) and bring to the boil with 1 sliced onion, the sliced carrot, 1 clove crushed garlic, the bay leaf and the rosemary. Reduce the heat and simmer for about an hour. Add half the oil and simmer until the beans are tender. Drain the beans (reserve the stock).

Gently heat the rest of the oil in a large frying pan. Add the remaining sliced onion and cook very gently until softened. Stir in the remaining clove of garlic and the tomatoes. Cook for 5-10 minutes, then add the drained beans and heat through, adding a little of the stock if necessary. Season, and serve sprinkled with basil or parsley.

BHAJI MASOOR NI DHAL

THIS TASTY INDIAN RECIPE consists primarily of red lentils cooked with spinach and onions. The lentils thicken into a gravy to make a versatile dish which can be served with bread or rice, or on its own as a nourishing soup.

PREPARATION TIME: 15 MINUTES
COOKING TIME: 30 MINUTES

INGREDIENTS FOR SIX
400 g red lentils
750 ml (3 cups) water
1 medium-sized onion, peeled and chopped*
3 cloves garlic, sliced
8 curry leaves
2 green chillies, sliced lengthways
2 ml (½ teaspoon) turmeric
5 ml (1 teaspoon) salt
100 g spinach, shredded
45 ml (3 tablespoons) sunflower oil
5 ml (1 teaspoon) mustard seeds

Wash and drain the lentils. Bring the water to the boil in a saucepan, add the lentils, onion, garlic, curry leaves, chillies, turmeric, salt, spinach and 15 ml (1 tablespoon) of the oil. Cover the saucepan and cook for 15 minutes.

Heat the remaining oil in a small saucepan, add the mustard seeds and allow them to brown. Pour over the lentil curry, stir, and gently simmer for 10 minutes.

VEGETABLES AND SALADS

HARICOT BEAN CURRY

DRIED BEANS AND PULSES are largely responsible for the versatility of Indian cuisine. About 16 different types are available, and all can be stored for a considerable time without spoiling.

An important ingredient in this dish is asafoetida, a pungent reddish-brown resin.

PREPARATION TIME: 15 MINUTES
SOAKING TIME: OVERNIGHT
COOKING TIME: 2 HOURS

INGREDIENTS FOR SIX
500 g dried haricot beans
2 medium-sized onions, peeled and chopped*
90 ml sunflower oil
1 litre (4 cups) water
5 ml (1 teaspoon) turmeric
7 ml (1½ teaspoons) salt
5 ml (1 teaspoon) red chilli powder
10 ml (2 teaspoons) coriander seeds, crushed
5 ml (1 teaspoon) cumin seeds, crushed
2 medium-sized ripe tomatoes, chopped
30 ml (2 tablespoons) chopped coriander (dhania) leaves
2 ml (½ teaspoon) ground asafoetida
1 dried red chilli

Wash and soak the beans overnight in hot water. Then drain them, add the onions and 15 ml (1 tablespoon) of the oil, and boil (covered) in 1 litre (4 cups) of water for 1 hour 20 minutes. Add the turmeric, salt, chilli powder, coriander, cumin, tomatoes and coriander leaves, and mix well.

Heat the remaining oil in another small saucepan. Sprinkle the asafoetida over the hot oil and add the dried chilli. Leave to brown for a few seconds, then pour over the cooked beans. Stir and simmer the beans for 30 minutes, or until soft. Add extra water to achieve a flowing consistency.

SERVING SUGGESTIONS Always serve with a mixed fruit pickle*.
Serve with chapati*, puri* or toast.

VARIATION If you prefer, drop the asafoetida and red chilli, and substitute two 5 cm lengths of cinnamon stick or 5 ml (1 teaspoon) lovage seeds (ajmo).

SOYA NUT LOAF

SOYA BEANS have more food value than any of the other pulses; they contain the necessary fats and essential amino acids for an excellent protein. Although their preparation and cooking time is rather lengthy, soya beans are economical in that they provide many more portions per kilogram than either meat or fish.

PREPARATION TIME: 2½ HOURS
SOAKING TIME: OVERNIGHT
COOKING TIME: 30 MINUTES
PRE-HEAT OVEN TO 180°C

INGREDIENTS FOR FOUR TO SIX
150 g soya beans
750 ml (3 cups) water
30 ml (2 tablespoons) sunflower oil
25 g butter
1 medium-sized onion, peeled and chopped*
1 medium-sized carrot, coarsely grated
2 cloves garlic, crushed
2 medium-sized tomatoes, skinned* and chopped
30 ml (2 tablespoons) tomato paste
2 ml (½ teaspoon) dried thyme
Salt and freshly ground pepper
5 ml (1 teaspoon) brown sugar
125 ml (½ cup) large-flake oats
1 extra-large egg, lightly beaten
50 g Brazil-nuts, chopped
45 ml (3 tablespoons) chopped parsley
15 ml (1 tablespoon) soy sauce
Dry breadcrumbs

Soak the beans in water overnight, then cook them in the 750 ml (3 cups) water, partially covered, for 2 hours or until soft. Mash the cooked beans finely, using a potato masher or a food processor.

Heat the oil and butter in a frying pan, then add the onion, carrot and garlic, and allow them to soften.

Reduce the heat and add the tomatoes, tomato paste, thyme, salt, pepper and sugar. Cover the pan and simmer the mixture gently until the vegetables are soft (about 10 minutes).

Add this mixture to the mashed beans, then stir in the oats, egg, nuts, parsley and soy sauce.

Oil a loaf-shaped baking tin, 19 cm x 8 cm x 7 cm. Sprinkle the bottom and sides with dry breadcrumbs, shake out any excess crumbs, then spoon the soya mixture into the dish. Press it down evenly and smooth the top. Bake it in the pre-heated oven for 30 minutes. Turn the loaf out carefully on to a heated platter.

SERVING SUGGESTIONS Serve the loaf hot, cut into thick slices, with mashed potatoes*, green peas and a creamy mushroom sauce*.
Serve the loaf cold with a green salad*, mayonnaise* and wholewheat rolls.

STEWED LENTILS

LENTILS ARE ONE of the oldest foods known to man. They require little preparation, and they readily absorb the flavours of the meat, herbs or vegetables with which they are cooked.

PREPARATION TIME: 10 MINUTES
COOKING TIME: 1 HOUR

INGREDIENTS FOR FOUR
250 g brown lentils
30 ml (2 tablespoons) olive oil
1 small onion, peeled and finely chopped*
1 small carrot, peeled and chopped
2 cloves garlic, chopped
A sprig of fresh mint
Salt and freshly ground black pepper
15 ml (1 tablespoon) chopped parsley
25 g butter, softened

Carefully pick over the lentils, removing any stones and grit. Rinse thoroughly.

Heat the oil in a large pan, add the onion, carrot and garlic, and fry gently for a few minutes. Add the lentils and cover generously with fresh cold water.

Add the mint and season the mixture with salt and pepper. Cover the pan, bring it to the boil and simmer for 1 hour, after which time all the water should have been absorbed and the lentils should be tender.

Remove from the heat and stir in the parsley and butter. Serve immediately.

SERVING SUGGESTION Serve with meat or as a vegetarian dish.

LENTIL AND SAUSAGE SALAD

THIS HEARTY, wholesome dish can serve as an accompaniment to other dishes, or alternatively stand on its own as a light main course for lunch or supper.

PREPARATION TIME: 30 MINUTES
COOKING TIME: 40 MINUTES
COOLING TIME: 45 MINUTES

INGREDIENTS FOR SIX
250 ml (1 cup) lentils, rinsed and picked over
750 ml (3 cups) water
Salt
500 ml (2 cups) sliced Russian sausage
4 spring onions, trimmed and sliced (including half the green)
1 green pepper, seeded and finely chopped
200 ml vinaigrette*
1 clove garlic, peeled and crushed

For the garnish:
1 hard-boiled egg*, shelled and sliced
2 medium-sized cooked beetroots, peeled and sliced
45 ml (3 tablespoons) chopped parsley

Place the lentils in a saucepan with the water and a little salt. Bring to the boil over a high heat, then reduce the heat and simmer gently for 30 minutes or so, or until the lentils are tender (but they must not be mushy).

Rinse under hot water and drain well. Soak the Russian sausage in hot water for 5 minutes, and then skin and slice. Put the lentils into a bowl with the sausage, spring onions and green pepper, and pour over the vinaigrette (to which you have added the crushed garlic). Toss to mix well and leave to cool.

Mound the salad on a platter and garnish with slices of hard-boiled egg and beetroot. Sprinkle with the parsley.

SERVING SUGGESTION You can also arrange the salad attractively on separate serving plates, as a light course on its own. In this case, mound the salad on pale green butter lettuce leaves.

VARIATION Omit the sausage for an excellent vegetarian dish.

MAKING A MEAL OF VEGETABLES

Try one of these delightful departures from the meat-and-two-vegetables approach to family fare.

CABBAGE ROLLS WITH SPROUT STUFFING

STUFFED CABBAGE is a popular dish in Russia, Poland, Hungary and Germany, and there are a number of stuffings that can be used, including this delicious mushroom, rice and sprout mixture.

PREPARATION TIME: 45 MINUTES
COOKING TIME: 20 MINUTES
PRE-HEAT OVEN TO 180°C

INGREDIENTS FOR SIX

5 medium-sized mushrooms, finely sliced
3 spring onions, finely sliced
1 small green pepper, seeded and finely chopped
40 ml sunflower oil
250 g cooked rice*
125 g mung bean sprouts, steamed for 3 minutes
125 g alfalfa sprouts
A dash each of cayenne pepper, origanum, sage, salt and black pepper
12 large cabbage leaves, simmered for 6-8 minutes, then drained and cooled
500 ml (2 cups) tomato and onion sauce*

Sauté the mushrooms, spring onions and green pepper in the sunflower oil for 3 minutes. Add the rice, bean and alfalfa sprouts, cayenne pepper, origanum, sage, salt and pepper, and blend them well to make the stuffing. Place spoonfuls of the mixture on each cabbage leaf, which is then folded over to make a little parcel. Place the cabbage parcels seam side down (secured with toothpicks) in an oiled shallow pan. Pour the tomato and onion sauce over the cabbage rolls and bake for 20 minutes.

VARIATIONS Place a little sauerkraut on the bottom of the pan with some left-over chopped cabbage. Place the cabbage rolls on top of this, sprinkle with oil, cover with a little more sauerkraut (including any juice), and bake the dish until it is tender.

The stuffing may be varied to include chopped celery and lentil sprouts instead of mushrooms.

BRINJALS STUFFED WITH CURRIED VEGETABLES

SELECT FIRM, RIPE brinjals for this spicy and filling dish. The skin of these tasty vegetables should be smooth and shiny: a wrinkled skin indicates that the vegetable is past its prime.

PREPARATION TIME: 1 HOUR
COOKING TIME: 45 MINUTES
PRE-HEAT OVEN TO 180°C

INGREDIENTS FOR SIX

6 small or medium-sized brinjals, washed and sliced in half lengthways
Salt
100 ml melted butter
2 cloves garlic, peeled and finely chopped
A 1 cm piece of fresh green ginger, scraped and finely chopped
1 small onion, peeled and finely chopped*
2 ml (½ teaspoon) ground coriander
5 ml (1 teaspoon) garam masala or medium-hot Indian curry powder
6 fresh green beans, trimmed and cut into 2 cm pieces
250 g frozen peas
2 carrots, scraped and finely chopped
1 large potato, peeled and finely chopped
1 tin (410 g) skinned tomatoes, drained and coarsely chopped
45 ml (3 tablespoons) finely chopped coriander leaves
15 ml (1 tablespoon) finely chopped fresh mint
30 g pea flour or lentil (chana) flour
2 ml (½ teaspoon) ground cumin
A pinch of cayenne pepper
60 ml (¼ cup) water
50 g butter

Scoop the pulp out of the brinjals with a melon scoop, leaving each shell about 1 cm thick. Reserve the pulp. Sprinkle the shells with salt and place them (flesh side down) on paper towels. Chop the pulp finely and set aside.

Brush an oven-proof dish (large enough to contain the brinjal shells neatly) with a little of the melted butter. Heat 50 ml of the butter in a heavy-based frying pan, then add the garlic, ginger and onion. Stir-fry for 1 minute.

Stir in the ground coriander, chopped brinjal pulp and curry powder, and season lightly with salt. Stir-fry for 6-7 minutes. Add the beans, peas, carrots, potato and tomatoes, turn down the heat and allow to simmer for 5 minutes, stirring from time to time.

Remove the frying pan from the heat and stir in the chopped coriander leaves and chopped mint.

Rinse the brinjal shells and dry well with paper towels. Divide the vegetable mixture among the brinjal shells and smooth the tops.

Make a paste of the pea or lentil flour, cumin, cayenne pepper and water, then spread a little of the mixture evenly on the vegetable stuffing. Carefully fry the stuffed brinjal shells in the remaining melted butter, 1 or 2 at a time, until lightly browned on the bottom.

Arrange in the prepared oven-proof dish and dot with the 50 g butter. Cover with a lid or piece of aluminium foil and bake for 30 minutes.

Remove the aluminium foil or lid and then bake for a further 15 minutes, or until the vegetables are tender and lightly browned.

VARIATIONS Almost any fresh vegetables that are available can be used for stuffing the brinjals: cauliflower, broccoli, sweet potato and lima beans are all very suitable choices. Do not, however, omit the tomatoes as they are essential to the success of the dish.

VEGETABLE MEDLEY

A TOPPING OF SOUR CREAM, Cheddar cheese and paprika lifts this ratatouille out of the ordinary.

PREPARATION TIME: 1 HOUR
STANDING TIME: 1 HOUR
COOKING TIME: 40 MINUTES
PRE-HEAT OVEN TO 160°C

INGREDIENTS FOR FOUR

1 medium-sized brinjal, peeled and cubed
6 small baby marrows, pared and thinly sliced into rounds
Salt
45 g butter
45 ml (3 tablespoons) olive oil
2 large onions, peeled and chopped*
2-3 cloves garlic, crushed
1 stick celery, chopped
1 red pepper, seeded and diced
200 g mushrooms, rinsed and sliced
2 ml (½ teaspoon) each dried thyme, origanum and tarragon
3 medium-sized tomatoes, skinned* and chopped
Freshly ground black pepper
2 bay leaves
25 ml (5 teaspoons) finely chopped parsley
5 ml (1 teaspoon) brown sugar
125 ml (½ cup) sour cream (smetena)
150 g Cheddar cheese, finely grated
Paprika

Sprinkle the brinjal cubes and baby marrow slices with salt. Place a weight over these vegetables and leave for 1 hour. Rinse and pat dry with paper towels.

Heat two-thirds of the butter and oil in a large, heavy-based frying pan. Add the onion, garlic, celery, red pepper, mushrooms and herbs. Sauté until just softening (about 5 minutes). Transfer to a large oven-proof dish, with any juices from the pan.

Add the remaining third of the butter and oil to the pan and toss in the brinjal, marrows and tomatoes. Cook over a low heat for 10-15 minutes, until the marrow slices have softened and the tomatoes are reduced to a pulp. Tip the contents of the pan into the oven-proof dish.

Add salt, pepper, the bay leaves, parsley and sugar. Stir the ingredients until well mixed, then cover the dish securely with a lid or aluminium foil and then bake for about 30 minutes in the pre-heated oven.

Remove the oven-proof dish from the oven, uncover and take out the bay leaves. All the vegetables should have become soft and juicy but there should not be an excess of liquid.

Drizzle over the sour cream, and sprinkle the cheese evenly over the top. Dust with paprika and return to the oven for about 10 minutes, or until the cheese has melted.

VARIATION Omit the cheese and serve this vegetable medley as an accompaniment to grilled steak or fish.

GREEK SALAD

An OLD FAVOURITE on many restaurant menus, this traditional Greek dish offers a fresh and tasty combination of ingredients dominated by the sharp taste of feta cheese and olives.

PREPARATION TIME: 20 MINUTES

INGREDIENTS FOR SIX

1 lettuce
2-3 medium-sized tomatoes, cut into wedges
½ cucumber, sliced
1 large onion, peeled and thinly sliced*
1 green pepper, sliced
6 radishes, sliced
1 tin (400 g) artichoke hearts, drained and quartered (optional)
125 g ripe black olives
100 g feta cheese, cubed
2 ml (½ teaspoon) origanum
125 ml (½ cup) garlic dressing*

Place the rinsed, well-drained lettuce leaves in a salad bowl. Add the remaining prepared vegetables. Top with the cheese and sprinkle with the origanum. Toss in the dressing at the table, or just before serving.

SALAD NICOISE

THE SIMPLE INGREDIENTS that go into this delightful salad make it an ideal lunch dish for a hot day. Follow tradition by serving it with a light, dry, white wine and crusty French bread.

PREPARATION TIME: 30 MINUTES

INGREDIENTS FOR SIX

500 g green beans, trimmed, washed and dried
1 butter lettuce, washed and patted dry
1 medium-sized onion, peeled and finely sliced*
3 ripe medium-sized tomatoes, cut into wedges
125 ml (½ cup) black olives
1 tin (55 g) anchovy fillets, drained
2 tins (200 g each) tuna, drained and broken into chunks
2 hard-boiled eggs*, sliced
10 ml (2 teaspoons) chopped parsley

For the salad dressing:
125 ml (½ cup) olive oil
60 ml (¼ cup) sunflower oil
60 ml (¼ cup) red wine vinegar
1 clove garlic (optional)
Salt and freshly ground black pepper

Blanch* the beans for 4 minutes in rapidly boiling water and then immediately cool under cold running water. Drain and reserve.

Arrange the lettuce leaves on a large, round platter. Overlap them with the beans, onion rings, tomato wedges, olives, anchovies, tuna and hard-boiled eggs. Sprinkle with the chopped parsley.

To make the salad dressing, blend the oils, vinegar, garlic (if used), salt and pepper in a liquidizer (or beat thoroughly) and pour over the salad.

SALAD NICOISE *A light, simple salad for a hot summer's day.*

VEGETABLE CASSEROLE

THIS CASSEROLE is particularly suitable for a cold winter's evening around the fireside. It is equally tasty baked into a hot and nutritious pie.

PREPARATION TIME: 30 MINUTES
COOKING TIME: 1 HOUR
PRE-HEAT OVEN TO 180°C

INGREDIENTS FOR SIX

225 g green beans, trimmed, washed and cut into 2,5 cm pieces
2 medium-sized carrots, thinly sliced
2 sticks celery, sliced
½ medium-sized cauliflower, separated into florets
½ green or red pepper, cut into thin strips
2 baby marrows, thinly sliced
225 g shelled peas or 250 g frozen peas
1 medium-sized onion, peeled and sliced*
2 medium-sized tomatoes, skinned* and cut into wedges
150 ml vegetable stock*
30 ml (2 tablespoons) olive oil
2 cloves garlic, crushed
5 ml (1 teaspoon) salt
1 bay leaf
5 ml (1 teaspoon) basil
60 ml (¼ cup) grated Parmesan cheese
15 ml (1 tablespoon) finely chopped parsley

Layer all the vegetables in an oven-proof dish. Heat the stock with the olive oil, garlic, salt, bay leaf and basil. When the liquid boils, pour it over the vegetables. Cover the dish and bake for 1 hour. Sprinkle over the Parmesan cheese and the finely chopped parsley, and then serve the casserole immediately.

VARIATION Make the recipe into a vegetable pie by cooking the vegetables as above but using Cheddar cheese instead of Parmesan and covering with puff pastry*. Cut a slit in the pastry to allow the steam to escape and brush with a little beaten egg or milk. Bake at 200°C for about 15 minutes, or until the pastry is puffed and golden.

Pasta, Rice and Cereals

THE ROMAN GODDESS of agriculture, Ceres, gave her name to cereal, the edible grains that form the staple food of most of the world. But domestic use of cereal pre-dates the Romans by a few millenia – people have been eating grains for at least 8 000 years.

The staple cereal of more than half the world's population is rice, of which there are several varieties. Its wide availability has led to the development of countless regional and national ways of cooking it. South Africa has its own distinctive yellow rice dish, but has also taken over many other national favourites, such as creamy Italian risottos, Chinese fried rice and Indian pilaffs.

Although rice, like pasta, forms the basis of many hearty meal-in-one family dishes, it is often served as a side dish. Rice and pasta, both rich in carbohydrates, make tasty, substantial salads too.

Noodles, made from flour and water (sometimes with eggs added), have probably been around in most cultures for as long as people have been making flour from grains. Marco Polo returned to Italy from his expedition to China at the beginning of the 14th century with appetising tales of the various noodle dishes he had eaten there. By that time, pasta in many shapes was already the staple food in his home country, and today the wide variety of Italian pasta types with their delicious sauces and stuffings have become firmly ensconced in international cuisine.

Most of the grain recipes in this country were brought here by early immigrants, but no South African cookbook would be complete without recipes for the traditional grain staples of the sub-continent: samp and mealie meal porridge, which have been eaten locally for centuries.

THE ART OF COOKING PASTA, RICE AND CEREALS · *PAGE 214*

PASTA, RICE AND CEREAL RECIPES · *PAGE 216*

SPECIAL FEATURE
RIJSTTAFEL – EXOTIC MÉLANGE OF RICE AND SPICE · *PAGE 220*

The Art of Cooking Pasta, Rice and Cereals

Pasta or rice can supply the starchy part of a main course in place of potatoes, dumplings or pastry.

Pasta

Pasta simply means the paste or dough from which Italian noodles are made. The basis of pasta is flour from hard durum wheat, which grows particularly well in Italy. The flour is mixed with oil and water, and sometimes spinach purée and egg are added. The pasta is then moulded into various shapes and dried before being sold.

The commonest shapes are long threads (spaghetti and vermicelli), tubes (macaroni), narrow strips (tagliatelle) and sheets (lasagne). Pasta is also moulded into broad ribbons, short thin threads, butterflies, shells and several other fancy shapes.

Cooked pasta can be served as a simple side dish, tossed with a light coating of butter or olive oil, or can be made into a composite dish such as lasagne*.

But the most common way is to serve the cooked pasta with any one of an almost endless variety of special accompanying sauces. These sauces are mostly tomato-based, such as Napolitana sauce* (a simple, home-made tomato sauce flavoured with herbs) or Bolognese sauce* (tomatoes and meat). Cream is also a popular base for a pasta sauce.

Grated Parmesan cheese is an almost indispensible part of most pasta meals; use it for sprinkling over the top, or incorporate it into your sauce.

Cooking pasta

Allow 75-125 g uncooked pasta for each person. All pasta is boiled, but cooking time depends on size and freshness. Pasta should be just firm to the bite, or *al dente* as the Italians say.

For every 100-125 g pasta use 1 litre (4 cups) water and 10 ml (2 teaspoons) salt. Bring the water to the boil in a large saucepan, add the salt and put in the pasta. Do not break up the long strands of spaghetti, but hold them at one end and curl the strands gradually into the boiling water as they soften. Cook the pasta at a steady boil, uncovered, until just tender. Drain thoroughly in a colander and return to the pan with a large knob of butter or 15 ml (1 tablespoon) sunflower oil. Season with salt and pepper, and toss the pasta until it is well coated with the butter or oil.

Making Home-Made Pasta

Although a large variety of pasta is available pre-packed, it is much tastier if made at home.

These basic recipes are for making pasta by hand or with a pasta-making machine, and can be varied easily.

Basic pasta

Preparation Time: 45 minutes-1 hour
Resting Time: 30 minutes
Cooking Time: 3-5 minutes

Ingredients for Four to Six, or to Yield 400 g

240 g flour
5 ml (1 teaspoon) salt
2 eggs, lightly beaten
60 ml (¼ cup) warm water

To mix by hand, sift the flour and salt into a bowl. Lightly beat the eggs and water together, and pour into the middle of the flour. Mix together, then knead to make a stiff dough. Wrap well with plastic wrap and allow to rest for 30 minutes before rolling.

To mix in a food processor, place the flour and salt in the bowl of the food processor, and spin around to aerate. Add the eggs through the funnel and process together. Then gradually pour in the water and process until well mixed. If the dough seems to need it, add a little more water, but add it drop by drop as it is easier to work with the dough if it is slightly dry. Wrap well and leave to rest for 30 minutes.

To roll out the pasta by hand, work with a small amount at a time. Divide the dough into 4 pieces and keep each piece well wrapped in plastic wrap or a damp tea towel. Roll out one piece very thinly, then roll up loosely like a Swiss roll, and cut across to form ribbons of noodles. Repeat with the other pieces.

To roll out the pasta in a machine, divide the pasta into 4 pieces. Roughly flatten each piece into a square. Set aside 3 pieces and keep them well wrapped in plastic wrap or a damp tea towel. Flour the unwrapped piece of dough and pass it through the plain rollers of the machine, opened to the widest setting. It will come out in a roughly rectangular shape.

Tuck in any ragged edges and fold in 3 like a letter. Put through the machine again and repeat until you have a smooth sheet of dough. (Should the dough tear, flour it before putting it through the machine again.) Place the smooth sheet of dough between clean tea towels and repeat the process with the remaining 3 pieces of dough.

Turn the knob on the side of the machine down a notch, to bring the rollers a little closer together. Do not fold the sheets of dough, but now simply pass them through the machine, adjusting the setting each time to bring the rollers closer together.

When the sheet becomes too long to handle, cut it in half. Then pass each half through the machine until the narrowest setting is reached so that it is very thin. Place the sheets of dough on floured tea towels for about 10 minutes, just long enough to dry out the dough so that it will pass through the cutting blades easily. Do not allow the sheets of dough to become too dry, or they will be too brittle.

Pass the sheets through the blades, then dust the strands with flour to prevent them from sticking together.

You can cook the pasta ribbons fresh, or allow them to dry out, well separated, on tea towels so that they do not stick together during cooking. You can also freeze the pasta, well dusted with flour, in plastic bags.

Cook the pasta in a large, uncovered saucepan of salted boiling water. Home-made pasta cooks very quickly. Within a matter of minutes it will float to the top and be ready.

Drain very well and toss the noodles in a little best-quality oil or melted butter. Serve immediately with a suitable sauce (see the recipe section that follows for suggestions).

Spinach pasta

Spinach pasta is particularly tasty with cream-based sauces. The green mixture is also used for making lasagne noodles.

Use the basic recipe, substituting 100 g spinach leaves for one of the eggs.

Wash the spinach very well and remove any tough stalks and ribs. Cook the wet leaves in a heavy-based or non-stick saucepan until wilted.

Drain and rinse under cold running water. As soon as the spinach is cool enough to handle, squeeze out the excess moisture by hand. Chop and purée the spinach.

Follow the method for basic pasta and add the spinach at the same time as you add the egg.

Lasagne noodles

Use the spinach pasta recipe and cut the rolled-out sheets of pasta into squares. Cook in plenty of salted boiling water and drain well, separating the noodles on tea towels to prevent sticking. Use the noodles for the classic baked lasagne*.

Cannelloni cases
Use the basic pasta recipe and cut the rolled-out sheets of pasta into 12 cm squares. Cook until barely tender and drain well, separating the squares on tea towels to prevent sticking. These are then wrapped around a filling, covered with sauce and baked (see the recipe section that follows).

Ravioli
Ravioli are small pasta 'parcels' containing a filling of meat or spinach and cheese (see the recipe section for making the filling). For the pasta use the basic recipe. Divide the dough in 2, roll out into sheets and trim them to the same size. Place tiny spoonfuls of filling on one of the sheets at 5 cm intervals, leaving a 2,5 cm margin around the edge of the pasta.

Brush the dough with water around the spoonfuls of filling. Carefully place the second sheet of dough on top. Press it down well between the heaps of filling, so that the 2 sheets of dough stick together.

Cut between the rows of filling into neat squares. Place them well apart on floured tea towels until you cook them.

RICE

There are several kinds of rice. Polished rice is usually white, while unpolished rice (from which the bran has not been removed) is brown. Wild rice, grey-brown in colour, has a nutty taste and is the seed of an aquatic grass, not a grain. For savoury dishes, long-grain rice is best. Round-grain rice is suitable for risottos and puddings.

Cooking plain boiled rice
Allow 50-60 g uncooked rice for each person. Put the rice in a fine sieve and wash well in plenty of cold running water. Drain and put in a pan. Pour in enough cold water to cover the rice by 2,5 cm. Add salt to taste and cover the pan. Bring to the boil, stirring occasionally, and simmer undisturbed for 10-12 minutes, or until all the water is absorbed. Remove from the heat and leave, covered, for 10-12 minutes. The rice should be dry and fluffy.

Alternatively, measure out the rice in cups (200 g = 1 cup), and put into a sieve to wash under cold water. For each cup of rice allow 500 ml (2 cups) water. One cup of uncooked rice is enough for 4 servings.

Cooking yellow rice
Heat 40 g butter and 25 ml (5 teaspoons) sunflower oil, and add 200 g long-grain rice. Cook, stirring constantly, for about 10 minutes, or until transparent. While the rice is cooking, mix the following ingredients in 750 ml (3 cups) boiling water: 10 ml (2 teaspoons) turmeric, 5 ml (1 teaspoon) salt, 10 ml (2 teaspoons) sugar.

Pour this mixture on to the rice when it has become transparent, mix well with a fork, cover the pan lightly and turn the heat to low. After 15 minutes, scatter 125 ml (½ cup) seedless raisins on top of the rice. Cover the pan again and cook for 10-15 minutes more, or until all the water has been absorbed. Then lightly stir the rice and raisins together.

Instead of cooking on top of the stove, the rice and boiling water mixture can be cooked in a casserole in a 160°C oven for about 1 hour, or until the water has been absorbed. The raisins should be added 15 minutes before the end of the cooking time.

CEREALS

Cereal grains have been the essential staples of every civilisation. Whole grains are increasingly recommended by doctors and nutritionists as they are the source of many of our basic dietary requirements. Apart from rice, some of the most popular cereals are:

Maize (or mealies as we know it) was the staple food of the Incas and Aztecs and is the only cereal grain native to the Americas. Since its introduction to Europe, maize has travelled widely and is now grown all over the world. It can be used, ground into meal, in porridge, puddings, muffins and bread. Mealie kernels that have been stamped and broken into smaller pieces, known as samp or stampmealies, are a staple of the indigenous people of South Africa, who often cook samp with beans. Mealie rice is similar, although finer, and is used as a substitute for rice.

Millet, sorghum or *maltabella* is indigenous to Africa. It has a malty flavour and is used for making porridge, or ground into a flour that is used for making flat breads and griddle cakes.

Oats are an important breakfast food. Higher in protein and oil than other grains, oats are used to make porridge, biscuits, crunchies and bread. Whole oats from which the hulls have been removed – known as groats – were used for making porridge before the advent of quick-cooking oats (which are steamed and flaked by the packagers). Although groats are no longer widely available, they are still used in dishes such as kasha.

Sago and *tapioca* are starchy pellets that are very similar to one another. Sago starch comes from the stem of an Asian palm, while tapioca is derived from the root of the cassava plant.

Wheat has been the principal cereal grain of Europe and the Near East for thousands of years and is high in gluten-forming protein. Wheat is the principal grain from which bread flour is milled. A hard variety, durum wheat, is used for making pasta.

Pearl wheat is the whole grain from which some of the bran has been removed to allow better penetration of water, so that the wheat can be cooked and eaten in a similar way to rice. Cracked wheat has been milled in such a way that the whole grain is broken but the kernel is left intact, whereas crushed wheat is similarly milled into finer pieces. Semolina is also a wheat product, consisting of the hard part of the wheat, sifted out and used in its fine form or made into pellets known as couscous.

Crushed wheat, thin mealie meal, or sorghum porridge
To make any of these for six people, bring 1,5 litres (6 cups) water to the boil and add 300 g crushed wheat, thin mealie meal or sorghum. Simmer for about 15 minutes, stirring occasionally. Add 2 ml (½ teaspoon) of both salt and sugar. Serve with cream or milk.

Prunes which have been soaked overnight may be stirred into the porridge. Stewed apple or soaked dried fruit may be used, and cinnamon may be sprinkled on top of the porridge.

Oatmeal porridge
To make oatmeal porridge for six people, mix 250 g rolled oats or oatmeal in 250 ml (1 cup) cold water. Stir, then add 2 ml (½ teaspoon) salt and 625 ml (2½ cups) hot water. Bring to the boil, stirring occasionally. Cover and simmer for 20-30 minutes. When the porridge is cooked, pour in a little milk and a small piece of butter. Add honey to taste.

Fresh or stewed fruit, chopped nuts, wheat-germ and bran may be added.

Stywe pap
Stywe pap, also known as 'krummel pap' and 'putu', is a traditional South African dish that allows no half-measures – you either hate it or love it! To make stywe pap for six people, pour 300 g coarsely ground mealie meal and 2 ml (½ teaspoon) salt into a pot containing 750 ml (3 cups) boiling water, and stir well. Cover and turn the heat down to its lowest setting. After 20-30 minutes, turn off the heat and allow the mixture to cool slowly on the hot plate – about 20 minutes.

Serve with milk and sugar, or alternatively sugar and a lump of butter.

Cooking mealie rice
To cook enough mealie rice for six people, soak 250 g mealie rice overnight in 750 ml (3 cups) water. Rinse well, then add 750 ml (3 cups) water and bring to the boil. Turn the heat down to the lowest setting, cover the pan and cook for about 45 minutes, or until soft. Add salt to taste.

Mealie rice can be treated as rice and used with casseroles and stews.

It can also be eaten as a dessert – made like rice pudding.

Cooking pearl wheat
To cook pearl wheat for six, bring 900 ml water to the boil and add 150 g pearl wheat and salt to taste. Cook, covered, on a medium heat for 45 minutes-1 hour, or until tender and dry.

Add it to a casserole when cooked, or serve instead of rice and potatoes.

Use it as a salad with green peppers, onion, tomatoes and vinaigrette*.

PASTA, RICE AND CEREALS

CANNELLONI

SHEETS OF PASTA (or pancakes) are filled with a meat and spinach mixture, then baked with a tomato and béchamel sauce until hot and bubbly.

PREPARATION TIME: 3 HOURS
COOKING TIME: 20-30 MINUTES
PRE-HEAT OVEN TO 190°C

INGREDIENTS FOR SIX

1 small onion, peeled and finely chopped*
30 ml (2 tablespoons) sunflower oil
2 large cloves garlic, crushed
250 g frozen spinach, chopped
300 g lean beef, finely minced
Salt and freshly ground pepper
60 ml (¼ cup) freshly grated Parmesan cheese
30 ml (2 tablespoons) cream (optional)
2 eggs, lightly beaten
5 ml (1 teaspoon) dried origanum
12 cooked home-made cannelloni cases* (using 200 g basic pasta), or 12 pancakes* (lightly cooked on one side only)
375 ml (1½ cups) Napolitana sauce*
375 ml (1½ cups) béchamel sauce*
15 g butter

Gently fry the onion in half the oil until softened, but not browned. Stir in the garlic and spinach over a high heat until all the moisture has evaporated, then remove the contents from the saucepan.

Add the rest of the oil to the pan and stir in the minced beef. While cooking, stir continually to prevent lumps forming. Once the mince is lightly browned, stir in the spinach mixture and allow to cool slightly. Season to taste, then mix with half the Parmesan, the cream (if used) and eggs. Add the origanum and check seasoning.

Divide this filling between the cannelloni cases or pancakes (placing it on the cooked sides of the pancakes), then roll them up to form tubes. Pour a little of the strained Napolitana sauce over the bottom of an oblong oven-proof dish. Place the rolled-up pasta or pancakes on top. Cover with the béchamel sauce, then with the rest of the Napolitana sauce. Sprinkle with the rest of the Parmesan and dot with the butter. Bake for 20-30 minutes.

PASTITSIO *Easy to prepare, this traditional Greek dish comprises layers of noodles, meat and a rich cheese sauce.*

PASTITSIO

THIS GREEK NOODLE dish is guaranteed to become a firm family favourite. It also makes an excellent party dish. Be generous with freshly grated Parmesan cheese in the cheese sauce, and serve simply with a Greek salad*.

PREPARATION TIME: 1 HOUR
COOKING TIME: 1 HOUR
PRE-HEAT OVEN TO 190°C

INGREDIENTS FOR SIX TO EIGHT

1 large onion, peeled and chopped*
30 ml (2 tablespoons) sunflower oil
1 clove garlic, crushed
750 g lean beef mince
60 ml (¼ cup) beef basic stock*
1 tin (410 g) tomatoes
125 ml (½ cup) dry red wine
1 cinnamon stick
1 bay leaf
15 ml (1 tablespoon) chopped parsley
5 ml (1 teaspoon) dried origanum
Salt and freshly ground black pepper
500 g macaroni, halved and cooked*
750 ml (3 cups) cheese sauce*, using all Parmesan cheese or 50 g Parmesan and 50 g Cheddar
45 ml (3 tablespoons) grated Parmesan cheese

Gently fry the onion in the heated oil. Stir in the garlic, then add the beef mince, stirring all the time, until the meat has changed colour.

Add the stock, the chopped tomatoes, the juice from the tin and the wine. Stir this mixture until it comes to the boil. Then reduce the heat and simmer it very gently with the spices, herbs and seasoning. Allow the mixture to cook for about 45 minutes, or until it is very tender. Check the seasoning.

To assemble, mix the drained, cooked macaroni with the meat sauce. Turn into a large, oiled oven-proof dish.

Cover the mixture with the prepared cheese sauce and sprinkle over the grated Parmesan cheese.

Bake for 45 minutes, or until the surface is golden. After removing from the oven, allow the dish to stand for about 5-10 minutes before cutting into squares for serving.

VARIATION Use 750 g (2 large) brinjals, cubed, instead of the lean beef mince. Add more sunflower oil, if necessary, to sauté the brinjals. Cook gently until tender.

RAVIOLI

Squares of home-made pasta are filled with a meat, cheese and spinach mixture, cooked until tender and then served with Napolitana sauce.

PREPARATION TIME: 2¼ HOURS
STANDING TIME: 30 MINUTES FOR THE PASTA
COOKING TIME: 10 MINUTES

INGREDIENTS FOR SIX
15 g butter
1 small onion, peeled and finely chopped*
250 g veal, finely minced
250 g frozen spinach, chopped
2 eggs, lightly beaten
60 ml (¼ cup) freshly grated Parmesan cheese
Freshly grated nutmeg
Salt and freshly ground pepper
400 g home-made pasta*, rolled into sheets
750 ml (3 cups) Napolitana sauce*
Parmesan cheese for sprinkling

Heat the butter and add the onion. Cook gently until softened but not browned. Stir in the veal until it changes colour.

Cook the spinach separately over a high heat, stirring continually, until all the moisture evaporates.

Mix the meat mixture with the spinach, eggs and 60 ml Parmesan cheese. Add the nutmeg and season to taste.

Make and fill the ravioli*.

Drop the ravioli squares into a large saucepan of boiling, salted water and cook for about 10 minutes until tender. Drain well, and serve with the Napolitana sauce and a sprinkling of Parmesan.

VARIATION Instead of the veal, mix in 300 g ricotta or chunky cream cheese. You can serve this ravioli with Napolitana sauce or heat 60 g butter with 180 ml cream and 5 ml (1 teaspoon) dried sage.

SPAGHETTI WITH BOLOGNESE SAUCE

This is an excellent recipe for one of the most popular spaghetti sauces. A vital step is the slow simmering of the sauce, which helps to bring out the full flavour of all the ingredients.

PREPARATION TIME: 20 MINUTES
COOKING TIME: 1 HOUR

INGREDIENTS FOR SIX,
OR TO YIELD 1,25 LITRES (5 CUPS)
125 g smoked ham, chopped (optional)
1 large onion, peeled and chopped*
1 medium-sized carrot, scraped and chopped
2 sticks celery, chopped
45 ml (3 tablespoons) sunflower or olive oil
500 g lean beef mince
125 ml (½ cup) dry white wine
375 ml (1½ cups) beef basic stock*
30 ml (2 tablespoons) tomato paste
1 clove garlic, crushed
125 ml (½ cup) cream (optional)
250 g chicken livers (optional), sautéed in 15 g butter and roughly chopped
Freshly grated nutmeg
Salt and freshly ground black pepper
500 g spaghetti
Chopped parsley for garnish
Grated Parmesan cheese for sprinkling

To make the sauce, chop the ham (if used) and vegetables together very finely. Fry gently in a heavy saucepan in half the oil until softened, though barely browned.

Remove the mixture, add the rest of the oil, then the minced beef, and cook over a medium heat, stirring all the time to prevent lumps.

Add the wine and increase the heat. Allow to boil, and keep on stirring until the liquid has almost evaporated.

Mix in the softened vegetables, stock, tomato paste and garlic. Bring to the boil, then reduce the heat and simmer, half-covered, for 45 minutes – stirring from time to time.

If you are using cream, add it while the dish is simmering. You can also add the chicken livers (if used) at the simmering stage. Add nutmeg and season to taste.

Towards the end of the cooking time for the sauce, cook* the spaghetti. Drain well and sprinkle with the parsley.

Serve the sauce over the spaghetti and pass around grated Parmesan cheese for sprinkling over individual servings.

LASAGNE

Lasagne makes a useful family meal as it can be assembled well in advance and baked just before serving. It is a dish that is often mediocre but if properly prepared it can be delicious. It is advisable to use home-made or imported pre-cooked squares of pasta.

PREPARATION TIME: 2 HOURS
COOKING TIME: 40 MINUTES
PRE-HEAT OVEN TO 180°C

INGREDIENTS FOR SIX TO EIGHT
250 g lasagne sheets*, cooked
500 ml (2 cups) Bolognese sauce*
500 ml (2 cups) cheese sauce*
60 ml (¼ cup) freshly grated Parmesan cheese

Arrange one-third of the lasagne sheets in the bottom of a lightly oiled, oblong ovenproof dish. Spread with one-third of the Bolognese sauce and cover with one-third of the cheese sauce. Repeat this process twice more, ending with the cheese sauce.

Sprinkle over the grated Parmesan and bake for 30-40 minutes, or until golden. Leave the lasagne to stand at room temperature for 5-10 minutes before cutting into squares.

SERVING SUGGESTION Being a rich dish, lasagne needs only a green salad* as an accompaniment.

VARIATIONS Instead of the meat sauce, layer it with 750 ml (3 cups) Napolitana sauce* and then add a layer of sautéed sliced mushrooms, or drained flaked tuna, or cooked fish.

SPAGHETTI WITH PESTO SAUCE

When basil is in season, this fragrant, unforgettable sauce is an absolute must to accompany your pasta.

PREPARATION TIME: 20 MINUTES
COOKING TIME: 15 MINUTES

INGREDIENTS FOR FOUR TO SIX
500 g spaghetti, cooked*
375 ml (1½ cups) fresh basil leaves
2 cloves garlic
60 ml (¼ cup) olive oil
125 ml (½ cup) sunflower oil
30-60 ml (2-4 tablespoons) pine nuts
100 g freshly grated Parmesan cheese
Salt and freshly ground pepper

While cooking the spaghetti, purée the other ingredients in a food processor. If the sauce seems too thick, thin it down with more oil. The sauce should be thin enough to run off a spoon.

You can also thin down the pesto by adding 15 ml (1 tablespoon) of the hot spaghetti water before tossing the pesto with the well-drained, hot spaghetti. Serve immediately.

VARIATION You can use walnuts instead of pine nuts.

SPAGHETTI ALLA CARBONARA

A quickly prepared, delicious pasta dish flavoured with eggs, bacon and cream makes for a very filling lunch or supper. This dish is best served simply with a fresh green salad*.

PREPARATION TIME: 25 MINUTES
COOKING TIME: 10 MINUTES

INGREDIENTS FOR FOUR TO SIX
15 ml (1 tablespoon) olive oil
15 g butter
250 g rindless streaky bacon, diced
6 egg yolks
125 ml (½ cup) cream
500 g spaghetti, cooked*
150 g freshly grated Parmesan cheese
Salt and freshly ground pepper

Heat the oil and butter in a frying pan, and add the diced streaky bacon. Cook gently for about 5 minutes. Beat the egg yolks and cream together.

Drain the cooked spaghetti well, then mix it with the hot, cooked bacon, together with the fat from the pan. Mix in the egg and cream mixture, and add the grated Parmesan. Season the mixture and then serve immediately.

VARIATION Mix the sauce with other pasta – spaghettini, tagliatelle or fettucine.

PASTA, RICE AND CEREALS

Spaghetti Alla Vongole

Vongole in Rome, *capperozzoli* in Venice, *arselle* in Genoa and *telline* in Florence: all mean exactly the same thing – the small clams that are used throughout Italy to make soup or sauce for a variety of pasta dishes.

In South Africa, the dish is generally made with tinned mussels, although clams are available. Ensure that the clams or mussels are not preserved in vinegar nor smoked and preserved in oil; this can ruin the fine flavour of the sauce.

PREPARATION TIME: 10 MINUTES
COOKING TIME: 40 MINUTES

INGREDIENTS FOR FOUR

75 g butter
1 large onion, peeled and chopped*
2 cloves garlic, crushed
700 g (2-3 large) tomatoes, skinned and seeded*, or 1 tin (410 g) tomatoes
1 ml (¼ teaspoon) each dried basil and thyme
A good pinch of peperoncino (dried chilli pepper) or cayenne pepper, or a few drops of Tabasco (chilli sauce)
450 g spaghetti
1 tin (290 g) clams or black mussels
Salt (optional)

Melt 50 g of the butter in a large saucepan and fry the onion until soft (about 15 minutes). Lower the heat, stir in the garlic and cook for 2 minutes.

Add the tomatoes with any juice, and the herbs. Cook for a further 10-15 minutes, then stir in the pepper or Tabasco. Keep the sauce on a low heat, stirring occasionally, while you cook* the spaghetti.

When the spaghetti is almost ready, add the drained clams or black mussels to the tomato sauce and heat this mixture through gently.

To serve, drain the spaghetti in a colander and pile it into a serving bowl. Add the remaining butter and toss the spaghetti in it.

Taste the sauce, add salt if necessary, and serve separately.

SERVING SUGGESTION Serve a green salad* before or after this dish.

Spaghetti Napolitana

This is the familiar Italian dish of a fresh tomato sauce served over hot, well-drained spaghetti with a generous grating of Parmesan cheese and a grinding of black pepper. The dish lends itself well to a number of delicious variations.

PREPARATION TIME: 20 MINUTES
COOKING TIME: 1¼ HOURS

INGREDIENTS FOR SIX

500 ml (2 cups) Napolitana sauce*
1 tin (410 g) tomato purée
500 g spaghetti
100 g Parmesan cheese, grated
Chopped fresh parsley or basil for garnish

Prepare the Napolitana sauce, adding the tomato purée with the tomatoes and cooking for an extra 15 minutes. Towards the end of the cooking time for the sauce, cook* the spaghetti and drain it well.

Serve the pasta with the sauce, sprinkling each serving with grated Parmesan and chopped parsley or basil.

SERVING SUGGESTIONS Alternatively, you can serve the sauce or any of its variations over any kind of noodle (the broad tagliatelle noodles are particularly good).

VARIATIONS For a smoother sauce, press through a sieve or purée in a liquidizer or blender.

Add 125 ml (½ cup) cream to the sauce towards the end of the cooking time.

Add 1 tin (290 g) drained clams or mussels (in salt water, not smoked) to the sauce.

Add 500 g brinjal (1 large or 2 medium-sized), cubed and sautéed in sunflower oil, to the completed sauce.

Add 300 g mushrooms, sliced and sautéed in butter.

Add 250 ml (1 cup) cooked and mashed soya beans, or 1 tin (300 g) soya beans, drained and mashed.

Add 1 tin (200 g) drained, flaked tuna.

SPAGHETTI NAPOLITANA *One of Italy's most popular pasta dishes.*

Fettucine with Tuna, Mushroom, Tomato and Onion Sauce

This dish is quick and easy to prepare, and makes a filling supper followed by a tossed green salad*.

PREPARATION TIME: 30 MINUTES
COOKING TIME: 20-30 MINUTES

INGREDIENTS FOR SIX

2 medium-sized onions, peeled and thinly sliced*
30 g butter
30 ml (2 tablespoons) sunflower oil
1 clove garlic, crushed
300 g mushrooms, washed and sliced
1 large tin (825 g) tomatoes
15 ml (1 tablespoon) chopped parsley
5 ml (1 teaspoon) dried origanum
Salt and freshly ground black pepper
1 tin (200 g) tuna, drained
12 black olives
500 g fettucine, cooked*

For the garnish:
Chopped parsley
125 ml (½ cup) grated cheese (optional)

Gently sauté the sliced onions in the hot butter and oil until softened. Stir in the garlic, then the mushroom slices. Stir-fry over a brisk heat for about 5 minutes.

Chop the tomatoes and add them to the mixture, together with the juice from the tin, the herbs and seasoning. Simmer, uncovered, stirring occasionally, until the sauce is reduced and slightly thickened.

Add the tuna, broken into chunks, and the olives, and allow to heat through. Serve over hot, well-drained fettucine sprinkled with parsley and grated cheese (if used).

Noodle Salad

Pasta adds body to a salad, but because of its bland flavour it needs to be enriched with herbs and spices, and tossed with crunchy ingredients to provide a contrast in texture. This noodle salad is a combination of pasta, vegetables, fruit and nuts, bound with a creamy dressing.

PREPARATION TIME: 35 MINUTES
COOKING TIME: 30 MINUTES
CHILLING TIME: 4 HOURS

INGREDIENTS FOR SIX TO EIGHT
3 pineapple slices (fresh or tinned)
2 green apples, peeled and diced
30 ml (2 tablespoons) lemon juice
75 g seedless raisins
Boiling water
200 g egg noodles (preferably small elbow macaroni), cooked* and drained
30 ml (2 tablespoons) sunflower oil
1 stick celery, finely chopped
50-100 g hazelnuts, chopped
500 ml (2 cups) finely shredded cabbage
4 spring onions, trimmed and chopped
Salt and freshly ground pepper
Sugar

For the dressing:
125 ml (½ cup) thick mayonnaise*
125 ml (½ cup) sour cream (smetena)
5-10 ml (1-2 teaspoons) curry powder
30 ml (2 tablespoons) chutney

For the garnish:
Strips of tinned red pimento and/or sliced black olives
Shredded lettuce
Wedges of avocado and tomato

Dice the pineapple and dry on paper towels. Toss the diced apple in the lemon juice. Cover the raisins with boiling water, stand for 10 minutes, then drain.

Toss the noodles with the oil. Turn the mixture into a large bowl and add the pineapple, apple, raisins, celery, hazelnuts, cabbage and spring onions.

Mix the dressing ingredients and add to the salad, then season with salt, freshly ground black pepper and a little sugar. Cover the salad and refrigerate for at least 4 hours to allow the flavours to blend.

Pile the salad on to a large platter with the pimento and/or olives and surround it with shredded lettuce and wedges of avocado and tomato.

SERVING SUGGESTIONS Serve with a hot French loaf, or wholewheat bread*.

PASTA, RICE AND CEREALS

TAGLIATELLE WITH CREAM AND PARMESAN CHEESE

THIS SUBTLY FLAVOURED noodle dish is ideal for a lunch or supper that needs to be prepared at short notice. Rich and delicious, it is best complemented with a simple green salad*.

PREPARATION TIME: 10 MINUTES
COOKING TIME: 15 MINUTES

INGREDIENTS FOR FOUR TO SIX
500 g tagliatelle, cooked*
500 ml (2 cups) cream
80 g freshly grated Parmesan cheese
45 ml (3 tablespoons) chopped parsley
Freshly grated nutmeg
Salt and freshly ground black pepper

While cooking the tagliatelle, heat the cream, allowing it to reduce slightly. Mix the cream with the hot noodles, stir in the cheese, parsley and nutmeg, and then season to taste.

SERVING SUGGESTIONS If you like, pass around more Parmesan at the table.

VARIATION When simmering the cream, add 300 g button mushrooms, washed and thinly sliced.

BEEF CHOW MEIN

CHOW MEIN IS SURELY one of the best known of Chinese dishes. 'Chow' is the Chinese description for any stir-fried dish, while 'mein' means noodles. This recipe offers a delicious combination of tender beef, noodles and crisp vegetables, creating an interesting contrast in textures. It is advisable to put the beef in the freezer for about 30 minutes beforehand in order to make slicing easier.

PREPARATION TIME: 30 MINUTES
COOKING TIME: 15 MINUTES

INGREDIENTS FOR SIX
90 ml sunflower oil
500 g Chinese noodles (or egg noodles or spaghetti), cooked*
1 clove garlic, crushed
2 ml (½ teaspoon) grated fresh green ginger

BEEF CHOW MEIN *Stir-frying produces crisp vegetables and tender meat.*

100 g Chinese or ordinary cabbage, shredded, or table celery, sliced
3 spring onions, cut into 1 cm lengths
4 pieces tinned bamboo shoots, drained and cut into matchstick strips
500 g lean beef, shredded into matchstick strips and tossed with 15 ml (1 tablespoon) cornflour
75 g tinned black mushrooms, finely sliced
40 ml light soy sauce
30 ml (2 tablespoons) dry sherry
5 ml (1 teaspoon) sugar
Chopped spring onion for garnish

Stir 15 ml (1 tablespoon) of the oil into the cooked noodles and set aside.

Place a wok or heavy-based frying pan over a high heat and add 15 ml (1 tablespoon) of the oil. When the oil is hot, add the garlic, ginger, cabbage or celery, spring onions and bamboo shoots. Stir-fry the mixture for 2 minutes over a high heat, remove the mixture from the wok or pan and set aside.

Heat 30 ml (2 tablespoons) of the oil in the same wok or pan. When the oil is very hot, add the meat and mushrooms. Stir-fry for 1 minute, add the soy sauce, sherry and sugar, and stir-fry for another minute.

Remove the meat and mushrooms from the wok or pan (leaving the gravy behind) and set aside. Add the remaining 30 ml (2 tablespoons) oil to the gravy in the wok or pan, then add the drained noodles and stir-fry for 1½ minutes. When the noodles are heated through and browned all over by the gravy and oil, add half the meat and half the cooked vegetables. Stir-fry for 1 minute, then remove.

Place the remaining meat and vegetables in the wok or pan, warm through and combine with the noodle mixture. Transfer the noodle mixture to a heated shallow bowl. Garnish with the spring onion.

VARIATIONS Instead of beef, use boned chicken breasts, pork or shelled and de-veined prawns*.

~ RIJSTTAFEL – EXOTIC MÉLANGE OF RICE AND SPICE ~

The *rijsttafel* (Dutch for 'rice table') is a blend of Muslim, Hindu and Buddhist cuisine from the spice islands of Indonesia. The unique character of the *rijsttafel* stems not only from the variety of dishes offered but also from the clever and abundant use of spices.

MENU FOR EIGHT

Nasi Goreng
(Indonesian-style fried rice)

Udang Goreng Asam Manis
(sweet and sour prawns)

Ayam Kuning
(yellow chicken)

Satay Sapi Pedes
(hot beef satay)

Saus Kacang Tidak Pedes
(bland peanut sauce)

Sambal Goreng Terung
(peppery brinjal)
(optional)

Sambal Ketimum
(spicy cucumber)

Planning the meal

The following preparations can be made the day before you serve the *rijsttafel*:

Cook the rice for the nasi goreng and store it in the refrigerator. Measure and prepare all the other ingredients.

Make the sweet and sour sauce and refrigerate. Prepare vegetable garnishes and keep in a crisper.

Prepare and cook the yellow chicken and store, covered, in the refrigerator (the flavours develop and will be better the next day).

Prepare the skewered beef and place in the marinade covered with plastic wrap.

Prepare the peanut sauce.

HOW TO SET OUT A RIJSTTAFEL

The food
Rice
One or more dishes of meat, fish, chicken or egg
One or more vegetable dishes
One or more sauces or pickles
A bowl of fresh fruit

Setting the table
Knives are not used at a *rijsttafel*. Set a dessert spoon (right hand side) and two forks – one on either side of the dinner plate. A tall, frosty glass of beer is a popular accompaniment to the *rijsttafel*.

Arranging the food
A revolving tray (lazy Susan) simplifies the serving of the food. Place it in the middle of the table with the large bowl of rice in the centre and the other dishes and sauces around it.

Eating from the rijsttafel
Place a mound of rice in the middle of your plate and spoon small helpings from the dishes of your choice around the rice. Add sauces and pickles.

Quantities for recipes
As a generous rule, four people will eat well if the *rijsttafel* consists of rice (400 g), one chicken, one meat dish and one vegetable dish with sauces. For each additional couple, add an additional dish and a further 200 g rice.

NASI GORENG
PREPARATION TIME: 20 MINUTES
COOKING TIME: 30 MINUTES

800 g long-grain rice
2 litres (8 cups) water
20 ml (4 teaspoons) salt
2 chicken breasts, diced
50 ml sunflower oil
4 large onions, peeled and sliced*
4 cloves garlic, chopped
5 ml (1 teaspoon) ground coriander
5 ml (1 teaspoon) ground ginger
10 ml (2 teaspoons) anchovy paste (or pounded tinned anchovies), or shrimp paste
1-2 dried red chillies, crushed
50 ml soy sauce
200 g cooked shrimps or prawns
8 fried eggs or strips of omelette

Boil the rice in the water with the salt, and then allow to cool. Stir-fry the diced chicken breasts in the oil, add the onions and continue cooking over high heat until the onions brown.

Lower the heat and add the garlic, coriander, ginger, anchovy or shrimp paste and chillies. Sauté for 1 minute to develop the flavour in the spices. Add the soy sauce, shrimps (or prawns) and cooked rice.

Warm through while stirring all the time to prevent the rice from burning. Top the dish with fried eggs or strips of omelette.

UDANG GORENG ASAM MANIS
PREPARATION TIME: 40 MINUTES
COOKING TIME: 20 MINUTES

1 egg
30 ml (2 tablespoons) flour
12 medium-sized prawns, shelled, de-veined* and lightly salted
Sunflower oil for deep-frying

For the sweet and sour sauce:
10 ml (2 teaspoons) soy sauce
15 ml (1 tablespoon) cornflour mixed with 50 ml water
15 ml (1 tablespoon) tomato sauce*
50 ml vinegar
125 ml (½ cup) strong chicken stock*
40 g sugar
3 ml (¾ teaspoon) ground ginger
Salt and pepper

For the garnish:
Julienne* strips of carrot
Pieces of pineapple
Sweet green pepper strips

Mix the egg with the flour and dip the prawns in this batter. Deep-fry in the hot oil and then drain on a paper towel.

To make the sweet and sour sauce, bring all the ingredients except the salt and pepper to a gentle boil, stirring continuously. Taste and season with salt and pepper. Add the vegetables for garnish and pour the hot sauce over the prawns just before serving.

Ayam Kuning

Preparation Time: 20 minutes
Cooking Time: 1 hour

5 ml (1 teaspoon) ground coriander
3 ml (¾ teaspoon) ground ginger
10 ml (2 teaspoons) salt
1,5 kg chicken pieces
50 ml sunflower oil
10 ml (2 teaspoons) turmeric
1 medium-sized onion, peeled and sliced*
2 cloves garlic, chopped
5 ml (1 teaspoon) grated lemon rind
500 ml (2 cups) coconut milk
15 ml (1 tablespoon) lemon juice

Make a mixture of the coriander, ginger and salt. Rub it into the chicken pieces. Brown the chicken in the oil and then put on one side.
Add the turmeric, onion, garlic and lemon rind to the remaining oil in the pan. Sauté for 1 minute. Add the coconut milk and lemon juice, and stir to make a sauce.
Place the browned chicken portions in this sauce and simmer over a very gentle heat for 45 minutes, then serve.

VARIATION If fresh coconut milk is not available, pour boiling water over 80g desiccated coconut, allow to draw and squeeze out the liquid.

Satay Sapi Pedes

Preparation Time: 15 minutes
Marinating Time: at least 1 hour
Cooking Time: 5-10 minutes

500g boneless sirloin
1 small onion, peeled and chopped*
50 ml sunflower oil
5 ml (1 teaspoon) chilli sauce
30 ml (2 tablespoons) smooth peanut butter
5 ml (1 teaspoon) ground coriander
A pinch of ground ginger
30 ml (2 tablespoons) lemon juice

Cut the meat into small pieces (about 2 cm square). Sauté the onion in the oil until golden-brown. Remove the pan from the heat and set aside to cool. Mix the chilli sauce, peanut butter, coriander, ginger and lemon juice with the onions. Place the cubed meat in this mixture and marinate for at least 1 hour or overnight.
Thread the cubes of meat on fine bamboo skewers and grill quickly until just done.

Saus Kacang Tidak Pedes

Preparation Time: 10 minutes
Cooking Time: 10 minutes

45 ml (3 tablespoons) smooth peanut butter
125 ml (½ cup) water or plain drinking yoghurt
1 clove garlic, finely chopped
5 ml (1 teaspoon) anchovy paste (or pounded tinned anchovy), or shrimp paste
5 ml (1 teaspoon) brown sugar
15 ml (1 tablespoon) dark soy sauce
15 ml (1 tablespoon) lemon juice
5 ml (1 teaspoon) salt

Blend the peanut butter with the water or yoghurt over a medium heat until the mixture boils. Turn off the heat and add the rest of the ingredients. Serve luke-warm. This sauce is especially good with the skewered meat (satay).

Sambal Goreng Terung

Preparation Time: 15 minutes
Cooking Time: 15 minutes

2 medium-sized brinjals
5 ml (1 teaspoon) salt
15 ml (1 tablespoon) lemon juice
1 small onion, peeled and sliced*
30 ml (2 tablespoons) sunflower oil
5 ml (1 teaspoon) ground coriander
5 ml (1 teaspoon) brown sugar
1 dried red chilli, crushed
10 ml (2 teaspoons) anchovy paste

Slice the brinjals (with the skin) into 1 cm thick slices. Sprinkle with the salt and lemon juice.
Sauté the onion in the oil. Add the coriander, brown sugar, chilli and anchovy paste. Place the brinjal slices in this mixture, turn to coat and sauté for about 10 minutes in an open pan until cooked. A little water may be added to speed up the cooking and prevent burning. Be careful not to reduce the brinjal to a pulp.

Sambal Ketimum

Preparation Time: 10 minutes

1 large cucumber
½ dried red chilli, crushed
50 ml vinegar
5 ml (1 teaspoon) salt
50 ml water

Peel and slice the cucumber. Mix all the other ingredients together and add to the cucumber. Spicy cucumber is an important *rijsttafel* dish, as it cools the palate.

RICE SALAD

RICE, COOKED in a well-flavoured stock, is the basis of this tasty salad. Vinaigrette makes a tangy change from the more usual mayonnaise dressing.

PREPARATION TIME: 25 MINUTES

INGREDIENTS FOR FOUR
150 g rice, cooked* in 375 ml
   (1½ cups) chicken* or
   vegetable stock*
75 g stuffed olives, finely sliced
2 hard-boiled eggs*, diced
1½ sticks celery, finely sliced
1 dill pickle, chopped
½ small green pepper, chopped
1 small onion, peeled and finely
   chopped*
80 ml (⅓ cup) vinaigrette*

Put the rice in a medium-sized bowl and mix in the olives, eggs, celery, dill pickle, green pepper and onion. Pour over the dressing while the rice is still hot. Toss and set aside to cool.

SERVING SUGGESTION Serve on a bed of lettuce leaves surrounded with slices or wedges of tomato.

VARIATION Dress with mayonnaise*, using enough to bind all the ingredients together. Omit the hard-boiled eggs and add 75 g seedless raisins.

FRIED RICE

RICE IS AN ESSENTIAL accompaniment to most Oriental meals. This fried rice dish – cooked quickly in the Chinese manner – may also be served with many Western style roasts or stews.

PREPARATION TIME: 30 MINUTES
COOKING TIME: 10 MINUTES

INGREDIENTS FOR SIX
30 ml (2 tablespoons) sunflower oil
2 eggs, well beaten
200 g rice, cooked*
125 ml (½ cup) tiny frozen peas
   (petit pois)
125 ml (½ cup) mung bean
   sprouts
2 spring onions, sliced
15 ml (1 tablespoon) light soy
   sauce

Heat 15 ml (1 tablespoon) of the oil in a wok or heavy-based frying pan, add the beaten eggs and swirl them around in the pan until they are firm. Turn on to a board and, when slightly cooled, slice into thin strips and keep warm.

Heat the remaining oil in the pan, add the rice and fry gently. Add the peas, bean sprouts, spring onions and soy sauce, stir-fry briefly, then remove from the heat.

Pile the rice into a heated serving bowl and sprinkle the egg strips over the top.

VARIATION The egg yolks and whites may be cooked separately for a colourful mixed garnish of yellow and white.

SPINACH RICE

THIS IS A GREEK recipe that vegetarians could enjoy as a main course with a sprinkling of freshly grated Parmesan. It also makes a good accompaniment to roast lamb or lamb chops grilled with lemon juice and oil.

PREPARATION TIME: 15 MINUTES
COOKING TIME: 45 MINUTES

INGREDIENTS FOR SIX TO EIGHT
2 bunches (about 16) spring
   onions, chopped
60 ml (¼ cup) olive oil
900 g spinach leaves, blanched*
30 ml (2 tablespoons) chopped
   fresh dill, or 10 ml
   (2 teaspoons) dried dill
200 g rice
500 ml (2 cups) hot chicken*
   or vegetable stock*
Salt and freshly ground black
   pepper
Lemon wedges

Fry the spring onions very gently in the oil until they soften. Squeeze the excess moisture from the spinach leaves by hand, then chop them. Add the spinach to the softened onions and cook this mixture, stirring, for a few minutes. Add the dill and rice, and stir.

Pour in the stock and bring the mixture to the boil. Reduce the heat and simmer, tightly covered, for about 20 minutes. Remove the lid and continue to cook until the rice is tender and all the liquid has been absorbed. Season to taste. Serve the dish with lemon wedges to squeeze over it.

SAFFRON RICE

SAFFRON IS a highly prized (and expensive) spice that imparts a brilliant yellow colour and delicate flavour to a variety of dishes. This recipe is for a subtly flavoured rice dish which is sprinkled with cashew nuts fried in clarified butter.

PREPARATION TIME: 15 MINUTES
COOKING TIME: 45 MINUTES

INGREDIENTS FOR SIX
400 g rice (preferably basmati
   rice)
125 ml (½ cup) melted ghee*
30 ml (2 tablespoons) cashew
   nuts, halved
2 cinnamon sticks (about 5 cm
   each)
3 medium-sized onions, peeled
   and sliced*
7 ml (1½ teaspoons) salt
2 medium-sized carrots, scraped
   and grated
2 ml (½ teaspoon) saffron, soaked
   for 15 minutes in 125 ml
   (½ cup) warm milk
500 ml (2 cups) hot water

Sort and wash the rice several times, then allow to drain. Heat the ghee in a heavy-based saucepan and fry the cashew nuts in it until golden-brown. Remove the cashew nuts and set them aside.

Add the cinnamon to the ghee and brown for a few seconds, then place the onions in the pan and stir-fry for 5 minutes. Place the rice, salt, carrots and saffron (with milk) in the saucepan, and stir well. Add the hot water and cover the saucepan.

Simmer on a low heat for 20-30 minutes, or until the rice is tender. Stir with a fork, garnish with the nuts and serve warm.

SERVING SUGGESTIONS Saffron rice is admirably suited to the following dishes: prawn curry*, coastal Indian-style mussels* and kheema kebabs*.

CHICKEN PILAFF

PILAFFS ORIGINATE in north India. They are simple rice dishes with a base of chicken, red meat, fish or vegetables. Pilaffs add variety and interest to a plain menu and are easy to prepare. They can be frozen for up to two months.

PREPARATION TIME: 15-20 MINUTES
MARINATING TIME: 2 HOURS
COOKING TIME: 1¾ HOURS

INGREDIENTS FOR SIX
1,5 kg chicken pieces
A 5 cm piece of fresh green
   ginger, scraped
6 cloves garlic, peeled
5 ml (1 teaspoon) ground cumin
2 green chillies
15 ml (1 tablespoon) sunflower
   oil
7 ml (1½ teaspoons) salt
5 ml (1 teaspoon) turmeric
500 g rice
125 ml (½ cup) melted ghee*
   (or sunflower oil)
3 medium-sized onions, peeled
   and sliced*
2 medium-sized tomatoes,
   chopped
15 ml (1 tablespoon) coriander
   seeds, crushed
2 ml (½ teaspoon) chilli powder
4 sprigs coriander leaves, chopped

Wash the chicken pieces and pat them dry. Grind the ginger, garlic, cumin and green chillies to a paste (you could use a liquidizer). Add the sunflower oil, salt and turmeric to the paste, and rub well over the chicken. Leave the chicken to marinate for 2 hours.

Clean and wash the rice several times. Boil in salted water until just tender. Place the rice in a sieve and allow cold water to run through, then leave to drain.

Reserve 30 ml (2 tablespoons) of the ghee (or oil) and heat the rest in a large pot. Fry the onions until soft. Add the chicken pieces to the pot and cook, covered, for 10 minutes, then add the chopped tomatoes, the crushed coriander seeds and the chilli powder. Stir and cook, covered, for a further 5 minutes.

Add the rice to the pot and pour the reserved ghee (or oil) over the top. Sprinkle with the coriander leaves, cover the pot and simmer on a low heat for 1 hour 20 minutes. Stir well with a fork just before serving.

SERVING SUGGESTION Serve this pilaff with kachoomer* (salad) and red tomato chutney*.

VARIATION Use filleted fish such as kingklip in place of the chicken.

Pilaff with Lamb and Apricots

THIS PILAFF lends itself well to variations, and makes a good vehicle for leftovers, allowing you to use virtually any cooked and cubed meat or fish.

Preparation Time: 30 minutes
Cooking Time: 1½ hours

Ingredients for Six

15 ml (1 tablespoon) sunflower oil
2 large onions, peeled and sliced*
100 g butter
750 g lamb shoulder (or thick shoulder chops), boned and cut into 1 cm cubes
125 g dried apricots, coarsely chopped
400 ml beef basic* or chicken stock*
Salt and pepper
1 green pepper, seeded and coarsely chopped
2 cloves garlic, crushed
1-2 tomatoes, skinned*, seeded and chopped
60 ml (¼ cup) seedless raisins
100 g flaked almonds, lightly toasted*
400 g rice
1 litre (4 cups) water

Heat the oil in a large saucepan and sauté the sliced onions until golden. Transfer to a large bowl with a slotted spoon and add half the butter to the saucepan. Brown the lamb cubes over a fairly high heat in batches, transferring the meat to the bowl with a slotted spoon as it is browned. Do not overcook.

When all the meat is sufficiently browned, return it to the saucepan together with the onions, apricots and stock, and simmer (covered) for 1 hour, or until the meat is very tender. Season to taste with salt and pepper.

While the lamb is cooking, sauté the green pepper, garlic and tomatoes in the remaining butter for 4-5 minutes, and then stir in the raisins, almonds and rice.

Stir-fry for 2 minutes, or until the rice is slightly translucent, and add the water. Simmer for 10 minutes or so, until the water is absorbed. Season the rice to taste with salt and pepper.

Spread one-third of the rice mixture in an even layer in a large, oven-proof casserole and top with one-third of the lamb. Add another layer of rice and lamb, and continue until you have used up all the ingredients, ending with a layer of lamb (the rice layers should be fairly thick).

Cover and cook over a low heat until the rice is tender (about 20 minutes) and the dish is heated through.

Serving Suggestion Serve this lamb pilaff in the casserole in which it was cooked, accompanied only by a large bowl of natural yoghurt* and a cucumber salad with a mint dressing.

Mushroom Pilaff

MUSHROOMS FRIED with onions and spices provide an exquisite pilaff when combined with fried white rice. This dish makes a substantial and appetising meal or side dish.

Preparation Time: 15 minutes
Cooking Time: 35 minutes

Ingredients for Six

400 g rice
1 litre (4 cups) salted water
125 ml (½ cup) melted ghee* or butter
2 large onions, peeled and sliced*
5 ml (1 teaspoon) salt
2 cloves garlic, crushed
5 ml (1 teaspoon) cumin seeds, crushed
5 ml (1 teaspoon) coriander seeds, crushed
200 g button mushrooms, cut into quarters

Boil the rice in the salted water until just tender (about 12 minutes). Pour the rice into a sieve and allow cold water to run through, then set aside.

Heat half the ghee or butter in a heavy-based saucepan. Add the onions, salt, garlic, cumin and coriander, and fry until the onions are translucent. Then add the mushrooms, toss for 1 minute, remove from the pan and set aside.

Heat the remaining ghee or butter. Add the rice to the pan and fry well for 2-3 minutes. Spread the mushroom mixture over the top and cover the saucepan. Cook on a low heat for 15-20 minutes, then serve.

Risotto Milanese

RISOTTO IS THE ITALIAN way of preparing rich and creamy rice dishes. They can be as simple as the traditional *risotto Milanese* recipe offered here, or as elaborate as you choose to make them.

Preparation Time: 5 minutes
Cooking Time: 45 minutes

Ingredients for Six

50 g butter
1 medium-sized onion, peeled and finely chopped*
400 g rice
125 ml (½ cup) dry white wine
1 litre (4 cups) hot chicken stock*
A pinch of saffron
30 g soft butter
100 g freshly grated Parmesan cheese
Salt and freshly ground black pepper

Melt the 50 g butter in a heavy-bottomed saucepan. Stir in the onion and cook very gently, stirring often, until softened but not browned. Stir in the rice and cook for 1-2 minutes, stirring all the time.

Pour in the wine and allow it to boil rapidly until it is almost all absorbed. Pour in half the hot stock and cook, uncovered, until this, too, is almost absorbed.

Stir the saffron into the remaining hot stock and add to the rice. Once again, cook until the stock is almost absorbed. If the rice is not yet tender, add a little more stock and cook until the rice is soft. If necessary, keep adding a bit more stock until the rice is tender. Stir in the 30 g soft butter and the Parmesan, and season to taste. Serve immediately.

VARIATION Stir-fry 400 g shelled prawns* in the hot butter. Remove and set aside. You can add more butter if necessary when softening the onion. Try using a fish stock* instead of the chicken stock (add the prawn shells when making the fish stock to give it a prawn flavour). Return the prawns to the rice just before it is cooked so that they can heat through.

RISOTTO MILANESE *is a rich, delicious way of preparing rice.*

PASTA, RICE AND CEREALS

TABBOULEH

This is a variation of the Lebanese salad served as a starter with other Middle Eastern dishes. It is also suitable as a side dish to accompany cold meats or fish.

PREPARATION TIME: 1 HOUR
CHILLING TIME: OVERNIGHT

INGREDIENTS FOR SIX

180 ml boiling water
250 ml (1 cup) crushed wheat, millet or couscous
4 medium-sized onions, peeled and finely chopped*
60 ml (¼ cup) chopped parsley
250 ml (1 cup) chopped cucumber, or ½ English cucumber, chopped
45 ml (3 tablespoons) chopped mint
215 ml olive oil
30 ml (2 tablespoons) lemon juice
Salt and freshly ground black pepper
6 firm, ripe tomatoes
2 medium-sized onions, peeled and finely sliced*
250 ml (1 cup) diced cucumber, or ½ English cucumber, diced
125 ml (½ cup) black olives
1 green pepper, seeded and coarsely chopped
60 ml (¼ cup) wine vinegar
Lettuce leaves, well washed

Pour the boiling water over the crushed wheat, millet or couscous, allow to cool, then add the finely chopped onion, parsley, chopped cucumber, mint, 90 ml of the olive oil and the lemon juice, and season to taste. Refrigerate overnight.

Next, coarsely dice the tomatoes. Add the sliced onions, diced cucumber, olives, green pepper, vinegar and remaining 125 ml (½ cup) olive oil. Gently toss the ingredients and season with salt and pepper.

Line a platter with the lettuce leaves. Mound the grain mixture on top, pile on the tomato mixture and serve.

VARIATION Toss the grain mixture with the tomato mixture and add 300 g diced feta cheese.

TABBOULEH *A tasty, versatile salad from the Middle East.*

COUSCOUS

Couscous is the staple of north Africa, as rice is to the Chinese. The word has two meanings – the completed dish, and the cereal from which it is made, which is usually semolina but might also be barley, wheat or millet. Couscous made from semolina pellets is available from some speciality food shops as well as many health food stores.

PREPARATION TIME: 30 MINUTES
SOAKING TIME: OVERNIGHT
COOKING TIME: 1¾ HOURS

INGREDIENTS FOR SIX

250 g couscous, millet or cracked wheat
125 g haricot beans
125 g chick-peas
500 g chicken pieces
500 g lamb leg (chump) chops
1 large onion, peeled and sliced*
5 ml (1 teaspoon) salt
12 black peppercorns
25 g butter
2 ml (½ teaspoon) freshly ground black pepper
2 medium-sized carrots, scraped and diced
4 baby marrows, sliced
2 medium-sized tomatoes, skinned* and quartered
1 small green pepper, seeded and finely chopped
2 ml (½ teaspoon) celery salt
2 ml (½ teaspoon) cayenne pepper
2 ml (½ teaspoon) chopped thyme
2 ml (½ teaspoon) chopped parsley

Place the couscous, millet or cracked wheat, the beans and the chick-peas in separate basins, cover with cold water and leave to soak overnight.

Next day, drain the beans and place in a very large saucepan with the chicken, lamb, onion, salt and peppercorns. Cover with water, bring to the boil and remove the scum. Lower the heat and stew gently for 1 hour.

Meanwhile, drain the couscous, millet or wheat and pour it into a separate saucepan containing 500 ml (2 cups) salted boiling water. Stir the grain frequently as it boils to prevent lumps from forming; it will absorb almost all the liquid. After 15 minutes, reduce the heat to very low and stir in the butter and freshly ground pepper. Cover closely with a lid, or with aluminium foil, and leave it over the heat to soften and swell while you continue preparing the stew.

When the chicken and lamb have cooked for 1 hour, lift them from the pan and slice off all the meat, discarding the skin, fat and bones. Return the meat to the pan. Drain the chick-peas and add to the meat with the carrots, baby marrows, tomatoes and green pepper. Add the celery salt, cayenne pepper, thyme and parsley. Boil gently for a further 35 minutes. Taste and adjust the seasoning.

Just before serving, increase the heat under the couscous, millet or wheat and stir until it is very hot.

MUESLI

Muesli is a very nutritious meal which originated in Switzerland. It is traditionally a breakfast cereal, but can be eaten as a light meal at any time of day.

PREPARATION TIME: 10 MINUTES

INGREDIENTS FOR SIX

225 g rolled oats
50 g wheat germ
50 g digestive bran
50 g crushed wheat
50 g sunflower seeds
100 g sultanas

Weigh out the ingredients and mix them together well.

SERVING SUGGESTIONS Add grated apple and yoghurt or milk.

For a more porridge-like consistency, soak portions overnight in water.

VARIATIONS For an elegant presentation, cut a pineapple lengthways, leaving the leafy top on, and scoop out the flesh. Grate the flesh and add it to the muesli. Pile the muesli into the pineapple case and sprinkle with chopped nuts.

Add chopped dried fruit.

Substitute slivered, blanched* almonds for the sunflower seeds.

Add honey and chopped, fresh fruit.

Muesli can also be used in a variety of biscuit recipes calling for rolled oats.

Granola

Granola is a rich mixture of grains and other foodstuffs which provides vitamin B, vitamin E and calcium. It is good as a breakfast dish or as a filling between-meals snack.

Preparation Time: 15 minutes
Cooking Time: 30 minutes
Pre-heat Oven to 150°C

Ingredients for Eight
500 g rolled oats
50 g desiccated coconut
60 g wholewheat flour
50 g sesame seeds
50 g sunflower seeds
10 ml (2 teaspoons) brewer's yeast
125 ml (½ cup) sunflower oil
80 ml (⅓ cup) honey
15 ml (1 tablespoon) vanilla essence

Mix together all the dry ingredients. Heat the oil, honey and vanilla essence until the mixture is thin. Stir the liquid into the dry ingredients and spread on to a shallow, oiled pan. Do not smooth the mixture; rather leave it lumpy.

Bake until evenly browned, stirring every 10 minutes. Cool and store in the refrigerator, or a cool place, in a tightly covered container.

Serving Suggestions Serve with milk or yoghurt and stewed or fresh fruit.

Give children a small bag of granola to take to school.

Variations Add 60 g raisins after you have toasted the mixture.

You can also add 45 ml (3 tablespoons) soya flour for extra enrichment.

Kasha with Mushrooms and Onions

Kasha is a popular Russian dish of cooked buckwheat (the Polish version is made with barley). For this version, buy a box of groats at a supermarket or health food shop. Its nutty texture combines remarkably well with the fried mushroom and onion mixture.

Vegetarians will enjoy this dish as a meal on its own, especially if it is accompanied by a mixed salad.

Preparation Time: 15 minutes
Cooking Time: 1 hour
Pre-heat Oven to 180°C

Ingredients for Six to Eight
250 g groats
1 egg
60 g butter
500-750 ml (2-3 cups) boiling water
5 ml (1 teaspoon) salt
4 medium-sized onions, peeled and chopped*
300 g button mushrooms, chopped

Toss the groats in a bowl with the egg. Place in a large, ungreased and preferably non-stick frying pan, and cook (uncovered), stirring constantly, until the grains are lightly toasted and dry.

Place the mixture in a greased oven-proof dish with half the butter, 500 ml (2 cups) boiling water and the salt. Bake for 45 minutes, checking halfway through the cooking process to see that the grains are not too dry: if necessary, add more water. The kasha is cooked when the grains are tender and have absorbed the water.

While the kasha is cooking, sauté the chopped onions and mushrooms in the remaining butter. Before serving, toss the kasha with the onions and mushrooms, and check the seasoning.

Potato Gnocchi

Served with tomato sauce, potato gnocchi make a light supper dish on their own. They can also be served with any kind of grilled or fried meat.

Preparation Time: 45 minutes
Standing Time: 1 hour
Cooking Time: 20 minutes

Ingredients for Six
2 large, floury potatoes
Salt
15 g butter
1 egg yolk
250-300 g flour

Boil the potatoes in salted water until tender. Drain well and peel. Push the cooked potatoes through a metal sieve over a bowl. Add the butter, which will melt from the heat of the potatoes.

Stir in the yolk and a pinch of salt. Add 250 g flour gradually until the dough has a firm consistency – if necessary, add a little more flour. (You can mash the potatoes and mix the dough in a food processor.)

Break off small pieces of the dough and shape into sausage-like rolls, each about 2,5 cm long and 1 cm thick. Traditionally each piece is pressed with the thumb against the concave surface of a cheese grater to give the gnocchi the appearance of shells with ridged patterns on their backs. Place the gnocchi on a floured surface to prevent them from sticking together. Flour lightly and leave to dry for an hour or more.

Cook the gnocchi in batches (so that they do not stick together) in a large saucepan of boiling, salted water for about 20 minutes. The gnocchi will rise to the top as soon as they are cooked. Remove with a slotted spoon.

Serving Suggestion Serve with a meat sauce sprinkled with grated Parmesan.

Spinach Gnocchi

Although this Italian favourite makes a very good starter, it is often served as the main course of a light meal.

Preparation Time: 30 minutes
Chilling Time: 1 hour
Cooking Time: 30 minutes

Ingredients for Six
250 g frozen spinach
250 g ricotta or chunky cottage cheese
2 eggs, beaten
120 g flour
15 g butter
Salt and pepper
Grated nutmeg
15 ml (1 tablespoon) grated Parmesan cheese
60 ml (¼ cup) melted butter
Grated Parmesan cheese for sprinkling

Cook the spinach over a medium heat, stirring often, until all the moisture has evaporated. Stir in the ricotta or cottage cheese and cook briefly over a gentle heat.

Remove from the stove and mix in the beaten eggs, flour, butter, seasoning, nutmeg and the Parmesan. If the mixture seems too floppy, add a little more flour. Chill for 1 hour.

Shape into tiny balls with a spoon and drop them, a few at a time, into barely simmering water for about 5 minutes. When cooked, they rise to the top. Remove with a slotted spoon and drain.

Pour the melted butter over the gnocchi and serve hot. Pass around a bowl of grated Parmesan to sprinkle over each serving.

Semolina Gnocchi

Plenty of Parmesan cheese adds flavour to these tasty Italian morsels. These gnocchi are baked rather than boiled.

Preparation Time: 45 minutes
Chilling Time: 1 hour
Cooking Time: 20 minutes
Pre-heat Oven to 230°C

Ingredients for Four
625 ml (2½ cups) milk
5 ml (1 teaspoon) salt
A pinch of freshly grated nutmeg
125 g semolina
Freshly ground black pepper
2 eggs, beaten
125 g freshly grated Parmesan
60 g butter, melted

In a large, heavy-based saucepan, bring the milk, salt and nutmeg to the boil. Gradually stir in the semolina – pour it in slowly enough for the milk to remain boiling.

Keep stirring all the time (to prevent lumps from forming) until the mixture is very thick. When the semolina is absorbed, beat briskly until the mixture leaves the sides and bottom of the pot. Remove from the stove and beat in a grinding of pepper, the eggs and 100 g of the Parmesan cheese until well blended.

Spread the semolina mixture 1 cm thick on to a large buttered baking sheet, using a spatula dipped in hot water to smooth it down. Chill for 1 hour, or until firm.

Cut out small circles (about 3 cm across) with a pastry cutter, or simply cut into diamond shapes. Carefully lift them into a buttered baking dish, arranging them so that they overlap slightly. Drizzle over melted butter and sprinkle on the rest of the cheese. Bake for 20 minutes, or until crisp and golden. Serve immediately.

Eggs and Cheese

Eggs and cheese are among the most versatile and nutritious ingredients in the kitchen. Both are rich in first-class animal protein, fats, minerals and vitamins, and are popular in family meals as less expensive – but equally beneficial – substitutes for meat and poultry.

The egg is seen by many cultures as a symbol of life and fertility. Early Christians, borrowing from pagan tradition, regarded it as a symbol of rebirth and made hard-boiled, decorated eggs as Easter gifts – the precursors of today's chocolate eggs.

Most bird eggs are edible, from the fishy-tasting seagull egg to the weighty ostrich egg, but battery hen eggs are the most commonly consumed ones. Eggs are the perfect breakfast food, whether poached, boiled, fried, coddled, baked or scrambled. They can also be made into omelettes, soufflés and quiches, and are useful for coating fried food, thickening or emulsifying sauces, binding rissoles, glazing, and using in a host of baked goods.

Cheese is almost as universally useful and is used in all types of dishes, from starters to desserts. It is ideal for a snack, served with fruit, wine, bread or crackers, and combines particularly well with pasta and rice dishes.

The taste of tangy cheese also mixes superbly with many vegetables – and its protein content can elevate a vegetarian dish to a balanced meal.

South Africa produces a wide range of cheeses locally, many of which were previously available only as imports. A selection from other countries can also still be bought at speciality stores.

USEFUL FACTS ABOUT EGGS AND CHEESE · *PAGE 228*

EGGS AND CHEESE RECIPES · *PAGE 232*

SPECIAL FEATURES

BREAKFAST THE TRADITIONAL ENGLISH WAY · *PAGE 236*
MEAL-IN-ONE DISHES · QUICK MEALS WITH
EGGS AND CHEESE · *PAGE 244*

Useful Facts about Eggs and Cheese

Choosing, Storing and Cooking Eggs

Although South Africans appear to like eggs – we each consume 189 of them a year on average – we take them pretty much for granted.

Yet the egg is undeniably one of nature's most remarkable accomplishments. It comes to us pure and perfectly packaged, its contents untouched by human hands, with no chemicals or preservatives added. Its high-quality protein is amazingly complete, containing all the essential amino acids, those building blocks necessary for growth and general good health. With the exception of vitamin C, all the vitamins, including the rare sunshine-growth vitamin D, are present, plus 13 minerals, including iron, phosphorus and calcium.

The yolk of an egg is about 33 per cent fat, while the white is mainly water. The shell is porous and can be penetrated by air, water or odours. The air chamber between the shell and the inner lining at the larger end gets bigger with age.

Cooked on their own, eggs thicken and solidify at 60-68°C – temperatures considerably lower than the boiling point of water. When mixed with other ingredients, however, they solidify at higher temperatures.

Choosing Eggs

Price is affected by grade and size; the nutritive value of all eggs of like grade and size is the same. Grade refers to cleanliness, soundness of shell, thickness of albumen and size of air cells. Size is based on minimum mass per dozen. Extra-large eggs, more than 61 g each, are the most expensive; then large, 52-61 g, and medium, 43-51 g. If there is less than a 3 c price difference per dozen eggs between one size and the next smaller size in the same grade, the best buy will always be the larger size.

Grades 1 and 2 are the best for general use. Undergrade eggs are not strictly fresh, and are best used for scrambling and for combining with other ingredients. Size and colour do not affect quality.

Grade 1 eggs have very small air cells, a large amount of thick white and a firm, upstanding yolk. Out of the shell, Grade 1 eggs cover a small area. Grade 2 eggs spread a bit more, for the white is not as thick nor the yolk as high. Undergrade eggs cover a wide area, and have much thinner whites and flatter yolks.

Storing Eggs

Store eggs in a clean, cool place with the pointed end down. Do not wash unless absolutely necessary, and keep away from strong-smelling foods whose flavour might permeate the porous shell.

Eggs up to 1 week old when bought will keep for 2 weeks at normal room temperature – about 18°C – or up to 5 weeks in a refrigerator.

Store separated whites and yolks in a refrigerator in different containers. Pour a thin layer of milk or water over the yolks to prevent them from hardening.

Yolks are best used within 2 days; whites can be kept up to 4 days.

Take eggs out of the refrigerator and leave them at room temperature for 45 minutes before using. Very cold eggs will crack when boiled, and chilled whites cannot be whisked easily.

Egg whites freeze well, but egg yolks must first be beaten with a little salt or sugar before they are frozen.

How to Tell a Fresh Egg

If you put a fresh egg in a solution of salt and water (10 per cent salt), it will sink to the bottom. If it floats, it is stale. When broken into a bowl, a fresh egg has a rounded yolk and a firm white. A stale egg has a flat yolk and a runny white.

Tips for Cooking Eggs

The following are the five most popular methods of preparing eggs. The cardinal rule that applies to all of them is never to overcook eggs and never to use too high a temperature – doing so will make them hard and rubbery.

Boiled eggs

Although this is the simplest method of preparing an egg, it still has its pitfalls. One of the commonest problems is that the egg cracks while being boiled, and the white escapes into the water. This can usually be prevented by pricking a hole in the broad end of the egg – it is advisable to use a proper 'egg pricker' when doing this. Pricking the egg will allow the air bubble within the egg to escape during boiling. The fresher the egg, the smaller the air bubble; consequently a week-old egg is less likely to crack than a two-week-old one. Also remember that an egg at room temperature is less likely to crack than one that comes straight out of the refrigerator.

The two most common methods of boiling eggs are by warming up the water and eggs together, or introducing the eggs to the water when it is already simmering. In the first method, there is less chance of the eggs cracking.

If you warm up the water and eggs together, start timing from the moment the water boils, then lower the heat and allow to simmer for the following times: 3 minutes for soft-boiled eggs, 4 minutes for firm whites with soft yolks, and 10 minutes for hard-boiled eggs.

If you introduce the eggs when the water is simmering, time the cooking from the moment they are placed in the water. The following cooking times will apply: 3¾ minutes for soft-boiled eggs, 7 minutes for firm whites with soft yolks, and 12 minutes for completely hard-boiled eggs.

It is inadvisable to cook eggs in rapidly boiling water; doing so makes the whites hard and tough before the yolk is cooked. Eggs taste best when cooked in gently simmering water.

When cooking hard-boiled eggs, it is advisable to plunge them into cold water immediately after taking them out of the boiling water. Peel them underwater and allow to cool. Doing this prevents a dark ring from forming around the yolk. This ring is a compound of iron in the yolk and sulphur in the egg white; it is quite edible but looks unattractive.

Fried eggs

Despite its simplicity, a fried egg remains one of the most delicious of meals. However, few things are as disagreeable as a badly prepared fried egg – oily, discoloured and of rubbery consistency.

The taste of a fried egg will depend to some extent on the shortening that you use to cook it in. Butter is the most recommended medium for frying eggs, as it imparts a light-golden colour and a pleasant taste. Cooking oil is relatively tasteless and bacon fat will of course impart a slight bacon flavour.

Always fry eggs over a medium heat. The shortening should be hot but not smoking. Eggs can be broken directly into the frying pan, or alternatively broken into a cup and slid gently into the pan. When you slip the eggs in, the white should solidify at once but not bubble and burn at the edges. If it does, lower the heat. You can, if you wish, baste the eggs with fat from the pan while they are frying – this will give the yolk a shiny appearance.

The cooking time for a fried egg is usually from two to three minutes. When they are cooked, lift the eggs out of the pan with a perforated egg-lifter, preferably in the order in which they were put in. Place the eggs briefly on paper towels to drain off excess fat, then serve within two to three minutes.

You may, if you wish, add 5 ml (1 teaspoon) water to the shortening in the pan, then cover with a lid and steam the eggs. The yolk will be opaque rather than clear.

If you like the white of your fried egg crisp and slightly brown, increase the cooking temperature.

Scrambled eggs

Scrambled eggs are very versatile, being suitable for breakfast, a light lunch, or a modest supper.

The basic recipe for scrambled eggs is two eggs to which 25 ml (5 teaspoons) milk or water has been added, and some seasoning. Whisk the mixture and pour into a heavy-based frying pan in which 10 ml (2 teaspoons) butter has been melted. (The butter should be sizzling and bubbling.)

Scrambled eggs must never be cooked at high temperatures, otherwise they will become dry and crumbly. The right ratio of eggs to liquid is important as too much liquid stops the eggs from congealing and the liquid tends to separate.

When the mixture starts to congeal, stir lightly with an egg-lifter, but do not stir continuously. Cook until the mixture is firm but not dry. Well-prepared scrambled eggs should consist of big soft chunks – not a finely textured mixture.

For variety, you can fry tomatoes and onions, left-over meat or vegetables, pasta or rice in the pan before adding the egg mixture.

Omelettes

A basic omelette consists of egg, liquid, spices and a filling. The important point to remember when making an omelette is to use the right proportions of egg and liquid. If you use too little liquid the omelette will be tough and rubbery; if you use too much, the liquid will separate.

Use a pan with a rounded side and of a suitable size to allow about 5 mm depth of egg. For two or three eggs, this means a pan 15 cm in diameter.

It is advisable to use butter for frying. Butter will give the omelette a very characteristic flavour and colour. It is best to use unsalted or clarified butter* since salted butter can cause the omelette to stick to the pan.

The butter in the frying pan should bubble and be slightly brown before you pour in the egg mixture. The darker the butter, the darker the final omelette will be.

It is best to fry a number of smaller omelettes instead of making one big one. The smaller they are, the lighter will be their texture. The best omelettes are made with water rather than with milk. The fat in milk tends to give them rather a tough consistency.

You should not add salt to the egg mixture before frying since it tends to toughen the texture of the omelette. Seasoning should be done just before folding.

If you are using a warm filling, ensure that it has been sufficiently heated before being folded into the omelette.

Poached eggs

Although this is probably the least used method for cooking eggs, a poached egg is particularly enjoyable if properly prepared.

When poaching eggs, boil about 5 cm of liquid in a saucepan, then lower to simmering before you break the eggs and slide them in. Eggs are normally poached in water, but you can also use tomato juice, milk, meat extract or soup. If you are using water, the addition of lemon juice or vinegar will enhance the flavour. The liquid should not contain salt.

A metal poaching ring is normally placed in the saucepan and the broken egg poured into it. The ring ensures that the egg keeps its shape, but it is not absolutely essential. A few drops of vinegar added to the water will help prevent the white from spreading.

The egg should be simmered for three to five minutes. Lift it out of the liquid with a perforated egg-lifter, drain and serve hot.

Poached eggs are delicious served on toast or buttered bread, and covered with a cheese sauce.

UNCOMMON EGGS

If you are an adventurous cook, you might like to try cooking with some of the more exotic eggs that are sometimes available from speciality shops.

Bantam eggs

These eggs are delicious because bantam hens are not reared in batteries and the eggs retain their natural flavour. They are used like hen eggs except that, being smaller, more of them are needed in scrambled eggs or omelettes.

Duck eggs

These are richer than other eggs, the yolks having a more oily texture. They are excellent boiled, scrambled or used in an omelette. Duck eggs are larger than hen eggs, and three of them in an omelette are enough for two people.

Duck egg omelette

PREPARATION TIME: 10 MINUTES
COOKING TIME: 5 MINUTES

INGREDIENTS FOR TWO
*30 ml (2 tablespoons) peeled and finely chopped onion**
1 clove garlic, chopped
15-30 ml (1-2 tablespoons) desiccated coconut
15 ml (1 tablespoon) cold water
3 duck eggs
30 ml (2 tablespoons) sunflower oil
Salt
2 ml (½ teaspoon) cayenne pepper

Mix the onion, garlic, coconut and water, and beat thoroughly with the eggs. Pour the oil into a pan and proceed as for usual omelettes*, sprinkling over the salt and cayenne pepper during cooking.

USING EGGS IN COOKING

1 Eggs make a substantial and nutritious meal on their own or can be used in other dishes, both sweet and savoury, in the various ways listed below.
2 The capacity that eggs have to coagulate when heated makes them ideal for binding loose, crumbly ingredients together – for example, poultry stuffing and croquettes. Mixed with breadcrumbs or flour, eggs form a crisp coating that protects fried foods from very hot fat. Fritters that are dipped in beaten egg before being fried will absorb virtually no oil.
3 Beaten eggs are invaluable as a thickening agent, being used to thicken custards, sauces, soups, fruit curds and tart fillings. A useful rule of thumb is that one medium-sized egg will thicken 275-300 ml liquid. Care should be taken not to heat the mixture to which the egg has been added for too long as the liquid will tend to separate out, with the egg forming a tough clot.
4 A particularly useful quality of egg yolks is that they act as emulsifiers – blending oil and other liquids, as in mayonnaise*. The addition of vinegar or lemon juice stabilises the emulsion.
5 A beaten egg white will give a pleasing gloss to pastries; raw pie crusts do not become soggy from the moisture in the filling when they are painted with beaten egg white.
6 Egg whites that have been whisked to a fine foam are the main ingredient of meringues*, soufflés* and light sponge cakes.
7 Because eggs are rich in many nutrients, they are ideal for increasing the nutritional value of other foods. They can be mixed with vegetables, pastas, grain and bread, and even a fruit drink becomes a complete meal with the addition of a raw egg.
8 Lightly beaten egg white or crushed egg shells can be added to broths and jellies to remove solids and to clarify the liquid. The whites solidify in the warmed liquid, trapping small particles, and this white solid is strained off. Similarly, food particles also adhere to crushed egg shells introduced to the liquid, and they too are strained off.
9 When making sweets, the addition of egg white prevents crystallisation.
10 Hard-boiled eggs* are widely used as an attractive and nutritious garnish. They may be used halved or quartered, or the yolk may be rubbed through a sieve, and the white cut into strips.

Ostrich eggs

For an unusual and surprisingly tasty dish, try serving your guests ostrich egg. In the ostrich-farming district of Oudtshoorn, scrambled ostrich egg is traditionally served with a dollop of 'moskonfyt', obtained by boiling hanepoot 'must' to a syrupy thickness. Alternatively, you might like to try hard-boiled ostrich egg. In theory, you can serve as many people with one ostrich egg as you would be able to with 24 hen eggs.

An uncooked ostrich egg in its shell will keep for four to six weeks in the refrigerator.

Scrambled Ostrich Egg

PREPARATION TIME: 5 MINUTES
COOKING TIME: 10 MINUTES

INGREDIENTS FOR EIGHT
1 whole ostrich egg
Water or skim milk (half the volume of the egg)
Salt and freshly ground black pepper
30 g butter

Make a 1,5 cm hole in one end of the egg (this is done by repeatedly chipping with a sharp screwdriver). Shake the egg over a bowl until the shell is empty. If the egg is very fresh, and a hole is made at either end, you will be able to blow the egg out.

Beat the egg and water (or skim milk) with salt and pepper to taste. Heat the butter until bubbly and pour in the egg mixture.

When the egg begins to cook, use a large spoon to lift slabs of it and fold them over (do not use a fork for stirring the mixture).

When the egg is properly cooked – and still moist – remove from the pan and transfer to heated plates. Serve the scrambled egg immediately.
Note: Kept in a closed glass jar in the refrigerator, the egg mixture will remain fresh for a week.

Quail eggs

Quail eggs are useful as a garnish or simply as a pre-meal appetiser. As an hors d'oeuvre, hard-boiled quail eggs can be attractively served in a tasty nest of rosti*. Use 4 eggs per person and boil them for 2½ minutes.

Turkey eggs

These are very similar to duck eggs and can be treated in the same way.

A GUIDE TO POPULAR CHEESES

Cheese is made of milk curds, which are produced from milk by the action of heat or rennet, the latter being an enzyme extracted from the lining of calves' stomachs. When a cheese is eaten unripened, it is soft and creamy, like cream cheese and cottage cheese. A short period of ripening results in a firmer but still easily spread cheese, such as Brie or Camembert, while longer periods of ripening produce semi-hard and hard cheeses.

Semi-hard cheeses are ideal for cutting and for including on a cheeseboard. Hard cheeses, which contain very little moisture, are good for grating. Some cheeses lend themselves particularly well to specific uses: they may make a good melting cheese or cooking cheese, but are not necessarily the kind you would serve at a cheese and wine party or with dessert and coffee.

Once cheese has been ripened it reaches its peak, which passes fairly quickly. It is best to buy cheese fresh, preferably from a shop which will cut it for you from a large block. Pre-cut pieces go stale more quickly.

Do not buy cheese that has cracks running from the edges or is darker in colour in the middle – this indicates that it is stale and drying out. Avoid cheese that is 'sweating', because it has been stored at too high a temperature and the flavour may be impaired.

Foil-wrapped soft cheese should feel soft, not rubbery, when the wrapping is gently pressed.

Cheese is best bought in small quantities for quick use, but it can be stored. To prevent it from drying out, wrap it in aluminium foil or wax paper and store it in a plastic bag or box, in a cool pantry or in the refrigerator.

If you do keep it in the refrigerator, remember to take the cheese out at least an hour before it is to be eaten to bring it to room temperature. With all food, cold suppresses flavour, and this is particularly true of cheese.

Hard or semi-hard cheese will keep for up to two weeks in a refrigerator and soft or cream cheese for five to seven days. If you have any odds and ends of cheese left over, grate them for use in cooking and store in a covered jar.

Most cheeses can be used for cooking, but hard or semi-hard cheeses that grate easily are best, such as Parmesan, Cheddar, Wensleydale, Gruyère and Emmenthal. For fondues, Gruyère and Emmenthal are traditionally used (although Cheddar is also good).

When melting cheese in a pan keep the heat low, or the cheese will be tough and stringy. If you use cheese as a topping for a cooked dish, do not add it until the last 5-10 minutes of cooking – long enough for it to melt. Feta cheese makes a delicious topping for steaks and grilled fish, and mozzarella is excellent melted over a vegetable casserole.

The following are some of the more popular and well-known cheeses available in South Africa. Some are produced locally while others are imported.

Bel paese

This is an ivory-coloured, soft-textured cheese originating in Italy: 'bel paese' means 'beautiful country'. It is a table cheese with a maturation period of about two months.

Blaauwkrantz

A local blue-veined, Roquefort-type cheese. It is very granular and has a sharp, tangy, salty taste. Blaauwkrantz cheese reaches full maturity in about five months.

Brie

Brie has a mild, piquant taste and is one of the most popular table cheeses available. It has been made in France since the 8th century – originally in the province of La Brie, east of Paris. When ripe, Brie should feel supple but not runny. A piece cut from a whole cheese has a better flavour than a packaged wedge. Its maturation period is two to six weeks.

Caerphilly

A British buttermilk cheese made from skimmed milk. It is best eaten when slightly immature. It melts well and is popular in cheese dishes.

Camembert

This is a popular table cheese having a mild, pleasant flavour. Its surface is covered with edible white mould which turns brownish on maturing. The maturation time is two to six weeks, by which time it should have a soft, creamy texture.

Cheddar

This popular cheese is used both as a table cheese and for cooking. It has a rich, nutty flavour that becomes sharper as it matures – a period of two to six months. Cheddar is a light straw colour and has a firm texture; mature Cheddar is covered with red wax and is more granular than ordinary Cheddar.

Cheshire

This is a crumbly, nutty cheese that can be red, white or blue – the South African version is white. It has a tangy, salty aftertaste and can be used both for cooking and as a table cheese. Cheshire matures in one to four months.

Cottage

Cottage cheese has a mild, slightly sour taste and is used both as a table cheese and for cooking. It is available either in a 'chunky' form or with a smooth texture, and can be bought with various added ingredients, such as onion, chives, asparagus or garlic. It is best eaten fresh.

Cream

Rich, creamy, soft and mild, this cheese is popular for both cooking and table use. Eaten fresh, it is delicious mixed with chopped raw vegetables or nuts and raisins, and is also an essential ingredient of American cheesecake*.

Danish Blue

This sharp, salty Danish cheese has a high fat content and a crumbly texture. The name covers a selection of excellent blue cheeses of which 'Danablu' is the most renowned. Others are 'mycella', which has a milder taste, and 'blucreme', which is smoother and creamier than 'Danablu'.

Drakensberg
A local semi-soft cheese, dark yellow in colour and having a soft creamy texture. It has a rich flavour and a maturation period of between three weeks and six months.

Edam
A pleasantly mild, slightly salty-tasting cheese that is usually encased in red or yellow wax. It is light yellow and should have a slightly elastic texture. Edam can be used both for cooking and as a table cheese. It takes from one month to a year to mature.

Emmenthal
The most distinctive aspect of this ivory-coloured cheese is its large holes. It has a sweet flavour that grows fuller with age and is excellent both for the table and for cooking. A Swiss cheese, it is made in large wheel shapes that are cut up into segments.

Esrom
This is a Danish cheese modelled on the French cheese Port Salut; however, it is stronger and has holes. It is often used in smorgasbord recipes, as well as being used as a table cheese.

Feta
Crumbly and salty, this cheese was originally made from ewe's milk by shepherds in the mountain regions near Athens. It is used a lot in Greek cooking, especially in salads. Feta cheese can be made less salty by soaking in milky water.

Fontina
A rich, firm Italian cheese made in the Piedmont region. It has a natural brown rind and melts very well. It is traditionally used in *fonduta* – a fondue served with white truffles.

Gloucester
This hard English cheese has a rich creamy colour and a mellow flavour. In terms of taste it is fairly similar to Cheddar. Manufactured in cylindrical shapes, this cheese is popular for cooking and is often used in sandwiches and salads.

Gorgonzola
Imported from Italy, this blue-veined cheese is pleasantly sharp in flavour. Gorgonzola should be springy to the touch and blue-grey in colour. Most Gorgonzolas have a musty smell but this should never be too strong.

Gouda
Originating in the town of Gouda, north of Rotterdam, this sweetmilk cheese is the archetypal Dutch cheese – a golden wheel with a yellow or red wax protective skin. It has a mild flavour and is used mainly as a table cheese.

Gruyère
This Swiss cheese has a fairly smooth rind and is ivory-yellow with tiny pinprick holes spaced far apart. It should have a waxy rather than a velvety surface. Gruyère is the main ingredient of the classic cheese fondue because of its fine melting qualities.

Havarti
A cheese with a mild, creamy taste which becomes sharper on maturing. It is used mainly as a table cheese and takes from three weeks to six months to mature. Havarti has a creamy colour with a soft texture.

Jarlsberg
This Norwegian cheese has a sweet, nutty flavour similar to Emmenthal. It has a thick natural rind covered with yellow wax and its interior contains irregularly shaped, rounded holes.

Leicester
Orange in colour and shaped like a millstone, this English cheese is firm-bodied with a mild flavour and a moist, flaky texture. It is particularly popular for making cheese sauces.

Limburger
Originally imported from Belgium and Germany, this cheese is now also made in South Africa. It has a reddish-yellow surface and a creamy-yellow interior. The flavour is strong and pungent.

Liptauer
A soft cheese from Hungary that is manufactured from sheep's and cow's milk. This cheese also comes with added ingredients, such as capers, onions, mustard and spices.

Mozzarella
Mozzarella, originating in southern Italy, is white and soft, and has a compact, elastic texture. It is ideal for pizzas and is best eaten fresh.

Muenster
A pungent-smelling and strong-tasting cheese, muenster is traditionally eaten with rye bread, caraway seeds and chopped onions. It is made in various sizes and has an orange-red rind.

Parmesan
The correct name for this famous Italian cheese is 'Parmigiano Reggiano'. It is used extensively for cooking and keeps for years, growing harder and fuller as it ages. Pre-packaged ground Parmesan is a poor substitute for the freshly grated product. The cheese is a light to dark straw colour depending on age.

Pecorino
This imported cheese is used both as a table cheese and for grating – often in place of Parmesan. Pecorino is round, hard and white with a yellow or red crust when mature. It has a strong, pungent, salty taste.

Pizzarella
A loaf-shaped, semi-soft cheese that is made locally. It has a slightly sour taste and is used mainly for cooking.

Pont L'Évêque
This French cheese is square, soft and fat, with a shiny, golden or reddish, salty rind. It is made from unpasteurised milk and has a strong taste and aroma. It comes packed in small boxes.

Port Salut
Similar to Saint Paulin, Port Salut is an orange-skinned French cheese with a velvety smooth texture. This small, round, whole-milk cheese is semi-hard and is usually mildly pungent.

Provolone
Mild, with a sharp, salty taste, provolone can be used both as a table cheese and for cooking. Most provolones are smoked and are available in a cylindrical form. The cheese has a firm texture with a thin, cream-coloured rind.

Ricotta
Slightly sweeter than cottage cheese, ricotta is a creamy, white, fresh cheese made from whey. It is used mainly as a table cheese, being popular as a diet food. It is ideal for mixing with fruit and raisins.

Roquefort
This renowned French cheese is creamy with green-blue veins. The texture is smooth and firm, and it has a pungent smell. It takes about six months to reach full maturity. It is excellent in salad dressings.

Saint Paulin
This French cheese is smooth and mild when young, becoming stronger in flavour as it ripens. It has a bright orange skin.

Stilton
This famous English cheese is of two types – white and blue, the blue being the more popular. Blue Stilton should be creamy ivory with green-blue veining throughout. White Stilton is sold when fairly young, but the blue variety requires about six months to develop.

Tilsit
This is a tasty, semi-soft cheese with a sharp aftertaste. It has a maturing period of one month to a year and is used mainly as a table cheese. It is a light straw colour with small, evenly spread holes.

Wensleydale
This cheese is of two varieties, blue and white. It has a slightly sharp taste and is mostly used as a table cheese. Wensleydale has a short maturation period of three weeks. In Yorkshire, where it originates, it is a traditional accompaniment to apple pie.

EGGS BENEDICT

THIS INTERNATIONAL FAVOURITE consists of poached eggs and ham on toasted soft rolls, topped with Hollandaise sauce.

PREPARATION TIME: 15 MINUTES
COOKING TIME: 40 MINUTES

INGREDIENTS FOR SIX

6 extra-large eggs
3 English muffins or soft, round rolls, or 6 slices bread
Butter for spreading
6 slices cooked ham*

For the Hollandaise sauce:
175 g butter
15 ml (1 tablespoon) grape vinegar
30 ml (2 tablespoons) lemon juice
3 egg yolks
2 ml (½ teaspoon) castor sugar
Salt and freshly ground pepper

First make the sauce. Put the butter into a small saucepan over a gentle heat and leave it to melt slowly. Put the vinegar and lemon juice into a second saucepan and bring to the boil. Blend the egg yolks, sugar and a little salt in a liquidizer, gradually adding the lemon juice and vinegar, and pepper.

When the butter starts to boil, pour it very slowly (with the liquidizer still switched on) into the yolk mixture until all the butter has been added and the sauce has thickened. Turn the sauce into a basin and keep it warm by standing the basin in a saucepan of hot water.

To poach the eggs, bring a frying pan of water to the boil. Reduce to a simmer and slip in 3 eggs for poaching, one at a time. When they are set to your liking (about 3 minutes), lift them out with a slotted spoon and leave to drain well on a plate lined with paper towels. Poach the remaining eggs in the same way. Meanwhile, split and toast the muffins, rolls or bread and spread them with butter. Top each with a slice of ham and a poached egg. Spoon over warm Hollandaise sauce and serve.

VARIATION Before assembling the eggs Benedict, cover the ham with 30 ml (2 tablespoons) sherry or Marsala, top with aluminium foil and warm it through in a 120°C oven for 10 minutes.

If you do not have a liquidizer, use a conventional Hollandaise sauce*.

EGGS FLORENTINE

QUICK AND EASY to prepare, this supper or luncheon dish consists of a bed of cooked spinach topped with eggs and covered with a cheese sauce.

PREPARATION TIME: 40 MINUTES
COOKING TIME: 20 MINUTES
PRE-HEAT OVEN TO 190°C

INGREDIENTS FOR FOUR

1 kg fresh spinach
Salt and freshly ground black pepper
45 g butter
8 eggs
40 g grated Parmesan cheese

For the sauce:
55 g butter
40 g flour
500 ml (2 cups) milk
Salt and pepper
150 g Cheddar or Gruyère cheese, grated
5 ml (1 teaspoon) French mustard (optional)

Cook the spinach with about 100 ml water until tender, then drain well. Chop it roughly and season.

Melt 30 g of the butter, stir in the spinach and allow to heat through. Turn the spinach and butter mixture into a buttered, shallow gratin or baking dish and spread evenly over the base.

To make the sauce, melt the butter, stir in the flour and cook for 1-2 minutes without browning. Gradually beat in the milk and bring to the boil, stirring all the time to make a smooth sauce. Season and stir in the grated cheese and mustard (if used). Cook over a gentle heat for 1 minute.

Make 8 depressions in the spinach with the back of a spoon. Gently break an egg into each one, season and spoon over the sauce.

Sprinkle with Parmesan cheese and dot with the remaining 15 g butter. Bake for 15-20 minutes.

SERVING SUGGESTIONS This dish is especially good when served with crusty bread or rice tossed in butter.

VARIATIONS Use poached* or hard-boiled* eggs, cover with a cheese soufflé* mixture and bake at 200°C for 30 minutes.

INDA NU SAKH *A perfect blend of spices goes into these curried eggs.*

INDA NU SAKH

THIS SIMPLE INDIAN DISH consists of hard-boiled eggs doused with a curry sauce with onions and tomatoes. It is a superb light meal.

PREPARATION TIME: 30-40 MINUTES
COOKING TIME: 30 MINUTES

INGREDIENTS FOR FOUR TO SIX

8 eggs
30 ml (2 tablespoons) chopped coriander leaves for garnish

For the sauce:
60 ml (¼ cup) sunflower oil
1-1½ green chillies, chopped
8 curry leaves, fresh or dried (optional)
2 onions, peeled* and grated or finely chopped*
4 tomatoes, halved and grated on coarse side of grater
3 ml (¾ teaspoon) turmeric
5 ml (1 teaspoon) cumin seeds, crushed
10 ml (2 teaspoons) coriander seeds, crushed
5 ml (1 teaspoon) salt

Boil the eggs for 10-12 minutes, cool under cold running water, and shell. Set aside.

To make the sauce, heat the oil in a shallow pan and add the chopped chillies and curry leaves (if used). Brown for 10 seconds, then add the grated or chopped onion to the pan and stir the mixture well. Cook for 3 minutes.

Pour the grated tomato into the pan and add the remaining spices and salt. Stir, cover the saucepan and simmer for 20 minutes, or until the vegetables are soft and blended with the spices. Cut the eggs in half lengthways and arrange in the saucepan. Cook for 3 minutes. Garnish with the coriander leaves and serve immediately.

SERVING SUGGESTIONS Serve with a helping of rice or hot roti* and fresh pickle.

BAJI AUR INDA

BAJI, THE INDIAN TERM for spinach, is used frequently in Indian cuisine. This spinach egg scramble is a soft-textured vegetable dish dressed with a delicious mixture of spices and eggs.

PREPARATION TIME: 20 MINUTES
COOKING TIME: 20 MINUTES

INGREDIENTS FOR FOUR
30 ml (2 tablespoons) sunflower oil
15 ml (1 tablespoon) butter
6 cloves garlic, peeled and crushed finely
2 medium-sized onions, peeled and sliced*
200 g spinach, shredded
1 green chilli, finely chopped
2 ml (½ teaspoon) turmeric
5 ml (1 teaspoon) salt
4 eggs, beaten

Heat the oil and butter in a shallow frying pan. Add the crushed garlic and fry for 10 seconds, then place the onions in the pan and fry until golden (2-3 minutes).

Add the spinach, chilli, turmeric and salt, and stir well. Cover the pan and simmer on a medium heat for 15 minutes. Pour the beaten eggs on to the spinach. Fry (stirring) until the eggs are firm.

SERVING SUGGESTIONS Serve with a warm roti*. Alternatively, serve as a filling for a rolled-up roti*, or cold on toast with a spoonful of sweet fruit pickle.

OEUFS MEULEMEESTER

THIS DISH, which derives its name from a family of restaurant owners in Bruges, is a traditional north Belgian method of serving eggs. It has long been a favourite with Belgian families, and should find broad appeal in this country too.

PREPARATION TIME: 20 MINUTES
COOKING TIME: 10 MINUTES
PRE-HEAT OVEN TO 200°C

INGREDIENTS FOR FOUR
8 eggs
15 g butter
7 ml (1½ teaspoons) chopped chervil
7 ml (1½ teaspoons) chopped parsley
2 ml (½ teaspoon) French mustard
100-125 g prawns, shelled and de-veined*
275-300 ml thin cream
Salt and freshly ground pepper
30 ml (2 tablespoons) grated Cheddar cheese

Boil the eggs for 10-12 minutes. Hold them under cold running water until cool. Shell them carefully, chop coarsely and set aside.

Put the butter, chopped chervil and parsley, mustard, prawns and cream into a medium-sized saucepan. Season and stir well with a wooden spoon. Stir in the chopped eggs and heat through, stirring.

Grease an oven-proof dish and pour in the mixture. Sprinkle with the grated cheese and bake in the top of the pre-heated oven for about 10 minutes, or until the top is golden-brown. Serve very hot.

EGG SALAD

A BED OF CRISP GREENS is topped with halved hard-boiled eggs, mayonnaise and strips of anchovy fillets.

PREPARATION TIME: 20 MINUTES

INGREDIENTS FOR FOUR
6-8 eggs
1 crisp butter lettuce
1 bunch tender young spinach or watercress
200 ml well-flavoured, home-made mayonnaise*
6-8 anchovies, drained and thinly sliced
15 ml (1 tablespoon) freshly chopped parsley, or 6 fresh chives, chopped

Boil the eggs for 10-12 minutes, then cool under cold running water. Shell the eggs and halve them lengthways.

Wash the greens and remove the tough stalks. Dry the leaves thoroughly before arranging them in a shallow salad bowl. Arrange the egg halves side by side, cut side down, over the greens.

Just before serving, spoon the mayonnaise over the eggs and garnish the tops with strips of anchovy. Sprinkle with parsley or chives and serve immediately.

OEUFS EN COCOTTE À LA CRÈME

THERE ARE MANY WAYS of serving *oeufs en cocotte* – eggs baked in small dishes. When *à la crème* is added to the name, this indicates the classic version, which is simply eggs baked with cream.

This recipe for a perfect light breakfast dish can easily be varied.

PREPARATION TIME: 5 MINUTES
COOKING TIME: 8 MINUTES
PRE-HEAT OVEN TO 200°C

INGREDIENTS FOR FOUR
15 g butter
Salt and freshly ground pepper
4 eggs
60 ml (¼ cup) thick cream
Boiling water

Put a dab of butter and a tiny pinch of salt and pepper in the bottom of each of 4 small oven-proof *cocotte* dishes. Break an egg into each and season the tops with more salt and pepper. Pour 15 ml (1 tablespoon) cream over each egg and add a further dab of butter.

Place the 4 *cocottes* in a roasting tin, and then pour round them enough boiling water to come halfway up the sides of the dishes.

Place in the pre-heated oven and bake for 7-8 minutes, until the white has just set (shake a *cocotte* to see if the white is still liquid) and the yolks are still runny. Eat this dish as soon as possible.

VARIATIONS Instead of using cream in this dish, try adding cooked asparagus tips, shrimps, cooked chicken breast or chopped fried mushrooms under the eggs.

OEUFS EN COCOTTE *Eggs baked in cream make excellent breakfast fare.*

Fillings for Sweet and Savoury Pancakes

Sweet fillings
Serve the basic pancakes with honey, syrup or sugar and lemon juice, or scoops of ice cream. Alternatively, you can fill the pancakes with sliced fresh berries, or poached fruit moistened with liqueur-flavoured syrup, and serve them with whipped cream.

The pancakes can also be rolled up on a plate sprinkled with desiccated coconut. This is particularly tasty with pancakes rolled around bananas that have been split in half lengthways and then sprinkled with a little lemon juice in order to prevent discoloration.

Savoury fillings
Pancakes can be rolled up around a wide variety of savoury fillings, placed in a buttered oven-proof dish and topped with a cheese sauce* and extra grated cheese. Sprinkle over dry breadcrumbs, dot with butter, and bake for 20 minutes at 200°C until bubbly and golden.

Instead of rolling the pancakes, you can also sandwich open pancakes with two fillings of your choice to form a 'cake'. Place in an ovenproof dish, pour over the cheese sauce, sprinkle with breadcrumbs and bake until golden, then cut into wedges for serving.

The amounts that are given here for the suggested fillings are enough to fill 12 pancakes.

Asparagus pancakes Wrap the prepared pancakes around 12 fat cooked asparagus spears – you can use either fresh or tinned. If the asparagus spears are very slim, use 2 or 3 per pancake.

Mushroom pancakes Heat 30 g butter and sauté 300 g finely chopped mushrooms in it over a high heat until all the moisture has evaporated. Stir in 30 ml (2 tablespoons) sour cream (smetana) and salt, pepper and dill or chives.

Spinach pancakes Cook 300 g frozen chopped spinach over a fairly brisk heat until all the moisture has evaporated. Add salt and pepper, and mix in 60 ml (¼ cup) smooth cottage cheese.

Tuna or salmon pancakes Mix a tin of drained, mashed tuna or salmon with 125 g savoury cottage cheese. Add a squeeze of lemon juice, salt and freshly ground black pepper to the mixture.

Pancakes

PANCAKES LEND THEMSELVES exceptionally well to a large variety of sweet or savoury fillings. They may be made a day or two ahead of time and refrigerated (well covered), or frozen for later use.

PREPARATION TIME: 10 MINUTES
CHILLING TIME: 1 HOUR
COOKING TIME: 15 MINUTES

INGREDIENTS FOR 12 PANCAKES
100 g flour
A pinch of salt
3 eggs
250 ml (1 cup) milk, or half milk and half water
15 ml (1 tablespoon) melted butter or sunflower oil (optional)
Butter for frying

Sift together the flour and salt. Beat in the eggs and milk to make a smooth batter. Chill for at least 1 hour.

Just before making the pancakes, stir in the 15 ml (1 tablespoon) melted butter or oil, if used.

Heat a frying pan (one with a non-stick surface is best) until very hot and swirl some butter around in it before pouring in a thin layer of batter. Once browned and set, flip the pancake over to lightly brown the other side. Keep warm over a bowl of boiling water while you complete cooking the rest of the pancakes.

Scotch Eggs

IN THE LAND of their origin, Scotch eggs are part of the traditional and, to foreigners, staggering Scots breakfast, which also includes porridge, bacon, fried eggs, flat sausage, black, white and fruit puddings and hot scones and jam. In South Africa, Scotch eggs are served hot with gravy, or cold with salads.

PREPARATION TIME: 20 MINUTES
COOKING TIME: 10 MINUTES

INGREDIENTS FOR SIX
7 eggs
350 g sausage meat
20 ml (4 teaspoons) finely chopped parsley or sage
Finely grated rind of 1 lemon
1 ml (¼ teaspoon) grated nutmeg
1 ml (¼ teaspoon) dried marjoram, basil or savory
Salt and freshly ground black pepper
100-125 g dried breadcrumbs
Refined peanut or sunflower oil for deep-frying

Boil 6 of the eggs for 10-12 minutes, then allow them to cool under cold running water. Shell carefully, and put the whole eggs on one side.

Put the sausage meat into a bowl with the finely chopped parsley or sage, the lemon rind and nutmeg. Add the marjoram, basil or savory (these herbs greatly improve the flavour).

Season the mixture with salt and freshly ground black pepper, and work all these ingredients well into the sausage meat with your hands.

Make a coating for each hard-boiled egg out of the sausage meat, working it round the eggs with wet hands to form an even layer.

Roll the covered eggs in the remaining egg (beaten), and then in the dried breadcrumbs.

Heat the oil in a deep frying pan. When the oil has just started to smoke – at 180-190°C – carefully put in 3 coated eggs and fry for 4-5 minutes, or until they turn deep golden.

Turn the eggs as they cook so that they brown evenly. Remove with a slotted spoon, drain on paper towels, and repeat with the remaining 3 eggs.

SERVING SUGGESTION Eat hot with gravy* or cold, halved lengthways, with a green salad*.

VARIATIONS For a cheesy version of Scotch eggs, mix 250 g grated Cheddar with 30 g flour, 5 ml (1 teaspoon) salt, 5 ml (1 teaspoon) Worcestershire sauce, a beaten egg and 30 ml (2 tablespoons) milk. Using wet hands, coat 6 hard-boiled* eggs with the cheese mixture, then roll in dried breadcrumbs. Refrigerate the crumbed eggs for an hour or so to allow the crumbs to set. Fry in hot oil until golden.

To make baked Scotch eggs, rather than deep-fried ones, place the prepared eggs on an oiled baking sheet. Drizzle with oil and bake at 200°C for 30 minutes, or until golden-brown and the meat is cooked through.

Eggs Mornay

SLICED OR WHOLE hard-boiled eggs are quickly baked in a creamy cheese sauce. This is a wonderfully easy dish that will be enjoyed by the whole family.

PREPARATION TIME: 40 MINUTES
COOKING TIME: 30 MINUTES
PRE-HEAT OVEN TO 200°C

INGREDIENTS FOR FOUR
8 extra-large eggs

For the sauce:
50 g butter
50 g flour
500 ml (2 cups) milk
Salt and freshly ground black pepper
250 g mature Cheddar cheese, grated
5 ml (1 teaspoon) prepared mustard
25 g breadcrumbs

Boil the eggs in water for 10-12 minutes. Drain, cool under cold running water and shell the eggs. Halve them lengthways and arrange them, cut side down, in a shallow oven-proof or gratin dish.

To make the sauce, melt the butter, stir in the flour and cook for 1-2 minutes without browning. Gradually stir in the milk and bring to the boil, stirring continually to make a smooth sauce. Season well.

Remove from the heat and add half the cheese and the mustard. Stir until the cheese has melted, and pour the sauce over the eggs. Sprinkle with the crumbs (mixed with the remaining cheese) and bake for 30 minutes.

SERVING SUGGESTIONS Serve with crusty bread or a green vegetable: spinach is particularly good.

VARIATIONS Instead of baking, you could grill until golden and bubbling.

Make a bed of mashed potato* or creamed spinach*. Lay the halved eggs on top, then spoon over the sauce.

Spring Rolls

These flavourful rolls are called 'spring rolls' in Shanghai and 'egg rolls' in the Canton region of China. But whatever you choose to call them, they are quite delectable with their savoury filling and crispy batter.

Spring rolls are delicious as part of a Chinese meal and make an unusual appetiser for an ordinary Western-style meal. They can be prepared early or even a day ahead, then dipped in batter and deep-fried just before they are served.

Preparation Time: 30 minutes
Standing Time: 2-3 hours
Cooking Time: 45 minutes

Ingredients for 12 Spring Rolls

For the batter:
40 g self-raising flour
100 ml water
A pinch of salt

For the pancakes:
125 g flour
A pinch of salt
1 egg
1 egg yolk
375 ml (1½ cups) soda water
15 ml (1 tablespoon) sunflower oil
Sunflower oil for frying

For the filling:
45 ml (3 tablespoons) sunflower oil
125 g minced meat
125 g shelled and de-veined* prawns, chopped
50 ml cornflour
5 ml (1 teaspoon) salt
4 spring onions, cut into 1 cm lengths
125 g bean sprouts
125 g mushrooms, sliced
7 ml (1½ teaspoons) sugar
25 ml (5 teaspoons) light soy sauce
1-2 ml (¼-½ teaspoon) five spice powder
30 ml (2 tablespoons) water

Make the batter by mixing together the flour, water and salt, and allowing the mixture to stand for 2-3 hours.

To make the pancakes, sieve the flour and salt into a bowl. Make a well in the centre, add the egg and egg yolk, and gradually stir in the soda water. Beat well until the mixture has a smooth consistency, then add the oil.

Allow the mixture to stand in the refrigerator for 30 minutes. Lightly oil a small frying pan, heat well, then pour in a little of the mixture, filling the pan quickly to make a thin, even pancake.

Cook for 1-2 minutes, then loosen the edges of the pancake with a knife and lift on to a paper towel (you can freeze the pancakes when cool).

Next, make the filling. Heat the oil in a wok or heavy-based frying pan, then sauté the minced meat until it is nearly cooked through.

Toss the prawns in a mixture of 5 ml (1 teaspoon) of the cornflour and the salt, then quickly stir-fry until they are quite firm. Then add the spring onions, bean sprouts, sliced mushrooms, sugar, soy sauce and five spice powder, and stir-fry for a further minute.

Mix the remaining 45 ml (3 tablespoons) cornflour together with the water, add to the pan and stir-fry for another minute. Turn out on to a dish and allow to cool completely.

To assemble the spring rolls, arrange the prepared pancakes on a flat surface with the light side facing upwards. Place a spoonful of the filling on each pancake, then fold over the ends to cover the filling and form a roll.

Heat 2,5 cm deep oil in a heavy-based frying pan (or use a wok). When it is hot, dip the rolls in the batter and fry 4 at a time, turning once, until they are crisp and golden. Drain and serve.

Serving Suggestion Place 2 spring rolls on each plate, together with lemon wedges and prawn crackers.

Variations You may leave out the minced meat and instead use an extra 125 g prawns (totalling 250 g prawns). Alternatively you can use meat only or slices of chicken in combination with the prawns instead of meat.

In place of bean sprouts, you can use sliced cabbage or alternatively bok choy (Chinese cabbage).

If you are unable to obtain five spice powder anywhere, substitute a combination of ground aniseed, fennel, cloves and cinnamon.

Minted Egg Pie *makes a special meal at a low cost.*

Minted Egg Pie

This recipe, which is extremely economical, is also perfectly delicious. The pie makes an ideal luncheon or supper dish served with a salad.

Preparation Time: 15 minutes
Cooking Time: 40 minutes
Pre-heat Oven to 220°C

Ingredients for Four

Shortcrust pastry* using 225 g flour
225 g cream cheese
50 g Cheddar cheese, finely grated
1 ml (¼ teaspoon) grated nutmeg
Salt and freshly ground pepper
4 eggs
20 ml (4 teaspoons) chopped fresh mint

Place a baking sheet in the middle of the pre-heated oven to get really hot.

Butter a deep (19 cm) pie plate and line* it with half the shortcrust pastry. Thoroughly mix the cream cheese, grated Cheddar, nutmeg and seasoning, and spread the mixture over the pastry.

Make 4 little nests and break the eggs into these hollows. Sprinkle thickly with the mint, and season again lightly. Cover with the rest of the pastry. Stand the plate on the baking sheet in the oven so that the bottom crust cooks, and bake for about 40 minutes. After 25 minutes, cover lightly with grease-proof paper to prevent over-browning. Cool before serving.

Serving Suggestion Make a salad accompaniment by mixing together 3 coarsely sliced heads of chicory with the inner hearts of 2 lettuces and ½ finely chopped onion*. Serve this salad with 150 ml home-made mayonnaise*.

Breakfast the Traditional English Way

What better way to start the day than with a full, hearty breakfast!
With proper organisation this traditional English
breakfast menu for six can easily be prepared within an hour.

Menu for Six

•

*Chilled Grapefruit**

*Whiskyed Porridge or Muesli**

*Baked Sausages,
Bacon and Eggs*
or
*Kippers with Scrambled Eggs**
or
*Smoked Haddock with
Egg Sauce*
or
Kedgeree

•

Herbed Crumbed Tomatoes

•

Toast, Scones and Butter*

•

*Selection of jams
and marmalades*

•

Tea or Coffee

Whiskyed Porridge

Preparation Time: 5 minutes
Soaking Time: overnight
Cooking Time: 10 minutes

Ingredients for Six
120 g porridge oats
1 litre (4 cups) milk
A pinch of salt
60 ml (¼ cup) honey
40 g butter
Whisky

Soak the oats overnight in the milk. In the morning, add a pinch of salt and cook gently, stirring often, until the porridge starts to boil and thicken. Stir in a little boiling water if it seems too thick.

Melt the honey and butter and pour into a jug. Serve the porridge, piping hot, in cereal bowls and pour over the honey-butter and a splash of whisky.

Herbed Crumbed Tomatoes

Preparation Time: 15 minutes
Cooking Time: 15 minutes
Pre-heat Oven to 180°C

Ingredients for Six
3 ripe red tomatoes, halved
Salt and freshly ground black pepper
Mild mustard
15 ml (1 tablespoon) melted butter
75 ml fresh breadcrumbs
15 ml (1 tablespoon) chopped parsley

Season the tomatoes lightly and spread with a little mustard. Melt the butter in a pan and stir in the crumbs. Cook until lightly browned. Stir in the parsley and press the mixture on top of each tomato half. Bake for 15 minutes, or until crisp and light golden.

Baked Sausages, Bacon and Eggs

Preparation Time: 5 minutes
Cooking Time: 30 minutes
Pre-heat Oven to 180°C

Ingredients for Six
6 sausages (pork, beef or boerewors)
12 rashers rindless bacon
6 eggs
90 ml melted butter

Prick the sausages and place them on the rack of a large grill pan in the oven. After 10 minutes, add the bacon. Five minutes later, add the eggs, each broken into an individual buttered oven-proof dish just large enough to hold it and covered with 15 ml (1 tablespoon) melted butter. After another 10 minutes, everything should be ready. Arrange on a large, heated platter.

HERBED CRUMBED TOMATOES

KIPPERS WITH SCRAMBLED EGGS

KIPPERS

Sadly, now that herring fishing is limited, the traditional kippers from Britain (Loch Fyne, the Isle of Man, Northumberland and East Anglia) are in short supply, and the only kind readily available in South Africa is the ginger-dyed variety.

If you are fortunate enough to chance upon some true kippers (split, dried and smoked herring), you should treat them as follows:

Slice the kipper flesh very thinly, using a sharp knife and cutting almost horizontally in the way that smoked salmon is sliced. Serve with bread and butter and lemon quarters.

Alternatively, make a Danish-style open sandwich with a nest of kipper slices arranged on a slice of buttered bread. Place a whole raw egg yolk in the middle, seasoned with freshly ground pepper. When you eat the sandwich, break the egg yolk with a fork and mix with the kipper.

All other varieties of kipper will need to be cooked. Buy them on the bone if you can, because the flavour is better than in fillets.

To jug kippers put them tail up into a heavy stoneware jug and pour boiling water in to cover them. Leave them for 5-10 minutes, depending on size, then drain them and serve hot with bread and butter.

To grill kippers arrange them skin side up on a rack in the grill pan. Cook them under a high heat until the skin begins to turn crisp, blisters and comes away from the flesh at the edges: this will take about 5 minutes. Serve at once – there is no need to grill the other side.

Another method is to arrange the kippers in pairs, skin side out, with plenty of butter between them, like a sandwich. Grill them for 5 minutes, then turn the pair over together to grill the other side for 5 minutes.

To fry kippers grease a frying pan, heat it and put in the kippers, skin side down. Cook over medium heat for 2-3 minutes, then turn and fry the other side for 2-3 minutes.

To bake kippers wrap them loosely in buttered aluminium foil, sealing the join and the ends well, and bake at 220°C. A single kipper will take about 5 minutes, and a pair sandwiched together with butter will take 10 minutes.

KEDGEREE

Preparation Time: 25 minutes
Cooking Time: 30 minutes

Ingredients for Six
500 g smoked haddock
Boiling water
80 ml (⅓ cup) clarified butter*
1 large onion, peeled and chopped*
175 g rice
5 ml (1 teaspoon) curry powder
40 g butter

For the garnish:
3 hard-boiled eggs*
15 ml (1 tablespoon) chopped parsley

Place the haddock, skin side up, in a wide, shallow pan, over a low heat. Pour over enough boiling water to barely cover the fish. Cook over a low heat for 10 minutes, without letting the water boil.

Remove the haddock (reserving the cooking liquid), discard the skin, and bone and flake the fish.

Meanwhile, heat the clarified butter in a large pan. Add the onion and cook gently until it begins to soften. Then raise the heat so that the onion browns slightly. Stir in the rice and, as it becomes transparent, add the curry powder. Cook for a minute or two, stirring all the time.

Pour in 600 ml of the water in which the haddock was cooked. Cover, and leave the rice to cook until tender – about 20 minutes. Check every 5 minutes and add more haddock liquid or water, if necessary, to prevent the rice from drying out.

While the rice is cooking, shell and either slice or quarter the eggs. When the rice is tender, mix in the haddock and let it heat through, adding enough butter to keep the mixture moist (dry kedgeree is the sign of a mean cook).

Pile on to a hot serving dish, decorate with hard-boiled eggs and parsley, and serve.

SMOKED HADDOCK WITH EGG SAUCE

Preparation Time: 35 minutes
Cooking Time: 20 minutes

Ingredients for Six
500 g smoked haddock
Boiling water

For the sauce:
2 eggs
600 ml milk
1 bay leaf
4 white peppercorns
2 sprigs parsley
50 g butter
50 g flour
1 ml (¼ teaspoon) grated nutmeg
Salt and pepper

Prepare the haddock in the manner described in the kedgeree recipe, but stop short of flaking it.

To make the sauce, put the eggs in a small pan and cover with cold water. Bring to the boil, then lower the heat and boil gently, to prevent cracking, for 10 minutes. Plunge the eggs into cold water and shell immediately. Separate the whites from the yolks and chop them separately into small pieces.

Put the milk with the bay leaf, peppercorns and parsley in a pan over a gentle heat. Remove when warm, put the lid on the pan, set aside to infuse for 15 minutes, then strain.

Melt the butter over the same gentle heat in a clean pan. Add the flour and nutmeg to the butter, and stir with a wooden spoon until smooth. Continue to cook gently for 2-3 minutes, stirring constantly.

Remove from the heat and add the strained, warm milk, stirring continuously. Return the pan to the heat and bring the sauce up to the boil, still stirring, then simmer for about 5 minutes, stirring from time to time.

When smooth, add the chopped egg whites, season generously with salt and pepper, and stir in half the chopped yolks. Coat the haddock with the sauce and serve immediately, sprinkled with the remaining chopped yolks.

A Selection of Omelette Fillings

One of the biggest advantages of the omelette is its great versatility. A wide variety of tasty fillings can be prepared separately and then spooned over the omelette before it is finally folded over.

No matter what filling you use, remember that an omelette is a dish that must be served immediately, otherwise it loses its lightness and becomes flat and heavy.

Mushroom Stir-fry 50 g thinly sliced mushrooms in 15 g hot butter. Add 15 ml (1 tablespoon) sour cream (smetena) and 5 ml (1 teaspoon) snipped chives.

Chicken liver Sauté 50 g chicken livers in hot butter until they are well browned outside but still pink inside. Add 15 ml (1 tablespoon) port and a pinch of thyme. Reduce this mixture over a high heat and then season to taste.

Three cheeses Mix together the following cheeses: 15 ml (1 tablespoon) cubed mozzarella, 15 ml (1 tablespoon) grated Parmesan and 15 ml (1 tablespoon) savoury cottage cheese.

Smoked oyster Mix 30 ml (2 tablespoons) chopped smoked oysters with 15 ml (1 tablespoon) cream cheese.

Tomato and herb Drizzle a thinly sliced, large ripe red tomato with 5 ml (1 teaspoon) good-quality olive oil and a pinch of dried origanum or 15 ml (1 tablespoon) torn fresh basil leaves.

Smoked salmon Mix 30 ml (2 tablespoons) chopped smoked salmon with 15 ml (1 tablespoon) cream cheese and a pinch of dried dill or 5 ml (1 teaspoon) chopped fresh dill.

Smoked snoek Mix 30 ml (2 tablespoons) flaked smoked snoek with 15 ml (1 tablespoon) thick sour cream (smetena). Alternatively, use flaked tuna.

Ham and cheese Mix 30 ml (2 tablespoons) chopped ham with 30 ml (2 tablespoons) chopped Gruyère cheese.

Sour cream and caviar Top the omelette with 15 ml (1 tablespoon) sour cream (smetena) and sprinkle over 15 ml (1 tablespoon) 'caviar'.

Sour cream and chives Spoon 15 ml (1 tablespoon) sour cream (smetena) over the omelette and sprinkle over 15 ml (1 tablespoon) finely chopped chives.

Basic French Omelette

A WELL-MADE OMELETTE is one of the quickest and best-tasting meals to make. Add a substantial filling to make a perfect luncheon or light supper dish.

PREPARATION TIME: 5 MINUTES
COOKING TIME: 5 MINUTES

INGREDIENTS FOR ONE
2 eggs
15 ml (1 tablespoon) water
10 ml (2 teaspoons) butter
Salt and freshly ground pepper

Beat the eggs with the water. Heat the butter in a suitable frying pan (the non-stick variety is best). When the butter has melted and the pan is hot, pour in the egg mixture. Keep lifting the edges to allow the liquid egg to run beneath.

Add the seasoning and allow to cook until the omelette starts to puff in the pan and the lower surface turns golden. Slide the omelette on to a warmed plate, deftly folding it over, and serve immediately.

Soufflé Omelette

YOU CAN MAKE a light, puffed omelette by separating the eggs and whipping the whites until stiff.

PREPARATION TIME: 5 MINUTES
COOKING TIME: 5 MINUTES
PRE-HEAT THE GRILL TO HOT

INGREDIENTS FOR ONE
2 eggs, separated
15 ml (1 tablespoon) water
Salt and freshly ground pepper
15 g butter
Chopped herbs for garnish

Beat the egg whites until stiff, then lightly beat the yolks in a separate bowl with the water and a little pepper. Fold the two together.

Heat the butter in a suitable omelette pan and use a spatula to spread the mixture evenly over the pan. Cook over a medium heat until golden-brown and very puffed, then place under the pre-heated grill for 2-3 minutes until set and slightly browned on top. Slide the omelette on to a warmed plate and fold over. Sprinkle with the herbs and salt and serve immediately.

Soufflé Jam Omelette

SWEET OMELETTES were very popular in English manor houses in Edwardian times. The cook could make them while the family and guests were eating the previous course. Still popular in England, these omelettes are not as well known in South Africa – although anyone who tastes them is sure to be won over.

PREPARATION TIME: 10 MINUTES
COOKING TIME: 5 MINUTES
PRE-HEAT THE GRILL TO VERY HOT

INGREDIENTS FOR FOUR TO SIX
4 egg yolks
30 ml (2 tablespoons) castor sugar
6 egg whites
1 ml (¼ teaspoon) salt
30 g butter
Castor sugar for sprinkling
15 ml (1 tablespoon) jam, warmed

Beat the egg yolks and castor sugar together. Whisk the egg whites with the salt until they have become stiff enough to stand up in peaks (this can be done well before the meal).

Just before cooking, quickly whisk the egg whites and salt again, and then stir them lightly into the beaten yolks while the butter is melting in a large omelette pan.

When the butter is very hot, pour in the egg mixture and cook for 3 minutes. Finish cooking the top by holding the pan under the hot grill for about 2 minutes, or until the omelette is well risen and golden.

Slide it on to aluminium foil sprinkled with castor sugar, carefully spread the warmed jam over it, and fold it in half by folding over the foil.

Slide the omelette from the foil on to a warm dish and serve at once, cut in wedges.

SERVING SUGGESTION A variety of jams can be used, such as an apricot* or strawberry jam*, or an imported cherry jam.

SOUFFLÉ JAM OMELETTE *A simple dessert that is bound to please.*

Omelette Arnold Bennett

THIS PERFECT MARRIAGE of haddock and Parmesan cheese took place in London's Savoy Grill. The name is a salute from one great artist to another – from Jean Baptiste Virlogeux, then the Savoy Hotel's *chef de cuisine*, to Arnold Bennett, the novelist who had immortalised Virlogeux as 'Roho' in his novel *Imperial Palace*, which was based on life at the Savoy Hotel.

Serve this dish as a light luncheon or supper dish, or as a snack before an evening at the theatre.

PREPARATION TIME: 15 MINUTES
COOKING TIME: 5 MINUTES
PRE-HEAT THE GRILL TO VERY HOT

INGREDIENTS FOR ONE
75 g cooked haddock, flaked
5 ml (1 teaspoon) grated Parmesan cheese
Salt and freshly ground pepper
2 eggs
15 ml (1 tablespoon) water
7 ml (1½ teaspoons) butter
15 ml (1 tablespoon) thick cream

Mix together the flaked haddock and cheese, season with salt and pepper, and then set aside.

Break the eggs into a bowl, add the water and season with a little pepper. Beat lightly with a fork.

Melt the butter in an omelette pan and, when it has become frothy, pour in the beaten eggs.

Cook over a medium heat until the omelette is only just set and still liquid in the middle. Salt lightly and transfer (unfolded) to an oven-proof plate.

Spread the haddock and cheese mixture over the top of the omelette and pour on the cream.

Slide under the very hot grill for a few minutes, until it is slightly browned and bubbling. Serve immediately.

SERVING SUGGESTIONS To make a more substantial meal, serve with grilled tomatoes or creamed spinach* and follow with a green salad*.

VARIATION Substitute smoked snoek for the haddock.

SPANISH OMELETTE *Potatoes and onions set in golden egg.*

Spanish Omelette

THIS LIGHT but solid-textured Spanish omelette makes a fine luncheon dish with a simple salad of lettuce, tomato and onion tossed at the table (Spanish-style) with a generous sprinkling of olive oil and a little vinegar. Add a slice of fresh, crusty bread and a glass of wine.

PREPARATION TIME: 15 MINUTES
COOKING TIME: 20 MINUTES

INGREDIENTS FOR FOUR
*2 medium-sized onions, peeled and finely chopped**
4 medium-sized potatoes, peeled and finely chopped
60 ml (¼ cup) olive oil
6 eggs, beaten
Salt and freshly ground black pepper
Finely chopped parsley for garnish

Use a very wide, heavy frying pan. Sauté the onions and potatoes very gently in the heated oil until they are soft but not browned. Pour in the beaten eggs and then cook until set.

Place a large oven-proof plate or baking sheet over the frying pan and invert the omelette on to it. Then slip the omelette carefully back into the pan to brown the other side.

Season lightly, sprinkle with parsley and serve immediately.

SERVING SUGGESTION Cut the omelette into individual wedges and then serve either hot or cold.

VARIATIONS Add any of the following ingredients to the softened onions and potatoes: peas, sliced mushrooms, spinach, tinned asparagus or fresh cooked asparagus, fresh or tinned artichoke hearts, chopped ham, anchovies, sliced chorizo sausage or garlic.

Piperade

THIS DISH originates in the Basque region of Spain. It combines creamy scrambled eggs with simmered onions, peppers and tomatoes – ingredients which abound in our country, and which provide a wonderful combination of flavours.

PREPARATION TIME: 10 MINUTES
COOKING TIME: 30 MINUTES

INGREDIENTS FOR FOUR
45 ml (3 tablespoons) olive oil
*2 medium-sized onions, peeled and thinly sliced**
2 cloves garlic, crushed
2 large sweet red peppers, thinly sliced
4 ripe red tomatoes, skinned and chopped*
2 ml (½ teaspoon) origanum
Salt and freshly ground black pepper
6 eggs, lightly beaten

Heat the oil in a frying pan and add the onions. Cook very gently until barely soft, then add the garlic and sliced peppers, and continue to cook gently until very soft. Add the tomatoes, origanum and seasoning.

Cook (covered) very gently for another 5-10 minutes. Pour in the beaten eggs and cook over a gentle heat, stirring, until the eggs are barely set and very creamy. Season to taste and serve.

STUFFED EGGS

Hard-boiled eggs* can be stuffed with a variety of fillings to make tasty snacks.

Shell 6 hard-boiled eggs and slice in half lengthways. To make the basic filling, remove the yolks and mash them with 30 ml (2 tablespoons) mayonnaise* and seasoning. Spoon or pipe the filling into the whites. If you like, mix in a little cream.

Devilled stuffing Mash the yolks with 50 g unsalted butter, and season with nutmeg and cayenne pepper.

Anchovy stuffing Pound 8 (drained) anchovy fillets to a paste and mix thoroughly with the basic egg filling.

Ham stuffing Dice 4 slices ham very finely and add to the basic egg filling.

Hints on Making Savoury Soufflés

A soufflé is simply a highly flavoured sauce or purée mixed with stiffly whipped egg whites which expand and puff in a really hot oven.

There is no mystery to making a good soufflé. Simply follow three easy rules: the basic sauce or purée must be fairly thick (like whipped cream), but soft enough to drop from a spoon; the egg whites must be stiffly whipped but not over-beaten and dry; and the whites should be folded, not beaten in.

A savoury soufflé dish need not have a paper collar, and the soufflé mixture can be left in the refrigerator for up to 2 hours before baking.

Bake at a high heat (200°C) so that it rises quickly and is soft inside but crisp and brown outside.

When ready, a soufflé should have increased by a half to two-thirds in volume, and should have risen above the edge of the dish. Shake it gently: if it wobbles all over, it is not done, and if just the middle wobbles, it is done to suit the French preference (a further 2-3 minutes' cooking makes it slightly firmer).

Even if the soufflé does not rise as high as you had hoped, it will still taste wonderful. The presentation trick is just to call it a savoury mould, and your guests will be none the wiser.

Soufflé Fillings

Asparagus soufflé Make a cheese soufflé using 75 g grated cheese. Spoon half the soufflé mixture into a prepared dish. Add 125 g cooked, chopped tender asparagus. Top this with the remaining soufflé mixture and bake it.

Salmon or tuna soufflé Flake or pound 225 g cooked fresh (or a tin of drained) salmon or tuna. Add this to the basic egg yolk sauce of the cheese soufflé recipe, with or without cheese. Season it well, then fold in the egg whites. Turn into a dish and bake it.

Smoked fish soufflé Flake or pound 225 g cooked smoked fish and stir this into the egg yolk mixture of the cheese soufflé. Fold in the remaining ingredients with a pinch of ground nutmeg, if liked. Turn this mixture into a soufflé dish and bake it.

Blue cheese soufflé Use 100 g blue cheese in the cheese soufflé recipe.

Cheese Soufflé

THIS IS A BASIC soufflé recipe which can be adapted to almost any fish or vegetable filling. See panel on left for suggestions for fillings.

This meal makes an inexpensive starter, or a light lunch or supper dish. Many people are intimidated by the idea of making soufflés but they are, in fact, easy to prepare.

PREPARATION TIME: 30 MINUTES
COOKING TIME: 25 MINUTES
PRE-HEAT OVEN TO 200°C

INGREDIENTS FOR FOUR
30 g butter
30 ml (2 tablespoons) flour
250 ml (1 cup) hot milk
Salt and freshly ground black pepper
4 egg yolks
A good pinch of dry mustard
A pinch of cayenne pepper
75-100 g mature Cheddar or Gruyère cheese, grated
5 egg whites
15 ml (1 tablespoon) fine dry breadcrumbs
15 ml (1 tablespoon) grated Parmesan cheese

Melt the butter, stir in the flour and cook for 1-2 minutes without browning. Add the milk and bring the mixture slowly to the boil, stirring continually to make a smooth, thick sauce.

Remove from the heat and beat in the seasoning, followed by the egg yolks, one at a time. Beat in the mustard and cayenne pepper with the grated Cheddar or Gruyère cheese.

Whisk the egg whites until they are stiff but not dry, and fold them into the soufflé mixture. Spoon the mixture into a 750 ml buttered oven-proof dish dusted all over with the breadcrumbs and grated Parmesan cheese. Bake the soufflé for about 25 minutes.

SERVING SUGGESTION Serve with a fresh green salad*.

VARIATIONS Pour the soufflé mixture into half-baked pastry or tartlet shells and bake at 200°C for 15 minutes until puffed and golden.

Pour the soufflé mixture over fillets of sole and bake until puffed and golden.

CHEESE BOUREKITAS *Spinach and potato fill these pastry crescents.*

Cheese Bourekitas

THIS EASY AND UNUSUAL recipe has won many admiring comments. Experiment with different fillings and textures to suit your own tastes and availability of ingredients.

PREPARATION TIME: 1 HOUR
COOKING TIME: 15-20 MINUTES
PRE-HEAT OVEN TO 180°C

INGREDIENTS FOR SIX TO EIGHT
250 ml (1 cup) sunflower oil
250 ml (1 cup) iced water
3 ml (¾ teaspoon) salt
480 g flour (or enough to make a firm dough)

For the potato filling:
4 large potatoes, peeled, boiled and mashed
3 eggs, beaten
120-150 g grated Parmesan cheese
Salt and pepper

For the spinach filling:
1 bunch spinach, stalks removed, washed, dried and finely shredded
15 ml (1 tablespoon) flour
2 eggs, beaten
100 g mozzarella cheese, grated
Salt and pepper

For the garnish:
1 egg, beaten
Parmesan cheese

Mix the oil, water and salt in a deep mixing bowl. Add the flour slowly and knead vigorously, then shape the dough into 4 cm balls. Allow the balls to rest for 15 minutes before rolling them out into thin discs on a floured board.

Mix the ingredients of each filling until smooth, and place 5 ml (1 teaspoon) of filling in the centre of each disc. Fill half of the discs with the spinach mixture and the rest with the potato mixture. Fold the discs into crescent shapes, brush the tops with beaten egg and sprinkle with Parmesan cheese.

Bake until golden (about 15-20 minutes) and serve immediately.

SERVING SUGGESTIONS This dish makes a tasty tea time snack or light snack before a midday or evening meal. It also tastes good when served at room temperature.

POTTED STILTON

THE VILLAGE OF STILTON in England gave its name to this most noble of cheeses. In 18th century England a number of cheeses were potted with spices and a 'glass of sack' (sherry). Although sherry benefits a mild cheese it is not the best for Stilton: if the Stilton is very dry, add a little port. Locally produced Blaauwkrantz, Rosetta or Gourmet Blue make less expensive substitutes for Stilton.

PREPARATION TIME: 10-15 MINUTES

INGREDIENTS TO YIELD ABOUT 275 G
225 g mellow Stilton
50 g unsalted butter, softened
1 ml (¼ teaspoon) ground mace
2 ml (½ teaspoon) freshly made English mustard
Clarified butter* (optional)

Mash the cheese with the butter, add the mace and mustard, and work to a cream. Pack into earthenware or china pots, making sure the cheese is well pressed down. To keep the cheese for any length of time, cover it with clarified butter.

VARIATIONS You can make potted cheese in this way with any mixture of left-over cheeses. If it seems too dry, mix in 30 ml (2 tablespoons) sherry.

To vary the flavour, add 1 ml (¼ teaspoon) curry powder or cayenne pepper in place of the mace and mustard.

MACARONI CHEESE

THE SECRET OF SUCCESS with macaroni cheese – always a good standby meal – is simply to be lavish with the strongly flavoured cheese sauce.

This dish is quick and easy to prepare and makes a popular and filling family meal.

PREPARATION TIME: 30-35 MINUTES
COOKING TIME: 20 MINUTES
PRE-HEAT OVEN TO 190°C

INGREDIENTS FOR FOUR
350 g macaroni
25 g fine home-made breadcrumbs
15 g butter, cut into pieces

For the sauce:
25 g butter
25 g flour
500 ml (2 cups) milk
Salt and freshly ground pepper
1 ml (¼ teaspoon) freshly grated nutmeg
100-125 g Cheddar cheese, grated

Bring a large pan of well-salted water to the boil, and put in the macaroni. Cook it for 15-20 minutes, or until just tender. Do not overcook, or it will not absorb the sauce. Drain well.

To make the cheese sauce, melt the 25 g butter in a medium-sized saucepan. Stir in the flour and let it cook for 2-3 minutes over a gentle heat. Gradually add the milk, stirring all the time with a wooden spoon to obtain a smooth, velvety sauce. Season, then add the nutmeg.

Let the sauce cook gently for 10-15 minutes, stirring from time to time, then add the cheese. When the cheese has melted, stir in the cooked, drained macaroni. Check the seasoning, and pour the mixture into a pie dish.

Sprinkle the top with the breadcrumbs, dot all over with the cut butter, and bake in the pre-heated oven for 20 minutes (or until golden-brown).

SERVING SUGGESTION Serve with baked tomatoes and a green vegetable or salad.

VARIATIONS Add a layer of sautéed tomatoes and onions in the middle.

Mix in 50 g chopped ham as an extra ingredient.

To make an even more substantial meal, pour the mixture over left-over fish.

ROULADES – FLUFFY SOUFFLÉ ROLLS

Roulades are light, fluffy soufflé rolls that lend themselves well to imaginative fillings. This recipe is for the basic roulade and three fillings, but any other savoury vegetable or seafood mixture, folded into a cream* or white sauce*, is also suitable for a filling. Roulades can be re-heated successfully and make good luncheon or supper dishes.

First make the soufflé base: melt 60 g butter in a saucepan, stir in 60 g flour and cook for 1 minute without browning. Gradually add 500 ml (2 cups) milk and cook, stirring constantly, in order to make a thick sauce.

Remove from the heat, stir in 5 ml (1 teaspoon) sugar, and season with salt and pepper. Lightly beat together 4 egg yolks, then beat them into the sauce. Whisk 4 egg whites until they are stiff, then fold them into the sauce.

Spread the soufflé mixture evenly into a greased, lined Swiss roll tin about 33 cm x 23 cm. Bake at 160°C for 40-45 minutes, or until golden.

Turn out the roulade on a sheet of wax or grease-proof paper, then peel off the lining paper. Keep warm.

Prepare the filling of your choice, then spread it over the roulade. Roll up the roulade from the long side and, if necessary, re-heat it for 10-15 minutes at 160°C. It should be served hot.

Fillings for roulades

Mushroom roulade Fry 1 large chopped onion* in 30 ml (2 tablespoons) sunflower oil and 30 g butter until soft. Add 400 g sliced mushrooms, and cook until the liquid has evaporated.

Remove from the heat, and stir in 30 ml (2 tablespoons) lemon juice and 125 ml (½ cup) sour cream (smetana). Season the mixture with salt and pepper. Serve the completed roulade with a further 125 ml (½ cup) sour cream for spooning on top of each of the individual servings.

Spinach roulade Heat 500 g cooked and chopped spinach with 30 g butter in a large saucepan. Stir in 10 ml (2 teaspoons) flour, and cook, stirring constantly, for 1 minute. Slowly add 250 ml (1 cup) cream or milk, and heat gently. Season well, then stir in a pinch of freshly grated nutmeg and 3 chopped hard-boiled* eggs (optional).

Haddock roulade Toss 500 g cooked and flaked smoked haddock in 10 ml (2 teaspoons) butter and 10 ml (2 teaspoons) flour, and cook, stirring constantly, for 1 minute.

Slowly add 250 ml (1 cup) cream or milk, and heat gently, stirring. Season well with salt and pepper, and stir in 30 ml (2 tablespoons) freshly chopped parsley. Garnish the completed roulade with a further 30 ml (2 tablespoons) fresh parsley.

EGGS AND CHEESE

QUICHES – QUICK AND TASTY SAVOURY TARTS

Quiches – open tarts with savoury fillings based on egg custard – make simple and thoroughly delicious meals served hot or cold. They also take very little time to prepare.

The first step is to line a quiche tin: roll out unsweetened shortcrust pastry* so that it fits a 23 cm loose-bottomed quiche tin. Prick the base.

Next make an egg custard: beat 3 eggs with 250 ml (1 cup) cream or sour cream (smetana) or half cream and half milk and 60 ml (¼ cup) grated Cheddar or Gruyère cheese, salt and pepper.

Place the filling of your choice in the pastry case, pour over the custard, then bake the quiche at 180°C for 35-45 minutes until set but not overcooked. The centre may be a little soft, but will settle further as the quiche cools slightly.

Asparagus quiche Fill the pastry case with egg custard and the contents of a 410 g tin of drained asparagus cuts.

Smoked haddock quiche Sprinkle the pastry case with 250 g cooked, flaked smoked haddock. Pour over egg custard, seasoned with salt, freshly ground black pepper and 5 ml (1 teaspoon) finely grated lemon rind, if desired.

Leek quiche Simmer 2 bunches (6-8) well-washed, sliced leeks in 50 g butter until they are soft (but not brown). Spoon this into the pastry case and cover with well-seasoned egg custard. Sprinkle the top with grated cheese.

Mushroom quiche Fill the pastry case with 300 g sliced mushrooms fried in 30 g butter. Top this with egg custard and sprinkle with grated cheese.

Onion quiche Fry 3-4 large sliced onions* in 50 g butter and 15 ml (1 tablespoon) sunflower oil until they are very soft. Spread the onions over the pastry case and top with egg custard, with or without grated cheese.

Prawn or crayfish quiche Fill the pastry case with 200 g cooked, de-veined* prawns or roughly chopped cooked crayfish. Cover with egg custard, flavoured with a hint of grated nutmeg.

Quiche Lorraine Coarsely chop 6 thin rashers streaky bacon and fry them for a minute so that the fat begins to run. Sprinkle the bacon in the pastry case, cover with egg custard and sprinkle the top with cheese. Add to the bacon 2-3 chopped spring onions sautéed in butter, if desired.

Smoked salmon quiche Arrange 175-200 g sliced smoked salmon in the pastry case. Cover with egg custard, flavoured with a little freshly chopped dill, if liked. Alternatively, garnish with sprigs of dill once baked.

Smoked snoek quiche Flake 250 g smoked snoek into the pastry case. Add a thinly sliced onion* (optional) sautéed in butter, then pour over egg custard and sprinkle with grated cheese, if desired.

Spinach quiche Cook 500 g spinach in 30 ml (2 tablespoons) water. Drain the spinach well, season and chop coarsely. Beat in 3 eggs, 125 ml (½ cup) cream, 250 g smooth cottage cheese and a sprinkling of grated nutmeg. Spoon this into a pastry case and bake until firm.

Tuna quiche Drain and flake a 200 g tin of tuna. Sprinkle the fish over a pastry case with 10 ml (2 teaspoons) capers or 3-4 chopped anchovies, if liked. Cover this with egg custard and bake.

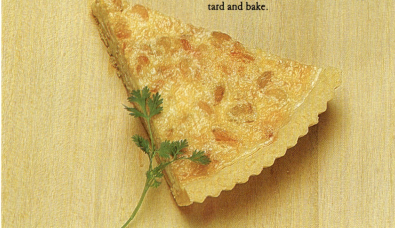

TYROPITA

THESE SMALL CHEESE PASTRIES are ideal to serve with drinks. They are also popular hors d'oeuvres – but make sure you have plenty of them on hand, as they are inclined to be consumed in surprisingly large quantities.

PREPARATION TIME: 45 MINUTES
COOKING TIME: 25 MINUTES
PRE-HEAT OVEN TO 180°C

INGREDIENTS FOR 24 PASTRIES

*500 g phyllo pastry**
250 ml (1 cup) melted butter
125 ml (½ cup) crumbled feta cheese
1 egg yolk
*30 ml (2 tablespoons) béchamel sauce**
Salt and freshly ground black pepper

Cut 24 strips (25 cm x 5 cm) from double layers of pastry and brush them with melted butter.

Mix together the feta cheese, egg and béchamel sauce, and then season with salt and pepper.

Place 5 ml (1 teaspoon) of the cheese mixture on one end of each strip and fold the pastry over it to form a small triangle (like folding samoosas*). Continue folding the pastry over in triangles down the full length of the strip, to make one multi-layered triangle.

Prepare the remaining strips of pastry in the same way.

Place the pastries on a buttered baking sheet, brush them with butter and bake them until they are golden (20-25 minutes). Serve hot.

SERVING SUGGESTION The pastries freeze very well, enabling you to prepare them well in advance. You should freeze them on a tray in one layer and, when frozen, place in a plastic bag and return to the freezer for use as required.

VARIATION For a different filling, the following variation is recommended: mix together 250 ml (1 cup) feta cheese, 30 ml (2 tablespoons) Parmesan cheese, 2 eggs, 30 ml (2 tablespoons) chopped parsley, a few scrapings of freshly grated nutmeg, and pepper. (If you use this filling recipe, omit the béchamel sauce.)

WELSH RAREBIT

THERE ARE ALMOST as many recipes for Welsh rarebit as there are cookbooks. This recipe is slightly more complicated than some, but it combines all the traditional ingredients, and is very tasty.

PREPARATION TIME: 15 MINUTES
COOKING TIME: 15 MINUTES

INGREDIENTS FOR SIX

30 g butter
250 ml (1 cup) beer
500 g Cheddar cheese, grated
1 egg, lightly beaten
5 ml (1 teaspoon) Worcestershire sauce
5 ml (1 teaspoon) salt
3 ml (¾ teaspoon) paprika
1 ml (¼ teaspoon) dry mustard, or a pinch of cayenne pepper
3 ml (¾ teaspoon) curry powder (optional)
6 slices hot, buttered toast

Melt the butter in the top of a double boiler and add the beer. When the beer is warm, slowly add the cheese and stir until melted. Beat slightly with a wire whisk, then add the egg and Worcestershire sauce.

Season to taste with the salt, paprika, mustard or cayenne pepper and curry (if used). Turn at once on to the hot, buttered toast and arrange the slices in a hot serving dish. Serve immediately.

SERVING SUGGESTIONS Welsh rarebit is also very good when spooned on to hot grilled tomatoes, or over crisply cooked cauliflower. Served this way, it makes a substantial and tasty luncheon or supper dish with fresh brown bread and a good salad.

VARIATION Welsh rarebit can also be made with milk or cream instead of beer. Substitute 200 ml creamy milk or cream for the beer and make in the usual way.

FRENCH TOAST

THE FRENCH NAME for this popular snack is *pain perdu*, literally 'lost bread' – for it is a delicious way of making use of slightly stale left-over bread.

PREPARATION TIME: 10 MINUTES
COOKING TIME: 10 MINUTES

EGGS AND CHEESE

INGREDIENTS FOR FOUR
8 slices French bread, or 4 slices of a larger loaf
3 eggs
125 ml (½ cup) milk
Butter for frying
Cinnamon sugar* for garnish

Prick the bread well with a fork. Beat the eggs and milk together and pour the mixture over the bread. Keep pricking and turning with a fork until the bread is saturated with the liquid.

Fry the slices in hot butter until golden-brown and serve immediately, sprinkling the toast with cinnamon sugar.

SERVING SUGGESTION Serve the toast American-style, with maple syrup and crisply grilled bacon.

PUFFY CHEESE TOAST

THIS IS A SUPER version of cheese toast. It lends itself to all sorts of variations to make an ideal light supper dish.

PREPARATION TIME: 15 MINUTES
COOKING TIME: 15 MINUTES
PRE-HEAT OVEN TO 220°C

INGREDIENTS FOR FOUR
200 g Cheddar or Gruyère cheese, grated
60 ml (¼ cup) savoury skim milk cheese
1 egg, beaten
1 ml (¼ teaspoon) dry mustard
15 ml (1 tablespoon) cream
Salt and freshly ground pepper
4 thick slices bread

Mix the ingredients, except for the bread, together to form a thick paste, and season. Spread the paste over the bread and bake on a buttered baking sheet for about 15 minutes, or until puffy and golden.

VARIATIONS Toast the bread under a hot grill on one side only. Spread the untoasted side with the cheese mixture and slide under the grill to brown.

Try sliced ham or grilled rashers of bacon under the cheese topping.

Make quick pizza toast by placing sliced tomatoes under the cheese mixture and crossing the top with fillets of anchovy. Add a pinch of origanum to the cheese mixture.

SPANAKOPITTA *This classic Greek spinach and feta cheese pie makes an excellent meal on its own.*

SPANAKOPITTA

THIS TRADITIONAL Greek recipe has become popular throughout the world. Now that phyllo pastry is available in speciality shops, even the novice can tackle it with confidence.

This dish may be made in advance, since it freezes well. If frozen, allow it to thaw before baking.

PREPARATION TIME: 40 MINUTES
COOKING TIME: 40 MINUTES
PRE-HEAT OVEN TO 175°C

INGREDIENTS FOR SIX
1 kg spinach
2-3 bunches spring onions
15 ml (1 tablespoon) salt
150 g butter
2 medium-sized onions, peeled and finely chopped*
2 extra-large eggs, beaten
200 g feta cheese, crumbled
Freshly ground black pepper
10 sheets phyllo pastry*

Wash, dry and finely chop the spinach (use a food processor if you have one). Chop the spring onions and place them in a colander in alternate layers with the spinach, sprinkling each layer with a little salt. Leave for 20 minutes.

Heat half the butter in a frying pan and add the chopped onions. Cook until they are transparent but not brown.

Squeeze out most of the moisture from the spinach and spring onion mixture. Place the vegetables in a mixing bowl and add the sautéed onion. In a separate bowl, add the crumbled feta cheese to the egg and season with black pepper. Blend the spinach and the cheese mixtures.

Melt the remaining butter. Butter a dish 25 cm x 25 cm x 4 cm, and lay one sheet of phyllo pastry in it, allowing the ends to overlap the dish. Brush with melted butter. While you are doing this, make sure that the rest of the pastry is covered all the time with a slightly dampened cloth or a sheet of plastic wrap to prevent it from drying out. Repeat the process until you have used 5 sheets of phyllo pastry.

Fill the pastry-lined dish with the spinach filling. Cover with a further 4 sheets of the phyllo pastry (remember to brush each layer with butter), cutting each piece of pastry to fit the exact size of the dish.

Fold the bottom layers of pastry over the top layers to tidy the edge. Brush the last piece of pastry with butter and overlap with the folded pastry. Make a diamond pattern, if desired, by cutting through the first 2-3 sheets of pastry with the tip of a sharp knife. Bake for 40 minutes.

VARIATIONS Spanakopitta may also be made in a rectangular dish or a round cake tin. If you use the latter, do not cut the pastry into a round shape, as the leaves must still overlap.

If fresh spinach is not available, substitute 1,5 kg frozen spinach, thawed.

Fresh dill makes a refreshing difference to the flavour, and 125 ml (½ cup) of freshly grated Parmesan cheese added to the spinach mixture will give it much additional character.

Quick Meals with Eggs and Cheese

Eggs and cheese are the basic ingredients of a number of exciting recipes that constitute quite substantial meals in themselves.

BAKED DEVILLED EGGS

THE IMAGINATIVE USE of interesting seasonings, and devilling the hard-boiled eggs, makes for a much more interesting dish than the popular sliced hard-boiled eggs baked in a cheese sauce.

PREPARATION TIME: 45 MINUTES
COOKING TIME: 20 MINUTES
PRE-HEAT OVEN TO 200°C

INGREDIENTS FOR SIX

6 eggs
15 ml (1 tablespoon) mayonnaise*
7 ml (1½ teaspoons) white wine vinegar
3 ml (¾ teaspoon) dry mustard
5 ml (1 teaspoon) Worcestershire sauce
3 ml (¾ teaspoon) salt
A dash of black pepper
A dash of paprika
30 ml (2 tablespoons) grated mature Cheddar cheese

For the sauce:
125 g butter
125 ml (½ cup) finely chopped onion*
30 ml (2 tablespoons) flour
2 ml (½ teaspoon) dry mustard
2 ml (½ teaspoon) salt
Freshly ground black pepper
375 ml (1½ cups) milk
125 ml (½ cup) grated mature Cheddar cheese
30 ml (2 tablespoons) grated Parmesan cheese for topping

Boil the eggs for 10-12 minutes, cool under cold running water, shell and halve lengthways. When the eggs are cold, remove the yolks carefully, and press through a sieve into a medium-sized basin. Add the mayonnaise, vinegar, mustard, Worcestershire sauce, salt, black pepper, paprika and grated Cheddar, and beat until smooth and fluffy. Insert the filling mixture into the hollow centres of the egg whites.

To make the sauce, heat the butter in a medium-sized saucepan, and sauté the onion until pale golden. Remove and set aside. To the left-over fat add the flour, mustard, salt and pepper, and stir until smooth. Gradually add the milk, stirring continuously, and bring to the boil. Remove from the heat, add the Cheddar cheese and onions, and stir until the cheese has melted.

Place the eggs, filled sides up, on a buttered oven-proof dish and cover with the cheese sauce. Sprinkle over the Parmesan and bake, uncovered, for 20 minutes.

SERVING SUGGESTION Serve hot from the oven with rounds of garlic bread*.

VARIATION Arrange a drained tin of asparagus, mushrooms or sweet corn on the bottom of the dish. You can use the liquid from the tin with milk to make up the liquid required for the sauce.

EGGS AND ASPARAGUS

EGGS AND ASPARAGUS complement each other extremely well. This dish, garnished with black pepper, makes a delicious light luncheon or supper.

PREPARATION TIME: 20-30 MINUTES
COOKING TIME: 5-10 MINUTES

INGREDIENTS FOR TWO

12 stalks cooked* or tinned asparagus
4 eggs, beaten
Salt and freshly ground black pepper
2 slices bread
40 g butter

Cut the asparagus into 1,5 cm lengths. Stir the asparagus pieces into the beaten eggs in a bowl, and season to taste.

Toast the bread and spread it with 15 g of the butter. Keep hot under the grill. Melt the remaining butter in a small, heavy-based saucepan. Pour in the egg and asparagus mixture and stir constantly with a wooden spoon over a moderate heat until it thickens to a creamy consistency.

Divide the mixture over the two slices of buttered toast and serve immediately.

SAVOURY BREAD AND BUTTER PUDDING

THIS IS AN old English supper dish that makes a very tasty meal. It can be refrigerated the day before, after the milk has been poured over the bread. It is then allowed to return to room temperature before being baked.

PREPARATION TIME: 20 MINUTES
COOKING TIME: 1½ HOURS
PRE-HEAT OVEN TO 180°C

INGREDIENTS FOR SIX

125 g soft unsalted butter
9 slices white bread
500 g mature Cheddar cheese, grated
45 ml (3 tablespoons) finely chopped spring onions
750 ml (3 cups) milk
6 large eggs, beaten lightly
A few drops of Tabasco (chilli sauce)
7 ml (1½ teaspoons) salt
5 ml (1 teaspoon) dry mustard

Set aside 30 g of the butter, then spread the remaining butter on the slices of bread. Remove the crusts and cut the bread into 1 cm cubes.

Arrange half the bread cubes in a well-greased 2,25 litre oven-proof dish and top with half the grated Cheddar cheese. Cover with the remaining cubes and then the remaining cheese.

Fry the spring onions in the reserved butter until softened. Beat together the milk, eggs, onions, Tabasco, salt and mustard, and pour this mixture over the cheese and bread. Place the dish in a pan of hot water and bake for about 1½ hours until it is set and golden.

SERVING SUGGESTION Serve hot with a bowl of chutney.

VARIATION Two large tomatoes, skinned* and chopped, may be sprinkled over the layers of bread before adding the sauce.

SHRIMP OMELETTE

ALTHOUGH SHRIMPS are one of the main ingredients in this recipe, you can vary it by using other shellfish.

PREPARATION TIME: 10 MINUTES
COOKING TIME: 2-3 MINUTES

INGREDIENTS FOR TWO TO THREE

6 eggs
15 ml (1 tablespoon) finely mixed chopped fresh parsley and chives
Salt and freshly ground black pepper
125 g shelled shrimps, coarsely chopped
1 spring onion, finely chopped
5 ml (1 teaspoon) flour
75 g butter

Place a serving dish under the grill at a low heat to warm.

Whisk the eggs in a bowl with the chopped herbs and seasoning until they are very light.

Stir in the chopped shrimps and the finely chopped spring onion. Sprinkle on the flour, and drop in 25 g of the butter, cut into small pieces.

Melt the remaining butter in a large omelette pan. When the butter starts to brown, pour in the egg mixture and cook quickly for 2-3 minutes, stirring it round a little and lifting the edges with a spatula to allow the butter to run underneath the omelette.

Place the heated serving dish beside the stove. Slide the omelette on to the dish, folding it in half as you do so.

Serve the omelette very hot. The butter will run out round the omelette in a golden pool – spoon it over each piece of omelette as you serve it.

VARIATIONS Add half a 410 g tin of whole kernel sweet corn, omitting the parsley and chives, and flavouring the egg with a pinch of nutmeg.

Substitute shelled and de-veined prawns*, coarsely chopped; crayfish, cleaned* and chopped; or perlemoen, prepared* and minced, for the shelled shrimps.

EGGS IN OVERCOATS

BEATEN EGG WHITES, or 'bird's milk' as the ancient Greeks called it, makes this combination of eggs and potatoes surprisingly light-textured. Served with salad, it provides an excellent light supper.

PREPARATION TIME: 30 MINUTES
COOKING TIME: 1¼ HOURS
PRE-HEAT OVEN TO 200°C

INGREDIENTS FOR SIX

6 large potatoes
75 ml hot milk
45 ml (3 tablespoons) chopped cooked ham*
30 ml (2 tablespoons) chopped parsley
50 g butter, softened
30 ml (2 tablespoons) thick cream
Salt and freshly ground black pepper
2 egg whites
6 eggs
15 ml (1 tablespoon) malt vinegar
30 ml (2 tablespoons) grated Cheddar cheese

Scrub the potatoes and prick them. Bake them in the pre-heated oven until cooked through (about 1 hour, depending on their size). Remove from the oven and allow to cool.

Lay the potatoes flat, and slice the top off each with a sharp knife. Scoop out the insides, and place in a bowl. Put the potato cases on one side.

Mash the scooped out potato with the hot milk until smooth. Mix in the ham, parsley, butter and cream, and season with salt and pepper.

Beat the 2 egg whites until stiff and stir into the potato mixture. Check the seasoning, and keep the mixture hot.

Lightly poach the whole eggs by sliding them into simmering water to which you have added the vinegar, but *no* salt. Lift out the eggs with a slotted spoon and drain them very carefully.

Half fill the potato cases with a layer of the mashed potato mixture.

Place a poached egg in each potato case, cover with the remaining mashed potato mixture and sprinkle the tops with the grated cheese.

Brown the cheese quickly in the top of the pre-heated oven or under a hot grill.

CRUSTLESS SAVOURY TART

THIS DISH has been evolved for the weight-conscious who love quiches – or for people who cannot eat pastry but love the filling. It can be cut as a normal tart since it sets firmly.

PREPARATION TIME: 15 MINUTES
COOKING TIME: 45 MINUTES
PRE-HEAT OVEN TO 180°C

INGREDIENTS FOR FOUR

4 slices cooked meat (such as ham, bacon or beef), diced
250 g savoury cottage cheese
25 g flour
5 ml (1 teaspoon) salt
Freshly ground black pepper
5 ml (1 teaspoon) dry mustard
15 ml (1 tablespoon) dried onion or 1 onion, peeled, finely chopped* and cooked
15 ml (1 tablespoon) chopped parsley, or 5 ml (1 teaspoon) dried parsley
4 large eggs
375 ml (1½ cups) milk
5 ml (1 teaspoon) Worcestershire sauce
A dash of paprika for the garnish

Grease a shallow 1,5 litre oven-proof dish. In a large bowl, mix together the meat, cottage cheese, flour, salt, pepper, mustard, onion and parsley. Beat in the eggs, milk and Worcestershire sauce and combine well. Pour into the greased dish and sprinkle with paprika. Bake for 45 minutes.

VARIATIONS Replace the meat with boned smoked snoek.

The mixture can be baked in small patty pans and served as cocktail snacks.

CRUSTLESS SAVOURY TART *A scrumptious choice for those watching their figures.*

BAKED EGGS IN SAUCERS

THIS SIMPLE, NOURISHING snack is a descendant of the old French *ramequin*, meaning a concoction of bread, eggs and cheese baked together in a mould.

Here saucers are used in place of the traditional ramekins. Replacing the cheese with mushrooms, as in this recipe, or with any of the other suggested toppings, makes an appetising variation on the original theme.

PREPARATION TIME: 10 MINUTES
COOKING TIME: 20 MINUTES
PRE-HEAT OVEN TO 180°C

INGREDIENTS FOR FOUR

75 g butter
4 thin slices white bread, with crusts removed
Salt and freshly ground black pepper
8 eggs
125 g mushrooms, washed, dried and sliced

Lightly grease 4 saucers (oven-proof glass ones would do well) with a little of the butter.

Melt 50 g of the butter in a small saucepan. Remove from the heat and dip each slice of bread quickly into the saucepan, coating both sides lightly with the melted butter. Allow any excess butter to run off back into the pan.

Press the bread into the saucers, sprinkle with salt and pepper, and bake in the pre-heated oven for 5 minutes.

Take the saucers out of the oven, and break 2 eggs into each one. Season with salt and pepper, and return the saucers to the oven for 8-10 minutes.

Meanwhile, fry the sliced mushrooms in the remaining butter in a small saucepan until all the moisture has completely evaporated.

Serve the eggs in the saucers, with the mushrooms on top.

VARIATIONS Top the eggs and mushrooms with 100 g grated Cheddar cheese and place under a hot grill just until the cheese is melted.

Instead of the sliced, fried mushrooms, top the cooked eggs with slices of fried tomato.

Slivers of lightly fried ham also make a delicious topping.

Pastries, Puddings and Desserts

MAN HAS PROBABLY always had a sweet tooth, but it is only in recent centuries that the idea of a sweet 'finale' to a meal has become an institution. In many countries, including South Africa, sweet and savoury dishes were served as part of the same course in the past. Stewed fruit with venison has long been a tradition in this country, while in England, for example, it was customary in the past to serve, say, quince pie and almond cream alongside roast beef.

Early pies often contained sweet and savoury fillings under the same pastry crust, a combination still found, but which is now less common than separate pies for savoury main courses and sweet desserts.

One should not, of course, serve a pie for both the main course and dessert. It is vital to select a dessert that complements your meal and is also suited to the weather. No matter how delicious a steamed pudding may be, it is unlikely to tempt your guests or family if served after a heavy meal or on a hot summer's day. A home-made ice cream or chilled fresh fruit is much more likely to find favour. Cape brandy pudding, on the other hand, is just the thing on a winter's night.

Appearance is often the key to the success of a dessert. Even at the end of the heartiest meal, few people are able to resist a beautifully presented dessert. Glass bowls are ideal if the dish itself is very pretty – for example, caramel oranges or fruit fools. Garnishes of citrus peel, fresh fruit, mint leaves or piped rosettes of cream can also do much to give a lift to something a little less inherently decorative.

HINTS ON PASTRIES, PUDDINGS AND DESSERTS · *PAGE 248*

PASTRIES, PUDDINGS AND DESSERTS RECIPES · *PAGE 258*

SPECIAL FEATURES

RICH AND DELICIOUS FRIDGE CAKES · *PAGE 270*
CONVERT DESSERT INTO A FROZEN ASSET · *PAGE 278*

USEFUL TIPS FOR PASTRIES, PUDDINGS AND DESSERTS

PASTRY

Some people shy away from making their own pastry, believing it to be too difficult an art to master. There is a knack to making pastry, but if you follow the general rules and are meticulous about measuring out proportions of ingredients, the results will be very rewarding.

PIES AND TARTS

A pie is made of two pastry layers enclosing a filling – or a filling in a deep container covered by a pastry lid.

A tart or flan is a flat pastry case containing a filling. Most tarts are open with no lid, but some have lids.

Tips for making sweet pies and tarts

Hard fruit which will take longer to cook than the pastry can be softened a little by cooking it gently for 5-6 minutes before filling the pie or tart.

Do not place a pastry lid on a hot pie filling. Allow the filling to cool first, or the pastry will become soggy.

Do not leave a final layer of sugar on top of any pie or tart filling but mix it in with the fruit. Otherwise the pastry lid or decorations will become soggy.

For tarts or flans with a custard filling, brush the base well with egg white before you add the filling. This seals the pastry and stops the custard mixture from leaking through.

Preparing savoury fillings

To prepare meat, trim off any gristle or excess fat and cut the meat into bite-sized pieces. It can also be minced. For game pies, joint the meat and cut it into pieces of a suitable size. Game can be mixed with other meats.

For pies with liquid added to the meat, coat the meat in seasoned flour. To do this, put 15 ml (1 tablespoon) flour and a good pinch of both salt and pepper into a plastic bag, add the pieces of meat and shake well. Tip the contents into the pie dish. The flour helps to thicken the liquid.

Prepare fish by cutting into bite-sized pieces. Coat the fish with seasoned flour. If using a bland fish, add chopped parsley or other chopped herbs to the seasoned flour.

Vegetables used as a savoury filling should be cut into cubes of about 2,5 cm, as they need to cook over the same period of time as the pastry. If necessary, blanch* hard vegetables first to ensure even cooking. A pie containing mainly vegetables needs to be well seasoned.

Assessing the amount of pastry

Most pie and tart recipes stipulate making the pastry with a particular mass of flour. If this is not identical to the amount given in the special pastry recipes on the following pages, adjust all the pastry ingredients in proportion.

For example, if a recipe calls for 'flaky pastry using 450 g flour', double all the ingredients listed in the flaky pastry recipe.

If you wish to assess the final mass of the pastry, it will be roughly the total of flour and fat.

Pastry ingredients

Pastry is basically flour and fat mixed with water, or sometimes milk and water. Other ingredients are added as flavouring or to ensure rising.

The proportions of the basic ingredients and the method of mixing are crucial to the texture of the pastry. Flour contains a sticky, elastic substance called gluten, which holds the dough together. Different mixing methods are used to control the gluten and vary the pastry texture. The type and amount of fat determines the richness and flavour.

Another vital ingredient is air, introduced during mixing and rolling. When the pastry is heated, the air expands, causing the pastry to rise and helping to make it light.

Flour Use cake flour to make sure the pastry has a fine, short texture and rises only a small amount when heated. Bread flour is not usually suitable, because it is high in gluten and would make the pastry rise too much and be too elastic, but it can be used in puff pastry.

Sieve the flour before use to make sure it is fresh, dry and free from lumps. If it has become damp, dry it in a warm place before using. Damp flour can make pastry heavy.

Fat Use fresh fat of good quality. If the fat is stale and has a slightly 'off' flavour, this will be even more pronounced in the cooked pastry.

Butter, lard, good dripping*, clarified fat*, margarine, vegetable fat and suet can all be used. Butter on its own produces rich pastry, and unsalted butter is best for puff pastry. For economical, well-flavoured, short pastry, use a mixture of lard and margarine, or margarine and vegetable fat. Lard used on its own can give a flavour that many people find unacceptable.

Salt A pinch of salt helps to develop the flavour of the pastry.

Baking powder is a chemical mixture (mainly sodium bicarbonate) that produces gas, and can be used with cake flour as a raising agent. It is needed only if the amount of fat used is less than half the amount of flour (although hot-water pastry needs no baking powder). Pastry containing too much baking powder goes stale quickly and has a dry taste. If you use baking powder, do not leave the pastry to stand – mix it quickly and bake immediately, because the raising agent begins to work at once.

Lemon juice Flaky, puff, strudel and rough puff pastries are rich; adding lemon juice counteracts the richness.

Egg yolk Adding an egg yolk enriches pastry and gives it a very short (crumbly) texture.

Hints for making pastry

When mixing and rolling pastry, the aim is to introduce as much air as possible so that the pastry will rise well when heated. The colder the air, the more it will expand during cooking.

Keep all utensils and ingredients as cool as possible, and wash your hands in cold water before you mix pastry. The exception to this rule is when you are making hot-water crust pastry, strudel pastry or phyllo pastry.

Mixing the dough

Sieve together the dry ingredients – flour, salt and baking powder (if used). This not only sifts out lumps, but also ensures even distribution.

Weigh out the correct amount of fat. Too much will make the pastry break easily; too little could make it hard and tough. Whichever method you use, the fat must be properly incorporated and distributed as evenly as possible, otherwise it will melt and run before it is absorbed into the flour during baking, giving tough, streaky pastry.

Mix in the water or other liquid with a broad-bladed knife, as a knife is cooler than your hands. Use water fresh from the tap – it is cooler and more aerated than water that has been standing.

Measure the amount of water carefully and add it gradually, because too much will spoil the texture of the pastry. Some flours absorb more water than others, so it is difficult to give the exact amount in a recipe.

When the dough is properly mixed it should be soft and elastic, and leave the side of the bowl clean.

Do not rub off any little pieces from your fingers into the pastry. This can result in rough spots and flecks when the pastry is rolled out.

Electric mixers and food processors can be used for mixing pastry. Carefully follow the manufacturer's instructions on timing.

Rolling pastry

If time allows, leave the lump of pastry to rest in a cool place for 10-20 minutes before rolling it out (unless it contains baking powder), particularly in hot weather. Pastry that gets overheated during handling will be tough.

Dredge the board and rolling pin with flour, but not the pastry. Too much flour rolled in can alter the ratio of flour to fat, particularly if you are making only a small quantity.

When rolling pastry, use short, quick, light strokes with even pressure from both hands. Always roll in a forward direction and lift the pin between strokes. Stop rolling just short of the edges to ensure a uniform thickness and avoid squeezing out air. Lift the edges lightly to check that the pastry is not sticking to the board. If it is, lightly dust beneath it with flour.

Do not handle pastry unless necessary. To move it or lift it on to a dish, turn it over a floured rolling pin. Unroll it on to a freshly dredged surface or across the surface of the dish. The rolled side of the pastry is the smoothest, and should be used for the pie surface.

Storing uncooked pastry

Unless it contains baking powder, pastry can be stored after mixing until ready for use. If sealed in a plastic bag, it will keep in a refrigerator for up to 3 days, whether in a lump or rolled out. It can be frozen for up to 3 months, but roll and shape it before freezing.

Shortcrust pastry, mixed to a crumb stage but with no liquid added, can be stored in a plastic bag or covered container in a refrigerator for up to 4 weeks. Use portions as required. It can also be frozen for up to 6 months.

Lining a shallow dish or flan ring

Grease the dish or ring, using a pastry brush or a piece of grease-proof paper and sunflower oil, butter or margarine. Alternatively, use a non-stick cooking spray to coat the dish or ring. Be particularly careful if using cheese pastry, which is likely to stick.

Roll out the pastry to the thickness required and a size large enough to allow for the depth as well as the width of the container, adding an extra 5 mm to allow for shrinkage during cooking.

Lift the pastry on a floured rolling pin and place it over the dish or ring. Press it into the container gently with the fingertips to fit it to shape, and to make sure there are no air bubbles trapped underneath.

To give a clean finish to the edges, roll the rolling pin across the top of the container, and the surplus bits of pastry will drop off.

If you need a lid, roll out the pastry to the same diameter as the dish. Fit as for covering a pie*.

Baking blind

A pastry case is baked blind – without a filling – if the filling needs little or no cooking or will be added later.

Prick the base of the pastry lining with a fork to let out the air. Cover the base with a circle of grease-proof paper or aluminium foil, and put in a temporary filling of dried beans or rice to prevent the pastry from rising.

Bake in the centre of an oven pre-heated to 190°C for about 15 minutes. When the pastry is cooked, take out the grease-proof paper or foil and the beans or rice (which can be used again), and put the case back into the oven for 2-3 minutes to dry out. Once the case is ready, proceed with the filling.

Filling a pie

Fill the dish or case to the rim and distribute the filling evenly. If the pie is to be covered, pile the filling up in the centre to support the lid.

If there is not enough filling to make a pile in the centre, put an egg cup or pie funnel in the bottom of the dish, in the middle, to raise the filling or, with savoury pies, use a large onion.

If the filling has been partially cooked before the lid is put on, make sure it is quite cool before you cover it with pastry. If it is warm, the pastry will become heavy and sodden.

Covering a pie

Prepare the pie covering before filling the pie dish. Roll out the pastry to the thickness required – usually no more than 5 mm – and an area roughly 2 cm larger all round than the top of the dish from rim to rim.

Invert the pie dish on to the pastry and cut away the spare pastry. Roll these trimmings into a strip about 2,5 cm wide.

After the pie dish has been filled, dampen the rim of the dish with a pastry brush dipped in cold water and then shaken, then line the moistened rim with the pastry strip. This forms the base of a double rim that provides a

GLAZING AND DECORATING PIES

Glazing a sweet pie
Brush the pie lid with cold water or milk, and sprinkle with castor sugar before you put it in the oven.

If you want to give it a more sparkling finish, take the pastry from the oven when it is almost baked and brush the lid with lightly beaten egg white, then dredge the lid with castor sugar.

Give the pastry a few more minutes in the oven to set the egg.

Glazing a savoury pie
To give the pie an attractive, shiny, golden-brown finish, make a wash from a well-beaten egg or a small amount of beaten egg or egg yolk diluted with an equal amount of milk or water. A wash of milk can be used on its own, but it does not give such a rich colour.

Brush the wash over the lid of the pie, usually before you bake it. Any decorations can be stuck down with the glaze, and then also brushed over with the glaze.

Pies that need long cooking, such as a game pie, should not be glazed before baking. Wait until the pie is almost cooked, quickly remove it from the oven and brush on the glaze, then return it to the oven to complete cooking.

Decorating a pie lid
To flake the edge, flour the first finger of your left hand and press it down lightly on the pastry rim. Using the back of a floured knife blade, make a mark beside your finger. Mark in the same way all round, using finger and knife blade alternately. This opens the edges and helps the pastry to rise.

Alternatively, you can scallop the edges by drawing the back of a floured knife blade upwards and inwards across the edges of the rim. Do this at 2,5 cm intervals, and at the same time press the pastry between the knife marks downwards and outwards with your thumb to form the scallop.

To make pastry leaves to decorate the lid, roll out the trimmings and divide them into strips about 3 cm wide. Cut the strips diagonally about every 4 cm to produce diamond shapes, and use the back of a knife to imitate vein markings.

To make a rose, cut two circles about 3 cm across from a strip of thinly rolled pastry. Roll another piece into a ball about 5 mm across. Put the circles one on top of the other and place the ball in the middle.

Fold the circles almost over the ball, sealing lightly. Turn the pastry over and cut a cross through the two outer layers into the centre of the ball with a sharp knife. Open out the two layers of each segment and fold them back to form a rose.

Dampen the decorations on the back with a wet pastry brush before placing them on the pie, or use the moist glaze to stick them in place. Do not cover the central steam vents with decorations.

good seal and lessens the risk of liquid boiling out of a pie.

Brush the pastry rim with water, lift the pastry lid on a floured rolling pin and lay it over the top of the dish. Gently press the two edges together.

Hold the pie dish in one hand and, with the other, trim off any excess pastry with a sharp knife. Hold the knife handle at a slight angle so that the trimmed edge slopes outwards from the rim. This allows for a little shrinkage during cooking.

Make two slits in the centre of the lid (over the pie funnel if there is one) to let steam escape.

Decorate* and glaze* the lid if desired, then seal or 'knock up' the edge of the pastry with the back of a floured knife blade held horizontally. Tap all round the edges with a slight lifting movement.

Shortcrust pastry

Shortcrust pastry should have a crisp, short (melt-in-the-mouth) texture. The pastry is usually baked at 190-220°C, depending on richness and size.

PREPARATION TIME: 10 MINUTES

INGREDIENTS TO LINE A 23 CM FLAN RING, TO LINE AND COVER AN 18 CM PIE PLATE, OR COVER A LITRE PIE DISH

225 g flour
2 ml (½ teaspoon) salt
50 g lard
50 g margarine
60 ml (¼ cup) cold water

Sieve the flour and salt into a bowl. Cut the fat into 1,5 cm cubes and distribute them evenly over the flour.

Rub the fat lightly into the flour with your fingertips, lifting up the mixture while rubbing to keep it as cool and aerated as possible. Continue rubbing until the mixture resembles fine breadcrumbs.

Make a well in the centre of the mixture and add the water gradually while you stir it in with a knife. Use just enough of the water to produce a soft (but not sticky) dough.

Turn out the dough on a floured surface and roll once only to the thickness required. The pastry will be heavy if you roll it too much.

Sweet shortcrust pastry

Flans and tarts to serve cold are sometimes made with sweet, enriched shortcrust pastry that can be rolled out very thinly. It is usually baked at 180°C.

PREPARATION TIME: 15 MINUTES

INGREDIENTS TO LINE TWO 18 CM FLAN RINGS

225 g flour
2 ml (½ teaspoon) salt
100 g butter
25 g castor sugar
2 extra-large egg yolks
30 ml (2 tablespoons) water

Prepare the flour and salt, and mix in the fat as for shortcrust pastry. Add the sugar and mix it in well.

Beat the egg yolks together and mix in the cold water, then make a well in the centre of the flour and stir in the egg and water mixture with a knife to produce a soft dough.

Turn out the dough on to a floured board and knead gently until it is pliable and free from cracks. Roll out once to the required thickness.

Flaky pastry

Flaky pastry is made up of thin, crisp layers with air in between. It is particularly suitable for pies to be served cold. It is usually baked at 220°C.

PREPARATION TIME: 30 MINUTES
STANDING TIME: 45 MINUTES

INGREDIENTS TO COVER AN 850 ML-1 LITRE PIE DISH, OR MAKE 10 SAUSAGE ROLLS OR 8 TURNOVERS

225 g flour
2 ml (½ teaspoon) salt
175 g butter or firm margarine, or a mixture of both
5 ml (1 teaspoon) lemon juice
100-125 ml cold water

Sieve the flour and salt into a bowl. Divide the fat into 4 equal portions.

Take one portion of fat, cut it into small pieces and rub it into the flour with your fingertips, lifting up the mixture while rubbing to keep it as cool and aerated as possible. Continue until the mixture resembles fine breadcrumbs.

Make a well in the centre of the mixture and add the lemon juice and just enough water to mix, with a knife, to a firm, elastic dough. Turn out the dough on a floured board and knead it until it is free from cracks.

Roll the dough into a strip 3 times as long as it is wide and about 2,5 cm thick. Take a second portion of the fat and, with a knife, flake it in even rows along two-thirds of the strip of pastry. Leave a clear strip about 2 cm wide at the edge. If the fat is too close to the edge, it will be squeezed out when you roll the pastry.

Fold one-third of the strip (the end with no butter) over to the middle. Then fold the other end (covered with butter) over that, so that the pastry is folded into 3 layers.

Leave the pastry to rest for 15-20 minutes in a cool place, then turn it so that an open edge is towards you.

Press the open edges together with a rolling pin to enclose the air. Then make ridges in 2 or 3 places by pressing with the rolling pin. This distributes the air and stops it from collecting in a large bubble that is difficult not to break when rolling.

Roll out the pastry again to a strip 3 times as long as its width, then flake on the third portion of fat in the same way as the second. Fold, rest, seal and ridge as before.

Repeat the whole process using the fourth portion of fat. Then roll out to the thickness required.

Sour cream flaky pastry

This pastry is made in much the same way as conventional flaky pastry, using cultured sour cream (smetena) in order to give it a tangy flavour suitable for savoury dishes.

Sour cream flaky pastry is usually baked at 190-220°C.

PREPARATION TIME: 15 MINUTES
STANDING TIME: 30 MINUTES

INGREDIENTS TO COVER TWO 850 ML-1 LITRE PIE DISHES, OR TO LINE AND COVER TWO 23 CM PIE DISHES

500 g flour
3 ml (¾ teaspoon) salt
250 g unsalted butter (refrigerator temperature)
250 ml (1 cup) sour cream (smetena)

Sieve the flour and salt together twice. Using a small, sharp knife, a pastry blender or a food processor, cut the butter into the flour. Continue until the mixture resembles breadcrumbs. Form a well in the centre of the flour and pour in the cultured sour cream, cutting it in with the knife until blended.

Gather the dough to form a ball and roll it out on a lightly floured board to form a rectangle 1 cm thick and 3 times as long as it is wide. With the short side of the rectangle in front of you, fold the lower third of the pastry up away from you and the upper third down towards you to form 3 layers. Turn the pastry half a turn so that the folded edges are on the sides and one of the open ends is facing you.

Roll the pastry again to a rectangle 1 cm thick. Fold the dough again and turn, then repeat the process of rolling and folding.

Place the pastry in a plastic bag and allow it to rest in the refrigerator for 30 minutes before using.

Puff pastry

Puff pastry is rich and very light. It is similar to flaky pastry, but lighter and with more layers, and is used for vol-au-vent cases. Bread flour can be used instead of cake flour.

This pastry is baked at a higher temperature than either flaky or rough puff – usually 230°C.

It is worth buying puff pastry ready mixed and frozen; the pastry will be ready for rolling once thawed. Note that the amount of pastry specified in recipes in this book is based on the quantity of flour; you will need more than 225 g frozen pastry for a recipe that specifies puff pastry using 225 g flour (see Assessing the amount of pastry*).

PREPARATION TIME: 40 MINUTES
STANDING TIME: 1 HOUR

INGREDIENTS TO LINE TWO 23 CM FLAN RINGS OR COVER A LITRE PIE DISH

225 g unsalted butter or firm margarine
225 g flour
2 ml (½ teaspoon) salt
5 ml (1 teaspoon) lemon juice
60-100 ml cold water to mix

PASTRIES, PUDDINGS AND DESSERTS

Pat the fat into a square and put it in a cool place to get firm, but not hard.

Sieve the flour and salt into a bowl. Make a well in the centre and add the lemon juice. Stir in enough water, using a knife, to form an elastic dough.

Turn out the dough on a floured board and knead it gently for 5-10 minutes until it is smooth and does not stick to your fingers.

Roll out the pastry to a strip large enough to enclose the fat. Place the fat in the middle of the pastry and fold the ends over it one at a time. Flatten the lump in 1 or 2 places with the rolling pin, then roll it out evenly and lightly into a long strip, taking care that the fat does not break through. Do not roll beyond the top and bottom edges.

Fold one-third of the length into the middle and press it down gently, then fold the other end over to form 3 layers, and press down gently. Do not seal the edges, as this could trap large air bubbles and cause the pastry to rise unevenly. Leave the pastry to rest in a cool place for 15 minutes.

Place the dough on the floured board so that an unsealed edge is towards you, then roll and fold again. Each rolling and folding is known as a turn, so this completes the second turn. Repeat the rolling and folding twice more so that you have completed 4 turns, then leave the pastry to cool again for about 10 minutes.

Roll and fold the pastry again 3 more times to give 7 turns in all. Roll out the pastry to the size and thickness required. Leave it in a cool place for 10 minutes before baking.

Rough puff pastry

Rough puff pastry is similar to flaky pastry, but has larger flakes and is not as light. It is usually baked at 220°C.

PREPARATION TIME: 20 MINUTES

INGREDIENTS TO COVER A 850 ML-1 LITRE PIE DISH, OR TO MAKE 12 SAUSAGE ROLLS OR 8 TURNOVERS

225 g flour
2 ml (½ teaspoon) salt
175 g firm margarine or butter, or a mixture of both
5 ml (1 teaspoon) lemon juice
100-125 ml cold water

Sieve the flour and salt into a mixing bowl. Add the fat in one lump, cover it with flour and then, with a knife or pastry blender, cut it into 1,5 cm cubes – each about the size of a hazelnut.

Make a well in the centre of the mixture and add the lemon juice, then stir in the water gradually with a knife, mixing lightly so that you do not break down the fat. Continue until the mixture is a firm, elastic dough.

Turn out the pastry on a floured board and press it into a lump, but do not knead it. Roll the pastry lightly into a strip about 3 times as long as it is wide and about 5 mm thick.

Fold one-third of the length into the middle, then the other end over the top to make 3 layers. Seal the open edges by pressing firmly with a rolling pin to enclose as much air as possible.

Turn the pastry so that a sealed edge is facing you, and make ridges in 2 or 3 places with a rolling pin. This distributes the air and stops it from collecting in a large bubble that will be difficult not to break when rolling.

Roll the pastry into a strip again, but be careful not to roll beyond the top and bottom edges, as this will press out air. Fold the pastry in 3 as before, then seal, turn and ridge again.

Repeat twice more the process of rolling out, folding, sealing, turning and ridging the pastry.

Roll out the pastry to the size and thickness required. Be very careful not to stretch it, as this will cause excessive shrinkage from the edge of the dish when baked.

Strudel pastry

Strudel pastry is made with warm ingredients – unlike most other pastries, which require cool ingredients and utensils. It is usually baked at 175-200°C.

PREPARATION TIME: 50 MINUTES
STANDING TIME: 30 MINUTES

INGREDIENTS FOR A STRUDEL 40 CM × 15 CM

225 g flour
A pinch of salt
2 eggs
3 ml (¾ teaspoon) lemon juice or vinegar
10 ml (2 teaspoons) butter
80-125 ml (⅓-½ cup) lukewarm water
60 ml (¼ cup) melted butter

> ### TIPS FOR COOKING PASTRY
>
> Always pre-heat the oven before baking pastry. If you put it into a cool oven, the fat will melt and run out before it is absorbed into the flour. This will make the pastry tough, greasy and of poor texture.
>
> Make sure the oven is not too hot, otherwise the pastry surface will set too quickly and form a crust that prevents full expansion of steam and air. This makes the pastry hard and biscuit-like. Place the pie or flan dish on a baking tray before you put it in the oven. It is then easier to remove when hot.
>
> The top of the oven is the hottest part and the bottom the coolest. It is usual to bake in the centre, but this may vary according to the make of oven. Follow the manufacturer's instructions for the baking position.
>
> If you have to open and close the oven door during baking, do it very gently. Avoid doing it before the pastry has set, because cold air may cause it to drop, particularly if the pastry is light. Puff pastry needs a very hot oven; do not put anything else in the oven at the same time.
>
> If the pastry starts to brown too quickly, wait until it has finished rising, then cover it with a sheet of aluminium foil.
>
> When baking a large pie in a small oven (or a pie that needs long cooking, such as a game pie), once the pie has reached the desired colour put a stiff collar of cardboard or a double collar of aluminium foil round the dish, and secure it with string. Lay foil or greaseproof paper on top of the collar.
>
> After cooking, leave the pudding or pie to cool slowly in a warm kitchen. If it cools too quickly in a draught or a cold room, it will be heavy.

Warm all the utensils you will be using.

Sieve the flour and salt into a bowl. Make a well in the centre of the flour and add the eggs and lemon juice or vinegar. Cut in the butter with a knife or rub it into the flour mixture with the fingertips until a crumb consistency is reached. Add just enough water to make a soft dough. Knead the dough well.

Bang the pastry on a board about 50 times (until it blisters, that is, shows small bubbles). Sprinkle the dough with flour, cover with a warmed pot, and allow it to rest for 30 minutes.

Prepare the filling for the strudel. When it is complete, proceed with the dough as follows.

Cover a table with a clean tablecloth. Work on a table which is easily accessible from all sides. Sprinkle the cloth with flour and rub it in with your hands. Roll out the pastry on the board, then transfer it to the tablecloth.

Brush the dough with a little melted butter, then, working under the sheet of dough with hands lightly clenched, stretch it with the knuckles, from the centre outwards. Work very gently, going around the table. Try not to tear the dough. It should stretch to about 1 square metre.

A fairly thick border will form and this must be cut off before you spread the filling on to the dough. Use the off-cuts to patch any holes you may have made. Brush the dough again with melted butter.

Choux pastry

Choux pastry is usually shaped through a forcing bag to make both sweet and savoury dishes, such as éclairs or cheese puffs. The pastry is very light and airy, and has a hollow centre.

During cooking – usually at 180-220°C – choux pastry puffs up to about three times its original size.

PREPARATION TIME: 15 MINUTES

INGREDIENTS TO MAKE 16-18 ÉCLAIRS OR ABOUT 20 CREAM PUFFS

65 g flour
1 ml (¼ teaspoon) salt
50 g butter
150 ml water
2 eggs, beaten

Sieve the flour and salt on to a sheet of grease-proof paper. Put the butter and water in a heavy-based saucepan and place over a low heat until the butter melts, then increase the heat and bring rapidly to the boil.

Remove the pan from the heat and pour in all the sifted flour, stirring quickly with a wooden spoon until the flour has been absorbed into the liquid.

Return the pan to a gentle heat, then cook for 2-3 minutes until the mixture is smooth and comes away from the side of the saucepan.

Cool the mixture for a few minutes, then beat in the eggs gradually. The pastry must be firm enough for piping, but not too stiff. If you are not going to use the pastry immediately, closely cover the saucepan with a sheet of moist grease-proof paper under the lid. This keeps the dough pliable.

Do not open the oven door while the pastry is cooking, otherwise it will be flat. When the pastry is cooked, split each puff open and leave it in the oven for 30-60 seconds to dry the inside.

Phyllo pastry

This pastry is made up of paper-thin layers. It is used in its native Greece for spinach or chicken pies and for baclava, and it lends itself well to other pies and strudels. Phyllo pastry can be kept in the freezer indefinitely or refrigerated for about a week. It is usually baked at 180-220°C.

Commercially available phyllo pastry is a good buy, since it is thinner than the sort that one could achieve at home. The recipes in this book that use phyllo pastry refer to bought sheets. When using the home-made kind, use roughly half the amount specified.

To use phyllo pastry, brush each layer with melted butter as you arrange it in a baking tin or dish. Allow 1-2 layers of home-made phyllo pastry under the filling and 2-3 layers for the topping, or follow the recipe.

PREPARATION TIME: 40 MINUTES
STANDING TIME: 15 MINUTES

INGREDIENTS TO YIELD 450 G
285 g flour
A pinch of salt
1 extra-large egg
150 ml water
5 ml (1 teaspoon) sunflower oil

Sieve the flour and salt into a bowl. Beat the egg, add the water and oil, and mix the liquid into the flour with a round-bladed knife. Using your hand, continue to mix the ingredients, adding a little more water if necessary to make a soft dough.

Lift the mixture in one hand and, with a flick of the wrist, throw the dough on a lightly floured board. Continue lifting and flicking the dough until it is very smooth and elastic. Place the dough in a clean, floured bowl, cover it and leave in a warm place for 15 minutes.

Flour a tea towel or large cloth spread on a table. Divide the dough in 4 and work with each portion separately as follows: roll out the pastry on top of the tea towel as thinly as possible. Flour your hand well and ease it under the pastry. Keeping the dough fairly flat, ease and gently stretch it with your hand, carefully working your way around until the pastry is paper-thin and you can see through it. Trim off any thick edges, then cover the pastry with a damp tea cloth. If you are not using it immediately, wrap it well and refrigerate.

Cream cheese pastry

This is a quick, simple pastry, suitable for use with sweet or savoury fillings. It is usually baked at 175-200°C.

PREPARATION TIME: 10 MINUTES
CHILLING TIME: 2-3 HOURS

INGREDIENTS TO LINE AND COVER A 28 CM PIE DISH, OR LINE TWO 26CM FLAN RINGS
250 g cream cheese
250 g unsalted butter
125 ml (½ cup) thick cream
350 g flour

Blend the cream cheese, butter, cream and flour in an electric mixer or by hand. Form the dough into a ball, wrap it in wax paper and chill in the refrigerator for 2-3 hours, or overnight.

Cheese pastry

You can make a cheese pastry using the shortcrust recipe. Use all butter or all margarine instead of lard and margarine, and add up to 125 g dry, strong cheese (grated) to the crumb mixture before you add the liquid. Mix to a paste with half water and half beaten egg.

Biscuit crumb crust

This is a trouble-free biscuit crust made from crushed dry biscuits – sweet or savoury – or cereal. It is bound with butter and baked for 8-10 minutes at 180°C before filling.

Use the biscuits of your choice, or follow the recipe recommendation.

PREPARATION TIME: 15 MINUTES

INGREDIENTS TO MAKE A 20 CM PIE CASE
200 g plain sweet or savoury biscuits
100 g butter, melted

Crush the biscuits with a rolling pin or in a food processor or blender. Tip the crumbs into a mixing bowl, then add the melted butter and mix the ingredients with a spoon until the crumbs adhere to each other.

Press the mixture evenly into a 20 cm loose-based, plain-sided flan ring or springform cake tin, working the crumb mixture up the sides of the tin in order to form a case.

JELLIES

The main thickening ingredient in jellies is gelatin, a natural animal substance that, when dissolved in hot liquid and added to other ingredients, cools to form a jelly.

Home-made clear jellies (as distinct from fruit jelly preserves) consist mainly of fruit juice, water, sugar and gelatin.

How to dissolve gelatin

Gelatin, widely used as a setting agent, is available in powder or leaf form, although powdered gelatin is more common.

Six sheets of leaf gelatin equal 25 g powdered gelatin. Both dissolve easily, but need careful handling to ensure good texture.

Use the correct proportions given in the recipe. Wash leaf gelatin in cold water, soak it in cold water for 15-20

VOL-AU-VENT

Vol-au-vents are cases made of puff pastry* which are baked, then filled with various mixtures bound together with a sauce. The tiny vol-au-vent cases favoured for cocktail snacks are known as bouchée cases.

A 500 g quantity of puff pastry makes one large 18 cm wide vol-au-vent case, eight 8 cm cases for individual servings, or 12-14 small bouchée cases for cocktail snacks.

For a large case, roll out the pastry to a 20 cm square. Using an 18 cm plate or lid as a guide, cut a circle with a sharp knife, held at an oblique angle to give a bevelled edge. Set the pastry upside down on a moist baking tray.

Brush the top of the pastry with a beaten egg and mark a 15 cm wide circle on the pastry with a knife. Cut through half the depth of the pastry, following the mark of this inner circle. Allow to rest for 15 minutes.

Bake the vol-au-vent case in the centre of a pre-heated oven at 230°C for about 20 minutes or until risen and brown, then reduce the heat to 180°C for a further 20 minutes.

When cooked, carefully ease out the pastry lid formed by the inner circle, and discard any soft pastry from the centre of the vol-au-vent.

Fill the case with 175-225 g diced chicken, salmon or prawns blended with 300 ml béchamel sauce*. Replace the lid.

Small vol-au-vent cases are made in a similar way. The pastry should be rolled out 1 cm thick and cut into 8 cm rounds, with lids 4 cm wide. Bake in a pre-heated oven at 230°C for 20 minutes. For bouchée cases, roll the pastry out 5 mm thick, and use 5 cm and 2,5 cm cutters for cases and lids respectively. Bake for about 15 minutes.

minutes until soft, then squeeze lightly to get rid of excess water.

Always add the powdered or leaf gelatin to the dissolvent liquid; do not pour the liquid on the gelatin. Heat gently – overheating will produce a gummy, unusable mass.

Gelatin that has been dissolved in milk will curdle if you allow the milk to boil.

Tips for making jellies

Jellies left to set in a cool place need slightly more gelatin than those set in a refrigerator. Increase the amount of gelatin by about one-third to compensate, or slightly reduce the quantity of liquid used.

Eat jellies within 24 hours of making. They tend to toughen if kept too long, especially in a refrigerator.

Make sure that jelly that is to be used for decoration is firm. Chop it evenly, but not too small, otherwise it will lose its sparkly effect.

Moulding and chilling

Aluminium, tin or tin-lined copper moulds give a sharper design and are more easily unmoulded than earthenware or porcelain ones.

Rinse the mould or dish under the cold water tap and shake off excess water before you fill it. Alternatively, you may spray the container with a non-stick cooking spray.

The water or spray makes it easier to unmould the pudding.

Before pouring a mixture into a mould or dish, stir gently to make sure that the ingredients are evenly distributed.

Be careful not to over-refrigerate – about 2-3 hours is generally enough setting time.

To unmould any chilled jelly pudding, dip the mould up to the rim in hot water for 5-10 seconds. Rinse the serving plate under the cold tap for a moment, shake off surplus water, then invert the plate over the mould before turning both plate and mould over together.

Give the mould a slight shake to free the jelly. The slightly moist plate allows you to slide the pudding to another position easily.

CREAM, MILK AND EGG PUDDINGS

Fools and ice creams generally have equal quantities of whipped cream and custard, combined with puréed fruit (in fools) or flavouring (in ice creams). The more you increase the proportion of cream to custard, the richer the dish.

Sorbets or water ices are sugar syrups flavoured with fruit juice, purée or other flavourings and sometimes thickened with egg whites.

Syllabubs are cream and sugar flavoured with wine, brandy or sherry. A trifle contains crystallised fruit or jam and sponge cake or sponge fingers, in addition to the syllabub ingredients.

Mousses are flavoured cream mixtures thickened with eggs and stiffened with gelatin. Flummeries are flavoured creams stiffened with gelatin and sometimes with oatmeal.

Hints for using cream

Always use good, fresh, thick cream. Never overwhip cream: it makes the final texture heavy and buttery. The cream is sufficiently whipped when it will remain in peaks when lifted up with the whisk.

For fools, mousses and ice creams, try to have the cream, custard and any fruit purée similar in consistency. If they are not, always add the thinner ingredient to the thicker one.

For a cream mixture stiffened with gelatin, such as a mousse, add the dissolved gelatin while it is still lukewarm. If you add the gelatin mixture when it is too hot, the cream will not be so light in texture. If you add it when it is too cold, it may stay in tiny lumps or specks.

Flummery

All husked cereals, if soaked and boiled, will set to make a kind of jelly. A properly made flummery has a smooth, jellied texture, a very white colour, and a delicious and distinctive flavour.

PREPARATION TIME: 10 MINUTES
SOAKING TIME: 48 HOURS
COOKING TIME: ABOUT 15 MINUTES
SETTING TIME: 1 HOUR

INGREDIENTS FOR SIX TO EIGHT
60 ml (¼ cup) fine oatmeal, or
75 ml cracked wheat
Juice of 2 oranges, strained
30 ml (2 tablespoons) castor sugar
150 ml cream
Finely grated rind of 2 oranges
60-80 ml (¼-⅓ cup) honey,
brandy or whisky
150 ml whipped cream for garnish

Soak the oatmeal or cracked wheat (in enough cold water to keep it covered) for 24 hours. Pour off the water, and cover the grain with about 1 litre (4 cups) fresh, cold water. Leave to stand for another 24 hours.

Stir well, and strain the liquid into a pan. Add the strained orange juice and the sugar, and boil, stirring frequently, for about 10 minutes, or until very thick. Allow to cool a little before stirring in the cream.

Pour into one large dish or into individual dishes, sprinkle with the grated rind and set aside until set.

To serve, top each dish with 10 ml (2 teaspoons) honey, brandy or whisky and a spoonful of whipped cream.

Tips for making custard

Many hot and cold desserts – for example, bread and butter pudding* – are based on custard.

Custard also makes a dish on its own – steamed, baked or as a sauce. The sauce can be made from commercial custard powder, but this does not give the same texture or flavour as home-made custard.

Always use fresh eggs and milk. For basic custard sauce or a baked custard, use 2 egg yolks or 1 whole egg to 250 ml (1 cup) milk.

Cook custard mixtures with just enough heat to thicken them without curdling. Do not allow them to boil.

Mild acids such as sherry or lemon juice should be added to custard slowly at the end of the cooking time, to prevent curdling.

Baked custard

This custard may be baked in small dishes and then unmoulded before serving. It may also be baked in one large dish.

HINTS FOR BEATING EGGS

Eggs are beaten to increase their volume by drawing in air. Use beaten eggs as soon as they are ready, before they lose their air.

When beating whole eggs by hand, break them into a bowl so that plenty of air can be taken in. Turn them over vigorously with upward movements of the fork, whisk or spoon. Stand the bowl on a damp cloth to stop it sliding about.

To mix egg yolks and sugar, beat the eggs first, add the sugar, then continue beating until the mixture drops in broad ribbons when the whisk is lifted out of it.

Always strain beaten eggs through a sieve before adding them to a smooth-textured dish such as a fool or custard. This removes any 'threads', specks or small particles of shell.

When making meringues, never use fresh egg whites for whisking, as they will not whisk to the necessary stiffness and volume. Use eggs that are at least 48 hours old, and ensure that they are at room temperature.

To whisk egg whites, use a clean, dry bowl that is deep and rounded enough for the whisk to be in constant contact with the whites.

Add a pinch of salt to the whites – this makes them stiffen more quickly and reduces whisking time.

Whisking is completed when the whites form stiff peaks when the whisk is lifted out of the bowl.

Folding in Use a metal spoon to fold beaten egg whites into a mixture. It will cause less air disturbance than a thicker, wooden spoon.

To fold in egg whites, pile them on top of the mixture and carefully draw part of the mixture from the bottom of the bowl over them, making sure they do not lose their air content. Continue doing this until all the whites are incorporated.

PREPARATION TIME: 30 MINUTES
COOKING TIME: 45 MINUTES
PRE-HEAT OVEN TO 180°C

INGREDIENTS FOR SIX

6 eggs
70 g sugar
A pinch of salt
1,5 litres (6 cups) milk
7 ml (1½ teaspoons) vanilla essence
Freshly grated nutmeg

Beat the eggs, sugar and salt until light and lemon-coloured.

Heat the milk in a saucepan until it feels warm when tested by placing a few drops on your hand. Add the lukewarm milk to the egg mixture with the vanilla essence and blend thoroughly.

Pour the custard into 6 individual oven-proof dishes, grate a little fresh nutmeg over each one and then allow the dishes to stand in a baking tin containing hot water.

Place the tin with the dishes in the oven and bake for 45 minutes, or until a knife inserted into the custard comes out clean.

Tips for making milk puddings

Milk puddings generally consist of the following ingredients: milk, a cereal (such as semolina or rice) and sometimes eggs and flavouring.

Cook milk puddings slowly and gently to produce a good, creamy texture. If the starchy contents are not thoroughly cooked, the pudding may end up being indigestible.

If adding eggs, wait until the pudding is thoroughly cooked, otherwise the heat needed for further cooking may curdle the eggs.

Let the pudding cool a little before you add the eggs, particularly if you are going to fold in stiffly whisked egg whites. Re-heat gently until the egg is cooked.

To give puddings a creamier texture you can, if you like, use half fresh milk and half evaporated milk.

You can make milk puddings in shapes and moulds, and turn them out on to a dish when cold and set. The proportion of cereal to milk for puddings made in this way needs to be greater than for soft puddings.

BATTERS

A batter is a mixture of flour, liquid (milk, water, oil or melted butter) and eggs. It is used for a number of purposes, including pancakes, puddings and fritters.

How to make a basic batter

Sieve the flour to remove any lumps and to incorporate air. Sieve any salt in the recipe along with the flour.

Make a well in the centre of the flour and break the egg into it. Pour a little of the liquid on to the egg and beat them together, gradually working in some of the flour. Continue slowly working in the liquid and flour, beating to incorporate air and give a smooth, creamy texture. Aim to have about one-third of the liquid left when all the flour is worked in.

Before you work in the rest of the liquid, dispose of lumps by beating well with a wire whisk for a minute or two. Lumps are more difficult to get rid of later. If the lumps are persistent, rub the mixture through a sieve.

Work in the rest of the liquid, beating continuously. The batter should have the consistency of thin cream.

If the batter has to stand for any time, stir it before use.

STEAMED PUDDINGS

It is simpler to steam puddings in a basin than using the traditional method of boiling them in a cloth.

Steaming is particularly suitable for puddings made with suet, such as Christmas pudding, as it makes them lighter and more digestible than when cooked by other methods. Steamed sponge puddings have a more feathery texture than oven-baked sponge cakes.

Puddings are covered during steaming to prevent water splashes or steam from entering the mixture and making it soggy. Follow recipes for instructions on steaming.

Preparing a basin for steaming

Grease the inside of the basin, using a pastry brush or piece of crumpled grease-proof paper.

Place any topping such as jam, sugar or currants at the bottom of the basin. Fill sponge and suet puddings to within 1,5 cm of the top, batter puddings about two-thirds full.

Cut out a square of grease-proof paper or aluminium foil for the basin cover, and grease one side with a brush, a piece of grease-proof paper or a flat-bladed knife. Place the square, greased side down, over the top of the basin and make a 1,5 cm pleat across the top to allow for expansion.

Tie the covering down with string wound twice around the basin under the rim, then looped over the top as a handle.

Re-heating steamed puddings

Most steamed puddings can be re-heated. To keep them moist, add 15 ml (1 tablespoon) milk to a jam or similar steamed sponge pudding, and 15 ml (1 tablespoon) milk or golden syrup to a suet mixture.

There is no need to cover the basin with grease-proof paper or foil. Steam in a steamer or over a saucepan of boiling water (with a plate or saucer covering the basin) for 20-30 minutes.

Alternatively, place the moistened pudding in a covered oven-proof dish and heat in the oven at 180°C for about 30 minutes.

Suet and sponge mixtures can also be sliced and fried gently in a little butter, then served with a sprinkling of sugar or golden syrup.

YOGHURT

Yoghurt is milk thickened and flavoured by a bacterial culture which grows in the milk under certain conditions.

As a milk product, yoghurt is rich in protein and essential vitamins. It is also easily digested.

During the yoghurt-making process, the bacteria which convert milk to yoghurt break down the milk protein, making it easy for the body to assimilate.

Yoghurt is not only eaten on its own, but is also often used instead of eggs or cream to thicken sauces, and in a multitude of sweet and savoury dishes.

Making your own yoghurt is easy and fun, as the bacteria do all the work. You can use any kind of milk – whole, non-fat, skim, dried, or tinned evaporated milk. Add yoghurt culture, keep it in a warm place, and in very little time you have fresh, home-made yoghurt.

Incubating yoghurt

There are several ways of incubating yoghurt, and there are even electric yoghurt-makers on the market. The best incubation temperature is 40-48°C, which can be achieved as follows:

Oven This method can be used for large quantities. Turn on your oven to the lowest setting, and if it is too hot, leave the door ajar.

Electric frying pan Fill the pan two-thirds full with water. Turn to the lowest temperature setting. Place the (covered) container of milk in the warmed water and allow to incubate for several hours.

Vacuum flask Pour hot water into a wide-mouthed flask, then set aside. Prepare the milk, empty out the water and add the milk mixture. Screw on the lid and leave overnight.

Insulated coolbox Pour the prepared milk into a container, then cover. Wrap a warm towel (warmed briefly in the sun or in a tumble drier) around the container. Place in the coolbox and cover to incubate. Incubation is aided by placing a bottle of hot water (with the lid screwed on tightly) in the box.

Basic yoghurt

This recipe uses a starter – a small amount of yoghurt containing the active yoghurt bacilli – and skim milk, whole milk or a mixture of evaporated milk and water. See Tips for making yoghurt*.

PREPARATION TIME: 10 MINUTES
COOKING TIME: 20 MINUTES
COOLING TIME: 30 MINUTES
STANDING TIME: 4 HOURS OR LONGER

INGREDIENTS TO YIELD 1,3 LITRES

1,25 litres (5 cups) skim or whole milk
60 ml (¼ cup) skim milk powder
15 ml (1 tablespoon) starter

Mix the milk and the powder, then heat to just below boiling point. Allow to cool to 43-46°C before adding the starter. Incubate* until it has reached the desired consistency, then refrigerate.

VARIATION Mix a 410g tin of evaporated milk with 560ml (2¼ cups) hot water and 80ml (⅓ cup) skim milk powder. Proceed in the same way as above.

Fruit yoghurt

Fruit yoghurts taste best if you add fruit after the yoghurt has been made. To make fruit yoghurt, purée enough fresh, frozen or tinned fruit to yield 500ml (2 cups). Add 100-125g sugar to the fruit. Soften 5ml (1 teaspoon) gelatin in 100ml water or fruit juice in a small bowl, then place the bowl over hot water to dissolve the gelatin. Cool the gelatin mixture, then add it to the fruit purée. Add the mixture to 1,25 litres (5 cups) yoghurt and place in the refrigerator for a few hours. This will yield about 1,8 litres fruit yoghurt.

For frozen fruit yoghurt, increase the gelatin to 20ml (4 teaspoons).

BUYING AND USING FRESH FRUIT

Fruit in season can provide enormous variety in the cook's repertoire. Whether it is eaten on its own, combined with other ingredients in salad or used in cooking, fruit adds colour and freshness to any meal.

When buying fresh fruit, it is advisable to choose underripe items and to allow them to ripen until ready to be eaten.

Large quantities of some fruits can be stored in the refrigerator, but with others it is advisable to buy just enough to use fresh. Modern commercial storage methods ensure that fruit reaches the consumer virtually ready to eat.

TROPICAL AND SUBTROPICAL FRUIT

Banana Use fresh or dried. It is usually eaten raw. Use in salad, fruit salad, baked desserts and flambés, or add to curries. The banana can be braaied, whole or halved, in its skin.

Custard apple Use fresh. It is not often available on the commercial market. The skin is hard and the flesh soft and white. Eat it fresh.

Date Use fresh or dried. The three chief commercial varieties are soft, juicy, large dates, dry, hard dates and the fibrous, broken, hard ones that are compressed into blocks and used mostly for cooking. Serve as hors d'oeuvres stuffed with cream cheese, or on a fruit platter with cheese; or use in baking, such as in a date and walnut loaf*.

Loquat (Japanese medlar, Japanese plum) Used mostly fresh, but also available tinned, the fruit grows in clusters. It is round, oval or pear-shaped, 2,5-7,5cm long, with a thick skin, large brown seed and soft, yellow, juicy flesh. Use in fruit salad or for jam.

Litchi Use fresh or tinned. The small, oval fruit has a hard, rough, red-brown shell, soft, white flesh and a large, brown stone. The flesh is translucent. Shell and stone, and use in fruit salad, or on its own as a fruit cup.

Mango Use fresh or tinned. The fruit is generally harvested before ripening and allowed to ripen under controlled conditions. It is mostly eaten fresh or used to make pickle, chutney or preserve, in which case either ripe or green mangoes are suitable. It is also available as a fruit juice.

Persimmon Eat fresh. This fruit is commercially marketed only on a small scale. Ripeness is very important, since immaturity means an unacceptable astringency. The ripe flesh is very sweet. Serve whole with lemon wedges. The purée can be used in fruit juices, gelatin desserts or ice cream.

Pineapple Use fresh, candied or tinned. Many different varieties are found – some are large, pale yellow and watery (Kaine), while others are smaller, bright yellow, sweeter and with a firmer flesh (Queen). Use fresh, in salads, especially fruit salad, in fruit drinks, or served on its own. A hollowed-out pineapple makes a popular tropical drink container. Pineapple is also used in some poultry dishes.

Prickly pear Eat fresh. This member of the cactus family is mostly home-grown, and commercial marketing is still on a very limited scale. The fruits are green, red, yellow or mauve, and covered in prickly spines. The skin has to be removed deftly with a sharp knife to avoid touching the spines. The flesh is usually a similar colour to the skin and full of hard seeds. Prickly pears are usually eaten raw, and taste best if kept ice cold in the refrigerator until serving time.

Pawpaw (papaw, papaya) Use fresh. Many large and small (papino) varieties are grown, with flesh colours ranging from pale yellow to bright reddish-orange. Use the pawpaw in fruit salads, on its own or puréed as a fruit drink. The unripe fruit can be cooked similarly to squash. The skin contains papaïn and can be used as a meat tenderiser.

Rhubarb Use fresh. Only the leaf stalk is edible. The green leaves are poisonous and must not be eaten. Cut off the leaves, then clean and chop the stems and cook them in a little water with

---

TIPS FOR MAKING YOGHURT

Clean all equipment thoroughly before you begin. Use glass, stainless steel or enamelled containers; do not use aluminium pots for heating.

Wash out the pot with cold water before you heat the milk; this makes it easier to clean afterwards.

Heat the milk to just below boiling point (this destroys bacteria which prevent the formation of yoghurt). Be careful not to scorch the milk, as this creates an unpleasant taste.

Allow the milk to cool to 43-46°C before adding the culture. If you do not have a thermometer, test the milk temperature by placing a few drops on your wrist. It should feel comfortably warm – not hot.

Remove the skin from the milk.

Add the starter – a small amount of yoghurt containing the active yoghurt bacilli. Choose a yoghurt with the flavour you like best to use for a starter. It must be fresh and unpasteurised, and at room temperature.

You may use a dried culture (available from health-food stores) instead of a starter. This will take up to 24 hours to incubate (rather than the 3-6 hours needed with a starter). Once you have made yoghurt from a dried culture, you can use some of the yoghurt as a starter for the next batch. With dried cultures, follow the packet instructions for amounts, since these may vary from one make to the next.

Do not add more starter than is mentioned in the recipe. Very little is needed, and adding too much will make the yoghurt lumpy and acidic.

The starter should be thoroughly blended with the milk. The best way to do this is to add a little of the milk to the starter, and stir gently but very well. Then add the remaining milk and again stir thoroughly. Warm the containers into which the milk will be poured. This hastens incubation.

Put the containers in a place where the yoghurt can incubate undisturbed.

Moving may lengthen the process, and may even cause lumps to form.

If you are using fresh milk and starter, incubation should take 3-4 hours before the milk begins to solidify. Gently tip the container to see if the milk has thickened. If it is custard-like, you can refrigerate it (it will continue to thicken, but the flavour will not get stronger).

The longer the yoghurt incubates, the stronger the flavour. For a sweet, mild yoghurt, incubate for 3-6 hours. If you want a stronger flavour, allow longer incubation before refrigerating.

For very sweet yoghurt, add 15-30ml (1-2 tablespoons) honey to the milk before heating.

If whey or water should form in chilled yoghurt, pour it off. Stirring it in will simply thin out the yoghurt.

Save a little yoghurt to use as a starter for the next batch. After one or two weeks, however, you should buy a fresh starter and begin again.

sugar, stick cinnamon and cloves. Eat the stewed rhubarb on its own, or cover it with pastry or a crumble topping and bake in the oven. Serve the rhubarb warm with thick cream.

Berries

The most important fruits of spring are the berries. They are all best eaten raw, but can be used in gelatin desserts, berry tarts and for preserves.

Cape gooseberry Use fresh or tinned. This small, yellow berry is enclosed in a husk shaped like a cape or lantern. It is made into preserves, jams and tarts, or eaten raw.

Cherry Use fresh, tinned or candied. In South Africa the bright red to blue variety predominates, although some yellow ones are also seen. Cherries are used decoratively, and, when plentiful, can also be used in meat dishes such as poultry or pork, as well as for desserts. They are also an ingredient of liqueurs and cherry brandy.

Mulberry Eat fresh or as jam. Grown on trees, this berry has been known since ancient times. The berries must be used as soon as possible after ripening. Pour a mixture of chartreuse, ginger syrup and orange juice over the fresh, sugared berries and serve as a dessert. They are good for jam if used early in the season when the pectin content is higher. The fruit is excellent for a mulberry sorbet.

Raspberry This berry of the same genus as the boysenberry, loganberry and youngberry is available fresh, tinned, as jam or preserves, or in fruit drinks. Grown as a creeper in the colder, winter-rainfall areas, the raspberry plant produces berries that ripen in summer rather than spring. Their taste is sweet, but the delightful flavour is easily destroyed by heat. The pectin content is high and the berries make fine preserves. Use fresh, in tarts, as a fresh fruit purée in gelatin desserts, or for raspberry wine.

Strawberry Use fresh, tinned or frozen, as jams or preserves. The cultivated variety is larger and has a longer season than the wild, wood strawberry, which has a superior flavour. The fruit is best served with fresh cream, or as a dessert with soft cream cheese. Use to make strawberry ice cream or sorbet, or for strawberry jam, which is traditionally served with scones and cream.

Summer Fruits

Many 'summer fruits' are actually available as early as spring, and cultivated varieties are marketed late into the summer season. The abundance of this fruit provides an incentive to preserve for winter. Most summer fruits are good for home bottling and preserving.

Apricot Use fresh, dried, tinned or as jam. The fruit is often marketed before being fully ripe. It is best eaten fresh, but large quantities are dried or processed. In cooking it can be used successfully with poultry or lamb, in a sorbet or gelatin dessert, in fresh fruit salad, or dried in a fruit compote.

Fig Use fresh, dried, tinned, as green fig preserve or ripe fig jam. Figs are not marketed commercially on a large scale. Different varieties are home-grown. The first figs are used for green fig preserves; ripe figs are used for jam. Sliced, fresh, ripe figs with sugar and Cointreau make an excellent dessert.

Granadilla (passion fruit) Use fresh, tinned or as fruit juice. This purple-skinned fruit with yellow pulp and black seeds grows on a creeper. Add the pulp to fruit salad or use in a fruit punch. It gives a delightful flavour to ice cream or sorbet.

Grape Use fresh, tinned, as jam, as fruit juice or, dried, as raisins. Many varieties are on the market: yellow, green, red, purple or black. Shapes range from small round, large round and small oval to long and elongated. Grapes may be preserved in brandy or liqueur. Many are grown specifically for wine-making, and the various cultivars form the base of many well-known wines such as riesling, chenin blanc, cabernet, shiraz and others.

Melon All melons have a high water content. After slicing or dicing they can be kept in the refrigerator for some time, but generally do not freeze well.

Netted melons, named because of the netted appearance of their skins, include the muskmelon and cantaloup or spanspek. The skins are usually cream to lightly coloured, the flesh pink to orange and the seeds white.

Green melons, winter melons or honeydew melons have smooth skins and green flesh, with seeds varying in colour from white to black. The ogen melon is a variety with a yellow and green striped skin.

Melons are mostly served fresh, as an hors d'oeuvre with Parma ham, in fruit salad or, in some African and tropical cuisines, in a cooked form similar to marrow.

Watermelon is used fresh, or as jam or preserves. The fresh watermelon is large, with a smooth, dark green to light green skin (used for melon and ginger jam) and bright pink flesh with black seeds. The wild variety has whiter flesh and a thicker skin, and is used mostly for preserves.

Pear Use fresh, tinned, candied, as fruit juice or dried. Many varieties, differing in colour, size and flavour, are available. Fresh pears make a delicious hors d'oeuvre when served with blue cheese, or a dessert when stewed in red wine.

Plum and prune plum Plums are used fresh, tinned, as jam or fruit juice. Many different varieties are grown, varying in colour from yellow to dark purple. The greengage is a green variety that is used for canning. Plums are best served fresh or stewed, and can be used with poultry or in gelatin desserts or sorbet, or as a base for fruit drinks.

The dark-leafed tree of the prune plum bears a fleshy plum that dries well; and although the fruit may be eaten raw, it is mostly used for drying. Prunes are used in meat dishes or as a fruit compote, and are very good marinated in liqueur or red wine.

Pomegranate Eat fresh. A native of Persia, the pomegranate tree was a traditional item in the home fruit orchard but it is very scarce today. The size of an orange, the pomegranate has large, bright red, fleshy, pipped seeds. Use fresh, or liquidized as a flavouring for fruit drinks, desserts or ice cream.

Sour fig (Hottentot's fig) The fruit of this wild succulent is fleshy or pulpy, and has a sourish taste if eaten raw. The fruits are available the year round. They are picked in the wild and preserved or dried. The sour fig is mostly found in the Cape Province and south coast of Natal.

Tree tomato Use fresh. Home-grown in colder areas, this plant takes 18 months to bear fruit. The fruit is stewed or used for cooking jam, which, because of the high pectin content, is excellent.

Winter Fruits

Apple Use fresh, dried, tinned or frozen. Many varieties are available: some are better for cooking, such as Granny Smith; others, such as Starking and Golden Delicious, are eating apples. Use the eating apples in salads. Wash well and dice with the peel: the bright yellow, red or green skins provide an interesting colour and texture variation in both vegetable and fruit salads. Use cooking apples for baking, stewing, apple sauce or purée.

Cherry guava These are small, round, purple or dark red guavas, used mostly for preserves.

Guava Use fresh, tinned or as fruit juice. This pale yellow, pear-shaped or round fruit with pink flesh and hard seeds has a characteristic musky smell and sweet but acidic flavour. It is an extremely good source of vitamin C, and the fruit juice has become popular as the first item on the breakfast menu. Use stewed guavas as a purée (extract the seeds) in desserts, ice creams or fruit juices. Guavas can also be used to make a fruit butter, or dried as a fruit roll.

Kiwi fruit (Chinese gooseberry) Use fresh, tinned or as fruit juice. First grown commercially in New Zealand, the fruit has a furry brown skin and a beautiful round pattern of black seeds in pale green pulp. The taste is slightly acidic, and it contains a high concentration of vitamin C. The kiwi fruit can be served on its own, cut in half and eaten from the skin with a spoon. Since it is still relatively expensive, the fruit is used mostly for decorative purposes (sliced into rounds).

Quince Use fresh, tinned, as jelly or as jam. One of the earliest known fruits, it was traditionally grown as a hedge round the fruit orchard. Quinces have a high pectin content and set into a good jelly. Though they can be eaten raw, grated with muesli for breakfast, or stewed, they are mostly used for jam, jelly or home-made preserves. Quinces can also be used to make fruit butter or dried as quince roll. In some eastern European countries they are cooked with beef, veal or chicken and onion. Quince jelly or stewed quinces are traditionally served with venison.

CITRUS

Citrus is traditionally winter fruit. Many types have, however, been cultivated to such an extent that they are available the year round.

The pith or white part inside the skin gives a bitter aftertaste and should be removed as much as possible if citrus is used in fresh salad or in cooking. If a recipe calls for the rind, peel off the outer layer thinly with a vegetable peeler. To use the fruit, remove the pith with a sharp knife. Ideally, the membranes separating the segments should also be removed.

All citrus peel dries well. Leave the peels to dry in the sun or oven. Citrus peel adds an interesting flavour to poultry, stews and fruit compote, and in baking.

Citron This fruit, which closely resembles the lemon, is grown for its peel, which is used in baking, sweets and preserves or to make candied peel. It is not generally available commercially.

Grapefruit Use fresh, tinned, frozen or as fruit juice. A white or pink variety is commonly available. Traditionally, grapefruit is served at breakfast or as an appetising fruit cup at the beginning of a menu with three or more courses. The fruit has a bitter taste and is not generally used as a dessert or after a meal.

Kumquat Use fresh or as preserves. A small, oval, orange-like fruit grown on a miniature tree, it tastes acid and bitter, and is not often eaten fresh. Preserved kumquats are a tasty accompaniment to ice cream, and so is kumquat liqueur. The preserves are made with a thick syrup, and the fruit is generally kept whole. Early in the season the fruit has a high pectin content and can be used for marmalade.

Lemon Use fresh, as lemon juice or as a fruit drink. Every kitchen should always be stocked with lemons. Lemon juice is the major flavouring ingredient for a good dressing. Grated lemon rind can be used to flavour desserts or in baking. Traditionally, home-made lemon syrup, lemon snow and lemon soufflé are items served when lemons are plentiful.

Lime Use fresh or as lime juice. The lime is a smaller, greener fruit than the lemon. It is usually also sweeter, and can be eaten on its own. A slice of lime in a gin and tonic or in many other drinks makes the drink all the more refreshing on a hot summer's day.

Naartjie (mandarin, tangerine) Use fresh, tinned or candied. Different varieties vary in size and shape. The peel may be thick or thin, coarse or fine. The peel dries well and makes an excellent flavouring for most cooking when fruit or curry is used. The fruit is best eaten raw, while the tinned product is often used with other citrus fruits in a fruit cup. If trimmed well, the bright orange segments add a nice splash of colour to many dishes.

Orange Use fresh, tinned, frozen, as fruit juice or as marmalade. Some oranges are more juicy or fleshy than others, and they can vary considerably in size. Some are bitter and others sweet. Oranges have a high pectin content and make good marmalade. Orange juice can be served fresh or used for cooking duck, in baking or in fruit desserts. The fruit can be served fresh in fruit salad or used for sorbet.

Pomelo Use fresh. The pomelo is larger than the grapefruit, has a thick skin and a bitter fibrous pulp. It is used mostly for preserves and marmalade.

Tangelo This cross between grapefruit and tangerine has a tapering shape, a bright orange skin and fleshy segments that taste best if eaten fresh.

A BUYER'S GUIDE TO NUTS

The term 'nut' is used not only to describe hard-shelled fruits but also some seeds. The peanut, for example, is actually the seed of an underground legume, but it is also covered by this description.

Nuts can be bought shelled or unshelled. Some, with very hard shells (such as pecan and Brazil-nuts), can be cracked more easily if left in boiling water for 15-20 minutes.

To remove the thin layer covering the white kernel of some nuts (almonds and walnuts for instance), a similar procedure can be followed to ensure effective blanching*. Some nuts are sold already blanched.

Nuts can be roasted or toasted* to enhance their flavour.

Salted nuts will not last as long as unsalted nuts. Store in airtight containers, away from heat and humidity.

Almond Available unshelled or shelled, roasted or raw, whole, slivered, ground or in almond paste. Almonds can be eaten as a snack or used in salads, baking, confectionery or as almond paste on a fruit cake.

Brazil-nut Available unshelled or shelled, whole, fresh or toasted. This nutritious nut is mostly eaten as a snack or used in salads or baking.

Cashew nut Available shelled, whole, salted or unsalted, roasted or raw. This nut grows as a protuberance at the end of an apple-like fruit. The shell must be removed by roasting before eating. Cashew nuts are served at cocktail time or in salads, baking and cashew butter.

Coconut Available fresh, whole or desiccated. This hard-shelled tropical fruit has a hairy exterior, firm white flesh inside and a white liquid known as 'coconut milk' in the cavity. The flesh can be eaten raw or dried; dried or 'desiccated' coconut is used in desserts, confectionery and baking. Different dishes can also be made from the coconut milk.

Hazelnut Available whole, unshelled or shelled. Hazelnuts keep well in shelled form. They are eaten whole or used in baking. Immature nuts can be preserved in brine and used in salads.

Macadamia nut Available shelled and whole. The nut is white, crisp and sweetish in flavour. Many claim it to be superior in taste to all other nuts. It is eaten whole or used in salads and baking.

Peanut (groundnut, monkey nut) Available unshelled or shelled, halved, whole, salted or unsalted, roasted or raw, or in peanut butter. The peanut is an important source of protein for many people. Numerous varieties have been developed with specific properties and for specific reasons. Peanuts are eaten whole or ground to a paste. Usually they are used only after they have been roasted. Peanut oil is extracted commercially.

Roast raw peanuts in a cool oven until dry. Use a bit of oil in the pan and leave the nuts until they are pale brown and the skin is brittle. As soon as the nuts have cooled, rub the skins off between your hands.

Pecan nut Available unshelled or shelled, fresh or roasted. It is rather difficult to remove the shells. Shelled pecan nuts go rancid quickly and should be kept refrigerated. Pecan nuts are traditionally used in baking, particularly for pecan pie and pecan cake, as well as in confectionery.

Pine nut Available shelled and whole. All pine-tree nuts are edible. Some, however, are smaller than others. Pine nuts are white, cream or yellow, and very soft in texture. They become more nutty in taste and appearance when they have been roasted. Use pine nuts in rice dishes, in stuffings, with spinach, pasta and Italian dishes, and also in confectionery. Pounded pine nuts, used as a thickener, go well with basil, anchovy, garlic, salt and oil to make a sauce for veal.

Pistachio nut Available whole, dyed pink, salted or unsalted. The pistachio has a fine green colour and mild flavour, although it may have a resinous aftertaste. It is used in cooking, for pâtés, stuffings and in a rice pilaff. Remove the skins by blanching* the nuts in salted water. Shelled pistachio nuts go rancid very quickly and should be kept refrigerated.

Walnut Available unshelled or shelled, halved or chopped. Walnuts can be eaten on their own or used in baking, stuffings, sweets or salads. They may also be pickled.

Apple Strudel

Contrary to the popular belief that *apfelstrudel* is an Austrian dish which originated in Vienna, it actually comes from Hungary. It was the Hungarians who first took their incredibly thin strudel dough from the great Turkish delicacy baclava and filled it with apples.

Today, however, the making of strudel has become an almost sacred rite in the city of Vienna, where it is said that a good strudel dough is one through which one's newspaper can be read.

Preparation Time: 1 hour for the filling;
50 minutes for the pastry
Standing Time: 30 minutes
Cooking Time: 30-35 minutes
Pre-Heat Oven to 200°C

Ingredients for Ten to Fifteen
Strudel pastry using 225 g flour
8 large apples (Granny Smith or winter pearmain)
180 g sultanas
60 ml (¼ cup) breadcrumbs
100 g sugar
10 ml (2 teaspoons) ground cinnamon
250 ml (1 cup) chopped almonds or other nuts
50 g butter, melted
30 ml (2 tablespoons) vanilla sugar**

First prepare the strudel pastry, then peel, core and thinly slice the apples. Wash the sultanas in hot water and dry well.

Sprinkle the breadcrumbs over the entire surface of the pastry. Pile the sliced apples along the top of the pastry to within 5 cm of each side.

Sprinkle the sultanas, sugar, cinnamon and nuts over the apples, and fold in the edges of the pastry.

Picking up two corners of the tablecloth on which you stretched the strudel pastry, allow the pastry to roll gently over on to itself, repeating this process until you have a cylinder resembling an elongated Swiss roll.

Gently slide it on to a greased baking sheet, and shape it into a horse-shoe curve. Brush with melted butter and sprinkle with a little water.

Bake for 20 minutes. Brush once more with butter, lower the temperature to 175°C and bake for a further 10 minutes, or until the strudel is golden.

Remove from the oven and dust with vanilla sugar.

Serving Suggestion Cut into wide, diagonal slices and serve with lightly whipped cream.

Variations Using the apple filling, simplify the whole procedure by making a cream cheese pastry*, rolling it out as thinly as possible, and proceeding as in the main recipe.

A sweet cream cheese or cherry filling is also delicious.

Apple Pie

Apple pie in its various forms is a dish that has been with us for a very long time. This recipe is for a deliciously simple pie flavoured with lemon rind and spice.

Preparation Time: 20 minutes
Cooking Time: 40 minutes
Pre-Heat Oven to 200°C

Ingredients for Six to Eight
*4 large Granny Smith apples
100-125 g sugar
5 ml (1 teaspoon) grated lemon rind
2 cloves, or 1 ml (¼ teaspoon) ground cinnamon or ground ginger
Shortcrust pastry* using 225 g flour
Castor sugar for sprinkling*

Peel, core and slice the apples. Mix the sugar, lemon rind and spice together.

Using a 26 cm pie dish, with a pie funnel placed in the centre if desired, arrange the apples and the sugar mixture in layers. Finish with a layer of apples.

Cover with the rolled-out pastry and make a small hole in the centre to allow the steam to escape.

Brush the top of the pie with cold water and sprinkle with a little castor sugar to give a crisp coating.

Bake in the pre-heated oven for 20 minutes, then reduce the heat to 190°C and bake for another 20 minutes, or until the apples are tender.

Serving Suggestions Serve warm with cream, custard* or caramel sauce*.

BAKEWELL TART *Jam, eggs and sugar make this tart a simple delight.*

Bakewell Tart

According to legend, this pudding was created in error by a cook at the town of Bakewell in the English Midlands who misunderstood her mistress's instruction that she should add butter, eggs and sugar to the pastry for a jam tart. Instead, she spread the mixed ingredients on top of the jam. The guests, needless to say, found the pudding delicious.

Preparation Time: 15 minutes
Cooking Time: 25-30 minutes
Pre-Heat Oven to 200°C

Ingredients for Four
Flaky pastry using 225 g flour, or shortcrust pastry* using 175 g flour
45 ml (3 tablespoons) strawberry jam*
3 eggs
75 g castor sugar
100-125 g butter, melted
75 g ground almonds*

Roll out the pastry to line* a 20 cm oval pie dish 5-8 cm deep. Trim the pastry flush with the edge of the dish.

Warm the jam gently in a saucepan and spread evenly over the pastry base. Beat the eggs and sugar until creamy, then stir in the melted butter and almonds, and pour the mixture over the jam.

Bake in the centre of the pre-heated oven for 25-30 minutes, or until the filling is set.

Serving Suggestion Serve hot with cream.

Tarte Aux Pommes

The following apple tart recipe from France combines the incomparable taste and texture of the cooking apple with a tasty, sweet shortcrust pastry.

Preparation Time: 40 minutes
Chilling Time: at least 2 hours
Cooking Time: 30-35 minutes
Pre-heat Oven to 180°C

Ingredients for Six to Eight
300 g sweet shortcrust pastry*
using 225 g flour

For the filling:
3 medium-sized cooking apples,
peeled, cored and sliced
30 ml (2 tablespoons) sugar
15 ml (1 tablespoon) water
3-4 crisp eating apples, peeled,
cored and thinly sliced
in crescents

For the glaze:
45 ml (3 tablespoons) apple jelly*,
apricot jam* or honey – the
latter melted with 10 ml
(2 teaspoons) lemon juice

First make the pastry, then wrap it in grease-proof paper and chill in the refrigerator for 2 hours.

Meanwhile, cook the prepared cooking apples gently with the sugar and water in a covered pan until the fruit makes a thick purée.

Roll out the pastry to line* a 25 cm flan ring. Prick the pastry base in several places with a fork.

Spread the apple purée over the base, and on it arrange a circle of closely overlapped slices of eating apple. One tip of each apple slice should touch the rim of the crust, and the other tip should point towards the centre of the flan. Fill the centre of this circle with a smaller circle of slices radiating from the centre of the flan.

Bake the tart in the centre of the pre-heated oven for 30-35 minutes, or until the crust is crisp and golden-brown and the apple slices soft. When the tart is cooked, remove it from the flan ring and stand it on a wire rack.

Warm the apple jelly and brush over the fruit; otherwise glaze with warmed, strained apricot jam, or the honey melted with lemon juice. Cool before serving.

PASTRIES, PUDDINGS AND DESSERTS

A Selection of Choux Pastry Favourites

Choux pastry* can be used for both savoury and sweet dishes. It puffs up to 3 or 4 times its original size, and must be placed straight into a hot oven so that the puffing up starts immediately. Only after about 10 minutes should the heat be reduced to prevent over-browning. The pastry must be baked until it is quite dry or else it will collapse when it is removed from the oven.

Cream Puffs

To form cream puffs, drop the choux pastry* from a teaspoon or tablespoon, depending on the size required, or force through a piping bag with a star nozzle, on to a greased baking sheet, leaving enough space for the puffs to expand. Bake them at 200°C for 10 minutes, then reduce the heat to 180°C and bake for anything up to a further 25 minutes, depending on the size of the cream puffs. Make sure that there are no moisture blisters on the puffs and also that they are firm to the touch. When they are cool, cut them horizontally with a sharp knife, remove any pieces of damp dough that may be inside, fill with a sweetened, whipped cream or crème pâtissière and dust the tops with icing sugar.

Crème Pâtissière

To make a crème pâtissière (confectioner's or baker's custard), scald* 375 ml (1½ cups) milk. In a separate saucepan, work together 4 egg yolks and 60 g sugar with a wooden spoon until the mixture is creamy and pale. Lightly mix in 30 g flour, then gradually stir in the scalded milk until the ingredients are well blended.

Place the saucepan over a low heat and stir the mixture constantly until it almost boils – do not allow it to boil. Strain, add a few drops of vanilla essence, then allow to cool (stirring occasionally to prevent a skin from forming).

Chocolate Éclairs

To make éclairs, follow the directions for making cream puffs but use a plain, round nozzle attached to a piping bag. Force the mixture through the bag into strips about as long as your middle finger. After baking, allow the éclairs to cool, slit them along one side and, using a piping bag with plain nozzle, fill them with sweetened cream. Coat them with chocolate glaze.

Chocolate Glaze

Combine 60 g butter with 15 ml (1 tablespoon) cocoa and 20 ml (4 teaspoons) water or milk, and heat to boiling. Remove from the heat and stir in 250 g sifted icing sugar. Cool the mixture a little before pouring it over the éclairs. The mixture will thicken as it cools.

Gâteau Saint-Honoré

Make a sweet shortcrust pastry* from 225 g flour, roll it out to a thickness of 5 mm and cut a circle 23-25 cm in diameter to form the base of the gâteau. Place this on a greased baking sheet. Brush a little cold water on the perimeter of the crust base, and then, using a piping bag fitted with a plain round nozzle, make a border of choux pastry*, about as thick as a man's thumb, around the edge of the pastry circle. Brush the choux pastry with an egg yolk mixed with a little water.

Bake the tart at 220°C for 20-25 minutes, or until the choux edge is brown. After removing from the oven, quickly cut a few slits in the choux ring to allow the steam to escape.

Meanwhile, make 18-20 small cream puffs*, each the size of a walnut. When the puffs are cool, make a hole in each of them and fill it with whipped cream.

Heat 75 g castor sugar in a small saucepan over a gentle heat until it turns golden. Dip the bottom of the puffs in this warm caramel syrup and arrange them around the edge of the gâteau. Drip the caramel over the puffs, working quickly before the syrup hardens. Fill the centre of the cake with whipped cream sweetened with castor sugar. Decorate with crystallised flowers*.

Profiteroles with Ice Cream and Hot Chocolate Sauce

To make profiteroles, force choux pastry* through a piping bag fitted with a plain nozzle. The portions should each be about the size of a walnut. Bake them as for cream puffs. When they are cool, and just before serving, fill them with small scoops of vanilla ice cream*. Serve them piled up on a serving dish – each serving consisting of two or three profiteroles covered with hot chocolate sauce.

To make the chocolate sauce mix a large tin (about 400 g) evaporated milk with 360 g sugar and 30 ml (2 tablespoons) cocoa, and bring to the boil over a medium heat. Cook the mixture for 3 minutes, stirring all the time. Remove from the heat and add 5 ml (1 teaspoon) vanilla essence and a pinch of salt. Beat for 1-2 minutes.

The sauce may be kept in a jar in the refrigerator and re-heated before use.

FIG TART

THIS TART is not to be missed during the fig season. If you do not have a fig tree in your garden, take a trip to the market – your effort will be well rewarded in making this delicious tart.

PREPARATION TIME: 30 MINUTES
COOKING TIME: 1 HOUR
PRE-HEAT OVEN TO 220°C

INGREDIENTS FOR SIX
Shortcrust pastry* using 225 g flour
12 ripe fresh figs
2 egg yolks
125 ml (½ cup) cream
30 ml (2 tablespoons) honey
15 ml (1 tablespoon) brandy
30 ml (2 tablespoons) icing sugar

Line* a 23 cm pie dish with the pastry and prick the base all over. Bake the shell for about 10 minutes, or until it has set (but not browned). Reduce the oven temperature to 180°C.

Peel the figs and cut across – almost right through – before arranging them in the bottom of the cooled, half-baked crust.

Beat together the egg yolks, cream, honey and brandy, and pour over the figs. Bake at 180°C for 40 minutes. Sift over the icing sugar and bake for another 10 minutes, or until set.

CAPE GOOSEBERRY FLAN

THE WORD 'CAPE' in the name of the cape gooseberry does not refer to any geographical area, but rather to its papery shell, which cloaks it like a cape. It is a delightful-tasting fruit but unfortunately has a very short season.

PREPARATION TIME: 45 MINUTES
CHILLING TIME: 1 HOUR
COOKING TIME: 20 MINUTES
PRE-HEAT OVEN TO 190°C

INGREDIENTS FOR SIX
For the pastry:
150 g flour, sifted
100 g butter
60 ml (¼ cup) sugar
1 egg
5 ml (1 teaspoon) finely grated lemon rind

For the pastry cream:
3 egg yolks
10 ml (2 teaspoons) flour
300 ml milk
60 ml (¼ cup) cream
60 ml (¼ cup) sugar
A pinch of salt

For the gooseberry topping:
250 ml (1 cup) water
125 g sugar
1 cinnamon stick
1 kg fresh gooseberries, or three 410 g tins

To make the pastry, place the flour, butter and sugar in a large bowl and cut in the butter with a knife, then quickly work in the egg and lemon rind. Chill the dough for about 1 hour.

Roll out the pastry to line* a greased 23 cm pie dish or a 26 cm loose-bottomed quiche tin. Cover the pastry with aluminium foil and weight with sugar beans or rice. Bake for 15-20 minutes. Remove the beans and foil, and allow to cool.

To make the pastry cream, beat the egg yolks with the flour. Scald* the milk and cream with the sugar in a heavy-based saucepan, add the pinch of salt, and gradually add the warm milk mixture to the yolk mixture, beating well all the time.

Return the mixture to the saucepan and cook over a gentle heat, stirring all the time, until the pastry cream has thickened. Pour into a bowl and allow to cool, stirring occasionally. When cool, pour into the pastry shell and smooth.

To make the gooseberry topping, boil the water, sugar and cinnamon for 3 minutes, then add the fresh gooseberries and simmer gently until the berries are tender. (Tinned gooseberries should not be added at this stage as they are already cooked and tender.) With a slotted spoon, remove the berries and allow to cool.

Meanwhile, boil the syrup until it has reduced to about 45 ml (3 tablespoons) and becomes a thickish glaze. Cover the pastry cream with the gooseberries (if using tinned ones, drain off their fluid) and gently coat them with the glaze.

VARIATION A vanilla instant pudding may be used if you need a quick version of pastry cream. Mix it with half milk and half cream, and flavour with 30 ml (2 tablespoons) brandy.

MELKTERT

POPULAR AS A SWEET SNACK with morning or afternoon tea or coffee, melktert may also be dressed up as a dessert.

PREPARATION TIME: 40 MINUTES FOR THE PASTRY; 30 MINUTES FOR THE FILLING
CHILLING TIME: 30 MINUTES FOR THE PASTRY
COOKING TIME: 25 MINUTES
PRE-HEAT OVEN TO 230°C

INGREDIENTS FOR SIX
Puff pastry* using 225 g flour
3 extra-large eggs, separated
50 g flour
20 ml (3 tablespoons) cornflour
50 g sugar
600 ml milk
1 cinnamon stick
15 g butter
Ground cinnamon for dusting

Roll out the pastry until it is very thin, and line a pie plate of 25 cm diameter. Ease the pastry into the plate to counteract possible shrinkage when baking. Slightly dampen the rim of the pastry and put additional strips around the edge, so that the filling will not run over.

Paint the inside edge of the pastry lining with 10 ml (2 teaspoons) of the egg whites. This will prevent the filling from pulling away from the crusts. Put the lined plate into a refrigerator while preparing the filling.

Mix the dry ingredients well (setting aside 1 tablespoon sugar), stir them into a paste with a little of the cold milk, and then add the rest of the milk and the cinnamon stick. Bring this mixture to the boil, stirring continuously.

When the mixture is well thickened and cooked, add the butter. Remove from the heat, then carefully add the egg yolks, first adding a little of the hot mixture to the yolks. Return to the heat for a minute, cooking slowly. Remove from the heat and cool slightly.

Meanwhile, beat the egg whites and reserved sugar until the mixture holds soft peaks, then fold thoroughly into the cooled milk mixture.

Spoon the filling into the cold lined pastry case, dust the top very lightly with cinnamon and bake the tart in the middle of the pre-heated oven for 10-15 minutes. Reduce the temperature to 180°C so that the soufflé can rise well and cook through. When it is golden, turn off the heat and leave it for 5 minutes more.

If the tart is not to be served immediately, take it out before the final 5 minutes so that the soufflé can puff again when being re-heated. If the tart is to be served after being frozen, defrost it before re-heating at 180°C.

SERVING SUGGESTIONS Melktert accompanied by a platter of colourful preserves or crystallised fruit makes an unusual and delicious dessert.

MINCE PIES

SMALL PIES filled with spicy fruit mincemeat and coated with sugar have been traditional Christmas fare for centuries. It was customary in the past to eat one for each of the 12 days of Christmas, to ensure 12 happy months ahead.

PREPARATION TIME: 50 MINUTES
COOKING TIME: 20 MINUTES
PRE-HEAT OVEN TO 220°C

INGREDIENTS TO YIELD 18-20 PIES
Shortcrust pastry* using 335 g flour, or puff pastry* using 450 g flour
450 g fruit mincemeat*
1 egg white
Castor sugar for sprinkling

Roll out the prepared pastry thinly and cut out 18-20 rounds, about 8 cm across, for the pie bases. Line 6,5 cm wide patty tins with these, and fill to about half their depth with the fruit mincemeat.

Cut out slightly smaller rounds for the pie covers. Dampen the rims of the pie bases with cold water and place the covers on top, pressing the edges together lightly to seal them. Make a small slit in the top of each pie, brush with the egg white and sprinkle with castor sugar.

Put the pies in the pre-heated oven and bake for about 20 minutes, or until a light golden-brown.

Remove from the oven and let them stand for 3-5 minutes before lifting them from the tins with a round-bladed knife. Put them on a wire rack to cool.

SERVING SUGGESTION Serve with cream or brandy butter*.

PASTRIES, PUDDINGS AND DESSERTS

Nut Tart

This rich, delicious tart is an ideal accompaniment to morning or afternoon tea, or alternatively it can be served with coffee to end a meal.

Preparation Time: 1 hour
Standing Time: 30 minutes
Cooking Time: 40 minutes
Pre-heat Oven to 180°C

Ingredients for Six
For the pastry:
115 g butter
100 g sugar
250 g flour, sifted
5 ml (1 teaspoon) baking powder
1 egg, beaten

For the filling:
125 g butter
125 g sugar
60 ml (¼ cup) milk
250 g almonds, with skins, coarsely chopped
3 ml (¾ teaspoon) vanilla essence
1 ml (¼ teaspoon) almond essence

Guava Tart *A liqueur-flavoured syrup adds a sheen to this tart that makes it a winner with guests.*

Guava Tart

Poached guavas make an excellent filling for a winter fruit tart. If fresh guavas are not available, you can always fall back on tinned ones. With its glazed finish and topped with whipped cream, this tart makes a most attractive dish.

Preparation Time: 15 minutes for the pastry; 40 minutes for the filling
Cooking Time: 20-30 minutes for the pastry; 20 minutes for the filling
Pre-heat Oven to 180°C

Ingredients for Six
Sweet shortcrust pastry* using 225 g flour
12 ripe guavas
250 ml (1 cup) water
250 ml (1 cup) red wine
250 ml (1 cup) honey
1 cinnamon stick
10 ml (2 teaspoons) gelatin
30 ml (2 tablespoons) port
15 ml (1 tablespoon) Van der Hum liqueur*
190 ml (¾ cup) natural yoghurt*

For the glaze:
15 ml (1 tablespoon) cornflour
30 ml (2 tablespoons) cold water
15 ml (1 tablespoon) Van der Hum liqueur*

Roll out the pastry to line* a 25 cm pie dish. Prick the base all over and bake the shell for 20-30 minutes, or until lightly browned.

Peel and halve the guavas. Bring the water, wine and honey to the boil, stirring occasionally. Add half the guavas and the cinnamon stick.

Reduce the heat and simmer gently (uncovered) for 5-10 minutes until just tender. Remove the guavas with a slotted spoon and repeat with the remaining fruit.

Strain the cooking syrup and set aside 190 ml (¾ cup) for the glaze. Store the remaining syrup in the refrigerator to use again for poaching fruits.

Reserve 16 guava halves for the topping, and purée the rest through a strainer to remove the pips.

Sprinkle the gelatin over the port in a small oven-proof dish. Place the dish in a pan of simmering water, stirring now and again until the gelatin is dissolved and the liquid clear. Fold the liqueur, yoghurt and dissolved gelatin into the purée of guavas. Spoon into the cooled baked crust.

Arrange the 16 reserved poached guava halves on top of the filling, cut-side facing down. To make the glaze, heat the reserved syrup. Mix the cornflour with the cold water until smooth. Stir into the heated syrup and keep stirring until thick, smooth and translucent. Stir in the liqueur and allow to cool slightly. Spoon over the guavas for a glazed finish. Chill the tart before serving.

Serving Suggestion Decorate with fresh mint, and serve with whipped cream.

Variations Use drained, tinned guavas for a quickly made tart. Thicken the syrup from the tin with 15 ml (1 tablespoon) cornflour or custard powder, and spoon over the guavas for a shiny finish.

You can also use a sponge flan as a base instead of the shortcrust pastry.

The guavas simply poached in the honey and wine make a light ending to any meal. Serve chilled with cream or natural yoghurt*.

To make the pastry, crumb the butter, sugar, flour and baking powder, and work in the beaten egg. Work the mixture into a firm dough and allow to stand for 30 minutes. Roll out to line* a greased, loose-bottomed quiche tin, 23 cm-25 cm in diameter. If the pastry is too crumbly to roll, add 10 ml (2 teaspoons) water to the dough – or more if necessary. Bake the pastry case blind* or prick well and bake for 8-10 minutes.

To make the filling, melt the butter and add the sugar, milk and almonds. Boil for 5 minutes over a low heat, stirring continuously. Remove from the stove and add the essences. Pour into the half-baked pastry shell, return to the oven and bake for a further 20-30 minutes. Serve at room temperature.

Variation For a nice change, use mixed nuts.

261

MAKING PIG'S EARS

Roll out 400 g ready-made puff pastry (sprinkling sugar instead of flour on the board) to a 30 cm x 35 cm rectangle.

Dredge it well with castor sugar. Trim the edges to make a rectangle. Roll up the two short edges of the pastry into the centre until they meet in the middle.

Cut the rolled pastry into 1 cm thick slices with a sharp knife.

Lay them, cut side down, on a baking sheet, leaving room for them to spread.

Flatten the pieces slightly with the heel of the hand or a wooden rolling pin dipped in sugar.

Chill for 1 hour, then sprinkle them lightly with more castor sugar and bake at 200°C for 15 minutes, or until they are puffed and golden-brown. Turn them if desired and bake for a further 2 minutes to crisp the second side. Cool the pig's ears on a wire rack.

BOW TIES

CHINESE CUISINE does not offer a wide variety of desserts. Bow ties, a restaurant favourite, are light, delicate confections that can be made in advance. You will need only a short time to complete the final stage on the day of serving.

PREPARATION TIME: 35 MINUTES
STANDING TIME: 30 MINUTES
COOKING TIME: 30 MINUTES

INGREDIENTS TO YIELD 80 BOW TIES
225 g flour
A pinch of salt
50 g cold butter, grated
Cold water to mix
Cornflour
Sunflower oil for deep-frying
250 ml (1 cup) golden syrup
30 ml (2 tablespoons) water
45 ml (3 tablespoons) lemon juice

Sieve together the flour and salt. Cut in the butter until the mixture is crumbly. Add water a little at a time, cutting it in with a knife to form a smooth, firm dough. Allow the dough to rest for 30 minutes in a cool place.

Roll the dough out paper thin on a board covered with sifted cornflour. (If you have a pasta machine, this will give you wonderfully thin strips.)

Using a sharp knife, cut the dough into rectangular shapes about 10 cm x 5 cm. Twist each rectangle in the middle to form a bow shape.

Heat deep oil in a pan or wok to medium heat and deep-fry the bow ties, 3 or 4 at a time, until they are golden on each side. Remove them and prepare for serving, or else remove, cool and freeze them, packed in a rigid plastic container.

To prepare the bow ties for serving, mix the golden syrup, water and lemon juice, and heat gently. Dip the bow ties in the syrup mixture one at a time, then drain them on a rack.

For the best results with frozen bow ties, re-fry the unthawed pastries very briefly in hot oil, just to crisp them, then dip them in the hot syrup mixture. The bow ties may also be defrosted and then dipped straight into the syrup mixture.

When completely cool, arrange them on a platter and cover them well with an airtight wrapping until serving time.

SERVING SUGGESTION Bow ties look wonderful arranged in circles on a large, round, clear tray. An attractive touch is to decorate the tray with hibiscus flowers.

VARIATION Use bottled ginger syrup instead of golden syrup.

PECAN NUT PIE

THIS DISH, with its buttery, sweet filling, is often referred to as 'Southern pecan pie', as it originates in the southern part of the United States, where pecan nuts are plentiful.

PREPARATION TIME: 15 MINUTES FOR THE PASTRY; 10 MINUTES FOR THE FILLING
CHILLING TIME: 30 MINUTES FOR THE PASTRY
COOKING TIME: 50 MINUTES
PRE-HEAT OVEN TO 180°C

INGREDIENTS FOR SIX TO EIGHT
Shortcrust pastry* using 225 g flour
125 ml (½ cup) melted butter
200 g sugar
250 ml (1 cup) golden syrup or maple syrup
A pinch of salt
4 eggs, lightly beaten
100 g pecan nuts

Line* a 26 cm pie dish with the pastry, fluting the edges, and chill the pastry case for 30 minutes.

To make the filling, combine the butter, sugar, syrup and salt. Stir in the eggs and nuts and pour the mixture into the prepared pie shell.

Bake for 50 minutes, or until a knife inserted in the centre comes out clean.

SERVING SUGGESTION Serve at room temperature with unsweetened cream, or with a scoop of vanilla ice cream*.

VARIATION For a pie filling which is not quite so sweet, reduce the amount of sugar used to 100 g, and add 15 ml (1 tablespoon) lemon juice.

DROP SCONES

ORIGINALLY A SCOTTISH SPECIALITY, these scones make an ideal snack or tea time treat. They are best served buttered, with a tasty fruit jam and whipped cream.

PREPARATION TIME: 5 MINUTES
COOKING TIME: 15 MINUTES

INGREDIENTS TO YIELD 15 SCONES
125 g flour
A pinch of salt
10 ml (2 teaspoons) baking powder
15 ml (1 tablespoon) castor sugar
1 extra-large egg
150 ml milk
30 ml (2 tablespoons) melted butter

Sieve the flour, salt, baking powder and castor sugar in a bowl. Stir in the egg and milk, and mix just enough to blend the ingredients, adding the melted butter just before cooking.

Fry spoonfuls of the mixture in a lightly oiled, flat, heavy-based frying pan (or on a griddle) until they are golden-brown on both sides.

SERVING SUGGESTION Keep the drop scones warm by wrapping them in a clean tea towel until serving.

GREEK CUSTARD PIE

THIS TRADITIONAL GREEK PIE, made with phyllo pastry, is typically very sweet and rich. It offers a delicious way to end a meal of some the simpler Greek-style dishes. Serve it with small cups of thick, sweet Greek or Turkish coffee. This pie recipe is for quite a large number of helpings, but bear in mind that it freezes well.

PREPARATION TIME: 1½ HOURS
COOKING TIME: 50 MINUTES
PRE-HEAT OVEN TO 180°C

INGREDIENTS FOR TEN TO FIFTEEN
For the syrup:
300 g sugar
1 cinnamon stick
5 ml (1 teaspoon) lemon juice
375 ml (1½ cups) water

PASTRIES, PUDDINGS AND DESSERTS

For the filling:
1,5 litres (6 cups) milk
145 g sugar
250 g butter
A strip of orange peel
180 ml cream of wheat, or first grade semolina
6 egg yolks, beaten

For the crust:
250 g butter, melted
500 g phyllo pastry* (use 285 g flour if making your own)

To make the syrup, boil the sugar, cinnamon stick, lemon juice and water together until thick and syrupy, and allow to cool.

To make the filling, heat the milk, sugar, butter and orange peel together. Just before the mixture reaches boiling point, add the cream of wheat, stirring all the time, until thick and creamy. Remove from the heat and allow to cool slightly before adding the beaten egg yolks.

Brush a deep, oblong baking tin (36 cm x 26 cm) with melted butter. Insert a sheet of the pastry to cover the bottom and sides of the tin. Brush the pastry with butter and repeat this process, using up to 8 sheets of commercially made pastry or 4 sheets of home-made pastry.

Pour the custard filling over the pastry and top it with the remaining 8-10 sheets of commercial pastry (or 4-5 sheets of home-made pastry), brushing each one in turn with the melted butter.

Brush the top with butter. Bake for about 50 minutes, or until golden-brown. Pour the cooled syrup over the hot pie.

SERVING SUGGESTION Serve this pie cut into squares while it is still warm or at room temperature. To freeze left-overs, wrap individual portions to take out as required.

AMERICAN CHEESECAKE

AMERICAN CHEESECAKE differs from the traditional English one in that it has a biscuit crust, as opposed to a pastry one, and a filling of cream cheese rather than one made from curds.

PREPARATION TIME: 50 MINUTES
COOKING TIME: 1 HOUR
COOLING AND CHILLING TIME: 2 HOURS FOR THE CRUST; 4 HOURS FOR THE FILLING
PRE-HEAT OVEN TO 180°C

AMERICAN CHEESECAKE *The tart taste of black cherries is a perfect foil for the creamy, savoury filling.*

INGREDIENTS FOR SIX TO EIGHT
For the crust:
1 packet (200 g) wheatmeal or digestive biscuits
30 ml (2 tablespoons) castor sugar
100 g butter, melted

For the filling:
250 g smooth cottage cheese and 250 g cream cheese, or 500 g cream cheese
125 g castor sugar
2 eggs, separated
125 ml (½ cup) sour cream (smetena)
30 ml (2 tablespoons) flour
5 ml (1 teaspoon) vanilla essence
5 ml (1 teaspoon) grated lemon rind

For the topping:
1 tin (425 g) cooked, stoned black cherries in syrup
30 ml (2 tablespoons) cornflour
5 ml (1 teaspoon) lemon juice
15 ml (1 tablespoon) castor sugar (optional)

To prepare the crust, reduce the biscuits to crumbs in a liquidizer, or put them in a paper bag or between 2 sheets of greaseproof paper and crush them into crumbs with a rolling pin.

Put the crumbs in a bowl, mix in the sugar and gradually blend in the melted butter until it is fully absorbed by the crumbs.

Spread the mixture over the base and sides of a well-greased 5 cm deep 24 cm flan dish, loose-bottomed cake tin or flan ring set on a baking tray. Use the back of a wooden spoon to press the crumbs into an even layer. Leave to set in the refrigerator for 2 hours.

For the filling, blend the cottage cheese (if used) to a smooth consistency with the cream cheese. Beat in the sugar and egg yolks, one at a time.

Stir in the sour cream, flour, vanilla essence and lemon rind, and then beat thoroughly until the mixture is smooth and glossy. Whisk the egg whites until stiff but not dry, and fold them carefully into the cheese mixture, using a metal spoon.

Spoon the filling into the prepared pie crust and bake in the centre of the pre-heated oven for 1 hour. Leave to cool at room temperature.

For the topping, put the cherries in a pan with their juice; if necessary, make this up with cold water to 175 ml. Reserve 30 ml (2 tablespoons) of the liquid and use it to blend the cornflour to a smooth paste in a small basin.

Add the lemon juice to the pan of cherries and bring to the boil over gentle heat. Stir in the cornflour paste and continue boiling for 5 minutes, stirring constantly until the mixture clears and thickens. Add castor sugar to taste.

Let the cherries cool slightly before spreading them over the top of the cheesecake. Chill in the refrigerator for at least 3 hours before serving.

VARIATIONS Top with a compote of crushed strawberries, tinned blueberries, pineapple or apricots, or with chocolate curls* or split almonds instead of the cherries.

Cape Brandy Pudding

This old Cape recipe was doubtlessly invented with cold winter's nights in mind! Delectable and filling, the date and nut pudding with its syrup topping is a must for your repertoire of desserts.

Preparation Time: 30 minutes
Cooking Time: 40-50 minutes
Pre-Heat Oven to 180°C

Ingredients for Six
250 g dates, stoned
5 ml (1 teaspoon) bicarbonate of soda
250 ml (1 cup) boiling water
115 g butter
200 g sugar
2 eggs, beaten
240 g flour
5 ml (1 teaspoon) baking powder
2 ml (½ teaspoon) salt
250 ml (1 cup) chopped walnuts

For the syrup:
250 g sugar
15 g butter
190 ml (¾ cup) water
5 ml (1 teaspoon) vanilla essence
A pinch of salt
125 ml (½ cup) brandy

Cut up the dates and divide them into two equal portions. Add the bicarbonate of soda to one half and pour over the boiling water. Stir to mix, then leave to cool.
Cream together the butter and sugar, add the beaten eggs and mix well.
Sieve together the flour, baking powder and salt, and fold these into the butter mixture.
Add the second portion of dates, together with the nuts. Then stir in the date and bicarbonate mixture, and mix all the ingredients thoroughly.
Turn the batter into one large ovenproof dish or two 22 cm tart plates. Bake for 40-50 minutes.
Meanwhile, make the syrup. Heat the sugar, butter and water together for 5 minutes. Remove them from the heat and stir in the vanilla essence, salt and brandy.
Pour the syrup over the hot tart when it is taken from the oven.

Serving Suggestion Serve hot or cold with whipped cream.

Cape Brandy Pudding *Try a traditional touch with this regional favourite.*

Bread and Butter Pudding

Slices of buttered bread are layered with fruit, then topped with a rich custard and baked until crisp and golden on top, yet meltingly soft inside. Made this way, with a dash of rum or brandy, the bread and butter pudding is suitable for any dinner party.

Preparation Time: 30 minutes
Standing Time: at least 30 minutes
Cooking Time: 55 minutes
Pre-Heat Oven to 160°C

Ingredients for Four
8 thin slices of buttered bread
45 g currants or sultanas, soaked for 15 minutes in 20 ml (4 teaspoons) rum or brandy
30 ml (2 tablespoons) candied peel*, chopped
4 extra-large eggs
300 ml milk
125 ml (½ cup) cream
100 g brown sugar
2 ml (½ teaspoon) ground cinnamon
A pinch of freshly grated nutmeg

Trim the crusts from the buttered bread and cut the slices in half (diagonally).
Arrange the bread slices in a buttered baking dish or soufflé dish, layering them with the currants or sultanas, any remaining rum or brandy and the chopped candied peel.
Beat together the eggs, milk, cream, sugar and cinnamon with a little freshly grated nutmeg. Pour over the bread in the dish and leave to stand for at least 30 minutes (or overnight).
Bake the dish for 55 minutes, or until set and golden-brown.

Serving Suggestion For a richer dish, pass around extra cream for spooning over each serving.

Variations Spread the bread with marmalade*, apricot jam* or lemon curd* as well as butter, or put sliced bananas between the layers.
For a family pudding, you could make the custard less rich: use 3 eggs to 500 ml (2 cups) milk and leave out the cream and candied peel.

Apple Crumble

This perennial favourite consists of layers of sliced apple, baked under a crisp sugary topping. The recipe is quick and easy to make, and lends itself well to a number of tasty variations. It is ideal for a spur-of-the-moment treat, since it requires no fancy ingredients.

Preparation Time: 30 minutes
Cooking Time: 30-40 minutes
Pre-Heat Oven to 180°C

Ingredients for Six
6 medium-sized green apples
75 g soft brown sugar
A pinch of ground cloves (optional)
5 ml (1 teaspoon) ground cinnamon (optional)
75 g sultanas (optional)
30 ml (2 tablespoons) water

For the crumble:
150 g butter
225 g cake or wholewheat flour
150 g soft brown sugar

Peel, core and thinly slice the apples into a medium-sized saucepan. Add the sugar, together with the spices and sultanas, if used, and the water.
Cover the saucepan and cook over a very gentle heat for about 3 minutes until the apples are soft. Turn into a well-buttered baking dish.
To make the topping, rub the butter into the flour, using your fingertips. When it all looks crumbly, add the sugar and stir the mixture well.
Sprinkle this topping over the apple filling, covering it completely. Do not press the topping down too much.
Bake the dish for 30-40 minutes until it is tinged with brown.

Serving Suggestions Serve with cream, custard* or scoops of vanilla ice cream*.

Variations Instead of all flour in the recipe, use half wholewheat and half porridge oats, or half flour and half muesli* breakfast cereal.
For a nut crumble, use three-quarters flour and one-quarter chopped nuts.
Vary the fruit, using poached apricot halves, or lightly cooked rhubarb segments.

PASTRIES, PUDDINGS AND DESSERTS

Crêpes Suzettes have long been popular for the citrus tang of the sauce.

CRÊPES SUZETTES

THESE PANCAKES with their citrus and liqueur sauce offer a delightful and surprisingly simple way to end a dinner party. The pancakes and the sauce can be made early, then baked in the oven just before they are served. Flame them at the dinner table for a special effect.

One of the secrets of making really good crêpes suzettes is to keep the pancakes as thin and light as possible.

PREPARATION TIME: 15 MINUTES
CHILLING TIME: 1 HOUR FOR THE PANCAKE BATTER
COOKING TIME: 15 MINUTES
PRE-HEAT OVEN TO 180°C

INGREDIENTS FOR FOUR TO SIX
75 g butter
5 ml (1 teaspoon) grated naartjie or orange rind
20-30 ml (4-6 teaspoons) castor sugar
175 ml strained naartjie or orange juice
30-45 ml (2-3 tablespoons) Van der Hum* or other citrus-based liqueur
12 pancakes*
30 ml (2 tablespoons) brandy

To make the sauce, melt the butter with the grated naartjie or orange rind and the castor sugar. Add the naartjie or orange juice and the Van der Hum.

Make the 12 pancakes, fold each of them in quarters and then arrange them neatly in an oven-proof dish. Heat the prepared sauce very gently and then pour it over the laid out pancakes.

Cover the dish and bake in the pre-heated oven for 15 minutes.

Warm the brandy and light it as you pour it over the crêpes.

WAFFLES

THESE TREATS are great fun to make at home if you have an electric waffle iron. Serve them piping hot, sandwiched with melted butter and syrup, and topped with whipped cream or ice cream.

PREPARATION TIME: 15 MINUTES
COOKING TIME: 30 MINUTES

INGREDIENTS FOR SIX
250 g flour
10 ml (2 teaspoons) baking powder
2 ml (½ teaspoon) salt
15 ml (1 tablespoon) sugar
3 eggs, separated
75 ml melted butter
375 ml (1½ cups) milk

Sieve the flour with the baking powder, salt and sugar. Beat the egg yolks with the melted butter and milk. Make a well in the centre of the dry ingredients and pour in the beaten liquids. Combine these ingredients but do not overblend. Fold the stiffly beaten egg whites into the batter until they are just blended.

Heat the waffle iron. Pour in enough batter to cover about two-thirds of the surface. Close the lid and cook the batter for about 4 minutes. The waffle is cooked when there is no more steam coming from the iron. If you lift the lid and it sticks, leave for another minute.

MALVA PUDDING

THIS IS A FAVOURITE with visitors to Boschendal restaurant in the historic Franschhoek valley.

PREPARATION TIME: 35 MINUTES
COOKING TIME: 45 MINUTES
PRE-HEAT OVEN TO 180°C

INGREDIENTS FOR SIX
200 g sugar
2 eggs
15 ml (1 tablespoon) apricot jam*
150 g flour
5 ml (1 teaspoon) bicarbonate of soda
A pinch of salt
15 g butter
5 ml (1 teaspoon) vinegar
100 ml milk

For the sauce:
200 ml cream
100 g unsalted butter
150 g sugar
100 ml hot water

Beat the sugar and eggs well in a food processor until thick and lemon-coloured, and add the jam.

Sieve together the flour, bicarbonate of soda and salt. Melt the butter and add the vinegar. Add this butter/vinegar mixture and the milk to the egg mixture alternately with the flour. Beat well and bake in a covered oven-proof dish for 45 minutes.

Melt together the ingredients for the sauce and pour them over the pudding as it comes out of the oven.

LEMON PUDDING

CENTURIES AGO, lemons were especially valued for their 'zest' – the aromatic oil obtained from the peel – which was used in perfumes and as a flavouring. The zest is used in this pudding. As the dessert is cooking, it separates to give a layer of sponge over a base of tangy lemon curd.

PREPARATION TIME: 25 MINUTES
COOKING TIME: 45 MINUTES
PRE-HEAT OVEN TO 170°C

INGREDIENTS FOR FOUR TO SIX
100-125 g sugar
50 g butter
15 ml (1 tablespoon) boiling water
50 g flour
Juice and grated rind of 1 large lemon
2 eggs, separated
225 ml milk

Cream together the sugar and butter, adding the boiling water to make the mixture workable. Stir in the flour, lemon juice and rind.

Whisk the egg yolks in the milk and add to the creamed mixture, a little at a time. Beat the egg whites until stiff and fold them into the mixture.

Pour the pudding into a buttered 1 litre pie dish and stand it in a roasting tin half filled with warm water. Bake in the pre-heated oven for 45 minutes.

SERVING SUGGESTION Serve hot on its own, or cold with a little cream.

Pastries, Puddings and Desserts

Banana Fritters

The basic directions for cooking and serving fritters were recorded some 500 years ago, and they still apply, although today we are more adventurous with the fillings. One of the most popular types of fritter has a banana filling – this particular recipe is given a slightly exotic flavour through the use of rum.

Preparation Time: 25 minutes
Standing Time: 1 hour
Cooking Time: 15-20 minutes

Ingredients for Four to Six
3 large ripe bananas, peeled
30 ml (2 tablespoons) sugar
60 ml (¼ cup) rum
5 ml (1 teaspoon) vanilla essence
100-125 g flour
5 ml (1 teaspoon) baking powder
1 ml (¼ teaspoon) salt
30 ml (2 tablespoons) melted butter
175 ml milk
1 egg white, whisked until stiff
Sunflower oil for frying

Cut the bananas in half lengthways, then cut each half in three or four pieces. Arrange the pieces in one layer in a shallow dish. Mix together the sugar, 45 ml (3 tablespoons) of the rum and the vanilla essence, and pour over the bananas. Leave for 1 hour, turning the fruit occasionally.

To prepare the batter, sieve the flour, baking powder and salt into a large bowl. Stir in the melted butter and the remaining 15 ml (1 tablespoon) rum. Add the milk a little at a time, beating well after each addition until the batter is perfectly smooth. Leave to stand for 1 hour. Fold in the whisked egg white to give the batter the consistency of thick cream.

Dip the banana pieces into the batter a few at a time and allow to drain until only thinly coated. Pour a 5 cm layer of oil into a deep pan and heat it to 190°C – a cube of bread should turn golden-brown in about a minute. Fry the pieces 4-5 at a time until golden-brown. Drain on paper towels and keep hot until all are ready.

Serving Suggestion Serve sprinkled with vanilla sugar*.

Variation Leave out the rum for an everyday family pudding.

Chinese Toffee Apples *Their appeal goes further than sheer visual delight: the flavour and texture are memorable.*

Chinese Toffee Apples

This is a true Pekinese dessert, more correctly named Drawn Thread Apple, which refers to the thin threads of toffee which form as the apple pieces are removed from the pan. This spectacular course is worth the last-minute preparation involved; if you cook it over a portable gas burner it is a fascinating and dramatic operation for your guests to watch.

Preparation Time: 15 minutes
Cooking Time: 20 minutes

Ingredients for Six
2 medium-sized green apples, peeled and cored
Sunflower oil for frying

For the batter:
115 g flour
15 ml (1 tablespoon) cornflour
250 ml (1 cup) water
10 ml (2 teaspoons) sunflower oil

For the toffee:
10 ml (2 teaspoons) sunflower oil
400 g sugar
250 ml (1 cup) warm water
30 ml (2 tablespoons) sesame seeds

Cut the apples into quarters and then into eighths.

To make the batter, sieve the flour and cornflour into a bowl, and then gradually add the water and oil. Stir until the mixture is smooth.

Drop the apple pieces into the batter, then drain off the excess batter and fry them in deep, hot oil for 3-4 minutes until they are golden-brown. Drain the pieces on paper towels.

To make the toffee, heat the oil in a pan or wok, add the sugar and warm water, and stir until the mixture boils. Continue stirring rapidly.

After about 5 minutes the mixture will foam and look as if it is going to crystallise. Stir it for another 2-3 minutes until the toffee turns a light golden-brown.

Remove the saucepan from the heat immediately and add the sesame seeds and apple slices, making sure that the slices are completely coated. Transfer the apples to lightly oiled serving dishes and place them quickly on the table.

Serving Suggestions Place a glass bowl filled with iced water and ice cubes on the table. Using chopsticks, each guest pulls the apple slices apart, then plunges them into the iced water. The syrup turns into a brittle glaze which cracks easily when bitten into.

Make sure you have plenty of ice cubes in the bowl or else the hot toffee will soon warm the water.

Variations You may use 2 large bananas, cut into chunks, instead of the sliced apples.

Alternatively, make the dessert from 1 apple and 1 banana.

Queen's Pudding

This layered pudding of fresh breadcrumbs, thick jam and golden meringue wears its title easily, for there are many who claim it is the most royal of puddings.

Preparation Time: 30 minutes
Cooking Time: 40 minutes
Pre-heat Oven to 180°C

Ingredients for Four to Six
150 g fresh white breadcrumbs
30 ml (1 tablespoon) castor sugar
Grated rind of 1 lemon
575-600 ml milk
50 g butter
4 large egg yolks
30 ml (2 tablespoons) raspberry* or apricot jam*

For the meringue:
4 large egg whites
100-125 g castor sugar

Put the breadcrumbs, castor sugar and lemon rind into a mixing bowl.
Heat the milk and butter in a saucepan over a low heat until the butter has melted and the milk is lukewarm.
Pour the warm milk and butter mixture on to the breadcrumb mixture and leave to stand for 10 minutes to absorb the milk. Beat in the egg yolks.
Grease a 1 litre pie dish and pour in the crumb mixture. Bake in the centre of the pre-heated oven for 30 minutes, or until just firm on the top.
Warm the jam so that it spreads easily, and very gently spread it over the pudding without breaking the surface.
To make the meringue topping, whisk the egg whites until they form stiff peaks and, using a metal spoon, gently fold in the castor sugar.
Pile the meringue over the pudding and return to the oven for a further 10 minutes, or until the meringue is lightly browned and crisp.

Serving Suggestion Serve the pudding hot with cream.

Semolina Pudding

Semolina pudding has a fine, unusual texture. Served piping hot with fresh cream it makes a delightful dessert for a cold winter's day.

Preparation Time: 5 minutes
Cooking Time: 40 minutes

Ingredients for Four
100 g butter
150 g semolina (cream of wheat)
45 ml (3 tablespoons) desiccated coconut
250 ml (1 cup) milk
500 ml (2 cups) warm water
150 g sugar
A few drops of almond or vanilla essence
15 ml (1 tablespoon) toasted poppy seeds
250 ml (1 cup) fresh cream, whipped until thick and fluffy

Heat the butter in a heavy-based saucepan. Place the semolina and coconut into the saucepan and cook, tossing constantly with a wooden spoon, for 15 minutes over a medium heat.
Take care not to allow the semolina to stick to the bottom of the saucepan and burn. The semolina should cook to a golden colour.
Add the milk, warm water, sugar and almond essence to the semolina and stir the mixture well.
Cover the saucepan and cook the mixture over a medium heat for 15 minutes. Stir it up with a fork. The semolina will expand as it absorbs the liquid.
Serve warm in individual glass bowls. Sprinkle the dish with the poppy seeds and serve with a generous helping of cream.

Serving Suggestion This pudding may also be re-heated over a low heat when necessary. Sprinkle it with a few drops of water and stir with a fork.
Semolina pudding may also be served with stewed fruit.
Alternatively, serve the pudding with scoops of rum and raisin ice cream.

Variations For a richer pudding, more butter may be added.
Instead of sprinkling with the poppy seeds, top the pudding with toasted flaked almonds.

Rice Pudding

This is one of the most popular milk puddings as it is easy to make and appealing to children and adults alike. It is often made from left-over cooked rice.

Preparation Time: 15 minutes
Cooking Time: 2 hours
Pre-heat Oven to 170°C

Ingredients for Four to Six
50 g rice
575-600 ml milk
75 g castor sugar
15 g butter, cut into flakes
2 ml (½ teaspoon) grated nutmeg
2 eggs, separated

Boil the rice in just enough water to cover it – about 150 ml – for 5 minutes. Drain the rice if necessary and put it in a buttered 1 litre oven-proof dish. Stir in the milk and 50 g of the sugar. Dot with the butter and sprinkle over half the nutmeg. Bake for about 1 hour.
Remove the dish from the oven, cool for 5 minutes, then beat the egg yolks lightly into the rice. Return to the oven for another 30 minutes.
Meanwhile, whisk the egg whites with the remaining sugar until they are stiff but not dry.
Remove the pudding from the oven and let it cool for 5 minutes. Fold in the beaten egg whites and sprinkle with the remaining nutmeg. Return the dish to the oven for 15 minutes to set the egg whites.

Sago Pudding

This sago dessert is nothing like the dreaded version often served at boarding schools. Lightened with stiffly beaten egg whites, it is both appetising and wholesome.

Preparation Time: 45 minutes
Cooking Time: 1 hour
Pre-heat Oven to 180°C

Ingredients for Six
500 ml (2 cups) milk
100 g sago
60 ml (¼ cup) sugar
125 g butter
2 eggs, separated

Heat the milk to boiling point. Stir in the sago, sugar and 90 g of the butter. Stir to remove any lumps and cook for 25 minutes, stirring often.
Pour into a large bowl and mix in the beaten egg yolks and the rest of the butter. Fold in the stiffly beaten egg whites. Pour the mixture into a buttered oven-proof dish and place it in a pan of hot water. Bake for an hour, or until it is set.

Variations Use semolina, rice or tapioca instead of the sago.

Plum Crumble

Perhaps the crumble was considered too lowly to be awarded a place in standard cookery books, for though it has been a firm favourite in South Africa for many years, the first recorded appearance of this crumbled pastry is in an American recipe dating back only to the 1940s. There it is described as a 'crunch' which is used as a topping for a 'candy pie' containing either apples or peaches.

Preparation Time: 20 minutes
Cooking Time: 45 minutes
Pre-heat Oven to 180°C

Ingredients for Six
24 small cooking plums
175 g granulated sugar
30 ml (2 tablespoons) water

For the crumble:
175 g flour
1 ml (¼ teaspoon) salt
75 g butter
75 g castor sugar

Wash, halve and stone the plums. Put them in layers in an 850 ml pie dish and sprinkle each layer with the granulated sugar; then add the water.
Sieve the flour and mix it with the salt in a large mixing bowl. Rub in the butter lightly with the fingertips until the mixture resembles fine breadcrumbs. Stir in the castor sugar and mix well.
Spread the flour mixture over the plums, covering them completely. Immediately place the dish in the oven and cook for 45 minutes, or until golden-brown.

Serving Suggestions Serve with fresh whipped cream or custard*.

Vanilla Soufflé

Soufflés are a great deal easier to make than one is usually given to believe. Much of the work can be done beforehand. A hot soufflé, light and puffy on the outside, with a flavourful, slightly creamy centre, makes a delicious dessert.

Preparation Time: 1½ hours
Cooking Time: 30-35 minutes
Pre-heat Oven to 200°C

Ingredients for Four to Six
15 g butter
45 ml (3 tablespoons) sugar

For Mixture A (the bouillie):
30 ml (2 tablespoons) flour
125 ml (½ cup) milk
40 g sugar
4 egg yolks
50 g butter
30 ml (2 tablespoons) vanilla essence

For Mixture B:
5 egg whites
A pinch of salt
15 ml (1 tablespoon) sugar

Icing sugar for sprinkling

Butter the inside of a 1,5 litre soufflé dish thoroughly and roll the sugar around to coat the butter well. Knock out all excess sugar. Set aside.

To make the bouillie base of the soufflé, use the ingredients of Mixture A. Blend the flour and a little milk in a small saucepan until smooth, then beat in the rest of the milk and the sugar, and stir over a medium heat until the mixture boils.

Boil, stirring constantly, for 30 seconds (the sauce will be very thick). Remove from the heat and beat with an electric beater for about 2 minutes. Whisk in the egg yolks, one at a time, then beat in half the butter. Dot the sauce with the remaining butter to prevent a skin from forming while you beat the egg whites.

To complete the soufflé, use Mixture B. Beat the egg whites together with a pinch of salt until soft peaks form, then sprinkle on the sugar and beat until stiff.

Add the vanilla essence to Mixture A, then stir in a quarter of Mixture B. Gently fold in the rest of Mixture B with a metal spoon, distributing it evenly.

Turn the soufflé mixture into the prepared soufflé dish, leaving a space of at least 3 cm between the top of the dish and the mixture. Place the soufflé in the middle of the pre-heated oven and immediately turn down the heat to 190°C.

After 20 minutes, when the soufflé is starting to brown and puff, quickly sprinkle the top with a little icing sugar. Do not slam the oven door, or open it too far. Bake for another 10-15 minutes, then test with a skewer plunged into the soufflé through the side of the puff. The skewer should indicate a slight creaminess. If you prefer a drier centre, bake for a bit longer.

Serving Suggestions A soufflé should always be served as soon as it is ready. Thin cream or a light liqueur sauce makes a good accompaniment.

Variations To make a lemon soufflé, rub 1 or 2 sugar cubes over the surface of a ripe lemon and use this sugar for Mixture A. Add the grated rind of the lemon to the sauce, and use 60 ml (¼ cup) lemon juice instead of vanilla essence.

To make an orange soufflé, use sugar lumps rubbed over the skin of a ripe orange, and add the grated rind of the orange to Mixture A. Substitute 60 ml (¼ cup) Cointreau, Grand Marnier or orange juice for the vanilla essence.

To make a coffee soufflé, change the preparation of Mixture A (the boulli base) as follows: once you have blended the flour with a little milk, heat the rest of the milk with 15 ml (1 tablespoon) pure instant coffee and stir until the coffee has dissolved. Add the hot coffee to the flour paste and then proceed in the normal way. Substitute 45 ml (3 tablespoons) coffee liqueur for the vanilla essence.

An almond flavour is particularly appealing in coffee, orange and vanilla soufflés. Add 90 g ground almonds and 1 ml (¼ teaspoon) almond essence to the vanilla soufflé sauce at the same time as the vanilla essence. You could also use a mixture of flaked and ground almonds.

A chocolate soufflé requires a slightly different method, as chocolate is rather heavy. Dissolve 125 g dark chocolate in 30 ml (2 tablespoons) strong coffee and add this to a bouillie made of cornflour (not plain flour) and milk. Use 3 egg yolks in Mixture A, to 5 egg whites in Mixture B, then proceed in the normal way.

Golden Sponge Pudding

This delightful pudding pleases the eye and the hearty appetite today as much as it did in the 1880s, when golden syrup was first developed. The feather-light sponge has a toffee-coloured coating that streams with melted golden syrup.

Preparation Time: 20 minutes
Cooking Time: 2½ hours

Ingredients for Four to Six
75 g butter
75 g sugar
1 egg, beaten
175 g self-raising flour, sifted
1 ml (¼ teaspoon) salt
Milk
75-90 ml golden syrup

Cream the butter and sugar together until fluffy. Beat in the egg and fold in the flour and salt. Stir in enough milk to give the mixture a soft, dropping consistency.

Butter a 1 litre basin, and coat the inside well with syrup. Spoon in the mixture and prepare the basin for steaming*. Stand it in a large pan with enough boiling water to come halfway up the basin. Steam for 2½ hours, adding more boiling water to the pan as necessary to maintain the level. Turn the pudding out on to a hot plate.

Serving Suggestion Serve at once with custard*, cream or more melted syrup.

Variations You may replace the syrup with lemon curd* or marmalade*.

Plum Sponge Pudding

This infinitely adaptable family pudding is ideal for cooking in the oven at the same time as a main course. The filling can include any fruit in season – apples, rhubarb or gooseberries – as well as the plums used here.

Preparation Time: 20 minutes
Cooking Time: 50 minutes
Pre-heat Oven to 180°C

Ingredients for Four
50 g butter
50 g white sugar
75 g self-raising flour, sifted
1 egg, beaten
15 ml (1 tablespoon) water
15 medium-sized plums, washed, halved and stoned
75 g brown sugar

Cream the butter and white sugar together until fluffy. Add the flour and egg alternately, a little at a time, beating well after each addition. Stir in the water.

Put the plums and brown sugar in alternate layers in a buttered 850 ml oven-proof basin. Cover with the sponge mixture and bake in the centre of the pre-heated oven for about 50 minutes, or until the top of the sponge is springy to the touch.

Serving Suggestion Serve hot with custard* or cream.

Chocolate Pudding

This rich chocolate pudding creates its own fudge sauce beneath a cake-like upper layer. A topping of whipped cream further enhances its appeal.

Preparation Time: 15 minutes
Cooking Time: 1 hour
Cooling Time: 1 hour
Pre-heat Oven to 170°C

Ingredients for Six to Eight
100-125 g flour
10 ml (2 teaspoons) baking powder
1 ml (¼ teaspoon) salt
175 g granulated sugar
25 g plain chocolate, melted
30 g butter, melted
150 ml milk
50 g brown sugar
50 g castor sugar
45 ml (3 tablespoons) cocoa
175 ml cold water

Sieve together the flour, baking powder and salt into a bowl. Stir in the granulated sugar, melted chocolate and melted butter. Blend in the milk.

Pour the mixture into a buttered 850 ml oven-proof dish. Sprinkle the brown sugar, castor sugar and cocoa in separate layers over the top. Pour over the cold water.

Bake in the pre-heated oven for 1 hour (a layer of chocolate-fudge sauce will form under the sponge topping as the pudding cooks). Let the pudding cool for an hour before serving, but do not chill.

UPSIDE-DOWN WINTER PUDDING *Golden pear halves set with cherries decorate this hearty cold-weather pudding.*

UPSIDE-DOWN WINTER PUDDING

GLISTENING RED CHERRIES nestling in a wheel of pears give a festive air to this delicious baked pudding. Properly turned out, the pudding is a credit to the cook, yet is easy to make.

PREPARATION TIME: 25 MINUTES
COOKING TIME: 45 MINUTES
PRE-HEAT OVEN TO 180°C

INGREDIENTS FOR SIX
Melted butter
45 ml (3 tablespoons) treacle sugar or soft brown sugar
3 pears, peeled, halved and cored
6 glacé cherries, rinsed
100-125 g butter
80 ml (⅓ cup) golden syrup
60 ml (¼ cup) black treacle
1 egg, beaten
150 ml lukewarm milk
5 ml (1 teaspoon) bicarbonate of soda
225 g flour
5 ml (1 teaspoon) ground cinnamon
5 ml (1 teaspoon) ground ginger
75 g soft brown sugar

Line the base and side of a deep (20 cm), round cake tin with a layer of grease-proof paper, and brush over with melted butter. Sprinkle the base with the treacle sugar (or brown sugar).

Place the pears, cut side down, on the sugar, radiating from the centre of the tin. As you do so, tuck a cherry into the cavity of each pear half, where the core has been removed.

Put the 100-125 g butter, syrup and treacle in a small pan over a low heat until the butter has melted. Set to one side. Stir together the beaten egg, milk and bicarbonate of soda.

Sieve the flour, cinnamon and ginger into a mixing bowl and stir in the 75 g soft brown sugar.

Make a well in the centre of the dry ingredients and pour in the melted butter mixture and the egg mixture. Stir together and beat thoroughly. Then pour the mixture into the prepared cake tin.

Bake in the centre of the pre-heated oven for about 45 minutes, or until well risen and firm to the touch. Turn out the pudding on to a warmed plate and peel away the paper.

SERVING SUGGESTION Serve hot, cut in wedges, with cream or custard*.

ZABAGLIONE

ITALIANS REGARD this hot, golden froth, imbued with the distinctive flavour of Marsala, as a dessert as well as a restorative. Zabaglione originated in Sicily, where the local grapes are used to make the fortified Marsala wine.

If the dessert is to be eaten hot, it should be served immediately after being made. It can, however, be eaten cold if it is prepared slightly differently.

PREPARATION TIME: 10 MINUTES
COOKING TIME: 5 MINUTES

INGREDIENTS FOR FOUR
4 egg yolks
15 ml (1 tablespoon) castor sugar
90 ml Marsala, warmed to body temperature

Put the egg yolks and sugar in the top of a small double boiler, and whisk with a balloon whisk (or use an electric mixer) until the mixture thickens enough to fall from the whisk in a broad ribbon.

Set the pan over the bottom half of the double boiler, in which water is just simmering over a low heat. Make sure that the base of the top pan does not touch the hot water, or crusty grains will form in the mixture.

Add the warm Marsala and whisk the mixture continuously over a low heat until it rises and forms a creamy foam that has noticeably thickened. Serve the zabaglione at once.

SERVING SUGGESTION Pour the mixture into warmed individual glasses and serve with sponge finger biscuits.

VARIATIONS For a cold zabaglione, not quite authentic but nevertheless delicious and able to be kept for up to 3 days in a refrigerator, make as above, but take the top pan from the double boiler as soon as the mixture has thickened. Set it immediately in a large pan already half filled with ice cubes. Keep whisking the mixture vigorously until the zabaglione is quite cold, then fold into it 150 ml thick cream, whipped but not stiff. Chill in a refrigerator until serving time.

This cream version can also be made with sweet wine instead of the Marsala and used as a sauce with fresh strawberries, raspberries or sliced peaches.

~ Rich and Delicious Fridge Cakes ~

The big attraction of fridge cakes is that they are appealing to the eye and palate, yet relatively easy to make. Each of these recipes is adequate for about six people.

Youngberry Cream Flan

Preparation Time: 30 minutes
Cooling Time: 45 minutes or 10 minutes over iced water
Chilling Time: 6 hours or overnight

Biscuit crumb crust*
10 ml (2 teaspoons) gelatin
1 packet lemon jelly
125 ml (½ cup) orange juice
125 ml (½ cup) lemon juice
250 g cream cheese, or smooth cottage cheese
100 g castor sugar
1 tin (410 g) evaporated milk, chilled
1 tin (410 g) youngberries, drained
Whipped cream for garnish

Line a flan dish or loose-based flan ring with a biscuit crumb crust. Gently heat together the gelatin, lemon jelly, orange juice and lemon juice in a small saucepan until the gelatin has dissolved. Remove from the heat, and leave it to cool.

Cream together the cream cheese or smooth cottage cheese with the castor sugar. Beat in the cooled jelly mixture.

Whip the chilled evaporated milk until thick and beat into the cheese mixture. Fold in the drained youngberries and pour into the crumb shell. Chill, then decorate with whipped cream.

APRICOT YOGHURT TART

Walnut Cream Torte

Preparation Time: 45 minutes
Chilling Time: overnight

100 g walnuts
125 ml (½ cup) hot milk
100 g butter
100 g icing sugar, sifted
2 egg yolks
125 ml (½ cup) cold milk
45 ml (3 tablespoons) medium-dry or sweet sherry
30 sponge fingers
250 ml (1 cup) cream

Line the base of an 18 cm loose-based cake tin with a circle of grease-proof paper. Chop or grind the walnuts finely and toast them under the grill until lightly browned. Set aside 30 ml (2 tablespoons) for decoration and put the remainder in a mixing bowl. Pour over the hot milk and leave to cool.

Meanwhile, cream the butter with the icing sugar until soft and light. Beat in the egg yolks, then the cooled nut mixture, and blend thoroughly.

Pour the cold milk into a shallow dish with the sherry. Soak the sponge fingers in the cold milk mixture (a few at a time) and use about one-third of them to line the base of the tin. Spread with half the creamed nut mixture. Top with another row of sponge fingers soaked in milk, then the rest of the nut mixture.

Finish with the remaining soaked biscuits and cover with a circle of grease-proof paper. Put a smaller-sized cake tin or plate on top and weight it lightly. Chill overnight.

To serve, loosen the sides, remove the grease-proof paper and invert the cake onto a serving dish. Lightly whip the cream and swirl over the top and sides to cover completely. Sprinkle with the reserved toasted nuts and refrigerate until ready to serve.

Lemon Gâteau

Preparation Time: 30 minutes
Chilling Time: overnight

1 round trifle sponge
125 g butter
200 g castor sugar
4 eggs, separated
Grated rind and juice of 2 lemons
250 ml (1 cup) whipped cream

For the garnish:
Whipped cream
Glacé lemon slices (optional)

Split the trifle sponge into thin layers and place a layer in the base of a pudding basin or 18 cm cake tin.

In a large mixing bowl, cream the butter and castor sugar until pale and fluffy. Whisk in the egg yolks, little by little, beating well after each addition. Add the grated lemon rind and juice, beating in a little at a time.

Whisk the egg whites until stiff and fold them into the yolk mixture with a metal spoon. Fold in the whipped cream.

Spoon a layer of this lemon cream into the lined basin or tin and continue layering sponge cake and lemon cream, finishing with a layer of sponge.

Cover with aluminium foil and put a plate on top. Chill in the refrigerator overnight. Turn out and cut into slices and serve with cream, or turn out and cover with whipped cream, and decorate with glacé lemon slices (if used).

Apricot Yoghurt Tart

Preparation Time: 30 minutes
Cooling Time: 1 hour or 10 minutes over iced water
Chilling Time: 4 hours

200 g tennis or ginger biscuits, crushed
100 g butter, melted
25 g castor sugar
1 packet orange jelly
125 ml (½ cup) hot water
500 ml (2 cups) apricot yoghurt

For the garnish:
Whipped cream
Tinned apricot halves (optional)

Make a biscuit crumb crust* using the biscuits, melted butter and castor sugar. Press into a 22-24 cm loose-based flan tin or china flan dish.

Dissolve the jelly in the water. Cool until just beginning to set. Whisk in the yoghurt. Pour into the biscuit crust and chill until set. Decorate with whipped cream and apricot halves (if used).

Brazilian Tipsy Gâteau

Preparation Time: 30 minutes
Chilling Time: 4-5 hours or overnight

1 oblong trifle sponge
30 ml (2 tablespoons) brandy or sherry
250 g cream cheese
125 g smooth cottage cheese
125 g castor sugar
1 tin (200 g) mandarin oranges, drained and chopped

For the garnish:
Whipped cream flavoured with coffee essence
Toasted almond flakes

Line the base and long sides of a litre loaf tin with grease-proof paper or aluminium foil. Split the trifle sponge into thin layers and use them to line the base and sides of the tin. Reserve one layer of sponge for the top and crumble the trimmings into a bowl. Add the brandy or sherry.

Beat the two cheeses with the sugar and oranges. Spread half the cheese mixture in the tin, cover with the cake crumb mixture, another layer of cheese, and finally the layer of reserved sponge cake.

Cover with foil and weight down lightly. Chill for 4-5 hours, or overnight. Remove the foil and turn the cake out on to a dish. Carefully peel off the paper or foil. Thinly cover with the whipped cream and press toasted almond flakes around the sides.

Yoghurt and Banana Flan

Preparation Time: 30 minutes
Chilling Time: 4 hours

Biscuit crumb crust*, made with ginger biscuits
5 medium-sized bananas
30 ml (2 tablespoons) lemon juice
175 ml natural yoghurt*
10 ml (2 teaspoons) sugar
½ small tin evaporated milk, chilled
10 ml (2 teaspoons) gelatin
30 ml (2 tablespoons) water

For the garnish:
Banana slices dipped in lemon juice
Whipped cream

Make the biscuit crumb crust*. To fill, mash or liquidize the bananas. Stir in the lemon juice, yoghurt and sugar.

Whisk the evaporated milk, and when thick, fold into the banana mixture with the gelatin dissolved in the water. Decorate with slices of banana and rosettes of whipped cream. Chill until ready to serve.

Rum and Chocolate Gâteau

Preparation Time: 45 minutes
Chilling Time: overnight

50 g sugar
45 ml (3 tablespoons) water
30 ml (2 tablespoons) rum
100 g plain dark chocolate
100 g butter
100 g icing sugar, sifted
4 egg yolks
18 sponge fingers

For the garnish:
Grated chocolate curls*
Chopped walnuts (optional)

Dissolve the sugar in the water, then simmer for 5 minutes. Take off the heat and add the rum. Melt the chocolate in a bowl over a basin of gently simmering water.

Cream the butter with the icing sugar, then beat in the egg yolks, a little at a time. Stir in the melted chocolate.

To assemble the cake, divide the sponge fingers into three lots of 6 each. Dip the biscuits (one or two at a time) into the warm syrup, letting them soak for a moment.

Arrange a neat row of 6 biscuits on a serving dish and spread with a layer of the chocolate cream. Cover with a second layer of soaked biscuits and another of chocolate cream. Top with a final layer of soaked biscuits and any remaining syrup.

Spread the rest of the chocolate cream over the top and around the sides of the cake. Decorate with chocolate curls and chopped walnuts (if used), and chill overnight. Cut into thin slices and serve with cream. The slices will have a pretty striped appearance.

Strawberry Cream Cake

Preparation Time: 30 minutes
Cooling Time: 1-1½ hours or 20 minutes over iced water
Chilling Time: 6 hours

15 ml (1 tablespoon) gelatin
40 g castor sugar
A pinch of salt
60 ml (¼ cup) water
1 large tin (410 g) evaporated milk
125 ml (½ cup) cream
300 g strawberries, sliced

For the topping:
125 g biscuits, crushed
100 g butter, melted
15 ml (1 tablespoon) sugar

For the garnish:
Whipped cream
Small whole strawberries

In a medium-sized saucepan, mix the gelatin, castor sugar and pinch of salt with the water and the evaporated milk. Stir well and cook over a low heat, stirring continually, until the gelatin has dissolved.

Remove from the heat and chill, stirring occasionally, until the mixture thickens. This process takes about 1-1½ hours in the refrigerator, whereas if done over iced water it takes about 20 minutes, but a watchful eye must be kept on it.

Whisk the cream until thick and fold into the gelatin mixture with the sliced strawberries. Pour into a litre loaf tin, lined with a strip of grease-proof paper.

Top with a biscuit crumb mixture made from the crushed biscuits, melted butter and sugar. Chill until the mixture is firm, then turn out and decorate with whipped cream and small whole strawberries.

Variation Cover with 50 g lightly crushed toasted cornflakes tossed with 50 g finely chopped, blanched* almonds, 50 g sugar and 30 g melted butter.

RUM AND CHOCOLATE GÂTEAU

LEMON GÂTEAU

Pastries, Puddings and Desserts

Christmas Pudding

A MEAT STEW called 'girout', a dish served at every coronation from that of William the Conqueror to George V, is the ancestor of Christmas pudding, though it has gone through many changes since William's day.

Gradually the meat was phased out, prunes and sultanas were substituted for plums, and the modern Christmas pudding evolved.

Christmas puddings need to mature, and are all the better for being prepared several weeks or even months in advance. Store them in a well-ventilated, dry place, and steam a second time before serving.

This well-tried recipe makes three medium-sized puddings, light-textured, dark and delicious.

Preparation Time: 1 hour
First Cooking Time: 7 hours
(2¾ hours in a pressure cooker)
Maturing Time: at least 6 weeks
Second Cooking Time: 3 hours
(30 minutes in a pressure cooker)

Preparing Dried Fruit

Dried fruit provides a convenient way to serve fruit at all times of the year.

To prepare dried fruit for serving, it should be soaked, in enough water to cover it, for about 2 hours. The fruit will absorb water and plump out and become softer. The fruit may be eaten in this form or it may be stewed.

To stew dried fruit, place it in a saucepan with a little water (preferably the water in which it soaked), bring to the boil and simmer, covered, for 10 minutes. Sugar may be added if desired. Spices and lemon juice or peel, added when stewing, also give an enhanced flavour to the fruit.

The dried fruit may also be softened by soaking it in fortified wine or spirits. Particularly suitable are port, sherry or rum. Fruit liqueur may be sprinkled over the fruit for extra taste.

Dried fruit can be used in baking or making dishes such as bobotie or curry. You can boil chutneys from dried fruit, too, or make dried fruit sweets or jams.

Try serving dried apricot soup on a hot day: stew the apricots, liquidize them and add a dash of curry powder, fruit juice and cream or natural yoghurt*.

Ingredients for Three 700 g Puddings
225 g self-raising flour
225 g shredded suet
225 g fresh white breadcrumbs
225 g currants
350 g sultanas
350 g seedless raisins
225 g soft brown sugar
5 ml (1 teaspoon) salt
5-10 ml (1-2 teaspoons) ground mixed spice
100-125 g chopped mixed peel
100-125 g glacé cherries, rinsed and chopped
1 small carrot, peeled and grated
1 small apple, peeled and grated
6 eggs, beaten
Grated rind and juice of 1 orange
Grated rind and juice of 1 lemon
275-300 ml stout

Grease 3 litre-sized pudding basins. Mix the flour, suet, breadcrumbs, dried fruit and sugar together in a large bowl. Stir in the salt, mixed spice, mixed peel, glacé cherries, carrot and apple.

Mix together the eggs, orange and lemon juice, rind and stout, and add to the dry ingredients to give a soft, dropping consistency. Add more stout if necessary.

Divide the mixture between the prepared basins, leaving 5 cm headspace to allow for rising. Cover each basin for steaming* and place each in a saucepan of boiling water. Cover the saucepans with lids and steam for 7 hours. Top up with more boiling water as necessary to maintain the level.

Remove the basins from the pans and leave to cool. Re-cover with fresh greaseproof paper, foil or cloth and store in a cool, dry place for as long as possible.

Before serving, cover with fresh greaseproof paper, foil or cloth again and steam for another 3 hours. Remove the covering, invert the pudding on to a warmed plate and decorate with a sprig of imitation holly.

If using a pressure cooker, cook each pudding for 15 minutes without pressure (pre-steaming), then for a further 2½ hours at high pressure. Before serving, steam at high pressure for 30 minutes.

Serving Suggestion Warm a small wineglassful of brandy in a saucepan and, at the last moment, pour it over the pudding and set it alight. Serve with brandy sauce* or brandy butter*.

Dried Fruit Compote

A TASTY DISH to start the day, dried fruit compote consists of various alternative combinations of fruits.

Adding some fresh fruit, such as pineapple, or sprinkling the completed dish with nuts, gives a lovely flavour to the dried fruit. The compote may also be stewed with cinnamon and ginger.

Preparation Time: 20 minutes
Soaking Time: 2 hours
Cooking Time: 10 minutes

Ingredients for Six
12 dried peaches
16 dried apricots
10 prunes
10 dried apple rings
2 oranges, peeled and segmented
2 grapefruit, peeled and segmented
1 banana, peeled and sliced
30 ml (2 tablespoons) lemon juice
30 ml (2 tablespoons) brown sugar
40 g pecan nuts, chopped
200 ml natural yoghurt* (optional)

Soak the combined dried fruit for 2 hours in just enough water to cover. Bring the fruit to the boil in the soaking water and simmer, covered, for 5 minutes, or until tender. Remove from the heat and allow to cool slightly.

Toss the cooled fruit lightly with the remaining ingredients (except the nuts and yoghurt) and spoon into individual serving bowls.

Top with the nuts and pour the yoghurt (if used) over the compote.

Serving Suggestions Serve the compote warm for breakfast, or as a dessert with whipped cream and shredded lemon rind, or with zabaglione*. It may also be served cold, if you prefer.

Variations There are endless possibilities when assembling a fruit compote: for instance, raisins, sultanas, dried figs or dates may also be used.

Any fresh fruit in season may be added to the compote, or only dried fruit may be used. Be careful not to sweeten the fruit too much, as the concentration of sugar in dried fruit is higher than in fresh fruit because of dehydration.

Caramel Oranges

THIS SIMPLE yet attractive dessert calls for few ingredients, and can be prepared well in advance of the meal. The syrup, flavoured with Van der Hum liqueur, adds a delicious taste.

Preparation Time: 30 minutes
Cooking Time: 45 minutes
Chilling Time: 3 hours

Ingredients for Six
6 oranges
310 ml (1¼ cups) water
150 g sugar
190 ml (¾ cup) golden syrup
30 ml (2 tablespoons) lemon juice
30 ml (2 tablespoons) Van der Hum liqueur*
Sprigs of mint for garnish (optional)

Remove the rind from 2 of the oranges with a vegetable peeler, avoiding any of the white pith. Cut the rind into long, thin strips and bring to the boil in 120 ml of the water. Drain well.

In a fairly large saucepan, mix together the sugar, golden syrup and remaining 190 ml (¾ cup) water, then bring to the boil, stirring until the sugar has dissolved completely.

Boil (uncovered) for 10 minutes, then add the rind and continue to cook on a very low heat for another 30 minutes, or until the syrup has slightly thickened.

Remove from the stove and stir in the lemon juice and liqueur.

Peel all the oranges, including the 2 rindless ones, and remove any white membrane adhering to the fruit. Place them in an oven-proof bowl.

Pour the hot syrup over the oranges and stir them around from time to time while the syrup cools down. When the syrup is quite cool, pack the oranges into a jar, pour over the syrup and store in the refrigerator (the oranges taste better when chilled).

Serve in individual glass bowls and garnish with the caramelised orange rind. Alternatively, heap the oranges on a tall pedestal dish, decorating them with the peel and sprigs of mint.

Variation Slice the oranges into discs, pour over the syrup and serve with scoops of vanilla ice cream*.

PASTRIES, PUDDINGS AND DESSERTS

STUFFED APPLES *are baked with a choice of fillings and a sherry syrup.*

BAKED STUFFED APPLES

BAKED APPLES are a popular dish that can be combined with a number of different fillings. The sherry syrup adds an elegant touch to them all.

PREPARATION TIME: 10 MINUTES
COOKING TIME: 1 HOUR
PRE-HEAT OVEN TO 180°C

INGREDIENTS FOR SIX
6 large cooking apples
25 g butter
75 g castor sugar
100-125 ml sherry

Fillings (one of the following):
125 g dried apricots, chopped and mixed with 2 tablespoons (30 ml) clear honey
125 g fruit mincemeat*
125 g dried dates, chopped with 75 g nuts, and the juice of 1 lemon
75 g soft brown sugar mixed with 10 ml (2 teaspoons) ground nutmeg

Core the apples and score the skin round the middle of each. Stand them in a buttered, deep oven-proof dish. Fill the cavities with your chosen filling, put a knob of butter on each apple, and sprinkle thickly with castor sugar. Pour the sherry into the dish around the apples.

Bake in the pre-heated oven for 1 hour. Baste the apples occasionally with the sherry syrup.

SERVING SUGGESTION Serve hot or cold with cream or custard*.

NECTARINE FOOL WITH PISTACHIO NUTS

ALTHOUGH THIS RECIPE calls for nectarines, you may replace them with other fruit in season, such as strawberries, peaches or apricots.

PREPARATION TIME: 20 MINUTES
CHILLING TIME: 2 HOURS

INGREDIENTS FOR FOUR
4-5 large, very ripe nectarines
15 ml (1 tablespoon) lemon juice
1 ml (¼ teaspoon) ground cinnamon
250 ml (1 cup) thick cream
30 ml (2 tablespoons) castor sugar
50 g pistachio nuts, chopped (preferably unsalted)

Place the nectarines in a bowl, cover with boiling water and leave for 30 seconds to loosen the peels. Pour off the water and cover with cold water: the skins will now peel off easily.

Quarter the fruit off the pip and mix immediately with the lemon juice (to prevent discoloration) and cinnamon. Blend the fruit to a smooth purée, and pour into a glass bowl. Cover with plastic wrap and chill for at least 2 hours.

Whip the cream with the sugar until it holds soft peaks, then fold the cream into the fruit purée, mixing gently but thoroughly.

Spoon the nectarine fool into individual serving dishes and sprinkle with chopped unsalted pistachio nuts.

Unsalted pistachio nuts are sometimes hard to obtain. If you are able to buy only salted ones, shell them and allow to stand in boiling water for 10 minutes. Then peel off the skins and dry the nuts in a 120°C oven for 15 minutes.

VARIATIONS Hulled and wiped strawberries, or peeled and stoned peaches or apricots, are also suitable for this recipe. Flaked almonds go well with strawberries and apricots, while chopped pecans are good with yellow peaches.

If you are using fresh apricots which are a little hard, you may poach them in a sugar syrup* for about 10 minutes before making the purée.

STUFFED PEACHES

ITALIANS OFTEN end a meal simply with cheese or fresh fruit. But when peaches are in season they prepare this unusual and delicious dish of whole peaches stuffed with ground almonds and baked until beautifully tender in dry white wine.

PREPARATION TIME: 30 MINUTES
COOKING TIME: 30 MINUTES
PRE-HEAT OVEN TO 190°C

INGREDIENTS FOR SIX
6 firm ripe peaches (preferably a 'loose-pip' variety)
250 ml (1 cup) ground almonds
50 g butter
90 g castor sugar
2 egg yolks
125 ml (½ cup) dry white wine

Dip the peaches in boiling water to loosen the skins, then in cold water, and remove the skins. Halve the peaches and remove the pips. If you are not using a 'loose-pip' variety, the pips might be difficult to remove and may have to be cut out.

With a teaspoon, scoop out some of the pulp from the peaches. Mix the pulp with the ground almonds, butter, 50 g of the castor sugar and the egg yolks.

Divide the mixture into 12 equal portions, then fill each peach half with a portion of the mixture.

Reconstitute them into whole peaches by joining the halves with toothpicks. Arrange in a buttered oven-proof dish.

Pour over the white wine, sprinkle with the remaining castor sugar and then bake the peaches for 30 minutes, or until just tender, basting often.

Remove the toothpicks from the peaches before serving.

SERVING SUGGESTION Serve the peaches with a splash of Amaretto liqueur.

VARIATION Instead of sandwiching the peach halves together, fill each half and stud the filling with a flaked almond before baking.

PASTRIES, PUDDINGS AND DESSERTS

SPICED PEACHES *need time to absorb the heady brandy and spice flavour.*

SPICED PEACHES

GLOWING AMBER PEACHES in a brandied, spicy syrup make a very grand sweet to serve at a dinner party.

This recipe is an adaptation of an 18th century one. It is quick and simple to prepare. Keep the dish for 3 days before serving; by then the syrup will have fully penetrated the fruit. If you want to keep it longer, double the amount of brandy.

PREPARATION TIME: 15 MINUTES
COOKING TIME: 20 MINUTES
STANDING TIME: 3 DAYS

INGREDIENTS FOR SIX
6 ripe peaches
6 cloves
450 ml water
350 g sugar
1 cinnamon stick (5 cm), or 5 ml (1 teaspoon) ground cinnamon
1 ml (¼ teaspoon) ground mace
100-125 ml brandy

Put the peaches in boiling water for 2-3 minutes. Drain and peel them carefully.
Stud each with a clove.
Put the water, sugar, cinnamon stick and mace in a deep pan, and bring to the boil, stirring until the sugar has dissolved completely.
Add the peaches to this syrup and cook them gently for about 15-20 minutes, making sure that they are completely covered by the syrup during that time. The cooking ensures that the fruit will not discolour while it matures in the jar.
Lift the peaches carefully into a wide-mouthed, screw-top jar.
Remove the cinnamon stick from the syrup and stir in the brandy. Pour the syrup over the peaches and leave them to cool before covering tightly with the screw top. Stand in a cool place and keep for 3 days before using.

SERVING SUGGESTION Serve the spiced peaches in individual glass bowls and pass around a jug of thin cream.

FRESH FRUIT BRÛLÉE

FRUIT SALAD topped with liqueur-flavoured custard, whipped cream and a crunchy sugar coating makes an excellent finale for a dinner party.

PREPARATION TIME: 30 MINUTES
COOKING TIME: 10 MINUTES
CHILLING TIME: 45 MINUTES

INGREDIENTS FOR SIX
Juice of 1 lemon
Juice of 1 orange
2 peaches, peeled and sliced
2 bananas, peeled and sliced
2 pears, peeled and sliced
1 small pineapple, peeled and diced
250 ml (1 cup) seedless grapes
45 ml (3 tablespoons) Cointreau
75 ml white sugar
30 ml (2 tablespoons) cornflour
500 ml (2 cups) milk
15 ml (1 tablespoon) butter
6 egg yolks, lightly beaten
5 ml (1 teaspoon) vanilla essence
250 ml (1 cup) thick cream
Brown sugar

Pour the lemon and orange juice into a bowl, add the prepared fruits and mix gently together. Add 30 ml (2 tablespoons) of the liqueur.
Turn the fruit into a fairly deep flan dish, about 25 cm in diameter, or another suitable dish. Chill until needed.
Make a custard by first mixing the white sugar with the cornflour in a medium-sized saucepan. Gradually add the milk and cook together, stirring constantly, until the sauce is smooth.
Add the butter and, still stirring, continue to cook until the sauce is thick and smooth. Allow to boil for barely a minute, still stirring.
Add a little of the hot mixture to the egg yolks, then add to the saucepan and cook (while stirring) until the mixture reaches boiling point. Remove from the stove and stir in the vanilla essence.
Place a circle of grease-proof paper directly on the surface of the custard to prevent a skin forming.
Stir the remaining spoonful of liqueur into the cooled custard and pour it over the chilled fruits. Spread with the thick cream and chill once again.

Before serving, cover the topping with a thick layer of brown sugar, sieved first to ensure that there are no lumps. Slide under a pre-heated grill to allow the sugar to melt: watch carefully to avoid burning it (it does not matter if the cream starts to melt). You may return the brûlée to the refrigerator until ready to serve.

PINEAPPLE ROMANOFF

GENEROUS FLAVOURINGS of rum, Cointreau and Kirsch make this dessert rich enough to serve in small portions. Make sure that it has been properly chilled before serving.

PREPARATION TIME: 20 MINUTES
CHILLING TIME: AT LEAST 4 HOURS

INGREDIENTS FOR SIX
1 large pineapple (or 2 small ones), peeled and cut into 1 cm cubes
100 g icing sugar
45 ml (3 tablespoons) Cointreau
45 ml (3 tablespoons) white rum
250 ml (1 cup) thick cream
45 ml (3 tablespoons) Kirsch
Grated rind of 1 orange

Place the pineapple cubes in a bowl and sprinkle 60 g of the icing sugar over them. Add the Cointreau and rum, and cover with plastic wrap. Chill for at least 4 hours (or overnight).
About 1 hour before serving, whip the cream lightly with the rest of the icing sugar and flavour with the Kirsch. Pour over the pineapple pieces and toss gently to coat them evenly.
Spoon the mixture into a glass serving bowl, cover and chill until ready to serve. Sprinkle the grated orange rind over the dessert just before serving.

VARIATIONS This dessert is equally delicious if you substitute strawberries (carefully wiped) for the pineapple cubes, and Van der Hum liqueur* for the Cointreau.
Try mixing the two fruits.
You may also add flaked almonds with the orange rind.
Try making the dish from kiwi fruit, cubed and marinated in kiwi fruit liqueur or Cointreau: in this case, leave out the orange rind and sprinkle the completed dessert with flaked almonds.

PASTRIES, PUDDINGS AND DESSERTS

SUMMER FRUIT BOWL

THIS FRUIT SALAD is particularly attractive as well as being delicious. The Kirsch is an important ingredient as it serves to enhance and meld together the flavours of the various fruits.

PREPARATION TIME: 30 MINUTES

INGREDIENTS FOR SIX

3 oranges
1 pear
2 peaches
¼ sweet melon
1 slice watermelon
¼ Ogen melon
½ mango
125 ml (½ cup) grapes (preferably seedless)
125 ml (½ cup) strawberries (optional)
15 ml (1 tablespoon) Kirsch
Castor sugar (optional)
Fresh mint for garnish

Wash and dry the fruits where necessary. Squeeze the juice from 2 oranges and pour into a bowl. Peel and slice the pear and peaches, and toss gently in the orange juice.

Use a small scoop to cut out balls from the melons (or slice them) and add to the bowl. Next, peel the last orange and slice it into thin segments. Add to the bowl with cubes of mango, then add the grapes (halved and seeded if not the seedless variety) and the strawberries (if used).

Pour in the Kirsch and gently toss the fruit salad. If you think it necessary, add a light sprinkling of castor sugar (although the natural sweetness of the fruits should be sufficient).

Cover the bowl and chill until serving. Garnish with fresh mint and a few of the best strawberries (with their stalks) set aside for decoration.

SERVING SUGGESTION Serve with a bowl of sweetened whipped cream.

VARIATIONS Add stoned fresh cherries when available, or a sliced kiwi fruit.

SUMMER FRUIT BOWL *The pick of the season's crop in one dish.*

HOT WINTER FRUIT SALAD

THIS IS A particularly versatile fruit salad in that it can be served hot or uncooked if you so wish. Although it was devised as a pudding, it can also be used as an accompaniment to venison or as a brunch dish.

PREPARATION TIME: 20 MINUTES
STANDING TIME: OVERNIGHT
COOKING TIME: 40 MINUTES
PRE-HEAT OVEN TO 130°C

INGREDIENTS FOR SIX TO EIGHT

100 g dried apricots
125 g dried figs
100 g dried peaches
Boiling water
1 cinnamon stick
2 pears
2 bananas
Juice of 1 lemon
2 oranges
250 ml (1 cup) fresh cape gooseberries (or tinned if fresh ones are not available)
30 ml (2 tablespoons) Van der Hum liqueur*
30 ml (2 tablespoons) brandy

Pour enough boiling water over the dried apricots, figs and peaches to cover them completely, then add the cinnamon stick and leave the fruit to soak overnight.

The next day, peel the pears and bananas, and slice them thinly. Toss the sliced fruit in the lemon juice and the juice of one of the oranges.

Place in an oven-proof bowl with the plumped dried fruit and the soaking liquid. Add the remaining orange, peeled and thinly sliced, and the berries. Pour the liqueur and brandy over the fruit, and cover the dish tightly with a lid or aluminium foil.

Bake the salad for 40 minutes, or until heated through. Remove the cinnamon stick before serving.

SERVING SUGGESTION Serve with dollops of sour cream (smetena) and pass around a bowl of brown sugar for sprinkling over the top of individual servings.

VARIATION The salad can also be served as is without cooking it, either at room temperature or chilled in the refrigerator until ready to serve.

FROSTED FRUIT AND CRYSTALLISED FLOWERS

Fruit and flowers can be given a light 'frosting' of sugar and used to garnish cakes or desserts. This should not be confused with crystallised fruit, which is first candied before being coated with a sugar syrup.

To frost fresh fruit such as small bunches of grapes, plums, strawberries or other berries for a garnish, dip them into beaten egg white, then into castor sugar. Dry the fruit on a rack.

The same method can be used to crystallise flowers such as violets, primroses or rose petals.

Alternatively, you can frost fruit and crystallise flowers using a sugar syrup, but you need a light hand for this method.

First prepare a syrup of sugar and water, letting it boil until it hardens when dropped into cold water.

Take the syrup off the heat, submerge petals or flower heads into it for a minute (with violets, you can dip a little posy at a time) and then dry them in a sieve, sprinkling them well with icing sugar.

Use fruit, frosted by this second method, at once. Flowers or petals may be stored for a few days in an airtight container.

ORIENTAL FRUIT SALAD

THIS IS AN IDEAL DESSERT for a Chinese menu. The ginger gives this fruit salad a pleasantly tangy flavour – while the contrast in the colours of the litchis and mandarin oranges provides it with plenty of visual appeal.

PREPARATION TIME: 10 MINUTES

INGREDIENTS FOR SIX

1 tin (560 g) litchis
1 tin (310 g) mandarin oranges
Juice of 1 lemon
Juice of 1 orange
30 ml (2 tablespoons) chopped ginger in syrup

Drain the tinned litchis and mandarin oranges well, and place the fruit in a bowl with the lemon juice, orange juice and chopped ginger. Chill this fruit salad well before serving.

SERVING SUGGESTION Serve with a jug of thin cream.

PASTRIES, PUDDINGS AND DESSERTS

SUMMER FRUIT PLATTER

THE INTERESTING COMBINATION of fresh fruits in this platter will prove popular amongst young and old alike. It is an ideal lunch or supper dessert during South Africa's hot summer months.

PREPARATION TIME: 30 MINUTES

INGREDIENTS FOR SIX

1 melon
1 pineapple
4 nectarines
8 apricots
Juice of 1 lemon
250 g grapes
Fresh mint for garnish

Peel and slice the melon and pineapple. Quarter the nectarines, halve the apricots, and brush the nectarine wedges with the lemon juice. Next, snip the grapes into small bunches. Arrange the fruits on an attractive platter, then cover and chill until ready to serve. Garnish with fresh mint.

SERVING SUGGESTION Serve with a bowl of thick, natural yoghurt* sweetened with honey.

VARIATION Add fresh plums (halved), granadillas (halved), mangoes (sliced) or whole fresh berries.

WINTER FRUIT SALAD

ALL THE INGREDIENTS for this fruit salad are usually readily available during South Africa's winter months. The flavour of the salad is delicious and well balanced – neither too sweet nor too tart.

PREPARATION TIME: 20 MINUTES

INGREDIENTS FOR SIX

3 oranges
2 bananas
1 green apple
1 red apple
1 yellow apple
1 pear
½ papino
½ pineapple
15 ml (1 tablespoon) Van der Hum liqueur*

Pour the juice of 2 of the oranges into a bowl. Peel and slice the third orange into thin segments. Peel and slice the bananas and toss in the orange juice.

Wash and core the apples (do not peel them, as the different colours of the skins look attractive). Slice the apples thinly and toss in the juice.

Add cubes of pear, papino and pineapple, and pour in the liqueur. Gently toss the salad, then cover and chill until ready to serve.

SERVING SUGGESTION Pass around a jug of thin cream.

VARIATION You may also add the pulp of 2-3 granadillas.

ORANGE AND GRAPEFRUIT SALAD WITH CARAMEL

THIS RECIPE combines two citrus favourites with a topping of delicious, smoothly textured caramel sauce. The chilled fruit and hot sauce make for a pleasant juxtaposition of temperatures.

PREPARATION TIME: 30 MINUTES
COOKING TIME: 10 MINUTES

INGREDIENTS FOR SIX

4 oranges
2 pink grapefruit
30 ml (2 tablespoons) Van der Hum liqueur*
200 g sugar
125 ml (½ cup) water
2 ml (½ teaspoon) cream of tartar

Remove the rind of the brightest orange with a peeler, being careful not to remove any of the pith. Cut the rind into long, thin strips and blanch* in boiling water, then strain and set aside.

Peel the fruit and slice it thinly, arranging the segments in overlapping circles on a serving plate. Pour over the liqueur, cover and chill well.

Just before serving, bring the sugar, water and cream of tartar to the boil, stirring only until the sugar dissolves. Add the blanched peel and allow to boil, without stirring, until the syrup turns golden.

Pour the syrup over the chilled fruit immediately and serve.

SERVING SUGGESTIONS This salad is delicious served with scoops of ice cream or citrus-flavoured sorbets.

GRANADILLA ICE CREAM MOULD

THIS IS A LIGHT and easy ice cream which needs no beating after chilling. The granadilla juice and ground almonds provide a different and delicious flavour.

PREPARATION TIME: 30 MINUTES
FREEZING TIME: AT LEAST 8 HOURS

INGREDIENTS FOR EIGHT

Non-stick spray or sweet almond oil
250 ml (1 cup) finely ground almonds
6 eggs, separated
100 g castor sugar
250 ml (1 cup) cream
250 ml (1 cup) granadilla juice, without pips
30 ml (2 tablespoons) grated orange rind

Spray a 1,5 litre mould or bowl with non-stick spray, or grease with sweet almond oil. Roll the ground almonds around in the bowl, coating it evenly. Tip out and retain the surplus.

Beat the egg whites until frothy, then add the sugar and beat until stiff and glossy. Whisk the yolks until they are frothy, light and lemon-coloured, and fold into the egg white mixture.

Whisk the cream until it is really thick, then fold in the granadilla juice and orange rind. Fold the cream mixture lightly into the egg mixture, mixing it thoroughly. Turn the ice cream into the mould and sprinkle the top with the remaining ground almonds. Freeze for 8 hours or longer.

SERVING SUGGESTION Remove the ice cream from the freezer about 20 minutes before serving. Turn out on to a glass or silver platter, garnishing with cream rosettes and finely shredded orange rind.

VARIATIONS Substitute finely crushed Marie or tennis biscuits for the almonds.

For a light and delightful lemon ice cream, increase the castor sugar to 210 g, and use 125 ml (½ cup) lemon juice (in place of the granadilla juice) and 30 ml (2 tablespoons) grated lemon rind (in place of the orange rind). Prepare as in the original recipe and garnish the turned out ice cream with thin slices of lemon, topping it with a sprig of mint.

VANILLA ICE CREAM

A TIME-HONOURED FAVOURITE throughout the world, this ice cream lends itself to variation and may be flavoured with any one of dozens of tasty extras.

PREPARATION TIME: 10 MINUTES
COOKING TIME: 20 MINUTES
FREEZING TIME: 5 HOURS

INGREDIENTS FOR FOUR TO SIX

4 extra-large egg yolks
125 g sugar
A pinch of salt
500 ml (2 cups) thin cream
10 ml (2 teaspoons) vanilla essence
Non-stick spray or sweet almond oil

Whisk the egg yolks with the sugar and salt until light and lemon-coloured. Scald* the cream and whisk it into the egg mixture. Pour this custard into the top of a double boiler and stir over a medium heat until the mixture thickens sufficiently to coat a wooden spoon.

Strain into a bowl and add the vanilla essence. Cover with aluminium foil or plastic wrap and freeze for 2 hours, then remove the ice cream from the freezer and whisk with a hand beater or electric beater until light and mushy. Pour it into a mould well greased with non-stick spray or sweet almond oil, or into an ice cream container. Cover and freeze for 2-3 hours.

VARIATIONS For a coffee ice cream, dissolve 15 ml (1 tablespoon) pure instant coffee in the hot custard and reduce the vanilla essence to 5 ml (1 teaspoon).

For a chocolate ice cream, grate 4-6 squares dark chocolate into the hot custard and stir until completely dissolved. Add a little more sugar to taste.

For a strawberry ice cream, add 250 ml (1 cup) crushed strawberries (well washed and hulled) to the ice cream before freezing. Add more sugar to taste.

To make honey and nut ice cream, substitute 125 ml (½ cup) honey for the sugar and add 125 g chopped mixed nuts (unsalted).

To make banana ice cream, blend 3 ripe bananas with 15 ml (1 tablespoon) lemon juice to a smooth purée and then beat well into the semi-soft ice cream (made without vanilla essence).

PASTRIES, PUDDINGS AND DESSERTS

ICE CREAM *Fill parfait glasses with scoops of praline and dark chocolate ice cream for a treat with broad appeal.*

DARK CHOCOLATE ICE CREAM

THIS RICH ICE CREAM can be the basis for many a delicious pudding, and is also very appealing on its own. Buy a good-quality dark chocolate to achieve the optimum results. The ice cream holds its shape very well and is therefore ideal for setting in moulds.

PREPARATION TIME: 45 MINUTES
COOKING TIME: 10 MINUTES
FREEZING TIME: 5 HOURS

INGREDIENTS FOR SIX

50 g sugar
125 ml (½ cup) water
250 g dark chocolate
3 egg yolks
400 ml thick cream
30 ml (2 tablespoons) chocolate or coffee liqueur
Sweet almond oil or non-stick spray

Combine the sugar and water in a saucepan and bring to the boil, stirring all the time. Boil for 3 minutes, then remove from the heat and leave to cool for 15 minutes.

Grate the chocolate into the syrup and pour into a blender. Cover and blend at high speed for 10 seconds, or until smooth and well mixed. Set the blender at a medium-high speed and add the egg yolks, one by one, blending until the mixture is smooth.

Beat the cream until it forms soft peaks and fold into the chocolate mixture with the liqueur.

Lightly coat a lidded mould with sweet almond oil or non-stick spray and pour in the ice cream. Cover and freeze for 5 hours before serving.

Remove the ice cream from the freezer and leave to stand for 10 minutes to soften before turning out on to a plate. If you wish, you can turn out the ice cream well in advance, cover with foil, then return it to the freezer.

SERVING SUGGESTIONS Decorate with chopped nuts (pecans, walnuts or flaked almonds are suitable) or rosettes of cream. Serve with more liqueur.

Alternatively, instead of unmoulding the ice cream, form it into scoops and serve it on its own or with scoops of other home-made ice creams in tall parfait glasses. Decorate with wafers.

VARIATIONS Instead of the liqueur, add 10 ml (2 teaspoons) vanilla essence to the ice cream and fold 50 g chopped pecans or walnuts into the mixture before freezing.

Add Van der Hum liqueur* to the ice cream in place of the coffee or chocolate liqueur, decorate with rosettes of cream flavoured with Van der Hum and top with pieces of preserved orange peel.

Use rum instead of the liqueur and fold in 50 g chocolate chips with the cream before freezing the mixture. Decorate the completed ice cream with rosettes of cream studded with chocolate chips.

PRALINE ICE CREAM

MAKE THIS NUTTY ice cream a day ahead to allow it time to set properly. The lemon juice adds an interesting tang.

PREPARATION TIME: 30 MINUTES
COOKING TIME: 30 MINUTES
FREEZING TIME: 8 HOURS

INGREDIENTS FOR SIX TO EIGHT
Non-stick spray

For the praline:
125 g sugar
30 ml (2 tablespoons) lemon juice
125 g almonds, blanched* and coarsely chopped

For the custard:
4 extra-large egg yolks
125 g sugar
A pinch of salt
500 ml (2 cups) thin cream
250 ml (1 cup) thick cream
10 ml (2 teaspoons) almond-flavoured liqueur or brandy

To make the praline, place the sugar and lemon juice in a saucepan over medium heat and stir until the sugar has dissolved completely. Boil gently until the sugar caramelises to a light brown colour.

Add the almonds and stir until they are well coated with caramel and slightly browned. Do not allow it to get too brown, or the praline will be bitter.

Pour the mixture on to a baking sheet that has been well coated with a non-stick spray and leave to cool. When the praline is cold and hard, pound it finely.

To make the custard, whisk the egg yolks with the sugar and salt until light and lemon-coloured. Scald* the thin cream and whisk it into the egg mixture. Pour this custard into the top of a double boiler and stir over a medium heat until the mixture thickens sufficiently to coat a wooden spoon. Add the praline to the custard, pour it into a bowl and leave to cool.

Cover and freeze until half set (about 2 hours), then whip the thick cream and beat it into the semi-frozen custard, together with the liqueur. Pour into a well greased mould, and freeze for 4-6 hours.

SERVING SUGGESTION Turn out the mould, or scoop balls of ice cream into a chilled bowl, and garnish with flaked almonds.

~ Convert Dessert into a Frozen Asset ~

Ice cream desserts are year-round favourites. These delicious puddings can be created quickly and easily, using either bought or home-made ice creams or sorbets. The more complicated confections can be made in advance.

Floral Ice-Bowl

A floral ice-bowl can be a visually dazzling container for a meal-ender. It is relatively easy to make, and it can be used again and again.

Spray the inside of a metal baking tin (about 30 cm square) with non-stick spray (it helps if you chill the tin first) and then fill with water to a depth of about 3 cm. Place in the freezer, making sure the baking tin is horizontal, and allow to freeze solid (about 4 hours).

Spray the outside of another smaller baking tin with non-stick spray and place it in the centre of the first tin, on top of the iced square, leaving a border at least 5 cm wide all around. Place a weight inside this tin so that it does not float.

Arrange sprigs of colourful bougainvillea, full-blown roses and so on, around the smaller container, but no higher than the edge of the outer baking tin. Fill with water and freeze solid (about 3 hours).

When well frozen, remove both tins and you will have an attractive ice-bowl.

Use it as a container for balls of assorted sorbets — decorate with mint sprigs, strawberries or any appropriate garnish just before serving. Place the ice-bowl on a silver tray or glass dish.

Iced Truffles

PREPARATION TIME: 40 MINUTES
COOKING TIME: 15 MINUTES
FREEZING TIME: 3-4 HOURS

INGREDIENTS FOR 30-36 TRUFFLES
Non-stick spray or sweet almond oil
375 ml (1½ cups) chopped pecan nuts, almonds or mixed unsalted nuts
1 litre (4 cups) ice cream (such as chocolate*, nut*, strawberry*, banana* or coffee*)
350 g dark chocolate, broken into small pieces
125 g butter
Foil bonbon cups or cookie cups

Coat a baking sheet with non-stick spray or sweet almond oil and place in the freezer. Spread the chopped nuts on a piece of wax paper. Make balls of ice cream with a large melon-ball scoop, then roll the ice cream balls immediately in the nuts and put on to the baking sheet in the freezer. Freeze for 2 hours, or until really hard.

Melt the chocolate and butter in a double boiler until smooth. Using a skewer or fork, dip the ice cream truffles into the chocolate mixture and return to the baking sheet, working quickly. When the chocolate is hard, cover with plastic wrap. Freeze for at least another hour.

Place the truffles in small, foil bonbon cups or arrange 3-4 in a cookie cup. Cover with plastic wrap until ready to serve.

VARIATIONS Appropriate garnishes can be pressed into the chocolate as it sets on the truffles (for example, a piece of glacé ginger if you have used ginger ice cream, a small nut or a piece of glacé fruit).

LIQUEUR ICE CUPS

Liqueur Ice Cups

PREPARATION TIME: 30 MINUTES
FREEZING TIME: 2 HOURS

INGREDIENTS FOR SIX TO EIGHT
12-16 chocolate cups (bought)
One or more assorted liqueurs such as Cointreau, chocolate mint, coffee, Van der Hum* or Drambuie
500 ml (2 cups) chocolate* or vanilla* ice cream
Assorted garnishes, such as chocolate vermicelli, chopped nuts, and self-hardening chocolate sauce
12-16 small fluted foil cups (optional)

Fill each chocolate cup with 5-10 ml (1-2 teaspoons) liqueur (about ⅓ full). Top with scoops of ice cream made with a large melon-ball scoop. Arrange the cups in a container and freeze until ready to serve (about 2 hours maximum).

If you wish, put the chocolate cups into small fluted foil cups and garnish.

VARIATION Instead of buying the chocolate cups, you can make them yourself. Melt 500 g dark chocolate in a bowl over a pot of gently simmering water until soft (do not allow the water to touch the bowl). Using the back of a small spoon, carefully smear the chocolate inside a double layer of small paper cups — the innermost one coated on the inside with non-stick spray. Immediately set them on a tray in the freezer for 30 minutes, or until hard, then peel away the paper cups from the outside of the chocolate and fill with the liqueur and ice cream. Put in the freezer until ready to serve. Garnish before serving.

Brandied Honey Creams

PREPARATION TIME: 30 MINUTES
FREEZING TIME: 8 HOURS

INGREDIENTS FOR EIGHT TO TEN
8 egg yolks
125 ml (½ cup) warmed honey
500 ml (2 cups) thick cream
125 ml (½ cup) brandy
100 ml thin cream

Whisk the egg yolks in a warmed bowl until light and lemon-coloured. Then, whisking all the time (by hand or with an electric mixer), drizzle in the warm honey. Beat for 5 minutes.

Whip the thick cream and brandy together until lightly thickened, then fold into the egg-yolk mixture. Spoon into individual dessert glasses or ramekins. Cover with plastic wrap and freeze.

Serve straight from the freezer with the thin cream served separately.

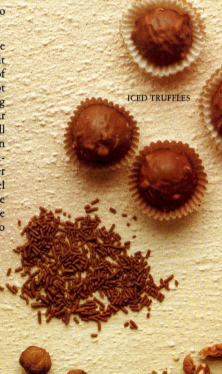

ICED TRUFFLES

TRIPLE CHOCOLATE BOMBE

PREPARATION TIME: 20 MINUTES
FREEZING TIME: 4 HOURS

INGREDIENTS FOR SIX TO EIGHT
A 20cm diameter trifle sponge
Non-stick spray or sweet almond oil
60 ml (¼ cup) brandy
60 ml (¼ cup) Van der Hum liqueur* (or any orange-flavoured liqueur)
1 litre (4 cups) dark chocolate ice cream*, softened
50 g pecan nuts, chopped and toasted*
1 litre (4 cups) chocolate mousse*

For the garnish:
15 ml (1 tablespoon) cocoa
30 ml (2 tablespoons) grated chocolate
125 ml (½ cup) cream, lightly whipped
A few drops vanilla essence

Slice the sponge horizontally into 3 layers and line a well-greased steel or glass mixing bowl with one of the layers. (To facilitate turning out the bombe, grease the bowl well with non-stick spray or almond oil and then place a strip of grease-proof paper across the base and up the opposite sides of the bowl, leaving two 'handles' above the edge of the bowl.) Combine the brandy and liqueur, and brush this first layer generously with one-third of the mixture.

Mix together the ice cream and the pecan nuts, adding a little of the liqueur mixture if you wish. Spoon the ice cream evenly over the first layer and then cover with a second sponge cake slice. Brush the top of the second slice with another third of the liqueur mixture and then spoon on the mousse. Cover this with the third slice of sponge-cake and sprinkle it with the last third of the liqueur mixture. It is important to work quickly. Cover with aluminium foil and freeze for 4 hours.

When the bombe has frozen firm, invert on to a plate, cover briefly with a hot cloth and then gently ease the bombe out of the bowl, using the two paper 'handles'.

Dust with the cocoa and sprinkle with the grated chocolate. Serve with the lightly whipped cream, flavoured with vanilla essence.

VARIATIONS Coffee-flavoured or chocolate mint liqueur could be substituted for the orange liqueur, and appropriate garnishes, such as grated, coffee-flavoured chocolate, or mint crisp, could be used as a garnish.

The bombe could also be decorated with rosettes of whipped cream.

BAKED BANANA ALASKA

PREPARATION TIME: 45 MINUTES
COOKING TIME: 2-3 MINUTES
PRE-HEAT OVEN TO 220°C

INGREDIENTS FOR SIX
A 12cm × 20cm trifle sponge
60 ml (¼ cup) semi-sweet sherry
3 medium-sized, ripe bananas
3 extra-large egg whites
80 g castor sugar
3 ml (¾ teaspoon) cream of tartar
1 litre block vanilla ice cream*, frozen hard
100 g pecans, coarsely chopped, or flaked almonds, toasted*

Slice the sponge cake in half horizontally and place half on a wooden board (keep the rest of the sponge for use on another occasion). Sprinkle with the sherry.

Peel the bananas and slice in half lengthways. Beat the egg whites until they begin to stiffen, then fold in the castor sugar and cream of tartar. Beat until stiff.

Place the ice cream neatly on the sponge cake, trimming the sponge to fit. Working swiftly, arrange the bananas neatly on the ice cream and sprinkle with the nuts and a little more sherry if you wish. Using a rubber spatula, cover the ice cream and sides of the sponge base completely with the egg-white mixture, making sure there are no holes in this meringue covering. Sprinkle with a little castor sugar and place immediately in the pre-heated oven. Turn off the lower heat and leave for 2-3 minutes under the grill until the peaks are just browned. Serve immediately.

SERVING SUGGESTION This dessert needs no accompaniment and is served sliced like a loaf of bread. A garnish of toasted* almonds would be attractive if you have used almonds in the dish.

VARIATIONS Tinned apricots marinated in a little rum (in this case, sprinkle the sponge with rum instead of sherry) are good substitutes for the bananas, as are pears (with a marbled chocolate-and-vanilla ice cream as the base).

CASSATA

PREPARATION TIME: 50 MINUTES
FREEZING TIME: 10 HOURS

INGREDIENTS FOR EIGHT TO TEN
250 ml (1 cup) mixed glacé fruits, finely chopped
60 ml (¼ cup) glacé cherries, halved
125 ml (½ cup) mixed unsalted nuts, coarsely chopped
30 ml (2 tablespoons) brandy or Van der Hum liqueur* (optional)
Non-stick spray or sweet almond oil
1 litre (4 cups) vanilla ice cream*
500 ml (2 cups) chocolate ice cream*
5 ml (1 teaspoon) vanilla essence
250 ml (1 cup) thick cream, or 250 ml (1 cup) thin cream beaten to soft peaks
15 ml (1 tablespoon) castor sugar

For the garnish:
Whipped cream
A few whole hazelnuts

Combine the glacé fruit, cherries and nuts in a bowl and pour over the brandy or liqueur (if used). Leave to stand while assembling the cassata.

Coat a 2 litre loaf tin or 2 smaller tins with non-stick spray or sweet almond oil. Spread a thick layer of vanilla ice cream evenly around the tin(s). Return immediately to the freezer to harden (about 1 hour).

Layer the chocolate ice cream evenly on the vanilla ice cream. Return to the freezer again until firm (about 1 hour).

Mix the fruit and nuts with the vanilla essence, cream and castor sugar to taste. Fill the centre of the cassata with the cream mixture, cover with aluminium foil and freeze for 8 hours, or until very firm.

To unmould, turn the container over on to a dish and cover the loaf tin with a cloth which has been wrung out in hot water, to help ease the cassata out. Decorate with cream rosettes and hazelnuts.

SERVING SUGGESTION Serve sliced like a loaf of bread in 2cm slices. Allow to soften slightly before slicing.

CASSATA

PASTRIES, PUDDINGS AND DESSERTS

PARFAITS AND SUNDAES

Parfaits, moulded from rich ice cream flavoured with liqueur, coffee, or fruit purée, and sparkling sundaes, made from scoops of ice cream layered with fresh fruit, toasted nuts, rich chocolate sauce* and fresh cream, make the most delectable treats imaginable.

BANANA SPLIT

As the name suggests, this dessert is made from bananas split lengthways. The bananas are sandwiched with scoops of 2 or 3 differently flavoured ice creams, then smothered with piped whipped cream and sprinkled with flaked toasted nuts, splinters of chocolate or glacé fruit.

PEACH MELBA

Created originally for the famous singer, Dame Nellie Melba, this dessert may be made from white or yellow peaches, peeled and lightly poached in syrup, then cooled and split in half. The halves are perched on top of scoops of ice cream in wide-rimmed champagne or dessert glasses, then coated with a carmine-coloured sauce made from puréed raspberries or youngberries, sweetened with icing sugar and topped with piped cream and spikes of angelica.

ICE CREAM SUNDAE

This dish can be as simple or sophisticated as you please. For a simple version, top scoops of ice cream with a melted chocolate sauce*. For a more exotic sundae, top the sauce with whipped cream, toasted nuts or chopped praline*.

STRAWBERRY SORBET

FRESH STRAWBERRIES, puréed with orange juice and flavoured with a liqueur, make a delicious sweet sorbet.

PREPARATION TIME: 30 MINUTES
STANDING TIME: 2 HOURS
FREEZING TIME: 7-8 HOURS

INGREDIENTS FOR SIX
425 g strawberries, hulled
250 g sugar
190 ml (¾ cup) orange juice
90 ml lemon juice
30 ml (2 tablespoons) Van der Hum liqueur*

Mix the fruit with the sugar, orange juice and lemon juice, and set aside for 2 hours. Purée and add the Van der Hum. Freeze until firm (about 3 hours). Whisk well, then re-freeze (about 2½ hours). When firm, whisk again and freeze until ready to serve (about 2 hours).

SERVING SUGGESTIONS Serve scoops of sorbet in individual dishes and decorate with fresh mint and strawberries.

VARIATIONS Instead of using strawberries, make the sorbet with sweet melon, watermelon or yellow cling peaches.

LEMON SORBET

THIS IS A VERY refreshing dessert with a sweet-sharp flavour. It is ideal for serving at an elegant dinner between courses to freshen the palate.

PREPARATION TIME: 20 MINUTES
STANDING TIME: 30 MINUTES
FREEZING TIME: 5 HOURS

INGREDIENTS FOR FOUR TO SIX
4 large juicy lemons
130 g sugar
30 ml (2 tablespoons) Van der Hum liqueur*
60 ml (¼ cup) water

Peel the fruit, removing all the pith and seeds, and dice. Purée in a food processor with the rest of the ingredients, then leave to stand for 30 minutes.

Pour into a shallow, freezer-proof container. Freeze until mushy, then process again until smooth. Re-freeze until set. If frozen very hard, allow to soften at room temperature for 10 minutes before serving.

SERVING SUGGESTIONS Decorate this lemon sorbet with some candied peel* or fresh mint leaves.

KHULFI

KHULFI-WALLAHS or professional ice cream makers of India are second to none. They use fresh tropical fruits, nuts of all kinds, and flavourings such as rose petals, saffron and cardamom to make deliciously unusual ice creams.

PREPARATION TIME: 30 MINUTES
COOKING TIME: 45 MINUTES
FREEZING TIME: 3 HOURS

INGREDIENTS FOR FOUR TO SIX
1,5 litres (6 cups) milk
1 tin (400 g) condensed milk
30 ml (2 tablespoons) cold milk
30 ml (2 tablespoons) cornflour
85 g sugar
30 ml (2 tablespoons) water
25 ml (5 teaspoons) slivered almonds
15 ml (1 tablespoon) pistachios or other nuts, chopped
30 ml (2 tablespoons) crushed cornflakes

Using a heavy-bottomed saucepan, bring the 1,5 litres (6 cups) milk and the condensed milk to boiling point. Simmer for about 20 minutes – stir continuously because the mixture burns very easily.

Make a smooth paste with the 30 ml (2 tablespoons) cold milk and cornflour, then add 100 ml of the warm milk to it. Stir and then add to the milk in the saucepan.

Stir again and simmer the mixture for about 30 minutes, until it is thick. A thin film of milk may form at the top – simply stir it into the mixture as this occurs. Remove the pan from the heat.

In a small pot heat the sugar and water, and boil rapidly until the syrup turns light brown. Remove from the heat, allow to cool slightly and then stir it into the milk mixture while it is still liquid. Pour into a freezer container and allow to semi-freeze. Stir well again, mixing in half the nuts and half the cornflakes. Freeze until solid and serve in individual bowls. Decorate with the remaining nuts and cornflakes.

CRÈME CARAMEL

THIS IS ONE of the most popular desserts in homes and restaurants alike. It is simple to make and can keep for 3-4 days in the refrigerator.

PREPARATION TIME: 25 MINUTES
COOKING TIME: 30-45 MINUTES
CHILLING TIME: 4-6 HOURS
PRE-HEAT OVEN TO 140°C

INGREDIENTS FOR SIX
75 ml sugar
15 ml (1 tablespoon) water
3 eggs
500 ml (2 cups) milk
A pinch of salt

Melt 60 ml (¼ cup) of the sugar with the water in a pan over a hot plate until the mixture melts and turns light brown. Do not stir the mixture or disturb it in any way until it has turned a good caramel colour. Be careful not to let it become too dark, however, as it will be bitter.

Pour the caramel into a straight-sided oven-proof dish or deep 20 cm cake tin. Swirl it around so that it coats the bottom and sides of the container, then set aside.

Beat the eggs and mix with the milk. Add the salt and remaining sugar, and pour this mixture into the caramel-lined container. Stand the container in a *bain-marie*, making sure that the water in the larger dish is warm. Bake for 30-45 minutes, depending on the depth of the dish. It is done when a knife inserted in the centre comes out clean. Do not allow the water in the *bain-marie* to boil as this will make the custard watery.

Allow the crème caramel to cool, adding cold water to the *bain-marie* during the cooling period. Chill in the refrigerator until the custard is quite firm – say, 4-6 hours, but overnight is even better.

Crème caramel can be served at room temperature directly from the dish. Run a knife around the edge to loosen the caramel and turn it out on to a dish which has a rim at least 1 cm high.

VARIATION Add 30 ml (2 tablespoons) strong coffee to the egg and milk mixture to make a delicious coffee custard.

To make a richer, firmer crème caramel to serve ten people, use 9 eggs, 1 litre (4 cups) milk and sugar to taste.

PASTRIES, PUDDINGS AND DESSERTS

CRÈME BRÛLÉE *Crunchy caramel bedecks a rich, creamy custard.*

CRÈME BRÛLÉE

THIS IS A RICH RELATION of crème caramel*: being made with cream it is not only more expensive but is also very rich and filling. The custard dessert with its crunchy caramel topping is fairly simple to make but is always considered to be something special.

PREPARATION TIME: 15 MINUTES
COOKING TIME: 40-50 MINUTES
CHILLING TIME: 4-6 HOURS
PRE-HEAT OVEN TO 140°C

INGREDIENTS FOR SIX
600 ml cream
70 g white sugar
A 2 cm piece of vanilla pod, or 7 ml (1½ teaspoons) vanilla essence
4 egg yolks
100 g brown sugar for topping

Heat the cream in a double boiler and stir in the sugar. If using the vanilla pod, add it to the cream. Continue to stir until all the sugar has dissolved.

In a large mixing bowl, beat the egg yolks until they are thick and light in colour. Pour the hot cream over the yolks, stirring vigorously.

If using vanilla essence, add it after the cream and yolks are mixed.

Strain the mixture into an oven-proof dish about 23 cm x 15 cm x 5 cm (or 6 individual dishes), and place it in a larger pan containing a 3 cm depth of hot water.

Bake for about 40-50 minutes. Allow to cool before placing the custard in the refrigerator to chill well (allow about 4-6 hours).

Before serving, cover the entire surface with a thin layer of the brown sugar. Set the dish on a bed of cracked ice to prevent the custard from being re-heated, then place it under a pre-heated grill until the sugar has melted and caramelised.

This dish can be served immediately or kept in the refrigerator until it is needed – not more than 2-3 hours.

VARIATION Stewed fruit may be added before the dish is baked to make an even more exotic dessert.

ICED COFFEE SOUFFLÉ

THIS DESSERT will be a delight for anyone who enjoys the flavour of coffee. Be careful not to allow the milk to boil, or the flavour will be spoilt.

PREPARATION TIME: 20 MINUTES
COOKING TIME: 20 MINUTES
CHILLING TIME: 3 HOURS

INGREDIENTS FOR SIX
15 ml (1 tablespoon) gelatin
500 ml (2 cups) milk
15 ml (1 tablespoon) pure instant coffee
3 eggs, separated
60 g castor sugar
125 ml (½ cup) cream

Prepare a 15 cm soufflé dish by tying a 'collar' of double thickness wax paper around the dish, making it stand 8-10 cm above the rim of the dish.

Sprinkle the gelatin on 50 ml of the milk and allow to stand for 10 minutes. Dissolve the coffee separately in 100 ml of the milk, then add the rest of the milk and heat to about body temperature. Put 60 ml (¼ cup) of this warm milk into the gelatin/milk mixture and stir to dissolve.

Beat the egg yolks with the sugar until light and lemon-coloured, then pour in the warm coffee/milk mixture, beating all the time. Return the mixture to the saucepan and stir over a medium heat until it is sufficiently thick to coat a wooden spoon. Do not allow to boil.

Add the gelatin/milk mixture and stir. Strain into a bowl and leave to cool, then cover and chill. Whisk the cream to the soft peak stage and whisk the egg whites until they are stiff.

When the soufflé has almost set, fold in half the cream and all the egg white, and turn into the prepared soufflé dish. Chill until set, then remove the paper 'collar' and decorate with the rest of the cream.

SERVING SUGGESTIONS If you are able to obtain little coffee-bean chocolates, use these (with rosettes of cream) to decorate the soufflé. Soufflés can also be made in smaller individual soufflé dishes.

VARIATION Reduce the milk by 30 ml (2 tablespoons) and soak the gelatin in 30 ml (2 tablespoons) coffee liqueur before dissolving in the milk.

BLANCMANGE

BLANCMANGE (literally 'white food') began in the Middle Ages as a potage of finely chopped chicken, rice and almond milk. Today blancmange refers to the light and creamy pudding described here.

PREPARATION TIME: 20-30 MINUTES
INFUSING TIME: 1 HOUR
CHILLING TIME: 4-5 HOURS

INGREDIENTS FOR FOUR
275-300 ml milk
Thinly peeled rind of 1 lemon
30 ml (2 tablespoons) gelatin
50-75 g castor sugar
275-300 ml thin cream
50 g ground almonds
45 ml (3 tablespoons) brandy

Put the milk and lemon rind in a covered saucepan. Stand on very low heat for 1 hour, stirring occasionally. Strain off the milk and dissolve the gelatin in a little of it. Add the gelatin mixture to the rest of the milk and stir in the sugar until it dissolves.

Mix in the cream and ground almonds, and stir the mixture until it is almost cold. Stir in the brandy and pour into a prepared mould*. Chill until completely set (about 4-5 hours) before turning out.

MAKING SOUFFLÉ COLLARS

An iced soufflé or fancy mousse is traditionally made in a dish wrapped in a paper collar which is removed before serving. This gives the illusion that the soufflé has risen magically in the refrigerator.

To make the collar, cut two equal strips of grease-proof paper or aluminium foil, long enough to fit around the dish with an overlap of about 5 cm, and deep enough to stand 8-10 cm above the rim of the dish.

Brush one side of one sheet with a light coating of sunflower or sweet almond oil. With this side inside, wrap the collar of paper around the dish. Pin or tape it in place. Wrap the second sheet over the first and fasten

Fill the dish with sweet soufflé or mousse so that the mixture comes above the rim of the dish, but is held in place by the collar of paper. Chill it until it is set.

To remove the collar, run a warmed knife blade around the soufflé between the two layers of paper, then carefully peel off the paper.

HONEYCOMB CREAM

WHEN PREPARING this light and simple dessert, take care not to overcook once you have added the egg yolks and sugar to the milk. When prepared properly, the top part of the pudding will have a spongy texture, with jelly underneath.

PREPARATION TIME: 20 MINUTES
COOKING TIME: 5 MINUTES
CHILLING TIME: 2 HOURS

INGREDIENTS FOR SIX
500 ml (2 cups) milk
2 eggs, separated
45 ml (3 tablespoons) sugar
20 ml (4 teaspoons) gelatin
30 ml (2 tablespoons) cold water
60 ml (¼ cup) hot water
5 ml (1 teaspoon) vanilla essence

Scald* the milk, then beat the egg yolks with the sugar and add the hot milk slowly to this mixture, stirring continuously. Cook the mixture for 1 minute and remove from the heat.

Soak the gelatin in the cold water for 5 minutes, then add the hot water. Add the gelatin and vanilla essence to the egg, sugar and milk mixture. Beat the egg whites until stiff and fold into the mixture. (It will look as if it has curdled.) Pour into a prepared mould*. Chill to set (about 2 hours).

SERVING SUGGESTION Serve with cream.

GAAJAR HALVA

THIS IS ONE of the traditional Indian sweetmeats known as halvas, which are made especially on festive occasions. It consists mainly of grated carrots cooked with milk, sugar and nuts – making a very tasty pudding. The halva can be stored in the refrigerator for up to 5 days.

PREPARATION TIME: 25 MINUTES
COOKING TIME: 1 HOUR 20 MINUTES

INGREDIENTS FOR SIX
75 g butter
7 medium-sized carrots, scraped and grated
30 ml (2 tablespoons) coarsely chopped almonds
140 g sugar
1 litre (4 cups) milk
30 ml (2 tablespoons) sultanas
5 dates, pitted and sliced
5 ml (1 teaspoon) cardamom seeds, crushed
2 ml (½ teaspoon) vanilla essence

Heat the butter in a heavy saucepan. Add the carrots and nuts, and toss for 7-10 minutes on a medium heat. Add the sugar and milk, stir, and simmer on a medium heat for 1 hour, stirring occasionally. Do not cover the saucepan, as the moisture should evaporate.

Add the sultanas, dates, cardamom seeds and vanilla essence. Stir and simmer the mixture gently for a further 10 minutes: the resulting texture will be grainy and moist.

SERVING SUGGESTION Serve warm in individual bowls, either on its own or with whipped cream.

LEMON MOUSSE

THIS IS A RICH and extravagant dessert in the old-fashioned tradition. For the best results, choose lemons that are fresh and firm. Using fruit that is past its prime will spoil the effect.

PREPARATION TIME: 35 MINUTES
SETTING TIME: 4-5 HOURS

INGREDIENTS FOR FOUR
10 ml (2 teaspoons) gelatin
45 ml (3 tablespoons) water
3 eggs, separated
150 g castor sugar
Juice and grated rind of 2 ripe lemons
250 ml (1 cup) thick cream, lightly whipped
45 ml (3 tablespoons) flaked almonds

Put the gelatin and water into a small saucepan and leave to soak for 10 minutes. Combine the egg yolks and sugar in a bowl and beat until light, lemon-coloured and thick, and then beat in the strained lemon juice and rind.

Slowly warm the gelatin mixture and stir until the gelatin is completely dissolved. Add it to the egg mixture, mixing gently but well. Leave until it starts to set.

Beat the egg whites until stiff but not too dry, and then fold into the egg yolk mixture with half the whipped cream.

Turn into a serving dish, cover with plastic wrap and leave to set in the refrigerator (about 4-5 hours).

When completely set, decorate with the rest of the whipped cream and the almonds.

SERVING SUGGESTION The mousse can also be placed in individual serving dishes and will then take half the time to set. It can be made ahead and frozen. Defrost overnight and decorate when defrosted.

CHOCOLATE MOUSSE

WITH A LITTLE CARE, you can make a chocolate mousse that beats any you may be served in a restaurant.

PREPARATION TIME: 30 MINUTES
CHILLING TIME: 3 HOURS

INGREDIENTS FOR SIX
150 g dark chocolate
3 eggs, separated
15 ml (1 tablespoon) castor sugar
250 ml (1 cup) cream
15 ml (1 tablespoon) cognac or coffee liqueur

Break the chocolate into a bowl and set it over another bowl of hot water. Stir until it melts, then leave to cool to room temperature. Beat the egg whites until stiff, then (using the same beater) lightly whisk the sugar and cream together.

Lastly, whisk the egg yolks lightly and add to the chocolate with the cognac or liqueur. Mix the ingredients until well blended and smooth.

Stir a quarter of the beaten egg white into the chocolate mixture and fold the chocolate mixture into the rest of the egg white, then fold in the cream which has been whisked until it forms soft peaks. Spoon the mousse into dessert glasses or pudding bowls and chill (covered with plastic wrap) for 3 hours.

SERVING SUGGESTIONS Decorate with chocolate curls*, a rosette of cream and flaked almonds or chopped pecan nuts.

VARIATIONS Make the mousse with Van der Hum liqueur* and add the grated rind and strained juice of 1 orange. Decorate with rosettes of cream topped with pieces of preserved orange peel.

Use white chocolate instead of dark.

GRANADILLA MOUSSE

THE FRESH, SHARP TASTE of the granadillas blends very effectively with the sugar, cream and eggs to make a smooth and delicious mousse.

PREPARATION TIME: 30 MINUTES
COOKING TIME: 20 MINUTES
CHILLING TIME: 4-6 HOURS

INGREDIENTS FOR SIX
20 granadillas
190 g sugar
15 ml (1 tablespoon) gelatin
60 ml (¼ cup) cold water
60 ml (¼ cup) boiling water
250 ml (1 cup) thick cream
3 egg whites

Squeeze out the granadilla pulp and remove the pips by straining. Place the pulp in the top of a double boiler with the sugar, and heat gently, stirring until the sugar has dissolved completely.

Soften the gelatin in the cold water, then add the boiling water and stir until the gelatin has completely dissolved. Strain into the granadilla mixture and leave to cool and set slightly.

Whisk the cream until thick (it should stand in soft points) and whisk the egg whites until stiff.

Fold the cream and egg whites into the cooled granadilla and gelatin mixture. Spoon the mousse into individual dessert glasses. Cover with plastic wrap and refrigerate for at least 4 hours.

SERVING SUGGESTIONS Decorate each mousse with rosettes of cream flavoured with Cointreau, and sprinkle on a little grated orange rind.

Instead of making individual desserts, spoon the mousse into a glass serving bowl and decorate it, once set, with cream and a sprinkling of flaked almonds.

Alternatively, spoon the mousse into scooped out granadilla shells and freeze until firm. Serve 2-3 per person.

Syllabub

TO THE ELIZABETHANS, the syllabub was a frothy drink made by milking directly from the cow into a cup of ale, wine or cider. But by the 18th century the name had come to be applied to a number of creamy whips, often thickened with a variety of fresh fruit juices.

One of the most popular was this confection of sweetened wine laced with brandy and whipped cream (sharpened by the juice of a lemon or a Seville orange), which can be eaten as a pudding in its own right, or used as a topping for trifle*.

PREPARATION TIME: 25-30 MINUTES
STANDING TIME: OVERNIGHT (8 HOURS)
CHILLING TIME: 2 HOURS

INGREDIENTS FOR SIX
150 ml sweet white wine
15 ml (1 tablespoon) medium-sweet sherry
30 ml (2 tablespoons) brandy
1 lemon, or 1 Seville (bitter) orange (or a sweet orange if preferred)
150 ml water
60 ml (¼ cup) castor sugar
275-300 ml thick cream

Pour the wine, sherry and brandy into a large basin.

Remove the rind of the lemon or orange, leaving the white pith intact, and reserve half the rind for a garnish.

Squeeze the juice from the lemon or orange and add it to the wine, with the remaining half of the rind. Leave this mixture to stand overnight, then remove and discard the rind.

Boil the reserved rind in the water, simmering for 2 minutes to remove its bitter taste. Drain off the water, then cut the rind into shreds.

Stir the sugar into the wine mixture until it dissolves, then add the cream and whip with a hand whisk until the mixture forms soft peaks. Spoon it into 6 wine glasses.

Stand the finished syllabub in the refrigerator for 2 hours. Before serving, decorate each syllabub with the shredded lemon or orange rind.

SERVING SUGGESTIONS The syllabub may also be used as a topping for fruit – fresh, poached or stewed dried fruit.

Trifle

RICH CREAM DISHES were the delight of the 18th century. Among them was a frivolous confection of biscuits or cake, soaked in dry white wine or sherry, topped with custard or syllabub, and decorated with almonds, ratafia cakes, jelly or crystallised fruits and flowers. This was known as a trifle.

The following updated version of a 1790 recipe brings you close to the dish's exciting origins. Fresh strawberries or sliced peaches can be used instead of jam.

Preparation needs to begin the day before so that the flavours in both the base and the syllabub can blend fully.

PREPARATION TIME: 40 MINUTES
COOKING TIME: 25 MINUTES
SETTING TIME: OVERNIGHT
CHILLING TIME: 2 HOURS

INGREDIENTS FOR EIGHT TO TEN

For the base:
100-125 g macaroons, or 8-10 slices of sponge cake*
45 ml (3 tablespoons) brandy
150 ml dry white wine
*45-60 ml (3-4 tablespoons) thin raspberry or strawberry jam**
575-600 ml thin cream
2 eggs, beaten
2 egg yolks, beaten
30 ml (2 tablespoons) castor sugar

For the topping:
Syllabub* and prepared shreds of orange or lemon rind
75 g blanched* almonds (optional)

Arrange the macaroons or slices of sponge cake on the bottom of a large glass dish. Spoon over the brandy and as much of the wine as they will soak up. Then carefully spread the macaroons or slices of sponge cake with the jam.

Bring the cream almost to boiling point, and stir it well into the beaten eggs and egg yolks. Pour into the top pan of a double boiler and set this over the bottom pan of hot water, taking care that the water does not touch it.

Keep the double boiler simmering and stir the custard until it thickens (about 15-20 minutes). Remove from the heat and stir in the sugar until dissolved.

Leave until almost cold before pouring over the macaroons or slices of sponge cake. Set in a cold place overnight. Begin making the syllabub, which also needs to stand overnight.

The next day, spread the syllabub carefully over the trifle and chill for 2 hours. Just before serving, sprinkle the blanched almonds (if used) and shredded lemon or orange rind on top.

VARIATION Top the trifle with whipped cream instead of the syllabub. In this case, decorate the top with crystallised flowers*.

TRIFLE *Layered in a glass dish, this traditional feast of a dessert is a temptation to the eye as well as the tastebuds.*

Meringues

There are many variations of meringue but all are based on the same ingredients – sugar and egg whites. Each type calls for a different preparation.

Make sure that bowls and utensils are thoroughly clean since any grease or foreign bodies will prevent the meringue from becoming stiff. Make sure the egg whites are at room temperature.

Use glass, stainless steel or, if available, a copper bowl for best results. An electric mixer is ideal and takes the effort out of making meringues, but if necessary a balloon whisk may be used, although it requires endurance.

To make small meringues, beat 4 egg whites with a pinch of salt until soft peaks form. Add 250 g castor sugar gradually, about 30 ml (2 tablespoons) at a time. Continue to beat the mixture until stiff peaks form or until there is no sign at all of sugar granules. Using a piping bag with a star nozzle, pipe mounds on to a greased and floured baking sheet – 8-10 cm is the ideal size for small meringues. Bake the meringues at 100°C for 2-2½ hours. At the end of the cooking time, loosen them from the tin, turn them on their sides and then leave them in the oven while it cools down. Store the meringues in an airtight tin (they will last about 2 weeks).

For a meringue with a chewy centre, add only half the amount of sugar, 30 ml (2 tablespoons) at a time, and beat the mixture until it is stiff. Then fold the rest of the sugar into the mixture with a metal spoon and proceed as above.

Either serve the meringues individually or sandwich them together with whipped cream.

Meringue Shells and Discs

Use the same recipe as for small meringues. Mark a circle on a greased and floured baking sheet (baking paper is ideal) about 23-25 cm in diameter. Using a piping bag with a plain nozzle, fill in the circle with meringue: starting in the centre, make a coil until the entire circle has been filled.

To make a shell, pipe a thick coil around the edge to form a raised border. For a disc, leave off the border. Dust with castor sugar. Bake at 120°C for 50-60 minutes. When the shell or disc is cool and dry, fill or sandwich with fruit and piped cream.

Meringue shells or discs can be made up to a week before you intend using them and stored in an airtight tin.

Hazelnut Meringues

Spread 100 g hazelnuts on a baking sheet and roast them at 180°C for about 15 minutes. Remove them from the pan, place them in a dry tea towel. Fold the towel over the nuts and rub them well to remove their skins. Do not worry if a few stubborn skins are left. Grind the nuts in a food processor or mincer.

Beat 4 egg whites until soft peaks form, then gradually add 225 g castor sugar and beat until the meringue is stiff. Fold in the nuts, 3 ml (¾ teaspoon) vinegar and 5 ml (1 teaspoon) vanilla essence.

Make the mixture into two 23 cm shells as above or make small meringues about 2 cm in diameter. If making circles, bake them at 130°C for 50-60 minutes – if making small meringues, bake at 140°C for 50-60 minutes, or until they feel firm and dry.

Sandwich the small meringues together with sweetened whipped cream.

Snow Eggs

A VERY DELICATE DESSERT of gently poached egg white, this is ideal to serve after a heavy meal. The dish is far easier to make than most people imagine it to be.

PREPARATION TIME: 30 MINUTES
COOKING TIME: 30 MINUTES

INGREDIENTS FOR SIX

4 egg whites
100 g sugar

For the soft custard:
500 ml (2 cups) milk
A 3 cm piece of vanilla pod, or 5 ml (1 teaspoon) vanilla essence
4 egg yolks
100 g sugar
10 ml (2 teaspoons) flour

Beat the egg whites until they begin to form soft peaks, then gradually add the sugar and beat the mixture until stiff peaks are properly formed and all the sugar has dissolved.

Heat a shallow pan of water until it is simmering. Using a wet spoon, form the meringue into egg shapes and slip them off the spoon into the simmering water.

Poach the snow eggs for about 2 minutes, then turn them and poach the other side for 2 minutes. Remove them from the water with a slotted spoon and leave them to dry on paper towels while you make the sauce.

To make the soft custard, scald* the milk with the piece of vanilla pod (if using essence, add it after the custard has been cooked). Allow the milk to stand for 10 minutes to absorb the vanilla flavouring.

Beat the egg yolks and gradually add the sugar until the mixture is smooth and creamy. Sprinkle the flour over the egg mixture and fold it in.

Gradually pour the scalded milk into the egg mixture. Return this to the saucepan and cook over a gentle heat, stirring all the time (this may be done in a double boiler). Cook until the mixture coats the back of a wooden spoon.

If the sauce has been cooking over direct heat, remove it as soon as the mixture reaches boiling point.

Strain the custard into a bowl and stir it occasionally until it has cooled.

SERVING SUGGESTIONS Serve the snow eggs on a bed of soft custard, or pour the soft custard over the snow eggs and sprinkle with toasted, sliced almonds or grated chocolate.

Alternatively, arrange sliced fresh fruit or berries in a shallow dish and arrange the snow eggs on top.

Meringue Gâteau

IF YOU HAVE a sweet tooth, this recipe is a perfect way to indulge it. If possible, the actual assembly of the gâteau should be done during a cool part of the day, otherwise it will be sticky work.

PREPARATION TIME: 1 HOUR
COOKING TIME: 50-60 MINUTES
CHILLING TIME: AT LEAST 3 HOURS
STANDING TIME: AT LEAST 30 MINUTES BEFORE SERVING

INGREDIENTS FOR SIX TO EIGHT

225 g plain dark chocolate
120 ml water
500 ml (2 cups) thick cream
3 thin meringue discs* (23 cm in diameter), using the amount of meringue mixture described in the recipe for small meringues
Chocolate curls* or chocolate vermicelli for garnish

Break or chop the chocolate into small pieces, put it into the top of a double boiler with the water and dissolve it over a pan of gently simmering water. Pour the chocolate into a bowl and allow to cool.

Whip the cream until it begins to thicken, then add the chocolate and continue beating until it is thick. Put the mixture in the refrigerator for 10 minutes.

To assemble, lay a meringue disc on a serving platter and spread it with some of the chocolate mixture. Place a second meringue disc on top, spread the chocolate mixture on it, then repeat the process with the last meringue disc.

Spread the top and sides of the assembled cake with the remaining chocolate mixture. Decorate with the chocolate curls or vermicelli and allow to stand in the refrigerator for at least 3 hours – preferably overnight – before using.

Remove the cake from the refrigerator at least 30 minutes before serving.

CHIFFON TART

THIS IS A FAVOURITE item at traditional South African teas, and is also an ideal dessert – served in a meringue shell with a decorative rose of whipped cream.

PREPARATION TIME: 45 MINUTES
CHILLING TIME: 24 HOURS
SETTING TIME: 1½ HOURS

INGREDIENTS FOR SIX
1 tin (200 g) evaporated milk
10 ml (2 teaspoons) gelatin
15 ml (1 tablespoon) warm water
2 eggs, separated
80 g sugar
70-90 ml chopped citron* or green fig preserve*
30 ml (2 tablespoons) chopped walnuts or pecan nuts
1 baked meringue shell* or biscuit crumb crust*

Place the evaporated milk in the refrigerator for 24 hours to thicken it, then shake the tin well. Beat the contents with a hand beater until stiff.

Dissolve the gelatin in the warm water. Beat the egg yolks with half the sugar until fluffy and add to the milk.

Lightly combine the milk/egg mixture with the cooled gelatin. Add the preserve and the nuts.

Whip the egg whites and remaining sugar until the mixture is very stiff. When the milk/egg mixture begins to thicken, fold in the egg whites.

Pour this mixture into the baked meringue shell or crumb crust.

Allow the tart to set in the refrigerator (about 1½ hours).

If you have used a meringue base the chiffon tart should preferably be eaten on the same day since the meringue rapidly becomes soggy.

VARIATIONS Instead of chilling and whipping the evaporated milk, make a custard by boiling the milk with half the sugar. Add this mixture to the whipped egg yolks and then add the dissolved gelatin. When this has cooled, add the nuts, preserve and, lastly, the egg whites whipped with the remaining sugar.

Replace the citron or green fig preserve with pieces of Chinese preserved ginger to vary the flavour.

PAVLOVA *Fresh fruit in season and whipped cream nestle in a delectable case of chewy meringue.*

PAVLOVA

THIS DISH IS ONE of Australia's most popular desserts. It consists of a crispy meringue crust with a thick marshmallow texture inside. The centre of the meringue case is filled with a mixture of whipped cream and a selection of fruit in season. To give the Pavlova an extra special touch, you may lightly frost the fruit.

PREPARATION TIME: 45 MINUTES
COOKING TIME: 1 HOUR
PRE-HEAT OVEN TO 140°C

INGREDIENTS FOR SIX
For the meringue:
4 egg whites
180 g castor sugar
60 g granulated sugar
15 ml (1 tablespoon) cornflour
3 ml (¾ teaspoon) lemon juice

For the filling:
250 ml (1 cup) cream, whipped until soft peaks form
100 g fresh strawberries, washed and hulled, or 100 g seedless grapes
100 g stoned cherries or plums
4 ripe apricots, or 2 nectarines, peeled, stoned and cut into slices
Pulp of 2 granadillas

Beat the egg whites until soft peaks form, then gradually add the castor sugar, beating the mixture well until all the sugar has dissolved. Fold the combined granulated sugar and cornflour into the meringue with the lemon juice.

Mark a 23 cm circle on grease-proof paper, grease it with butter and dust it with cornflour. Shake off the excess cornflour and fill in the circle with about one-third of the meringue mixture.

Place the rest of the meringue in a piping bag fitted with a star nozzle. Pipe the mixture decoratively around the edge of the Pavlova to form a rim. Bake the meringue for 1 hour.

If you would prefer a crisp texture throughout the meringue ring, then bake for an extra 45 minutes.

Fill the meringue case with most of the whipped cream and the prepared fruit, and then decorate it with the remaining cream and a few strawberries or small clusters of grapes.

SERVING SUGGESTION Garnish with frosted grape clusters and plums. Dip the fruit in beaten egg white, then into castor sugar and allow to dry.

VARIATION You can make a simpler yet still traditional Pavlova by topping the baked meringue shell only with whipped cream and granadilla pulp.

PASTRIES, PUDDINGS AND DESSERTS

APRICOT SAUCE

THE DELICATE, PERFUMED FLAVOUR of ripe apricots, captured in jam, is present in this simply made sauce.

PREPARATION TIME: 10-15 MINUTES

INGREDIENTS FOR FOUR
45-60 ml (3-4 tablespoons) apricot jam*
30 ml (2 tablespoons) sugar
90 ml dry white wine

Gently heat the jam with the sugar and wine in a small saucepan for about 10 minutes, stirring from time to time to blend throughly. Rub through a sieve to rid the sauce of apricot skin.

SERVING SUGGESTIONS Serve the sauce hot with milk puddings or cold with ice cream.

VARIATION To make marmalade sauce, simply substitute marmalade* for the apricot jam. Serve hot with steamed sponges and milk puddings.

APRICOT SHERRY SAUCE

THIS QUICK SAUCE adds a tang to many desserts. To save time, you could make it a day ahead and re-heat it before serving.

PREPARATION TIME: 10 MINUTES
COOKING TIME: 20 MINUTES

INGREDIENTS FOR FOUR TO SIX
1 tin (420 g) apricot halves or 450 g poached apricots
125 ml (½ cup) syrup from the apricots
60 ml (¼ cup) sugar
10 ml (2 teaspoons) cornflour
60 ml (¼ cup) semi-sweet sherry
2 ml (½ teaspoon) grated lemon rind

Drain the apricots and retain the syrup. Blend the apricots to a smooth purée and place in a saucepan with the syrup and sugar. Bring to the boil on medium heat.

Meanwhile, blend the cornflour and sherry until smooth, and add to the simmering sauce. Stir until the sauce thickens and starts to bubble, then add the lemon rind and serve.

SERVING SUGGESTIONS Serve with steamed puddings or vanilla ice cream*.

BRANDY BUTTER

BRANDY BUTTER has become a traditional Christmas side dish to serve with Christmas pudding and warm mince pies.

PREPARATION TIME: 10 MINUTES

INGREDIENTS FOR FOUR
100-125 g soft, unsalted butter
30 ml (2 tablespoons) castor sugar
60 ml (¼ cup) brandy

Cream the butter and sugar together thoroughly until fluffy and pale. Work in the brandy, a few drops at a time, beating well after each addition, until completely absorbed.

SERVING SUGGESTIONS Serve the brandy butter well chilled, either piled into a small dish or formed into small balls. Apart from being served with Christmas pudding* and mince pies*, it is also good with other steamed puddings.

BRANDY SAUCE

THE FLAVOUR THAT brandy imparts to this sauce can make a party piece of a steamed sponge or suet pudding. Brandy sauce may also be served with Christmas pudding* or mince pies* in place of the more traditional brandy butter.

PREPARATION TIME: 25 MINUTES

INGREDIENTS FOR FOUR TO SIX
10 ml (2 teaspoons) cornflour
275-300 ml milk
10 ml (2 teaspoons) castor sugar
2 egg yolks, beaten
60 ml (¼ cup) brandy

Mix the cornflour to a paste with 30 ml (2 tablespoons) of the milk. Heat the rest of the milk in a saucepan until it just reaches boiling point. Remove from the heat and stir in the cornflour paste. Bring to the boil, and boil for 5 minutes (stirring constantly).

Stir in the sugar and leave the sauce to cool for 5 minutes. Stir in the beaten egg yolks and brandy.

Put the pan over another pan of boiling water and stir continuously until the sauce thickens. Take great care that it does not boil, or it will curdle.

CUSTARD

MILK AND EGGS were always on hand in the farmhouse kitchen, and it was quite natural for the farmer's wife to combine them in warm, nourishing dishes.

Synthetic preparations cannot be compared with true custard, which is made from milk thickened with eggs. Serve it with steamed or baked puddings, pies, tarts or stewed fruits.

PREPARATION TIME: 20 MINUTES

INGREDIENTS FOR SIX
3 egg yolks
15 ml (1 tablespoon) vanilla sugar*, or 15 ml (1 tablespoon) castor sugar and 2 ml (½ teaspoon) vanilla essence
5 ml (1 teaspoon) cornflour
375 ml (1½ cups) hot milk

Beat the egg yolks, vanilla or castor sugar and cornflour together in a bowl until well blended.

Gradually stir some of the hot milk into the eggs and sugar, then add the mixture to the rest of the hot milk.

Pour the sauce into the top of a double boiler, and set over the bottom pan of simmering water.

Using a wooden spoon, stir the mixture constantly over a gentle heat until it thickens just enough to coat the back of the spoon.

If vanilla essence is being used, stir it into the thickened sauce. Strain the custard before serving.

SERVING SUGGESTIONS Serve the sauce hot or cold. If you wish to serve it cold, cover the cooked custard and stir it occasionally as it cools, to prevent a skin from forming. Refrigerate (covered) until needed.

CUSTARD *This classic is delicious served simply with a dried fruit compote.*

Caramel Sauce

IN THIS DELICIOUS RECIPE, caramel syrup is the basis of a creamy sauce that is particularly good when chilled and served with ice cream or apple dishes.

PREPARATION TIME: 1 HOUR

INGREDIENTS FOR FOUR
100-125 g sugar
80 ml boiling water
150 ml thick cream

Put the sugar in a small saucepan. Add 30 ml (2 tablespoons) of the water and set the pan over a low heat, stirring until the sugar has completely dissolved. Bring the mixture to the boil, and boil it rapidly until it becomes a deep golden colour (this will take 2-3 minutes).

Quickly remove the pan from the heat and pour in the remaining 50 ml boiling water. Put the pan over a low heat and dissolve the caramel mixture without allowing it to boil. This may take 15-20 minutes. When the caramel has dissolved, leave it to become cold before stirring it into the cream.

If you wish, you may whip the sauce to thicken it slightly.

Chocolate Sauce

ENJOY THIS DELICIOUS SAUCE over your favourite flavour of ice cream or stir it into a cup of hot milk on a cold winter's evening. It can be stored in the refrigerator for up to a week.

PREPARATION TIME: 35 MINUTES

INGREDIENTS FOR FOUR
100 g dark chocolate
180 ml water
30 ml (2 tablespoons) cream

Break the chocolate into pieces and place them in a saucepan with the water. Simmer for about 5 minutes until the chocolate has melted completely.

Stir the sauce, and cover it, then simmer it, stirring occasionally, on a low heat for about 25 minutes, or until the sauce has reduced and thickened.

Stir the cream into the thickened sauce to make a good consistency, adding more if necessary.

Fresh Strawberry Sauce

ALTHOUGH THIS RECIPE calls for the sauce to be chilled before serving, it could also be re-heated and served hot as a variation.

In either case, however, the sauce should be allowed to stand for a few hours for the flavours to stabilise. The sauce can also be successfully frozen.

PREPARATION TIME: 30 MINUTES
CHILLING TIME: 4 HOURS

INGREDIENTS FOR SIX
100 g sugar
60 ml (¼ cup) water
500 g strawberries, wiped, hulled and sliced
Grated rind and juice of 1 orange
30 ml (2 tablespoons) Curacao liqueur

Place the sugar and water in a saucepan, and bring to the boil, stirring constantly until the sugar has completely dissolved.

Boil the syrup for another 5 minutes, then remove from the heat and leave to cool slightly.

Blend the strawberries to a smooth purèe with the grated orange rind and orange juice. Add the cooled syrup and then the Curacao to the fruit purèe.

Pour the sauce into a jug or bowl and allow to cool. Cover and chill for at least 4 hours before serving.

SERVING SUGGESTIONS Serve with ice cream, hot vanilla soufflé*, steamed puddings or poached fruit.

VARIATIONS A simpler sauce can be made by blending the strawberries with the sugar syrup and leaving out the orange juice and liqueur.

A fresh raspberry sauce can be made in the same way. In this case, substitute Cointreau for the Curacao.

To make a mulberry sauce, wash the mulberries and drain well, then remove and discard the stalks. Omit the liqueur from this sauce.

LEMON SAUCE *makes a fragrant topping for a golden sponge pudding.*

Lemon Sauce

THIS LEMON SAUCE is ideal for sharpening the flavour of steamed fruit puddings or sponge puddings. It is fragrant and tasty, and very simple to prepare. It may be served hot or cold.

PREPARATION TIME: 20 MINUTES

INGREDIENTS FOR FOUR TO SIX
100-125 g castor sugar
20 ml (4 teaspoons) cornflour
1 ml (¼ teaspoon) salt
250 ml (1 cup) water
Finely grated rind of 1 lemon
25 g butter, cut into small pieces
45 ml (3 tablespoons) lemon juice

Put the sugar, cornflour and salt in a saucepan, and stir in the water a little at a time to make a smooth paste. Stir in the finely grated lemon rind and place the pan over a low heat.

Cook gently, stirring all the time, until the mixture simmers and thickens. Continue simmering for about a minute longer, then remove from the heat. Beat in the butter pieces, one at a time, and stir in the lemon juice.

Rum Butter

ROMANTIC TALES of rum smuggling play a part in the history of rum butter. English legend has it that a woman who took a broken cask of the illicit cargo found that it had dripped into the sugar and butter stored on her larder shelf.

To such a happy accident, it is claimed, we owe this rich blend of rum and brown sugar with butter and spices. Serve it with warm mince pies* or any steamed pudding containing dried fruits.

PREPARATION TIME: 15-20 MINUTES

INGREDIENTS FOR FOUR TO SIX
225 g soft, unsalted butter
100-125 g soft brown sugar
1 ml (¼ teaspoon) freshly grated nutmeg
2 ml (½ teaspoon) lemon juice
45-60 ml (3-4 tablespoons) rum

Cream the butter until it is fluffy, then beat in the sugar, nutmeg and lemon juice.

Add the rum carefully, drop by drop, beating in each drop thoroughly before adding the next so that the butter mixture does not curdle.

Breads, Cakes and Biscuits

THE BREAD WE EAT in South Africa is very much in the European tradition of leavened breads, although many people also enjoy such unleavened Eastern breads as puri.

Leavening, which makes dough light and spongy, has been practised since the Iron Age. The Celts of Spain and France used the froth from fermenting beer as a leavening agent, and through the centuries yeasts from many other fermentation processes have been used. French immigrants to South Africa even used must (mos) to leaven their dough early during the wine-making season – from which tradition we inherited mosbolletjies, a baked treat still enjoyed today.

The dividing line between bread and cake is thin, although cakes are more likely to contain sugar, eggs and fruits. Cakes developed from the enriched breads made by the Romans. Today there is a flourishing tradition of special cakes for celebrations, for example, birthday cakes, wedding cakes, Christmas cakes and Easter simnel cakes.

Biscuits developed even earlier than cakes. Originally they were mostly rusks, which are baked twice and account for the name 'biscuit' – derived from the French *bis cuit* ('twice cooked'). Today biscuits are no longer baked in the same way (some fridge biscuits are not baked at all), and there is a far greater and tastier variety from which to choose.

NOTES ON BAKING BREADS, CAKES AND BISCUITS · *PAGE 290*

BREADS, CAKES AND BISCUITS RECIPES · *PAGE 296*

SPECIAL FEATURES

PETITS FOURS – SMALL, SWEET AND SCRUMPTIOUS · *PAGE 302*
THE DECORATIVE ART OF ICING · *PAGE 310*

Notes on Baking Breads, Cakes and Biscuits

Breads

There is nothing to beat the taste and texture of home-baked bread, so strikingly different from commercially produced loaves. Baking your own bread is not necessarily cheaper than buying it, but the satisfaction of eating the home-made product certainly makes the effort involved worth your while.

Ingredients for Bread-Making

Flour

All the wheat flours are suitable for bread-making, since they have a high content of gluten, the substance that gives bread its volume and texture.

Wholewheat flour, as its name suggests, contains the whole grain, including the bran. Brown bread flour is similar, but has had some of the coarsest bran removed. White bread flour has had even more of the whole grain extracted to give a lighter baked product, while cake flour, the lightest of the flours, is the most refined of all.

A wholewheat flour used on its own to make bread will give a dense loaf full of healthy fibre. Wholewheat or brown bread flour will not give as large a volume or as light a texture as white flour. Wholewheat and brown bread flour can be mixed with an equal quantity of white bread or cake flour, or even with more than half, to give a bread of lighter texture, colour and taste.

Brown bread flour does not keep as well as white, especially after the bag has been opened, so it is best to buy only as much as you can use up quickly. Keep flour in the bag in which you buy it, remembering to mark it with the date of purchase. Keep it on a cool, dry shelf or put it, still in its bag, inside a stoneware jar or other special flour jar. Once the bag is opened, use up brown flour within 1 month and white within 3 months. When storing new flour, do not mix it with old flour.

For bread-making, weigh out the flour you will need in advance, and put

it in a large, warm mixing bowl in a warm place to come up to room temperature, or a little above.

You may substitute different types of flour, such as soya or rye flour, or rolled oats or bran for part of the wheat flour. Wheat germ, nuts and seeds – such as sunflower, sesame, poppy or linseed – may also be added with the dry ingredients to give an interesting texture and flavour.

Yeast

The raising agent usually used in bread is yeast: a single-celled organism, *Saccharomyces cerevisiae,* which is visible only under a microscope. Hundreds of thousands of these organisms are compressed together to make crumbly, putty-like blocks of greyish-cream fresh yeast or dried yeast.

Yeast feeds on carbohydrates – that is, starches and sugars. When mixed in dough and given the right conditions of warmth, moisture and food, it ferments, growing rapidly and giving off carbon dioxide, which permeates the dough, making it spongy in texture. It takes time for the yeast to carry out the process, which is why the mixed dough is left to rise once or twice before baking. During fermentation, alcohols and acids are produced which develop flavour. The longer the fermentation time, the better the flavour.

It is not necessary to use up fresh yeast immediately. It will keep for up to 5 days in a cool place if wrapped in a plastic bag or in a plastic box with a tightly fitting lid, or for up to 3 weeks in the refrigerator. To store yeast in a freezer, wrap each cube in aluminium foil and freeze for up to 3 months.

Dried yeast (baker's yeast – not brewer's yeast or tonic yeast) is widely available from grocers, health-food shops and large supermarkets. Provided that it is kept in an airtight container and in a cool place, dried yeast will remain active for up to 6 months.

Always check whether the amount given in your recipe refers to fresh or dried yeast. A useful conversion to remember is that 15 ml (1 tablespoon) dried yeast is equal to a 25 g cake of fresh yeast.

The amount of yeast needed varies according to the type of dough being made. Wholewheat bread, brown bread and enriched breads need more yeast than white bread.

Both fresh and dried yeast need creaming with warm liquid – water or milk – before being added to the flour. Fresh yeast will cream easily in 30-45 ml (2-3 tablespoons) liquid. Dried yeast is best whisked with a fork into about 150 ml liquid and then left in a warm place for 10 minutes, or until frothy.

Liquids – warm water or milk

Water, milk or a mixture of both are the liquids used in bread. The amount needed will vary depending on what kind of bread is being made and what kind of flour is being used. Enriched doughs, for example, are usually mixed to a softer consistency than ordinary bread dough.

The temperature of the liquid is important: 40°C is warm enough to start fresh yeast fermenting quickly. The liquid will feel gently warm to the touch, but it is best to use a thermometer to test the temperature. Do not have the liquid warmer than 43°C, or it will start to kill the yeast. For dried yeast you can use hotter water – 1 part boiling water mixed with 2 parts cold water gives the correct temperature.

Salt

The flavour in bread is developed partly by salt, but salt also slows down the fermentation process, and too much can kill the yeast. Do not exceed the amount of salt recommended in the recipe you are using.

Salt should never come into direct contact with yeast as it withdraws all the yeast's natural moisture, which is why the salt is always mixed with the flour before the yeast mixture is added.

The usual proportion of salt to give the right amount of flavour to bread is 10 ml (2 teaspoons) to every 500 g flour. Enriched breads and sweet buns do not need as much, so always follow the amounts given in recipes.

Sugar

Traditionally, this was always creamed with the yeast in order to activate it. However, too much sugar can kill some of the yeast cells, which gives the bread a more yeasty taste than most people like, so be careful not to exceed the amount that is recommended in the recipe.

Some recipes now recommend that the yeast is creamed with liquid alone, and sugar is omitted completely.

Fat

Butter, margarine or lard rubbed into the flour in varying amounts enriches the dough, giving the bread a softer crumb and helping to keep it fresh.

Eggs

Added to enriched doughs, eggs give a richer colour and flavour, increase the food value, add to the lightness and prolong storage time.

Fruit

When adding dried fruits, such as sultanas or currants, to a dough, prepare well in advance by covering them with boiling water, leaving them to stand for about 1 hour. Then drain the fruit well and spread it on paper towels in a warm place to dry a little. The fruit will not only be plumper and juicier, but will also be much less likely to burn during the baking process.

MIXING THE DOUGH

Always work in a warm kitchen when using yeast. Make sure that the dry ingredients are at room temperature or a little above, the liquids warm to the touch, the mixing bowls warmed, and any baking tins and sheets warmed and lightly greased. Do not let any draughts of cold air reach the dough – especially when it starts to rise.

Basic method

To make dough for plain breads, sieve the flour and salt together, rub in the fat and pour in the yeast mixture and any remaining liquid. Mix the ingredients vigorously, first with a wooden spoon and then with the hands, until all the flour has been fully incorporated. This standard method is used with both fresh and dried yeast.

Ferment and dough method

This is a two-stage mixing process used in the making of high-quality enriched breads. Mix the yeast first with the combined liquids, some of the sugar, and a little of the flour.

Leave this mixture to ferment for up to 30 minutes. By the end of this time the yeast has become very active, and the rest of the flour, the enriching fat, sugar and fruit are added.

Kneading

This action develops the gluten in the flour, changing the soft, sticky mixture into a firm and springy dough that will hold a shape.

To knead the dough, put it on a lightly floured working surface, hold it in place with one hand and, with the other, take hold of part of the edge, stretch it away from you and then fold it back to the centre and push it down with the ball of the hand or a fist.

Turn the dough round a little and repeat the stretching, folding and pushing. Keep this up for 5-10 minutes.

The dough will then have a smooth, silky feel, an even texture and a firmly elastic consistency.

The dough hook of an electric mixer will knead the dough quickly. Use it at a low speed, following the manufacturer's instructions.

Storing surplus dough

If you have mixed and kneaded more dough than you want to bake, store the surplus, unrisen and well wrapped in plastic, in a refrigerator for up to 2 days.

Unrisen dough can also be deep-frozen satisfactorily for 3 months but will deteriorate after that. Divide the dough into the quantities needed for individual loaves, pack each portion in an oiled plastic bag and seal. Use a bag large enough to allow the dough to rise later. When the dough is needed, take a bag from the freezer, unseal it and then re-seal it loosely. Allow the bag of dough to rise overnight in the refrigerator, or give it 3-4 hours at normal room temperature. Knock back, shape and prove (see ensuing sections) in the usual way.

Rising

When the dough has been kneaded to an even, springy texture, it must be left to stand to give the yeast time to work. Cover the dough during rising, both to keep it warm and to prevent a hard skin from forming over it. Put the dough in a clean bowl and cover it with a sheet of lightly oiled plastic, plastic wrap or a slightly dampened cloth or tea towel.

If you like, you can put the dough inside an oiled plastic bag and fold the bag loosely, or put it in a lightly oiled plastic box with a lid. Use a large container, because the dough must rise until double in bulk. When it is ready, it will spring back if pressed lightly with a floured finger.

The time it takes for the dough to reach this condition and size will vary, depending on the temperature of the place where you put it to rise. It will take about 1 hour in a warm place such as the warming drawer of an oven or in the sun. At room temperature it will take 2 hours. In a cooler place it will take 4-6 hours, and if you put it in a refrigerator it will take about 12 hours.

Placing the dough in a refrigerator is useful if you want to cook fresh rolls for breakfast or coffee-time the next day. Allow the dough to come to room temperature before shaping, proving (final rising) and baking.

Knocking back

Risen dough contains pockets of gas unevenly distributed through it, and it will have become soft. It has to be restored to an even, springy texture. Turn it out of its bowl or other container on to a clean working surface.

The dough will no longer be sticky, so only a very little flour, if any, will be needed on the working surface. Too much flour on the dough at this stage could leave streaks in the bread and on the crust.

Knock out the gas pockets from the dough with the side of your hand or fist, then knead it quickly until it is smooth and firmly elastic again.

SHAPING

The dough is now ready for shaping. You can bake it in a loaf tin, in a round earthenware pot or on a flat baking sheet.

Divide or weigh off the dough into the number of pieces you require, then cover them with oiled plastic sheets or a dampened cloth and leave them for 5 minutes: this will make them easier to shape.

As you mould the dough to the required shape, stretch and pull it to give a smooth, tight outer skin over the top and sides, with the ends being tucked in underneath.

If the loaf is to be baked in a tin or pot, mould it to an appropriate shape, fit it into the warmed and greased container and cover it for the final rising.

You can of course make various traditional shapes instead of opting for a plain tin loaf.

Split tin loaf

When the shaped loaf has been rising in its tin for 25 minutes, make a cut 1,5 cm deep from end to end along the centre of the loaf with a very sharp blade. Put the loaf back to rise for a further 15 minutes before baking.

Vienna loaf

Mould the dough into a fat sausage shape, place it on a warm, greased baking sheet, cover it and put it to rise. After 25 minutes use a very sharp blade to make cuts diagonally along the loaf, 5 mm deep and 4 cm apart. Put the loaf back to rise for a further 15 minutes before baking.

Round loaf

Shape the dough into a smooth ball and place it on a warmed and greased baking sheet. Cover the loaf and put it to rise for 40 minutes.

French loaf

Shape the twice risen, well-kneaded dough into loaves as long as your baking tray (about 45 cm) or use special baking pans shaped for French loaves. With a sharp knife cut diagonal slashes about 1 cm deep at 5 cm intervals on top of the loaves. Dissolve 5 ml (1 teaspoon) salt in 125 ml (½ cup) water and brush the glaze on the loaves. Leave to rise until double in bulk. (Use 1 kg flour to yield 3 loaves.)

Bridge rolls

Divide the dough into 25-40 g pieces. Roll each piece under the slightly cupped palm of your hand to make a sausage shape with tapering ends. Place the rolls on a warmed and greased baking sheet, and put them to rise until they have doubled in size before baking.

Rolls

Divide the dough into pieces weighing 40-50 g. Roll each piece under the cupped palm of your hand until it forms a smooth, round ball. Place the rolls on a warmed and greased baking sheet, and put them to rise until they have doubled in size before baking.

Final rising or proving

Once the dough has been shaped, it must be left to rise again so that it will have a light, spongy texture. Cover it in the same way as for the first rising, so that a hard skin does not form over it. Put it in a warm place. The dough needs to rise for 30-40 minutes until it doubles in volume again.

During or at the end of the final rising, you can brush over the bread with one of several finishes to give the kind of crust you prefer.

For a soft crust, brush over the bread lightly with sunflower oil or dust it over lightly with flour. To give a crisp crust, dissolve 1 ml (¼ teaspoon) salt in 30 ml (2 tablespoons) water and brush the bread over lightly with the mixture. Brushing over with a mixture of milk and sugar will give a rich brown crust, and a light glaze of beaten egg or egg white will give a shiny finish.

If the bread is coated with a sticky glaze, such as beaten egg, part of the way through the final rising, leave it uncovered to finish rising, but make sure that it is in a warm place free of draughts.

Poppy or sesame seeds sprinkled over white bread before it is baked will give it a crunchy coating, and cracked wheat sprinkled over brown bread will produce the same effect.

BAKING

Bread must always be put into a hot oven in order to kill all the yeast. Bake at the temperature given in the recipe.

Rolls will take 15-20 minutes to bake, 500 g loaves about 35 minutes, and 1 kg loaves about 50 minutes. When the bread is ready, it will be well browned with its sides shrunken away from its container, and it will give a hollow sound if you tap it underneath with your knuckles.

If the underneath is not quite as crusty as you would like it, invert the loaf in its tin for a final 5 minutes' baking.

Remove cooked bread from its tin or baking sheet immediately you take it out of the oven. Put it on a wire rack to cool so that air can circulate round it. If the bread is left in the tin, it will go soggy round the edges. The bread must be completely cold before it is put in a bread bin.

GARLIC OR HERB BREAD

Slice a long French loaf or a shorter oval one almost completely through. Then spread the slices thickly with a herb* or garlic butter*. Spread some butter over the top of the bread.

Wrap the loaf in aluminium foil and bake it at 200°C for about 20 minutes, or until it is piping hot. Then open the foil and bake the bread for a further 5-10 minutes to ensure that it becomes golden and crusty.

MELBA TOAST

Slice bread thinly – about 5 mm thick – and dry out the slices slowly in the oven at 160°C until golden and crisp.

To make small Melba toasts for cocktail snacks, use slices of French bread.

The bread will be easier to slice if it is slightly stale.

CAKES

The dividing line between bread and cake is hard to draw. Cakes today are distinguished by the large amount of sugar in them, by the high fat content, which gives them a rich, melting texture, and by the fact that they are raised by eggs instead of yeast.

INGREDIENTS FOR CAKE-MAKING

Flour

Recipes for cakes use cake flour mixed with baking powder or sometimes self-raising flour. In this book, when the ingredients list simply 'flour', cake flour is referred to.

Keep the flour in the packet in which you bought it, remembering to mark on it the date of purchase. Store the flour in a cool, dry cupboard or put it, still in its packet, in a stoneware jar or other special flour container.

Cake flour will keep unopened for 9 months in these conditions, and for 3 months once it has been opened. Self-raising flour will keep for 6 months unopened, and for 2 months opened.

Use up one batch of flour before you open the next, and, when storing, do not mix new flour with old.

Fat

This can be butter (either salted or unsalted), margarine, lard, vegetable fat or oil. Sometimes a mixture of fats is used. Butter gives the best flavour, especially to a sponge without strong flavourings added, but many people prefer to use margarine for reasons of economy and health.

Remember to take the fat out of the refrigerator well before you want to use it. You can mix the cake much more quickly with fat that has softened at room temperature.

Sugar

If a recipe recommends castor sugar, try to use this whenever possible, and do not be too ready to substitute granulated sugar, which is more difficult to cream thoroughly. It produces a cake of a coarser texture, and can give a spotty appearance to the surface of the baked cake. If you have no castor sugar, you can grind granulated sugar in a blender or food processor for a few seconds to give it a finer texture.

Eggs

These must be fresh to give the cake good flavour and lightness. Break each egg into a cup and add it to the mixture before you break open the next. This avoids all danger of adding a stale egg to your cake mixture or to the other eggs.

Make sure that you bring the eggs into the warm kitchen well before you make your cake. An egg that is much colder than the ingredients to which you add it will make the mixture curdle. Sometimes a creamed cake mixture curdles when eggs are added too quickly. You can avoid this by beating into the mixture, with each egg, 5 ml (1 teaspoon) of the flour that has been weighed out for the cake; or you can remedy curdling that has already occurred by stirring 5-10 ml (1-2 teaspoons) of flour from the weighed ingredients into the cake mixture.

Milk

Measure out milk carefully where a recipe gives an exact amount. Do not exceed the amount recommended, as too much milk can make a cake heavy. If you are short of milk, use a mixture of milk and water, which will give just as satisfactory a result.

Dried fruit

Currants, raisins and sultanas often need washing to make them clean enough to add to a cake. Weigh out the amount you need into a colander or sieve and pour plenty of boiling water through the fruit. Shake off as much water as you can, and dry the fruit well on paper towels or a tea towel. Leave the fruit to become completely cold before adding it to the cake. Warm, wet fruit will produce a heavy cake.

Rinse and dry glacé cherries, crystallised fruit and candied peel in the same way to remove excess sugar. If the fruit is too sugary, it will sink to the bottom of the cake. Cherries are less likely to sink if you halve or quarter large ones and roll in a little flour before adding them to a cake mixture.

Raising agents

Self-raising flour already contains the required amount of raising agent. Raising agents that you add during mixing a cake include:

Air This is the principal raising agent in a cake. It is introduced into the mixture by sieving the flour, by creaming the fat and sugar together until light, and by beating in whole eggs or whisked egg whites. The air incorporated in the mixture expands during baking to give the cake an airy, spongy texture.

Baking powder This must be measured exactly. Too much of it will make small cakes and biscuits dry. Too much in a large cake will give it a flat taste. Baking powder should be sieved thoroughly with the flour.

Cream of tartar and bicarbonate of soda These must be mixed very thoroughly into the flour in the amounts specified in your recipe. It is usual to use 2 parts cream of tartar to 1 part bicarbonate of soda. Take care to keep to these proportions. Too much soda, for example, gives a soapy taste and dark colour.

Buttermilk, or sour milk, with bicarbonate of soda An old-fashioned combination rarely used today.

Vinegar or lemon juice, mixed with bicarbonate of soda This was an economical raising mixture used a great deal in Europe during World War 2 to replace eggs in a cake mixture.

Different Types of Cake Mixture

Creamed mixtures

These are based on a mixture of equal quantities of fat and sugar. Use a wooden spoon to work the fat and sugar together until combined, then beat vigorously until the mixture becomes pale and fluffy.

The beating is easier if the mixing bowl and the fat are at room temperature, but on no account allow the fat to become oily as this would produce a heavy cake. A hand-held or other electric mixer will cream the mixture quickly and thoroughly.

Eggs, flour and flavouring are added to the creamed mixture. The amounts vary according to whether the cake is a light sponge type with an open, airy texture, or a closer, more substantial cake, perhaps rich with fruit.

With some modern, soft fats, there is no need for a separate creaming stage. All the ingredients are put in a mixing bowl together and beaten until thoroughly combined. This quick and easy method is not suitable for all cakes, however, so use it only when it is recommended in the recipe.

Melted-fat mixtures

This method is used mostly for cakes containing syrup or treacle. Heat the fat gently with the sweetening ingredients before adding it to the dry ingredients. Mix the fat and sweetening together thoroughly as they melt, and take care not to let the mixture come to the boil.

Sieve the flour and raising agent thoroughly together, and combine them carefully with the melted ingredients to make sure that no lumps form in the mixture. The amount of fat used is generally half, or less than half, the amount of flour.

Rubbed-in mixtures

This method is used for very plain mixtures, such as scones. The amount of fat used is half, or less than half, the amount of flour. Sieve the flour, salt and raising agent together well before adding the fat.

Then rub in the fat thoroughly with the fingertips until it is completely blended and the mixture resembles breadcrumbs.

Mix in any other dry ingredients that are required, such as sugar, spices or dried fruit, at this stage, and then finally stir in enough liquid to bind the mixture satisfactorily together.

Whisked mixtures

Sponges are the cakes most commonly made by this method. A true sponge consists only of eggs, sugar and flour. For its light, spongy texture, it depends on the air beaten into the eggs. The eggs and sugar should be beaten together with a wire whisk until they form a pale, thick mixture.

When this has become thick enough, a ribbon of the mixture that is trailed from the whisk over the surface will lie there for a few seconds before it starts sinking in.

To speed up the whisking process, place the mixing bowl over a pan of hot, but not boiling, water while you beat the mixture. You can use a hand-held or other electric mixer to whisk the mixture quickly.

When the eggs and sugar have been properly whisked, gently fold in the sifted flour with a metal spoon until it has been completely incorporated. Beating or roughly mixing in the flour would drive out much of the air that the whisking process has introduced and will tend to spoil the light, fluffy texture of the cake. Use a metal spoon to fold in the flour; this implement cuts through the whisked mixture with the least amount of disturbance.

Baking Cakes

Always prepare the cake tins you need before starting to mix the cake. Many cake mixtures must be put in the oven as soon as they are mixed, and will be spoiled if they are kept waiting while a tin is lined.

If you are using non-stick baking ware, you should follow the manufacturer's instructions for preparing the tins for baking.

Brush over other tins with a pastry brush dipped in sunflower oil, or rub them over lightly with a little butter or margarine on a piece of grease-proof paper. Another method is to coat the tin with a non-stick cooking spray.

Rich cakes or delicate mixtures should be put into lined tins. For lining, use grease-proof paper, aluminium foil rubbed over with sunflower oil or butter, or a non-stick baking paper. Lining a tin helps prevent burning during cooking.

To line a square or oblong tin, cut a square or oblong sheet of paper large enough to cover the base and sides of the tin. Make a cut from each corner of the paper towards the centre, and fit the paper into the tin, overlapping the cut edges at the corners.

To line a round tin, cut a circle of paper to fit the base and a long strip to go all round the side but slightly deeper than the tin. Make small cuts along the bottom edge of the strip so that when it is fitted into the tin, the cut edges lie neatly on the base of the tin. Lay the cut-out circle of paper over the base, covering the cut flap.

Baking Tips to Bear in Mind

1 Set out all the ingredients and utensils that you will be needing before you actually start mixing.
2 Prepare the cake tins before you start mixing.
3 Switch on the oven at the required temperature and arrange the shelves where you will need them.
4 Measure the ingredients accurately.
5 Do not beat a cake or mix it too much after you have added the flour, or the cake will be heavy.
6 If you are making fruit cake, add the fruit last if possible. It is a good idea to dust the fruit with a little of the weighed flour so that it does not form lumps.
7 When you are making a cake in sandwich tins, divide the mixture as equally as you can between the baking tins so that the cake layers will all be ready together.
8 Avoid opening the oven door while the cake is baking.

Give any cake that requires long baking, such as a rich fruit cake, extra protection by tying a double layer of thick brown paper round the outside of the tin, or fitting a double layer of brown paper between the tin and the lining paper. This prevents the formation of a dry, heavy crust during the long baking.

To give a crisp coating to sponge cakes, dredge the greased tin with 5 ml (1 teaspoon) castor sugar mixed with 5 ml (1 teaspoon) flour. Toss the mixture round the tin to coat all the greased surface, then tip out the surplus.

When the cake mixture is ready, pour it or scoop it into the prepared tin, or into paper baking cases if you are making small cakes. Smooth the top of the mixture, and make a slight depression with the back of a spoon in the centre of a large cake. This will level out as the cake bakes; it prevents the cake from rising to a peak.

Small cakes are usually baked near the top of the oven, but place large cakes in the middle of the oven, where they are less likely to brown too quickly. If a cake is browning too much before it is due out of the oven, cover it lightly with a square of grease-proof paper or aluminium foil. This will prevent further browning.

Do not open the oven door unneccessarily while your cake is baking. An inrush of cold air can check the rising of the cake, or cause it to rise unevenly. If you have to open the oven, do it slowly and close the oven door gently afterwards.

To test whether small cakes or sponges are ready, press the centre very lightly with a fingertip. If the cake springs back after your touch, it is cooked.

To test whether a large, rich cake is ready, run a warmed, bright-metal skewer into the centre of the cake. If it comes out clean, the cake is cooked. Large, rich cakes also shrink from the sides of the tin when cooked.

Cooling and storing

When the cake is baked enough, take the tin from the oven and leave the cake in it for 5-10 minutes. Then remove the cake from the tin and stand it on a cake rack in a draught-free place to cool. The paper that is used to line the tin should be left on until the cake has cooled.

The one exception to these rules is a Swiss roll, which must be taken from the oven and immediately turned from its tin on to sugared paper laid on a damp tea towel. Peel away the paper that lined the baking tin, trim the edges off the sponge, and roll it up while it is still warm. When it is cold, unroll it, spread on the filling and roll it up again.

When the cake is cold, store it in an airtight tin. Large, rich cakes that need to mature can be wrapped in aluminium foil before being put in a tin.

THE ALTITUDE FACTOR

The success of one's baking efforts can be affected by a number of factors – one of them being altitude. The further one lives above sea level, the greater the adjustments to the recipe.

If you live at about 1 000 metres above sea level (for example, the Karoo) decrease each teaspoon (5 ml) baking powder by ½ ml and increase each cup liquid (250 ml) by 20 ml.

If you live at an altitude of about 1 600 metres (for example, the Transvaal Highveld and Orange Free State), decrease each teaspoon (5 ml) baking powder by 1 ml and increase each cup (250 ml) liquid by 35 ml.

If you live at about 2 300 metres (for example, Lesotho and the Drakensberg), the adjustments required are much more extensive: decrease each teaspoon (5 ml) baking powder by 2 ml; increase each cup (250 ml) liquid by 50 ml; decrease each cup (250 ml) sugar by 20 ml; decrease each cup (250 ml) shortening (butter, lard or fat) by 20 ml; for sponge cakes add ½ an egg for every 4 eggs used; for rich fruit cakes increase the temperature by 5 per cent and decrease the baking time by 20 per cent.

BISCUITS

Some of the earliest biscuits were what we would call rusks, being twice-cooked bread – hence their name, which comes from the French *bis cuit* ('twice cooked'). Biscuits of the Middle Ages were always cooked twice; the second cooking was to dry them out thoroughly.

MAKING BISCUITS

A true biscuit makes a decided snapping noise when it is broken in half. Many so-called biscuit recipes make a softer product, which is a cookie rather than a true biscuit.

Use fresh ingredients to give your biscuits the best flavour. Biscuit dough is much firmer than that used for cakes – more the consistency of pastry. It may be made by the rubbing-in, creaming or melted-fat methods.

Some biscuits are shaped into small walnut-sized pieces with the hands. Others are stamped out with pastry cutters from a rolled-out sheet of dough or cut from a 'sausage' of dough.

In hot weather, a biscuit mixture containing a high proportion of fat to flour may be too soft to handle easily. Wrap it in grease-proof paper and leave it in the refrigerator for 10-20 minutes to make it easier to roll out or shape.

Roll dough to an even thickness, and stamp out biscuits of equal size that will all bake in the same time.

Bake the biscuits in the centre of the oven, as this helps to give them even baking and colouring. If you want to bake 2 trays of biscuits at once, put one tray on the shelf above the other and, halfway through the baking time, change over the trays. You may also need to give each tray a quarter-turn if the biscuits at one side are browning faster than the rest.

When the biscuits are cooked, take them from the oven, leaving them on the baking tray to cool a little before moving them to a wire rack to cool completely. Do not put them away in a tin or box until they are cold.

Never store biscuits in the same tin as a cake or they will absorb moisture from the cake and lose their crispness. Biscuits are never as crisp again as when they are freshly baked, but they will keep fairly well for a few days in a tin or box with a tightly fitting lid.

ICING

As well as giving an attractive finish, many icings are of practical use. On cakes they help to prevent drying out, and on rather bland sweet breads and biscuits they add extra flavour.

Tint them delicately with food colouring if you wish, and flavour them to taste with, for example, vanilla, coffee, chocolate or orange.

Butter icing or butter cream

This icing is suitable for light cakes, such as sponge*, chocolate*, coffee or orange cakes.

PREPARATION TIME: 10 MINUTES

INGREDIENTS TO YIELD 400 G, OR TO COVER THE TOP AND SIDES OF A 20 CM CAKE

125 g butter, softened (but not oily)
250 g icing sugar, sifted
15 ml (1 tablespoon) milk
Flavouring

Beat the butter until it is pale, then gradually beat in the sifted icing sugar until the mixture has become fluffy. Add the milk (in order to make it easier to spread) and then work in a little flavouring.

Fondant icing

Use fondant for glazing petits fours* or light fruit cakes such as Dundee cake* or cherry cake*.

This icing may also be used to fill chocolates, poured into moulds to make sweets, or used as a syrup glaze into which you dip cherries or strawberries to make friandises.

PREPARATION TIME: 45 MINUTES
COOKING TIME: 15 MINUTES
STANDING TIME: 24 HOURS

INGREDIENTS TO YIELD 500 G, OR TO COVER THE TOP AND SIDES OF A 20 CM CAKE

500 g sugar
250 ml (1 cup) water
60 ml (¼ cup) liquid glucose (obtainable at pharmacies), or a pinch of cream of tartar dissolved in 5 ml (1 teaspoon) water
Flavouring and/or colouring

Heat the sugar and water in a large, heavy-based saucepan until the sugar dissolves. Add the liquid glucose or cream of tartar.

Bring the mixture to the boil and boil it rapidly without stirring until it reaches the soft-ball stage* (115 °C). (If sugar crystals form on the sides of the saucepan while boiling, wash them down with a pastry brush dipped in water.) Remove the saucepan at once from the heat.

Allow the bubbles to subside and, from a height of about 40 cm, pour the mixture slowly on to a dampened tray or a marble slab. Do not scrape the excess from the saucepan. Let the mixture cool, at least until it holds a fingerprint momentarily.

With a sugar scraper (or a paint-removing tool, metal spatula or wooden spoon) lift and fold the mixture over on itself, always from the edges towards the centre. Repeat the process, working the fondant vigorously, until it becomes opaque. It will do this suddenly and may become hard to handle. If it does, invert a bowl over it for a few minutes; the humidity will soften it. Now work small pieces at a time with your hands, until the fondant becomes smooth. Dust your hands with icing sugar if necessary. Pack the pieces into an airtight container and store in a cool place for at least 24 hours before using.

When needed, heat the required amount over hot water in a double boiler, beating it constantly until it melts. Add the desired flavouring or colouring, then spread it at once, since this icing tends to harden rapidly. If it does harden, the icing will need re-heating. Alternatively, you may add a few drops of boiling water to make it easier to handle.

To ice a cake, place it on a rack with a plate below. Cover the cake with the icing, and re-use any icing that may drip on to the plate.

Easy fondant

This icing will be suitable for all the applications that have been described under fondant icing.

PREPARATION TIME: 20 MINUTES

INGREDIENTS TO YIELD 600 G, OR TO COVER THE TOP AND SIDES OF A 23 CM CAKE

500 g icing sugar
60 ml (¼ cup) liquid glucose
1 egg white
Flavouring and/or colouring

Sieve the icing sugar into a bowl. Make a well in the centre and add the glucose, egg white and flavouring. (If the glucose is stiff, melt it slowly over hot water.) Beat the mixture, drawing the icing sugar into the centre until the mass is a stiff paste.

Turn on to a board which has been lightly dusted with icing sugar and knead it into a smooth mixture. If you are adding colouring, mix a little into the paste when starting to knead the mixture.

When smooth, heat the fondant over hot water in a double boiler, beating it constantly until it melts. Use it at once, as it hardens rapidly. If it does harden, either re-heat it or add a few drops of boiling water to make it easier to handle. Use in the same way as you would ordinary fondant.

VARIATION Another way of using this fondant to ice a cake is as follows: after kneading the fondant until it is smooth, roll out the icing thinly into a circle large enough to cover the cake. Wrap it around the rolling pin, then unroll over the cake. Mould the icing with your hands so that it covers the cake smoothly and snugly. Neaten the edge with a sharp knife.

Frosting

This icing is best used with flavoured, light cakes, such as chocolate*, lemon*, orange or coffee cakes.

PREPARATION TIME: 10 MINUTES
COOKING TIME: 15 MINUTES

INGREDIENTS TO YIELD ABOUT 300G, OR TO COVER THE TOP AND SIDES OF A 20 CM CAKE

250g castor sugar
60ml (¼ cup) water
1ml (¼ teaspoon) cream of tartar dissolved in 5ml (1 teaspoon) water
1 egg white
Flavouring

Put the sugar and water in a heavy-based pan, and place the pan over a low heat. Allow the sugar to dissolve without stirring. Add the cream of tartar to the sugar syrup.

Bring the mixture to the boil, then boil without stirring until it reaches the soft-ball stage* (116°C). Just before the syrup is ready, whisk the egg white in a large, heatproof bowl until it has become stiff.

Remove the syrup from the heat and allow the bubbles to subside. Pour the syrup in a thin stream into the egg white, whisking all the time. Whisk until opaque, then mix in the flavouring. Allow to cool slightly before using.

Fudge icing

Suitable for firm cakes, this particular icing may be used for coffee, mocha or chocolate* cakes.

PREPARATION TIME: 15 MINUTES
COOLING TIME: 30 MINUTES
COOKING TIME: 30 MINUTES

INGREDIENTS TO COVER THE TOP AND SIDES OF A 23 CM CAKE

500g castor sugar
300ml water
50g unsalted butter
30ml (2 tablespoons) golden syrup
Flavouring

Put all the recipe ingredients in a saucepan and stir over a gentle heat (without boiling) until the castor sugar has completely dissolved.

Then bring the icing mixture to the boil, and boil until it reaches the soft-ball stage* (117°C).

Remove the saucepan from the heat and leave the mixture to cool. Add the flavouring and then beat with a wooden spoon until it is thick. Use immediately since the icing sets fairly quickly.

Basic glacé icing

Use this icing for any of the following: cherry cake*, nut cake, light fruit cake, éclairs* or cupcakes.

PREPARATION TIME: 10 MINUTES
COOKING TIME: 10 MINUTES

INGREDIENTS TO COVER THE TOP AND SIDES OF A 23 CM CAKE, OR TO GLAZE 12 ÉCLAIRS

140g icing sugar
15-30ml (1-2 tablespoons) water

Sieve the icing sugar into a stainless steel saucepan. Add 15ml (1 tablespoon) of the water. Stir over medium heat and cook until the icing is soft and will coat the back of a wooden spoon (add a bit more water if necessary – not too much since it must not be too runny). Allow to cool slightly before pouring it over the cake or éclairs.

VARIATIONS Melt about 150g unsweetened chocolate with a very little water until it is smooth. Flavour glacé icing with 3ml (¾ teaspoon) vanilla essence. Mix this with the melted chocolate, beating it well, then use it immediately.

Alternatively, sieve 20ml (4 teaspoons) cocoa with the icing sugar and proceed as for basic glacé icing.

Royal icing

Royal icing is suitable for icing elaborate birthday and wedding cakes. It can be used for tube work and flower making.

PREPARATION TIME: 20 MINUTES

INGREDIENTS TO YIELD 250G, OR TO COVER THE TOP AND SIDES OF A 25 CM CAKE

200-250g icing sugar
1 egg white (at room temperature)
A few drops of acetic acid (vinegar) or a squeeze of lemon juice
Colouring and/or flavouring

Sieve the icing sugar twice. Place the egg white and the acetic acid or lemon juice in a bowl and beat gently with a fork. Add the icing sugar gradually until the texture of the mixture is as required (see below). Beat well.

For latticing or lettering, pull a spoon or spatula through the icing – if the peak that forms is soft, the texture is correct. For flower-making, scrollwork or basket-weaving, the peak must stand quite stiffly. The few drops of lemon juice will keep the icing pliable. Add colouring and/or flavouring as desired.

VARIATION If you require a larger quantity, increase the amount of egg white and add icing sugar accordingly.

Honey butter frosting

This delicious frosting can be used to cover a Victoria sponge*, a light honey cake, nut cake or lemon* cake.

PREPARATION TIME: 15 MINUTES

INGREDIENTS TO COVER THE TOP AND SIDES OF A 22 CM CAKE

90g butter
170g icing sugar, sifted
15ml (1 tablespoon) honey
15ml (1 tablespoon) lemon juice

Beat the butter until soft and then gradually beat in half the icing sugar. Beat in the honey and lemon juice and then the rest of the icing sugar.

POINTS TO WATCH WHEN ICING

1 Do not ice a cake until it is cold, or the icing will melt and run off.
2 Brush off any loose crumbs.
3 Ideally, the surface to be iced should be flat. If it is a large cake, trim the top to level it, or turn the cake upside down and ice the base.
4 For delicate-textured cakes, such as sponges, use icing of a very soft consistency that will spread without pulling lumps out of the cake.
5 If cakes or biscuits are to be sandwiched with a filling as well as iced, put the filling in first.
6 To coat a cake with soft icing, stand the cake on a wire rack with a large plate beneath the rack. Pour the icing over the cake and let it find its own level. As it trickles down the sides, spread it with a palette knife to cover the sides completely (it is easier if you warm the knife by dipping it into hot water from time to time).
7 To coat a cake with butter icing, stand the cake on a flat board or alternatively a large, upturned plate. Using a round-bladed knife, coat the sides of the cake first, spreading the icing as evenly as possible. Pile the rest of the icing on the cake and spread it to the edges. Mark a pattern on it with a fork, knife or confectioner's comb.

Making a Five-Strand Plaited Loaf

Divide the dough into 5 equal pieces and roll each into a long strand no more than 1,5 cm thick. Moisten one end of each strand with water, stick all the moist ends together and spread the strands slightly apart, like the fingers on a hand. Think of the strands as numbered 1-5 from one side to the other and, each time a strand is moved, re-number it according to the position it now occupies.

Lift strand 2 over 3, strand 5 over 2, and then strand 1 over 3.

Repeat the numerical sequence, again and again, until you reach the ends of the strands.

Moisten these ends very slightly with water and seal them together.

Crusty White Bread

A TRADITIONAL WHITE loaf, this bread is full of flavour and character and is ideal for sandwiches, toast or snacks.

PREPARATION TIME: 25-35 MINUTES
RISING TIME: 3¾ HOURS
COOKING TIME: 45 MINUTES
PRE-HEAT OVEN TO 220°C

INGREDIENTS FOR 2 SANDWICH LOAVES, 4 FRENCH LOAVES, OR 20 ROLLS
750 g white bread flour
10 ml (2 teaspoons) salt
25 g butter
15 ml (1 tablespoon) dried yeast, or 25 g fresh yeast
5 ml (1 teaspoon) sugar
450 ml warm water

Sieve the flour and salt into a mixing bowl. Rub in the butter. Mix the yeast, sugar and 45 ml (3 tablespoons) of the warm water and allow to stand for 10-15 minutes, or until the mixture becomes frothy. Add this to the flour with the rest of the warm water, and blend well.

Knead well for 5-10 minutes to make a stiff, springy dough. Shape the dough into a ball. Put it back into the clean bowl, cover it with plastic wrap or a clean towel and leave in a warm place to rise for about 2 hours.

Turn out the dough and knead it again until it is smooth. Re-shape it into a ball, put it back into the bowl, cover and leave to rise again for 1 hour.

Shape the dough to fit into 2 loaf tins, each having a capacity of 1 litre. Cover these with a sheet of greased plastic and leave them to rise in a warm place for 45 minutes. Bake for 45 minutes.

VARIATIONS For French loaves, divide the dough into 4 pieces. Shape them into 4 rolls or sticks as long as your baking tray. Make diagonal slashes about 5 mm deep at 5 cm intervals on top of the loaves. Brush them with 15 ml (1 tablespoon) salt dissolved in 100 ml water and bake at 190°C for about 30 minutes.

For rolls, shape the dough into twists, crescents, rounds or whatever shape you like. Brush them gently with beaten egg and sprinkle some with poppy or sesame seeds, then bake them at 180°C for 20 minutes.

Milk Bread

A BEAUTIFULLY QUICK bread to make, white, fine and very light-textured, milk bread is delicious buttered and served with cheese or pâté.

PREPARATION TIME: 30 MINUTES
RISING TIME: 40 MINUTES
COOKING TIME: 40-45 MINUTES
PRE-HEAT OVEN TO 180°C

INGREDIENTS FOR 1 LARGE LOAF
400 g flour
5 ml (1 teaspoon) salt
225 ml warm milk
15 ml (1 tablespoon) dried yeast, or 25 g fresh yeast
15 ml (1 tablespoon) sugar
1 large egg, beaten
15 ml (1 tablespoon) sunflower oil

Sieve the flour and salt into a mixing bowl. Stir 60 ml (¼ cup) of the warm milk into the yeast with the sugar and allow to stand for 10 minutes, or until it is frothy.

Stir the activated yeast into the flour with the remaining milk, the egg and the oil. Beat well for 4-5 minutes and shape the dough into a sausage. Place in a 1 litre greased loaf tin. Cover with a sheet of greased plastic and leave in a warm place for the dough to rise – about 40 minutes. Bake for 40-45 minutes, or until crisp.

VARIATIONS To make this a herb bread, add 5 ml (1 teaspoon) dried mixed herbs to the dough and, just before baking, sprinkle the loaf with fennel seeds.

For a cheese loaf, add 250 ml (1 cup) grated mature Cheddar to the dough and sprinkle with more grated cheese halfway through baking.

For a fruit loaf, add 100 g seedless raisins to the dough. When baked, brush with a sugar glaze consisting of 30 ml (2 tablespoons) milk mixed with 30 ml (2 tablespoons) castor sugar.

Since milk bread makes very good toast, bake it under a tin to give slices a neat shape suitable for toasting. Put the dough into the tin in the normal way and allow it to rise in a warm place until it is just below the top of the tin. Place a greased and warmed baking sheet over the tin, then carefully turn the baking sheet and tin over together. Allow the dough to rise for another 5 minutes before baking. Bake with the baking sheet under the tin in the pre-heated oven for 30-35 minutes.

You can also use milk bread dough to make a plaited loaf*.

If you like, sprinkle poppy seeds liberally on the loaf to give a deliciously nutty flavour.

Soda Bread

THIS IS AN IRISH speciality which, years ago, would have been cooked over a peat fire in a shallow iron cooking pot. It is not a loaf for keeping, as it is made without yeast, rather like a scone mixture. Nevertheless, it is delicious sliced straight from the oven and topped with butter and honey or cheese.

PREPARATION TIME: 15 MINUTES
COOKING TIME: 30 MINUTES
PRE-HEAT OVEN TO 200°C

INGREDIENTS FOR 1 LOAF
250 g wholewheat flour
250 g cake flour
5 ml (1 teaspoon) salt
10 ml (2 teaspoons) bicarbonate of soda
50 g butter
10 ml (2 teaspoons) sugar (optional)
250-375 ml (1-1½ cups) buttermilk, or fresh milk stirred with 15 ml (1 tablespoon) cream of tartar

Stir the flours, salt and bicarbonate of soda together in a mixing bowl. Rub in the butter until the mixture resembles fine crumbs. Stir in the sugar (if used) and then enough buttermilk or milk mixture to make a soft dough. Turn the dough on to a floured board and shape it into a round loaf 5-7 cm thick.

Transfer the loaf to a baking sheet and cut a large, deep cross on top. Bake for about 30 minutes until the bread sounds hollow when tapped on the bottom.

For a crusty finish, cool the loaf on a wire rack, or, for a softer crust, wrap the loaf in a clean tea towel to cool.

VARIATIONS Add a handful of currants to the basic dough.

Use 500 g cake flour, omitting the wholewheat flour.

BREADS, CAKES AND BISCUITS

BROWN BREAD

PEOPLE HAVE BEEN making bread for well over 8 000 years. By the Roman period, eating white bread carried social distinction, and the rougher, darker kinds were left for the poorer classes. It was not until recently that doctors and dieticians started to value and recommend the natural bran that brown bread flour retains.

PREPARATION TIME: 25 MINUTES
RISING TIME: 1 HOUR 35 MINUTES
COOKING TIME: 35-40 MINUTES
PRE-HEAT OVEN TO 230°C

INGREDIENTS FOR 1 LARGE LOAF
450 g brown bread flour
7 ml (1½ teaspoons) salt
15 ml (1 tablespoon) sunflower oil
5 ml (1 teaspoon) brown sugar
350 ml warm water
10 ml (2 teaspoons) dried yeast, or 15 g fresh yeast
Brown bread flour for sprinkling

Mix the flour and salt together on a working surface or in a large mixing bowl. Rub in the oil and make a well in the centre.

Dissolve the sugar in the water. If using dried yeast, dissolve it in 150 ml of the sugar water. Mix fresh yeast to a paste with 30 ml (2 tablespoons) of the sugar water. Allow the yeast to stand for 10 minutes, or until frothy. Add the rest of the sugar water and pour into the well.

Mix vigorously to blend in the flour, then knead for 5 minutes to make a smooth, elastic dough. Shape it into a ball and put in a warm, greased bowl. Cover with a sheet of greased plastic and set in a warm place to rise for 1 hour.

Turn out the risen dough on to a working surface and knock out any air. Mould the dough into a ball and put it on a warmed, greased baking sheet. Cover with the plastic and put back to rise in a warm place for 35 minutes, cutting a cross in it 1,5 cm deep with a sharp blade after 20 minutes and sprinkling with flour. Bake in the pre-heated oven for 35-40 minutes.

VARIATION To make brown bread rolls, shape pieces of dough into rolls and place on a buttered baking sheet. Allow to rise in a warm place for 15 minutes. Bake in a 200°C oven for about 20-25 minutes.

WHOLEWHEAT BREAD *Easy to make and packed with goodness.*

WHOLEWHEAT BREAD

THIS NO-KNEAD BREAD is very easy to make and very wholesome. A thick slice of it, freshly baked, buttered and topped with cheese, is a meal on its own.

PREPARATION TIME: 15 MINUTES
RISING TIME: 1 HOUR
COOKING TIME: 1-1¼ HOURS
PRE-HEAT OVEN TO 200°C

INGREDIENTS FOR 1 LOAF
15 ml (1 tablespoon) dried yeast or 25 g fresh yeast
625 ml (2½ cups) warm water
15 ml (1 tablespoon) honey
500 g wholewheat flour
15 ml (1 tablespoon) sunflower oil
10 ml (2 teaspoons) salt

Dissolve the yeast in 125 ml (½ cup) of the warm water. Stir in the honey and allow this mixture to stand for about 10 minutes, or until it is frothy.

Place the flour in a large bowl. Stir in the oil, salt and dissolved yeast. Add the remaining warm water and mix well together. Spoon into a well-oiled 24 cm x 12 cm loaf tin.

Cover the tin with plastic wrap and a tea towel and place it in a warm place for about 1 hour, or until the bread has risen to the top of the tin.

Bake for 1 hour, or until browned. Turn out the bread on to a baking sheet and return it to the switched-off oven for 15 minutes to ensure that it is baked through.

Leave the loaf to cool on a wire rack. For a softer crust, cover the loaf with a tea towel while cooling.

VARIATIONS Substitute 250 ml (1 cup) rolled oats for 130 g of the flour.

Use 190 ml (¾ cup) seeds – a mixture of sunflower, sesame and linseeds – instead of the equivalent amount of flour. Sprinkle the top of the bread with poppy seeds before baking.

OATMEAL BREAD

A PLEASANT NUTTY TASTE and chewy texture are given to this bread by the oatmeal – an unusual ingredient in bread these days but one that was quite extensively used in past centuries by English and Scottish bakers.

The recipe given here has been adapted from that used for many years by a family in Lancashire, England. They called it monastery bread.

PREPARATION TIME: 30 MINUTES
RISING TIME: 1¾ HOURS
COOKING TIME: 1 HOUR
PRE-HEAT OVEN TO 235°C

INGREDIENTS FOR 1 LOAF
125 g fine oatmeal
350 g wholewheat flour
125 g white bread or cake flour
7 ml (1½ teaspoons) salt
7 ml (1½ teaspoons) brown sugar
15 ml (1 tablespoon) dried yeast, or 25 g fresh yeast
About 450 ml warm water
Fine oatmeal for coating

Mix together the oatmeal, wholewheat flour, white flour and salt on a working surface or in a large mixing bowl. Make a well in the centre. Whisk together the sugar, yeast and 300 ml of the water and allow to stand for about 10 minutes, or until it has become frothy.

Pour the yeast mixture into the well. Draw in the flour gradually and mix well together, adding more of the water to work up a dough. Knead the dough well, then shape into a ball and put in a warmed and greased bowl.

Cover with a sheet of greased plastic and set in a warm place to rise for 45 minutes. Turn out the dough on to a working surface and knock out all the bubbles. Knead into a ball again, put back into the bowl, cover with the plastic and put back to rise for a further 15 minutes.

Turn out the risen dough on to a working surface and mould it to fit a warmed and greased 23 cm x 14 cm loaf tin. Roll the shaped dough in oatmeal before putting it in the tin.

Cover the tin with the greased plastic and put in a warm place to rise for 45 minutes. Bake in the pre-heated oven for 45 minutes-1 hour.

297

Sandwiches and School Lunches

A good packed lunch should include a protein, a hearty sandwich, a fruit or raw vegetable and a drink. School lunches can be made fun as well as wholesome. Add a surprise – a small packet of nuts and raisins, a container of fresh fruit salad or a home-baked biscuit. Use suitably sized airtight containers.

For the protein Pack in one of the following: a crumbed chicken drumstick*; a hard-boiled egg*; a stuffed egg*; a Scotch egg*; a fish croquette*; or a wedge of cheese. Alternatively, include the protein in the sandwich.

For the sandwich Use wholewheat bread* or try a compromise of one slice white and one slice brown.

For the filling
Layer thin slices of meat or chicken and lettuce between bread slices spread with mayonnaise* and a little mild mustard.

Mix flaked tuna with mayonnaise* and a squeeze of lemon juice. Add lettuce to the sandwich.

Mix flaked smoked snoek with savoury cottage cheese. Add lettuce to the sandwich.

Chopped hard-boiled egg* is tasty mixed with mayonnaise*. Use the filling with lettuce.

Peanut butter is appetising and rich in protein.

Spread bread with mayonnaise* and chutney for extra flavour. Sandwich together with slices of cheese and lettuce.

Savoury cottage cheese combines well with sliced tomato and cucumber.

Mix cream cheese with chopped dried apricots or dates and nuts.

Mashed avocado mixed with savoury cottage cheese, or slices of avocado brushed with lemon juice plus lettuce and tomato, make a tasty change.

For the drink
Freeze a small bottle of milk or fruit juice or water (only three-quarters full, to allow for expansion). When packed with a lunch it will still be refreshingly cold at break time.

For cold weather, fill a small thermos flask with warm milk and honey or tea, or a nourishing winter soup.

Rye Bread

CENTURIES AGO in central Europe, rye bread was considered rough peasant food. Nowadays it has become a speciality bread and its firm texture and very distinctive flavour make it ideal for open sandwiches.

There is a wide variety of rye breads, from the darkest pumpernickel to light ryes. The higher the proportion of rye flour used, the closer the texture of the loaf.

Traditionally, rye bread is made with a sour dough starter to give it a characteristic taste, but this is by no means essential.

PREPARATION TIME: 30 MINUTES
RISING TIME: 2 HOURS
COOKING TIME: 40-45 MINUTES
PRE-HEAT OVEN TO 200°C

INGREDIENTS FOR 2 MEDIUM-SIZED LOAVES
400 g rye flour
400 g white bread flour
15 ml (1 tablespoon) caraway seeds
15 ml (1 tablespoon) salt
15 ml (1 tablespoon) dried yeast, or 25 g fresh yeast
10 ml (2 teaspoons) brown sugar
575 ml warm water
5 ml (1 teaspoon) black treacle

Mix the flours with the caraway seeds and salt in a large mixing bowl. Stir the yeast, sugar and 100 ml of the warm water together and leave for 10 minutes, or until frothy.

Make a well in the middle of the flour mixture and drop in the treacle, activated yeast mixture and enough warm water to make a soft, slightly sticky dough. Mix thoroughly, cover with plastic wrap and leave in a warm place to rise for 1 hour.

Turn the dough out on to a working surface and knead it until it is really smooth and elastic. Put it back into the bowl, cover and leave to rise for a further 30 minutes.

Turn it out, cut the dough in half and knead both halves into sausage shapes as long as your baking tins, or put the loaves straight on to greased baking sheets.

With a sharp knife or scissors blade, make incisions about 5 mm deep the whole length of each loaf or slash 4-5 times across the top of the dough. Sprinkle the surface with a little more rye flour.

Cover the loaves and leave them to rise to the top of the tins, or for about 30 minutes. Bake the bread for 40-45 minutes.

VARIATION For a lighter rye bread, you can leave out the caraway seeds, replace the sugar and the treacle with 15 ml (1 tablespoon) honey, and use 600 g white bread flour to 250 g rye flour.

Mealie Bread

THIS DELECTABLE bread deserves to be served more often in restaurants. Farmers' wives traditionally serve it thickly buttered with yellow farm butter. If mealies are not available, you can use tinned, well-drained whole kernel corn.

PREPARATION TIME: 20 MINUTES
COOKING TIME: 1¼ HOURS
PRE-HEAT OVEN TO 180°C

INGREDIENTS FOR 1 SMALL LOAF
500 g fresh mealie kernels cut from the cob, or 2 tins (410 g each) whole kernel corn, well drained
2 extra-large eggs
5 ml (1 teaspoon) salt
A pinch of pepper
10 ml (2 teaspoons) sugar
A pinch of nutmeg
125 ml (½ cup) buttermilk or plain drinking yoghurt
125 ml (½ cup) milk
60 g flour
5 ml (1 teaspoon) baking powder

Place all the ingredients in a food processor, or mince the mealies, add the rest of the ingredients and mix.

Line the base of a small, well-greased loaf tin (about 22 cm x 10 cm x 5 cm) with wax paper, grease the paper, and pour in the mixture. Bake for 1¼ hours, or until nicely browned.

SERVING SUGGESTIONS Serve mealie bread warm and thickly buttered.

Pitta Bread

THIS IS A MIDDLE EASTERN 'pocket' bread which is ideal for eating with a variety of fillings. The recipe is not nearly as complicated to make as a first glance at the instructions may suggest.

PREPARATION TIME: 50 MINUTES
RISING TIME: 2½ HOURS
COOKING TIME: 10 MINUTES
PRE-HEAT OVEN TO 250°C

INGREDIENTS FOR 8 PITTA BREADS
7 ml (1½ teaspoons) dried yeast, or 12,5 g fresh yeast
375 ml (1½ cups) warm water
5 ml (1 teaspoon) sugar
500 g flour
2 ml (½ teaspoon) salt
30 ml (2 tablespoons) sunflower oil

Dissolve the yeast in 125 ml (½ cup) of the warm water. Stir in the sugar and allow to stand for about 10 minutes, or until the mixture is frothy.

Sieve the flour and salt into a bowl. Make a well in the centre and pour in the yeast mixture. Gradually stir in the remaining 250 ml (1 cup) warm water and the oil to form a firm dough.

Knead the dough for about 15 minutes (or do it in 2 or 3 batches in seconds in a food processor) until the dough is smooth and elastic. Place the dough in an oiled bowl, turning to coat it with the oil. Cover with plastic wrap and leave to rise for about 2 hours, or until double in bulk. Punch down and knead lightly on a floured board.

Divide the dough into 8 pieces and roll them out into 5 mm thick rounds on a floured board. Dust the pieces with flour and arrange them on a floured cloth. Cover with another floured cloth and leave to rise in a warm place for about 20 minutes.

Heat the oven to 250°C and leave it on for at least 15 minutes once the temperature is reached. When the breads have risen, put oiled baking sheets into the oven to get really hot, being careful not to let the oil burn. Then carefully place the risen rounds on to the hot baking sheets and sprinkle them with water to stop them browning. Bake for 6-10 minutes without opening the oven, until they are well puffed but still pale. Cool on wire racks. When split, the breads will be hollow.

Fresh Plum Kuchen

KUCHEN, TRANSLATED LITERALLY from German, means 'cake' but the word has come to encompass a variety of yeast-raised confectionery.

This dough can either be risen and shaped on the same day or, if preferred, left to rise overnight. The cake will keep well for up to a week.

Preparation Time: 45 minutes
Rising Time: 2 hours
Cooking Time: 40 minutes
Pre-heat Oven to 180°C

Ingredients for 1 Cake

For the yeast pastry base:
1 extra-large egg
45 ml (3 tablespoons) cold milk
Hot water
15 ml (1 tablespoon) dried yeast, or 25 g fresh yeast
45 g castor sugar
45 g soft butter
250 g flour
1 ml (¼ teaspoon) salt

For the topping:
30 g butter, melted
1 kg prune plums, stoned and halved
150 g granulated sugar mixed with 5 ml (1 teaspoon) cinnamon

Break the egg into a measuring cup, add the cold milk, then make this up to 150 ml with hot (not boiling) water. Pour the liquid into a large mixing bowl and then add the yeast.

Stir until the yeast has dissolved. If dried yeast is being used, add 5 ml (1 teaspoon) of the sugar. Allow to stand for 10 minutes or until frothy.

Add the butter, sugar, flour and salt. Beat with a wooden spoon or electric beater for 5 minutes, or until the dough is smooth and stretchy, and leaves the bowl clean when pulled away from it. If it is still a little sticky at this point, add an extra 15 ml (1 tablespoon) flour and beat it in. Leave the dough in the same bowl and cover it with a damp tea towel or plastic wrap. Allow the dough to rise in a warm kitchen for about 1 hour, or until it has doubled in bulk.

Press the dough down, knead it for about 2 minutes and then allow it to rise for a further 30 minutes. The dough is then ready to be used.

Roll out the risen dough to a thickness of 1 cm. Place it in a lightly greased, shallow tin, about 35 cm x 25 cm. Allow the dough to rise for 30 minutes, then spread it with the melted butter. Arrange the plums, skin side down, over the surface in neat rows. Sprinkle them with the cinnamon sugar.

Leave for 10 minutes, then bake in a 180°C oven for 40 minutes. Cut the cake into squares and serve at room temperature.

VARIATIONS Stoned apricots can be used instead of plums.

To allow the dough to rise overnight, use the following method. After the dough has risen for 1 hour and then been kneaded for 2 minutes, place it in a large greased plastic bag. Tie it loosely and place it on the lowest shelf of a refrigerator. The next day, remove the dough and allow it to stand at room temperature for about 1 hour before you use it.

BREAD WITH DRIED FRUIT *This fruity, enriched bread is ideal for special occasions.*

Bread with Dried Fruit

THIS RECIPE is for a bread that is particularly suitable for special occasions such as Easter and Christmas. It has a rich, fruity texture and a firm, nutty crust.

Preparation Time: 30 minutes
Rising Time: 1½ hours
Cooking Time: 35 minutes
Pre-heat Oven to 180°C

Ingredients for 1 Large Loaf

275 g flour
5 ml (1 teaspoon) salt
20 g butter
25 g sugar
2 ml (½ teaspoon) ground mixed spice
1 large egg, beaten
150 ml warm water
12 ml (2½ teaspoons) dried yeast, or 20 g fresh yeast
225 g currants
100-125 g sultanas
25 g mixed peel, chopped

Sieve the flour and salt on to a working surface or into a large mixing bowl. Rub in the butter and make a well in the centre. Mix the sugar and spice together – reserving 5 ml (1 teaspoon) sugar if you are using dried yeast – and put into the well.

Combine the beaten egg with the warm water. If you are using dried yeast, dissolve the reserved sugar and the yeast in 100 ml of the egg/water mixture. If using fresh yeast, use 45 ml (3 tablespoons) of this mixture to blend the yeast to a smooth paste and allow to stand for 10 minutes.

Stir the rest of the egg/water mixture into the yeast mixture. Pour this over the sugar in the well, mix vigorously to blend, then knead well to make a smooth, elastic dough. Mix together the currants, sultanas and mixed peel, and knead lightly into the dough.

Mould the dough into a round or long shape and put on a greased baking sheet or in a greased 900 g loaf tin. Cover with a sheet of greased plastic and put in a warm place to rise for 1½ hours. Bake in the pre-heated oven for 35 minutes.

BREADS, CAKES AND BISCUITS

BAGELS

A GOOD HOME-BAKED bagel, light and crisp, is a favourite Jewish treat. New Yorkers love their bagels thickly spread with real cream cheese and then topped with layers of smoked salmon – the ultimate way to enjoy them.

PREPARATION TIME: 45 MINUTES
RISING TIME: 2 HOURS
COOKING TIME: 20 MINUTES
PRE-HEAT OVEN TO 200°C

INGREDIENTS FOR 12 BAGELS
60 ml (¼ cup) sunflower oil
30 ml (2 tablespoons) sugar
2 ml (½ teaspoon) salt
250 ml (1 cup) warm water
7 ml (1½ teaspoons) dried yeast, or 12,5 g fresh yeast
1 egg, beaten
450 g flour

Mix the oil, sugar and salt with the warm water. Stir in the yeast and leave this mixture for about 10 minutes, or until it is frothy. Beat in the egg.

Sieve the flour into a bowl and stir in the yeast mixture. Knead well together for 10-15 minutes on a floured board until the dough is smooth. Cover and leave to rise until it is double in bulk (about 2 hours). Punch the dough down and knead it again until it is smooth and elastic.

Divide it into about 12 equal portions. Roll each piece into a sausage shape and form it into a ring, moistening the ends and pinching them well together. Cover the rings and leave them to rise in a warm place for about 10 minutes.

Drop them into a pot of rapidly boiling water, one at a time, and cook them for a few minutes until each one rises to the top. Remove with a slotted spoon and place on an oiled baking sheet.

Bake the bagels in the pre-heated oven for about 20 minutes, or until they are golden and crisp.

BRIOCHES

ONE OF THE DELIGHTS of a French breakfast is the brioche: crisp and golden on the outside, and meltingly light in the mouth. The recipe given here is equally suitable as a crust for pies and pâtés or for wrapping meats, and for small or large loaves. Brioche dough can be made in advance and kept in the refrigerator for a day before use.

PREPARATION TIME: 40 MINUTES
RISING TIME: 2¾ HOURS
COOKING TIME: 10-25 MINUTES
PRE-HEAT OVEN TO 230°C

INGREDIENTS FOR 18-20 SMALL, OR 4 LARGE BRIOCHES
15 ml (1 tablespoon) dried yeast, or 25 g fresh yeast
15 ml (1 tablespoon) sugar
90 ml warm milk
450 g flour
5 ml (1 teaspoon) salt
4 eggs, beaten
225 g butter, soft but not oily
A little beaten egg to glaze

Mix the yeast and sugar with the milk and set aside for 10 minutes, or until frothy.

BRIOCHES and CROISSANTS *Golden treats that give a lift to breakfast or brunch.*

Sieve the flour and salt together into a large mixing bowl, pour in the yeast mixture and the beaten eggs, and beat vigorously with a wooden spoon. The dough will be soft and sticky at first, and should be beaten for 5 minutes or more until it has become smooth, elastic and slightly shiny in appearance.

Mix in the butter, a little at a time, until the dough is smooth and glossy. Shape the dough into a ball and place in a warmed, lightly buttered bowl. Cover with greased plastic wrap and stand in a warm place to rise for about 2 hours, or until it has trebled in bulk.

Tip the dough on to a lightly floured working surface and knock out all the air. (If you wish to store the dough, do so at this stage. Shape it into a ball, place it in a buttered bowl, cover and put in the refrigerator.) Divide the dough into 18-20 pieces, each with a mass of about 50 g. Mould each piece to fit a small fluted tin, warmed and lightly buttered. The dough should come about one-third of the way up the tin.

Alternatively, you can divide the dough into 4 larger pieces and mould them to fit larger fluted tins or small loaf tins.

Put the tins on a baking sheet, cover with a sheet of greased plastic and stand the dough in a warm place for about 45 minutes, or until it has risen to fill the tins. Brush over the beaten egg and bake in the pre-heated oven until golden-brown. Allow 10 minutes' baking for small brioches, or 20-25 minutes for 4 large ones. Eat as soon as possible after baking.

VARIATION For covering a pie, roll out the brioche dough instead of dividing it into pieces. Roll it to no more than 5 mm in thickness, fit it over the warm pie filling, brush it with beaten egg and stand in a warm place to rise for 45 minutes-1 hour. Brush again with beaten egg and bake for about 15 minutes at 230°C.

Hot Cross Buns

IT IS SAID that, in medieval times, bakers marked all their loaves with a cross to ward off evil spirits and encourage the bread to rise. In England, this practice was condemned as 'popish' during the 17th century and dropped. Only buns made on Good Friday continued to bear a cross, in token of the Crucifixion.

PREPARATION TIME: 40 MINUTES
RISING TIME: 2½-2¾ HOURS
COOKING TIME: 6-7 MINUTES
PRE-HEAT OVEN TO 240°C

INGREDIENTS FOR 15 BUNS
For the ferment:
10 ml (2 teaspoons) dried yeast, or 15 g fresh yeast
7 ml (1½ teaspoons) sugar
About 275 ml warm water
1 large egg, beaten
50 g flour

For the dough:
100-125 g currants
25 g sultanas
25 g chopped, candied lemon peel*
450 g flour
5 ml (1 teaspoon) salt
10-15 ml (2-3 teaspoons) ground mixed spice
75 g butter
75 g sugar
Grated rind of 1 lemon
Golden syrup (heated) for glazing

To make the ferment with the dried yeast: Dissolve the yeast with the sugar in 100 ml of the warm water and allow to stand for 10 minutes, or until frothy. Add the beaten egg and enough of the remaining warm water to give 275-300 ml liquid. Mix this with the 50 g flour, cover and put in a warm place for 30 minutes.

To make the ferment with fresh yeast: Combine the beaten egg with enough warm water to give 275-300 ml liquid. Whisk in the yeast, sugar and flour, cover and put in a warm place for 30 minutes.

Before starting to mix the dough, rinse the currants, sultanas and candied lemon peel with hot water, and spread on a paper towel in a warm place to drain.

Sieve the flour, salt and spice into a large mixing bowl, rub in the butter and make a well in the centre. Put the sugar and grated lemon rind in the well and pour on the ferment. Gradually draw in the flour and mix vigorously, then knead to a smooth, elastic dough.

Carefully work in the warm, moist currants, sultanas and candied lemon peel. Shape the dough into a ball, put it in a warm, greased bowl, cover with a sheet of greased plastic and allow to rise in a warm place for 1 hour.

Turn out the dough and knead to knock out any air bubbles and give the dough an even texture. Shape it into a ball again, put back into the bowl, cover and allow to rise for another 30 minutes.

Turn out the dough on to a working surface and divide into 15 pieces (each 75 g). Shape them into balls and leave to rest for 5 minutes (covered with the plastic) on the working surface.

Roll out the balls into 8 cm discs and place on lightly greased baking sheets. Cut each disc into quarters, cutting right through the dough but leaving the quarters touching each other so that the dough has a well-marked cross on it as it rises.

Cover the buns with a sheet of greased plastic and put in a warm place to rise for 40 minutes. Bake in the pre-heated oven for 6-7 minutes, and brush hot golden syrup over the buns as soon as they are taken from the oven.

VARIATION The cross on each bun can be made with shortcrust pastry* to which water has been added until it is soft enough to pipe through a nozzle. Instead of cutting the discs of dough, pipe a cross of the pastry on to each bun before baking.

Croissants

TO MOST PEOPLE the croissant is as French as the Arc de Triomphe. But the Viennese, not the French, invented it when Vienna defeated the invading Turks in 1686. The invaders had tunnelled their way under the city walls and it was the all-night bakers who raised the alarm and so saved the day.

When the bakers were asked to create a 'commemorative confection', they devised a pastry-like bread roll shaped like the crescent emblem on the defeated enemy's flag. The roll's popularity spread to Italy and then to France, where the French adopted the croissant as their own.

Choose the coolest part of the day to make croissants, as the batter tends to become unmanageable in high temperatures.

PREPARATION TIME: 45 MINUTES
RESTING AND RISING TIME: 1¼ HOURS
COOKING TIME: 10 MINUTES
PRE-HEAT OVEN TO 230°C

INGREDIENTS FOR 12 CROISSANTS
450 g flour
5 ml (1 teaspoon) salt
25 g butter
1 large egg, beaten
215 ml warm water
5 ml (1 teaspoon) sugar
15 ml (1 tablespoon) dried yeast, or 25 g fresh yeast
175 g butter, cut in pieces
A little beaten egg to glaze

Sieve the flour and salt into a large mixing bowl, rub in the 25 g butter and make a well in the centre.

Mix together the egg, water, sugar and yeast, and allow to stand for 10 minutes, or until frothy. Pour into the well, mix vigorously to blend well, then knead to a smooth dough.

Cover the bowl with plastic wrap and put in a cold place for the dough to rest for 10 minutes.

Follow the directions alongside for shaping croissants, then cover with greased plastic wrap and allow to rise in a warm place for 40 minutes, brushing lightly with beaten egg after 20 minutes.

Place the prepared croissants in the pre-heated oven and bake for about 10 minutes. Bake lightly so that you can re-heat the croissants without fear of browning them too much.

VARIATIONS Brush the triangles of dough with melted butter and sprinkle generously with sugar and cinnamon. Then roll them up and proceed as in the main recipe.

Brush the triangles of dough with melted butter and warmed runny honey. Sprinkle with about 125 ml (½ cup) finely chopped walnuts. Roll the triangles up and allow the dough to rise. Brush with the beaten egg and sprinkle with sesame seeds, then bake as usual.

Another variation is to wrap a square of bitter chocolate inside each croissant.

Shaping Croissants

Roll out the dough to a rectangle about 38 cm x 15 cm. Dot the butter pieces over two-thirds of it, starting from a short side.

Fold the unbuttered third over the centre third, and the remaining third over these two.

Roll out the dough again to a rectangle the same size as before and fold in three in the same way as before, but without buttering. Wrap loosely in plastic wrap and put in a refrigerator to rest for 10 minutes.

Repeat the rolling out and folding for a third time, wrap the dough again and put in a refrigerator to rest for 15 minutes.

Roll out the dough evenly to make a strip 60 cm x 20 cm and 3 mm thick. Mark along one long edge at 10 cm intervals. Mark along the opposite edge after 5 cm and then at 10 cm intervals. Cut across the strip from mark to mark to give 11 large triangles and a small one at each end; join these two small triangles to make another large one.

Roll up each triangle firmly from the short side to the pointed tip, then roll with the palm of your hand to make it slightly longer. Curve the rolls into crescents and place on a lightly greased baking sheet.

Petits Fours – Small, Sweet and Scrumptious

A *petit four* really means 'a little something from the oven'.
Nowadays, however, the term includes a comprehensive selection of small fancy items,
some of which would seem to belong more in the realm of confectionery than of pastry-making.

The fundamental skill of making petits fours lies in the ability to cope with sugar and sugar syrups. The syrup used is a solution of sugar and water, combined in varying ratios which determine different textures ranging from soft and toffee-like to extremely hard and brittle.

You will need a good sugar thermometer and a smooth surface on which to work (such as a large marble slab). Other requirements are: the basic equipment for biscuit-making, a selection of piping bags and nozzles, a heavy-based, deep saucepan, one or two sizes of good-quality baking sheets and a rectangular cake tin (36 cm x 20 cm x 5 cm).

Sponge Fingers

Preparation Time: 15 minutes
Cooking Time: 15 minutes
Pre-heat Oven to 170°C

Ingredients for 50 Sponge Fingers
4 eggs, separated
100g sugar
2 drops orange essence
100g flour
Icing sugar for dusting

Combine the egg yolks and sugar. Whisk until thick and pale – when the whisk is lifted out, the mixture should fall from it in a thick ribbon which lies on the surface briefly. Add the orange essence.

Sieve the flour and fold into the yolk mixture, using a metal spoon. In another bowl, whisk the egg whites until stiff. Fold a quarter of the beaten whites into the yolk mixture and then gently fold in the rest of the egg white, avoiding overmixing.

Using a piping bag with a plain nozzle, pipe 8-10 cm strips on to a greased baking tray, leaving them room to spread. Work quickly as the batter spoils if it stands for too long. Dust each biscuit with sifted icing sugar and bake for 15 minutes – do not let the biscuits brown. Allow to cool on a rack.

Macaroons

Preparation Time: 20 minutes
Cooking Time: 15-20 minutes
Pre-heat Oven to 180°C

Ingredients for 26 Macaroons
200g ground almonds
250g sugar
2 ml (½ teaspoon) vanilla sugar*
or 1 ml (¼ teaspoon) vanilla essence
2 egg whites
Water for brushing
Icing sugar for dusting

Place the almonds in a bowl, pounding them with a pestle as the sugar is gradually added. Add the vanilla sugar or essence and, little by little, the egg whites. The dough should be firm enough to knead.

Mix or knead well and divide the dough into small balls (about 3 cm in diameter is ideal, but the size can be varied).

Oil a sheet of grease-proof paper (or use non-stick baking paper) and place on a biscuit tray. Place the almond balls on the paper and flatten them slightly, allowing room for them to spread.

Brush the surfaces of the macaroons with water. Dust with a little icing sugar. Bake in the middle of the pre-heated oven for 15-20 minutes. If using grease-proof paper, place the paper on a well-dampened tea towel as the macaroons come out of the oven. As soon as the paper is moist, quickly remove the biscuits.

Tiles

Preparation Time: 20 minutes
Cooking Time: 4 minutes
Pre-heat Oven to 220°C

Ingredients for 32 Tiles
50g flour
100g icing sugar
100g flaked almonds
1 ml (¼ teaspoon) vanilla essence
1 egg
2 egg whites

Sieve the flour and icing sugar into a bowl, mix together with a wooden spoon, and add the almonds. Mix in the vanilla essence, egg and egg whites, and allow the mixture to stand for 10 minutes.

Drop teaspoonfuls of this batter on a greased baking sheet and spread into flat rounds with a wet fork. Bake for 4 minutes, or until the edges are light brown. Remove at once from the baking sheet and drape over a rolling pin to give them a curved shape. Allow to cool and harden.

If the biscuits harden before they are removed from the baking sheet, return them to the oven for a few minutes to soften.

Rum Truffles

Preparation Time: 30 minutes
Chilling Time: 4 hours

Ingredients for 30 Truffles
500g dark chocolate
125 ml (½ cup) cream
About 30 ml (2 tablespoons) rum
Chocolate vermicelli, grated chocolate or cocoa powder for coating

Melt the chocolate over hot (not boiling) water. Whip the cream and pour the melted chocolate slowly into the whipped cream. Continue beating until they are well combined and add rum to taste.

Allow to chill in the refrigerator for 4 hours, or until the mixture is of a rolling consistency. Roll into small balls, then roll the truffles in the vermicelli, grated chocolate or cocoa powder.

Return the rum truffles to the refrigerator until served.

PETITS FOURS GLACÉS

Petits Fours Glacés

Preparation Time: 2 hours 20 minutes
Cooking Time: 50-55 minutes
Cooling Time: 45 minutes
Pre-heat Oven to 180°C

Ingredients for 30 Petits Fours

For the Genoese sponge:
4 eggs
125 g sugar
125 g flour
A pinch of salt
60 g butter, melted and cooled

For the butter cream:
5 egg yolks
125 g sugar
100 ml water
250 g butter, softened

Flavouring (any one of these):
15 ml (1 tablespoon) instant coffee dissolved in 30 ml (2 tablespoons) water; 125 ml (½ cup) praline*; 30 ml (2 tablespoons) liqueur; or 15 ml (1 tablespoon) grated lemon rind

125 ml (½ cup) smooth apricot jam*

For the light sugar syrup:
160 ml water
500 g sugar

1 kg fondant icing*
Chocolate frills* or glacé cherries and angelica for decoration

First make the sponge cake. Whisk the eggs and sugar together in a large bowl. Place the bowl over a saucepan of hot (not boiling) water. Beat the mixture with an electric beater (or whisk) until it is thick and pale in colour and falls from the whisk to form a thick ribbon of batter on the surface. This requires about 10 minutes with an electric beater or 20 minutes by hand.

Remove the bowl from the heat and beat for a few more minutes until the mixture has cooled slightly. Sieve the flour with the salt 3 times and add, bit by bit, to the egg mixture alternately with the melted butter, starting and ending with flour. Be sure to fold the flour very gently, using a metal spoon. Pour the batter into a buttered and floured rectangular cake tin (about 36 cm x 20 cm x 5 cm). Bang the tin on the table to expel air bubbles.

Bake in the pre-heated oven for 20-25 minutes. Place the tin on a cake rack to cool for 5 minutes, then turn the cake out of the tin and allow it to cool completely.

To make the butter cream filling, whisk the egg yolks until they are thick, foamy and pale (about 8 minutes with an electric beater). Over a medium heat, dissolve the sugar in the water to form a syrup. Cook until the syrup reaches the thread stage* (106-112°C on a sugar thermometer). Pour the hot syrup into the whisked yolks in a thin stream, beating all the time, and continue to beat until the mixture is cool. It will be thick and fluffy.

In a separate bowl, cream the butter with a wooden spoon and gradually add the egg mixture, beating well with the wooden spoon until all the egg mixture has been added. Add the flavouring of your choice.

With a sharp knife, halve the sponge horizontally and fill with the butter cream, reserving some of the butter cream for decorating the petits fours. Cut the cake into the desired shapes – circles, squares, triangles or ovals – making sure they are small (about 4 cm in diameter).

Now coat each cakelet with apricot glaze: warm the jam over low heat and strain it through a fine sieve. Spear each cakelet with a fork and use a paint brush or pastry brush to apply the warm glaze.

Before applying the fondant icing, prepare a light sugar syrup by putting the water into a heavy-based saucepan and pouring in the sugar. Place over a medium heat, and stir with a wooden spoon until the sugar dissolves. Increase the heat and bring to the boil without stirring or shaking. Allow to boil for 10 minutes. Arrest the cooking by placing the saucepan in a bowl of icy water. Store in a screw-top jar.

Place the fondant icing in a bowl over hot water on a low heat. When it begins to melt, stir in about 30 ml (2 tablespoons) of the light sugar syrup. Continue to stir the fondant over the hot water, adding more syrup if necessary until the fondant coats the back of a spoon.

Place the little jam-glazed petits fours on a wire rack, coat each by pouring fondant icing over it, and decorate with lacy chocolate frills or butter cream garnished with glacé cherries and angelica.

Variations Fill with smooth apricot jam* instead of butter cream.

A small ball of marzipan* can be placed on top of each glazed petit four and a nut inserted into that. It may then be finished with a glaze of basic glacé icing* or coated with flavoured and coloured fondant.

Brandy Snaps

Preparation Time: 20 minutes
Cooking Time: 8-10 minutes
Pre-heat Oven to 170°C

Ingredients for 20 Brandy Snaps

60 g butter
50 g castor sugar
30 ml (2 tablespoons) golden syrup
60 g flour, sifted
A pinch of salt
3 ml (¾ teaspoon) ground ginger
5 ml (1 teaspoon) grated lemon rind
45 ml (3 tablespoons) brandy

For the filling (optional):
250 ml (1 cup) cream
30 g icing sugar, sifted
15 ml (1 tablespoon) brandy

Melt the butter, sugar and syrup over a moderate heat, stirring until the sugar dissolves. Allow the mixture to cool and then gradually beat in the flour, salt, ginger, lemon rind and brandy. Beat until smooth.

Drop teaspoonfuls of the batter on a well-greased baking tray – they tend to spread, so keep them well spaced. Bake for 8-10 minutes, or until golden-brown. Roll each brandy snap around the buttered handle of a wooden spoon, doing so as quickly as possible.

If the snaps harden before you are able to curl them, return them briefly to the oven until soft. Once you have curled the snaps around the handle, leave them there and place on a wire rack until cool. It is advisable to have 3-4 wooden spoons handy.

To make the filling, beat the cream until thick, add the icing sugar and beat to form stiff peaks. Fold in the brandy. Carefully pipe the cream into the brandy snaps and serve immediately.

BRANDY SNAPS AND MACAROONS

BREADS, CAKES AND BISCUITS

MOSBOLLETJIES

IT WAS ONCE CUSTOMARY during the wine-making season at the Cape to use fresh must as a leavening agent for must buns, which became widely known by their Afrikaans name, mosbolletjies. When must was not available, the yeast was made from raisins.

PREPARATION TIME: 1½ HOURS
STANDING TIME: 2 DAYS
COOKING TIME: 1 HOUR
PRE-HEAT OVEN TO 180°C

INGREDIENTS FOR 50 BUNS
250 g raisins with seeds
750 ml (3 cups) cold water
2 ml (½ teaspoon) dried yeast, or 5 g fresh yeast
60 ml (¼ cup) warm water
2,5 kg flour, sifted
500 g sugar
7 ml (1½ teaspoons) salt
15 ml (1 tablespoon) aniseed
250 g butter, melted (margarine, vegetable fat or lard may be used instead)
750 ml (3 cups) lukewarm milk, or an equal mixture of milk and water

For the glaze:
1 egg yolk, beaten with a pinch of sugar and 15 ml (1 tablespoon) milk

Crush the raisins and place in a saucepan with the cold water. Boil for 10 minutes, then allow to cool until lukewarm. Pour into a glass jar or enamel container with a well-fitting lid.

Dissolve the yeast in the warm water and stir into the raisin mixture. Stir well together and leave in a warm place for 24-48 hours, or until the raisins have risen to the top. Strain the raisin liquid (must).

Stir 250 g of the flour into the must to form a smooth batter. Leave in a warm place for 3-4 hours, or until it is well fermented.

Sieve together the rest of the flour, the sugar and salt, and add the aniseed. Form into a stiff dough with the must and flour mixture, the melted butter and enough of the milk (or milk and water) to make a stiff dough. Knead very well together (it is ready when a piece of the dough cut with a knife shows evenly distributed air bubbles).

Cover well and leave in a warm place overnight, or until the dough doubles in bulk. It is not necessary to knead it again.

Carefully shape the dough into buns and pack into greased deep loaf pans. Lightly cover and allow to rise in a warm place until doubled in bulk. Brush with the egg yolk, sugar and milk glaze, bake for 1 hour, then turn out and break apart.

SERVING SUGGESTION Serve hot, spread with butter. The buns can be toasted the next day. To keep them for a long time, make rusks by drying the buns out in a very slow oven (about 140°C). Store in an airtight container.

VARIATION Add 2 beaten eggs along with the melted butter and liquid.

PIZZA

THE PIZZA is a popular and inexpensive dish that is both tasty and filling. It lends itself to a multitude of variations. This is a traditional Italian recipe.

PREPARATION TIME: 40 MINUTES
RISING TIME: 20 MINUTES
COOKING TIME: 20 MINUTES
PRE-HEAT OVEN TO 240°C

INGREDIENTS FOR FOUR TO SIX
For the dough:
15 ml (1 tablespoon) dried yeast, or 25 g fresh yeast
2 ml (½ teaspoon) sugar
125 ml (½ cup) warm water
200 g flour
1 ml (¼ teaspoon) salt
15 ml (1 tablespoon) sunflower oil

For the topping:
250 ml (1 cup) Napolitana sauce*, or 4 tomatoes, skinned* and chopped
150 g mozzarella cheese, grated
100 g Parmesan cheese, grated
6 anchovy fillets, or 10 slices salami
12 ripe black olives
6 fresh button mushrooms, sliced
3 slices Parma ham, cut in strips
1 small sweet red, green or yellow pepper (if available), sliced
2 cloves garlic, crushed
5 ml (1 teaspoon) dried origanum
15 ml (1 tablespoon) sunflower oil

Mix the yeast and sugar with the warm water in a large bowl. Allow to stand for 10 minutes, or until frothy.

Sieve half the flour into the bowl, add the salt, then stir until smooth. Gradually mix in enough of the remaining flour to form a stiff dough. Add the oil and knead well until the dough is smooth and elastic.

Leave for about 20 minutes before rolling out to fit a large, well-oiled 23 cm pizza pan.

To make the topping, spread the dough with the Napolitana sauce* or the tomatoes. Sprinkle with the grated mozzarella and Parmesan cheese. Top with anchovy fillets (or slices of salami), ripe black olives, sliced mushrooms, strips of Parma ham and strips of sweet pepper (if used).

Add the crushed garlic and origanum. Drizzle with the oil and bake on the lowest shelf of the pre-heated oven for about 20 minutes, or until the crust is lightly browned and crisp, and the topping is piping hot.

PIZZA *A recipe that will have everyone clamouring for more.*

VARIATIONS You can fold the round of pizza dough over to enclose the filling and bake for about 30 minutes, or until golden. In this case prepare a mixture of 1 egg, 45 ml (3 tablespoons) grated Parmesan cheese and 250 g ricotta – or chunky cream cheese mixed with 30 ml (2 tablespoons) cream and rubbed through a sieve – and smear this mixture on half the dough. Cover with a layer of thinly sliced salami and a sprinkling of tiny cubes of mozzarella cheese before folding and baking.

To make a deep-dish pizza, brush a 23 cm layer cake tin with oil and sprinkle with cornflour. Press the dough in to fit, pushing it firmly up the sides. Mix 250 g grated mozzarella cheese with 100 g grated Parmesan. Set aside 125 ml (½ cup) of this to sprinkle on top. Add 250-375 ml (1-1½ cups) Napolitana sauce* to the remaining cheese and use to fill the pizza. Add any of the ingredients suggested for the flat pizza before sprinkling the reserved cheese on top. Bake at 230°C for 25 minutes.

PURI

Bread or rice is eaten daily in most Indian homes. Puri, an easy-to-make, light bread, is dough rolled into a disc and deep-fried to a pale colour. The discs have a tendency to puff out like a ball – in spite of the fact that they contain no raising agent. They can be stored in a covered container for about three days.

Preparation Time: 30 minutes
Cooking Time: 20 minutes
Ingredients for 20 Puri
140 g white bread flour
140 g cake flour
5 ml (1 teaspoon) salt
125 ml (½ cup) melted butter
50 ml milk
80 ml (⅓ cup) water
750 ml (3 cups) sunflower oil for deep-frying

Sieve the flours and salt together, then rub in the melted butter to form a crumbly texture. Meanwhile, heat the milk and water in a saucepan but do not allow to boil. Cool slightly and add to the flour mixture, then mix to form a soft dough.

Knead well for 3-5 minutes, then divide the dough into 20 balls. Roll each ball between your palms and press flat. Flour a board very lightly and roll each disc to a 10 cm diameter. Place on a tray.

Heat the oil to a medium temperature (about 180°C) in a deep saucepan – a cube of day-old bread will turn golden in 1-1¼ minutes. Place 3 puri in the oil and fry for 30 seconds on either side. If the puri have been rolled evenly, they should puff up immediately into a hollow ball. Remove from the oil and place on paper towels.

Serving Suggestions Puri can be served hot or cold. Serve this light bread with Indian vegetable or lentil dishes, or with a layer of jam for tea.

SWEDISH TEA RING

This type of tea or coffee cake was formerly baked in every Swedish home once a week, and in such quantity that it would last the entire week. It was made into small buns and also in many different shapes, one of which, certainly the most impressive, is the tea ring.

Preparation Time: 30 minutes
Rising Time: 2½ hours
Cooking Time: 35 minutes
Pre-heat Oven to 160°C
Ingredients for 1 Large Cake
20 ml (4 teaspoons) dried yeast, or 30 g fresh yeast
60 ml (¼ cup) warm water
60 g sugar
180 g butter
10 ml (2 teaspoons) crushed cardamom seeds, or 5 ml (1 teaspoon) ground cardamom seeds
2 ml (½ teaspoon) salt
190 ml (¾ cup) milk, scalded*
1 egg
420-500 g flour, sifted

For the filling:
30 g softened butter
100 g sugar, mixed with 10 ml (2 teaspoons) cinnamon
125 g raisins

Mix the yeast in the warm water with 5 ml (1 teaspoon) of the sugar and allow to stand for 10 minutes, or until frothy. Mix together the butter, remaining sugar, cardamom, salt and hot milk, and cool until lukewarm. Add the egg, yeast mixture and 300 g of the flour. Beat this mixture thoroughly. Add, a little at a time, enough of the remaining flour to make a soft dough.

Turn out the dough on a lightly floured surface and knead until smooth and elastic – about 10 minutes.

Place the dough in a lightly buttered bowl, and turn it over once to grease its surface. Cover and allow to rise in a warm place until it is double in bulk – about 1½ hours. When it is light, punch down, turn out on a lightly floured surface and knead lightly.

Roll out the dough into a rectangle (about 60 cm x 25 cm). Spread the surface with the 30 g softened butter and sprinkle it with the cinnamon sugar. Sprinkle over the raisins. Roll up, Swiss roll fashion, and shape it into a ring on a large buttered baking sheet. Leave it whole or cut slits about 2 cm deep at 3 cm intervals with a sharp knife or scissors blade.

Allow the ring to rise in a warm place until it is double in bulk – about 40 minutes-1 hour. Bake for 30-35 minutes, or until golden-brown.

SCONES

The name 'scone' is believed by some to come from the Gaelic word *sgonn*, meaning 'large mouthful'. Whether plain or flavoured, scones have long been a tea time favourite. Quickly made, they are ideal for serving to unexpected guests.

Preparation Time: 15 minutes
Cooking Time: 15 minutes
Pre-heat Oven to 220°C

Ingredients for About 24 Scones
125 g butter
500 g self-raising flour
1 ml (¼ teaspoon) salt
2 eggs
125-150 ml milk

Rub the butter into the flour with your fingertips until the mixture looks like breadcrumbs. Add the salt. Mix in the beaten eggs and the milk to make a soft dough, adding more milk if necessary.

Pat or roll out the dough lightly until it is about 1,5 cm thick, and cut into 4 cm rounds with a pastry cutter. Bake in the pre-heated oven for 12-15 minutes.

Variations Use wholewheat flour, or a mixture of wholewheat and cake flour, adding 10 ml (2 teaspoons) baking powder.

Make cheese scones by mixing in 50 g mature Cheddar cheese, grated, and 1 ml (¼ teaspoon) dry mustard before the eggs and milk. Serve hot and buttered.

For another variation, add 5-10 ml (1-2 teaspoons) finely chopped chives to the basic recipe. These herb scones are best served with soup.

You can sweeten plain scones by adding 15 ml (1 tablespoon) sugar to the basic mixture before the milk.

To make fruit scones, add 50 g sugar and 100 g sultanas to the basic mixture.

Scones *This tea time standby never fails to please.*

Black Forest Cake

It has been said that there are almost as many variations of this famous German cake as there are trees in the Black Forest itself. A lot of work goes into making this recipe but it is certainly well worth the trouble involved.

Preparation Time: 2 hours
Cooking Time: 30-45 minutes
Chilling Time: 24 hours
Pre-heat Oven to 160°C

Ingredients for 1 Cake

For the meringue layers:
8 extra-large egg whites
A pinch of salt
A pinch of cream of tartar
300 g sugar
125 g ground almonds
25 ml (5 teaspoons) cornflour
25 ml (5 teaspoons) flour

For the butter cream:
250 g sugar
180 ml water
8 egg yolks
500 g soft butter

For the praline:
150 g sugar
80 g almonds (with skins)

For the Kirsch flavouring:
30 ml (2 tablespoons) Kirsch

For the mocha flavouring:
15 ml (1 tablespoon) instant coffee
10 ml (2 teaspoons) cocoa
Water

Grated chocolate curls* (for decoration)

To make the meringue layers, trace 4 circles on grease-proof paper each having a diameter of 23 cm. Grease and flour the circles and lay the paper on biscuit trays. (Alternatively, make the circles on non-stick baking paper.)

Combine the egg whites with the salt and beat until soft peaks form. Add the cream of tartar, beat for 30 seconds and slowly add three-quarters of the sugar, one tablespoon at a time, until the meringue is stiff.

Mix the ground almonds, cornflour, flour and the remaining sugar, and gently fold this mixture into the meringue, using a metal spoon. Spread the meringue on to the 4 prepared circles.

Bake the circles for 30 minutes. (You could try baking 2 circles for 45 minutes so that the meringues will have different textures.) Gently remove the paper and allow the meringues to cool.

To make the butter cream, boil the sugar and water for 10 minutes. Meanwhile, beat the egg yolks until they are thick. Pour the sugar syrup over the yolks, beating gently. Cream the butter and add the egg mixture to the creamed butter. Chill until it is of a spreading consistency.

To make the praline, melt the sugar in a heavy frying pan. When golden, add the nuts and cook until the smell of the nuts becomes noticeable (30 seconds-1 minute), then pour the mixture on to an oiled slab or tin. Allow it to cool, then pulverise it in a blender or food processor. Mix the praline into a quarter of the butter cream.

Flavour another quarter of the butter cream by mixing the Kirsch into it.

To make the mocha flavouring, mix the instant coffee with the cocoa, moisten this with a few drops of water to make a thick paste and use it to flavour the remaining half of the butter cream.

To assemble the cake, place a circle of meringue on a serving platter. Spread it with mocha butter cream. Place a second meringue layer on that, spread it with Kirsch butter cream, cover with the third meringue circle, spread with praline butter cream, cover with the last meringue round and spread the top and sides with the remaining mocha butter cream. Cover the cake with grated chocolate curls and refrigerate for 24 hours before serving.

Variations Halve the meringue recipe and make 3 thin meringue circles. Make 2 chocolate rounds by beating together 4 eggs with 180 g sugar until thick and creamy (about 10 minutes). With a metal spoon gently fold in 180 g sifted flour and 10 ml (2 teaspoons) cocoa. Divide between 2 buttered and floured 23 cm cake tins and then bake for 1 hour. Layer them alternately with the meringue circles and the butter cream.

In place of the butter cream, use 500 ml (2 cups) whipped cream and a 410 g tin of drained black cherries.

Black Forest Cake *Layer upon layer of rich filling combine to make this cake scrumptious.*

Madeira Cake

Madeira cake derives its name from the practice in 19th century England of serving this rich sponge cake with a glass of Madeira wine. The cake is a true test of a cook's skill, since it must not be too dry.

Preparation Time: 15 minutes
Cooking Time: 1½-1¾ hours
Pre-heat Oven to 170°C

INGREDIENTS FOR 1 CAKE
225 g self-raising flour
1 ml (¼ teaspoon) salt
175 g butter
175 g castor sugar
4 eggs
2 strips candied citron peel

Sieve the flour and salt together. Cream the butter and sugar together until pale and fluffy. Beat in the eggs, one at a time, adding 15 ml (1 tablespoon) of the flour with each egg.

Fold in the rest of the flour thoroughly and spoon the mixture into a greased and lined cake tin, 18 cm in diameter. Bake in the pre-heated oven for 30 minutes, then place the two strips of citron peel on top of the cake. Bake the cake for a further 30 minutes, then reduce the oven temperature to 150°C and bake for a further 30-45 minutes.

VARIATION Grated lemon rind may be added to the basic mixture to give the cake a tangy lemon flavour.

CARROT CAKE

CARROT CAKE MAY be served with or without the rich icing as it is quite sweet on its own. It has become increasingly popular with young and old alike. One of its advantages is that it keeps well.

PREPARATION TIME: 40 MINUTES
COOKING TIME: 45 MINUTES FOR THE TRIPLE LAYER CAKE; 1¼ HOURS FOR THE TUBE CAKE
PRE-HEAT OVEN TO 180°C

INGREDIENTS FOR 1 LARGE CAKE
375 g flour
10 ml (2 teaspoons) baking powder
10 ml (2 teaspoons) bicarbonate of soda
5 ml (1 teaspoon) ground cinnamon
3 ml (¾ teaspoon) salt
375 g sugar
4 eggs, lightly beaten
375 ml (1½ cups) sunflower oil
5 ml (1 teaspoon) vanilla essence
750 ml (3 cups) grated carrots
250 ml (1 cup) chopped walnuts
250 ml (1 cup) chopped pineapple

For the cream cheese icing:
250 g firm cream cheese
125 g butter
500 g icing sugar
5 ml (1 teaspoon) vanilla essence

In a large bowl, sieve together the flour, baking powder, bicarbonate of soda, cinnamon and salt. Add the sugar.

Make a well in the centre and add the eggs, oil and vanilla essence. Combine the mixture well.

Stir in the carrots, walnuts and pineapple. Mix well. Butter and flour a 25 cm tube pan or three 23 cm sandwich tins. Bake for 1¼ hours if making a tube cake or 45 minutes if making 3 layers.

Allow the cake to cool for at least 15 minutes before turning it out of the pan or tins.

To make the icing, cream the cheese and butter together. Slowly beat in the icing sugar and vanilla essence. If the icing is soft, refrigerate until it is of a good spreading consistency. Ice the cake when it has cooled thoroughly.

VARIATION To make this carrot cake less expensive, you can omit the nuts and pineapple.

BASIC BUTTER CAKE

THIS EXCELLENT basic butter cake mixture, tender and moist, can easily be varied to suit many other types of cake. The cake may also be iced. It will keep even longer than usual if it is well wrapped in aluminium foil or plastic wrap and then stored in an airtight tin.

PREPARATION TIME: 30 MINUTES
COOKING TIME: 1-1¼ HOURS
PRE-HEAT OVEN TO 180°C

INGREDIENTS FOR 1 CAKE
150 g soft butter
180 g castor sugar
5 ml (1 teaspoon) vanilla essence
3 extra-large eggs
200 g flour
8 ml (1¾ teaspoons) baking powder
45 ml (3 tablespoons) hot water

For the topping:
Milk
Castor sugar

Cream the butter well, then add the sugar, a tablespoon at a time, beating it thoroughly after each addition until the mixture has become light and fluffy. Add the vanilla essence.

In a small bowl, beat the eggs lightly and add them slowly to the creamed butter mixture.

Sieve together the flour and baking powder. Add these dry ingredients alternately with the hot water to the creamed mixture, starting and ending with the flour.

Butter and flour any of the following tins: a 23-25 cm tube pan, a 20 cm round loose-bottomed tin or a 23 cm x 12 cm loaf tin. Pour in the batter. For a really good finish, paint the surface with milk and sprinkle it with castor sugar (omit this step if using a tube tin as it is inverted for serving).

Bake for about 1 hour; the exact time will depend on the type of baking tin being used. If the cake is not baked after the hour, reduce the heat to 170°C and bake for a further 15 minutes if necessary.

To test whether the cake is done, gently press the centre of the cake – if it is ready, the cake will spring back at once; if not, a faint impression will remain. The sides of the cake will have shrunk slightly from the sides of the tin when it is done.

Remove the cake from the oven and allow it to stand in the tin for 5 minutes. Turn out on to a wire cooling rack.

VARIATIONS For a slightly richer cake, use warm milk instead of the hot water.

For a cherry cake, cut 100 g glacé cherries in halves or quarters. Mix these with the flour and proceed as in the basic recipe. The grated rind of half a lemon will improve the flavour. The cake can be iced with a plain glacé icing*.

For a dried fruit cake, plump 200 g dried fruit by covering it with boiling water and allowing it to soak for 15 minutes. Drain and dry well, then stir this into the cake mixture with the flour.

For a walnut cake, add 100 g chopped walnuts and 3 ml (¾ teaspoon) ground cinnamon to the cake batter.

For a marble cake, divide the basic mixture into two. Leave one half plain, and to the other half add 30 ml (2 tablespoons) cocoa mixed to a paste with 15 ml (1 tablespoon) hot water. Put this into the tin in alternate spoonfuls.

LEMON CHIFFON CAKE

LIGHT AND DELICIOUS, this lemon chiffon cake may be eaten plain or dressed up in many guises to make a fancy dessert.

The secret of success with a chiffon cake is to use a baking tin which has never been greased. Because of its fine texture, the cake should also not be cut with a knife – split it using 2 forks.

PREPARATION TIME: 40 MINUTES
COOKING TIME: 1 HOUR 10 MINUTES
PRE-HEAT OVEN TO 160°C

INGREDIENTS FOR 1 CAKE
280 g flour, sifted
380 g sugar
10 ml (2 teaspoons) baking powder
5 ml (1 teaspoon) salt
125 ml (½ cup) sunflower oil
5 egg yolks
125 ml (½ cup) water
60 ml (¼ cup) lemon juice
10 ml (2 teaspoons) grated lemon rind
7-9 egg whites
3 ml (¾ teaspoon) cream of tartar
Icing sugar for dusting

All ingredients should be at room temperature. Have ready a 25 cm circular tube pan or chiffon tin, ungreased.

Sieve together the flour, sugar, baking powder and salt in a large bowl. Make a well in the centre.

In a separate bowl, beat the oil, egg yolks, water and lemon juice until they are of a smooth consistency. Add the lemon rind. Add this to the flour mixture and beat very well.

In another mixing bowl, beat the egg whites until soft peaks have formed. Add the cream of tartar and then beat until the egg whites have become very stiff and have lost their gloss.

Pour the egg yolk mixture over the egg whites and gently fold together, using a metal spoon. Pour into the tin and bake for 1 hour 10 minutes.

Remove from the oven, and allow the tin to hang, upside down, over the neck of a bottle until it is completely cold. Then, with a sharp, thin knife, cut the chiffon cake out of the tin and dust it lightly with the icing sugar.

Chocolate Chiffon Cake

This cake, sliced horizontally into 4, is often used as a substitute for Black Forest cake. It forms a suitable base for a variety of desserts. As with other chiffon cakes, it should be baked in a tin which has never been greased.

Preparation Time: 40 minutes
Cooking Time: 1 hour
Pre-heat Oven to 180°C

Ingredients for 1 Cake

50 g cocoa
180 ml boiling water
220 g flour
8 ml (1¾ teaspoons) bicarbonate of soda
440 g sugar
5 ml (1 teaspoon) salt
125 ml (½ cup) sunflower oil
7 egg yolks
10 ml (2 teaspoons) vanilla essence
7 egg whites
3 ml (¾ teaspoon) cream of tartar

Combine the cocoa and boiling water, and allow to cool. Sieve the flour, bicarbonate of soda, sugar and salt into a bowl. Make a well in the centre and add the oil, egg yolks, the cooled cocoa mixture and the vanilla essence. Beat until smooth.

Beat the egg whites until soft peaks form. Add the cream of tartar and beat until very stiff and the whites have lost their gloss.

Pour the egg yolk mixture over the egg whites and fold in gently with a metal spoon. Pour into an ungreased 25 cm circular tube pan or chiffon tin. Bake for 50 minutes. Increase the temperature to 190°C and bake for a further 10 minutes.

Remove from the oven and hang the tin upside down over the neck of a bottle until it is completely cold. Using a sharp thin knife, gently cut around the edges of the tin to loosen the cake.

Chocolate Cake

This moist, rich cake with its delicious fudge icing flavoured with cocoa and chocolate is bound to become a party favourite. It will keep for up to a week in an airtight container.

Preparation Time: 1 hour
Cooking Time: 35 minutes
Pre-heat Oven to 180°C

Ingredients for 1 Cake

225 g flour
10 ml (2 teaspoons) baking powder
2 ml (½ teaspoon) bicarbonate of soda
1 ml (¼ teaspoon) salt
50 g cooking or plain chocolate
225 ml milk
150 g butter
275 g dark, soft brown sugar
3 eggs
15 ml (1 tablespoon) black treacle or golden syrup
5 ml (1 teaspoon) vanilla essence

For the fudge icing:
450 g granulated sugar
150 ml milk
100-125 g butter
15 ml (1 tablespoon) golden syrup
20 ml (4 teaspoons) cocoa
50 g cooking or plain chocolate

Sieve together the flour, baking powder, bicarbonate of soda and salt.

Put the chocolate with the milk into a small saucepan over a low heat and stir occasionally until the chocolate has melted. Remove the pan from the heat and allow the mixture to cool.

Cream the butter and sugar together until fluffy. Beat in the eggs, one at a time, adding a little of the flour mixture alternately with each egg. Stir in the treacle or syrup and vanilla essence, and fold in the remaining flour. Mix well, then stir in the cooled chocolate and milk mixture to make a thick batter.

Divide the mixture among 3 greased sandwich tins, 18 cm in diameter, or two 23 cm sandwich tins, and bake in the pre-heated oven for 30-35 minutes. Turn out the cakes on to a rack to cool.

To make the icing, put the sugar, milk, butter, syrup, cocoa and chocolate into a heavy-based pan. Heat gently until the sugar has dissolved, then bring to the boil and cook to the soft-ball stage*.

Leave to cool for 10 minutes, then beat until the icing is thick enough to spread. Sandwich the cake layers together with the icing, and spread it over the top and sides of the cake, swirling it with a knife.

Dundee Cake

Dundee cake is a fruit cake recognisable by the almonds which decorate the top. Rum, brandy or sherry can be added at the cook's discretion in place of some of the lemon or orange juice.

Preparation Time: 20 minutes
Cooking Time: 1¾-2 hours
Pre-heat Oven to 150°C

Ingredients for 1 Cake

175 g butter
175 g soft brown sugar
4 eggs
225 g flour, sifted
1 ml (¼ teaspoon) salt
25 g ground almonds
175 g sultanas
100-125 g currants
50 g mixed chopped candied peel*
50 g glacé cherries, chopped
Juice and grated rind of ½ lemon
Juice and grated rind of ½ orange
25 g whole almonds, blanched*

Cream the butter and sugar together until light and fluffy. Beat in the eggs, one at a time. Mix the sifted flour, salt and ground almonds, fold into the butter mixture and mix well. Stir in the remaining ingredients (except the almonds).

Grease a 20-23 cm cake tin and line it with a double layer of grease-proof paper. Spoon the mixture into the tin and smooth the top, hollowing the centre slightly.

Arrange the blanched almonds on top and bake in the pre-heated oven for 1¾-2 hours. Do not open the oven door during the first 30 minutes. If the cake is browning too much towards the end of the cooking time, cover it lightly with a piece of grease-proof paper or aluminium foil.

Allow the cake to cool completely before wrapping in foil and storing in an airtight tin, where it will keep for many weeks.

Dundee Cake *Cherries add a splash of colour to this fruity cake.*

BOILED FRUIT CAKE

A BIG ADVANTAGE of this cake is that it keeps well for weeks, even months. In fact, keeping it a week or two undoubtedly improves the flavour.

PREPARATION TIME: 30 MINUTES
COOKING TIME: 1 HOUR 10 MINUTES
PRE-HEAT OVEN TO 160°C

INGREDIENTS FOR 1 CAKE
150 g butter
250 ml (1 cup) water
200 g sugar
150 g sultanas
150 g currants
150 g mixed candied peel*
150 g seedless raisins
125 ml (½ cup) brandy
250 g flour
10 ml (2 teaspoons) baking powder
5 ml (1 teaspoon) bicarbonate of soda
5 ml (1 teaspoon) mixed spice
3 ml (¾ teaspoon) ground cinnamon
3 ml (¾ teaspoon) ground ginger
2 extra-large eggs, lightly beaten

In a large saucepan, bring the butter, water, sugar, sultanas, currants, mixed peel, raisins and brandy to the boil.

Meanwhile, sieve the flour, baking powder, bicarbonate of soda and spices into a large mixing bowl. Add the boiled fruit mixture to the flour mixture and blend well. Fold in the eggs. Pour the mixture into a lined and greased loaf tin, 23 cm x 12 cm, or a 20 cm deep round tin (if you use a non-stick tin with a fine coating of non-stick cooking spray, it will not be necessary to line the tin), and bake for about 1 hour 10 minutes. Test after 1 hour. Leave the cake in the tin for 10 minutes, then turn it out. When the cake is cool, wrap in aluminium foil and store.

VARIATION For a richer cake, add the following to the boiling fruit mixture: 100 g each of glacé cherries, glacé pineapple, glacé or preserved figs, watermelon konfyt, chopped dates and preserved ginger. After the eggs have been added, fold in 200 g chopped nuts. Bake for 1½ hours in 2 loaf tins (the extra ingredients will double the amount of cake made).

GINGERBREAD CAKE

GINGERBREAD CAKE with butter is a delightful tea time snack. It freezes well, making it ideal for unexpected guests.

PREPARATION TIME: 10 MINUTES
COOKING TIME: 1 HOUR
PRE-HEAT OVEN TO 175°C

INGREDIENTS FOR 1 CAKE
320 g flour
5 ml (1 teaspoon) ground cinnamon
5 ml (1 teaspoon) ground ginger
2 ml (½ teaspoon) ground cloves
2 ml (½ teaspoon) salt
125 g butter
125 g sugar
250 ml (1 cup) golden syrup
10 ml (2 teaspoons) bicarbonate of soda
250 ml (1 cup) boiling water
2 eggs, lightly beaten

Sieve together the flour, cinnamon, ginger, cloves and salt. Combine the butter, sugar and syrup. Dissolve the bicarbonate of soda in the boiling water, then add it to the butter mixture. Add the eggs and the dry ingredients. Pour the mixture into a greased and floured loaf tin, 23 cm x 12 cm, and bake for 1 hour.

VARIATION The gingerbread may be baked in 2 small loaf tins for 45 minutes.

RICH FRUIT CAKE

THIS CAKE MUST MATURE for at least 2 months. It may be kept for as long as 18 months if it is treated with brandy every 2 months during that period. It will then be even more delicious. This is an ideal recipe for a Christmas or wedding cake.

PREPARATION TIME: 1½ HOURS
STANDING TIME: 24 HOURS
COOKING TIME: 3½-4 HOURS
MATURING TIME: AT LEAST 2 MONTHS
PRE-HEAT OVEN TO 125°C

INGREDIENTS FOR 3 CAKES
OF 2 KG (20 CM DIAMETER)
300 g seeded raisins, sliced
1 kg seedless raisins
300 g prunes, soaked and cut in small pieces
500 g cherries, halved or quartered
250 g sliced candied pineapple
1,4 kg candied citrus peel* (citron, orange, lemon)
300 g walnuts or pecan nuts
15 ml (1 tablespoon) grated orange rind
125 ml (½ cup) orange juice or brandy
500 g butter
400 g white sugar
200 g brown sugar
10 eggs, beaten
15 ml (1 tablespoon) vanilla essence
600 g flour
7 ml (1½ teaspoons) salt
15 ml (1 tablespoon) baking powder
15 ml (1 tablespoon) ground cinnamon
10 ml (2 teaspoons) ground cloves
5 ml (1 teaspoon) ground allspice
10 ml (2 teaspoons) ground mace or nutmeg
90 ml brandy

Combine the fruit, peel, nuts and orange rind, and then pour the orange juice or brandy over the mixture. Leave it to stand for 24 hours.

Cream the butter, add the white and brown sugar, cream well and then add the beaten eggs. Add this to the fruit mixture, followed by the vanilla essence. Sieve together the flour, salt, baking powder and spices, twice, then fold into the fruit mixture and stir well by hand – do not beat.

Line 3 cake tins (20 cm diameter) with 3 layers of baking paper (or buttered grease-proof paper) each. Divide the cake mixture among the 3 tins. Bake for 3½-4 hours in the pre-heated oven (place a pan of water in the oven on the bottom rack). To test whether the cakes are done, insert a knife into the centre of each – if it comes out clean, the cakes are cooked.

Remove the cakes from the oven and while they are still hot pour 30 ml (2 tablespoons) brandy over each one. Leave the cakes to cool in the tins before removing them, but do not remove the lining paper. Store the cakes wrapped in plastic wrap or aluminium foil in tightly closed containers.

Pour brandy over the cakes once or twice during their maturing time.

SWISS ROLL

THE BASIC SWISS ROLL is filled with smooth apricot jam, but it can be dressed up with various other fillings and made in many flavours. A true Swiss roll is traditionally made without any baking powder and relies entirely on well-beaten eggs for the necessary leavening. In this recipe, however, baking powder is used so that the inexperienced cook will be able to make the roll with little trouble.

PREPARATION TIME: 20 MINUTES
COOKING TIME: 15 MINUTES
PRE-HEAT OVEN TO 200°C

INGREDIENTS FOR 1 ROLL
100 g flour
1 ml (¼ teaspoon) salt
5 ml (1 teaspoon) baking powder
5 eggs
180 g sugar
5 ml (1 teaspoon) vanilla essence
30 ml (2 tablespoons) boiling water
Sugar for sprinkling
Smooth apricot jam*

Sieve together the flour, salt and baking powder. Beat the eggs and sugar together very well (about 10 minutes), then gently fold in the flour mixture. Add the vanilla essence and boiling water.

Pour the mixture into a greased tin, 38 cm x 25 cm, which has been lined with buttered grease-proof paper. Bake for 12-15 minutes.

Turn out the cake on to a damp tea towel that has been sprinkled with sugar. Trim the edges of the cake, then roll it up with the tea towel. Cool it, unroll it gently, removing the tea towel, and fill the cake with smooth apricot jam, or with the filling of your choice. Then gently roll up the cake once again.

VARIATION Use 200 g ground almonds or walnuts in place of the flour. Omit the boiling water. Fill the cake with coffee-flavoured whipped cream.

~ The Decorative Art of Icing ~

No celebration cake is complete without a tasty and attractive icing.
With a little bit of practice, and the right equipment,
you will be able to turn ordinary cakes into works of art.

Christmas Cake

Icing Time: 20 minutes

20 cm round fruit cake (rich fruit cake*, boiled fruit cake*, or Dundee cake* baked without the almond decoration)
A little smooth apricot jam*
700 g marzipan*
600 g easy fondant icing*
Red ribbon
Green ribbon
1-2 sprigs imitation holly

Brush the cake with a little apricot jam that has been warmed. Cover the top with the marzipan.

Roll the easy fondant icing very thinly and mould the sheet of icing with your hands to fit the cake smoothly and snugly. Neaten the bottom edge with a sharp knife.

Tie the ribbons around the cake so that they overlap slightly and end in bows. Position the holly in the centre of the cake.

Heart Cake

Icing Time: 30 minutes

Victoria sponge sandwich* or basic butter cake* baked in 2 heart-shaped layer tins
800 g butter icing*
Tiny fresh flowers
Thin ribbon

Sandwich the cooled cakes with butter icing, then cover completely with the same icing. With a star nozzle, pipe a decorative border around the edges of the cake.

Top with a posy of fresh flowers and a bow of thin, curly ribbon.

Decorated in a pale pink, this makes a pretty cake for a young girl's party, or a romantic Valentine's Day surprise.

Party Cake

Icing Time: 20 minutes

Lemon chiffon cake*
300 g frosting*
Fresh flowers

Cover the cake with the boiled white frosting. Use a spatula to swirl the frosting decoratively. Fill the centre hole of the cake with a posy of fresh flowers. This cake must be decorated on the day of the celebration as the boiled frosting loses its lustre if made too far in advance.

Birthday Cake

Icing Time: 30 minutes

20 cm round fruit cake (rich fruit cake*, boiled fruit cake*, or Dundee cake* baked without the almond decoration)
600 g easy fondant icing*
Sugar roses*
250 g royal icing*
Pastel-coloured ribbon

Cover the cake with a layer of easy fondant icing. Position a few sugar roses (moulded out of the easy fondant icing) on top of the cake.

With a star nozzle, pipe a decorative border of royal icing around the top and bottom circumference of the cake. Pipe rosettes on top of the cake to hold tiny candles. Tie the pastel-coloured ribbon around the cake.

BIRTHDAY CAKE

Sugar Roses and Leaves

Preparation Time: 40 minutes

600 g easy fondant icing*
Colouring (optional)

Divide up the icing and knead in the appropriate colouring, unless you prefer to leave the flowers white.

Roll out the icing thinly. Cut out leaf and rose petal shapes. With a small, sharp knife, mark out the veins in the leaf shapes.

To make the roses, build them out of the cut-out rose petals.

Allow the leaves and shaped flowers to harden on grease-proof or non-stick paper. Once hardened, lift off gently.

Store in an airtight container and use to decorate cakes for special occasions.

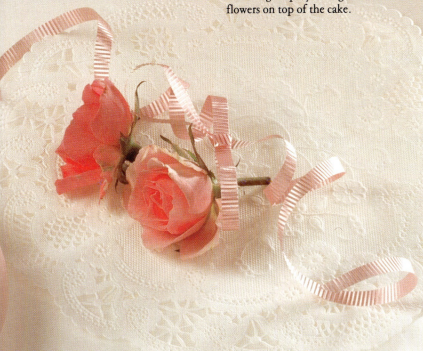

Wedding Cake

Icing Time: 45 minutes

Rich fruit cake* baked in 3 round tins of graduated sizes
A little smooth apricot jam*
1,4 kg marzipan*
1,2 kg easy fondant icing*
250 g white royal icing*
White ribbon
White sugar roses*, or fresh white rosebuds or tiny white flowers

Cover each cake layer with the warmed jam, the marzipan and easy fondant icing. Stack the cakes directly one on top of the other to form 3 tiers.

Use a star nozzle to pipe a decorative border of royal icing around the edges of each layer. Tie a ribbon around each layer.

Arrange a posy of sugar roses or fresh flowers on top of the cake.

Chocolate Celebration Cake

Preparation Time: 15 minutes for the filling
Assembly and Icing Time: 30 minutes
Chilling Time: 2 hours

750 ml (3 cups) cream, well chilled
375 ml (1½ cups) sifted icing sugar
180 ml sifted cocoa
5 ml (1 teaspoon) vanilla essence
1 ml (¼ teaspoon) salt
5 ml (1 teaspoon) gelatin
30 ml (2 tablespoons) cold water
Chocolate chiffon cake*
Chocolate roses and leaves*

Beat the chilled cream with the icing sugar, cocoa, vanilla essence and salt until stiff enough to hold its shape. Refrigerate.

Sprinkle the gelatin over the cold water to soften, then heat it over hot water, stirring until the gelatin has dissolved. Allow the mixture to cool slightly.

Cut a 2,5 cm thick slice from the top of the cake and set it aside. Carefully hollow out enough cake to leave a 2,5 cm thick wall of cake around the centre hole, a 2,5 cm thick outer circumference, and a 2,5 cm thick base to the cake. Set aside 300 ml of the cake crumbs.

Fold the cooled gelatin into 500 ml (2 cups) of the chocolate cream and use this mixture to fill the hollowed-out cavity. Replace the lid of the cake.

Mix the cake crumbs with 125 ml (½ cup) of the chocolate cream and use this mixture to fill the centre hole of the cake.

Cover the cake with the rest of the chocolate cream and decorate with chocolate roses and leaves. If you like, you can pipe a decorative border of chocolate cream.

Refrigerate the cake until well chilled, before slicing.

Train Cake

Assembly and Icing Time: 1 hour

A little smooth apricot jam*
2 small loaf cakes (made with basic butter cake mixture*)
1 Swiss roll*
800 g chocolate, melted
Halved wafer biscuits for windows, or small quantity of white royal icing*
Icing sugar
A few chocolate peppermint creams, or a medium-sized candle
Popcorn (optional)
Round basic butter biscuits* or round chocolate biscuits
Small candles (to represent years)

With the jam, sandwich the 2 loaf cakes together vertically and join on to the end of the Swiss roll – they form the main front and back sections of the train engine. Coat with melted chocolate.

For the windows in the engine-driver's cabin, use halved wafer biscuits or pipe appropriate window shapes with white royal icing. If using wafer biscuits, these can be embedded while the chocolate coating is still soft, or alternatively stuck on later using a little icing sugar mixed with water.

To make the chimney, stack up a few chocolate peppermint creams, melting the bottoms slightly so that they adhere to one another. Alternatively, use a candle for the chimney – when lit it will give an appropriate visual effect. If you want to create 'smoke' above the peppermint creams, stick pieces of popcorn together with icing sugar and water, and stick this cluster on top of the chimney.

To make the wheels, use round, painted basic butter biscuits* or round chocolate biscuits and stick these to the sides of the engine with icing sugar and water. You can use white royal icing to pipe the spokes and outline the shape of the wheel.

A very appealing final touch is to place a row of paper-covered or brightly painted shoe boxes behind the engine and down the length of the table to represent the trucks. They are also very convenient for holding sweets, biscuits and other party 'goodies'. Again, use biscuits to represent the wheels of the trucks.

SIMNEL CAKE *This Easter cake, covered with tasty almond paste, is rich in fruit – and in tradition.*

SIMNEL CAKE

IN ENGLAND, MOTHERS whose daughters went into service as cooks in the late 1600s looked forward to the fourth Sunday in Lent. It was then that the girls came home bearing the proof of their cooking skills – a rich and delicious fruit cake enriched with almond paste, and called a simnel cake. These cakes always improved with keeping and were traditionally eaten at the end of the Lenten Fast, when they were sometimes known as Easter cakes.

Simnel cake keeps well in an airtight tin for two weeks or more.

PREPARATION TIME: 30 MINUTES
COOKING TIME: 1½-2 HOURS
PRE-HEAT OVEN TO 140°C

INGREDIENTS FOR 1 CAKE

For the almond paste:
150 g castor sugar
150 g ground almonds
1 egg, beaten
2 ml (½ teaspoon) almond essence

125 g butter
125 g soft brown sugar
3 eggs, beaten
150 g flour
1 ml (¼ teaspoon) salt
5 ml (1 teaspoon) ground mixed spice (optional)
350 g mixed raisins, currants and sultanas
50 g chopped mixed peel
Grated rind of ½ lemon
A little smooth apricot jam*
A little beaten egg for glazing

To make the almond paste, mix together the sugar and ground almonds, and add enough beaten egg to give a fairly soft consistency. Add the almond essence and knead until the paste is smooth and pliable. Roll out one-third of the almond paste to make an 18 cm circle. Reserve the remainder for topping the cooked cake.

Cream the butter and brown sugar together until fluffy. Beat in the eggs, a little at a time. Sieve the flour, salt and mixed spice (if used) together, and add to the butter mixture alternately with the dried fruit, peel and grated rind, mixing well.

Put half the mixture into a greased and lined 18 cm cake tin and cover with the circle of almond paste. Add the rest of the cake mixture and smooth the top, hollowing the centre slightly. Bake in the pre-heated oven for 1½-2 hours. Leave to cool in the tin.

When the cake is cold, remove from the tin and brush over the top with apricot jam. Form 11 small balls from the reserved almond paste and roll out the rest to cover the top of the cake. Lay it on the jam, set the balls round the edge and brush all the top with a very little beaten egg. Return the cake to the oven for about 10 minutes at 180°C for the almond paste to brown.

VARIATION If you like, you can decorate the centre of the cake with coloured marzipan Easter eggs.

VICTORIA SPONGE SANDWICH

THIS SPONGE CAKE, named after Queen Victoria, was originally filled with various preserves or fruit. Nowadays raspberry or apricot jam is usually substituted for the preserves or fruit.

PREPARATION TIME: 15 MINUTES
COOKING TIME: 25 MINUTES
PRE-HEAT OVEN TO 190°C

INGREDIENTS FOR 1 CAKE
250 g butter
250 g castor sugar
4 eggs
250 g self-raising flour, sifted
2 ml (½ teaspoon) vanilla essence
Raspberry* or apricot jam*

Cream together the butter and sugar until pale and fluffy. Beat in the eggs, one at a time, adding 10 ml (2 teaspoons) of the flour with the second egg. Fold in the rest of the flour and the vanilla essence.

Divide the mixture equally between 2 greased 23 cm sandwich tins. Bake for 20-25 minutes. Cool, inverted on a wire rack, removing the tins after 10 minutes. Sandwich the cakes together with the raspberry or apricot jam.

VARIATIONS For a tangy sponge, use lemon rind in the sponge and sandwich together with lemon curd.

Make 20 cupcakes with the mixture instead of a cake, baking for 10-15 minutes, or until golden-brown.

DATE AND WALNUT LOAF

THIS BASIC TEA BREAD is just as delicious served plain as with a thin layer of fresh butter. It keeps well if sealed in plastic wrap and stored in an airtight tin.

PREPARATION TIME: 15 MINUTES
COOKING TIME: 1 HOUR
PRE-HEAT OVEN TO 180°C

INGREDIENTS FOR 1 LOAF
250 g dates, chopped
5 ml (1 teaspoon) bicarbonate of soda
250 ml (1 cup) boiling water
15 g butter
1 egg, beaten

250 g flour, sifted
80 g walnuts, chopped
3 ml (¾ teaspoon) baking powder
250 g sugar
3 ml (¾ teaspoon) salt

Mix together the dates, bicarbonate of soda, boiling water and butter. Allow to cool slightly.

Add the egg, flour, nuts, baking powder, sugar and salt. Gently mix together and pour the mixture into a greased and floured 23 cm x 15 cm loaf tin.

Bake for 1 hour. Allow to cool in the tin for 5 minutes, then turn out on to a wire rack to cool.

BANANA LOAF

ALWAYS A GOOD STANDBY, these tasty loaves can be made a few at a time and then frozen. The banana loaf provides an ideal way to make use of bananas that have become soft and discoloured.

PREPARATION TIME: 15 MINUTES
COOKING TIME: 1 HOUR
PRE-HEAT OVEN TO 180°C

INGREDIENTS FOR 1 MEDIUM-SIZED LOAF
125 g butter
180 g sugar
2 eggs, well-beaten
5 ml (1 teaspoon) vanilla essence
250 g flour
5 ml (1 teaspoon) bicarbonate of soda
3 ml (¾ teaspoon) salt
45 ml (3 tablespoons) soured milk
3 large bananas, well mashed

Cream the butter well, then gradually beat in the sugar, the beaten eggs and the vanilla essence. Sieve together the flour, bicarbonate of soda and salt, and add the dry ingredients alternately with the milk and well-mashed bananas.

Turn the mixture into a greased loaf tin, about 23 cm x 12 cm, and bake for 1 hour – a knife inserted into the loaf should come out clean.

SERVING SUGGESTION Banana loaf is delightful when it is simply served sliced and buttered.

VARIATION Add 125 ml (½ cup) chopped walnuts to the mixture.

BABA AU RHUM

THIS FAMOUS FRENCH dessert has found favour the whole world over. It is said to have been the creation of a Polish king who named it after his favourite hero in the *Tales of a Thousand and One Nights*. More precisely, what the creator of this dish did was to invent a new way of serving *kugelhupf*, an old, well-established central European cake, by soaking it in a rum syrup.

PREPARATION TIME: 25 MINUTES
RISING TIME: 1½ HOURS
COOKING TIME: 20 MINUTES FOR THE BABAS;
40 MINUTES FOR THE SYRUP
PRE-HEAT OVEN TO 210°C

INGREDIENTS FOR EIGHT TO TEN
15 ml (1 tablespoon) dried yeast, or 25 g fresh yeast
60 ml (¼ cup) luke-warm milk
A pinch of sugar
250 g flour, sifted
4 eggs, lightly beaten
3 ml (¾ teaspoon) salt
15 ml (1 tablespoon) sugar
180 g soft butter
120 g currants

For the rum syrup:
200 g sugar
375 ml (1½ cups) water
125 ml (½ cup) rum

Mix the yeast with the milk and add the pinch of sugar. Allow to stand for 10 minutes, or until frothy.

Place the flour in a large mixing bowl and make a well in the centre. Add the eggs, salt, the 15 ml (1 tablespoon) sugar and the yeast mixture. Mix this well and then beat it in the bowl for a few minutes. Cover and allow to rise in a warm place until it is double in bulk – about 45 minutes.

Stir down the mixture and add the butter and currants. Beat it in the bowl for another 4 minutes. Fill 8-10 well-greased muffin or dariole moulds to one-third full and allow to rise until the batter doubles again in bulk (about 45 minutes).

Bake for 10 minutes. Reduce the heat to 180°C and bake until the babas are golden-brown. Turn them out on to a wire rack and cool them to lukewarm.

While they are cooling, make the rum syrup. Simmer the sugar and water together for 35-40 minutes, or until the liquid is syrupy. Add the rum.

Place the babas in a deep dish, prick them all over with a skewer and pour the hot rum syrup over them. Baste them until most of the syrup is absorbed.

SERVING SUGGESTION Serve at room temperature with whipped cream.

VARIATION Omit the currants and bake the dough in a round-bottomed ring mould – the dish is then called a savarin.

VETKOEK

THESE TRADITIONAL fried cakes can add interest to a breakfast or serve as a tasty nibble between meals.

PREPARATION TIME: 40 MINUTES
COOKING TIME: 5-10 MINUTES

INGREDIENTS FOR ABOUT 20 CAKES
240 g flour
10 ml (2 teaspoons) baking powder
15 ml (1 tablespoon) sugar
2 ml (½ teaspoon) salt
2 eggs, beaten
125 ml (½ cup) water or milk
Fat or sunflower oil for frying

Sieve the flour and baking powder together, and add the sugar. Mix together the beaten eggs and the water or milk, then gradually add this mixture to the dry ingredients. The batter should be fairly stiff.

Heat enough fat or oil for shallow- or deep-frying until it is hot but not smoking. Dip a tablespoon into the hot fat or oil and then use it to drop spoonfuls of the batter into the frying pan. Fry until the cakes brown on all sides.

Allow the vetkoek to drain well on a wire rack over a bowl.

SERVING SUGGESTION Serve with jam or honey for breakfast or supper – it makes a good alternative to bread.

BABA AU RHUM *A French favourite redolent with rum.*

Koeksisters

THE SWEET TASTE of these attractively plaited dough cakes makes them a great favourite in South Africa. The secret of their success, some claim, is in preparing the syrup a day ahead and chilling it before dipping the koeksisters.

PREPARATION TIME: 1 HOUR
CHILLING TIME: 2 HOURS, OR OVERNIGHT, FOR THE SYRUP
STANDING TIME: 30 MINUTES-1 HOUR
COOKING TIME: 50 MINUTES

INGREDIENTS FOR 40 KOEKSISTERS
For the syrup:
1 kg sugar
500 ml (2 cups) water
2 pieces fresh green ginger (each 5 cm), peeled and crushed
2 ml (½ teaspoon) cream of tartar
A pinch of salt
Grated rind and juice of ½ lemon

For the dough:
500 g flour
2 ml (½ teaspoons) salt
30 ml (2 tablespoons) baking powder
55 g butter, grated
1 egg
250-375 ml (1-1½ cups) milk or water
Sunflower oil for deep-frying

To make the syrup, put all the ingredients in a saucepan. Heat (stirring) until the sugar has completely dissolved. Cover the mixture and boil for 1 minute.

Remove the saucepan lid and boil the syrup for a further 5 minutes, but do not stir it.

Remove the syrup from the stove and allow it to cool for at least 2 hours in a refrigerator, or preferably overnight.

To make the dough, sieve together the dry ingredients and rub in the grated butter with your fingertips, or cut it in with a pastry cutter.

Beat the egg, add 250 ml (1 cup) of the milk or water and mix lightly with the dry ingredients to a soft dough. Add more milk or water if the dough is too stiff. Knead well until small bubbles form under the surface of the dough. Cover with a damp cloth and allow to stand for 30 minutes-1 hour. Roll out the dough to a thickness of 1 cm, then form koeksisters in either of the following ways:

Cut strips 1 cm wide and twist 2 strips together, or plait 3 strips together, cutting the twisted or plaited lengths at 8 cm intervals and pinching the ends together. Alternatively, cut the dough into 8 cm x 4 cm pieces. Cut 2 vertical slits in each piece, reaching to 1 cm from the end. Plait the 3 strips that have been formed and pinch together the loose ends.

Heat 7-8 cm deep oil to 180-190°C – a cube of day-old bread should turn golden-brown in a minute. Fry the koeksisters for 1-2 minutes, or until golden-brown, then turn them over with a fork and fry until golden-brown on the other side.

Remove the koeksisters with a lifter or slotted spoon, drain them for a moment on paper towels and then plunge them into the cold syrup for 1-2 minutes. Stand the container of syrup in a bowl of ice so that the syrup will stay cold.

Remove the koeksisters from the syrup with a lifter or slotted spoon, allowing the excess syrup to flow back into the basin, then drain them slightly on a wire rack.

VARIATIONS For a lighter dough, use sour milk or buttermilk, or add lemon juice to the water. For a more cake-like texture, add 2 well-beaten eggs to the milk and 2 ml (½ teaspoon) grated nutmeg.

Without eggs the koeksisters have more of a doughnut consistency.

Adding 5-10 ml (1-2 teaspoons) glycerine to the syrup will give the koeksisters a shiny appearance when coated.

Boston Brownies

BROWNIES ARE MOIST, chewy cakes found throughout the United States. Their names, and brownie recipes, differ from area to area – but Boston brownies are among the best.

Take care not to overcook brownies, or they will become dry and brittle.

PREPARATION TIME: 15 MINUTES
COOKING TIME: 25-30 MINUTES
PRE-HEAT OVEN TO 180°C

INGREDIENTS FOR 15 BROWNIES
50 g butter
200 g soft brown sugar
1 egg, beaten
5 ml (1 teaspoon) vanilla essence
100-125 g flour
1 ml (¼ teaspoon) salt
2 ml (½ teaspoon) baking powder
100-125 g walnuts or pecan nuts, chopped

Melt the butter in a medium-sized saucepan over a low heat. Add the sugar and stir well. Draw the pan off the heat and let the mixture cool for 1 minute, then add the egg and vanilla essence.

Sift the flour, salt and baking powder together, and stir these ingredients into the butter mixture. Add the chopped nuts and mix well.

Grease a 28 cm x 18 cm tin and spread the mixture in it evenly. Bake in the pre-heated oven for 25-30 minutes, or until a light crust has formed on top. Cool in the tin for 15 minutes, cutting into 15 squares after about 5 minutes.

BOSTON BROWNIES *and* ALMOND BISCUITS *Excellent companions.*

Almond Biscuits

BISCUITS ARE a useful standby and these tasty almond strips are certain to become firm favourites.

PREPARATION TIME: 20 MINUTES
CHILLING TIME: 4 HOURS
COOKING TIME: 20-25 MINUTES
PRE-HEAT OVEN TO 180°C

INGREDIENTS FOR 40 BISCUITS
200 g castor sugar
3 eggs
125 g soft butter
A pinch of salt
1 ml (¼ teaspoon) almond essence
360 g flour, sifted
250 g almonds, chopped

Beat the sugar and eggs together very well, then add the butter, salt and almond essence. Add the sifted flour and mix into a soft dough.

Add the almonds and refrigerate the biscuit mixture for 4 hours.

Roll the biscuit mixture into long strands about 2,5 cm in thickness. Bake the strips on a greased biscuit tray for about 15 minutes, or until they have become a pale golden colour.

Cut the strips into 6 cm lengths. Return them to the oven and bake for a further 5-10 minutes until crisp.

BREADS, CAKES AND BISCUITS

BOEREBESKUIT

ONCE FOUND on every Afrikaans housewife's shelves, this biscuit is traditionally made with home-made sweet yeast ('soetsuurdeeg') or salt-rising yeast. But commercial yeast may also be used.

PREPARATION TIME: 1 HOUR
RISING TIME: 9 HOURS
COOKING TIME: 1 HOUR
PRE-HEAT OVEN TO 180°C

INGREDIENTS FOR 50 RUSKS
For the ferment:
22 ml (4½ teaspoons) dried yeast, or 37,5 g fresh yeast
7 ml (1½ teaspoons) sugar
500 ml (2 cups) lukewarm water
60 g flour

500 g butter or 250 g butter and 250 g vegetable fat
300 ml milk and 50 ml water, boiled
7 ml (1½ teaspoons) salt
2,5 kg sifted flour
Melted butter for brushing

Dissolve the yeast with the sugar in the water, sprinkle over the flour, stir, cover and keep in a warm place to ferment for 1-2 hours. The mixture must be frothy.

Melt the butter (or butter mixture) in the milk and water mixture, add the salt and allow to cool until lukewarm. Put the 2,5 kg flour into a deep basin and make a hollow in the middle. Pour the lukewarm milk mixture and the yeast mixture into the hollow. Blend with a wooden spoon to a stiff dough. Add lukewarm water if necessary.

Knead the dough very well, taking care that it is not exposed to draughts or allowed to get cold. Spread a little melted butter over the dough. Cover the basin with plastic wrap, and wrap it up warmly in a heavy blanket. Leave the dough to rise to double its bulk in a warm place for 3-4 hours.

When well-risen, roll pieces of dough into long rolls of 4 cm diameter. Cut off 4 cm pieces and pack them closely together in greased deep loaf pans. Brush with melted butter. Cover the pans lightly and leave the pieces to rise in a warm place until they are double in bulk (about 3 hours).

Bake for 1 hour in the pre-heated oven. When they have cooled, break the rusks into portions, place on wire racks and dry in a very cool oven with the door ajar.

BUTTERMILK RUSKS

THIS IS A VARIATION on boerebeskuit – the traditional yeast-baked rusk which formed the staple diet of the Boer commandoes – and is much simpler to make. If the rusks are to be kept for a long time do not substitute margarine for the butter.

PREPARATION TIME: 40 MINUTES
COOKING TIME: 45-55 MINUTES
DRYING TIME: 4-5 HOURS, OR OVERNIGHT
PRE-HEAT OVEN TO 180°C

INGREDIENTS FOR 36 RUSKS
375 g butter
500 g sugar
2 extra-large eggs
1,5 kg self-raising flour
30 ml (2 tablespoons) baking powder
500 ml (2 cups) buttermilk or plain drinking yoghurt

Cream the butter and sugar together very well. Add the eggs, one at a time. Sift the flour and baking powder together, and add this to the creamed mixture, using a fork to mix. Add the buttermilk or yoghurt, using a little milk to rinse out the carton. Mix well with a fork and then knead lightly.

Pack lightly rolled, golf ball sized buns of the dough into greased bread pans close together, and bake for 45-55 minutes. Place the pans in the middle of the oven, with a sheet of brown paper on the top shelf to protect the buns from becoming browned too quickly.

Remove the paper after the buns are well risen and cooked through, to brown the tops. Reduce the heat to the lowest possible setting. Turn out the buns on to cake racks, cool them and separate them, using 2 forks. Pack them on wire racks or on cooled oven racks – air must circulate. Place them in the cool oven, leaving the door ajar, for 4-5 hours, or overnight, to dry out.

VARIATION If no buttermilk or yoghurt is available, fresh milk curdled with lemon juice or white vinegar may be used.

BUTTERMILK RUSKS *A classic recipe from Ouma's kitchen.*

OLD-FASHIONED SOETKOEKIES

IF YOU HAVE CHILDREN, be sure to make a large quantity of 'soetkoekies' as they are guaranteed to 'disappear' very quickly.

PREPARATION TIME: 1½ HOURS
STANDING TIME: 1 HOUR
COOKING TIME: 15 MINUTES
PRE-HEAT OVEN TO 200°C

INGREDIENTS FOR 200 BISCUITS
960 g flour
2 ml (½ teaspoon) salt
7 ml (1½ teaspoons) bicarbonate of soda
10 ml (2 teaspoons) cream of tartar
10 ml (2 teaspoons) ground cinnamon
5 ml (1 teaspoon) ground cloves
400 g sugar
230 g butter
2 eggs
125-200 ml water or sweet wine
5 ml (1 teaspoon) grated orange rind
50 almonds, blanched* and split (optional)

Sieve together the flour, salt, bicarbonate of soda, cream of tartar, cinnamon and cloves. Add the sugar and mix well.

Grate the butter and work it into the dry ingredients using your fingertips.

Beat the eggs thoroughly in a separate bowl, adding 30 ml (2 tablespoons) of the water or wine and the orange rind.

Add the egg mixture gradually to the dry mixture and blend it with enough of the remaining water or wine to form a soft dough, which may be rolled easily. Knead well and allow to stand for 1 hour or longer.

Cut off a portion of the dough for rolling, leaving the rest in a cool place. Roll it to a 3 mm thickness and cut out rounds with a biscuit cutter dipped in flour. Put a halved almond (if used) on the centre of some of the biscuits for variety.

Lift the biscuits with a spatula on to greased baking sheets, placing them about 2,5 cm apart. Bake them for 15 minutes. Remove the biscuits with a spatula, place them on a wire rack and leave to cool.

Store the biscuits in a tin with a tight-fitting lid to keep them crisp. They will also keep dry in a covered earthenware jar.

315

The Art of Painting Biscuits

Painted butter biscuits are ideal for festive occasions and make delightful gifts or treats for children's birthday parties.

To make the 'paint', beat an egg yolk and blend in enough red, green or yellow food colouring to reach the colour intensity desired. Mix yellow and red to get orange. The mixture thickens on standing, so beat in drops of water to maintain a good brushing consistency.

With a small paintbrush, brush the coloured egg yolk on to the unbaked biscuits. Brush the surface completely to the edges. Paint the biscuits in one colour, or be imaginative and work out adventurous designs. After baking, you can accentuate the shapes with outlines of piped icing.

Bake the biscuits for about 8 minutes at 190°C until they are set but not browned. Baking for too long darkens and spoils the brightness of the baked colours.

Basic Butter Biscuits

IDEAL FOR A PLAIN biscuit or for jam or date squares, this recipe is also suitable for a sweet pie crust. It keeps well in a refrigerator for up to 2 weeks, wrapped in grease-proof paper.

PREPARATION TIME: 30 MINUTES
CHILLING TIME: 1 HOUR
COOKING TIME: 10 MINUTES
PRE-HEAT OVEN TO 200°C

INGREDIENTS FOR 80 BISCUITS
250 g butter
375 g sugar
360 g flour
15 ml (1 tablespoon) baking powder
A pinch of salt
2 extra-large eggs, beaten
5 ml (1 teaspoon) vanilla essence

Cream the butter and sugar together. Sieve the dry ingredients and add them to the creamed mixture alternately with the beaten eggs, then add the vanilla essence. Allow this mixture to rest in the refrigerator for at least 1 hour before rolling it out (about 5 mm thick). Cut out desired shapes, place them on lightly greased biscuit trays and bake for 8-10 minutes.

Oblietjies

OBLIETJIES ARE ROLLED WAFERS that were made by the Huguenots in special oblietjie irons. If you do not have such an iron (they are quite rare nowadays), you can utilise two frying pans in the manner described.

PREPARATION TIME: 30 MINUTES
COOKING TIME: 1 HOUR

INGREDIENTS FOR 30 OBLIETJIES
110 g butter
225 g castor sugar
2 eggs
5 ml (1 teaspoon) ground cinnamon
2 ml (½ teaspoon) salt
250 g flour
250 ml (1 cup) sweet sherry

Cream the butter and sugar together. Beat each egg and add it to the creamed mixture, beating well after each addition. Add the cinnamon and salt to the flour, and sieve the mixture twice. Add the flour mixture alternately with the sherry to the creamed mixture. Blend well.

The batter should not be thinner than pancake batter. Heat the oblietjie iron or a heavy-based frying pan, and grease it lightly with fat.

Put a little batter – about 10 ml (2 teaspoons) – on one side of the iron, or in the pan. If using an oblietjie iron, close the 2 sections and put the iron on the stove. If using a pan, compress the batter with another pan and leave this pan resting on the oblietjie while cooking.

After 2-3 minutes turn the iron, or if using a pan, turn over the oblietjie. Remove it from the heat when the batter is light brown on both sides.

With a fork, roll the oblietjie or wafer like a pancake or shape it like a trumpet, then allow it to cool. Store the oblietjies in an airtight container.

SERVING SUGGESTION Serve plain or with whipped cream or any other filling.

OBLIETJIES *Light and airy wafers add a touch of tradition.*

Muesli Biscuits

FILL THE BISCUIT TIN with these easy-to-make biscuits textured with muesli.

PREPARATION TIME: 20 MINUTES
COOKING TIME: 12-15 MINUTES
PRE-HEAT OVEN TO 180°C

INGREDIENTS FOR ABOUT 30 BISCUITS
120 g flour
2 ml (½ teaspoon) baking powder
2 ml (½ teaspoon) salt
125 g butter
200 g soft brown sugar
1 egg
2 ml (½ teaspoon) vanilla essence
15 ml (1 tablespoon) milk
150 ml muesli*

Sieve together the flour, baking powder and salt. Cream the butter and sugar together until fluffy, then beat in the egg, vanilla essence and milk until smooth. Gradually add the flour mixture and stir in the muesli. Place tablespoonfuls on a baking sheet and bake for 12-15 minutes.

Ginger Snaps

THESE CRISP BISCUITS with their tangy flavour keep well if stored in an airtight tin. They are excellent for making biscuit crumb crusts*.

PREPARATION TIME: 30 MINUTES
CHILLING TIME: 1 HOUR
COOKING TIME: 15-20 MINUTES
PRE-HEAT OVEN TO 180°C

INGREDIENTS FOR 80 BISCUITS
120 g butter
175 g brown sugar
1 egg, beaten
80 ml (⅓ cup) golden syrup
320 g flour
3 ml (¾ teaspoon) salt
8 ml (1¼ teaspoons) ground ginger
3 ml (¾ teaspoon) bicarbonate of soda
125 ml (½ cup) milk

Cream together the butter and sugar well, and add the beaten egg. Add the syrup. Sieve together all the dry ingredients except the bicarbonate of soda. Mix the bicarbonate of soda with the milk. Fold the dry ingredients into the creamed butter and sugar mixture, then add the milk and bicarbonate mixture.

Wrap the dough in wax paper and allow it to rest in a refrigerator for 1 hour. Roll it out about 5 mm thick, working very quickly as the dough softens fast. Cut into 5 cm rounds and place on a greased baking sheet. Bake them for 15-20 minutes, or until lightly browned. Cool them slightly before removing them from the baking sheet.

Chocolate Chip Cookies

THESE ALL-AMERICAN favourites are very easy to make and they will appeal to adults and children alike.

PREPARATION TIME: 20 MINUTES
COOKING TIME: 12 MINUTES
PRE-HEAT OVEN TO 190°C

INGREDIENTS FOR 30 BISCUITS
125 g soft butter
70 g castor sugar
65 g dark soft brown sugar
2 ml (½ teaspoon) salt
2 ml (½ teaspoon) vanilla essence
1 egg
2 ml (½ teaspoon) bicarbonate of soda
185 g flour, sifted
100 g dark chocolate, chopped
100 g pecan nuts, chopped

Cream together the butter, castor and brown sugar, salt and vanilla essence until the mixture is light and fluffy. Beat in the egg and bicarbonate of soda. Gradually add the flour and mix well together. Fold in the chocolate and nuts.

Drop tablespoonfuls of the mixture well apart on to well-buttered baking sheets. Flatten the tops slightly and bake for 12 minutes, or until they are firm to the touch and lightly browned. Cool the cookies on wire racks.

Crunchies

THESE CRISPY BISCUITS are especially suitable for those who are seeking recipes containing no eggs.

PREPARATION TIME: 15 MINUTES
COOKING TIME: 15 MINUTES
PRE-HEAT OVEN TO 160°C

INGREDIENTS FOR 35 CRUNCHIES
180 g butter
30 ml (2 tablespoons) golden syrup
5 ml (1 teaspoon) bicarbonate of soda
125 g flour
180 g oatmeal
250 g sugar
80 g coconut

Heat together the butter and syrup. When the mixture boils, add the bicarbonate of soda. Sieve the flour into a large bowl, and mix in the oatmeal, sugar and coconut. Add the butter mixture to the dry ingredients and mix with the hands.

Press the mixture evenly into a greased Swiss roll tin, 38 cm x 25 cm, and bake for 15 minutes. Allow it to cool for 3 minutes and then cut into squares.

Leave the crunchies for another 10 minutes, then remove from the pan and allow to cool completely on a wire rack.

VARIATION Add 250 ml (1 cup) chopped nuts to the dry ingredients.

Shortbread

SHORTBREAD IS ALWAYS a temptation to the appetite, and here is an easy recipe. Traditionally, this melt-in-the-mouth Scottish treat is presented at the table as a flat round cake which is cut into wedges.

PREPARATION TIME: 15 MINUTES
COOKING TIME: 45 MINUTES
PRE-HEAT OVEN TO 160°C

INGREDIENTS FOR 2 ROUNDS
(24 CM DIAMETER)
CUT INTO 32 SERVINGS
500 g butter
250 g granulated sugar
750 g flour
20 ml (4 teaspoons) castor sugar (optional)

Soften the butter and knead it with the granulated sugar and flour into a smooth dough. Press the dough into two 24 cm loose-bottomed flan tins, prick well all over and cut into wedges.

Bake the rounds in the centre of the oven for 45 minutes and re-cut after baking. If you wish, sprinkle with castor sugar while still warm.

VARIATIONS To make individual shortbread biscuits, form the dough into rolls of 5 cm or less in diameter. Roll these in plastic wrap or aluminium foil sheets and refrigerate them until the dough is firm. Slice across the rolls of dough for biscuits 5 mm thick. With a spatula lift the biscuits on to an ungreased baking sheet and place it on the middle shelf of the oven. Bake the biscuits for 15 minutes at 180°C. If you are baking 2 sheets simultaneously, they will need to be alternated on the 2 shelves every few minutes to prevent the biscuits from overbaking.

In order to make very fine-textured biscuits replace 150 g of the flour with 150 g cornflour.

For almond biscuits, replace 150 g of the flour with 150 g cornflour and add almond essence to taste.

SHORTBREAD *Let butter melt in your mouth the Scottish way.*

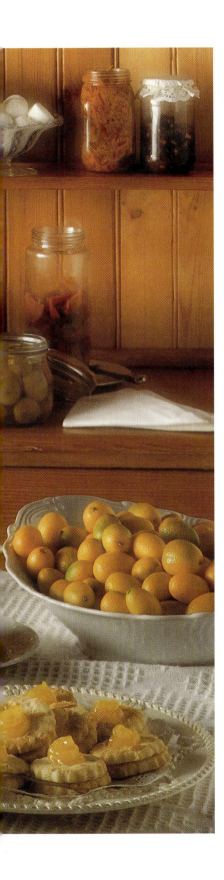

Preserves, Jams, Pickles and Sweets

ALONG WITH DRYING and curing, bottling was an important way of preserving food before the days of refrigeration in South Africa. Fruit and vegetables could be made into preserves, jams and pickles to be enjoyed out of season.

Local cooks used methods brought from Europe and the East, but also developed some distinctly South African delicacies, such as sour fig preserve.

In spite of the advent of freezing, these time-tested methods are still useful in reaping the benefits of seasonal gluts of fruit and vegetables – and delicious, home-made preserves and jams, potted in attractive containers, make delightful presents.

Many people avoid making preserves because they believe it is too difficult. If instructions are followed to the letter, however, preserving is not beyond the average cook's skills. It is important to be meticulous: the time spent on preparing preserves is wasted unless they are correctly packed and stored.

As in Europe, many of the pickle and chutney recipes that have become popular in South Africa were introduced from the East. The main preservative used is vinegar, yet, strangely enough, we derived the word 'pickle' from the Germanic word *pekel,* which means brine!

Sweets are fun to make and the home-made varieties are excellent at celebrations – whether you actually serve them to your guests or hand them over as gifts. They offer plenty of scope for the cook to become a real culinary artist.

SKILLS FOR PRESERVING, POTTING AND SWEET-MAKING · *PAGE 320*

PRESERVES, JAMS, PICKLES AND SWEETS RECIPES · *PAGE 326*

SPECIAL FEATURES

BOTTLE UP A PRESENT OF PRESERVES · *PAGE 330*

CHOCOLATE – A SWEET CONFECTION FROM A BITTER BEAN · *PAGE 336*

Skills for Preserving, Potting and Sweet-making

Jam, Fruit Jelly and Marmalade

Bruised and crushed fruit boiled quickly in a sugar syrup appeared under the name jam – a slang word dating from Elizabethan times – in 18th century cookery books. It had begun to take the place of the thick and paste-like 'tartstuffs' of earlier days. Fruit juice boiled to a jelly with sugar was stored in pots and served in slices to garnish winter cream dishes.

The original marmalade was quince jelly, introduced from Portugal. It took its name from *marmelo,* the Portuguese word for 'quince'. Later, citrus fruits began to be used, particularly oranges.

In the past, jam-making had to be undertaken during the short period when the fruit season was at its height. Today, with a freezer to store fruit in prime condition, jam-making can be spread out for a longer period.

The equipment you need

A heavy-based preserving pan of good-quality aluminium or stainless steel, wide to allow for evaporation and deep enough to prevent the jam from boiling over. The heavy base prevents burning. A lip for pouring may be useful.

Copper and brass pans are not suitable for making preserves, as the acid in the fruit reacts with the metal.

If you have no preserving pan, use a heavy-based 4-4,5 litre saucepan for making small quantities of jam.

Scales.

Nylon sieves.

Wooden spoon for stirring. Buy a long-handled jam-making spoon in order to reduce the risk of hot jam splashing your hands and arms.

Knives and peelers with stainless-steel blades, which do not discolour the fruit.

Heat-proof measuring jug.

Jam jars and covers. Plastic-coated screw tops are the most expensive covers, but are useful if storage conditions are not ideal. Otherwise use ordinary screw-on lids, or rounds of plastic wrap or cellophane tied down with fine string.

A layer of paraffin wax to seal the surface of the jam. Alternatively, seal with rounds of paper dipped in brandy.

A wide-necked funnel for filling jam jars is useful but not essential.

A sugar thermometer is useful for checking jam temperature to ascertain setting point, but it is not essential.

For making fruit jelly you will need a jelly bag for straining the juice from the fruit. You can buy flannel/nylon jelly bags, with or without dripstands.

Alternatively, make your own bag from a square of white cotton or flannel, four to six layers of butter muslin, or a white cotton pillowcase. For a home-made dripstand, tie each corner of the bag to the legs of an upturned stool and put a plastic or china bowl underneath to catch the juice.

For making marmalade, a juice extractor is useful but not essential. The fruit can be minced in a mincing machine after the juice has been squeezed out, but the finished marmalade tends to have a paste-like texture. The slicer on a food processor is useful for shredding peel.

Facts about preserving

Preserving food is one of the best ways to make use of any surpluses or gluts of fruit or vegetables, whether home-grown or bought.

When preserving food, the aim is to take it at its peak quality and nutritive value, and to keep it at that point. The main preserving agents used today are sugar, salt, vinegar and alcohol.

Methods of preserving include jam-making, pickling, drying, smoking and the more recent techniques of heat processing and freezing.

Successful preserving depends on using fresh food of the best quality available. Whether you use home-grown or bought food, process it as soon as possible. Choose fruits that are firmly ripe, and vegetables that are mature but not overblown or overripe.

Preservatives are not effective unless applied in the correct quantities and manner. Time spent on preparing preserves is wasted unless they are correctly packed and stored.

Jam

Jam is crushed fruit boiled to a thick consistency and preserved by impregnation with sugar.

Pectin, a substance in fruit that reacts with acid when heated, is the jellying, or setting, agent. Fruits vary in their pectin and acid content.

Jam is made by first cooking the fruit to a pulp, then adding sugar and boiling until the mixture is ready to set. For the best colour and flavour, simmer slowly before adding the sugar and boil rapidly afterwards. Underboiling causes runny jam, overboiling makes it sticky.

The amount of sugar used is crucial. Too little and the jam will ferment and be runny. Too much and the jam will crystallise and be dark and sticky.

The final yield from good, well-set jam should be about 5 kg for each 3 kg sugar used.

A guide to good jam-making

Good jam is bright in colour, well set but easy to spread, and has the true, distinct flavour of the fruit used.

Make fairly small quantities of jam at a time in case you do not like the flavour or get a poor result.

Never make more than 5 kg final mass at any time. The less time spent in cooking the jam, the better its colour and flavour.

Choose firmly ripe fresh fruit, picked dry. Do not use wet fruit as the water will account for some of its mass, and kilogram for kilogram it will have less pectin and acid than dry fruit. This may affect the set and flavour of the jam.

Prepare the fruit, removing stalks or any bruised portions, and wash if necessary. Stone cherries and leave whole, but halve and stone plums, apricots, peaches and greengages.

Put the fruit in a large, heavy-based pan, with any acid required in the recipe. Do not overfill the pan, or the jam may spill over during boiling. It should be about one-third full of fruit.

Add water only if the recipe says so. Fruit in a deep pan will need less water than fruit in a shallow pan where evaporation is quicker.

Do not add water to soft, juicy fruits such as strawberries and raspberries.

Bring the fruit to the boil, then simmer it gently to break down the skin and tissues, and to extract the pectin. Fruits with tough skins, such as plums, may need to simmer for 30-45 minutes.

Do not cover the pan unless the recipe says so. Evaporation of the water content is essential.

If you need to test the jam for its pectin content (see Pectin, acid and testing for setting point*), do so before you add the sugar.

Do not use brown sugar unless specified, as it affects the flavour.

Carefully weigh out the amount of sugar to be added and warm it in a pre-heated oven at a temperature of 110°C. Warm sugar dissolves more quickly than cold. Never add the sugar too soon to fruits. Sugar toughens their skins, and no amount of boiling will soften them.

Add the sugar gradually, stirring continually until it has dissolved, then bring the jam to boiling point.

Do not let the jam boil before the sugar has dissolved. The set will be poor and the texture grainy.

If you are using granulated sugar, add a nut of butter or a few drops of glycerine during boiling. This cuts down the amount of scum.

After the jam has been boiling for a few minutes, remove from the heat and test for setting point. Jam reaches setting point after boiling for anything from three minutes to an hour, depending on the kind of fruit.

Remove any scum with a stainless-steel slotted or perforated spoon once the jam is finished. Do not remove during cooking – it is wasteful.

Cool the finished jam in the pan for 5-6 minutes before potting, to prevent the fruit from rising – especially if making strawberry or cherry jam.

Before potting, stir the jam gently to distribute the fruit.

Never leave the jam in the pan longer than necessary: it may stain the metal.

Using frozen fruit in jam

Deep-frozen fruit is likely to have lost some of its original pectin content.

To compensate, use more fruit. Increase the quantity given in the recipe by 10 per cent – for example, add an extra 250 g to 2,5 kg.

Alternatively, use the amount of fruit given and decrease the sugar by 10 per cent. For example, use 2,25 kg sugar instead of 2,5 kg.

Do not attempt to make strawberry conserve (jam containing whole fruit) with frozen strawberries. The fruits will collapse and become mushy.

FRUIT JELLY

Fruit jelly is fruit juice boiled to a thick consistency and preserved with sugar. It should have a clear, bright colour and true flavour. As in jam, the setting agent is the pectin in the fruit, which reacts with acid when heated.

Because only the juice is used, the same mass of fruit yields less jelly than jam. Low-pectin fruits are not suitable for jelly-making: so much pectin and acid would have to be added to ensure setting that the true flavour of the fruit would be lost.

The final yield can be estimated in the same way as for jam – about 5 kg for each 3 kg of sugar used. But the total quantity of sugar is not given in the recipe, as it depends on the quality and quantity of juice. It is generally apportioned according to the amount of juice produced – usually 500 g for every 600 ml.

Points to note in jelly-making

Wild fruits such as Catawba grapes are often used in jelly-making. As the yield of jelly is low for the amount of fruit used, wild fruit helps to keep down the cost. Damaged or bruised fruit, or windfalls, can be used as long as the unsound parts are cut away.

Crab apples make a jelly of delicious colour and flavour, but cooking-apple jelly is rather insipid. Cloves, lemon, ginger, or geranium leaves improve the flavour. Apple juice is a good base for herb jellies.

In general, fruit jelly is made in the same way as jam, except that the pulped fruit is strained and only the juice boiled with the sugar. Follow the guide given for jam-making, but note the following points.

There is no need to peel apples. Remove any stalks and leaves. Cut large plums and apples into chunks to reduce cooking time.

Most fruits used in jelly making are best cooked in water – follow the amount that is given in the recipe. Tough-skinned fruits, such as plums, usually need more water than soft fruits, such as loganberries.

Gentle cooking to break down the fruit takes longer than for jam. The fruit must be thoroughly pulped to release the pectin and acid. Pulping may take 30 minutes to 1 hour.

Before pouring the pulped fruit into the jelly bag to strain it, scald the bag with boiling water.

Allow the juice to drip through the bag into a large bowl for 2-4 hours or longer if needed. Follow the guidance in the recipe.

Never squeeze the jelly bag to hurry things up. If you do, the jelly will be cloudy because some of the fruit tissues will be forced into it.

Finish making the jelly within 24 hours of it being strained. Prolonged standing will cause the juice to lose pectin and become dark. If you have to leave the juice for a time, be sure that you cover the bowl with butter muslin or a tea towel.

If the juice is thick and sticky it should set well. If it is thin and watery, simmer for 10-15 minutes to remove some of the excess water before you continue cooking.

If you are in doubt, use the pectin test to help you to decide the setting quality. Add pectin if necessary.

Measure the quantity of juice to determine how much sugar to use.

PECTIN, ACID AND TESTING FOR SETTING POINT

When using a good jam recipe it is rarely necessary to measure the pectin content of the fruit. If low-pectin fruits are included, they are normally blended with high-pectin fruits to achieve the right balance. Similarly, acid is usually included in the ingredients if low-acid fruits are used.

High-pectin fruits are: cooking apples, quinces, gooseberries, plums, loganberries, lemons, grapefruit, oranges with pips, and loquats.

Medium-pectin fruits are: fresh apricots, greengages and raspberries.

Poor-pectin fruits are: cherries, ripe pears, rhubarb, peaches, strawberries and ripe figs.

Fruits low in acid are: sweet apples, sweet cherries, ripe quinces, peaches, strawberries, raspberries, and pears.

The pectin test
Check the pectin content of the fruit after it has been simmered to a pulp but before you add the sugar.

Put 5 ml (1 teaspoon) juice from the pan into a small glass jar and let it cool for a minute or two.

Add 15 ml (1 tablespoon) methylated spirits to the cooled juice; shake the two well together.

After 1 minute, a transparent clot should form.

If the clot is large and jelly-like, the pectin content is high. No extra pectin is needed.

If the clot is less firm and perhaps in two or three lumps, the pectin content is medium, but sufficient.

If there is no clot, or if there are a lot of very small ones, the pectin content is low. Extra pectin is needed.

Adding pectin
Pectin can be bought from a pharmacy. Add it according to the maker's instructions before returning the pan to the heat. Do not use too much pectin as it will spoil the flavour.

A simpler way of adding pectin to strawberry jam is to put in a grated cooking apple and 10 ml (2 teaspoons) lemon juice for each 500 g strawberries. The apple does not affect the flavour.

Adding acid
Put in any acid included in the recipe before you start cooking the fruit.

As a guide, for each 1,5 kg fruit, one of the following acids is normally used in the quantity given:
Lemon juice – 25 ml (5 teaspoons).
Citric or tartaric acid – 2 ml (½ teaspoon).
Redcurrant or gooseberry juice – 125 ml (½ cup).

Testing for setting point
After the jam has been boiling for some minutes, use one of the following three simple tests to see if it has reached setting point. Remove the pan from the heat first, or the jam may go past setting point and be overboiled.

The flake test
1 Dip a clean wooden spoon in the jam.
2 Remove it and hold it over the jam, twisting it round once or twice to cool the jam adhering to the spoon.
3 Let the jam fall from the edge of the spoon. If the drops run together and form flakes that hang on the spoon edge for 15-30 seconds, the jam has reached setting point.

The cold saucer test
1 Chill a saucer in the refrigerator for 1 minute.
2 Put 5 ml (1 teaspoon) jam on the saucer and let it cool for 1 minute.
3 Push the surface of the cooled jam with your fingertip. If it wrinkles, the jam has reached setting point.

The thermometer test
1 Stir the jam.
2 Dip the thermometer in hot water, then sink the bulb end in the jam.
3 If the temperature is 105°C, the jam has reached setting point.

Bring the juice to the boil before you add the warmed sugar. Stir continually and do not let the juice reboil while the sugar dissolves.

Jelly usually reaches setting point after 20-40 minutes' boiling. Reduce the boiling rate as setting point approaches, or the finished jelly may be full of air bubbles.

Test for setting point. The flake or thermometer tests are the most reliable.

Once setting point is reached, dip a large, stainless-steel spoon in boiling water, then shake well. With the pan off the heat, use the spoon to take the scum off the jelly – it will cling to the hot spoon.

To remove the last bits of scum, use a piece of grease-proof paper with torn edges. Draw it across the jelly surface to the side of the pan, where the scum will stick.

Pot the jelly immediately (see Potting, sealing and storing*). Left too long, it will start to set in the pan.

Marmalade

Marmalade, like jam, is jellied boiled fruit that is preserved by being impregnated with sugar, but generally only citrus fruits are used.

Thick marmalade mostly contains every part of the fruit but the pips. Jelly marmalade – made from the juice of citrus fruits – can either be left clear or else contain shreds of the peel.

In citrus fruits, most of the pectin is in the pips and white inner skin, or pith. Despite their acidity, citrus fruits (except lemons) cannot produce enough acid to ensure setting, and more has to be added.

The pith of bitter oranges becomes translucent when cooked, whereas the pith of sweet oranges, lemons and grapefruit remains opaque. This is why marmalade made with a mixture of citrus fruits looks cloudy although the flavour is unaffected.

The final yield for marmalade can be estimated in the same way as for jam – 3 kg sugar yields about 5 kg marmalade. But you will generally need much less fruit than for a similar amount of jam. Jelly marmalade needs more fruit than thick marmalade to produce a given amount.

Points to note when making marmalade

Most marmalade is made from bitter oranges, distinguished by their rough outer skins.

The methods for making thick marmalade and marmalade jelly are basically the same as for making jam and fruit jelly, but note the following.

Choose firm fruit of good colour and heavy in relation to its size.

Use the fruit as soon as possible, or else freeze it for use at a later date.

Wash the fruit well before use and scrub if necessary. There is no need to soak overnight to soften the peel.

Prepare the fruit by cutting it in half and squeezing the juice and pips into a bowl, then shred the peel and put it in the pan with the water.

Next strain the juice into the pan, add the acid, and put the pips and tissue in a muslin bag tied to the pan handle. Hang well into the water.

If you cut away some of the thick pith when shredding the peel, put it in the muslin bag with the pips.

For jelly marmalade, put some of the shredded peel in a muslin bag and hang it in the pan during cooking. If you wish, stir this peel into the jelly when potting.

Because of their thick skins, citrus fruits need longer cooking and more water than fruits used in jam-making. Pulping generally takes 2-3 hours.

Make certain that the peel is well cooked. It should disintegrate when squeezed between finger and thumb.

Lift out the bag of pips between two spoons and squeeze it gently over the pan before you stir in the warmed sugar. For an Old English marmalade, replace half the white sugar with brown sugar. Or use white sugar and add 15 ml (1 tablespoon) black treacle for every 500 g marmalade in the given yield.

Marmalade usually reaches setting point after 15-45 minutes' boiling. Use the flake or cold saucer method to test.

Remove the scum as soon as possible after the marmalade reaches setting point, otherwise it clings to the peel.

Cool for 5-10 minutes, then stir to distribute the fruit before potting*. This prevents the peel from rising in the jars.

Using frozen fruit in marmalade

You can freeze freshly bought citrus fruits for use at a later date. To freeze whole, scrub well, dry and pack in plastic bags. Alternatively, cut the fruit up and cook to a pulp first, so that only the final boiling with sugar has to be done after thawing.

Always use extra fruit – 10-15 per cent more than the recipe specifies – to offset pectin loss during freezing.

PICKLES, CHUTNEYS AND RELISHES

Pickles are vegetables or fruit preserved in spiced vinegar, with their shape and texture retained as far as possible.

Some vegetables, such as onions and cauliflowers, need to be salted before being pickled; this is known as brining*. It reduces the moisture content of the vegetable, and so ensures a crisp texture.

Most pickles are best left to mature for at least 6-8 weeks.

Chutneys are vegetables or fruit cooked to a smooth pulp and preserved in vinegar, salt and spices. They are often made from a blend of fruit and vegetables. Because the fruit and vegetables are not used whole, chutney can be made from damaged specimens, as long as unsound parts are cut away.

Relishes are vegetables or fruit preserved in vinegar, salt and spice, but the texture is different from chutney. The ingredients are coarsely chopped.

Some relishes are cooked and others are made with raw ingredients. They are made, bottled and stored in the same ways as pickles and chutneys.

The equipment you need

A stainless-steel, aluminium or enamel saucepan. Do not use copper or brass pans; the vinegar will react with the metal and taint the preserve.

For chutney, use a heavy-based aluminium or stainless-steel saucepan.

Nylon sieves.

Wooden spoons.

Stainless-steel knife.

Kitchen scales.

Measuring jug.

Jars with airtight screw tops or clip-on lids, made of plastic or plastic-coated. Never allow metal to come into contact with the pickles while preparing or bottling, as the vinegar will corrode it.

MAKING PICKLES

Pickles are simple to make and store. Many vegetables can be pickled cold and raw, or lightly cooked.

POTTING, SEALING AND STORING JAM, JELLY AND MARMALADE

Jam, fruit jelly and marmalade are potted and stored in the same way.

Sterilising jars and bottles
1 Thoroughly wash the jars in hot water and mild detergent, rinse and drain on a clean towel.
2 Warm the dry jars in the oven for about 20 minutes at 110°C. A convenient way to do this is to place the jars in the pre-heated oven when you are warming the sugar.

Filling and sealing
1 Fill the jars to the brim with the hot, finished jam, jelly or marmalade. It will shrink during cooling.

Tilt jelly jars while filling them, so that the jelly runs down the side – this prevents air bubbles from forming. Once the jelly jar is filled, do not move or tilt it until the jelly has set.

2 If covering with cellophane or plastic wrap, melt a disc of wax on the jam surface after filling. This seal keeps the jam in good condition.
3 Seal the jars while the jam is hot – do not leave it to become lukewarm before sealing, as this encourages the growth of mould. You can tie down cellophane or plastic wrap tightly once the jam is cold and set, and the jars are easier to handle.
4 If using plastic-coated screw tops, put on as soon as a jar is filled. No wax disc is needed.
5 Label each sealed and covered jar with the contents and date.
6 Store in a dry, cool and dark place. Damp causes mould to grow on the surface, heat makes the contents shrink, and too much light may fade the colour. Most preserves will keep 6-12 months in good conditions.

Sweet pickles are generally made from fruits such as peaches, crab apples or pears, or sweet vegetables such as marrows. They are cooked gently in a syrup of vinegar and sugar.

Malt vinegar can give pickles a better flavour. Cider vinegar can be used in fruit pickles, but white vinegar is generally used because the brown vinegar colours the pickles. Brown vinegar is best used for pickled onions.

Choose fresh, young vegetables and firmly ripe, undamaged fruits.

Wash, drain and cut up the vegetables or fruit according to the instructions in the recipe.

Brine* (salt) the vegetables if necessary. Wash and drain well.

For sweet pickles, dissolve the sugar in the vinegar and cook the vegetables or fruit gently until just tender. Undercook a little rather than overcook, as they will go on softening in the hot vinegar.

Always pot hot and sweet pickles immediately. Never leave pickles standing in a saucepan for longer than necessary.

Potting and sealing pickles

Use clean jars – warmed for cooked pickles – and leave about 2,5 cm headspace above the pickles. For raw pickles, drain off any water that collects at the bottom of the jar before adding the vinegar.

Use cold spiced vinegar for raw pickles and hot spiced vinegar for cooked pickles. Cover the pickles with the vinegar to give a topping of at least 1,5 cm. Vinegar evaporates during storage, and any vegetables or fruit that become uncovered will discolour.

Cover and seal the jars at once. Tops must be airtight, or the vinegar will evaporate and the contents dry out.

Store in a cool, dark, dry place.

For fruit pickles, keep surplus sweetened vinegar in a jar so that you can top up as necessary. Some fruits absorb the vinegar as they mature.

Making spiced vinegar

Use whole spices whenever possible. Ground spices make the vinegar look cloudy and muddy.

To each 1 litre (4 cups) vinegar, add 25 g mixed pickling spice (obtainable from most supermarkets or grocers). Or add the following spice mixture:
15 ml (1 tablespoon) cloves
15 ml (1 tablespoon) mace
15 ml (1 tablespoon) allspice
10 cinnamon sticks (about 5 cm each)
A few peppercorns
1-2 pieces dry root ginger

Leave to steep for 6-8 weeks. The spices will gradually sink to the bottom of the bottle, so give the bottle a shake from time to time.

Strain to remove spices before use.

Alternatively, put the spices in a muslin bag and hang them in the vinegar to steep. You need not strain the vinegar before use.

Quick spiced vinegar

If you want spiced vinegar for immediate use, make it as follows:

Put the vinegar and spices in a basin and place it in a pan of cold water. The water should be halfway up the basin.

Cover the basin with a lid or plate and bring the water to the boil.

Take the saucepan from the heat and let it stand until the vinegar is cold.

Strain to remove spices before use.

Brining

There are two methods, soaking in salt solution or layering in dry salt for 12-24 hours. For both methods use coarse salt. Table salt may make the pickle cloudy.

To soak in brine, dissolve 200 g salt in 2 litres (8 cups) water and immerse the prepared vegetables in the solution. Put an upturned plate over the vegetables to keep them immersed.

For dry salting, spread a layer of the prepared vegetables on a large dish and sprinkle liberally with salt. Add other layers if necessary, sprinkling with salt.

MAKING CHUTNEY

Good chutney should have a mellow flavour and a fairly smooth texture. Apples, plums, beetroot and red or green tomatoes are commonly used as bases for chutneys.

Chutney adds interest and zest to many dishes – for example, cold meats, curries, casseroles, sandwiches and cheese snacks. You may alter the flavouring of the chutney to suit your taste, but keep to the proportions given.

Make small amounts of chutney if using a new recipe, or if you are inexperienced. If the flavour is not to your taste you can adjust it in the next batch that you make.

Wash and prepare the vegetables and fruit as necessary. Cut them up as directed, or finely chop or mince them to ensure a smooth texture.

Soften onions and any other tough vegetables by cooking them gently in a little water in a covered pan.

Add the other ingredients as directed (the sugar is not usually added until cooking is nearly completed). Continue cooking with the lid off – evaporation is an essential part of cooking.

If you use plain vinegar rather than ready-spiced vinegar, add the spices to the fruit or vegetables. Put ground spices directly into the saucepan; if using whole spices, tie them to the pan handle in a muslin bag and hang the bag well into the mixture.

Brown sugar is normally used to give a good flavour and dark, rich colour. But use white sugar if you prefer it, or if you want a light colour. White vinegar and white sugar help to keep the bright colour of red tomato chutney, for example.

Long, gentle simmering – up to 2 hours – will always give the best results. In order to test when the chutney is ready, tilt the saucepan and draw a wooden spoon through the mixture. It should leave a completely clean path in the bottom of the pan, with no traces of liquid.

Potting and sealing chutneys

Pot into clean, warm jars while hot. Fill jars to within 1,5 cm of the top and cover tightly with airtight plastic or plastic-coated (never metal) lids.

Store in a cool, dry, dark place. Leave to mature for 6-8 weeks, or as recommended in the recipe.

Check the bottles from time to time. If the chutney is shrinking, the cover is not airtight and the moisture is evaporating.

If loose liquid collects on the top of the chutney after a few weeks, it has not been cooked enough. Bring it to the boil again and cook gently until the liquid disappears.

SAUCES AND KETCHUPS

Sauce is liquidized fruit or vegetables with vinegar and spices added to flavour and preserve it.

Ketchup is usually the juice of two vegetables preserved and flavoured with vinegar and spices. It is normally more highly concentrated and seasoned, and thinner in consistency, than sauce.

The equipment you need

In general, the equipment is the same as for pickles, chutneys and relishes.

In place of jars, use bottles with corks or screw tops. Sterilise* them in the same way as jam jars. Use new corks, and submerge them in boiling water for 10 minutes before use. This sterilises them and also softens them.

Use plastic or plastic-coated screw tops to prevent corrosion by the vinegar.

MAKING SAUCES AND KETCHUPS

Like pickles, chutneys and relishes, sauces and ketchups are used as accompaniments or flavourings.

Use fresh, firm, sound fruit and vegetables.

Finely chop the ingredients to give quicker cooking.

Cook the fruit and vegetables to a pulp in an open pan to allow evaporation.

Sieve the pulped mixture.

Cook the mixture again if instructed in the recipe, adding any ingredients specified. The final consistency should be between that of thin and thick cream.

Bottling and sealing sauces and ketchups

Fill clean, dry, warm bottles to within 2,5 cm of the top and seal immediately.

Sauces made from ingredients with a low acid content, such as ripe tomatoes and mushrooms, must be sterilised* after bottling. This prevents fermentation.

Store in the same way as jams.

Sterilised sauces and ketchups will keep for several months and can be opened and re-opened during that time. Use unsterilised sauces and ketchups fairly quickly once opened.

Sterilising sauces and ketchups

Sterilise low-acid sauces and ketchups immediately after bottling.

If the bottles are sealed with corks, tie the corks down to prevent them from blowing out.

If the bottles are sealed with screw caps, tighten them, then give a half turn back.

Use a deep saucepan, and make a false bottom of slatted wood, folded newspaper or straw.

Stand the prepared bottles on the false bottom, making sure that they do not touch each other or the sides. Use small pads of newspaper to keep them apart if necessary.

Add enough cold water to reach the bottom of the corks or screw tops.

Heat the water to 77°C. If you do not have a thermometer, heat slowly for about 1 hour until tiny bubbles are rising continually from the bottom of the pan.

Keep the water at this temperature for about 30 minutes.

Remove the bottles from the pan and tighten the tops or push down the corks.

Rub a thin film of paraffin wax over each cork and bottle-top to provide an airtight seal.

FLAVOURED VINEGARS

Flavoured vinegar has herbs, fruit or vegetables steeped in it for periods varying from several days to several weeks, according to the recipe. It is then strained and bottled.

Herb and vegetable vinegars can be used to flavour salads, cold meats, casseroles or grills. Vegetable vinegars are usually made from such distinctly flavoured vegetables as horseradish, cucumbers or celery.

Fruit vinegars are usually made from soft fruits such as raspberries. Use them as a flavouring in a sauce, or dilute them to make a hot drink.

Use wine vinegar and fresh, firm, sound fruit or vegetables for the most successful results.

Bottling and storing vinegars

Bottle into clean, warm, dry bottles in the same way as sauces. There is no need to sterilise the bottles.

Store in a dark place to prevent loss of colour.

SWEETS

Sweets are fun to make, and are highly acceptable as presents.

Always take great care in the kitchen when making sweets. Never leave boiling syrup unattended, particularly when young children are about.

Equipment for sweet-making

Large, heavy-based saucepans of stainless steel, aluminium or tinned copper. Enamel pans will not withstand the high temperature needed.

A sugar thermometer, which should be clearly marked and register up to 200°C. If you have no sugar thermometer, follow the water tests*.

A marble slab is useful for shaping and cooling many sweets, particularly fondant* and barley sugar. If you have no marble slab, pour the mixture into a baking tin. Never pour syrup directly on to a laminated surface or wood, as it will stick to it.

Long-handled, flat-based wooden spatulas, which are better than metal for beating or stirring. Keep two different sizes handy and use these utensils only for sugar work.

Pastry brushes. Keep one brush exclusively for brushing down the sugar crystals from the pan and another for oiling tins.

A sugar scraper is ideal for fondant-making. Or use a plastic or metal spatula instead.

Baking tins for setting sweets such as fudge or coconut ice. You may use loaf tins or foil baking cases instead.

Sweet moulds, which are sold in sheets of several small moulds. If you have no moulds, spoon small amounts of the mixture on to a baking tray.

Kitchen scales to measure out the ingredients exactly.

Scissors. Some sweet mixtures, such as barley sugar, have to be cut up with scissors.

Fine nylon sieve for sieving icing sugar.

Wax paper for lining and dividing boxes or containers of home-made sweets and chocolates.

Rice paper: edible paper for lining baking trays on which sticky mixtures such as nougat are placed.

INGREDIENTS FOR SWEET-MAKING

Sugar Mass for mass, all refined sugars are equally sweet. However, the finer the sugar, the faster it dissolves and the sweeter it seems.

Granulated sugar has a medium-sized, white sparkling crystal and is 99,9 per cent pure sucrose. It is the most popular and widely used refined sugar, as well as the cheapest. It is used in many sweets, for example butterscotch, marshmallows, coconut ice, fruit fondants and jujubes.

Castor sugar dissolves more quickly than granulated sugar. In uncooked sweetmeats, such as marzipan, it gives a smoother texture.

Icing sugar is made by grinding sugar crystals to a fine powder. It is used in uncooked peppermint-cream mixtures, in truffles, and for coating marshmallows and other sweets.

Cube sugar is produced from granulated sugar, moistened and moulded into neat shapes. It is used in barley sugar.

Soft brown sugars are all finely grained refined sugars, but they range in colour from creamy-beige to dark brown. They give a rich flavour to such sweets as treacle toffee.

Golden syrups vary in flavour and colour. They are made from the liquid left after refined sugar has been crystallised. They enrich the flavour of honeycomb and toffee apples.

Treacles are thinner, darker and less refined than syrups, and have a flavour close to that of cane molasses. They are used for making some toffees and boiled sweets.

Vanilla sugar You can easily make your own by burying a whole vanilla pod in an airtight jar of castor sugar. Stir occasionally to move the pod around. The sugar will be ready after 1 week. Top up the jar as the sugar is used. The pod should last for months. Vanilla sugar gives a delicious flavour to fudge.

Liquid glucose This is less sweet than sugar. A glossy appearance is given to such sweets as nougat if some liquid glucose is added. It also keeps fondants in a soft, uncrystallised state.

Stock syrup Use very small amounts for moistening fondant mixtures that are too dry. Make a quantity to store in a well-stoppered bottle. Dissolve 100-125 g granulated sugar in 80 ml (⅓ cup) warm water as for sugar boiling. Boil to 105°C, then leave to cool.

Fat When fat is needed in sweet-making, it is best to use unsalted butter. Use margarine only when the quantity of fat required is very small. Too large a quantity of margarine will separate from the toffee or other sweets. For greasing tins use sunflower oil. Apply it with a pastry brush for a thin, overall film.

Cream and milk These must be fresh. Evaporated milk is sometimes used, but it may curdle if the cooking process is too long.

Cream of tartar or tartaric acid Some sweet recipes use this to reduce the tendency of sugar to re-crystallise. Measure it carefully, as too much can make sweets too soft and sticky.

Chocolate Both dark and milk chocolate are used in sweet-making. For very sweet fillings, such as fondant mixture, dark chocolate provides a contrast.

Flavouring and colouring

Use good-quality flavourings and colourings and never tip them straight from the bottle, as they are very concentrated. Pour the flavouring or colouring on to a marked measuring spoon, or dip a skewer into the bottle and shake off one drop at a time.

Blanching, roasting and toasting nuts

Nuts are usually blanched and skinned before use in sweets and other dishes. For some recipes they are then roasted.

Place the nuts in a bowl, cover with boiling water and allow to stand for a minute or two. Drain off the water; the skins will then peel off easily. Almonds can be bought ready blanched.

To roast or toast nuts, spread the blanched nuts on a baking sheet or Swiss-roll tin. Place the tin in the oven, pre-heated to 180°C, until the nuts are golden-brown. This will take 5-10 minutes. Check after 5 minutes, as nuts can burn rapidly.

Tips for Making Sweets

Measure the ingredients accurately.

Make sure that there is no grease on kitchen scales or cooking utensils – this could spoil the sugar syrup.

If nuts are to be coated, warm them in a low oven (130°C) for 10 minutes while the toffee is boiling. The toffee will then stick to them more easily.

When finishing off sweets, mould or cut them in small, neat sizes.

Use cellophane to wrap sweets such as toffees, toffee apples and nougat, which tend to go sticky when exposed to air.

When packing sweets in boxes as gifts, use wax paper to separate the layers and rows. Foil and paper cases make pretty, protective wrappings for some sweets, such as chocolates.

When packing boiled sweets in jars or tins, put a crumpled plug of wax paper at the bottom and top to prevent the sweets from being tossed about.

Toffee

PREPARATION TIME: 15 MINUTES
COOKING TIME: 15-20 MINUTES
COOLING TIME: 1 HOUR

INGREDIENTS TO YIELD 600 G
120 g unsalted butter
450 g sugar
30 ml (2 tablespoons) warm water
30 ml (2 tablespoons) white vinegar
60 ml (¼ cup) golden syrup, or 30 ml (2 tablespoons) each of syrup and treacle

Melt the butter in a fairly large pan, stir in the sugar and remove the pan from the heat. Add the water, vinegar and syrup, or syrup and treacle. Stir over low heat until the sugar dissolves, taking care not to let the mixture boil. Then bring to boiling point. Boil steadily until the small-crack stage* (132-143°C).

Pour the toffee into a well-buttered rectangular tin, measuring 28 cm x 18 cm. Leave the toffee to cool. As soon as it has begun to set, mark it into squares with a knife. When it is quite cold, break the squares up and wrap each one in cellophane.

Store in a jar or airtight tin.

Caramel

PREPARATION TIME: 15 MINUTES
COOKING TIME: 20 MINUTES
SETTING TIME: 6 HOURS

INGREDIENTS TO YIELD 550 G
250 ml (1 cup) evaporated milk
125 ml (½ cup) cream
100 g brown sugar
100 g granulated sugar
190 ml (¾ cup) golden syrup
1 ml (¼ teaspoon) salt
5 ml (1 teaspoon) vanilla essence
25 g butter

Combine the evaporated milk and cream, and reserve 100 ml of the mixture. Combine the rest with the brown and granulated sugar, syrup and salt in a heavy-based saucepan. Bring to the boil over a medium heat, stirring all the time until the sugar dissolves. Boil, stirring all the time, to the soft-ball stage* (112-118°C).

Gradually stir in the remaining milk and cream mixture, ensuring that the syrup boils all the time. Boil, stirring, to the firm-ball stage* (118-120°C).

Remove from the stove and beat in the vanilla essence and butter quickly. Pour the mixture into a well-greased 22 cm x 12 cm loaf tin and allow to cool completely at room temperature.

Cut the caramel into pieces, using a knife dipped into hot water.

VARIATIONS Add 90 g grated cooking chocolate with the remaining milk and cream mixture.

Add 250 ml (1 cup) coarsely chopped pecan nuts or almonds just before pouring the mixture into a pan to set.

Butterscotch

PREPARATION TIME: 50 MINUTES
SETTING TIME: 30 MINUTES

INGREDIENTS TO YIELD 450 G
450 g sugar
150 ml hot water
1 ml (¼ teaspoon) cream of tartar
75 g unsalted butter
1 ml (¼ teaspoon) vanilla essence

Put the sugar and water into a heavy-based saucepan. Dissolve the sugar, following the rules for sugar boiling*.

Add the cream of tartar and boil to the soft-ball stage* (112-118°C). Remove from the heat and add the butter in small pieces. Return to the heat and continue to boil to the small-crack stage* (132-143°C).

Remove the pan from the heat, stir in the vanilla essence and pour the mixture into a well-oiled tin, 28 cm x 18 cm.

When the butterscotch has almost set, mark it into rectangles with a sharp knife. When cold, break the squares apart and wrap each in shiny metallic paper.

RULES FOR SUGAR BOILING

1 Measure the sugar and water accurately. Excess water takes longer to boil off, which can be detrimental.
2 Heat the sugar and water gently and do not let the mixture boil until every grain of sugar has dissolved.
3 During the dissolving process, stir the mixture very carefully with a wooden spatula. Stir right to the bottom and corners of the pan, keeping the tip of the spatula under the liquid to avoid splashing.
4 Brush down the sides of the saucepan from time to time with a clean pastry brush dipped in warm water. This prevents crystals from forming on the side of the pan and dropping back into the mixture.
5 Never stir boiling syrup unless specifically directed to do so – as, for example, when milk is used.
6 It is essential to boil the sugar and water mixture on which most sweets are based to the temperature given in each individual recipe. If the temperature is too high, the mixture will burn, and if too low, it will not set properly. Measure the temperature with a sugar thermometer or use the water tests*.
7 If using a sugar thermometer, warm the bulb by dipping it in hot water before immersing it in the syrup. Hold the thermometer upright and read it at eye level.
8 Take the sugar thermometer out of the saucepan of syrup and place it in a jug of hot water.
9 When the correct temperature is reached, remove the pan from the heat and place it on a damp cloth. This will prevent any further cooking.
10 Check the accuracy of your thermometer by placing it in water that has just come to the boil. The boiling point of water is 100°C at the coast. This drops by 1°C for every 300 m above sea level, so take this into consideration. You will also have to adjust the temperature of sugar syrups accordingly for altitudes above sea level: use the water test* in conjunction with your thermometer to test the syrup for readiness.

Water tests without a thermometer
If you have no sugar thermometer, use these water tests. Remember that temperatures will be affected by altitude (see point 10).

Fill a small bowl with cold water. Remove the pan of sugar mixture from the heat, take 2 ml (½ teaspoon) of the mixture and drop it into the water. Leave for 1 minute, and test between forefinger and thumb to see which of the following stages it has reached.

Thread At 106-112°C the syrup in the water will form a fine thread between finger and thumb if they are pressed on it and then pulled apart.
Soft ball At 112-118°C the syrup in the water will form a soft ball which can be squashed flat. As the temperature goes towards the higher end of this stage, the ball will become slightly firmer. This is the appropriate temperature for fondants and fudges.
Firm ball At 118-120°C the syrup in the water will form a firm but pliable ball. This is the temperature for marshmallows and caramels.
Hard ball At 121-130°C the syrup dropped into water forms a ball which holds its shape when pressed.
Small crack At 132-143°C the syrup will separate into threads that will snap cleanly. This stage is used for toffee.
Hard crack At 149-159°C the mixture dropped into cold water forms threads which are hard and brittle. This stage is used for hard toffees and rock.
Caramel At 160-177°C the syrup becomes a golden colour and is used for praline or caramel sauce.

FRESH APRICOT JAM

THIS TASTY, tart and aromatic jam should be golden in colour and not too sweet. An old Cape favourite, apricot jam is enjoyable with scones or as a filling for pastries. Traditional jam tarts are also made with apricot jam.

PREPARATION TIME: 10 MINUTES
COOKING TIME: 1 HOUR

INGREDIENTS TO YIELD 3 JARS OF 500 ML
1 kg halved and stoned apricots
80 ml (⅓ cup) water
750 g sugar (or 1 kg sugar if using green fruit)

Place the apricots and water in a saucepan, and poach, covered, until tender.

Remove from the heat and add the sugar. Heat slowly, stirring occasionally, until all the sugar has dissolved.

Boil rapidly, uncovered, for about 40-45 minutes, skimming the foam from the surface with a slotted spoon. Do not boil on too high a heat as the jam burns easily, becoming dark. The jam is ready when marble-sized bubbles issue from the bottom. (Do not stir against the bottom towards the end of cooking – this may dislodge any burnt jam at the base of the saucepan.) Test the jam for setting point*.

Pour into hot sterilised jars and seal (see Potting, sealing and storing jam*).

VARIATIONS The fruit may be minced to make smooth apricot jam. If the fruit is very ripe, the jam will be naturally smooth.

A few crushed apricot stones added while cooking give a nutty flavour.

A tot of Van der Hum liqueur* will give an enriched flavour to apricot jam – add the liqueur after the jam has cooled for about 10 minutes (before potting).

To make dried-apricot jam, add 1 kg dried apricots to 1,5 litres (6 cups) boiling water and leave to soak for 10 minutes. Simmer, covered, over a low heat until tender. Remove from the heat. Add 2,5 kg sugar and the juice of 2 lemons, and stir until all the sugar has dissolved. If you wish, you can add 100 g crushed pecan nuts or almonds at this stage. Return the saucepan to the heat and boil the mixture fairly rapidly for about 20 minutes, testing the jam for setting point*. Skim the foam from the surface. Pot as above.

FIG JAM

THIS RECIPE is for ripe fig jam, as opposed to the traditional green fig preserve. Its golden-brown colour and fruity taste have long been popular.

PREPARATION TIME: 10 MINUTES
COOKING TIME: 40 MINUTES

INGREDIENTS TO YIELD 2 JARS OF 500 ML
1,5 kg ripe figs
250 ml (1 cup) water
60 ml (¼ cup) lemon juice
750 g sugar

Peel the figs, then place the fruit in a large saucepan with the water and simmer, covered, until tender (about 5-10 minutes). Remove from the heat.

Add the lemon juice and sugar, and stir until the sugar has dissolved. Boil, uncovered, until ready, testing the jam for setting point*. Skim to remove the foam from the surface. Bottle the jam in hot, sterilised jars and seal immediately (see Potting, sealing and storing jam*).

GRAPE JAM

GRAPE JAM has long been one of the most popular jams in the Cape. It is quite sweet, lasts very well and provides a good way to use up a glut of ripe grapes.

PREPARATION TIME: 20-30 MINUTES
COOKING TIME: 30-40 MINUTES

INGREDIENTS TO YIELD 3 JARS OF 500 ML
1 kg black or green grapes
75 ml water
750 g sugar
20 ml (4 teaspoons) lemon juice

Remove the grapes from their stems, halve them and remove the seeds.

Place the grapes and the water in a heavy-based saucepan and simmer, covered, until the fruit is tender (about 5-10 minutes). Remove from the heat.

Add the sugar and lemon juice, and heat slowly, stirring occasionally, until all the sugar has dissolved. Boil rapidly, uncovered, until ready, testing the jam for setting point*. Skim any foam from the surface.

Pour the jam into hot, sterilised bottles and seal immediately (see Potting, sealing and storing jam*).

MELON AND GINGER JAM *Try a home-made version of this indigenous classic.*

MELON AND GINGER JAM

THIS TRADITIONAL South African recipe must rank as one of the most economical ways of making jam. If you are not keen on ginger there are a number of delicious variations that can be made using watermelon. 'Konfyt' watermelon is usually available most of the year round.

PREPARATION TIME: 30 MINUTES
STANDING TIME: OVERNIGHT
COOKING TIME: 50 MINUTES

INGREDIENTS TO YIELD 5 JARS OF 500 ML
2 kg peeled, diced and pitted 'konfyt' watermelon
Grated rind of 2 lemons
625 ml (2½ cups) lemon juice
250 g crystallised ginger, chopped, or 25 g ground ginger
2 kg sugar

Place the melon, lemon rind, lemon juice, ginger and sugar in a heavy-based pan, and leave overnight.

The next day, bring the pan slowly to the boil and continue to boil gently for 35-40 minutes, testing the jam for setting point*. Pour the jam into hot, sterilised jars and seal (see Potting, sealing and storing jam*).

VARIATIONS Vary this recipe by substituting any of the following for the ginger:

1 kg grated pineapple to make melon and pineapple jam.

1 kg peeled and grated quince to make melon and quince jam.

2 kg peeled and chopped guavas to make melon and guava jam.

2 kg chopped ripe figs to make melon and fig jam.

In all the above variations follow the original method.

SLICED PEACH JAM

THIS RECIPE is for peach slices in syrup – an attractive and delicious way to use up a glut of fruit. The slices should be shiny and not too sweet.

PREPARATION TIME: 40-55 MINUTES
COOKING TIME: 35 MINUTES
PRE-HEAT OVEN TO 110°C

INGREDIENTS TO YIELD 2-3 JARS OF 500 ML
*1 kg yellow cling peaches
25 ml (5 teaspoons) salt
2,6 litres water
1 kg sugar
20 ml (4 teaspoons) lemon
juice*

Halve, stone and peel the peaches. Mix the salt with 2,5 litres (10 cups) of the water and soak the peaches in this brine solution for 10-15 minutes to prevent discoloration. Drain well and rinse quickly in fresh water.

Slice the peaches 3-5 mm thick, then place in a heavy-based saucepan. Add the remaining 100 ml water and poach the fruit, covered, until the slices are just soft (about 5 – 10 minutes). Remove the saucepan from the heat.

Warm the sugar slightly in the oven so that it will dissolve more quickly, then add it to the peaches with the lemon juice. Stir until all the sugar has dissolved.

Boil, uncovered, over a medium heat until the peach slices are translucent and shiny, and the syrup is thick (this will take about 20-30 minutes). Test the jam for setting point*.

Bottle in hot, dry, sterilised jars and seal immediately (see Potting, sealing and storing jam*).

VARIATIONS If peaches are ripe or slightly damaged you can make smooth peach jam instead. Peel the peaches, remove the stones and cut in pieces. Calculate 750 g sugar per 1 kg fruit, and 20 ml (4 teaspoons) lemon juice per 1 kg fruit. Poach the fruit, covered, in a little water until soft. Purée the fruit, add the sugar and stir until dissolved, then boil the mixture until it is ready, testing the jam for setting point*. Bottle in hot, dry, sterilised jars and seal immediately as above.

You may add 10 ml (2 teaspoons) whisky to each jar of jam if you like.

ALL-THE-YEAR-ROUND JAM

ALL-THE-YEAR-ROUND jam is so called because it is made from nuts and dried fruits which are obtainable at any time.

PREPARATION TIME: 45 MINUTES
STANDING TIME: OVERNIGHT
COOKING TIME: 20 MINUTES

INGREDIENTS TO YIELD 4 JARS OF 500 ML
*100 g whole almonds
500 g prunes
500 g seedless raisins
600 ml water
500 g soft brown sugar*

Blanch* and chop the almonds and place them in a bowl with the prunes and raisins. Pour on the water and leave overnight.

The next day, strain off the juice. Remove the prune stones and chop the prunes and raisins. Place the strained juice in a large, heavy-based pan and heat gently. Add the sugar, stirring continuously until it is dissolved, then add the fruit and nuts.

Bring the mixture to the boil and cook rapidly, stirring occasionally, for about 20 minutes. Test for setting point*. Pot and seal (see section on Potting, sealing and storing jam*).

LEMON CURD

LEMON CURD is probably descended from the curd tarts of the 17th century in Europe. More than 200 years were to pass before it occurred to anyone that lemon tart filling might be delicious if spread on bread and butter.

PREPARATION TIME: 20 MINUTES
COOKING TIME: 30-40 MINUTES

INGREDIENTS TO YIELD 2 JARS OF 500 ML
*Juice and finely grated rind
of 4 medium-sized lemons
250 g butter
500 g castor sugar
5 eggs, beaten*

Mix all the ingredients in a food processor, then pour into a pan and cook over a medium heat. Stir all the time until the mixture boils. Bottle in hot, sterilised jars (see Potting, sealing and storing jam*).

This curd has a shelf life of 2 weeks, but will keep for up to a month in a refrigerator.

RASPBERRY JAM

THE CHIEF GLORY of raspberry jam lies in its bright red colour and its flavour of fine, fresh fruit. Be careful, therefore, not to overcook it, or a brown, sticky concoction will result.

Neither water nor pectin is required in making this delicious jam. Its colour and sharp-sweet taste make it particularly suitable as a filling for cakes, such as Victoria sponge sandwich* or Swiss roll*.

PREPARATION TIME: 45 MINUTES
COOKING TIME: 20 MINUTES
PRE-HEAT OVEN TO 110°C

INGREDIENTS TO YIELD 9 JARS OF 500 ML
*2,75 kg sugar
2,75 kg raspberries*

Put the sugar in an oven-proof bowl and place it in the middle of the pre-heated oven for 10 minutes. Doing this helps the sugar to dissolve when it is added to the fruit.

Carefully pick over the raspberries and wash them if necessary, draining well. Place the fruit in a large, heavy-based saucepan and simmer gently for about 10 minutes, or until the raspberries are tender and the juice is running.

Take the saucepan off the heat and stir in the warmed sugar until it is completely dissolved. This will take about 5 minutes.

Put the pan back on the heat, bring to the boil and cook rapidly for about 5 minutes, testing for setting point*.

Cool for 3 minutes, stir to distribute the fruit, then bottle (see Potting, sealing and storing jam*).

RASPBERRY JAM *Its colour and flavour are ideal with a fluffy Swiss roll.*

Strawberry Jam

An easy way to preserve a glut of strawberries, this jam is an all-time favourite. It should be deep red and shiny, with the taste of the fruit recognisable.

Preparation Time: 10 minutes
Standing Time: overnight
Cooking Time: 35 minutes

Ingredients to Yield 2 Jars of 500 ml
1 kg cleaned and hulled
  strawberries
750 g sugar
30 ml (2 tablespoons) lemon juice

Layer the strawberries with the sugar in a stainless-steel saucepan and leave overnight, or for several hours.

The next day, heat the fruit and sugar very slowly, stirring to ensure that all the sugar dissolves. Add the lemon juice.

Boil rapidly, uncovered, stirring occasionally to prevent burning, for about 35 minutes until the jam is ready. Test the jam for setting point*.

Skim the surface of the jam with a slotted spoon to remove the foam and pour into hot, dry, sterilised jars. Seal the jars immediately (see Potting, sealing and storing jam*).

VARIATION Strawberry conserve is easier to make than jam and does not set as stiffly, because the lemon juice is omitted. Ideally, the fruit must remain whole with a shiny syrup. Use good-quality strawberries of even size. Clean and hull the strawberries and add 1 kg sugar per 1 kg fruit. Follow the same procedure as for the jam, but boil the mixture for only 5 minutes. Remove it from the heat and leave the fruit, covered, in a cool place or refrigerator for 2 days. Then boil again for 15 minutes. Bottle and seal. Use the conserve for fillings in tarts and cakes.

Quince Jelly

Quinces, the golden apples that to the ancient Greeks symbolised love and happiness, have been grown in many countries since Roman times.

This recipe, with its sweet lemon fragrance, goes well with pork, venison and other strongly flavoured meats. It can also be served with scones or buttered bread.

Preparation Time: 1½-2 hours
Straining Time: about 4 hours
Cooking Time: 35 minutes
Pre-heat Oven to 110°C

Ingredients to Yield 2 Jars of 500 ml
1 kg quinces
1 litre (4 cups) water
500 g sugar
Juice of 2 lemons

Wash the quinces, chop them roughly and place in a large, heavy-based pan with enough water to just cover them. Bring to the boil, cover and simmer for 1-1½ hours until very soft.

Ladle the fruit and liquid into a sterilised jelly bag (see Points to note in jelly-making*) and leave to strain for 4 hours.

Do not squeeze the bag or allow it to touch the liquid which has been strained into the bowl – this would make the jelly cloudy. The yield of strained juice should be about 600 ml. If it is not, adjust the amount of sugar to be used, in proportion.

Place the sugar in an oven-proof dish in the middle of the oven to warm through for 10-15 minutes.

Warm the quince juice in a pan and add the lemon juice. Stir in the warmed sugar until dissolved. Bring the jelly to the boil and cook rapidly for about 35 minutes, testing for setting point*. Skim if necessary, and bottle (see Potting, sealing and storing jelly*).

VARIATIONS Make apple jelly from 1 kg Granny Smith or other cooking apples. Cut the apples in chunks with the peel and pips. Cover with cold water and boil until soft. Strain the juice and measure it in order to calculate the amount of sugar: use 200 g sugar for every 250 ml (1 cup) juice. Proceed as for quince jelly adding the juice of 2 lemons. (Yield: 4 jars of 500 ml)

To make loquat jelly, wash 1 kg loquats and remove the stones. Cover with water and boil until the loquats are very soft. Proceed as in previous recipes, using 150 g sugar for every 250 ml (1 cup) juice, and adding the juice of 2 lemons. (Yield: 2-3 jars of 500 ml)

For grape jelly, add 1 kg green or sour grapes to a pot containing 1 litre (4 cups) water. Boil for 30 minutes, then strain through a jelly bag. Measure the juice and add 150 g sugar and the juice of 1 lemon for every 250 ml (1 cup) juice produced. Slowly bring this mixture to the boil, stirring until the sugar dissolves, then boil vigorously for 30 minutes, testing for setting point*. (Yield: 2 jars of 500 ml).

To make mint jelly with apple pectin, cut 1 kg green apples into chunks with the peel and pips. Squeeze the juice from 1 lemon, and add 1 litre (4 cups) water. Boil the apples in this liquid until very soft. Strain as in quince jelly and measure the juice. Add 200 g sugar for every 250 ml (1 cup) juice, and 125 ml (½ cup) mint leaves. Boil until the jelly is well flavoured. Remove the mint leaves and continue to boil the jelly for about 50 minutes, testing for setting point*. (Yield: 2-3 jars of 500 ml) For a fresh green colour, you may add a few drops of vegetable colouring.

Serve mint jelly with roast lamb. The other jellies go particularly well with venison or ham. They may be eaten with scones* and cream as well.

After the juice has been extracted, the fruit pulp may be mixed with sugar and boiled again to make a tasty, thick jam known as a fruit butter. Use 225-350 g sugar per 500 g pulp.

All-The-Year-Round Marmalade

A fresh fruit marmalade that can be made at any time of the year is a bonus if you miss the short season for Seville oranges, or if you have not made enough to carry you through the year. This marmalade has a good, sharp flavour, provided that the lemons and grapefruit are not outweighed by the sweet oranges.

Remember that the thicker the skin of the citrus fruit, the higher the pectin content and therefore the better the marmalade sets. It is also advisable to choose fruit that still has a touch of green in it.

Navel and Valencia oranges are particularly good, as they seldom have pips.

Preparation Time: 1-1½ hours
Cooking Time: 2 hours 50 minutes

Ingredients to Yield 7-8 Jars of 500 ml
1,5 kg mixed lemons, grapefruit,
  sweet and bitter oranges, made
  up as available
3 litres water
2,75 kg sugar

Scrub the fruit and cut in half. Squeeze out the juice and pips into a basin. Cut the peel into thin strips or chunks, as preferred.

Put the cut peel and any soft pulp into a large, heavy-based pan with the water. Strain in the juice. Put the pips into a muslin bag and tie this to the handle of the pan so that it hangs well down in the water. Cook gently for 2 hours, or until the peel is tender.

Lift out the bag of pips and squeeze it between 2 spoons over the pan before discarding. Add the sugar and stir until it dissolves completely.

Bring to the boil and boil hard until setting point* is reached (about 40 minutes). Remove any scum and leave the marmalade to stand for 5-8 minutes, then stir well to distribute the peel. Pot and seal (see Potting, sealing and storing marmalade*).

VARIATIONS To make sweet orange marmalade, use 1,5 kg navel oranges, 1 lemon, 3 litres water and 2,5 kg sugar. Follow the recipe for all-the-year-round marmalade.

Use the same proportions to make naartjie marmalade.

Fruit Mincemeat

Originally, mincemeat was actually made with minced meat – usually beef or tongue – mixed with dried fruit. This mixture was highly spiced and preserved with brandy or another spirit. Today, the meat is replaced by beef suet, and the mixture contains apples.

Mincemeat is better if it matures for a week or two before use. It will remain fresh and juicy for up to six months if covered with a plastic top or screw-on lid to prevent it from drying out.

Preparation Time: 45 minutes
Standing Time: 2-3 days

Ingredients To Yield About
6 Jars of 500 ml
750 g cooking apples
500 g seedless raisins
500 g sultanas
250 g currants
250 g chopped candied peel*
500 g soft brown sugar
500 g shredded suet, finely
  chopped

PRESERVES, JAMS, PICKLES AND SWEETS

50 g flaked or chopped almonds
Juice and grated rind of 2 lemons
2 ml (½ teaspoon) ground mixed spice
60 ml (¼ cup) brandy, whisky or rum

Wash, peel, core and chop the apples. Combine with the raisins, sultanas, currants and candied peel. Mince coarsely and place in a mixing bowl.

Add the sugar, suet, almonds, lemon juice, lemon rind and spice. Mix well.

Cover the bowl with a tea towel and leave for 2-3 days. Stir the mixture well 2-3 times a day. Add the brandy or other spirit. Bottle as you would jam (see Potting, sealing and storing jam*).

PLUM SAUCE

A THICK, FRUITY SAUCE always goes well with cold meats or poultry. Plums are particularly useful for sauces because they have a sweet-sharp flavour that blends well with spices. For this sauce, a mixture of plum varieties can be used.

PREPARATION TIME: 15 MINUTES
COOKING TIME: 1 HOUR 10 MINUTES
MATURING TIME: 1 MONTH

INGREDIENTS TO YIELD ABOUT 850 ML
1 kg plums, washed and dried
250 g sugar
600 ml malt vinegar
5 ml (1 teaspoon) salt
5 ml (1 teaspoon) ground ginger
2 ml (½ teaspoon) cayenne pepper
8 cloves

Cut the plums up roughly and put into a large, heavy-based pan with the stones. Add the remaining ingredients, stir well over a gentle heat until the sugar dissolves, then bring to the boil.

Reduce the heat and simmer for 30 minutes, stirring occasionally. Rub the mixture through a sieve, ensuring all the purée goes through. Wash the pan and return the purée. Simmer for 40 minutes, stirring occasionally, until the sauce has the consistency of whipping cream.

Bottle and seal the sauce (see Bottling and sealing sauces and ketchups*), and keep for at least 1 month before using.

TOMATO SAUCE

THIS IS THE BEST KNOWN of all the traditional sauces of Western cuisine. Well-made tomato sauce or ketchup, as it is also known, is a universally popular complement to almost any meal. Bacon, eggs, sausages, meats and savouries all take on a new and benevolent glow in its sweet-sharp company.

PREPARATION TIME: 50 MINUTES
STANDING TIME: 2-3 HOURS
COOKING TIME: 2-3 HOURS

INGREDIENTS TO YIELD 750 ML
5 ml (1 teaspoon) whole allspice
1 cinnamon stick (5-8 cm long)
3-4 blades mace
600 ml distilled white vinegar, or 300 ml white vinegar and 300 ml tarragon vinegar
2,75 kg ripe tomatoes, washed and sliced
30 ml (2 tablespoons) salt
5 ml (1 teaspoon) paprika
250 g sugar

Tie the allspice, cinnamon stick and mace in a muslin bag, and put this bag in a pan with the vinegar. Bring to the boil, then remove from the heat, cover and leave to infuse for 2-3 hours.

Meanwhile, put the tomatoes in a large, heavy-based pan and simmer for about 30 minutes until pulpy.

Rub the tomato pulp through a sieve into a bowl, clean out the pan and return the strained pulp to it.

Add the salt and paprika, and cook gently, uncovered, for 1 hour, stirring occasionally, until thick. Add the sugar and the vinegar, stirring continuously until the sugar dissolves. Continue cooking slowly for another hour until the sauce takes on the consistency of thick cream.

Pour into hot bottles, leaving about 2,5 cm space at the top, and seal immediately (see Bottling and sealing sauces and ketchups*). This sauce does not keep well unless sterilised (see Sterilising sauces and ketchups*). It does not need to mature and can be used at once.

FRUIT VINEGAR

ORIGINALLY, FRUIT VINEGAR was prepared as a sauce to serve with plain steamed puddings.

However, it can also form the basis of a refreshing sherbet drink – you simply dilute it to taste with soda water – or it can be used to make a hot drink to ease a cold or soothe a sore throat.

PREPARATION TIME: 5 MINUTES
STANDING TIME: 4-5 DAYS
COOKING TIME: 30 MINUTES
MATURING TIME: 2 WEEKS

INGREDIENTS TO YIELD 2 JARS OF 500 ML
500 g ripe soft fruit, such as boysenberries or raspberries, with leaves and stalks discarded
575-600 ml wine vinegar
450 g granulated or brown sugar

Crush the fruit with a wooden spoon or vegetable masher until it is pulpy. Stir the vinegar into the fruit.

Cover the bowl with a clean cloth draped over a wire cake rack or 2-3 pieces of clean wood, to prevent it from sagging into the bowl. Secure the cloth with elastic. Leave, covered, for 4-5 days, stirring the mixture once or twice daily.

Scald a clean cloth in boiling water, wring out and strain the fruit through it.

Measure the juice into a saucepan. The yield should be about 600 ml. If it is not, adjust the amount of sugar to be used, in proportion. Add the sugar, heat gently, stirring until the sugar has dissolved completely, then bring to the boil and boil gently for 10 minutes.

Pour into clean, dry sauce bottles, filling to 1,5 cm below the cap. Seal securely and label (see Bottling and sealing sauces and ketchups*).

Store the fruit vinegar for 2 weeks in a cool, dark place before using.

TOMATO SAUCE *Make your own version of this ubiquitous condiment.*

~ BOTTLE UP A PRESENT OF PRESERVES ~

Preserves, or *stukkonfyt*, are a traditional South African delicacy consisting of whole fruit, or large segments of fruit, boiled in syrup until saturated. When bottled, with a decorative cloth cover over the lid and a neatly hand-written label, they make very attractive gifts.

CITRON PRESERVE

PREPARATION TIME: 30 MINUTES
SOAKING TIME: OVERNIGHT
COOKING TIME: 2½ HOURS

INGREDIENTS TO YIELD 3 JARS OF 500 ML
1 kg green citrons
1,5 litres (6 cups) boiling water
750 g sugar
Paraffin wax for sealing

Scrape the citrons with a grater or remove the rind very thinly with a sharp knife, so that just the shiny green outer skin containing the bitter oil glands is removed. Cut open the citrons and remove the flesh using a sharp-edged teaspoon. Discard this flesh or keep it to make a pungent jelly (see Fruit jelly*). Cut the skins into quarters and leave overnight in a deep basin with enough water to cover. Because the skins are light and will float to the top, weigh them down with a heavy plate and a weight.

Discard the water and weigh the fruit skins. The mass should be about 750 g. If it is not, adjust, in proportion, the quantity of sugar to be used in making the syrup. Parboil the fruit by immersing it, piece by piece, in a pot containing the 1,5 litres (6 cups) boiling water so that the temperature of the water is not reduced. When a skewer or sharpened matchstick easily pierces the pieces, lift them out with a draining spoon. Pour the cooking water through a strainer lined with a piece of damp muslin to clarify it for use in the syrup.

Measure 1,25 litres (5 cups) of this water (top up with fresh water if necessary) and bring to the boil. Slowly add the sugar, then turn the heat lower and stir frequently until a thin syrup has developed. Then boil rapidly and add the fruit slowly so that the temperature is not reduced. (If the syrup has any impurities it should be strained through muslin and brought to the boil again before the fruit is added.)

Turn the heat down and cook slowly so that the syrup does not thicken too soon, otherwise the fruit will be hard and tough.

When the syrup boils in small bubbles – after 45 minutes-1 hour – test a little of the syrup on a saucer. If the syrup, after rapid cooling, is as thick as cooling dessert jelly, the pan is ready to be removed from the heat. Stir the preserve very gently for a minute or two so that there is no foam on top, then place in dry sterilised jars.

When the syrup and fruit have cooled, insert a knife down the inside of the glass jars to let any air bubbles escape. Pour a little melted paraffin wax over the top of the preserve to make airtight seals, and screw on the lids when the wax is cold (see Potting, sealing and storing jam*). Store, preferably in a cool, dark place.

KUMQUAT PRESERVE

WATERMELON PRESERVE

PREPARATION TIME: 30 MINUTES
SOAKING TIME: OVERNIGHT IN LIME SOLUTION; 2 HOURS IN FRESH WATER
COOKING TIME: 1½-2 HOURS

INGREDIENTS TO YIELD 4 JARS OF 500 ML
1 kg watermelon or 'konfyt' watermelon peel
25 ml (5 teaspoons) slaked lime, or 45 ml (3 tablespoons) bicarbonate of soda
7 litres water
1 kg sugar
20 ml (4 teaspoons) lemon juice
A pinch of salt
A 4 cm piece of fresh green ginger, bruised

To obtain the watermelon peel, cut a melon into slices, then remove and discard the soft flesh. Peel off the hard, thin outer rind and discard. Cut the remaining white, fleshy peel into squares and prick well on both sides.

Soak the peel overnight in a solution made from the lime (or bicarbonate of soda) and 5 litres of the water. This ensures that the preserve is tender yet crisp. Rinse the peel thoroughly, soak in fresh water for 2 hours, then drain.

WATERMELON PRESERVE

Place the pieces in boiling water one at a time so that the water does not stop boiling. Boil, uncovered, until just tender (20-30 minutes) – test by piercing the peel with a matchstick.

To prepare the syrup, combine the sugar, 2 litres (8 cups) water, lemon juice, salt and ginger in a saucepan over a low heat. When all the sugar has dissolved, bring the mixture to the boil. Place the peel in the boiling syrup and boil rapidly until the pieces are tender and translucent and the syrup thick (1-1½ hours).

Pack the peel into hot, dry sterilised bottles, fill the bottles with the syrup and seal immediately (see Potting, sealing and storing jam*).

VARIATION The fruit may also be boiled in syrup over a period of a few days. Boil for 30 minutes on the first day and leave to cool. The next day, remove the fruit from the syrup and bring the syrup to the boil. Add the pieces of peel one by one (to ensure that the syrup does not stop boiling) and boil for 30-40 minutes. Repeat the process the following day but boil until ready for bottling.

SOUR FIG PRESERVE

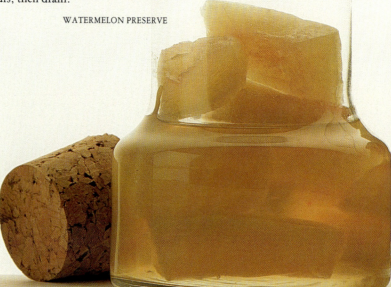

Orange Preserve

Preparation Time: 1 hour
Standing Time: 30 minutes
Soaking Time: overnight
Cooking Time: 1½ hours

Ingredients to Yield 4 Jars of 500 ml
1 kg oranges (not too ripe)
Salt
2,5 litres (10 cups) water
1,25 kg sugar
20 ml (4 teaspoons) lemon juice
A 4 cm piece of fresh green ginger
Peel of ½ naartjie

Grate the rind very thinly from the oranges (this helps the syrup to penetrate the fruit), then rub the oranges with salt to prevent discoloration. Leave to stand for 30 minutes. Place the oranges in a basin and pour boiling water over them. Leave to stand until the water has cooled, then rinse in cold water and leave to soak overnight in fresh, cold water to remove any bitter taste. Drain off the water.

Remove the pips by cutting a deep, narrow cross at the base of each orange. Roll the orange gently between your hands and squeeze out the pips. Place the oranges in boiling water and continue boiling until the skin is soft (about 20 minutes). Test by piercing with a matchstick – the skin must be soft. Then, either leave the oranges whole, or halve or quarter them.

Prepare the syrup by boiling the 2,5 litres (10 cups) water and pouring it over the sugar in a saucepan. Add the lemon juice, ginger and naartjie peel, and bring the syrup to the boil, stirring to dissolve the sugar. Add the fruit and boil until the oranges are translucent and the syrup thick (about 1 hour).

Skim the foam from the preserve. If the syrup is ready before the fruit, add some thin syrup and boil again. If the oranges are ready and the syrup too thin, remove the fruit and boil only the syrup; add the fruit when the syrup is ready and bring back to the boil.

Pack the oranges into hot, dry, sterilised jars. Fill with syrup, covering the fruit completely, and seal immediately (see Potting, sealing and storing jam*).

VARIATION To make whole naartjie preserve, use 1 kg tight-skinned naartjies.

To make grapefruit preserve, use 1 kg grapefruit with firm peels and follow the above recipe – leaving out the ginger and naartjie peel from the ingredients.

Green Fig Preserve

Preparation Time: 1 hour
Soaking Time: overnight
Cooking Time: 1¼ hours

Ingredients to Yield 4 Jars of 500 ml
1 kg green figs
15 ml (1 tablespoon) slaked lime
2,5 litres (10 cups) water
1,25 kg sugar
20 ml (4 teaspoons) lemon juice

Scrape the figs with a knife and make a cross on the rounded, bottom end of each fig. Make a lime solution by stirring the slaked lime into the 2,5 litres (10 cups) water and soak the figs in it overnight. This ensures that the preserve will be tender yet crisp. Rinse thoroughly in fresh water and leave to soak for 15 minutes.

Drain and then boil in a fresh batch of water (enough to cover the fruit) for about 15 minutes, or until just tender. Remove the figs (reserving the cooking water), and allow to drain and cool slightly in a colander.

Prepare a syrup by pouring 2 litres (8 cups) of the water in which the figs were boiled into a saucepan containing the sugar. Add the lemon juice and bring the syrup to the boil, stirring to dissolve the sugar.

Squeeze the excess water from each fig. Place them, one at a time, in the boiling syrup, ensuring that the syrup does not stop boiling. Boil, uncovered, until the figs are tender and translucent and the syrup is thick. Spoon the figs and syrup into hot, dry, sterilised bottles and seal immediately (see Potting, sealing and storing jam*).

Kumquat Preserve

Preparation Time: 30 minutes
Cooking Time: 45 minutes

Ingredients to Yield 4 Jars of 500 ml
1 kg kumquats (not overripe)
1 kg sugar
2 litres (8 cups) water
20 ml (4 teaspoons) lemon juice

Place the kumquats in a saucepan and cover with boiling water. When cool, drain off the water and pour over boiling water again. Drain once more, remove the kumquats and cut a cross in the bottom of each fruit. Place in boiling water and boil until the fruit is just tender – about 15 minutes (test for tenderness by piercing with a matchstick). Drain, then squeeze the pips from the fruit – in doing so you will also remove some of the excess water.

Prepare the syrup by bringing the sugar, 2 litres (8 cups) water and lemon juice to the boil. Add the kumquats and boil for about 45 minutes, or until the fruit is translucent and the syrup is thick and reduced by almost half.

Pack the fruit into hot, sterilised jars, fill with the syrup and seal (see Potting, sealing and storing jam*).

Sour Fig Preserve

Preparation Time: 2 hours
Soaking Time: overnight
Cooking Time: 2 hours

Ingredients to Yield 3 Jars of 500 ml
1 kg sour figs
100 g salt
6 litres water
1 kg sugar
1 cinnamon stick

Top the sour figs, rinse well and soak overnight in a brine solution made from the salt and 5 litres of the water to clean the fruit thoroughly. Drain and rinse again, then peel thinly.

Make a syrup with the sugar, remaining 1 litre (4 cups) water and cinnamon. Bring to the boil and add the fruit. Boil until the fruit is shiny and the syrup is thick (1½-2 hours).

Bottle immediately in hot, dry, sterilised jars and seal (see Potting, sealing and storing jam*).

CITRON PRESERVE

ORANGE PRESERVE

GREEN FIG PRESERVE

PRESERVES, JAMS, PICKLES AND SWEETS

HERB VINEGAR *Aromatic herbs impart subtle flavour to plain vinegar.*

HERB VINEGAR

UNTIL FIFTY YEARS ago, many country people in Europe fermented their own vinegars from cowslips, dandelions and rhubarb, leaving them to mature for a year or so in a cask before using.

Probably few people make these pleasant, tangy vinegars nowadays, though their close equivalents, herb vinegars, still remain firm favourites. Use them to give an extra lift to home-made pickles, salad dressings and savoury sauces.

PREPARATION TIME: ABOUT 10 MINUTES
STEEPING TIME: 2-3 WEEKS
MATURING TIME: 2-4 WEEKS

INGREDIENTS TO YIELD 600 ML
100-175 g freshly gathered tarragon, sage, rosemary, mint, basil or other herb
About 600 ml white wine vinegar

Pick the herbs just before they flower. Wash the leaves and the tender parts of the stalks, put them in a large jar, then bruise them with a wooden spoon.

Top up the jar with the white wine vinegar, cover with a cloth and leave to steep for 2-3 weeks. If you are using a clear glass jar, stand it in a dark cupboard to prevent any colour loss.

Strain the vinegar through a piece of clean muslin. Place a fresh, washed sprig of the herb in the bottle before sealing the vinegar (see Bottling and sealing sauces and ketchups*).

Leave the vinegar to mature for 2-4 weeks before use.

SERVING SUGGESTIONS Use herb vinegars in dressings such as vinaigrette*, avocado dressing* and ravigote sauce*, or for pickled cucumbers*. Herb vinegar made from tarragon is good for making tomato sauce* or pickled sweet peppers*.

PICKLED CUCUMBERS

PICKLED CUCUMBERS are very easy to make at home. Remember not to marinate in aluminium or chipped enamel pots – use only glass, ceramic or stainless-steel containers.

When sealing the jars, place a round of wax paper over the opening before screwing on the top.

PREPARATION TIME: 30 MINUTES
STANDING TIME: 4 HOURS
COOKING TIME: 10 MINUTES

INGREDIENTS TO YIELD 6 JARS OF 500 ML
2 kg pickling cucumbers
250 g salt
Ice cubes
Iced water
100 g sugar
*750 ml (3 cups) strong herb vinegar**
60 ml (¼ cup) dill seeds
18 peppercorns

Wash the cucumbers and cut into pieces if you prefer a smaller pickle. Place the cucumbers in a deep dish and sprinkle the salt over them. Cover with ice cubes and iced water and leave to stand for 4 hours. Drain and rinse thoroughly.

Add the sugar to the herb vinegar in a stainless-steel saucepan and stir to dissolve. Add the cucumbers, heat slowly and boil, uncovered, for 5-6 minutes.

Add 10 ml (2 teaspoons) dill seeds and 3 peppercorns to each clean, hot pickling jar, and then fill with the cucumbers and boiling vinegar. Seal immediately (see Potting and sealing pickles*).

PICKLED RED CABBAGE

PICKLED CABBAGE has been eaten since the 18th century at least, when its sharp, near-lemony flavour led explorer Captain Cook to believe, erroneously, that preserved cabbages fermented with juniper berries were a preventive against scurvy.

Pickled cabbage loses its crispness after 10-12 weeks' storage. This recipe may equally be used for white cabbage.

PREPARATION TIME: 30 MINUTES
STANDING TIME: 24 HOURS
MATURING TIME: AT LEAST 1 WEEK

INGREDIENTS TO YIELD 1,75-2,25 KG
1 firm red cabbage
100-175 g coarse salt
*450-600 ml spiced malt or white vinegar**

Remove any discoloured leaves from the cabbage, cut it into quarters and wash well. Cut away the tough inner stalk, and shred the cabbage. Layer the cabbage and salt in a basin, ending with a layer of salt. Leave for 24 hours.

Rinse thoroughly in cold water and drain well. Pack the cabbage loosely into jars, cover with the cold, spiced vinegar and seal at once (see Potting and sealing pickles*). Leave to mature for at least 1 week.

PICKLED SWEET PEPPERS

THIS IS A TASTY relish to serve with grilled pork or lamb. Pickled sweet peppers may also be used in any recipes that call for pimentos.

PREPARATION TIME: 15 MINUTES
STANDING TIME: OVERNIGHT
COOKING TIME: 10-15 MINUTES

INGREDIENTS FOR 4 JARS OF 500 ML
1 kg green peppers
500 g sweet red peppers
500 g salt
4 litres cold water
Boiling water
750 ml (3 cups) tarragon vinegar
3 ml (¾ teaspoon) salt
15 ml (1 tablespoon) mustard seeds
1 ml (¼ teaspoon) cayenne pepper
4 cloves
4 peppercorns
1 clove garlic, crushed
1 bay leaf
50 g sugar

Remove the stems, seeds and pith from the peppers. Dissolve the 500 g salt in the cold water and soak the peppers overnight in this brine solution. Drain and rinse in fresh water.

Pour boiling water over the peppers and allow to stand for 2-5 minutes. Drain, remove the skins and pack into clean jars.

Heat the vinegar and add all the remaining ingredients. Pour over the peppers and seal (see Potting and sealing pickles*).

332

PICKLED ONIONS AND CARROTS

TRY THIS EASY RECIPE for pickled onions and carrots – a deliciously crunchy treat that makes an admirable gift.

PREPARATION TIME: 20 MINUTES
MATURING TIME: 1 WEEK

INGREDIENTS TO YIELD 2 JARS OF 500 ML
500 g pickling onions, peeled
100 g carrots, cut into thick chips
4 fresh green chillies
10 ml (2 teaspoons) salt
10 black peppercorns
250 ml (1 cup) white vinegar
60 ml (¼ cup) cold water

Wash and drain the vegetables. Mix in the chillies, salt and peppercorns. Place the mixture in clean jars and cover with the mixed vinegar and water. Seal (see Potting and sealing pickles*), shake the bottles and leave for 1 week.

PICKLED ONIONS

ONE OF THE MOST POPULAR relishes must be pickled onions. Not only are they eaten with cold meats, but they provide a tasty complement to snacks such as cheese and crusty bread.

Small pickling onions can be grown or bought, or else shallots may be used instead. If the onions are packed in cold vinegar, they will remain beautifully crisp during storage.

People with a sweet tooth may add 10 ml (2 teaspoons) soft brown sugar to each 500 ml jar of pickled onions.

PREPARATION TIME: 1½-2 HOURS
SOAKING TIME: 36 HOURS
MATURING TIME: 6-8 WEEKS

INGREDIENTS TO YIELD 5 JARS OF 500 ML
2,75 kg pickling onions
1 kg coarse salt
10 litres water
1,5 litres (6 cups) spiced vinegar*

Place the onions, unpeeled, in a brine made by dissolving 500 g of the salt in 5 litres of the water. Cover with a plate, to keep the onions below the surface of the brine, and leave to soak for 12 hours.

The next day, drain the onions. Place them in a large bowl and scald them in boiling water for 1 minute. Drain, then top, tail and peel them.

Prepare a second solution of brine by dissolving the remaining 500 g salt in the remaining 5 litres water and leave the peeled onions to soak in it, covered with a plate, for a further 24 hours. Then remove the onions and drain thoroughly.

Pot in clean bottles or jars, pour over the cold, spiced vinegar and seal (see Potting and sealing pickles*). Leave to mature for 6-8 weeks.

MIXED FRUIT PICKLE

PICKLES ARE ENJOYED by most people, but they are especially important to any Indian meal. Dried fruits blended with golden syrup and spices make an exceptional sweet pickle.

Be sure you allow this pickle to stand in glass jars – not in metal or plastic, which will be corroded by the spices.

PREPARATION TIME: 45 MINUTES
MATURING TIME: 5 DAYS

INGREDIENTS TO YIELD 2-3 JARS OF 500 ML
500 g mixed dried fruit
250 ml (1 cup) malt vinegar
15 ml (1 tablespoon) dry mustard
15 ml (1 tablespoon) chilli powder
15 ml (1 tablespoon) turmeric
20 ml (4 teaspoons) salt
8 cloves garlic, peeled and halved
250 ml (1 cup) sunflower oil
5 ml (1 teaspoon) cloves
15 ml (1 tablespoon) black peppercorns
125 ml (½ cup) golden syrup

Wipe the dried fruit with a damp cloth. Slice the fruit into strips about 6 mm thick and place in a mixing bowl.

Pour the vinegar into a separate bowl and stir in the mustard, chilli powder, turmeric, salt and garlic. Add the vinegar mixture and the remaining ingredients to the fruit and mix thoroughly.

Bottle the mixture in pickle jars (see Potting and sealing pickles*) and allow to mature for 5 days.

SERVING SUGGESTION This sweet pickle is ideal with vegetable or lentil dishes.

PICCALILLI

PICCALILLI, a good way of making use of end-of-season garden produce, goes well with various cold meats. Use equal quantities of vegetables in order to make up the total amount.

PREPARATION TIME: 45 MINUTES
STANDING TIME: 24 HOURS
COOKING TIME: 15-20 MINUTES
MATURING TIME: 6-8 WEEKS

INGREDIENTS TO YIELD 6-7 JARS OF 500 ML
2,75 kg prepared vegetables: cucumber (or gherkin) and marrow in 1,5 cm cubes; green beans, strung and in 2,5 cm slices; small onions, peeled*; small green tomatoes, sliced; cauliflower sprigs
500 g coarse salt
15 g turmeric
25 g dry mustard
25 g ground ginger
175 g sugar
1 litre (4 cups) white vinegar
40 g flour or cornflour

Spread the vegetables on a large dish and sprinkle the salt over them. Put a plate on top, weight it, and leave for 24 hours. The next day, thoroughly drain, wash and rinse the vegetables.

Using a wooden spoon, stir the spices and sugar into most of the vinegar (reserve 50 ml) in a large pan. Heat gently, stirring until the sugar has fully dissolved. Add the vegetables and then simmer gently for 10-15 minutes, or until the required texture is reached. This depends largely on individual taste, but the vegetables must be whole.

Blend the flour (or cornflour) with the remaining vinegar and add to the pan. Bring the mixture to the boil, stirring carefully. Simmer for 2-3 minutes. Pot and seal (see Potting and sealing pickles*) and then leave for 6-8 weeks.

PICCALILLI *Crunchy vegetables in a sharp pickle.*

Apple, Date and Walnut Chutney

This recipe makes a sweet, nutty chutney that is a good accompaniment to pork and ham, a bright topping for cocktail snacks, and a delicious addition to cheese sandwiches of all kinds.

Preparation Time: about 50 minutes
Cooking Time: 1½ hours
Maturing Time: 2-3 weeks

Ingredients to Yield 5 Jars of 500 ml

500 g peeled and chopped onions*
125 ml (½ cup) water
1 kg peeled, cored and chopped cooking apples
750 g dates, stoned and chopped
100 g walnuts, chopped
5 ml (1 teaspoon) salt
5 ml (1 teaspoon) ground ginger
5 ml (1 teaspoon) cayenne pepper
600 ml vinegar
250 g sugar

Put the onions in a large, heavy-based pan with the water. Bring to the boil and simmer until soft.

Add the apples and continue cooking gently for 15-20 minutes.

Put in the dates, walnuts, salt, spices and half the vinegar. Cook, stirring occasionally, until the mixture thickens.

Add the sugar and the rest of the vinegar, stirring until the sugar dissolves. Continue to simmer until the chutney becomes very thick.

Stir occasionally. Pot and seal (see Potting and sealing chutneys*). Leave to mature for 2-3 weeks.

APPLE, DATE AND WALNUT CHUTNEY *A relish made from a popular combination.*

Green Tomato Chutney

The tomato, a native of tropical America, made its European debut in the middle of the 16th century and was erroneously hailed as an aphrodisiac – hence its early name of love apple or *pomme d'amour*.

This chutney is a good way of using green tomatoes and goes well with cold meats and cheeses. It is also served with or added to various curried dishes.

Preparation Time: about 30 minutes
Cooking Time: about 2 hours
Maturing Time: 6 weeks

Ingredients to Yield 4-5 Jars of 500 ml

1,75 kg green tomatoes, washed and chopped
750 g peeled and chopped onions*
500 g peeled, cored and chopped cooking apples
600 ml vinegar
8 red chillies
25 g whole dried ginger
250 g seedless raisins or chopped dates
10 ml (2 teaspoons) salt
500 g sugar

Put the chopped tomatoes, onions and apples in a large, heavy-based pan with half the vinegar. Bring to the boil, then simmer gently for about 30 minutes, or until everything is tender.

Tie the chillies and whole dried ginger in a muslin bag, bruise with a hammer, and add to the pan with the raisins or chopped dates. Cook, stirring from time to time, until the mixture thickens (about 1 hour).

Add the salt, sugar and the rest of the vinegar, stirring well until the sugar dissolves. Continue cooking, pressing the bag of spices occasionally with a wooden spoon, until the mixture is very thick. Remove the muslin bag before potting and sealing (see Potting and sealing chutneys*). Leave to mature for 6 weeks.

Lemon Chutney

This tart chutney is an excellent accompaniment to any Indian food. It is a delicious way to make use of lemons when they are plentiful.

Preparation Time: 30 minutes
Standing Time: 2 hours
Cooking Time: 35-45 minutes

Ingredients to Yield 2 Jars of 500 ml

8 lemons
250 g onions, peeled and sliced*
30 ml (2 tablespoons) salt
500 ml (2 cups) white vinegar
500 g sugar
100 g seedless raisins
15 ml (1 tablespoon) mustard seeds
A 4 cm piece of fresh green ginger
2 ml (½ teaspoon) cayenne pepper

Wash the lemons and slice them thinly (with the peel). Remove all the pips. Sprinkle the lemon and onion slices with the salt and leave for 2 hours.

Place the lemon and onion in a saucepan, add the remaining ingredients and boil until the lemon peel is soft (about 30 minutes).

Bottle in warm, dry jars and seal (see Potting and sealing chutneys*).

Red Tomato Chutney

It seems a pity to turn sound, ripe red tomatoes into chutney, but if there is a glut in your garden, or they are especially cheap in the shops, capitalise on the plethora to make this versatile companion to fish, cheese and meats.

Preparation Time: 30-40 minutes
Cooking Time: 1½-2 hours
Maturing Time: 3-5 weeks

Ingredients to Yield 4 Jars of 500 ml

2,5 kg peeled and chopped ripe tomatoes
500 g peeled and chopped onions*
30 ml (2 tablespoons) salt
10 ml (2 teaspoons) paprika
1 ml (¼ teaspoon) cayenne pepper
300 ml spiced distilled or malt vinegar*
350 g sugar

Put the tomatoes and onions in a large, heavy-based pan. Bring to the boil, then simmer for 20-30 minutes until soft. Add the salt, spices and half the vinegar, and cook gently for about 45 minutes.

APRICOT BLATJANG

APRICOT BLATJANG, one of the original Cape recipes, is a tangy, slightly tart chutney. It is easy to make, and complements many dishes.

PREPARATION TIME: 15 MINUTES
COOKING TIME: 1¼ HOURS

INGREDIENTS TO YIELD 6 JARS OF 500 ML
2 kg ripe apricots
1 large onion, peeled and chopped*
1 clove garlic, crushed
500 g seedless raisins
400 g sugar
1 ml (¼ teaspoon) cayenne pepper
5 ml (1 teaspoon) salt
10 ml (2 teaspoons) ground ginger
5 ml (1 teaspoon) dry mustard
500 ml (2 cups) vinegar

Halve and stone the apricots. Mix all the ingredients in a stainless-steel saucepan and bring slowly to the boil. Simmer, uncovered, for 45 minutes-1 hour, stirring occasionally.

When thick and shiny, bottle in clean, hot jars and seal immediately (see Potting and sealing chutneys*).

SERVING SUGGESTIONS Chutneys offer a good way to liven up a meat dish. Try making cold meat sandwiches with chutney or use on cold snoek or pickled fish.

VARIATION For date chutney, combine 1,5 kg stoned and chopped dates, 1 kg sugar, 10 ml (2 teaspoons) ground ginger, 1,25 litres (5 cups) vinegar, 250 g peeled* and minced onions, 1 clove garlic, minced, 5 ml (1 teaspoon) cayenne pepper and 2 ml (½ teaspoon) salt, and boil together in a saucepan until the mixture is thick and shiny — about 30 minutes. Bottle the chutney in clean, hot jars (the yield will be about 4-5 jars of 500 ml) and seal (see Potting and sealing chutneys*).

MANGO ATJAR *This Malay condiment is perfect with a mild mutton curry.*

MANGO ATJAR

ATJARS MAY BE MADE by pickling various vegetables or fruits to add piquancy to food. The Cape Malay recipes are generally milder than those from the Far East. Mango atjar has a lovely flavour and can be served with a great variety of foods. Try serving it with a mutton curry* on a cold winter's day.

Atjar differs from chutney in that the fruit and spices are boiled until soft but the fruit is kept in chunks, whereas chutney has the consistency of thick jam.

Be careful when cutting up the mangoes – they are very slippery and you could cut your fingers.

PREPARATION TIME: 30 MINUTES
COOKING TIME: 45 MINUTES

INGREDIENTS TO YIELD 3 JARS OF 500 ML
1,5 kg peeled and stoned mangoes (as green and hard as possible), cut in 2 cm chunks
500 ml (2 cups) white vinegar
250 g sugar
200 g almonds, blanched* and chopped
2 onions, peeled and sliced*
60 ml (¼ cup) fresh green ginger, peeled and chopped
5 ml (1 teaspoon) cayenne pepper
5 ml (1 teaspoon) mustard seeds
2 cloves garlic, crushed
5 peppercorns
5 ml (1 teaspoon) salt

Combine all the ingredients and boil until the mango chunks are soft, but still whole. Bottle in clean hot jars (see Potting and sealing chutneys*).

CHOCOLATE GINGER LITCHIS

THESE UNUSUAL confections have an Oriental flavour and add special interest to a Chinese meal. They also offer a wonderful way to end a Western meal, accompanied by good strong coffee.

The chocolate ginger litchis must be kept in the refrigerator and should be eaten within two to three days.

PREPARATION TIME: 40 MINUTES
STANDING TIME: 1 HOUR

INGREDIENTS TO YIELD ABOUT 24 CONFECTIONS
1 tin (420 g) stoned litchis
60 g drained preserved ginger
200 g dark chocolate
15 g solid white vegetable shortening, or 10 ml (2 teaspoons) sunflower oil
Cornflour

Drain the litchis and let them stand upside down on paper towels for 1 hour, or until they are dry, patting them with paper towels to dry them thoroughly. Cut the ginger into slivers and stuff each litchi with a sliver of ginger.

Melt the chocolate over hot water together with the shortening or oil. Stir and then remove from the heat.

Place a little cornflour in a bowl. Add the litchis and toss to coat lightly. Dip each litchi into the chocolate, using a fork.

Place each chocolate-coated litchi on a baking tray lined with wax paper, making sure that all parts of the litchis are coated with the chocolate. If there are gaps or thin patches, allow the chocolate coating to harden and then dip a second time.

Refrigerate. If you wish, dribble the remaining chocolate decoratively over the top of each coated litchi.

SERVING SUGGESTIONS For a Chinese meal, pile the chocolate litchis into a bowl. Supply a set of chopsticks to enable your guests to help themselves, and serve China tea.

For a Western meal, place each chocolate in a little paper case and arrange on a glass sweet dish.

VARIATION Special dipping chocolate is now available in many shops. If this is used there is no need to add shortening or oil to the chocolate.

Chocolate – A Sweet Confection from a Bitter Bean

Chocolate knows no cultural or geographical boundaries.
It is enjoyed virtually everywhere in the world and eaten in a variety of forms –
from the simple survival slab in a soldier's backpack to the expert mouldings of a master confectioner.

Hints on Using Chocolate for Decoration and Sweet-making

Different purposes require different types of chocolate. Bitter chocolate (not readily available in South Africa) is used for baking, as is cooking chocolate, which is also used in desserts and for home-made chocolates. Couverture chocolate, which has extra cocoa fat, is used for coating, sculpting and lattice-making.

Melting chocolate The best method of melting chocolate is to cut half the quantity into small pieces and to grate the other half. Place the pieces in a bowl over hot (not boiling) water and stir all the time until the chocolate has melted. Remove from the heat and gradually add the grated chocolate. Melted in this way the chocolate should have a good sheen. Do not allow any water, steam or other moisture to come into contact with the chocolate, as this will make it hard.

Flavouring and colouring If you are flavouring chocolate, use only oil-based flavourings – a water-based one will ruin it. If you are colouring white chocolate, use only paste or powder colouring and do so sparingly. Use an egg-poaching pan for melting small amounts of chocolate that have to be coloured in different shades. If the chocolate becomes too thick, add very small quantities of white margarine.

Storage Always keep chocolate in a cool, dark place.

Making chocolates in moulds Melt the required amount of cooking chocolate and pour it into chilled moulds. Tap the moulds gently on the work-surface to dispel any air bubbles and to ensure that the chocolates have an even base. Place the moulds in the refrigerator until the chocolates are firm, then gently tap them out of the moulds and allow to return to room temperature before storing. The moulds should be cleaned and dried immediately after use.

If different colours are required to highlight shape and design, use a good-quality, fine paintbrush to apply the decorations or fill the indentations in the moulds before the main-colour chocolate is poured into the moulds.

Chocolate clusters Melted cooking chocolate can be mixed with nuts, raisins or coconut (or a combination) to make clusters. Stir well to coat, then place spoonfuls of the mixture on to wax paper and allow to set. These keep well in an airtight container for up to 4 weeks.

Chocolate leaves Wash and dry rose leaves or any other leaves which have a ribbed underside (plastic or cloth leaves may also be used). Melt the required amount of cooking chocolate and, using a paintbrush, coat the underside of the leaves with the melted chocolate. Make quite sure that the chocolate is thick; it may be necessary to give the leaf 2 coats, allowing the first coat to set for a few minutes before applying the second coat.

Place the leaves, chocolate side up, on a tray in the refrigerator to set, then gently peel off the leaves.

Chocolate roses Take apart a plastic or cloth rose and coat each petal with melted cooking chocolate in the same way as for chocolate leaves. It will be easier to peel off the petals later if you do not brush the chocolate quite to the edges. Once the chocolate has set in the refrigerator and been removed from the petal, assemble the rose, using melted chocolate as an adhesive.

Chocolate frills Melt cooking chocolate, pour it on a marble slab or baking sheet and spread it into a thin layer with a metal spatula. Allow to cool and set in the refrigerator or a cool place. When it has set, position the spatula at a low angle against the chocolate and gently push the blade: a thin layer of chocolate will curl into a roll or frill.

Grated chocolate curls Rub a large block of chocolate against the coarse side of a grater, using long strokes to form the curls. These are ideal for decorating puddings or the sides and tops of cakes.

Chocolate filigree or fans Draw a pattern on a strip of cardboard or paper. Place wax paper over the design. Melt couverture chocolate and pour it into a small paper piping bag. Cut a tiny hole in the tip of the bag. Hold it over the paper and, squeezing gently, pipe chocolate over the design. Slide the design along under the wax paper if you wish to repeat it. Work quickly, as the chocolate soon hardens.

Allow the chocolate to set in the refrigerator. Remove it from the paper by holding the paper on the edge of a table and slowly and gently pulling the paper down and away from the chocolate, allowing the filigree to fall into your waiting hand. Keep chilled.

Strawberry Chocolate Box

Preparation Time: 45 minutes
Chilling Time: 4-6 hours

Ingredients for Six

For the filling:
160 g dark cooking chocolate
15 ml (1 tablespoon) brandy
2 eggs, separated
125 ml (½ cup) cream

For the casing:
125 g dark cooking chocolate
15 g white vegetable fat

For the topping:
500 g strawberries
65 ml strawberry jam
10 ml (2 teaspoons) brandy
125 ml (½ cup) cream

First make the filling. Chop up the chocolate and place it in the top of a double boiler. Melt over hot, not boiling, water. Remove from the heat, cool slightly and gradually add the brandy and egg yolks.

Whip the cream lightly and fold it into the chocolate mixture. Beat the egg whites until soft peaks form; fold half the whites into the chocolate mixture, then gently fold in the rest.

To make the casing, lightly grease a deep cake tin 15-18 cm square. Line the tin by placing 2 strips of aluminium foil across each other in the tin. Each piece of foil must be the full width of the tin. Allow the edge of the foil to droop over the sides of the tin to make it easy to remove the chocolate case when set.

Break the 125 g chocolate in the top of a double boiler, with the vegetable fat. Stir over hot, not boiling, water until melted. Cool and pour into the foil-lined tin. Swirl the chocolate around the tin to coat the sides and base, trying to keep the top edges as even as possible. The chocolate should come about 3,5 cm up the sides of the tin.

Place in the refrigerator for about a minute. Remove and swirl the chocolate remaining in the base of the tin around once more to create a second layer – this will strengthen the box. Refrigerate until set (about 5-10 minutes).

Pour the chocolate filling in the prepared chocolate box, return it to the refrigerator and allow to set (about 4-6 hours).

To make the topping, wash and hull the strawberries. Place the jam and brandy in a small saucepan and melt over a gentle heat to form a glaze.

Whip the topping cream and place in a piping bag with a large star tube. Carefully lift the chocolate box from the tin, gently peel away the foil and place the box on a serving dish.

Place the strawberries in the centre of the box and coat them with the jam glaze. Pipe cream decoratively around the edge of the box. Refrigerate until ready to serve.

Variation Tinned cherries may be used instead of the strawberries. In this case, omit the glaze.

Mixed Chocolates

Preparation Time: 1½ hours
Setting Time: 30 minutes

Ingredients to Yield about 1 kg
300 g cooking chocolate
100 g marzipan*
100 g glacé cherries
50 g glacé pineapple
100 g coconut ice*
50 g crystallised ginger
100 g Brazil-nuts
200 g easy fondant*, flavoured with fruit and/or peppermint, and cut into 1,5 cm cubes or set in small moulds

Break up the chocolate and place it in a bowl over a saucepan of hot water set on a low heat. Stir the chocolate often with a wooden spoon until it melts, and then remove the pan from the heat.

Meanwhile, roll out the marzipan. Completely cover and seal each of the cherries with a piece of the marzipan. Cut the pineapple and coconut ice into cubes about 1,5 cm square. Cut a strip off each piece of ginger to use for decorating the ginger chocolates.

Place some wax paper on a cooling rack. Using 2 skewers – one in each hand to lift the chocolates – dip the coconut ice, pieces of ginger, nuts and fondants in turn into the melted chocolate.

Tap the skewers on the bowl edge to remove the excess chocolate. Put a piece of ginger on each of the ginger chocolates and place the sweets on the rack for 30 minutes to harden.

Dip the cherries coated in marzipan and the pineapple cubes into the chocolate, and place them on the cooling rack so that the chocolate drips down the sides and evenly coats and seals them.

When quite cold, place the sweets in paper cases and arrange in a chocolate box.

Variations Use dark chocolate for dipping some of the fillings.

You can substitute any of the following for fillings: cubes of Turkish delight*, marshmallows* or caramels*.

Chocolate-Coated Ice Cream Balls

Preparation Time: 1 hour
Chilling Time: 8 hours, or overnight

Ingredients to Yield 40 Balls
15 ml (1 tablespoon) gelatin
30 ml (2 tablespoons) water
45 ml (3 tablespoons) liqueur
1 litre vanilla ice cream (use a very hard variety)
250 g dark cooking chocolate
120 g white vegetable fat

Sprinkle the gelatin over the 30 ml water and allow to stand for 5 minutes. Dissolve over a pan of hot water and allow to cool before adding the liqueur.

Put the ice cream into the bowl of a food processor. Add the cooled gelatin mixture and beat until just combined. (It is important that the gelatin is quite cool but still liquid when added to the ice cream and that it be beaten in as quickly as possible, otherwise the gelatin will form lumps in the ice cream.)

Put the ice cream into a container and freeze for several hours, or overnight, until it is quite firm.

Place a baking tray in the freezer until it is very cold. Working very quickly with a melon-ball scoop, form balls of ice cream, place them on the tray and return to the freezer. When the balls are firm, remove them from the freezer and push wooden toothpicks (frilled ones are attractive) into each at a slight angle and return them to the freezer.

Put the chocolate and vegetable fat in the top of a double boiler over hot, not boiling, water until melted. Allow to cool slightly, then pour the chocolate mixture into a small drinking glass and dip the ice cream balls into it, coating them well. Put the chocolate-coated balls on to a cold tray and return to the freezer until firm.

Variation Wash 500-750 g strawberries but do not hull them. Dry them well. Holding each strawberry by its stalk, dip it about three-quarters deep into the chocolate coating and allow to dry on wax paper.

PRESERVES, JAMS, PICKLES AND SWEETS

MARZIPAN

Because marzipan is soft and pliable, it is ideal for moulding sweets or for decorating or icing cakes.

PREPARATION TIME: 1 HOUR

INGREDIENTS TO YIELD 700 G

350 g ground almonds
175 g icing sugar, sifted
175 g castor sugar
7 ml (1½ teaspoons) lemon juice
A few drops of almond essence
1 egg, lightly beaten
Sifted icing sugar for sprinkling
A few drops of red, green and yellow food colouring (optional)
A few dates, walnuts and glacé cherries for the sweets (optional)
A few cloves for the oranges and lemons (optional)

Put the ground almonds, icing sugar and castor sugar together in a mixing bowl. Add the lemon juice and the almond essence. Stir in enough of the beaten egg to make a fairly dry paste. Turn it on to a board lightly sprinkled with sifted icing sugar and knead it until it is smooth.

If you are colouring the marzipan for making shapes, divide into 4 sections; leave one plain and colour the remaining pieces red, green and yellow by adding a few drops of colouring and kneading the marzipan with your hands.

Sweets You can make sweets very quickly by placing a small piece of coloured paste in a stoned date, sandwiching a piece between 2 halves of a shelled walnut, or partially enclosing a glacé cherry in a piece of uncoloured paste, leaving a small section of the cherry showing at the top.

Cauliflowers Partially enclose a piece of uncoloured paste, the size of a hazelnut, in green paste flattened to the size of a 20 cent piece. Mark the top with the point of a skewer to represent the flower, and press round the green 'leaves', shaping them with the side of the skewer.

Oranges and lemons To obtain an orange paste, knead some of the red paste into some of the yellow. Shape the appropriate colour to resemble an orange or a lemon, and press a clove into one end for the stalk. Roll the sweet over a coarse grater to mark the surface.

Strawberries Shape a strawberry in red paste and pit the surface with the point of a cocktail stick. Make tiny leaves with green paste. Press 4 leaves into the end of the strawberry, using a cocktail stick.

Icing To ice a fruit cake with marzipan, first glaze the cake with a little heated and strained smooth apricot jam*. Roll out the kneaded marzipan (5 mm-1 cm thick) into the shape of the top of the cake, then lift it with your rolling pin and ease it on to the surface of the cake.

MARSHMALLOWS

The sweet-tasting root of the marshmallow plant used to be the main ingredient of this sweetmeat, but nowadays only the name survives in the recipe. Until the 18th century the plant was greatly esteemed for its medicinal properties, and a syrup of marshmallows was recommended to cure sore throats, hoarseness and all lung complaints.

The first reference to marshmallows prepared as a sweetmeat instead of as a medicine was in 1884. This version is delicately flavoured with vanilla essence.

PREPARATION TIME: 45 MINUTES
COOLING AND DRYING TIME: 36 HOURS

INGREDIENTS TO YIELD 800 G

150 ml water
30 ml (2 tablespoons) gelatin
5 ml (1 teaspoon) vanilla essence
450 g sugar
200 ml warm water
225 ml liquid glucose
1 egg white
45 ml (3 tablespoons) cornflour
45 ml (3 tablespoons) icing sugar, sifted

Place the 150 ml water, gelatin and vanilla essence in a small bowl set over a saucepan of water. Heat gently over a low heat to dissolve the gelatin, then take the pan off the heat. Leave the bowl on top of the pan to keep the mixture warm.

Dissolve the sugar in the 200 ml warm water in a fairly large pan over a low heat, then gently stir in the liquid glucose with a wooden spoon. Stop stirring and let the mixture boil to the firm-ball stage* (118°C). Remove the pan from the heat.

Pour the still-warm gelatin mixture into a heat-proof mixing bowl rinsed out with water to prevent sticking. Gradually trickle the sugar syrup into the gelatin mixture, whisking all the time. A balloon whisk gives the lightest blend, but an electric mixer saves hard work.

When the mixture is well thickened, beat in the egg white little by little. The mixture will become light and foamy.

Mix together the cornflour and icing sugar, and sprinkle some of this coating mixture over the base of an oiled 28 cm x 18 cm tin. Pour the marshmallow into the tin and leave for 24 hours.

MARZIPAN *Become a sculptor in the kitchen with this versatile – and delicious – almond sweet.*

PRESERVES, JAMS, PICKLES AND SWEETS

Dust a working surface and your fingers lightly with the coating mixture. Use a knife to lift a corner of the marshmallow, then pull it gently out of the tin on to the working area.

Using a hot, dry, sharp knife, cut the marshmallow into 2 cm squares. Dip the cut sides in the coating mixture, and leave to dry for about 12 hours. Pack in layers in an airtight tin.

JUJUBES

A PRICKLY TREE belonging to the buckthorn family, with the unlikely name of Zizyphus, is the bearer of a plum-like fruit which has the even more unlikely name of jujube.

In the early part of the 19th century the juice of this fruit was used to flavour little gelatin lozenges. Today, a jujube is simply a kind of fruit gum.

PREPARATION TIME: 30 MINUTES
SETTING TIME: OVERNIGHT

INGREDIENTS TO YIELD ABOUT 700 G

175 g dried apricots, soaked overnight
275-300 ml cold water
450 g sugar
50 g gelatin
150 ml warm water
10 ml (2 teaspoons) lemon juice
Castor sugar for coating

Place the apricots and the cold water in a medium-sized saucepan and cook until soft, then purée. This will yield about 275-300 ml thick purée. Return the purée to the saucepan, add the sugar and heat gently to dissolve.

Meanwhile, put the gelatin in a bowl containing the warm water and place the bowl over a saucepan filled with boiling water. Place the pan over a low heat until the gelatin has dissolved. Stir the gelatin and then the lemon juice into the prepared sugar syrup.

Rinse an 18 cm square sandwich tin under the cold tap and strain the mixture into it. Leave to set overnight. Cut into 2 cm squares with a hot knife and toss the jujubes in castor sugar.

SERVING SUGGESTION Serve in paper sweetcases and eat fairly soon, as jujubes do not store well.

FUDGE

FUDGE HAS LONG been a favourite homemade sweet. It is easy to prepare and makes an ideal contribution to a school fête, or any other fund-raising activity.

PREPARATION TIME: 1¼ HOURS
SETTING TIME: 3 HOURS

INGREDIENTS TO YIELD 900 G

900 g sugar
225 g butter
1 tin (410 g) evaporated milk
¼ of the milk tin of cold water
1 ml (¼ teaspoon) vanilla essence

Rinse out a 4 litre saucepan with cold water. Put in the sugar, butter, evaporated milk, water and vanilla essence.

Set the pan over a low heat until the sugar has dissolved completely. Stir the mixture occasionally, and from time to time brush the sides of the pan with warm water to make sure that sugar crystals do not form and drop into the mixture.

When the sugar has dissolved, bring the mixture to the boil, and boil rapidly until it reaches the soft-ball stage* (114°C).

Take the pan off the heat and allow the fudge to cool for 3 minutes, then beat it rapidly with a wooden spoon until the mixture thickens and feels rough.

Line a 20 cm square tin with wax paper. Pour in the fudge and, when it is beginning to set, mark in squares with a knife.

Cut the fudge into squares when it has cooled completely, and store it in an airtight tin.

COCONUT ICE

SIR FRANCIS DRAKE introduced coconuts to the people of England in this way: 'The said cochos hath a hard shell and a green huske over it, as hath our walnut... Within this hard shell is a white rine resembling in shewe very much, even as any thing may do, to the white of an egg when it is hard boyled.'

Coconut is a popular addition to many spiced and sweet recipes. A slab of coconut ice is something few children can resist, and is quick and easy to make.

PREPARATION TIME: 30 MINUTES
SETTING TIME: 2 HOURS

INGREDIENTS TO YIELD 1 KG

150 ml water and 150 ml milk, or 300 ml milk
900 g sugar
25 g butter
225 g desiccated coconut
5 ml (1 teaspoon) vanilla essence
A few drops of red colouring or cochineal

Pour the water and milk (or milk only) into a medium-sized saucepan with the sugar and butter, and heat it slowly until the sugar dissolves completely.

Bring the mixture to the boil and cook for 10 minutes, stirring from time to time, until it reaches the firm-ball stage* (120°C). Meanwhile, oil a shallow 20 cm square tin.

Remove the saucepan from the heat and add the coconut and vanilla essence. Beat the mixture briskly with a wooden spoon until it is fairly thick and creamy. Pour half the mixture into the oiled tin.

Add the colouring to the remaining half; do this quickly, as the texture will soon change, making it difficult for the colour to spread evenly. Pour the pink coconut mixture on top of the white and spread it over evenly.

Leave the coconut ice in a cool place until it is firm, and then cut it into narrow bars about 4 cm long.

Store the sweets in an airtight tin.

MEBOS

MEBOS IS AN OLD CAPE delicacy made from choice apricots. The characteristic salty-sweet taste makes a pleasant change from the sweetness of conventional dried fruit. Mebos may be eaten on its own, or used in fruit cakes or muffins, or for making mebos chutney.

PREPARATION TIME: 15 MINUTES
SOAKING TIME: 8 HOURS
DRYING TIME: 4-6 DAYS, OR
6 HOURS IN AN OVEN

INGREDIENTS TO YIELD 250 G

1 kg choice, well-ripened apricots
280 g salt
3,5 litres water
30 ml (2 tablespoons) lime
Sugar for dipping and packing

DRIED FRUIT ROLLS

Dried fruit rolls or 'smeer', as they are known in Afrikaans, offer an excellent way to use summer fruits such as quinces, peaches, apples, pears or pineapples.

The rolls can be made either from raw minced or puréed fruit, or from a mixture of cooked fruit and sugar. In both instances the fruit purée is then spread on grease-proof paper or plastic and left to dry out before being rolled up.

To make the rolls from raw fruit, choose ripe, healthy fruit. Peel it and remove any stones or pips. Mince the fruit (this gives the best texture) or purée it. Spread the minced or puréed fruit on sheets of grease-proof paper or plastic and leave to dry for one to four days. If you prefer a sweet product, spread honey over the fruit when it is dry, or dust it with castor sugar. Then roll it up. Pack the dried fruit rolls in plastic bags or airtight containers.

To make the rolls from cooked fruit, leave the skin on (except in the case of pineapple). Stone or seed if necessary, then cut the fruit into chunks. Simmer for a short while, preferably without water or, if water is needed, a very small amount. Mince the fruit or purée it, add sugar to taste, and spread and dry the fruit in the same way as for raw fruit rolls, omitting the honey or castor sugar.

Fruit rolls may also be dried in a cool oven (60°C) – but in this case the purée should not be spread on plastic.

Soak the apricots for 8 hours in a brine solution made from the salt and 2 litres (8 cups) of the water. Drain the fruit, and remove the skins and pips.

Shape the apricots into flat rounds, spread them on racks and dry for 4-6 days. Cover the fruit with muslin or thick mesh. Ensure that the air can circulate freely, and turn the fruit regularly. Bring inside at night or at the first hint of rain, as the humidity and drop in temperature will spoil the fruit.

The fruit may also be dried in a cool oven: 60°C for about 6 hours (a convection oven works particularly well).

When dry, soak the apricots for 5 minutes in a lime solution made by dissolving the lime in the remaining 1,5 litres (6 cups) water. Dry slightly and dip in sugar.

Pack the mebos in tins or boxes, layering the fruit with sugar.

Candied Angelica

Candied angelica is made from the stalks of the angelica herb. It has a very distinctive taste and is usually used as a decoration for cakes or desserts.

To candy angelica, blanch* the stalks of the fresh herb and peel off the outer skin. Cut the inner stems into shorter pieces.

Place the stems in a saucepan and cover with water. Bring to the boil and simmer, with a few vine leaves to keep them a bright green, until the stems feel soft when pressed and look transparent. Drain and discard the water.

Make a hot syrup of 200 g sugar and 250 ml (1 cup) water, and soak the stems in this syrup for 24 hours.

Remove the angelica from the syrup, boil the syrup to 102°C and pour again over the angelica. Leave the stems in the syrup for 24 hours.

Repeat this procedure three more times. Then boil the syrup to a temperature of 105°C, add the angelica and boil again. Leave the angelica to cool in the syrup. Remove from the syrup and leave to dry, or dry in a cool (80°C) oven. Store in airtight containers.

Tammeletjies

MALAY VENDORS sold tammeletjies on Cape Town streets many years ago, always finding enthusiastic customers. Today, however, these sweets are usually made only for feasts, where they appear in a number of guises: made with coconut, peas and 'pitjies' (pine kernels).

PREPARATION TIME: 15 MINUTES
COOKING TIME: 30 MINUTES

INGREDIENTS TO YIELD 400 G
400 g sugar
250 ml (1 cup) water
Almonds, desiccated coconut or pine kernels for flavouring (optional)

Boil the sugar and water until the mixture is a caramel colour, and continue boiling until it starts frothing. Add a sprinkling of chopped almonds, desiccated coconut or pine kernels (if used).

Pour the mixture into a well-greased flat pan, 23 cm square, and mark off squares or other shapes. Leave to cool, then cut.

Sesame Seed Bars

YOU CAN SERVE these delicious little bars with China tea after a Chinese meal, or after a Western meal with coffee. They keep well in an airtight tin.

PREPARATION TIME: 5 MINUTES
COOKING TIME: 15 MINUTES
PRE-HEAT OVEN TO 180°C

INGREDIENTS TO YIELD 25-30 BARS (6 CM x 3 CM)
50 g sesame seeds
400 g sugar
80 ml (⅓ cup) white vinegar
15 ml (1 tablespoon) water
225 g unsalted roasted peanuts, skinned and halved
Sunflower oil

Toast the sesame seeds by spreading them on a baking tray and baking in the oven for 5 minutes, or until golden-brown.

Combine the sugar, vinegar and water in a pan, and stir over a low heat until the sugar dissolves. Next, bring the mixture to the boil and (without stirring) boil for about 10 minutes until golden-brown, or to the hard crack stage* (154°C).

While this toffee is being prepared, oil an 18 cm × 28 cm baking tray. Sprinkle half the sesame seeds and all the peanuts over the base. Pour over the hot toffee, smoothing it evenly with an oiled spatula or spoon. Sprinkle over the remaining sesame seeds. Allow the toffee to cool a little before cutting it into bars (do this before it cools completely).

SERVING SUGGESTION Serve on an attractive shallow plate in one layer (otherwise the bars may stick to one another).

VARIATION Add 80 ml (⅓ cup) chopped seedless raisins to the halved peanuts.

Sugared Almonds

THIS DELICIOUS SNACK is ideal for serving as a sweet with coffee at the end of a meal. The sugared almonds can be stored for about two months in an airtight container.

PREPARATION TIME: 20 MINUTES
COOKING TIME: 40 MINUTES
PRE-HEAT OVEN TO 180°C

INGREDIENTS TO YIELD 350 G
250 g whole shelled almonds
500 g sugar
100 ml water
5 ml (1 teaspoon) ground cinnamon

Toast the shelled almonds in the oven for 5-7 minutes until pale golden-brown.

Place the sugar and water in a medium-sized saucepan and heat over low heat, stirring occasionally, until the sugar dissolves. Add the cinnamon and boil briskly until the syrup reaches the hard-ball stage* (121-130°C). Add the nuts quickly and stir until they are well coated. Remove from the heat and continue stirring until the syrup dries on the nuts. Turn on to a board and leave to dry.

Candied Peel

USED GENERALLY to enrich cake mixtures or fillings for pastries, candied peel is made from citrus fruits.

PREPARATION TIME: 30 MINUTES
SOAKING TIME: UP TO 3 DAYS
TOTAL COOKING TIME: 1 HOUR

INGREDIENTS TO YIELD ABOUT 250 G
Peel of 1 orange, 1 lemon and 1 grapefruit
200 g sugar
500 ml (2 cups) water

Wash the fruit and cut into sections. Scoop out the flesh and cut the peel into strips. Soak the peel overnight in water. (Grapefruit peel, however, should be soaked for 3 days, the water being changed daily.)

Drain the citrus peel and then boil the pieces in fresh water for 30 minutes, or until they are soft. Test with a skewer or cocktail stick.

Prepare a syrup with the sugar and 500 ml water. The syrup should cover the peel – if more is needed, you can double the quantities.

Bring the syrup to the boil and add the citrus peel. Boil again briefly, then allow the peel to cool in the syrup. Repeat this process 3-4 times then remove the peel and leave to dry.

VARIATION For a shiny product, glaze the peel. Prepare a syrup with 400 g sugar, 250 ml (1 cup) water and 1 ml (¼ teaspoon) cream of tartar. Boil the syrup to the soft-ball stage* (112-118°C). Dip the candied peel in this syrup and leave to dry. Keep the syrup hot while dipping the peel.

Peanut Brittle

PEANUTS, LIKE CHOCOLATE, vanilla, sweet corn, sweet potatoes, avocados and tomatoes, are native to Central and South America.

Peanut brittle, a simple concoction of nuts and sugar, is also Latin American in origin. There it is regarded as a food of the very poor. The sweet is highly nutritious since it contains a good balance of protein, fat and sugar. It is also relatively inexpensive, since peanuts are the cheapest nuts available.

PREPARATION TIME: 45 MINUTES
SETTING TIME: 20 MINUTES

INGREDIENTS TO YIELD 175 G
*175 g fresh peanuts, skinned, chopped and toasted**
200 g granulated sugar
125 g soft brown sugar
50 ml golden syrup
75 ml hot water
25 g unsalted butter
A pinch of bicarbonate of soda

Put the chopped peanuts in a warm place, such as the top of the stove or an airing cupboard, until required.

Place the sugars and the golden syrup in a fairly large, heavy-based saucepan with the hot water.

Heat gently, stirring until the sugar has dissolved completely.

Boil, without stirring, to the hard-crack stage* (154°C).

Remove the pan from the heat and stir in the butter, chopped peanuts and bicarbonate of soda.

Pour the mixture into a well-greased shallow tin, 25 cm x 15 cm, and leave to cool for 20 minutes.

When the toffee is beginning to set – after about 10 minutes – mark it out into squares with a sharp knife. When it is quite cold, break up the squares and wrap each one in cellophane.

Store in a cool dry place.

PRESERVES, JAMS, PICKLES AND SWEETS

Chinese Honey Nuts

These little sweetmeats look and taste delicious. Once you begin to eat them, it is difficult to stop! They are excellent served with drinks or as a sweet with after-dinner coffee.

Preparation Time: 5 minutes
Marinating Time: 2 hours
Cooking Time: 5 minutes

Ingredients for Six
250 g pecan or walnut halves
190 ml (¾ cup) honey
15 ml (1 tablespoon) lemon juice
5 ml (1 teaspoon) soy sauce
Castor sugar for coating
Sunflower oil for frying

Mix the pecans or walnuts, honey, lemon juice and soy sauce, and allow to stand for 2 hours, stirring occasionally to keep the nuts coated with the mixture.
Drain the nuts and toss them in castor sugar, coating them well. Heat just enough oil to cover the nuts, then add the marinated nuts and cook them until golden. Remove immediately and drain well.
Serving Suggestions Pile into a serving bowl or place each nut in a little paper case.

Chinese Honey Nuts, Turkish Delight and Nougat *Tastebud sensations from around the world.*

Turkish Delight

Traditional turkish delight should not be overly sticky or too strongly flavoured, and should have a shiny, firm-jellied appearance.

Preparation Time: 30 minutes
Standing Time: 12 hours

Ingredients to Yield 40-50 Squares (2 cm x 2 cm)
625 ml (2½ cups) water
50 g gelatin
750 g sugar
6 cinnamon or cassia sticks
5 ml (1 teaspoon) triple-strength rosewater (obtainable from pharmacies)
60 ml (¼ cup) shelled chopped pistachio nuts (optional)
Pink colouring (optional)
Non-stick cooking spray (optional)
Icing sugar for coating

Pour the water into a large, deep, heavy-based saucepan. Sprinkle over the gelatin and dissolve it on a low heat, stirring all the time. Add the sugar and continue to stir until it has dissolved.
Add the cinnamon or cassia and, still stirring, boil for 10 minutes until thick and clear. Remove from the heat and discard the cinnamon or cassia.
Add the rosewater and the pistachio nuts (if used). If you like your Turkish delight pink, colour with a few drops of pink colouring.
Pour the mixture into a 20 cm square tin, either wetted or coated with a non-stick cooking spray. Leave for 12 hours at room temperature until firm.
Turn the Turkish delight on to a board that has been generously coated with sifted icing sugar and sift more icing sugar over the top. Cut into small, neat squares with a sharp knife.
Roll the squares in more icing sugar and store in tins.

Nougat

A delicious, nutty sweet, nougat originated in France. It is particularly enjoyable served with coffee and liqueurs after dinner.

Preparation Time: 40 minutes
Cooking Time: 20 minutes
Setting Time: 24 hours
Pre-heat Oven to 180°C

Ingredients to Yield about 750 g
Rice paper
250 g sugar
100 ml runny honey
45 ml (3 tablespoons) corn syrup or liquid glucose
125 ml (½ cup) water
300 g almonds, blanched and toasted*
125 g whole hazelnuts, blanched and toasted*
2 egg whites, stiffly beaten
5 ml (1 teaspoon) vanilla essence

Line a 24 cm square tin with a layer of rice paper.
Put the sugar, honey, syrup (or liquid glucose) and water into a saucepan, and stir over a moderate heat until the sugar has dissolved completely.
Without stirring, cook the syrup until it reaches the small-crack stage* (143°C).
Meanwhile, heat the nuts for 5 minutes in the oven.
Take the hot syrup off the stove and gradually pour it over the stiffly beaten egg whites, beating all the time until very stiff. If you have difficulty in getting the mixture stiff enough, put the bowl over a pot of hot water and continue to beat. Add the vanilla essence and the warmed nuts.
Turn the nougat into the prepared tin and cover with a sheet of rice paper. Place a board and a heavy weight on top. Leave to set for a day.
Cut the slab of nougat into 4 cm squares or oblong pieces for serving. If necessary, store in the refrigerator.

341

PART 2
Entertaining

The word 'entertaining' is an all-embracing term that can refer to something as relatively effortless as having a few close friends around for a braai, or as daunting as a buffet supper for a few hundred people. Entertaining involves more than just knowing how to prepare food and drinks – it often calls for a knowledge of how to combine dishes to form well-balanced menus, and an awareness of how to save time and money through effective organisation. You will find all this information, and more, in the following pages. Remember that practice makes perfect. Entertaining in high style or for large numbers will probably give you butterflies the first time round, but once initiated, you will find yourself enjoying the occasion as much as your guests – which is as it should be!

Party Time

A party is a cook's ultimate challenge. Your family and very close friends may be indulgent of your culinary shortcomings but you obviously do not want to be shown up in front of a room full of guests! Moreover, catering for large numbers may confront you with problems with which you are unfamiliar. There is no cause for pre-party anguish provided that, in true scout fashion, you are well prepared and follow a few commonsense rules.

To begin with, if you are inexperienced in entertaining, start in a modest way. Think in terms of serving, say, a casserole rather than a saddle of venison, or a simple sorbet rather than a baked Alaska (which may all too easily come to soggy grief if left for a few extra seconds under the grill).

The simpler dishes make sound economic sense, especially when you have many mouths to feed. And that leads to a second basic rule for party entertaining: cater within your budget. There is no point in cooking in order to impress if the expense leaves the household on starvation rations for the next six weeks!

The third golden rule for party-givers is to choose dishes that can be made well in advance and then stored in the refrigerator. That could mean a cold soup, or cold meats and salads, in high summer; or in chillier weather a quiche or pie that needs no more than heating up 10 minutes before serving.

A party is a time for enjoyment, so why spend it slaving over a hot stove when you could be enjoying the company of your friends?

BREAKFASTS

When it comes to entertaining friends, most people think solely in terms of lunch or dinner, neglecting the gastronomic potential of a hearty social breakfast. A breakfast party will not involve you in a great deal of preparation and is an economical way of entertaining. Here are some menu suggestions:

MENU 1

Fresh fruit in season
Chilled fruit juice

•

Basic French omelette
with one of the following fillings:
Ham and cheese
Creamed mushrooms
Crispy fried bacon
Sour cream and 'caviar'

•

Croissants, wholewheat bread
Butter, jam, honey

•

Coffee

MENU 2

Tall glasses of freshly squeezed orange juice

•

Eggs Benedict
or
Omelette Arnold Bennet

•

Toast
Butter, marmalade, strawberry jam

•

Tea

BRUNCHES

An early lunch or a combination of breakfast and lunch is a pleasant and not too demanding way of entertaining over the weekends. The hostess has plenty of time to devote to her guests since many of the usual dishes served can be prepared the day or evening before. Possible brunch menus include:

MENU 1

Chilled fresh fruit in season

•

Kedgeree
Spanish omelette
Herbed crumbed tomatoes

•

Oatmeal bread

•

Butter, fig jam, marmalade

•

Filter coffee

MENU 2

Chilled grapefruit with Van der Hum liqueur

•

Cheese bourekitas

•

Hot spinach and bacon salad

•

Drop scones with honey and butter

•

Coffee

MENU 3 OUTDOOR BRUNCH

Ambrosia skewers (served cold)

•

Scrambled eggs
Boerewors
Devilled kidney skewers
Creamed mushrooms on toast

•

Selection of white and wholewheat rolls

•

Butter, melon and ginger jam, quince jelly

•

Coffee

PLANNING A LUNCH OR DINNER PARTY MENU

The two most important issues to consider when planning a menu are: what food will your guests enjoy eating, and what can you produce with the skills, time, money and space you have available?

The dietary restrictions, preferences and lifestyles of your guests are of paramount importance. For example, somebody you have invited may be a diabetic, allergic to seafood, strictly kosher or a vegetarian.

Be realistic when you are planning a menu, bearing in mind your budget, cooking skills (or lack of them), the size of your kitchen and oven, the amount of time you will have for preparation beforehand and how much help you can count on.

When choosing the food, ask yourself the following questions:

Is it nutritionally balanced?

Is there a good colour harmony and/or contrast?

Is there enough contrast in texture? (For example, the crisp texture of toasted almonds juxtaposes well with the soft texture of poached apples.)

What different shapes are involved? Strive for interesting combinations of shapes and sizes.

Do the flavours of the various dishes blend and complement each other?

Traditionally, menus can consist of quite a number of different courses. Today, most of us settle for the three-course menu, with perhaps a little sorbet or salad between courses. The most common menu format is:

Starter
Soup
Fish
Main course
Dessert
Cheese

The following are three modern variations that could be considered:

Fish starter
Small salad
Meat dish
Cheese

•

Soup
Small salad
Fish dish
Dessert

•

Hot vegetable starter
Sorbet
Meat dish
Cheese
Dessert

Although in South Africa cheese is usually served at the end of the meal, it is worth noting that the French always serve it before the dessert because the red wine enjoyed with a meaty main course is an excellent accompaniment to cheese.

When entertaining, the choice of a lunch or supper menu should not only be a question of combining a number of favourite courses. Thought should be given to how the various dishes are going to complement one another and also whether they are suitable for the time of year. For example, a hot malva pudding could be an

Bright, contrasting colours can be used to good effect to create a sunny and cheerful atmosphere for your breakfast table.

ideal dessert for a winter's evening, but perhaps not the best choice for a summer luncheon. Furthermore, take care not to combine too many rich or very filling dishes. Another very important consideration is the availability of vegetables, fruit or game.

The following lunch, supper and formal dinner menus should provide a useful guide when you are planning your meal.

SPRING

LUNCH

Fresh green asparagus tips with Maltaise sauce

•

Fish with paprika cream sauce
Noodles tossed in poppy seeds
Green salad made of young spinach leaves with vinaigrette

•

Guava tart and cream

EVENING BRAAI

Lettuce and chicken liver salad

•

Fish in newspaper with crayfish and prawn sauce
or
Grilled baby chicken with barbecue sauce
Garlic bread
Green salad

•

Dom Pedro

PARTY TIME

FORMAL SUPPER

Fresh globe artichokes with Hollandaise sauce

•

Lemon sorbet

•

Crown roast of lamb
Individual rosti
Green beans with herbs

•

Camembert in phyllo pastry

•

Coffee
Liqueur ice cups

SUMMER

LUNCH

Chilled cucumber soup

•

Chicken breasts with apricots and almonds
Rice and Greek salad

•

Summer fruit bowl

CHINESE SUPPER

Won ton soup

•

Chinese steamed sweet and sour fish

•

Stir-fried beef with oyster-flavoured sauce
Chinese noodles

•

Chinese toffee apples

•

Chinese tea

FORMAL SUPPER

Avocado with crayfish

•

Individual watercress salads

•

Stuffed boned chicken
Napolitana sauce
Baked potatoes with sour cream topping
Glazed marrow

•

Strawberries and cream

•

Coffee

AUTUMN

LUNCH

Avocado soup (served hot)

•

Brinjals stuffed with curried vegetables

•

Rice and sambals

•

Chilled fresh fruit with yoghurt

INFORMAL SUPPER

Taramasalata
Pita bread

•

Individual green salads
Tagliatelle with cream and Parmesan cheese

•

Crêpes suzette

FORMAL SUPPER

Grilled black mussels and French bread

•

Fennel, tomato and mushroom salad

•

A SEASONAL GUIDE TO FRESH PRODUCE

One's choice of food when entertaining should be dictated by the vegetables and fruit that are available at the time. Here is a seasonal guide to various popular vegetables and fruits in South Africa.

SPRING

Vegetables Beetroot, cabbage, carrots, cauliflower, celery, garlic, leeks, onions, parsley, asparagus, radishes, spinach, turnips, broccoli, brinjals and baby marrows.
Fruit Bananas, guavas, lemons, naartjies and oranges.

SUMMER

Vegetables Cucumbers, garlic, lettuce, marrow, mealies, onions, pumpkin, gem squash, hubbard squash, butternut, tomatoes, green beans and baby marrows.
Fruit Apricots, bananas, watermelons, pawpaws, peaches, pineapples, plums, strawberries, sweet melons, pears, nectarines and grapes.

AUTUMN

Vegetables Avocados, beetroot, cabbage, carrots, cauliflower, celery, leeks, onions, potatoes, sweet potatoes, pumpkin, spinach, tomatoes, broccoli and brinjals.
Fruit Apples, bananas, grapefruit, guavas, lemons, naartjies, oranges, pawpaws, pears and grapes.

WINTER

Vegetables Avocados, beetroot, cabbage, carrots, cauliflower, celery, leeks, onions, potatoes, sweet potatoes, pumpkin, radishes, spinach, tomatoes and turnips.
Fruit Apples, bananas, grapefruit, guavas, lemons, naartjies, oranges, pawpaws and pears.

PARTY TIME

Roast duck with grapefruit
Roast potatoes
Creamed spinach

•

Cheese platter

•

Coffee and Chinese honey nuts

WINTER

LUNCH

Meal-in-one fish soup

•

Caesar salad

•

Lemon pudding with cream

EASTERN SUPPER

Samoosas (served with pre-dinner drinks)

•

Indian chicken soup
(Murgh aur khaddu haleem)

•

Mutton curry
Chapati (roti)
Sambals
Rice

•

Oriental fruit salad

•

Coffee

FORMAL SUPPER

Butternut soup

•

Grapefruit sorbet

•

Roast saddle of venison
Cumberland sauce
Stir-fried vegetables
Individual moulds of saffron rice

•

Cheese platter

•

Cape gooseberry flan and fresh cream

•

Coffee

Sophisticated accessories and angular china provide this formal supper for autumn months with a cool, classical ambience.

BUFFETS

Self-help from a buffet table has become a popular method of service in restaurants worldwide. There are many reasons why this is such an excellent service system, both commercially and at home. The food can be displayed to good advantage on the table, and because the food is massed together it tends to look impressive. The guests can choose only what they like to eat, and can dish out portions appropriate to personal liking.

The flower arrangement on a buffet table should be big and bold, and candles for evening functions may be used to add extra atmosphere. For large functions, the height of dishes may be varied by placing boxes of various sizes under the tablecloth. Food can be dramatically displayed on mirrors, slabs of stone, banana leaves, or a bed of ice.

In order to make self-service as easy as possible, the plates, utensils and food should be arranged on the table in a logical sequence.

The following two menus could be considered for a buffet lunch or supper:

HOT WINTER BUFFET

Smoked snoek paté
Wholewheat bread

•

Tomato bredie
Chicken pie
Rice
Green beans
Glazed sweet potatoes
Tossed salad

•

Malva pudding
Spiced peaches and cream

•

Coffee

COLD FISH BUFFET

'Caviar', egg and onion starter

•

Cape salmon in aspic with Malay dressing
Seafood salad with melon and lemon cream sauce
Baby marrow salad served on a bed of lettuce
Cold asparagus with herb mayonnaise
Tomato and onion salad

•

Fruit salad brûlée

•

Coffee

CHILDREN'S BIRTHDAY PARTIES

Possibly the most important consideration when planning a child's birthday party is the age of the child. The following are some rough guidelines to parties for different age groups.

The one-year-old
This party is more for adults than for children, so make sure you cater well for the mothers.

The two-year-old
Invite as few children as possible! The party should be short and sweet. Keep the food very simple. Mothers will accompany their toddlers, so again you will have to provide something for them.

The three-year-old
Keep the numbers restricted to a manageable number. Children of this age love an interesting cake. Provide toys to keep them busy – they are not yet ready for organised games.

The four- and five-year-old
They love parties! Allow them to play a part in the planning, preparation and organisation. Simple group games will be popular. Provide savoury as well as sweet foods.

The primary school child
A birthday is a real event for younger primary school children. Not only will a party be given for close friends at home, but the whole class may have to be treated to a cake at school. They adore games, songs, a puppet or video show. Children in this age group may prefer to ask only friends of the same sex as themselves.

THE TABLE
Use a paper or plastic cloth in bright, cheerful colours; provide paper plates and glasses and plenty of paper serviettes. Cake boxes for after the party 'take-aways' are a useful idea.

GAMES
Hide and seek, treasure hunt, blind man's buff, prick the balloon, musical chairs, team games and races are all enjoyable possibilities.

PARTY MENU FOR VERY YOUNG CHILDREN

A birthday cake with candles amounting to the age of the child
Small cakes or biscuits
Savoury snacks, such as popcorn, potato crisps, peanuts (not for children under three), cocktail sausages and cheese cubes
Jelly and custard
Ice cream
Fruit juice or cool drinks
Sweets

PARTY MENU FOR PRIMARY SCHOOL CHILDREN

Iced birthday cake
(Use the basic butter cake recipe)
Painted biscuits
Chocolate chip cookies
Potato chips
Hot sausage rolls
Cheese cubes
Yoghurt and banana flan
Chocolate-coated ice cream balls
Fudge
Fruit juice or cool drinks

TEENAGE PARTIES

Teenagers are very aware of themselves and the image they have among their peer group, so the success or failure of a teenage party can assume life-or-death proportions for the person who is holding it. Be prepared for much chopping and changing of both the guest list and the menu. Tears on the day and a general gloom that everything will be a disaster are all part of the average teenage party scenario.

The food at a teenage party need not be very elaborate as teenage girls are usually very weight-conscious and teenage boys will eat anything. In fact, teenagers are easily embarrassed by a mother 'fussing' and trying to show off her culinary achievements. Simple snacks, plenty of soft drinks and perhaps punch, and some hot food, such as lasagne or curry and rice, are all that is needed. A buffet-style presentation is usually the best method of serving the food.

The following menus could be considered:

MENU 1

Vegetable crudités and chips with one or more of the following dips:
Avocado dip
Cream cheese dip
Tuna dip

•

Traditional Italian pizza
Tossed salad

•

Dark chocolate ice cream

MENU 2

Vegetable crudités with smoked snoek dip

———•———

*Bobotie baked in a pumpkin
Rice
Apricot blatjang
Cucumber sambal
Kachoomer*

———•———

Banana split

TWENTY-FIRST BIRTHDAYS

Traditionally, this birthday is celebrated in a more formal manner, and family and friends of all age groups may be present. A special toast will be proposed by one of the parents or a family friend of the person who is celebrating his/her birthday. This may be followed by a short answering speech.

The person whose birthday is being celebrated will act as host together with his/her parents.

Many people prefer to celebrate their twenty-first birthday with only a few close friends. Here is a suitable menu for the occasion:

Vegetable terrine (served chilled)

———•———

*Greek lamb with yoghurt
Baked potatoes
Greek salad*

———•———

Strawberry or lemon sorbet

———•———

Coffee served with miniature chocolate éclairs

WEDDINGS

A couple's wedding is usually the most important social event of their lives. It should, therefore, be carefully planned so as to ensure that it is remembered with happiness.

Down the ages, set procedures have evolved as to who does what before and during the wedding – and also who pays for what. Nowadays, however, etiquette is becoming much more fluid, and arrangements will depend on the size and type of wedding and reception, and the financial capabilities of the people involved.

THE WEDDING RECEPTION

The reception can take many forms, such as a champagne brunch, luncheon party, morning or afternoon

Warm colours and candlelight create a relaxed and informal atmosphere that is well suited to the teenage party.

tea, cocktail party, cheese and wine reception, buffet-type reception, or a formal sit-down dinner.

If it is a sit-down occasion, the main table must be set on one side only, so that the bridal party faces the guests. Place-cards on the bridal table will prevent any confusion as to who sits where. The usual arrangement is for the bride to sit on the left of the groom in the centre. Next to the bride sit the bride's father, groom's mother, minister or friend. Next to the groom sit the bride's mother, groom's father and master of ceremonies.

THE WEDDING CAKE

Traditionally, this is a rich, dark, fruit cake, iced in white or pastel shades. It is advisable to arrange for a special small table on which to display the wedding cake. At the reception, after the speeches, the bride and groom together make the first token cut in the cake, leaving the caterers to cut the cake into small slices to be handed round to guests.

THE MENU

In keeping with the occasion, wedding food should look delicate and pretty, but the choice of food will depend largely on one's budget and personal tastes. Usually if the guests have travelled a long way, or if it is a farm reception, quite a substantial meal may be served.

If you choose to have a cocktail reception, it is advisable to have at least five different types of snacks to eat – both hot and cold. Allow 5-8 individual snacks per person. Among the most popular hot snacks are: mushrooms baked with garlic butter; tiny hot sausage rolls; tiny quiches (mushroom, asparagus, shrimp or olive); bacon-wrapped chicken livers; fish croquettes; and cocktail sausages with mustard.

Possible cold snacks are: vegetable crudités and bread or biscuits with dips; chicken liver pâté with port; marinated calamari (antipasto); smoked salmon; marinated mushrooms (antipasto); and salted or spiced nuts.

If, however, you have opted for a sit-down lunch or supper, the following menus are among the many possible options.

BUFFET-STYLE GARDEN RECEPTION IN SUMMER

*Individual salmon mousses
with cucumber sauce*

•

*Cold smoked chicken
Vitello tonnato
Rice salad served on lettuce leaves surrounded by
sliced tomatoes*

•

*Granadilla ice cream mould
Cream puffs*

•

Coffee

SIT-DOWN DINNER IN AUTUMN OR WINTER

Fish terrine with sour cream sauce

•

*Chicken pie
Yellow rice
Onions à la Monégasque
Buttered green beans*

•

Cucumber and radish salad

•

Walnut cream torte

•

Coffee

BUFFET WEDDING BREAKFAST

*Fresh orange juice with sparkling wine
Snacks:
Parma Ham and melon
Smoked salmon nibbles*

•

*Eggs Florentine
Oeufs en cocotte à la crème
Bacon-wrapped chicken livers
Ham crescents
Grilled tomato halves
Creamed mushrooms*

•

*Wholewheat bread,
crusty white bread, croissants*

•

Butter, grape jam, marmalade, strawberry jam

•

*Wedding cake
Coffee*

CHRISTMAS

In households that celebrate Christmas – and even in many that do not – this is usually the most important and festive social event of the annual calendar for young and old alike. Traditionally held at home, the Christmas lunch or dinner is essentially a family occasion at which as many members as possible are brought together. Consequently, when deciding on a Christmas menu, it is best to choose dishes that are likely to be enjoyed by all age groups.

The following two menus – one for a sit-down dinner, and the other for an out-of-doors lunch – could be considered.

MENU FOR A SIT-DOWN CHRISTMAS DINNER

*Chilled melon with port
or
Individual cucumber and prawn mousses*

•

*Roast turkey with two stuffings
Bread sauce
Roast potatoes
Peas with chopped fresh mint
Green salad with vinaigrette*

•

*Cold Christmas pudding
Mince pies*

•

Coffee

ALL-FISH MENU FOR AN OUT-OF-DOORS CHRISTMAS LUNCH

*Smoked snoek pâté served in
scooped-out lemons*

•

*Trout parcels with almonds
Garlic bread
Fennel, tomato and mushroom salad
Green salad*

•

*Fresh fruit on a mound of chipped ice
Vanilla ice cream with fresh strawberry sauce*

•

Iced coffee

NEW YEAR'S EVE PARTIES

New Year's Eve is the one time of year when even the most constrained of us tend to 'let go' and carouse to our full potential!

If you are to have music and dancing at your party, the most obvious way of entertaining would be a buffet supper – the more elaborately decorated the table the better.

The following are a few menu suggestions from which to choose:

FISH DISHES
'Caviar', egg and onion starter
Fresh mussels on the half-shell
Salmon mousse with cucumber sauce
Fish Mauritian
Smoked trout
Fish bobotie

HOT AND COLD MEAT AND POULTRY DISHES
Moussaka
Beef stroganoff
Devilled shoulder of lamb
Vitello tonnato
Greek chicken
Chicken stew with orange and tomato
Turkey salad with cheese and sesame seeds

SALADS
Marinated artichokes and mushrooms (antipasto)
Baby marrow salad
Beetroot salad
Coleslaw
Fennel, tomato and mushroom salad
Brinjals à la Greque

DESSERTS
Cape gooseberry flan
Fig tart
Gâteau Saint-Honoré
Triple chocolate bombe
Apricot yoghurt tart
Pavlova
Rum and chocolate gâteau

COCKTAIL PARTIES

Cocktail parties are a popular social event. Some of the advantages of this type of function are that a large number of people can be accommodated in a relatively small space, minimal cutlery and crockery is needed, guests can move around and mix easily, and the party usually does not go on for more than a few hours.

When preparing a room (or rooms) for a cocktail party, remove all unnecessary furniture and ornaments, and supply plenty of large ashtrays and absorbent coasters. Check the ventilation – a few burning candles will help to purify the air of cigarette smoke. Arrange for more than one serving point for the food as well as the drinks. Make sure you have plenty of extra glasses.

Hot as well as cold snacks should be supplied – you should allow five to eight individual snacks per person,

Freshness and beauty should be the keynotes at a wedding reception. Flowers, lace table cloths and scalloped china help to achieve this.

depending on the size of the food morsels being served. The following are some suggestions for hot and cold snacks to provide at a cocktail party:

HOT
Samoosas
Sausage rolls
Tiny quiches
Cheese beignets
Fish croquettes
Cocktail sausages
Mustard

COLD
Dips and vegetable crudités or biscuits
Pâtés
Blini with 'caviar'
'Caviar' tart
Taramasalata
Chopped herring
Toasted salted nuts
Sliced meats
Marinated olives (antipasto)

LIQUOR LIST FOR A TWO-HOUR COCKTAIL PARTY FOR 25 GUESTS

Vodka	1 bottle of 750 ml
Cane	1 bottle of 750 ml
Gin	1 bottle of 750 ml
Whisky	3 bottles of 750 ml
Brandy	2 bottles of 750 ml
Dry vermouth (white)	1 bottle of 750 ml
Sweet vermouth (red)	1 bottle of 750 ml
Campari	1 bottle of 750 ml
Sherry – dry	½ bottle of 750 ml
– medium	½ bottle of 750 ml
Dry white wine	6-8 bottles
Red wine	2-3 bottles
Beer	12 dumpies/cans
Apple juice	12 small
Club soda	6 litres
Tonic water	4 litres
Ginger ale	2 litres
Cola drink	3 litres
Mineral water (sparkling)	2 litres
Tomato juice	6 small bottles
Angostura bitters	1 small bottle

Bottle store services available
Free hiring of glasses
Free ice
A trained barman and/or waiters can be hired for an evening
Unopened bottles may be returned and money will be refunded

Check list
Ice bucket and tongs
Water jugs
Tot measures
Bottle openers
Corkscrews
Serviettes
Ashtrays
Matches
Coasters
Lemon slices
1 large bucket of ice (10 litres)
Olives
75 glasses – assume 3 drinks per guest

CHEESE AND WINE PARTIES

The ever-popular cheese and wine party can serve a number of different purposes. It may be used by a group of serious gourmets to actually *taste* an exciting new wine or a selection of cheeses, but usually it is an informal occasion akin to a cocktail party, with the same sort of advantages.

The quantities of food and drink provided in the list below would be enough for a cheese and wine party for about 50 people:
Allow half a bottle of wine per person
About 24 soft drinks to cater for those who do not drink alcohol
1 kg Cheddar cheese
1 kg Gouda cheese
1 kg mixed processed cheeses
250 g Blaauwkrantz
250 g Camembert or Brie
250 g Drakensberg
250 g cottage cheese
6 packets of assorted biscuits
2 dips with chips
1-2 pâtés of your choice
6 bunches of spring onions
6 bunches of radishes
500 g nuts
500 g raisins
500 g pickled gherkins
500 g black olives
500 g green olives
500 g butter
Serviettes

Optional extras
4 hot quiches
60 hot sausage rolls
4 hot apple pies
1 litre (4 cups) cream

CATERING FOR LARGE NUMBERS

To cater successfully for large numbers of guests, it is essential to plan beforehand to the last detail. Plan well in advance – the advantage of doing this is that all impractical ideas will be sifted out in good time, and you will also have a chance to consider new ideas, recipes and possible shortcuts. When catering for large numbers, it is useful to plan under the following headings:

GUEST LIST
An up-to-date guest list with addresses and telephone numbers is a must. It will also be invaluable for future functions and, in the case of a wedding, for writing 'thank-you' letters after the reception. The guest list can be used to allocate seating.

INVITATIONS
The more of an 'occasion' that your party is, the stronger the argument for having written invitations. The following details should always be listed on an invitation:
Who the host/hostess is
Who is being invited
Address and telephone number of host/hostess (a map may be handy if the address is difficult to find)
Date, day of the week and time of the function
Type of function and dress expected

A FINAL MENU
Remember, it is wiser to settle for fewer, but better-prepared dishes rather than offer a large spread of indifferent food. Not only will the presentation be more attractive, the organisation will be more manageable as well. Analyse each dish under the following headings (examples are given below them):

Dish	Any accompaniments	Garnish	Served on	Eaten on/with
Salmon mousse	Cucumber sauce	Cucumber slices	Large glass platter	Fish plates Fish knives and fish forks

BAR REQUIREMENTS
Decide what will be served before, during and after the meal. Do not forget small details, such as corkscrews and bottle openers, chilling facilities for wine, ice, mixers and lemon slices.

HIRING SERVICES
When organising a large function, especially out of doors, it is reassuring to know that there are some very professional hiring services available. They are naturally centered in the cities, but most will deliver quite far afield.

Apart from the usual supplies of cutlery, crockery, glasses, trays, tablecloths, tables and chairs, some also offer:
Big and small marquees in the colour of your choice
Dance floors which can be placed over swimming pools
Special lighting for discotheques
Special décor touches
Canopies and pergolas
Covered walkways to connect buildings to each other
Braziers and heaters to warm large areas
Carveries and spitroasts
Warming ovens
Bains-marie
Portable toilet facilities
Temporary overnight lock-up-storage

Contact the hire specialists in your area for details and quotes.

CREATING ATMOSPHERE

Make a note of what colours are already present in the reception room, and bear this in mind when selecting colours for the tablecloths, napkins and flowers. If there are lots of empty corners, it may be advisable to obtain indoor plants.

SOUND REQUIREMENTS

If there are going to be speeches at the function, make sure properly functioning microphone equipment is available. If there is to be music, decide whether you are going to have a band, discotheque or your own sound system.

ARRANGING THE RECEPTION ROOM

Be sure to obtain a floor plan from the hotel or hall that clearly indicates where the kitchen, toilets, entrances, exits and bandstand are situated. Use this to decide on the placing of the main table as well as the arrangement of service or buffet tables and the seating of the guests. By looking at the floor plan of the room you will immediately be able to see what the best arrangement is.

FOOD QUANTITIES

If you are doing the catering yourself, the following is a guide to the food and drink that you could consider serving, and the amounts of each that you will need to cater for about 100 people.

Apples (for apple pies) – 14 kg
Bacon (2 rashers each) – 4,5 kg
Beans (dried lima or butter) – 5 kg
Beans (fresh green) – 10 kg
Beans (frozen green) – 7 kg
Beef (roast, boned) – 18-20 kg
Beef (fried mini steaks) – 15 kg
Beef (for stews) – 15 kg
Beef (T-bone steaks) – 25 kg
Beetroot (for salad) – 4 kg
Bread – 7 loaves
Bread rolls – 110
Broccoli (frozen) – 9 kg
Brussels sprouts (frozen) – 9 kg
Butter (with bread) – 2 kg
Butter (with rolls) – 1 kg
Butter (for sandwiches) – 1,5 kg
Butter (for vegetables) – 500 g
Carrots (frozen) – 9 kg
Cauliflower (frozen) – 9 kg
Champagne or sparkling wine for a toast – 17 bottles
Cheese (grated for sandwiches) – 3,5 kg
Chicken (as the only main course) – 20 roast chickens
Chicken (with other meat) – 8-10 roast chickens
Chicken (for small cocktail pies) – 5 chickens
Chicken (for large pies) – 10-12 chickens
Chicken (for stews) – 15 chickens
Coffee (instant) – 500 g
Cool drinks – 18-20 litres
Corn (frozen whole kernel) – 7 kg
Cream (for coffee) – 1,5 litres
Custard – 5 litres
Eggs – 105
Fish (skinned and filleted) – 15 kg
Fruit juice (frozen concentrate) – 8 tins of 340 ml
Fruit juice (tinned) – 8 tins of 1,3 kg
Fruit salad – 3,5 kg prepared fruit (15 litres)
Gravy – 3 litres
Ham (as only main course) – 18 kg
Ham (for sandwiches) – 6 kg
Hamburgers – 5 kg mince makes 100 hamburgers
Ice cream (as only dessert) – 15 litres
Ice cream (with other desserts) – 8 litres
Jelly (with other desserts) – 12 packets of 80 g
Lamb (roast leg) – 10 legs of 2,5 kg
Macaroni (for macaroni cheese) – 4 kg
Meatballs (small cocktail) – 2,5 kg mince
Milk (for coffee) – 6 litres
Milk (for tea) – 4 litres
Mutton (chops) – 15 kg
Noodles (as a side dish) – 3,5 kg
Olives – 6 tins of 800 g
Peas (frozen) – 7 kg
Pineapples (cubed) – about 10
Pork (lean chops) – 12 kg
Pork (roast boned loin) – 18 kg
Potatoes (for salad) – 4 kg
Rice – 2,5 kg
Sausage – 12 kg
Schnitzels (veal or chicken) – 12 kg
Soup – 25 litres
Spaghetti (with Bolognese sauce) – 5 kg
Spinach (frozen) – 9 kg
Strawberries – 15 kg
Sugar for tea and coffee – 1-1,5 kg
Teabags – 80
Tongue (as main course) – 18 kg
Turkey (roast) – 36 kg
Wine – 30-50 bottles of 750 ml

GENERAL HINTS

Cold chicken is actually best served either at room temperature or lukewarm. If it is at all possible, try and cook the chickens on the day they are to be served. Refrigerated cooked chicken tends to become dried out and tough.

Cold roast beef is easy to prepare, and refrigerates well. You can give the meat added colour and flavour by rubbing it well beforehand with various spices or herbs, paprika and black pepper. Refrigerate the roast beef until it is cold, then slice paper thin pieces on a bread or bacon slicer.

Leg of lamb Remove the hip bone in order to facilitate carving and leave the shank bone uncut so as to provide a 'handle'.

Rice can be pre-cooked and kept in heat-resistant cooking bags. These may be frozen, then defrosted on the day. Defrost by placing the cooking bags in a large container and then pouring boiling water over two or three times. This will heat the rice if steamers or oven space are not available.

Hard-boiled eggs are easily peeled after being dunked under cold running water straight after cooking. The contraction of the hot shells in the cold water will loosen them from the egg white. To shell an egg easily, crush the shell in a band around the middle and peel it away. The remaining shell will come off easily in two halves.

Tongue Place cooked tongue immediately in cold water and peel off the skin. The tongue may now be placed back into the cooking liquid. This procedure ensures a soft, juicy result.

Pasta may be cooked well in advance. After it has been cooked, rinse the pasta under running cold water, oil lightly and keep in sealed plastic bags in the refrigerator.

Meringues To stop the base of a Pavlova from going soft, spread melted white chocolate over it. This coating of chocolate insulates the meringue against the dampness of the cream.

Serving Wine

GRAPE CULTIVARS

There are about 120 varieties or 'cultivars' of grape officially designated for use in the making of wine in South Africa, but only a few of these are important to the industry in terms of volume. Each variety has certain characteristics which the skilled winemaker will use to create a wine of a desired style.

WHITE CULTIVARS

Chenin blanc

By far the most widely grown wine grape is chenin blanc, also known as steen. It accounts for more than 30 per cent of South Africa's wine grapevines.

Its great popularity is due to its vigorous growing habits, its prolific yield and its versatility. Chenin blanc grapes are used for natural wines ranging from extra-dry to sweet, noble late harvests. They are used for making sherries, ports and jerepigos, and are distilled into wine spirits or spirits that are made into brandy.

Palomino

Formerly known as white French, this is the grape from which almost all Spanish sherry is made. While it is also used for this purpose in South Africa, its popularity has declined. This cultivar is used extensively for brandy.

Palomino is the second most widely used wine-grape variety, making up almost 14 per cent of the total. As a natural wine, it is usually of low acidity, and is seldom bottled on its own (it is sometimes used for blending).

Cape riesling or South African riesling

Nearly all the grapes of this variety are used to produce dry table wine. Although popular, it accounts for only about 2,3 per cent of the wine vine acreage.

Rhine riesling or weisser riesling

This famous German cultivar has not, on the whole, transplanted well to other lands. Wine growers and makers have had to contend with the problem of an excess 'terpine' or oily character which develops in wines made from this grape.

Recently, however, they seem to have overcome the problem and have produced wines of some distinction, ranging from dry to semi-sweet. Although not widely grown in South Africa, Rhine riesling is gaining in popularity.

Colombar

Also spelled colombard, this variety has long been favoured in Cognac and Armagnac for making the famous brandies of those names. In the Robertson district it was once popular for the production of 'rebate brandy'. During the late 1960s colombar was first made into a fragrant, fresh table wine.

Some producers bottle it as a cultivar wine, but it is used mainly for its crispness as a blending component, and for distilling into good-quality brandy. Colombar accounts for about six per cent of the wine vine population and ranks fourth in the number of vines planted for white wines.

Hanepoot or muscat d'Alexandrie

This versatile variety is not only a popular table and wine grape but is also dried for high-quality raisins, and is the basis for most pure grape juice products.

Used judiciously in blending, white hanepoot imparts a delightful muscat flavour to table wines. It comes in varying degrees of sweetness, ranging from dry wines to fortified sweet dessert wines. White hanepoot ranks third in the number of white wine vines planted.

Gewürztraminer

Believed to have been originally cultivated in Austria, gewürztraminer has a firmly established reputation as one of the world's quality cultivars. Grown in Alsace, it produces fragrant, spicy, full-flavoured wines with great depth of character.

Although the variety produced in South Africa is not as full-flavoured, a number of wines have been marketed, particularly in off-dry or semi-sweet styles. The best examples of these wines echo the fragrance and spiciness of their European counterparts.

Plantings of this newcomer to South Africa presently represent about one per cent of the total, but its popularity is growing among wine farmers.

Sauvignon blanc

Although representing less than one per cent of the wine grape vines in South Africa, the popularity of this cultivar is rapidly increasing. It is at home in Bordeaux, where – in combination with sémillon and muscadelle (not to be confused with the South African muscadel) – it makes the driest of dry Graves and luscious sweet Sauternes and Barsacs. In the Loire region it produces the best Sancerres and wines such as Pouilly Fumé.

In South Africa, sauvignon blanc is best grown in cool climates with a limited yield. Also known as blanc fumé, two styles of wine have been made from sauvignon blanc in South Africa: one with no wood contact, and the other partly fermented in wood, or wood-matured, or both. Some wines of excellent quality have been made in each style.

Clairette blanche

Seldom bottled on its own, this variety produces light, flowery wines of low acidity, used mainly for blending.

Sémillon or green grape

It is believed by some that what is known as green grape in South Africa is not the same as the sémillon of France. However, most people today accept it as a clone of sémillon. The variety has been known in South Africa from early times, when it was the most common cultivar. Today, however, it is seldom bottled on its own. It is favoured as a blending component, particularly in the sweeter styles of table wines.

Bukettraube

This comparatively new cultivar, developed in Germany and introduced to South Africa quite recently, makes fragrant wines with a delicate muscat character which seem to show up best as semi-sweets.

Kerner

Although a white variety, kerner is a cross between Rhine riesling and trollinger, a red cultivar. Though it is very sparsely planted, dry and semi-sweet styles of acceptable quality have been made from this variety.

Chardonnay

Considered to be the most noble of white cultivars, chardonnay makes the great white classics of Burgundy. This is the grape of Chablis and one of the permitted Champagne varieties. Chardonnay has achieved great success in California and, latterly, in Australia.

While some fine examples of chardonnay have been produced on a small scale in South Africa, not all of them are yet commercially available.

RED CULTIVARS

Cinsaut
Formerly known as hermitage, this is the basis for the bulk of South Africa's mass-produced red table wines. Wine made from this grape varies considerably in style, depending on where and how it is grown.

Cinsaut produces light- to medium-bodied wines which are ready to drink while still young. For this reason it is sometimes used for blending with other wines that are harder and take longer to mature. Although it is the third most common wine grape in South Africa, representing about 11 per cent of the total number of vines, its popularity is declining.

Pinotage
This cultivar originated in South Africa, where it was developed in the 1920s by Professor Abraham Perold. Its name derives from its forebears, the variety being a cross between pinot noir and cinsaut (hermitage).

The first commercially bottled pinotage was of 1959 vintage. Since then it has been planted in all regions. Pinotage makes medium- to full-bodied wines, usually with a very distinctive varietal character. Though sometimes used as a blending component, it is usually bottled on its own.

Cabernet sauvignon
This cultivar is the basis of the finest Bordeaux clarets. One must be patient to enjoy it at its best; when young, its wines are hard, tannic and astringent, but with time they bloom into the noblest of beverages.

Cabernet sauvignon has adapted well in most wine-producing countries. In Bordeaux it is blended mainly with cabernet franc, merlot, malbec and petit verdot. Although there is a trend in South Africa towards making this style of wine, a fair amount of cabernet sauvignon is bottled as straight cultivar wine.

Shiraz
Known in South Africa for many years, this grape produces medium- to full-bodied wines with a recognisable varietal character, described by some as smoky.

Pinot noir
This is the grape that makes the great Burgundian reds of the Côte d'Or. Although it has not generally adapted well to other climates, it has attracted some attention in South Africa in recent years – particularly from estate producers. Good, light- to medium-bodied wines have been made from it.

Zinfandel
This grape, which may be the same as the Italian variety primitivo, is one of the most favoured cultivars in California. It makes well-balanced, medium-bodied, fruity wines. As yet there are only a few examples in South Africa.

Merlot
Excellent as a blending ingredient with cabernet sauvignon, merlot matures much sooner than cabernet. Some very good wines have been made from it in South Africa, mainly through blending.

Other cultivars
There are many other varieties grown in South Africa on a small scale, including a number of port varieties such as tinta barocca, tinta roriz and souzao.

Cabernet franc has been bottled on its own, but its main role is that of a blending component. The same is true for grenache. Gamay, the grape of Beaujolais, is grown, and small quantities of malbec and petit verdot have been planted for blending purposes.

STORING WINE

A wine cellar need not be a sophisticated, fully fledged, underground cellar complete with cobwebs. Any storage area that is vibration-free, enjoys a reasonably cool and constant temperature, and is relatively dark and well ventilated will do.

One of the factors responsible for the bottle maturation of wine is the interaction of the wine in the bottle with the air trapped between the wine and the cork. If the wine is vibrated, more of it comes into contact with the air in a given time, and this tends to accelerate maturation – thus reducing the optimum life of the wine.

Fluctuations in temperature, while undesirable, are not all that important if they are gradual, and do not range between extremes of hot and cold. Usually the pulp sleeves in which many wines come packed insulate them against temperature variations.

High temperatures speed up chemical reactions and are to be avoided, since they reduce the lifespan of the wine. Strong light can also affect wine adversely because of its influence on the wine's protein content.

Bottles should be stored horizontally so that the corks are kept moist and tight. A dry cork shrinks, allowing air to enter the bottle and spoil the wine. Good ventilation reduces the likelihood of mould forming on the corks, which could contaminate the wine.

Contrary to popular belief, white wines can benefit from being laid down, but their bottle life will depend on the fixed acid and sugar content. If left to lie for too long, a wine low in acid will lose its freshness and tang, making it taste flat and uninteresting.

Ideally one should be able to open a bottle from each batch of stored wine every six months or so and monitor the wine's progress. Experience will show when a wine has reached its peak, or whether it would benefit from further maturation.

WINE IN SOUTH AFRICA

Within two months of arriving at the Cape, Jan van Riebeeck asked for a variety of seeds and plants to be sent out from the Netherlands. Included in his list were 'vines, which ought to thrive as well on the local hill slopes as they do in Spain or France'.

The response was somewhat tardy: the first vines arrived more than two and a half years later, in December 1654. By February 1659 Van Riebeeck was able to enter in his journal: 'Today, praise be to God, wine was made for the first time from Cape grapes....'

Van Riebeeck was the first of many who helped to shape the wine industry. Commander (later Governor) Simon van der Stel was an enthusiastic wine-farmer, as were the French Huguenots. Building on what had been achieved, Hendrick Cloete, who in 1778 had bought Groot Constantia, the wine estate established by Van der Stel, became famous for his wines in the royal courts of Europe.

The Napoleonic wars brought further good fortune to Cape wines. With the traditional wine suppliers cut off by the war, Britain encouraged production at the Cape – in British hands since 1806 – with preferential tariffs.

The ready market and lack of competition had a disastrous effect on quality. Cape wines and brandies soon acquired a thoroughly bad reputation – so bad that, when the preferences were abolished in 1861, the export trade collapsed. In 1886 another disaster struck: *phylloxera vastatrix*, the dreaded louse which had already ravaged the vineyards of Europe. Only with the development of *phylloxera*-resistant rootstock did the industry begin to recover.

So vigorous was the recovery that by 1904 over-production was at its highest ever: wine was being sold for £3 a leaguer (577 litres) and less. Trying to prevent the total ruin of the industry, the government made £50 000 available for the establishment of co-operative wineries.

In 1918 the KWV (Ko-operatieve Wijnbouwers Vereniging van Zuid-Afrika), the body that now controls all aspects of wine production in South Africa, came into being. The first years were difficult: between 1921 and 1923 more than 50 million litres of wine were literally poured down the drain because there was no market for it. But over the years the KWV – backed by legislation – gained strength.

Production began to increase once more, this time in a more orderly fashion. South Africa today produces about 900 million litres of wine a year, of which 85 per cent comes from the 70 co-operative cellars around the country.

The Wine of Origin Seal

In line with the practice adopted in the foremost wine-producing countries of Europe – such as Italy, France, Germany and Spain – South Africa introduced its own 'wine of origin' legislation in the early 1970s.

Based on the principle that soil and climate are major contributors to the character of a wine, the winelands were demarcated into a number of regions, areas and wards in descending order of size. In addition, the smallest unit of origin (the estate) was defined.

The system of certification assures the consumer only that the information provided on the bottle label is correct: the certification is not a claim of quality (except in the case of a superior appellation). Similarly, a wine that has not been certified is not necessarily of poor quality.

Certification is made in respect of five aspects: origin, vintage, cultivar, whether it is an estate wine, and whether the Wine and Spirit Board considers it to be of superior quality.

ORIGIN This is indicated by a blue band on the seal, and certifies that all the grapes used in making the wine came from the region, area or ward specified on the label.

VINTAGE The vintage is indicated by a red band, and certifies that a minimum of 75 per cent of the grapes for that wine were picked during the harvest year specified on the label.

CULTIVAR The green band on the seal certifies that a certain minimum proportion of the cultivar indicated on the label, as specified in the regulations, is contained in the bottle (for example, cabernet sauvignon).

ESTATE Subject to certain conditions which define an estate, a producer can have his wine certified as an estate wine if all the grapes from which the wine was made were grown, and the wine was wholly produced, on the estate specified on the label. The regulations permit the wine to be bottled and matured elsewhere.

SUPERIOR If the Wine and Spirit Board considers a wine to be of outstanding quality, it will grant the wine a superior appellation. This is now indicated by the issue of a gold seal (as shown here) with the words 'Superieur – Superior' inscribed on it. These words used to appear below the green band on the ordinary white seal.

To qualify for a superior seal, the wine has to achieve a mean score of at least 7,5 points out of 9 when tasted 'blind' by the board's tasting committee, which then passes its recommendation to the board for confirmation.

Serving Wine

The sole purpose of any conventions relating to the serving of wine should be the enhancement of its enjoyment. Since an appreciation of wine depends on the senses of sight, smell and taste, all three need to be taken into account when wine is served.

SERVING TEMPERATURE

White, rosé and sparkling wines taste crisper and more refreshing when cool, but take care not to chill them to the point where the release of the aromatic substances is inhibited. Placing these wines in a refrigerator for an hour or two before serving is usually sufficient to cool them to between 10°C and 12°C. A natural sweet wine, such as a special or noble late harvest, also benefits from cooling.

To maintain the low temperature during serving, place the bottle in any one of a number of specially designed insulators, or in an ice bucket. If allowed to stand in an ice bucket for too long, however, the temperature can drop to below the desired level.

Red wine is traditionally served at 'room temperature'. However, room temperature on a hot summer's day in South Africa is unlikely to be the same as room temperature in mid-winter, and if red wines are very slightly chilled on a hot day they will come to no harm. It is more important that all the elements in the wine remain in harmony; if it is served too warm, one can detect the emission of the volatile alcohol.

BREATHING AND DECANTING

To breathe or not to breathe – this has long been a point of controversy, and still is. There are those who believe a red wine should be opened and allowed to stand for anything up to 24 hours before serving, while others say this can be detrimental to the wine.

At 'blind' tastings conducted in South Africa and overseas to try to resolve the issue, it was concluded that younger wines were more likely to benefit from aeration, while older wines lost some of their bouquet. Decanting provides a greater degree of aeration.

An older wine – particularly one that has thrown a sediment – should be stood upright for a day or two before serving to allow any suspended particles time to settle. The wine should be carefully decanted in one continuous pouring action up to the point when sediment is seen approaching the neck of the bottle. It is easier to watch the movement of sediment if a light is placed behind the bottle.

SERVING ORDER

As a general rule, whites – except when they are sweet – precede reds. Dry goes best before semi-sweet, and delicate whites before the more full-flavoured varieties. Serve the best wines first and, particularly in the case of reds, young before old. Sweet wines, whether natural or fortified, seem to fit in best at the end of a meal, being served with dessert, nuts or certain kinds of cheese.

SERVING ETIQUETTE

Cut the plastic or lead sheath at the top of the bottle with a sharp knife just below the ridge at the top. Remove and discard the top of the sheath, and then wipe the neck of the bottle clean with a suitable cloth or napkin. Pull out the cork and then wipe the neck once again.

There are several conventions to be followed when serving wine on a formal occasion, but only a few if the entertaining is on an informal basis. When you are formally entertaining a small group at home, pour the wine (before the food is served) from the guests' right side.

Start with the female guest seated to the right of the host and continue clockwise until all the female guests have been served. Then, starting with the man sitting to the right of the hostess, serve all the men. In this situation the host does not sample the wine first, as he is presumed to be *au fait* with its condition.

In a restaurant, all the procedures should be carried out in full view of the host, who should be shown the bottle before it is opened, given it to feel the temperature (in the case of a chilled wine) and shown the cork after it has been pulled (this enables him to check its condition). A little wine is then poured into the host's glass for him to taste and approve before the guests are served (again from their right side, and always beginning with the women).

WINE WITH FOOD

Much has been written on the correct wines to be drunk with certain dishes, and wine purists have been known to raise an eyebrow if someone steps out of line. In reality there is no such thing as one wine being correct for a particular dish, while another is taboo. There is no hard and fast rule to be followed slavishly.

However, to maximise the pleasure that can be derived from wine with food, the two should complement each other. Delicate dishes should be accompanied by delicate wines, while more robust fare goes better with fuller wines. Similarly, sweet wines are best suited to desserts. The following are merely suggestions: let your own palate be your guide.

APÉRITIFS

There is very little to equal a good dry sparkling wine, preferably Champagne, to stimulate the taste buds. Lightly chilled sherry also makes a good apéritif.

STARTERS AND SOUPS

Antipasto or hors d'oeuvres Dry or slightly off-dry white, for example chenin blanc (steen), Cape riesling or blanc de noir.
Artichokes Dry white, for example Cape riesling, colombar or blended wine.
Asparagus Dry white, for example unwooded sauvignon blanc (blanc fumé) or colombar.
Avocado with seafood Dry or slightly off-dry white, for example, Cape riesling, chenin blanc (steen), chardonnay or sauvignon blanc (blanc fumé).
Caviar Sparkling wine (brut).
Consommés Extra dry or dry sherry.
Gazpacho Extra dry or dry sherry.
Herring or rollmops Dry to off-dry white, depending on the style of dish.
Chilled melon Special or noble late harvest.
Minestrone Dry blanc de noir, rosé or light red.
Oysters Dry white, for example chardonnay, unwooded sauvignon blanc (blanc fumé) or sparkling wine (brut).
Parma ham with melon or figs Medium- to full-bodied dry or off-dry white, for example wooded sauvignon blanc (blanc fumé), Rhine riesling, gewürztraminer, bukettraube, blanc de noir or rosé.
Patés – fish or smoked fish Dry white, for example colombar, Cape riesling or blanc de noir.
Patés – liver Full-flavoured dry or off-dry white, for example chenin blanc (steen), Cape riesling, Rhine riesling, blanc de noir, rosé or light red.
Seafood soup Full-bodied dry or slightly off-dry white, for example chardonnay, Rhine riesling or wooded sauvignon blanc (blanc fumé).
Smoked fish – angelfish, mackerel or snoek Full-bodied dry white, for example wooded sauvignon blanc (blanc fumé), chardonnay or Rhine riesling.
Smoked fish – salmon, trout or eel Full-flavoured dry white, for example sauvignon blanc (blanc fumé), Cape riesling, chenin blanc or blanc de noir.
Snails (escargots) Full-flavoured dry or off-dry white, such as Rhine riesling, gewürztraminer, bukettraube, chenin blanc (steen), or rosé, light red or sherry.
Taramasalata Dry white, for example colombar, chenin blanc or Cape riesling.
Terrines See patés.

FISH AND SEAFOODS

Crayfish and crab Depending on how the dish is prepared and whether served hot or cold: dry to off-dry white, for example chardonnay, sylvaner, hárslevelü, sauvignon blanc (blanc fumé), Rhine riesling, Cape riesling, colombar or sparkling wine.
Fish – white (angelfish, Cape salmon, hake, kabeljou, kingklip, sole, steenbras and stumpnose) Delicate dry or slightly off-dry white, for example colombar, Cape riesling, chenin blanc (steen) or sylvaner.
Fish – pelagic or game fish (anchovy, maasbanker, harder, snoek, tunny, and yellowtail) Medium- to full-bodied dry, or off-dry, white, depending on how the dish is prepared, for example chenin blanc (steen), sauvignon blanc (blanc fumé), chardonnay, Rhine riesling or hárslevelü, or blanc de noir or rosé.
Mussels and clams – white See Perlemoen.
Mussels and clams – black Dry or slightly off-dry white, for example colombar, Cape riesling, Rhine riesling or sauvignon blanc.
Paella Robust dry white, blanc de noir, rosé or light red.
Perlemoen (abalone) Dry or off-dry white, for example chardonnay, unwooded sauvignon blanc (blanc fumé), Cape riesling, Rhine riesling or a delicate blended wine.
Prawns and shrimps Medium-bodied dry or slightly off-dry white, for example chardonnay, sauvignon blanc (blanc fumé), Cape riesling or colombar.
Squid (calamari) Dry or off-dry white, for example Cape riesling, chenin blanc (steen), colombar or sylvaner.
Trout Delicate dry white, for example Cape riesling, sylvaner or chenin blanc (steen).

MEAT

Beef With roasts serve almost any medium-bodied red, as well as blends; with stews and casseroles serve medium- to full-bodied reds, for example blended wines, pinotage or shiraz; and with steaks serve medium- to full-bodied reds, for example cabernet sauvignon or well-aged pinotage.
Lamb and mutton With roasts serve medium-bodied reds, Bordeaux-style blends, cabernet sauvignon or a fuller pinot noir; with stews and casseroles serve the same types but fuller-bodied (also shiraz or pinotage); and with grilled meat serve tinta barocca, cinsaut, pinotage or blended medium-bodied reds.
Pork If roasts are accompanied by apple sauce, serve a full-flavoured gewürztraminer, bukkettraube, muscat blend or off-dry rosé; otherwise a full-bodied dry or off-dry white or any light red, for example cinsaut.
Ham and gammon Dry, full-bodied rosé or light- to medium-bodied red, for example cinsaut, tinta barocca, pinot noir or blended wine.
Venison Fullest-bodied reds, cabernet sauvignon, shiraz, pinotage or Burgundy-style.
Rabbit A robust red blend (pinotage or shiraz) goes well with a spicy stew.
Liver, kidneys and sweatbreads Medium-bodied pinotage, shiraz, blended wine, full-bodied cinsaut, tinta barocca or merlot.

CURRIES

Full-bodied semi-sweets, for example gewürztraminer, Rhine riesling, bukettraube, chenin blanc (steen), colombar, stein, late harvest or semi-sweet rosé.

POULTRY

Chicken and turkey With cold meat serve dry to off-dry white or blanc de noir, rosé or a light red. Serve the same types with grilled meat, but choose slightly more robust wine. With roast or pot-roast serve full-bodied, off-dry white, for example chenin blanc (steen), Rhine riesling, rosé or a light- to medium-bodied red.
Duck and goose Fruity white, from dry to semi-sweet, depending on the style of dish. If reds are preferred, pinot noir, tinta barocca, pinotage or well-aged shiraz.
Game birds These need good red wines to set them off, for example full-bodied Burgundy-style, pinot noir, cabernet sauvignon, well-aged shiraz or pinotage.

PASTA, PIES AND PIZZAS

Choose the wines according to the fillings or sauces used. Refer to the appropriate section.

DESSERTS

For desserts served cold, choose anything from chilled doux sparkling wine to late harvest, special late harvest or noble late harvest. For hot desserts, select sweet sherry, muscadel, sweet hanepoot or port. These wines also go well with nuts.

Drinks for all Occasions

~ Teas, Coffees and Soft Drinks ~

For a departure from the everyday, try tea or coffee in a different guise: a spiced Indian tea (masala chai), Turkish coffee or an Italian cappuccino. Alternatively, try an exotic soft drink such as a Malay boeboer or Gedat milk, or an Indian lassi or keri sherbet.

ICED TEA

PREPARATION TIME: 15 MINUTES
COOLING TIME AND CHILLING TIME: 45 MINUTES

INGREDIENTS FOR FOUR
20 ml (4 teaspoons) China or Ceylon tea leaves
800 ml boiling water
10-20 ml (2-4 teaspoons) sugar (optional)
45-60 ml (3-4 tablespoons) dark rum (optional)
4 slices lemon
4 ice cubes
4 sprigs fresh mint

Put the tea leaves in a jug and pour on the boiling water. Add the sugar (if used). Leave to stand for 10 minutes, then strain into another jug.

When cool, place the jug in the refrigerator and leave until very cold.

Add the rum (if used) and stir well to mix thoroughly. Place a slice of lemon and an ice cube in each of 4 glasses and pour in the tea.

Garnish each glass of iced tea with a sprig of fresh mint and serve immediately.

VARIATIONS Make a sun-brewed tea with 6 tea bags to 1 litre (4 cups) cold water. Place the tea bags and the water in a jar with 2 cinnamon sticks and 1 clove. Screw the lid on tightly and leave the jar in the hot sun for a few hours to brew gently. Pour the tea into tall glasses over lots of ice cubes. Add a slice of lemon and a sprig of fresh mint to each glass.

Use rooibos tea instead of China or Ceylon tea, and leave out the rum.

MALAY VERMICELLI BOEBOER

PREPARATION TIME: 10 MINUTES
SOAKING TIME: 30 MINUTES
COOKING TIME: 1 HOUR

INGREDIENTS FOR EIGHT
35 g sago
125 ml (½ cup) water
50 g butter
150 g fine vermicelli, broken into small pieces (available from speciality Indian stores)
8-10 cardamom pods
3 cinnamon sticks (about 2,5 cm each), bruised or whole
2 litres (8 cups) milk
400 g sugar
A few drops of rose-water to flavour (optional)

Soak the sago in the water for 30 minutes.

Meanwhile melt the butter in a saucepan and gently brown the vermicelli in the butter, stirring it around constantly to prevent it from sticking.

Add the cardamom pods and cinnamon, then the milk, sago and sugar.

Simmer the mixture slowly, stirring occasionally, until it is thick and creamy. If desired, add rose-water to taste. (Rose-water is available from some pharmacies.)

Serve hot or cold.

VARIATIONS More sago may be added for a thicker consistency.

Grated (unsalted) nuts and coconut may also be added to vary the flavour of the boeboer.

KERI SHERBET

PREPARATION TIME: 30 MINUTES
CHILLING TIME: 30 MINUTES

INGREDIENTS FOR SIX TO EIGHT
4 ripe mangoes
60 ml (¼ cup) sugar
750 ml (3 cups) milk
500 ml (2 cups) water
A small pinch of salt
10 ml (2 teaspoons) cumin seeds, roasted in a pan for 2 minutes, then pounded to a powder
A pinch of saffron threads, soaked in 30 ml (2 tablespoons) milk for 15 minutes
500 ml (2 cups) khulfi* or vanilla ice cream*

Peel the mangoes and cut the fruit from the stone. Take care when cutting the mangoes, since they are slippery and you could cut your fingers. Place the mango flesh and sugar in a liquidizer or blender, and purée.

Add the milk and water to the fruit.

Pour the diluted fruit purée into a medium-sized bowl and season the mixture with the salt and powdered cumin seeds. Add the saffron threads and the milk in which they have been soaking.

Stir the mixture well and pour into tall glasses.

Allow the glasses of sherbet to cool in a refrigerator for about 30 minutes. Place a generous helping of khulfi or vanilla ice cream over the top of each glass of sherbet and serve immediately.

VARIATION If you prefer a thinner consistency of sherbet, you may mix in more water: the recipe can take up to 125 ml (½ cup) extra.

LASSI

PREPARATION TIME: 15 MINUTES

INGREDIENTS FOR FOUR

625 ml (2½ cups) natural yoghurt*
  or buttermilk
30 ml (2 tablespoons) sugar
375 ml (1½ cups) crushed ice
15 ml (1 tablespoon) slivered almonds
15 ml (1 tablespoon) finely chopped
  pistachio nuts
5 ml (1 teaspoon) raisins

Place the yoghurt or buttermilk in a deep bowl. Stir in the sugar until it dissolves. Add the crushed ice and allow the yoghurt to chill until the ice melts.

Using a whisk, beat the chilled yoghurt until it becomes fluffy and foamy. Add the almonds, pistachio nuts and raisins. Stir the mixture well and serve it immediately in glasses.

SERVING SUGGESTION Lassi may also be served as a cool sauce with pilaff* or Indian rice dishes.

COFFEE WITH A DIFFERENCE

Iced coffee
It is best to make iced coffee with freshly brewed coffee, which has a better flavour than left-over coffee. To make iced coffee for one person, pour 150 ml freshly made filter coffee into a tall glass filled with ice cubes (the ice will melt and chill the coffee). Sweeten with 5 ml (1 teaspoon) sugar – use more or less to taste – and add 15 ml (1 tablespoon) brandy or coffee-flavoured liqueur (optional). Top with a scoop of ice cream and garnish with a swirl of whipped cream. Serve immediately.

Cappuccino
To make this Italian-style coffee, whisk milky strong coffee until it is very frothy. Add sugar to taste and sprinkle chocolate powder or ground cinnamon over the top.

Turkish coffee
For each serving of Turkish coffee heat together 10 ml (2 teaspoons) finely ground coffee with 5 ml (1 teaspoon) sugar and 125 ml (½ cup) water. When the froth starts to rise, remove from the heat and stir. Repeat this twice. Serve the coffee very hot in tiny cups. Do not stir, as the grounds must settle at the bottom of the cup – but spoon some of the froth on to each cup of coffee. If you like your Turkish coffee very sweet, add more sugar initially.

GEDAT MILK

PREPARATION TIME: 5 MINUTES
COOKING TIME: 10 MINUTES
STANDING TIME: 20 MINUTES

INGREDIENTS FOR EIGHT TO TEN

2 ml (½ teaspoon) cardamom pods
  pounded or bruised
1 cinnamon stick (5 cm), slightly
  bruised
1 litre (4 cups) milk
A pinch of salt
20 ml (4 teaspoons) sugar
A few drops of rose-water

Tie the cardamom and cinnamon in a muslin bag. Leave this spice bag in half the milk for about 5 minutes, then heat the milk to boiling point with the spice bag, salt and sugar. Remove from the heat. Cover the saucepan with a lid and allow the spices to draw for at least 15 minutes, then remove the bag.

Add the remaining milk to the boiled milk. Strain, add a few drops of rose-water and serve in very small glasses.

MASALA CHAI

PREPARATION TIME: 10 MINUTES

INGREDIENTS FOR FOUR

750 ml (3 cups) water
500 ml (2 cups) milk
6 thin slivers of washed fresh green
  ginger, pounded
2 ml (½ teaspoon) tea masala (available
  at Indian stores), or a pinch of freshly
  ground pepper
4 cardamom pods, partly split
2 blades citronella grass, cut into pieces
  (optional)
15 ml (1 tablespoon) tea leaves
40 ml (8 teaspoons) sugar

Place the water in a deep saucepan. Add the milk and bring to the boil. Watch constantly to prevent it from boiling over.

Add the ginger, tea masala or pinch of pepper, cardamom pods and citronella grass (if used) and simmer the mixture gently on a medium heat for about 3 minutes to extract the flavour.

Add the tea leaves and stir in the sugar. Bring the mixture to the boil and then simmer for a few minutes until the tea turns a caramel colour.

Remove from the heat and strain the tea into a teapot.

HERBAL AND BUSH TEAS

Either fresh or dried herbs may be used to make herbal teas. Generally 25 g fresh herbs are used for 1 litre (4 cups) boiling water. This quantity may, however, be varied to taste. For dried herbs, use the same quantities as you would of other teas.

The fresh green leaves of the following plants make excellent tea: basil, camomile, dandelion, dill, fennel, geranium, lavender, lemon balm, lemon verbena, marjoram, mint, origanum, rosemary, sage, savory and thyme.

To make the tea, place the fresh leaves or sprigs in a warm earthenware or china teapot and pour on the required amount of boiling water. Leave to stand for about 10 minutes, then strain into teacups. If you are using dried herbs or hard seeds, it is often advisable to add them to the right measure of water in a pot and allow them to simmer for at least 20 minutes.

Herbal teas may be served hot or cold, with honey or lemon juice, but not milk and sugar.

Ordinary Ceylon teas may be mixed with any of the following: rose geranium, peppermint and honey, leaf buchu or lemon verbena.

Herb teas are a valuable ingredient in fruit punches or non-alcoholic drinks, mixed with fruit juices, squashes, soda water and/or ginger ale (served ice cold). Garnish with a borage flower, mint leaf or twig of lemon thyme, together with slices of lemon, orange, cherries, granadilla and/or strawberries.

The following herb tea blends are recommended: rosemary, lavender and lemon balm in equal quantities; thyme and rosemary in equal quantities; sage, rosemary, hyssop and peppermint in equal quantities; marjoram with twice the amount of thyme.

One of the best-known South African bush teas is rooibos tea, derived from a leguminous shrub with needle-like leaves.

Rooibos tea is a refreshing beverage which contains very little tannin and no caffeine, and is rich in minerals. It is brewed as you would Ceylon tea, or boiled in the water (you may add milk and sugar before you boil the tea). It can be drunk alone, or with honey, lemon or milk and sugar. Always use a strainer if loose tea, not a tea bag, is used. Keep left-over tea as a basis for fruit drinks or iced tea. Rooibos tea is also suitable as a cooking liquid for meat.

Honeybush tea is another popular bush tea. It tastes best if it is allowed to simmer until a dark extraction is obtained. Then strain and serve it with hot milk and sugar. Alternatively, the tea may be boiled with the milk and sugar.

~ Children's Party Drinks ~

These drinks have been selected especially to tempt young party-goers.
But the emphasis on healthy fruit and milk drinks
should ensure that their parents are equally happy with the choice.

Mixed Fruit Drink

Preparation Time: 20 minutes
Standing Time: 30 minutes

Ingredients to Yield about 1,5 litres
125 ml (½ cup) granadilla pulp
125 ml (½ cup) lemon juice
500 ml (2 cups) orange juice
250 ml (1 cup) grated pineapple
250 ml (1 cup) grated guava
375 ml (1½ cups) sugar syrup*

Mix all the ingredients and allow to stand for 30 minutes.

Serving Suggestion Dilute with iced water and serve with crushed ice.

Variation Flavour the sugar syrup with ginger.

Milk Shakes

Preparation Time: 10 minutes

Ingredients for One
250 ml (1 cup) milk
150 ml ice cream
5 ml (1 teaspoon) flavouring syrup
1 scoop of ice cream for the topping

Combine the milk, 150 ml ice cream and flavouring syrup in a blender or food processor (or use a rotary hand beater) and whisk until frothy. Pour into a glass, top with the remaining ice cream and serve with a straw.

Variations To make a banana milk shake, substitute 2 ripe, mashed bananas for the flavouring syrup.
To make a fruit shake, substitute 60 ml (¼ cup) fruit juice for the flavouring syrup.
Natural yoghurt* makes a delicious substitute for the initial 150 ml ice cream in the basic recipe. The extra ice cream topping may be omitted in this case.
If using home-made fruit syrups* to flavour the milk shake, use 45 ml (3 tablespoons) in place of the flavouring syrup.

Guava Drink

Preparation Time: 10 minutes
Cooking Time: 30 minutes

Ingredients to Yield 1 litre
1 kg ripe guavas
1 litre (4 cups) water
200 g sugar
30 ml (2 tablespoons) lemon juice

Halve the guavas, cover them with the water and simmer (covered) until tender. Strain the liquid through a double layer of cheesecloth.
Add the sugar and lemon juice (use less sugar if the juice is very sweet) and stir to dissolve the sugar. Chill before serving.

Serving Suggestion Dilute with chilled lemonade, cold water or soda.

Hot Chocolate

Preparation Time: 10 minutes

Ingredients for One
250 ml (1 cup) milk
60 ml (¼ cup) grated chocolate

Heat the milk with the chocolate. Stir until the chocolate has melted completely, and allow the mixture to get very hot (but do not let it boil).
Whisk until very frothy, then pour into a large mug.

GINGER BEER

VANILLA MILK SHAKE

DRINKS FOR ALL OCCASIONS

Old-Fashioned Lemonade

PREPARATION TIME: 5 MINUTES
COOKING TIME: 12 MINUTES

INGREDIENTS TO YIELD 1 LITRE

4 juicy lemons, scrubbed
700 g sugar
10 ml (2 teaspoons) citric acid
10 ml (2 teaspoons) tartaric acid
1 litre (4 cups) boiling water

Using a potato peeler, peel the lemons very thinly to remove only the coloured rind (not the pith).

Squeeze the juice from the lemons into a large basin and add the sugar and the citric and tartaric acids.

Pour the boiling water into a medium-sized saucepan, add the lemon rind and boil for 2 minutes. Remove from the heat, then strain the water over the lemon juice and sugar mixture. Stir to dissolve the sugar. Strain the lemonade, pour into clean screw-top bottles and close securely.

If stored in a cool place, this lemonade will keep for several weeks.

SERVING SUGGESTION Dilute with hot or cold water to taste, and add a half slice of lemon or orange or a twist of finely cut peel to each glass.

Ginger Beer

PREPARATION TIME: 45 MINUTES
COOLING TIME: 45 MINUTES
FERMENTATION TIME: 3-4 DAYS

INGREDIENTS TO YIELD 4,5 LITRES

25 g fresh green ginger
1 lemon, scrubbed
450 g sugar
25 g cream of tartar
4,5 litres boiling water
25 g wine yeast or baker's yeast

Bruise the ginger by folding it in a clean cloth and pounding it with a hammer to release the flavour.

Using a potato peeler, peel the rind very thinly from the lemon. Squeeze the juice from the lemon.

Put the ginger, sugar, cream of tartar and lemon rind into a large plastic bucket. Pour on the boiling water – in two lots, if necessary. Add the lemon juice and stir well. Leave until the liquid has cooled to 21°C.

Cream the yeast with a little water in a small bowl and stir it into the liquid. Cover the bucket with a clean cloth draped over a wire cake rack or 2 or 3 pieces of clean wood to prevent sagging. Secure the cloth with elastic, and leave in a warm place for 24 hours. Skim off the froth and, without disturbing the sediment too much, use a jug to bale the 'beer' into strong bottles.

Alternatively, strain the 'beer' and pour it through a funnel into the bottles. Close the bottles with corks and tie the corks down with string or fine florist's wire, leaving a little play on the tie.

Store the bottles in a cool place and examine them frequently. If fermentation is vigorous, loosen the strings or wires slightly to relieve the pressure in the bottles, until fermentation quietens down.

The ginger beer is ready for drinking in 2-3 days.

Fruit Syrups

Commercially prepared blackcurrant syrup is widely known, loved by children and valued for its high vitamin C content. Similar fruit syrups can easily be made at home using fruits – such as strawberries, raspberries, boysenberries, mulberries or loganberries – that are too soft and ripe for other preserving methods.

When preparing the syrup, keep the heating to a minimum in order to retain the fresh fruit flavour. Most fruits will yield their juices when treated as described below. However, when using boysenberries it may be advisable to add water to the mashed fruit – up to 300 ml water for each 500 g berries.

With really ripe fruit, the juice yield should be satisfactory, but juice yields can be improved by adding pectinase – a pectin-destroying enzyme. Pectinase is quite difficult to obtain, but you might try a specialist store that stocks wine-making equipment, or alternatively order it through your chemist. Use 2 ml (½ teaspoon) to each 2,5 kg fruit.

Wash the fruit if necessary, remove any leaves and stalks, place the fruit in a large heat-proof bowl and crush with a wooden spoon or vegetable masher.

Cover the bowl with a clean cloth and secure with elastic to prevent sagging (if necessary, put a wire cake rack on top of the bowl). Leave to stand for 2-3 days in a cool pantry or cupboard.

Bring a pan of water to the boil and place the bowl of fruit over the pan. Heat gently until the juice runs freely.

Scald a clean cloth, wring it out and strain the extract through into a measuring jug. Add sugar in the proportion of 350 g for each 600 ml juice. Stir in the sugar without heating, but if it is slow to dissolve, pour the juice and sugar into a saucepan and heat gently.

Pour the syrup through a funnel into sauce bottles. Screw the caps on tightly and label. Store in a refrigerator and use as required.

The syrup will keep for up to 6 weeks. If you wish to store the bottles longer, they need to be sterilised* in the same way as for sauces and ketchups. Label and store in a cool, dark place or a refrigerator. Syrups can be deep-frozen in cartons; stir well when fully thawed.

Serve diluted to taste with iced water or lemonade for a summer drink.

STRAWBERRY MILK SHAKE

GUAVA DRINK

~ Cocktails – A Taste of Glamour ~

Whether you are wanting to unwind after a hard day at work, or get a social occasion off the ground, cocktails can be one of the most enjoyable and dependable ways of achieving your aim. The following selection of cocktail recipes should provide you and your friends with a variety of interesting 'lift-offs'.

Many cocktails are extravagantly decorated, sometimes with tiny paper umbrellas or decorative swizzle sticks, and with edible garnishes or sliced fruit or cherries.

Some garnishes are traditionally part of the drink, such as the olive or lemon twist with a martini. To make twists of lemon or lime, thinly peel the rind off the fruit and cut it into pieces about 1 cm by 2 cm. Twist the piece of rind before placing it in the glass or, if you like, rub it along the rim.

To frost a cocktail glass with salt or sugar, invert it and dip the rim firstly into egg white and then into the salt or sugar. Allow this frosting to set hard in the refrigerator, and be careful not to disturb it when pouring in the cocktail.

Unless otherwise stipulated, the quantities given here are for one person.

BEACHCOMBER

½ tot Cointreau
2 tots rum
Juice of ½ lemon
2 dashes maraschino liqueur

Shake the ingredients with crushed ice and serve in a champagne glass.

BETWEEN THE SHEETS

½ tot brandy
½ tot Cointreau or triple sec
½ tot rum
A dash of lemon juice (optional)

Shake the ingredients well with ice and pour into a cocktail glass.

BLACK RUSSIAN

1 tot vodka
1 tot Tia Maria or Kahlua

Fill a tumbler with ice, add the ingredients and stir.

BLOODY MARY

A dash of lemon juice
A dash of Tabasco (chilli sauce)
5 ml (1 teaspoon) Worcestershire sauce
Salt and freshly ground black pepper
1 tot vodka
Tomato juice

Half fill a mixing glass with ice, and add the lemon juice, Tabasco, Worcestershire sauce, salt and a grinding of black pepper.

Stir well, then add the vodka and top up with tomato juice. Stir again and pour into a tall glass.

DAIQUIRI

1 tot white rum
½ tot lime juice
2 ml (½ teaspoon) sugar
1 cherry

Shake the rum, lime juice and sugar well with ice, and pour into a chilled cocktail glass.

Serve garnished with the cherry.

DRY MARTINI

2 tots gin
1 tot vermouth
A twist of lemon or an olive

Add the gin and vermouth to a mixing glass half filled with ice cubes.

Stir carefully, and strain into a chilled cocktail glass before the ice starts to melt.

Serve with the twist of lemon or olive.

KIR

A glass of dry white wine
A splash of crème de cassis

Simply add the crème de cassis to the glass of white wine and add ice if desired.

MARGARITA

1 tot tequila
½ tot Cointreau
½ tot fresh lemon juice
5 ml (1 teaspoon) sugar

Shake the tequila, Cointreau, lemon juice and sugar well together with ice and pour into a cocktail glass that has been frosted* with salt.

MANHATTAN

2 tots rye whiskey
1 tot sweet vermouth
A dash of Angostura bitters
1 maraschino cherry

Mix the whiskey, vermouth and dash of bitters together with ice in a mixing glass, then pour the mixture into a cocktail glass.

Decorate with the cherry.

MINT JULEP

5 ml (1 teaspoon) icing sugar
6 mint leaves
Soda water
2 tots bourbon whiskey

Mash together the icing sugar, mint leaves and a little soda in a tall glass. Add the bourbon and fill up the glass with soda water.

NEGRONI

1 tot Campari
½ tot gin
½ tot red Martini
A dash of Angostura bitters
A slice of orange

Mix the Campari, gin, Martini and dash of bitters together in a tumbler.

Garnish with the slice of orange.

PINA COLADA

2 tots white rum
2 tots pineapple juice
10 ml (2 teaspoons) coconut milk
   (preferably fresh)
2 dashes Angostura bitters
A pinch of salt
A slice of orange
A hollowed pineapple husk
   (optional)
Lemon slices
Glacé cherries

Mix the rum, pineapple juice, coconut milk, bitters and salt together, add the orange slice and pour into the hollowed pineapple husk or a large goblet.

Decorate the pina colada with the slices of lemon and glacé cherries.

PINK LADY

1 tot gin
½ tot fresh lemon juice
2 dashes grenadine
½ egg white
A sprig of mint

Shake the gin, lemon juice, grenadine and egg white well with ice, then pour into a cocktail glass. Decorate with the sprig of mint.

PRAIRIE OYSTER

1 egg
A dash of Worcestershire sauce
1 tot brandy

Break the egg into a tumbler, making sure that the egg yolk is kept intact. Gently blend the Worcestershire sauce and brandy with the egg white.

SAMBA SURPRISE

2 tots Maracuja
Lemonade
Soda water
A slice of lemon

Pour the Maracuja over crushed ice in a tall glass and top up the glass with equal quantities of lemonade and soda water.

Garnish with the lemon slice.

SCREWDRIVER

1 tot vodka
Orange juice

Put 2 or 3 ice cubes into a tall glass. Add the vodka, then the orange juice and stir well.

SIDECAR

1 tot brandy
1 tot Cointreau
1 tot lemon juice
A twist of lemon

Shake the brandy, Cointreau and lemon juice with ice, and pour into a cocktail glass. Garnish with the twist of lemon.

STINGER

1 tot brandy
1 tot white crème de menthe

Shake the ingredients well with ice and pour into a cocktail glass filled with crushed ice.

TEQUILA SUNRISE

1 tot tequila
Orange juice
5 ml (1 teaspoon) grenadine

Place a few ice cubes in a tall glass and pour over the tequila and orange juice.

Add the grenadine, which will permeate down through the mixture.

FRESH TOMATO COCKTAIL

INGREDIENTS TO YIELD 1 LITRE
7 medium-sized tomatoes, chopped
500 ml (2 cups) water
10 ml (2 teaspoons) salt
1 medium-sized onion, peeled and
   sliced*
6 drops Tabasco (chilli sauce) (optional)
2 sticks celery, or 3 ml (¾ teaspoon)
   celery seeds
3 ml (¾ teaspoon) pepper
15 ml (1 tablespoon) sugar
3 ml (¾ teaspoon) Worcestershire sauce
   (optional)
3 bay leaves, or 3 lemon leaves
10 ml (2 teaspoons) lemon juice
Parsley and lemon slices for garnish

Mix all the ingredients except the lemon juice and garnish, then heat to boiling point. Simmer the mixture for 30 minutes until cooked, then remove from the heat and rub through a sieve.

Add the lemon juice and leave until ice-cold. If necessary, dilute the cocktail with a little iced water.

Decorate each glassful with parsley and slices of lemon.

TOM COLLINS

1 tot gin
Juice of 1 lemon
5 ml (1 teaspoon) sugar
A dash of Angostura bitters
Soda water
A slice of lemon

Put the gin, lemon juice, sugar, bitters and some soda water into a tall glass and stir the mixture until the sugar has dissolved.

Top up with soda water, stir again, and decorate the lip of the glass with the lemon slice.

WHISKY SOUR

2 tots whisky
1 tot lemon juice
2 ml (½ teaspoon) sugar
½ egg white (optional)
A slice of orange and a cherry

Shake the ingredients well with ice and pour into a tumbler. Decorate with the slice of orange and cherry. Using the egg white makes the cocktail light and frothy.

WHITE LADY

1 tot gin
½ tot Cointreau
½ tot fresh lemon juice
5 ml (1 teaspoon) sugar
1 cherry

Shake the gin, Cointreau, lemon juice and sugar with ice, then pour into a cocktail glass which has been frosted* with sugar. Garnish with the cherry on a cocktail stick.

~ AFTER-DINNER DRINKS AND PUNCHES ~

End a dinner party with one of the firm restaurant favourites – Dom Pedro or Irish coffee – or with a home-made liqueur. Punches, on the other hand, make good drinks for large numbers – whether they are hot or cold, with or without alcohol.

DOM PEDRO

PREPARATION TIME: 10 MINUTES

INGREDIENTS FOR ONE
250 ml (1 cup) vanilla ice cream*
15 ml (1 tablespoon) cream
30 ml (2 tablespoons) whisky

Blend the ingredients together in a liquidizer or food processor (for a very short time) and pour into a champagne glass. Serve with a short straw.

VARIATIONS Use a coffee liqueur instead of the whisky.

IRISH COFFEE

PREPARATION TIME: 10 MINUTES

INGREDIENTS FOR SIX
250 ml (1 cup) cream
180 ml Irish whiskey
30 ml (2 tablespoons) soft brown sugar
750 ml (3 cups) strong hot coffee

Whip the cream in a chilled bowl until it holds soft peaks. Pour 30 ml (2 tablespoons) whiskey into each of 6 Irish coffee glasses (250 ml size), add 5 ml (1 teaspoon) brown sugar and top with hot coffee. Give each coffee a brief stir, then divide the cream among the glasses (pour the cream over the back of a teaspoon so that it rests on top of the coffee).

VARIATION Substitute Van der Hum* or other liqueurs for the whiskey.

ADVOKAAT

PREPARATION TIME: 15 MINUTES
CHILLING TIME: 30 MINUTES

INGREDIENTS FOR FOUR
6 egg yolks
200 g sugar
2 ml (½ teaspoon) vanilla essence
250 ml (1 cup) brandy

Beat the egg yolks, sugar and vanilla essence until thick and lemon-coloured. Gradually add the brandy, beating constantly until the mixture acquires the consistency of cream. Chill and serve in wine glasses.

VAN DER HUM LIQUEUR

PREPARATION TIME: 15 MINUTES
STANDING TIME: 1 MONTH

INGREDIENTS TO YIELD 1,75 LITRES
5 cloves
2 pieces dry naartjie peel
1 small cinnamon stick
2 ml (½ teaspoon) freshly grated nutmeg
1 litre (4 cups) brandy
500 ml (2 cups) sugar syrup*
250 ml (1 cup) gin

Mix the cloves, naartjie peel, cinnamon and nutmeg into the brandy, then pour into a bottle, cork and seal with wax. Leave for a month, then strain the flavoured brandy and mix in the sugar syrup and gin.

MILK PUNCH

PREPARATION TIME: 10 MINUTES
COOKING TIME: 10 MINUTES

INGREDIENTS FOR FOUR
600 ml milk
12 sugar cubes, or 50 g sugar
Rind of ½ small lemon, thinly peeled, with all pith removed
1 egg yolk, beaten
30 ml (2 tablespoons) brandy
60 ml (¼ cup) dark rum

Put 15 ml (1 tablespoon) milk on one side and pour the remainder into a 1 litre saucepan. Add the sugar and lemon rind. Simmer over a low heat for 10 minutes to extract the lemon flavour. Remove from the heat and discard the rind.

Put the egg yolk in a bowl and add the 15 ml cold milk. Whisk together and, still whisking, slowly add the brandy and rum. Whisk this mixture into the heated milk until frothy. Serve at once in warmed mugs.

VAN DER HUM LIQUEUR

GLÜHWEIN

DRINKS FOR ALL OCCASIONS

SANGRIA

PREPARATION TIME: 10 MINUTES

INGREDIENTS FOR SIX
750 ml (1 bottle) red wine
50 ml brandy
Juice of 2 lemons
Juice of 2 oranges
Castor sugar
175 ml (1 small bottle) soda water
6 ice cubes
2-3 orange slices

Use a tall glass jug large enough to hold all the ingredients – about 1,5 litres in capacity.

Pour the wine into the jug, and add the brandy, lemon juice and orange juice. Stir well, then, still stirring, add the sugar, 5 ml (1 teaspoon) at a time, to taste.

Keep the jug in a cool place and, just before serving, add the soda water and the ice cubes. Float the orange slices on top.

LOVING CUP

PREPARATION TIME: 20 MINUTES

INGREDIENTS TO YIELD 6,5 LITRES
450-700 g sugar, according to taste
1 litre (4 cups) water, warmed
1,5 litres (2 bottles) sherry
1,5 litres (2 bottles) Marsala
750 ml (1 bottle) port
750 ml (1 bottle) claret
Juice of 6 lemons
750 ml (1 bottle) champagne, sparkling wine or sparkling cider

Determine the amount of sugar to use from the sweetness of the wines.

Put the sugar in a medium-sized saucepan and add the water. Stir over a gentle heat to dissolve the sugar. Pour the sugar syrup into a punch bowl and add the sherry, Marsala, port, claret and lemon juice. Stir well and surround with crushed ice until required.

Just before serving, add the champagne, sparkling wine or sparkling cider.

VARIATION For additional flavouring, add 1-2 ml (¼ - ½ teaspoon) of any of the following during preparation: freshly grated nutmeg, cinnamon or ginger, chopped fresh borage, verbena or mint, thinly peeled lemon or orange rind.

FRUIT PUNCH

PREPARATION TIME: 45 MINUTES
COOKING TIME: 10 MINUTES

INGREDIENTS FOR TEN TO TWELVE
3 apples, peeled and sliced
3 oranges, peeled and sliced
2 bananas or peaches, peeled and sliced
125 g grapes, halved and with the pips removed
125 g fresh or tinned cherries, stoned
1 litre (4 cups) water
450 g sugar
Juice of 3 lemons
Juice of 3 oranges
600 ml ginger ale
300 ml cold tea (without milk)
600 ml soda water
12 ice cubes

Place the apples, oranges, bananas or peaches, grapes and cherries in a 3 litre bowl.

Put the water in a medium-sized saucepan and add the sugar, lemon juice and orange juice. Heat gently until the sugar is dissolved, then boil for 5 minutes, stirring with a wooden spoon. Pour the syrup over the fruit in the bowl and leave until cool.

Just before the punch is required, add the ginger ale, cold tea, soda water and ice cubes.

SERVING SUGGESTION Serve in goblets, ladling a little fruit into each.

GLÜHWEIN

PREPARATION TIME: 5 MINUTES
COOKING TIME: 15 MINUTES

INGREDIENTS FOR SIX TO EIGHT
300 ml water
4-6 cloves
A 5 cm cinnamon stick
A 5 cm piece of lemon rind
75 g castor sugar
750 ml (1 bottle) red wine

Put the water in a large saucepan. Add the cloves and cinnamon, and simmer for 5 minutes. Add the lemon rind and sugar and heat gently, stirring to dissolve the sugar.

Pour in the bottle of wine and heat until the liquid starts to steam (it must not boil). Remove the spices and serve the wine as hot as possible in heat-proof glasses or mugs.

LOVING CUP

PART 3

The Practical Cook

Cooking is not so much a science as it is an art. As with any artistic endeavour, the success of one's efforts will depend not only on skill and ability, but also on the more basic elements such as the utensils and equipment at one's disposal and a thorough knowledge of the 'fundamentals'. This part of the book looks at the practical considerations which collectively form the cornerstone of a properly organised and efficiently run kitchen. Here you will find useful information on important basics, such as buying food and making the most of it, storage, freezing, safety, cooking implements and kitchen appliances. There are also invaluable charts describing how to prepare, package and cook all types of food before freezing. No matter what your level of experience, you are sure to find many useful tips and information in the following pages.

The Practical Cook

KEEPING FOOD FRESH

When you are buying food, bear in mind that it may not be as fresh as you think, perhaps having been stored for some time already. Always look for quality, and buy small quantities often, rather than buying occasionally and in bulk.

The most efficient way to store potatoes, squashes, pumpkin and onions is to keep them in a cool, well-ventilated cupboard.

Wrap green vegetables in plastic bags that have been punched with a few holes to allow ventilation and prevent sogginess, then refrigerate.

Tomatoes, carrots and most other vegetables can be kept in loosely tied perforated plastic bags, as long as the contents are checked regularly for soggy or discoloured spots – if this happens the vegetables should be used immediately or thrown away. Vegetables take up less space in the refrigerator packed this way than if kept in airtight plastic boxes.

Cucumbers, peppers and brinjals are best kept unwrapped in the salad drawer of the refrigerator.

Do not wash or cut fruit or vegetables before storing them, and leave peas and beans in their pods until just before cooking.

Fresh fruit is best stored in a cool, slightly moist place, such as the bottom of the refrigerator. Again, it is best wrapped loosely in perforated plastic bags and checked regularly for mould.

Dairy foods should always be kept cool and well covered, as they absorb odours easily. Wipe cartons and plastic or glass bottles with a clean cloth before storing them in the refrigerator. Cheese, although best kept in the refrigerator, should be allowed to return to room temperature before being served.

Eggs are best bought weekly and kept at room temperature.

Meat will keep overnight in a cool place and for up to three days in a refrigerator, but smaller cuts such as chops or steaks should be eaten after two days in the refrigerator.

Mince and offal are best eaten after a day; fish should be eaten on the same day it is bought or else stored for not more than a day in the refrigerator.

Buy pre-cooked meats on the day you want to eat them. If possible, insist that the meat slices are freshly cut at the time you buy them.

Ready-frozen food is best bought at the last possible moment when shopping, and then put straight into the freezer when you arrive home.

Frozen vegetables survive thawing and re-freezing fairly well, but pre-prepared dishes, meat, fish and ice creams should not be allowed to thaw before they are put in the freezer.

Ideally, you should eat food when it is very fresh. Even a day or two in the refrigerator can rob fruit or vegetables of some of their nutrients; the longer that fresh produce is stored before being eaten, the greater the loss of nutritional value.

SHELF LIFE OF FOOD

Although tinned foods can be kept quite safely for years, it is best to use them within a year of purchase. Date each tin when you buy it and rotate your stock, using tins from the back of the shelf first.

Store tinned food in a cool, dry cupboard, and never buy tins with bulging ends. Slight dents and rust on the outside of tins do not affect the inside, but they, too, are best avoided.

Once opened, most food can be left in the tin, covered, and stored in the refrigerator for up to three days. However, tomato products, fruit and fruit juices are best decanted into non-metal containers before refrigerating, as the acid in the food may react with the metal and give the food a metallic flavour.

Tinned meats keep for up to three years, but are best eaten long before that. Fish in oil will last for five years, fish in tomato sauce for 12 months, and fruit and vegetables for up to two years.

Cereals are best stored in well-sealed containers, and should be regularly checked for weevils or other insects. An effective method of preventing any potential infestation is to place sealed containers of the cereal in a freezer for 48 hours. This treatment will kill any existing eggs or insects.

Herbs and spices keep indefinitely if sealed in jars and stored in a dark cupboard. If they are left open in cardboard packets, or in plastic or glass containers in direct light, they lose their flavour very quickly. Spices are generally best bought as whole seeds, as these retain their flavour better than ground spices do.

Dried fruit and most nuts keep indefinitely if well preserved. Dried fruit may dry out a little, but it can always be reconstituted. Nuts should be kept in airtight containers, otherwise they may become rancid.

Sugar will keep indefinitely and, although in some conditions it may harden to form a lump, it can still be used in cooking or simply broken down in a blender or food processor.

Syrup and honey will keep indefinitely. Should they crystallise, warm them before use to restore a smooth, runny consistency.

Jams keep well if they are sealed, but once opened they may grow mouldy on the surface. If this happens, simply scrape the mould off – the jam underneath can safely be eaten. If you have an ant problem, keep jams in the refrigerator.

Coffee and tea should be used as fresh as possible; vacuum-packed sachets of coffee beans or tea should keep their flavour for up to a year. Instant coffee should be used within three months for the best flavour.

Mixes and miscellaneous packets, such as instant pudding, cake mixes and so on, usually keep well for about six months, and some will keep longer, depending on how long they have sat on the shop shelf. Ideally, they are best used as soon as possible.

LEFT-OVERS

Some cookery books encourage one to plan meals so accurately that there are no left-overs, but this is not always possible. Do not aim to produce left-overs, but if anything does remain uneaten use it as the basis of another meal – carcasses for stock, vegetables for soup or omelettes, scraps of meat for a cottage pie or a spaghetti sauce.

One of the problems of storing left-overs is that they tend to dry out. To prevent this, lightly wrap meat, poultry and fish before storing them in the refrigerator. Cool cooked food as quickly as possible and pack it into the refrigerator well wrapped or sealed in airtight plastic containers.

Do not cut, slice or mince left-overs until just before you need them.

Since food that has already been cooked often lacks flavour, try a bit of seasoning on your left-overs. Always trim off the fat from cold meat that is to be used in prepared dishes as it does not taste very nice re-heated. Trim off discoloured parts or tough fibres from vegetables before re-using them.

Many people living alone find it easier to cook for two separate meals at the same time. If you do this, remember to cool the food for the second meal as quickly as you can. You may place the food container in a bowl of iced water, but do not place hot food in the refrigerator, where it might raise the temperature of other foods stored there. Once cooled, cover the food and store it in the refrigerator.

When you re-heat food, be sure you do so thoroughly. Food that is partly cooked, left to cool slowly and then warmed again rather than heated through thoroughly, can cause gastric upsets.

Prevent this by following a few simple rules: to re-heat soups or stews, bring them to the boil slowly, then boil thoroughly for five minutes. For casseroles and prepared dishes such as lasagne, cover and heat through in a 180°C oven for at least 30 minutes, then uncover and leave for five to ten minutes to crisp the top.

CONVENIENCE FOOD

If you enjoy entertaining and eating well but you do not have the time to spend hours shopping, then convenience foods are a must.

Out-of-the-tin cookery fools few – it is usually instantly recognisable – but the clever use of fresh convenience foods ensures reasonably quick meals that seem home-made. It costs a bit more to feed people this way, but it is certainly cheaper than eating out.

Make sure that you have something in stock that can be produced in an emergency – a tin of asparagus to blend with stock and cream to make into soup, a frozen quiche or pizza for a starter or lunch, a ready-made chicken Kiev that just needs frying, baby peas and even instant potato or noodles tossed with melted butter. These all make good meals that can be complemented with a finale of cheese or fresh fruit.

Appearance is important. You can cut the cost of convenience food by serving a slightly smaller amount to each person and adding a large bowl of crisp salad, fresh bread and neatly curled butter twists.

LABELS

It pays to give special attention to the labels on the foods you buy to ensure that you get the best value for money.

Manufacturers are required by law to itemise all ingredients, in descending order of the proportions (by mass) in which they were used in the manufacturing process. In other words, the ingredient listed first is the one in greatest quantity. If, for example, a tin of stewing steak lists tomatoes as the first of the ingredients on the label, it will not be as good a buy as another brand that shows steak first.

The grade of a product is shown on the main body of the label, usually in fairly bold print. The top grades such as 'fancy' or 'extra choice' mean that the contents are cut in even sizes. The lower grades, from 'choice' to 'sub-standard', are made from the same top-quality ingredients but have been cut into uneven shapes or sizes during processing. These lower grades are ideal for cooking, for making purées or for feeding children – they are unlikely to worry unduly about the varying sizes of individual pieces!

The contents of packet foods are listed in descending order of the final dried mass. This does not always give an accurate picture of the contents, but it does tell you what preservatives (if any) or additives have been used, and whether it contains 100 per cent real meat or some soya substitute.

Some manufacturers sell ranges of tinned fruit packed in natural juices, which are far tastier and healthier than the more traditional sugar syrup.

Other manufacturers supply ranges of tinned foods without salt or without sugar, and these products are ideal for people who are following special diets for health reasons.

FREEZING

Freezing is the simplest and quickest way of preserving food at its peak. If properly carried out, it is perfectly safe and will keep the food close to its original state. Properly frozen foods can be kept for months and, in some cases, for years.

The major component of most food is water, which, when frozen, turns to crystals. The faster the freezing, the smaller the crystals and the less damage to the cell walls of the food. Slower freezing means larger crystals, which tend to spoil the quality of the food.

A domestic freezer stores food at a temperature of about minus 18°C. It is also capable of bringing a specified quantity of fresh food (usually about 10 per cent of the freezer's total capacity) down to this temperature within 24 hours.

If too much fresh food is placed in a freezer at once, it will take much longer for the food to freeze right through. This could affect the quality of the food and possibly make it less safe to eat.

A frozen-food storage compartment inside a refrigerator will not freeze food successfully but only store frozen food for short periods. The star-rating is used to show how long food can be kept; one star indicates one week, two stars up to one month and three stars up to three months.

It is important to wrap food that is to be kept in the freezer. The most versatile and cheapest form of freezer packaging is plastic bags. It is best to use heavy-duty

FREEZING MEAT

Meat (storage time in brackets)	Preparation and packaging	Thawing
Joints (beef 8 months; lamb, pork and veal 6 months)	Wrap in heavy-duty plastic bags, seal well and label.	Thaw thoroughly before cooking, preferably in a refrigerator. Allow 5 hours per 500 g in a refrigerator, or 2 hours per 500 g at room temperature.
Cutlets, chops, hamburgers, meatballs, steaks and cubed meat (3 months)	Pack in suitable quantities. Separate cutlets, chops, hamburgers, meatballs and steaks with wax paper. Pack in plastic bags or rigid containers.	These small cuts can be cooked frozen over gentle heat.
Minced meat and sausage meat (3 months)	Pack in small quantities in plastic bags or rigid containers.	Thaw in a cool place for 1½ hours or a refrigerator for 3 hours, or cook from frozen.
Offal and sausages (1-3 months)	Clean and trim offal. Pack in small quantities in plastic bags.	Thaw in a cool place for 1½ hours or a refrigerator for 3 hours.
Hare, rabbit (6 months)	Wrap each joint in plastic wrap and pack several portions in heavy-duty plastic.	Thaw in wrapping in the refrigerator for 2-3 hours.
Venison (up to 12 months)	Freeze well-hung meat in joints or cutlets. Wrap joints in plastic wrap and plastic bags. Pack cutlets individually.	Thaw in wrapping in the refrigerator for 5 hours.

FREEZING FISH

Fish (storage time in brackets)	Packaging	Thawing
Whole fish (6 months)	Pack tightly in heavy-duty plastic.	Thaw large fish loosely wrapped in the refrigerator for about 6 hours. Small whole fish may be cooked frozen over low heat.
Fillets, steaks (6 months)	Wrap each piece in wax paper, then pack in suitable portions in heavy-duty plastic.	Thaw in wrapping in a refrigerator for about 3 hours.

FREEZING POULTRY AND GAME BIRDS

Poultry	Preparation and packaging	Thawing
(Chicken 12 months; duck 4-6 months; game birds 6-8 months; goose 4-6 months; turkey 6 months; giblets 3 months; livers 3 months)	Wrap whole birds in heavy-duty plastic. Trim bones from joints and wrap individually before packing in heavy-duty plastic. Pieces for pies and casseroles may be packed in rigid containers. Pack giblets and livers separately in plastic bags.	Thaw in wrapping in the refrigerator: a whole bird for 8 hours; joints and pieces for 2-3 hours. Thaw livers and giblets in wrapping in the refrigerator for 2 hours.

freezer bags; avoid the temptation to economise by buying thinner 'bread' bags as they tear easily.

More fragile items, such as meringues, are best packed in rigid containers. Lidded plastic boxes and empty plastic margarine, cottage cheese and ice cream containers can all be successfully used for storing food in the freezer.

Aluminium foil dishes with lids are ideal for freezing pre-cooked or made-up dishes and take up less space than freezer-proof casseroles.

Sheets of wax paper, aluminium foil and plastic wrap are invaluable for separating chops, steaks, pancakes and cookies but are not recommended for wrapping for long-term storage as they tend to split.

Whatever way you package foods for the freezer, remember to seal, label and dry each item before it goes into the cabinet so that, once frozen, it is easy to identify and remove.

Used carefully, a freezer will preserve just about every known perishable, with the exception of a few items such as mayonnaise, jelly, lettuce and cucumber.

FREEZING TECHNIQUES

Apart from freezing food in containers or wrappings, the following methods may also be employed:

Open-freezing is used for some fruits and vegetables. The food is cleaned and dried, then placed in a single layer on a tray lined with wax paper. Place the tray in the freezer until the food is firm, then pack in rigid containers or strong plastic bags.

A dry sugar pack or sugar-freezing is used for some fruits. For 2 kg fruit, mix 3 ml (¾ teaspoon) ascorbic acid powder with 500 g sugar. Toss the fruit in the sugar mixture before freezing – either freeze in containers or open-freeze*.

Sugar syrups may be used for freezing fruit. Choose from one of three strengths: light syrup, made from 250 g sugar and 500 ml (2 cups) water; medium syrup, made from 400 g sugar and 500 ml (2 cups) water; or heavy syrup, made from 500 g sugar and 500 ml (2 cups) water. Boil the water, add it to the sugar, and stir until the sugar has dissolved.

Allow about 250 ml (1 cup) sugar syrup for every 500 g fruit.

FREEZING MEAT

If you plan to buy a large quantity of fresh meat for freezing, check first that you have plenty of room in the freezer. Remember that meat should be fast-frozen before storing, and in most deep-freezers only a limited amount can be frozen at a time.

If you cannot freeze everything at once, keep the remainder in the refrigerator until it can be frozen.

Bulk-buying whole or half carcasses of meat can bring enormous savings, but these will be wasted if the meat is not of good quality or if you do not eat it all.

Check 'special offer' bulk buys of meat carefully. Packs of delicious lamb chops nestling against a leg joint could be hiding a layer of fatty cuts underneath. It is impossible to tell from the outside what the quality of packs of meat really are, so you should shop at a reliable butcher or try samples of the goods before spending a lot of money.

The wisest course of action is to buy from a reliable butcher when the price is favourable. A quick, regular turnover of a variety of meats is more economical than buying large stocks of lamb or beef, which can become monotonous.

Whenever possible, bone meat before freezing. Bones take up space and are likely to tear protective wrappings. Use the bones to make stock or soup. Also trim off any excess fat since it tends to become rancid if frozen for a long period.

Pack steaks, chops, schnitzels and similar items individually, then overwrap the total so that you can separate them as needed.

If you are buying frozen meat, avoid punctured packages or brittle white fat – this indicates that they have been frozen for too long.

It is possible to roast joints of under 3 kg straight from the freezer, but it takes a long time and you will find it difficult to ensure a moist, tender result. It is best to thaw all larger joints slowly in the refrigerator before cooking so that they do not lose too much liquid.

If you are in a hurry, speed up the process by thawing the meat at room temperature. Never be tempted to thaw meat in hot water: it will lose its flavour as well as its nutrients.

Small cuts can be grilled straight from the freezer. Allow about two minutes on each side at maximum heat, then 10-15 minutes at a lower heat, or until cooked through. Casseroles, hamburgers, meatballs, sausages and offal can all be cooked from the frozen state. Be sure to allow them enough time to be thoroughly cooked in the middle.

FREEZING FISH

Commercially frozen fish is usually very reasonably priced, particularly if you find special offers.

If you are fortunate enough to buy fish straight from the boat or have a fisherman in the family, it is well worth freezing your own fish. Clean, prepare and freeze it within three hours of being caught, and keep it for up to nine months.

Small fish can be frozen whole, but larger fish need to be cut into fillets or cutlets, then wrapped in individual sheets of freezer wrap. Whether you freeze fish whole or in portions, it should first be overwrapped in two plastic bags so that it does not contaminate the freezer with a fishy smell.

Smoked or oily fish freeze well, but they have a shorter freezer life – about two months. Raw or cooked shellfish also freeze well but they should not be kept in the freezer for more than a month.

It is preferable to cook all prepared fish from the frozen state. It takes a few minutes longer, but the flavour and texture are best this way.

FREEZING EGGS

Eggs are so readily available that there is little point in freezing them. Whole eggs in their shells expand and burst in the freezer, so, if you do have a glut, break them into a bowl and mix gently until well combined. Stir in 2 ml (½ teaspoon) salt or sugar to every 6 eggs and freeze in small lidded containers. This egg mixture will be useful for baking – 45 ml (3 tablespoons) is equivalent to 1 large egg.

You can also separate whites and yolks; freeze whites in a lidded container as they are, but add a pinch of salt or sugar to the beaten egg yolks before freezing – 15 ml (1 tablespoon) yolk and 30 ml (2 tablespoons) white equal 1 large egg.

Eggs can be frozen for up to 10 months. Never freeze cooked or stale eggs.

FREEZING POULTRY AND GAME BIRDS

Poultry and game birds freeze very well, but to save money do not buy them for the freezer at Christmas time, when the festive demand has pushed up the price.

Buy whole chickens and cut them into portions yourself. Even taking into account the wastage on a whole bird (wing tips for instance), it is still cheaper to buy chickens whole and portion them yourself than to buy ready-cut pieces.

If, however, you want to save time, buy ready-cut portions for freezing. They have a shorter freezer life and are more liable to 'freezer burn' (white spots on the surface) than a whole chicken because of the number of cut surfaces. They do cook more quickly, however, particularly portions of boned chicken breasts, which can be flash-fried in butter in a matter of minutes.

To pack fresh poultry or game birds, pluck* and bleed them, and cool as quickly as possible in a bowl of ice. Draw*, wash and hang them to dry, then refrigerate for 24 hours. Joint or leave them whole, then pack them, keeping giblets separate as they have a shorter freezer life. Put the whole birds or portions into plastic bags, expel all air, then seal, label and freeze.

The coverings of ready-frozen bought packs of chicken should be checked for tears and, if necessary, the packs should be overwrapped in a new plastic bag.

Although it is technically possible to roast chicken from the frozen state, it is not advisable to do so. There have been many instances of people suffering food

FREEZING FRUIT

Fruit	Preparation and packaging
Apples	Peel, core and slice, dropping slices into cold water with lemon juice or vinegar added. Blanch* for 1-2 minutes, cool in iced water. Drain well. Open-freeze* or sugar freeze*. Pack in plastic bags or rigid containers, leaving 1 cm headspace. *Purée:* prepare as for slices. Stew in a minimum of water, add sugar to taste. Cook until soft and beat to a smooth pulp. Cool before packing in rigid containers, leaving 1 cm headspace.
Apricots	Plunge into boiling water for 30 seconds and peel. Remove stones and halve or slice. Freeze in a medium sugar syrup* and add 1 ml (¼ teaspoon) ascorbic acid or 30 ml (2 tablespoons) lemon juice to each 500 ml (2 cups) syrup. Pack in rigid containers, leaving 1 cm headspace.
Boysenberries, loganberries, mulberries, raspberries, strawberries and youngberries	Open-freeze* or sugar-freeze*. Pack in plastic bags or rigid containers. *Purée:* Press through a nylon sieve and sweeten to taste with castor sugar. Pack in rigid containers. Use for fools and mousses.
Cape gooseberries	Wash and dry. Open-freeze* until firm and pack or cover with sugar syrup* in rigid containers, leaving 1 cm headspace. *Purée:* stew in a minimum of water, pass through a nylon sieve and sweeten to taste. Cool and freeze in rigid containers. Use for sauces and fools.
Grapefruit	Peel, removing all pith. Divide into segments and sugar-freeze*: layer the sugar and segments in rigid containers. Alternatively, freeze in heavy sugar syrup*. Pack in rigid containers, leaving 1 cm headspace.
Greengages	Wash in cold water, halve and remove stones. Pack as for apricots.
Lemons	Open-freeze* slices or grated rind until firm then pack into plastic bags. Alternatively, cover with sugar syrup*, or freeze squeezed juice.
Melons	Cut in half and remove seeds. Cut flesh into cubes or balls. Freeze in sugar syrup*. Pack in rigid containers, leaving 1 cm headspace.
Oranges	Freeze and pack segments as for grapefruit; freeze juice and rind as for lemon. Seville oranges can be frozen whole in plastic bags. Use thawed for marmalade, allowing extra fruit to counterbalance loss of pectin. (See Using frozen fruit in marmalade*)
Peaches	Peel and stone peaches, cut in half or slice; brush immediately with lemon juice to prevent discoloration. Freeze and pack in sugar syrup* as for apricots. Alternatively, sugar-freeze*, or purée peeled and stoned peaches, add 15 ml (1 tablespoon) lemon juice and 125 g sugar to each 500 g prepared fruit. Pack in rigid containers.
Pineapple	Peel and cut into slices or chunks. Pack in rigid containers, separating with non-stick paper or a double thickness of cellophane. Sugar-freeze* or freeze in sugar syrup*, including any pineapple juice from the preparation. Pack in rigid containers, leaving 1 cm headspace. Mix crushed pineapple with sugar, allowing 125 g castor sugar to 375 g prepared fruit; pack in rigid containers.
Plums	Wash, halve and remove stones. Freeze as for apricots.
Rhubarb	Wash, trim and cut into 2 cm lengths. Open-freeze* until firm and pack in plastic bags, or blanch* for 1 minute, drain and cool. Sugar-freeze* and pack in plastic bags. Do not use aluminium containers for packing. Alternatively, freeze in a heavy sugar syrup*. Pack in rigid containers, leaving 1 cm headspace. *Purée:* stew in a little water, sweeten to taste and press through a nylon sieve; cool and pack in rigid containers, leaving 1 cm headspace.

poisoning from undercooked chicken roasted in this way, and it is almost impossible to tell whether or not a frozen bird has been cooked right through. What is more, you could turn a plump, moist chicken into a tough bird as the outside will invariably be overcooked long before the inside is thawed.

Chicken portions can be cooked straight from the freezer, but make sure that they are cooked right through. Ideally, thaw chicken and game birds in the refrigerator overnight; you will then have minimal loss of liquid and maximum flavour.

FREEZING BAKED GOODS

Baked cakes, biscuits, pies, pastries, pizzas, scones and bread all freeze well. Cakes in particular need extra-careful handling when packing for the freezer. The best way is to lift the cake on to a metal baking tray and freeze it, uncovered, until quite hard; then lift it off the tray and pack it in a plastic bag, excluding as much air as possible before sealing. Small cakes and pastries can be frozen in the same way.

Fragile pastry shells can be baked and frozen for a short time if filled with crumpled paper towels, then packed carefully in a lidded container so that the shells are not crushed.

Protect the tops of pies with an inverted paper or aluminium pie plate when freezing. Freeze pizzas flat until solid, then stack, interleaving each one with a square of plastic and overwrapping the batch.

FREEZING UNBAKED GOODS

Bread, creamed cakes and fruit cakes (not whisked sponges) can be frozen before baking. However, they are best baked first, then frozen, as the raising agent tends to lose some of its effectiveness in the freezer.

Sausage rolls, pies, pizzas, pastries and quiches are ideal for freezing unbaked, as are slabs of raw shortcrust, flaky or puff pastry dough.

The easiest way to keep unbaked pastry in the freezer is to roll it out to the size or shape required, fill it if preferred, and then open-freeze*. When firm, pack into a lidded container.

Discs of ready-rolled pastry for flan cases or pie toppings can be stacked with wax paper between the layers, then overwrapped and frozen.

Bake ready-shaped pastry straight from the freezer. Alternatively, thaw a disc of rolled pastry and press it into a flan case, then bake.

FREEZING COOKED DISHES

Most prepared meat, fish and vegetable dishes can be successfully frozen, and if treated carefully they will taste as good, if not better, once re-heated. To ensure the best possible flavour for pre-cooked dishes, follow these few simple guidelines.

FREEZING VEGETABLES

Vegetables	Preparation and packaging	Cooking
Artichokes (globe)	Remove coarse outer leaves and stalks; trim tops and stems or freeze hearts only. Wash in cold water, with lemon juice or vinegar added. Blanch* for 7 minutes in water, cool and drain. Pack in rigid containers.	Cook frozen in boiling salted water for 10 minutes, or until leaves are tender and easily removed.
Asparagus	Remove woody parts, cut into even lengths, and wash well. Grade into thick and thin stems. Blanch* thin stems for 2 minutes; thick ones for 4 minutes. Cool and drain. Pack in rigid containers, or wrap small bundles in wax paper or aluminium foil.	Cook frozen in boiling salted water for 5-8 minutes.
Baby marrows	Select young baby marrows. Wash, trim off ends and cut into 1 cm slices or leave whole. Blanch* for 1 minute (sliced) or 4 minutes (whole), cool and drain. Alternatively, sauté in a little butter, cool quickly. Pack in rigid containers, leaving 1 cm headspace.	Cook frozen in butter.
Beans (broad, green, runner)	Wash well. Shell broad, trim green and slice runner beans. Blanch* for 2 minutes, cool and pack in plastic bags.	Cook frozen in boiling salted water: whole beans and broad beans 7-8 minutes; sliced beans for 5 minutes.
Broccoli	Trim off woody parts and outer leaves. Wash in salted water; divide into small sprigs and grade in sizes. Blanch* for 3-5 minutes, cool and drain. Open-freeze* until firm. Pack in rigid containers.	Cook frozen in boiling salted water for 5-8 minutes.
Brussels sprouts	Choose small, compact sprouts. Remove outer leaves and wash thoroughly. Grade into sizes. Blanch* for 3 minutes, cool and drain. Open-freeze* until firm. Pack in plastic bags.	Cook frozen in boiling salted water for 8 minutes.
Cabbages (green and red)	Choose young, crisp cabbages. Wash thoroughly, shred finely, blanch* for 1 minute, cool and drain. Pack in plastic bags.	Cook frozen in boiling salted water for 4 minutes, or stir-fry for 2-3 minutes.
Carrots	Choose young carrots. Remove tops, wash and scrape, leave whole. Blanch* for 3 minutes, cool and drain. Open-freeze* until firm. Pack in plastic bags.	Cook frozen in boiling salted water for 8 minutes.
Cauliflower (storage time: 6 months)	Choose firm, compact, white cauliflower. Wash and break into florets. Blanch* for 3 minutes in water with lemon juice or vinegar added, cool and drain. Pack in plastic bags or in rigid containers.	Cook frozen in boiling salted water for 8-10 minutes.
Celery	Use crisp, young stalks; remove stem bases and leaves. Cut into 2,5 cm lengths. Blanch* for 2-3 minutes, cool and drain. Open-freeze* until firm. Pack in plastic bags.	Add to stews and casseroles while still frozen, 10 minutes before serving. Alternatively, cook in boiling salted water from frozen for 5-6 minutes. Drain and toss in butter or coat with cheese sauce.
Mealies	Freeze fresh, young mealies only. Remove husks and threads. Blanch* for 6-8 minutes, cool and dry. Open-freeze* until firm, then wrap or pack individually in wax paper or aluminium foil.	Cook frozen mealies in boiling salted water for 4-5 minutes, or until tender.

FREEZING VEGETABLES

Vegetables	Preparation and packaging	Cooking
Mushrooms (storage time: 3 months)	Wipe clean. Mushrooms more than 2,5 cm wide should be sliced. Sauté in butter, cool quickly and pack in rigid containers, leaving 1 cm headspace.	Cook frozen mushrooms in butter, or add to stews and casseroles.
Parsnips	Trim, peel and cut into quarters, or slice and dice. Blanch* for 2 minutes, cool and drain. Pack in plastic bags or rigid containers.	Cook frozen in boiling salted water for 5-10 minutes.
Peas	Shell young peas. Blanch* for 1 minute, shaking the basket to distribute heat evenly. Cool, drain and open-freeze* until firm. Pack in plastic bags.	Cook frozen in boiling salted water for 5-7 minutes.
Potatoes	Not entirely successful as they lose texture. Freeze small new potatoes whole. Blanch* for 4 minutes, cool, drain and pack in plastic bags. *Chips:* peel, wash and dry, cut into even-sized chips. Fry in deep fat for 3 minutes. Drain on paper towels and cool quickly. Pack in plastic bags. Mashed potato toppings on pies freeze well.	Cook frozen new potatoes in boiling salted water for 15 minutes. Thaw chips partially at room temperature for 30-60 minutes. Deep-fry for 3 minutes.
Spinach	Select young leaves, trim off stalks. Wash thoroughly and drain. Blanch* small quantities for 2 minutes. Cool and press out excess moisture. Pack in rigid containers, leaving 1 cm headspace.	Cook frozen spinach in melted butter for 7 minutes.
Tomatoes	Best frozen as purée or juice. *Purée:* skin, core and simmer in their own juice for 5 minutes, or until soft. Pass through a nylon sieve or liquidizer; cool and pack in rigid containers in quantities suitable for use. *Juice:* wash, quarter and core tomatoes. Simmer for 5-10 minutes. Press through a nylon sieve and add 5 ml (1 teaspoon) salt to every litre (4 cups) juice. Cool and pack in rigid containers.	Use frozen purée in sauces, soups and stews, or with pasta. Thaw juice in container in the refrigerator and serve chilled.
Turnips	Trim, peel and dice young turnips. Blanch* for 2½ minutes, cool and drain; pack in plastic bags. *Mashed:* cook until tender, drain and mash; freeze in rigid containers, leaving 1 cm headspace.	Cook frozen diced turnips in boiling salted water for 5-10 minutes. Heat mashed turnips in a double boiler with butter and seasoning.

Use seasonings sparingly during cooking, especially garlic and herbs; when re-heating, check and adjust the flavour if necessary.

Wine and alcohol can lose their flavour during freezing, so use half during cooking and add the remainder when re-heating.

The moisture content of dishes tends to reduce slightly during the freezing period, so add a little extra liquid when re-heating.

Undercook casseroles by about 20 minutes before freezing, as they will need additional cooking before they are served.

If you wish to freeze cooked dishes, cool them quickly by standing them in a bowl of iced water. Freeze as soon as they are cold.

Sauces, particularly cream sauces, may separate. Turn them into a pan and heat gently, whisking all the time, and they will become smooth again.

Always check that the middle of a dish of re-heated frozen food is piping hot before serving.

FREEZING FRUIT

Few fruits can be frozen whole and served 'fresh', so do not get carried away to the extent that you freeze everything and deny yourself the pleasure of eating really fresh fruit. Freeze fruit only when you find bargain produce in good condition.

During defrosting, the colour and texture of most fruit changes, but peeled and sliced or puréed fruit freezes well and can be used later for all sorts of dishes.

Freeze only fruit that is of top quality, and then not too much at a time. Overripe fruit can be made into purées, then used in mousses, ices, jellies or soufflés.

Peel, seed, slice or cut any fruit you do not want to freeze whole. Fruits that discolour should be dipped into a solution of lemon juice or ascorbic acid and water: 1 g or 3 ml (¾ teaspoon) ascorbic acid powder in 1 litre (4 cups) water.

Fruit can be frozen in several ways: open-frozen* raw without sugar or syrup; or in a dry sugar pack*; in sugar syrups* of various strengths; or stewed, puréed or juiced, with or without sugar.

Grated citrus peel freezes very well, as do slices of lemon, for use in drinks or as garnishes.

Most fruit will freeze well for six months or longer, but it is best used sooner.

FREEZING VEGETABLES

Vegetables, with the exception of some salad ingredients, are among the best produce to freeze – as long as they are harvested or bought and frozen when young and tender, and as soon as possible after picking.

Do not make the mistake of filling your freezer with things that no one wants to eat regularly. Vegetables that are well worth freezing are peas, beans, baby marrows, artichoke hearts, asparagus cuts for soup, corn on the cob, spinach, chopped tomatoes for sauces or stews, and blanched slices of pepper.

It is not necessary to blanch vegetables for the freezer if you intend to keep them there only for a day or two, but for longer periods spend a few minutes preparing them properly and they will freeze better.

Blanching* preserves the nutrients as well as the colour and texture of vegetables – this can be done quite quickly in boiling water, steam or oil.

Cook vegetables from the frozen state in a minimum of water or stock, or just heat them through in butter in a frying pan until tender. This way they keep all their flavour and texture.

Blanching vegetables for freezing Prepare them in the usual way, cutting if necessary. Bring a 5 litre pan of water to the boil and immerse 500 g vegetables into the water (best contained in a wire blanching basket). Allow two minutes for small vegetables and up to six minutes for larger items such as artichokes. Lift out, drain and plunge the vegetables into iced water for as long as they were blanched. Drain well, cool, pat dry, pack, seal, label and freeze at once.

Freezing Prepared and Pre-cooked Dishes

Food (storage time in brackets)	Method	Thawing and serving
Biscuits unbaked (6 months)	Shape dough into cylinders about 5 cm wide and wrap in aluminium foil or plastic. Shape soft mixtures on to a paper-lined tray, freeze, then pack carefully in rigid containers, separating layers with paper.	Slightly thaw rolls of uncooked dough, slice and bake. Shaped biscuits can be cooked from frozen state but will need 3-5 minutes more cooking time.
baked (2 months)	Pack as for shaped soft biscuits before freezing.	Cooked biscuits may be crisped in a warm oven after thawing.
Bread and rolls (4 weeks)	Wrap in plastic bags.	Thaw in wrapper at room temperature (3 hours for 750 g or overnight in refrigerator). May be thawed in oven at 150°C for about 30 minutes, but this causes it to go stale quickly. Sliced bread may be toasted or fried from frozen state.
Cakes (6 months – iced cakes lose quality after 2 months)	Use less essence and spice than usual. Fill cakes with cream, but not jam, before freezing. Wrap unfilled layer cakes separately or separate with wax paper or cellophane; pack in aluminium foil or plastic. Freeze iced cakes unwrapped until icing has set, then wrap in foil or cellophane and pack in boxes to protect icing.	Cream-filled cakes are best sliced while frozen. Unwrap iced cakes before thawing so that paper does not stick to icing. Leave plain cakes in wrapping and thaw at room temperature: allow 1-2 hours for plain layer cakes and small cakes; 4 hours for iced cakes.
Ice cream (home-made 3 months, commercial 1 month)	Wrap bought ice cream in moisture-proof bags; freeze home-made ice cream in moulds or waxed containers, and overwrap with plastic.	Place in refrigerator for 30 minutes to soften.
Meat dishes (2 months)	Cook for a slightly shorter time than usual to allow for re-heating. Do not season heavily. Make sure meat is completely immersed in gravy or sauce. It is better to add potatoes, rice, noodles, garlic and celery at time of serving. Pack in rigid foil containers; or freeze in foil-lined casserole, remove and pack in plastic bags.	Turn frozen food out of container into saucepan to re-heat. Pre-formed foil-lined dishes may be re-heated in oven in original casserole for 1 hour at 200°C reducing heat if necessary to 180°C for last 40 minutes.
Meat loaves, pâtés, terrines (1 month)	Make in usual way, taking care not to season or spice heavily. When cold, remove from tins or moulds and wrap in plastic to freeze.	Thaw in wrapping for 6-8 hours, or overnight in refrigerator.
Pancakes unfilled (2 months)	Stack pancakes between layers of grease-proof paper or cellophane, wrap conveniently sized stacks in aluminium foil or plastic.	Thaw in wrapping at room temperature for 2-3 hours, or overnight in refrigerator. To thaw quickly, unwrap, spread out pancakes and thaw at room temperature for about 20 minutes. Heat individual pancakes in a lightly greased frying pan for 30 seconds each side. Or heat stack of pancakes wrapped in foil in oven at 190°C for 20-30 minutes.
filled (1-2 months)	Choose fillings which are suitable for freezing. Do not season heavily. Pack filled pancakes in foil containers, seal and overwrap.	Remove overwrapping, place frozen pancakes in foil container, unopened, in oven at 200°C for about 30 minutes.
Pastry uncooked (3 months)	Make as usual and roll out to size required. Line foil plates or pie dishes, freeze unwrapped, remove from pie dishes if necessary and wrap in plastic. Roll out pastry lids and separate with wax paper before wrapping in plastic. Stack, separating the layers with two sheets of wax paper, place on cardboard and wrap. Single or double crust fruit pies may be frozen uncooked with the filling in place, ready for baking. Do not make slits in the top crust before freezing. Wrap in aluminium foil or plastic bags when frozen solid.	Return pie shells to original dishes. Thaw pastry lids at room temperature before fitting on filled pies. Pie cases can be baked frozen (oven-proof glassware should be left to stand at room temperature for 10 minutes before baking). Add 5 minutes to baking time. Place unwrapped fruit pies in oven at 200°C for 40-60 minutes. Slit tops of crusts when beginning to thaw.
cooked (pastry cases and fruit pies 6 months; meat pies 3 months)	Bake pies in foil containers and cool quickly. Wrap in aluminium foil or plastic. Tops may be protected with an inverted foil dish before wrapping.	Thaw at room temperature; pies for 2-4 hours. Re-heat in oven.
Pizzas unbaked (3 months)	Prepare to baking stage. Wrap in aluminium foil or plastic. Freeze and overwrap.	Remove wrapping and place frozen pizza in cold oven set at 230°C, bake for 30-35 minutes.
baked (2 months)	Wrap in aluminium foil or plastic and freeze as for unbaked pizza.	Remove wrapping. Heat in oven at 180°C for 15 minutes.

SAFETY IN THE KITCHEN

The kitchen is potentially the most dangerous room in the house. Although toddlers and the elderly are most vulnerable, anyone can be the victim of a serious kitchen accident.

The safest kitchen layout is one that has the sink, working top and stove in an unbroken line, and at the same time eliminates the potential danger of spillage from hot pans. Stoves should be sited in a draught-free area, never under a window or near an inward-opening door. A heat-resistant working surface on one or both sides of the stove-plates gives a safe resting place for hot pots and dishes.

Keep wall-hung cupboards away from the area above the stove, as it is so tempting to lean over the stove to reach for something on a shelf above – a practice which can easily lead to burns.

All shelves should be easily accessible without having to climb on a chair. Ideally, they should be far enough off the floor to prevent dust and dirt from accumulating under them.

Many accidents are caused by poor lighting. Working surfaces, storage areas, the stove, sinks and even floors should be brightly lit.

Floors should be level and preferably have a non-slip surface. Always mop up spills immediately, particularly oil or grease, which, apart from being messy, can be dangerously slippery.

Young children are best kept out of the kitchen, but this is not always possible. It is essential, however, to insist that they sit or play away from the working area in a spot where they can be watched.

Keep pan handles turned towards the back of the stove so that they can not be pulled off, and keep plastic bags, bleaches, oven cleaners and all household poisons out of reach, preferably locked away.

Sharp knives and trailing flex are other great temptations to toddlers, so keep them well out of reach. Rounded corners on working surfaces and tables reduce the risk of bruising, and tables without cloths help to prevent boisterous children from pulling hot food over themselves.

Wires and plugs should be checked regularly to see that they have not been dangerously damaged. Always read manufacturers' instructions when using electrical gadgets, and have the gadgets serviced regularly.

If you smell gas, do not on any account look for the leak with a lighted match. Check all pilot lights – if they are working but the smell persists, switch off the gas at the mains and call in an expert.

Fire is a major hazard in kitchens, so keep a small fire-extinguisher in an easily accessible place. If pans of fat or grill pans catch alight, never try to extinguish them with water. Smother small flames with a handful of salt and larger flames with a lid or a large, damp cloth. Aerosol cans will explode if they get too hot, so always keep them in a cool place.

Keep a first aid kit in the kitchen for emergencies.

Basic Kitchen Utensils

There is practically no limit to the number of different kitchen utensils you can buy, but the following list should provide a good basic supply.

KNIVES

The most important tools in a kitchen are undoubtedly knives. To begin a collection, buy these three shapes:
French or cook's knife This has a wide, tapering, triangular blade of high-carbon stainless steel. When buying, hold it to see that it is properly weighted and check that its blade is wide and rather heavy near the handle but tapers to a triangle at the point. This is an ideal shape for cutting, slicing and chopping.
Slicing knife This has a fairly thin, supple blade and a round or pointed end. It is used to cut meat, poultry and so on, from paper-thin slivers to thick slices.
Peeling knife This has a small, triangular blade a bit like a miniature cook's knife.

There are many other shapes and sizes that can be added to these basics, for example, a boning knife, a bread knife with a serrated edge, a ham knife and a cleaver. Your choice will depend on the type of cooking and preparation you do.

Good knives need a wooden chopping board with a bit of 'give'. If you use knives on a plastic or laminated working surface, they will soon be ruined.

SAUCEPANS

These are available in a multitude of types, shapes, sizes and colours. You will probably find that no particular type suits every need, and that instead of a set you will choose various types of pans.

Heavy-gauge aluminium pans are reliable and are good conductors of heat. They are light-weight, easy to clean and hard-wearing, and should last a lifetime. Do not leave food to stand too long in aluminium, as the metal can react badly with the food.

Enamelled cast-iron pans are often more attractive and make good 'oven-to-table' ware. Do not drop them, as they chip or even break. Sometimes the enamelled interior becomes stained – if this happens, soak the pan overnight in a solution of biological washing powder. They are not ideal for sauces, which tend to stick.

Stainless steel is elegant, good-looking in a clinical way, easy to clean, light and popular. The edges on some pans get hotter than the centre, which means care must be taken that the edges do not scorch.

French chefs swear by copper pans, which, although they look good, are not very practical. The brass handles get very hot and the tin lining wears badly – this lining has to be replaced regularly, so that the copper underneath does not react with the foods being cooked.

Non-stick saucepans will not last a lifetime, but they do greatly simplify cooking. Remember never to use metal implements in them to stir or whisk, as this will damage the non-stick surface.

CASSEROLES AND ROASTING TINS

Cast-iron enamelled ware looks most attractive, but the less expensive temperature-resistant glassware is really more practical as you can use it in the freezer, on top of the stove, in the oven, or in a microwave cooker.

Roasting and baking tins should be solid enough not to buckle. When setting up a kitchen, the following starter collection will be useful: a meat-roasting tin, a quiche tin with loose base, and, depending on how much use you will get out of them, a selection of bread and cake tins.

MISCELLANEA

Other useful items for your kitchen are: a good-quality balloon whisk, a small electric hand-whisk, a kitchen fork or two, a fish slice or egg-lifter, a variety of kitchen spoons, a spatula, a pair of tongs for frying and braaing, scissors, a potato peeler, a grater, a pepper mill, a garlic press, a sieve, a colander or salad basket/spinner, kitchen scales, a calibrated measuring jug, a set of measuring spoons, a tin/bottle opener, a rolling pin, mixing bowls, a kettle and a toaster.

Beyond Basics

PRESSURE COOKERS

Pressure cookers cut cooking time drastically – they will cook a stew in 20-30 minutes and soups in less than 10 minutes, as well as speeding up more delicate dishes such as baked custards, fish and vegetables.

The latest models do not hiss while cooking, and are better designed and easier to handle than the early versions. There are several types to choose from, but it is important to look for one with a high, domed lid and three different pressure options, as this gives you the most versatile performance. More expensive models have timers and fitted baskets and trays.

Remember that the variety of food that can be prepared in a pressure cooker does not end with the manufacturer's instruction leaflet. Many other recipes can be adapted to make the most of your pressure cooker in summer and winter.

There are two basic points to remember when using a pressure cooker: use a liquid that will give off steam,

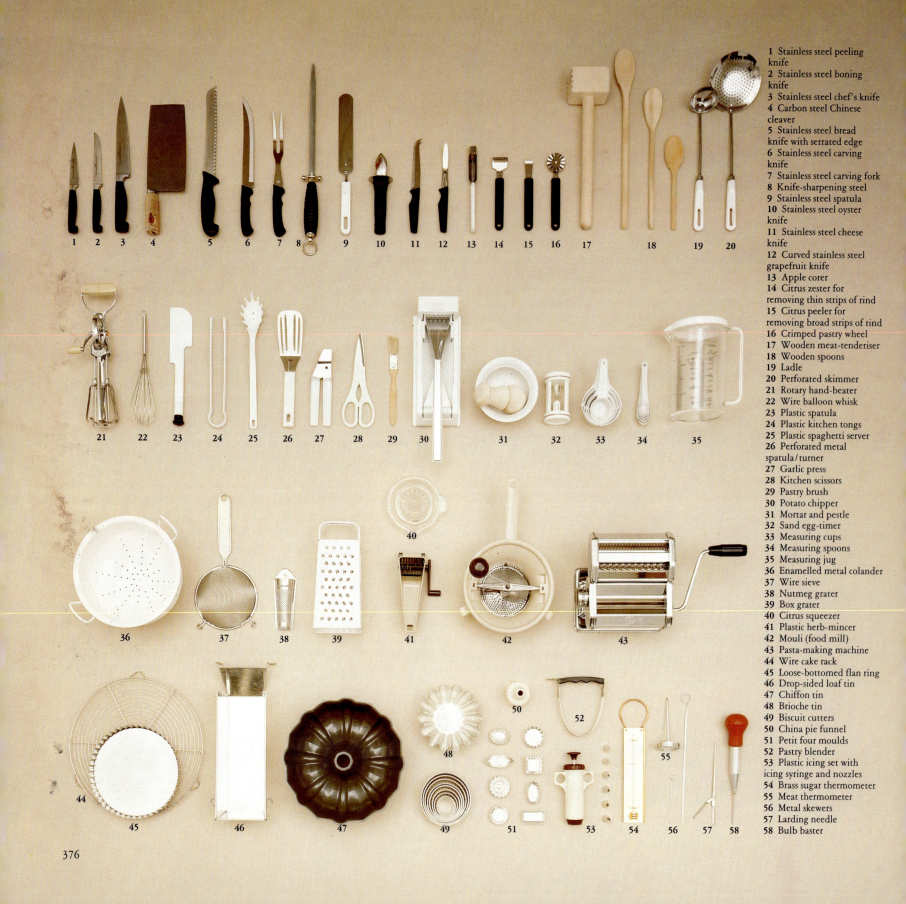

such as water, milk, stock or wine, but do not use fat or oil only; and remember not to fill the cooker more than two-thirds full of solids or half full of soup, milk pudding, stew or fruit mixtures.

CLAY POTS

Modern meat or chicken bricks and terracotta cooking pots are sophisticated versions of an ancient cooking method which supposedly originated among North American Indians. They wrapped raw food, fish, game or sweet corn in wet clay, put it in the fire and left it there until the clay was baked. It was then cracked open and the feathers or skin pulled off with the clay.

Nowadays specially designed pots for cooking chicken, meat, fish or vegetables are available. They give food a golden succulence without mess. The pot is usually soaked in water before use. This ensures that the moisture is retained in the food, and, as a result, little fat or liquid has to be added during cooking.

WOKS

Woks are bowl-shaped steel pans that are used traditionally for Chinese cooking.

You can braise, fry, poach, boil or steam all kinds of food in a wok. The sides of the pan get as hot as the bottom, so food is cooked very quickly at very high temperatures. This seals in flavour and retains the crispiness, vitamins and colour that are inevitably lost with prolonged cooking.

There are many types of wok, but the basic, cheap, steel models produce the best results because they can be brought to the very high temperature needed for wok cooking. Non-stick and electric models often cannot reach this temperature and, although they are safer and much easier to keep clean, they do not produce a fully authentic result.

Woks need to be used over a high and easily variable heat, so gas is by far the best fuel for this type of cooking. If you cook with electricity, look for a wok with a flat bottom: heat the electric plate or ring to high before starting, then control the temperature by sliding the wok on and off the heat.

Supports for woks with round bases are sometimes supplied with the pan, but they can be difficult to use. It is advisable not to leave the pan on the support without holding the pan with one hand.

FOOD PROCESSORS

More compact and lighter than most freestanding electric mixers, food processors are popular because they are simple to operate and take much of the hard work out of food preparation.

They usually consist of revolving steel cutters in an enclosed plastic bowl with a funnel leading into it through which extra ingredients can be added.

Plastic blades and special steel discs are often part of the basic unit, or can be bought separately, for mixing, rubbing in, creaming, grating, shredding or cutting.

Some processors have a motor unit on which a chopping unit, mixing bowl or blender goblet can be fixed. Most food processors work at either one or two speeds, and some also have a 'burst' or 'pulse' position, which switches the motor on in short, sharp bursts.

Food processors are highly versatile machines and very quick. At the flick of a switch they can cope with cake mixes, bread doughs, pastries, soups, batters, pâtés, minced meats and soups.

The knives, cutters, discs and bowl are quick and easy to change and wash, and some manufacturers make a storage rack as an optional extra.

Food processors cannot mix large quantities at a time, but they work so fast that it is no trouble to process two or three batches of the same mixture one after the other. They do not whisk egg whites or cream quite as efficiently as a mixer, and cakes tend to have a slightly closer texture if you over-process them by as much as a second. They do, on the other hand, speed up all the long and tedious chopping, slicing and grating jobs.

LIQUIDIZERS (BLENDERS)

Liquidizers – or blenders as they are also called – vary in power, price and design. Some models are part of a bigger mixer, others are freestanding, but in both cases stainless-steel, motor-driven cutters are enclosed in a goblet of glass or plastic, usually marked off in pints or litres, with a lip and handle for easy pouring.

A lid fits on top of the goblet, and some models have a removable central cap in the lid so that you can add extra ingredients while the motor is switched on. Larger models often have removable blades, which make them easier to wash and dry.

The smaller goblet blenders have a capacity of about 500 ml (2 cups), and the larger ones hold about 1 litre (4 cups) and can cope with bigger, drier mixes.

Liquidizers will purée fruit, vegetables, baby foods, soups and drinks at the flick of a switch. Many will also chop vegetables and fresh herbs, grind nuts and biscuits, make breadcrumbs, and mix fish and meat pâtés. Many cooks even use them to make mayonnaise.

Be sure to give your full concentration to the task whenever you use a liquidizer. Put the cap on tightly and remember not to prod food inside the goblet while the machine is switched on. *Never* put your fingers inside the goblet once it is attached to the motor.

It is best to only half-fill a liquidizer, in order to save overloading the motor. For the same reason it is best to run them for no more than a minute at a time, then switch off for a short rest. If the machine labours, the mixture may be too dry, so add a little more liquid if possible or push the food further down on to the blades with the handle of a wooden spoon.

Always cut or break food into small cubes or slices before feeding it into the goblet, as this stops the blades jamming, thereby causing the motor to burn out.

MIXERS

Electric mixers, whether hand-held or attached to a bowl that sits on the working surface, take much of the hard work out of baking and food preparation. Freestanding mixers have very powerful motors with up to 12 speed-variations. They can tackle a wide range of mixing, beating and whisking tasks and will cope with large quantities of heavy mixtures.

Most machines are sold with beaters and a whisk, and sometimes a dough hook. Extra attachments may include slicers, shredders, mincers, blenders, graters, peelers, bean-slicers, pea-shellers, tin-openers, pasta-makers, cream-makers, juice-extractors, separators, fruit-presses, coffee-grinders, knife-sharpeners or sieves. Handmixers do not have this range of extra available attachments, but they do have the advantage of being more portable.

The rechargeable type that runs off batteries can be used anywhere, but even electric models are light enough to be used wherever there is a plug.

Electric mixers will quickly and efficiently cope with all sorts of tedious beating, whisking and whipping jobs that take much longer by hand, and some can be bought with a liquidizer attachment.

COFFEE GRINDERS

The choice between electric and hand grinders is purely a personal one, as there is little difference in price. Grinding beans with a hand machine is fairly hard work, but such machines do have an attractive appearance. Electric grinders are quite noisy but will grind coffee beans effortlessly in seconds.

Some electric grinders can also be used for grinding small quantities of nuts and breadcrumbs, and for grinding ordinary sugar into castor sugar.

There are many types of electric coffee grinders on the market offering various facilities, such as an adjustment switch for the degree of fineness needed or a storage compartment for the beans. Some are operated by a press button or switch, while on others the motor is automatically started when the lid is put in place.

ELECTRIC FRYING PANS

These useful kitchen appliances look like large, square saucepans with legs, and have elements underneath and domed lids with air vents. Single people, young or old, can use them in place of a stove, and even large families will find them useful, energy-saving appliances that look attractive enough to use near the table.

An electric frying pan will hold cooked food at a set temperature without drying it out, until you are ready to serve it. Without the lid the pan can be used for frying, stir-frying or deep-fat frying. With the lid it becomes a small, self-contained oven which can be used for roast meats, roast potatoes, stews, casseroles, baked cakes and toasted sandwiches.

You can even take it outdoors with an extension cable to cook summer brunches.

There are two basic points to remember: always pre-heat the frying pan before use, and always remove the temperature control before washing.

Thermostats vary, so follow the manufacturer's instruction book initially and then, when you are used to the pan, alter the temperature to suit your style of cooking. Some models are available with non-stick lining, which make them even easier to use and clean.

SLOW-COOKERS

Slow-cookers – or electric casseroles, as they are also called – offer controlled, gentle cooking at far less cost than a conventional oven.

These appliances are ideal for people who are out all day because there is no risk that the casserole will boil dry. Even if you are delayed by several hours, food is kept hot without drying out. When entertaining there need be no last-minute problems such as food being spoilt if guests are late. A slow-cooker is perfect for a buffet or supper party because it keeps food piping hot.

Although slow-cookers do not save time, they do save fuel costs, avoid vitamin loss and evaporation, cut down shrinkage, bring out the flavour of food, and tenderise more economical cuts of meat.

The cooker stands on the working surface and can be plugged into any 15-amp power socket. An integral heating element ensures gentle, even heat which cuts out the need for stirring.

Some models have a removable inner casserole which can be placed under the grill or in the oven for browning. It can also be used as a serving dish, which means less washing up afterwards.

On most slow-cookers the control is by a high or low switch – low for cooking up to 12 hours, high for up to six hours. Some models automatically switch from high to low when the correct working temperature has been reached. Whichever temperature you select, it will be high enough to destroy harmful bacteria and maintain the correct heat throughout cooking.

Slow-cookers are ideal for winter foods such as soups, stews, preserves and puddings, but are just as useful in warmer weather for stuffed vegetables, vegetable stews, spaghetti sauces, savoury rice or curry.

All cooking, with the exception of yoghurt-making, is done with the lid on. The condensation forms a liquid seal, which prevents evaporation.

Choose a model that is large enough for your needs and the type of dishes you plan to cook. A large-capacity model is ideal when bulk-cooking for the freezer; a deep model is needed to take a pudding basin or a whole chicken.

Read the manufacturer's instructions before using and check whether pre-heating on high is advised. Always leave 2-3cm between food and the lid, and make sure that a basin or bowl used inside the pot does not touch the sides of the cooker.

Do not use a slow-cooker to re-heat frozen or refrigerated foods – they need a higher temperature to make sure that all bacteria are killed.

DEEP-FAT FRYERS

The advantage of an electric deep-fat fryer is that it is safer to use than a chip pan filled with oil. The thermostatic control makes sure that the oil is heated to exactly the right temperature. The result is crispy, golden food and very little smell or mess.

Many models have a replaceable filter in the lid to reduce smells even further, an important factor if your kitchen is close to your eating area. The built-in element heats the oil quickly and safely, saving time and energy.

Electric deep-fat fryers are available in a variety of different sizes, but it is best to choose the right capacity model for your needs. They range from 1,7 litre to 4 litre capacity.

The baskets in some can be lowered into the oil and raised again while the lid is in place, which cuts out splashing and smell. Others have a 'viewer' which lets you see the cooking food without lifting the lid.

Deep-fat fryers are also obtainable with non-stick interiors and timers. Some can be used as large saucepans for boiling or preserving.

If you like fried foods it is worth having a fryer, but follow a few sensible rules to prevent accidents. Never fill the pan more than two-thirds full of oil, and do not leave it unattended. Always heat the oil very gently, and never let it reach the point of hazing or smoking.

Do not overcrowd the pan during frying, as this lowers the temperature and makes food fatty and soggy. The aim of deep-frying is to seal food into a crisp coating so that all the flavour is captured within.

OVENS

There are many different types of oven available. Free-standing models have some advantages over built-in, split-level ones: you usually get more features for your money in a smaller space, and you can take them with you more easily when you move. On the other hand built-in, split-level stoves look neater, and having an oven at a more convenient height is an advantage.

Smaller, table-top ovens are very portable, as they operate off an ordinary 15-amp socket and are relatively cheap to run. Some have grills, and some are big enough to take a large turkey or up to six sponge sandwich cakes. The only drawback is that you need a separate hob or ring for frying and simmering.

Conventional electric ovens usually have two heating elements: one at each side of the base, or one in the roof and one in the base. Gas ovens have burners at the back of the base. In all such ovens the middle heats up to the temperature you select, while the top gets slightly hotter. Fan ovens, however, give a uniform heat throughout, which means that the bottom and top shelves cook at the same temperature all the time.

The choice between a conventional electric oven or a fan oven depends on the type of cooking you do. If you normally use the oven to cook two or more dishes at a time, a conventional oven would probably be more suitable because the variation in heat from the top to the bottom of the oven allows you to cook dishes at the same time that need different cooking temperatures.

If, however, you want to do a lot of batch cooking, a fan oven is a great asset. You get a greater cooking capacity because you can fill all the shelves with, for example, sponge cakes or pizzas, and they should all cook at about the same rate. This means you do not have to switch trays from shelf to shelf.

Another bonus with a fan oven is that you can reduce cooking time by about 10 minutes per hour and use a slightly lower (10-40°C) temperature setting, thus cutting running costs. Fuel consumption is also less than for a conventional oven because fan ovens need no pre-heating (except for very sensitive dishes such as soufflés); in addition they are usually cleaner to use, and it is possible to open the door of a fan oven without disturbing the contents.

When you are deciding what is best for your needs, look at ceramic hobs, which give a clean look because of the entirely flat stove-top. They do take a little getting used to after radiant rings and you may have to buy new pans with a thicker base, as thinner-bottomed ones may buckle. Ceramic hobs sometimes take longer to heat up, and some cook more slowly than radiant rings, but they are easy to clean, using the special preparations supplied by most manufacturers.

Rotisseries cook joints of meat and poultry more quickly and cleanly than conventional roasting, and are worth having if you roast meat regularly.

Auto-timers are standard equipment on many stoves these days, and pan thermostats, which keep a pan and its contents at a set temperature automatically, are also available.

Ovens with non-stick or self-cleaning interiors are a great asset, as are doors that open in the right direction and stay open without being held, then shut again firmly and securely.

MICROWAVE OVENS

Microwave cooking is fast, economical and clean. Microwaves are electro-magnetic waves of very short length and high frequency. They are absorbed by the moisture molecules in food, which vibrate, causing the food to heat up and cook.

Microwaves are reflected off metals, preventing them from reaching the food, but pass through materials such as glass, pottery, wood, paper and most plastics. Even the basic microwave cookers save on washing up because you can cook food in the serving dishes.

Microwave ovens cook food from the inside out: thinner, less dense food cooks fastest, and the more food you put into the oven the longer it takes to cook.

The microwave oven is one of the safest appliances in the kitchen. Both the oven and cooking containers remain cool, so there is little danger of burning yourself, and the microwaves are retained in the oven. With the various safety catches built into the doors, there is no chance of the energy being switched on when the door is open.

There is a wide variety of microwave ovens available, from small, simple models with just an on/off switch and one power setting, to larger ovens with several power settings, rotating turntables, defrost controls, temperature probes, and conventional browning elements fitted into the roof of the oven. Others offer both microwave and conventional cooking facilities in one.

When you are comparing models before buying, check the price against features offered. Remember that microwave ovens may be much bigger externally than they seem in a large showroom: measure the space you have available and note the position of the vents. If they are at the back you cannot push the oven against a wall; if they are at the top the oven must not be squeezed under a shelf.

Make sure that the door opens the way you find most convenient, and that the internal dimensions are big enough to take the food you plan to cook.

You will find that fish and vegetables are particularly easy to cook in a microwave oven. Some dishes, such as Yorkshire pudding and choux pastry, are not successful, nor are tougher cuts of braising or stewing meat, which do not have sufficient cooking time in a microwave to become tender.

Irregularly shaped joints and pieces of food should be boned or tied into neat shapes to get the best results, and if you prefer a browner finish to meat, first seal it by browning it in a pan, or brush with a seasoning mixture before cooking.

For pies and pastries, brush with a little diluted yellow food colouring or sprinkle with brown sugar. Cakes and tarts can be iced or piped with cream to cover the pale colour.

DISHWASHERS

There is nothing like a dishwasher to take the drudgery out of washing up. It does a better job than a pair of hands, giving a hotter, more thorough wash and more efficient drying.

For a family, buy the biggest machine you can afford as children seem to create large quantities of dirty dishes. Obviously a couple will not want as big a model, unless they do a lot of entertaining. There are machines for 6, 10, 12 or 14 table settings. They vary in height from ones that slide under the work surface to slightly taller models.

Most have a variety of washing cycles, rinses and plate-warming settings, but a normal wash (whether the machine takes hot or cold water) is usually about 1½ hours.

Some dishwashers are easier to load than others, and some have a salt dispenser which helps give the glass and cutlery an added sparkle in hard-water areas.

When you choose a dishwasher make sure that the filters and the soap and salt dispenser are easy to get at and operate.

Look for a model with simple controls and well-designed racks that take a variety of large and small items.

Check the number of programmes: while you do not often need a vast number, it is useful to have a rinse-and-hold facility so that you can rinse off loose dirt from dishes which must wait until the machine is full for their proper wash. A programme for glasses and one for lightly soiled items is useful too. Economy programmes will save electricity and time.

Check after-sale service arrangements before you buy; and make sure that the plumbing and drainage in your kitchen will take the extra load and that the water pressure is high enough for the machine to function efficiently.

REFRIGERATORS

Refrigerators are long-life kitchen appliances – having few moving parts they are far less likely to go wrong than a washing machine or dishwasher – so it is important to think carefully about your future needs as well as your present ones.

Size is obviously a key factor, and refrigerators offer more choice in this respect than most other appliances. Look for an arrangement of shelf and door storage that suits the items you will want to store, and decide whether you wish to spend money on such extra features as automatic defrosting or iced-drink dispensing.

Bear in mind that if you already own a freezer you can make do with a 'larder' fridge, that is, one with minimal (if any) frozen food storage space.

If you are buying only a refrigerator and hope to add a freezer later, look at models which stack one above the other. In this way you can plan your kitchen knowing that you will not need more floor space once you can afford the freezer.

FREEZERS

Freezers come in three basic types: the chest, the upright, and the kind that is combined with a refrigerator. Some have quick-freeze switches, thermostatic temperature settings, and warning and interior lights. Some are finished with a stove-enamelled exterior, others with acrylic enamel or laminate. Interior finishes include enamelled steel, stainless steel, aluminium and occasionally plastic.

In general, freezers vary in capacity from about 100 litres to about 600 litres. As a rough guide, 10 kg frozen food takes up 25 litres of space. When choosing a freezer, bear in mind that a large one does not cost twice as much as a small one, but that it is uneconomical to run a half-empty freezer. For a family of four, a good size to consider is a 270 litre freezer.

It is not imperative that you keep your freezer in the kitchen; site it anywhere that is cool and dry, with a convenient electric socket and a floor strong enough to take the weight. Here is a guide to the three basic types:

Chest freezers are usually the cheapest to buy and run, and need defrosting less frequently than other models. Although they would seem to invite frozen fingers and slipped discs (you have to lean down into them and often burrow to find packets at the bottom), they are worth considering if you plan to shop in bulk. They take large parcels with little wastage of space and, if packed carefully, they hold more per litre capacity than an upright freezer.

Choose a model with a counterbalanced lid so that it will not fall on your head, and buy a variety of small baskets and containers, as the larger ones can be rather heavy to lift out.

Upright freezers look like wardrobes and may have either one or two doors. They take up less floor space than chest freezers, and the shelves inside make storage easier. Some have shelves in the door and some have pull-out drawers instead of shelves.

A front-opening freezer can be more expensive to run than a chest, as cold air 'falls out' of the cabinet every time the door is opened. The solution is to open the door as little as possible and to shut it again fast.

If space is a problem you can buy a table-top freezer, but they tend to be more expensive than larger models.

Refrigerator freezers have the two appliances built together, running off one socket outlet. They are convenient to use, being so close together, but often the freezer section is the upper half of the cabinet with the refrigerator down below, whereas it is more sensible to have them the other way round to reduce bending.

Glossary

A

à la grecque In the Greek style. Vegetables, particularly mushrooms and artichokes, cooked in olive oil and/or stock, with coriander seeds and other seasonings, and served cold.

al dente The phrase refers to the texture of food, particularly pasta, which is properly cooked but still firm to the bite.

anoint To smear over oil or an oily liquid.

antipasto Italian starters, which often consist of marinated vegetables and seafoods and slices of salami or other cold meats.

arrowroot A starch made from the root of a plant of the same name. It is used to thicken sauces.

aspic A clear jelly made from the cooking juices of meat, poultry or fish. It is used to coat or mould cold food, as a garnish or as a salad.

atjar A Malay condiment of blended fruit and spices, similar to chutney but containing chunks of whole fruit.

au gratin A method of finishing a cooked dish by covering it with sauce, and sprinkling over breadcrumbs and/or grated cheese, then browning it under the grill or in the oven.

avocado ritz An hors d'oeuvre usually consisting of half a raw avocado, filled with a cooked shellfish mixture.

B

bain-marie A large pan of hot water in which a smaller pan or other container is placed for cooking food or keeping it warm. It can also refer to a double boiler: a two-part saucepan with a top pan fitted to a lower one that holds simmering water.

bake blind To bake a pastry case without its filling.

bard To wrap lean meat, game or poultry with strips of pork fat or fatty bacon to prevent the flesh from drying out during cooking.

baste To spoon juices over food during cooking to prevent it from drying out.

bean curd A soft-textured curd, also known as tofu, made from curdled soya milk which, in turn, is made from puréed soya beans and water. It is often used in Chinese and Japanese cooking.

beat Mixing food to introduce air, to make it lighter and fluffier, using a wooden spoon, hand whisk or electric mixer.

beurre manié (kneaded butter) Flour and butter worked to a paste, used to thicken soups, sauces and stews.

beurre noir A sauce for fish or brains made by frying butter until dark brown (not black) and adding parsley, vinegar, capers and seasoning.

beurre noisette A sauce of melted butter, cooked until nut-brown, and seasoned.

bind To add egg, fat or liquid to a mixture, such as a pâté, rissole or stuffing mixture, to hold it together.

biriani An Indian dish of meat, fish or chicken with rice, lentils, eggs and spices.

blanch To immerse food briefly in boiling water in order to soften it (for example, vegetables); to skin it (as with tomatoes or nuts); to rid it of excess salt or very strong flavours; or to kill enzymes before freezing.

blanquette A white stew, made of veal, poultry or rabbit, with a creamy sauce.

blatjang See chutney.

blend To combine ingredients with a spoon, beater, food processor or blender to achieve a uniform mixture.

blini A pancake made of buckwheat flour and served with caviar and sour cream.

blood heat Food at this temperature (37°C) feels lukewarm to the touch.

boil Cooking in liquid at boiling point, that is the temperature at which the liquid evaporates when bubbling.

bouchée A small puff pastry case, baked blind and filled with a savoury or sweet filling.

bouillie French for pulp or porridge, also used to describe the thick sauce which forms the base of a soufflé.

bouquet garni A small bunch of herbs (often consisting of thyme, parsley, marjoram and a bay leaf) tied together with string or placed in a small muslin bag. It is used to flavour soups and stews and is discarded before serving.

braise To cook food slowly, covered, in a minimum of liquid after it has been browned in fat.

bredie A Malay stew of meat and vegetables, subtly spiced and cooked slowly in a minimum of liquid.

brine A salt-water solution used for pickling and preserving meat, fish or vegetables.

brioche Soft bread made of a rich yeast dough that has been slightly sweetened.

brown Searing the outer surface of meat to seal in the juices. Also used to refer to cooking other foods until they are brown.

brûlé(e) Applied to dishes such as cream custards that are finished with a caramelised sugar glaze.

buttermilk A sourish liquid left over from churned cream when butter is being produced.

C

canapé An appetiser made of biscuits or small slices of fresh, fried or toasted bread topped with a savoury mixture.

cannelloni Large pasta tubes stuffed with savoury fillings.

capers The pickled flower buds of the Mediterranean caper bush, used in sauces and as a garnish.

caramelise To heat sugar until it turns brown and syrupy.

casserole A cooking pot with a lid, made of oven-proof material. It also refers to a slow-cooked stew of meat, poultry, fish and/or vegetables.

challah Bread, usually plaited, traditionally eaten on the Jewish sabbath.

chill Cooling food, without freezing it, in a refrigerator.

chutney An Indian relish, cooked or uncooked, of fruits or vegetables and spices, served with curries or other foods.

cinnamon sugar Sugar flavoured by the addition of ground cinnamon: use 5-10 ml (1-2 teaspoons) for every 250 ml (1 cup) sugar.

clarified butter Butter that has been cleared of impurities or sediment by melting and straining.

clarify To clear fat by heating and filtering. Alternatively, clearing consommés and jellies with beaten egg white or broken eggshell.

cocotte A small oven-proof dish used for baking individual mousses, soufflés or egg dishes.

coddle To cook food, particularly eggs, slowly in simmering water.

colander A perforated metal or plastic basket used for draining away liquid.

compote Fresh or dried fruit cooked in syrup, often flavoured with spices such as cloves or cinnamon.

conserve Whole fruit preserved by boiling in sugar. It is used like jam.

coral Orange shellfish roe.

court-bouillon Liquid used for poaching fish, made from water and wine or vinegar, flavoured with herbs and vegetables.

crackling Crisp skin of pork obtained by frying, rendering or roasting.

cream To work together a mixture such as fat and sugar with a wooden spoon until light and fluffy, like whipped cream.

crème fraîche Cream that has been allowed to mature but not sour.

crêpe A thin pancake.

croquette Cooked food, such as chopped meat, fish, chicken or vegetables, moulded in an oval or cork shape, dipped in egg and crumbs, and deep-fried.

croûtons Small cubes of fried bread used to garnish soups and dishes that have sauces.

crudité Raw vegetables or fruit, served as an appetiser or snack, often with sauces for dipping the food.

GLOSSARY

cuisine minceur The phrase, meaning 'slimming cookery', was coined by the French chef Michel Guérard, whose imaginative cooking concentrated on the lightness, freshness and simplicity of foods to cut down kilojoules.

curd The semi-solid part of curdled milk. Lemon curd is lemon rind and juice cooked with sugar, eggs and butter to a spreading consistency.

curdle To cause fresh milk or a sauce or other liquid to separate into solids and liquids by overheating or by adding acid (such as lemon juice or vinegar). Alternatively, to cause creamed butter and sugar in a cake recipe to separate by adding the eggs too rapidly.

cure To preserve meat or fish by drying, smoking or salting.

D

Danish 'caviar' Lumpfish roe.

dariole A small round or oval mould, or the food made in it; usually puddings, pastries or pâtés.

deep-fry To fry food by immersing it in hot fat or oil.

deglaze To scrape browned, solidified cooking juices off the bottom of a roasting or frying pan with the help of a liquid such as wine, stock, cream or brandy.

demerara A soft brown sugar produced in the West Indies and nearby countries.

devil To prepare meat, fish or poultry with sharp, hot seasonings before grilling or roasting.

dice To cut into small cubes.

dough A mixture of flour, water, milk and/or egg, sometimes enriched with fat, which is firm enough to knead, roll and shape.

draw To disembowel.

dredge To coat food lightly with flour, icing sugar or other fine powders.

dress To pluck, draw and truss poultry or game birds. Alternatively, to pour salad dressing over a salad.

dripping Fat that runs from meat or poultry during roasting, or animal fat rendered down.

drizzle To moisten with droplets of, say, oil.

dumplings Small balls of dough, stuffing or vegetable mixture, which are steamed or poached. They are used to garnish soups and stews. The term also refers to fruit encased in dough and baked.

dust To sprinkle flour, sugar, spice or seasoning lightly over food.

E

éclair A light, oblong of choux pastry split lengthways and filled with cream, usually topped with chocolate icing.

en croûte Food encased in pastry.

escalope A thin slice of meat, usually veal, which is beaten flat and shallow-fried, often after being coated with breadcrumbs.

F

fines herbes A mixture of finely chopped fresh herbs: parsley, chervil, tarragon and chives.

flake Separating cooked fish into individual flaky slivers. Alternatively, grating chocolate or cheese into small slivers.

flambé Flamed, for example food tossed in a pan to which burning brandy or other alcohol is added.

flan An open pie or tart filled with fruit or a savoury mixture.

florentine Of fish and eggs: served on a bed of buttered spinach and coated with a cheese sauce. Alternatively, a thin biscuit made of nuts, glacé fruit and chocolate.

fluff To fluff with a fork, as for cooked rice: lift the rice lightly with the fork and toss to separate the grains.

fold in To envelop one mixture or ingredient into another with a metal spoon or spatula, so that air does not escape. Cut through the mixture with the spoon or spatula, slide it along the bottom of the bowl, then lift and turn the mixture over the ingredient to be folded in. Continue until blended.

fondue A Swiss dish of melted cheese with Kirsch and white wine, into which cubes of bread are dipped at the table. Also a number of other preparations in which morsels of food are impaled on forks and then cooked at the table in a pot of oil, stock, wine or other liquid (kept hot on a portable burner). The food may then be dipped in a variety of sauces.

fool An English cold dessert made of fruit purée folded into whipped cream or custard.

freeze Solidifying or preserving food by storing it in a freezer at a temperature of 0°C or less.

French dressing A mixture of oil, vinegar (or lemon juice), salt and pepper, sometimes flavoured with herbs and garlic. (Also known as vinaigrette.)

fricassee A white stew of chicken, veal or rabbit and vegetables, first fried in butter and cooked in stock, then completed with cream and egg yolks.

frikkadels, fricadelles Meatballs made of minced meat, fresh breadcrumbs and seasonings, then poached in stock or shallow-fried.

fritto-misto Italian for 'mixed fry', it may consist of meat and vegetables, coated with batter and deep-fried; or of sliced chicken breast, brains, sweetbreads, artichokes and mozzarella (alla Fiorentina); fried seafood (di mare); or sliced brinjals, baby marrows and mozzarella (di verdure).

frost To coat a cake with an icing made of icing sugar. Alternatively, to dip the rim of a glass in egg white, then in castor sugar (or salt), and chill until set. Fruit is also frosted with egg white and sugar.

fry, deep See deep-frying.

frying pan A long-handled, shallow pan used for frying food.

fry, shallow See shallow-frying.

G

galantine A dish of boned and stuffed poultry, game or meat glazed with aspic and served cold.

game chips Thin rounds of potato, fried until very crisp. Often served with roast venison and game birds.

garam masala A mixture of hot spices and herbs lightly sprinkled over Indian food at the end of cooking.

garnish To enhance a dish with edible decorations.

ghee Clarified butter used in Indian cooking.

giblets Edible internal organs of poultry and game birds, including the liver, heart, gizzard and neck.

glaze A glossy finish given to food by coating it with beaten egg, milk, sugar syrup or aspic after cooking.

gnocchi Small dumplings made from semolina, potato, spinach or choux pastry.

gratin The French term for a crust.

H

halaal, halal Food that is prepared according to Muslim dietery laws.

hang To suspend meat or game birds from hooks for a period to tenderise and mature the flesh.

haricot A variety of green bean or the dried seed of this plant.

hash A fried dish consisting of chopped meat, potatoes and other vegetables.

hoisin sauce A thick, soy-based barbecue-type sauce used in Chinese cooking.

hors d'oeuvre Hot or cold appetisers served at the beginning of a meal.

hull To remove the green leafy cup (calyx) and stalk from berries.

I

infuse To extract flavour through immersion and soaking in hot water (such as spices, herbs or tea): the resulting liquid is called an infusion.

J

joint A prime cut of meat for roasting. Alternatively the word means to divide meat, poultry or game into individual pieces.

jugged Meat or fish dishes stewed in a covered pot.

julienne Thin, straw-like strips of vegetables, often used as a garnish or in clear soup.

junket A sweet dessert made from flavoured milk which has been set with rennet.

K

kebab Meat cubes marinated and grilled on a skewer. Also refers to fish, poultry, fruit and/or vegetables prepared in the same way.

kichel A thin, sweet biscuit, usually spread with a savoury mixture, eaten on the Jewish sabbath and other holidays.

kitke A plaited loaf of bread that is traditionally eaten on the Jewish sabbath. Also known as challah.

kneaded butter See beurre manié.

kosher Food prepared in accordance with Orthodox Jewish dietary laws.

GLOSSARY

L

lard To thread strips of fat (lardons) through lean meat, using a special larding needle, to prevent it from becoming too dry during roasting.

lardons Strips of fat threaded through lean meat to keep it moist during roasting (see lard). Anchovies are also sometimes used as lardons.

legumes Vegetables from plants with seed pods, such as beans and peas.

lentils The small seeds of a legume. They are used in soups, stews, curries, purées and salads.

liaison A thickening for sauce or soup, for example egg yolk and oil in mayonnaise, or a starch such as flour or cornflour in a sauce.

M

macedoine A mixture of cubed fruit or vegetables, cooked or raw.

macerate To soften food by steeping it in liquid.

marinade A blend of oil, wine or vinegar, herbs and spices used to tenderise and flavour meat, poultry or fish. Other ingredients are often added or substituted.

marinate To soak foods in liquid to make them more tender or to flavour or preserve them. See marinade.

marinière Of mussels: cooked in white wine and herbs, and served on the half shell. Of fish: cooked in white wine and garnished with mussels.

Marsala A sweet Italian wine drunk as an apéritif or used in cooking.

masala A mixture of spices and herbs used in curries.

mask To cover food with sauce.

meringue Whisked egg white and sugar, which is spooned or piped on top of sweet pies or into shapes and baked at a low temperature until crisp.

meunière A French term meaning 'in the style of the miller's wife'. It refers to fish coated in flour, fried in butter, and served with melted butter and a sprinkling of parsley and lemon juice.

molasses Uncrystallised syrup drained from crude, unrefined sugar.

mornay A cheese sauce used to coat fish, egg or vegetable dishes.

moules French for mussels.

mousse A smooth sweet or savoury mixture, enriched with cream, lightened with beaten egg whites, and, if necessary, stiffened with gelatin.

mull To heat and spice or flavour wine or ale.

mushrooms, dried Chinese Dehydrated mushrooms used in Chinese cooking.

N

noodles Flat ribbon pasta, made from flour, water and egg.

nouvelle cuisine A 'new' style of French cooking with the emphasis on simplicity, the ultimate freshness of ingredients and shorter cooking times. This imaginative, lighter, flourless cuisine rejects the richer aspects of traditional French cookery. The chef supervises the artistic arrangement of food on beautiful plates, which leave the kitchen under large silver covers.

O

offal Edible internal organs of animals.

P

paella A Spanish dish of saffron rice, chicken and shellfish, which is named after the shallow round pan in which it is cooked.

panada A thick sauce made with flour or bread which is used to bind ingredients (for example when making fish croquettes).

parboil Partially cooking food by boiling it for a short while.

parfait A frozen dessert made from eggs and cream and/or ice cream, with fruit.

pasta A paste made of flour and water, sometimes with eggs or other ingredients added, from which macaroni, spaghetti and other Italian noodles are made.

pasteurise A method of sterilising milk by heating it to 60-82°C to destroy bacteria.

pastry Dough made from flour, fat and water (sometimes with other ingredients), which is baked or deep-fried until crisp.

pâté A savoury mixture of finely chopped meat, game or poultry which is baked in a casserole or terrine, with or without a pastry case, and served cold. The name is also used for some mixtures that are not baked, such as fish pâtés.

patty A small, flat, round or oval cake of food, such as a potato cake or fish cake, which is served hot. Alternatively, a flat, individual pie which is served hot or cold.

pearl barley De-husked barley grains used in soups.

pectin A substance in some fruits and vegetables which causes jams and jellies to set. It is extracted for use with fruits or vegetables which have very little pectin.

petit four A tiny sponge cake, iced and decorated; small fruits coated in a sugar glaze; marzipan coloured and shaped to resemble miniature fruits and vegetables; and other small, sweet items.

petit pois Tiny, young, green peas.

pickle To preserve meat or vegetables in brine or vinegar mixtures. The pickled food is also known as a pickle.

pimento Sweet green or red peppers. Alternatively the spice called allspice.

pipe To force cream, meringue, icing, savoury butter, mashed potato or other pastes through a forcing bag fitted with a nozzle to decorate various dishes.

piquant Pleasantly sharp and appetising.

pistou The French Mediterranean pistou, similar to the Italian pesta, is a sauce made of garlic, basil, tomato and cheese. It may be served on spaghetti, or added to vegetable soup.

pith The white fibrous part of citrus peel, situated under the rind.

pluck To remove the feathers from poultry or game birds. It also means offal.

poach To cook gently by immersing food in simmering liquid.

pot-roast To cook food in steam, raised on a rack above a small amount of liquid in a covered pot.

praline Hot, caramelised sugar and browned almonds mixed together and left to set into a brittle sheet, which is then pounded in a mortar or broken into pieces for use as a flavouring.

preserve To keep food in good condition by treating it with chemicals, heat, refrigeration, pickling in salt or vinegar or boiling in sugar. It also refers to pieces of fruit suspended in a sugar syrup.

prove Causing dough to rise in a warm place before baking.

provencale In the Provence style, cooked with garlic and tomatoes.

pudding A baked or boiled sweet dessert. Alternatively, a boiled suet crust filled with meat or poultry.

pulp The soft, fleshy tissue of fruit or vegetables. Alternatively, to reduce food to a soft mass by crushing or boiling.

purée Raw or cooked food crushed to a very smooth texture by passing it through a sieve or blending in a blender or food processor. Alternatively, thick vegetable soup which is passed through a sieve or blended.

Q

quenelles Light, savoury dumplings made of meat or fish and used as a garnish or in a delicate sauce.

quiche An open tart with a savoury filling based on an egg and milk or cream custard.

R

ramekin A small baking dish for individual servings. Alternatively, a small pastry case with a cream cheese filling.

red tide This phenomenon, in which orange-coloured patches appear in the sea, is caused by the proliferation of microscopic plants known as phytoplankton. Sometimes these organisms multiply to such an extent that they cause the death of large numbers of fish. Red tide can also be fatal to people: a particular type of phytoplankton causes white or black mussels to become deadly poisonous without showing any signs of change. Although not all red tides are dangerous, it is wise not to take a chance.

reduce To concentrate or thicken a liquid by rapid boiling. To 'reduce by half' means to boil until half the liquid has evaporated.

refresh To freshen food, such as boiled or blanched vegetables, by placing it under cold running water.

relish A sharp or spicy sauce made with fruit or vegetables which adds a piquant flavour to other foods.

render To melt animal fat slowly to a liquid. It is then strained to eliminate any residue.

rennet A substance extracted from calves' stomachs and used to coagulate milk in cheese-making (also for making junket).

rice paper Edible, glossy white paper made from the pith of a tree grown in China. It is used in making sweets and other confections.

rigatoni Ribbed pasta.

rind The coloured, outer oily skin of citrus fruit which, when grated or thinly peeled, is used as a flavouring.

risotto Italian savoury rice, fried and then cooked in stock or tomato juice, with or without other ingredients added.

rissole A small roll or patty made of minced meat, sometimes with rice or vegetables, usually bound together with egg, then fried.

roast To cook in the oven with radiant heat, or on a spit over or under an open flame.

roe Milt of the male fish, called soft roe; eggs of the female fish, called hard roe; or shellfish roe, called coral because of its colour.

rotisserie A rotating spit used for roasting or grilling meat or poultry.

roulade A roll of meat, vegetables, chocolate cake, soufflé omelette or pastry.

roux Melted fat (usually butter) and flour mixed together and cooked to form the basis for savoury sauces.

rub in To mix flour or other dry ingredients with fat (usually butter) using the fingertips to give a crumbly rather than a smooth result.

S

saddle The undivided loin from a meat carcass.

salami Spiced Italian pork sausage, which is sold fresh, smoked or cooked.

saltpetre The chemical potassium nitrate, which is used in tiny amounts as a preservative in curing meat.

sambals Side dishes served with Indian or Malay dishes.

sauté Frying food rapidly in a small amount of fat until it is evenly browned, shaking the pan to toss and turn the contents. The food is either just browned or cooked through.

savoury rice The term refers to a number of different rice dishes, particularly risottos, or rice flavoured with fried onion, tomato and green pepper, or other ingredients. Commercially packaged savoury rice is also available.

scald To heat liquid, usually milk, to just below boiling point, until bubbles form around the edge of the pan. The word is sometimes used as an alternative to blanch.

schnitzel A slice of veal, often coated with crumbs before being cooked. See escalope.

score To make shallow cuts, preferably with a heavy knife, over the surface of fish or meat, such as steak, to tenderise it or to allow better penetration of heat.

sear To brown meat rapidly with fierce heat to seal in the juices.

seasoned flour Flour flavoured with salt and pepper.

seasoning Salt, pepper, spices or herbs, which are added to food to improve flavour.

shallow-frying To cook food in a little fat in a shallow pan.

shrip To shred vegetables by cutting thin shavings from them.

sift To pass flour or sugar through a sieve to remove lumps.

simmer To cook in liquid which is just below boiling point, with only a faint ripple showing on the surface.

skewer A metal or wooden pin used to hold meat, poultry or fish in shape during cooking, or to hold small pieces of food together during cooking.

skim To remove cream from the surface of milk, or fat or scum from broth, stews or jam.

slake Adding water (or other liquid) to a powder, such as lime or cornflour.

smetena, sour(ed) cream A commercially prepared product made from half cream and half skim milk which has been cultured sour (therefore lower in kilojoules than cream). A home-made substitute can be made by adding 30 ml (2 tablespoons) buttermilk to 125 ml (½ cup) skim milk and 125 ml (½ cup) cream. Keep at room temperature for 4-6 hours, then store in the refrigerator.

smoke To cure food, such as bacon or fish, by exposing it to wood smoke.

sorbet Water ice made with fruit juice or purée.

soufflé A baked sweet or savoury dish thickened with egg yolks and whipped egg whites.

soufflé dish A straight-sided circular dish used for cooking and serving soufflés.

souse To pickle food in brine or vinegar (for example, soused herring).

spit A revolving skewer or metal rod on which meat, poultry or game is roasted over a fire or under a grill.

starch Carbohydrate obtained from potatoes or cereals.

steam To cook food in the steam rising from boiling water.

steep To soak in liquid until saturated, or to remove an ingredient such as salt.

sterilise To destroy germs by exposing food to heat.

stir To mix with a circular movement, using a fork or spoon.

stir-fry A method of cooking favoured by the Chinese, in which finely chopped food is quickly stirred and tossed in a little oil over a high heat.

stock Liquid that has absorbed the flavour of the fish, meat, poultry and/or vegetables cooked in it.

strain To separate liquids from solids by passing them through a metal or nylon sieve or through muslin.

strudel Thin leaves of pastry dough, filled with fruit, nuts or savoury mixtures, which are rolled and baked.

stuffing A savoury mixture of bread or rice, herbs, fruit or minced meat, which is used to fill cavities in poultry, fish, meat or vegetables.

suet Fat around beef or lamb kidneys.

sweat To soften vegetables, particularly onions, by cooking them gently, covered, so that they release their juices but do not brown.

syrup A thick, sweet liquid made by boiling sugar with water and/or fruit juice.

T

tagliatelle Thin, flat egg noodles.

terrine An earthenware pot used for cooking and serving pâté. It also refers to the food cooked in the pot.

thickening A preparation such as flour, butter, egg yolk or cream used to thicken and bind sauces and soups.

truss To tie a bird or joint of meat in a neat shape with skewers and/or string before cooking.

tube pan A ring-shaped tin for baking cakes.

twist A thin sliver of lemon or lime rind, twisted and added to a drink.

U

unleavened bread Bread made without a raising agent which, when baked, is thin, flat and round.

V

vanilla sugar Sugar flavoured with vanilla by enclosing it with a vanilla pod in a closed jar.

velouté A basic white sauce made with chicken, veal or fish stock. It also describes a creamy soup.

vermicelli Very fine strands of pasta.

vinaigrette A mixture of oil, vinegar (or lemon juice), salt and pepper, sometimes flavoured with herbs and garlic.

vinegar A clear liquid, consisting mainly of acetic acid, that has been obtained through the fermentation of red or white wine, cider or malt beer.

vlek To open out an uncooked fish by cutting up along the backbone and through the head, leaving the entire spine attached to one side; the fish is then folded open like a book.

W

whey The watery liquid that separates out when milk or cream curdles.

whip To beat eggs until frothy; or cream until thick.

Y

yeast Fungus cells (*Saccharomyces cerevisiae*) used to produce alcohol fermentation or to cause dough to rise. Available fresh – in the form of a putty-like block, or dried – in the form of granules.

yoghurt Curdled milk which has been treated with harmless bacteria.

Z

zest The coloured, outer oily skin of citrus fruit which, when grated or thinly peeled, is used as a flavouring. It is also referred to as the rind.

Index

Page numbers in italics indicate that there is a photograph of the subject; page numbers in bold type indicate that the entry is to be found in the glossary.

A

À la grecque **380**
Abalone *see* Perlemoen
Accompaniments
  to fondues 105
  to Indian dishes 136
  to Malay dishes 101
Acid (testing for) 321
Advokaat (cocktail) 364
After-dinner drinks 364
Aïoli 176
Alaska, baked banana 279
Alcohol, cooking with 109
Alcohol in freezing 373
Al dente **380**
Alfalfa 187
Alikreukel 57
Allspice *130*
All-the-year-round
  jam 327
  marmalade 328
Almond(s) 257
  recipes:
    biscuits *314*
    broccoli with 192
    chicken breasts with apricots and 140
    chicken with (var.) 133
    sugared 326
    trout with 71
Amadumbe 186
Ambrosia skewers (braaied) *163*
American barbecue lamb chops 154
American cheesecake *263*
Anchovy *recipes:*
  and egg and onion starter (var.) 23
  and potato bake (var.) 66
  butter 179
  fingers 21
  stuffing for eggs 239
  tuna baked with garlic and 67
Andalusian soup (gazpacho) *44*
Angel fish 55
Angelica, candied 340

Aniseed 130
Anoint **380**
Antipasto(s) *31*, **380**
Apéritifs 357
Apple(s) 256
  freezing 371
  recipes:
    and raisin stuffing 178
    baked stuffed 273
    Chinese toffee 266
    crumble 264
    date and walnut chutney 334
    jelly (var.) 328
    open roast chicken with 146
    pie 258
    rum-soaked, with roast goose 145
    sambal 101
    sauce 170
    strudel 258
    tarte aux pommes 259
Applemint 199
Apricot(s) 256
  freezing 371
  recipes:
    blatjang 335
    chicken breasts with almonds and 140
    chutney 335
    dried, wrapped in bacon 21
    jam, dried (var.) 326
    jam, fresh 326
    mebos 339
    pilaff with lamb and 223
    sauce 286
    sherry sauce 286
    stuffing 179
    yoghurt tart 270
Arnold Bennett, omelette 239
Arrowroot **380**
  sauces thickened with 167
Artichoke(s), globe 186
  freezing 372
  preparing and serving 189
  recipes:
    with Spanish chicken (var.) 146
Artichoke(s), Jerusalem 186
  braised 195
  soup 43
Asafoetida 130
  in haricot bean curry 209
Asparagus 186
  freezing 372

  preparing and serving 188
  recipes:
    and eggs 244
    in cheese sauce 188
    pancakes 234
    quiche 242
    soufflé 240
    soup, creamed 45
Aspic *37*, **380**
  salmon in, with Malay dressing 64
Atjar **380**
  mango *335*
Aubergine *see* Brinjal
Au gratin **380**
Auto-timers 378
Avgolemono 40
Avocado(s) 184
  recipes:
    dip 28
    dressing 178
    making the most of 16
    ritz **380**
    sauce 170
    sauce, yellowtail with 70
    soup 44
Ayam kuning (yellow chicken) *221*

B

Baba au rhum *313*
Baby marrow(s) 184
  freezing 372
  recipes:
    in cheese sauce 188
    salad 188
Bacon 82
  and eggs with baked sausages 236
  and leek with baked potato 203
  and sausage fondue 104
  and spinach salad, hot *18*
  chicken livers (or prunes or dried apricots) wrapped in 21
  mixed grill 85
Bagels 300
Bain-marie **380**
Baji aur inda (spinach egg scramble) 233
Baked(-ing)
  blind 249, **380**
  breads, cakes and biscuits 290 (*see also* Bread(s); Cake(s); Biscuits)
  freezing baked goods 372
  recipes:
    banana Alaska 279
    beans and pork 120
    chicken and potatoes 146
    custard 253
    devilled eggs 244
    eggs in saucers 245
    fish, whole 62
    fish with tomato and onion sauce 61
    meat in golden pastry parcels 112
    onions 200
    potatoes 203
    prawns with garlic butter 72
    sausages with bacon and eggs 236
    stuffed apples 273
    stuffed fish, whole 65
    tuna with anchovies and garlic 67
Bakewell tart *258*
Bamboo shoot 184
Banana(s) 255
  and yoghurt flan 271

  baked Alaska 279
  braaied, in their skins 163
  fritters 266
  loaf 313
  split 280
Bantam eggs 229
Barbecue *see* Braai(-ed/-ing)
Barbecue sauce 170
Barbecue spare ribs 157
Barbel 59
Bard 84, **380**
Barley
  and brisket soup *41*
  chicken with mushrooms and 147
Barley, pearl **382**
Barnacles *see* Limpets
Basic brown sauce 166
Basic butter biscuits 316
  painting *316*
Basic butter cake 307
Basic glacé icing 295
Basic stock 36
Basil 199
Bass 59
Baste **380**
Batter(s) 254
  how to make a basic 254
Bay leaves *131*, 198
Beachcomber (cocktail) 362
Beans(s) 187
  curd **380**
  freezing 372
  storage 368
  recipes:
    baked, and pork 120
    broad, with butter 190
    butter, with tomato 208
    curry 209
    green, bredie 94
    green, provencale 176
    green, with herbs 190
    haricot, curry 209
    haricot of mutton 101
    matar aur baïgan sakh (vegetable casserole) 190
    soup 50
    sousboontjies 208
Bearnaise sauce 170
Beat **380**
Béchamel sauce 166
Beef 82 (*see also* Steak)
  braaing 151

INDEX

buying 82
carving 86, 87
cooking methods 83
cooking times 85
cuts 83
cuts for braaing 151
serving hints 353
stews 86 (see also Casseroles and stews)
uses for cuts 83
recipes:
and noodles 121
and tomato pie 91
bobotie 114
braaied whole fillet 156
bubble and squeak 192
burgers, braised, with vegetables 121
chow mein 219
corned 89
cornish pasties 91
fillet of, in brioche *112*
fondue bourguignonne *104*
frikkadels 114
giema curry 102
hamburgers (braaied) 156
hashed, with tomatoes 120
kheema kebabs *103*
loaf 89
olives *90*
pot-au-feu 86
pot-roast brisket with prunes 88
pot-roast of 85
roast, and Yorkshire pudding 88
saltimbocca alla Romana *93*
satay sapi pedes (hot beef satay) *221*
smoke roasted 69
stew with parsley dumplings *121*
stir-fried, with oyster-flavoured sauce *91*
stroganoff 89
Beef sausage(s)
smoke roasting 69
Beetroot 186
borsch (soup) *43*
salad 191
sweet and sour 191
Bel paese cheese 230
Bergamot 199
Berries 256
Between the sheets (cocktail) 362
Beurre manié (kneaded butter) **380**
Beurre noir 168, **380**
Beurre noisette 168, **380**
Bhaji masoor ni dhal 208
Biltong 119
Bind **380**
Binding sauce 167
Birds, game *see* Poultry and game birds
Biriani **380**
chicken 137

mutton 101
Birthday cake *310*
Birthday parties for children 348
Birthday parties, twenty-first 349
Biscuit(s) 294, 314
freezing 374
icing 294
making 294
painting 316
recipes:
almond *314*
basic butter *316*
boerebeskuit 315
Boston brownies *314*
buttermilk rusks *315*
chocolate chip cookies *317*
crunchies *317*
ginger snaps *317*
muesli *316*
oblietjies *316*
shortbread *317*
soetkoekies, old-fashioned *315*
Biscuit crumb crust 252
Blaauwkrantz cheese 230
Black Forest cake *306*
Black mussels, grilled 24
Black Russian (cocktail) *362*
Blacktail 55
Blanch(-ing) **380**
nuts 324
vegetables 184, 373
Blancmange 281
Blanquette **380**
Blanquette de veau 92
Blatjang *see* Chutney
Blend **380**
Blenders 377
Blini **380**
with caviar *22*
Blintzes, smoked salmon 24
Blood heat **380**
Bloody Mary (cocktail) *362*
Blue cheese or Roquefort dressing 178
Blue cheese soufflé filling 240
Bobotie *114*
fish *64*
Boeboer, Malay vermicelli *358*
Boerebeskuit 315
Boerewors 118
smoke roasting 69
Boerpampoen *see* Pumpkin
Boil(-ed/-ing) **380**
meat 85
mutton 86
salad dressing 176
sugar (rules for boiling) 325
vegetables 184
Bolognese sauce, spaghetti with *217*
Bombe, triple chocolate *279*
Boned(-ing)
chicken *128*

fish 54, 58
poultry 124
stuffed, chicken *128*
Borage 198
Borsch *43*
Boston brownies *314*
Bouchée **380**
Bouillie **380**
Bouquet garni 199, **380**
Bourekitas, cheese 240
Bow ties *262*
Boysenberries, freezing 371
Braai, evening menu 346
Braai(-ed/-ing)
choosing the meat for 151
fish 152
in foil 152
marinades 153
meat and poultry 152
step-by-step guide to 150
suitable cuts for 151
traditional pot cooking 153
recipes:
ambrosia skewers *163*
American barbecue lamb chops *154*
bananas in their skins *163*
barbecue spare ribs *157*
butterflied leg of lamb *155*
crayfish *161*
devilled kidney skewers *154*
fish in newspaper *160*
hamburgers *156*
herbed chicken *156*
husaini kebabs *159*
Indonesian lamb kebabs *159*
kofta kebabs *158*
mixed vegetables in foil *162*
mushrooms on skewers *161*
mussels on skewers *160*
onions baked in coals *161*
pork satay kebabs *158*
potatoes baked in coals *162*
prawns teriyaki *161*
salt ribs *159*
sosaties *154*
spicy chicken kebabs *159*
T-bone steak *156*
trout parcels *157*
whole beef fillet *156*
whole marinated fish *157*
whole mealies or sweetcorn *162*
yellowtail cubes with citrus marinade *160*
Brains 117
buying and preparing 83
Braised(-ing) 85, **380**
cuts suitable for 83
recipes:
beefburgers with vegetables *121*
chicken, Malay *134*
chicken with sweet potato and pumpkin *147*

guinea fowl 144
Jerusalem artichokes 195
lamb with spinach *120*
vegetables 184
Brandied honey creams *278*
Brandy butter 286
Brandy pudding, Cape *264*
Brandy sauce 286
Brandy snaps *303*
Brawn 86, 116
Brazil-nut 257
Bread 290
baking 292
bridge rolls 291
freezing 374
French loaf 291, *296*
garlic or herb 292
ingredients for 290
kneading 291
knocking back 291
Melba toast 292
mixing the dough 291
plaited loaf *296*
rising or proving 291
rolls 291
rolls, freezing 374
round loaf 291
shaping 291
split tin loaf 291
storing surplus dough 291
Vienna loaf 291
recipes:
and butter pudding *264*
and butter pudding, savoury *244*
bagels *300*
banana loaf *313*
brioches *300*
brown *296*
chapati *136*
croissants *301*
crusty white *296*
date and walnut loaf *312*
hot cross buns *301*
mealie *298*
milk *296*
mosbolletjies *304*
oatmeal *297*
pitta *158*, *298*
pizza *304*
puri *305*
rye *298*
sandwiches and school lunches *298*
sauce 171
scones *305*
soda *296*
wholewheat *297*
with dried fruit *299*
Breakfast
English 236
party menus 344
wedding 350

Bream *see* Kurper
Bredie(s) 94, **380**
green bean *94*
pumpkin *94*
tomato *95*
waterblommetjie *95*
Brie cheese 230
Brine(-ing) **380**
for pickles 323
preserving meat in 89
Brinjal(s) 186
storage 368
recipes:
à la grecque *189*
and chicken and noodle casserole *146*
dip *28*
matar aur baïgan sakh (vegetable casserole) *190*
parmigiana (var.) *191*
pastitsio (var.) *216*
sambal goreng terung (peppery brinjal) *221*
spaghetti Napolitana with (var.) *218*
spiced *188*
stuffed *189*
pastitsio (var.) *216*
Brioche *300*, **380**
fillet of beef in *112*
Brisket *recipes:*
and barley soup *41*
pot-roast, with prunes *88*
Broad beans 184, 187
with butter *190*
Broccoli 184
freezing 372
recipes:
alla parmigiana *191*
soup (var: cauliflower) *45*
with almonds *192*
Broth, Scotch 40
Brown **380**
Brown stock 36
Brownies, Boston *314*
Brûlée **380**
crème *281*
fresh fruit *274*
Brunch – party menus 344
Brussels sprouts 186
freezing 372
Bubble and squeak *192*
Buckwheat pancakes (blini) with caviar *22*
Buffet 348
menus 348
wedding reception *350*
Bukettraube 354
Bulk-buying 370
Buns, hot cross *301*
Burgers
beef-, braised, with vegetables 121

INDEX

Bush tea 359
Butter 168
  beurre noir 168
  beurre noisette 168
  biscuits, basic 316
  cake, basic 307
  clarified 169
  clarified (ghee) 168, 169, **380**
  icing or cream 294
  melted (sauce) 168
  meunière 168
  savoury 168, 179
Butter beans 187
  with tomato *208*
Butterflied leg of lamb (braaied) *155*
Buttermilk **380**
  rusks *315*
Butternut squash 187
  braaied *161*
  braised chicken with sweet potato and (var.) *147*
  soup (var: pumpkin) *47*
  stuffed *192*
Butterscotch 325

CHINESE MENUS

STARTERS
Chicken wings *21*
Paper-wrapped chicken *133*

SOUPS
Chicken stock *36*
Hot and sour soup *138*
Won ton *41*

MAIN COURSES
Beef chow mein *219*
Cabbage *185*
Chicken with cashew nuts *133*
Fried rice *222*
Peking duck *139*
Spicy red lamb ribs *100*
Spring rolls *235*
Steamed sweet and sour fish *61*
Stir-fried beef with oyster-flavoured sauce *91*
Stir-fried chicken and vegetables *132*
Stir-fried vegetables *138*
Watercress salad *206*
Whole marinated red roman *138*

DESSERTS
Bow ties *262*
Chinese honey nuts *341*
Chinese toffee apples *266*
Chocolate ginger litchis *335*
Fried ice cream balls *139*
Oriental fruit salad *275*

C

Cabbage(s) 184
  Chinese 185
  freezing 372
  recipes:
  bubble and squeak *192*
  creamed *192*
  red, pickled *332*
  red, stewed *205*
  rolls with sprout stuffing *210*
  stuffed leaves (var: dolmades)
Cabernet franc 355
Cabernet sauvignon 355
Caerphilly cheese 230
Caesar salad *196*
Cakes 292, 314 (*see also* Biscuits)
  baking tips 293
  cooling and storing 293, 372, 374
  freezing 372, 374
  fridge *see* Fridge cakes
  icing 294, 310
  ingredients for 292
  mixtures 293
  wedding 350
  recipes:
  baba au rhum *313*
  banana loaf *313*
  basic butter *307*
  Black Forest *306*
  birthday *310*
  carrot *307*
  cherry (var.) *307*
  chocolate *308*
  chocolate celebration *311*
  chocolate chiffon *308*
  Christmas *310*
  date and walnut loaf *312*
  Dundee *308*
  fresh plum kuchen *299*
  fruit, boiled *309*
  fruit, rich *309*
  gingerbread *309*
  heart *310*
  koeksisters *314*
  lemon chiffon *307*
  Madeira *306*
  party *310*
  scones *305*
  simnel *312*
  Swedish tea ring *305*
  Swiss roll *309*, *327*
  train *311*
  vetkoek *313*
  Victoria sponge sandwich *312*
  wedding *311*
Calamari 57
  preparing *75*
  recipes:
  fried *75*
  grilled *75*
  stewed *75*
Calf (*see also* Veal)
  liver with onions *117*
  offal 83
Camembert cheese 230
  en croûte *33*
Canapé **380**
Candied angelica 340
Candied peel 340
Cannelloni 216, **380**
  cases 215
Cantaloup 256
Cape brandy pudding *264*
Cape gooseberries 256
  flan *260*
  freezing 371
Cape lamb pie *103*
Cape riesling 354
Cape salmon 55
  in aspic with Malay dressing *64*
Caper(s) **380**
  sauce *171*
  sauce (var: Hollandaise) *173*
Cappuccino 359
Caramel 325
  crème *280*
  fillet steak *89*
  oranges *272*
  sauce *287*
Caramelise **380**
Caraway seed 130
Cardamom *130*
Carp 59
Carrot(s) 185
  freezing 372
  storage 368
  recipes:
  and onions, pickled *333*
  and tomato soup *48*
  cake *307*
  glazed *193*
  salad *193*
  sambal *101*
  sweet and sour (var.) *191*
Carving meat 86, 87
Carving poultry 125
Cashew nuts 257
  chicken with *133*
Cassata 279
Casseroles and stews (*see also* Bredies; Hotpots) 86, **380**
  cuts suitable for 83
  freezing 372
  recipes:
  beef and noodles *121*
  beef stew with parsley dumplings *121*
  braised beefburgers with vegetables *121*
  braised lamb with spinach *120*
  calamari *75*
  chicken, brinjal and noodle *146*
  chicken casserole with 20 cloves of garlic *132*
  chicken stew with orange and tomato *135*
  chicken with spring vegetables *147*
  fish and noodle *79*
  fish stew with red wine *77*
  green bean bredie *94*
  guinea fowl *144*
  hashed beef or lamb with tomatoes *120*
  Irish stew *99*
  lamb casserole with orange *99*
  Lancashire hotpot *120*
  lentils *209*
  matar aur baïgan sakh (vegetable casserole) *190*
  mussel ragout *71*
  oxtail *116*
  pigeons *145*
  pork and baked beans *120*
  pumpkin bredie *94*
  seafood *76*
  tomato bredie *95*
  veal (blanquette de veau) *92*
  vegetable *211*
  venison, with sour cream *109*
  waterblommetjie bredie *95*
Cassia 130
Catering for large numbers 352
Cauliflower(s) 185
  freezing 372
  recipes:
  cheese *194*
  soup *45*
  spiced *194*
Caviar
  and egg and onion starter *23*
  and egg bites *20*
  blini with *22*
  omelette filling *238*
  tart *23*
  with baked potatoes *203*
Cayenne pepper 130
Celeriac 185
Celery 185, 199
  freezing 372
  recipes:
  and mushroom and walnut stuffing *179*
  sauce *171*
  sticks, stuffed *20*
Celery seeds 130
Ceramic hobs 378
Cereals 215
  maize 215
  maltabella 215
  mealie meal, thin 215
  mealie rice 215
  millet 215
  oats 215
  sago 215
  sorghum 215
  storage 368
  tapioca 215
  wheat 215
  recipes:
  cooking mealie rice 215
  cooking pearl wheat 215
  crushed wheat porridge 215
  mealie rice 215
  oatmeal porridge 215
  sorghum porridge 215
  stywe pap 215
  thin mealie meal porridge 215
  whiskyed porridge *236*
Challah **380**
Chapati (roti) *136*
Chardonnay 354
Chasseur sauce *171*
Chateaubriand steak 82
Chaud-froid sauce *167*
Chayote *see* Cho-cho
Cheddar cheese 230
  fondue *105*
Cheese
  and eggs, quick meals with 232, 244
  and wine parties 352
  guide to 230
  storage 368
  recipes:
  American cheesecake *263*
  and ham omelette filling *238*
  beignets *21*
  blue, soufflé filling *240*
  bourekitas (pastries) *240*
  broccoli parmigiana *191*
  camembert en croûte *33*
  cauliflower with *194*
  cream cheese bites *20*
  cream cheese dip *29*
  Liptauer, dip *28*
  macaroni *241*
  omelette filling *238*
  Parmesan, broccoli with *191*
  pastry 252
  quiches *242*
  sauce *171*
  soufflé *240*
  spanakopitta (spinach pie) *243*
  Swiss fondue *105*
  tagliatelle with cream and Parmesan *219*
  toast, puffy *243*
  topping, fish and potatoes with *79*
  turkey salad with sesame seeds and *143*
  tyropita (pastries) *242*
  vegetables with cheese and potato topping (var.) *79*
  Welsh rarebit *242*
  whirls *21*
Cheese, cream
  bites *20*

INDEX

dip *28*
Cheese sauce 171
    asparagus in 188
    baby marrows in 188
Cheesecake, American *263*
Chenin blanc 354
Cherry 256
Cherry cake (var.) 307
Cherry guava 256
Chervil 199
Cheshire cheese 230
Chestnut stuffing 179
Chicken
    boning *128*
    braaing 152
    freezing 370, 371
    general guide to roasting 125
    meal-in-one dishes 146
    roasting (frozen) 371
    serving hint (cold) 353
    smoke roasting 68
    recipes:
    and brinjal and noodle casserole 146
    ayam kuning (yellow chicken) 221
    baked, and potatoes 146
    biriani 137
    braaied herb chicken 156
    braised, with sweet potatoes and pumpkin *147*
    breasts (var.) 93
    breasts with apricots and almonds 140
    casserole of, with spring vegetables 147
    casserole with 20 cloves of garlic 132
    Chinese stock 36
    chop suey 109
    chow mein (var.) 219
    devilled *129*
    egged, breaded and roasted *126*
    fricassee with sherry 129
    Greek *132*
    grilled, with lemon and herb marinade 140
    kesar masala murghi (chicken in saffron gravy) 136
    Kiev *134*
    liver and lettuce salad 18
    liver omelette filling 238
    liver pâté *30*
    liver puffs 21
    livers, chopped 31
    livers, wrapped in bacon 21
    Malay braised 134
    murgh aur khaddu haleem (chicken and pumpkin soup) 42
    open roast, with orange juice and apples 146
    oven-fried crumbed 134
    paper-wrapped *133*
    peri-peri 135
    pie *137*
    pilaff 222
    pot-roasted 128
    roast baby, with rice and raisin stuffing *127*
    roast stuffed 126
    roast, with herb butter stuffing under the skin 179
    salad 140
    satay kebabs (var.) 158
    smoke roasting 68
    sooki murghi (spicy chicken) 136
    soup (cock-a-leekie) 42
    soup (murgh aur khaddu haleem) 42
    Spanish, with rice 146
    spicy kebabs *159*
    stew with orange and tomato 135
    stir-fried, and vegetables 132
    stock 36
    stuffed boned 128
    wings, Chinese *21*
    with cashew nuts *133*
    with mushrooms and barley 147
Chick-pea(s) 187
    dip *28*
Chicory 185
    and orange salad 195
Chiffon cake
    chocolate 308
    lemon 307
Chiffon tart 285
Children's birthday parties 348
Children's party drinks 360
Chill **380**
Chilled grapefruit 16
Chilled melon 16
Chilli 185
Chilli powder *130*
Chinese
    beef chow mein 219
    bow ties 262
    cabbage 185
    chicken stock 36
    chicken wings 21
    chocolate ginger litchis 335
    fried ice cream balls 139
    gooseberry *see* Kiwi fruit
    honey nuts *341*
    hot and sour soup *138*
    menu 138, 346
    Oriental fruit salad 275
    Peking duck *139*
    spicy red lamb ribs 100
    spring rolls 235
    steamed sweet and sour fish 61
    stir-fried beef with oyster-flavoured sauce 91
    stir-fried chicken and vegetables 132
    stir-fried vegetables 207
    toffee-apples 266
    watercress salad 206
    whole marinated red roman 138
    won ton soup 41
Chips
    fish and *60*
    game 203
Chives 199
    baked potatoes with sour cream and 203
    omelette filling 238
Cho-cho 186
Chocolate(s) 336
    clusters 336
    curls and frills 336
    filigree or fans 336
    hints on using 336
    leaves and roses 336
    recipes:
    and rum gâteau *271*
    bombe, triple 279
    cake 308
    celebration cake 311
    chiffon cake 308
    chip cookies 317
    -coated ice cream balls 337
    éclairs 259
    fondue 105
    ginger litchis 335
    glaze 259
    hot drink 360
    ice cream (var.) 276, *277*
    mixed 337
    mousse 282
    pudding 268
    sauce 287
    soufflé 268
    sponge pudding 268
    strawberry chocolate box 337
Chokka *see* Squid
Chops
    kassler rib, with mustard sauce 107
    lamb, American barbecue 154
    lamb, portmanteau'd 100
Chop suey 109
Choux pastry 251
Chow mein, beef 219
Christmas cake 310
Christmas menus 350
Christmas pudding 272
Chutney **380**
    making 323
    potting and sealing 323
    recipes:
    apple, date and walnut *334*
    apricot blatjang 335
    lemon 334
    mango atjar *335*
    tomato, green 334
    tomato, red 334
Cider, cured ham in 107
Cinnamon 130, *131*
Cinnamon sugar **380**
Cinsaut 355
Citron 257
Citron preserve *330*
Citrus 257
    marinade; yellowtail cubes with 160
    sauce; sweet and sour beetroot with 191
Clairette blanche 354
Clarified
    butter (ghee) 168, 169, **380**
    fat or dripping 169
Clarify **380**
Clarifying soups, stocks and broths with egg 229
Clay pots 377
Clear stock 36
Cloves *130*
Cock-a-leekie soup 42
Cocktail, crayfish 24
Cocktail parties 351
Cocktail reception 350
Cocktails 362
    beachcomber 362
    between the sheets 362
    black Russian 362
    bloody Mary 362
    daiquiri 362
    dry martini 362
    kir 362
    Manhattan 362
    margarita 362
    mint julep 362
    negroni 362
    pina colada 363
    pink lady 363
    prairie oyster 363
    samba surprise 363
    screwdriver 363
    sidecar 363
    stinger 363
    tequila sunrise 363
    Tom Collins 363
    whisky sour 363
    white lady 363
Coconut 257
Coconut ice 339
Cocotte **380**
    oeufs en cocotte à la crème *233*
Coddle **380**
Coffee
    grinders 377
    storage 368
    recipes:
    cappuccino 359
    ice cream (var.) 276
    iced 359
    Irish 364
    soufflé 268, 281
    Turkish 359
Colander **380**
Coleslaw 193
Colombar 354
Composed salad
    crayfish (var.) 24
    grapefruit 17
Compote **380**
    dried fruit 272, 286
Conserve **380**
Conserve, strawberry (var.) 328
Convenience food 369
Cookies *see* Biscuits; Cakes
Cooking poultry 125
Cooking times for meat 85
Cooking vegetables 184
Cooking with wine 109
Coral **380**
Coriander 130
Corned beef 89
Cornish pastries 91
Cottage cheese 230
Cottage pie 115
Country herb stuffing 181
Courgette *see* Baby marrow(s)
Court-bouillon 55, **380**
Couscous 224
Cowpeas 187
Crab 57
Crackling **380**
Crayfish 58
    preparing 74
    recipes:
    and prawn sauce 172
    boiling 58, 74
    braaied 161
    cocktail 24
    grilled 74
    Newburg 73
    omelette (var.) 244
    quiche 242
    salad (var.) 24
    sauce 168
    thermidor 74
Cream **380**
    hints for using 253
    puddings 253
    recipes:
    cake, strawberry 271
    puffs 259
    sauce 167
Cream cheese
    bites 20
    dip *28*
    pastry 252
    lemon, seafood salad with melon and 76
Creamed perlemoen 72
Creamed spinach 206
Cream, sour, and dill dressing 178
Cream, soured (smetena) **383**
Crème brûlée *281*
Crème caramel 280
Crème fraîche 169, **380**
Crème pâtissière 259

INDEX

Crêpe **380**
Crêpes suzettes *265*
Croissants *301*
Croquette(s) **380**
   fish 21
   potato 203
Croûtons 39, **380**
Crown roast of lamb 97
Crudité 29, **380**
Crumble
   apple 264
   plum 267
Crunchies 317
Crushed wheat porridge 215
Crustless savoury tart 245
Crystallised flowers 275
Cucumber(s) 185
   storage 368
   recipes:
   and prawn mousse 16
   and radish salad 195
   and yoghurt dip 29
   boats 21
   pickled 332
   raita 136
   sambal 101
   sambal ketimum *221*
   sauce (var: Hollandaise) 173
   sauce with salmon mousse *25*
   soup, chilled *45*
Cumberland sauce 171
Cumin 130
Curd **381**
   lemon 327
Curdle **381**
Cure **381**
Curing a ham 107
Curry(-ies/-ied)
   leaves *131*
   mayonnaise 177
   powder *131*
   recipes:
   bhaji masoor ni dhal 208
   giema 102
   haricot bean 209
   mayonnaise sauce 177
   mutton 102, *335*
   Parsi dhansak (mutton) *102*
   pickled fish 61
   prawn 73
   sauce 62, 172
   sauce, fish in 62
   south Indian fish 63
   vegetables; brinjals stuffed with 210
Custard
   tips for making 253
   recipes:
   baked 253
   crème pâtissière 259
   pie, Greek 262
   sauce *286*
Custard apple 255

D

Dahi (yoghurt sauce) 177
Daiquiri (cocktail) 362
Dairy foods – storage 368
Dandelion 185
Danish blue cheese 230
Danish caviar **380**
Dariole **380**
Dassie *see* Blacktail
Date 255
   and apple and walnut chutney *334*
   and walnut loaf 312
Deep-fat fryers 378
Deep-frying **381**
Deglaze **381**
Demerara **381**
Demi-glace sauce 166
Denning vleis 100
Desserts (*see also* Chocolate(s); Fridge cakes; Ice cream; Pastries; Puddings)
   useful tips 248
   recipes:
   apple crumble 264
   apple pie 258
   apple strudel 258
   apricot sauce 286
   apricot sherry sauce 286
   baba au rhum *313*
   baked banana Alaska 279
   baked custard 253
   baked stuffed apples *273*
   bakewell tart *258*
   banana fritters 266
   banana split 280
   blancmange 281
   bow ties 262
   brandied honey creams 278
   brandy butter 286
   brandy sauce 286
   bread and butter pudding 264
   Cape brandy pudding *264*
   cape gooseberry flan 260
   caramel oranges 272
   caramel sauce 287
   cassata 279
   cheesecake, American 263
   chiffon tart 285
   Chinese toffee-apples 266
   chocolate éclairs 259
   chocolate glaze 259
   chocolate ice cream *277*
   chocolate mousse 282
   chocolate pudding 268
   chocolate sauce 287
   choux pastry favourites 259
   Christmas pudding 272
   cream puffs *259*
   crème brûlée *281*
   crème caramel 280
   crème patissière 259
   crêpes suzettes 265
   crystallised flowers 275
   custard (sauce) 286
   dried fruit 272
   dried fruit compote 272, *286*
   drop scones 262
   fig tart 260
   floral ice bowl 278
   fresh fruit brûlée 274
   fresh strawberry sauce 287
   fried ice cream balls 139
   frosted fruit and crystallised flowers 275
   gâteau Saint-Honoré 259
   gaajar halva 269
   golden sponge pudding 268, *287*
   granadilla ice cream mould 276
   granadilla mousse 282
   Greek custard pie 262
   guava tart *261*
   hazelnut meringues 284
   honeycomb cream 282
   hot winter fruit salad 275
   ice cream 276
   ice cream sundae 280
   iced coffee soufflé 281
   iced truffles *278*
   khulfi (Indian ice cream) 280
   lemon mousse 282
   lemon pudding 265
   lemon sauce 287
   lemon sorbet 280
   liqueur ice cups *278*
   malva pudding 265
   melktert 260
   meringues *284*
   meringue gâteau 284
   meringue shells and discs 284
   mince pies 261
   nectarine fool with pistachio nuts 273
   nut tart 261
   orange and grapefruit salad with caramel 276
   Oriental fruit salad 275
   frozen parfaits 280
   Pavlova *285*
   peach melba 280
   pecan nut pie 262
   pig's ears *262*
   pineapple Romanoff 274
   plum crumble 267
   plum sponge pudding 268
   praline ice cream *277*
   profiteroles with ice cream and hot chocolate sauce 259
   queen's pudding 267
   rice pudding 267
   rum butter 287
   sago pudding 267
   semolina pudding 267
   snow eggs 284
   spiced peaches 274
   strawberry sorbet 280
   stuffed peaches 273
   summer fruit bowl 275
   summer fruit platter 276
   sundaes 280
   syllabub 283
   tarte aux pommes 259
   trifle 283
   triple chocolate bombe 279
   upside-down winter pudding 269
   vanilla soufflé 268
   waffles 265
   winter fruit salad 276
   zabaglione 269
Devilled(-ing) **381**
   chicken 129
   eggs, baked 244
   eggs, stuffing 239
   lamb kidneys 117
   lamb kidneys, skewered 154
   shoulder of lamb 96
Dhania phoodini chatni (coriander mint chutney) 136
Dice **381**
Dill 199
   and mustard dressing 178
   and sour cream dressing 178
Dill seeds 131
Dips 28
   ideas for dipping, 29
   recipes:
   avocado 28
   brinjal 28
   chick-pea 28
   cream cheese 28
   Liptauer cheese 28
   smoked oyster 29
   smoked snoek 29
   tuna 29
   yoghurt and cucumber 29
Dolmades 17, 21
Dom Pedro 364
Dough **381**
Dough, bread *see* Bread
Drakensberg cheese 231
Draw(-ing) **380**
   game birds 125
   poultry 124
Dredge **381**
Dress **381**
Dressing(s) 168 (*see also* Mayonnaise; Sauces; Vinaigrette)
   avocado 178
   boiled 176
   for simple green salad 197
   French *see* Vinaigrette
   garlic 177
   Malay; Cape salmon in aspic with 64
   minted yoghurt sauce 177
   mustard and dill 178
   Roquefort cheese 178
   sesame 178
   sour cream and dill 178
Dried fruit *see* Fruit, dried; Mincemeat, fruit
Drink(s) 358
   after-dinner 364
   cocktails 362
   for children's parties 360
   punches 364
   wine *see* Wine
   recipes:
   bush teas 359
   cappuccino (coffee) 359
   cocktails *see* Cocktails
   Dom Pedro 364
   fruit punch 365
   fruit syrups 361
   Gedat milk 359
   ginger beer *361*
   glühwein 365
   guava 360
   herbal teas 359
   hot chocolate 360
   iced coffee 359
   iced tea 359
   Irish coffee 364
   keri sherbet 358
   lassi 335
   loving cup 365
   Malay vermicelli boeboer 358
   milk punch 364
   milk shake 360
   mixed fruit drink 360
   old-fashioned lemonade 361
   sangria 365
   teas 359
Dripping 86, **381**
Drizzle **381**
Drop scones 262
Drying herbs 198
Dry martini (cocktail) 362
Duck 125
   freezing 370
   roasting, guide to 125
   recipes:
   Peking 139
   roast, with grapefruit 140
   roast, with orange and Van der Hum *141*
   terrine of, with orange *32*
Duck eggs 229
   omelette 229
Dumplings 39, **381**
   liver 39
   matzo 39
   parsley 181
   parsley, with beef stew *121*
   semolina 181
   suet 181
Dundee cake *308*
Dust **381**

INDEX

E

Éclair(s) **381**
    chocolate 259
Edam cheese 231
Eel 55
Egg(s) 228, 368
    bantam 229
    boiled 228
    choosing 228
    cooking 228
    duck 229
    freezing 370
    fried 228
    hard-boiled; serving hint 353
    hints for beating 253
    omelettes 229
    poached 229
    puddings 253
    quail 230
    scrambled 229
    smoke roasting 69
    storing 228
    turkey 230
    uncommon 229
    using – in cooking 229
    recipes:
    and asparagus 244
    and bacon with baked sausages 236
    and caviar and onion starter 23
    and caviar bites *20*
    and cheese, quick meals with 244
    and lemon fish 67
    and lemon sauce 173
    avgolemono (soup or sauce) *40*
    baji aur inda (spinach egg scramble) 233
    baked, devilled 244
    baked in baked potatoes 203
    baked in saucers 245
    Benedict 232
    Florentine 232
    garnishes for soup 39
    inda nu sakh (eggs in curry sauce) 232
    in overcoats 245
    mornay 234
    oeufs en cocotte a la crème 233
    oeufs meulemeester 233
    omelettes *see* Omelettes
    ostrich 230
    pie, minted *235*
    piperade 239
    salad 233
    sauce, with smoked haddock 237
    Scotch 234
    scrambled (piperade) 239
    scrambled (ostrich) 230
    stuffed *21*, 239
Egged, breaded and roasted chicken *126*
Eggplant *see* Brinjal
Electric frying pans 377
Elf 55
Emmenthal cheese 231
    turkey salad with sesame seeds and cheese (var.) *143*
En croûte **381**
Endive 185
English breakfast 236
Entrecôte steak 82
Escalope **381**
Espagnole sauce 166
Esrom cheese 231
Evening braai menu 346

F

Fan ovens 378
Fennel 185, 198
    and tomato and mushroom salad 195
Fennel seeds *131*
Fenugreek *131*
Feta cheese 231
Fettucine, cooking *see* Pasta, cooking
Fettucine with tuna, mushroom, tomato and onion sauce 218
Fig 256
    and melon jam (var.) 326
    and Parma ham (var.) 20
    green, preserve *331*
    jam 326
    sour *see* Sour fig
    tart 260
Fig leaves, stuffed (var.) *17*
Filet mignon 82
Fillet(s)
    caramel 89
    of beef in brioche *112*
    of pork, papered *106*
    of steak 82
    steaks, ostrich *145*
Fines herbes **381**
Firm ball 325
Fish 54 (*see also* Caviar; Crayfish; Finger food; Mussels; Prawns; Perlemoen; Seafood; Shellfish; Shrimps)
    baking 55
    boning and filleting 54, *58*
    braaing 55, 152
    buying fresh 54
    cooking in parcels 55
    cooking methods 54, 57
    deep-frying 54
    filleting *58*
    freezing 54, 370, 371
    freshwater 59
    grilling 55
    guide to common sea fish 55
    pie fillings 248
    poaching 55
    preparing 54, *58*
    shallow-frying 54
    skinning 54, *58*
    steaming 55
    stock 36
    storage 368
    tips for cooking 57
    recipes:
    and chips *60*
    and noodle casserole 79
    and potatoes with cheese topping 79
    baked, with tomato and onion sauce 61
    baked, with vegetables 78
    bobotie 64
    Boulangère 78
    Cape salmon in aspic with Malay dressing 64
    Chinese steamed sweet and sour 61
    chopped herring 27
    croquettes 21
    curried, pickled 61
    egg and lemon 67
    gefilte 76
    gesmoorde snoek 65
    grilled 61
    grilled sole 67
    in curry sauce 62
    Indian curry 63
    in newspaper (braaied) *160*
    in pastry 78
    kedgeree 237
    kippers 237
    Mauritian 63
    meal-in-one fish soup 49
    meunière 62
    oven-fried, and chips 60
    pastes, smoked 25
    peri-peri (var.) *135*
    pickled 61
    pie 78
    pilaff (var.) *222*
    poached sole with mushrooms 67
    poached trout 70
    roe pâté 27
    salmon mousse with cucumber sauce *25*
    Sandveld snoek 65
    smoke roasted 68
    smoked, and baked potato 203
    smoked fish soufflé filling 240
    smoked salmon blintzes 24
    smoked snoek and potato bake 66
    smoked snoek pâté 27
    sole Véronique 66
    soup, meal-in-one 49
    south Indian curry 63
    stew with red wine 77
    terrine with sour cream sauce *26*
    trout parcels (braaied) *157*
    trout with almonds 71
    tuna baked with anchovies and garlic 67
    whole baked 62
    whole baked stuffed 65
    whole marinated (braaied) *157*
    whole marinated red roman 138
    with paprika cream sauce 63
    yellowtail cubes with citrus marinade (braaied) *160*
    yellowtail with avocado sauce 70
Five spice powder *131*
Flake **381**
Flaky pastry 250
Flambé **381**
Flan **381**
    lining a ring 249
    recipes:
    cape gooseberry 260
    yoghurt and banana 271
    youngberry cream 270
Floral ice bowl 278
Florentine **381**
    eggs 232
Flour 248, 290, 292
    freezing 374
    seasoned **383**
Flowers, crystallised 275
Fluff **381**
Flummery 253
Fold in **381**
Fondant icing 294
Fondue(s) 104, **381**
    accompaniments 105
    bacon and sausage 104
    beef bourguignonne *104*
    Cheddar 105
    chocolate 105
    French Canadian 105
    Mongolian fire pot 104
    sausage and bacon 104
    seafood 104
    Swiss cheese 105
    Turkish lamb 104
    vegetable 104
Fontina cheese 231
Food processors 377
Fool 253, **381**
    nectarine, with pistachio nuts 273
Freeze **381**
Freezers 379
Freezing 369
    baked goods 372
    cooked dishes 372, 374
    eggs 371
    fish 370
    fruit 371
    herbs 198
    meat 370
    poultry and game birds 370, 371
    unbaked goods 372
    vegetables 372, 373
French
    Canadian fondue 105
    dressing **381**
    loaf 291, 296
    toast 242
Fresh produce – seasonal guide 346
Fricassee **381**
    chicken, with sherry 129
Fridge cakes 270
    apricot yoghurt tart 270
    Brazilian tipsy gâteau 271
    lemon gâteau 270
    rum and chocolate gâteau 271
    strawberry cream cake 271

INDEX

walnut cream torte 270
yoghurt and banana flan 271
youngberry cream flan 270
Fried
  calamari 75
  ice cream balls 139
  fish and chips *60*
  oven-, fish and chips *60*
  perlemoen 72
  rabbit, young *111*
  rice 222
Frikkadels 114, **381**
Fritters
  banana 266
  pumpkin 205
  sweet corn 197
  sweet potato (var.) 205
Fritto-misto **381**
Frost **381**
Frosted fruit 275
Frosting 295
Frozen food
  storage 368
  thawing 370
Fruit
  buying and using fresh 255
  freezing 371
  frosted 275
  seasonal guide 346
  storage 368
  syrups 361
  tropical and subtropical 255
  recipes:
  ambrosia skewers (braaied) *163*
  brûlée 274
  drink, mixed 360
  gums (jujubes) 339
  jelly 320
  mincemeat 328
  Oriental salad 275
  pickle, mixed 333
  punch 365
  salad (brûlée) 274
  salad, hot winter 275
  summer bowl 275
  summer platter 276
  vinegar 329
  winter salad 276
Fruit, dried
  preparing 272
  storage 368
  recipes:
  bread with *299*
  compote 272, *286*
  mebos 339
  mincemeat *see* Mincemeat, fruit
  rolls 339
Frying 84 (*see also* Fried)
  cooking times 85
  cuts suitable for 83
Frying pan **383**
Fudge 339
Fudge icing 295

G

Gaajar halva 282
Galantine 128, **381**
Galjoen 56
Gamay grape 355
Game chips 203, **381**
Gammon 82, 83
  steaks in puff pastry 113
Garam masala 131, **381**
Garlic 185
  baked potatoes with 203
  bread 292
  butter 179
  butter with baked prawns 72
  chicken casserole with 20 cloves of 132
  salad dressing 177
  tuna baked with anchovies and 67
Garnish **381**
Gâteau
  Brazilian tipsy 271
  lemon 270
  meringue 284
  rum and chocolate *271*
  Saint Honoré 259
Gazpacho *44*
Gedat milk 359
Gefilte fish 76
Gem squash 187
  stuffed 195
Gesmoorde snoek 65
Gewürztraminer 354
Ghee 168, **381**
Giblets **381**
Giema curry 102
Ginger *131*
  and melon jam *326*
  beer *361*
  litchis, chocolate 335
  snaps 317
Gingerbread cake 309
Glaze(-d/-ing) **381**
  carrots 193
  marrow 197
  meat 37
  pies 249
  sweet potatoes 206
Gloucester cheese 231
Glühwein *365*
Gnocchi **381**
  potato 225
  semolina 225
  spinach 225
Goat – choosing and preparing 84
Golden sponge pudding 268, *287*
Goose 125
  freezing 370
  roasting 125
  roast, with rum-soaked apples *145*

Gooseberry, cape *see* Cape gooseberry
Gorgonzola cheese 231
Gouda cheese 231
Granadilla (passion fruit) 256
  ice cream 276
  mousse 282
Granola 225
Grape 256
  cultivars 354
  jam 326
Grapefuit 257
  and orange salad 276
  freezing 371
  preserve (var.) 331
  roast duck with 140
  salad *17*
  sorbet (var.) 280
Gratin **381**
Greek
  avgolemono (soup) 40
  chicken *132*
  custard pie 262
  dolmades 17, *21*
  lamb with yoghurt 98
  moussaka 111
  pastitsio 216
  salad 211
  spanakopitta (spinach pie) 243
  taramasalata (fish roe pâté) 27
Green bean(s) 185
  bredie 94
  provencale 176
  with herbs 190
Green fig preserve *331*
Green grape 354
Green salad 197
Green tomato chutney 334
Grill, mixed 85
Grilled(-ing) 84
  cooking times 85
  cuts suitable for 83
  recipes:
  black mussels 24
  calamari 74
  chicken with lemon and herb marinade 140
  crayfish 74
  fish 61
  frozen meat 370
  sole 67
Gruyère cheese 231
  turkey salad with sesame seeds and *143*
Guava 256
  and melon jam (var.) 326
  drink 360
  tart 261
Guinea fowl
  roasting 125
  recipes:
  braised *144*
  casserole *144*

H

Haddock
  kedgeree 237
  quiche 242
  roulades *241*
  smoked, with egg sauce 237
Hake 56
Halaal **381**
Ham 82, 83
  carving 87
  cooking (in cider) 107
  curing 107
  recipes:
  and cheese omelette filling 238
  and mushrooms with baked potatoes 203
  and veal pie 93
  crescents *21*
  cured, in cider 107
  Parma, and melon or fig wrap *20*
  pinwheels *21*
  stuffing for eggs 239
Hamburgers
  braaing 156
  braised, with vegetables 121
Hamburgers, frozen 370
Hanepoot wine 354
Hang **381**
Hanging gamebirds 125
Hanging poultry 124
Hard ball 325
Hard crack 325
Harder 56
Hare – choosing and preparing 84
Haricot **381**

> **GREEK MENUS**
>
> STARTERS
> Dolmades 17, *21*
> Taramasalata (fish roe pâté) 27
> Tyropita (pastries) 242
>
> SOUP
> Avgolemono *40*
>
> MAIN COURSES
> Brinjals à la Grecque 189
> Greek chicken *132*
> Greek salad 211
> Lamb with yoghurt 98
> Leg of lamb in phyllo 113
> Moussaka 111
> Pastitsio 216
> Spanakopitta (spinach pie) 243
> Spinach rice 222
>
> DESSERT
> Greek custard pie 262

bean 187
bean curry 209
of mutton 101
Hash **381**
Hashed beef or lamb with tomatoes 120
Havarti cheese 231
Hazelnut 257
Heart – buying and preparing 83
Heart cake 310
Herb(s) *198*
  drying 198
  freezing 198
  storage 368
  recipes:
  and lemon marinade with grilled chicken 140
  bouquet garni 199
  butter 179
  country, stuffing 181
  mayonnaise sauce 177
  oils 169
  tea 359
  vinegar 332
Herbed chicken (braaied) *156*
Herbed crumbed tomatoes 236
Herbed prune stuffing *180*
Herbed vinaigrette 178
Herring, chopped 27
Herring rollmops 30
Hing 130
Hoisin sauce **381**
Hollandaise sauce 173
Honey
  storage 368
  recipes:
  and nut ice cream (var.) 276
  butter frosting 295
  creams, brandied 278
  nuts, Chinese 341
Honeycomb cream 282
Honeydew melons 256
Honeyed lamb 97
Hors d'oeuvres **381** (*see also* Starters, snacks and savouries)
Horseradish 131
  creamed *105*
  mayonnaise sauce 177
  sauce 173
  sauce (var: Hollandaise) 173
  vinaigrette 178
Hot and sour soup *138*
Hot cross buns 301
Hotpot, Lancashire 120
Hotpots 86 (*see also* Casseroles and stews)
Hottentot's fig 256
Hubbard squash 187
Hull **381**
Hummus *see* Chick-pea dip
Hungarian fish with paprika cream sauce 63
Husaini kebabs and sas sauce 159

INDEX

I

Ice cream
freezing 374
recipes:
baked banana Alaska 279
banana (var.) 276
banana split 280
cassata 279
chocolate (var.) 276
chocolate-coated balls 337
coffee (var.) 276
dark chocolate 277
fried balls 139
granadilla 276
honey and nut (var.) 276
iced truffles 278
khulfi 280
lemon (var.) 276
liqueur ice cups 278
nut (praline) 277

INDIAN MENUS

STARTER
Samoosas 22

SOUP
Murgh aur khaddu haleem (chicken and pumpkin soup) 42

MAIN COURSES
Accompaniments 136
Baji aur inda (spinach egg scramble) 233
Bhaji masoor ni dhal (lentil stew or soup) 208
Chicken biriani 137
Chicken pilaff 222
Coastal Indian-style mussels 72
Cucumber raita 136
Fish curry 63
Haricot bean curry 209
Inda nu sakh (eggs in curry sauce) 232
Kachoomer (salad) 208
Kesar masala murghi (chicken in saffron gravy) 136
Kheema kebabs 103
Matar aur baïgan sakh (vegetable casserole) 190
Mushroom pilaff 223
Parsi dhansak (mutton curry) 102
Pilaff with lamb and apricots 223
Prawn curry 73
Sooki murghi (spicy chicken) 136
South Indian fish curry 63
Spiced brinjals 188

Chapati (bread) 136
Puri (bread) 305

DESSERTS
Gaajar halva 282
Khulfi (ice cream) 280

parfaits 280
peach melba 280
praline 277
strawberry (var.) 276
sundaes 280
triple chocolate bombe 279
vanilla 276
Iced coffee 359
Iced tea 359
Iced truffles 278
Icing 294, 310
basic glacé 295
birthday cake 310
butter 294
chocolate celebration cake 311
Christmas cake 310
easy fondant 294
fondant 294
heart cake 310
party cake 310
royal 295
sugar roses and leaves 311
train cake 311
wedding cake 311
Inda nu sakh (eggs in curry sauce) 232
Indian
baji aur inda (spinach egg scramble) 233
bhaji masoor ni dhal (lentils) 208
chapati 136
chicken biriani 137
chicken pilaff 222
cucumber raita 136
dahi (yoghurt sauce) 177
dhania phoodini chatni (coriander mint chutney) 136
dishes: accompaniments to 136
fish curry 63
haricot bean curry 209
inda nu sakh (eggs in curry sauce) 232
kachoomer (salad) 208
kesar masala murghi (chicken in saffron gravy) 136
khajoor ni chatni (date and tamarind chutney) 136
kheema kebabs 103
khulfi (ice cream) 280
matar aur baïgan sakh (vegetable casserole) 190
murgh aur khaddu haleem (chicken and pumpkin soup) 42
mussels, coastal Indian-style 72
parsi dhansak (mutton curry) 102
poppadums 136
puri 305
samoosas 22
sooki murghi (spicy chicken) 136
spiced brinjals 188

Indonesian lamb kebabs with yoghurt sauce 159
Infuse **381**
Irish coffee 364
Irish stew 99
Italian
antipasto 31, **380**
broccoli parmigiana 191
cannelloni 215, 216, **380**
fettucine with tuna, mushroom, tomato and onion sauce 218
gnocchi 225
minestrone (soup) 46
osso bucco (veal) 96
saltimbocca alla Romana (veal schnitzels or beef steaks) 93
semolina gnocchi 225
spaghetti alla carbonara 217
spaghetti alla vongole 218
spaghetti Napolitana 218
spaghetti with Bolognese sauce 217
spaghetti with pesto sauce 217
spinach gnocchi 225
tripe Venetian style 118
vitello tonnato (veal with tuna sauce) 92
zabaglione 269

ITALIAN MENUS

STARTER
Antipasto 31

SOUP
Minestrone 46

MAIN COURSES
Broccoli Parmigiana 191
Cannelloni 216
Fettucine with tuna, mushrooms, tomato and onion sauce 218
Lasagne 217
Osso bucco (veal) 96
Pizza 304
Potato gnocchi 225
Ravioli 217
Risotto Milanese 223
Saltimbocca alla Romana 93
Semolina gnocchi 225
Spaghetti alla carbonara 217
Spaghetti alla vongole 218
Spaghetti Napolitana 218
Spaghetti with Bolognese sauce 217
Spaghetti with pesto sauce 217
Spinach gnocchi 225
Tagliatelle with cream and Parmesan cheese 219
Tripe Venetian style 118
Vitello tonnato 92

DESSERT
Zabaglione 269

J

Jam
making 320
pectin, acid and setting point 321
potting, sealing and storing 322
storage 368
using frozen fruit in 321
recipes:
all-the-year-round 327
all-the-year-round marmalade 328
apple jelly (var.) 328
apricot 326
apricot, smooth (var.) 326
fig 326
grape 326
grape jelly (var.) 328
lemon curd 327
loquat jelly (var.) 328
melon and ginger 326
mint jelly (var.) 328
peach, sliced 327
quince jelly 328
raspberry 327
strawberry 328
Jarlsberg cheese 231
Jellies 252
how to dissolve gelatin 252
moulding and chilling 253
Jelly, fruit 320
making 321
pectin, acid and setting point 321
potting, sealing and storing 322
recipes:
apple (var.) 328
grape (var.) 328
loquat (var.) 328
mint (var.) 328
quince 328
Jerusalem artichoke(s) see Artichoke(s), Jerusalem
Jewish
bagels 300
challah **380**
chopped chicken liver 31
chopped herring 27
gefilte fish 76
kichel **381**
kitke **381**
matzo dumplings 39
pot-roast brisket with prunes 88
Joint(-ing) **381**
poultry and game birds 124
rabbit and hare 84
Jugged **381**
kippers 237
Jujubes (fruit gums) 339
Julienne **381**
Junket **381**

K

Kabeljou 56
Kachoomer (salad) 208
Kale 186
Kasha 225
Kassler rib chops with mustard sauce 107
Kebab(s) 158, **381**
hints on making 158
husaini, and sas sauce (braaied) 159
Indonesian lamb, with yoghurt sauce (braaied) 159
kheema 103
kofta (braaied) 158
meat for 152
pork satay, and peanut sauce (braaied) 158
spicy chicken (braaied) 159
Kedgeree 237
Keri sherbet 358
Kerner 354
Kesar masala murghi (chicken in saffron gravy) 136
Ketchup 323
Khajoor ni chatni (date and tamarind chutney) 136
Kheema kebabs 103
Khulfi (Indian ice cream) 280
Kichel **381**
Kid – buying and preparing 84
Kidney(s)
buying and preparing 83
recipes:
and steak pie 115
devilled lamb 117, 154
mixed grill 85
Kidney beans see Haricot beans
Kiev, chicken 134
Kingklip 56
cocktail (var.) 24
pilaff (var.) 222
Kippers 237
Kir (cocktail) 362
Kitchen 375
utensils 375, 376
Kitke **381**
Kiwi fruit 256
Romanoff (var.) 274
Kneaded butter **381**
Knives 375
Koeksisters 314
Kofta kebabs (braaied) 158
Kohlrabi 186
Konfyt see Preserves
Kosher **381**
Krummelpap see Stywe pap
Kumquat 257
preserve 331
Kurper 59

391

L

Labels 369
Lamb
    carving 87
    choosing 82
    cooking times 85
    cuts 83
    offal 83
    serving hint 353
    stews 86
    uses for cuts 83
    recipes:
    braised, with spinach 120
    butterflied leg (braaied) 155
    Cape lamb pie 103
    casserole with orange 99
    chops, American barbecue
        (braaied) 154
    chops in phyllo 112
    chops, portmanteau'd 100
    crown roast 97
    devilled kidneys 117
    devilled kidney skewers
        (braaied) 154
    devilled shoulder of 96
    fondue, Turkish 104
    frikkadels 114
    Greek, with yoghurt 98
    hashed, with tomatoes 120
    honeyed 97
    husaini kebabs and sas sauce
        (braaied) 159
    Indonesian kebabs with yoghurt
        sauce (braaied) 159
    kheema kebabs 103
    Lancashire hotpot 120
    leg, carving 87
    leg, in phyllo 113
    mixed grill 85
    pie, Cape 103
    pilaff with 223
    roast saddle of 96
    roast stuffed shoulder of 96
    smoke roasting 69
    spicy red ribs 100
Lancashire hotpot 120
Langoustine 58
Lard(-ing) 124, **382**
Lasagne noodles 214
    recipe 217
Lassi 359
Leaves, chocolate 336
Leaves, sugar (icing) 311
Leek(s) 185
    and bacon with baked potatoes
        203
    quiche 242
    vinaigrette 196
Left-overs 368
Leg of lamb
    carving 87

serving hint 353
recipes:
    butterflied (braaied) 155
    in phyllo 113
Leg of mutton, stuffed 98
Legumes **382**
    dried 187 (see also Sprouts)
Leicester cheese 231
Lemon(s) 257
    freezing 371
    recipes:
    and herb marinade with grilled
        chicken 140
    avgolemono (soup or sauce) 40
    butter 179
    chiffon cake 307
    chutney 334
    cream sauce; seafood salad with
        melon and 76
    curd 327
    fish; egg and 67
    gâteau 270
    mousse 282
    pudding 265
    sauce 287
    sorbet 280
    soufflé 268
Lemonade, old-fashioned 361
Lemon balm 199
Lemon thyme 199
Lentils
    and sausage salad 209
    bhaji masoor ni dhal 208
    stewed 209
Lettuce 185
    and chicken liver salad 18
Lima bean 186
Limburger cheese 231
Lime 257
Limpets 58
Lining a pie plate 249
Liptauer cheese 231
    dip 28
Liqueur
    ice cups 278
    Van der Hum 364
Liquidizers 377
Liquor list for cocktail party
    352
Litchi(s) 255
    chocolate ginger 335
Liver
    buying and preparing 83
    recipes:
    calf, in mixed grill 85
    calf, with onions 117
    chicken, and lettuce salad 18
    chicken, omelette filling 238
    chicken, pâté 30
    chicken, puffs 21
    chicken, wrapped in bacon 21
    chopped calf (var.) 31
    chopped chicken 31

dumplings 39
Loaf
    banana 313
    beef 89
    date and walnut 312
    plaited 296
    soya nut 209
Loganberries – freezing 371
Loquat 255
    jelly (var.) 328
Lovage 199
Loving cup 365
Lunch menus 346, 347

MEAL IN A HURRY MENUS

This selection of recipes can be
prepared in an hour or less.

SOUPS
Avgolemono 40
Avocado 44
Cauliflower 45
Pumpkin 47

MAIN COURSES
Baked devilled eggs 244
Baked prawns with garlic butter 72
Bubble and squeak 192
Chicken breasts with apricots and
    almonds 140
Chicken salad 140
Chicken with cashew nuts 133
Crayfish Newburg 73
Devilled chicken 129
Egg salad 233
Eggs and asparagus 244
Devilled lamb kidneys 117
Fish and noodle casserole 79
Fish meunière 62
Greek salad 211
Grilled calamari 75
Grilled crayfish 74
Grilled sole 67
Hot spinach and bacon salad 18
Lettuce and chicken liver salad 18
Macaroni cheese 241
Mushroom salad 200
Oeufs meulemeester 233
Omelettes (various fillings) 238
Pancakes (various fillings) 234
Pepper steak 90
Piperade 239
Poached sole with mushrooms 67
Prawns baked with garlic butter 72
Saltimbocca alla Romana 93
Shrimp omelette 244
Spaghetti carbonara 217
Stir-fried beef with oyster-flavoured
    sauce 91
Stir-fried chicken and vegetables 132
Stuffed tomatoes 207
Toad-in-the-hole 119
Wiener schnitzel 93

M

Macadamia nut 257
Macaroni cheese 241
Macaroni cooking see Pasta cooking
Macaroons 302
Mace see Nutmeg
Mackerel 56
Madeira cake 306
Maize 215
Malay dishes (see also Indian)
    accompaniments to Malay dishes
        101
    apple sambal 101
    bobotie 114
    braised chicken 134
    chicken biriani 137
    carrot sambal 101
    cucumber sambal 101
    denning vleis 100
    giema curry 102
    green bean bredie 94
    mutton biriani 101
    mutton curry 102
    onion sambal 101
    pumpkin bredie 94
    sosaties 152, 154
    tomato bredie 95
    waterblommetjie bredie 95
Malbee grape 355
Maltabella 215
Maltaise sauce (var.) 173
Malva pudding 265
Mandarin see Naartjie
Mango 255
    atjar 335
    chutney 335
    keri sherbet 358
Manhattan (cocktail) 362
Margarita (cocktail) 362
Marinade(s) 153, **382**
    citrus; yellowtail cubes with 160
    for antipasto 31
    lemon and herb, with grilled
        chicken 140
Marinate(d) **382**
    pork spare ribs 106
    red roman, whole 138
    whole fish (braaied) 157
Marinière **382**
Marjoram 198
Marmalade 322
    pectin, acid and setting point
        321
    potting, sealing and storing 322
    making 322
    recipes:
    all-the-year-round 328
    naartjie (var.) 328
    orange (var.) 328
Marrow (vegetable) 186
    glazed 197

stuffed 197
Marrow bones – buying and
    preparing 83
Marsala **382**
Marsala sauce 174
Marshmallows 338
Martini, dry (cocktail) 362
Marzipan 338
Masala **382**
Masala chai 359
Mask **382**
Matar aur baïgan sakh (vegetable
    casserole) 190
Matzo dumpling 39
Mauritian fish 63
Mayonnaise 177
    aïoli (garlic) 176
    curry 177
    herb 177
    horseradish 177
    sauces based on 177
    seafood 177
    tartar sauce 177
    Thousand Island dressing 177
Mealie(s) 186
    freezing 372
    recipes:
    bread 298
    whole (braaied) 162
Meal-in-one dishes (see also
    Casseroles and stews)
    baked chicken and potatoes 146
    baked devilled eggs 244
    baked eggs in saucers 245
    baked fish with vegetables 78
    beef and noodles 121
    beef stew with parsley
        dumplings 121
    braised beefburgers with
        vegetables 121
    braised chicken 147
    braised lamb with spinach 120
    brinjals stuffed with curried
        vegetables 210
    cabbage rolls with sprout
        stuffing 210
    chicken, brinjal and noodle
        casserole 146
    chicken with mushrooms and
        barley 147
    crustless savoury tart 245
    eggs and asparagus 244
    eggs in overcoats 245
    fish and noodle casserole 79
    fish and potatoes with cheese
        topping 79
    fish Boulangère 78
    fish in pastry 78
    fish pie 78
    fish soup 49
    Greek salad 211
    hashed beef or lamb with
        tomatoes 120

INDEX

Lancashire hotpot 120
open roast chicken with orange juice and apples 146
pork and baked beans 120
salad Niçoise *211*
savoury bread and butter pudding 244
shrimp omelette 244
Spanish chicken with rice 146
vegetable casserole 211
vegetable medley 210
Meat 82 (*see also* Bacon; Beef; Bredies; Casseroles and stews; Game birds; Gammon; Goat; Ham; Hare; Lamb; Marrow bones; Mutton; Offal; Pork; Poultry; Rabbit; Sausages; Steak; Veal; Venison)
boiling 85
braaing 150
braising 85
brawn 86
bredie 94
bulk-buying 370
buying hints 82
carving 86, 87
choosing 82
cooking 84
cooking, salted 89
cooking times 85
cooking with wine 109
cuts 83
cuts for braaing 151
dripping 86
freezing 369, 370, 374
frying 84
grades 82
gravy 86
grilling 84
hotpots 86
loaves – freezing 374
mixed grill 85
pie fillings 248
pot-roasting 85
preparing – hints on 82
preserving – in brine 89
pressed 86
re-heating 86
roasting 84
salted – cooking 89
stews 86, 120
storage 368
tenderising 82
uses for cuts 83
wine served with 357
Meatballs
frozen 370
recipes:
braised beefburgers 121
frikkadels 114, **381**
kheema kebabs *103*
kofta kebabs *158*
Turkish lamb fondue 104

Mebos 339
Mediterranean seafood stew 76
Melba toast 292
Melktert 260
Melon 256
chilled 16
freezing 371
recipes:
and ginger jam *326*
and Parma ham 20
seafood salad with lemon cream sauce and 76
Melted butter (sauce) 168
Melton Mowbray pie *108*
Menus
braai 346
breakfast *236*, 344
brunch 344
buffet 348
children's parties 348
Chinese *138*, 346
Christmas 350
dinner 345
for large numbers 352
formal supper 346, *347*
lunch 346, *347*
New Year's Eve 351
planning a party 344
rijsttafel *220*
seasonal 346
teenage parties 348
traditional English breakfast *236*
twenty-first birthday 349
wedding reception *350*
Meringue(s) *284*, **382**
freezing 370
keeping 353
recipes:
chiffon tart 285
discs and shells *284*
gâteau 284
hazelnut 284
Pavlova *285*
Merlot 355
Meunière **382**
butter 168
fish 62
Microwave ovens 379
Milk
bread 296
cream and egg puddings 253
gedat 359
puddings 253, 254
punch 364
shakes *360*
Millet 215
couscous 224
Minced meat
cuts suitable for 83
storage 368
recipes:
bobotie *114*
Bolognese sauce 217

braised beefburgers 121
cottage pie 115
frikkadels 114
giema curry 102
kheema kebabs *103*
kofta kebabs *158*
moussaka 111
pastitsio *216*
samoosas 22
spring rolls 235
Turkish lamb fondue 104
Mincemeat, fruit 328
pies 260
Mince pies 260
Minestrone soup 46
Mint and pineapple sauce 174
Minted egg pie *235*
Minted yoghurt sauce 177
Mint julep (cocktail) 362
Mint sauce 168
Minute steak 82
Mixed fruit pickle 333
Mixed grill 85
Mixed spice 131
Mixers 377
Molasses **382**
Mongolian fire pot 104
Monkfish 56
cocktail (var.) 24
Mornay **382**
Mosbolletjies 304
Moulding and chilling 253
Moules marinière (mussels) 71
Moussaka 111
Mousse **382**
chocolate 282
cucumber and prawn 16
granadilla 282
lemon 282
salmon, with cucumber sauce *25*
Mousseline sauce (var.) 173
Mozzarella cheese 231
broccoli alla parmigiana 191
omelette filling 238
Muenster cheese 231
Muesli 224
biscuits 316
Mulberry(-ies) 256
freezing 371
Mull **382**
Mung bean 187
Murgh aur khaddu haleem (chicken and pumpkin soup) 42
Muscat d'Alexandrie 354
Mushroom(s) 185
freezing 373
recipes:
and celery and walnut stuffing 179
and ham with baked potato 203
baked with garlic butter (var.) 16
chicken with barley and 147

creamed 197
fettucine with tuna 218
kasha with 225
omelette filling 238
on skewers (braaied) 161
pancakes 234
pilaff 223
poached sole with 67
quiche 242
roulades 241
salad 200
sauce 174
snails in 16
spaghetti Napolitana with 218
stuffed 200
Muskmelon 256
Muslim (*see also* Malay dishes)
halaal **381**
Mussel(s) 58
cleaning and opening 71
recipes:
coastal Indian-style 72
grilled black 24
moules marinière 71
on skewers (braaied) 160
ragout 71
spicy fried *see* coastal Indian-style
Musselcracker 56
Mustard 130, 131, 185
and dill dressing 178
rabbit with 111
sauce 174
sauce (var: Hollandaise) 173
Mutton
braaing 151
bredies 94
choosing 82
cooking methods 83
cooking times 85
cuts 83
cuts for braaing 151
offal 83
uses for cuts 83
recipes:
biriani 101
bobotie *114*
boiled 86
curry 102, *335*
frikkadels 114
giema curry 102
green bean bredie 94
haricot of 101
kheema kebabs *103*
parsi dhansak (curry) *102*
pumpkin bredie 94
salt ribs 154
stuffed leg of 98
tomato bredie *95*
waterblommetjie bredie 95

N

Naartjie (mandarin, tangerine) 257
peel 131
preserve (var.) 331
Napolitana sauce 176
Nasi goreng (Indonesian-style fried rice) 220
Negroni (cocktail) 362
Newburg crayfish 73
New Year's Eve parties 350
Noodles 214
the art of cooking 214
recipes:
and chicken and brinjal casserole 146
and fish casserole 79
beef and 121
beef chow mein *219*
lasagne 217
salad 218
Nougat *341*
Nouvelle cuisine **382**
sauces thickened by reduction (in the manner of) 168
Nut(s)
blanching, roasting and toasting 324
buyer's guide 257
storage 368
recipes:
Chinese honey *341*
tart 261
Nutmeg and mace 130, 131

INDEX

O

Oatmeal 215
  bread 297
  muesli 224
  porridge 215
Oblietjies 316
Octopus 58
Oeufs en cocotte a la crème 233
Oeufs meulemeester 233
Offal **382** (*see also* Brain; Feet; Heart; Kidney; Liver; Marrow bones; Sweetbread; Tongue; Tripe; Trotters)
  choosing and preparing 83
  frozen 370
  storage 368
Okra 186
Olives, beef or veal 90
Omelette(s)
  Arnold Bennett 239
  basic French 238
  fillings 238
  shrimp 244
  soufflé 238
  soufflé jam 238
  Spanish 239
Onion(s) 185
  peeling, slicing and chopping 201
  recipes:
    à la Monégasque 201
    and carrots, pickled 333
    and caviar and egg starter 23
    and sage stuffing 181
    and tomato salad 266
    baked 200
    baked in coals 161
    bubble and squeak 192
    creamed button 201
    kasha with 225
    pickled 333
    quiche 242
    salad 201, 206
    sambal 101
    sauce 174
    soup 46
    tripe and 118
Open-freezing 370
Open roast chicken with orange juice and apples 146
Orange(s) 257
  freezing 371
  recipes:
    and chicory salad 195
    and grapefruit salad 276
    caramel 272
    chicken stew with tomato and 135
    lamb casserole with 99
    marmalade (var.) 328
    preserve 331

    roast duck with Van der Hum and *141*
    soufflé (var.) 268
    terrine of duck with *32*
Orange juice
  open roast chicken with apples and 146
Oriental fruit salad 275
Origanum 198
Osso bucco 96
Ostrich eggs 230
Ostrich, fillet steaks of *145*
Oven-fried crumbed chicken 134
Oven-fried fish and chips 60
Oven-roasting – cuts suitable for 83
Ovens 378
Ox offal 83
Oxtail
  buying and preparing 83
  recipes:
    soup 51
    stew 116
Ox tongue 83, 117
Oyster(s) 58
  cleaning and serving 24
  dip, smoked 29
  -flavoured sauce, stir-fried beef with *91*
  omelette filling 238
  soup 50

P

Packet foods 369
Paella 77, **382**
Palomino grape 354
Panada 167, **382**
Pancake(s) 234
  freezing 374
  recipes: 234
    crêpes suzettes *265*
    fillings 234
    potato 204
Pan thermostats 378
Paper-wrapped chicken 133
Papered fillets of pork 106
Paprika 130, 131
  cream sauce, fish with 63
Parboil **382**
Parfaits 280, **382**
Parma ham and melon or fig 20
Parmesan cheese 231
  broccoli alla Parmigiana 191
  omelette filling 238
  semolina gnocchi 225
  tagliatelle with 219
Parmigiano Reggiano *see* Parmesan cheese
Parsi dhansak (mutton curry) 102
Parsley 198
  recipes:
    butter 179
    dumplings 181
    dumplings, beef stew with *121*
    sauce 174
Parsnip 186
  balls *202*
  recipes:
    freezing 373
Parties 344
  breakfasts *344*
  brunches 344
  buffets 348
  catering for large numbers 352
  cheese and wine 352
  children's birthday 348
  Christmas 350
  cocktail 351
  dinner 344
  formal suppers 346, *347*
  lunch 344
  New Year's Eve 350
  teenage *348*
  weddings 349, *351*
Partridge – roasting 125
Party cake 310
Passion fruit *see* Granadilla
Pasta
  214, **382**
  cooking 214
  making home-made 214
  storage 353
  recipes:
    basic 219
    beef and noodles 121
    beef chow mein 219
    cannelloni 215, 216
    chicken, brinjal and noodle casserole 146
    fettucine with tuna, mushrooms tomato and onion sauce 218
    lasagne 214, 217
    noodle salad 218
    noodles and fish casserole 79
    pastitsio 216
    ravioli 215, 217
    spaghetti alla carbonara 217
    spaghetti alla vongole 218
    spaghetti Napolitana 218
    spaghetti with Bolognese sauce 217
    spaghetti with pesto sauce 217
    spinach 214
Pastes, smoked 25
Pasteurise **382**
Pastitsio 216
Pastries (*see also* Desserts; Pies; Tarts)
  freezing 372, 374
  useful tips 248, 251
Pastry 248, **382**
  assessing the amount 248
  baking blind 249, **380**
  covering a pie 249
  filling a pie 249
  freezing 372, 374
  glazing and decorating pies 249
  hints for making 248
  ingredients 248
  lining a shallow dish or flan ring 249
  parcels, meat baked in *112*
  mixing the dough 248
  rolling 249
  storing uncooked 249
  useful tips 248, 251
  recipes:
    biscuit crumb crust 252
    brioche 300, **380**
    cheese 252
    choux 251
    cream cheese 252
    fish in (sour cream flaky) 78
    flaky 250
    phyllo 252
    puff 250
    rough puff 251
    shortcrust 250
    sour cream flaky 250
    strudel 251
    sweet shortcrust 250
Pâté **382**
  freezing 374
  recipes:
    chicken liver 30
    smoked snoek 27

    taramasalata (fish roe) 27
    tuna (var.) 27
    venison 31
Patty **382**
Pavlova 285
  keeping crisp 353
Pawpaw 255
Pea(s) 186
  dried 187
  freezing 373
  split 187
  storage 368
  recipes:
    creamed 202
    soup with mint 40
    split pea soup 48
Peach(es)
  freezing 371
  recipes:
    chicken breasts with pine nuts and (var.) 140
    jam, sliced 327
    melba 280
    spiced 274
    stuffed 273
Peanut 257
  brittle 340
  sauce, pork satay kebabs and 158
  saus kacang tidak pedes (bland peanut sauce) 221
Pear 256
Pearl barley **382**
Pecan nut 257
  pie 262
Pecorino cheese 231
Pectin 321, **382**
Peel, candied 340
Peking duck 139
Pepper 131
  steak 90
Peppers (capsicum) 185
  skinning 203
  storage 368
  recipes:
    pickled 332
    salad 203
    stuffed 202
    sweet, pickled 332
Peppermint 199
Peri-peri 131
  chicken 135
  fish (var.) 35
  prawns 73
  prawns (var.) 35
  sauce 174
Periwinkle 59
Perlemoen 59
  cleaning 72
  recipes:
    creamed 72
    fried 72
    omelette (var.) 244
Persimmon 255

INDEX

Petit pois **382**
Petits fours *302*, **382**
    glacés *303*
Petit verdot grape 355
Pheasant – roasting 125
Phyllo pastry 252
    lamb chops in 112
    leg of lamb in 113
Piccalilli 333
Pickle **382**
Pickled
    cucumbers 332
    curried fish 61
    herring 30
    mixed fruit 333
    onions 333
    onions and carrots 333
    peppers, sweet 332
    red cabbage 332
Pickles
    making 322
    potting and sealing 323
Pickling spices 131, 323
Pies 248
    covering 249
    decorating 249
    filling 249
    freezing 372
    glazing 249
    tips for making 248
    recipes:
    apple 258
    beef and tomato 91
    Cape lamb 103
    chicken *137*
    cottage 115
    fish 78
    Greek custard 262
    mince 260
    pecan nut 262
    pork (Melton Mowbray) *108*
    steak and kidney *115*
    veal and ham 93
Pigeons
    roasting 125
    stewed 145
Pig's ears *262*
Pilaff
    chicken 222
    mushroom 223
    with lamb and apricots 223
Pilchard 56
Pimento *130*, **382**
Pina colada (cocktail) 363
Pineapple 255
    freezing 371
    recipes:
    and melon jam (var.) 326
    and mint sauce 174
    Romanoff 274
Pine nut(s) 257
    chicken breasts with apricots and (var.) 140

Pink lady (cocktail) 363
Pinotage 355
Pinot noir 355
Pipe **382**
Piperade 239
Piquant **382**
Pistachio nut 257
Pistou **382**
Pith **382**
Pitta bread *158*, 298
Pizza(s) *304*
    freezing 372, 374
    wine served with 357
Pizzarella cheese 231
Plaited loaf *296*
Plucking **382**
    game birds 125
    poultry and game birds 124
Plum(s) 256
    freezing 371
    recipes:
    crumble 267
    kuchen 299
    sauce 329
    sponge pudding 268
Poach(-ed/-ing) **382**
    eggs 229
    fish 55
    recipes:
    sole with mushrooms 67
    trout 71
Pomegranate 256
Pomelo 257
Pommes gratin dauphinois 205
Pont l'Évêque cheese 231
Poppadums 136
Poppy seeds 131
Pork
    braaing 151
    choosing 82
    cooking methods 83
    cooking times 85
    cuts 83
    cuts for braaing 151
    offal 83
    uses for cuts 83
    recipes:
    and baked beans 120
    barbecue spare ribs (braaied) *157*
    chop suey 109
    cutlets in white wine (var.) 93
    kassler rib chops with mustard sauce 107
    marinated spare ribs 106
    Melton Mowbray pie *108*
    papered fillets of *106*
    pot-roast cushion of, with apple and prune stuffing 106
    satay kebabs and peanut sauce *158*
    sausages 118
    smoke roasting 69

Porridge – cooking 215
Porridge, whiskyed 236
Porterhouse steak 82
Portmanteau'd lamb chops 100
Port Salut cheese 231
Portuguese chicken peri-peri 135
Pot-au-feu 86
Pot cooking 153
Potato(es) 186
    freezing 373
    recipes:
    and fish with cheese topping 79
    baked – variations 203
    baked and stuffed – variations 203
    baked chicken and 146
    baked in coals 162
    baked, smoked snoek and 66
    bubble and squeak 192
    chips and fish 60
    croquettes 203
    eggs in overcoats 245
    game chips 203
    gnocchi 225
    mashed 186
    oven-fried fish and chips 60
    pancakes 204
    pommes gratin dauphinois 205
    roast 186
    rosti *204*
    salad 204
    soufflé 203
Potjiekos 153
Pot-roast(-ing) 85, **382**
    beef 85
    brisket with prunes 88
    chicken 128
    cushion of pork with apple and prune stuffing 106
    cuts suitable for 83
Potted shrimps 27
Potted Stilton 241
Potting, sealing and storing 322, 323
Poultry and game birds 124
    boiling 125
    boning 124, *128*
    braaing 152
    buying 124
    carving 125
    choosing 124, 125
    cooking 125
    drawing 124, 125
    freezing 370, 371
    hanging 124, 125
    jointing 124
    larding 124
    plucking 124, 125
    poussin 125
    preparing 124, 125
    roasting 125
    stock 36
    storage 368
    stuffing 124
    trussing 124
    turkey 125
    recipes see Chicken; Duck; Goose; Guinea fowl; Ostrich; Partridge; Pheasant; Pigeon; Poussin; Quail; Turkey
Poussin – roasting 125
Prairie oyster (cocktail) 363
Praline 306, **382**
    ice cream 277
Prawns 59
    de-veining and shelling 73
    recipes:
    and crayfish sauce *172*
    and cucumber mousse 16
    baked with garlic butter 72
    chop suey 109
    chow mein (var.) 219
    cocktail (var.) 24
    curry 73
    omelette (var.) 244
    peri-peri 73 (var.) 135
    potted (var.) 27
    quiche 242
    ragout (var.) 71
    risotto Milanese (var.) 223
    teriyaki (braaied) *161*
    udang goreng asam manis (sweet and sour prawns) 220
Preserves 320, **382**
    citron *330*
    grapefruit (var.) 331
    green fig *331*
    kumquat *331*
    naartjie (var.) 331
    orange *331*
    sour fig *331*
    watermelon *330*
Preserving 320 (see also Chutney; Fruit, dried; Jam; Jelly; Ketchups; Marmalade; Mincemeat; Pickles; Potting; Preserves; Relish)
    bottling and sealing 323
    equipment 320
    making spiced vinegar 323
    meat in brine 89
    potting and sealing 322, 323
Pressed meat 86
Pressure cookers 375
Prickly pear 255
Profiteroles with ice cream and hot chocolate sauce 259
Prove(-ing) 291, **382**
Provencale **382**
Provolone cheese 231
Prune plum 256
Prunes
    pot-roast brisket with 88
    stuffing, herbed *180*
    wrapped in bacon 21
Pudding(s) 248, **382**
    batter 254
    Christmas 272
    cream, milk and egg 253, 254
    flummery 253
    hints for beating eggs 253
    hints for using cream 253
    preparing a basin for steaming 254
    reheating 254
    steamed 254
    tips for making custard 253
    tips for making milk puddings 254
    recipes:
    baked custard 253
    bread and butter 264
    Cape brandy *264*
    chocolate 268
    Christmas 272
    golden sponge 268, *287*
    lemon 265
    malva 265
    plum sponge 268
    queen's 267
    rice 267
    sago 267
    savoury bread and butter 244
    semolina 267
    steamed 254
    upside-down winter *269*
Puff pastry 250, 251
    gammon steaks in 113
    steak in 112
Pulp **382**
Pumpkin 187 (see also Hubbard squash; Squash)
    boerpampoen 187
    braised chicken with sweet potato and *147*
    bredie 94
    fritters 205
    purée 205
    soup 47
    soup (murgh aur khaddu haleem) 42
Punch(es) 364
    fruit 365
    glühwein *365*
    loving cup *365*
    milk 364
    sangria 365
Purée **382**
Puri 305

INDEX

Q

Quail – roasting 125
Quail eggs 230
Queen's pudding 267
Quenelles **382**
Quiches *242*, **382**
 tiny *21*
Quick bites *20*
Quince 257
 and melon jam (var.) *326*
 jelly *328*

R

Rabbit
 choosing and preparing 84
 jointing 84
 recipes:
  fried young *111*
  with mustard *111*
Radish 185
 and cucumber salad *195*
Ragout, mussel 71
Raisin and apple stuffing *178*
Raisin and rice stuffing *127*
Ramekin **382**
Raspberries 256
 freezing 371
Raspberry jam *327*
Ratatouille 207
Ravigote sauce *178*
Ravioli 215, 217
Red cabbage
 pickled *332*
 stewed *205*
Red roman 56
 whole marinated *138*
Red steenbras 56
Red tide **382**
Red tomato chutney *334*
Reduce **382**
Red wine sauce 166
Refresh **382**
Refrigeration 368
Refrigerators 379
Relish **382**
Render **382**
Rennet **382**
Rhine riesling 354
Rhubarb 255
 freezing 371
Ribs
 barbecue spare *157*
 kassler chops with mustard sauce *107*
 marinated spare *106*
 salt (braaied) *154*
 spicy red lamb *100*

Rice 215
 cooking plain 215
 cooking yellow 215
 rijsttafel *220*
 savoury *381*
 serving hint 353
 recipes:
  and raisin stuffing *127*
  brown, and water chestnut stuffing *179*
  fried *222*
  nasi goreng (Indonesian-style fried rice) *220*
  pudding 267
  risotto Milanese *223*
  saffron *222*
  salad *222*
  Spanish chicken with *146*
  spinach *222*
Rice paper **382**
Ricotta cheese 231
Riesling 354
Rigatoni **383**
Rijsttafel *220*
Rind **383**
Risotto **383**
 Milanese *223*
Rissole 333, **383** (*see also* Frikkadels)
Roast(-ed/-ing) 84, **383**
 beef and Yorkshire pudding 88
 beef, carving 86, 87
 chicken, egged, breaded *126*
 chicken, frozen 371
 chicken, general guide to 125
 chickens, baby, with rice and raisin stuffing *127*
 chicken, stuffed *126*
 chicken with herb butter stuffing *179*
 cooking times 85
 crown roast of lamb *97*
 duck with grapefruit *140*
 duck with orange and Van der Hum *141*
 frozen meat 370
 game birds 125
 goose with rum-soaked apples *145*
 lamb, carving 86, 87
 lamb, stuffed shoulder of *96*
 nuts *324*
 open roast chicken with orange juice and apples *146*
 poultry and game birds 125
 saddle of lamb *96*
 saddle of venison *110*
 standing rib, carving 87
 turkey with two stuffings *142*
 venison, saddle of *110*
Rocket 199
Rock lobsters *see* Crayfish
Roe **383**

pâté 27
Rollmops, herring 30
Rolls *see* Bread
Roosterkoek 153
Roquefort cheese 231
Roquefort or blue cheese dressing *178*
Rosemary 198
Roses and leaves
 chocolate *336*
 sugar (icing) *311*
Rosti *204*
Roti *see* Chapati
Rotisserie 378, **383**
Rough puff pastry 251
Roulade(s) *241*, **383**
Roux **383**
Royal icing 295
Rub in **383**
Rules for sugar-boiling 325
Rum
 and chocolate gâteau *271*
 baba au rhum *313*
 butter *287*
 roast goose with rum-soaked apples *145*
Rump steak 82
Rum truffles *302*
Rusks, buttermilk *315*
Russian
 beef stroganoff 89
 blini with caviar 22
 kasha 225
 sausage and lentil salad 209
Rye bread 298

S

Saddle **383**
 of lamb, roast *96*
 of venison, roast *110*
Safety in the kitchen 375
Saffron 131
 rice *222*
Sage 198
 and onion stuffing *181*
Sago 215
 pudding 267
Saint Paulin cheese 231
Salad
 asparagus 188
 baby marrow 188
 bacon and hot spinach *18*
 beetroot *191*
 Caesar *196*
 carrot *193*
 chicken *140*
 chicken liver and lettuce *18*
 chicory and orange *195*
 coleslaw *193*
 cucumber and radish *195*
 egg *233*
 fennel, tomato and mushroom *195*
 fresh fruit (brûlée) *274*
 grapefruit *17*
 Greek *211*
 green *197*
 hot spinach and bacon *18*
 hot winter *275*
 kachoomer *208*
 lentil and sausage *209*
 lettuce and chicken liver *18*
 mushroom *200*
 nicoise *211*
 noodle *218*
 onion *201*
 orange and grapefruit *276*
 Oriental fruit *275*
 pepper *203*
 potato *204*
 rice *222*
 seafood, with melon and lemon cream sauce *76*
 sousboontjies *208*
 sweet and sour beetroot with citrus sauce *191*
 tomato and onion *206*
 turkey, with cheese and sesame seeds *143*
 watercress *206*
 winter fruit *276*
Salad burnet 198
Salad dressings *see* Dressings
Salami **383**
Salmon (*see also* Cape salmon)
 mousse with cucumber sauce *25*
 smoked, serving *27*

 smoked, blintzes *24*
 smoked, nibbles *20*
 smoked, omelette filling *238*
 smoked, quiche *242*
 soufflé (var.) *240*
Salmon trout parcels (var.) *157*
Salsify 185
Salt 131
Salted meat – cooking 89
Saltimbocca alla Romana (veal schnitzels or beef steaks) 93
Saltpetre **383**
Salt ribs (braaied) *154*
Sambal(s) **383**
 apple *101*
 carrot *101*
 cucumber *101*
 goreng terung (peppery brinjal) *221*
 ketimum (spicy cucumber) *221*
 onion *101*
Samba surprise (cocktail) *363*
Samoosas 22
 folding *22*
 meat *22*
 vegetarian *22*
Sandveld snoek 65
Sandwich (cake), Victoria sponge *312*
Sandwiches 298
 toasted (braaied) *153*
Sangria 365
Sas sauce, husaini kebabs and *159*
Satay kebabs and peanut sauce *158*
Satay sapi pedes (hot beef satay) *221*
Sauce(s) 166, 170, 286, 323 (*see also* Desserts; Dressings; Mayonnaise; Vinaigrette)
 bottling and sterilising 323
 equipment 166
 freezing 373
 keeping and re-heating roux-based 167
 making 323
 rescuing roux-based 167
 thickening 166, 167, 168
 recipes:
  aïoli *174*
  apple *170*
  avgolemono *40*
  avocado *170*
  barbecue *170*
  basic brown 166
  Bearnaise *170*
  béchamel 166
  beurre noir 168
  beurre noisette 168
  binding 167
  Bolognese 217
  bread *171*
  caper *171*
  caper (var: Hollandaise) *173*
  celery *171*

INDEX

chasseur 171
chaud-froid 167
cheese 171
coating 167
crayfish 168
crayfish and prawn *172*
cream 167
creamed horseradish 105
cucumber (var.) 173
Cumberland 171
curry 62, 105, 172
dahi (yoghurt) 177
egg and lemon 173
egg, with smoked haddock 237
Espagnole 166
green herb 105
Hollandaise 173
horseradish 173
horseradish (var: Hollandaise) 173
Maltaise (var.) 173
marsala 174
melted butter 168
meunière 168
mint 168
mint and pineapple 174
minted yoghurt 177
mousseline (var.) 173
mushroom 105, 174
mustard 105, 174
mustard (var: Hollandaise) 173
Napolitana 176
olive 105
onion 174
parsley 174
peri-peri 174
pesto 217
plum 329
ravigote 178
red wine 166
suprême 167
sweet-sour *174*
tartar 177
tomato *329*
Toulouse (var.) 173
velouté 167
vinaigrette 178
white 166
Saucepans 375
Sausage(s) 83
 choosing and preparing 83
 for braaing 152
 frozen 370
 smoke roasting 67
 recipes:
 and bacon fondue 104
 and lentil salad 209
 baked, with bacon and eggs 236
 boerewors 118
 pork 118
 sausage rolls *33*
 toad-in-the-hole *119*
Saus kacang tidak pedes (bland peanut sauce) 221
Sauté **383**
Sauvignon blanc 354
Savouries *see* Starters, snacks and savouries
Savoury
 bread and butter pudding 244
 butters 179
 fillings 248
 rice **383**
 tart, crustless *245*
Scald **383**
Schnitzel **383**
 veal (saltimbocca alla Romana) 93
 Wiener 93
School lunches 298
Scones 305
 drop 262
Score **383**
Scotch broth 40
Scotch eggs 234
Screwdriver (cocktail) 363
Seafood (*see also* Fish) 54, 57, 78
 recipes:
 baked prawns in garlic butter 72
 braaied crayfish 161
 coastal Indian-style mussels 72
 crayfish cocktail 24
 crayfish Newburg 73
 crayfish thermidor 74
 creamed perlemoen 72
 fondue 104
 fried calamari 75
 fried perlemoen 72
 grilled black musels 24
 grilled calamari 75
 grilled crayfish 74
 mayonnaise 177
 meal-in-one fish soup *49*
 moules marinière 71
 mussel ragout 71
 mussels on skewers (braaied) 160
 oyster soup *50*
 paella 77
 peri-peri prawns 73
 potted shrimps 27
 prawn curry 73
 salad with melon and lemon cream sauce 76
 smoked oyster dip 29
 stew 76
Sear **383**
Seasonal guide to fresh produce 346
Seasoned flour **383**
Seasoning(s) **383**
 frozen 373
Sea urchin 59
Seeds for sprouting 187 (*see also* Sprouts)
Sémillon grape 354
Semolina
 dumplings 181

gnocchi 225
pudding 267
Sesame dressing 178
Sesame seed(s) *131*
 bars 340
 turkey salad with cheese and *143*
Setting point for jams, jellies and marmalade 321
Shad 55
Shallot 185
Shallow-frying **383**
Shelf life of food 368
Shellfish 57 (*see also* Crayfish; Mussels; Prawns; Perlemoen; Seafood; Shrimps)
Sherbet, keri 358
Shiraz 355
Shortbread *317*
Shortcrust pastry 250
Shortcrust pastry, sweet 250
Shrimp(s) 59
 cocktail (var.) 24
 omelette 244
 potted 27
 ragout (var: Mussel) 71
Shrip **383**
Sidecar (cocktail) 363
Sift **383**
Silverfish 56
Simnel cake *312*
Simmer **383**
Sirloin of steak 82
Skate 56
Skewer **383**
Skim **383**
Slake **383**
Slow-cookers 378
Small crack 325
Smetena (soured cream) **383**
Smoke **383**
Smoked
 fish pastes 25
 fish soufflé (var.) 240
 haddock with egg sauce 237
 oyster dip 29
 salmon 27
 salmon blintzes 24
 salmon nibbles *20*
 salmon omelette filling 238
 salmon quiche 242
 snoek and potato bake 66
 snoek dip *29*
 snoek omelette filling 238
 snoek pâté 27
 snoek quiche 242
Smoke roasting 67
 recipes:
 beef 69
 boerewors and beef sausage 69
 chicken 68
 eggs 69
 fish 68

pork and lamb 69
Smoking oven 151
Smoorsnoek (gesmoorde snoek) 65
Snacks *see* Starters, snacks and savouries
Snails
 in garlic butter (var.) 16
 in mushrooms 16
Snoek 57
 recipes:
 dip, smoked 29
 fingers 20
 gesmoorde 65
 Sandveld 65
 smoked, and potato bake 66
 smoked, omelette filling 238
 smoked, pâté 27
 smoked, quiche 242
Snow eggs 284
Soda bread 296
Soetkoekies, old-fashioned 315
Soft ball 325
Sole
 recipes:
 grilled 67
 poached, with mushrooms 67
 Véronique 66
Sooki murghi (spicy chicken) 136
Sorbet **383**
 grapefruit (var.) 280
 lemon 280
 strawberry 280
Sorghum 215
 porridge 215
Sorrel 186
Sosaties
 braaing 154
 meat for 152
Soufflé(s) 240, **383**
 hints on making savoury 240
 making collars 281
 recipes:
 asparagus (var.) 240
 baked potato 203
 blue cheese (var.) 240
 cheese 240
 chocolate (var.) 268
 coffee (var.) 268
 iced coffee 281
 jam omelette *238*
 lemon (var.) 268
 omelette 238
 orange (var.) 268
 salmon (var.) 240
 smoked fish (var.) 240
 tuna (var.) 240
 vanilla 268
Soufflé dish **383**
Soup(s) 36, 40 (*see also* Dumplings; Stocks)
 clarifying with egg 229
 cuts suitable for 83
 garnishes 38

 serving 38
 thick 38
 thin 37
 recipes (cold):
 avocado 44
 borsch (beetroot) *43*
 carrot vichyssoise with mint 42
 chilled cucumber *45*
 gazpacho *44*
 Jerusalem artichoke 43
 vichyssoise 51
 vichyssoise, chilled carrot, with mint *42*
 recipes (hot):
 avgolemono 40
 avocado (var.) 44
 bean 50
 borsch (beetroot) *43*
 brisket and barley *41*
 butternut (var.) 47
 cauliflower 45
 chicken and pumpkin (murgh aur khaddu haleem) 42
 cock-a-leekie 42
 cream of asparagus 45
 hot and sour *138*
 Japanese thin 37
 Jerusalem artichoke 43
 meal-in-one fish 49
 minestrone 46
 murgh aur khaddu haleem (chicken and pumpkin) 42
 mussel (var.) 71
 onion 46
 oxtail *51*
 oyster *50*
 pea, with mint 40
 pumpkin 47
 pumpkin and chicken (murgh aur khaddu haleem) 42
 Scotch broth 40
 spinach 46
 split pea 48
 tomato and carrot 48
 vegetable 49
 vichyssoise 51
 won ton *41*
Sour(ed) cream (smetena) **383**
 and chives, baked potatoes with 203
 and dill dressing 178
 flaky pastry 250
 sauce; fish terrine with *26*
Sour fig 256
 preserve *331*
Sousboontjies 208
Souse **383**
Sou-sou *see* Cho-cho
South African riesling 354
South Indian fish curry 63
Souzao grape 355
Soya bean(s) 187
 spaghetti Napolitana with 218

397

INDEX

sprouts 187, 191
Soya nut loaf 209
Spaghetti
    cooking *see* Pasta cooking
    alla carbonara 217
    alla vongole 218
    Napolitana *218*
    with Bolognese sauce 217
    with pesto sauce 217
Spanakopitta (spinach pie) *243*
Spanish
    chicken with rice 146
    omelette 239
    paella 77
Spanspek 256
Spare ribs
    barbecue 157
    pork, marinated 106
Spiced brinjals 188
Spiced cauliflower 194
Spiced peaches *274*
Spiced vinegar 323
Spices *130*
    storage 368
    whole or ground 368
Spicy chicken kebabs 159
Spicy red lamb ribs 100
Spinach 186
    baji aur inda (spinach egg scramble) 233
    freezing 373
    pasta 214
    recipes:
    and bacon salad, hot *18*
    braised lamb with 120
    creamed 206
    gnocchi 225
    pancakes 234
    quiche 242
    rice 222
    roulades 241
    soup 46
    spanakopitta (spinach pie) *243*
    stuffed leaves (var.) 17
Spinach beet (Swiss chard) 186
Spit **383**
Split peas 187
    soup 48
Sponge fingers 302
Sponge sandwich (cake), Victoria 312
Spring rolls 235
Sprout(s)
    growing and using 191
    seeds for sprouting 187
    recipes:
    stuffing with cabbage rolls 210
Squash 187 (*see also* Butternut squash; Gem squash; Table queen squash)
Squid 59
Standing rib roast – carving 87
Starch **383**

Starters, snacks and savouries (*see also* Dips)
    antipasto *31*
    filled cases 21
    making the most of avocados 16
    quick bites 20
    recipes:
    anchovies, egg and onion (var.) 23
    anchovy fingers 21
    avocado dip 28
    avocados 16
    bacon-wrapped chicken livers (or prunes or dried apricots) 21
    blini with caviar 22
    camembert en croûte *33*
    caviar, egg and onion 23
    caviar tart 23
    caviar with blini 22
    cheese beignets 21
    cheese whirls 21
    chicken liver pâté with port *30*
    chicken liver puffs 21
    chilled grapefruit 16
    chilled melon 16
    Chinese chicken wings 21
    chopped herring 27
    chopped liver 31
    composed crayfish salad 24
    composed grapefruit salad 17
    crayfish cocktail 24
    cream cheese bites 20
    cucumber and prawn mousse 16
    cucumber boats 21
    dolmades (stuffed vine leaves) 17, 21
    egg and caviar bites 20
    finger foods *20*
    fish croquettes 21
    fish roe pâté (taramasalata) 27
    fish terrine with sour cream sauce 26
    for cocktail party 352
    grilled black mussels 24
    ham crescents 21
    ham pinwheels 21
    herring rollmops 30
    hot spinach and bacon salad *18*
    lettuce and chicken liver salad *18*
    oysters; cleaning and serving 24
    Parma ham and melon or fig 20
    potted shrimps 27
    quiches, tiny 21
    salmon mousse with cucumber sauce 25
    samoosas 22
    sausage rolls 33
    smoked fish paste 25
    smoked salmon – serving 27
    smoked salmon blintzes 24
    smoked salmon nibbles 20
    smoked snoek pâté 27

    snails in garlic butter (var.) 16
    snails in mushrooms 16
    snoek fingers 20
    stuffed cabbage leaves (var.) 17
    stuffed celery sticks 20
    stuffed eggs 21
    stuffed fig leaves (var.) 17
    stuffed spinach leaves (var.) 17
    taramasalata 27
    terrine of duck with orange *32*
    vegetable terrine 19
    venison pâté 31
    venison tart (var.) 31
Steak(s)
    braaing 151
    chateaubriand 82
    choosing 82
    cuts for braaing 151
    entrecôte 82
    filet mignon 82
    fillet 82
    minute 82
    porterhouse 82
    rump 82
    sirloin 82
    T-bone 82
    tenderising 82
    recipes:
    and kidney pie *115*
    braaing T-bone 156
    fillet, caramel 89
    in puff pastry 112
    ostrich fillet *145*
    pepper 90
    T-bone (braaied) 156
Steam **383**
Steamed(-ing)
    fish 55
    fish, Chinese sweet and sour 61
    puddings 254
    vegetables 184
Steenbras, red 56
Steep **383**
Sterilise(-ing) **383**
    jars and bottles 322
    sauces and ketchups 323
Stewed
    lentils 209
    pigeons 145
    red cabbage *205*
Stewing, cuts suitable for 83
Stews *see* Casseroles and stews
Stilton cheese 231
Stilton, potted 241
Stinger (cocktail) 363
Stir **383**
Stir-fried beef with oyster-flavoured sauce 91
Stir-fried chicken 132
Stir-fried vegetables, Chinese 139, 207
Stir-fry **383**
Stir-frying vegetables *139*, 184, 207

Stock 36, **383** (*see also* Soup)
    clarifying with egg 229
    cooking in a pressure cooker 37
    cuts suitable for 83
    main types 36
    making 37
    storing 37
    recipes:
    aspic 37
    basic 36
    brown 36
    chicken and other poultry 36
    chicken, Chinese 36
    clear 36
    cubes 37
    cuts suitable for 83
    fish 36
    household 36
    meat glaze 37
    vegetable 37
    white 36
Storing
    food 368
    vegetables 84
    wine 355
Strain **383**
Strawberries 256
    freezing 371
Strawberry
    chocolate box 337
    conserve 328
    cream cake 271
    ice cream 276
    jam 328
    Romanoff (var.) *274*
    sorbet 280
Stroganoff, beef 89
Strudel **383**
Strudel, apple 258
Strudel pastry 251
Stuffed
    apples, baked *273*
    boned chicken 128
    brinjals 189
    butternuts *192*
    eggs *21*, 239
    gem squash 195
    leg of mutton 98
    marrow 197
    mushrooms 200
    peaches 273
    peppers 202
    tomatoes 207
    whole baked fish 65
Stuffing 169, **383**
    making and using 169
    recipes:
    apple and prune, with pot-roast cushion of pork 106
    apple and raisin 178
    apricot 179
    brown rice and water chestnuts 180

    celery, mushroom and walnut 179
    chestnut 179
    chicken 126
    country herb 181
    herb butter, roast chicken with 179
    herbed prune *180*
    poultry and game birds 124
    rice and raisin *127*
    sage and onion 181
    turkey with two stuffings *142*
Stumpnose 57
Stywe pap 215
Subtropical fruit 255
Suet **383**
    dumplings 181
Sugar
    -freezing 370
    roses and leaves (icing) *311*
    rules for boiling 325
    storage 368
    syrups 370
Summer fruit(s) 256
    bowl *275*
    platter *276*
Summer savory 199
Sundaes 280
Supper menus
    Chinese 346
    Eastern 347
    formal 346, *347*
    informal 346
Suprême sauce 167
Sweat **383**
Swede 187
Swedish tea ring 305
Sweet and sour
    beetroot with citrus sauce 191
    fish, Chinese steamed 61
    prawns (udang goreng asam manis) *221*
    sauce 174
Sweetbreads, buying and preparing 83
Sweet corn 186
    fritters 197
    whole (braaied) *162*
Sweet potato(es) 187
    braised chicken with pumpkin and *147*
    fritters (var.) 205
    glazed 206
Sweet shortcrust pastry 250
Sweets
    making 324
    rules for sugar-boiling 325
    recipes:
    butterscotch 325
    caramel 325
    Chinese honey nuts *341*
    chocolate *see* Chocolate
    coconut ice 339

fudge 339
jujubes (fruit gums) 339
marshmallows 338
marzipan *338*
mebos 339
nougat *341*
peanut brittle 340
sesame seed bars 340
sugared almonds 340
tammeletjies 340
toffee 325
Turkish delight *341*
Sweets (desserts) *see* Desserts
Swiss chard (spinach beet) 186
Swiss cheese fondue 104
Swiss roll 309, *327*
Syllabub 283
Syrup(s) **383**
　fruit 361
　storage 368
　sugar 370

T

Tabbouleh 224
Table queen squash 187
Tagliatelle **383**
　with cream and Parmesan cheese 219
Tamarind 131
Tammeletjies 340
Tangelo 257
Tangerine *see* Naartjie
Tapioca 215
Taramasalata (fish roe pâté) 27
Tarragon 198
Tart(s)
　tips for making 248
　recipes:
　apricot yoghurt 270
　Bakewell 258
　caviar 23
　chiffon 285
　crustless, savoury 245
　fig 260
　guava *261*
　melktert 260
　nut 261
Tartar sauce 177
T-bone steak 82
　braaing 156
　Tea
　bush 359
　herbal 359
　iced 358
　storage 368
Teenage parties *348*
Tenderising steak 82
Tequila sunrise (cocktail) 363
Terrine(s) **383**
　freezing 374
　recipes:
　fish, with sour cream sauce 26
　of duck with orange *32*
　vegetable *19*
Thickening **383**
Thin mealie meal porridge 215
Thread 325
Thyme *199*
Tiger fish 59
Tiles 302
Tilsit cheese 231
Tinned foods
　labels 369
　storage 368
Tinta barocca 355
Tinta roriz grape 355
Toad-in-the-hole *119*
Toasted sandwiches (braaied) 153
Toast, fluffy cheese 243
Toast, French 242
Toasting nuts 324
Toast, Melba 292
Toffee 325

Toffee apples, Chinese *266*
Tomato(es) 186
　freezing 373
　skinning and seeding *48*
　storage 368
　recipes:
　and beef pie 91
　and carrot soup *48*
　and onion salad 206
　and onion sauce (Napolitana sauce) 176
　bredie 95
　butter beans with *208*
　chicken stew with orange and *135*
　chutney (red and green) 334
　cocktail, fresh 363
　green, chutney 334
　hashed beef or lamb with 121
　herbed crumbed *236*
　kachoomer (salad) 208
　Napolitana sauce 176
　red, chutney 334
　salad 206
　sauce *329*
　stuffed 207
Tom Collins (cocktail) 363
Tongue
　buying and preparing 83
　serving hint 353
　recipes:
　ox tongue 117
　Toulouse sauce (var: Hollandaise) 173
　Train cake 311
Tree tomato 256
Trifle *283*
Tripe
　buying and preparing 83
　recipes:
　and onions 118
　and trotters 84
　Venetian style *118*
Triple chocolate bombe 279
Tropical and subtropical fruit 255
Trotters
　and tripe 84
　buying and preparing 83
Trout 59
　parcels (braaied) 157
　poached 71
　with almonds 71
Truffles, rum 302
Trussing **383**
　poultry and game birds 124
Tube pan **383**
Tuna 57
　baked with anchovies and garlic 67
　dip 29
　fettucine with 218
　pancakes 234
　quiche 242

soufflé (var.) 240
spaghetti Napolitana with 218
Turkey 125
　freezing 370, 371
　roasting 125
　recipes:
　puff 143
　salad with cheese and sesame seeds 143
　with two stuffings 142
Turkey eggs 230
Turkish coffee 359
Turkish delight *341*
Turkish lamb fondue 104
Turmeric 131
Turnips 186
　freezing 373
Twenty-first birthday 349
Twist 362, **383**
Tyropita (cheese pastries) 242

VEGETARIAN MENUS

SOUPS
Chilled cucumber *45*
Gazpacho *44*
Jerusalem artichoke 43
Minestrone *46*
Pea soup with mint 40
Vegetable soup 49

MAIN COURSES
Baby marrows in cheese sauce 188
Bhaji masoor ni dhal (lentil stew) 208
Brinjals stuffed with curried vegetables 210
Broccoli alla Parmigiana 191
Broccoli with almonds 192
Butter beans with tomato 208
Cabbage rolls with sprout stuffing 210
Greek salad 211
Haricot bean curry 209
Hot vegetable platter 206
Kasha with mushrooms and onions 225
Lentil salad (var.) 209
Macaroni cheese 241
Matar aur baïgan sakh (vegetable casserole) 190
Mixed vegetables with cheese topping (var.) *79*
Mushroom pilaff 223
Noodle salad 218
Soya nut loaf 209
Spaghetti Napolitana *218*
Spaghetti with pesto sauce 217
Spinach gnocchi 225
Stuffed brinjals 189
Stuffed butternuts *192*
Stuffed gem squash 195
Stuffed mushrooms *200*
Stuffed peppers 202
Stuffed tomatoes 207
Vegetable casserole 211
Vegetable medley 210

U

Udang goreng asam manis (sweet and sour prawns) 221
Unleavened bread **383**
Upside-down winter pudding *269*
Utensils 375, *376*

V

Van der Hum liqueur 364
　roast duck with orange and *141*
Vanilla 131
　ice cream 276
　soufflé 268
Vanilla sugar **383**
Veal
　choosing 82
　cooking methods 83
　cooking times 85
　cuts 83
　offal 83
　stews 86
　uses for cuts 83
　recipes:
　and ham pie 93
　blanquette de veau 92
　cordon bleu (var: Wiener schnitzel) 93
　cutlets in white wine 93
　olives 90
　osso bucco 96
　schnitzels (saltimbocca alla Romana) 93
　vitello tonnato (with tuna sauce) 92
　Wiener schnitzel 93
Vegetable(s) 184 (*see also* Herbs; Salads; Sprouts and specific vegetables, e.g. Carrots; Potatoes)
　blanching 184, 373
　boiling 184
　braising 184
　comprehensive guide to 184
　cooking 184
　freezing 372, 373
　growing and using sprouts 191
　herbs 198
　legumes 187
　preparing 184
　pulses 187
　seasonal guide to 346
　seeds for sprouting 187
　steaming 184
　stir-frying 184, *207*
　storing 184, 368
　suitable for dipping 29
　that should be cooked 186

399

used raw or cooked 184
recipes:
and stir-fried chicken 132
braised beefburgers with 121
brinjals stuffed with curried 210
casserole 211
casserole of chicken with
   spring vegetables 147
Chinese stir-fried *139, 207*
fondue 104
medley 210
mixed, in foil (braaied) 162
pie (var: casserole) 211
platter, hot 206
ratatouille 207
savoury pie filling 248
soup 49
soup (minestrone) *46*
stir-fried *207*
stir-fried chicken and 132
stock 37
terrine *19*
Velouté 167, **383**
Venetian-style tripe *118*
Venison
   choosing and preparing 84
   recipes:
   casserole with sour cream 109
   pâté 31
   roast saddle of *110*
Vermicelli **383**
   boeboer, Malay 358
Vetkoek 313
Vichyssoise
   chilled carrot, with mint *42*
   hot or chilled 51
Victoria sponge sandwich (cake) 312
Vinaigrette 178, **383**
   avocado dressing (var.) 178
   blue cheese dressing (var.) 178
   herbed (var.) 178
   horseradish (var.) 178
   hot with egg (var.) 178
   ravigote sauce (var.) 178
   Roquefort dressing (var.) 178
Vinegar **383**
   flavoured 324
   fruit 329
   herb *332*
   spiced 323
Vine leaves 187
   stuffed (dolmades) 17, *21*
Vitello tonnato (veal with tuna
   sauce) *92*
Vlek **383**
Vol-au-vent(s) 252

W

Waffles 265
Walnut 257
   and apple and date chutney *334*
   and date loaf 312
   cream torte 270
   celery and mushroom stuffing
      179
Waterblommetjie(s) 187
   bredie 95
Water chestnut and brown rice
   stuffing 180
Watercress 186
   salad 206
Watermelon 256
   preserve 330
Watermint 199
Water test 325
Wedding cake 311, *350*
Wedding reception 349, *351*
Weevils in food 368
Weisser riesling 354
Welsh rarebit 242
Wensleydale cheese 231
Wheat 215 (*see also* Bread; Cake;
   Flour; Wholewheat)
   recipes:
   couscous 224
   Tabbouleh *224*
Whey **383**
Whip **383**
Whiskey sour 363
Whiskyed porridge *236*
White lady (cocktail) 363
White sauce 166
White stews 86
White stock 36
Wholewheat bread 297
Wiener schnitzel 93
Wine
   breathing and decanting 356
   grape cultivars 354
   cooking with 109
   freezing 373
   history of in S.A. 355
   serving 354
   serving etiquette 356
   serving order 356
   serving temperature 356
   storing 355
Winter fruit(s) 256
   salad 276
Winter savory 199
Woks 377
Won ton(s)
   how to make *41*
   soup 41

Y

Yeast 290, **383**
Yellow rice 215
Yellowfish 59
Yellowtail 57
   cubes with citrus marinade
      (braaied) *160*
   with avocado sauce *70*
Yoghurt 254, **383**
   basic 254
   fruit 255
   incubating 254
   tips for making 255
   recipes:
   and banana flan 271
   and cucumber dip 29
   basic 254
   dahi (sauce) 177
   fruit 255
   Greek lamb with *98*
   sauce (dahi) 177
   sauce; Indonesian lamb kebabs
      with 159
   sauce, minted 177
   tart, apricot 270
Yorkshire pudding
   roast beef and *88*
   toad-in-the-hole *119*
Youngberry(-ies)
   cream flan 270
   freezing 371

Z

Zabaglione 269
Zest **383**
Zinfandel 355
Zucchini *see* Baby marrows

Acknowledgments

Reader's Digest acknowledges with thanks the assistance provided by the following individuals and companies in providing kitchen utensils, appliances and other items for photographs in this book:

The Antiquarian
Arena Interiors
Bath Tiles (CTPS)
Binnehuis Interiors (Pty) Ltd
Boardmans Cape Town
Bygones Antiques
Collectors Corner
Country Matters
Defy Major Appliances
Düykers Gallery
Etcetera Gift Boutique (Pty) Ltd
Falkirk Industries (Pty) Ltd
Vivia Ferreira
Arthur J Foster (Pty) Ltd
Mr K Harcourt-Wood
The Inside Shop
Ncamekile Kokane
Knysna Oyster Company
La Maree
Marilyn Lilley
Martha's Vineyard
Metropole Hotel
Miscellania
Morris the Butcher
Ramola Parbhoo
Hym Rabinowitz
Wm Spilhaus Silverware (Pty) Ltd
Stuttafords Ltd
Tedelex
Thorn EMI Kenwood
Villeroy and Boch (Luxembourg)

We would like to thank the following individuals and organisations for providing practical advice:
Egg Control Board
Dave Finlayson
Ernest Gacias
KWV Paarl
Meat Board
Gonaseelan Moodley
Sue Pitt

We would like to thank the following companies for providing food for recipe testing purposes:
All Gold Foods
Blossom Margarine
Colman's Foods
County Fair Foods (Pty) Ltd
Farmer Brown
Gilbey Distillers and Vintners
   (Pty) Ltd
Lawry's Spices of Southern
   California
Moir's
Robertsons (Pty) Ltd
Sasko Perfection Flour
Stellenbosch Farmers' Winery
Tastic Rice
Van Riebeeck Dairies (Pty) Ltd

The illustration on page 8 has been reproduced by courtesy of the Council of the City of Cape Town.

The table of mass volume equivalents of dry and solid ingredients is reproduced under the Government Printer's Copyright Authority 8359 of 20 May 1985 and with acknowledgments to the Homemaking Division of the Department of Education and Culture.